# OFF TO WAR
The Virginia Volunteers in the War with Mexico

or

# FUERA DE GUERRA
La Virginia Volentarios en la Guerra con Mexico

William Page Johnson, II

HERITAGE BOOKS
2006

## HERITAGE BOOKS
*AN IMPRINT OF HERITAGE BOOKS, INC.*

**Books, CDs, and more—Worldwide**

For our listing of thousands of titles see our website at
www.HeritageBooks.com

Published 2006 by
HERITAGE BOOKS, INC.
Publishing Division
65 East Main Street
Westminster, Maryland 21157-5026

Copyright © 2002 William Page Johnson, II

All rights reserved. No part of this book may be reproduced or transmitted in any form or by any means, electronic or mechanical, including photocopying, recording or by any information storage and retrieval system without written permission from the author, except for the inclusion of brief quotations in a review.

International Standard Book Number: 978-1-58549-767-3

VIRGINIA VOLUNTEERS IN MEXICO

*Acknowledgements*

Special recognition is due to the very capable staff of the Virginia Room, Fairfax City Regional Library. Suzanne Levy, Brian Conley, Anita Ramos, Kate Depret-Guillaume and Karen Moore all took an active interest in this project. They were always ready to assist me with my many telephone calls and frequent visits.

# OFF TO WAR

*Preface*

All wars have heroes. Those individuals who excel at command or through self-sacrifice accomplish heroic deeds. The war with Mexico was no exception. It was an incubator for the future leaders of that most terrible conflict - the American Civil War. Among the Virginians who career rise began with the Mexican War are such notable figures as:

- Major Jubal A. Early, (Major Gen., C.S.A.)
- Captain Robert E. Lee, (Command Gen., C.S.A.)
- Captain James L. Kemper, (Brig. Gen, C.S.A & Virginia Governor)
- Lieutenant Thomas J. Jackson, (Lt. Gen., C.S.A.)
- Lieutenant George Thomas, (Major Gen., U.S.A.)

The Virginia regiment produced its share of political leaders as well:

- William Mallory Levy, U.S. Congressman - Louisiana
- James Lawson Kemper, Governor of Virginia
- James Taylor Craig, Attorney General of Virginia
- Henry Erskine, Virginia Senator
- Harvey Black, Virginia Delegate
- Jubal Anderson Early, Virginia Delegate
- Henry Erskine, Virginia Delegate
- Kenton Harper, Virginia Delegate
- Benjamin R. Linkous, Virginia Delegate
- James Francis Preston, Virginia Delegate
- Charles Augustus Ronald, Virginia Delegate
- James Thrift, Virginia Delegate

We know a good deal about these men. History has recorded much of the minutia of their lives. However, this book is not about them. This book is about those Virginians who served that are now all but forgotten. Those Virginia citizens who left hearth and home to fill the ranks as private soldiers and serve their country. It is an attempt to tell the story of their lives, before, during and after the war with Mexico. Sadly, in some cases all that remains is their official service record. In other cases a small window is opened into their lives.

VIRGINIA VOLUNTEERS IN MEXICO

*Illustrations and Photographs*

**Map of Westward Expansion 1815-1846**
University of Texas Library Webpage
http://www.lib.utexas.edu/maps/historical/mexican_1815-1845.jpg
Austin, TX

**Map of Mexican War**
University of Texas Library Webpage
http://www.lib.utexas.edu/maps/historical/mexican_1846-1847.jpg
Austin, TX

**Proclaimation of Virginia Governor**
November 18, 1846
Montgomery Dent Corse Papers
Lloyd House Library
Alexandria, VA

**Flag of Petersburg Union Volunteers**
Virginia Historical Society Library
Richmond, VA

**Certificate of Discharge and Disability
of Pvt. Samuel Ellis**
Mexican War Pension File SC #816
National Archives and Records Administration
Washington, DC

**Pvt. Harvey M. Black**
Virginia Polytechnic Institute & State University Library
Special Collections, Black Family Papers - Ms74-003
Blacksburg, VA

**Pvt. James Lawrenson Bryan**
VMI Archives - ACCNUM 1862
Virginia Military Institute
Lexington, VA

**Pvt. John Thomas Day**
Fairfax County Photo Archives
Fairfax City Regional Library
Fairfax, VA

OFF TO WAR

**Major Jubal Anderson Early**
Virginia Historical Society
Richmond, VA

**Cpl. Benjamin Franklin Ficklin**
VMI Archives - ACCNUM 2341
Virginia Military Institute
Lexington, VA

**Sgt. Charles Franklin Force**
Confederate Veteran Magazine, © 1896, v. 4, p. 390,
Nashville, TN.

**Pvt. Thomas W. Gaines**
Library of Virginia
Richmond, VA

**Pvt. Robert Davison Gardner**
Robertson, James I., $4^{th}$ Virginia Infantry,
© 1988, H.E. Howard, Inc.
Lynchburg, VA

**$1^{st}$ Lt. Thomas Stuart Garnett**
Chalpa, John D, $48^{th}$ Virginia Infantry,
H.E. Howard, Inc.
Lynchburg, VA

**Col. John Francis Hamtramck**
Daguerreotype ca. 1847, Unknown Artist
Amon Carter Museum - P1981.65.3
Ft. Worth, TX

**$2^{nd}$ Lt. William Henry Harmon**
Virginia Grand Lodge A.F.& A.M.
Richmond, VA

**Pvt. Edwin T. Lucado**
Courtesy of James S. Lucado
Dallas, TX 75229

**$2^{nd}$ Lt. Thomas M. Moore**
Courtesy of Edgar & Nancy Pritchard
Fairfax, VA

## VIRGINIA VOLUNTEERS IN MEXICO

**2nd Lt. Peter Archibald Peterson**
Sketches and Portraits of the Virginia Conference
Methodist Episcopal Church, South
Lafferty, John J., D.L., © 1890, Richmond, VA

**Pvt. John Poe, Jr.**
Virginia Fire and Police Museum
200 West Marshall Street
Richmond, VA

**1st Lt. George Alexander Porterfield**
Armstrong, Richard L., 25th Virginia Infantry and 9th Battalion Virginia Infantry, © 1990 H.E. Howard, Inc.
Lynchburg, VA.

**Pvt. Thomas Robinson Satterfield**
Senior Pastors of the First United Methodist Church
http://www.firstumc.net/Ministers/History%20of%20Ministers.htm
321 Oak Street
DeKalb, IL

**1st Sgt. Henry H. Tillson**
*Baltimore Sun, November 3, 1906,* p. 7,
Baltimore, MD

**2nd Lt. David Addison Weisiger**
Alabama Department of Archives and History
Montgomery, AL

OFF TO WAR

*Abbreviations*

| | |
|---|---|
| A.T. | Arizona Territory |
| abt. | about |
| Actg. | Acting |
| Adjt. | Adjutant |
| a.k.a. | Also Known As |
| apptd. | appointed |
| Arty. | Artillery |
| Asst. | Assistant |
| AWOL | Absent Without Leave |
| b. | born |
| BLW | Bounty Land Warrant |
| Brig. | Brigade |
| bro. | brother |
| Btln. | Battalion |
| Btry. | Battery |
| bur. | buried |
| Bvt. | Brevet |
| c. | circa |
| C.H. | Court House |
| c/o | Care of |
| Capt. | Captain |
| capt. | captured |
| Cav. | Cavalry |
| Cem. | Cemetery |
| Cert. | Certificate |
| Co. | company or county |
| Col. | Colonel |
| complex. | complexion |
| cor. | corner |
| Cpl. | Corporal |
| CSA | Confederate State of America |
| d. | died |
| DVS | Disabled Volunteer Soldiers |
| dau. | daughter |
| Dept. | Department |
| desc. | description |
| det. | Detached or detailed |
| Dist. | District |
| Div. | Division |
| div. | divorced |
| Dr. | Doctor |
| enl. | Enlisted |
| F-cap | Forage Cap |
| Genl. | General |

## VIRGINIA VOLUNTEERS IN MEXICO

| | |
|---|---|
| Hosp. | Hospital |
| Hvy. | Heavy |
| IC | Invalid Claim |
| Inf. | Infantry |
| IOOF | International Order of Odd Fellows |
| K.T. | Kansas Territory |
| KIA | Killed In Action |
| LIC | Light Infantry Company |
| Lt. | Lieutenant |
| m. | married |
| m/1 | married $1^{st}$, $2^{nd}$ $3^{rd}$, etc. |
| Maj. | Major |
| mbr. | Member |
| Med. | Medical |
| Mex. | Mexico or Mexican |
| m-i-l | mother-in-law |
| mos. | months |
| N. | North |
| Natl. | National |
| NFR | no further record |
| No. | Number |
| occ. | occupation |
| OWIA | Old War Invalid Claim |
| phys. | physical |
| pd. | paid |
| P.O. | Post Office |
| pr. | pair |
| pres. | present |
| prom. | Promoted |
| Ret. | Retail |
| Pt. | Point |
| Pvt. | Private |
| QM | Quartermaster |
| Qtrs. | Quarters |
| recd. | received |
| Regt. | Regiment |
| Regtl. | Regimental |
| res. | reside(s) |
| Rev. | Reverend |
| rt. | right |
| SA | Survivor Application |
| SC | Survivor Claim |
| Sec. | Secretary |
| Sgt. | Sergeant |
| s-i-l | son in law |
| Soc. | Society |

OFF TO WAR

| | |
|---|---|
| St. | Street |
| Surg. | Surgeon |
| trans. | transferred |
| USA | United States of America |
| USCT | United States Colored Troops |
| USMA | United States Military Academy |
| USS | United States Ship |
| U.Va. | University of Virginia |
| VMI | Virginia Military Institute |
| Vols. | Volunteers |
| w. | wife |
| w/ | with |
| WA | Widow Application |
| WC | Widow Claim |
| wd. | wound |
| wded. | wounded |
| wid. | widow |
| yrs. | years |

# VIRGINIA VOLUNTEERS IN MEXICO

## Medical Ailments

|  |  |
|---|---|
| *Apoplexy* | Stroke |
| *Bilious* | Excess bile |
| *Blood on the Brain* | Aneurysm |
| *Bone Eryesylis* | ? |
| *Bright's Disease* | Kidney Disease |
| *Cerebral Apoplexy* | Stroke |
| *Cerebral Embolism* | Blood clot in brain |
| *Cerebral Lesion* | Brain damage of some type |
| *Cholera* | Intestinal bacterial disease |
| *Congestion of the Brain* | Water on the brain |
| *Congestion of the Lungs* | Pneumonia |
| *Consumption* | Tuberculosis |
| *Cystitis* | Urinary Tract Infection |
| *Debility* | Abnormal weakness |
| *Delirium Tremens* | Delirium w/ alcoholism |
| *Derangement of the Heart* | Heart Attack? |
| *Dropsy* | Swelling of abdomen |
| *Dysentery* | Intestinal inflammation |
| *Endocarditis* | Swelling of the heart |
| *Erysipelas* | Infectious disease of the skin |
| *Fistula* | Abscess or unclosed wound |
| *Fistula in Ano* | Hemmoroids |
| *Gangrene* | Dead or rotting flesh |
| *Hemorrhage of the Bowels* | Bleeding from the bowels |
| *Intemperance* | Alcoholism |
| *Ischisrectal Celluitis* | Pelvic Inflammation? |
| *Locomotor Ataxia* | Paralysis assoc. w/ syphillis |
| *Malaria* | Disease w/spasms, chills, etc. |
| *Marasmus* | Gradual emaciation |
| *Nephritis* | Kidney Disease |
| *Neuralgia* | Acute nerve pain |
| *Non Compos Mentis* | Not Mentally Competent |
| *Paralysis* | Loss of motor & sensory function |
| *Paresis* | Loss of motor function |
| *Phthisis* | Difficulty breathing |
| *Pneumonia* | Any form of lung inflammation |
| *Pulmonary Consumption* | Heart disease |
| *Rupture* | Hernia |
| *Scarlet Fever* | Acute infectious disease of skin |
| *Senile Debility* | Progressive mental feebleness |
| *Softening of the Brain* | Loss of mental function |
| *Smallpox* | Contagious disease of the skin |
| *Strictum* | Contraction of a part of the body |
| *Stricture of the Urethra* | Contraction of the urethra |

## OFF TO WAR

| | |
|---|---|
| *Thrombosis* | Obstruction of blood circulation |
| *Tuberculosis* | Disease of the lungs |
| *Turpidity of Liver* | Cloudiness of liver |
| *Typhoid Fever* | Waterborne disease of intestines |
| *Uremia* | Impurities in blood |

# VIRGINIA VOLUNTEERS IN MEXICO

*Primary Sources*

*Company Muster Rolls of the 1st Regiment Virginia Volunteers, Mexican War*, Record Group 94, National Archives and Records Administration, Washington, D.C.

*Compiled Service Records of 1st Regiment of Virginia Volunteers, Mexican War*, Record Group 94, National Archives and Records Administration, Washington, D.C.

*Court-Martial Proceedings, Mexican War*, Records of the Office of the Judge Advocate General(Army), Record Group 153, National Archives & Records Administration, Washington, D.C.

*Descriptive Roll of Soldiers Discharged...*, Record Group 94, Entry 57, National Archives and Records Administration, Washington, D.C.

*Letter Book, 1st Regiment Virginia Volunteers, Mexican War*, Record Group 94, National Archives and Records Administration, Washington, D.C.

*Pension Files, Mexican War*, Record Group 94, National Archives and Records Administration, Washington, D.C.

*Secondary Sources*

Eisenhower, John S.D., *So Far from God: The U.S. War with Mexico*, Random House, New York, NY, © 1989

McCaffrey, James M., *Army of Manifest Destiny: The American Soldier in the Mexican War*, New York University Press, New York, NY, © 1992.

Nardo, Don. *The Mexican-American War*, Lucent Books., San Diego, CA, © 1991.

Wallace, Lee A., Jr., *The First Regiment of Virginia Volunteers 1846-1848*, The Virginia Magazine of History and Biography, v. 77 (1969), p. 46-77.

White, Virgil D., *Index to Mexican War Pension Files*, National Historical Publishing Company, Waynesboro, TN, © 1989.

Robinson, Cecil, ed. The View from Chapultepec: Mexican Writers on the Mexican-American War. Univ. of Arizona Pr., 1989.

Additional primary and secondary sources were utilized and are so noted.

# OFF TO WAR

### A Brief Overview of the War

Of all the major wars in which our country has been engaged perhaps none was more controversial and more significant than the Mexican War, fought between the United States and Mexico 1846 - 1848. Subsequent to this war the borders of the United States would be expanded by one third, incorporating all of the present southwest and the modern states of Arizona, California, Nevada, New Mexico, Texas & Utah.

The origins of the conflict date back to the 1820's. Following Mexico's independence from Spain in 1821 the Mexican government encouraged the colonization of their border regions by Americans. At the time Texas belonged to the Mexican State of Coahuila and in contrast to California, Arizona and New Mexico, Texas was largely uninhabited. The Mexican government, hoping to stabilize their borders offered hugh tracks of land, as much as 4,000 acres, to individual families in exchange for citizenship. New colonization laws were enacted by the Mexican government which were extremely generous to new settlers. While the American government, in its own territory, fixed a price of two pesos per acre payable in four years, the Mexican government fixed a price of *one peso for 144 acres of land payable over six years.* This was the equivalent of less than one cent per acre!

Between 1821 and 1835 an estimated 38,000 people moved into the area of Texas. The stream of settlers was so great that Texas was rapidly becoming a pseudo American province. Alarmed, Mexican officials first reduced then eliminated the number of immigrants permitted into the area. Mexican troops were sent to the border in an effort to enforce the new policy. This did little to slow the expansion however. By 1835, there were nearly five times as many Americans (30,000) as Mexicans (8,000) living in the region.

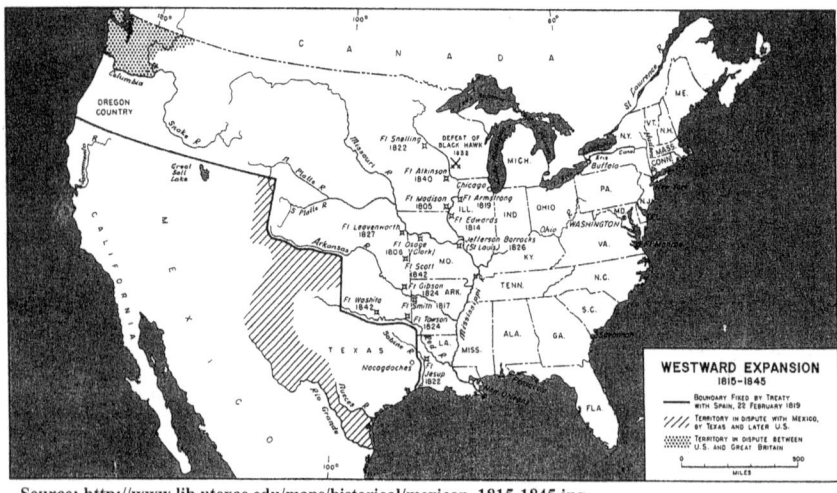

Source: http://www.lib.utexas.edu/maps/historical/mexican_1815-1845.jpg

In a true clash of cultures, Native Americans and Mexicans had already occupied the area being settled by the Americans for centuries, each with their own unique customs and ways of life. Most Mexicans were devout Catholics. The American settlers, who were primarily farmers from Kentucky,

## VIRGINIA VOLUNTEERS IN MEXICO

Tennessee, Arkansas and Missouri, brought with them their own variety of ethnic and religious backgrounds. In addition they brought something else – slavery. Although the Mexican government officially banned slavery they did little to enforce this ban in the border areas.

Even though they were the newcomers, many Americans viewed Mexicans as ignorant, indolent and conniving. The Native Americans, too, were viewed with disdain. Many Americans labeled them as simple savages to be avoided or eliminated altogether.

This view was part of the doctrine of *Manifest Destiny*, which was the belief that the people of the United States were destined to expand not only their borders but to extend the boundaries of freedom to others by imparting their idealism and belief in democratic institutions to those who were incapable of self-government. Those people who were perceived as being incapable of self-government were essentially all non-whites. In truth, *Manifest Destiny* was an expression of a genuine ideal on the part of Americans. But it was also a justification for expansion at the expense of the native population. As the population of the United States grew and the economy developed, the desire to expand into new territory also grew. In Texas, armed confrontation and revolt began in the early 1830's as American settlers, frustrated by Mexican rule, began to demand better representation from Mexico City. Instead of support, Mexican General Antonio Lopez de Santa Anna not only abolished local rule in 1835, he dissolved the

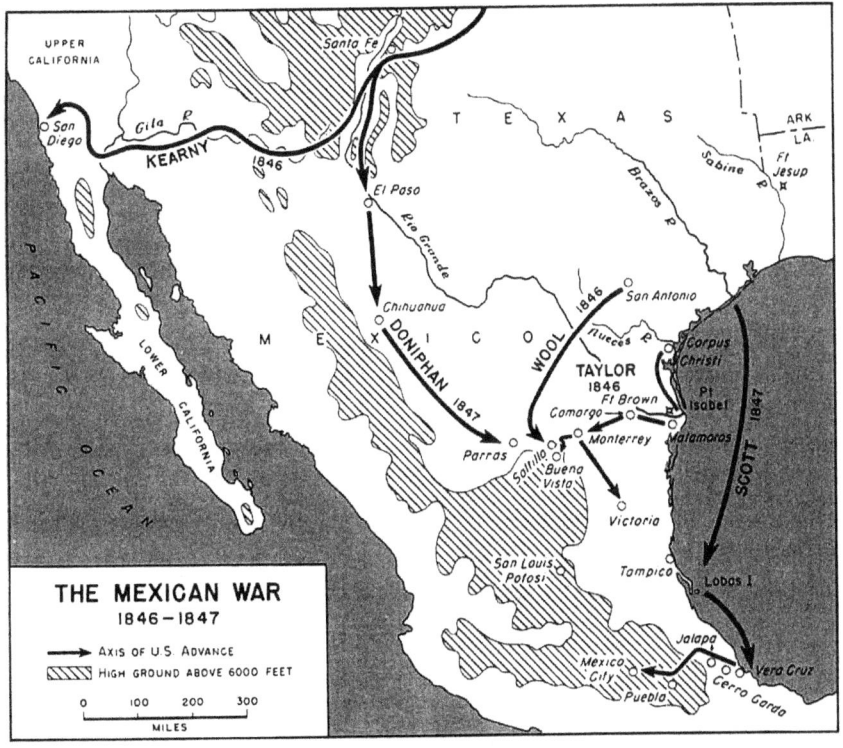

Source: http://www.lib.utexas.edu/maps/historical/mexican_1846-1847.jpg

## OFF TO WAR

Mexican Congress and declared himself dictator. The American settlers in Texas pledged to fight against Santa Anna and declared their independence from Mexico on March 2, 1836. A brief armed struggle known as the Texas War of Independence ensued. At the Battle of the Alamo on March 6, 1836, 187 Texas defenders were massacred by an opposing Mexican army estimated at 20,000. A little more than a month later however, Texas won its independence with a crushing defeat of the Mexican army at the Battle of San Jacinto near present-day Houston, on April 21, 1836. General Santa Anna was captured and secured his freedom by signing a treaty officially recognizing the Republic of Texas.

In spite of their Mexican citizenship and recent independence, most Texans remained loyal to the United States. After securing its independence a state of near anarchy prevailed in many areas of the young Texas republic. In September 1836 Texans voted overwhelming in favor of annexation by the United States. However, U.S. President Martin Van Buren rejected the idea. Constitutional concerns, fear of war with Mexico, and the existence of slavery in the Texas republic were the main obstacles to annexation.

In 1841, Texas President Sam Houston tried in vain to push the annexation issue. With the War of 1812 still very much a recent event, Great Britain opposed the annexation of Texas by the U.S. Hoping to curb U.S. expansion Great Britain began trade negotiations with the Texas Republic in 1843. The following year U.S. President John Tyler, fearing a Texas alliance with the British, proposed annexation. In June 1844 the annexation of Texas was defeated in the U.S. Senate. The annexation of Texas then became a central issue of the presidential election of 1844. James K. Polk, of Tennessee, who favored annexation, was elected. On February 28, 1845, by joint resolution of the U.S. Congress, and subject to ratification by the people, Texas was annexed into the United States. Texas was formally admitted to the Union as the 28$^{th}$ State on December 29, 1845.

While a Republic, Texas had claimed the Rio Grande River as its boundary. The adjacent Mexican State of Tamaulipas claimed the area north of the Rio Grande River to the Nueces River as the correct boundary. Mexico consequently not only refused to recognize the annexation of Texas into the United States, but further did not recognize the Rio Grande as the boundary between the two countries. Mexico had previously warned that they would consider the annexation of Texas a declaration of war. Adding insult to injury, in November 1845 U.S. President Polk, through his emissary John Slidell, offered Mexico up to $25 million dollars for the purchase of the California and New Mexico territories. Insulted by the offer the Mexican officials refused to see Slidell. In January 1846, after the failure of the Slidell mission, President Polk ordered General Zachary Taylor and 4,000 men to the mouth of the Rio Grande River to defend Texas from invasion and reinforce the American boundary claim. Taylor, who had been camped on the Nueces River, arrived at the Rio Grande on March 28, 1846. This action was viewed by some in the United States as a provocation for war. On April 25, 1846 Mexican troops crossed north of the Rio Grande and ambushed a small detachment of American cavalry. Sixteen Americans were killed. The news of the ambush did not reach President Polk until May 9$^{th}$, nearly two weeks later. Upon hearing the news on May 11$^{th}$ he addressed a joint session of Congress and asked for a declaration of war proclaiming that Mexico had "invaded our territory and shed American blood on American soil." In reality, Mexico had as good a claim as the United States to the disputed territory. After significant debate the U.S. Congress declared war on Mexico on May 13, 1846. In the meantime the Mexican army twice more crossed the Rio Grande to engage the Americans but were repulsed. These engagements would come to be known as the Battles of Palo Alto on May 8$^{th}$ and Resaca de la Palma on May 9$^{th}$.

The losses at Palo Alto and Resca de la Palma shocked the Mexican leadership. Their well-trained army of 32,000, eight times larger than the American force of 4,000, had been soundly defeated. The losses caused open revolt between competing factions within the Mexican government. The revolt spread to the Mexican army where mass defections occurred. By the summer of 1846 Mexico was in a state of near anarchy. In August 1846, with disaster looming General Santa Anna returned to Mexico from exile in Cuba. With the assurance to help negotiate a settlement, he was permitted to pass through the American naval blockade stationed along the Mexican coast. Unfortunately, no negotiations occurred and Santa Anna once again assumed dictatorial command of the Mexican government and the army.

## VIRGINIA VOLUNTEERS IN MEXICO

In the meantime, the United States, taking full advantage of the intense turmoil in Mexico, continued to marshall their forces for war. In of small but vocal opposition from an abolitionist faction in the northeast, Americans generally support the war. Nearly all 36 states in the Union made its volunteer forces available for Mexican service. Within a few short months the American forces in Mexico swelled to 100,000. While there was widespread support for the war, some states experienced difficulty in recruiting volunteers. There were two primary reasons for this. First, general economic conditions were good. Second, many Americans feared the annexation of Texas would lead to an expansion of slavery. This was especially true in New England.

In prosecuting the war with Mexico the United States had essentially two goals. First, to expand its borders. Under the doctrine of *Manifest Destiny* American expansion into the western territory claimed by Mexico was fully justified. Second, after the rebuff of the Slidell mission invasion would force Mexico to accept the loss of the territory.

The actual war with Mexico was fought in three separate actions. The occupation of New Mexico, the California revolt and the overland campaign in Mexico.

In June 1846, General Stephen W. Kearny set out with about 1,700 troops from Fort Leavenworth, Kans., to capture New Mexico. In August, the expedition captured the town of Santa Fe. Kearny left the area in command of Col. Alexander Doniphan and his voluteer force from Missouri and pushed west across the desert to California.

Also, in June 1846, a group of American settlers led by U.S. Army officer John C. Fremont revolted against the Mexican government in California. This rebellion became known as the Bear Flag Revolt because of the portrayal of a grizzly bear on the settlers' flag. In July, U.S. naval forces under Commodore John D. Sloat captured the California town of Monterey and occupied the San Francisco area. On December 6, Kearny led about 100 troops in the bloody Battle of San Pasqual near San Diego. Reinforcements from San Diego helped save the small American army. In January 1847, U.S. troops under Kearny and Commodore Robert F. Stockton of the Navy won the Battle of San Gabriel near Los Angeles. This victory completed the American conquest of California.

In northeastern Mexico, General Zachary Taylor had driven the Mexicans across the lower Rio Grande to Matamoros in the two battles of Palo Alto and Resaca de la Palma. On May 18, 1846, Taylor crossed the river and occupied Matamoros. After waiting for new troops, he moved his army up the river to Camargo and then marched against the important city of Monterrey. Monterrey fell on September 24$^{th}$ after a fierce battle. Before the end of the year, Taylor had occupied Saltillo and Victoria, important towns in northeastern Mexico. However, Mexico still refused to negotiate with the United States.

In December 1846, Col. Alexander W. Doniphan led about 850 troops south from Santa Fe to capture the Mexican city of Chihuahua. Passing through El Paso his force defeated a Mexican army at El Brazito on Christmas Day. Continuing south Doniphan's army won the furious Battle of the Sacramento, fought just outside Chihuahua on Feb. 28, 1847. The Americans occupied the city on March 1$^{st}$.

Polk and his advisers decided to land an army at Veracruz, on the east coast, and strike a blow at Mexico City. Many of Taylor's best troops were ordered to join Major General Winfield Scott, who was placed in charge of the new campaign. President Santa Anna personally commanded the Mexican Army. He learned of the American plans and immediately led a large army of between 16,000 to 20,000 men against Taylor. Taylor's force of about 5,000 men defended a narrow mountain pass against Santa Anna near a rancho named Buena Vista in the mountains beyond Saltillo. In a two day battle fought February 22-23, 1847, the American forces defeated the Mexicans and established their permanent hold on northeastern Mexico.

As a result of these victories General Taylor became a national hero. It has been suggested that President Polk reduced the number of troops assigned to Taylor because he was concerned over the General's increasing popularity and his potential as a future political revial. Taylor would indeed be elected U.S. President in 1848 principally because of his popularity arising from the Mexican War.

General Scott, with a force of about 10,000 men, landed near Veracruz on March 9, 1847. Twenty days later he captured the city, and on April 8$^{th}$ he began his advance toward the Mexican capital. The American army stormed a mountain pass at Cerro Gordo on April 17$^{th}$ and 18$^{th}$ and pushed on. Near

## OFF TO WAR

Mexico City, American troops fought and won the battles of Contreras and Churubusco on August 19th and 20th. The Mexican Army was superior in numbers but poorly equipped and poorly led. After a two weeks' armistice in which peace neogiations proved futile the Americans resumed the offensive and won victories at Molino del Rey on September 8th, and stormed and captured the hilltop fortress of Chapultepec on September 13th. On the following day the Americans marched into Mexico City.

Despite all the American victories, Mexico refused to negotiate a peace treaty. In April 1847, Polk had sent Nicholas P. Trist, Chief Clerk of the Department of State, to join Scott's army in Mexico and attempt to open diplomatic negotiations with Santa Anna. When the armistice of August failed, the President recalled Trist. But Santa Anna resigned shortly after Scott entered the Mexican capital. Mexico established a new government, and it feared that it might lose even more territory if it did not accept the American demands. In fact many Americans wanted to annex all of Mexico. At the request of the Mexican leaders and General Scott, Trist agreed to remain in Mexico against Polk's orders and negotiate a settlement.

A peace treaty was signed on February 2, 1848, at the village of Guadalupe-Hidalgo, near Mexico City effectively ending the war. The treaty required Mexico to give up only the disputed territory. The United States paid Mexico $15 million for this territory, known as the Mexican Cession. In a speech in December 1848, President James K. Polk spoke of the resolution to the conflict, *"Texas was a natural and almost indispensable part of our territory. Fortunately it has been restored to our homeland."*

### The Aftermath

Subsequent to the Mexican War the United States gained more than 525,000 square miles of additional territory. This intensified the quarrels over slavery. Here was new territory. Was it to be slave or free? The Compromise of 1850 made California a free state and established the principle of "popular sovereignty." That meant letting the people of a territory decide whether it would be slave or free. However, popular sovereignty later led to bitter disagreement and became one of the underlying causes of the American Civil War.

In 1853, the United States purchased a small strip of land in northeastern Mexico along the southern border of present-day Arizona and New Mexico. The Gadsden Purchase, as it came to be known, gave an additional 29,640 square miles to the United States.

The Mexican War gave training to many officers who later fought in the Civil War. These included Jefferson Davis, Ulysses S. Grant, Stonewall Jackson, Stephen Kearney, Robert E. Lee, George B. McClellan, George Gordon Meade and William T. Sherman.

### Mobilization in Virginia

Ten days after the declaration of War, Virginia Governor William Smith issued a proclamation on May 23, 1846 calling for 30 companies of volunteers. Recruitment in Virginia started immediately. Governor Smith also appointed the officers to staff the newly created regiment. Selected were Colonel John Francis Hamtramck, of Jefferson County; Lt. Colonel Thomas Beverly Randolph, of Warren County; Major Jubal Anderson Early, of Franklin County. All of these men were graduates of the United States Military Academy, West Point, New York.

Among the first to offer the services of their militia companies were Captains Robert Scott, Jr. and Captain Edward C. Carrington, both of Richmond, and Captain Montgomery D. Corse, of Alexandria.

The Alexandria men were particularly successful in their recruitment efforts. Patriotism was running high owing to the recent retrocession of Alexandria back to Virginia.[1] However, elsewhere in

---

[1] Alexandria had been part of the District of Columbia until it was retroceded back to Virginia March 20, 1847.

## VIRGINIA VOLUNTEERS IN MEXICO

Virginia, as in the rest of the country, economic prosperity was a huge deterrent to raising a volunteer

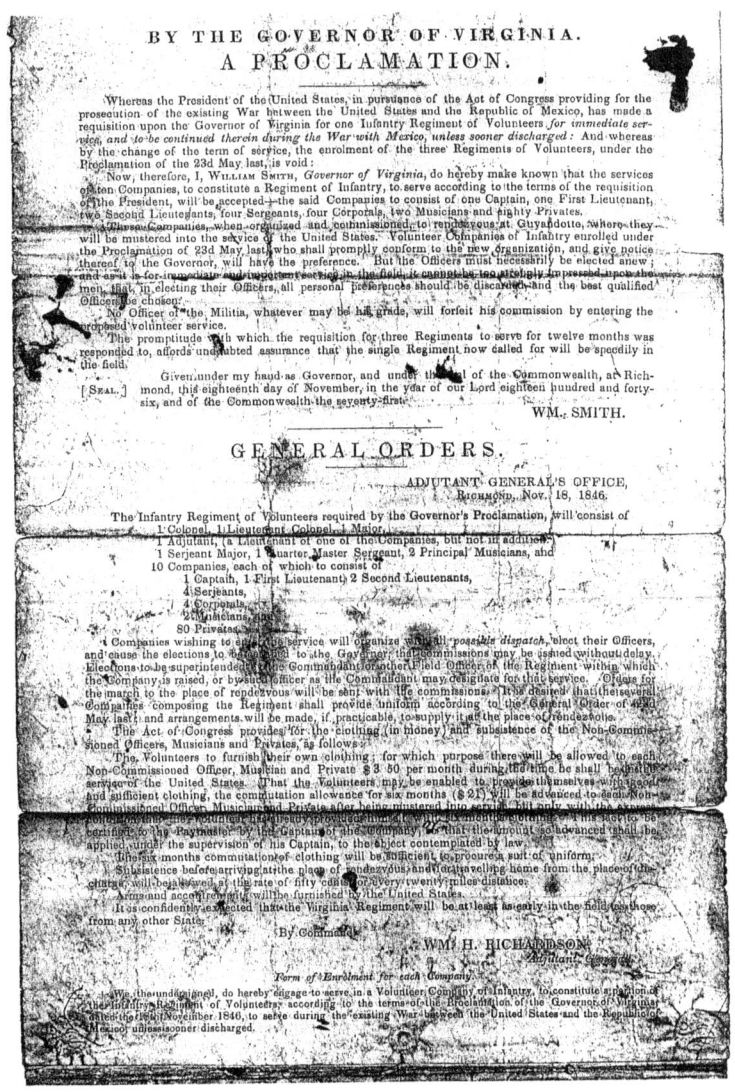

Source: Lloyd House Library, M.D. Corse Papers, Alex., VA

force. Another factor hindering recruitment was the size of the population in some communities. Many

## OFF TO WAR

areas within the state attempted to raise and equip volunteers for the war but were not successful because of these factors. To make matters worse the War Department notified Governor Smith in July that existing conditions in Mexico did not warrant the use of any additional volunteers. As the summer worn on it became apparent that the war would take longer to prosecute and more troops would be needed. Consequently, on November 16, 1846 Governor Smith issued a second call for volunteers. The new organization was to comprise a single regiment of ten volunteer companies *"for immediate service"* in Mexico. Each company was to consist of 93 officers and men. Ultimately, in response to this call companies were organized and accepted from Augusta, Berkeley, Caroline, Fairfax, Jefferson, and Montgomery counties and the cities of Alexandria, Lynchburg, Petersburg, Portsmouth and Richmond.

The initial rendezvous point for the Virginia regiment was to be the town of Guyandoyte, Virginia (now WV) on the Ohio River. Because of the poor condition of the roads in the interior of Virginia and because most of the volunteers were from the eastern part of the State, Guyandoyte was later abandoned in favor of Fort Monroe, Virginia on the Chesapeake Bay.

Each Virginia Volunteer accepted for service in the Mexican War had to be between 18 and 45 years of age and *"in physical strength and vigor."* Each man was required to pass muster consisting of a cursory exam by the regimental surgeon. Each volunteer was initially required to furnish his own uniform and equipment consisting of a musket, a navy blue cloth cap, a navy jacket and pair of pantaloons (trousers), 2 pairs of bootees, 2 pair of woolen socks, 2 cotton shirts, 2 flannel shirts, 1 great coat (overcoat), cartridge box, waist belt and cross belt. Once mustered an initial allowance of $21 was offered. Thereafter, a monthly clothing allowance of $3.50 was authorized. Clothing and accoutrements were subsequently deducted from the soldier's monthly pay as they were supplied. A "commutation" allowance of fifty cents per twenty miles to the rendezvous point was also granted.

Individual companies were ranked in order of their acceptance into the service of the United States. The first company so accepted was designated company "A", the next company "B", and so on. Company commanders too, were granted seniority based on their companies' acceptance into service. Initially, this was the source of no small debate within the regiment.

Captain Robert G. Scott, Jr. had initially offered the services of his company, the *Richmond Grays*, on May 22$^{nd}$ a day before Governor Smith issued his first call for volunteers. The Grays were not accepted for service until November 19$^{th}$ three days after the governors second call. They were the first of the Virginia volunteers officially mustered for service and as such were designated Company "A."

Captain Montgomery D. Corse, an affluent Banker and Merchant from Alexandria, had organized a company from that city after the May call for volunteers. His was also among the first to offer its services to the Commonwealth. The Company was officially organized on November 20, 1846 in Alexandria by Corse, completing its organization by early December. On December 12, 1846 the company was escorted to the Potomac River by two additional militia units, the *Mount Vernon Guards* and the *Ringold Cavalry*. They boarded the steamer *Phoenix* and sailed down the Potomac to Aquia Creek. From there they boarded a train for Richmond at which place they arrived on December 13$^{th}$. They were greeted by a large crowd at the station and were escorted to the Union Hotel by the *Public Guard* and subsequently accepted for service as Company "B."

In early December two companies were organized from the Shennandoah valley. On December 11$^{th}$ Captain Kenton Harper, editor of the *Staunton Spectator*, organized a company from Augusta County. At about the same time Captain James F. Preston mobilized the local militia into service. Both of these companies received no letter designation. Harper's company became known as the *Grenadier's* and Preston's company was designated simply the *Light Infantry Company*.

Captain Smith Pyne Bankhead, son of an U.S. Army General, organized a company from the Fredericksburg area beginning December 18, 1846. Recruiting was slow until Lt. Washington L. Mahan, a native of Philadelphia, arrived with fifty recruits from his native city. They had evidently completed their organization by December 30$^{th}$--the day they arrived in Richmond and were designated Company "C."

In Petersburg, Virginia two companies were raised. William M. Robinson organized the first - *The Petersburg Union Volunteers*. Robinson was the son of a prominent Physician and a close

## VIRGINIA VOLUNTEERS IN MEXICO

acquaintance of the writer Edgar Allan Poe. This company arrived in Richmond on January 7, 1847 and was designated Company "D." Members of this company could be distinguished from all others by a red ribbon they had adopted as a badge or cockade.[2] On January 28th the officers of this command were presented swords from the people of Petersburg. In addition, the ladies of Petersburg presented the company with a flag. This flag now resides in the collection of Virginia Historical Society and is the only known Virginia flag from the Mexican War. The second company accepted from Petersburg was the *Petersburg Mexican Volunteers*, subsequently known as Company "E." Their Captain was a 29-year old Petersburg lawyer, Fletcher Harris Archer who had organized the company on December 3, 1846.

The tidewater region of Virginia was also represented in the regiment. Portsmouth Physician John P. Young organized a volunteer company from the City of Portsmouth and surrounding Norfolk County

Flag of the Petersburg Union Volunteers (aka City Guards).
Photo credit: Virginia Historical Society, Richmond, VA

---

[2] Petersburg was dubbed the "The Cockade City of the Union," which is usually shortened to "The Cockade City," by President James Madison in 1813. The Petersburg Militia was in the habit of wearing an ornamental cockade or badge on their hats. Searching for something complimentary to say, Madison proclaimed Petersburg the *Cockade City of the Union*, analogous to the ornament of the Union.

# OFF TO WAR

as well. This company was accepted for service on January 8, 1847 as became Company "F."

Two days after the United States declared war on Mexico, Richmond lawyer, Edward C. Carrington, Jr., the son of U.S. Army general of the same name, completed the organization of a company of volunteers from that city. They were not immediately accepted because the Governor had yet to issue a call for volunteer forces. Carrington's company was accepted for service on November 19th and designated Co. "G."

In northeastern Virginia two companies were organized. In Berkeley County (now in West Virginia), the 29 year-old editor of the *Martinsburg Gazette*, Ephraim Alburtis organized men from the town of Martinsburg and surrounding Berkeley County into a company of volunteers. The core of this company was made up of the local Berkeley County militia known as the *Independent Blues*. They arrived in Richmond on December 31st and were designated Co. "H." The other company from northeastern Virginia was organized in Jefferson County (now in West Virginia) by a 37 year old stonemason from Charlestown, John William Rowan. With the aid of a committee of prominent citizens funds were solicited from the community to purchase equipment for the new company. Men from the county began to enroll in this company on December 1, 1846. The *Alexandria Gazette* reported on the recruitment activities of this company:

> "We learn that Lieut. Lawrence Washington, of this company, is a descendant of the family of the great George Washington, and that the Orderly Sergeant is a lineal descendant of Lord Fairfax."[1]

On January 4, 1847 the company had completed its organization and prepared to leave Charlestown for Fort Monroe, VA. The company received an official sendoff from a large gathering of citizens at the Jefferson county courthouse. After several speeches by dignitaries they boarded a train for Harper's Ferry, VA where they transferred to "packet" boats[3] and traveled down the C & O canal to Georgetown. From Georgetown the company made its way to Richmond arriving there on January 6, 1847. On arrival John S. Gallaher, their state senator and the father of Pvt. John S. Gallaher, of Martinsburg presented the men to Virginia Governor William Smith. Rowan's company became Co. "K." While in Richmond, Rowan's company was quartered at the Union Hotel.[4]

On December 12th Richmond resident William B. Archer began to organize a company of volunteers in that city. Dubbed the *Marshall Guard* and subsequently known as Company "I," they completed their organization and were accepted for service on February 25th.

On the morning of January 3rd the companies of Scott, Carrington, Corse, and Bankhead boarded a steamer for Fort Monroe, Virginia, the final assembly point. As they approached the wharf at City Point to pick up Capt. William Archer's company, Pvt. Arthur McNulty of Co. G fell overboard and was drowned. He became the regiment's first causality.[2] The conditions at Fort Monroe were less than ideal. Sleeping quarters were insufficient to house all of the men. There was also a lack of adequate drinking water and shortages of food and other supplies. As consequence of these cramped conditions disease began to be a problem. On February 12, 1847 Peter Booker (Bougher) of Winchester became the first member of Co. K to die of disease. Two days later, two more members of Co. K, William Kirk, of Loudoun Co., and William Bryant of Richmond, also died. Initially, the stay at Ft. Monroe was to have been brief while the necessary transport ships to Mexico were acquired. However, the regiment was not

---

[3] **Packet Boats** were either canal or river boats used to transport passengers and goods in the 19th c.
[4] **The Union Hotel** was located on the southwest corner of 19th and Main Streets, facing on Main. It was built in 1817 by Dr. John Adams and designed by Richmond's first architect Otis Manson. It was used by the Medical College of Virginia when that instution was established in Richmond in 1838. After 1845 it reopened as the United Sates Hotel. During the Civil War it was used as a hospital and was known as General Hospital No. 10. After the war, it was for many years, the home of Richmond Theological Seminary from which developed the present Virginia Union University. In its latter years was the home of Richmond Methodist Mission. The building was razed in 1911. Present site is numbered 1821-3-5 East Main Street.

## VIRGINIA VOLUNTEERS IN MEXICO

adequately equipped when they reached Ft. Monroe. The anticipated uniforms and equipment were not yet available. Thus the companies were forced to remain at Ft. Monroe nearly three weeks. At least fifteen members of the regiment would die while at Ft. Monroe awaiting transport to Mexico.

Because of the conditions at Ft. Monroe no additional companies were sent there. Instead. the regiment was split into two battalions. Cos. A, B, C, E, G and the Grenadier's (Scott, Corse, Bankhead, F.H. Archer, Carrington, and Harper) were designated first battalion. The second battalion consisted of those companies still in Richmond and still in the process of organizing. Namely Cos. D, F, H, I, K and the Light Infantry Company (Robinson, Young, Alburtis, W.B. Archer, Rowan and Preston).

Finally, the necessary uniforms and equipment arrived and on January 26th the first battalion, under the command of Lt. Col. Randolph, was ordered to Mexico. Cos. A, C, E and Grenadiers embarked on the transport *May Flower*. Cos. G and B who sailed on the transport *Victory* quickly followed them on January 28th.

By the first week of February the second battalion, excluding W.B. Archer's company who were still in Richmond, were in quarters at Ft. Monroe awaiting transport. They too had to wait for uniforms and equipment. On February 19th Col. Hamtramck turned over command of the second battalion to Major Early. Col. Hamtramck then traveled overland to New Orleans, presumably to arrange for the arrival of the regiment. The necessary equipment and uniforms for the second battalion arrived on February 22, 1847. On that date companies F, H and K sailed for Mexico on the barque *Exact*. The company of William Archer arrived at Ft. Monroe on February 25th. On March 1st companies D, I and the Light Infantry Company boarded the transport *Sophia Walker* and set sail.

The voyage to Mexico was extremely unpleasant for most of the Virginians. The weather was rough and many of the men suffered from seasickness. Small Pox, Mumps and Typhoid Fever were also prevalent. Four members of the regiment, Pvts. Alexander Dyes, James Moss, Merrett W. Boatright and William Yopp, died enroute to Mexico and were buried at sea. Commissary Captain James L. Kemper recorded the death of Pvt. Alexander Dyes in his diary:

> "Today we witnessed what to most of us a scene as impressively solemn as novel. One poor volunteer, Young's Company, died last night. Today while the heavens were shrouded in black, while the sea rolled in awful wildness, and the wind whistled mournfully through the shrouds and the ship's timbers creaked and the rain beat over us, we committed the corpse to its long home in the watery deep."[3]

At least one of the ships, the *May Flower,* appears to have stopped in Havana, Cuba before reaching Mexico.[4]

The first Virginia troops in Mexico were those of the first battalion which arrived at Point Isabel on February 18, 1847. Shortly afterward Capt. Carrington wrote home from Point Isabel, Texas in a letter dated February 21, 1847:

> "I have met a good many Mexicans of the lower class here. They appear from their action to be very sluggish and indolent; yet they're fully as large and muscular, it seems to me, as our men. We all arrived safely - no sickness, except mumps and sea sickness."[5]

They did not know it at the time but the Virginia Volunteers had arrived in Mexico just as active campaigning in the north was ending. The final battle being fought at Buena Vista on February 22nd-23rd. Lt. Col. Randolph was ordered to immediately proceed with his command up the Rio Grande to Camargo, Mexico and then overland to Monterrey. The same route taken by Gen. Taylor nearly a year before. Randolph reached Camargo on March 2nd. On March 7th he left with four companies to escort a wagon train to Monterrey. The second battalion, under the command of Major Early, arrived at Point Isabel on March 10th. They followed Randolph to Camargo on about March 18th. Col. Hamtramck, who had been delayed in New Orleans arrived at Point Isabel on March 21st. He proceeded to Camargo and arrived there on March 27th. On the same day Lt. Col. Randolph and his command returned from Monterrey.

## OFF TO WAR

On April 4th the entire regiment under the command of Col. Hamtramck left Camargo for Monterrey. On April 13th the regiment arrived at China [Chee-Na]. Lt. Col. Randolph and companies B, C, F, G, K and the Light Infantry Co. were left to garrison the town. On April 16th Col. Hamtramck, with the remainder of the regiment resumed the march to Monterrey. Shortly afterwards, Col. Hamtramck, who had become ill on the march from Camargo, turned over command of the regiment to Major Early. The Virginia volunteers under Major Early arrived in Monterrey on the morning of April 21. A camp was established just outside of the town.

Several weeks later the Virginia regiment was ordered into Monterrey proper to relieve the 1st Ohio Regiment of Volunteers. Captain Scott was ordered to post his company at the Citadel known as the *"Black Fort"* located about 1,000 yards from the town. Captain Scott was evidently extremely unhappy with this posting it being so far from the relative luxury of the town of Monterrey. On the evening of May 17th after being ordered to post his company in the Black Fort Capt. Scott left his company in command of Lt. John J. Fry and went into Monterrey. While there he evidently got drunk and was late in returning to the Fort. The incident was reported to Major Early. Later that summer Capt. Scott was court-martialed on three separate charges: 1) Gross Neglect and Violation of Duty, 2) Conduct Prejudicial to Good Military Order and Discipline, 3) Conduct Unbecoming an Officer and a Gentleman. He was convicted on all charges and sentenced to be privately reprimanded. He was the highest-ranking Virginia volunteer to be court-martialed during the Mexican War. [See Scott, Robert G. for full transcript of court-martial].

Meanwhile, the garrison at China also experienced some misfortune. Two officers, 2nd Lieutenants Washington L. Mahan, of Co. C, and Carlton R. Munford, of Co. G, participated in a duel. On May 18th Lt. Mahan reported to Capt. John P. Young, in his quarters, that he had seen a body of forty mounted-armed Mexicans one to two miles from China. This was in the presence of several other officers, including Lt. Munford. Lt. Munford then stated that he did not believe Lt. Mahan and called him *"a damned liar."* Munford further stated that he had previously caught Mahan telling lies. The story Lt. Mahan told, of his having seen this armed force created considerable excitement within the camp. Shortly afterward, on the morning of the 20th of May 1847, the two men met again in the tent of Capt. Young with several other officers present. Lt. Mahan came in with his sword in his hand. He complimented Lt. Munford on his sword. Lt. Munford replied that he (Lt. Mahan) was not fit to carry a sword and that he would disgrace any sword that could be placed in his hands and that he did not consider him a fit associate for the officers of the detachment. Privately, Capt. Young suggested to Lt. Mahan that he had been *"grossly insulted"* and that he *"could no longer appreciate him as an Officer or a Gentleman, unless he resented"* how Lt. Munford had insulted him. Lt. Mahan then went to speak with Capt. Bankhead on the matter. Bankhead advised him not to escalate the trouble and Mahan agreed he would not. At about this time Lt. Munford came into the room and again insulted Lt. Mahan in the presence of Capt. Bankhead, Lts. Garnett and Coleman. Lt. Mahan then challenged Lt. Munford to fight him with weapons. To which challenge Lt. Munford agreed. All efforts of Capt. Bankhead, Capt. Young and Lt. Garnett to induce Lt. Munford to retract his statements and to settle the matter peaceably proved futile. The duel took place on the evening of the 20th of May 1847 at the foot of a small mountain on the Camargo Road one half mile from China. Both men armed with muskets advanced to within thirty-five paces and fired simultaneously. Lt. Mahan was struck with *"slug"* in his chest and a *"ball"* in the left axcilla that came out left of the spinal column, he died on the 1st of June 1847. Lt. Munford was struck with eight buckshot and died some thirty hours later.

When word of this incident reached Mahan's father, a letter of petition from several *"concerned citizens"* in Philadelphia was sent to President James K. Polk, charging that Capts. Bankhead, Young and Lt. Thomas S. Garnett were *"guilty of a manifest violation of military duty, in aiding abetting and countenancing by their presence, the fatal meeting between Lts. Mahan & Munford."* The President evidently agreed and a Court of Inquiry was held at Buena Vista, Mexico 01/03/1848.[6] The Court of Inquiry subsequently found no evidence of wrongdoing or complicity in the deaths of Lts. Mahan and Munford.

In March 1847 Captain Henry Fairfax of Fairfax County, Virginia organized a "13th" company for service from Virginia. Henry Fairfax was the son of Thomas Cary Fairfax (9th Lord Fairfax), whose

## VIRGINIA VOLUNTEERS IN MEXICO

family originally controlled a vast amount of land comprising most of present-day northern Virginia. In addition to coming from a wealthy and prestigious family, Henry Fairfax had also attended the United States Military Academy at West Point, NY. The initial organization of the Fairfax company occurred at Fairfax C.H. on March 1, 1847. The men recruited were primarily from Fairfax County, Virginia. On March 16$^{th}$ the company arrived in Alexandria, VA The *Alexandria Gazette* reported that:

> "The company is composed of fine looking, athletic young men, and will challenge a favorable comparison with any yet formed."[7]

The following morning they boarded the steamer *Phoenix* and crossed the Potomac River and went into quarters at Ft. Washington, MD to await transports to Mexico. On April 1$^{st}$ the company re-crossed the Potomac and traveled by train from Washington, D.C. to Relay House, Maryland[5] where they spent the night. The next morning they boarded trains to Cumberland, Maryland, the terminus of the railroad at that time. Arriving at Cumberland on the evening of April 2$^{nd}$ the Fairfax company attracted the attention of the local newspaper the *Cumberland Civilian*. The paper reported on their arrival and hinted at the difficulties the company faced in securing passage to Mexico:

> "Capt. Henry Fairfax's Company, comprising the 13$^{th}$ Company of Virginia Volunteers, arrived in Cumberland on Friday night, and proceeded en route to Pittsburg [sic] on Saturday morning...Their fine spirits and excellent behavior seem to have attracted the attention of the young men on the route from Washington, if we may judge from the number who joined them at different points. Although in almost every respect unprepared for the field, yet the company started at a minute's warning, thereby demonstrating that they are 'ready.' We have no doubt that in the event of a collision with the enemy they will also prove themselves 'rough.' It is only to be hoped that under Gen. Taylor's standard they will receive better treatment than they have from the President of the United States."[8]

On the morning of April 3$^{rd}$ the company left Cumberland and went overland by *"road wagons"* to Brownsville, Pa. and the Ohio River. The men continued their journey by boat down the Ohio River past Pittsburgh, Pa. to the Mississippi River and down to New Orleans, La. At New Orleans they boarded the barque *Baring Brothers* and sailed to Point Isabel. They reached Point Isabel by April 28th. From there they were ordered to join Major Early and the rest of the Virginia regiment at Monterrey. On May 4$^{th}$ the company left for Monterrey. On May 9$^{th}$ they reached Camargo and rested there several days. The resumed the march for Monterrey on May 12$^{th}$ arriving there on May 21$^{st}$.

On about the first of June Lt. Col. Randolph was ordered to move with the first battalion to Buena Vista. Shortly afterward, on June 22$^{nd}$ the second battalion under Major Early received orders to join the regiment at Buena Vista. Arriving on June 25$^{th}$ they were brigaded together with the 1$^{st}$ North Carolina Volunteers and 2$^{nd}$ Mississippi Volunteers. Col. Robert Treat Paine commanded the North Carolina regiment.[6] The Mississippi regiment was under the command of Col. Jefferson Davis.[7] Until this moment

---

[5] **Relay House.** The first trains on the B&O railroad were horse drawn wagons. The distance between Baltimore, Md. and Ellicott's Mills, Md. was too great for a single team of horses. And so, a fresh team, or *"relay"* team, was acquired halfway between the two towns.

[6] **Robert Treat Paine:** a U.S. Representative from North Carolina; b. Edenton, Chowan County, N.C., 02/18/1812; attended private schools and grad. Washington (now Trinity) College, Hartford, Conn.; studied law; was admitted to the bar and practiced; held several local offices; owned and operated shipyards and engaged in the shipping business; member of the State house of commons in 1838, 1840, 1844, 1846, and 1848; served as colonel of a North Carolina regiment during the Mexican War; War Governor of Monterrey, Mexico, in 1846; member of the Mexican Claims Commission after the war; elected as a candidate of the American Party to the Thirty-fourth Congress (March 4, 1855-March 3, 1857); moved to Austin County, Tex., in 1860 and engaged in agricultural pursuits; died in

## OFF TO WAR

the Virginia regiment had never been entirely together at any one place while in Mexico for more than just a few days.

In August another unfortunate incident occurred. Several members of the Virginia volunteers became involved in a mutiny with members of the North Carolina and Mississippi regiments. Col. Paine of the North Carolina regiment was a strict disciplinarian well known was meting out severe punishments to those guilty of infractions. Consequently, many members of his command were dissatisfied with his leadership. On the evening of August 15$^{th}$ a group of four or five men threw stones at Col. Paine's tent. When Paine came out of his tent the men ran. He ordered them to halt. They refused and continued to run in the direction of the Virginia camp, cursing after him as they went. He warned them to halt or he would open fire. One man jeered at him *"fire then God damn you."* Paine fired his pistol wounding two of the men with one shot. One man, from the North Carolina regiment, fell mortally wounded. The other man, Pvt. Thomas F. King, of the Virginia regiment was wounded in the hand by the same bullet as it exited the first man. Several men, including King, were later identified, court-martialed and dishonorably discharged.

While in Mexico, the Virginians spent the better part of their service at Buena Vista and Saltillo. Buena Vista was the site of the fierce battle that had been fought there in February 1847. The area where they were camped was situated at an elevation of 5,200 feet, in the Anahuac region ("country by the waters" in the Aztec language), a term describing the great central plateau of Mexico. The climate was dry and hot in the summer, but the winters mild, with lots of sunshine. The average annual temperature was approximately 65 degrees Fahrenheit. Two mountain chains bordered the region, the Sierra Madre Oriental and the Sierra Madre Occidental. Saltillo is located on the plateau of the Sierra Madre Occidental, near Monterrey.

While in camp the Virginians fell into a seemingly endless regimen of drill and guard duty. The letter of Lt. James M. Wade to his brother Charlie Wade while at Camargo, Mexico, March 28, 1847, describes a typical day:

> *"At day light reveille beats at which we all must attend or be arrested. Drill for an hour. Breakfast. Drill again for two hours. Prepare for and eat dinner. Drill again two hours in the evening. Rest for an hour. When retreat beats eat our supper and rest until nine o'clock when tattoo beats. We then with pleasure throw ourselves upon our downy blankets sometimes spread on a board with our overcoats under our heads there in sweet and sometimes undisturbed slumber, rest our wearied limbs and then the next day we run the same gauntlet."*

During the day, officers and enlisted men were permitted to enter the town of Saltillo located five miles north of Buena Vista. Because of this companies were occasionally posted at Saltillo to keep order. Saltillo is located near the *Arteaga*, an area of pine and oak forests, mountains, and green hills.

Clearly, the Virginians, owing to their late entry into the war were largely relegated to garrison duty. This duty, however, was inherent with its own dangers. While stationed at China, Mexico several

---

Galveston, Tex., February 8, 1872; interment in Brenham Cemetery, Brenham, Tex. (from Congressional Biography).

[7] **Jefferson Davis**: b. Fairview, Christian County (now Todd), Kentucky, 06/03/1808; grad. USMA, West Point, NY 1828; served in Black Hawk War 1832; m/1 Taylor 1835 (dau. of Zachary Taylor); m/2 Varina Howell 1845; elected twenty-ninth congress (03/04/1845 – 06/1846) resigned to command Mississippi Regt. In Mexican War; apptd. U.S. Senate to fill unexpired term of Sen. Jesse Speight; subsequently elected to U.S. Senate (08/10/1847-09/10/1851), resigned; unsuccessful candidate for Gov. of Miss. 1851; apptd. Sec. of War (1853-1857) by Pres. Franklin Pierce; elected U.S. Senate (03/04/1857-01/21/1861), resigned with other secessionist Senators; elected Pres. of Confederate States of America (1861-1865); captured by Union troops at Irwinville, Ga. 05/10/1865; imprisoned at Ft. Monroe, Va. and indicted for treason; was paroled into the custody of the court in 1867; d. New Orleans, La. 12/05/1889 and bur. Hollywood Cem., Richmond, Va.

## VIRGINIA VOLUNTEERS IN MEXICO

members of the regiment were reported as having been *"assassinated by the Mexicans."* The Virginians too, were not beyond depredations as witnessed by the following letter:

*Head Quarters, Buena Vista*
*October 15th 1847*

*To Col. Hamtramck*
*Comdg. Infantry Brigade*

*Colonel:*
*It is reported to the Commanding General that some men from your command leave camp nightly to plunder the inhabitants of the neighboring ranchos. Gabriel Narvo says that a party from, it is supposed, the Mississippi Regiment, took out of his pen last night a fat hog. On another evening they went to a rancho and killed a hog, but not liking it, left it. They also steal fowls &c.*
*The Commanding General directs that you will make strict inquiry in order to ascertain who the thieves are, and have them severely punished.*
*Very Respectfully*
*I am Yr. Obdt. Servt.*
*Irwin McDowell, A.A.G.*

Col. Hamtramck made his reply on the back of the same letter:

*Major Price will institute a thorough inquiry into the facts reported for the purpose of ascertaining if any one of his Regiment has been guilty of the outrage complained of and report.*
*John F. Hamtramck*
*Comdg. Infantry Brigade*

While the Virginia volunteers were not engaged in any offensive operations there were routinely called on to quell minor rebellions. Bands of guerilla fighters often disguised as Comanche Indians operated in the area. One such incident occurred on Nov. 20$^{st}$. A small party of guerillas had raided the village of Agua Nueva twelve miles south of Buena Vista. Several Mexican civilians had been killed. In response, Col. Hamtramck ordered four companies to pursue the criminals. They were unsuccessful.

By the late fall of 1847 the lack of active combat; the boredom associated with camp life and the ever-present specter of sickness were beginning to take a toll in the Virginia camp. A sign of the growing frustration of the Virginia troops was an increase of both desertions and court-martials. Court-martials were convened for a variety of offences. The most common offences were Neglect of Duty, Disobedience of Orders, Sleeping on Post, Absence Without Leave, and Desertion. If found guilty of an offence a solider was likely to be sentenced to forfeit his pay for a month or more, be confined in the provost guardhouse, and/or be made to perform hard labor with a ball and chain attached to his leg. Usually the more serious the infraction the more severe the punishment. For example, Pvt. Henry Gordon who was court-martialed and found guilty of desertion was sentenced:

> *"...to stand on the head of a barrel two (2) hours each day for one month with a ball and chain weighing 18 pounds attached to his leg...to forfeit his pay proper, and afterward to be kept in confinement in the Provost Guard during the continuance of the war with Mexico. Then to be marked with the letter 'D', one and a half inch long, on the left hip, with india ink, and to be dishonorably discharged from the service."*

Pvt. James F. Simmons was found guilty of the theft of $97.50 from a trunk in his captain's tent. He was court-martialed, found guilty and sentenced:

## OFF TO WAR

*"...to forfeit all pay and allowances due him. To be confined in irons in the Provost Guard for one week. To be "<u>bucked</u>" two hours each day of said week from 3 to 5 o'clock P.M. To stand on the head of a barrel each day of said week from 7 to 9 o'clock A.M. To have one side of his head shaved, his face blacked, the letter "T" branded on his right hip. And at the end of the week to be <u>drummed out of service</u>."*

The final company to join the regiment was that of William A. Talbot of Lynchburg and William A. Scott of Dinwiddie County. By July of 1847 Talbot had raised a partial company of about 70 men at Lynchburg but lacked the minimum number of 93 to be accepted for service. At about the same time Scott was attempting to raise a company of volunteers from Amelia, Nottoway and Lunenburg counties. However, by the end of the summer Scott had only about 25 men in his company. The two companies were merged into one with Talbot as captain and Scott as first lieutenant. Talbot's company arrived at Buena Vista in January 1848 and was designated Co. "M."

In February 1848 Gen. Wool ordered that the town of Parras de la Fuente ninety miles west of Saltillo be garrisoned to protect Mexican civilians from bandits operating in that vicinity. Captain Harper led his own company as well as Cos. B, D, K on the expedition. While there two members of the garrison Pvts. Moses Hurt and Israel Peck, both of the Light Infantry Company, were *"assassinated"* by bandits. The criminals were later captured and executed with the blessings of the local Mexican authorities.

In February 1848 the war with Mexico was clearly coming to an end. News of the ratification of the Treaty of Guadalupe-Hildago, actually ending the war, reached the Virginia volunteers on June 9th. Col. Hamtramck ordered artillery salutes to commence at noon in honor of the peace. Evidence of the level of the celebration that occurred is manifest in the medical discharge, on account of deafness, of Pvt. Samuel Ellis. Years later when applying for a pension he explained:

*"I lost my hearing at China, Mexico about the last of May 1847 in this manner: We were firing salutes and it was my duty to ram the cartridge and spring the cannon. The report of said cannon destroyed my hearing entirely for about a month and then my hearing, in part, returned. But not sufficiently for me to perform my duty.... I was treated by my regimental surgeon and discharged for deafness and chronic diarrhea;"*

The Virginia volunteers remained in Mexico until July 1848 when they boarded transport ships and returned to Virginia by way of Fort Monroe where they were mustered out of service. From there they made their way to their homes. As they did so, whole communities turned out to honor their return. Picnics and parties of all degrees were common throughout all of Virginia in the late summer and fall of 1848.

For many, wanderlust was now a way a life. In 1849, the year following the war gold was discovered in California - now a territory of the United States. Many former soldiers migrated to California. In at least one instance they organized themselves into a military style company in the quest for gold. Lts. Robert Keeling, Lawrence Washington, Vincent Geiger and John Gallaher helped organize the Charles Town Mining Co. and led an expedition of approximately 100 men to the gold fields of northern California.

As you might expect, a significant number of the men who served in the Virginia volunteers during the Mexican War also served in the Civil War.

### Epilogue

Although the Virginia regiment was never engaged in battle they suffered as greatly as any other regiment sent to Mexico. Most American deaths that occurred while in Mexico were due to diseases. Measles, Smallpox, Typhoid and Malaria were extremely common.

## VIRGINIA VOLUNTEERS IN MEXICO

However, for enduring these hardships the Virginia Volunteers were eligible receive a federal Bounty Land Warrant (BLW) and a federal Pension. Bounty Land Warrants were available to veterans immediately upon discharge. They were redeemable for 160 acres of any unclaimed federally owned land anywhere in the United States. In order to receive his land a veteran had to send a request to the Department of the Interior in Washington, D.C., along with proof of his service, usually a discharge certificate. Unfortunately, many veterans were cheated out of their claims by unscrupulous land speculators who acted as *agents* in the claim process. These agents would typically understate the value of the land and/or charge the veterans and a high fee for filing their claim. Many veterans received nothing at all.

In addition to the Bounty Land Warrants, disabled Virginia veterans were eligible to receive federal pensions immediately on discharge from the service. Widows of men who were killed or died in service and orphaned children under the age of sixteen were also eligible. Eventually, after heavy lobbying of Congress by the Mexican War veterans themselves the Mexican War Pension Act became law on January 29, 1887. This act authorized for all veterans who were disabled by illness, war wounds or service-connected injuries a general pension. Both veterans and widows were eligible to receive $8 per month but had to give proof of service and proof of disability. After 1900 the monthly pensions were increased to $12, then $20 per month. The majority of pension recipients applied within the first three years of the pension's availability. Mexican War pension claims were accepted until 1926.

The following information is typical of what may be found in BLW and pension applications for Mexican War service. The files contain significant biographical information on each soldier. They may also yield a clue as to where the veteran settled after the war. The BLW file typically contains the veterans discharge (as proof of service) and reveals whether or not the veteran sold his warrant or redeemed it. In pension files, a *"survivor's application"* (SA), or *"survivor's claim"* (SC) typically shows the veteran's name, rank, military unit, period of service, residence at time of mustering-in, residence at time of application, birthplace, age or date of birth, and, when the claim was made on the basis of need, a list of property. Most pension files also contain a physical description of the soldier. Usually the veteran had to submit to a physical examination by a doctor, who in turn submitted a report attached to the pension claim. In addition, the veteran was normally required to obtain affidavits from at least two individuals who were able to attest to his service. A *"widow's application"* (WA), or *"widow's claim"* (WC), shows most of the same information about the veteran as well as the widow's name, age, residence at time of application, maiden name, date and place of marriage, and date and place of her husband's death. An application of a child or heir gives essentially the same biographical information. The bounty land warrant and pension files are stored in Record Group 94 in the National Archives, in Washington, D.C.

In 1874 the National Association of Veterans of the Mexican War (NAVMW) was created with the purpose of securing a federal pension for needy veterans, preserving battlefields and the establishment of a national Mexican War monument. The NAVMW which existed from 1874 until 1910 achieved only one of those objectives - the Mexican War Pension Act of 1887. Information about the NAVMW is sketchy but it appears that they were organized into state chapters with delegates attending a national convention held annually in a different city. The NAVMW published the *Vedette*, a monthly journal devoted to the interests of the survivors of the Mexican War. Subscriptions were available at $1 per year.[9] Beginning in 1887, this publication also routinely included blank *Survivor* applications for Mexican War pensions. Because a great many Mexican War veterans belonged to the NAVMW many existing pension applications originated from this publication. The NAVMW also issued its members a small bronze medal honoring their military service. This medal was the only such honor most Mexican War veterans received as Congress never authorized such a medal. The final meeting of the NAVMW occurred in Indianapolis, IN in 1910.

Another veterans' organization was the Aztec Club of 1847. It was founded in Mexico City on October 12, 1847 by officers of the U.S. Army. The club is still in existence today.

In 1989 the Descendants of Mexican War Veterans (DMWV) was founded in Dallas, Texas. According to their official website they have declared themselves the heir in spirit to the National

## OFF TO WAR

Association of Veterans of the Mexican War. The DMWV has incorporated the original NAVMW seal into its own and has adopted many of the veterans' unrealized goals.

### Echoes

Today, several places in Virginia and take their name directly from the War with Mexico. In Highland County, Virginia which was organized in 1847, the County seat is the town of *Monterey*, named in honor of the American victory at the Mexican city of the same name. Similarly, the independent City of Buena Vista, located in Rockbridge County, is undoubtedly linked to the battle which occurred at that Mexican city. The extinct community of Matamoros in Montgomery Co., Virginia probably also takes its name from the period.

# VIRGINIA VOLUNTEERS IN MEXICO
## Statistics and Facts

| **US Troops** | | **Virginia Vols.** | |
|---|---|---|---|
| Regular Army | 30,954 | Regular Army | ---- |
| Volunteers | 73,776 | Volunteers | 1,348 |
| Navy | 7,500 | Navy | ---- |
| Total Troops | 112,230 | Total Troops | 1,348 |

| **Casualties** | | | |
|---|---|---|---|
| Battles Deaths | 1,753 | Battle Deaths | ---- |
| Other Deaths | 11,550 | Other Deaths | 97 |
| Wounds | 4,152 | Wounds | ---- |

**Average age of the Virginia Volunteers at enlistment:** 25

**No. Virginia Vols. of Mex. War to serve in Civil War:**

| United States | 45 | 3.3% |
|---|---|---|
| Confederate States | 268 | 19.8% |
| **Total** | 313 | 23.1% |

**Top Occupation of Virginia Volunteers:**

| Farmer | 104 | Physician | 12 |
|---|---|---|---|
| Laborer | 51 | Plasterer | 11 |
| Carpenter | 34 | Blacksmith | 10 |
| Clerk | 22 | Cooper | 8 |
| Lawyer | 18 | Miller | 7 |
| Shoemaker | 16 | Printer | 7 |
| Tailor | 15 | Saddler | 7 |
| Painter | 14 | Teacher | 7 |

**Last Known Surviving Virginia Volunteer:**
Pvt. Uriah Jackson Rose died January 18, 1926, age 98

**Cemetery w/ the Largest Number of Virginia Volunteer Interments:**
Blandford Cemetery, Petersburg, Virginia    41

## OFF TO WAR

### A War of Firsts

The first foreign war of the United States.

The first war anywhere in the world to be photographed.

The first war in which steamboats played an important role.

The first war in which newspaper correspondents regularly reported from battles.

The first war in which graduates of the U.S. Military Academy at West Point participated.

# OFF TO WAR

Colonel John Francis Hamtramck
1st Virginia Volunteers

## VIRGINIA VOLUNTEERS IN MEXICO

### The 1st Virginia Volunteer Infantry in the War with Mexico 1846-1848

#### Field & Staff

Colonel John Francis Hamtramck

Lt. Colonel Thomas B. Randolph

Major Jubal Anderson Early

Adjutant, 2nd Lt., David Addison Weisiger

Surgeon, Dr. William H. I'Anson

Assistant Surgeon, Dr. James H. Bell

Quartermaster, Captain, James Lawson Kemper

Commissary Captain, Henry Erskine

Sgt. Major, Thomas E. Watkins

Qtr. Mstr. Sgt., Charles Thompson

Qtr. Mstr. Sgt., John H. Hunter

Principal Musician, John Cunnigham

Principal Musician, Thomas A. Farley

# VIRGINIA VOLUNTEERS IN MEXICO

## Muster Roll of Company A, 1st Virginia Volunteer Infantry
### a.k.a. Captain Robert G. Scott's Co.
### *Richmond Grays*, (Richmond)
### Mexican War 1846-1847

Scott, Robert G., Jr., Capt.
August, Thomas P., 1st Lt.
Gravatt, William, 2nd Lt.
Bodeker, Charles, 2nd Lt.
Tillson, Henry R., 1nd Sgt.
Watkins, Thomas E., 2nd Sgt.
Raux, Emile, 3rd Sgt.
Flournoy, Peter C., 4th Sgt.
Cox, James T., 1st Cpl.
Winn, James, 2nd Cpl.
Hecht, Frederick, 3rd Cpl.
Currie, Stephen C., 4th Cpl.
Craft, John C., Drummer
Templeton, James, Fifer

Atherton, John, Pvt.
Barker, James W., Pvt.
Barziza, Edgar A., Pvt.
Bilson, Andrew J., Pvt.
Bohannan, Abner J., Pvt.
Bridgewater, Charles, Pvt.
Brown, Charles H., Pvt.
Buchannan, Milo, Pvt.
Chaille, John, Pvt.
Corbin, Layfayette, Pvt.
Davis, James L., Pvt.
Doyle, John, Pvt.
Dreury, Jesse C., , Pvt.
Ellis, John W., Pvt.
Faulkner, Josiah, Pvt.
Francis, William, Pvt.
Fry, Joshua D., Pvt.
Garnett, James J., Pvt.
Haley, Woodson, Pvt.
Hall, Frederick, Pvt.
Hallman, Peter F., Pvt.
Hatcher, Edmund J., Pvt.
Hawkins, William R., Pvt.
Hilliard, Richard, Pvt.
Hohn, John, Pvt.
Jewett, Noah, Pvt.
Johnson, Almon, Pvt.
Jones, John A., Pvt.
Krishmann, Anthony, Pvt.
Lottier, Lewis, Pvt.
Maule, Lewis, Pvt.
McKinney, Meridith C., Pvt.
McMann, John, Pvt.
Merryman, Pulaski P., Pvt.
Montero, Andrew A., Pvt.

Pierce, Dorastus, Pvt.
Poe, John, Jr., Pvt.
Poe, Thomas, Pvt.
Potts, John H., Pvt.
Quinn, Martin, Pvt.
Roane, William A., Pvt.
Rolberg, Henry, Pvt.
Scott, John H., Pvt.
Spillman, James W., Pvt.
Stagg, James, Pvt.
Velines, Charles H., Pvt.
Whitlow, James I., Pvt.
Winston, Thomas B., Pvt.
Wrenn, Louis, Pvt.
Wrenn, Robinson B., Pvt.
**Died**
Guthrow, William, Pvt.
Spooner, Samuel J., Pvt.
**Discharged**
Donnan, Robert C., 2nd Lt.
Fry, John J., 2nd Lt.
Ball, Thomas C., 4th Cpl.
Ficklin, Benjamin F., 4th Cpl.
Bowyer, Michael, Pvt.
Burton, William, Pvt.
Cardwell, James, Pvt.
Crump, Andrew C., Pvt.
Daws, Louis, Pvt.
Deemer, Nicholas, Pvt.
Gibson, John W., Pvt.
Hogg, William C., Pvt.
Howard, Alexander, Pvt.
King, John H., Pvt.
Malone, Marshall, Pvt.
Michael, Carl, Pvt.
Norvell, George W., Pvt.
Rucks, Stephen C., Pvt.
Winston, William J., Pvt.
Woodson Martin R., Pvt.
**Deserted**
Brown, Edward, Pvt.
Dockerty, George, W., Pvt.
Dopleb, Reynold, Pvt.
Gates, Vincent, Pvt.
Love, James, Pvt.
McArthur, John D., Pvt.
Plumb, William, Pvt.
Provost, James, Pvt.
Rodecker, William, Pvt.
Whitlock, William W., Pvt.

## Muster Roll of Company B, 1st Virginia Volunteer Infantry
### a.k.a. Montgomery D. Corse's Co. (Alexandria)
### *Alexandria Volunteers*[10]
### Final Muster Roll - Mexican War 1846 –1848

Corse, Montgomery D., Capt.
Higdon, John S., 1st Lt.
Douglas, James S., 2nd Lt.
Minor, William G., 2nd Lt.
Young, John T., 1st Sgt.
Jenkins, William, 2nd Sgt.
Force, Charles F., 3rd Sgt.
Fenwick, Benedict J., 4th Sgt.
McPhail, Dougald, 1st Cpl.
Maxwell, William, 2nd Cpl.
Cawood, Charles H., 3rd Cpl.
Mitchell, Robert, 4th Cpl.

Acton, John, Pvt.
Ashton, Gurdon C., Pvt.
Baker, Charles A., Pvt.
Bloxham, William P., Pvt.
Booth George, W., Pvt.
Bramblett, McHenry, Pvt.
Brown, James W., Pvt.
Brown, John, Pvt.
Carney, Noah, Pvt.
Carpenter, Fayette D., Pvt.
Carter, John E., Pvt.
Chichester, Thompson, Pvt.
Compton, James, Pvt.
Davis, William K., Pvt.
Dorsey, Benjamin, Pvt.
Fegan, Thomas, Pvt.
Ferguson, Robert, Pvt.
Fisher, Isaiah, Pvt.
Ford, Joseph W., Pvt.
Goodrich, John F., Pvt.
Hall, William, Pvt.
Hunter, Zachariah P., Pvt.
Hutchings, George W., Pvt.
Jones, John J., Pvt.
Jones, Richard, Pvt.
Lotts, John, Pvt.
Marmon, Washington, Pvt.
Martin, Peter, Pvt.
Mathews, Robert, Pvt.
Minor, Albert G., Pvt.
Moody, George A., Pvt.
Mooney, George S., Pvt.
Moorlick, Michael, Pvt.

Mullen, Charles, Pvt.
Murphy, Daniel, Pvt.
Owens, William W., Pvt.
Reinhardt, Michael, Pvt.
Reisinger, Daniel, Pvt.
Snyder, George R., Pvt.
Stephenson, James E., Pvt.
Sullivan, Andrew, Pvt.
Swann, Benjamin, Pvt.
Thompson, William, Pvt.
Tibbets, Charles D., Pvt.
Tridle, John, Pvt.
Van Sant, James R., Pvt.
West, Covington, Pvt.
White, Philip, Pvt.
**Died**
Waters, Benjamin G., 2nd Lt.
Moore, Silas, 2nd Cpl.
Belt, John C., Pvt.
Felts, John, Pvt.
Gordon, Henry, Pvt.
Heninger, John H., Pvt.
Shaw, Elias, Pvt.
**Deserted**
Bangs, John W., Pvt.
Doyle, William, Drummer
Farrow, Joseph S., Pvt.
Hoffmaer, Frederick, Pvt.
Howard, Jacob, Pvt.
Mullen, Robert, Pvt.
Self, Thomas, Pvt.
Weeks, John, Pvt.
**Discharged**
Ashby, Turner W., 1st Lt.
Dulany, John S., 4th Cpl.
Brooks, John, Pvt.
Caddis, Henry, Pvt.
Carr, Hampton, Pvt.
Coppedge, Thomas L., Pvt.
Fisher, Amos T., Pvt.
Fowler, James H., Pvt.
Green, Jesse C., Pvt.
Keilholtz, John, Pvt.
Naugle, William H., Pvt.
Orrison, Albert W., Pvt.
Poston, John F., Pvt.

VIRGINIA VOLUNTEERS IN MEXICO

**Muster Roll of Company C, 1st Virginia Volunteer Infantry
a.k.a. Captain Smith P. Bankhead's Co. (Caroline Co.)
Final Muster Roll - Mexican War 1846-1848**

Bankhead, Smith P., Capt.
Garnett, Thomas S., 1st Lt.
Coleman, Robert F., 2nd Lt.
Battaile, Lawrence, 2nd Lt.
Barrell, George F., 1st Sgt.
Good, Jonathan, 2nd Sgt.
Little, Moses A., 3rd Sgt.
Collins, Albert G., 4th Sgt.
Blondell, Theodore, 1st Cpl.
Hesser, Theodore, 2nd Cpl.
Millholland, John, 3rd Cpl.
Carter, John W., 4th Cpl.
Waugh, Frederick, Drummer

Albertson, Harvie, Pvt.
Black, Thomas C., Pvt.
Bradley, Michael, Pvt.
Brown, Alexander L., Pvt.
Cain, Benjamin, Pvt.
Campbell, Lewis, Pvt.
Carroll, Franklin, Pvt.
Chase, Robert, Pvt.
Clarke, William T., Pvt.
Clayton, Jasper S., Pvt.
Davis, Thomas, Pvt.
Fields, Richard, Pvt.
Finnall, William, Pvt.
Graham, Thomas M., Pvt.
Hall, George, Pvt.
Hart, John L., Pvt.
Hawthorn, Joel B., Pvt.
Haywood, Joseph, Pvt.
Hillard, Joseph, Pvt.
Hood, Benjamin, Pvt.
Hurston, Thomas H., Pvt.
Jennings, William, Pvt.
Jones, George, Pvt.
Keiter, Isaac, Pvt.
Lawson, Lewis, Pvt.
Leckie, John, Pvt.
Lewis, Charles, Pvt.
Lewis, Joseph, Pvt.
Mahan, Thomas T., Pvt.
McGathey, Levi, Pvt.
Merritt, Edwin P., Pvt.
Miller, John, Pvt.
Nicholson, Lemuel, Pvt.
Otter, William, Pvt.
Palmer, William L., Pvt.

Piper, Joseph F., Pvt.
Roach, John, Pvt.
Saddler, Frederick A., Pvt.
Shelton, John, Pvt.
Sorrell, Harrison, Pvt.
St. Clair, Francis, Pvt.
Taylor, John, Pvt.
Taylor, Thomas, Pvt.
Wall, Alexander A., Pvt.
Wall, James L., Pvt.
Wallace, Robert, Pvt.
Wallace, William W., Pvt.
White, James E., Pvt.
**Died**
Mahan, Washington L., 2nd Lt.
Fagunders, Jacob H., Pvt.
Heays, John, Pvt.
Johns, Elhanan, Pvt.
Love, Hugh, Pvt.
McFarland, Samuel, Pvt.
Sampson, William, Pvt.
Taliaferro, John R., Pvt.
Turner, Francis L., Pvt.
**Discharged**
Mason, Thomas S., 2nd Lt.
Coghill, Thomas B., 3rd Sgt.
Andrews, John W., Pvt.
Brown, Charles B., Pvt.
Bullard, James, Pvt.
Burruss, John S., Pvt.
Calhoun, John, Pvt.
Carmichael, Andrew, Pvt.
Franklin, Layfayette, Pvt.
Jackson, Nathaniel, Pvt.
Landrum, John, Pvt.
McPhelin, Peter, Pvt.
Morgan, David W., Pvt.
Riddle, Alexander, Pvt.
Sampson, William, Pvt.
Simmons, James F., Pvt.
Widdifield, George W., Pvt.
**Deserted**
Major, Henry, 3rd Cpl.
Briggs, William S., Pvt.
Brown, Joseph, Pvt.
Davis, Thomas, Pvt.
Hillard, Joseph, Pvt.
Jones, George, Pvt.
Otter, William, Pvt.

OFF TO WAR

Muster Roll of Company D, 1st Virginia Volunteer Infantry
a.k.a. Captain William M. Robinson's Co.
*Petersburg Union Volunteers,* (Petersburg)
Final Muster Roll - Mexican War 1846-1848

Robinson, Wm. M., Capt.
Bryan, James L., 1st Lt.
McGowan, Wm. G., 2nd Lt.
Collier, Benjamin W., 1st Sgt.
Winfield, Benj. F., 2nd Sgt.
Baldwin, James B., 3rd Sgt.
Rivers, James W., 4th Sgt.
Pebworth, Nathaniel, 1st Cpl.
Burns, Harman T., 3rd Cpl.
Fisher, John W., 4th Cpl.

Allen, Richard Farrar, Pvt.
Anderton, Isaac A., Pvt.
Britt, William H., Pvt.
Clanton, Williamson S., Pvt.
Clemments, Francis D., Pvt.
Comann, Fitzwilliam J., Pvt.
Crocket, William S., Pvt.
Davis, James H., Pvt.
Duncan, George, Pvt.
Franklin, James, Pvt.
Foster, Lewis H., Pvt.
Fowlkes, Calvin B., Pvt.
Hart, J.B., Pvt.
Henderson, Alexander, Pvt.
Hammond, Rodolphus, Pvt.
Harrison, George W., Pvt.
Howle, William T., Pvt.
James, William H., Pvt.
Johnstone, James H., Pvt.
Lanier, John T., Pvt.
Loomis, Ralph J., Pvt.
Maynard, Mendoza, Pvt.
McCollum, Daniel, Pvt.
Moore, James M., Pvt.
Moyler, John, Pvt.
Moss, John J., Pvt.
Martin, William D., Pvt.
Nicholson, David W., Pvt.
Noel, Landon, Pvt.
Payne, William T., Pvt.
Payne, Edward F., Pvt.
Payne, Robert F., Pvt.
Perkinson, George W., Pvt.
Procise, Thomas, Pvt.
Procise, Joseph D., Pvt.
Ralls, George N., Pvt.
Smiley, Theodore B., Pvt.
Spooner, Charles C., Pvt.

Spaulding, James J., Pvt.
Smith, Albert A., Pvt.
Smith, Calvin N., Pvt.
Smith, J.B., Pvt.
Smith, William B., Pvt.
Tudor, Richard, Pvt.
Totty, John, Pvt.
Towner, Thomas H., Pvt.
Vaden, Robert H., Pvt.
Wigden, Thomas, Pvt.
Wyatt, John, Pvt.
Wilkins, Benjamin, Pvt.
**Died**
Adams, Joseph C., Pvt.
Archer, Edwin C., Pvt.
Gray, Benjamin H., Pvt.
Holloway, Cornelius, Pvt.
Lundie, Thomas Y., Pvt.
Phipps, Robert H., Pvt.
Stuart, William W., Pvt.
**Discharged**
Shands, Aurelius R., 2nd Lt.
Rives, William F., 2nd Sgt.
Stith, Drury B., Fifer
Adams, St. Lawrence, Pvt.
Bentley, Hartwell, Pvt.
Crowder, James B., Pvt.
Heath, William, Pvt.
Garrett, Wesley B., Pvt.
Gibbs, Joseph F., Pvt.
Goodwin, Robert A., Pvt.
Hobgood, Edward, Pvt.
Hobgood, John R., Pvt.
Jordan, Alexander, Pvt.
McCarthy, Dennis, Pvt.
Murdaugh, J.W., Pvt.
Newell, Benjamin C., Pvt.
Poynts, James W., Pvt.
Rittenburg, Alfred, Pvt.
Shepherdson, William N., Pvt.
Vaughan, Alfred J., Pvt.
Wills, Armistead B., Pvt.
Wells, John H., Pvt.
**Deserted**
Cheatzom, Joseph D., Pvt.
Hamlin, Richard, Pvt.
Hudgins, John W., Pvt.
Womack, James, Pvt.

# VIRGINIA VOLUNTEERS IN MEXICO

## Muster Roll of Company E, 1st Virginia Volunteer Infantry
## aka Captain Fletcher Harris Archer's Co.
### *Petersburg Mexican Volunteers*, (Petersburg)
### Final Muster Roll - Mexican War 1846-1848

Archer, Fletcher Harris, Capt.
Pegram, Franklin, 1st Lt.
Weisiger, David A., 2nd Lt.
Peterson, Peter A., 2nd Lt.
Pollard, Peyton, 1st Sgt.
Scott, Thomas, 2nd Sgt.
Wilson, Samuel G., 3rd Sgt.
Jackson, Andrew, 1st Cpl.
Drinkard, Charles B., 2nd Cpl.
Foley, James S., Jr., 3rd Cpl.
Cock, Harrison C., 4th Cpl.

Alley, William E., Pvt.
Atkins, James H., Pvt.
Barnes, James H., Pvt.
Brown, James C.N., Pvt.
Cain, Nathaniel D., Pvt.
Cargill, Nathaniel E., Pvt.
Carter, Joseph L., Pvt.
Donnan, James M., Pvt.
Doudge, Soloman B., Pvt.
Eagle, Robert N., Pvt.
Eanes, James C., Pvt.
Fewqua, Robert F., Pvt.
Fitzgerald, Edward W., Pvt.
Fust, Richard, Pvt.
Goodwin, Archibald B., Pvt.
Goodwin, Arthur M., Pvt.
Graham, Isaac T., Pvt.
Harris, Hamlin E., Pvt.
Henderson, John F., Pvt.
Hughes, Hezekiah, Pvt.
Judkins, William N.B., Pvt.
Knox, Samuel T., Pvt.
Lahmeyer, John H., Pvt.
Landes, Samuel, Pvt.
Lightfoot, William T., Pvt.
Lunsford, James, Pvt.
Martin, James, Jr., Pvt.
Marye, George B.P., Pvt.
McCaleb, Thomas J., Pvt.
McGee, Fleming C., Pvt.
McIntosh, Joseph, Pvt.
Moore, William H., Pvt.
Parr, George B., Pvt.

Partin, Edward G., Pvt.
Peterson, William T., Pvt.
Price, Edward T., Pvt.
Prichard, Samuel H., Pvt.
Prichett, William L., Pvt.
Ricaud, Benjamin, Pvt.
Robinson, James A., Pvt.
Seymore, Richard, Pvt.
Shields, David F., Pvt.
Simpson, Robert, Pvt.
Smith, James, Pvt.
Smith, Samuel, Pvt.
Spotswood, Edward J., Pvt.
Tenain, John E., Pvt.
Thompson, John W., Pvt.
Traylor, Richard B., Pvt.
Vaiden, Mordica, Pvt.
Watkins, Edward, Pvt.
Wells, William J., Pvt.
Westmore, Richard H., Pvt.
White, Joseph L., Pvt.
Wilkinson, Joseph, Pvt.
Williams, George W., Pvt.
**Died**
Brichett, Alexander E., Pvt.
Choate, Jesse C., Pvt.
**Discharged**
Bailey, Richard A., 4th Sgt.
Bain, George S., Pvt.
Ballow, James T., Pvt.
Brevitt, Joseph P., Pvt.
Dunn, James A., Pvt.
Galloway, Joseph, Pvt.
Greenhow, Thomas B., Pvt.
Harrison, Joseph N., Pvt.
Hoy, Francis, Pvt.
Lipscomb, George B., Pvt.
Long, Napoleon B., Pvt.
Loomis, Charles F., Pvt.
Robertson, James B., Pvt.
Vernon, William A.C., Pvt.
Williams, Edward, Pvt.
**Transferred**
Farley, Thomas A., Pvt.
I'Anson, William H., Pvt.

# OFF TO WAR

## Muster Roll of Company F, 1st Virginia Volunteer Infantry
## a.k.a. Captain John P. Young's Co. (Portsmouth)
## Final Muster Roll - Mexican War 1846-1848

Young, John P., Capt.
Cooke, John K., 1st Lt.
Blamire, Edward J., 2nd Lt.
Levy, William M., 2nd Lt.
Lappin, John, 1st Sgt.
James, Joseph H., 2nd Sgt.
Councill, Eugene D., 3rd Sgt.
Benson, Francis L., 4th Sgt.
Misley, John, 1st Cpl.
Dyes, Nathaniel, 2nd Cpl.
Webster, Henry, 3rd Cpl.
Jones, Sparrell, 4th Cpl.

Aldridge, William M., Pvt.
Bames, John, Pvt.
Benton, Jesse, Pvt.
Brigham, James S.A., Pvt.
Burdine, John, Pvt.
Butt, James W., 1st Sgt.
Callaghan, Thomas, Pvt.
Callis, Bailey, Pvt.
Caterson, James, Pvt.
Cherry, William, Pvt.
Cohen, Lewis, Pvt.
Conner, John, Pvt.
Corden, Elijah, Pvt.
Creekmur, Charles J., Pvt.
Cunningham, Frederick A., Pvt.
Donnell, John S., Pvt.
Forbes, John P., Pvt.
Gayle, Benjamin, Pvt.
Grimes, James, Pvt.
Grimes, Joshua, Pvt.
Hawkins, Nathaniel B., Pvt.
Howell, Richard S., Pvt.
James, William D., Pvt.
Johnson, Richard E., Pvt.
Lamb, Samuel, Pvt.
Lawrence, Christopher, Pvt.
Manning, William W., Pvt.
McCrady, Jeremiah, Pvt.
Miller, Samuel W., Pvt.
Morse, Daniel, Pvt.
Norfleet, Christopher, Pvt.

Orton, George W., Pvt.
Parker, Francis W., Cpl.
Pitts, Virginius L., Pvt.
Reed, William, Pvt.
Reynolds, Samuel, Pvt.
Shelling, John, Pvt.
Spencer, John, Pvt.
Spratt, James W., Pvt.
Tabb, Augustus G., Pvt.
Totten, Samuel, Pvt.
Turner, Henry, Pvt.
White, William, Pvt.
Whitson, James, Pvt.

**Died**
Rogers, Nathaniel G., 4th Sgt.
Boykin, Joseph, Pvt.
Dyes, Alexander, Pvt.
Gilmore, Charles, Pvt.
Joiner, William M., Pvt.
Moore, James E., Pvt.
Moss, James, Pvt.
Peel, Richard, Pvt.
Spratt, John T., Pvt.
Waples, Isaac, Pvt.

**Discharged**
Montague, Richd. T., 1st Cpl.
Boothe, Zerah, Pvt.
Beatty, Samuel J., Pvt.
Cherry, David, Pvt.
Edwards, Henry K., Pvt.
Haslay, John W., Pvt.
Moyer, John, Pvt.
Nottingham, William T., Pvt.
Peed, James W., Pvt.
Shinn, Thomas, Pvt.
Stewart. Edward G., Pvt.
Wilson, Francis S., Pvt.

**Transferred**
Pollard, James D., Pvt.
Williamson, Andrew, Pvt.

**Deserted**
Hinchman, John E., Pvt.
Miller, James, Pvt.

VIRGINIA VOLUNTEERS IN MEXICO

## Muster Roll of Company G, 1st Virginia Volunteer Infantry
### a.k.a. Captain Edward C. Carrington's Co. (Richmond)
### Final Muster Roll - Mexican War 1846-1848

Carrington, Edward C., Capt.
Porterfield, George A., 1st Lt.
Williamson, Henry W., 2nd Lt.
Dunn, Thomas H., 2nd Lt.
Peck, William F, 1st Sgt.
Murphy, William W., 2nd Sgt.
Womack, Abram N., 3rd Sgt.
Fitzhugh, Layfayette, 4th Sgt.
Starke, Richard, 1st Cpl.
Powell, Robert, 2nd Cpl.
Diddep, Archibal W., 3rd Cpl.
Grimes, Benjamin A., 4th Cpl.
Starke, Henry, Drummer

Alexander, George W., Pvt.
Armstrong, Richard, Pvt.
Banks, Albert A., Pvt.
Barry, Robert, Pvt.
Brown, John G., Pvt.
Burnett, Richard C., Pvt.
Carter, Zacariah, Pvt.
Coleman, John H., Pvt.
Converse, Farmer, Pvt.
Didlake, Andrew J., Pvt.
Fitzgugh, John H., Pvt.
Giles, George N., Pvt.
Goodwin, Henry, Pvt.
Gooslby, Thomas, Pvt.
Grant, William, Pvt.
Graves, John R., Pvt.
Hammond, Charles, Pvt.
Hoskins, Joseph, Pvt.
Hoskins, William A., Pvt.
Hubbard, George W., Pvt.
Hudnall, William, Pvt.
Jones, William A., Pvt.
Kidd, William E., Pvt.
Kolp, Henry, Pvt.
Lennox, John, Pvt.
Lynch, Joseph N., Pvt.
Minor, Philip B., Pvt.
Montgomery, Benjamin, Fifer
Neese, John M., Pvt.
Newhall, Charles G., Pvt.
O'Neil, Felix, Pvt.
Pavo, John, Pvt.
Powell, Edward, Pvt.

Price, Williamson C., Pvt.
Pullen, Romulus F., Pvt.
Sandifer, James, Pvt.
Schwitzer, Stephen, Pvt.
Scott, Joseph P., Pvt.
Snead, Samuel M., Pvt.
Waller, Thomas B., Pvt.
Ward, Nicholas, Pvt.
Watson, John F., Pvt.
Webster, Archibald, Pvt.
Williams, John W., Pvt.
Williams, William H.H., Pvt.

**Died**
Munford, Carlton R., 2nd Lt.
Barker, William, Pvt.
Driscoll, John A., Pvt.
Jones, Edward, Pvt.
Leard, Samuel, Pvt.
McAllister, William T., Pvt.
McNulty, Arthur, Pvt.
Woodruff, Hiram, Pvt.

**Discharged**
Lewellen, John R., 2nd Lt.
Akin, Edward, Pvt.
Beadles, Lewis J., Pvt.
Bradley, Philip A., Pvt.
English, John, Pvt.
King, Thomas F., Pvt.
Langford, William, Pvt.
Montgomery, Charles H., Pvt.
Moore, John, Pvt.
Otey, Van R., 1st Cpl.
Pleasants, Samuel S., Pvt.
Shell, John H., Pvt.
Simmons, Wesley C., Pvt.
Waller, John P., Pvt.
Wells, William H., Pvt.
Winfree, Thomas, Pvt.

**Deserted**
Kurt, John, 1st Sgt.
Ellis, Joseph, Pvt.
Fielder, Martin D., Pvt.
Gray, Layfayette W., Pvt.
Philips, Robert H., Pvt.
Riley, William, Pvt.
Wade, John, Pvt.
Wharton, Benjamin T., 4th Cpl.

# OFF TO WAR

## Muster Roll of Company H, 1st Virginia Volunteer Infantry
### a.k.a. Captain Ephraim G. Alburtis' Co.
### *Independent Blues*, (Berkeley Co.)
### Final Muster Roll - Mexican War 1846-1848

Alburtis, Ephraim G., Capt.
Otho, H. Harrison, 1st Lt.
Pollock, Robert, 2nd Lt.
Poisal, Daniel, 2nd Lt.
Maxwell, Edward W., 1st Sgt.
Reed, John C., 2nd Sgt.
Coontz, Thornton, 3rd Sgt.
Sherrard, William, 4th Sgt.
Keef, John W., 1st Cpl.
Miller, John Mc., 2nd Cpl.
Vanlier, John, 3rd Cpl.
Hooven, William, 4th Cpl.

Bennett, Anderson, Pvt.
Blessing, John H., Pvt.
Brown, John, Pvt.
Brown, William J., Pvt.
Cain, William C., Pvt.
Creamer, John Q., Pvt.
Crowl, Jacob, Pvt.
Dobb, Carlise, Pvt.
Dunn, William W., Pvt.
Erwin, Charles, Pvt.
Evans, James, Pvt.
Free, Henry S., Pvt.
Gainor, Robert, Pvt.
Gallaher, John S., Pvt.
Gordon, Aaron K., Pvt.
Grove, Lewis H., Pvt.
Hagan, Arthur, Pvt.
Harwood, James D., Pvt.
Heck, David, Pvt.
Heller, Josiah, Pvt.
Hodges, George, Pvt.
Hood, John W., Pvt.
Hooser, Francis W.M., Pvt.
Hunter, John H., Pvt.
Jamison, John, Pvt.
Johnson, Joseph, Pvt.
Kimley, William, Pvt.
Lewis, James, Pvt.
Loftin, Charles, Pvt.
Magee, Bernard, D., Pvt.
Mansford, Robert, Pvt.
Mason, Thompson, Pvt.
McCommack, William, Pvt.

McMinn, Joseph, Pvt.
Moore, Richard G., Pvt.
Ott, John H., Pvt.
Peace, James, Pvt.
Pentony, James, Pvt.
Reese, Jeremiah R., Pvt.
Rinor, Jacob, Pvt.
Robbins, George T., Pvt.
Seigler, William, Pvt.
Shank, Jacob, Pvt.
Shoemaker, William L., Pvt.
Sorber, William, Pvt.
Stewart, John P., Pvt.
Vanmetre, Abram G., Pvt.
Vauhorn, John C., Pvt.
Weast, George L., Pvt.
Williams, John R., Pvt.
Winter, Richard, Pvt.

**Died**
Blondell, Benjamin W., Fifer
Duffey, Andrew, Pvt.
Klein, Charles H., Pvt.
McCorkle, Alexander C., Pvt.
Prather, Socrates, Pvt.
Reamy, John T., Pvt.
Stephens, Richard H., Pvt.

**Discharged**
Chambers, George W., 2nd Lt.
Gray, David W., 2nd Lt.
Page, William H., 2nd Cpl.
Beales, John A., Pvt.
Blakney, George W., Pvt.
Brown, Peter A., Pvt.
Done, William D., Pvt.
Griffin, Andrew M., Pvt.
Heilfeinstein, Jacob H., Pvt.
Jones, John, Pvt.
Kisinger, Otho, Pvt.
Muny, John, Pvt.
Nopie, William, Pvt.
Peare, John, Pvt.
Vaden, Paskil, Pvt.
Whiteman, Charles, Pvt.
Wilhelm, Henry, Pvt.

**Deserted**
McGuire, Patrick, Pvt.

# VIRGINIA VOLUNTEERS IN MEXICO

## Muster Roll of Company I, 1st Virginia Volunteer Infantry
### a.k.a. Captain William B. Archer's Co.,
### *The Marshall Guard*[11] (Richmond)
### Final Muster Roll - Mexican War 1846-1848

Archer, William B., Capt.
Shumaker, Lindsay B., 1st Lt.
Keeling, Robert R., 2nd Lt.
Kellam, James S., 2nd Lt.
Scott, James A., 1st Sgt.
Crawford, Samuel, 2nd Sgt.
Henderson, Burton, 3rd Sgt.
Binford, John G., 4th Sgt.
Noble, Moses G., 1st Cpl.
Richardson, John, 2nd Cpl.
Hobson, Joseph M., 3rd Cpl.
Riggins, John J., 4th Cpl.

Acree, Edward H., Pvt.
Alexander, James, Pvt.
Austin, Augustus L., Pvt.
Baker, Jackson, Pvt.
Bailey, Richard B.H., Pvt.
Barnett, Anderson N., Pvt.
Bowles, Robert, Pvt.
Burks, William A., Pvt.
Cantor, Sydney S., Pvt.
Custer, Henry, Pvt.
Dixon, Henry, Pvt.
Ellett, Joseph E., Pvt.
Ellis, Obadiah, Pvt.
Gough, William, Pvt.
Goulden, Henry L. Pvt.
Green, Henry S., Pvt.
Hammons, Henry, Pvt.
Hayden, Franklin G., Pvt.
Harland, James, Pvt.
Henderson, Thomas D., Pvt.
Hogden, Ivory P., Pvt.
Hurst, Rhoten, Pvt.
Jennings, James, Pvt.
Jones, Charles R., Pvt.
Jones, Richard, Pvt.
Kennon, James, Pvt.
Kidd, William, Pvt.
Mills, William J., Pvt.

Neighbours, James, Pvt.
Russell, Ellerson, Pvt.
Spencer, John S., Pvt.
Stone, Augustus, Pvt.
Talley, Miles, Pvt.
Taylor, George, Pvt.
Taylor, William L., Pvt.
Walker, Benjamin J., Pvt.
Watson, John, Pvt.
Willis, John H., Pvt.
Woodrah, Joseph J., Pvt.
Wyatt, William C., Pvt.

**Died**
Boatright, Merrett W., Pvt.
Marshall, Charles H., Pvt.
Murray, James, Pvt.
Salmon, Charles G., Pvt.
Sweeney, William B., Pvt.

**Discharged**
Allen, William R., 2nd Lt.
Sandige, Joseph E., 1st Sgt.
Adams, Bartlett P., Pvt.
Clark, John A., Pvt.
Clark, Robert, Pvt.
Clarke, James L., Pvt.
Evans, John G., Pvt.
Francis, William T., Pvt.
Garrison, William B., Pvt.
Gennett, Samuel, Pvt.
Hannah, Musty, Pvt.
Holland, Thomas, Pvt.
Horne, Nicholas R., Pvt.
Howle, James, Pvt.
Logwood, Andrew J., Pvt.
Martin, William A., Pvt.
Snead, Jesse L., Pvt.
Weisiger, James L., Pvt.

**Deserted**
Marshall, Andrew J., Pvt.
Stanfield, Henderson, Pvt.
Wallace, Robert, Pvt.

# OFF TO WAR

## Muster Roll of Company K, 1st Virginia Volunteer Infantry
### a.k.a. Captain John William Rowan's Co. (Jefferson Co.)
### Final Muster Roll - Mexican War 1846-1848

Rowan, John William, Capt.
Avis, John, 1st Lt.
Washington, Lawrence B., 2nd Lt.
Gallaher, John W., 2nd Lt.
Ball, Lewis D. 1st Sgt.
Copeland, James R., 2nd Sgt.
Kendall, William, 3rd Sgt.
Poland, John F., 4th Sgt.
Heafer, Richard W., 1st Cpl.
Glasscock, David B., 2nd Cpl.
Harry, James, M., 3rd Cpl.
Douglass, Thos. H., Drummer

Baker, James H., Pvt.
Baker, William A., Pv. K
Ball, James B., Pvt. t., Co
Bateman, James W., Pvt.
Beam, Emanuel, Pvt.
Birkit, William, Pvt.
Boughn, Peter, Pvt.
Bradford, Benjamin H., Pvt.
Bragg, William F., Pvt.
Brock, John P., Pvt.
Cabell, Henry L., Pvt.
Cole, Fayette, Pvt.
Copenhafer, Andrew J., Pvt.
Davy, Henry, Pvt.
Evans, Joseph, Pvt.
Everett, Joseph L., Pvt.
Fairfax, George William, Pvt.
Gibson, Carter, Pvt.
Grandberry, John, Pvt.
Hampton, Joseph L., Pvt.
Heflin, John M., Pvt.
Henning, Joseph, Pvt.
Herrington, Dennis, Pvt.
Hillard, William, Pvt.
Hogan, John F., Pvt.
Howell, John V., Pvt.
Howell, Morriss B., Pvt.
Hurst, Stephen D., Pvt.
Jones, Joseph, Pvt.
Kennedy, John T., Pvt.
Kile, George W., Pvt.

Lancaster, Beverley W., Pvt.
Mack, George W., Pvt.
McClure, William C., Pvt.
McKay, Pilate, Pvt.
McKinney, James W., Pvt.
Miller, Peter, Pvt.
Mindenall, Elijah L., Pvt.
Neighbors, Christopher, Pvt.
Seabright, James C., Pvt.
Sheets, John William, Pvt.
Shelling Barnardt, Pvt.
Shinault, James, Pvt.
Shipman, William P., Pvt.
Shryock, James F., Pvt.
Thompson, James, Pvt.
Vonreason, Henry G., Pvt.
Wall, Treadwell S., Pvt.
Watson, David H., Pvt.
Whiting, John B., Pvt.
Wood, Andrew J., Pvt.

**Died**
Booker, Peter, Pvt.
Bryant, William, Pvt.
Bush, Vance W., Pvt.
Gallenar, Henry, Pvt.
Kirk, William, Pvt.
McCrory, Thomas, Pvt.

**Discharged**
McCormick, William, 2nd Lt.
Duke, James W., 2nd Sgt.
English, John M., 3rd Sgt.
Cunningham, John, Fifer
Barr, Cornelius P., Pvt.
Carlin, Cornelius, Pvt.
Ellis, Samuel, Pvt.
French, Charles, Pvt.
Gover, William C., Pvt.
Harding, John A.B., Pvt.
Meyer, Joseph, Pvt.
Thompson, Charles M., Pvt.
Waddell, Charles, Pvt.

**Deserted**
Satterfield, Thomas R., Pvt.

# VIRGINIA VOLUNTEERS IN MEXICO

## Muster Roll of Company L, 1st Virginia Volunteer Infantry
### a.k.a. *Fairfax's Co., Thrift's Co., 13th Co.* (Fairfax Co.)
### Final Muster Roll - Mexican War
### March 18th, 1847 - July 27th, 1848

Thrift, James, Capt.
Dulaney, James H., 1st Lt.
Herbert, Upton H., 2nd Lt.
Moore, Thomas, 2nd Lt.
Bishop, Charles, 1st Sgt.
Waldon, James F., 2nd Sgt.
Thrift, Benjamin F., 3rd Sgt.
Burke, Abdon L., 4th Sgt.
Davis, Augustus, 1st Cpl.
White, George W., 2nd Cpl.
Moore, John L., 3rd Cpl.
Day, James, 4th Cpl.

Ballenger, John, Pvt.
Brown, Andrew, Pvt.
Brown, Samuel, Pvt.
Bruce, Winfield S., Pvt.
Byrnes, John, Pvt.
Churchill, James, Pvt.
Dantt, William T., Pvt.
Day, John, Pvt.
Dyer, Robert, Pvt.
Dykes, Joel R., Pvt.
Evans, Henry, Pvt.
Evans, John, Pvt.
Gately, Patrick, Pvt.
Givens, James E., Pvt.
Griffith, James, Pvt.
Gunnell, John R., Pvt.
Hagan, William, Pvt.
Haines, Charles F., Pvt.
Hamilton, Edward L., Pvt.
Jenkins, William H., Pvt.
Kerr, George, Pvt.
Kitchen, Caleb, Pvt.
Lakeman, Abner J., Pvt.
Lindsay, Opie, Pvt.
Mansell, James J., Pvt.
McDonald, John A., Pvt.
Millan, James R., Pvt.
Mills, Armistead S., Pvt.
Mills, Henry, Pvt.
O'Bannon, Dagobert B., Pvt.
Patterson, Charles, Pvt.

Ratcliffe, Thomas, Pvt.
Richards, George F., Pvt.
Richards, Henry C., Pvt.
Richards, John R., Pvt.
Robey, William, Pvt.
Sheckles, Samuel, Pvt.
Smith, Abijah B., Pvt.
Smith, James L., Pvt.
Stark, Ebenezer E., Pvt.
Waugh, John, Pvt.
Wilson, Frances S., Pvt.
Wren, Charles B., Pvt.
Wright, John T., Pvt.

**Died**
Fairfax, Henry, Capt.
Mills, Mahlon, Pvt.
Mills, Robert, Pvt.
Trott, Samuel, Pvt.
West, Charles, Pvt.

**Discharged**
Richard, Young, 2nd Lt.
Barnard, John B. F., Pvt.
Bennett, John A., Pvt.
Berry, Thomas, Pvt.
Clemments, James H., Pvt.
Conroy, James J., Pvt.
Corrie, William W., Pvt.
Creamer, Jacob, Pvt.
Dean, James, Pvt.
Deneal, James C., Pvt.
Eaton, Henry, Pvt.
Fenwick, Maury, Pvt.
Hull, John, Pvt.
Kelly, William, Pvt.
Kennedy, Charles, Pvt.
McCoy, George M., Pvt.
Steward, James, Pvt.
Tuttle, Joseph, Pvt.
West, James, Pvt.

**Deserted**
Bryant, Richard, Cpl.
Allen, William, Pvt.
Gardner, James, Pvt.
Newall, James, Pvt.

OFF TO WAR

Muster Roll of Company M, 1st Virginia Volunteer Infantry
a.k.a. Captain William A. Talbott's Co. (Lynchburg)
Final Muster Roll - Mexican War 1846-1848

Talbott, William A., Capt.
Scott, William A., 1st Lt.
Pleasants, William H., 2nd Lt.
Folks, Robert W., 2nd Lt.
Stagg, John F., 1st Sgt.
Johnson, Joseph A., 2nd Sgt.
Willis, Richard D., 3rd Sgt.
Flagg, Thomas, G., 4th Sgt.
Brown, William C., 1st Cpl.
Edmundson, Upton A., 2nd Cpl.
Featherstone, John R., 3rd Cpl.
Lee, Robert W., 4th Cpl.
Vallett, Francis, Musician
Wilkes, Reuben B., Musician

Boswell, William C., Pvt.
Booker, William T., Pvt.
Breeden, Bartlett, Pvt.
Burke, William H., Pvt.
Beck, Jacob, Pvt.
Bowers, Samuel, Pvt.
Brown, Jesse P., Pvt.
Carney, George W., Pvt.
Chick, George W., Pvt.
Cropp, Alexander J., Pvt.
Clark, John, Pvt.
Crowder, A.M., Pvt.
Comerford, John, Pvt.
Cotton, John, Pvt.
Donevant, William E., Pvt.
Dixon, Charles C., Pvt.
Etheridge, Nelson C., Pvt.
Eustace, D.M., Pvt.
Eaves, James H., Pvt.
Fraizer, John D., Pvt.
Folks, Algernon R., Pvt.
Foster, Elijah, Pvt.
Garther, Edward, Pvt.
Goodwin, John L., Pvt.
Golden, George W., Pvt.
Goodwyn, Washington, Pvt.
Hammock, Lewis, Pvt.
Halsey, George W., Pvt.
Humphreys, John R., Pvt.
Jones, Thomas R., Pvt.
Johnson, Francis A., Pvt.
Johnson, John A., Pvt.
Jenkins, John, Pvt.
Jones, Edward W., Pvt.
Johnson, William H., Pvt.

Lucado, Edwin T., Pvt.
Miller, Jacob G., Pvt.
Miller, John, Pvt.
Marable, Thomas F., Pvt.
Manson, Josiah, Pvt.
Meador, Albert, Pvt.
Moss, James O., Pvt.
Nicholson, John W., Pvt.
Organ, John T., Pvt.
Outland, Richard W., Pvt.
Olcott, Henry B., Pvt.
Pinnell, Joseph J.W., Pvt.
Parrish, William N., Pvt.
Phillips, Robert H., Pvt.
Pevenlly, Anthony, Pvt.
Powers, Walter, Pvt.
Robertson, D.S., Pvt.
Stafford, William H., Pvt.
Savage, Paul L., Pvt.
Scott, William H., Pvt.
Smith, James, Pvt.
Tiffin, Joseph, Pvt.
Wingfield, Albert G., Pvt.
Wilson, Peter H., Pvt.
Warden, James, Pvt.
Whitlock, Robert A., Pvt.
Wills, William, Pvt.
Wilks, Benjamin W., Pvt.
Williams, Thomas R., Pvt.
Willis, Ira, Pvt.
Yates, William M., Pvt.

**Died**
Bowen, Jesse P., Pvt.
Johnson, William H., Pvt.
Waterman, James A., Pvt.

**Discharged**
Astrop, Robert F., 2nd Lt.
Wallace, Sterling L., 3rd Cpl.
Bain, James H.H., Pvt.
Bradley, Jesse P., Pvt.
Hammond, Otis, Pvt.
Muloy, Francis P., Pvt.
White, David M., Pvt.
Wiglesworth, Ed L., Pvt.

**Deserted**
Diamond, John, Pvt.
Dillard, John Q.A., Pvt.
Taylor, John, Pvt.
Thorpe, Henry, Pvt.

# VIRGINIA VOLUNTEERS IN MEXICO

## Muster Roll of Harper's Light Infantry Co., 1st Virginia Volunteer Infantry
### a.k.a. Captain Kenton Harper's Co. (Augusta Co.)
### Final Muster Roll - Mexican War 1846-1848

Harper, Kenton, Capt.
Kinney, Robert Henry, 1st Lt.
Geiger, Vincent Epley, 2nd Lt.
Harmon, William Henry, 2nd Lt.
Allen, George W., 1st Sgt.
Ball, Charles H., 2nd Sgt.
Blackburn, William, 3rd Sgt.
Merritt, Christian Garber, 4th Sgt.
Poage, Alpheus W., 1st Cpl.
Chase, Abel D., 2nd Cpl.
Tar, Abram, 3rd Cpl.
Harlan, George, 4th Cpl.

Alexander, George, Pvt.
Bailey, John, Pvt.
Bibelby, James, Pvt.
Bickle, William O., Pvt.
Bishop, Joseph M., Jr., Pvt.
Carroll, William, Pvt.
Cole, Richard, Pvt.
Dubecq, John, Pvt.
Dunlap, William, Pvt.
Eyrse, William G., Pvt.
Fisher, Addison, Pvt.
Goens, William, Pvt.
Gordon, Archibald A., Pvt.
Graham, James S., Pvt.
Gregory, Augustus A., Pvt.
Harrow, Morgan, Pvt.
Helms, Samuel, Pvt.
Hull, William H., Pvt.
Hulvey, Guy H., Pvt.
Illick, Jacob, Pvt.
Johnson, Isaac W., Pvt.
Johnson, Richard, Pvt.
Johnson, Samuel, Pvt.
Knowles, John, Pvt.
Kurtz, Isaac, Pvt.
Lavall, Owen C., Pvt.
Logan, John J., Pvt.
Long, William, Pvt.
Mellon, Alexander C., Pvt.
Pelter, James T., Pvt.
Robertson, William C., Pvt.
Searl, Samuel, Pvt.
Shackelford, Andrew J., Pvt.
Skeen, William E., Pvt.
Sly, William M., Pvt.
Smead, Robert L., Pvt.
Smith, Jonathan, Pvt.
Steel, John H., Pvt.
Stoffer, Daniel A., Pvt.
Taylor, William G., Pvt.
Terrell, Greenberry B., Pvt.
Wade, Samuel P., Pvt.
Wilson, Samuel W., Pvt.

**Died**
Imboden, Benjamin F., 4th Cpl.
Bowles, John, Pvt.
Brown, James B., Pvt.
Grove, Alexander, Pvt.
Hurt, Moses, Pvt.
Lambert, Henry, Pvt.
Long, Jacob, Pvt.
Peck, Israel, Pvt.
Simes, Miles, Pvt.
Terrell, Lewis K., Pvt.

**Discharged**
Clarke, Lewis H., 2nd Cpl.
Britt, George W., Pvt.
Brown, Preston, Pvt.
Crist, Andrew, Pvt.
Emerson, John, Pvt.
Eyrse, James W., Pvt.
Ferguson, William, Pvt.
Gladwell, Valentine, Pvt.
Goens, James, Pvt.
Hoffman, Arington, Pvt.
Miller, William, Pvt.
Noon, Hugh D., Pvt.
Parent, John S., Pvt.
Peer, John, Pvt.
Powers, James, Pvt.
White, Cyrus C., Pvt.

# OFF TO WAR

## Muster Roll of Preston's Co. of Grenadiers, 1st Virginia Volunteer Infantry
### a.k.a. Capt. James Francis Preston's Co. (Montgomery Co.)
### Mexican War 1846-1847

Preston, James Francis, Capt.
Gardner, Fleming, 1st Lt.
Stanger, Henry S., 2nd Lt.
Wade, James M., 2nd Lt.
Newlee, Robert G., 1st Sgt.
Moyers, James Harvey, 2nd Sgt.
Linkous, Benjamin R. 3rd Sgt.
Bowers, Patterson, 4th Sgt.
Keister, George A., 1st Cpl.
Willis, Charles S., 2nd Cpl.
Henderson, William T., 3rd Cpl.
Tucker, George W., 4th Cpl.
Sheaf, George W., Drummer

Akers, Wyatt, Pvt.
Argabright, John, Pvt.
Austin, Robert, Pvt.
Barnett, Thomas R., Pvt.
Barringer, John A., Pvt.
Bennett, William G., Pvt.
Black, Harvey, Pvt.
Blackard, Joel, Pvt.
Boles, William T., Pvt.
Campbell, George, Pvt.
Carter, Alexander, Pvt.
Chandler, Greenbery, Pvt.
Clifton, Andrew J., Pvt.
Clingenpeel, Pleasant H., Pvt.
Collins, Henry, Pvt.
Collins, John, Pvt.
Cox, John W., Pvt.
Davis, Jehu, Pvt.
Dudley, George B., Pvt.
Falconer, George, Pvt.
Falconer, John F., Pvt.
Foukhowitzer, John N., Pvt.
Gaines, Thomas W., Pvt.
Gardner, Robert Davison, Pvt.
Gibson, John, Pvt.
Gilmore, Thomas, Pvt.
Henderson, Thomas, Pvt.
Howard, Tazewell, Pvt.
Howell, Lorenzo D., Pvt.
Jackson, Charles, Pvt.
Johnson, Charles Y., Pvt.
Johnson, William R., Pvt.
Jones, Benson W., Pvt.
Kipps, Michael, Pvt.
Lee, Charles, Pvt.
Miller, Joseph, Pvt.
Minnick, John H., Pvt.
Moore, Philip A., Pvt.
Murray, Lewis, Pvt.
Pendergrass, Sylvester G., Pvt.
Phillips, Alexander, Pvt.
Ronald, Charles A., Pvt.
Roop, Byrd, Pvt.
Shell, Henry B., Pvt.
Simpkins, William D., Pvt.
Simpson, James R., Pvt.
Stevens, Crawford B., Pvt.
Stevens, Harvey B., Pvt.
Stuart, John H., Pvt.
Talley, Crofford A., Pvt.
Tankersley, George W., Pvt.
Taylor, George William, Pvt.
Tucker, William, Pvt.
Wall, Harvey, Pvt.
Young, John L., Pvt.

**Died**
Davis, James P., 3rd Cpl.
Black, William A., Pvt.
Harmon, Daniel, Pvt.
Lindsey, Stephen, Pvt.
Linkous, William B., Pvt.
Manson, John L., Pvt.
Muirhead, James W., Pvt.
Starr, John W., Pvt.
Trump, James N., Pvt.
Weeks, James, Pvt.
Yopp, William, Pvt.

**Discharged**
Bridges, Morgan M., Pvt.
Brittle, William, Pvt.
Elliott, Curtis, Pvt.
Farris, Jeremiah, Pvt.
Lawrence, John E., Pvt.
Lee, James, Pvt.
Linkous, Crockett, Pvt.
Lorton, Robert, Pvt.
McDaniel, Reuben, Pvt.
Roop, Crocket, Pvt.
Rose, Uriah
Silvers, William, Pvt.
Short, Calvin R., Pvt.
Stow, Lemuel C., Pvt.
Taylor, James C., Pvt.

**Deserted**
Cassaday, John N., Pvt.

# VIRGINIA VOLUNTEERS IN MEXICO

## Muster Roll of Recruits, 1$^{st}$ Virginia Volunteer Infantry

### Mexican War 1846-1847

Tymeson, J.P., 1$^{st}$ Cpl.
Ayers, William, Pvt.
Bowyer, John P., Pvt.
Boyer, Silas, Pvt.
Brigedine, John, Pvt.
Carter, James J., Pvt.
Castleman, Nathaniel Green, Pvt.
Charlton, Walter D., Pvt.
Cowen, George W., Pvt.
Crafton, James E., Pvt.
Crane, John H., Pvt.
Crossley, John, Pvt.
Davis, Charles P., Pvt.
Dodge, Richard, Pvt.
Duckwiler, Daniel, Pvt.
Dudley, Winston P., Pvt.
East, John, Pvt.
Ewald, Stephen, Pvt.
Gallager, John, Pvt.
Garnett, John, Pvt.
Green, John, Pvt.
Grubb, Hiram, Pvt.
Grubb, James, Pvt.
Hamilton, Alfred A., Pvt.
Hines, William S., Pvt.
Jackson, Robert, Pvt.
Johnson, John, Pvt.
Johnson, Vincent, Pvt.
King, John, Pvt.
Kisner, Ashford, Pvt.
Mays, Mortimer N., Pvt.
Merrick, John W., Pvt.
Moore, William, Pvt.
Ourey, Robert V., Pvt.
Painter, James C., Pvt.
Painter, Stewart D., Pvt.
Philips, Alfred, Pvt.
Pickett, Rufus, Pvt.
Pulman, William, Pvt.
Reed, John D., Pvt.
Riley, David, Pvt.
Sanders, Robert H., Pvt.
Shepherd, J. Newton, Pvt.
Shriver, William, Pvt.
Sinclair, James H., Pvt.
Sine, Lorenzo D., Pvt.
Sira, Nicholas, Pvt.
Smith, Edmond P., Pvt.
Stout, William, Pvt.
Talbert, William R., Sgt.

Talley, Crawford A., Pvt. *
Taylor, Jordon, Pvt.
Thomson, James, Pvt.
Wade, Reuben A., Pvt.
Warden, John M., Pvt.
Warden, Johnson B., Pvt.
Weaver, Isaac, Pvt.
Wilbourn, William R., Pvt.
Wolford, William R., Pvt.
Young, Christopher Clarke, Pvt.
Young, George W., Pvt.
**Died**
Conrad, Henry K., Pvt.
Krumbein, Henry, Pvt.
**Discharged**
Cooper, Albert, Pvt.
Crafton, G. Washington, Pvt.
Evans, Montgomery, Pvt.
Ford, James B., Pvt.
Shepperson, George C.P., Pvt.
Terrell, John J., Pvt.
Thornton, Henry F., Pvt.
Williams, Isaac D., Pvt.
**Deserted**
Colin, William, Pvt.


* See Preston's Co.

OFF TO WAR

**Acree, Edward H.**, Pvt., Co. I; b. c. 1820; enl. Mex. War service 02/15/1847 Richmond, VA, age 27; pres. 02/1847; pres. 04/1847; in confinement 06/1847; pres. 08/1847; pres. 10/1847, pay stopped for: 3 cotton shirts-$1.72, 3 pr. drawers-$1.06$^{1/2}$, 1 pr. shoes-$1.22, 1 pr. socks-$.24$^{1/2}$, 1 cap-$.95$^{1/2}$; pres. 12/1847, pay stopped for: 1 pr. socks-$.24$^{1/2}$, 1 jacket-$2.66, 2 cotton shirts-$.86; pres. 02/1848; pres. 04/1848; pres. 08/1848, pay stopped for: 1 pr. shoes-$1.22, BLW sent to Richmond, VA; c. 1860 res. Ashland, Hanover Co., VA, age 41, occ. Carpenter;[12] Civil War service enl. Pvt., Co. K, 56$^{th}$ VA Inf., 08/06/1861 at Mechanicsville, VA, AWOL 08/31/1861, pres. 10/1861, captured Ft. Donelson, d. 04/06/1862 of pneumonia at Indianapolis, Ind., bur. Green Lawn Cem., reinterred Crown Hill Cem.[13]

**Acton, John**, Pvt., Co. B; enl. 11/20/1846, Alexandria, VA, age 20; pres. 06/1847; pres. 08/1847; pres. 10/1847, pay stopped for: 2 pr. shoes-$2.44, 3 cotton shirts-$1.29, 1 pr. overalls-$2.28, 2 pr. socks-$.49, 2 pr. cotton drawers-$.71; pres. 12/1847, pay stopped for: 1 pr. overalls-$2.28, 1 cap-$.95$^{1/2}$, 2 flannel shirts-$1.80, 2 pr. socks-$.49, 1 blanket-$2.22; pres. 02/1848; pres. 04/1848; pres. 08/1848, pay stopped for: 1 bayonet scabbard-$.56, 1 waist belt-$.21, 1 waist belt plate-$.12, BLW sent to Alexandria, VA

**Adams, Bartlett P.**, Pvt., Co. I; b. Richmond, VA;[14] m. Hyphasia Cook, 12/1840, Garysburg, Northampton Co., NC; enl. Mex. War service 01/10/1847 Richmond, VA, phys. desc. age 27, b. Richmond, VA, occ. Butcher, 5'8", dark hair, dark eyes, light complexion;[14] pres. 02/1847; pres. 04/1847; discharged 05/15/1847 for disability at camp near Monterey, Mex.; c. 1850 res. Henrico Co., VA, age 30, occ. Butcher, w. Henrietta (28), dau. Sarah E. (8), dau. Mary A. (4);[15] c. 1860 res. Richmond, Henrico Co., VA, age 38, occ. Clerk, w. Hyphasia (38), dau. Sarah E. (17), dau. Mary A. (13), dau. Alice J. (9), dau. ??? (3);[16] d. 12/11/1886, *"consumption,"* 712 17$^{th}$ St., Richmond, VA, bur. Shockoe Hill Cemetery, Richmond, VA;[14] wid. Hyphasia; WC #214 02/26/1887 filed from 712 17$^{th}$ St., Richmond, VA; since discharge res. Richmond, VA; Four children, two of which are Mollie Adams and Alice Adams Johnston;[14] (HCA d. 07/17/1905, bur. Oakwood Cemetery, Richmond, VA).[14]

**Adams, Joseph C.**, Pvt., Co. D; enl. Mex. War service 01/04/1847, Petersburg, VA, age 22; pres. 02/1847; pres. 04/1847; pres. but sick 04/1847; d. 07/20/1847 Buena Vista, Mex.

**Adams, St. Lawrence**, Pvt., Co. D; b. 12/19/1827, Philadelphia, Pa., son of David & Elizabeth Adams;[17, 18]enl. Mex. War service 12/20/1846, Petersburg, VA, age 19; pres. 02/1847; absent 04/1847 sick, sent from Camargo, Mex. to Hosp. Matamoros, Mex. 03/29/1847; discharged 06/05/1847 Monterey, Mex. on Surgeon's Certificate of Disability; m Harriet Andrews 09/07/1858, Petersburg, Va;[17] c. 1860 res. Petersburg, Dinwiddie Co., VA, age 32, occ. none listed, w. Harriet (21);[19] Civil War service enl. Pvt., Co. C, 18$^{th}$ Btln. VA Arty, 06/01/1861 at Petersburg, VA, pres. through 06/30/1862, discharged 08/31/1862;[20] conscripted 01/01/1863 as Pvt., Co. D, 12$^{th}$ Va. Inf. at Petersburg, VA, b. 1828, res. Plum St., Petersburg, VA between Cross and Canal Sts., illiterate, joined regt. 08/14/1863, absent sick 04/1864;[21] SC #5231, filed from Petersburg, Dinwiddie Co.; phys. desc. 5'8", light complexion, blue eyes, grayish hair, occ. Huckster; Pvts. John Totty & Thomas J. McCaleb gave affidavit in pension claim;[17] d. 06/05/1887, *"pneumonitis,"* bur. Blandford Cem., Sq. 4, Sec. 31, Ward D, Petersburg, VA;[22, 23] wid. Harriet, WC #4387, 03/22/1888, filed from Petersburg, Dinwiddie Co., VA; (HAA d. 10/15/1896).[22]

**Aiken, James H.**, Pvt., Co. E; b. c. 1824, Petersburg, VA; enl. Mex. War service 11/30/1846 Petersburg, VA, age 23; pres. 04/1847; pres. 06/1847; absent 08/1847 furloughed 07/24/1847 for 3 mos. due to the death of his father;[24] a request for discharge was sent to the Sec. of War in order that Pvt. Aiken may attend to his fathers estate.[24] This in turn was forwarded to Col. Hamtramck who argued against the discharge, *"His furlough was consented to only in consideration of the state of his affairs, consequent upon the death of his father, with the assurance that two months would be all he would require, at which time he would certainly return."*[25] absent 10/1847 furloughed 3 mos.; absent 12/1847 on furlough; desc., age 23, 5'7", light complexion, light eyes, light hair, occ. Farmer; discharged 01/15/1848, by order Sec. of

## VIRGINIA VOLUNTEERS IN MEXICO

War;[26] m. Josepha Allevia Cunningham 05/12/1853 St. Charles, St. Charles Co., Mo.;[27, 28] SC #84, 02/12/1887 filed from Broadway St., Hannibal, Marion Co., Mo.; phys. desc. 5'7" light complexion, light hair, bluish-gray eyes; since discharge res. Wyandotte, KS, Warren Co., St. Charles Co., and Marion Co., Mo.; d. 06/09/1893, *"heart failure,"* Montgomery City, Montgomery Co., Mo.;[27] wid. Josepha A., WC #8844, 06/19/1893, filed from Prospect Ave., Buffalo, Erie Co., NY; (JAA b. 08/06/1834, d. 08/09/1911).

**Akers, Wyatt**, Pvt., *Preston's Co.*; b. 12/16/1828, Montgomery Co., VA, son of James & Eliza (Thompson) Akers;[29, 30] enl. Mex. War service 12/06/1846 Montgomery Co., VA, age 20; pres. 04/1847; sick 06/1847; sick 08/1847; pres. 10/1847, pay stopped for: 1 jacket-$2.66, 2 pr. socks-$.49, 1 cap-$.95$^{1/2}$; pres. 12/1847, pay stopped for: 1 pr. overalls-$2.28, 1 pr. shoes-$1.22, 1 pr. drawers-$.35$^{1/2}$, 2 blankets-$4.44; pres. 02/1848; pres. 04/1848, pay stopped for: 1 pick & brush-$.12; pres. 07/1848; BLW sent to Christiansburg, VA c/o Fleming Gardner; c. 1850 res. Montgomery Co., VA, age 22, occ. Farmer;[31] c. 1860 res. Christiansburg, Montgomery Co., VA, age 32, occ. Farmer, w. Julia (23), dau. Laura J. (5), son General Wade (4), son David G. (1), dau. Not Named (6/12);[32] m. Julia Ann Muncy, 03/30/1861, Floyd Co., VA;[30] Civil War service a Wyatt M. Akers, enl. Pvt., Capt. A.E. Reed's Co., Hvy. Arty. 03/24/62, pd. $50 bounty, trans. to Co. B, 19$^{th}$ Btln. VA Hvy. Arty., 04/12/1862 at Richmond, VA, discharged 08/31/1862 under Conscription Act;[33] SC #7790, 03/07/1887, filed from Floyd Co., VA; phys. desc. 6'2$^{1/2}$", dark complexion, black eyes, black hair, occ. Farmer;[30] since discharge res. Montgomery Co., and Floyd Co., VA;[30] wid. Julia A., WC #16084, 04/11/1914, filed from Tindall, Floyd Co., VA; BLW #4044f-160-47; d. 01/16/1914, *"cystitis,"* near Basham, Tindall, Floyd Co., VA;[34] Lists children Liza Akers b. 04/1864, Harry Akers b. 03/1863, Lou Emma Akers b. 04/1864, Aicha Lu Akers b. 05/1865, Bailey R. Akers b. 04/1866, H.W. Akers b. 03/1867, Furley Mary Akers b. 04/1868;[34] (JMA b. 12/25/1836, Locust Grove, Floyd Co., VA; d. 1923).[34]

**Akin, Edward**, Pvt., Co. G; enl. Mex. War service 12/07/1846 Richmond, VA, age 22; absent 06/1847 left sick in Hosp. at Monterey, Mex.; discharged 08/11/1847 Monterey, Mex., on Surgeon's Certificate of Disability, due to *"chronic diarrhea."*[35]

**Albertson, Harvey**, Pvt., Co. C; b. 01/11/1826 Philadelphia, Pa.; enl. U.S. Navy 08/10/1841 at Philadelphia Navy Yard as 2$^{nd}$ Class Cabin Boy, served on Battleship *U.S.S. North Carolina*, trans. Steam Frigate *U.S.S. Missouri "which sailed to Gibraltar and was there destroyed by fire 08/26/1843,"* sailed to Boston, Mass. on *U.S.S. Ohio*, trans. to Sloop of War *U.S.S. Plymouth*, discharged 08/30/1847 at Philadelphia, Pa., enl. Mex. War service 12/30/1846, Bowling Green, VA, age 20, occ. Sailor; pres. 06/1847; pres. 08/1847, pay stopped for: 1 cap-$.95$^{1/2}$, 2 pr. socks-$.49, 2 cotton shirts-$.86, 2 woolen shirts-$1.80, 1 pr. shoes-$1.22; pres. 10/1847, pay stopped for: 2 pr. socks-$.49, 2 pr. drawers-$.71, 1 pr. pants-$2.28, 2 woolen shirt-$1.80, 1 pr. shoes-$1.22;, 1 great coat-$6.93$^{1/2}$; pres. 12/1847, pay stopped for: over pay 1.22, 1 pr. pants-$2.28, 1 pr. shoes-$1.22; pres. 04/1848, pay stopped for: 1 flannel shirt-$.90, 1 pr. shoes-$1.22; 1 jacket-$2.66, 1 pr. shoes-$1.50, 1 haversack-$.20$^{3/4}$, 1 india rubber canteen-$.27; pres. 08/1848, BLW sent to Philadelphia, Pa., c/o John Hancock; Went West *"worked his way down the Mississippi until he reached Pensacola, Fla.,"* enl. U.S. Navy 06/01/1849 at Pensacola, Fla. as Ordinary Seaman, treated for diarrhea at Pensacola Naval Hosp. 1849, discharged 09/30/1849 as *"incurable,"* admitted Pittsburgh, Pa. Hosp. 1850, diarrhea, Philadelphia, Pa. Hosp. in summer 1850, Broadway, N.Y. in winter 1850. Went to California Spring 1851. Returned to Philadelphia, Pa. 1853. Resided Philadelphia 1853-1858. Resided California 1858-1867; took oath of allegiance near Sacramento, Calif. during Civil War. Returned to Philadelphia, Pa. 1867;[36] SC #9630, 04/05/1887 filed from 2221 S. Broad St., Philadelphia, PA; Pvt. John Roach, of 2212 Hare St., Philadelphia, Pa. and Pvt. Thomas S. Mahan of 1912 Jefferson St., Philadelphia, Pa. gave affidavits in Pension Claim;[37] OW IA #23006, rejected.

## OFF TO WAR

**Alburtis, Ephraim Gaither**, Capt., Co. H; b. 07/06/1817;[38] Editor of the *Martinsburg Gazette*; m. Mary C. Swartz 12/20/1842, Williamsport, MD;[39] enl. Mex. War service 11/21/1846, Matrinsburg, VA; pres. 04/1847; pres. 06/1847; pres. 08/1847; pres. 10/1847; pres. 12/1847; pres. 02/1848; absent 03/14/1848 on furlough; honorably discharged 06/20/1848; mbr. and *Standard Bearer*, Palestine Encampment No. 9, Knights Templar, Martinsburg, VA;[40] c. 1860 res. Martinsburg, Berkeley Co., VA, age 43, occ. Clerk of the Circuit Court, w. Mary C. (34), dau. Mary L. (14), dau. Nancy (12), dau. Rosa (10), dau. Josina (9), dau. Amelia (7), son James L. (3), dau. Jane R. 7/12;[41] Civil War service enl. as a Capt., Co. B, Wise Artillery 10/1859, resigned 01/25/1862 by reason of ill health, employed as Clerk in Qtr. Master Dept.; d. 03/21/1875, bur. Green Hill Cem., Martinsburg, WV;[42] c. 1880 wid. Mary C. (54) res. Martinsburg, Berkeley Co. WV, dau. Rosalie (25), dau. Amelie (23), dau. Jane (19), dau. Eva (16), s-i-l John Mattingly (46) Machinist, dau. Marie Mattingly (30);[43] d. 03/21/1875, Martinsburg, WV, bur. Green Hill Cem. Martinsburg, WV;[39, 44, 45] wid. Mary C., WC #3037 11/17/1887, file from Martinsburg, Berkeley Co., WV; Edward W. Maxwell and John W. Keef gave affidavits in pension claim;[39] (MSA b. 11/02/1825, Martinsburg, VA, d. 08/28/1897);[39] bro. Capt. William Alburtis, 2nd U.S. Inf. KIA at the Battle of Vera Cruz.[46]

**Aldridge, William M.**, Co. F; b. 10/08/1826, Simpson's, Floyd Co., VA; enl. Mex. War service 09/01/1847 Fayette C.H., VA; went from Fayette C.H. to Staunton, VA;[47] mustered 01/27/1848, age 20, from Regtl. Depot; pres. 02/1848; absent 04/1848 on extra duty at Hosp. in Saltillo, Mex.; pres. 08/1848, BLW sent to Portsmouth, VA c/o E.T. Blamire; m/1 Lucy Ann Aldridge 11/08/1849, Copper Hill, Floyd Co., VA (1st cousins);[47, 48] c. 1860 res. Floyd Co., VA, age 33, occ. Farmer, w. Lucy A. (29), dau. Joanna (6), son Asa H. (4), Isaac M (2), Mary C. (6 mos.);[49] SC #6946, 05/19/1887, filed from Simpsons, Floyd Co., VA; states since discharge res. Fayette C.H. 12 mos. and for the last 28 years about $1^{1/2}$ miles north of Simpsons P.O., Floyd Co., VA;[47] phys. desc. 5'8", light complexion, light hair, blue eyes;[47] Wyatt Akers gave affidavit in pension claim;[47] (LAA b. 05/06/1835, d. 04/07/1889, bur. Salem Church Cemetery, Floyd Co., VA); m/2 Letitia A. Williams Hudson; 11/12/1895, Franklin C.H., Franklin Co., VA;[47, 50] applied for a pension increase 1897 and lists children: Joanna, age 43, Asa H., age 41, Isaac M., age 39, Mary C., age 37, Lucy J., age 35, Laura, age 33, John H.C., age 31, Octavia, age 29, Ballis, age 27, Gertrude, age 22;[47] c. 1900 res. Locust Grove District, Floyd Co., VA, age 73, w. Lutitia A. (62);[51] (LAWA b. 08/02/1837, d. 06/13/1911, bur. Salem Church Cemetery, Floyd Co., VA;[45] *"stricken down helpless on the 8th day of June 1912;"*[47] d. 08/14/1914, *"apoplexy,"* at the home of his son John H.C. Aldridge; bur. Salem Church, *"of which he was a member many years ago,"* Floyd Co., VA[47]

**Alexander, George**, Pvt., LIC; b. 03/1825 near Waynesboro, Augusta Co., VA;[52] enl. Mex. War service 12/12/1846 Staunton, VA, age 19; pres. 06/1847; pres. 08/1847; pres. 10/1847, pay stopped for: 1 forage cap-$.95$^{1/2}$, 1 wool jacket-$2.66, 1 pr. overalls-$2.28, 3 cotton shirts-$1.29, 2 pr. shoes-$2.44, 2 pr. socks-$.49, 1 pr. drawers-$.35$^{1/2}$, 1 blanket-$2.22; absent 12/1847, sick in quarters, pay stopped for: 1 pr. socks-$.24$^{1/2}$, 1 pr. shoes-$1.22, 1 pr. overalls-$2.28, 1 pr. drawers-$.35$^{1/2}$; pres. 04/1848, pay stopped for: 1 cotton shirt-$.43; pres. 07/1848, pay stopped for: 1 cartridge box belt plate-$.10, 1 gun sling-$.16, 1 pick & brush-$.12, 1 screw driver-$.07, 1 wiper-$.20; BLW sent to Staunton, VA; c. 1850 res. Augusta Co., VA, age 21, occ. Painter;[53] m. Margaret Southard, 08/08/1851, Staunton, Augusta Co., VA;[52] Civil War service enl. Pvt., Co. A, 4th Va. Inf., 02/08/1863, age 39, wded. 05/03/1863, gunshot wd. in right knee, at Battle of Chancellorsville, right leg amputated 05/05/1863;[54] SC # 72, 03/11/1887, filed from Staunton, Augusta Co., VA; phys. desc. 5'5", light complexion, grey eyes, light hair, occ. House Painter;[52] lists dau. Florence K. Alexander; (MSA d. 09/21/1891);[52] d. 05/28/1911, *"fractured hip, the result of a fall;"* bur. Thornrose Cemetery, Staunton, VA[52]

**Alexander, George W.**, Pvt., Co. G; b. 03/27/1827 New Kent Co., VA;[55] enl. Mex. War service 11/18/1846 Richmond, VA, age 18; pres. 06/1847; Court-martialed 07/18/1847, Buena Vista,

# VIRGINIA VOLUNTEERS IN MEXICO

Mex. *Charge #1: Unsoldierlike Conduct; Specification: In this that Private Alexander of Company G, Virginia Regiment, did on the 30$^{th}$ of May 1847, whilst on the march from China to this place, at the town of Cadareyta, take without the knowledge of the owners, and with felonious intent various articles of clothing and one Daguerretype [sic] likeness, and sold the same, converting the money to his own use. To which charge and specification the prisoner pleaded "Not Guilty." The Court after mature deliberation with testimony adduced, are of the opinion that the charge and specification is not sustained in this that there is no evidence whatever of the taking, or sale of the clothing by the prisoner and converting the same to his own use, and that the possession of the Daguerretype[sic] likeness, only raises a suspicion of the theft of the clothes, which is not sustained; and that although they are compelled to find him Guilty of selling the likeness, and converting the proceeds to his own use - his long confinement has sufficiently punished him, and they therefore recommend his discharge from further confinement;* pres. 08/1847; pres. 10/1847, pay stopped for: 1 pr. overalls-$2.28, 2 shoes-$2.44, 2 pr. socks-$.49, 1 forage cap-$.95$^{1/2}$; pres. 12/1847, 1 pr. shoes-$1.22, 2 pr. drawers-$.71, 1 pr. pants-$2.28, 1 cap-$.95$^{1/2}$; pres. 02/1848; pres. 04/1848, pay stopped for: 1 blanket-$2.22; pres. 08/1848, pay stopped for: 1 gun sling-$.16; BLW sent to Richmond, VA; m. Virginia Harras 11/05/1855, Raleigh, NC; c. 1880 res. South Grant District, Cabell Co., WV, age 53, occ. Farming, Virginia (46) Keeping House, son George A. (21) Farming;[56] SC #22052, 09/13,1889, filed from Milton, Cabell Co., WV; Theoderick Nunnally of 725 South End of Cherry St., Richmond, VA gave affidavit in pension claim; d. 08/12/1890 *"affliction of the bladder,"* Cabell Co., WV;[57] wid. Virginia, WC #9675, 02/24/1891, filed from Milton, Cabell Co., WV; (VHA b. 12/28/1828, on 05/01/1891 res. Buffington St., Guyandoyte, WV, d. 03/20/1919).[57]

**Alexander, James**, Pvt., Co. I; m. Elizabeth Joy, 02/28/1839, Richmond, Henrico Co., VA;[58] enl. Mex. War service 02/22/1847 Richmond, VA, age 30; pres. 02/1847; pres. 04/1847; in confinement 06/1847; in confinement 08/1847; pres. 10/1847, pay stopped for: 3 flannel shirts-$2.70, 3 pr. drawers-$1.06$^{1/2}$, 1 pr. shoes-$1.22, 2 pr. socks-$.49; Court-martialed 10/04/1847, Buena Vista, Mex. *Charge #1: Gross Neglect of Duty; Specification: In this that he, the said Private James Alexander, Co. I, Va. Regt. Vols., being regularly mounted on Guard at Camp Buena Vista, Mexico on or about the 1$^{st}$ of September 1847, and being posted as a sentinel at the Provost Guard between the hours of 9 & 11 o'clock P.M., did suffer Wm. Lalock, a prisoner confined at the Provost Guard, to pass his post and thereby escape. To which charge and specification the prisoner pled Not Guilty. Private Jno. C. Swively, Co. A, 1$^{st}$ Dragoons, a witness for the prosecution, being duly sworn, says: On or about the 1$^{st}$ of September 1847, four prisoners, including myself, went to the post of the sentinel stationed at the Provost Guard and called for the supernumerary to go out with us. We passed a few paces over the Sentinels post and three of us halted. The fourth, Wm. Lalock, went on and did not return. It was dark and I did not see who was on post, but someone was on post. The first call for tatto[sic] had just beaten. The supernumerary had not joined us when Lalock left us. Question by the Prisoner: Did you hear the supernumerary say to you, 'go on. I will be there presently?' Answer: I heard someone say so, but do not know who it was. Private Andrew Montero, Co. A, Va. Regt. Vols., a witness for the prosecution, being duly sworn, says: I was supernumerary of the Guard at the Provost on or about the 1$^{st}$ of Sept. 1847. I was called to go out with some prisoners while tatto was being beaten. I went out and joined three who were beyond the Sentinels post some paces and returned with them. Wm. Lalock was not of the party. The prisoner was on post when I went out and when I returned. I know that Lalock escaped that night. The prisoner called to me to come to his post after I returned with the three prisoners and said to me that Lalock had gone out and had not returned. I replied that I reckconed [sic] that Lalock had not escaped as he had not gone out with me. I took the prisoners musket and walked his post while he went to see if Lalock had escaped. He said to me when he came back that Lalock was gone, that he was not in his tent. We immediately*

## OFF TO WAR

*called for the Sergeant of the Guard and repeated the circumstances. Question by the Court: Did you hear anyone call for the supernumerary about tatto on the night specified. Answer: Yes, and I supposed it was the prisoner on post that called. I said something, but do not recollect what, to let him know that I heard his call. Question by the Prisoner: Did you come to my post with the four prisoners without your musket and tell them to go on that you would join them immediately? Answer: No. I was seated some distance from the Guard Tent when I heard the call. Question by the Prisoner: Did I not say when you went out that four prisoners went out with you? Answer: No. You said so when I returned. Private Wm. H. Boyer, Co. B, 4$^{th}$ Ark., a witness for the defence, being duly sworn, says: On or about the 1$^{st}$ of Sept. 1847 four prisoners including myself, went to the Sentinels Post at the Provost Guard and called for the Supernumerary to go out with us. The Supernumerary went for his gun and then joined of some six or eight paces beyond the Sentinels Post. We went to the ____ but returned with the Supernumerary. The call for tatto had beaten. Question by the Court: Was the prisoner on post when you passed? Answer: I do not know whether the prisoner was on post. There was someone on post. Question by the Court: Was the Supernumerary present when you passed the Sentinels Post? Answer: He was present when I passed, but the others three were in advance of me. Question by the Judge Advocate: Do you know that the Supernumerary saw the man that escaped after he crossed the Sentinels Post? Answer: The Supernumerary and myself joined the three prisoners that were in advance. I saw Lalock go off and the Supernumerary was nearer him than I was. Private E.D. Worler, Co. K, N.C. Regt. Vols., a witness for the defence, being duly sworn, says: On the night that Lalock escaped, I was out with a Supernumerary before and saw four prisoners coming. Lalock in advance and the Supernumerary some ten paces behind him. Shortly after I returned to the guard I head the prisoner say to the Supernumerary that four prisoners had gone out with him and but three had returned. The Supernumerary replied that only three went out with him. Question by the Court: Was the night dark or so dark that you could not see plainly ten paces? Answer: I was so light that I could distinguish persons at ten paces. The prisoner testified in his own defence: I halted the prisoners as they came up to my post, but they proceeded two or three paces beyond it. The Supernumerary said, 'Go on and I will join you.' I then considered the men under his charge and let them go. After deliberation the Court found the prisoner Not Guilty;* in confinement 12/1847, pay stopped for: 1 flannel shirt-$.90, 1 pr. shoes-$1.22, 1 pr. socks-$.24$^{1/2}$, 1 cap-$.95$^{1/2}$, 1 pr. pants-$2.28, 1 jacket-$2.66; Court-martialed 12/03/1847 Buena Vista, Mex. *"Charge #1: Violent and Disorderly Conduct; Specification: In that the said Pvt. James Alexander, Co. I, Va. Regt. Vols., did on or about the morning of the 28$^{th}$ of November 1847 at the Hacienda take without permission a piece of beef from the butcher or butchers, and refused to pay for the same and when spoken to about it did curse and otherwise abuse said butchers and did come away without paying for it. This at or near the Hacienda, Buena Vista, Mexico. Pleaded: Not Guilty. Pvt. Henry Christ, Co. B, 4$^{th}$ Arty. a witness for the prosecution being duly sworn says sometime last month I was at the Butchers' Shop at the Ranch. Two men came in, one of them was the prisoner.[He] took up a beef tongue and asked me whether the Butcher was in or not. I told him I thought he was behind the house. He then went off with the tongue and the Butcher came in presently and went out after him. I do not know what took place afterwards. Question by the prisoner: Did you see me purchase any other meat at the ranch on that day? Answer: No, I did not. Question by the prisoner: Did you see me have any other meat at the Ranch on that day? Answer: I did Not. The other man who was with him had a quarter of mutton on his arm. Question by the prisoner: Did I pay for the mutton or not? Answer: I did not see him nor do I know whether he did or not. Question by the Court: Did you hear any of the conversation between the Prisoner and the Butcher after the Butcher went after him? Answer: No. I did not. Question by the Court: You say you heard the Prisoner enquire for the Butcher. Do you know if he paid the Butcher or not? Answer: I do not know...Not Guilty;*[59] pres. 02/1848, 1 pr. shoes-$1.22, 1 pr. overalls-$2.28, 1 blanket-$2.22;

pres. 04/1848; pres. 08/1848, pay stopped for: 2 swivals-$.40, 1 screw driver-$.25, 1 gun sling-$.16, BLW sent to Richmond, VA; d. *"in the county of Botetourt in Virginia sometime during the year 1862 while engaged as a stone mason at or near the Jackson River for the James River and Kanawha Canal Company;*[60] wid. Elizabeth, WC #611, 04/16/1887, filed from 415 N. 7th St., Richmond, Henrico Co., VA; Augustus Stone and Charles R. Jones gave affidavits in pension claim;[58] (EJA b. 04/20/1821, Yorkshire, England).[58]

**Allen, George Henry**, Co. C; b. 09/12/1816? near Dumfries, Prince William Co., VA;[61] enl. Mex. War service 08/30/1847, Warrenton, VA, age 20; pres. 04/1847, joined company 01/27/1848 from Regtl. Depot; pres. 08/1848, BLW sent to Centreville, Fairfax Co., VA; c. 1860 res. Warrenton, Fauquier Co., VA, age 38, occ. Fencer;[62] Civil War service *Henry Allen* enl. Pvt., Co. K, 17th Va. Inf., 04/22/1861 at Warrenton, VA, age 35, occ. Laborer, absent 04/30/1862 sent to Richmond, VA Hosp., *"neuralgia,"* trans. 05/14/1862 to Lynchburg Hosp., discharged 07/22/1862 as over age;[63] c. 1870 res. Upperville, Fauquier Co., VA, age 47, occ. Laborer;[64] m. Alcinda Mathie 09/09/1879, near Thoroughfare, Prince William Co., VA; c. 1880 res. Gainesville Dist., Prince William Co., VA, age 60, occ. Boarder, listed as *"married;"*[65] SC #5530, 04/18/1887, filed from Warrenton, Fauquier Co., VA, *"...was engaged in no battles except attacking Indian Stampeders when possible;"*[66] phys. desc. 5'3½", fair complex., gray eyes, gray hair, occ. Gardner; d. 02/15/1902 near Waterfall, Prince William Co., VA, *"He was a very small shrunken man of no attraction whatever for women in late years and there is no suspicion that he lived with any other woman after leaving claimant. He boarded around and died in* [the] *house of Mrs. Schwartz. I called upon her but she was away from home. I believe that Col. Berkeley's*[8] *idea that* [the] *soldier left home on account of claimant mother is correct, although she would not acknowledge it;"*[67] wid. Alcinda, WC #13173, 03/24/1902, filed from Waterfall, Prince William Co., VA; *"...a sample of a 'poor white' of Virginia. She lives in a small cabin on the estate of Col. Berkeley;"*[67] (AMA b. 1847 Loudoun Co., VA, d. 03/19/1924 *"pneumonia,"* near Thoroughfare, Prince William Co., VA)

**Allen, George W.**, 1st Sgt., LIC; b. c. m. Lucy Ann Coyner, 09/10/1835, Augusta Co., VA;[68] enl. Mex. War service 12/07/1846 Staunton, VA, age 38; pres. 06/1847; pres. 08/1847; pres. 10/1847, pay stopped for: 1 forage cap-$.95½, 1 wool jacket-$2.66, 1 pr. overalls-$2.28, 1 pr. shoes-$1.22, 3 pr. socks-$.73½, 2 cotton shirts-$.86, 1 flannel shirt-$.90, 1 pr. drawers-$.35½, 1 blanket-$2.22; absent 12/1847 on detached service as Clerk in Actg. Asst. Adjt. Genl. office since 11/08/1847, pay stopped for: 1 pr. overalls-$2.28, 1 cotton shirts-$.86; pres. 04/1848, Actg. Sgt. Major of Parras Battalion; pres. 04/1848, pay stopped for: 1 cotton shirt-$.43; pres. 07/1848, pay stopped for: 1 bed sack-$.60, 1 ball screw-$.12; BLW sent to Waynesborough, VA; c. 1850 res. Augusta Co., VA, age 42, occ. Farmer, w. Lucy A. (39), son Frances S. (13), dau. Mary J. (11), son James W. (10), dau. Sarah J. (8), dau. Elizabeth V. (7), dau. Margaret E. (5).[69]

**Allen, Richard Farrar**, Pvt., Co. D; b. 03/08/1825, Prince Edward Co., VA;[70] enl. Mex. War service 09/01/1847, Petersburg, VA, age 22; pres. 04/1848, pay stopped for: 1 blanket-$2.22; Prince Edward C.H., VA; m/1 Eliza M. date/place unknown, (EMA d. *"childbirth,"* 04/03/1857, Prince Edward Co., VA);[70] m/2 Martha Jane Tisdale 04/03/1859, Lunenburg Co., VA;[70] SC #5492, 04/28/1887, filed from Worsham, Prince Edward Co., VA; phys. desc. b. Prince Edward Co., VA 1825, 6'0", fair complexion, dark eyes, auburn hair, occ. at enl Student now Planter, lists children Mary Alice Allen b. 12/31/1854, Eliza Allen 04/02/1857;[70] d. 11/25/1905 *"pneumonia, resulting from a fall;"*[71] wid. Martha J., WC #14392, 12/18/1905, filed from Felden, Prince Edward Co., VA (MJA b. 01/20/1835, d. 06/08/1908).[71]

**Allen, William A.**, 2nd Lt., Co. I; enl. Mex. War service 02/15/1847 Richmond, VA; pres. 02/1847; pres. 04/1847; absent 06/1847 on furlough; resigned 07/15/1847.

---

[8] Edmund Berkeley (1824-1915) was Lt. Col. of 8th Virginia Infantry, C.S.A.

OFF TO WAR

**Allen, William**, Pvt., Co. L; b. 1821; enl. Mex. War service 03/15/1847 Fairfax C.H., age 26; pres. 06/1847; deserted 08/16/1847 from camp Buena Vista, Mex.[72]

**Alley, William E.**, Pvt., Co. E; b. 12/1829, son of Thomas & Nancy Alley;[45, 73] enl. Mex. War service 11/28/1846 Petersburg, VA, age 18; pres. 04/1847; pres. 06/1847; pres. 08/1847; pres. 10/1847, pay stopped for: 1 pr. overalls-$2.28, 2 pr. shoes-$2.44, 4 pr. stockings-$.98, 2 cotton shirts-$.86, 2 flannel shirts-$1.80, 1 cap-$.95$^{1/2}$, 1 overcoat-$6.93$^{1/2}$; pres. 12/1847, pay stopped for: 1 jacket-$2.66, 1 pr. pants-$2.28, 1 pr. shoes-$1.22, 1 cotton shirt-$.43, 2 flannel shirts-$1.80, 2 pr. drawers-$.35$^{1/2}$, 1 blanket-$2.22; pres. 02/1848; pres. 04/1848, pay stopped for: 2 cotton shirts-$.88; c. 1850 res. Petersburg, Dinwiddie Co., VA, age 19, occ. Saddler;[74] c. 1860 res. Templeton, Prince George Co., VA, age 30, occ. Harness Maker, w. M.B. (32), dau. L.E. (6), son E.J. (4);[75] SC #17077, 09/18/1888; d. 09/1893, *Uremia*, bur., Blandford Cem., Sq. 2, Sec. 10, Ward R Petersburg, VA;[76] wid. Mary B., WC #9347 11/24/1893, both from VA

**Anderton, Isaac A.**, Pvt., Co. D; enl. Mex. War service 01/04/1847, Petersburg, VA, age 25; pres. 02/1847; pres. 04/1847; pres. 06/1847; pres. 08/1847, pay stopped for: 1 cap-$.95$^{1/2}$, 1 pr. pants-$2.28, 2 cotton shirts-$.86; pres. 10/1847, pay stopped for: 1 pr. pants-$2.28, 2 flannel shirts-$1.80, 1 pr. drawers-$.35$^{1/2}$, 3 pr. socks-$.73$^{1/2}$, 1 pr. shoes-$1.22; pres. 12/1847, pay stopped for: 1 pr. pants-$2.28, 1 pr. shoes-$1.22, 1 blanket-$2.22; pres. 04/1848, pay stopped for: 1 cotton shirt-$.43; Hicks Ford, Greensville Co., VA; Civil War service enl. Pvt., Co. K, 16$^{th}$ Va. Inf. 05/11/1861 at Petersburg, VA, Co. trans. to artillery service 03/18/1862, Pvt., Branch's Field Arty., pres. through 08/1862, captured 09/1862 Sharpsburg, MD, paroled (no date), pres. 12/1862 through 10/1864, detailed 08/31/1864 as Ambulance Driver, captured 04/02/1865 Petersburg, VA, sent to Hart's Island, NY Harbor, released on oath 06/20/1865, desc. res. Greensville Co., VA, 5'10", grey eyes, brown hair, light complexion;[77, 78] m/ Eliza V. Edwards 01/14/1866, Greensville Co., VA;[79] SC #40, 02/17/1887, filed from Hicksford (Emporia), Greensville Co., VA; phys. desc. at enl., age 28, occ. Farmer, 5'10", fair complexion, blue eyes;[79] d. 10/26/1886 Greensville Co., VA;[79] wid. Eliza V., WC #2517, 07/28/1887, filed from Hicksford, Greensville Co., VA; lists son W.A. "Gus" Anderton and *"three or four other children;"*[80] (EVA b. 05/30/1844, near Brink, Greensville Co., VA, d. 10/12/1927).[80]

**Andrews, John W.**, Pvt., Co. C; b. c. 1823, Philadelphia, Pa., enl. Mex. War service 12/30/1846, Bowling Green, VA, age 23; pres. 06/1847; pres. 08/1847, pay stopped for: 1 cap-$.95$^{1/2}$, 2 pr. socks-$.49, 2 cotton shirts-$.86, 2 woolen shirts-$1.80; pres. 10/1847, pay stopped for: 2 pr. socks-$.49, 2 pr. drawers-$.71, 1 jacket-$2.66, 1 pr. pants-$2.28, 2 cotton shirt-$.86, 2 woolen shirt-$1.80, 2 pr. shoes-$2.44, 1 blanket-$2.22, 1 knapsack & straps-$1.10; pres. 12/1847, pay stopped for: 1 pr. socks-$.24$^{1/2}$, 1 pr. pants-$2.28, 2 woolen shirts-$1.80; discharged 01/30/1848, Buena Vista, Mexico on Surgeon's Certificate, physical desc. age 24, 5'10", dark complexion, grey eyes, dark hair, occ. Stonecutter.[26]

**Argabright, John**, Pvt., *Preston's Co.*; enl. Mex. War service 11/28/1846 Montgomery Co., VA, age 19; pres. 04/1847; absent 06/1847 on detached service as Waggoner in QM Dept. since 05/01/1847; absent 08/1847 on detached service in the QM Dept., to receive $25 in addition to his pay as a soldier; pres. 10/1847, pay stopped for: 1 jacket-$2.66, 1 pr. overalls-$2.28; pres. 12/1847, pay stopped for: 1 cap-$.95$^{1/2}$; pres. 02/1848; pres. 04/1848; pres. 07/1848, pay stopped for: 1 jacket-$2.37, 1 gun sling-$.18; BLW sent to Christiansburg, VA c/o Fleming Gardner; c. 1850 res. Montgomery Co., VA, age 23, occ. Carpenter;[81] c. 1860 res. Giles Co., VA w/ Green Chandler (also of 1$^{st}$ Va. Vols.) occ. Laborer.[82]

**Arbogast, Nicodemus**, Pvt., LIC; *Not on Muster Rolls*; b. 10/12/1826 Pendleton Co., VA; m. Mary Simmons, Braxton Co., VA; c. 1860 res. Clay Co., WV, age 36, w. Mary (34), dau. Edith (11), Margaret (7), America (6), Sarah (5), Rocksena (5), George (1); c. 1870 res. Clay Co., WV age 44, w. Mary (41), Edath (21), Sarah D. (15), Roccenith (15), George F. (13), Jonathan J. (8) Francis M. (3) Watson (2); m. Mahala Margaret (Hanes) Jeffrey 11/1875; 1880, res. Pleasant District, Clay Co., WV, age 55, occ. Farmer, w. Margaret (33) Keeping

## VIRGINIA VOLUNTEERS IN MEXICO

House, son Thomas J.(Jeffers) (17), son Francis (15), son George (15), son Watson (12), dau. Ann E. (7), son John (10), son Michael (4), son Shiloerah (2);[83] SA #25665, 01/24/1914, from WV; d. 07/02/1915, bur. Elkhurst, WV.[84]

**Archer, Edwin C.**, Pvt., Co. D; enl. Mex. War service 01/14/1847, Petersburg, VA, age 44; pres. 02/1847; d. 03/16/1847 *"off Brasos Island."*

**Archer, Fletcher Harris**, Capt., Co. E; b. 02/06/1817, Petersburg, VA, son of Allen & Prudence (Whitworth) Archer; grad. U.VA 1841 (Law);[85] enl. Mex. War service 11/29/1846 Petersburg, VA, age 29; pres. 04/1847; pres. 06/1847; pres. 08/1847; pres. 10/1847; pres. 12/1847; pres. 02/1848; pres. 04/1848; m/1 Elizabeth Ann Eppes Allen, 05/23/1849, Petersburg, VA, (EAEA d 04/22/1851, Petersburg, VA);[85, 86] Civil War service enl. Capt., Co. K, 12$^{th}$ Va. Inf., 05/04/1861 at Petersburg, VA, occ. lawyer, resigned 09/1861, apptd. Lt. Col., 5$^{th}$ Btln. Inf., declined reelection, late 1862 apptd. Maj. 3$^{rd}$ Btln. VA Reserves, prom. Lt. Col. 1863, wded. 06/16/1864 in Battle of Petersburg, VA, wded. 04/06/1865 Sayler's Creek, VA, paroled at Appomattox, VA;[21, 87] m/2 Martha Georgiana Morton Barksdale, 03/31/1863; Councilman, City of Petersburg 1879-1881; Mayor of Petersburg, VA 1881-1882;[85] SC #37, 03/10/1887, filed from Petersburg, Dinwiddie Co., VA; phys. desc. 5'6", gray eyes, black hair, lists daughter Eliza Ann Eppes Archer b. 01/13/1851, *Mayfield*,[88] Dinwiddie Co., VA;[86] d. 08/1902, *Softening of the Brain*, Petersburg, VA;[21] bur. Blandford Cem., Sq. 4, Sec. 16, Ward R, Petersburg, VA;[89] wid. Martha G., WC #13244, 09/15/1902, filed from 247 High Street, Petersburg, Dinwiddie Co., VA; (MGA b. 06/16/1827, Charlotte Co., VA).[90]

**Archer, William B.**, Capt., Co. I; m. Mary Marshall, dau. of Thomas, 01/1837;[91] Democrat;[92] enl. Mex. War service 11/15/1846, Richmond, VA; pres. 02/1847; AWOL 04/1847, from 04/29/1847; Court-martialed 05/17/1847, Monterey, Mexico *Charge #1: Insubordinant*[sic] *Conduct; Specification: In this that he the said Captain William B. Archer, did, on or about the 5$^{th}$ day of May 1847 in the City of Monterey, Mexico, write and cause to be delivered to Col. J.F. Hamtramck, his commanding officer, a certain letter in the words and figures following , to wit: Monterey, Mexico, May 5$^{th}$ / 47 Col. J.F. Hamtramck: Dear Sir: The public rebuke given me today by yourself has caused me much annoyance, believing as I do that is was uninvited, as I had told you the day before yesterday that it was my purpose if well enough to go out today to camp to stay. Yesterday, I was confined almost the whole day to my bed and under the medical direction of Dr. Madison of the Army. This morning though very unwell, I determined to go to Camp and when I met you I was in pursuit of a horse to ride out being unable to take the walk. Public reprimands, however delicately given, in the presence of officers of the other Regts. Are at all times painful but especially so to one who has <u>ceased to be a boy</u>. In stopping in Monterey I have neither consulted my pleasure nor my interest. So long as I shall remain in the Virginia Regt., I respectfully request that when you think my conduct merits reproof, you will take some other method than the one adopted today. With high respect, your obedient servant. Wm. B. Archer. Charge #2: Disrespectful Conduct Towards his Commanding Officer; Specification: In this that he, the said Captain William B. Archer, did, on or about the 5$^{th}$ day of May 1847, at the City of Monterey, Mexico, write and cause to be delivered to Colonel J.F. Hamtramck, his commanding officer, a certain letter in the words and figures following to wit* [see above letter] *Charge #3: Conduct Prejudicial to Good Order and Military Discipline; Specification: In this that he, the said Captain William B. Archer, did, on or about the 5$^{th}$ day of May 1847, at the City of Monterey, Mexico, write and cause to be delivered to Colonel J.F. Hamtramck, his commanding officer, a certain letter in the words and figures following to wit* [see above letter] *Charge #4: Absence Without Leave; Specification: In this that the said Captain William B. Archer was absent from his company and camp near Monterey, Mexico from the 29$^{th}$ day of April 1847 until the afternoon of the 30$^{th}$ day of April 1847, without leave from his commanding officer; Specification #2: In this that the said Captain William B. Archer, did absent himself from his company and camp*

OFF TO WAR

*near Monterey, Mexico, on the afternoon of the 30th of April 1847, without leave from his commanding officer and did remain absent without leave until on or about the afternoon of the 6th day of May 1847; Charge #5: Gross Neglect and Violation of Duty; Specification #1: In this that the said Captain William B. Archer was absent from his company and camp near Monterey, Mexico from the 29th day of April 1847 until the afternoon of the 30th day of April 1847, without leave from his commanding officer and did fail, during that time to perform any duty whatsoever with his company or command, and did absent himself from muster of his company on the 30th day of April 1847, although particularly informed of his duty in regard thereto and admonished to be present on that occasion by Major J.A. Early, his commanding officer. Specification #2: In this that the said Captain William B. Archer was absent from his company and camp near Monterey, Mexico from the 29th day of April 1847 until the afternoon of the 30th day of April 1847, without leave from his commanding officer and did fail, during that time to perform any duty whatsoever with his company or command, but spent the said time in the Town of Monterey, Mexico in idleness or amusement. Charge #6: Violation of the 42nd Article of War; Specification: In this that Captain William B. Archer, did, without leave from his commanding officer, lie out of camp near Monterey, Mexico, during the nights of the 29th and 30th days of April, and the 1st, 2nd, 3rd, 4th and 5th days of May 1847, and did lie during the said nights of the 29th and 30th of April and of the 1st, 2nd, 3rd, 4th, and 5th of May 1847, in the Town of Monterey, Mexico away from his company and command. To which charges and specifications the accused pleaded as follows: 1st Charge: Not Guilty; Specification: Guilty; 2nd Charge: Not Guilty; Specification: Guilty; 3rd Charge: Not Guilty; Specification: Guilty; and the 4th, 5th and 6th Charges and Specifications: Not Guilty; The accused requested of the Court that Fletcher H. Archer be allowed to assist the accused in his defense. The request was granted. Major J.A. Early, Va. Regt., was called as a witness for the prosecution. Other witnesses were requested to leave the Court room after which Maj. Early was duly sworn and said: On the 21st of April I arrived at this place with a portion of troops under my command from carriages, by the way of China, a portion of which troops was a company of Virginia Volunteers commanded by Capt. Archer. The day previous to my arrival Capt. Archer was complaining and not doing duty with his company. After remaining in town a short time I marched with my command to the camp at the Walnut Springs near Genl. Taylor's Head Quarters. A short time after arriving at the place designated for the camp of my command I ascertained that Capt. Archer was not present with the command and was informed that he had been taken very sick after leaving town and had returned. Two or three days after, I came into town and saw Capt. Archer at which time he informed me that he had been taken very sick on the march from town to my camp and had to return. I then informed Capt. Archer that his stopping was right under the circumstances but that he must go down to camp as soon as he was able to do so, as I wanted him with his company. He told me that he desired to do so – to go to his company – and that he would do so as soon as he was able. At that time he was out walking in the streets somewhere. I came into town a day or two after again and saw Capt. Archer and asked him how he was getting. He informed me that he was not well but that he intended to come to camp very shortly. I told him again that I wished him to do so as soon as possible. At that time I saw him in the streets again and he appeared to me to be well, at least sufficiently so to go to camp, but relying upon his own sense of duty, I did not order him to do so. I came into town again before the 29th and saw Capt. Archer and he told me that he was coming down to camp the next day. At that time I don't recollect that he complained of being unwell. On the 29th of April I came to town and saw Capt. Archer again, he not having moved down to camp, and had a conversation with him in which I told him that he must come down to camp that evening – that his company would be mustered on the next day and that it was necessary for him to be there at the muster and that his muster rolls must be made out. He told me that these would all be attended to and that he would come down there*[sic] *that evening, or at any rate he would be down there next morning before the muster. At that time he stated*

## VIRGINIA VOLUNTEERS IN MEXICO

*to me that he might be detained in town until the next morning by circumstances which he then related. I told him then that he must come down that evening. At night of the 29$^{th}$ having ascertained that Capt. Archer had not gone to camp I caused Lt. R.H. Keeling, the ranking officer on duty with Capt. Archer's company to make out the muster rolls of his company according to directions which I gave him. On the morning of the 30$^{th}$ ascertaining that Capt. Archer had not yet gone to camp at the time designated for the muster of the battalion under my command, I mustered Capt. Archer's company under the command of Lt. Keeling and Capt. Archer was not present at the muster. About one o'clock on the 30$^{th}$, I saw Capt. Archer ride into camp. Shortly after he came to my tent and I informed him that as he had not come down I had been compelled to muster him as absent without leave. He stated at that time that he did not know that it was so necessary for him to be there, but that he could obviate all difficulty and turned to Lt. Gardner of the Va. Regt., who was at my tent at the time, and asked him to give him that communication that he had given him the day before, Lt. Gardner went immediately to his quarters and Capt. Archer very shortly afterwards handed me a letter which was addressed to me and did purported to be a resignation of his commission. After reading the letter I informed Capt. Archer that if he was determined to resign it was necessary for him to address his letter to Maj. Bliss, Assistant Adjutant General,*[William Wallace Smith Bliss, 1815-1853, son-in-law of General Taylor; and for whom Fort Bliss, El Paso, Texas is named] *and handed him the letter addressed to me. In a short time he left my tent and went towards the officers tents of his own company, and I saw him no more until the afternoon of the 6$^{th}$ of May, at which time I saw him in the camp of the battalion under my command. I then had some conversation with Capt. Archer with regard to his absence in which he said that he didn't understand if that he had been absent without leave, that he had in the first place tendered his resignation to me and according to my direction had afterwards sent it to Maj. Bliss and that for the last five days he had regarded himself as out of service. I told him then that his resignation did not release him from service until it was accepted. I then gave him permission to come in town on the next day for the purpose of having his baggage brought to camp, and in the evening after his return I arrested him.* Lt. R.H. Keeling, Va. Regt., Co. J.F. Hamtramck, Va. Regt., Col. Mitchell, all testified in the proceedings. Dr. T.C. Madison, U.S.A. testifies that the accused was suffering from and attack of *"strictum"* and *"diarrhea."* *After deliberation the Court found the accused on the 1$^{st}$ Charge: Not Guilty, and Specification: Guilty; 2$^{nd}$ Charge: Not Guilty, and to the Specification: Guilty; 3$^{rd}$ Charge: Not Guilty, and to the Specification: Guilty; 4$^{th}$ Charge: Guilty, and to the Specifications: Guilty; 5$^{th}$ Charge: Not Guilty, and to the Specification: Guilty except the words 'but spent time in town of Monterey, Mexico in idleness or amusement;' 6$^{th}$ Charge: Guilty; and to the Specification: Guilty. The Court did not award any punishment in this case as it is satisfactory to the Court from the evidence admitted that Capt. Archer was unable to do any duty during the period referred to in the charges and specifications and was ignorant of the precise course he should have pursued in order to comply strictly with army regulations.*[93] absent 06/08/1847 on furlough in Richmond; Col. Hamtramck wrote of Capt. Archer, *"I have the honor to report that Capt. Wm. B. Archer(Company I), procurred*[sic] *sick leave while in Monterey, and that he left with the expectation of having it extended by the Department, I am told declaring that he would not return again, but would hold on to his commission as long as possible, and I am induced to report the fact with the hope that he will be ordered to rejoin his company or resign;"*[94] AWOL 08/1847 since 08/02/1847; placed on report for *"neglecting to make his periodical report to the Head Quarters of his* [Company] *while on leave of absence and I have further the disagreeable duty of again reporting Capt. W.B. Archer, Co. I, Va. Regt. Vols., Lieut. Pegram, Co. E, Va. Regt. Vols., Lieut. L. Washington, Co. K, Va. Regt. Vols. absent without leave."*[95] AWOL 10/1847; AWOL 12/1847; AWOL 02/1848; pres. 04/1848; pres. 08/1848; c. 1850 res. Hanover Co., VA, age 31, occ. not listed, w. Marietta;[96] [In the 1854 election for the U.S. House of Representatives in the 7th District of Illinois, Democratic

OFF TO WAR

candidate James C. Allen defeated Republican William B. Archer 8,452 to 8,451; Civil War service a W.B. Archer served on the Board of Enrollment as a Commissioner from the state of Illinois from 05/1863 to 0/1865][97]

**Armstrong, Richard**, Pvt., Co. G; enl. Mex. War service 12/02/1846 Richmond, VA, age 21; pres. 06/1847; pres. 08/1847; pres. 10/1847, pay stopped for: 1 pr. overalls-$2.28, 2 cotton shirts-$.86, 1 pr. drawers-$.35$^{1/2}$, 1 shoes-$1.22, 2 pr. socks-$.49, 1 forage cap-$.95$^{1/2}$; pres. 12/1847, 1 pr. shoes-$1.22, 2 pr. drawers-$.71, 1 pr. pants-$2.28, 1 cap-$.95$^{1/2}$; pres. 02/1848; pres. 04/1848; pres. 08/1848, BLW sent to Louisa Co. C.H., VA; c. 1850 res. Lousia Co., VA, age 25, occ. Farmer.[98]

**Ashby, Turner Wade**, 1$^{st}$ Lt., Co. B; b. 08/11/1811, son of Thomson & Ann (Menefee) Ashby; m. Elizabeth Smith Gregory abt. 1831; c. 1835 appointed 2$^{nd}$ Lt., 2nd Regt. o Cav., 5$^{th}$ Brigade, 2$^{nd}$ Div. VA Militia;[99] enl. 11/20/1846, Alexandria, VA; absent 06/1847 left camp, Buena Vista, Mex., 06/22/1847 on recruiting service in VA; absent 08/1847 on recruiting service in VA; absent 10/1847 on recruiting service; absent 12/1847 on recruiting service; absent 02/1848 on recruiting service; discharged 02/23/1848 by order of Sec. of War; c. 1856 Major of Militia Btln. in Alexandria, VA; Postmaster of Alexandria, VA prior to 1861; SC #173, 02/19/1881, from VA; d. 04/20/1893, *General Debility* Alexandria, VA, bur. Ivy Hill Cem., Alex., VA;[100] 1$^{st}$ cousin of Brig. Gen. Turner Ashby, C.S.A.

**Ashton, Gurdon C.**, Pvt., Co. B; enl. 12/12/1846, Alexandria, VA, age 21; pres. 06/1847; pres. 08/1847; pres. 10/1847, pay stopped for: 2 pr. socks-$.49, 1 cotton shirt-$.43, 1 pr. shoes-$1.22, 1 pr. overalls-$2.28, 1 cap-$.95$^{1/2}$, 2 flannel shirts-$1.80; pres. 12/1847, pay stopped for: 1 pr. cotton drawers-$.71, 2 pr. socks-$.49, 1 pr. shoes-$1.22, 1 blanket-$2.22; pres. 02/1848; pres. 04/1848, pay stopped for: 1 jacket-$2.66; pres. 08/1848, pay stopped for: 1 wiper-$.20, BLW sent to Washington, DC; m. Helen A. Harrison 1/20/1853, Washington, D.C.;[101] res. Washington, D.C. 1855-1881; c. 1855 occ. Merchant, res. 500 MD Ave., Washington, D.C.;[102] d. 06/06/1869 in Canada; wid. Helen W. WC #3393, 06/17/1887 from D.C, (*HWA* d. 10/22/1891, Washington, D.C.).[103]

**Ashworth, Parks Edward**, Pvt., Co. I; b. 08/07/1827, near Wylliesburg, Charlotte Co., VA, son of Anderson and Susan Ashworth;[104] enl. Mex. War service 08/24/1847 Ft. Monroe, VA, age 20; pres. 02/1848, joined co. 01/26/1848; pres. 02/1848, joined co. 01/26/1848; pres. 04/1848, pay stopped for: 1 jacket; pres. 08/1848, BLW sent to Lunenburg, VA; c. 1850 res. Lunenburg Co., VA, age 24, occ. Farmer;[105] m. Martha Ann Wooten, 12/20/1852, Granville Co., NC;[104] c. 1860 res. Pleasant Grove, Lunenburg Co., VA, age 33, w. Martha A. (27), son John P. (5), dau. Ann E. (4), dau. Louisa (2);[106] Civil War service a P.A. Ashworth, age 36, was conscripted at Camp Lee and assigned as Pvt., Co. K, 23$^{rd}$ Va. Inf. 05/16/1864, in hosp. 07/26/1864 Charlottesville, VA, diarrhea, trans. to hosp. in Lynchburg, VA, in hosp. 12/1864 at Petersburg, VA, discharged 02/09/1865 for disability, phys. desc. 5'7", dark complexion, dark eyes, paroled 04/22/1865 at Burkeville, VA;[107] SC #7672, 03/07/1887, filed from Plantersville, Lunenburg Co., VA; phys. desc. 5'5", blue eyes, black hair, occ. Farmer; d. 09/19/1919, *"old age and paralysis,"* Rehoboth, Lunenburg Co., VA, bur. *"at his home,"* Lunenburg Co., VA;[108] wid. Martha A., WA #20557, 09/18/1919, filed from Ontario, Charlotte Co., VA; BLW #62616-160-47; Lists children Marshall Pegram Ashworth, b. 10/28/1853, Ann Udora Ashworth, b. 09/04/1855, Laura Wooten Ashworth, b. 03/05/1858, Eddie Lee Ashworth, b. 12/09/1860, Parker Anderson Ashworth, b. 08/26/1863, George Gordon Ashworth, b. 04/15/1866, Ida Jackson Ashworth, b. 01/05/1868, Eula Spergeon Ashworth, b. 06/02/1871, Ellie May Ashworth, b. 02/28/1875, Charlie Sim Ashworth, b. 06/16/1878;[108] d. Ontario, Charlotte Co. VA, 09/04/1919; (MWA b. 07/23/1832, d. 11/15/1919, bur. on estate of Charles S. Ashworth, Ontario, Lunenburg Co., VA)[108]

**Ashworth, William A.**, Pvt., Co. I; enl. Mex. War service 08/09/1847 Richmond, VA, age 21; pres. 02/1848, joined co. 01/26/1848; pres. 04/1848, 1 jacket, 1 blanket; pres. 08/1848,BLW sent to Lunenburg, VA; m. Permelia A. Bailey 02/01/1849, Lunenburg Co., VA;[109, 110] c. 1850

VIRGINIA VOLUNTEERS IN MEXICO

res. Lunenburg Co., VA, age 25, occ. Laborer, w. Permelia (23), dau. Ellen (6/12);[111] c. 1860 res. Pleasant Grove, Lunenburg, Co., VA, age 34, occ. Carpenter, w. Permelia A., (37), dau. Ann S. (10), son Wm. W. (8), dau. Mavis F. (5), dau. Dura S. (3), dau. Isabella B. (3/12);[112] Civil War service Pvt., Co. K, 23rd Va. Inf. 05/02/1861 at Keysville, VA, for 1 yr., absent sick 12/1861 at Winchester, VA, reenlisted for war 02/1862, pres. through 12/1864;[107] Struck by lightning July 30, 1874;[110] SC #9629, 03/28/1887, filed from Plantersville, Lunenburg Co., VA; phys. desc. age 61, [1887], b. Charlotte Co., VA; 5'8", light complexion, blue eyes, dark hair, occ. Farmer; *""Department of Interior, Bureau of Pensions Dear Sir: I inlisted*[sic] *as a recrute*[sic] *for the VA Regiment which was in Mexico at that time and we were held at Fort Monroe as the Detachment from August 1847 to about December 1847 which we was put in charge of Lieutenant Pegram and shipped to Mexico on a vesal*[sic] *by the name of John G. Colly and was landed at Brasazs or Santeago* [sic] *about the 12th of January 1848. Lieutenant Pegram then took us from there to Buena Vista to the VA Regiment. We arrived there about the latter part of January 1848. On our arrival there we, the Detachment, were distributed between the 13 old companies to fill up the vacancies. I became a member of Captain William B. Archer's company and remained a member of that company the remainder of the war. The Regiment was encamped round about Saltillo until peace was made about the last of May. Congress then passed an act that we should be returned back to our native state before being discharged. We took up march from Buena Vista about the 8th day of June 1848 and was brought to Brazas and put aboard a vesal called the Memphis and shipped from there to Fort Monroe landing there sometime in July 1848. There remained intell*[sic] *discharged the 3rd of August, Very Respectfully, Wm. A. Ashworth, Plantersville, Lunenburg Co., Virginia, October 23, 1893;*[110] Parks E. Ashworth and William H.H. Williams gave affidavit in pension claim; d. 03/13/1899;[113] wid. Permelia A., WC #11672, 04/06/1899, filed from Eubon, Lunenburg Co., VA; (PBA b. 01/16/1823, d. 02/18/1902).[113]

**Astrop, Robert F.**, 2nd Lt., Co. M; enl. Mex. War service 09/08/1847, Forksville, Mecklenburg Co., VA; pres. 10/1847; pres. 11/1847; pres. 12/1847; pres. 02/1848; resigned 03/01/1848 at Saltillo, Mex.

**Atherton, John**, Pvt., Co. A; enl. Mex. War 12/01/1846 Richmond, VA, age 29; pres. 06/1847; pres. 08/1847; pres. 10/1847, pay stopped for clothing: 2 pr. shoes-$2.44, one pr. wool overalls-$2.28, 1 cap-.95$^{1/2}$; pres. 12/1847, pay stopped for clothing: 1 pr. Drawers-$.35$^{1/2}$, 1 blanket-$2.22; pres. 02/1848; pres. 04/1848; 07/1848, pay stopped for: musket sling-$.16; BLW sent to, Baltimore, MD

**August, Thomas Pearson**, 1st Lt., Co. A; enl. 11/18/1846, Richmond, VA, age 25; pres. 12/1846–04/1847; pres. 06/1847 in arrest 06/1847, appointed Adjutant of the Regt. 06/1847 by order of Col. Hamtramck; pres. 08/1847 commanding company, relieved of duty as Regt. Adjutant to take command of company; pres. 10/1847 commanding the company in the absence of Capt. Scott; under arrest 12/1847; under arrest 02/1848; pres. 04/1848; c. 1850 res. Richmond, VA, age 28, single, occ. Lawyer;[114] c. 1853 mbr. Knights Templar, Richmond Encampment No. 2, Richmond, VA;[40] c. 1860 res. 2nd Ward, Richmond, VA, age 38, single, occ. Lawyer;[115] Civil War service apptd. Col. 15th Va. Inf. 07/01/1861, occ. Lawyer, wded. 07/01/1862 at Malvern Hill, VA, absent wded. until detached as Commandant of Conscript Camp, Raleigh, NC, 07/1864, retired from service 12/31/1864, *photograph*;[116, 117] member of the Richmond BAR, d. 07/31/1869, Richmond, VA;[118] bur. Hollywood Cem., Sect. 0, Lot 1, Richmond, VA.[119]

**Austin, Augustus L.**, Pvt., Co. I; b. 09/08/1820, son of Alexander & Elizabeth Austin;[45] enl. Mex. War service 01/10/1847 Lynchburg, VA, age 26; pres. 02/1847; pres. 04/1847; pres. 06/1847, prom. 2nd Cpl. 06/15/1847; pres. 08/1847, prom. 1st Cpl.; pres. 10/1847, reduced to ranks from 1st Cpl. 10/14/1847 by order of court-martial, pay stopped for: 3 flannel shirts-$2.70, 3 cotton shirts-$1.72, 3 pr. drawers-$1.06$^{1/2}$, 1 pr. shoes-$1.22, 1 pr. socks-$.24$^{1/2}$, 1 cap-$.95$^{1/2}$; pres. 12/1847, pay stopped for: 1 pr. shoes-$1.22, 1 pr. pants-$2.28, 1 blanket-

OFF TO WAR

$2.22, 2 cotton shirts-$.86, 2 flannel shirts-$1.80, 1 jacket-$2.66; pres. 02/1848, pay stopped for: 1 pr. shoes-$1.22; pres. 04/1848, pay stopped for: 1 jacket; pres. 08/1848, BLW sent to New London, Campbell Co., VA; c. 1850 res. Campbell Co., VA, age 30, single, occ. Tutor;[120] Civil War service Pvt., Co. B, 11th Va. Inf. enl. 04/25/1861, age 40, occ. Farmer, in hosp. 10/1861 w/ typhoid, detailed as a baggage guard 01/1862, discharged 08/25/1862;[121] d. 05/11/1865, bur. Austin Family Cem., Rt. 625, Campbell Co., VA.[45]

**Austin, Robert**, Pvt., *Preston's Co.*; b. Charlotte Co., VA;[122] enl. Mex. War service 01/07/1847 Roanoke, VA, age 27; pres. 04/1847, prom. Fifer; absent 06/1847 left as Hospital Attendant in Monterey, Mex. since 06/22/1847; absent 08/1847 on detached service as a Hospital Attendant in Monterey, Mex.; pres. 10/1847, reduced to ranks from Fifer 10/01/1847 (regtl. order No. 111), pay stopped for: 1 cotton shirt-$.43, 1 belt plate-$.10, 1 musicians sword belt plate-$.10; pres. 12/1847, pay stopped for: 1 pr. overalls-$2.28, 1 pr. shoes-$1.22; pres. 02/1848; absent 04/1848 on detached service as Hospital Attendant; pres. 04/1848; pres. 07/1848, pay stopped for: 1 jacket-$2.37; BLW sent to Salem, VA; m. Nancy Elizabeth Mills, 12/05/1855, Copper Hill, Floyd Co., VA;[122] c. 1860 res. Floyd C.H., VA, age 44, occ. Farmer, illiterate, w. Nancy E. (23), son James P. (2), son Wm. T. (2);[123] d. 06/22/1879, *"heart disease,"* Graysville, Floyd Co., VA;[122] wid. Nancy, WC #408, 04/08/1887, filed from Graysville, Floyd Co., VA; Lists children Gemima Austin b. 09/23/1865, Sarah A. Austin b. 06/13/1868, Octavia Ann Austin b. 01/19/1871, Permelia J. Austin b. 10/03/1873, Mary E. Austin b. 07/09/1878;[122] (NMA b. 02/18/1834, near Copper Hill, Floyd Co., VA, d. 03/25/1901).[122]

**Avis, John**, 1st Lt., Co. K; b. 07/09/1818, Charlestown, Jefferson Co., VA;[124] enl. Mex. War service Jefferson Co., VA 12/01/1846; pres. 06/1847; pres. 08/1847; pres. 10/1847; pres. 12/1847; pres. 04/1848; pres. 07/1848; m/1 Imogene Little date/place unknown; c. 1850 res. Charlestown, Jefferson Co., VA, age 32, occ. Shoemaker, w. Imogene (22), son James L. (6), son John L. (3), son Braxton D. (6/12);[125] (ILA d. 03/09/1853);[124] m/2 Mary O'Neill, b. 04/10/1854, Frederick, Frederick Co., MD;[124] c. 1860 res. Charles Town, Jefferson Co., VA, age 42, occ. Jailer;[126] was Deputy Sheriff in charge of Abolitionist John Brown during his trial. Was kind to John Brown for which kindness Brown left Avis his Sharp's rifle in his Will;[127] Slave Dealer at Winchester, VA 1860; Civil War service apptd. Capt., Co. K, 5th Va. Inf., 05/09/1861, resigned 06/09/1862, apptd. Provost Marshall Staunton, VA 04/1865, phys. desc. 5'7", fair complex., light hair, blue eyes; postwar res. Charles Town, WV, occ. Town Sergeant, Mayor, Justice of the Peace, Superintendent of Jefferson Co. Poor House;[128] c. 1880 res. Charles Town, Jefferson Co., WV, age 62, occ. Keeps Bowl. Tol, w. Mary (45) Keeping House, son Clegit (17), dau. Maggie (15), son John (10), dau. Ardelia (9), son Walter (7);[129] phys. desc. age 65 [1883], 5'8" or 9", light complexion, light eyes, light hair, occ. Justice of the Peace, occ. at enl. saddler and shoemaker;[124] d. 09/03/1883, bur. Edge Hill Cem., Charlestown, WV; wid. Mary O., WC #1313 04/28/1887, filed from Charleston, Jefferson Co., WV; John W. Rowan and John W. Gallaher gave affidavit in pension claim;[124] (MOA b. 09/23/1835);[124] Raymond Parks, (304) 725-1062. Has photo of Capt. John Avis. Rhody Johnson 715 Painted Bunting Ln., Vero Bch., FL 32963 (561) 234-7396. (304) 647-9905.

**Ayers, William**, Pvt., *Recruit Co.*, enl. Mex.War service 02/16/1848 Charlestown, VA, age 19; pres. 04/1848; pres. 06/1848; BLW sent to Lebanon, Pa.

**Bacon, Waddy, S.**, Pvt., Co. I; b. 12/02/1827, near Lunenburg C.H., Lunenburg Co., VA, son of Gillee M. and Mary A. (Street) Bacon;[130] enl. Mex. War service 08/09/1847 Ft. Monroe, VA, age 19; absent 02/1848, on detached service in QM Dept., joined the co. 01/26/1848; absent 04/1848 on extra duty in Commissary Dept.; pres. 08/1848, pay stopped for: 1 pick & brush-$.12, 1 wiper-$.20, BLW sent to Lunenburg C.H., VA; Civil War service enl. Pvt., Co. K, 5th Va. Cav. 03/20/1864 at Richmond, VA, AWOL thru 10/15/1864, NFR, conscripted Co. F, 53rd Va. Inf. 03/10/1864 at Richmond, VA, prom. Cpl. 05/01/1864, wded. 04/07/1865 Sailor's Creek, VA, admitted Hosp. Farmville, VA, paroled as a POW by 04/21/1865;[131] m. Inez Street, 11/17/1880, San Marino, Dinwiddie Co., VA;[130] phys. desc. age 60 [1888], 5'8", dark

62

## VIRGINIA VOLUNTEERS IN MEXICO

complexion, grey eyes, grey hair, occ. Farmer;[130] since discharge res. California 1848-1857, Central America 1857-1860, Virginia 1860-1876, Wyoming Territory until recently;[130] *"Injury to left humerus by gunshot in the Confederate service. He also received a fracture of right tibia in 1852 while mining for gold in California;"*[130] SC #18574, 02/24/1888, filed from Petersburg, Dinwiddie Co., VA; d. 07/13/1903, bur. Bacon Family Cem., Rt. 671, Giles Co., VA;[132, 133] wid. Inez S., WC #17238, 08/15/1903, filed from Narrows, Giles Co., VA; (ISB b. 02/03/1846, d. 12/11/1912, Shumate, Giles Co., VA).[132]

**Bailey, John G.**, Pvt., Co. LIC; enl. Mex. War service 08/07/1847 Staunton, VA, age 21; pres. 04/1848, joined co. from regtl. depot 01/26/1848, pay stopped for: 1 blanket-$2.22; pres. 04/1848, pay stopped for: 1 cotton shirt-$.43; pres. 07/1848, pay stopped for: 1 screw driver-$.07, 1 wiper-$.20; BLW sent to Staunton, VA; m. Elizabeth Smith, 12/27/1848, Augusta Co., VA;[134] c. 1850 res. Augusta Co. VA, age 24, occ. Laborer, w. Elizabeth J. (20), son John H. (5/12);[135] w. Elizabeth J., WC #2082, 03/01/1887, from VA; d. 11/20/1859, Staunton, VA, *"...the deceased came to his death by poison, either taken by himself or administered by someone..."*[136] [pension file not found].

**Bailey, Richard A.**, 4th Sgt., Co. E; b. 03/17/1820, King William Co., VA [discharge states Hanover Co., VA];[137] enl. Mex. War service 11/30/1846 Petersburg, VA, age 26; pres. 04/1847; discharged 06/05/1847 Monterey, Mex. for disability; phys. desc., age 26, 6'3", light complexion, blue eyes, light hair, occ. Blacksmith;[138] m/1 Martha Jane Bailey, date/place unknown, divorced 03/09/1855, St. Louis, Mo.;[139] m/2 Eliza Jane Wood 05/08/1856, Hermann, Gasconade Co., Mo.; admitted 09/13/1885 National Soldiers Home, Milwaukee, WI, *"rupture left side and partial blindness;"* SC # 4301, 05/14/1887, filed from North-Western Branch, National Home for D.V.S., Milwaukee, WI, wife and family resided 139 South Bay St., Milwaukee, WI; d. 12/07/1898 National Soldiers Home, Milwaukee, WI, *"remains taken to Forest Home Crematory December 9, 1898 by Son-in-law;"* wid. Eliza J., WC #11594, 12/31/1898, filed from Baltimore, MD, *"temporary residence;"* Lists children Cliffie, Richmond, and Flora Bailey.

**Bailey, Richard B.H.**, Pvt., Co. I; enl. Mex. War service 01/10/1847 Lynchburg, VA, age 27; pres. 02/1847; pres. 04/1847; pres. 06/1847; pres. 08/1847; in confinement 04/1848 in provost guard; in confinement 10/1847, pay stopped for: 3 pr. drawers-$1.06$^{1/2}$, 3 cotton shirts-$1.72, 2 pr. shoes-$2.44, 1 pr. pants-$2.28, 1 overcoat-$6.93$^{1/2}$, 1 cap-$.95$^{1/2}$, 1 pr. socks-$.24$^{1/2}$; Court-martialed 11/15/1847 Buena Vista, Mex. *Charge #1: Conduct Prejudicial to Good Order and Military Discipline; Specification #1: In this that the said Private Richard H. Bailey, of Company I, Virginia Volunteers, did on or about the night of the 25$^{th}$ of October cut or stab with a knife Wm. A. Burks, a private in the same company. This after the said Private Burks had retired for sleep. The said Private Bailey wishing to play cards in the tent with two men of company K of same Regiment and Private Burks making objection. Specification #2: In this that the said Private R.H. Bailey did, on or about the night of the 25$^{th}$ of October bring into his tent in his company liquor in cups and did there with members of Company K, of the same regiment drink and become intoxicated. All this at the camp of his regiment near the Hacienda of Buena Vista, Mexico, on or about the 25$^{th}$ of October 1847. To which charges and specifications the prisoner plead Guilty. Pvt. Joseph Elliott, Co. I, Va. Regt., a witness for the defense, being duly sworn, says: On the night of the 25$^{th}$ of last month we put out our light at Taps and Burks and I went to sleep. When I woke up some time in the night I found some drinking and gambling going on in the tent. The prisoner Bailey went out and brought some liquor which was drunk. He then wanted to go and bring some more. Burks told him he had plenty the prisoner called Burks 'a damned rascal.' Burks replied back he was a 'damned son of a bitch.' The prisoner then raised the knife and cut Burks on the shoulder. I think he made more than one blow but struck him but once. Question by the Court: What kind of knife was it the prisoner used? Answer: It was a common butcher's knife. After deliberation the Court found the prisoner guilty. Sentenced him to be kept at hard labor in charge of the*

## OFF TO WAR

Provost Guard for the period of three (3) months;[140] in confinement 12/1847, pay stopped for: 1 pr. shoes-$1.22, 1 blanket-$2.22, 2 flannel shirts-$1.80, 1 jacket-$2.66; in confinement 02/1848; in confinement 04/1848; pres. 08/1848, pay stopped for: 1 musket complete & accoutrements complete-$16.15, BLW sent to Lynchburg, VA.

**Bain, George Spillman**, Pvt., Co. E; b. 1828, Newbern, Craven Co., NC, son of Rev. Geo. A. & Frances M. Bain;[141, 142] enl. Mex. War service 11/30/1846 Petersburg, VA, age 18; absent 04/1847 sick in China, Mex. since 04/18/1847; discharged 06/05/1847 Monterey, Mex. for disability; phys. desc. 5'8", light complexion, blue eyes, light hair, occ. Clerk;[141] m Anna W. Christian, 07/15/1851, Petersburg, VA;[141] c. 1870 res. Petersburg, VA, age 41, occ. Book Keeper, w. Anna W. (35) Keeping House, son Edward G. (16) At School, son Thomas (14) Clerk in Tobacco Warehouse, son George (3), son Charles (7/12);[143] d. 10/30/1880, *"no contagious disease,"* Williamsburg, James City Co., VA, bur. Blandford Cem., Sq. 2, Sec. 11, Ward B, Petersburg, VA;[142] w. Anna W., WC #1383, 03/04/1887, field from 141 Mercer Street, Petersburg, VA; (AWB b. 09/16/1834, d. 06/02/1899).[141]

**Bain, James H.H.**, Pvt., Co. M; enl. Mex. War service 10/22/1847, Ft. Monroe, VA, age 18; pres. 09/1847; discharged 11/05/1847 at Ft. Monroe, VA on writ of habeas corpus.

**Baker, Charles A.**, Pvt., Co. B; enl. 11/20/1846, Alexandria, VA, age 19; pres. 06/1847; pres. 08/1847; pres. 10/1847, pay stopped for: 2 pr. shoes-$2.44, 2 flannel shirts-$2.70, 1 pr. overalls-$4.56, 2 pr. socks-$.49, 2 pr. cotton drawers-$.71, 4 cotton shirt-$1.72, 1 overcoat-$ 6.99, 1 jacket-$2.66, 1 cap-$.95$^{1/2}$, 1 blanket-$2.22; pres. 12/1847, pay stopped for: 2 pr. socks-$.49, 1 pr. overalls-$2.28, 1 blanket-$2.22; pres. 02/1848, pay stopped for: 1 flannel shirts-$.90, 1 pr. shoes-$1.22; pres. 04/1848 pay stopped for: 1 jacket-$2.66; pres. 08/1848, pay stopped for: 1 bayonet scabbard-$.56, 1 waist belt-$.21, 1 waist belt plate-$.10, BLW sent to Alexandria, VA

**Baker, Jackson**, Pvt., Co. I; b. 10/10/1815;[144] enl. Mex. War service 02/23/1847 Richmond, VA, age 29; pres. 02/1847; pres. 04/1847; pres. 06/1847, sick; pres. 08/1847 sick; pres. 10/1847 sick, pay stopped for: 2 pr. drawers-$.71, 1 blanket-$2.22, 2 pr. socks-$.49; discharged 12/07/1847 on Surgeon's Certificate of Disability; c. 1860 res. Richmond, VA, age 40, occ. Laborer, wid. Ann F. (23), son George W. (1/12);[145] SC #142, 02/10/1887, filed from Elko, Henrico Co., VA; phys. desc. age 72 [1887], 5'6", fair complexion, black eyes, light hair, occ. at enl. Hotel Keeper;[144] since discharge res. Elko, Henrico Co., VA;[144] lists daughter Mattie Baker;[144] (AFB d. 07/10/1904);[144] d. 07/11/1904.[144]

**Baker, James H.**, Pvt., Co. K; enl. Mex. War service Frederick Co., VA 12/09/1846, age 19; pres. 06/1847; pres. 08/1847; pres. 10/1847, pay stopped for: 1pr. shoes-$1.22, 1 pr. overalls-$2.28, 4 pr. drawers-$1.42, 5 pr. socks-$1.22$^{1/2}$, 4 cotton shirts-$1.72, 1 cap-$.95$^{1/2}$; pres. 12/1847, pay stopped for: 1 jacket-$2.66, 1 pr. overalls-$2.28, 1 pr. boots-$1.22, 1 blanket-$2.22; pres. 04/1848; pres. 07/1848, pay stopped for 1 screw driver-$.25, 1 wiper-$.20, 1 gun sling-$.18; BLW sent to Winchester, Frederick Co., VA; Pvt. Baker evidently wrote home to his mother relating an inaccurate picture of his condition while in Mexico in the hopes of securing a discharge. In response to these pleadings a family friend wrote the Adjutant General of the U.S. Army, Roger Jones, hoping to secure Pvt. Baker's release. *"...Mrs. Baker received a letter from her son stating that being in wretched health and entirely unable to attend to his duties as a soldier, he wishes to return home if only to die with his mother."* [146]Adjt. Gen. Jones forwarded this letter to Col. Hamtramck by way of the Sec. of War, William L. Marcey. Several months later Col. Hamtramck responded thusly, *"...Baker, about whom you honored me with a letter, and some others have written home with the hope of procuring their discharge and represented their cases different from the reality. Baker is in excellent health, a tall, strong, able man. I must therefore report against procuring his discharge..."*[147]

## VIRGINIA VOLUNTEERS IN MEXICO

**Baker, William A.**, Pvt., Co. K; enl. Mex. War service Jefferson Co., VA 12/01/1846, age 38; sick 06/1847; pres. 08/1847; pres. 10/1847, pay stopped for: 1pr. shoes-$1.22, 2 pr. socks-$.49, 1 pr. drawers-$.35$^{1/2}$, 1 pr. overalls-$2.28, 2 cotton shirts-$.86; pres. 12/1847, pay stopped for: 1 jacket-$2.66, 1 pr. overalls-$2.28, 1 pr. boots-$1.22, 1 pr. socks-$.24$^{1/2}$, 2 pr. drawers-$.71, 1 blanket-$2.22, 1 cap-$.95$^{1/2}$, 1 cotton shirt-$.43, 2 flannel shirts-$1.80; pres. 04/1848, pay stopped for: 1 pr. pants-$2.28; pres. 07/1848, pay stopped for 1 breast plate-$.10; BLW sent to Charlestown, Jefferson Co., VA; Voted against secession at Hillsboro, Loudoun Co., VA, *"Was true and loyal to the U.S. Government during the entire time from 1860-1866 and was a Union man and so known for that period;"*[148] SC #200, 09/26/1885, filed from Purcellville, Loudoun Co., VA; *"Was ruptured and received injury to right hand by being thrown from a wagon* [and striking a big rock] *while on a detail for getting wood for use in camp in Buena Vista near Saltillo, Mexico about July 1848;"*[148] phys. desc. 5'7$^{1/2}$", dark complexion, dark (now grey) hair, grey eyes, occ. Dentist at enl. also;[148] John W. Gallaher and Richard W. Heafer gave affidavits in pension claim;[148] *"Baker was employed about the wagons. At Buena Vista, Mexico teams of said wagons were almost entirely wild Mexican mules, very vicious, and running away with wagons at every opportunity;"*[148] admitted c. 1889, National Soldiers Home, Elizabeth City Co., Hampton, VA;[148] filed for pension increase in 1893 from Keep Tryst, Washington Co., MD;[148] d. 08/04/1897, Hillsboro, Loudoun Co., VA;[148] [pension file in custody of Department of Veterans Affairs].

**Baldwin, James W.**, 3$^{rd}$ Sgt., Co. D; b. 03/01/1825, Montrose, Susquehanna Co., Pa;[149] enl. Mex. War service 12/11/1846, Petersburg, VA, age 21; pres. 02/1847; pres. 04/1847; pres. 06/1847, reduced to ranks 06/16/1847 by order of Col. Hamtramck; pres. 08/1847, pay stopped for: 1 spring vice-$.35$^{1/2}$, 1 pr. shoes-$1.22; pres. 10/1847, pay stopped for: 1 pr. pants-$2.28, 2 pr. socks-$.49, 1 overcoat-$6.93$^{1/2}$; pres. 12/1847, pay stopped for: 1 jacket-$2.66, 1 pr. pants-$2.28, 1 pr drawers-$.35$^{1/2}$, 1 pr. shoes-$1.22, 1 blanket-$2.22; sick 04/1848, pay stopped for: 1 cap-$.95$^{1/2}$, 1 bayonet scabbard-$.50, 1 belt plate-$.10, 1 cartridge box belt & plate-$.10, 1 musket & bayonet-$13.00; pres. 08/1847, BLW sent to Petersburg, VA; Civil War service Pvt., Co. B, 8$^{th}$ California Vols., enl. Sacramento, Calif. 11/1/1864, discharged 11/1/1865;[149] res. California 1848 – 1875, res. Bradford, Pa. 1876-1881, res. Washington, D.C. 1882-1887;[149] SC #12648, 09/17/1887, from DC, res. 923 F St., NW, Washington, D.C.; SA #23667, 07/09/1891, from VA

**Ball, Charles H.**, 2$^{nd}$ Sgt., LIC; enl. Mex. war service 11/27/1846 Staunton, VA, age 27; pres. 06/1847; pres. 08/1847; pres. 10/1847, pay stopped for: 1 forage cap-$.95$^{1/2}$, 1 wool jacket-$2.66, 1 pr. overalls-$2.28, 2 pr. socks-$.49; pres. 12/1847, pay stopped for: 1 pr. socks-$.24$^{1/2}$, 1 blanket-$2.22, 1 pr. shoes-$1.22, 1 pr. overalls-$2.28, 1 cotton shirt-$.43, 1 pr. drawers-$.35$^{1/2}$; pres. 04/1848, pay stopped for: 1 pr. shoes-$1.22; pres. 04/1848, pay stopped for: 1 cotton shirt-$.43; pres. 07/1848, pay stopped for: 1 flannel shirt-$.77$^{1/2}$, 1 gun sling-$.16, 1 screw driver-$.07; BLW sent to Staunton, VA; c. 1850 res. Augusta Co., VA, age 30, occ. Confectioner;[150] c. 1860 res. Charlottesville, VA, age 40, occ. Saddler, w. Harriet (33), dau. Mary E. (6), George C. (4), dau. Malvania (1), Kate N. (1).[151]

**Ball, James B.**, Pvt., Co. K; enl. Mex. War service Frederick Co., VA 12/01/1846, age 20; pres. 06/1847; pres. 08/1847; pres. 10/1847, prom. 3$^{rd}$ Cpl. from Pvt. 09/17/1847; pres. 12/1847, pay stopped for: 1 jacket-$2.66, 2 pr. overalls-$4.56, 2 pr. boots-$2.44, 1 pr. socks-$.24$^{1/2}$, 2 pr. drawers-$.71; pres. 04/1848, reduced to ranks 04/01/1848; pres. 07/1848; BLW sent to Charlestown, Jefferson Co., VA

**Ball, Lewis D.**, 1$^{st}$ Sgt., Co. K; enl. Mex. War service Clarke Co., VA 12/09/1846, age 27; pres. 06/1847, prom. 2$^{nd}$ Sgt. from 3$^{rd}$ Sgt. 05/31/1847; pres. 08/1847; pres. 10/1847, reduced to ranks from 2$^{nd}$ Sgt. at his own request; pres. 12/1847, pay stopped for: 2 pr. overalls-$4.56, 2 pr. boots-$2.44, 3 pr. socks-$.73$^{1/2}$, 2 pr. drawers-$.71, 1 blanket-$2.22, 1 cap-$.95$^{1/2}$; pres. 04/1848, prom. 1$^{st}$ Sgt. 01/1848; pres. 07/1848; BLW sent to Washington City; c. 1850 res.

OFF TO WAR

Clarke Co., VA, age 30, occ. Painter;[152] c. 1860 res. Front Royal, Warren Co., VA, age 36, occ. Painter.[153]

**Ball, Thomas C.**, Pvt., Co. A; enl. 11/18/1846 Richmond, VA, age 37; pres. 12/1846-04/1847; pres. 06/1847; pres. 08/1847, prom. 4$^{th}$ Cpl. 08/23/1847; sick 02/1848; discharged 03/16/1848 on Surgeon's Certificate of Disability.

**Ballenger, John**, Pvt., Co. L; b. 1819, Fairfax Co., VA, son of John & Ann Ballenger;[154] enl. Mex. War service 03/09/1847 Fairfax C.H., age 28; pres. 06/1847; sick 08/1847; pres. 10/1847, pay stopped for: 1 pr. pants-$2.28, 1 forage Cap .95; 1 pr. Shoes 1.22; pres. 12/1847, pay stopped for: 1 jacket-$2.66, 1 pr. pants-$2.28, 2 flannel shirts-$1.80, 3 cotton shirts-$1.29, 1 blanket-$2.22, 3 pr. drawers-$1.06$^{1/2}$, 1 pr. socks-$.24$^{1/2}$; pres. 02/1848; 04/1848; pres. 07/1848; BLW sent to Daysville P.O., Loudoun Co., VA; m. Ann E. Gregg, 12/21/1854, Loudoun Co., VA;[154] c. 1860 res. Goresville, Loudoun Co., VA, age 41, occ. Farmer, w. Annie E. (29), son James W. (4), dau. Sarah A. (2);[155] SC #10551, 07/06/1887, from OH.

**Ballow, James T.**, Pvt., Co. E; enl. Mex. War service 12/01/1846 Petersburg, VA, age 23; pres. 04/1847; discharged 06/05/1847 Monterey, Mex. for disability; c. 1850 res. Petersburg, VA, age 24, occ. Carpenter, w. Lavinia (18), dau. Victoria (1), Elizabeth Hardy (96);[156] c. 1860 res. Petersburg, VA, age 39, occ. Carpenter, w. Larissa (29), son Othello (9), dau. Isabella (5), dau. Mary A. (2), dau. Victoria (9).[157]

**Bangs, John W.**, Pvt., Co. B; enl. 12/20/1846, Alexandria, VA, age 19; deserted 01/24/1847, Fort Monroe; m. Adelphia Jenkins, 12/14/1850, Washington, D.C.[158]

**Bankhead, Smith Pyne**, Capt., Co. C; b. 08/28/1823, Ft. Moultrie, SC; son of James Monroe & Anne (Pyne) Bankhead; attended Georgetown Univ. and the Univ. of VA;[159] enl. 12/01/1846, Bowling Green, VA, age 23; pres. 06/1847; sick 08/1847; absent 10/1847 on recruiting service in VA from 10/12/1847; absent 12/1847 on recruiting service in VA; a letter of petition from several *"concerned citizens"* in Philadelphia, Pa. was sent to President James K. Polk, charging that Capt. Bankhead, Capt. John P. Young and Lt. Thomas S. Garnett were *"guilty of a manifest violation of military duty, in aiding abetting and countenancing by their presence, the fatal meeting between Lts. Mahan & Munford;* "[160] (see Munford, Carlton Radford, Lt.) absent 04/1848 on recruiting service in VA; *California 49er,* in Memphis, Tennessee by 1851, founded the *Memphis Whig* newspaper, served as Memphis City Attorney;[159] c. 1860 res. Memphis, TN, occ. Lawyer; Civil War service organized Bankhead's Tennessee Battery 05/1861 (Co. B, Tenn. Light Arty.); prom. Major of Artillery 04/01/1862, at Battle of Shiloh, Chief of Artillery of Polk's Corps; prom. Col. 11/13/1862 Trans-Mississippi Department; Spring 1863 commanded San Antonio, Texas Post; apptd. Acting Brig. Gen. 05/30/1863 in command the Third Sub-Dist. of Texas between the Colorado and San Antonio Rivers, by Maj. Gen. John B. Magruder;[161] never confirmed by the President Jeff. Davis; rank reverted to Col. which rank was not confirmed until January 14, 1865 to rank from June 15, 1864; m. Adeline Garth date unknown; occ. Lawyer; murdered on Main Street, Memphis, Tennessee, March 30, 1867, died age 43 from effects of a blow on head per Cemetery record; obit. appeared in *Memphis Daily Appeal* 04/02/1867;[162] bur. Elmwood Cem., Lot 67, Memphis, TN;[163, 164] brother of U.S. Navy Capt. John Pyne Bankhead, who commanded the USS Monitor 09/1862 -12/1862 when it sank off Hatteras, NC, and Union Bvt. Brig. Gen. Henry Clay Bankhead. 1$^{st}$ Cousin of Maj. Gen. John Bankhead Magruder, C.S.A. *Note: Smith Bankhead's grandfather, General James Bankhead (1756-1785) may have engaged in a duel at Old Vauter's Church, Essex County, VA in 1785.*[165]

**Banks, Albert A.**, Pvt., Co. G; b. 07/21/1826 Clarksville, Mecklenburg Co., VA;[166] enl. Mex. War service 11/28/1846 Richmond, VA, age 20; pres. 06/1847; pres. 08/1847; pres. 10/1847, pay stopped for: 1 blanket-$2.22, 1 pr. overalls-$2.28, 1 cotton shirt-$.43, 1 pr. drawers-$.35$^{1/2}$, 2 shoes-$2.44, 3 pr. socks-$.73$^{1/2}$, 1 forage cap-$.95$^{1/2}$; pres. 12/1847, 1 blanket-$2.22, 1 pr. pants-$2.28, 1 cap-$.95$^{1/2}$, 1 overcoat-$6.93$^{1/2}$, 1 pr. socks-$.24$^{1/2}$; in confinement 02/1848, pay stopped for: 1 pr. pants-$2.28, 1 jacket-$2.66, 1 pr. shoes-$1.22; Court-martialed

## VIRGINIA VOLUNTEERS IN MEXICO

02/14/1848, Buena Vista, Mex., *Charge #1: Absence Without Leave; Specification: In this that he, Pvt. Albert Banks, Co. G, Va. Regt. of Vols., did absent himself from camp without permission on Saturday, the 5th of Feby. And remain absent until Sunday, the 6th of Feby. 1848. All this at Camp Buena Vista, Mexico. Charge #2: Neglect of Duty; Specification: In this that he Pvt. Albert Banks, Co. G, Va. Regt. of Vols., did fail to appear at Inspection and Dress Parade on Sunday the 6th of February 1848, although he was in camp at the time the company formed. All this at Camp Buena Vista, Mexico. To which the accused pleaded Guilty to Charge #1 and Specification and Not Guilty to Charge #2 and Specification. Sergt. J.J. Peck, Co. G, Va. Regt. of Vols., a witness for the prosecution being duly sworn, says: I am Orderly Sergt. of Co. G, Va. Regt. The accused was absent from parade and inspection on the evening of the 6th of February 1848. Question by the Judge Advocate: Was the accused in Camp or not at the time the company was formed on that evening? Answer: He was in Camp. I saw him on the company road about an hour before the company was formed. Pvt. Andrew Didlick, Co. G., Va. Regt. Vols., a witness for the defense being duly sworn was interrogated as follows: Question by the prisoner: Was I not asleep in my tent at the time of evening parade and inspection last Sunday week? Answer: I saw the prisoner lying down in his tent apparently asleep on that evening just before Inspection. I tried to wake him up and he spoke to me, and if I am not mistaken, told me that he was unwell. After deliberation the court found the accused Guilty of all Charges and Specifications. Sentenced him to forfeit five ($5) dollars of his pay and to be kept on Police Duty in his company for one month;*[167] in confinement 04/1848; pres. 08/1848, pay stopped for: 1 ramrod-$.63, 1 cartridge box plate-$.10; BLW sent to Lynchburg, VA; Civil War service 2nd Lt., Co. B, 28th Va. Inf., enl. 05/15/1861 Craig Co., VA, age 21, occ. Teacher, absent 07/1861 –12/1861 sick at home, resigned 02/14/1862;[168] Pvt., Co. K, 60th Va. Inf., conscripted 01/28/1863 in Craig Co., VA, pres. until under arrest for AWOL 02/1864, pres. 04/1864 until captured at Berryville, VA, 07/20/1864, sent to Elmira, NY, where he took the oath of allegiance and was released, phys. desc. 5'8", blue eyes, light hair, res. Philadelphia, Pa.;[169] m. Emma Deyerle 06/27/1872, Wytheville, Wythe Co., VA;[166] SC #14572, 03/12/1887, from Newton, Catawba Co., NC; served a five year apprenticeship in Lynchburg, VA with Printer, Charles W. Stotham;[170] *"I was living in Lynchburg when I went to Richmond, VA and joined Carrington's Co. G, 1st Virginia Regiment; "* pensioner states his disability occurred at Newport, Tennessee December 20, 1886: *"I am a printer by trade and have lost the use of my right hand from rheumatism (partially). Cannot set type;"* several months later pensioner states *"disability incurred at Hendersonville, North Carolina on or about 23rd day December 1886 after several days of hard drinking an attack of accute*[sic] *rheumatism during which he lost his mind;"*[171] discharged as *"recovered"* from Western North Carolina Insane Asylum May 19, 1887;[166] since discharge res. Lynchburg, and Salem, VA, Asheville, Hendersonville and Newton, NC; d. 08/04/1901.[166]

**Barker, James W.**, Pvt., Co. A; enl. Mex. War service 12/01/1846 Richmond, VA, age 20; pres. 12/1846 - 04/1847; pres. 06/1847; pres. 08/1847; pres. 10/1847, pay stopped for clothing: 1 pr. wool overalls-$2.28, 1 cap-$.95$^{1/2}$, 4 pr. stockings-$.98, 2 flannel shirts-$1.80, 1 pr. shoes-$1.22; on detached service 12/1847 as Waggoner in QM Dept., pay stopped for clothing: 2 pr. shoes-$2.44, 1 blanket-$2.22; on detached service 02/1848 detailed as wagoneer in QM Dept.; on detached service 04/1848 as waggoneer in QM Dept.; BLW sent to Henrico Co., VA

**Barker, William**, Pvt., Co. G; enl. Mex. War service 11/18/1846 Richmond, VA, age 31; d. 06/12/1847 Monterey, Mex.; SA #16803, 09/30/1887, wid. Margaret A., WC #5075, 05/25/1888, both from VA; also served in 4th US Arty.

**Barnard, John B.F.**, Pvt., Co. L; b. 1821; pres. 06/1847; discharged 08/30/1847 at Saltillo, Mex. on surg. cert.;[72] m. Abby Sibley 10/20/1847, Danielsonville, CT; res. 30 First St., Greenbush, NY; c. 1855 res. Greenbush, Rensselaer Co., NY, age 35, occ. Express Agent, b. Mass., w. Abba V. (35), b. Maine, dau. Caroline M.F. (4), b. Mass., son George S. (2), b. Mass.;[172] d.

OFF TO WAR

12/21/1875 Greenbush, Rensselaer Co., NY, bur. Greenbush Cemetery, Greenbush, NY; w. Abby S., WC #1427, 05/27/1887, filed from Greenbush, Rensselaer Co., NY.

**Barnes, James H.**, 2nd Cpl., Co. E; b. 02/07/1816 Brunswick Co., VA;[173] m/1 _____ Street (1st wife d. 06/08/1842);[174] enl. Mex. War service 12/01/1846 Petersburg, VA, age 30; pres. 04/1847; pres. 06/1847; pres. 08/1847, prom. 4th Cpl.; pres. 08/1847; pres. 10/1847, pay stopped for: 1 pr. overalls-$2.28, 2 pr. stockings-$.49, 1 cap-$.95$^{1/2}$; pres. 12/1847, prom. 3rd Cpl., pay stopped for: 1 jacket-$2.66, 1 pr. pants-$2.28, 1 pr. shoes-$1.22, [illegible], 1 blanket-$2.22; pres. 02/1848, prom. 2nd Cpl., pay stopped for: 1 jacket-$2.66; pres. 04/1848; c. 1860 res. Morven, Amelia Co., VA, age 42, occ. Farmer, w. Ann E. (40), dau. Henrietta (18); Civil War service Capt., Co. H, 44th Va. Inf. enl. as 2nd Lt. 06/08/1861 Amelia C.H., VA, pres. 8/1861 through 4/1862, prom. 1st Lt. 12/12/1861, elected Capt. 5/01/1862, wded. 06/27/1862 at Gaines Mill, VA, wded. 12/13/1862 Fredericksburg, VA, pres. 1/1863 through 6/1863, ordered to arrest deserters and to recruit 08/22/1863, resigned 12/19/1863;[175] m/2 Ann E. Bailey 12/20/1866, Amelia Co., VA;[173] c. 1870 res. Lodore, Amelia Co., VA, age 53, occ. Farmer, w. Ann (27), son Henry (1), son William (2);[176] member Amelia Co. Board of Supervisors 1872;[177] Superintendent of the Poor Amelia Co., VA, 1888, 1893;[177, 1739] SC #4600, 05/09/1887, filed from Amelia C.H., Amelia Co., VA; since discharge res. Petersburg, VA to 1853 since then res. in Amelia Co., VA; David A. Weisiger and James M. Donnan gave affidavits in pension claim; d. 04/15/1897;[173,] wid. Annie E., WC #11212, 05/07/1897, filed from Amelia C.H., Amelia Co., VA; (AEB b. 04/18/1837, Amelia C.H., Amelia Co., VA, d. 02/20/1915, *"cancer,"* near Amelia C.H., Amelia Co., VA).

**Barnes, John**, Pvt., Co. F; enl. Mex. War service 11/23/1846, Portsmouth, VA, age 18; pres. 06/1847; pres. 08/1847; pres. 10/1847, pay stopped for: 2 pr. overalls-$4.56, 4 cotton shirts-$1.72, 1 forage cap-$.95$^{1/2}$; 5 pr. socks-$1.22$^{1/2}$, 2 pr. drawers-.71, 1 pr. shoes-$1.22; pres. 12/1847; pres. 01/1848, pay stopped for: 1 pr. overalls-$2.28, 1 infantry jacket-$2.66, 1 cotton shirt-$.43; pres. 04/1848; pres. 08/1848, pay stopped for: 1 brush & pick-$.12, 1 gun sling-$.18, 1 wiper-$.20, 2 cotton shirts-$.88, 1 blankets-$2.25, 1 pr. shoes-$1.16, 1 forage cap-$.83, BLW sent to Portsmouth, VA c/o E.T. Blamire.

**Barnett, Anderson M.**, Pvt., Co. I; b. 05/01/1813, Lexington, Rockbridge Co., VA;[178] enl. Mex. War service 01/10/1847 Lynchburg, VA, age 33; pres. 02/1847; pres. 04/1847; pres. 06/1847; pres. 08/1847, prom. 4th Cpl. resigned as 4th Cpl. 08/26/1847; absent 10/1847, pay stopped for: 4 cotton shirts-$1.72, 2 flannel shirts-$1.80, 3 pr. drawers-$1.06$^{1/2}$, 1 pr. shoes-$1.22, 1 pr. pants-$2.28, 1 overcoat-$6.93$^{1/2}$, 1 cap-$.95$^{1/2}$, 1 pr. socks-$.24$^{1/2}$, 1 jacket-$2.66; pres. 12/1847, pay stopped for: 1 pr. shoes-$1.22, 1 jacket-$2.66, 1 pr. pants-$2.28, 2 cotton shirts-$.86; pres. 02/1848; pres. 04/1848; pres. 08/1848; BLW sent to Lexington, VA; c. 1860 res. Grayson C.H., Grayson Co., VA, age 45, occ. Tailor, w. Elizabeth (47);[179] Civil War service Pvt., French's Battery, Giles Arty., enl. 04/01/1862 at Great Bridge, age 55 yrs., discharged 11/10/1862 at Camp Stuart w/ *"valvular disease of the heart;"*[180] SC #3943, 03/30/1887, filed from Hampton Cross Roads, Grayson Co., VA; d. 10/12/1899.[178]

**Barnett, Thomas R.**, Pvt., *Preston's Co.*; b. 03/1826, son of Robert & Mary Barnett;[181] enl. Mex. War service 12/06/1846 Montgomery Co., VA, age 20; absent 04/1847 left sick in Hosp. at Ft. Monroe, VA since 03/16/1847; pres. 06/1847; sick 08/1847; pres. 10/1847, pay stopped for: 1 pr. socks-$.24$^{1/2}$, 1 flannel shirt-$.90, 1 cotton shirt-$.43; pres. 12/1847, pay stopped for: 1 jacket-$2.66, 1 pr. overalls-$2.28, 1 pr. shoes-$1.22, 1 pr. socks-$.24$^{1/2}$, 1 cap-$.95$^{1/2}$, 1 pr. drawers-$.35$^{1/2}$, 1 blankets-$2.22; pres. 02/1848; pres. 04/1848; pres. 04/1848; pres. 07/1848, pay stopped for: 1 pr. shoes-$1.22; BLW sent to Christiansburg, VA c/o Fleming Gardner; Thomas R. Barnett, age 29 yrs., 10 mos., 23 days, occ. Blacksmith, m. Eliz Linkinhoker, 01/17/1856, Montgomery Co., VA;[181] c. 1860 res. Alleghany Springs, Montgomery Co., VA, age 34, occ. Blacksmith, w. Elizabeth (26), dau. Emma J. (3), dau. Olivia (2), dau. Ann (1), dau. Not Named (8/12);[182] Civil War service Pvt., 4th Va. Inf. enl. 10/17/1864, NFR;[54] c. 1870 res. Alleghany Springs, Montgomery Co., VA, age 45, *"Since died,"* wid. Elizabeth (37), dau.

68

## VIRGINIA VOLUNTEERS IN MEXICO

Emma J. (13), dau. Olivia (12), dau. Ann E. (11), dau. Betty (10), son Joseph (9), son George E. (7), son William (1), James F. (4/12).[183]

**Barr, Cornelius B.**, Pvt., Co. K; b. c. 1822, Winchester, VA, son of Robert and Araminta B. Barr;[184] enl. Mex. War service Frederick Co., VA 12/24/1846; discharged 03/30/1847 at Camargo, Mex. on Surgeon's Certificate of Disability; m. Mary Frances Grimm 05/17/1855, Winchester, Frederick Co., VA; c. 1860 res. Winchester, Frederick Co., VA, age 37, occ. Master Bricklayer, w. Frances (25), dau. Ida (4), son Henry (2), son Charles (6/12);[185] Civil War service Pvt., Co. A, 5$^{th}$ Va. Inf. enl. 07/04/1861 at Winchester, discharged 10/02/1861, ordered to report to Capt. J.C. Booth at Fayettville, NC *"fully acquainted with building furnaces;"*[128] c. 1870 res. Winchester, Frederick Co., VA, age 47, occ. Brick Mason, w. Mary F. (37), dau. Ida (14), son Henry B. (12), son Charles (10), dau. Minnie (8), dau. Kate (6), son John W. (4), dau Bettie (2);[186] SC #123, 02/15/1887, filed from 611 E. 11$^{th}$ St., Wilmington, New Castle Co., DE; phys. desc. age 64 [1887], 5'8$^{1/2}$", fair complexion, blue eyes, mixed hair, occ. bricklayer;[184] d. 05/31/1894, *"paresis,"* 1315 King St., Wilmington, DE, bur. Riverview Cemetery, Wilmington, DE;[187] wid. Mary Frances, WC #10799, 06/01/1894, filed from 1315 King St., Wilmington, New Castle Co., DE; (MGB b. 01/26/1834, d. 1902).[187]

**Barrett, George F.**, 1$^{st}$ Sgt., Co. C; enl. Mex. War service 12/30/1846, Bowling Green, VA, age 23; pres. 06/1847, prom. 2$^{nd}$ Sgt. 06/16/1847; pres. 08/1847, prom. 1$^{st}$ Sgt. 08/25/1847, pay stopped for: 1 cap-$.95$^{1/2}$, 2 pr. socks-$.49, 2 cotton shirts-$.86, 2 woolen shirts-$1.80, 1 pr. shoes-$1.22, 1 knapsack & straps-$1.10; pres. 10/1847, pay stopped for: 2 pr. socks-$.49, 1 pr. pants-$2.28, 1 cotton shirt-$.43; pres. 12/1847, pay stopped for: 1 pr. pants-$2.28, 2 blankets-$4.44; pres. 04/1848, pay stopped for: 1 jacket-$2.66, 1 pr. pants-$2.28, 1 haversack-.20$^{3/4}$, 1 india rubber canteen-$.27; pres. 08/1848, BLW sent to Washington City, DC; Civil War service Pvt., Co. E, 1$^{st}$ Va. Inf., enl. 04/22/1861, age 38, occ. painter, co. was disbanded abt. May 1862; c. 1870 a George Barrett res. 4$^{th}$ Ward, Washington, D.C.;[188] 1874 occ. Painter res. 1421 T St., NW, Wash., D.C.[189]

**Barringer, John A.**, Pvt., *Preston's Co.*; b. 08/09/1829 Montgomery Co., VA, son of Jacob and Araminta (Goodwin) Barringer;[48] enl. Mex. War service 12/14/1846 Montgomery Co., VA, age 19; pres. 04/1847; pres. 06/1847; pres. 08/1847; pres. 10/1847, pay stopped for: 1 pr. overalls-$2.28, 3 pr. socks-$.73$^{1/2}$, 1 cotton shirt-$.43; sick 12/1847, pay stopped for: 1 jacket-$2.66, 1 pr. overalls-$2.28; pres. 02/1848; pres. 04/1848; pres. 07/1848; pres. 08/1848, pay stopped for: 1 pr. shoes-$1.16, 1 brush & pick-$.12; BLW sent to Floyd C.H., VA; m. Triphena Sowers, 01/29/1849, Floyd Co., VA;[190] c. 1860 res. Greasy Creek, Floyd Co., VA, age 30, occ. Farmer, w. Triphena (36), dau. Sabra (9), dau. Sarah A. (7), son William (5), dau. Mary (3), dau. Virginia (8/12);[191] Civil War service Pvt., Co. D, 54$^{th}$ Va. Inf., enl. 03/24/1862 at Abingdon, VA, listed as MIA at Missionary Ridge on 11/25/1863 but was captured on 11/27/1863 at Ringold, Ga., apparently a deserter, sent to Chattanooga and released on oath of allegiance sent north of the Ohio, phys. desc. fair complex., dark hair, blue eyes, 5'10";[192] c. 1870 res. Floyd C.H., VA, age 40, occ. Miller, w. Trifana (46), dau. Sabra Ann (20), son William (16), dau. Mary (13), dau. Sarah Ann (18), dau. Anna Laura (6), dau. Arbilla (3), dau. Dorthea M. (1), adopted dau. Morilla Green Jett (9);[193] phys. desc. at enl. age 18, occ. Farmer, florid complexion, black hair, blue eyes, 5'10";[190] since discharge res. Floyd Co., VA;[190] d. 02/02/1876, bur. Barringer Cem., Burk's Fork, Floyd Co., VA;[190, 192] wid. Triphena, WC #508, 04/05/1887, filed from Burk's Fork, Floyd Co., VA; Charles A. Ronald gave affidavit in pension claim;[190] (TSB b. 07/07/1824, d. 11/18/1892, *"cancer,"* bur. Barringer Cem. Burk's Fork, Floyd Co., VA).[48, 190]

**Barry, Robert**, Pvt., Co. G; enl. Mex. War service 11/25/1846 Richmond, VA, age 24; pres. 06/1847; pres. 08/1847; pres. 10/1847, pay stopped for: 1 blanket-$2.22, 1 pr. overalls-$2.28, 1 cotton shirt-$.43, 3 flannel shirts-$2.70, 1 pr. drawers-$.35$^{1/2}$, 1 shoes-$1.22, 4 pr. socks-$.98, 1 forage cap-$.95$^{1/2}$; pres. 12/1847, pay stopped for: 1 overcoat-$6.93$^{1/2}$, 1 pr. shoes-

OFF TO WAR

$1.22, 1 pr. pants-$2.28, 1 pr. socks-$.24$^{1/2}$; pres. 02/1848, pay stopped for: 1 jacket-$2.66; pres. 04/1848, pay stopped for: 1 pr. shoes-$1.22; pres. 08/1848; BLW sent to Richmond, VA

**Barziza, Edgar A.**, Pvt., Co. A; enl. Mex. War service 12/01/1846 Richmond, VA, age 21; pres. 12/1846 - 04/1847; pres. 06/1847; pres. 08/1847; pres. 10/1847, pay stopped for clothing: 1 pr. wool overalls-$4.56,1 cap-$.95$^{1/2}$, 4 pr. stockings-$.98, 1 wool jacket-$2.66, 1 cotton shirts-$.43, 2 flannel shirts-$1.81; pres. 12/1847, pat stopped for: 1 pr shoes-$1.22; pres. 02/1848, pay stopped for clothing: 1 pr. wool overalls-$2.28; pres. 04/1848; 07/1848, pay stopped for: musket sling-$.56, pick & brush-$.12, screw driver-$.25, [illegible]; BLW sent to Williamsburg, VA

**Bateman, James W.**, Pvt., Co. K; enl. Mex. War service Jefferson Co., VA 01/20/1847, age 19; pres. 06/1847; pres. 08/1847; pres. 10/1847, pay stopped for: 2 pr. shoes-$2.44, 5 cotton shirts-$2.15, 2 pr. drawers-$.71, 2 pr. socks-$.49, 1 pr. overalls-$2.28, 1 greatcoat-$6.93$^{1/2}$; pres. 12/1847, pay stopped for: 1 jacket-$2.66, 1 pr. overalls-$2.28, 1 pr. boots-$1.22, 1 pr. socks-$.24$^{1/2}$, 1 pr. drawers-$.35$^{1/2}$, 1 cap-$.95$^{1/2}$, 1 cotton shirt-$.43, 2 flannel shirts-$1.80; pres. 04/1848, pay stopped for: 1 flannel shirt-.90, 1 gun sling-$.18; pres. 07/1848, pay stopped for: 1 wiper-$.20; BLW sent to Harper's Ferry, Jefferson Co., VA; c. 1850 res. Harper's Ferry, VA, age 21;[194] c. 1860 res. Bolivar, Jefferson Co., VA, age 39, occ. Laborer, w. Ann, (24), son Stephen (7), son James (5), son Julian (3).[195]

**Battaile, Lawrence**, 2$^{nd}$ Lt., Co. C; enl. Mex. War service 12/13/1846, Bowling Green, VA, age 21; pres. 06/1847; pres. 08/1847, pay stopped for: 1 cap-$.95$^{1/2}$, 2 pr. socks-$.49, 2 cotton shirts-$.86, 2 woolen shirts-$1.80; pres. 10/1847, pay stopped for: 2 pr. socks-$.49, 1 jacket-$2.66, 1 cotton shirt-$.43, 1 woolen shirt-$.90, 1 pr. shoes-$1.22, 1 great coat-$6.93$^{1/2}$, 1 blanket-$2.22; pres. 12/1847, pay stopped for: 2 pr. drawers-$.71, 2 pr. socks-$.49, 1 pr. pants-$2.28, 1 pr. shoes-$1.22, 1 blanket-$2.22; pres. 04/1848, prom. 2$^{nd}$ Lt. 04/17/1848, pay stopped for 1 pr. shoes-$1.22, 1 haversack-$.20$^{3/4}$, 1 india rubber canteen-$.27; pres. 08/1848, BLW sent to Griffinsburg, Culpeper Co., VA

**Beadles, Lewis J.**, Pvt., Co. G; enl. Mex. War service 11/28/1846 Richmond, VA, age 22; pres. 06/1847; sick 08/1847; discharged 09/11/1847 on Surgeon's Certificate of Disability.

**Beales, John A.**, Pvt., Co. H; enl. Mex. War service 11/21/1846, Berkeley, VA, age 24; pres. 04/1847; discharged 05/09/1847 at camp near Monterey, Mex. on Surgeon's Certificate of Disability.

**Beam, Emanuel**, Pvt., Co. K; b. c. 1820, Milford, Page Co., VA;[196] enl. Mex. War service Frederick Co., VA 01/01/1847, age 20; pres. 06/1847; pres. 08/1847; pres. 10/1847, pay stopped for: 1 pr. overalls-$2.28, 2 pr. drawers-$.71, 2 pr. socks-$.49, 2 cotton shirts-$.86, 1pr. shoes-$1.22, 1 cap-$.95$^{1/2}$; pres. 12/1847, pay stopped for: 1 pr. overalls-$2.28, 1 blanket-$2.22; pres. 04/1848, pay stopped for: 1 pr. pants-$2.28, 1 pr. shoes-$1.22; pres. 07/1848; BLW sent to Winchester, VA; m. Sarah _____, c. 1850, Sparta, [Mauzy] Rockingham Co., VA;[196] SC #5788, 03/22/1887, filed from Mt. Crawford, Rockingham Co., VA; John P. Brock gave affidavit in pension claim;[196] since discharge res. Mays, Franklin Co., Pa., Cedar Point, Page Co., Lacy Spring and Mt. Crawford, Rockingham Co., VA;[196] d. 1889.[196]

**Beatty, Samuel J.**, Pvt., Co. F; b. c. 1804, Washington Co., MD; enl. Mex. War service 01/22/1847, Portsmouth, VA, age 43; pres. 06/1847; pres. 08/1847; absent 10/1847 sick, pay stopped for: 1 pr. overalls-$2.28, 1 cotton shirt-$.43, 2 flannel shirts-$1.80, 1 pr. shoes-$1.22, 2 pr. socks-$.49, 2 pr. drawers-.71, 1 forage cap-$.95$^{1/2}$; absent 12/1847 sick; discharged 01/07/1848 Buena Vista, Mex. on Surgeon's Certificate of Disability; desc., age 43, 5'8", dark complexion, hazel eyes, grey hair, occ. Tailor; discharged 01/07/1848 Buena Vista, Mexico, on Surgeon's Certificate of Disability;[26] m. Ann Frances Furrow, 1849, Montgomery Co., VA;[197] c. 1850 res. Montgomery Co., VA, age 50, occ. Tailor, w. Ann (23).[198]

**Beck, Jacob**, Pvt., Co. M; b. c. 1810, VA, son of Elizabeth Beck; m. Sarah Summers 12/22/1834, Augusta Co., VA;[199] enl. Mex. War service 09/01/1847, Petersburg, VA, age 43; pres. 09/1847; pres. 11/1847; pres. 12/1847; pres. 02/1848, pay stopped for: 2 flannel shirts-$1.80;

## VIRGINIA VOLUNTEERS IN MEXICO

pres. 04/1848; pres. 08/1848, pay stopped for: 1 musket-$13.00, 1 cartridge box belt-$.21, 1 cartridge box belt plate-$.10, 1 waist belt-$.21, 1 waist belt plate-$.10, 1 bayonet scabbard-$.56, 1 bayonet-$1.44, 1 pick & brush-$.12, 1 screw driver-$.07, 1 wormer-$.20; BLW sent to Petersburg, VA; c. 1850 res. Augusta Co., VA, age 40, occ. Farmer, w. Sarah (38), son William A. (13), son Andrew D.S. (11), son Alexander (7), son John S.B. (3), dau. Anna A.V. (5), mother? Elizabeth (58);[200] c. 1860 res. Staunton, Augusta Co., VA, age 49, occ. Farmer, w. Sarah (49), son William A. (23), son Andrew D.S. (20), son Alexander L. (18), dau. Anna A.V. (15), son John S.B. (12), dau. Rose (6), dau. Lilley (6), dau. Elizabeth (9);[201] [Civil War service a Jacob Beck served as Pvt., Co. H, 5$^{th}$ Btln. Inf. Local Defense;][202] c. 1870 res. Craigsville, Augusta Co., VA, age 59, occ. Farmer, w. Sarah (58), son John S.B. (23), dau. Rose A. (15), dau. Lilla A. (15);[203] d. 10/21/1876, aged 66, Augusta Co., VA[204]

**Belt, John C.**, Pvt., Co. B; enl. 12/26/1846, Alexandria, VA, age 28; sick 06/1847, left in hosp. Monterey, Mex. 06/01/1847; d. 07/01/1847 in hosp. at Monterey, Mex.

**Bennett, Anderson**, Pvt., Co. H; enl. Mex. War service 01/06/1847, Berkeley, VA, age 20; pres. 04/1847; pres. 06/1847; pres. 08/1847; pres. 10/1847, pay stopped for: 1 forage cap-$.95$^{1/2}$, 1 pr. pants-$2.28, 4 cotton shirts-$1.72, 3 flannel shirts-$2.70, 1 pr. drawers-$.35$^{1/2}$, 4 pr. socks-$.98, 1 greatcoat-$6.93$^{1/2}$, 1 jacket-$2.66; pres. 12/1847; pres. 02/1848, 1 pr. drawers-$.35$^{1/2}$, 1 pr. shoes-$1.22; pres. 04/1848; pres. 07/1848, pay stopped for: 1 gun sling-$.16, 1 waist belt plate-$.10, 1 screw driver-$.25, 1 wiper-$.20, BLW sent to Philadelphia, Pa.; Civil War service an Anderson D. Bennett enl. as Pvt., Co. H, 76$^{th}$ Pa. Inf.

**Bennett, John A.**, Pvt., Co. L; b. 1813; enl. Mex. War service 03/18/1847 Fort Washington, age 34; discharged 04/29/1847 by order Adj. Genl.[72]

**Bennett, William G.**, Pvt., *Preston's Co.*; b. 1827, son of David M. & Prudence Bennett;[205] enl. Mex. War service 12/06/1846 Montgomery Co., VA, age 19; pres. 04/1847; sick 06/1847; pres. 08/1847; pres. 10/1847, pay stopped for: 1 jacket-$2.66, 1 pr. overalls-$2.28, 1 pr. shoes-$1.22, 2 pr. socks-$.49, 1 flannel shirt-$.90, 1 cotton shirt-$.43, 1 pr. drawers-$.35$^{1/2}$, 1 cap-$.95$^{1/2}$; pres. 12/1847, pay stopped for: 1 jacket-$2.66, 1 pr. overalls-$2.28, 1 pr. shoes-$1.22; pres. 02/1848; sick 04/1848; pres. 07/1848, pay stopped for: 1 screw driver-$.07, 1 wiper-$.13; BLW sent to Christiansburg, VA c/o Fleming Gardner; m. Nancy Ann McDonald, 05/01/1851, Montgomery Co., VA;[206, 207] c. 1850 res. Montgomery Co., VA, age 24, occ. Farmer; c. 1860 res. McDonald's Mills, Montgomery Co., VA, age 36, occ. Farmer, w. Nancy A. (25), son Edward (7), son William H. (5), dau. Martha J. (3), son George McD. (1);[208] Civil War service Pvt., Co. E, 4$^{th}$ Va. Inf. enl. 11/01/1864;[54] d. 03/16/1868, Montgomery Co., VA;[206] wid. Nancy Ann, WC #3135, 12/19/1887, filed from McDonald's Mill, Montgomery Co., VA; Michael Kipps gave affidavit in pension claim;[206] (NMB b. 08/29/1833, Montgomery Co., VA, d. 12/19/1899).[206]

**Benson, Francis L.**, 4$^{th}$ Sgt., Co. F; b. c. 1826 Portsmouth, Norfolk Co., VA;[209] enl. Mex. War service 01/15/1847, Portsmouth, VA, age 31; prom. 4$^{th}$ Cpl. date unknown; pres. 06/1847; pres. 08/1847, prom. 3$^{rd}$ Cpl.; pres. 10/1847, pay stopped for: 1 pr. overalls-$2.28, 4 cotton shirts-$1.72, 1 flannel shirt-$.90, 4 pr. socks-$.98, 3 pr. shoes-$3.66, 2 pr. drawers-.71, 1 overcoat-$6.93$^{1/2}$; pres. 12/1847; pres. 02/1848, pay stopped for: 1 blanket-$2.22, 1 forage cap-$.95$^{1/2}$, 1 pr. overalls-$2.28; pres. 04/1848; pres. 03/01/1848 4$^{th}$ Sgt.; pres. 08/1848, pay stopped for: 1 shoes-$1.16, BLW sent to Norfolk, VA; c. 1850 res. Norfolk Co., VA, age 37, occ. Plasterer, w. Mary A. (20), son James (13);[210] Civil War service 2$^{nd}$ Sgt., Co. K, 9$^{th}$ Va. Inf., enl. as Pvt. 04/20/1861 at Portsmouth, VA, prom. 2$^{nd}$ Sgt. 08/15/1862, detailed as Hosp. Steward and 09/15/1862 through 02/1864, at Winchester and Petersburg, VA, discharged 02/28/1864;[211] SA #173, 02/04/1887, filed from Portsmouth, Norfolk Co., VA; phys. desc. age 70 (1886), 5'8", dark complexion, gray eyes, dark hair, occ. Plasterer;[209] John K. Cooke, 809 Dinwiddie St., Portsmouth, VA, gave affidavit in pension claim; d. 10/27/1901, Cedar Grove Cem., Portsmouth, VA

## OFF TO WAR

**Bentley, Hartwell**, Pvt., Co. D; enl. Mex. War service 01/23/1847, Richmond, VA, age 29; pres. 04/1847; absent 06/1847, left sick in Hosp. Monterey, Mex. 06/22/1847; discharged about 08/01/1847 Monterey, Mex. on Surgeon's Certificate of Disability, due to *"chronic headache."*[212]

**Benton, Jesse**, Pvt., Co. F; enl. Mex. War service 12/20/1846, Portsmouth, VA, age 27; absent 06/1847 left sick in Hosp. Camargo, Mex. 04/04/1847; absent 08/1847 sick at Camargo, Mex. since 04/04/1847; absent 10/1847 sick at Camargo, Mex. since 04/04/1847; absent 12/1847 sick at Camargo, Mex.; absent 02/1848 sick in Camargo, Mex.; absent 04/1848 sick in Camargo, Mex.; absent on final roll 08/1848.

**Berry, Thomas**, Pvt., Co. L; b. 1831, son of Thomas & Elizabeth (Silmone) Berry; enl. Mex. War service 03/01/1847 Fairfax C.H., age 19; discharged 03/24/1847 by order of Adj. Genl.;[72] c. 1850 res. Alexandria, VA, age 18, occ. Ship's Carpenter;[213] c. 1860 res. Alexandria, VA, age 29, occ. Cooper;[214] c. 1870 res. Alexandria, VA, age 37, occ. Ship's Carpenter, mother? Elizabeth (61), sister? Margaret (22).[215]

**Bibey, James B.**, Pvt., LIC; b. c. 1823, Middle River, Augusta Co., VA;[216] enl. Mex. War service 08/09/1847 Staunton, VA, age 24; pres. 04/1848, joined the co. 01/26/1848 from the regtl. depot, pay stopped for: 1 pr. overalls-$2.28, 1 blanket-$2.22, 2 cotton shirts-$.86; pres. 04/1848, pay stopped for: 1 cotton shirt-$.43; pres. 07/1848, pay stopped for: 1 pick & brush-$.12; BLW sent to Staunton, VA; c. 1850 res. Augusta Co., VA, age 28, occ. Farmer;[217] m. Mary Shue, date unknown, Augusta Co., VA;[216] SC #165, 02/11/1887, filed from Staunton, Augusta Co., VA; phys. desc. age 64 [1887], 6'1", fair or ruddy complexion, blue eyes, dark hair, occ. Laborer;[216] d. 05/1889 Augusta Co., VA, age 65 yrs., 2 mos., 25 days.[218]

**Bickle, William O.**, Pvt., LIC; enl. Mex. War service 12/07/1846 Staunton, VA, age 24; pres. 06/1847; pres. 08/1847; pres. 10/1847, pay stopped for: 1 forage cap-$.95$^{1/2}$, 1 wool jacket-$2.66, 1 pr. overalls-$2.28, 2 cotton shirts-$.86, 5 pr. socks-$1.32$^{1/2}$, 1 pr. shoes-$1.22; pres. 12/1847, pay stopped for: 1 pr. socks-$.24$^{1/2}$, 1 pr. shoes-$1.22, 1 pr. overalls-$2.28; pres. 04/1848, reduced to ranks from 1$^{st}$ Cpl. 04/04/1848 by sentence of garrison court-martial, pay stopped for: 1 pr. overalls-$2.28, 1 pr. shoes-$1.22; pres. 04/1848, pay stopped for: 1 cotton shirt-$.43; pres. 07/1848, pay stopped for: 1 gun sling-$.16; BLW sent to Staunton, VA; c. 1850 res. Augusta Co., VA, age 28, occ. Carriage Maker;[219] Civil War service Pvt., Co. C, 1$^{st}$ Ohio Inf., res. 3 N. Augusta St., Staunton, Va;[220] d. 04/22/1897.[221]

**Bilson, Andrew J.**, Co. A; enl. Mex. War 11/18/1846 Richmond, VA, age 31; pres. 12/1846-04/1847; pres. 06/1847; pres. 08/1847; pres. 10/1847, pay stopped for clothing: 2 cotton shirts-$1.72, 2 pr. wool overalls-$4.56, 1 cap-$.95$^{1/2}$, 3 pr. shoes-$3.66, 3 pr. stockings-$.73$^{1/2}$, 2 flannel shirts-$1.80, 1 great coat-$6.93$^{1/2}$; in confinement 12/1847, pay stopped for clothing: 1 pr. wool overalls-$2.28, 2 pr. drawers-$.71, 1 musket complete-$13.00, 1 cartridge box-$1.10, 1 cartridge box belt & plate-$.70, 1 bayonet-$.50, scabbard & belt-$.56; pres. 02/1848, pay stopped for: 1 pr. shoes-$1.22; 1 pick & brush-$.12; 1 pr. wool overalls-$2.28, 1 blanket-$2.22; on detached service 04/1848 in QM Dept., Saltillo, Mex. since 03/21/1848; 07/1848, pay stopped for: 1 pr. shoes-$1.16; BLW sent to Richmond, VA; m/ Lucy Jane Welsh 08/16/1849 Williamsburg, VA; c. 1850 res. Williamsburg, VA, age 20, w. Lucy J. (20), dau. Virginia M. (6/12);[222] d. 07/14/1867, *"bronchitis,"* Baltimore, MD; bur. Green Mount Cemetery, Area J, Lot 47, Baltimore, MD; wid. Lucy Jane, WC #2772, 09/10/1887, filed from 1223 N. Gilmore St., Baltimore, MD; (LJB b. 01/01/1830 Williamsburg, VA, d. 07/28/1899).[223]

**Binford, John G.**, 4$^{th}$ Sgt., Co. I; b. c. 1827, Goochland Co., VA, son of Thomas & M. Binford;[224]enl. Mex. War service 12/01/1846 Richmond, VA, age 19; pres. 02/1847; pres. 04/1847; pres. 06/1847, reduced from 2$^{nd}$ Cpl. 06/15/1847; pres. 08/1847; pres. 10/1847, pay stopped for: 1 cotton shirt-$.43, 3 flannel shirts-$2.70, 1 pr. pants-$2.28, 1 pr. shoes-$1.22, 1 pr. socks-$.24$^{1/2}$, 1 cap-$.95$^{1/2}$, 1 pr. drawers-$.35$^{1/2}$; pres. 12/1847, pay stopped for: 2 pr. socks-$.49, 1 jacket-$2.66, 1 pr. pants-$2.28, 1 pr. shoes-$1.22, 1 blanket-$2.22; pres.

VIRGINIA VOLUNTEERS IN MEXICO

02/1848; pres. 04/1848, prom. 4$^{th}$ Cpl. 03/25/1848, prom. 4$^{th}$ Sgt. 04/20/1848; pres. 08/1848, BLW sent to Goochland C.H., VA; c. 1850 res. Goochland Co., VA, age 20, occ. Farmer;[225] m/1 Nettie Wallace,date/place unknown; c. 1860 res. Augusta Co., VA, age 30, occ. Manager on Rail Road, w. Hettie (27), dau. Kate (5), son Thomas H. (3);[226] (NWB d. 1869 or 1870, Wytheville, VA);[224] m/2 Lucy W. Brown, 01/26/1874, Covington, Alleghany Co., VA;[224] d. 11/13/1884, Craigsville, Augusta Co., VA; [224, 227] wid. Lucy W., WC #3213, 04/18/1887, filed from Craigsville, Augusta Co., VA; (LBB b. 07/04/1849, Covington, Alleghany Co., VA, d. 08/20/1919, Portsmouth, VA, bur. Oak Grove Cemetery, Norfolk, VA).[224]

**Birkitt, William**, Pvt., Co. K; enl. Mex. War service Loudoun Co., VA 12/24/1846, age 24; pres. 06/1847; pres. 08/1847; pres. 10/1847, pay stopped for: 1 pr. overalls-$2.28, 5 cotton shirts-$2.15, 1pr. shoes-$1.22, 3 pr. drawers-$1.06$^{1/2}$, 4 pr. socks-$.98, 2 flannel shirts-$1.80, 1 cap-$.95$^{1/2}$; pres. 12/1847, pay stopped for: 1 jacket-$2.66, 1 pr. overalls-$2.28, 1 pr. boots-$1.22, 3 pr. socks-$.73$^{1/2}$; pres. 04/1848, pay stopped for: 1 pick & brush-$.12, 1 gun sling-$.18; pres. 07/1848; BLW sent to Hillsborough, Loudoun Co., VA; c. 1860 res. Hillsborough, Loudoun Co., VA, age 34, occ. Tailor;[228] m. Margaret Ann (Fritz) Taylor, 04/11/1872, Loudoun Co. VA;[229, 230] phys. desc. 5'10', dark complexion, grey eyes, dark brown hair, occ. Tailor;[230] d. 07/13/1878, *"chronic malaria and diarrhea,"* Eastern State Hospital, Williamsburg, VA;[230] wid. Margaret A., WC #3448, 09/23/1887, from VA; (MAB b. 02/14/1826, m/1 Joseph Taylor, 09/13/1848, JT d. 02/13/1870, MAB d. 09/04/1892).[230]

**Bishop, Charles**, 1$^{st}$ Sgt., Co. L; b. 1822; enl. Mex. War service 03/01/1847 Fairfax C.H., age 25; pres. 08/1847, prom. 3$^{rd}$ Sgt. from 4$^{th}$ Sgt.; pres. 10/1847, pay stopped for: 1 W Jacket-$ 2.66, 1 pr. Pants-$2.28, 1 F cap-$.95.; pres. 12/1847, prom. 1$^{st}$ Sgt. from 3$^{rd}$ Sgt. 11/04/1847, pay stopped for: 1 pr. Pants 2.28, 2 F Shirts 1.80, 7 Ct Shirts 3.01, 1 Blanket 2.22, 3 prs. Drawers 1.86, 2 prs. Socks .49; pres. 02/1848, pay stopped for: 1 Jacket-$2.66; pres. 04/1848; pres. 07/1848, pay stopped for: 1 brush & pick-$.12, 1 screw driver-$.25, 6 buttons-$.10, 1 waist belt-$.21, 1 waist belt cleat-$.10, 1 bayonet-$1.44, 1 cartridge box-$1.10, 1 bayonet scabbard-$.56, 1 wiper-$.20; BLW sent to Washington City.

**Bishop, James H.**, Co. C; b. 10/02/1825 Lunenburg Co., VA;[231] enl. Mex. War service 08/09/1847, Lunenburg Co., VA, age 21; pres. 04/1848, joined company 01/27/1848 from Regtl. Depot, pay stopped for: [illegible]; pres. 08/1848, BLW sent to ___ Oaks, Lunenburg, VA; m. Sarah F.T. Bowers, 03/10/1851, Lunenburg Co., VA; [231, 232] c. 1860 res. Pleasant Grove, Lunenburg Co., VA, age 34, occ. Farmer, w. Sarah F. (29), son Peter B. (6), dau. Anna G. (3);[233] c. 1870 res. Lunenburg C.H., VA, age 45, occ. Farmer, w. Sarah F. (39), son Peter B. (17), son Joseph H. (9), son James A. (5), son Thomas F. (3), dau. Sarah B. (1);[234] SC #5499, 03/18/1887, filed from Non-Intervention P.O., Lunenburg Co., VA, Children named in pension claim Joseph H., Peter B. & James A.; Pvts. John W. Overby and Edward W. Goodwyn gave affidavit in pension claim; d. 04/08/1894, Lunenburg Co., VA.[231]

**Bishop, Joseph M., Jr.**, Pvt., LIC; enl. Mex. War service 01/05/1847 Charlottesville, VA, age 25; pres. 06/1847; pres. 08/1847; pres. 10/1847, pay stopped for: 1 forage cap-$.95$^{1/2}$, 1 wool jacket-$2.66, 1 pr. overalls-$2.28, 2 pr. shoes-$2.44, 4 cotton shirts-$1.72, 3 pr. socks-$.73$^{1/2}$; pres. 12/1847, pay stopped for: 1 pr. socks-$.24$^{1/2}$, 1 blanket-$2.22, 1 pr. overalls-$2.28, 2 cotton shirts-$.86, 2 flannel shirts-$1.80, 2 pr. drawers-$.71; pres. 04/1848, to forfeit 1 mos. pay by sentence of Garrison court-martial, pay stopped for: 1 pr. shoes-$1.22; pres. 04/1848, pay stopped for: 1 cotton shirt-$.43; pres. 07/1848, pay stopped for: 1 flannel shirt-$.77$^{1/2}$, 1 blanket-$2.25, 1 bayonet-$1.44, 1 gun sling-$.16, 1 pick & brush-$.12, 1 screw driver-$.07, 1 wiper-$.20; BLW sent to Charlottesville, VA; m. Fanny McGoath, 09/29/1858, Albemarle Co., VA;[235] c. 1860 res. Charlottesville, Albemarle Co., VA, age 33, occ. Overseer, w. Fanny (24), son William (10/12);[236] c. 1870 res. Scottsville, Albemarle Co., VA, age 39, occ. Farmer, (illiterate), w. Fannie (35), son William (11), son Shedrack (9), son Joseph (5), dau. Isabella (3), son John (1).[237]

OFF TO WAR

**Black, Harvey**, Hospital Steward, *Preston's Co.*; b. 08/27/1827, Blacksburg, VA, son of Alexander & Elizabeth (McDonald) Black; enl. Mex. War service 11/24/1846 Montgomery Co., VA, age 19; pres. 04/1847; absent 06/1847, on detached service as a Hospital Ward Master since 05/10/1847, prom. 4th Cpl. 05/25/1847; absent on detached service as Hospital Ward Master, prom. 3rd Cpl.; absent 10/1847, on detached service as Hospital Steward; pres. 12/1847, prom. Hosp. Steward; pres. 02/1848; absent 04/1848 on detached service; pres. 07/1848, pay stopped for: 1 gun sling-$.18, 1 wiper-$.13; BLW sent to Blacksburg, VA; c. 1850 res. Montgomery Co., VA, age 23, occ. Physician;[238] m. Mary J. Kent 09/07/1852, Blacksburg, Montgomery Co., VA;[239, 240] c. 1860 res. Blacksburg, VA, age 34, occ. Physician, w. Mary (24), son Kent (7), dau. Elizabeth (5), son Alexander (3), son Charles W. (11/12);[241] Civil War service enl. Regtl. Surgeon, 4th Va. Inf., 05/04/1861, served the entirety of the war;[54] c. 1870 res. Blacksburg, VA, age 43, occ. Physician, w. Mary J. (34), son Kent (17), dau. Elizabeth (15), son Alexander (13), son Charles W. (11);[242] phys. desc. at enl. 6', fair complexion, grey eyes, dark hair, occ. Medical Student;[239] d. 10/19/1888, *"kidney disease,"* St. Luke's Home For the Sick, Richmond, VA, bur. Westview Cemetery Blacksburg, VA;[239, 54] wid. Mary J., WC #10827, 02/25/1890, filed from Blacksburg, Montgomery Co., VA Black assisted in the operation on General "Stonewall" Jackson after he had been wounded at the Battle of Chancellorsville. He was a founder and was on the first Board of Visitors of the Virginia Agricultural and Mechanical College, now Virginia Tech; Board Member, Southwestern Lunatic Asylum in Marion, 1887-1888; mbr. Virginia House of Delegates 1885 - 1887. Kept a Mexican War Diary (1847-1849); (MKB b. 04/27/1836, d. 05/18/1911, Blacksburg, Montgomery Co., VA).[239]

Photo credit: VPI Library, Blacksburg, VA

**Black, Thomas C.**, Pvt., Co. C; enl. Mex. War service 12/29/1846, Bowling Green, VA, age 21; pres. 06/1847; pres. 08/1847, pay stopped for: 1 cap-$.95[1/2], 2 pr. socks-$.49, 2 cotton shirts-$.86, 2 woolen shirts-$1.80, 1 pr. shoes-$1.22, 1 pr. drawers-$.35[1/2]; pres. 10/1847, pay stopped for: 2 pr. drawers-$.71, 1 jacket-$2.66, 1 pr. pants-$2.28, 2 woolen shirts-$1.80, 1 pr. shoes-$1.22; pres. 12/1847, pay stopped for: 1 pr. pants-$2.28, 1 pr. shoes-$1.22, 1 blanket-$2.22; pres. 04/1848, pay stopped for: 1 india rubber canteen-$.27; pres. 08/1848, BLW sent to Philadelphia, Pa.

**Black, William A.**, Pvt., *Preston's Co.*; enl. Mex. War service 12/07/1846 Pulaski Co., VA, age 19; d. 02/04/1847 at Ft. Monroe, VA; *"congestion of the brain;"*[243] bur. Ft. Monroe, VA, *"with the honors of war and the company testified their regard for him by erecting a stone to his memory costing $17."*[244]

**Blackaby, John**, Pvt., *Recruit Co.*, enl. Mex. War service 01/01/1848 Christiansburg, VA, age 19; pres. 02/1848; pres. 06/1848; BLW sent to Washington, D.C.

**Blackard, Joel**, Pvt., *Preston's Co.*; b. Smyth Co., VA enl. Mex. War service 11/28/1846 Montgomery Co., VA, age 27; pres. 04/1847; sick 06/1847; pres. 08/1847; pres. 10/1847, pay stopped for: 3 pr. socks-$.73[1/2], 1 cotton shirt-$.43, 1 cap-$.95[1/2]; pres. 12/1847, pay stopped for: 1 pr. overalls-$2.28, 1 pr. shoes-$1.22, 1 pr. drawers-$.35[1/2], 1 blanket-$2.22; pres. 02/1848; pres. 04/1848; pres. 07/1848, pay stopped for: 1 jacket-$2.37, 1 gun sling-$.18; BLW sent to Blacksburg, VA; c. 1850 res. Blacksburg, Montgomery Co., VA, age 30, occ. Pump Maker;[245] c. 1860 res. Giles Co., VA, occ. Pump Borer, age 40;[246] Civil War service enl.

VIRGINIA VOLUNTEERS IN MEXICO

as a Lt. Co. D, 7$^{th}$ Va. Inf. 05/31/1861, at Giles C.H., prom. Capt. 04/26/1862, KIA 06/30/1862 at Frayser's Farm, VA

**Blackburn, Thomas**, Pvt., Co. A; *Not on Muster Rolls*; wid. Augusta, WC #8786, 02/02/1889, from MO.

**Blackburn, William Allen**, 3$^{rd}$ Sgt., LIC; b. Spotsylvania Co., VA, 08/02/1818, son of Thomas R. & Mary A. Blackburn;[247] enl. Mex. War service 12/07/1846 Staunton, VA, age 25; pres. 06/1847, prom. 3$^{rd}$ Sgt.; pres. 08/1847; pres. 10/1847, pay stopped for: 2 forage cap-$1.91, 1 wool jacket-$2.66, 1 pr. overalls-$2.28, 3 pr. socks-$.73$^{1/2}$, 2 cotton shirts-$.86; pres. 12/1847, pay stopped for: 1 blanket-$2.22, 1 pr. overalls-$2.28; pres. 04/1848; pres. 04/1848, pay stopped for: 1 gun sling-$.16; BLW sent to Staunton, VA; c. 1850 res. Augusta Co., VA, age 29, occ. Carpenter;[247] c. 1860, age 39, occ. Carpenter, w. Mary A. (31), dau. Mary E. (9), son John H. (8), dau. Alice V. (5), son Thomas R. (4), son Albert B. (8/12);[248] Civil War service enl. 04/17/1861 at Staunton, VA as 2nd Lt., Co. L, 5th Va. Inf., C.S.A.; won West Augusta Guard shooting medal 09/24/1858; on sick furlough 03/28/1862; dropped from roll 04/17/1862;[128] d. Augusta Co., 11/24/1904, bur. Bethlehem Lutheran Church Cemetery.[249]

**Blakney, George W.**, Pvt., Co. H; b. 06/26/1829; enl. Mex. War service 11/21/1846, Berkeley, VA, age 19; discharged 01/23/1847 Richmond, VA by writ of habeas corpus; m. Mary Jane (date unknown); Civil War service Pvt., Co. B, 67$^{th}$ VA Militia (Berkeley Co.) trans. as Pvt., Co. A, 11$^{th}$ Va. Cav., 10/07/1861; d. 03/23/1894, bur. St. Joseph's Catholic Cem., Berkeley Co., WV.[45]

**Blamire, Edward Thurston**, 2$^{nd}$ Lt., Co. F; b. 04/17/1808; m. Lucretia F. Browne, 02/05/1834, Norfolk Co., VA;[250] enl. Mex. War service 11/23/1846, Portsmouth, VA; pres. 06/1847; pres. 08/1847; absent 10/1847 on detached service as Provost Martial since 10/23/1847; pres. 12/1847 returned to company 12/20/1847; pres. 02/1848; pres. 04/1848; pres. 08/1848; m. Mary Elizabeth Nathaniel c. 1850;[45] c. 1850 res. Portsmouth, Norfolk Co., VA, age 40, occ. Customs Inspector, w. Elizabeth (47), dau. Kate (15), son Jarvis (12), son Edward (9);[251] c. 1853 mbr. Knights Templar, Portsmouth Encampment No. 5, Portsmouth, VA;[40] Civil War service Capt., Co. C, 16$^{th}$ Va. Inf., enl. 04/20/1861 at Portsmouth, VA, age 57, rcvd. Commission 07/01/1861, dropped 05/01/1862 at reorganization;[77] d. 1870, (Masonic emblem) bur. Cedar Grove Cem., Portsmouth, VA.[45]

**Blessing, John H.**, Pvt., Co. H; b. 09/18/1828, Maryland;[252, 253] enl. Mex. War service 12/27/1846, Berkeley, VA, age 18; pres. 04/1847; pres. 06/1847; pres. 08/1847; pres. 10/1847, pay stopped for: 1 forage cap-$.95$^{1/2}$, 1 pr. pants-$2.28, 4 cotton shirts-$1.72, 3 flannel shirts-$2.70, 1 pr. drawers-$.35$^{1/2}$, 1 pr. shoes-$1.22, 4 pr. socks-$.98, 1 greatcoat-$6.93$^{1/2}$, 1 jacket-$2.66; pres. 12/1847, pay stopped for: 1 pr. pants-$2.28, 1 pr. shoes-$1.22, 1 pr. socks-$.24$^{1/2}$, 1 cotton shirt-$.43; pres. 02/1848, pay stopped for: 1 jacket-$2.66, 1 blankets-$2.22; absent 04/1848, on extra duty as a Teamster in the QM Dept. since 04/09/1848; pres. 07/1848; BLW sent to Boonsboro, MD; m. Susan Weddle, 06/23/1852, Greencastle, Franklin Co., Pa.;[254] Civil War service Pvt., Co. F, 13$^{th}$ Md. Inf., discharged 05/29/1865, Baltimore, MD; SC #8888, 02/04/1887, filed from Mt. Carroll, Carroll Co., IL; phys. desc. age 57 [1885], fair complexion, blue eyes, light hair, occ. Cooper;[254] d. 12/09/1888, *"pneumonia, 60 years, 2 mos., 24 days,"* Mt. Carroll, IL[252, 253] wid. Susan, WC #6252, 04/8/1887, filed from Mt. Carroll, Carroll Co., IL; (SWB b. 01/07/1831, d. 03/05/1813, *"Dropsy,"* Mt. Carroll, Carroll Co., IL, bur. Mt. Carroll, IL).[252, 253]

**Blondell, Benjamin W.**, Fifer, Co. H; enl. Mex. War service 12/30/1846, Berkeley, VA, age 18; d. 02/28/1847 Ft. Monroe, VA

**Blondell, Theodore A.**, 1$^{st}$ Cpl., Co. C; b. Maryland; enl. Mex. War service 12/08/1846, Bowling Green, VA, age 23; pres. 06/1847, prom. 3$^{rd}$ Cpl. 06/07/1847, pres. 08/1847, prom. 2$^{nd}$ Cpl. 08/25/1847, pay stopped for: 1 pr. drawers-$.35$^{1/2}$, 1 cap-$.95$^{1/2}$, 2 pr. socks-$.49, 2 cotton shirts-$.86, 2 woolen shirts-$1.80, 2 pr. shoes-$2.44; pres. 10/1847, pay stopped for: 2 pr.

OFF TO WAR

socks-$.49, 1 pr. drawers-$.35$^{1/2}$, 1 jacket-$2.66, 1 pr. pants-$2.28, 2 cotton shirts-$.86, 2 woolen shirts-$1.80, 1 pr. shoes-$1.22, 1 great coat-$6.93$^{1/2}$; 1 blanket-$2.22; pres. 12/1847, prom. 1$^{st}$ Cpl. 12/16/1847, pay stopped for: 2 cotton shirts-$.86, 1 pr. shoes-$1.22, 1 blanket-$2.22; pres. 04/1848, pay stopped for: 2 pr. pants-$4.56, 1 pr. shoes-$1.22; 1 pr. shoes-$1.50, 1 india rubber canteen-$.27, 1 jacket-$2.66; pres. 08/1848, BLW sent to Bowling Green, Caroline Co., VA; c. 1850 res. Bowling Green, Caroline Co., VA, age 23, occ. Carriage Maker;[255] c. 1860 res. Abingdon, Washington Co., VA, age 33, occ. Master Carpenter, w. Sarah (23);[256] c. 1870 res. Gladesville, Wise Co., VA, age 45, w. Sarah (34), son Freeman W. (7), dau. Mary E. (6), dau. Josephine (4), son Abner (2), son Ezra (11/12);[257] c. 1890 owned the land in the vicinity of the Town of Appalachia, Wise Co., VA[258]

**Bloxham, William Preston**, Pvt., Co. B; b. VA c. 1824, son of William & Polly Bloxham;[259] enl. 12/05/1846, Alexandria, VA, age 22; pres. 06/1847, on extra duty in QM Dept.; in confinement 08/1847; absent 10/1847, on detached service w/ QM Dept., pay stopped for: 4 cotton shirt-$1.72, 1 flannel shirt-$.90, 1 pr. overalls-$4.56, 1 jacket-$2.66, 1 overcoat-$6.93$^{1/2}$, 1 cap-$.95$^{1/2}$; on extra duty 12/1847 since 12/11/1847 as Teamster in QM Dept., pay stopped for: 1 pr. shoes-$1.22, 2 pr. overalls-$4.56, 2 flannel shirts-$1.80, 2 cotton shirts-$.86, 1 blanket-$2.22; on extra duty 02/1848 as teamster in QM Dept. since 12/11/1847, pay stopped for: 1 pr. overalls-$2.28; on extra duty 04/1848 as teamster in QM Dept. since 12/11/1847; pres. 08/1848, pay stopped for: 1 pick & brush-$.12, 1 waist belt plate-$.10, BLW sent to Alexandria, VA; m/1 Mary bef. 1870; c. 1870 res. Falls Church, Fairfax Co., VA, age 46, occ. Engineer on Steamship, w. Mary (42);[260] m/2 Georgia B. Veitch, 10/10/1883, Alexandria, VA;[261] SC #225, 02/09/1887, wid. Georgia R., WC #11645 dated 5/9/1899, both from VA bur. Alex. Meth. Prot. Cem.[45]

**Bodeker, Charles**, 2$^{nd}$ Lt., Co. A; enl. 11/25/1846 Richmond, VA, age 24; pres. 12/1846 – 04/1847; pres. 06/1847; pres. 08/1847, prom. 2$^{nd}$ Lt. from 4$^{th}$ Sgt. 08/20/1847; Court-martialed 03/28/1848 Buena Vista, Mex. *Charge #1: Conduct Prejudicial to Good Order and Military Discipline; Specification: In this that 2$^{nd}$ Lt. Charles Bodeker, Va. Regt. of Vols., being in a state of intoxication, did disturb the peace and quiet of the Camp of his Regt., by riotous and disorderly conduct. This at Buena Vista, Mexico, on or about the 3$^{rd}$ of February 1848. Charge #2: Ungentlemanly and Unofficerlike Conduct; Specification: In this that the said 2$^{nd}$ Lt. Charles Bodeker, Va. Regt, did, while in a state of intoxication, wantonly assault certain soldiers of his Regt. When remonstrated with by a superior officer, did call the said superior officer 'a damned son of a bitch' or words to that effect. This at the Camp of his Regt., at Buena Vista, Mexico, on or about the 3$^{rd}$ of February 1848. Charge #3: Riotous and Disorderly Conduct; Specification: In this that the said 2$^{nd}$ Lt. Charles Bodeker, Va. Regt., being in a state of intoxication, did at a public house in Saltillo, Mexico, commit a most violent assault upon Sergt. Tillson of his Regt. by throwing plates at his head and otherwise demean himself in a most disorderly and unbecoming manner. This on or about the 19$^{th}$ of January 1848. Charge #4: Drunkenness; Specification: In this that the said 2$^{nd}$ Lt. Charles Bodeker, Va. Regt., has upon repeated occasions, namely at Saltillo, on or about the 19$^{th}$ of January 1848, and on the 3$^{rd}$ of February 1848, become intoxicated, by drinking to a degree which rendered him utterly forgetful or regardless of his duties and his character as an officer. To which charges and specification the accused pleaded Not Guilty. The accused objected to the inclusion of the 4$^{th}$ charge and specification on the grounds that said charge was already covered in the first charge. The court agreed and the 4$^{th}$ charge was thrown out. Captain W.A. Talbot, Va. Regt. of Vols., a witness for the prosecution being duly sworn, says: I came in camp about a week after I arrived. Lt. Bodeker came into my tent one afternoon. There were several officers present. I do not remember who. He was intoxicated at the time and I requested Lt. Scott of my company, in a low tone of voice, to endeavor to get Mr. Bodeker to leave. Lt. Bodeker heard the remark which I did not intend he should, and left my tent, about dark. The same evening a mail arrived in camp and while waiting at the Post*

## VIRGINIA VOLUNTEERS IN MEXICO

*Office, and I think Capt. Thrift and myself and some other officers were in conversation. Lt. Bodeker came down to the officer and spoke to the officers, etc. I returned the salutation, he replied, 'You are no gentleman,' as well as I remember, evidently intending it for me, I made no reply, however and this is about all I know in reference to the first charge and specification. I reference to the $2^{nd}$ charge and specification. I saw Lt. Bodeker strike a soldier of the Regt. on the same day in Camp at the Post Office. I do not know who the soldier was, whether he gave any provocation to Lt. Bodeker or not. This is about all I know in reference to the charges. Mr. Bodeker came to me the next morning and said he was very sorry for what he had said to me, and I forgave him very cheerfully. Question by the Judge Advocate: Was Lt. Bodeker in a state of intoxication at the time you have stated you saw him strike a soldier? Answer: I thought he was. Question by the Accused: Do you know of your own knowledge whether the man the accused struck was a soldier? Answer: He had on a soldier's uniform and I had seen the man before in the Regt. but his name or to what company he belonged I do not know? Question by the Accused: Was there not a very large crowd at the door of the Post Office and was Lt. Bodeker in the crowd making his way into the Post Office? Answer: There was a crowd present and we were standing near the door of the office and this occurrence took place after he had got through the crowd to where I was, and had made the remark to me, as I have mentioned. Question by the Accused: Did not the man of whom you have spoken press against Lt. Bodeker, or push him, before he struck him? Answer: Not to my knowledge. There was, as there usually is about the Post Office, a considerable pushing and crowding towards the door of the office. $2^{nd}$ Lt. James S. Douglas, Va. Regt., a witness for the prosecution being duly sworn, says: On the morning of the day specified in the charges and specifications, I was walking in the direction of the Quarter Masters Office with Capt. Thrift when they were opening the mail. There was a large crowd collected around the door. As we were approaching the door, we were joined by Lt. Bodeker. I did not want him to go down to the office as he was a little intoxicated at the time. I wanted him to remain with me, not wishing him to expose himself before the men as he was laughing and talking as men do when under the influence of liquor. I remained a short distance off. Lt. Bodeker refused to remain with me, but went down to where the crowd was. In a short time I heard some angry words, or some one quarrelling in the crowd and went up to the crowd and saw Lt. Bodeker in the crowd standing by Capt. Talbot and Capt. Thrift, who appeared to be endeavoring to pacify him. I went up to the place where he was standing and endeavored to get him off he refused and I finally laid hands on him and by that means got him off. This is about all I know in reference to the matter. Sergeant H.H. Tillson, Co. A, Va. Regt. of Vols., a witness for the prosecution being duly sworn, says: In Saltillo, at the time alluded to, I was so much intoxicated myself and have so little recollection of what occurred as to be unable to state with any distinctness what took place between Lt. Bodeker and myself. Question by the Judge Advocate: Do you recollect the fact of the accused throwing a plate or plates at your head on that occasion in Saltillo? Answer: I have know[sic] recollection of anything of the kind. Capt. J. Thrift, Va. Regt. of Vols., a witness for the prosecution being duly sworn, says: On or about the $3^{rd}$ of February last I know that a mail arrived on that day in Camp and that while Lt. Douglas and myself were on our way to the office we were joined by Lt. Bodeker, who appeared to be intoxicated. Soon after I had got to the tent door, I heard some altercation between Lt. Bodeker and Capt. Talbot, who was near me. I do not recollect what is was now. There was a large crowd around the tent door and much loud talking as is usual. Capt. Talbot, Capt. Stith [Thrift?]and myself and some others were immediately in front of the door. Lt. Bodeker, I think, was immediately behind me. I heard a scuffle and upon looking around I saw Lt. Bodeker apparently in the act of striking some one. I did not see whom he struck, or struck at. Nor do I know whether he had any provocation or not. Soon after I heard another scuffle and looking round I saw Lt. Bodeker and a soldier, they had clinched. I immediately separated them. Soon after that Lt. Douglas took Lt. Bodeker away. This is about all I know about it.*

OFF TO WAR

*Question by the Accused: Will you state how long Lt. Bodeker has been under arrest and what has been the character of that arrest? Answer: He has been under arrest nearly two months and has been confined to his tent nearly all the time except a short time he has had the privilege of the camp.* The accused submitted a written defense to the court. *After deliberation the court found the accused Guilty of Charge and Specification #1; Guilty of Charge and Specification #2; and Not Guilty of Charge and Specification #3. He was sentenced to be publically*[sic] *reprimanded in the order of the commanding general. The court considered this lenient in consideration of the long and close confinement of the accused and his inexperience in service. Head Quarters, Army of Occupation, Monterey, Mexico, April 14$^{th}$, 1848 The finding of the Court, in the case of 2$^{nd}$ Lt. Charles Bodeker, Va. Vols. is hereby approved. The commanding General cannot, however, refrain from observing that the interest of the service would have been better promoted, if the court had pronounced a sentence of a severer nature, as a decisions, like the present, are wholly inadequate to abate an evil habit, which prevails to an alarming extent in the Army of Occupation. It is evident, from the testimony recorded in the proceeding, that the accused was in a state of intoxication, according to the charges alleged against him, and while in the reprehensible condition, exposed himself to the view of a crowd of persons, composed of officers and privates. The Commanding General embraces this occasion, to call upon all commanders of Districts, Regiments and Posts, to exert their authority to arrest this pernicious vice of intoxication, which, in addition to the degradation that it entails upon its victim, is attended with other ruinous consequences, wholly incompatible with the due discharge of military duties. 2$^{nd}$ Lt. Charles Bodeker, Va. Vols., is released from arrest. John E. Wool, Brig. Genl., Commanding;*[262] under arrest 02/1848; pres. 04/1848; BLW sent to, Richmond, VA; c. 1860 an Augustus Bodeker, b. Hanover Germany, res. Charlottesville, Albemarle Co., age 42, occ. Druggist, w. Ann (32), dau. Pearl (8/12);[263] c. 1870 an Augustus Bodeker, b. Germany, res. Richmond, Henrico Co., VA, age 50, occ. Druggist, w. Anna (37), dau. Pearl (12), dau. Ruby (9).[264]

**Bohannan, Abner J.**, Pvt., Co. A; enl. Mex. War service 12/01/1846 Richmond, VA, age 32; pres. 12/1846; sick 04/1847 - 06/1847, in Hosp. at Camargo, Mex. since 04/04/1847; pres. 08/1847; pres. 10/1847, pay stopped for clothing: 2 cotton shirts-$.86, 2 pr. wool overalls-$4.56, 1 cap-$.95$^{1/2}$, 2 pr. stockings-$.49, 1 pr. shoes-$1.22; pres. 12/1847, pay stopped for clothing: 1 pr. wool overalls-$2.28, 2 pr. socks-$.49 pres. 02/1848, pay stopped for: 1 pr. shoes-$1.22; 1 jacket-$2.66, 1 pick & brush-$.12; sick 04/1848; 07/1848, pay stopped for: 1 bayonet sheath-$.56, musket sling-$.16, 1 pick & brush-$.12; BLW sent to Montague's Tavern, Essex Co., VA; c. 1850 res. Essex Co., VA, age 36, occ. Farmer, w. Mary (49), son George (13);[265] c. 1860 res. Mathews Co., VA, age 46, occ. Tailor;[266] Civil War service enl. Co. C, 59$^{th}$ Va. Inf. 01/03/1863 at Richmond, VA, prom. 5$^{th}$ Sgt. 03/01/1863, pres. until absent 12/31/1863 sick in Hosp. at Quitman, VA, d. 07/12/1864 at Chimborazo Hosp. from debility and dysentery, bur. Oakwood Cem., Richmond, VA[267]

**Bonner, James C.N.**, Pvt., Co. E; enl. Mex. War service 12/04/1846 Petersburg, VA, age 23; pres. 04/1847; pres. 06/1847; pres. 08/1847; pres. 10/1847, pay stopped for: 2 pr. stockings-$.49, 1 cap-$.95$^{1/2}$; pres. 12/1847, pay stopped for: 1 jacket-$2.66, 1 pr. pants-$2.28, 1 flannel shirts-$.90, 1 pr. drawers-$.35$^{1/2}$, 1 blanket-$2.22; pres. 02/1848; absent 04/1848 sick in Hosp.; c. 1850 res. Raleigh, Wake Co., NC age 22, occ. None, b. VA, res. in Hotel;[268] m. Elizabeth A. Ashley 01/11/1854, Raleigh, Wake Co., NC;[269] d. 05/10/1878;[269] wid. Elizabeth A., WC #944, 05/18/1887, filed from Raleigh, Wake Co., NC; (EAB b. 11/19/1830, d. 10/27/1908).[269]

**Booker, Peter**, Pvt., Co. K enl. Mex. War service Richmond Co., VA 01/06/1847, age 20; d. 02/12/1847 Ft. Monroe, VA

VIRGINIA VOLUNTEERS IN MEXICO

**Booker, William T.**, Pvt., Co. M; enl. Mex. War service 06/20/1848 Richmond, VA, age 18; pres. 09/1847; pres. 11/1847; pres. 12/1847; pres. 02/1848, pay stopped for: 1 greatcoat-$6.93$^{1/2}$; pres. 04/1848; pres. 08/1848; BLW sent to Richmond, VA
**Boothe, Zerah**, Pvt., Co. F; b. c. 1802, Randolph Co., VA; enl. Mex. War service 01/22/1847, Portsmouth, VA, age 37; court-martialed 06/23/1847 Buena Vista, Mex., *Charge #1: Conduct Unbecoming a Soldier; Specification: "in that Pvt. Zarah Booth, Co. F, 1$^{st}$ Virginia Regiment, on the 18$^{th}$ day of June 1847 was in a state of intoxication and while so uttered insulting and abusive language towards his superior officer, Lt. Levy;" Charge #2: Violation of the 9$^{th}$ Article of War; Specification: In that Pvt. Zarah Booth, Co. F, 1$^{st}$ Virginia Regiment, on the 18$^{th}$ day of June 1847 came into the quarters of Lt. Levy at Buena Vista in a state of intoxication and uttered abusive language towards Lt. Levy and when ordered by him out of his presence and did refuse to go and attempted to strike him before several men of the company;"*[270] pres. 06/1847; pres. 08/1847; pres. 10/1847, fined 09/1847 1 mos. pay by order of genl. court-martial, pay stopped for: 1 pr. overalls-$2.28; pres. 12/1847; discharged 01/28/1848 Buena Vista, Mex., on Surgeon's Certificate of Disability; desc. at discharge, age 45, 5'10", dark complexion, dark eyes, black hair, occ. Tanner; discharged 01/28/1848 on Surgeon's Certificate of Disability.[26]
**Boatright, Merrett W.**, Pvt., Co. I; enl. Mex. War service 02/15/1847 Richmond, VA, age 18; pres. 02/1847; d. 03/08/1847 at sea on board the transport ship *Sophia Walker.*
**Boswell, William C.**, Pvt., Co. M; b. 01/03/1826, Lunenburg Co., VA;[271] enl. Mex. War service 09/06/1847 Yatesville, VA, age 21; pres. 10/1847; pres. 11/1847; pres. 12/1847; pres. 02/1848, pay stopped for: 1 blanket-$2.22, 2 cotton shirts-$.86, 2 flannel shirts-$1.80; pres. 04/1848; pres. 08/1848, pay stopped for: 1 waist belt plate-$.10, 1 thumb vice-$.35; BLW sent to Yatesville, Lunenburg Co., VA; m. Mary Armistead Burwell, 08/20/1851, Mecklenburg Co., VA;[271] c. 1870 res. Pittsylvania Co., VA, age 43, occ. Farmer, w. Mary A. (38), dau. Nancy R. (17), son Thomas T. (14), son John L. (12), son William (10), son Henry (8), dau. Lucy (5), son Chaney (17);[272] SC #8059; 02/25/1887, filed from 304 N. Green St., Baltimore, MD; since discharge res. Henry Co., VA, Danville, VA and Baltimore, MD;[271] phys. desc. age 81 [1907], 6'0", fair complexion, grey eyes, auburn hair, occ. Farmer;[271] lists children Nannie Ravenscroft Boswell b. 03/28/1853, Thomas Taylor Boswell b. 10/13/1855, John Louis Boswell b. 03/19/1857, Henry Harrison Boswell b. 06/28/1861, Lucie Seawell Boswell b. 07/29/1864, Mary Armistead Boswell b. 03/11/1871;[271] d. 06/13/1907, *"uremia and chronic nephritis,"* Baltimore, MD, bur. Woodlawn Cemetery, Baltimore, MD;[273] wid. Mary A., WC #14741, 06/21/1907, filed from 3712 Springdale Ave., Forest Park, Baltimore, MD; (MBB b. 05/31/1831, d. 12/10/1911).[273]
**Bowen, Abraham**, Pvt., LIC; *Not on Muster Rolls;* c. 1860 res. Weston, Lewis Co., VA, age 45, occ. Cabinet Maker, w. Hester (35), dau. Sarah F. (16) *deaf & dumb,* dau. Mary C. (14), son Noah D. (12), dau. Harriett L. (9), son William C. (6), son John T. (4) *deaf & dumb,* son Benjamin W. (3), dau. Agnes B. (1);[274] SA #7537, 04/14/1887, from WV.
**Bowen, Jesse P.**, Pvt., Co. M; enl. Mex. war service 09/10/1847 Forksville, VA, age 23; pres. 10/1847; pres. 11/1847; pres. 12/1847; pres. 02/1848; d. 04/28/1848 in Hosp. at Saltillo, Mex., pay stopped for 1 blanket-$1.22, 1 pr. shoes-$1.22;
**Bowers, Patterson**, 4$^{th}$ Sgt., *Preston's Co.*; b. 03/10/1825, Montgomery Co., VA;[275] enl. Mex. War service 12/07/1846 Montgomery Co., VA, age 21; pres. 04/1847; pres. 06/1847, prom. 4$^{th}$ Sgt. 05/25/1847; pres. 08/1847; pres. 10/1847, pay stopped for: 1 pr. overalls-$2.28, 1 pr. shoes-$1.22, 2 pr. socks-$.49, 2 flannel shirts-$1.80, 3 cotton shirts-$1.29; pres. 12/1847, pay stopped for: 1 pr. overalls-$2.28, 1 pr. drawers-$.35$^{1/2}$, 1 blankets-$2.22; pres. 02/1848; pres. 04/1848; pres. 07/1848, pay stopped for: 1 jacket-$2.37, 1 spring vise-$.35; BLW sent to Christiansburg, VA c/o Fleming Gardner; m/1 Elizabeth M. Graves, 12/1852, Wythe Co., VA, (EGB d. 01/1853, Wythe Co., VA);[275] m/2 Moriah L. _____, date/place unknown;[275] SC #17367, 04/28/1888, filed from Santa Ana, Los Angeles Co., CA; since discharge res.

OFF TO WAR

Wytheville, VA, Tyler, TX, and Los Angeles, Ca. for the last 30 years; Harvey Black gave affidavit in pension claim;[275] d. 10/01/1898, Santa Anna, CA, bur. Fairhaven Memorial Park, Lawn R, Lot 129, Space 1, Santa Ana, CA.[276]

**Bowers, Samuel**, Pvt., Co. M; enl. Mex. War service 09/10/1847 Brickland, VA, age 25; pres. 11/1847; pres. 12/1847; pres. 02/1848; pres. 04/1848, pay stopped for: 1 pr. shoes-$1.22; pres. 08/1848, pay stopped for: 1 musket-$13.00, 1 waist belt-$.21, 1 waist belt plate-$.10, 1 bayonet scabbard-$.56; BLW sent to Brickland, Lunenburg Co., VA

**Bowles, John**, Pvt., LIC; b. Ireland, c. 1824; enl. Mex. War service 11/27/1846 Staunton, VA, age 24; d. 05/03/1847 at China, Mex. of dysentery.

**Bowles, Robert**, Pvt., Co. I; enl. Mex. War service 10/10/1847 Lynchburg, VA, age 28; pres. 04/1848; pres. 02/1847; pres. 04/1847; absent 06/1847, on extra duty as a Teamster in QM Dept.; pres. 08/1847; absent 10/1847 on extra duty in QM Dept., pay stopped for: 2 flannel shirts-$1.80, 1 cotton shirt-$.43, 1 pr. drawers-$.35$^{1/2}$, 1 pr. shoes-$1.22, 1 pr. socks-$.24$^{1/2}$, 1 cap-$.95$^{1/2}$; in confinement 12/1847, pay stopped for: 2 pr. pants-$4.56, 1 pr. shoes-$1.22, 1 blanket-$2.22, 2 pr. drawers-$.35$^{1/2}$, 1 jacket-$2.66; Court-martialed 11/15/1847 Buena Vista, Mex. *Charge #1: Disobedience of Orders; Specification: In this that he Pvt. Robert Bowles, Co. I, Va. Regt., Teamster in the Quarter Master Dept., Va. Regt., did on or about the 3$^{rd}$ day of Nov. 1847, clandestinely bring intoxicating liquor into the wagon yard of the Quarter Master Dept. attached to the VA Vol. Camp. This in violation of his known duty and of orders which he repeatedly received; Charge #2: Disorderly Conduct; Specification: In this that he the said Pvt. Robert Bowls, Co. I, Va. Regt., did on or about the 3$^{rd}$ day of Nov. 1847 introduce into the wagon yard of the Quarter Masters Dept. attached to the Va. Regt. intoxicating liquors and did on or about the 3$^{rd}$ and 4$^{th}$ days of Nov. 1847 retail or otherwise furnish the same to the soldiers of the Va. Regt. to the prejudice of good order and military discipline. To which charges and specification the prisoner plead Not Guilty. George Faulkner, Wagon Master, Quarter Master Dept., Va. Regt, a witness for the prosecution, being duly sworn, says: I had told the prisoner frequently that he was suspected of bringing liquor into the yard for the men in the Regt. and that if he did so and I found it out I should report him. I went to the wagon yard one morning about the 3$^{rd}$ of this month and I found some liquor under the bunk of the prisoner in his tent. The liquor was in a small goat skin and I reported it to Lt. Harrison. The goat skin of liquor was in the water bucket belonging to the prisoners wagon. The prisoner had been previously warned about bringing liquor into camp. He was confined but I did not see him after I found the liquor in his tent and before he was confined. William R. Johnson, Teamster, Va. Regt., a witness for the prosecution, being duly sworn, says: I saw a skin of liquor in the wagon of the prisoner on the evening of the 3$^{rd}$ at the wagon yard of the Va. Regt. after he came from town. Though I do not know who it belonged to. Question by the Judge Advocate: Was the prisoner in town on that day with his wagon? Answer: Yes! He had been to town with his wagon that day. I do not know how long he had been back before I saw the liquor then. The prisoner stated to the court that the liquor was in his wagon until he found it there when he went to get his bucket out at night and that he intended by putting it in his tent to find out who was responsible. The court deliberated and found the prisoner guilty on all charges and specifications. Sentenced him to forfeit twenty ($20) dollars of his pay as a Teamster and to be returned to duty in his company;*[277] pres. 02/1848, pay stopped for: 1 pr. shoes-$1.22; pres. 04/1848; pres. 08/1848, pay stopped for: 2 pr. shoes, BLW sent to Liberty, VA; c. 1860 res. Peaksville, Bedford Co., VA, w. Martha A. (34), dau. Judy A. (16), son Caleb (8);[278] wid. Martha A., WC #409, 03/18/1887, from VA; [pension file missing].

**Bowles, William Thomas**, Pvt., *Preston's Co.*; b. 09/28/1828, Blacksburg, Montgomery Co., VA, son of Peter & Nancy (Hale) Bowles;[279] enl. Mex. War service 12/06/1846 Montgomery Co., VA, age 18; pres. 04/1847; pres. 06/1847; pres. 08/1847; pres. 10/1847, pay stopped for: 1 jacket-$2.66, 3 pr. socks-$.73$^{1/2}$, 2 cotton shirts-$.86, 1 pr. drawers-$.35$^{1/2}$, 1 cap-$.95$^{1/2}$;

## VIRGINIA VOLUNTEERS IN MEXICO

pres. 12/1847, pay stopped for: 1 pr. overalls-$2.28, 1 blanket-$2.22; pres. 02/1848; pres. 04/1848; pres. 07/1848, pay stopped for: 1 brush & pick-$.13; BLW sent to Blacksburg, VA; c. 1850 res. Montgomery Co., VA, age 22, occ. Laborer;[280] Civil War service Cpl., Co. L, 4th Va. Inf. 07/16/1861, absent sick 09/1861 through 04/1862, reduced to ranks 04/23/1862; absent 04/30/1862 through 10/31/1862 detailed as ambulance driver; wded. 05/03/1863 at Chancellorsville, VA, assigned to Pioneer Corps. 01/01/1864, captured 02/06/1865 at Petersburg, VA and paroled;[54] m. Mary Elizabeth Burkett 02/04/1866, Montgomery Co., VA;[279] SC #19599, 01/15/1889, filed from Bond, Douglas Co., KS; since discharge res. Montgomery Co., VA 10$^{1/2}$ yrs., Miller & Lafayette Cos., Mo. 1$^{1/2}$ yrs., Montgomery Co., VA 8 yrs., Gallia Co., OH 2 yrs., Montgomery Co., VA 13 yrs., Douglas Co., KS since 1883;[279] d. 01/04/1900, near Lone Star, Douglas Co., Kan.;[279] wid. Mary E., WC #12177, 03/05/1900, filed from Lone Star, Douglas Co., KS; (MBB b. 09/23/1844, Montgomery Co., VA, d. 04/22/1922);[279] dau. Lulu North Edmondson wrote to the Veterans Administration 05/04/1961 inquiring on her father's Mexican War service.[279]

**Bowyer, John Preston**, Pvt., *Recruit Co.*, VMI class of 1849 from Fincastle, VA;[281] enl. Mex. War service 10/01/1848 Washington, VA, age 25; absent 04/1848 on recruiting service; pres. 06/1848; BLW sent to Richmond, VA, c/o R.D. Hughes; d. at sea enroute to California.

**Bowyer, Michael**, Pvt., Co. A; enl. Mex. War 12/14/1846, age 27; pres. 12/1846; pres. 04/1847, pay stopped for 1 cartridge Box, 2 belts-waist & cross, 1 canteen, 1 cartridge box plate & 2 belt plates; pres. 06/1847; AWOL 08/1847, since morning of 08/31/1847; sick 10/1847, pay stopped for clothing: 2 cotton shirts-$1.72, 1 pr. wool overalls-$2.28, 1 cap-$.95$^{1/2}$, 1 pr. shoes-$1.22, 2 pr. stockings-$.49, 1 wool jacket-$2.66, 1 great coat-$6.93$^{1/2}$; discharged 11/24/1847 at Buena Vista, Mex., on Surgeon's Certificate of Lunacy.

**Boyer, Silas**, Pvt., *Recruit Co.*, enl. Mex. War service 03/01/1848 Amherst C.H., VA; pres. 06/1848; BLW sent to Amherst C.H., VA

**Boykin, Joseph**, Pvt., Co. F; enl. Mex. War service 12/29/1846, Jerusalem, VA, age 23; absent 06/1847 left sick at Matamoros, Mex. 04/04/1847; d. date unknown Matamoros, Mex.

**Bradford, Benjamin Hellenius**,[282] Pvt., Co. K; b. 09/1826, son of Col. Benjamin R. & Hellen W. (Edmonds) Bradford;[283] enl. Mex. War service Jefferson Co., VA 01/05/1847, age 20; pres. 06/1847; pres. 08/1847; pres. 10/1847, pay stopped for: 1 pr. overalls-$2.28, 3 pr. drawers-$1.06$^{1/2}$, 4 pr. socks-$.98, 2 flannel shirts-$1.80, 1 pr. shoes-$1.22; pres. 12/1847, pay stopped for: 1 jacket-$2.66, 1 pr. overalls-$2.28, 1 pr. socks-$.24$^{1/2}$, 1 cap-$.95$^{1/2}$, 1 blanket-$2.22, 2 cotton shirts-$.86; pres. 04/1848, pay stopped for: 1 flannel shirt-$.90, 1 gun sling-$.18, 1 pr. shoes-$1.22, 1 cotton shirt-$.43, 1 pick & brush-$.12; pres. 07/1848, pay stopped for: 1 gun sling-$.18, 1 screw driver-$.25, 1 wiper-$.20; BLW sent to Farrowsville, Fauquier Co., VA; c. 1850 res. Fauquier Co., VA, age 23, occ. Clerk;[284] d. 05/11/1856, Markham, VA, of consumption, occ. School teacher.[283]

**Bradley, Jesse P.**, Pvt., Co. M; enl. Mex. War service 10/07/1847 Amelia, VA, age 28; pres. 11/1847; pres. 12/1847; discharged 12/12/1847 on Surgeon's Certificate of Disability; m. Elizabeth F. Clay, 07/01/1848, Amelia Co., VA;[285] c. 1850 res. Amelia Co., VA, age 31, occ. Harness Maker, w. Elizabeth F. (28).[286]

**Bradley, Michael**, Pvt., Co. C; enl. Mex. War service 12/29/1846, Bowling Green, VA, age 21; pres. 06/1847; pres. 08/1847, pay stopped for: 1 cap-$.95$^{1/2}$, 2 pr. socks-$.49, 2 cotton shirts-$.86, 2 woolen shirts-$1.80, 1 pr. shoes-$1.22; pres. 10/1847, pay stopped for: 2 pr. socks-$.49, 1 pr. pants-$2.28, 2 cotton shirts-$.86, 2 woolen shirts-$1.80, 2 pr. shoes-$2.44, 1 cartridge box plate-$.10; pres. 12/1847, pay stopped for: 2 pr. drawers-$.71, 1 jacket-$2.66, 1 pr. pants-$2.28, 1 pr. shoes-$1.22, 1 blanket-$2.22; pres. 04/1848, pay stopped for: 1 india rubber canteen-$.27; pres. 08/1848, BLW sent to Philadelphia, Pa.

**Bradley, Philip A.**, Pvt., Co. G; enl. Mex. War service 11/23/1846 Richmond, VA, age 21; absent 06/1847 left sick in Hosp. at Monterey, Mex.; discharged 08/11/1847 Monterey, Mex. on Surgeon's Certificate of Disability, due to *"chronic diarrhea."*[287]

OFF TO WAR

**Bragg, William F.**, Pvt., Co. K; enl. Mex. War service Jefferson Co., VA 12/29/1846, age 24; pres. 06/1847; pres. 08/1847; pres. 10/1847, pay stopped for: 1 pr. overalls-$2.28, 2 pr. shoes-$2.44, 1 cap-$.95$^{1/2}$, 1 cotton shirts-$.43, 2 pr. drawers-$.71, 2 flannel shirts-$1.80, 4 pr. socks-$.98; pres. 12/1847, pay stopped for: 1 jacket-$2.66, 1 pr. overalls-$2.28, 2 pr. socks-$.49, 2 pr. drawers-$.71; pres. 04/1848, pay stopped for: 1 pr. shoes-$1.22, 1 cap-$.95$^{1/2}$; pres. 07/1848; BLW sent to Charlestown, Jefferson Co., VA; Civil War Service enl. 06/18/1863, Capt., Co. A, 2$^{nd}$ Md. Cav., discharged 01/26/1864; enl. date unknown as 1$^{st}$ Lt., Co. F, 1$^{st}$ Potomac Home Brig.; Prom. 02/29/1864, Capt., Co. F, 1$^{st}$ Potomac Home Brig.; mustered out 06/28/1865;[288] SC #7569, 06/07/1887, from MD; [see Civil War pension claims, IC #601766, WC #410759].

**Bramblett, McHenry**, Pvt., Co. B; b. 05/13/1824 Campbell or Bedford Co., VA;[289] enl. 12/19/1846, Richmond, VA, age 18; pres. 06/1847; absent 08/1847, on detached service w/QM Dept. for six mos. from 08/01/1847, to receive $25 per mo. in addition to pay as soldier; pres. 10/1847, pay stopped for: 1 pr. shoes-$1.22, 2 cotton shirt-$.86, 1 pr. overalls-$2.28, 2 pr. socks-$.49; pres. 12/1847, pay stopped for: 2 pr. socks-$.49, 1 pr. overalls-$2.28, 2 pr. cotton drawers-$.71, 1 cap-$.95$^{1/2}$, 1 blanket-$2.22; pres. 02/1848; pres. 04/1848, pay stopped for: 1 jacket-$2.66, 1 pr. shoes-$1.22; pres. 08/1848, pay stopped for: 1 pick & brush-$12, 1 gun sling-$.06, BLW sent to Chambersburg, Bedford Co., VA; m. Louisa Marie Thomas 04/07/1862, Blount Co., TX;[289] Civil War service 1$^{st}$ Sgt., Co. D, Ragsdale's Cav. Btln.; c. 1870 res. Frio Co., TX, age 40, occ. Justice of the Peace, w. L.M. (36) b. MS., dau. Canby A. (5), Fannie T. (4), Ewell Presley (2);[290] c. 1880 res. Frio Co., TX, age 50, occ. Stock Raiser, w. Louisa A. (47), dau. Canby A. (15), Fannie I. (14), Ewell P. (11), Virginia F. (8), Hellen E. (6);[291] SC #17425, 11/15/1888, phys. desc. 5'7", light complexion, blue eyes, dark hair, occ. Farmer; *"I was entirely too old to be considered under the Conscription Law of the rebellion at which time I was Bald headed and Gray bearded;"*[292] d. 07/29/1907 *"locomotor ataxia,"* Big Foot, Frio Co., TX, bur. Long View Cemetery, Big Foot, TX;[293] wid. Louisa A., WA #18874, 12/11/1907, both from TX; children: Canby Alice b. 11/19/1864, Fannie Ida b. 03/30/1866, Virginia Florence b. 02/07/1871, Hellen Effie b. 08/06/1873.[293]

**Breeden, Bartlett**, Pvt., Co. M; b. 01/16/1827, Richmond, VA;[294] enl. Mex. War service 08/01/1847 Richmond, VA, age 18; pres. 09/1847; pres. 11/1847; pres. 12/1847; pres. 02/1848, pay stopped for: 1 greatcoat-$6.93$^{1/2}$, 1 pr. shoes-$1.22, 1 cotton shirt-$.43, 1 flannel shirt-$.90; pres. 04/1848; pres. 08/1848; BLW sent to Richmond, VA; c. 1850 res. Richmond, VA, age 28, occ. Public Guard;[295] m. Catherine A. Glenn, 08/15/1854, Richmond, Henrico Co., VA;[294] SC #19755, filed from Brusly Landing West Baton Rouge, Louisiana; phys. desc. 5'4" or 5", fair complexion, light hair, blue eyes, occ. laborer;[294] d. 11/19/1899;[296] wid. Catherine, WA #15932, 12/17/1900, filed from 3401 E. Marshall St., Richmond, VA; [a Bartlett B. Breeden served as a Pvt., Co. C, 1$^{st}$ VA Arty. (Young's Co.)]; (CGB b. 10/22/1831, Richmond, VA, m/1 11/15/1848, William T. Adams, he died 05/29/1851; d. 01/13/1901, Richmond, VA)[296]

**Brevitt, Joseph P.**, Pvt., Co. E; b. c. 1820, Baltimore, MD;[297] enl. Mex. War service 12/01/1846 Petersburg, VA, age 25, 5'8$^{1/2}$", light complexion, dark eyes, dark hair, occ. Hatter; absent 04/1847 sick in Matamoros, Mex. since 03/02/1847; discharged 06/05/1847 Monterey, Mex. for disability; Civil War service enl. Pvt. Co. D, 2$^{nd}$ Md. Inf. 06/18/1861, trans. Co. B date unknown, phys. desc. 5'8", light complexion, dark hair, dark eyes, discharged 07/17/1865;[297,288] SC #295, 02/04/1887, filed from National Soldiers Home, Elizabeth City Co., VA; Seeks pension due to *"rupture received in E. Tenn. In line of duty during fall of 1863. Injury to chest & collarbone was received at S. Norwalk, Conn. In 1882 by R.R. accident;"*[297] d. 10/21/1897, National Soldiers Home, Elizabeth City Co., VA, bur. Dayton National Cemetery, Plot: K 24 21, Dayton, Montgomery County, Ohio.[45,297]

## VIRGINIA VOLUNTEERS IN MEXICO

**Brichett, Alexander E.**, Pvt., Co. E, enl. Mex. War service 11/28/1846 Petersburg, VA, age 20; d. 01/18/1847 Fort Monroe, VA, *"nothing due sutler."*

**Bridges, Morgan M.**, Pvt., *Preston's Co.*; enl. Mex. War service 12/06/1846 Montgomery Co., VA, age 22; pres. 04/1847; discharged 05/05/1847 on Surgeon's Certificate of Disability; m. Susan Beverage 09/17/1849, Pocahontas Co., VA;[298] c. 1850 res. Pocahontas Co., VA, age 26, occ. Millwright, w. Susannah (16);[299] d. 02/22/1881, Bellevue, Clay Co., TX;[298] wid. Susan, WC #5889, 11/28/1888, filed from Bellevue, Clay Co., TX; (SBB b. 09/19/1834, Pocahontas Co., VA; d. 01/18/1903).[298]

**Bridgewater, Charles**, Pvt., Co. A; enl. Mex. War service 12/10/1846 Richmond, VA, age 23; pres. 12/1846 - 04/1847; pres. 06/1847; pres. 08/1847; pres. 10/1847, pay stopped for clothing: 2 cotton shirts-$.86, 1 pr. wool overalls-$2.28, 1 cap-$.95$^{1/2}$, 1 pr. shoes-$1.22, 2 pr. stockings-$.49, 2 flannel shirts-$1.80, 1 wool jacket-$2.66, 1 pr. drawers-$.35$^{1/2}$, 1 pr. wool overalls-$2.28, 1 great coat-$6.93$^{1/2}$; pres. 12/1847, pay stopped for clothing: 1 pr. wool overalls-$2.28, 1 pr. drawers-$.35$^{1/2}$, 1 pr. shoes-$1.22, 1 blanket-$2.22; on detached service 02/1848 as cook in hosp. at Saltillo, Mex. since 01/05/1848; pres. 04/1848, pay stopped for: 1 wool jacket; BLW sent to Richmond, VA

**Brigedine, John**, Pvt., *Recruit Co.*, enl. Mex. War service 05/02/1848 Richmond, VA; pres. 06/1848; BLW sent to Dunsville, Essex Co., VA

**Briggs, William Sheridan**, Pvt., Co. C; b. 07/04/1820, *Stoney Hill*, Falmouth, Stafford Co., VA, son of James McDonald & Charlotte Ashmore (Keith) Briggs;[300] enl. Mex. War service 12/12/1846, Falmouth, VA, age 26; deserted 01/02/1847 Richmond, VA; d. 1892.

**Brigham, James S.A.**, Pvt., Co. F; enl. Mex. War service 11/23/1846, Portsmouth, VA, age 40; pres. 06/1847; pres. 08/1847; pres. 10/1847, pay stopped for: 1 pr. overalls-$2.28, 2 pr. socks-$.49, 1 pr. shoes-$1.22, 2 pr. drawers-.71, 2 cotton shirts-$.86; pres. 12/1847; pres. 02/1848, pay stopped for: 2 cotton shirts-$.86, 1 pr. overalls-$2.28, 1 blanket-$2.22; pres. 04/1848; pres. 08/1848, pay stopped for: 1 musket complete-$13.00, 1 cartridge box, belt & plate-$1.90, 1 bayonet scabbard-$.56, 1 waist belt & plate-$.31, 1 brush & pick-$.12, 1 screw driver & wiper-$.44, 2 cotton shirts-$.88, 1 blankets-$2.25, BLW sent to Portsmouth, VA c/o E.T. Blamire.

**Britt, George W.**, Pvt., LIC; enl. Mex. War service 11/27/1846 Staunton, VA, phys. desc. age 22, 6'1", dark complexion, black eyes, black hair, occ. Miller;[301] pres. 06/1847; pres. 08/1847; discharged 10/19/1847 on Surgeon's Certificate of Disability, *"phthisis;"*[301] c. 1850 res. Rockbridge Co., VA, age 25, occ. Miller;[302] m. Elizabeth Ann Poe, 10/17/1854, Spring Hill, Augusta Co., VA;[301] c. 1870 res. Mt. Sidney, Augusta Co., VA, age 43, occ. Whiskey Inspector, w. Elizabeth;; d. 07/11/1871, *"apoplexy,"* Augusta Co., VA, age 46;[301, 303] wid. Elizabeth A., WC #50, 02/24/1887, filed from Staunton, Augusta Co., VA; (EPB b. 12/30/1829, Mt. Sidney, Augusta Co., VA).[301]

**Britt, William H.**, Pvt., Co. D; b. 03/26/1824 Sussex Co., VA;[304] enl. Mex. War service 12/29/1846, Petersburg, VA, age 20; pres. 02/1847; pres. 04/1847; pres. 06/1847; pres. 08/1847, pay stopped for: 1 cap-$.95$^{1/2}$, 1 pr. pants-$2.28, 2 cotton shirts-$.86, 1 pr. shoes-$1.22; pres. 10/1847, pay stopped for: 2 cotton shirts-$.86, 1 pr. drawers-$.35$^{1/2}$, 1 pr. socks-$.24$^{1/2}$; pres. 12/1847, pay stopped for: 1 cap-$.95$^{1/2}$, 1 jacket-$2.66, 1 pr. pants-$2.28, 1 pr drawers-$.35$^{1/2}$, 1 pr. socks-$.24$^{1/2}$, 2 pr. shoes-$2.44, 1 blanket-$2.22, 2 flannel shirts-$1.80; pres. 04/1848, pay stopped for: 2 sets picks & brushes-$.24, 1 pr. pants-$2.28, 1 pr. shoes-$1.22, 1 blanket-$2.22, 1 haversack-$.20$^{3/4}$; pres. 08/1847, BLW sent to Jarratt's Depot, Sussex Co., VA; m/1 Sarah Freeman 12/18/1848 Sussex Co., VA;[304] c. 1850 res. Sussex Co., VA, age 25, occ. Farmer, w. Sally (27);[305] c. 1860 res. Surrey Co., VA, age 32, occ. Laborer, w. Sarah (33), dau. Martha (9), dau. Mary (4), son James (2), son John (10/12);[306] Civil War service Cpl., Co. A, 1$^{st}$ Va. Inf. Btln., enl. as Pvt. 02/20/1862 at Petersburg, VA, pres. through 07/01/1862, prom. Cpl. 07/01/1862, AWOL 09/1862 through 02/28/1863, reduced to ranks, pres. 09/1863 through 12/1863 detailed as a Teamster, pres. 01/1864 through 02/1865, absent sick 03/10/1865 in Richmond Hosp., captured 04/02/1865 at Petersburg, VA, sent to Hart's Island, N.Y., released 06/20/1865, phys. desc. 5'7³/⁴", dark complex, dark hair, dark eyes, res. of Sussex Co., VA;³⁰⁷ c. 1870 res. Charles City Co., VA, age 45, occ. Carpenter, w. Sarah (45), dau. Martha (20), dau. Mary E. (16), son James (13);³⁰⁸ (SFB d. 07/11/1870 Charles City Co., VA), m/2 Rebecca Gill;³⁰⁴ SC #10744, 03/23/1897, filed from Roxbury, Charles City Co., VA; since discharge res. Sussex and Charles City Cos., VA; Pvts. John Totty and James M. Donnan gave affidavits in pension claim; d.11/14/1904.³⁰⁴

**Brittle, William**, Pvt., *Preston's Co.*; enl. Mex. War service 12/06/1846 Montgomery Co., VA, age 18; pres. 04/1847, reduced to ranks from Drummer 01/17/1847; absent 06/1847 left sick in hosp. in Monterey, Mex. since 06/22/1847; discharged 07/31/1847 at Monterey, Mex. on Surgeon's Certificate of Disability.

**Brock, John P.**, Pvt., Co. K; b. 05/17/1823, Lacey Springs, Rockingham Co., VA, son of Archibald & Sarah (Moyer) Brock;³⁰⁹ enl. Mex. War service Jefferson Co., VA 12/01/1846, age 24; prom. Sgt. Major 02/16/1847; pres. 04/1848, reduced to ranks at his own request from Sgt. Major 01/11/1848, pay stopped for: 1 jacket-$2.66, 1 pr. pants-$2.28, 1 blanket-$2.22; pres. 07/1848, pay stopped for: 1 brush & pick-$.12; BLW sent to Spartapolis, [now Mauzy] Rockingham Co., VA; c. 1850 res. Rockingham Co., VA, age 25, occ. Cattle Dealer;³¹⁰ m. Caroline Amanda Lincoln, 09/04/1851, Smith's Creek?, Rockingham Co., VA;³⁰⁹ c. 1860 res. Harrisonburg, VA, age 37, occ. Farmer, w. Caroline (29), son Charles (6), son John (4);³¹¹ Civil War service 10ᵗʰ Va. Cav., enl. 06/03/1861; pres. 6/61-9/61; resigned 09/26/1861; served as Commissary Officer 1862-1865;³¹² c. 1870 res. Harrisonburg, VA, age 40, occ. Farmer, w. Amanda (36), son Charles (14), dau. Sally (9), dau. Rebecca (5), dau. Not Named (9/12);³¹³ On list of registered voters Linville, Rockingham Co., VA 1871 -1872;³¹⁴ SC #4597, 04/23/1887, filed from New Market, Shennandoah Co., VA; Lists children Charles A. Brock, b. 03/18/1854, Abraham Edwin Brock, b. 04/17/1856, Arezona F.V. Brock, b. 05/13/1858, Sallie Ariminta Nannie Brock, b. 06/24/1863, Carrie L. Brock, b. 12/07/1865, Rebecca A.C. Brock, b. 02/20/1868, Edna Earl Dakota Brock, b. 08/24/1869, Hugh Willie Lincoln Brock, 04/29/1871;³⁰⁹ *"I was engaged with the said John P. Brock in trying to raise a company of volunteers in the county of Rockingham, VA for the Mexican War. We failed in raising the company, but John P. Brock left the county to join the Virginia regiment at Richmond...;"*³⁰⁹ d. 12/01/1892, New Market, VA, bur. Lincoln Cem., near Edom, Rockingham Co., VA³¹²,³¹⁵ wid. Caroline Amanda, WC #8956, 04/14/1893, filed from New Market, Shennandoah Co., VA; (CLB b. 10/09/1831, d. 05/05/1899).³¹⁵

**Brooks, John**, Pvt., Co. B; enl. 11/30/1846, Alexandria, VA, age 42; sick 06/1847, sent to hosp. Saltillo, Mex. 06/26/1847; discharged 07/31/1847 Buena Vista, Mex. on Surgeon's Certificate of Disability.

**Brown, Alexander L.**, Pvt., Co. C; enl. Mex. War service 08/09/1847, Lunenburg, VA, age 21; pres. 04/1848, joined company 01/27/1848 from Regtl. Depot, pay stopped for: [illegible]; pres. 08/1848, BLW sent to Lunenburg C.H., VA; c. 1850 res. Lunenburg Co., VA, age 23, occ. Farmer;³¹⁶ m/1 Abigail C. Rash, 11/22/1852, Lunenburg Co., VA;³¹⁷ m/2 Mary H. Rash, 09/12/1864, Lunenburg Co., VA;³¹⁸ [Civil War service an Alexander Brown served as a 1ˢᵗ Cpl., Staunton Hill Artillery, enl. 09/23/1861 in Charlotte Co., VA, absent 10/1864 in Hosp.; pres. 12/1864, NFR;⁷⁸ c. 1870 res. Brown's Store, Lunenburg, Co., VA, age 45, occ. Farmer, w. Mary H. (35), dau. Sallie A. (15), son Robert A. (12), dau. Mary E. (10), dau. Anna J. (5), dau. Emma I. (2);³¹⁹ d. 02/21/1884 Lunenburg Co., VA; wid. Mary H., WC #529, 03/18/1887, filed from Blackstone, Nottoway Co., VA, widow *"has 6 young children and no means, the oldest boy, 10 years of age;"* (MHB b. 09/10/1834 Lunenburg Co., VA).

**Brown, Andrew J.**, Pvt., Co. L; b. 1828; enl. Mex. War service 03/01/1847 Fairfax C.H., age 19; pres. 06/1847; pres. 08/1847; pres. 10/1847, pay stopped for: 1 pr. pants-$2.28; 1 forage cap-$.95; 1 pr. shoes-$1.22; pres. 12/1847, pay stopped for: 1 jacket-$2.66, 2 flannel shirts-$1.80, 2 cotton shirts-$.86, 1 blanket-$2.22, 2 pr. drawers-$.71, 2 pr. socks-$.49; pres. 02/1848, pay

VIRGINIA VOLUNTEERS IN MEXICO

stopped for: 1 pr Shoes 1.22, 1 Brush & Fork .12; pres. 04/1848, pay stopped for: 1 pr. Shoes 1.22; pres. 07/1848, pay stopped for: 1 Wiper .20; BLW sent to Andrew Brown, Washington City, D.C.; SC #14116, 12/17/1887, from D.C., res. 1215 E St., SE; c. 1890 dropped from Mex. War Pension roll recd. Pension for Civil War service.[320]

**Brown, Charles B.**, Pvt., Co. C; enl. Mex. War service 12/01/1846, Bowling Green, VA, age 19; discharged 06/16/1847, Monterey, Mex., on Surgeon's Certificate of Disability; m. Jane E.L. Jackson, 10/09/1848, Orange Co., VA;[321] c. 1850 res. Caroline Co., VA, age 22, occ. Tailor, w. Jane E.L. (21), dau. Mary J. (10/12);[322] c. 1860 res. Bowling Green, Caroline Co., VA, age 32, occ. Constable, w. Jane E.L. (31), dau. Mary J. (10), Clarinda (8), son Charles J. (6), son William W. (4), son Philip (1);[323] [Civil War service a Charles Barbour Brown served as a Lt., Co. I, 6$^{th}$ Va. Cav., KIA 06/09/1863 at Brandy Station, VA].[324]

**Brown, Charles G.**, Co. A; b. c. 1825 Richmond, VA; enl. Mex. War service 11/18/1846 Richmond, VA, age 21; pres. 12/1846 - 04/1847; pres. 06/1847; AWOL 08/1847, since morning of 08/31/1847; pres.10/1847, pay stopped for clothing: 2 cotton shirts-$.86, 1 pr. wool overalls-$2.28, 1 cap-$.95$^{1/2}$, 2 pr. stockings-$.49, 1 flannel shirt-$.90, 1 pr. shoes-$1.22, 1 wool jacket-$2.66; pres. 12/1847, pay stopped for clothing: 3 pr. socks-$.73$^{1/2}$, 1 pr. shoes-$1.22, 1 great coat-$6.93$^{1/2}$, 1 pr. drawers-$.35$^{1/2}$, 1 flannel shirt-$.90, 1 pr. wool overalls-$2.28, 1 blanket-$2.22; pres. 02/1848, pay stopped for: 1 blanket-$2.22, 1 pick & brush-$.12; pres. 04/1848, pay stopped for 1 wool jacket; 07/1848, pay stopped for: 1 musket-$13.00, cartridge box belt-$.60, 1 musket sling-$.16, 1 cartridge box belt plate-$.10, 1 brush-$.12, 1 wiper-$.20, 1 screw driver-$.25; BLW sent to ___sburg, VA; enl. Battery "F", U.S. Artillery at Baltimore, MD 05/27/1850, trans. to Battery "K" 11/10/1851, discharged 05/27/1855 at Ft. McHenry, MD Re-enl. 05/28/1855 in Co. D, 2$^{nd}$ U.S. Cav. at Baltimore, MD Prom. Cpl. 12/15/1855. Reduced to Pvt. 05/19/1857 Camp Verde, Tex., trans. to /Battery "A", 2$^{nd}$ U.S. Artillery 11/17/1857 Ft. Leavenworth, Kansas Territory, discharged 08/16/1860 Ft. Leavenworth, K.T.;[325] Civil War service Lt. of Artillery, Newbern, NC. Captured and exchanged date unknown. Prom. Capt. of Artillery served at Mobile, Ala.;[325] m. Sarah H. Wragg 07/28/1863 Mobile, Ala.;[326] Children dau. Hortense b. 1877, son Tudor age unknown; SC #6767, 04/07/1887, filed from 1422 S. Compton Avenue, St. Louis, Mo.; Physician's affidavit states 5'9", 125 lbs., *"right forefinger shot off 1856;"* d. 03/05/1895 1423 Sarah St., St. Louis, Mo., bur. St. Peter's Cem., St. Louis, Mo.,[327] wid. Sarah H., WC #9710 03/13/1895, both from MO. (SHB b. 07/28/1842 Mobile, Ala., d. 01/27/1930 St. Louis, Mo., bur. St. Peter's Cem., St. Louis, Mo.)

**Brown, Edward**, Pvt., Co. A; enl. Mex. War 12/14/1846, age 26; deserted 12/25/1846 at Richmond, VA

**Brown, James B.**, Pvt., LIC; enl. Mex. War service 11/27/1846 Staunton, VA, age 28; d. 06/24/1847 at Monterey, Mex. of fever; a letter from Asst. Surgeon, T.C. Madison to Lt. Thomas P. August, Co. A related the news. *"I regret to report the death of Pvt. B. Brown of Capt. Fairfax's Co. on the 24$^{th}$ of Hemorhage* [sic] *from the Bowels. His gun &c. were taken by Lt. Kinney."*[328]

**Brown, James W.**, Pvt., Co. B; enl. 12/21/1846, Richmond, VA, age 20; pres. 06/1847; pres. 10/1847, pay stopped for: 2 pr. shoes-$2.44, 3 flannel shirts-$2.70, 2 pr. overalls-$4.56, 1 jacket-$2.66, 4 pr. cotton drawers-$1.42, 1 cap-$.95$^{1/2}$; pres. 12/1847, pay stopped for: 1 pr. socks-$.24$^{1/2}$, 1 pr. overalls-$2.28, 1 blanket-$2.22; on extra duty 02/1848 in QM Dept. repairing tents &c. since 12/31/1847; on extra duty 04/1848 in QM Dept. repairing tents &c.; pres. 08/1848, pay stopped for: 1 musket & bayonet-$13.00, 1 bayonet scabbard-$.56, 1 cartridge box-$1.10, 1 cartridge box belt-$.60, 1 cartridge box belt plate-$.10, 1 waist belt-$.21, 1 pick & brush.12, 1 screw driver-$.07, 1 wiper-$.20, 1 gun sling-$.10, 1 waist belt plate-$.10, BLW sent to Front Royal, Fauquier Co., Va.[BLW lined out]; Left at Brasos Island 07/06/1848, AWOL.

85

OFF TO WAR

**Brown, John G.**, Pvt., Co. G; b. 12/28/1821 Richmond, VA, son of Edward & Anna Brown;[329] enl. Mex. War service 11/28/1846 Richmond, VA, age 25; pres. 06/1847; pres. 08/1847; pres. 10/1847, pay stopped for: 2 pr. overalls-$4.56, 1 cotton shirt-$.43, 1 pr. drawers-$.35$^{1/2}$, 2 shoes-$2.44, 3 pr. socks-$.73$^{1/2}$, 1 forage cap-$.95$^{1/2}$; pres. 12/1847, pay stopped for: 1 pr. shoes-$1.22, 1 blanket-$2.22, 1 pr. pants-$2.28, 1 pr. socks-$.24$^{1/2}$; pres. 02/1848; pres. 04/1848; pres. 08/1848, pay stopped for: 1 screw driver-.07, 1 gun sling-$.16, 1 cartridge box plate-$.10; BLW sent to Richmond, VA; m. Blanche Imboden, 03/25/1875, Pocahontas, Randolph Co., Ark.;[330] SC #11179, 08/22/1887, filed from 406 N. 3$^{rd}$ St., St. Louis, MO; d. 02/16/1907 *"thrombosis, attributed to gangrene,"* St. Anthony's Hosp., St. Louis, Mo., bur. St. Matthews Cemetery, St. Louis, Mo.;[329] wid. Blanche, WC #14941, 06/21/1897, filed from 3715 Wyoming St., St. Louis, MO; (BIB b. c. 1850, d. 07/09/1917).[331]

**Brown, John**, Lt., Va. Vols.; d. 01/1857.[332]

**Brown, John**, Pvt., Co. B; enl. 12/12/1846, Alexandria, VA, age 19; pres. 06/1847; in confinement 10/1847, pay stopped for: 4 cotton shirts-$1.72, 1 pr. overalls-$2.28, 1 jacket-$2.66, 2 pr. cotton drawers-$.71, 2 pr. shoes-$2.44, 1 pr. socks-$.24$^{1/2}$, 1 overcoat-$ 6.93$^{1/2}$; pres. 12/1847, pay stopped for: 1 flannel shirt-$.90, 1 pr. overalls-$2.28, 1 cap-$.95$^{1/2}$, 2 pr. socks-$.49, 1 cotton shirt-$.43, 1 blanket-$2.22; pres. 02/1848; pres. 04/1848, pay stopped for: 1 jacket-$2.66; pres. 08/1848, pay stopped for: 1 musket lock-$3.00, 1 bayonet scabbard-$.56, 1 waist belt-$.21, 1 waist belt plate-$.10, BLW sent to Alexandria, VA

**Brown, John**, Pvt., Co. H; enl. Mex. War service 01/06/1847, Berkeley, VA, age 35; pres. 04/1847; pres. 06/1847; pres. 08/1847; pres. 10/1847, pay stopped for: 1 pr. pants-$2.28; pres. 12/1847, pay stopped for: 1 forage cap-$.95$^{1/2}$, 1 jacket-$2.66, 1 flannel shirt-$.90, 1 pr. shoes-$1.22, 2 pr. socks-$.49; pres. 02/1848; pres. 04/1848; pres. 07/1848, pay stopped for: 1 brush & pick-$.12, 1 wiper-$.20, 1 pr. shoes-$1.16, BLW sent to Philadelphia, Pa.

**Brown, Joseph**, Pvt., Co. C; enl. Mex. War service 12/29/1846, Bowling Green, VA, age 38; deserted 01/12/1847 Fort Monroe, VA

**Brown, Peter A.**, Pvt., Co. H; enl. Mex. War service 01/11/1847, Alexandria, VA, age 22; absent 04/1847 left in Hosp. at China, Mex. 04/16/1847; absent 06/1847, left as an Attendant in Hosp. at Monterey, Mex. 06/22/1847; sick 08/1847; discharged 10/16/1847 Buena Vista, Mex. on Surgeon's Certificate of Disability.

**Brown, Preston**, Pvt., LIC; enl. Mex. War service 12/28/1846 Scottsville, VA, age 28; absent 06/1847 sick in quarters; discharged 08/01/1847 on Surgeon's Certificate of Disability.

**Brown, Samuel**, Pvt., Co. L; b. 1828; enl. Mex. War service 03/01/1847 Fairfax C.H., 19; absent 06/1847 sick in hospital at Saltillo, Mex.; pres. 08/1847; pres. 10/1847, pay stopped for: 1 pr. shoes-$1.22; pres. 12/1847, pay stopped for: 2 pr. pants-$4.56, 1 pr. shoes-$1.22, 2 flannel shirts-$1.80, 2 cotton shirts-$.86, 2 pr. drawers-$.71; pres. 02/1848, sick in qtrs., pay stopped for: 1 pr. Shoes 1.22, 1 Jacket 2.66, 1 Bayonet Scabbard .50, 1 bayonet scabbard plate-$.10, 1 Brush & Pick .12; absent 04/1848 sick in hosp.; pres. 07/1848, pay stopped for: 1 Waist Belt .21, 1 Waist Belt Plate .10; BLW sent to Charles Bishop c/o Samuel Brown, Washington City, D.C.

**Brown, William C.**, 1$^{st}$ Cpl., Co. M; enl. Mex. War service 07/15/1847 Richmond, VA, age 20; pres. 09/1847; pres. 11/1847, reduced to 2$^{nd}$ Cpl. from 4$^{th}$ Sgt.; pres. 12/1847; pres. 02/1848; pres. 04/1848, pay stopped for: 1 pr. shoes-$1.22, 2 cotton shirts-$.86; pres. 08/1848, prom. 1$^{st}$ Cpl., pay stopped for: 1 musket-$13.00, 1 cartridge box-$1.10, 1 waist belt-$.21, 1 waist belt plate-$.10, 1 thumb vise-$.35, 1 bayonet scabbard-$.56, 1 screw driver-$.07, 1 wormer-$.20; BLW sent to Richmond, VA

**Brown, William J.**, Pvt., Co. H; enl. Mex. War service 01/06/1847, Berkeley, VA, age 18; pres. 04/1847; absent 06/1847, left sick in Hosp. at Monterey, Mex. 06/22/1847; absent sick 08/1847 at Monterey, Mex.; absent 10/1847 sick in Hosp. at Monterey, Mex.; in confinement 12/1847, pay stopped for: 1 forage cap-$.95$^{1/2}$, 1 jacket-$2.66, 1 pr. pants-$2.28, 2 cotton shirts-$.86, 1 pr. shoes-$1.22, 2 pr. socks-$.49; pres. 02/1848, pay stopped for: 1 forage cap-

## VIRGINIA VOLUNTEERS IN MEXICO

$.95$^{1/2}$, 2 jackets-$5.32, 1 pr. pants-$2.28, 2 cotton shirts-$.86, 3 pr. drawers-$1.06$^{1/2}$, 1 pr. shoes-$1.22, 2 pr. socks-$.49; pres. 04/1848; pres. 07/1848, pay stopped for: 1 waist belt plate-$.10, BLW sent to Philadelphia, Pa.

**Bruce, Winfield Scott**, Pvt., Co. L; b. 04/03/24 in Fauquier Co., VA, son of Reuben & Mariah Bruce; enl. Mex. War service 04/02/1847 Harper's Ferry, VA, age 23; pres. 06/1847; pres. 08/1847; pres. 10/1847, pay stopped for: 1 pr. Pants 2.28; 1 pr. Shoes 1.22; pres. 12/1847, pay stopped for: 1 jacket-$2.66, 1 pr. pants-$2.28, 2 pr shoes-$4.56, 1 flannel shirt-$.90, 5 cotton shirts-$2.15, 1 blanket-$2.22, 4 pr. drawers-$1.42, 2 pr. socks-$.49; pres. 02/1848, pay stopped for: 1 pr. Shoes 1.22, 1 Jacket 2.66, 1 Brush & Fork .12; pres. 04/1848, pay stopped for: 1 Blanket 2.25, 1 pr. Shoes 1.22, 4 Cotton Shirts 1.76; pres. 07/1848, pay stopped for: 1 Brush & Pick .12; BLW sent to W.S. Bruce, Warrenton, Fauquier Co., VA; m/1 Artemecia Fox, 02/03/1849, Fauquier Co., VA;[333] m/2 Martha F. Bruce 01/13/1852, Rappahannock Co., VA;[334] c. 1860 res. Sperryville, Rappahannock Co., VA, age 33, occ. Carpenter, w. Martha (29);[335] Civil War service enl. Co. B, 6$^{th}$ Va. Cav. "Rappahannock Cavalry," 5/8/1861 as a Cpl., promoted to Sgt. 7/26/1861. Under arrest 5 - 6/62. with Gen. Trimble on 10/8/1862. Hip dislocated in fall from horse 11/20/1862. wded. 10/1/1863. Reported as a deserter 2/28/1865 but on final roll 3/21/1865.[324] c. 1870 res. Sperryville, Rappahannock Co., VA, age 43, occ. Carpenter, w. Martha (40), son Landon H. (3), father Reuben (78), mother Mariah (68);[336] SC #4044, 03/17/1887, d. 03/11/1912, *"valvular lession of the heart,"* Sperryville, Rappahannock Co., VA, wid. Martha F., WC #15814, 04/23/1912, (*MFB* d. 03/18/1918, Sperryville, Rappahannock Co., VA), both from VA

**Bryan, James Lawrenson**, 1$^{st}$ Lt., Co. D; b. 1824, Cambridge, MD; son of James Bryan & Emily LeCompte; graduate VMI 1843; enl. Mex. War service 12/22/1846, Petersburg, VA; pres. detached 02/1847 Actg. Assistant of Commissary & Subsistance to the detachment on board the ship *Sophia Walker*; pres. 04/1847 rejoined company 03/27/1847; pres. 06/1847, apptd. Adjutant *pro tem* 06/19/1847 by order of Col. Hamtramck; pres. 08/1847; pres. 10/1847; pres. 12/1847; pres. 04/1848; pres. 08/1848; doctor; Episcopal clergyman; m. Anne Aurelia Pattison, 12/07/852, St. Peters Episcopal Church, Baltimore, MD;[281,]

Photo courtesy: VMI Archives, Lexington, VA

[337] SC #7746, 02/01/1887, filed from Cambridge, Dorchester Co., MD; *"Affiant was studying medicine in Baltimore at date of enlistment. He was born in Cambridge, MD, his age is 78 yrs. next August. His occupation has been a practicing Physician part of the time, Superintendent of Public School of Dorchester County, Principal of a Military Academy and Minister of the Protestant Episcopal Church;"*[337] phys. desc., age 62, 6'0", brown complexion, iron gray hair, dark eyes, since discharge res. Baltimore, MD 2 yrs., Lakeville, MD 5 yrs., Taylor's Island, MD 2 yrs., Cambridge until death;[337] d. 11/06/1904, Cambridge, MD;;[338, 281] WC #13900, 11/23/1904, filed from 122 Mill St., Cambridge, Dorchester Co., MD; list *"eight living"* children D'Arcy Pattison Bryan b. 03/09/1855, William Lewis Herndon Bryan b. 11/15/1858, Mary Virginia Bryan b. 01/14/1861, Guy Lee Byran b. 03/23/1854, Lay Bryan b. 07/16/1870, Nora Bryan b. 10/05/1871, Emily Sherwood Bryan b. 04/10/1874, Frank Otis Bryan b. 09/29/1856 – Julian L. Bryan, deceased; (AAB b. 01/07/1836 Taylor's Island, Dorchester Co., MD, d. 05/08/1919).

**Bryant, Richard**, 2$^{nd}$ Cpl., Co. L; b. 1822; enl. Mex. War service 03/01/1847 Fairfax C.H., VA, age 25; pres. 06/1847; deserted 08/16/1847 from camp Buena Vista, Mex.[72]

OFF TO WAR

**Bryant, William**, Pvt., Co. K; enl. Mex. War service Richmond, VA 01/05/1847, age 20; d. 02/14/1847 at Ft. Monroe, VA.
**Buchannan, Milo**, Pvt., Co. A; enl. Mex. War service 11/28/1846 Richmond, VA, age 24; pres. 12/1846 - 04/1847; pres. 06/1847; pres. 08/1847; pres. 10/1847 pay stopped for clothing: 1 cap-$.95$^{1/2}$, 4 pr. stockings-$.98, 1 pr. wool overalls-$2.28, 1 pr. drawers-$.35$^{1/2}$, 1 pr. shoes-$1.22; pres. 12/1847; pres. 02/1848, pay stopped for: 1 pr. shoes-$1.22; pres. 04/1848; BLW sent to Uttica, Oneida Co., New York.
**Bullard, James**, Pvt., Co. C; b. c. 1820, King George Co., VA, son of Reuben & Lucy Bullard;[339] enl. Mex. War service 12/18/1846, Fredericksburg, VA, age 23; discharged 06/16/1847 Monterey, Mex. on Surgeon's Certificate of Disability; c. 1860 res. Clifton, King George Co., VA, age 40, occ. Farmer, w. Ellen (25), dau. Mary (7), son James (5), dau. Lucy L. (2);[340] c. 1870 res. Passabytanzy, King George Co., VA, age 50, occ. Farmer, w. Ellen (38), dau. Mary (17), son James (16), dau. Lucy (13);[341] d. 10/10/1878, King George Co., VA *"'dropsy."*[342]
**Burdine, John**, Pvt., Co. F; m. Francisco Dowers 09/07/1842 Villa Carlos, Spain;[343] enl. Mex. War service 12/24/1846, Portsmouth, VA, age 37; pres. 06/1847; absent 08/1847 sick; absent 10/1847 on detached service in QM Dept., pay stopped for: 1 bayonet-$1.44, 1 bayonet scabbard & frog-$.50, 1 belt & plate-$.66, 3 cotton shirts-$1.29, 1 pr. overalls-$2.28, 2 pr. shoes-$2.44, 1 forage cap-$.95$^{1/2}$, 2 pr. socks-$.49, 2 pr. drawers-.71, 1 flannel shirt-$.90; absent 12/1847 on daily duty in QM Dept.; pres. 02/1848, pay stopped for: 1 waist belt & plate-$.35; pres. 04/1848; pres. 08/1848, pay stopped for: 1 gun sling-$.18, 1 infantry jacket-$2.57, 2 cotton shirts-$.88, BLW sent to Washington, D.C.; d. 1849 or 1851 *"drowned,"* at Pensacola, Fla.;[343] wid. Francisco, WC #3952, 08/01/1887, filed from Washington Asylum, or Alms House, Washington, DC; adjudged *"insane"* by decree of DC Superior Court 06/17/1892;[343] (FDB d. 1897).[343]
**Burke, Adolphus T.**, Pvt., Co. I; enl. Mex. War service 08/09/1847 Ft. Monroe, VA, AGE 22; pres. 02/1848, joined co. 01/26/1848; pres. 04/1848, pay stopped for: 1 blanket; pres. 08/1848, BLW sent to Pleasants Grove, Lunenburg Co., VA; m. Jane Crafton, 09/28/1848, Lunenburg Co., VA;[344] [Civil War service an Adolphus T. Burke served as a Cpl., Co. G, 10$^{th}$ Miss. Inf.][202]
**Burke, Abdon Lee**, 4$^{th}$ Sgt., Co. L; b. 11/19/1824, Loudoun Co., VA, son of Ethelbert & \_\_\_\_ (Lee) Burke;[345] enl. Mex. War service 03/02/1847 Fairfax C.H., age 22; pres. 08/1847, prom. 3$^{rd}$ Cpl. from Pvt.; pres. 10/1847, pay stopped for: 1 forage cap-$.95; pres. 12/1847, pay stopped for: 1 pr. Pants 2.28, 1 F Shirt .90, 2 C Shirts .86, 1 Blanket 2.22, 2 pr. Drawers .71, 2 pr. Socks .24, 1 dragoon overcoat-$8.75; pres. 02/1848, pay stopped for: 1 Jacket 2.66, 1 Bayonet Scabbard.50; pres. 04/1848, sick in Qtrs., pay stopped for: 1 Blanket 2.25, 1 pr. Shoes 1.16, 2 Cotton shirts .88; BLW sent to Capt. Thrift c/o Abdon L. Burke, Fairfax Court House, Fairfax Co., VA; BLW #34888 for 160 ac., 1847; m. Anna Eliza Shrader 07/02/1855;[345] served in Civil War (US), 1$^{st}$ Lt., LIC, 25$^{th}$ U.S.C.T. & Co. H, 3$^{rd}$ Wis. Inf.; IC #167094; d. 6/9/1914; WA #20229 "Ann E." dated 7/10/1914 rcvd. from NE; [pension filed not found].
**Burke, William H.**, Pvt., Co. M; enl. Mex. War service 07/01/1847 Richmond, VA, age 31; pres. 09/1847; pres. 11/1847; pres. 12/1847; pres. 02/1848; pres. 04/1848; pres. 08/1848, pay stopped for: 1 cartridge box belt plate-$.10, 1 pick & brush-$.12, 1 screw driver-$.07; BLW sent to Richmond, VA; c. 1850 res. Richmond, VA, age 34, occ. Printer.[346]
**Burks, William A.**, Pvt., Co. I; enl. Mex. War service 01/10/1847 Lynchburg, VA, age 22; pres. 04/1847; absent 06/1847, left in Monterey, Mex. 06/22/1847 supposed that he deserted; pres. 08/1847, rejoined the co. 07/05/1847; absent 10/1847, pay stopped for: 2 flannel shirts-$1.80, 3 pr. drawers-$1.06$^{1/2}$, 1 pr. pants-$2.28, 1 pr. shoes-$1.22, 1 cotton shirt-$.43, 1 blanket-$2.22, 1 cap-$.95$^{1/2}$, 1 pr. socks-$.24$^{1/2}$, 1 jacket-$2.66; pres. 12/1847, pay stopped for: 1 pr. socks-$.24$^{1/2}$, 1 cotton shirt-$.43, 2 flannel shirts-$1.80, 2 pr. drawers-$.71, 1 flannel shirt-$.90; pres. 02/1848, pay stopped for: 1 pr. shoes-$1.22, 1 flannel shirt-$.90, 1 pr. overalls-

## VIRGINIA VOLUNTEERS IN MEXICO

$2.28; absent 04/1848 on furlough in Saltillo, Mex.; pres. 08/1848, BLW sent to Lynchburg, VA

**Burnett, Richard C.**, Pvt., Co. G; enl. Mex. War service 11/28/1846 Richmond, VA, age 18; pres. 06/1847; pres. 08/1847; pres. 10/1847, pay stopped for: 2 pr. overalls-$2.28, 3 cotton shirts-$1.29, 1 pr. drawers-$.35$^{1/2}$, 2 shoes-$2.44, 3 pr. socks-$.73$^{1/2}$, 1 forage cap-$.95$^{1/2}$; sick 12/1847, pay stopped for: 1 pr. shoes-$1.22, 1 blanket-$2.22, 2 pr. socks-$.49; pres. 02/1848, pay stopped for: 1 cartridge box belt-$.70, 1 brush & pick-$.12, 1 pr. shoes-$1.22; pres. 04/1848; pres. 08/1848; BLW sent to Old Church, Hanover Co., VA

**Burns, Harman T.**, 2$^{nd}$ Sgt., Co. D; enl. Mex. War service 12/29/1846, Petersburg, VA, age 28; pres. 02/1847; pres. 04/1847; pres. 06/1847, prom. 3$^{rd}$ Sgt. 06/16/1847; pres. 08/1847; pres. 10/1847, prom. 2$^{nd}$ Sgt., pay stopped for: 1 pr. pants-$2.28, 3 cotton shirts-$1.29, 2 pr. socks-$.49; pres. 12/1847, pay stopped for 1 cap-$.95$^{1/2}$, 1 pr. pants-$2.28, 2 pr drawers-$.71, 1 blanket-$2.22; absent 04/1848, detailed as QM Sgt. 02/25/1848, by order of Capt. Harper commanding Parras Battalion, pay stopped for: 1 haversack-$.20$^{3/4}$; pres. 08/1847, BLW sent to Washington City, DC.

**Burruss, John S.**, Pvt., Co. C; enl. Mex. War service 12/13/1846, Bowling Green, VA, age 20; discharged 05/15/1847 Matamoros, Mex. on Surgeon's Certificate of Disability.

**Burton, William**, Pvt., Co. A; enl. Mex. War service 12/01/1846 Richmond, VA, age 28; discharged 04/28/1847 for disease by order of Maj. Gen. Taylor.

**Bush, Vance W.**, Pvt., Co. K; enl. Mex. War service Richmond, VA 01/20/1847, age 31; pres. 06/1847; sick 08/1847; d. 09/20/1847 at Buena Vista, Mex.

**Butt, James W.**, 1$^{st}$ Sgt., Co. F; enl. Mex. War service 11/23/1846, Portsmouth, VA, age 28; pres. 06/1847; pres. 08/1847; pres. 10/1847, pay stopped for: 1 pr. overall-$2.28, 2 pr. socks-$.49, 1 pr. shoes-$1.22, 1 forage cap-$.95$^{1/2}$; pres. 12/1847; pres. 02/1848, 2 pr. drawers-$.71, 2 pr. socks-$.49; pres. 04/1848, reduced to ranks from 1$^{st}$ Sgt. 04/01/1848; pres. 08/1848, pay stopped for: 2 cotton shirts-$.88, BLW sent to Portsmouth, VA c/o E.T. Blamire.

**Byrnes, John**, Pvt., Co. L; b. 1814; enl. Mex. War service 03/15/1847 Alexandria, VA, age 33; pres. 06/1847; pres. 08/1847; pres. 10/1847; pres. 12/1847, to forfeit 1 mos. pay by sentence of general court-martial, pay stopped for: 1 jacket-$2.66, 1 pr. pants-$2.28, 1 cap-$.95$^{1/2}$, 1 pr. shoes-$1.22, 2 flannel shirts-$1.80, 1 cotton shirts-$.43, 2 pr. drawers-$.71, 1 pr. socks-$.24$^{1/2}$; pres. 02/1848, pay stopped for: 1 Blanket 2.22; pres. 04/1848, pay stopped for: 2 Flannel Shirts 1.55; pres. 07/1848; BLW sent to Capt. Thrift c/o John Byrnes, Fairfax Court House, Fairfax Co., VA

**Cabell, Henry L.**, Pvt., Co. K; b. 12/25/1828 Lynchburg, Campbell Co., VA;[347] enl. Mex. War service Frederick, VA 12/09/1846, age 18; pres. 06/1847; sick 08/1847; absent 10/1847 on detached service in QM Dept., Actg. Post QM in Saltillo, Mex.; absent 12/1847 on detached service in QM Dept. as Actg. Post QM, pay stopped for: 1 pr. boots-$1.22, 2 pr. socks-$.49, 1 cap-$.95$^{1/2}$, 1 blanket-$2.22, 2 flannel shirts-$1.80; absent 04/1848 on detached service in QM Dept. in Saltillo, Mex.; pres. 07/1848; BLW sent to Winchester, VA; c. 1850 res. Winchester, Frederick Co., VA, age 21, occ. None Listed;[348] m. Annie W. Cabell, 06/13/1855, Nelson Co., VA;[347] c. 1860 res. Tye River Warehouse, Nelson Co., VA, age 31, occ. M.D., w. Annie W. (28), son Henry L. (1);[349] c. 1870 res. Winchester, Frederick Co., VA, age 41, occ. Physician, w. Annie (38), dau. Sallie L. (9), son Charles G. (7), dau. Ellen C. (5), son Samuel J. (2);[350] (AWC d. 12/26/1872, Newtown, VA); SC #9913, 04/22/1887, filed from Cedarville, Warren Co., VA; since discharge res. Winchester, and Howardsville, VA, Buckhannon, Upshur Co., WV, Frederick Co., VA, and lastly Warren Co., VA;[347] Andrew J. Copenhaver gave affidavit in pension claim.[347]

**Caddis, Henry**, Pvt., Co. B; enl. 12/01/1846, Alexandria, VA, age 30; sick 06/1847; pres. 08/1847; discharged 10/12/1847 Buena Vista, Mex. on Surgeon's Certificate of Disability; [a Henry Caddis m. Mary Putt 01/18/1853, Starke Co., OH][351]

89

OFF TO WAR

**Cain, Benjamin**, Pvt., Co. C; enl. Mex. War service 12/29/1846, Bowling Green, VA, age 35; pres. 06/1847, one mos. pay stopped by order of regtl. court-martial; pres. 08/1847, pay stopped for: 1 cap-$.95$^{1/2}$, 2 pr. socks-$.49, 2 cotton shirts-$.86, 2 woolen shirts-$1.80; pres. 10/1847, pay stopped for: 2 pr. socks-$.49, 2 pr. drawers-$.71, 1 pr. pants-$2.28, 2 cotton shirt-$.86, 1 pr. shoes-$1.22; pres. 12/1847, pay stopped for: 1 jacket-$2.66, 1 pr. pants-$2.28, 2 woolen shirts-$1.80, 1 pr. shoes-$1.22, 1 blanket-$2.22; pres. 04/1848, pay stopped for: 1 pr. shoes-$1.50, 1 india rubber canteen-$.27; pres. 08/1848, BLW sent to Lap, PO, Lancaster Co., Pa.

**Cain, Nathaniel D.**, Pvt., Co. E; b. Prince Geo. Co., VA, son of Nicholas R. & Frances A. Cain;[352] enl. Mex. War service 12/08/1846 Petersburg, VA, age 26; pres. 04/1847; pres. 06/1847; pres. 08/1847; pres. 10/1847, pay stopped for: 2 pr. overalls-$2.28, 2 pr. shoes-$2.44, 4 pr. stockings-$.98, 2 cotton shirts-$.86, 2 pr. drawers-$.71, 1 cap-$.95$^{1/2}$; pres. 12/1847, [illegible]; pres. 02/1848; pres. 04/1848; c. 1850 res. *"Rail Road Shanty,"* Dinwiddie Co., VA, age 32, occ. Overseer on R.R.;[353] m. Virginia Sarah Farley, 04/29/1873, Petersburg, VA;[354, 355] d. 08/24/1879, *Dysentery*, Petersburg, VA, bur. Blandford Cem., Sq. 4, Sec. 11, Ward D, Petersburg, VA;[356,] wid. Virginia S., WC #1123, 03/09/1887, filed from 555 Washington St., Petersburg, Dinwiddie Co., VA; (VSC b. 09/03/1844, Nottoway Co., VA)[354]

**Cain, William Coulson**, Pvt., Co. H; b. 03/11/1815, Montgomery Co., VA;[357] m. Jane Maria VanSickel, 06/14/1835, Philadelphia, Pa.;[357] enl. Mex. War service 01/01/1847, Berkeley, VA, age 31; pres. 04/1847; pres. 06/1847; pres. 08/1847; pres. 10/1847, pay stopped for: 1 pr. pants-$2.28, 1 cotton shirt-$.43, 1 pr. shoes-$1.22, 2 pr. socks-$.49; pres. 12/1847; pres. 02/1848; pres. 04/1848; pres. 07/1848, BLW sent to Philadelphia, Pa.; (JVC d. 06/12/1854, Philadelphia, Pa.);[357] m/2 unknown (unknown wife d. 1880, Coatsville, Chester Co., Pa.);[357] SC #419, 03/02/1887, filed from National Soldiers Home, Elizabeth City Co., Hampton, VA; since discharge res. 1223 Howard St., 426 N. 8$^{th}$ St., and 1036 Mechanic St., Philadelphia, Pa.; National Soldiers Home, Dayton, OH; and National Soldiers Home, Elizabeth City, VA[357]

**Calhoun, John**, Pvt., Co. C; enl. Mex. War service 12/18/1846, Fredericksburg, VA, age 43; discharged 06/16/1847 Monterey, Mex. on Surgeon's Certificate of Disability;

**Callaghan, Thomas**, Pvt., Co. F; enl. Mex. War service 01/10/1847, Portsmouth, VA, age 36; pres. 06/1847; pres. 08/1847; pres. 10/1847, pay stopped for: 1 pr. overalls-$2.28, 2 cotton shirts-$.86, 1 pr. shoes-$1.22, 2 pr. drawers-.71; pres. 12/1847; pres. 02/1848, pay stopped for: 2 flannel shirts-$1.80, 1 pr. overalls-$2.28, 1 pr. shoes-$1.22; pres. 04/1848; pres. 08/1848, BLW sent to Portsmouth, VA c/o E.T. Blamire.

**Callis, Bailey**, Pvt., Co. F; enl. Mex. War service 01/28/1847, Portsmouth, VA, age 35; pres. 06/1847; pres. 08/1847; in confinement 10/1847, pay stopped for: 1 pr. overalls-$2.28, 2 cotton shirts-$.86, 2 pr. socks-$.49, 1 pr. shoes-$1.22; pres. 12/1847; pres. 02/1848, pay stopped for: 1 blanket-$2.22, 1 pr. shoes-$1.22; pres. 04/1848; pres. 08/1848, pay stopped for: 1 musket complete-$13.00, 1 cartridge box & belt complete-$1.90, 1 bayonet & scabbard-$1.56, 1 waist belt & plate-$.31, 1 brush & pick-$.12, 1 screw driver-$.25, 1 wiper-$.20, 1 jacket-$2.37; BLW sent to Portsmouth, VA c/o E.T. Blamire.

**Campbell, George**, Pvt., *Preston's Co.*; enl. Mex. War service 12/07/1846 Montgomery Co., VA, age 30; pres. 04/1847; pres. 06/1847; pres. 08/1847; pres. 10/1847, pay stopped for: 3 pr. socks-$.73$^{1/2}$, 1 flannel shirt-$.90, 1 cotton shirt-$.43; absent 12/1847, on detached service altering company clothing since 11/28/1847, pay stopped for: 1 jacket-$2.66, 1 pr. overalls-$2.28, 1 pr. shoes-$1.22; pres. 02/1848, pay stopped for: 1 pr. shoes-$1.22; pres. 04/1848; pres. 07/1848, pay stopped for: 1 screw driver-$.07; BLW sent to Christiansburg, VA c/o Fleming Gardner.

**Campbell, Lewis**, Pvt., Co. C; enl. Mex. War service 12/30/1846, Bowling Green, VA, age 19; sick 06/1847; pres. 08/1847, pay stopped for: 1 cap-$.95$^{1/2}$, 2 pr. socks-$.49, 2 cotton shirts-$.86, 2 woolen shirts-$1.80, 1 knapsack & straps-$1.10; pres. 10/1847, pay stopped for: 2 pr. socks-$.49, 2 pr. drawers-$.71, 1 pr. pants-$2.28, 1 cotton shirt-$.43, 3 pr. shoes-$3.66, 1 great

## VIRGINIA VOLUNTEERS IN MEXICO

coat-$6.93$^{1/2}$; Court-martialed 11/24 & 25/1847 Buena Vista, Mex. *Charge #1: Desertion; Specification: In this that Pvt. Lewis Campbell, Co. C, Va. Regt. Vols. Whilst a prisoner in the Quarter Guard of the Va. Regt. on the 12$^{th}$ of Nov. 1847 did desert the service of the United States, and was apprehended on the 13$^{th}$ of Nov. 1847 by Capt. Thrift, VA. Regt., nine miles more or less east of Saltillo on the road to Monterey. Charge #2: Conduct Prejudicial to Good Order and Military Discipline; Specification: In this that Pvt. Lewis Campbell, Co. C, Va. Regt., whilst a prisoner in the Quarter Guard, Va. Regt., did break his arrest and did then desert the service of the United States. This at Camp Buena Vista, Mexico on the 12$^{th}$ of Nov. 1847. To which charges and specifications the prisoner plead Not Guilty. Sergt.J.R. Goode, Co. C, Va. Regt. Vols. A witness for the prosecution being duly sworn says: I was Sergt. of the Qtr. Guard of the Va. Regt. on the 12$^{th}$ of Nov. The prisoner Campbell was a prisoner in charge of the guard when I mounted guard on that day. He was sent to camp to get his dinner and he left then without any authority and I've not see him again until he was brought back to camp on the morning of the 14$^{th}$ I think. Captain James Thrift, Va. Regt. of Vols., a witness for the prosecution being duly sworn says: I found the prisoner, Private Lewis Campbell, on the Monterey road on the 13$^{th}$ of Nov. last. I was in pursuit of a man from my company who had deserted and when at a Ranch some 12 miles below Saltillo, I saw Campbell passing along the road from Monterey towards Saltillo. Supposing that probably he had some connection with the man who had deserted from my company, I arrested him and sent him to Saltillo in charge of some men who I had with me. When I asked him what he was doing away from camp, he told me he had got drunk and that he had gone down the road with some Mexicans the day before, as far as the Rinconada Pass. I am certain he had been some distance further on, as I saw his tracks. Thinking he had some connection with this man of mine who had gone off, I was anxious to trace it out. I observed the track of this man some two or three miles further down the road below the Ranch where I first saw him. He told me also that he was going back to camp when I first questioned him. The prisoner was found Not Guilty of Desertion but Guilty of Absence Without Leave. Sentenced: to forfeit two (2) months pay and to be kept on extra police duty in his company for the period of two months."*[358] in confinement 12/1847, in provost guard, pay stopped for: 2 pr. drawers-$.71, 1 pr. pants-$2.28, 3 woolen shirts-$2.70, 1 pr. shoes-$1.22, 1 blanket-$2.22; pres. 04/1848, fined 2 mos. pay by order of genl. court-martial, pay stopped for: 1 jacket-$2.66, 1 cotton shirt-$.43, 1 jacket-$2.66, 1 pr. shoes-$1.50; 1 haversack-$.20$^{3/4}$, 1 india rubber canteen-$.27; pres. 08/1848, BLW sent to Philadelphia, Pa.; m. Hanah M. Lukens 07/05/1855 Philadelphia, Pa.; Civil War service Co. C, *Rushes Lancers*, 6$^{th}$ Pa. Cav.; enl. 05/1861, discharged 10/21/1861; SC #17691, 05/09/1888, filed from Welsh Rd., Holmesburgh, Philadelphia, PA; since discharge res. in City of Philadelphia, Pa., phys. desc. 5'11$^{1/2}$", light complex., gray eyes, gray hair, occ. Laborer; widower by 03/07/1898, *"no children."*[359]

**Cantor, Sydney S.**, Pvt., Co. I; enl. Mex. War service 01/25/1847 Lynchburg, VA, age 37; pres. 02/1847; pres. 04/1847; pres. 06/1847; pres. 08/1847; absent 10/1847, pay stopped for: 2 pr. drawers-$.71, 2 flannel shirts-$1.80, 1 pr. shoes-$1.22, 4 cotton shirts-$1.72, 1 pr. pants-$2.28, 1 cap-$.95$^{1/2}$; pres. 12/1847, pay stopped for: 1 pr. pants-$2.28, 1 pr. shoes-$1.22, 1 blanket-$2.22, 1 pr. drawers-$.35$^{1/2}$, 1 jacket-$2.66; pres. 02/1848; pres. 04/1848; pres. 08/1848, pay stopped for: 1 pick & brush-$.12, 1 wiper-$.20, BLW sent to Washington, D.C.

**Cardwell, James**, Pvt., Co. A; enl. Mex. War service 12/11/1846 Richmond, VA, age 26; pres. 12/1846 - 04/1847; pres. 06/1847; sick 08/1847; discharged 10/16/1847 at Buena Vista, Mex. on Surgeon's Certificate; m. Lucy A. Lambert 03/12/1849, Hanover Co., VA;[360] c. 1850 res. Hanover Co., VA, age 30, occ. Machinist, w. Lucy A. (25);[361] c. 1860 res. Negrofoot, Hanover Co., VA, age 40, occ. Carpenter, w. Lucy A. (35), dau. Juila L. (9), son John W. (7), son James H. (5), son Thomas W. (2);[362] Civil War service Pvt., Co. C, 15$^{th}$ Va. Inf., enl. 04/23/1861 at Ashland, VA, discharged 0721/1862, age 45, above the age of the Conscription Act;[116] c. 1870 res. Hewlett's, Hanover Co., VA, age 53, occ. Miller, w. Lucy (45), Julia S.

(18), son John W. (16), son Marcellus (15), dau. Mary L. (13), son Robert Lee (5), son Charles (3), dau. Cetia (1);[363] d. 07/26/1885 *"at his home in Hanover Co., VA;"*[360] wid. Lucy A., WC #2421, 07/07/1887, filed from 841 N. 17th St., Richmond, VA; (LAC b. 03/24/1825 Hanover Co., VA).

**Cargill, Nathaniel E.**, Pvt., Co. E; enl. Mex. War service 11/30/1846 Petersburg, VA, age 25; pres. 04/1847; pres. 06/1847; absent 08/1847 on detached service in Insp. Genl. Dept. since 08/28/1847; absent 10/1847 on detached service Insp. Genl. Dept.; absent 12/1847 on detached service Insp. Genl. Dept.; absent 02/1848 on detached service Insp. Genl. Dept. absent 04/1848 on detached service Insp. Genl. Dept.

**Carlin, Cornelius**, Pvt., Co. K; enl. Mex. War service Frederick Co., VA 12/19/1846, age 19; sick 06/1847; discharged 07/29/1847 at Buena Vista, Mex. on Surgeon's Certificate of Disability.

**Carmichael, Andrew**, Pvt., Co. C; enl. Mex. War service 12/29/1846, Bowling Green, VA, age 29; pres. 06/1847; discharged 07/30/1847, Buena Vista, Mex. on Surgeon's Certificate of Disability.

**Carney, George W.**, Pvt., Co. M, enl. Mex., War service 12/04/1847 Norfolk, VA, age 24; pres. 04/1848, pay stopped for: 1 pr. shoes-$1.22, 2 cotton shirts-$.86, 1 blanket-$2.22; pres. 08/1848, pay stopped for: 1 musket & accoutrements complete-$16.22, $30 fee for desertion; BLW sent to Norfolk, VA

**Carney, Noah**, Pvt., Co. B; enl. 12/05/1846, Alexandria, VA, age 24; pres. 06/1847; pres. 08/1847; pres. 10/1847, pay stopped for: 2 pr. shoes-$2.44, 1 pr. overalls-$2.28, 2 pr. socks-$.73[1/2], 2 cotton shirts-$.86, 1 cap-$.95[1/2], 1 pr. cotton drawers-$.71; pres. 12/1847, pay stopped for: 1 blanket-$2.22; pres. 02/1848, pay stopped for: 1 pr. overalls-$2.28, 1 jacket-$2.66; pres. 04/1848; pres. 08/1848, pay stopped for: 1 wiper-$.20, BLW sent to Occoquan, Prince Wm., Co., VA

**Carpenter, Fayette D.**, Pvt., Co. B; enl. 12/26/1846, Alexandria, VA, age 21; pres. 06/1847; pres. 08/1847; pres. 10/1847, pay stopped for: 2 pr. shoes-$1.22, 2 flannel shirts-$2.70, 1 cotton shirt-$.43, 1 pr. overalls-$2.28, 1 pr. socks-$.24[1/2], 2 pr. cotton drawers-$.71, 1 blanket-$2.22; pres. 12/1847, pay stopped for: 1 cap-$.95[1/2], 1 pr. shoes-$1.22; pres. 02/1848; pres. 04/1848, pay stopped for: 1 jacket-$2.66; pres. 08/1848, pay stopped for: 1 pick & brush-$.12, 1 screw driver-$.07, BLW sent to Upperville, Fauquier Co., VA

**Carr, Hampton**, Pvt., Co. B; enl. 12/06/1846, Alexandria, VA, age 28; sick 06/1847; absent 08/1847, discharged on 07/31/1847 Surgeon's Certificate of Disability.

**Carrington, Edward Codrington, Jr.**, Capt., Co. G; b. 182(4)5, Halifax, VA; son of Gen. Edward C. and Eliza Henry (Preston) Carrington, U.S.A.; attended VMI (non-graduate); enl. Mex. War service 11/18/1846 Richmond, VA, age 21; absent 06/1847 on recruiting service in U.S. since 06/25/1847; absent 08/1847 on recruiting service; absent 10/1847, on detached service recruiting for regt.; absent 12/1847 on recruiting service; absent 02/1848 on recruiting service; absent 04/1848 on recruiting service; discharged 07/20/1848; Capt. Co. K, 1st Va. Regt.; m. 06/1848, Maria Antoinette Swope, of Augusta Co., VA, dau. of Washington Swope;[364] c. 1850 res. Botetourt Co., VA, age 25, occ. Lawyer;[365] Civil War service Capt., Co. A, DC Vols.; District Attorney for the District of Columbia during the Civil War;[366] res. in Washington, DC until his death, occ. lawyer, Carrington & Carrington;[367] d. 06/03/1892, *"Valvular Disease of the Heart,"* aged 67, *"Genl. USA,"* Washington, D.C., bur. Rock Creek Cem., Sec. 4B, Lot 51, Site 5, Washington, D.C.;[281, 368] brother of Major James McDowell Carrington, Charlottesville Artillery, C.S.A. ***Authors 2nd Cousin, 4x removed.***

**Carroll, Franklin**, Pvt., Co. C; b. 03/27/1827, Orange C.H., Orange Co., VA; enl. Mex. War service 12/13/1846, Fredericksburg, VA, age 19; pres. 06/1847; pres. 08/1847, pay stopped for: 1 cap-$.95[1/2], 2 pr. socks-$.49, 2 cotton shirts-$.86, 2 woolen shirts-$1.80, 1 pr. drawers-$.35[1/2], 1 pr. overalls-$2.28; pres. 10/1847, pay stopped for: 4 pr. socks-$.98, 2 pr. drawers-$.71; pres. 12/1847, pay stopped for: 1 pr. pants-$2.28, 1 blanket-$2.22; absent 04/1848, left

## VIRGINIA VOLUNTEERS IN MEXICO

sick in hosp. at Saltillo, Mex., pay stopped for: 1 jacket-$2.66, 1 pr. shoes-$1.22; 1 india rubber canteen-$.27, 1 cotton shirt-$.43; pres. 08/1848, BLW sent to [illegible]; SC #16233, 02/24/1887, filed from Albuquerque, Bernalillo Co., Territory of NM. claims *"lance wound to rt. knee and left wrist,"* since discharge res. Mexico, California and New Mexico, phys. desc. 5'7$^{1/2}$", dark complex., auburn hair, occ. Physician.

**Carroll, William K.**, Pvt., LIC; b. 05/31/1811;[369] m. Melvina Malcom, 11/18/1841, Pendelton Co., VA;[369] enl. Mex. War service 12/07/1846 Staunton, VA, age 19; absent 08/28/1847 on detached service as Orderly to Col. Randolph; pres. 10/1847, pay stopped for: 1 forage cap-$.95$^{1/2}$, 1 wool jacket-$2.66, 1 pr. overalls-$2.28, 1 pr. shoes-$1.22, 3 pr. socks-$.73$^{1/2}$, 2 cotton shirts-$.86; pres. 12/1847, pay stopped for: 1 blanket-$2.22, 1 pr. overalls-$2.28; pres. 04/1848, pay stopped for: 1 pr. shoes-$1.22; pres. 07/1848, pay stopped for: 1 bayonet scabbard-$.56, 1 waist belt-$.21, 1 waist belt plate-$.10, 1 gun sling-$.16; BLW sent to Staunton, VA; d. 1861, McDowell, Highland Co., VA; wid. Malvania, WC #14479, 04/04/1898, filed from Meadow Dale, Highland Co., VA; (MMC b. 03/1814, Monroe Co., VA).

**Carter, Alexander**, Pvt., *Preston's Co.*; enl. Mex. War service 12/06/1846 Montgomery Co., VA, age 18; pres. 04/1847; pres. 06/1847; absent 08/1847 on detached service in QM Dept., to receive $25 in addition to his pay as a soldier; pres. 10/1847, pay stopped for: 1 pr. overalls-$2.28, 3 pr. socks-$.73$^{1/2}$, 1 cotton shirt-$.43; pres. 12/1847, pay stopped for: 1 jacket-$2.66, 1 pr. overalls-$2.28, 1 cap-$.95$^{1/2}$, 1 pr. drawers-$.35$^{1/2}$, 1 blanket-$2.22; pres. 02/1848, pay stopped for: 1 pr. shoes-$1.22; pres. 04/1848, pay stopped for: 1 pick & brush-$.12; pres. 07/1848, pay stopped for: 1 screw driver-$.07, 1 wiper-$.13; BLW sent to Christiansburg, VA

**Carter, James J.**, Pvt., *Recruit Co.*, enl. Mex. War service 05/13/1848 Bowling Green, VA; pres. 06/1848; BLW sent to Bowling Green, Caroline Co., VA

**Carter, John E.**, Pvt., Co. B; b. 03/09/1815 Richmond, Henrico Co., VA;[370] enl. 12/22/1846, Richmond, VA, age 31; pres. 06/1847; sick 08/1847; pres. 10/1847, pay stopped for: 2 pr. shoes-$2.44, 4 pr. socks-$.98, 2 pr. cotton drawers-$.71, 2 cotton shirt-$.86; pres. 12/1847, fined 1 mos. pay by order (162) of genl. Court-martial, pay stopped for: 1 cap-$.95$^{1/2}$, 1 blanket-$2.22, 1 pr. overalls-$2.28, 1 pr. shoes-$1.22; pres. 02/1848, pay stopped for: 1 pr. shoes-$1.22; pres. 04/1848; pres. 08/1848, pay stopped for: 1 pr. shoes-$1.16, 1 musket-$13.00, 1 bayonet scabbard-$.56, 1 waist belt-.21, 1 waist belt plate-$.10, 1 gun sling-$.16, 1 pick & brush-$.12, 1 screw driver-$.07, 1 wiper-$.20, BLW sent to Richmond, VA; m/1 Unknown; m/2 Margaret J. Waddle 09/03/1855, Green Co. TN; SC #339, 02/07/1887, phys. desc. blue eyes, dark hair, occ. Farmer; Moved to Dandridge, Jefferson Co., TN after discharge and lived there 31 yrs. Moved to Leitchfield, KY in 1880;[370] d. 09/10/1888, Leitchfield, Grayson Co., KY; *"Had come to town and started home and only got a short distance when he apparently fell dead;"*[370] wid. Margaret, WC #5926, 11/16/1888, from KY (d. 01/1898).

**Carter, John W.**, 4$^{th}$ Cpl., Co. C; enl. Mex. War service 12/18/1846, Bowling Green, VA, age 24; pres. 06/1847; pres. 08/1847, pay stopped for: 1 cap-$.95$^{1/2}$, 2 pr. socks-$.49, 2 cotton shirts-$.86, 2 woolen shirts-$1.80, 1 pr. drawers-$.35$^{1/2}$, 1 pr. overalls-$2.28; pres. 10/1847, pay stopped for: 1 pr. socks-$.24$^{1/2}$, 1 pr. drawers-$.35$^{1/2}$, 1 jacket-$2.66, 1 pr. pants-$2.28, 1 woolen shirt-$.90, 1 blanket-$2.22; pres. 12/1847, prom. 4$^{th}$ Cpl 12/16/1847, pay stopped for: 2 pr. drawers-$.71, 2 pr. socks-$.49, 1 pr. shoes-$1.22; pres. 04/1848, pay stopped for: [illegible] 1 pr. shoes-$1.50; 1 india rubber canteen-$.27; pres. 08/1848, BLW sent to Stafford C.H., VA; c. 1850 res. Stafford Co., VA, age 30, occ. Quarrier, w. Catherine A. (28).[371]

**Carter, Joseph LaFayette**, Pvt., Co. E; b. 1827, Sussex Co., VA, son of Richard Carter;[45, 372] enl. Mex. War service 12/05/1846 Petersburg, VA, age 20; pres. 04/1847; pres. 06/1847; pres. 08/1847; pres. 10/1847, pay stopped for: 1 pr. overalls-$2.28, 2 pr. shoes-$2.44, 2 pr. stockings-$.49, 2 cotton shirts-$.86, 1 cap-$.95$^{1/2}$; pres. 12/1847, pay stopped for: 1 jacket-

OFF TO WAR

$2.66, [illegible], 2 pr. socks-$.49, 2 flannel shirts-$1.80, 1 blanket-$2.22; pres. 02/1848, pay stopped for: 1 pr. pants-$2.28, 1 pr. shoes-$1.22; pres. 04/1848; c. 1850 res. Dinwiddie Co., VA age 22, occ. Carpenter;[373] c. 1860 res. Petersburg, Dinwiddie Co., VA, age 40, occ. Carpenter, w. Mary (22);[374] Civil War service 2$^{nd}$ Sgt., Co. K, 12$^{th}$ Va. Inf., enl. 05/11/1861 Petersburg, VA, trans. 03/26/1862 to Branch's Field Arty., discharged 07/16/1862, over the age of Conscription Act.;[21, 77] c. 1870 res. Petersburg, Dinwiddie Co., VA, age 44, occ. Trucker, w. Eliza (35), son William J. (8), son Charles E. (7), son Richard A. (4), dau. Emma L. (2);[375] SC #13911, 01/24/1888, from VA; XC #896383; d. 03/14/1912, *Chronic Nephritis*, bur. Blandford Cem., Sq. 2, Sec. 6, Ward B, Petersburg, VA;[376] [pension file in custody of Department of Veterans Affairs].

**Carter, Zachariah**, Pvt., Co. G; enl. Mex. War service 11/18/1846 Richmond, VA, age 28; pres. 06/1847; pres. 08/1847; pres. 10/1847, pay stopped for: 1 pr. overalls-$2.28, 2 cotton shirts-$.86, 1 pr. drawers-$.35$^{1/2}$, 1 shoes-$1.22, 2 pr. socks-$.49, 1 great coat-$6.95$^{1/2}$, 1 forage cap-$.95$^{1/2}$; pres. 12/1847, pay stopped for: 1 cotton shirt-$.43, 2 flannel shirts-$1.80, 1 blanket-$2.22; pres. 02/1848; sick 04/1848; pres. 08/1848, pay stopped for: 1 waist belt-$.21, 1 waist belt plate-$.10, 1 scabbard & frog-$.56; BLW sent to Caroline Co. C.H., VA

**Castleman, Nathaniel Green**, Pvt., *Recruit Co.*, b. 01/18/1830, son of Alfred & Margaret Lucinda (Milton) Castleman;[377] enl. Mex. War service 01/09/1848 Charlestown, VA, age 18; pres. 02/1848; pres. 04/1848; pres. 06/1848; BLW sent to Berryville, Clarke Co., VA; *California 49er*, moved to Calif. 1849.[378]

**Caterson, James**, Pvt., Co. F; enl. Mex. War service 01/22/1847, Portsmouth, VA, age 36; absent 06/1847 left sick Hosp. Monterey, Mex. 06/03/1847; pres. 08/1847; pres. 10/1847, pay stopped for: 2 pr. shoes-$2.44, 2 pr. drawers-.71, 2 pr. socks-$.49, 1 forage cap-$.95$^{1/2}$, 1 pr. overalls-$2.28, 2 cotton shirts-$.86; pres. 12/1847; pres. 02/1848, pay stopped for: 1 blanket-$2.22, 1 pr. socks-$.24$^{1/2}$, 1 infantry jacket-$2.66, 1 pr. shoes-$1.22; pres. 04/1848; pres. 08/1848, pay stopped for: 1 bayonet scabbard & frog-$.56,1 waist belt & plate-$.31, 1 brush & pick-$.12, 1 screw driver-$.25, 1 blanket-$2.25, BLW sent to Portsmouth, VA c/o E.T. Blamire.

**Cassaday, John N.**, Pvt., *Preston's Co.*; enl. Mex. War service 12/06/1846 Montgomery Co., VA, age 35; absent 04/1847,*"left in Richmond, and has not since joined his company...;"* absent 06/1847 left in Richmond, VA; AWOL 08/1847, *"(Note: The circumstances attending this man's absence is that as to* [illegible] *his company* [illegible] *he has no intention of deserting. If, however, he shall not have joined his company before next muster he will be reported as a deserter.)"*; deserted 10/1847, *"This man was left in Richmond, VA when the company left that place his commander did not suppose he intended to desert, but as he has failed to join his company he is now reported as a deserter."*

**Cawood, Charles H.**, 3$^{rd}$ Cpl., Co. B; enl. 12/12/1846, Alexandria, VA, age 22; pres. 06/1847; sick 08/1847; pres. 10/1847, pay stopped for: 1 pr. overalls-$2.28, 1 pr. socks-$.24$^{1/2}$, 1 pr. shoes-$1.22, 2 flannel shirts-$2.70, 2 pr. cotton drawers-$.71, 4 cotton shirt-$1.72, 1 overcoat-$ 6.99, 1 jacket-$2.66, 1 cap-$.95$^{1/2}$, 1 blanket-$2.22; pres. 12/1847, pay stopped for: 2 flannel shirts-$1.80, 1 pr. overalls-$2.28, 1 cap-$.95$^{1/2}$, 1 pr. socks-$.24$^{1/2}$; pres. 02/1848, pay stopped for: 1 pr. shoes-$1.22; pres. 04/1848, prom. 3$^{rd}$ Cpl. 04/18/1848; pres. 08/1848, BLW sent to Piscataway, Prince George's Co., MD

**Chaille, John**, Pvt., Co. A; enl. Mex. War service 12/30/1846 Richmond, VA, age 30; pres. 12/1846 - 04/1847; pres. 06/1847; pres. 08/1847; in confinement 10/1847, pay stopped for clothing: 1 pr. wool overalls-$2.28, 1 cap-$.95$^{1/2}$, 1 pr. shoes-$1.22, 2 cotton shirts-$.86; Court-martialed 11/08/1847, Buena Vista, Mex. *Charge #1 Conduct to the Prejudice of Good Order and Military Discipline; Specification 1$^{st}$: In this that the Private John Chaille, on or about the 26$^{th}$ of October 1847, at Buena Vista, Mexico, did feloniously take and fraudulently appropriate to his own use one purse containing twenty five dollars more or less in gold and silver, the property of A.A. Montero, a private of Co. A, Virginia Regt.; Specification 2$^{nd}$ In*

## VIRGINIA VOLUNTEERS IN MEXICO

*this that he the said Private John Chaille, Co A, Virginia Regt. Volunteers, between the first and the twenty-seventh of October 1847 at Buena Vista, Mexico, did keep for sale and did reputedly sell, between those dates, liquor to the soldiers of his company and regiment; To which charge and specifications the prisoner pleaded Not Guilty to the Charge and 1$^{st}$ Specification and Guilty to the 2$^{nd}$ Specification; Pvt. A.A. Montero, Co. A, Virginia Regt. of Volunteers, a witness for the prosecution being duly sworn says: On the night of the 27$^{th}$ or 26$^{th}$ of October 1847, I sat down to play a game of cards in the prisoners tent with a purse containing twenty-eight dollars. At Taps I left off playing as I commenced without loaning anything and loaned the prisoner five dollars after which I returned to my tent and did not miss my purse until Reveille. On missing my purse I went over to the prisoners tent and enquired if he had seen anything of it. He gave me no satisfaction and I repaired to the tent of one of the which had been engaged in playing at the game of cards and on returning from his tent I saw the prisoner throwing out into the sink of the company with his hands I took no further notice of this at the time, later one of the men of the company told me that he had seen a purse at the sink which answered the description I had given of mine. I then went to the sink and brought the purse which was the one I had lost on the preceding evening. The man, Pvt. Curry, who was the man who had first seen it there told me he had dug it out from the sink. I went with the purse to the prisoner and openly before the company accused him of stealing my money. He did not remark at the time but exhibited what I considered evidence of guilt. Some hours afterwards when excited by liquor he made a cowardly attack on me. Question by the Judge Advocate: Was the prisoner sitting anywhere near you on the evening referred to or was he sitting opposite to you? Answer: He was sitting directly opposite me and in front of the door of the tent. He could not have taken my purse while I was sitting down, the time I suspect him of taking it was when I left the tent as I had to pass close by him and he got up to untie the door of the tent. He might then very easily have extracted it from my pocket. Question by the prisoner: Did you not say in the morning when you first came to my tent that you suspected Robinson Wren of taking your purse? Answer: I did say so at first but <u>his</u> conduct afterwards at the sink caused me to lose sight of anyone else and to suspect the prisoner. Question by the prisoner: Did you not remark to me at that time that Robinson Wren sat next to you and his pressing very hard against you and then suddenly starting up and leaving the tent? Answer I did make this remark to him in the morning when I first saw the prisoner and before I saw him at the sink and my purse being found their. This as I have stated caused me to suspect the prisoner. Question by the prisoner: Did you not state to the company that your purse contained one ten-dollar gold piece and ten or twelve dollars in silver and then afterwards state to Sergt. Jamison that it contained two ten dollars gold pieces and some silver? Answer: I do not recollect positively what I told Sergt. Jamison my purse contained. I can swear that I had in my purse when I lost it one ten-dollar gold piece and thirteen dollars in silver besides the five dollars I loaned the prisoner that night. Question by the Court: What time did you loan the prisoner the five dollars? Answer: Just before I got up to leave the tent. Question by the Court: Did you lend him this money out of your purse? Answer: No. It was in the stake I had on the table. Question by the Court: When you found your purse in the morning was it the same spot you saw the prisoner throwing dirt? Answer: It was as near the spot as I could identify from the distance I saw him in the act of throwing the dirt. Question by the Court: Do you know whether you had the purse after you left the tent? Answer: No. I do not. I went immediately to my tent and went to sleep. Question by the Court: Was there any money in the purse when you found it? Answer: No. Private S.C. Curry, Co. K, Va. Regt., a witness for the prosecution, being duly sworn says: I found a purse at the sink of the Company 'A' one morning two or three weeks ago which purse Pvt. Montero claimed as his after I had found it. I saw the prisoner at the sink on that morning before I found the purse. One end of it was sticking out tho' I can't say that there had been any dirt <u>thrown</u> upon it. Pvt. J.H. Scott, Co. K, Va. Regt. of Volunteers, a witness for the prosecution, being duly sworn says: I went into my*

## OFF TO WAR

*tent where the prisoner and several other men were playing at cards about 2 o'clock in the morning of that day. I saw money about the amount of fifteen or twenty dollars. I heard the prisoner Chaille remark when I first went into the tent that he only had fifty (.50) cents. He played and lost this. After that I saw him with this money. The prisoner has been in the habit of carrying his money in a bag I don't think he got this money out of the bag. Question by the Judge Advocate: Did you see the prisoner at anytime after you came in the tent on that evening with a purse of money and after he said he had but fifty cents? Answer: I saw him have a purse of money after he said he had but fifty cents. Question by the Judge Advocate: Where did the prisoner produce the purse from? Answer: The pulled it out from about his person. Question by the Judge Advocate: Was this after the playing at cards had ceased? Answer: Yes! There were two others in the tent but the company he had been playing with had dispersed. Question by the Judge Advocate: Do you know if this purse belonged to the prisoner, or do you know if it was the one found in or near the sink the next morning? Answer: I never saw the prisoner with a purse before. He is in the habit of carrying his money in a small bag, but I cannot say that it was the same purse that was found at the sink the next morning. Question by the Judge Advocate: Did you see the purse that was found at the sink? Answer: Yes! I did see it after it had been found. Question by the Judge Advocate: Did you examine the purse, the evening before that the prisoner showed you? Answer: No! I did not examine it particularly. Question by the Prisoner: Was there any person in the tent except yourself when I showed you the purse as you have stated? Answer: There was not. I meant that two others belonged in the tent but they were not in it at this time. Question by the Prisoner: When you came to the tent on that evening were you not pretty well intoxicated? Answer: I had been drinking in the far part of the evening but was not under the influence of liquor when I went into the tent. Question by the Prisoner: Did you or not state to me the day after the affair that you did not think I had the money? Answer: He asked me the opinion of the company generally. I told him it was not of the opinion of many in the company that he had the money. He asked me my opinion I replied I did not think he had, but if I was called upon I should tell the truth. Question by the Court: You have stated you saw the purse that was brought from the sink, did that purse correspond with the one the prisoner showed you on the night before? Answer: I was about the same length and corresponded as nearly as I could judge with the one the prisoner had shown me the night before. 1$^{st}$ Lt. T.P. August, Va. Regt., a witness for the defense, being duly sworn, says in answer to the following: Question by the Prisoner: What has been my character for honesty since you have known me? Answer: I never heard or knew anything against the character of the prisoner until charges were alleged against him by a man in the company which I am in command of. I knew him slightly in Richmond before he joined the company. Private John Poe, Co. A, Va. Regt. Vols., a witness for the defense, being duly sworn, says in answer to the following: Question by the Prisoner: What has been my character for honesty since you have known me? Answer: The prisoner he always maintained the character of an honest man since I have known him, which has been only since we have been in the company together. Pvt. Milo Buchannan, Co. A, Va. Regt. Vols., a witness for the defense, being duly sworn, says in response to the following: Question by the Prisoner: Did I not borrow from Private Jewit some money on the night of the 26$^{th}$ of October 1847 after you had gone to bed? Answer: As to the date I am not positive, but he did come to my tent between tatto[sic] and taps on the night previous to the purse being found and borrowed some money from Private Jewit. Question by the Prisoner: What amount of money did Pvt. Montero state to you that he had lost? Answer: Twenty-two dollars and a half. Question by the Judge Advocate: What was the amount of money the prisoner borrowed at the time referred to? Answer: Ten dollars. He had borrowed two dollars and a half before from another messmate. Question by the Court: Was the money loaned in gold or silver? Answer: It was in silver. Question by the Judge Advocate: What character has the prisoner in the company for himself previous to this? Answer: It has been good as far as I know. After*

# VIRGINIA VOLUNTEERS IN MEXICO

*deliberation the court found the prisoner: Guilty of the Charge and Specification #2 and Not Guilty of Specification #1. He was sentenced to forfeit two (2) months pay and to be kept at hard labor in charge of the Provost Guard for the period of one month;*[379] in confinement 12/1847, pay stopped for clothing: 1 pr. drawers-$.35$^{1/2}$; pres. 02/1848, pay stopped for: 1 pr. shoes-$1.22, fined $14.00 by order (#27) of genl. court-martial; pres. 04/1848; 07/1848, pay stopped for: 1 pick & brush-$.12, 1 screw driver-$.25, 1 wiper-$.20; BLW sent to Richmond, VA

**Chambers, George W.**, 2$^{nd}$ Lt., Co. H; b. 01/21/1828, Frederick Co., MD;[380] [tombstone says 01/06/1829];[381] enl. Mex. War service 12/20/1846, Berkeley, VA; phys. desc. 5'11", light complexion, gray eyes, auburn hair, occ. Printer;[382] pres. 04/1847; pres. 06/1847; pres. 08/1847; Court-martialed 09/20/1847 Buena Vista, Mex. *Charge #1: Disobedience of Orders; Specification: In this that the said Lt. George W. Chambers, did, after having been frequently notified to do so in accordance with orders of the Commander of the Regiment, Col. Hamtramck, fail to attend reveille roll call. This at Buena Vista, Mexico, on or about the 2$^{nd}$ day of September 1847. Charge #2: Using Insulting and Disrespectful Language to his Commanding Officer; Specification: In this that the said Lt. Geo. W. Chambers, did, at Buena Vista, Mex., on the morning of the 2$^{nd}$ of September 1847, when remonstrated with by his Captain for his frequent failures to attend reveille roll call, and when informed that if he neglected again he would be reported, replied 'You may report and be damned, I am as independent as you are' or words to that effect. To which the accused plead Guilty to the first charge and specification and Not Guilty to the second charge and specification. Captain E.G. Alburtis, of the Va. Regt. Vols., a witness for the prosecution being duly sworn, says: I attended reveille roll call on the morning of the 2$^{nd}$ Sept. 1847 and found Lt. Chambers absent. I went t6o his tent and found him in bed. I awoke him and afterwards conversed with him in relation to his frequent neglect of duty. I spoke to him kindly upon the subject and stated to him that if the neglect occurred again I should be compelled to report him. He replied that I might report and be damned that he was as independent as I. Question by the Judge Advocate: Had the prisoner been ordered previous to the 2$^{nd}$ of September to attend reveille roll call at all times. Answer: He had. Lt. Robert Pollock, Va. Regt. Vols., a witness for the prosecution being duly sworn, says: I know that Lt. Chambers did not attend reveille roll call on the morning of the 2$^{nd}$ September 1847. There is a Regimental order for all officers to attend reveille roll call at all times. After deliberation the court found the accused Guilty of all charges and specifications and sentenced him to be publically reprimanded in orders by the Commanding Officer of the Regiment and to be suspended from rank and pay for one calendar month;*[383] absent 10/1847, suspended without pay or rank for 1 mo. by order of genl. court-martial 10/25/1847; pres. 12/1847; discharged 02/29/1848 by order of Genl. Wool; Editor of the *Valley Democrat*, New Market, VA beginning 12/08/1849;[384] c. 1850 res. Shennandoah Co., VA, age 22, occ. Editor;[385] m. Frances A. Cutshaw, 11/11/1857, Baltimore, MD;[380] c. 1860 Mayor, Harper's Ferry, VA; c. 1860 res. Harper's Ferry, Jefferson Co., VA, age 32, occ. Merchant, w. Fannie (24), dau. Metta (1);[386] Civil War service Capt. Co. K, 2$^{nd}$ Va. Inf., enl. Harper's Ferry 05/03/1861, resigned 04/14/1862;[387] c. 1880 res. Bolivar, Jefferson Co., WV, age 52, occ. Printer, w. Frances A. (45), son Wilford C. (16), dau. Minnie (20);[388] SC #12914, 05/06/1887, filed from Harper's Ferry, Jefferson Co., WV; since discharge res. in Harper's Ferry, VA 1848-1850, New Market, VA, 1580-1852, Harper's Ferry since then; d. 02/03/1908, *"cerebral embolism,"* Bolivar, Jefferson Co., WV, bur. Harper's Cem., Harper's Ferry, WV;[381, 382] wid. Frances A., WC #14927, 02/18/1907, filed from cor. Bloomingdale Rd. and Baker St., Baltimore, MD; Lists children Meta Hunt Chambers, b. 04/28/1859, Minnie H. Chambers, b. 11/18/1860, Caroline M. Chambers, b. 01/12/1867, Benjamin L. Chambers, b. 02/12/1868;[382] (FCC b. 02/20/1835, d. 02/16/1923).[382]

**Chandler, Greenbery**, Pvt., *Preston's Co.*; b. Franklin Co., VA c. 1829, son of Moses & Elizabeth (Hodges) Chandler; enl. Mex. War service 12/06/1846 Montgomery Co., VA, age

OFF TO WAR

18; pres. 04/1847; pres. 06/1847; sick 08/1847; pres. 10/1847, pay stopped for: 1 jacket-$2.66, 1 pr. overalls-$2.28, 2 pr. socks-$.49, 3 cotton shirts-$1.29, 1 pr. drawers-$.35$^{1/2}$; pres. 12/1847, pay stopped for: 1 pr. overalls-$2.28; pres. 02/1848, pay stopped for: 1 pr. shoes-$1.22; pres. 04/1848; pres. 07/1848; BLW sent to Christiansburg, VA c/o Fleming Gardner; m. Elizabeth Fisher 07/04/1855; res. Giles Co. c. 1860, occ. Carpenter, res. w/ John Argabright (also of 1$^{st}$ Va. Vols.);[389] Civil War service enl. Sgt., Co. H, 36$^{th}$ Va. Inf. 04/18/1862 at Giles C.H., pres. until 02/1863 when detached in Dublin, VA, prom. to Lt. 04/09/1863, wded. 06/05/1864 at Piedmont, VA, d. 06/06/1864 at Staunton Hosp., bur. Thornrose Cemetery, Staunton, VA[390]

**Charlton, Walter D.**, Pvt., *Recruit Co.*, enl. Mex., War service 01/03/1848 Christiansburg, VA, age 18; pres. 02/1848; pres. 04/1848; pres. 06/1848; BLW sent to Christiansburg, VA

**Chase Abel Dustin**, 2$^{nd}$ Cpl., LIC; b. 10/18/1826, Baltimore, MD;[391] enl. Mex. War service 11/27/1846 Staunton, VA, age 20; pres. 08/1847; pres. 10/1847, pay stopped for: 1 forage cap-$.95$^{1/2}$, 1 wool jacket-$2.66, 2 pr. overalls-$4.56, 2 pr. shoes-$2.44, 3 cotton shirts-$1.29, 3 pr. socks-$.73$^{1/2}$, 1 pr. drawers-$.35$^{1/2}$; pres. 12/1847, pay stopped for: 1 pr. shoes-$1.22; pres. 04/1848, prom. 2$^{nd}$ Cpl. 12/07/1847; pres. 07/1848; BLW sent to Staunton, VA; m. Nancy McCoy, *"a citizen of the Chickasaw Nation,"* 04/24/1860, Virginia Hill, near Old Fort Washita,[9] Indian Territory;[391] SC #9073, 02/04/1887, filed from Healdton, Pickens Co., Chickasaw Nation, Indian Territory; phys. desc. 5'9", dark complexion, black eyes, black hair;[391] since discharge res. Staunton, VA to 1859 when he moved to Indian Territory;[391] d. 05/15/1909, Ardmore, Carter Co., OK, bur. Rose Hill Cemetery, Ardmore, OK;[392] wid. Nancy, WC #15304, 07/17/1909, filed from Ardmore, Carter Co., OK; Lists children: Grove E. Chase b. 02/01/1861, Chagris, Indian Territory, Emma Chase Bates b. Robbers Roost, Indian Territory, Ruth Chase Newton b. Cornish, Indian Territory, Callie Chase Blake b. Marietta, Indian Territory;[392] (NMA b. 02/05/1842, Doaksville, Choctaw Nation, Indian Territory, d. 6/08/1919).[392]

**Chase, Robert**, Pvt., Co. C; enl. Mex. War service 12/29/1846, Bowling Green, VA, age 21; phys. desc. 5'10$^{1/2}$", light complex., blue eyes, light hair, occ. Butcher; sick 06/1847; pres. 08/1847, pay stopped for: 1 cap-$.95$^{1/2}$, 2 pr. socks-$.49, 2 cotton shirts-$.86, 2 woolen shirts-$1.80, 1 pr. drawers-$.35$^{1/2}$; pres. 10/1847, pay stopped for: 2 pr. socks-$.49, 1 jacket-$2.66, 1 pr. pants-$2.28, 3 cotton shirts-$1.29, 2 woolen shirts-$.90, 2 pr. shoes-$2.44, 1 blanket-$2.22, 1 brush & picker-$.12; pres. 12/1847, pay stopped for: 1 cotton shirt-$.43, 1 pr. shoes-$1.22, 1 blanket-$2.22; pres. 04/1848, pay stopped for: 1 pr. shoes-$1.22; 1 haversack-$.20$^{3/4}$, 1 india rubber canteen-$.27, 1 pr. shoes-$1.50; pres. 08/1848, BLW sent to Philadelphia, Pa.; m. Mary Stratton 03/04/1849 Emory M.E. Church, 18$^{th}$ St., Philadelphia, Pa.; Civil War service 2$^{nd}$ Sgt. Co. H, 31$^{st}$ Pa. Inf. enl. 08/21/1861 Philadelphia, Pa., occ. Shoemaker, wded. left shoulder *"ball having passed near the head of the humerus and downwards"* 05/31/1862 at the Battle of Fair Oaks; discharged 09/19/1862; rcvd. Invalid Pension #10273 for wd. sustained; c. 1880 res. Bristol, Bucks Co., Pa., age 53, occ. Shoemaker, w. Mary (47), son Winsfield (19), dau. Frances A. (24), son Reuben (14), son William (9), grand. dau. Everline (6);[393] SC #10391, 06/21/1887, filed from Bristol, Bucks Co., Pa., stated since discharge he had lived in Philadelphia, Pa. 14 yrs. and Bristol, Pa. 25 yrs.; d. 04/08/1888, *"consumption,"* Bristol, Bucks Co., Pa., *"funeral paid by Post;"* wid. Mary, WC #4919, 05/05/1888, both from PA; (MSC b. 08/13/1831, Gloucester, NJ, d. c. 1901).

**Cheatzom, Joseph D.**, Pvt., Co. D; enl. Mex. War service 12/21/1846, Petersburg, VA, age 18; pres. 02/1847; absent 04/1847 left sick in Hosp. Port Isabel, Tex. 03/18/1847; absent 06/1847

---

[9] **Fort Washita** was constructed by the U.S. Army in 1841 to safeguard the Choctaw and Chickasaw Indians from marauding Plains Indians. Located near Durant and Madrill, Oklahoma the fort remained in operation until about 1870. The fort is now owned by the Oklahoma Historical Society and is in the process of being restored.

## VIRGINIA VOLUNTEERS IN MEXICO

reported as having returned home on 60 day furlough, from May 10$^{th}$ - July 10$^{th}$ by authority & order unknown; deserted 07/10/1847 while on furlough at Pittsburgh, Pa.

**Cherry, David**, Pvt., Co. F; enl. Mex. War service 01/18/1847, Portsmouth, VA, age 22; pres. 06/1847; absent 08/1847 sick; discharged 09/11/1847 Buena Vista, Mex. on Surgeon's Certificate of Disability; m. Chloe Lewis 10/1849, Norfolk Co., VA;[394] Civil War service enl. 02/28/1862 at Deep Creek, Norfolk Co., VA as Pvt., Co. H, 61$^{st}$ Va. Inf., age 44, deserted 05/10/1862? at Portsmouth, VA, d. 11/10/1868 Deep Creek, Norfolk Co., VA;[394] listed on Confederate Roll of Honor;[395] wid. Chloe, WC #3785, 05/14/1887, filed from 5 Mariner Street, Norfolk, Norfolk Co., VA (CC b. 06/02/1829 Camden, NC).[394]

**Cherry, William**, Pvt., Co. F; enl. Mex. War service 12/28/1846, Portsmouth, VA, age 21; pres. 06/1847; pres. 08/1847; pres. 10/1847, pay stopped for: 1 pr. overalls-$2.28, 1 forage cap-$.95$^{1/2}$, 4 cotton shirts-$1.72, 4 pr. socks-$.98, 2 pr. shoes-$2.44, , 2 pr. drawers-.71; pres. 12/1847; pres. 02/1848, pay stopped for: 1 pr. overalls-$2.28, 1 blanket-$2.22, 1 infantry jacket-$2.66, 1 pr. shoes-$1.22, 1 brush & pick-$.12; pres. 04/1848; pres. 08/1848, pay stopped for: 2 cotton shirts-$.88, BLW sent to Portsmouth, VA c/o E.T. Blamire; wid. Caroline F., WC #2829, 05/01/1887, from VA

**Chichester, Thompson M.**, Pvt., Co. B; enl. 12/01/1846, Alexandria, VA, age 30; sick 06/1847; sick 08/1847; pres. 10/1847, pay stopped for: 2 pr. socks-$.49, 1 pr. shoes-$1.22, 2 pr. cotton drawers-$.35$^{1/2}$; pres. 12/1847, pay stopped for: 1 pr. socks-$.24$^{1/2}$, 1 pr. shoes-$1.22; pres. 02/1848, pay stopped for: 1 cap-$.95$^{1/2}$; pres. 04/1848, 1 pr. shoes-$1.22; pres. 08/1848, pay stopped for: 1 bayonet scabbard-$.56, 1 cartridge box-$1.10, 1 cartridge box belt-$.60, 1 cartridge box plate-$.10, 1 waist belt-$.21, 1 waist belt plate-$.10, 1 pick & brush-$.12, 1 screw driver-$.07, 1 wiper-$.10, BLW sent to Alexandria, VA; SC #575, 02/21/1887, filed from National Soldiers Home, Dayton, OH. States he was born on a farm in Fairfax Co., VA and that he is 70 yrs. of age, 5'7", fair complexed, blue eyes, black hair. He worked as a laborer in Woods and Plesant Cos., WV and was admitted to the National Soldiers Home 05/07/1881; d. 07/12/1889, *"res. of Wood Co., WV,"* bur. Lot H 6 6, Dayton National Cemetery, Dayton, OH.

**Chick, George Washington**, Pvt., Co. M; b. 08/28/1827, Campbell Co., VA;[396] enl. Mex. War service 08/01/1847 Lynchburg, VA, age 19; pres. 09/1847; pres. 11/1847; pres. 12/1847; pres. 02/1848; pres. 04/1848, pay stopped for: 1 blanket-$2.22; pres. 08/1848; BLW sent to Lynchburg, VA; Sgt., Capt. Tracy's Co., 2$^{nd}$ Btln. Calif. Inf. enl. 05/12/1851 discharged 06/13/1851, California Indian Wars; m. Mary Swope, 10/09/1872, Monterey Co., CA;[396] SC #18979, 12/24/1887, filed from *"10 miles east of"* Hollister, San Benito Co., CA; states that *"from Ft. Monroe, VA went in a sailing vessel, John G. Colly with his company and 50 more recruits;"*[396] phys. desc. age 62 [1889], 5'8", light complexion, gray eyes, light hair, occ. Brick Mason;[396] lists children William Chick b. 1881; Lottie M. Chick b. 1886, Frances E. Chick b. 1891, Veda L. Chick b. 06/26/1894;[396] d. 07/19/1899, Paicines, San Benito Co., CA;[397] wid. Mary, WA #15308, 09/30/1899, filed from Hollister, San Benito Co., CA;[397] (MSC b. 05/18/1855, Scotland Co., MO.)[397]

**Choate, Jesse C.**, Pvt., Co. E; enl. Mex. War service 11/26/1846 Petersburg, VA, age 21; d. 04/05/1847, Matamoros, Mexico Hospital of diarrhea.[398]

**Churchill, James**, Pvt., Co. L; b. 1818; enl. Mex. War service 03/01/1847 Fairfax C.H., age 29; sick 06/1847; sick 08/1847; Court-martialed 10/20/1847 *Charge#1: Sleeping On Post; Specification: In this that he, the said Private James Churchill, 13$^{th}$ Co., Va. Regt., being regularly posted, or stationed on Post No. 9 at 1 o'clock A.M. did lay down and sleep on or near his post. This at Saltillo, Mex. on or about the 15$^{th}$ of Oct. 1847. To which charge and specification the prisoner pled Guilty. The prisoner made the following remarks to the Court in his defense. I was not detailed for guard till 7 o'clock in the evening and went on post immediately. I went on picket after being relieved, between 9 & 12 o'clock and had been drinking during the day. After deliberation the Court found the prisoner Guilty of the charge*

OFF TO WAR

*and specification and sentenced him to forfeit one months pay and to perform company police duty for one month in addition to his usual duties;*[399] pres. 10/1847, to forfeit $ 7 by sentence of genl. court-martial, pay stopped for: 1 W. Jacket 2.66, 1 pr. Pants 2.28, 1 F Cap .95, 1 pr. Shoes 1.22, 1 F shirt .90; Court-martialed 11/20/1847 Buena Vista, Mex. *Charge #1: Desertion; Specification 1$^{st}$: In this that he, Private James Churchill of the 13$^{th}$ Co., Va. Regt. of Vols. Did desert the service of the United States at Saltillo, Mexico on or about the 12$^{th}$ November 1847. Specification 2$^{nd}$: In this that he, Pvt. James Churchill, of the 13$^{th}$ Co., Va. Regt. of Vols., did desert from Saltillo, Mexico, his company station, on the 12$^{th}$ of Nov. 1847 and proceed to Monterey and remain there until he was arrested on the 14$^{th}$ of Nov. intending thereby to escape from the service of the United States. To which charges and specifications the prisoner pleaded: Guilty. Sentenced: To forfeit three months pay and to be kept at hard labor with a ball and chain attached to his leg, in the Provost Guard for the period of three months;*[400] in confinement 12/1847, to forfeit 3 mos. pay by sentence of general court-martial, pay stopped for: 1 pr. pants-$2.28, 1 cotton shirt-$.43; in confinement 02/1848, to forfeit 3 mos. pay by sentence general court-martial, pay stopped for: 1 pr. pants-$2.28, 1 cotton shirt-$.43, 1 blanket-$ 2.22, 1 flannel shirt-$.90, 1 overcoat-$6.93; pres. 04/1848; pres. 07/1848, pay stopped for: 1 pr. Shoes 1.16; BLW sent to Greenport, Long Island.

**Clanton, Williamson S.**, Pvt., Co. D; b. 12/18/1825, Sussex Co., VA, son of Williamson & Sally Clanton;[401] enl. Mex. War service 12/21/1846, Petersburg, VA, age 21; pres. 02/1847; pres. 04/1847; pres. 06/1847, pay stopped for: 1 bayonet *"lost through negligence;"* pres. 08/1847, pay stopped for: 1 cap-$.95$^{1/2}$, 2 cotton shirts-$.86, 2 pr. shoes-$2.44; pres. 10/1847, pay stopped for: 1 jacket-$2.66, 1 pr. pants-$2.28, 1 pr. drawers-$.35$^{1/2}$, 2 pr. socks-$.49, 1 pr. shoes-$1.22; pres. 12/1847, pay stopped for: 1 pr drawers-$.35$^{1/2}$, 1 pr. socks-$.24$^{1/2}$, 1 blanket-$2.22; pres. 04/1848, pay stopped for: 1 set of picks & brushes-$.12, 1 cotton shirt-$.43, 1 cartridge box belt & plate-$.10; pres. 08/1847, BLW sent to Henry P.O., Sussex Co., VA; c. 1850 res. Sussex Co., VA, age 24, occ. None Listed;[402] c. 1860 res. Sussex Co., VA, age 34, occ. None Listed;[403] Civil War service Pvt., Co. A, 41$^{st}$ Va. Inf.; enl. 05/24/1861 at Sussex C.H., occ. Clerk; desc. 5'8", dark eyes, dark hair, reenlisted 3/62, recvd. $50 bounty; medical discharge 05/02/1862;[404] SC #13372, 02/17/1887, filed from Henry, Sussex Co., VA, since discharge res. Sussex Co., *"except in Petersburg 1853- 1856;"* phys. desc. , age 21, occ. farmer, b. Sussex Co., 5'8", black hair, hazel eyes, dark complexion; d. c. 1900.[401]

**Clark, John A.**, Pvt., Co. I; enl. Mex. War service 02/25/1847 Richmond, VA, age 42; pres. 02/1847; pres. 04/1847; discharged 05/15/1847 for disability at camp near Monterey, Mex.

**Clark, John**, Pvt., Co. M; enl. Mex. War service 11/10/1847 Fort Monroe, VA, age 26; pres. 11/1847; pres. 12/1847; pres. 02/1848, pay stopped for: 1 blanket-$2.22; pres. 04/1848, pay stopped for: 1 pr. shoes-$1.22, 1 cap-$.95$^{1/2}$; pres. 08/1848, pay stopped for: 1 pick & brush-$.12, 1 wormer-$.20, 1 pr. shoes-$1.22; BLW sent to Norfolk, VA

**Clark, Robert**, Pvt., Co. I; enl. Mex. War service 11/20/1846 Richmond, VA, age 25; pres. 02/1847; absent 04/1847, left sick at Matamoros, Mex. 04/01/1847; pres. 06/1847 sick; absent 08/1847 sick; discharged 10/17/1847 on Surgeon's Certificate of Disability, pay stopped for: 2 flannel shirts-$1.80, 2 pr. drawers-$.71.

**Clarke, William T.**, Pvt., Co. C; enl. 08/09/1847 Lunenburg Co., VA, age 22; pres. 04/1848, joined the company 01/27/1848, pay stopped for: 1 jacket-$2.66; pres. 08/1848, BLW sent to Pleasant Grove, Lunenburg Co., VA

**Clarke, James L.**, Pvt., Co. I; enl. Mex. War service 02/05/1847 Richmond, VA, age 27; pres. 02/1847; pres. 04/1847, reduced to ranks from 3$^{rd}$ Sgt. 04/10/1847; pres. 06/1847 sick; pres. 08/1847 sick; discharged 10/17/1847 on Surgeon's Certificate of Disability, pay stopped for: 2 flannel shirts-$1.80, 1 cap-$.95$^{1/2}$; d. 11/1_/1872, age 52; bur. Hollywood Cem., Sect. S.G. R.[119]

**Clarke, Lewis H.**, 2$^{nd}$ Cpl., LIC; b. 11/01/1824, Waynesboro, Augusta Co., VA;[405] enl. Mex. War service 12/19/1846 Staunton, VA, age 22; absent 06/1847 sick; discharged by 08/1847 at

# VIRGINIA VOLUNTEERS IN MEXICO

Monterey, Mex. on Surgeon's Certificate of Disability; m/1 Belinda Barrott, 12/16/1849, Urbana, OH;[405] c. 1850 res. Urbana, Champaign Co. OH, age 25, occ. Farmer, w. Belinda (21);[406] (BBC d. 10/30/1854);[405] m/2 Julia V. Taylor, 10/16/1856, Urbanna, OH;[405] SC #20324, 05/09/1895, filed from Delaware, Delaware Co., OH; disabled while unloading ammunition boxes from wagon injuring his back;[405] since discharge res. in Virginia until 1848, Champaign Co., OH 1848-1865, McLean Co., IL 1865-1872, Champaign Co., OH 1872-1878, Delaware Co., OH since then, occ. Tanner;[405] d. 07/02/1897, *"paralysis,"* 229 Union St. Delaware, Delaware Co., OH;[407] wid. Julia V., WC #10936, 09/09/1897, filed from 229 Union St., Delaware, Delaware Co., OH; (JTC b. 01/06/1834, Urbana, OH, d. 05/08/1916).[407]

**Clayton, Jasper S.**, Pvt., Co. C; b. New Market, Caroline Co., VA c. 1825; enl. Mex. War service 12/18/1846, Bowling Green, VA, age 20; pres. 06/1847; pres. 08/1847, pay stopped for: 1 cap-$.95$^{1/2}$, 2 pr. socks-$.49, 2 cotton shirts-$.86, 2 woolen shirts-$1.80; pres. 10/1847, pay stopped for: 1 pr. socks-$.24$^{1/2}$, 1 pr. drawers-$.35$^{1/2}$, 1 jacket-$2.66, 1 pr. pants-$2.28, 1 woolen shirt-$.90, 1 blanket-$2.22; pres. 12/1847, pay stopped for: 1 pr. pants-$2.28, 1 pr. shoes-$1.22; pres. 04/1848, pay stopped for: 1 haversack-$.20$^{3/4}$, 1 india rubber canteen-$.27, 1 pr. shoes-$2.25; pres. 08/1848, BLW sent to Bowling Green, Caroline County, VA; c. 1850 res. Hanover Co., VA, age 23, occ. Farmer;[408] c. 1870 res. Chester, Chesterfield Co., VA, age 44, occ. Farmer, w. Ann (40), George B. (37), Maria (30);[409] c. 1880 res. Manchester, Chesterfield Co., VA, age 52, w. Annie F. (50), niece Ada M. McCrarey (13), niece Rowena Clayton (10), son Thomas H. Clements (25);[410] SC #6032, 02/24/1887, phys. desc. 5'5", dark complex., brown eyes, dark hair, occ. Farmer; stated house burned 01/11/1893; m/2 Clevie Knight 04/16/1899, Richmond, VA; d. 01/22/1904, Chesterfield Co., VA; wid. Clevie K., WA #17519, 03/12/1904, filed from 1914 Bainbridge St., Manchester, VA; states she has a child *"not yet fours old;"* claim abandoned;(CKC b. 06/17/1878, Chesterfield Co., VA).

**Clemments, Francis D.**, Pvt., Co. D; enl. Mex. War service 12/28/1846, Petersburg, VA, age 23; pres. 02/1847; pres. 04/1847; pres. 06/1847; pres. 08/1847, pay stopped for: 1 cap-$.95$^{1/2}$, 1 pr. pants-$2.28, 2 cotton shirts-$.86, 1 pr. shoes-$1.22; pres. 10/1847, pay stopped for: 1 jacket-$2.66, 2 cotton shirts-$.86, 1 pr. drawers-$.35$^{1/2}$, 2 pr. socks-$.49, 1 blanket-$2.22; pres. 12/1847, pay stopped for: 1 pr. pants-$2.28, 1 overcoat-$6.93$^{1/2}$; pres. 04/1848, pay stopped for: 1 haversack-$.20$^{3/4}$; pres. 08/1847, BLW sent to Hicks Ford, Greensville Co., VA

**Clemments, James C.**, Pvt., Co. L; b. 01/28/1831, Washington, D.C.;[411] enl. Mex. War service 04/01/1847 Relay House, MD, age 18; pres. 06/1847; sick 08/1847; pres. 10/1847, to forfeit $3.50 per sent. of garrison court-martial, pay stopped for: 1 F Cap .95, 1 pr Pants 2.28, 1 pr. Shoes 1.22; pres. 12/1847, pay stopped for: 2 pr shoes-$2.44, 1 flannel shirt-$.90, 2 cotton shirts-$.86, 1 overcoat-$6.93$^{1/2}$, 1 blanket-$2.22, 2 pr. drawers-$.71, 2 pr. socks-$.49; pres. 02/1848, to forfeit half mos. pay by sentence of general court-martial, pay stopped for: 1 jacket-$2.66; discharged 03/17/1848 at Saltillo, Mex. on Surgeon's Certificate of Disability;[72] m/1 Mary Ann Pagan date unknown; m/2 Margaret Catherine Jarvis, Norfolk Co., VA 08/15/1860;[411] SC #18232, 04/02/1889, filed Natchez, Adams Co., MS, *"I was just 16 years old at enlistment. On about the 1$^{st}$ of April 1847 the Co. of Va. Vols. Passed through Washington, D.C. enroute to the seat of war. I got on the train at Washington with said Co. and proceeded with them to the Relay House, nine miles from Baltimore, MD And was there enrolled that night by Captain Henry Fairfax. The next morning proceeded with the said Co. to Cumberland, MD By R.R. thence by road wagons to Brownsville, Pa., thence by steamboat to Pittsburg, Pa. to New Orleans. La. I gave my age as 18 years when I was enrolled. I went with said Co. from New Orleans to Brazos Santiago, Texas on the Bark **Baring Brothers**...;"* d. 08/16/1900, Washington, D.C.; wid. Margaret C., WC #13918, 10/29/1910, from VA, res. 622 Cooke St., Portsmouth, VA, c. 1916 moved to Wash., D.C. res. 1858 Ingleside Terrace, d.

## OFF TO WAR

11/27/1918, Wash, D.C.[411]; named children Margorie C. Clemments and Archibald D. Clemments.

**Clifton, Andrew J.**, Pvt., *Preston's Co.*; enl. Mex. War service 12/07/1846 Montgomery Co., VA, age 18; pres. 04/1847; pres. 06/1847; d. 08/21/1847 at Buena Vista, Mex., *"of Consumption,"* pay stopped for: 2 pr. socks-$.49, 1 cotton shirt-$.43, 1 canteen-$.27, 1 haversack-$.20$^{3/4}$.

**Clingenpeel, Pleasant H.**, Pvt., *Preston's Co.*; enl. Mex. War service 01/06/1847 Montgomery Co., VA, age 19; pres. 04/1847; pres. 06/1847; sick 08/1847; d. 09/08/1847 in hosp. at Buena Vista, Mex., pay stopped for: 1 pr. overalls-$2.28, 2 pr. socks-$.49, 1 flannel shirt-$.90, 1 cotton shirt-$.43, 1 canteen & strap-$.27, 1 haversack-$.20$^{3/4}$, 1 pr. wiper-$.15, 1 brush & pick-$.12, 1 gun sling-$.08, 1 breast plate-$.10.

**Cock, Harrison C.**, 1$^{st}$ Cpl., Co. E; b. 1820 Prince Geo. Co., VA, son of Walter Cocke;[412] enl. Mex. War service 11/30/1846 Petersburg, VA, age 26; pres. 04/1847; pres. but sick 06/1847, prom. 3$^{rd}$ Cpl.; pres. 08/1847 prom. 2$^{nd}$ Cpl.; pres. 10/1847, pay stopped for: 1 pr. overalls-$2.28, 2 pr. shoes-$2.44, 3 pr. stockings-$.73$^{1/2}$, 1 cap-$.95$^{1/2}$; pres. 12/1847, prom. 1$^{st}$ Cpl., pay stopped for: 2 flannel shirts-$1.80, [illegible] 1 blanket-$2.22; pres. 02/1848, pay stopped for: 1 pr. pants-$2.28; absent sick in qtrs. 04/1848; d. 03/23/1850, *Ulceration of Stomach*, bur. Blandford Cem., Sq. 3, Sec. 7, Ward C, Petersburg, VA[412]

**Coghill, Thomas Benjamin**, 3$^{rd}$ Sgt., Co. C; b. c. 1822, Caroline Co., VA, son of William and Nancy (Samuel) Coghill; enl. Mex. War service 12/13/1846, Bowling Green, VA, age 24; discharged 06/16/1847 on Surgeon's Certificate of Disability; m. Bettie A. Beazley of Caroline Co., VA, 08/27/1854;[413] Lt. Col. VA militia; occ. Farmer, 1860, Flippo's Store, VA; Civil War service enl. 5/61 Capt. Co. G, 30$^{th}$ Va. Inf.; absent sick several times during 1861, resigned due to ill health 04/02/1862, d. 01/1866, *consumption*.[414]

**Cohen, Lewis**, Pvt., Co. F; enl. Mex. War service 01/25/1847, Portsmouth, VA, age 21; pres. 06/1847; pres. 08/1847; pres. 10/1847, pay stopped for: 1 pr. overalls-$2.28, 3 pr. shoes-$3.66, 2 forage caps-$1.91, 7 cotton shirts-$3.01, 3 pr. socks-$.73$^{1/2}$, 2 pr. drawers-.71, 1 overcoat-$6.93$^{1/2}$; pres. 12/1847; pres. 02/1848, pay stopped for: 2 pr. overalls-$4.56, 2 pr. shoes-$2.44, 1 blanket-$2.22, 1 infantry jacket-$2.66; pres. 04/1848; pres. 08/1848, pay stopped for: 1 gun sling-$.18, 2 cotton shirts-$.88, 3 pr. shoes-$3.48, 1 blanket-$2.25, 2 forage caps-$1.66, BLW sent to Portsmouth, VA c/o E.T. Blamire; [c. 1870 res. Oak Forest, Cumberland Co., VA, age 43, occ. Ret. Dealer, w. Dora both born Prussia.][415]

**Cole, Fayette**, Pvt., Co. K; b. 08/17/1817, Lacy Spring, Rockingham Co., VA, son of Jacob Cole;[416, 417] enl. Mex. War service Richmond, VA 01/26/1847, age 27; pres. 06/1847; pres. 08/1847; pres. 10/1847, pay stopped for: 2 flannel shirts-$1.80, 2 pr. drawers-$.71, 1 blanket-$2.22; pres. 12/1847; pres. 04/1848, pay stopped for: 1 jacket-$2.66, 1 pick & brush-$.12, 1 gun sling-$.18; pres. 07/1848, pay stopped for: 1 cartridge box plate-$.10, 1 cartridge box belt plate-$.10, 1 bayonet scabbard & frog-$.56; BLW sent to Spartapolis, [now Mauzy] Rockingham Co., VA; c. 1850 res. Rockingham Co., VA, age 32, occ. Laborer;[418] m. Susan Jane Gentry 11/27/1851, Greene Co., VA;[417] c. 1860 res. Harrisonburg, Rockingham Co., VA, age 40, occ. Farmer, w. Julia (33), son William (7), dau. Hannah (5), dau. Mary (2);[419] Civil War service Pvt., Co. D, 9$^{th}$ Btln. VA Reserves;[202] SC #7176, 04/12/1887, filed from Bazine, Ness Co., KS; phys. desc. age 70 [1887], 5'9", dark complexion, dark eyes, dark hair, occ. Farmer; since discharge res. Rockingham Co., VA, 23 yrs., Layfayette Co. and Jackson Co., Mo., 8 yrs., Ness Co., KS since then;[417] d. 04/8/1899, Bazine Township, Ness Co., KS;[416, 420] wid. Susan J., WC #12571, 05/09/1899, filed from Bazine, Ness Co., KS; (SJG b. 12/15/1833, Green Co., VA).[420]

**Cole, Richard**, Pvt., LIC; b. 12/12/1824 Greenbrier Co., VA, son of Thomas Cole;[421] enl. Mex. War service 12/12/1846 Staunton, VA, age 22; pres. 08/1847; pres. 10/1847, pay stopped for: 1 forage cap-$.95$^{1/2}$, 1 wool jacket-$2.66, 1 pr. overalls-$2.28, 1 pr. shoes-$1.22, 2 pr. socks-

## VIRGINIA VOLUNTEERS IN MEXICO

$.49, 2 cotton shirts-$.86; pres. 12/1847, pay stopped for: 2 pr. socks-$.49, 1 blanket-$2.22, 1 pr. shoes-$1.22, 1 pr. overalls-$2.28, 1 cotton shirt-$.43; pres. 04/1848, pay stopped for: 1 pr. shoes-$1.22; pres. 07/1848, pay stopped for: 1 wiper-$.20; BLW sent to Falling Spring, Greenbrier Co., VA; [a Richard Cole m. Sarah Jane Kennard 02/03/1856, Melville, Butler Co., OH;[421] Civil War service enl. Cpl., Co. I, 167$^{th}$ Ohio Inf., 05/02/1864, discharged 09/08/1864, Hamilton, Ohio;[421] SC #543, 02/26/1887, filed from Batesville, Ripley Co., IN; d. 11/24/1894, New Point, Decatur Co., IN;[422] wid. Sarah J., WC #9754, 06/15/1893, filed from New Point, Decatur Co., IN; Lists two sons Edward V. Cole and Corey W. Cole;[422] (SKC b. 04/02/1828, d. 05/10/1903).[422]

**Coleman, Addison**, Pvt., Co. I, enl. Mex. War service 08/19/1847 Ft. Monroe, VA, age 19; pres. 02/1848, joined co. 01/26/1848; pres. 04/1848, pay stopped for: 1 blanket; pres. 08/1848, pay stopped for: 1 bayonet scabbard & frog-$.56, 1 waist belt-$.21, 1 waist belt plate-$.10, BLW sent to Lunenburg C.H., VA

**Coleman, John H.**, Pvt., Co. G; enl. Mex. War service 12/02/1846 Richmond, VA, age 27; pres. 06/1847; pres. 08/1847; pres. 10/1847, pay stopped for: 2 pr. overalls-$4.56, 1 pr. drawers-$.35$^{1/2}$, 1 shoes-$1.22, 2 pr. socks-$.49, 1 forage cap-$.95$^{1/2}$; pres. 12/1847, pay stopped for: 1 pr. shoes-$1.22, 1 flannel shirt-$.90, 1 cotton shirt-$.43, 2 pr. drawers-$.71, 1 pr. pants-$2.28; pres. 02/1848; sick 04/1848; pres. 08/1848; BLW sent to Cumberland Co. C.H., VA

**Coleman, Robert F.**, 2$^{nd}$ Lt., Co. C; enl. Mex. War service 12/01/1846, Fredericksburg, VA, age 23; pres. 06/1847; pres. 08/1847; pres. 10/1847; pres. 12/1847 commanding the company; absent 04/1848 on furlough on account of ill health; wid. Ellen D., WC #7215, 07/23/1890, from DC.; 1890 *"Ellen, wid. Robert"* res. 13 E St., NW, Wash., D.C.[423]

**Colley, John**, *Gray's Co.*; *Not on Muster Rolls*, SA #14550, 06/24/1887, from VA

**Collier, Benjamin W.**, 2$^{nd}$ Lt. Co. D; b. 11/03/1823 Greensville Co., VA;[424] enl. Mex. War service 01/04/1847, Petersburg, VA, age 24; pres. 02/1847; pres. 04/1847; pres. 06/1847, prom. 2$^{nd}$ Lt. 06/07/1847, pay stopped for 1 bayonet scabbard, 1 knapsack, 1 haversack, & 1 canteen lost 05/31/1847; pres. 08/1847; pres. 10/1847; pres. 12/1847; absent 04/1848 detailed as QM & Commissary Sgt. w/ Parras Battalion; pres. 08/1848, BLW sent to Hicks Ford, Greensville Co., VA; m/1 Mary E. Wingate (WWC d. 12/1862), m/2 Anna Maria Stockard 11/26/1863, Oxford, Layfayette Co., MS;[425] SC #1220, 03/07/1887, filed from Oxford, Layfayette Co., MS; d. 10/12/1893; wid. Anna Maria, WC #9153, 12/04/1893, filed from Oxford, Layfayette Co., MS; No children; (AMC b. 02/14/1830, m/2 M.M. Whitfield 05/11/1897, Oxford, MS, marriage annulled 11/23/1897 on grounds AMC was *"non compos mentis"*(not mentally competent), d. 11/29/1910, bur. St. Peter's Cemetery, Oxford, MS.)[425]

**Colin, William**, Pvt., *Recruit Co.*, enl. Mex. War service 07/29/1847 Petersburg, VA, age 25; deserted.

**Collins, Albert G.**, 4$^{th}$ Sgt., Co. C; enl. Mex. War service 12/18/1846, Fredericksburg, VA, age 27; pres. 06/1847, prom. 2$^{nd}$ Cpl. 06/16/1847; pres. 08/1847, prom. 1$^{st}$ Cpl., 1 pr. drawers-$.35$^{1/2}$, 1 cap-$.95$^{1/2}$, 2 pr. socks-$.49, 2 cotton shirts-$.86, 2 woolen shirts-$1.80; pres. 10/1847, pay stopped for: 4 pr. socks-$.98, 1 pr. drawers-$.35$^{1/2}$, 1 jacket-$2.66, 1 pr. pants-$2.28, 1 pr. shoes-$1.22, 1 blanket-$2.22; pres. 12/1847, prom. 4$^{th}$ Sgt. 12/16/1847, pay stopped for: 2 pr. socks-$.49, 1 pr. pants-$2.28, 1 pr. shoes-$1.22; pres. 04/1848, pay stopped for: 1 haversack-$.20$^{3/4}$, 1 india rubber canteen-$.27; pres. 08/1848, BLW sent to Fredericksburg, VA; m. Emily P. Bozel, 11/29/1837, Fredericksburg, VA[426]

**Collins, Henry**, Pvt., *Preston's Co.*; b. 06/10/1821, Montgomery Co., VA;[427] enl. Mex. War service 12/06/1846 Montgomery Co., VA, age 26; pres. 04/1847; pres. 06/1847; pres. 08/1847; pres. 10/1847, pay stopped for: 1 pr. overalls-$2.28, 1 pr. socks-$.49, 1 flannel shirt-$.90, 1 cotton shirt-$.43, 1 pr. drawers-$.35$^{1/2}$, 1 blanket-$2.22; pres. 12/1847, pay stopped for: 1 jacket-$2.66; pres. 04/1848, pay stopped for: 1 pick & brush-$.12; pres. 07/1848, pay stopped for: 1 jacket-$2.37, 1 pr. shoes-$1.22, 1 pick & brush-$.12, 1 gun sling-$.18; BLW sent to Christiansburg, VA c/o Fleming Gardner; m. Malinda Lee, 02/01/1849, Montgomery

# OFF TO WAR

Co., VA;[428] c. 1850 res. Montgomery Co., VA, age 29, occ. Farmer, w. Malinda (23, dau. Eliza J. (7/12);[429] c. 1860 res. Christiansburg, Montgomery Co., VA, age 37, occ. Farmer, w. Malinda (35), dau. Eliza Jane (10), dau. Mary F. (8), son Robert H. (6), son John A. (4), son James M. (2);[430] c. 1870 res. Christiansburg, Montgomery Co., VA, age 50, occ. Farmer, w. Malinda (42), dau. Mary F. (19), son Henry R. (16), son John W. (14), son James M. (12), dau. Rebecca A. (9), son Joseph (7), son Charles T. (4), dau. Malinda C. (1);[431] SC #8472, 03/07/1887, filed from Montgomery Co., VA; since discharge res. Montgomery Co., VA;[427] Wyatt Akers and Charles Willis gave affidavits in pension cliam;[427] d. 08/23/1899.[427]

**Collins, John**, Pvt., *Preston's Co.*; b. 08/25/1822, Montgomery Co., VA;[432] enl. Mex. War service 12/06/1846 Montgomery Co., VA, age 23; absent 04/1847 left sick in hosp. at Camargo, Mex. since 04/04/1847; pres. 06/1847; pres. 08/1847; pres. 10/1847, pay stopped for: 2 pr. socks-$.49; absent 12/1847, on detached service in QM Dept., pay stopped for: 1 jacket-$2.66, 1 pr. overalls-$2.28; absent 02/1848 on detached service as Teamster in QM Dept.; absent 04/1848, on detached service as a Teamster; pres. 07/1848, pay stopped for: 1 gun sling-$.18; BLW sent to Christiansburg, VA c/o Fleming Gardner; m. Amy J. Folds, 10/29/1867, Huntsville, Madison Co., AL;[432] occ. Carpenter;[432] SC #4609, d. 05/01/1889, Gadsden, AL;[433] wid. Amy J., WC #6728, 08/05/1889, filed from 341 S. 5th St., Gadsden, Etowah Co., AL; (AFC b. 11/30/1842, Jasper, Ga.; d. 10/29/1907).[433]

**Comann, Fitzwilliam J.**, Pvt., Co. D; enl. Mex. War service 01/05/1847, Petersburg, VA, age 23; pres. 02/1847; pres. 04/1847; pres. 06/1847, pay stopped for 1 bayonet *"lost through negligence"* 03/22/1847; pres. 08/1847, pay stopped for: 1 cap-$.95$^{1/2}$, 2 cotton shirts-$.86; pres. 10/1847, pay stopped for: 1 pr. pants-$2.28, 2 flannel shirts-$1.80, 2 pr. drawers-$.71, 2 pr. socks-$.49, 1 pr. shoes-$1.22; pres. 12/1847, pay stopped for: 1 jacket-$2.66, 1 pr. pants-$2.28, 1 cotton shirt-$.43, 1 pr drawers-$.35$^{1/2}$, 1 blanket-$2.22; pres. 04/1848, pay stopped for: 1 set of picks & brushes-$.12, 1 pr. pants-$2.28, 1 pr. shoes-$1.22; pres. 08/1847, BLW sent to Smokey Ordinary, Brunswick Co., VA; c. 1860 res. Tazewell C.H., Tazewell Co., VA in the "Virginia Hotel," age 31, occ. Tailor;[434] Civil War service Pvt., Co. C, 37th Va. Inf. enl. 06/31/1861 at Richmond, VA, on detached service 01/1862 – 03/1862, captured 03/23/1863 Kernstown, VA and sent to Ft. Delaware, sent to Aikens Landing 06/09/1862, exchanged 08/05/1862;[435] Pvt., Co. I, 16th Va. Cav. enl. 10/09/1862 in Tazewell Co., VA, detailed as provost guard 04/01/1864, Tailor for officers 12/31/1864.[436]

**Colton, John**, Pvt., Co. M; enl. Mex. War service 11/23/1847 Norfolk, VA, age 37; pres. 11/1847; pres. 12/1847; pres. 02/1848, pay stopped for: 1 flannel shirt-$.90; pres. 04/1848, pay stopped for: 1 blanket-$2.22, 1 pr. shoes-$1.22, 2 cotton shirts-$.86; pres. 08/1848, pay stopped for: 1 musket & accoutrements complete-$16.22, 1 pr. shoes-$1.22; BLW sent to Norfolk, VA

**Comerford, John**, Pvt., Co. M; b. 01/05/1825, Ireland;[437] enl. U.S. Navy 1846, Norfolk, VA? served as a Landsman on *U.S.S. Saratoga*;[437] enl. Mex. War service 11/04/1847 Norfolk, VA, age 21; pres. 11/1847; pres. 12/1847; pres. 02/1848, pay stopped for: 1 overcoat-$6.93$^{1/2}$; pres. 04/1848, pay stopped for: 1 pr. shoes-$1.22, 1 cap-$.95$^{1/2}$; pres. 08/1848; BLW sent to Norfolk, VA; m. Mary Ann Jackson, 1855, Portsmouth, Norfolk Co., VA;[437] (MJC d. 1855);[437] Civil War service enl. Pvt., Co. I, 4th CA Inf., 02/08/1862, discharged 02/11/1865; SC #14533, 02/24/1888, filed from San Bernardino, San Bernadino Co., CA; IO #498971; *"Disability incurred at Fort Mojave in Arizona on or about the 20th day of August 1864. While on duty became short of water and nearly perished on the desert near Ft. Mojave while in the Union service fighting for our country;"*[437] *"In the month of August 1864 I was stationed at Ft. Mojave, Arizona Territory. I was 1st Lt., Co. I, 4th Regt. Calif. Inf. John Comerford was a Private in said co. The same month he was out with an Exploring Party and got separated from his comrades and he came very near dying of thirst for the want of some water. His comrades met some Indians, gave them their canteens and sent them for some water. When the Indians returned with the water some of the Party went back and found John Comerford*

## VIRGINIA VOLUNTEERS IN MEXICO

*nearly naked for he had taken nearly all his clothes off and laying on the ground. His tongue was swollen, all black and sticking out of his mouth. The first water they gave him made him appear as though he was mad. It was about 25 miles to the Fort, and the Party was 2 days getting Comerford back to the Fort. It was some two months before he was returned to duty. After he got better he was reported as a Hospital Steward for Dr. Stark, Regimental Surgeon;"*[437] since discharge res. San Bernadino Co., CA, occ. Painter;[437] d. 1891, National Soldiers Home, Los Angeles, CA?[437]

**Compton, James**, Pvt., Co. B; enl. 12/10/1846, Alexandria, VA, age 21; pres. 06/1847; absent 08/1847 left sick 06/01/1847 in hosp. at Monterey, Mex.; pres. 10/1847, pay stopped for: 1 pr. overalls-$2.28, 1 pr. shoes-$1.22, 5 pr. socks-$1.22$^{1/2}$, 2 pr. cotton drawers-$.71, 2 flannel shirts-$1.80, 4 cotton shirt-$1.72; pres. 12/1847, pay stopped for: 1 cap-$.95$^{1/2}$, 1 jacket-$2.66, 2 pr. cotton drawers-$.71, 1 pr. overalls-$2.28, 1 blanket-$2.22; pres. 02/1848, pay stopped for: 1 pr. shoes-$1.22; pres. 04/1848, pay stopped for: 2 flannel shirts-$1.80; pres. 08/1848, pay stopped for: 1 gun sling-$.16, BLW sent to Alexandria, VA

**Conner, John**, Pvt., Co. F; enl. Mex. War service 01/22/1847, Portsmouth, VA, age 24; pres. 06/1847; pres. 08/1847; in confinement 10/1847, fined 1 mos. pay by order of genl. court-martial, pay stopped for: 1 pr. overalls-$2.28, 2 cotton shirts-$.86, 2 pr. drawers-.71, 1 blanket-$2.22, 1 forage cap-$.95$^{1/2}$; pres. 12/1847; pres. 02/1848, pay stopped for: 1 blanket-$2.22, 1 pr. shoes-$1.22, 1 pr. socks-$.24$^{1/2}$; pres. 04/1848, $6.97 due him from 10/31/1847 muster roll; pres. 08/1848, pay stopped for: 1 gun sling-$.18, BLW sent to Philadelphia, Pa.

**Conrad, Henry K.**, Pvt., *Recruit Co.*, enl. Mex. War service 12/31/1847 Charlestown, VA, age 18; pres. 02/1848; pres. 04/1848; d. 05/22/1848 at Mill Creek Branch near Ft. Monroe, VA, *"whilst bathing. Was found two days after and buried."*

**Conroy, James J.**, Pvt., Co. L; b. c. 1828; enl. Mex. War service 03/01/1847 Fairfax C.H., VA, age 19; sick 06/1847; pres. 08/1847; pres. 10/1847, to forfeit $3.50 by sentence of garrison court-martial. pay stopped for: 1 pr. Pants 2.28, 1 pr. Shoes 1.22 sick 12/1847, pay stopped for: 1 pr. pants-$2.28, 1 cap-$.95$^{1/2}$, 1 pr. shoes-$1.22, 2 cotton shirts-$.86, 1 blanket-$2.22, 2 pr. drawers-$.71, 1 pr. socks-$.24$^{1/2}$; desc., age 19, 5'4$^{1/2}$", dark complexion, blue eyes, dark hair, occ. Carpenter;[26] discharged 02/25/1848 at Saltillo, Mex. on Surgeon's Certificate.[72]

**Converse, Farmer**, 3$^{rd}$ Cpl., Co. G; enl. Mex. War service 12/05/1846 Richmond, VA, age 34; pres. 06/1847, prom. 3$^{rd}$ Cpl.; pres. 08/1847; pres. 10/1847, pay stopped for: 2 pr. overalls-$4.56, 2 cotton shirts-$.86, 1 flannel shirt-$.90, 2 pr. drawers-$.71, 2 shoes-$2.44, 5 pr. socks-$1.22$^{1/2}$, 2 forage cap-$1.91; sick 12/1847, reduced to ranks at his own request, pay stopped for: 1 pr. shoes-$1.22, 1 blanket-$2.22, 2 pr. socks-$.49; sick 04/1848, pay stopped for: 1 brush & pick-$.12; pres. 04/1848; pres. 08/1848; BLW sent to [illegible].

**Cook, Charles J.**, Co. F; m. Lucy _____ c. 1843, Halifax Co., North Carolina;[438] enl. Mex. War service 08/17/1847 Petersburg, VA, age 26; pres. 02/1848, joined from regtl. depot; pres. 04/1848, 1 mos. pay and 3 days clothing money due him; pres. 08/1848, pay stopped for: 1 cartridge box belts & plates complete-$1.90, 1 bayonet scabbard-$.56, 1 waist belt & plate-$.31, 1 bayonet-$1.44, 2 infantry jackets-$4.75, 3 blankets-$6.75, 2 pr. shoes-$2.32, 3 cotton shirts-$1.32, BLW sent to Fort Monroe, VA; d. 1848 Norfolk, VA;[438] WC #629, 05/05/1887 filed from Boydton, Mecklenburg Co., VA; phys, desc. 5'7", b. New York City, fair skin, blue eyes, light hair, *"a circus man."*[438]

**Cooke, John K.**, 1$^{st}$ Lt., Co. F; b. 12/11/1812, son of Mordecai Cooke;[45] enl. Mex. War service 11/23/1846, Portsmouth, VA; pres. 06/1847, in command of the company until 06/28/1847; absent 08/1847 on detached service as Provost Marshall since 07/16/1847; pres. 10/1847; absent 12/1847 sick; pres. 02/1848; pres. 04/1848 in command of the company; pres. 08/1848; m. Fanny (b. 03/18/1818; d. 01/22/1867); c. 1853 mbr. and *Generalissimo* of Portsmouth Encampment No. 5, Knights Templar, Portsmouth, VA;[40] d. 02/06/1887, bur. Cedar Grove Cem., Portsmouth, VA [listed as Capt. w/ CSA marker]

OFF TO WAR

**Coontz, Thornton**, (aka Koontz, Koonce) 3rd Sgt., Co. H; b. 12/16/1821; enl. Mex. War service 11/29/1846, Berkeley, VA, age 26; pres. 04/1847; pres. 06/1847, prom. 1st Cpl.; pres. 08/1847; pres. 10/1847, pay stopped for: 1 forage cap-$.95$^{1/2}$, 1 pr. pants-$2.28, 2 flannel shirts-$1.80, 1 pr. drawers-$.35$^{1/2}$, 1 pr. shoes-$1.22, 2 pr. socks-$.49, 1 jacket-$2.66; pres. 12/1847, pay stopped for: 1 pr. shoes-$1.22, 1 pr. socks-$.24$^{1/2}$, 1 pr. pants-$2.28, 1 blanket-$2.22; pres. 02/1848, pay stopped for: 1 jacket-$2.66, 2 pr. drawers-$.71, 1 pr. shoes-$1.22, 2 pr. socks-$.49; absent 04/1848, sick in Hosp., prom. 3rd Sgt. 02/29/1848; pres. 07/1848, BLW sent to Shepherdstown, VA; c. 1850, res. Goochland Co., VA, age 30, occ. Laborer;[439] c. 1860 res. Vancleavesville P.O., Berkeley Co., VA, age 40, occ. Laborer;[440] Civil War service enl. 2nd Sgt., Co. F, 1st Va. Cav. 04/18/1861 Shepardstown, VA, pres. through 02/13/1862, discharged overage (no date), reenl. as a substitute for Robert K. Wilson, pres. through 8/1864, paroled 04/1865 at Salisbury, NC; d. 05/12/1886, bur. Elmwood Cem., Shepherdstown, WV.[441]

**Copeland, James R.**, 2nd Sgt., Co. K; b. 06/26/1822, Hillsboro, Loudoun Co., VA;[442] enl. Mex. War service Jefferson Co., VA 12/01/1846, age 22; pres. 06/1847, prom. to 1st Cpl. from 2nd Cpl.; pres. 08/1847, prom. 4th Sgt.; pres. 10/1847, prom. 3rd Sgt., pay stopped for: 1 pr. overalls-$2.28, 2 pr. shoes-$2.44, 1 cotton shirt-$.43, 2 pr. socks-$.49, 1 flannel shirt-$.90, 1 cap-$.95$^{1/2}$; pres. 12/1847, pay stopped for: 1 jacket-$2.66, 2 pr. overalls-$4.56, 2 pr. boots-$2.44, 1 pr. socks-$.24$^{1/2}$, 2 pr. drawers-$.71; pres. 04/1848, prom. 2nd Sgt., pay stopped for: 1 jacket-$2.66, 1 pr. pants-$2.28, 1 flannel shirt-$.90, 2 gun slings-$.36, 1 pick & brush-$.12, 1 pr. shoes-$1.22; pres. 07/1848, pay stopped for: 1 pick & brush-$.12, 1 screw driver-$.25; BLW sent to Charlestown, Jefferson Co., VA; m/1 Nancy Ann Preston, 01/09/1851, Purcellville, Loudoun Co., VA;[443, 442]c. 1860 res. Snickersville, Loudoun Co. VA, age 28, occ. Laborer, w. Nancy (25), dau. Mary (7), dau. Ann E. (5), son David H. (4), son Thomas F. (4), son George E. (3), dau. Lydia Ann (4/12);[444] Civil War service Pvt., Co. C, 35th Btln. Va. Cav., age 46, capt. 10/21/1862 at Bollington, paroled 10/25/1862 sent to Aiken's Landing; captured 01/29/1864, Hillsboro, VA, sent to Wheeling, WV, then to Camp Chase, OH 03/04/1864; trans. to Ft. Delaware 03/14/1864; released 06/19/1865; desc. 5'8", fair, blue eyes, dark hair;[445] c. 1870 res. Loudoun Co., VA, age 46, occ. Carpenter, w. Nancy (45), dau. Mary J. (18), son George (12), dau. Lydia (10), son James D. (8), dau. Rosanna L. (4);[446] (NPC d. 11/09/1876, Round Hill, VA, bur. Ketoctin Baptist Church Cem., Round Hill, VA); m/2 Harriet A.M. Butts, 10/09/1877, Loudoun Co., VA;[447, 442] SC #538, 02/24/1887, filed from Round Hill, Loudoun Co., VA; (HBC d. 12/25/1897, Round Hill, VA, bur. Ketoctin Baptist Church Cem., Round Hill, VA); m/3 Elizabeth A. Sowers 03/10/1898, Leesburg, Loudoun Co., VA;[448] d. 05/29/1901, near Round Hill, Loudoun Co., VA, bur. Ketoctin Baptist Church Cemetery, Round Hill, VA; wid. Elizabeth A., WC #13070, 06/19/1901, filed from Round Hill, Loudoun Co., VA; (ESC b. 08/13/1835, Bethel, Clarke Co., VA, m/1 William B. Sowers who d. 12/31/1891).[448]

**Copenhaver, Andrew Jackson**, Pvt., Co. K; b. 12/18/1827, Winchester, Frederick Co., VA;[449]enl. Mex. War service Frederick Co., VA 12/09/1846, age 19; pres. 06/1847; pres. 08/1847; pres. 10/1847, pay stopped for: 2 cotton shirts-$.86, 2 pr. overalls-$4.56, 2 pr. shoes-$2.44, 2 pr. drawers-$.71, 4 pr. socks-$.98, 2 flannel shirts-$1.80, 1 cap-$.95$^{1/2}$; pres. 12/1847, pay stopped for: 1 jacket-$2.66, 1 pr. overalls-$2.28, 1 pr. boots-$1.22, 1 pr. socks-$.24$^{1/2}$, 2 pr. drawers-$.71, 1 blanket-$2.22, 1 flannel shirt-$.90; pres. 04/1848, pay stopped for: 1 bed sack-$1.07$^{1/2}$, 1 pick & brush-$.12, 1 gun sling-$.18; pres. 07/1848, pay stopped for: 1 cartridge box plate-$.10, 1 gun sling-$.18, 1 pick & brush-$.12, 1 screw driver-$.25; BLW sent to Winchester, Frederick Co., VA; m. Matilda C. Brown 08/08/1851, Harper's Ferry, Jefferson Co., WV;[449] [Civil War service enl. 05/27/1861 Pvt., Co. A, 8th Va. Cav. at Marion, Smyth Co., VA; AWOL 9/30 – 10/21/1864; took oath of allegiance 03/31/1865; postwar occ. Farmer, Tazewell Co., VA;[450]] c. 1870 res. Winchester, Frederick Co., VA, age 42, occ. Blacksmith, w. Matilda (37);[451] SC #8101, 02/04/1887, Kent St., Winchester, Frederick Co., VA; phys. desc. age 59 [1886], 5'6", grey eyes, brown hair, dark complexion, occ.

## VIRGINIA VOLUNTEERS IN MEXICO

Blacksmith;[449] since discharge res. Clarksburg, Harrison Co., WV, Gallipolis, OH, 13 or 14 mos., Winchester, VA since then;[449] d. 09/05/1899, Winchester, Frederick Co., VA;[452] wid. Matilda C., WC #11909, 11/03/1899, filed from 420 Kent St., Winchester, Frederick Co., VA; (MBC b. 08/29/1830, Winchester, Frederick Co., VA).[452]

**Coppedge, Thomas L.**, Pvt., Co. B; enl. 12/19/1846, Richmond, VA, age 27; sick 06/1847; pres. 08/1847; discharged 07/31/1847 Monterey, Mex. on Surgeon's Certificate of Disability; m. Marthy Mourning 03/22/1853, Lincoln, Mo.;[453] wid. Martha A., WC #768, 02/16/1887, from MO.

**Cooper, Albert**, Pvt., *Recruit Co.*, enl. Mex. War service 08/05/1847 Brunswick C.H., VA, age 25; discharged 08/23/1847 by Surgeon.

**Corbin, Lafayette**, Pvt., Co. A; b. 04/01/1824, Culpeper Co., VA, son of Jameson & Mary Nelson (Mason) Corbin;[454] enl. Mex. War service 11/18/1846 Richmond, VA, age 22; pres. 12/1846 - 04/1847; pres. 06/1847; pres. 08/1847; pres. 10/1847, pay stopped for clothing: 3 cotton shirts-$1.29, 1 pr. wool overalls-$2.28, 1 cap-$.95$^{1/2}$, 2 pr. shoes-$2.44, 2 pr. stockings-$.49, 2 flannel shirts-$1.80, 1 pr. drawers-$.35$^{1/2}$, 1 wool jacket-$2.66, 1 great coat-$6.93$^{1/2}$; pres. 02/1848; pres. 04/1848, pay stopped for: 1 cap; BLW sent to Falmouth, Stafford Co., VA; c. 1850 res. Stafford Co., VA, age 26, occ. Clerk;[455] m. Catherine S.M. 03/02/1852, Stafford Co., VA; c. 1857 res. Stafford Co.;[456] c. 1860 res. Fauquier Co., VA, age 36, occ. Farmer, Catherine (28), dau. Mary F. (7), son Thomas B. (3), son Richard L. (1);[457] c. 1870 res. Upperville, Fauquier Co., Va. w. Catherine S.M. (37), dau. Mary F. (17), son Thomas B. (13), son Randall B. (8), dau. Ellen A. (6), son Lafayette (3);[458] Catherine, *"widow of Lafayette,"* res. Washington, D.C. 1876-1902; d. 12/26/1867 *"chronic diarrhea, dyspepsia and derangement of the heart,"* Stafford Co., VA; wid. Catherine S.M., WC #618, 03/02/1887, filed from 501 H St., S.W., Washington, DC. Children Mary Fannie b. 12/10/1852, res. Fauquier Co., VA; Thomas B. b. 01/24/1857, res. Washington, D.C.; Major Richard b. 02/22/1859, res. Stafford Co., Randall B. b. 09/10/1861, res. Washington, D.C.; Ella Amelia b. 04/11/1864, res. Washington, D.C.; Lafayette Montague b. 04/10/1867, res. Washington, D.C.[459]

**Corder, Elijah**, Pvt., Co. F; enl. Mex. War service 01/22/1847, Portsmouth, VA, age 23; pres. 06/1847; pres. 08/1847; pres. 10/1847, pay stopped for: 1 pr. overalls-$2.28, 2 cotton shirts-$.86, 1 forage cap-$.95$^{1/2}$, 4 pr. socks-$.98, 2 pr. shoes-$2.44, 2 pr. drawers-.71, 1 flannel shirt-$.90, 1 Infy. Jacket-$2.66; pres. 12/1847; pres. 02/1848, pay stopped for: 1 pr. overalls-$2.28, 1 flannel shirt-$.90, 1 cotton shirt-$.43, 1 blanket-$2.22, 2 pr. socks-$.49, 1 bed sack-$1.07; pres. 04/1848; pres. 08/1848, pay stopped for: 1 bayonet scabbard & frog-$.56, 1 gun sling-$.18, 6 cotton shirts-$2.64, 2 blankets-$4.50, BLW sent to Portsmouth, VA c/o E.T. Blamire.

**Cornwell, William P.**, Co. B; *Not on Muster Rolls*, SA #21948, 08/09/1889, from KY

**Corrie, William W.**, Pvt., Co. L; b. 1828; enl. Mex. War service 04/01/1847 Alexandria, VA, age 19; pres. 06/1847; sick 08/1847; discharged 10/16/1847 at Saltillo, Mex. on Surgeon's Certificate of Disability.[72]

**Corse, Montgomery Dent**, Capt., Co. B; b. 03/14/1816, Alexandria, DC, son of John & Julia (Granville) Corse; enl. 11/20/1846, Alexandria, VA; pres. 06/1847; pres. 08/1847; pres. 10/1847; pres. 12/1847; pres. 02/1848; pres. 04/1848; pres. 08/1848; *California 49er*, organized the Sutter Rifles Militia Co. 1849; Civil War service Brig. Gen., C.S.A.; m. Elizabeth Beverley 11/22/1862; SC #832, 02/09/1887, from VA d. 02/11/1895, *Debility Incident to Old Age*, Alex., VA, bur. St. Paul's Episcopal Cemetery, Alexandria, VA[100]

**Councill, Eugene Deans**, 3$^{rd}$ Sgt., Co. F; b. 12/19/1824, Carrsville, Isle of Wight Co., VA, son of Joseph Godwin & Judith Yates (McClenney) Councill;[460] enl. Mex. War service 11/23/1846, Portsmouth, VA, age 22; absent 06/1847 sick in camp; pres. 08/1847; pres. 10/1847, pay stopped for: 1 pr. overalls-$2.28, 2 pr. socks-$.49, 1 forage cap-$.95$^{1/2}$; 2 pr. shoes-$2.44, 1 pr. drawers-.35$^{1/2}$, 1 blanket-$2.22; pres. 12/1847; pres. 02/1848, pay stopped for: 1 pr. overalls-

OFF TO WAR

$2.28, 1 pr. shoes-$1.22; pres. 04/1848, prom. 03/01/1848 3$^{rd}$ Sgt.; pres. 08/1848, pay stopped for: 2 shirts-$.88, 1 pr. shoes-$1.16, BLW sent to Portsmouth, VA c/o E.T. Blamire.

**Cowen, George W.**, Pvt., *Recruit Co.*, enl. Mex. War service 04/18/1848 Wytheville, VA; pres. 06/1848; BLW sent to Wytheville, VA [a George W. Cowan served during the Civil War as 1$^{st}$ Lt., Co. A, 7$^{th}$ Tenn. Inf.; c. 1870 res. Newbern, Pulaski Co., VA, age 43, occ. Plasterer, w. Nancy (33), son William M. (15), dau. Sarah R. (13), son James M. (4), dau. Monnote (2), son George S. (4./12), mo. Elizabeth (76)]$^{461}$

**Cox, James T.**, 1$^{st}$ Cpl., Co. A; b. Caroline Co., VA 1826; enl. Mex. War service 11/21/1846 Richmond, VA; pres. 12/1846 - 04/1847, when sick in hosp. at Monterey, Mex. since 04/25/1847; sick in quarters 06/1847; pres. 08/1847, prom. 1$^{st}$ Cpl. 08/23/1847; pres. 10/1847, pay stopped for clothing: 2 cotton shirts-$.86, 2 pr. wool overalls-$4.56, 1 cap-$.95$^{1/2}$, 4 pr. stockings-$.98, 1 wool jacket-$2.66, 1 pr. shoes-$1.22, 2 pr. drawers-$.71; pres. 12/1847 - 02/1848, pay stopped for: 1 pr. shoes-$1.22, 1 pr. wool overalls-$2.28; sick 04/1848, pay stopped for: 1 wool jacket; 07/1848 pay stopped for: bayonet sheath-$.56, waist belt-$.21, belt plate-$.10; BLW sent to, Miller's Tavern, Essex Co., VA; m. Keziah H. Gay 01/24/1850, Henrico Co., VA; enl. Civil War service Pvt., Co. A., 46$^{th}$ Va. Inf. 07/30/1863; pres. 12/63; pres. 2/64; granted 15 days home furlough in Henrico Co.; admitted Petersburg Hosp. w/ diarrhea 06/03/1864; returned to duty 08/21/1864; pres. 8/64; pres. 10/64; pres. 2/65; desc. 5'11", black eyes, dark hair, occ. Farmer;$^{462}$ d. 04/27/1870, *a Police Man killed in the Capital Disaster,*$^{"10}$ bur. Hollywood Cem., Richmond, VA, Sect. F, Lot 27;$^{119, 463}$wid. Keziah H., WC #4331, 03/30/1888, filed from 409 N. 2$^{nd}$ St., Richmond, VA; (b. 03/23/1826, d. 04/11/1902, bur. Hollywood Cem., Sect F, Lot 27).$^{119}$

**Cox, John W.**, Pvt., *Preston's Co.*; b. c. 1820, NC, son of Ross & Anna (Wade) Cox, m. Cynthia (Newton) Lester 06/01/1843 Floyd Co., VA;$^{464}$ enl. Mex. War service 12/06/1846 Floyd Co., VA, age 27; pres. 04/1847, pay stopped for: 1 waist belt, 1 waist belt plate, 1 bayonet scabbard & frog; pres. 06/1847; absent 08/1847 on detached service in QM Dept., to receive $25 in addition to his pay as a soldier; absent 10/1847, on detached service in QM Dept., pay stopped for: 1 jacket-$2.66, 1 pr. shoes-$1.22, 2 pr. socks-$.49, 2 cotton shirts-$.86, 1 pr. drawers-$.35$^{1/2}$, 1 cap-$.95$^{1/2}$; pres. 12/1847, pay stopped for: 1 jacket-$2.66, 1 pr. overalls-$2.28, 1 pr. socks-$.24$^{1/2}$, 1 pr. drawers-$.35$^{1/2}$, 1 blanket-$2.22; pres. 02/1848, pay stopped for: 1 cap-$.95$^{1/2}$, 1 pr. shoes-$1.22; pres. 04/1848, pay stopped for: 1 pick & brush-$.12; pres. 07/1848, pay stopped for: 1 cap-$.95$^{1/2}$ 1 pr. shoes-$1.16, 1 cartridge box belt-$.70, 1 cartridge box belt plate-$.10,1 brush & pick-$.12, 1 gun sling-$.18, 1 screw driver-$.07, 1 wiper-$.07; BLW sent to Rocky Mount, VA c/o William R. Johnson; c. 1850 res. Floyd Co., VA, age 30, occ. None, b. NC, w. Cinthia (35) b. NC can not read or write, dau. Susan (4); [Civil War service a John W. Cox b. 1821; enl. Pvt., Co. F, 6$^{th}$ Va. Inf. 05/13/1861 Princess Anne Co., VA for 1 yr.; absent sick 11/23/61 to 3/62; Discharged 05/06/1862 on Surgeon's Certificate of Disability]$^{465}$ d. 06/1862 Jeffersonville, WV;$^{464}$ wid. Cintha, WC #628, 04/09/1887, file from Posey, Floyd Co., VA; phys. desc. b. NC, 5'6", black hair, blue eyes, light complexion.$^{464}$ (CNLC m/l Jacob Lester who d. 02/17/1842, Floyd Co., VA) $^{464}$

**Craft, John C.**, Drummer, Co. A; enl. Mex. War 12/14/1846, age 18; pres. 12/1846 – 04/1847; pres. 06/1847; detached service 08/1847, with Regtl. Band since 05/01/1847; pres. 10/1847, pay stopped for clothing: 2 cotton shirts-$.86, 2 pr. shoes-$2.44, 1 wool jacket-$2.66, 1 pr.

---

$^{10}$ The **Capitol Disaster** refers to the collapse of the balcony on the third floor of the Capitol on April 27, 1870. A hotly disputed Richmond mayoral election case being argued in front of the Supreme Court of Appeals drew a large crowd of spectators to the court room on the third floor, and the overflow, about 100 persons, crowded into the gallery above. As one eye-witness said, ". . . there was a loud report, like the explosion of a gun. The gallery gave way and fell to the main floor, then the main floor went down with a terrific crash." The floor, which had been weakened by the removal of a partition, collapsed under the weight of the crowd, killing 62 people and injuring 251.

VIRGINIA VOLUNTEERS IN MEXICO

wool overalls-$2.28, 1 cap-.95$^{1/2}$, 4 pr. stockings-$.98, 1 pr. drawers-$.35$^{1/2}$; pres. 02/1848, pay stopped for: 1 pr. shoes-$1.22; pres. 04/1848; 07/1848, pay stopped for: 1 pr. shoes-$1.16; BLW sent to, Richmond, VA
**Crafton, George Washington**, Pvt., *Recruit Co.*, enl. Mex. War service 08/09/1847 Lunenburg C.H., VA, age 21; discharged 08/23/1847 by Surgeon; m. Mary Barnes, 05/01/1852, Lunenburg Co., VA[466]
**Crafton, James E.**, Pvt., *Recruit Co.*, enl. Mex. War service 08/17/1847 Petersburg, VA, age 19; pres. 02/1848; absent 04/1848 sick; SA #22936, 08/08/1890, from VA
**Cramer, John I. or J.**, *Not on Muster Rolls*, wid. Sarah A., WC #5872, 09/25/1888, from PA.
**Crane, John H.**, Pvt., *Recruit Co.*, enl. Mex. War service 01/01/1848 Charlestown, VA, age 20; pres. 02/1848; pres. 04/1848; pres. 06/1848; BLW sent to Charlestown, Jefferson Co., VA; c. 1850 res. Charlestown, Jefferson Co., VA, age 23, occ None Listed;[467] [Civil War service a John Crane, b. c. 1826, enl. Pvt., Co. C, 5$^{th}$ Va. Cav., at Danville, VA 03/13/1862; pres. 1/64; absent sick w/ rheumatism in Richmond Hosp. 4/64 – 7/64; deserted; nfr];[131] SC #16616, 12/22/1887, from VA
**Crawford, Samuel G.**, 2$^{nd}$ Sgt., Co. I; b. 01/13/1822, New London, Campbell Co., VA,[468] son of Samuel Leake & Charlotte (Austin) Crawford; enl. Mex. War service 10/10/1847 Lynchburg, VA, age 21; pres. 02/1847; pres. 04/1847; pres. 06/1847, prom. 3$^{rd}$ Sgt. 06/16/1847; pres. 08/1847; absent 10/1847, pay stopped for: 3 pr. drawers-$1.06$^{1/2}$, 2 cotton shirts-$.86, 1 cap-$.95$^{1/2}$, 1 pr. socks-$.24$^{1/2}$, 1 pr. pants-$2.28; pres. 12/1847, pay stopped for: 2 pr. shoes-$2.44, 1 pr. socks-$.24$^{1/2}$, 1 jacket-$2.66, 1 pr. pants-$2.28, 1 blanket-$2.22, 2 cotton shirts-$.86; 2 flannel shirts-$1.80, 1 pr. drawers-$.35$^{1/2}$; pres. 02/1848; pres. 04/1848; 08/1848, prom. 2$^{nd}$ Sgt., BLW sent to New London, Campbell Co., VA; m/1 Julia A. Perkins 01/12/1854, Fluvanna Co., VA, (JAC b. 1833, d. 06/07/1860 Fluvanna Co., VA, bur. Fluvanna Co., VA);[469] Civil War service a Samuel Crawford enl. Pvt., Co. C, 20$^{th}$ VA Btln. Hvy. Arty. 03/10/1862; a res. of Botetourt Co., VA; desc. 5'9", light complex., brown hair, grey eyes; absent sick 9/62; AWOL 10/62; returned to duty and pres. thru 4/65; captured 04/06/1865 at Farmville; sent to Pt. Lookout, MD; took oath and released 06/24/1865;[470] m/2 Sallie Ragland (Perkins) Winston, 01/24/1867, place unknown, (SRC b. 01/12/1831, m/1 Bicherton Winston, d. 01/08/1868, Poindexter, VA?);[469] m/3 Harriett Elizabeth Perkins, (aka "Hattie B." or "Hattie Bet"), 06/08/1870, *"Empire House, Washington City, D.C.;"*[469] c. 1870 res. Trevillians, Louisa Co., VA, age 47, occ. Farmer, w. Hattie B. (28), dau. Mary A. (14), son William (12), m-i-l Martha Perkins (63);[471] SC #8407, 03/27/1893, filed Louisa C.H., Louisa Co., VA; since discharge res. Louisa Co., VA; phys. desc. age 86 [1907], fair complexion, grey eyes, black hair, occ. mechanic;[468] lists children William N. Crawford, b. 05/28/1856 *("by 1$^{st}$ marriage")*, Lottie M. Crawford, b. 09/07/1874, Powhattan Perkins Crawford, b. 02/01/1878, Johnson W. Crawford, b. 01/23/1882, *("by last marriage")*;[468] d. 07/29/1907, *"old age and acute indigestion,"* Green Springs, Louisa Co., VA age 85;[469, 472] wid. Hattie B., WC #15006, 08/28/1907, filed from Louisa C.H., Louisa Co., VA; OW IA #13437 rejected; (HBC b. 10/12/1841, near Watkinsville, VA, d. 08/17/1817, Richmond, VA, bur. Louisa, VA).[469]
**Creamer, Jacob Q.**, Pvt., Co. L; b. 1804; enl. Mex. War service 03/01/1847 Fairfax C.H., VA, age 43; sick 06/1847; discharged 08/30/1847 at Saltillo, Mex. on Surgeon's Certificate of Disability.[72]
**Creamer, John Q.**, Pvt., Co. H; enl. Mex. War service 11/21/1846, Berkeley, VA, age 22; pres. 04/1847; pres. 06/1847; pres. 08/1847; pres. 10/1847, pay stopped for: 1 forage cap-$.95$^{1/2}$, 1 pr. pants-$2.28, 3 cotton shirts-$1.29, 1 pr. drawers-$.35$^{1/2}$, 1 pr. shoes-$1.22, 3 pr. socks-$.73$^{1/2}$, 1 jacket-$2.66; in confinement 121/1847, pay stopped for: 1 pr. pants-$2.28, 1 pr. shoes-$1.22, 1 pr. socks-$.24$^{1/2}$; pres. 02/1848, pay stopped for: 1 cotton shirt-$.43, 1 flannel shirt-$.90, 1 pr. shoes-$1.22, 1 blanket-$2.22; pres. 04/1848; pres. 07/1848, pay stopped for: 2 gun slings-$.48, 3 brush & picks-$.36, 2 cartridge box plate-$.20, 2 cartridge box belt plates-$.20, 2 bayonet scabbards & frogs-$1.12, 2 waist belts-$.42, 2 waist belt plates-$.20, 1 musket

OFF TO WAR

complete-$13.00, 1 cartridge box-$1.10, BLW sent to Martinsburg, VA; c. 1850 res. Martinsburg, Berkeley Co., VA, age 24, occ. Cooper.[473]

**Creekmur, Charles J.**, Pvt., Co. F; b. 09/14/1828, Norfolk Co., VA; enl. Mex. War service 11/11/1847, Portsmouth, VA, age 18; pres. 06/1847; pres. 08/1847; pres. 10/1847, pay stopped for: 1 pr. overalls-$2.28, 4 cotton shirts-$1.72, 4 pr. socks-$.98, 1 pr. shoes-$1.22, 2 flannel shirts-$1.80, 1 blanket-$2.22; pres. 12/1847; pres. 02/1848, pay stopped for: 1 forage cap-$.95[1/2], 1 pr. overalls-$2.28; pres. 04/1848; pres. 08/1848, pay stopped for: 1 cartridge box belt & plate-$1.90, 1 waist belt plate-$.10, 1 gun sling-$.18, 1 pr. shoes-$1.16, 1 blanket-$2.25, 2 cotton shirts-$.88, BLW sent to Portsmouth, VA c/o E.T. Blamire; m. Elizabeth J. Mills 01/16/1850, Portsmouth, Norfolk Co., VA;[474] c. 1850 res. Nansemond Co., VA, age 22, occ. Merchant Tailor, w. Elizabeth (18);[475] c. 1860 res. City of Portsmouth, VA, age 31, occ. Clerk, w. Elizabeth (27), dau. Anna F. (5);[476] Civil War service enl. Pvt., Co. K, 9th Va. Inf.,04/20/1861 at Portsmouth, occ. Clerk; discharged spring 1862 at Pinner's Pt., Norfolk Co.;[211] SC #9709, 02/04/1887, filed from 312 East Main St., Norfolk, Norfolk Co., VA; states he returned to Virginia from Mexico by ship *"Herman;"* since discharge res. Portsmouth, Norfolk, Richmond and Petersburg, VA, and Philadelphia, Pa.;[474] phys. desc. age 57 (1885), 5'9", light complexion, blue eyes, light hair, occ. Bookkeeper, at enlistment occ. was Farmer;[474] names daughter Rose C. Isaacs;[474] Francis L. Benson and Virginius L. Pitts give affidavits in pension claim;[474] filed for a pension increase 02/01/1900 and states he is a *"Collector"* [Life Insurance Agent] for Security Mutual Life Insurance Co.;[474] d. 12/06/1901 Norfolk, VA,[477] bur. Cedar Grove Cemetery, Portsmouth, VA; wid. Elizabeth J., WC #12719, 12/23/1901, 28th St. Park Place, Norfolk, Norfolk Co., VA; states her husband was employed in *"Gentleman's Clothing;"* from VA;[477] (EJC b. 01/05/1834 Bell's Mill, Norfolk Co., VA, d. 01/10/1907).[477]

**Crist, Andrew H.**, Pvt., LIC; b. 06/28/1826, Greenbrier Co., VA;[478] enl. Mex. War service 11/30/1846 Staunton, VA, age 20; sick 08/1847; discharged 09/13/1847 on Surgeon's Certificate of Disability; m. Elizabeth Jane McClintic, 10/30/1851, Frankfort, Greenbrier Co., VA;[478] Civil War service Pvt., Co. C, 135th VA Militia;[202] Pvt., Co. K, 14th Va. Cav., enl. 01/29/1862 Blue Sulphur Springs, VA, absent 04/1862 on leave, absent 06/1862 sick, discharged 07/16/1862 over age of conscription;[479] POW Camp Chase, Ohio 08/1862 – 09/1862, age 36;[480] c. 1860 res. Lewisburg, Greenbrier Co., VA, age 37, occ. Farmer, w. Elizabeth J. (23), son Robert M. (8), Herbert (2), Lucy (1/12);[481] c. 1870 res. Lewisburg, Greenbrier Co., WV, age 44, occ. Tailor;[482]c. 1880 res. Springfield Dist., Monroe Co., WV, single, age 53, occ. Tailor;[483] SC #16732, 07/05/1888, filed from Hinton, Summers Co., WV; since discharge res. Greenbrier Co., Monroe Co., and Summers Co., WV;[478] phys. desc. at enl. age 20, 5'7", dark complexion, black hair, gray eyes., occ. Tailor;[478] d. 05/23/1889, Hinton, Summers Co., WV, bur. Hinton Burying Ground;[484] wid. Elizabeth J., WC #8151, 06/25/1891, filed from Doudton, Pendleton Co., KY; OW IA #20835 rejected; (EMC b. 05/26/1828).[484]

**Crocket, William S.**, Pvt., Co. D; enl. Mex. War service 01/25/1847, Petersburg, VA, age 18; pres. 02/1847; pres. 04/1847; pres. 06/1847; pres. 08/1847, pay stopped for: 1 cap-$.95[1/2], 1 pr. pants-$2.28, 2 cotton shirts-$.86, 1 pr. shoes-$1.22; pres. 10/1847, pay stopped for: 1 cap-$.95[1/2], 1 jacket-$2.66, 1 pr. pants-$2.28, 2 flannel shirts-$1.80, 4 cotton shirts-$1.72, 1 pr. drawers-$.35[1/2], 2 pr. socks-$.49, 1 pr. shoes-$1.22, 1 blanket-$2.22; pres. 12/1847, pay stopped for: 1 pr. pants-$2.28, 2 cotton shirts-$.86, 1 pr drawers-$.35[1/2], 2 pr. socks-$.49, 1 pr. shoes-$1.22, 1 blanket-$2.22, 1 overcoat-$6.93[1/2]; pres. 04/1848, pay stopped for: 1 set of picks & brushes-$.12, 1 cap-$.95[1/2], 1 pr. pants-$2.28, 1 blanket-$2.22, 1 pr. shoes-$1.22; pres. 08/1847, BLW sent to Petersburg, VA; c. 1850 res. Petersburg, Dinwiddie Co., VA, age 21, occ. None, w. Mary (23).[485]

**Cropp, Alexander J.**, Pvt., Co. M; enl. Mex. War service 08/07/1847 Lynchburg, VA, age 29; pres. 09/1847; pres. 11/1847, reduced to ranks from 3rd Cpl.; pres. 12/1847; pres. 02/1848; sick 04/1848; pres. 08/1848; BLW sent to Farersville, VA

VIRGINIA VOLUNTEERS IN MEXICO

**Crossley, John**, Pvt., *Recruit Co.*, enl. Mex. War service 01/03/1848 Alexandria, VA , age 39; pres. 02/1848; pres. 04/1848; pres. 06/1848; BLW sent to Alexandria, VA

**Crowder, Armstead Mann**, Pvt., Co. M; b. 02/09/1821;[486] enl. Mex. War service 09/07/1847 Nottoway, VA, age 26; pres. 10/1847; pres. 11/1847; pres. 12/1847; sick 02/1848; pres. 04/1848; pres. 08/1848; BLW sent to Nottoway C.H., VA; m. Bethany Jane Bell, 03/23/1854, Knox Co., TN;[486, 487] SC #535, 02/11/1887, filed from Andersonville, Anderson Co., TN; Richard D. Willis gave affidavit in pension claim;[486] d. 11/05/1904, Andersonville, TN;[488] wid. Bethany Jane, WC #13963, 11/16/1904, filed from Clinton, Anderson Co., TN; (BBC b. 07/31/1837, d. 12/19/1906).[488]

**Crowder, James B.**, Pvt., Co. D; enl. Mex. War service 01/05/1847, Petersburg, VA, age 24; pres. 02/1847; pres. 04/1847; absent 06/1847 left sick in Hosp. Monterey, Mex. 06/22/1847; discharged 07/31/1847 Monterey, Mex. on Surgeon's Certificate of Disability.

**Crowl, Jacob**, Pvt., Co. H; enl. Mex. War service 12/19/1846, Berkeley, VA, age 30; pres. 04/1847; pres. 06/1847; pres. 08/1847; pres. 10/1847, pay stopped for: 1 forage cap-$.95$^{1/2}$, 1 pr. pants-$2.28, 3 cotton shirts-$1.29, 2 flannel shirts-$1.80, 2 pr. socks-$.49, 1 blanket-$2.22; pres. 12/1847, pay stopped for: 1 pr. pants-$2.28, 1 cotton shirt-$.43, 1 pr. drawers-$.35$^{1/2}$, 1 pr. shoes-$1.22, 2 pr. socks-$.49; pres. 02/1848, pay stopped for: 1 cotton shirt-$.43, 2 pr. drawers-$.71, 1 pr. shoes-$1.22; pres. 04/1848; pres. 07/1848, pay stopped for: 2 gun slings-$.48, 2 brush & picks-$.24, 1 waist belt-$.21, 1 bayonet scabbard & frog-$.56, BLW sent to Martinsburg, VA; [a Jacob Crowl m. Emily Daylong 02/16/1850, Berkeley Co., VA][489]

**Crump, Andrew C.**, Pvt., Co. A; enl. Mex. War service 12/14/1846 Richmond, VA, age 22; discharged 06/02/1847 for disease by order Maj. Gen. Taylor.

**Cunningham, Frederick A.**, Pvt., Co. F; b. South Carolina; enl. Mex. War service 01/26/1847, Portsmouth, VA, age 19; pres. 06/1847; pres. 08/1847; pres. 10/1847, pay stopped for: 1 pr. overalls-$2.28, 3 pr. shoes-$3.66, 1 forage cap-$.95$^{1/2}$; 4 cotton shirts-$1.72, 6 pr. socks-$1.57, 1 overcoat-$6.93$^{1/2}$, 3 pr. drawers-1.06$^{1/2}$; pres. 12/1847; pres. 02/1848, pay stopped for: 1 forage cap-$.95$^{1/2}$, 1 pr. drawers-$.35$^{1/2}$, 1 infantry jacket-$2.66, 1 pr. shoes-$1.22, 1 bed sack-$1.07; pres. 04/1848, $.53 due him from 10/1847 muster roll; pres. 08/1848, pay stopped for: 1 bayonet scabbard-$.56, 1 gun sling-$.18, 4 shirts-$1.76, 2 blankets-$4.50, 2 pr. shoes-$2.32, BLW sent to Washington, D.C.; c. 1850 res. Portsmouth, VA, age 24, occ. Printer;[490] m. Margaret A. Okay, 04/03/1856, Washington, D.C.

**Cunningham, John**, Fifer, Co. K; enl. Mex. War service Jefferson Co., VA 01/01/1847, age 45; discharged 02/16/1847 when appointed Fife Major; c. 1850 res. Charlestown, VA, age 55, occ. Laborer, w. Mary (59).[491]

**Curry, Stephen C.**, Pvt., Co. A; m. Maria E. Mullen, 04/08/1841, Fredericksburg, VA;[492] enl. Mex. War service 11/18/1846 Richmond, VA, age 27; pres. 12/1846 - 04/1847; pres. 06/1847; pres. 08/1847; pres. 10/1847, pay stopped for clothing: 2 pr. wool overalls-$4.56, 1 cap-$.95$^{1/2}$, 1 pr. shoes-$1.22, 3 pr. stockings-$.73$^{1/2}$, 2 cotton shirts-$.86, 1 pr. drawers-$.35$^{1/2}$, 1 blanket-$2.22; pres. 12/1847, pay stopped for clothing: 1 pr. shoes-$1.22, 2 blanket-$4.44; 2 pr. drawers-$.71, 2 flannel shirts-$1.80, 2 pr. socks-$.49; pres. 02/1848, pay stopped for: 1 pr. wool overalls-$2.28, 1 pr. shoes-$1.22, 1 pick & brush-$.12; pres. 04/1848, prom. 4$^{th}$ Cpl. 03/19/1848, pay stopped for: 1 wool jacket; 07/1848, pay stopped for: musket sling-$.16; BLW sent to, Fredericksburg, VA; Civil War service 2$^{nd}$ Lt., Curtis' Arty.(Fredericksburg) 6/61–9/61;[493] wid. Maria E., WC #1773, 06/10/1887, from VA

**Custer, Henry**, Pvt., Co. I; enl. Mex. War service 01/10/1847 Richmond, VA, age 36; pres. 02/1847; pres. 04/1847; pres. 06/1847; pres. 08/1847; absent 10/1847, pay stopped for: 1 pr. drawers-$.35$^{1/2}$, 1 pr. pants-$2.28, 1 flannel shirt-$.90, 1 pr. socks-$.24$^{1/2}$; pres. 12/1847, pay stopped for: 1 pr. socks-$.24$^{1/2}$, 1 pr. pants-$2.28, 1 blanket-$2.22, 1 jacket-$2.66; pres. 02/1848; pres. 04/1848; pres. 08/1848; BLW sent to Rocky Mount, Franklin Co., VA; [Civil War service a Henry Custer enl. Pvt., Aldredge's Co., 47$^{th}$ Btln. Va. Cav. 10/29/1863; afterwards AWOL.][494]

OFF TO WAR

**Daniel, Theophilus**, Pvt., Co. M; b. c. 1826, son of Mabry & Rebecca Daniel;[495] enl. Mex. War service 09/10/1847, Forksville, VA, age 22; NFR; m. Susan Robinson 12/22/1853, Brunswick Co., VA;[496] c. 1850 res. Brunswick Co., VA age 22, occ. Overseer;[497] c. 1860, res. Brunswick Co. VA, occ. Laborer, age 34, w. Martha S. (32) children John E.W. (6) & Laura E. (9/12);[498] Civil War service enl. Pvt., Co. F, 12$^{th}$ Va. Inf. 04/01/1862 at Brunswick Co., VA discharged 05/10/1862 as overage;[21] conscripted as a Pvt., Co. G, 17$^{th}$ Va. Inf. 10/10/1863 in Brunswick Co., VA deserted 11/1863, absent in arrest at Petersburg, VA, re-arrested 01/15/1864, tried for desertion by court-martial at Petersburg, VA sentenced to be shot sent to the regiment at Kinston, NC, executed (shot) for desertion 04/07/1864 at Kinston, NC.[63, 63,499]

**Dantt, William T.**, Pvt., Co. L; b. 1828; enl. Mex. War service 03/01/1847 Fairfax C.H., VA, age 19; pres. 06/1847; pres. 08/1847; pres. 10/1847, pay stopped for: 1 F. Cap .95, 1 pr. Pants 2.28; pres. 12/1847, pay stopped for: 1 pr. shoes-$1.22, 1 flannel shirt-$.90, 1 blanket-$2.22, 3 pr. drawers-$1.06$^{1/2}$, 1 pr. socks-$.24$^{1/2}$; pres. 02/1848, pay stopped for: 1 jacket-$ 2.66; pres. 04/1848, pay stopped for: 2 Flannel Shirts 1.55; pres. 07/1848; BLW sent to William L. Dantt, Washington City, D.C.; m. Sarah E. Watson 3/13/1849, Washington, D.C.;[500] c. 1850 res. Alexandria, VA, age 21, occ. Laborer, w. Sarah (19);[501] Civil War service Pvt., President's Mounted Guard (Capt. Samuel W. Owen's D.C. Cavalry) 04/1861 – 07/19/1861;[502] c. 1863 occ. "*grocer and produce, H north cor 8$^{th}$ west, h do;'*"[503] c. 1865 occ. Carpenter, res. 520 N St. north;[504] c. 1869, occ. Grocer, res. 524 N. St. n.;[505] c.1870 occ. Grocer, 907 N St., N.W.[506]

**Danzy, Robert**, *Kellam's Co., Not on Muster Rolls*, wid. Eliza. J., WA #8370, 09/20/1889, from KY

**Davey, Henry**, Pvt., Co. K, enl. Mex. War service Jefferson Co., VA 12/27/1846, age 24; pres. 06/1847; pres. 08/1847, to forfeit 1 mos. pay by order of garrison court-martial; pres. 10/1847, pay stopped for: 1 pr. shoes-$1.22, 1 pr. overalls-$2.28, 1 cotton shirt-$.43, 2 pr. drawers-$.71, 3 pr. socks-$.73$^{1/2}$, 2 flannel shirts-$1.80, 1 greatcoat-$6.93$^{1/2}$, 1 blanket-$2.22, 1 cap-$.95$^{1/2}$; pres. 12/1847, pay stopped for: 1 jacket-$2.66, 1 pr. overalls-$2.28, 1 pr. socks-$.24$^{1/2}$, 1 cotton shirt-$.43, 1 flannel shirt-$.90; pres. 04/1848, pay stopped for: 1 jacket-$2.66, 1 pr. shoes-$1.22, 1 bed sack-$1.07$^{1/2}$, 1 cotton shirt-$.43; pres. 07/1848, pay stopped for: 1 cartridge box plate-$.10, 1 pick & brush-$.12, 1 screw driver-$.25; BLW sent to Charlestown, Jefferson Co., VA; c. 1850 res. Loudoun Co., VA, age 23, occ. Tailor;[507] Civil War service Pvt., Co. E, 68$^{th}$ Ill. Inf.; SC #10995, 07/21/1887, from AR; LW IC #605593 [see Civil War pension claim].

**Davis, Augustus**, 1$^{st}$ Corp., Co. L; b. 1828; enl. Mex. War service 03/01/1847 Fairfax C.H., VA, age 19; pres. 06/1847; pres. 08/1847; pres. 10/1847, prom. 3$^{rd}$ Cpl. from Pvt. 09/01/1847, pay stopped for: 1 pr. shoes-$1.22; pres. 12/1847, pay stopped for: 1 Jacket 2.66, 1 pr. Pants 2.28, 1 pr. Shoes 1.22, 2 cotton shirts-$.86, 1 Blanket 2.21, 3 pr. drawers-$1.06, 2 pr. socks-$.49; pres. 02/1848, pay stopped for: 1 Brush & Pick .12; pres. 04/1848, pay stopped for: 1 pr. Shoes 1.16, 2 Cotton Shirts .88; pres. 07/1848; BLW sent to Washington City, D.C.; m. Mary Stanley 9/29/1850, Washington, D.C.;[508] res. Washington, D.C. 1863-1890;[509] c. 1863 occ. Bricklayer, res. 492 I St., n.;[510] c. 1869 occ. Bricklayer, res. 574 H. St., n.;[511] c. 1870 res. 4$^{th}$ Ward, Washington, D.C.;[512] 1874 occ. Builder, res. 461 H St., NW, Wash., D.C.,[513] SC #8594, 03/22/1887, wid. Mary A., WC #7089, 04/07/1890, both from D.C.; [pension file not found].

**Davis, Charles P.**, Pvt., *Recruit Co.*, enl. Mex. War service 02/24/1848 Lynchburg, VA; pres. 06/1848; BLW sent to Lynchburg, VA

**Davis, James H.**, 1$^{st}$ Cpl., Co. D; enl. Mex. War service 01/04/1847, Petersburg, VA, age 28; pres. 02/1847; pres. 04/1847; pres. but sick 06/1847, prom. 2$^{nd}$ Cpl. 06/07/1847; pres. 08/1847, pay stopped for: 1 pr. wool pants-$2.28, 2 cotton shirts-$.86, 1 pr. shoes-$1.22; pres. 10/1847, pay stopped for: 3 pr. socks-$.73$^{1/2}$; pres. 12/1847, pay stopped for: 1 jacket-$2.66, 1 pr. pants-$2.28, 1 pr. socks-$.24$^{1/2}$, 1 cotton shirt-$.43, 1 pr. shoes-$1.22, 1 blanket-$2.22; pres. 04/1848; pres. 08/1847, BLW sent to Hicks Ford, Greensville Co., VA; m. Frances A. Snead 02/07/1850, Oak Grove Church, Northampton Co., NC;[514] c. 1850 res. Northampton

# VIRGINIA VOLUNTEERS IN MEXICO

Co., NC age 32, occ. Clerk, w. Frances A. (16), Sarah M. (19), Benjamin L. (21) Clerk;[515] [Civil War service a James H. Davis, b. c. 1821, Halifax Co., VA, enl. Pvt., Co. F. 38$^{th}$ Va. Inf. 06/04/1861 at Republican Grove, VA; absent on furlough 08/31/1861; discharged 11/19/1861 due to lung illness; desc. 6'0", light complex., light hair, blue eyes, occ. Farmer;[516] enl. Pvt., Co. I, 17$^{th}$ Va. Inf. 08/28/1863 at Richmond, VA, a res. of Halifax Co., captured 03/31/1865 at Dinwiddie C.H., VA; sent to Pt. Lookout, MD; released on oath 06/11/1865;][63] d. 03/14/1874 *"turpidity of liver,"* Shell Landing, Northampton Co., NC; wid. Fannie A., WC #5646 04/02/1887, filed from Wallace, Panola Co., MS; since discharge res. Northampton & Halifax Cos., NC 15 yrs. and Petersburg & Lynchburg *"a number of years;"* phys. desc. of soldier at enlistment 5'10", occ. Farmer, brown hair, brown eyes, dark complexion, age 22; Pvt. Lewis H. Foster gave affidavit; (FAD d. 04/19/1904).

**Davis, James L.**, Pvt., Co. A; a James L. Davis, of Richmond, VA, m. 07/1842, Eliza J. Thompson, dau. of John S. Thompson of Cumberland Co., VA;[517] enl. Mex. war service 12/31/1846 Richmond, VA, age 31; pres. until sick 04/1847 – 06/1847, in Hosp. at Matamoros sent there from Camargo, Mex. 04/02/1847; court-martialed 07/27/1847, *Charge #1: Neglect of Duty;* (he failed to report for guard duty); Charge 2, *Disobedience of Orders* (positively refused to report for duty by saying *"he would go under Guard, but not on Guard,"* plead not guilty to both charges; was sentenced to *"police his company parade ground and sinks for one month under supervision of an NCO and that $3.50 be stopped from his pay*; pres. 08/1847; fined $3.50 by order (#69) of regtl. court-martial 08/1847; sick 10/1847, pay stopped for clothing: 1 blanket-$2.22. 1 pr. wool overalls-$2.28, 1 cap-$.95$^{1/2}$, 1 pr. shoes-$1.22, 1 wool jacket-$2.66, 1 cotton shirts-$.43, 1 great coat-$6.93$^{1/2}$; in confinement 12/1847, pay stopped for clothing: 1 great coat-$6.93$^{1/2}$, 1 pr. drawers-$.35$^{1/2}$; Court-martialed 02/02/1847 Buena Vista, Mexico, *Charge #1, Violation of the Ninth Article of War; Specification #1: In this that he the said Private James L. Davis, Co. H, Va. Regt of Vols., on or about the 22$^{nd}$ of November 1847, did strike 2$^{nd}$ Lt. William Gravatt, of the Va. Regt., and offer violence against him whilst he, the said Lt. Gravatt, was in the execution of his office. This at Buena Vista, Mexico. Specification #2: In this that he the said Pvt. James L. Davis, Co. A, Va. Regt., did on or about the 22$^{nd}$ of November 1847, disobey the lawful command of 2$^{nd}$ Lt. William Gravatt, his superior officer, whilst on the march from Camp Buena Vista, Mexico to Agua Nueva, Mexico and did strike and offer violence against him whilst in the execution of his office. This at Buena Vista, Mexico. To which charge and specifications the prisoner pleaded Not Guilty. 2$^{nd}$ Lt. William Gravatt, Va. Regt of Vols., a witness for the prosecution being duly sworn, says: On the evening of the 22$^{nd}$ of November 1847, on the march from this Camp to Agua Neuva, after the Indians, I ordered Pvt. Davis, the prisoner, to take the step. He turned round to me and replied in a very abusive manner 'I have the step.' I told him a second time to take the step, that he did not have it. He again replied to me in a very abrupt manner that he 'had the step.' I then said to him 'damn you, do you know who you are talking to? I'll run my sword through you' The prisoner replied, 'Yes, God Damn you. I know whom I am talking to,' and as he said this, he jumped out of ranks and struck me with his musket across the hand and head. I do not recollect his striking me more than once, the musket was taken out of his hand by Corpl. Ball, and when I made at him with my sword he ran. Question by the Judge Advocate: When you ordered the prisoner to take step, did he at anytime obey your order? Answer: No. He did not. Question by the Court: On what occasion was this march you alluded to from Buena Vista to Agua Nueva? Answer: It was a command ordered by Col. Hamtramck after the Indians. Question by the Court: When you used the expression to the prisoner, :I'll run my sword through you', did you accompany it by any gesture by which to impress him with the idea that you would put your threat into execution? Answer: I think it probable I did. I intended to strike him. Question by the Court: Was it from the insolence of the prisoner towards you, or for his refusal to obey your order, that you threatened to rum him through? Answer: It was for both his insolence and his refusal to obey my order. After deliberation the*

OFF TO WAR

*court found the prisoner Guilty of the Charge and Specifications. Sentenced him to be confined in the Provost Guard with a ball and chain attached to his leg and kept at hard labor during the continuance of the war with Mexico and then be dishonorably discharged from service;*[518] in confinement 02/1848; in confinement 04/1848.

**Davis, James P.**, 3rd Cpl., *Preston's Co.*; enl. Mex. War service 12/01/1846 Montgomery Co., VA, age 19; absent 04/1847 left sick in hosp. at Ft. Monroe, VA since 02/27/1847; absent 06/1847 left sick in hosp. at Ft. Monroe, VA, prom. 3rd Cpl.; d. 03/03/1847 at Ft. Monroe, VA, *"of smallpox."*[243]

**Davis, Jehu**, Pvt., *Preston's Co.*; enl. Mex. War service 12/06/1846 Montgomery Co., VA, age 18; pres. 04/1847; pres. 06/1847; pres. 08/1847; pres. 10/1847, pay stopped for: 1 cotton shirt-$.43, 1 blanket-$2.22; absent 12/1847, on detached service as Wagoneer in QM Dept. since 12/11/1847, pay stopped for: 1 pr. overalls-$2.28, 2 pr. socks-$.49, 1 cap-$.95$^{1/2}$, 1 pr. drawers-$.35$^{1/2}$, 1 cotton shirt-$.43; absent 02/1848, on detached service as a Teamster in QM Dept., pay stopped for: 1 pr. shoes-$1.22; pres. 04/1848; pres. 07/1848, pay stopped for: 1 cap-$.95$^{1/2}$, 1 jacket-$2.37, 1 gun sling-$.18; BLW sent to Christiansburg, VA c/o Fleming Gardner.

**Davis, Thomas**, Pvt., Co. C; enl. Mex. War service 12/01/1846, Bowling Green, VA, age 43; deserted 01/02/1847 Richmond, VA

**Davis, William K.**, Pvt., Co. B; enl. 09/19/1847, Warrenton, VA, age 19; pres. 02/1848, 6 mos. clothing pd. in advance; pres. 04/1848; pres. 08/1848, BLW sent to Middleburg, Loudoun Co., VA

**Daws, Louis**, Pvt., Co. A; enl. Mex. War service 11/18/1846 Richmond, VA, age 24; pres. 12/1846 - 04/1847; sick in quarters 06/1847; pres. 08/1847; fined $ 5.00 by order (#72) of regtl. court-martial 08/1847; pres. 10/1847, pay stopped for clothing: 1 pr. wool overalls-$2.28, 1 cap-$.95$^{1/2}$, 4 pr. stockings-$.98, 2 flannel shirts-$1.80, 1 pr. shoes-$1.22, 1 great coat-$6.93$^{1/2}$; fined 10/1847 $7.00 by order (#103) of regtl. court-martial; pres. 12/1847, pay stopped for clothing: 1 pr. wool overalls-$2.28, 1 pr. drawers-$.35$^{1/2}$, 2 flannel shirt-$1.80, 1 pr. shoes-$1.22, 1 pr. socks-$.24$^{1/2}$, 1 blanket-$2.22; pres. 02/1848, pay stopped for: 1 pr. shoes-$1.22; detached service 04/1848 with QM Dept. in Saltillo, Mex. since 03/21/1848; in confinement 07/1848 to be dishonorably discharged from the service by order (#63) of a genl. court-martial is confined in the Provost Guard during the continuance of the war with Mexico; BLW sent to Richmond, VA

**Day, James**, 4th Corp., Co. L; b. 1825; enl. Mex. War service 03/16/1847 Alexandria., VA, age 22; pres. 06/1847; pres. 08/1847; pres. 10/1847, pay stopped for: 1 F Cap .95, 1 pr. Pants 2.28, 1 pr. Shoes 1.22; pres. 12/1847, pay stopped for: 1 jacket-$2.66, 1 pr. pants-$2.28, 1 pr shoes-$1.22, 2 flannel shirts-$1.80, 1 cotton shirts-$.43, 1 blanket-$2.22, 1pr. drawers-$.35$^{1/2}$, 2 pr. socks-$.49; pres. 02/1848; pres. 04/1848, pay stopped for: 1 pr. Shoes 1.16; pres. 04/1848; pres. 07/1848; BLW sent to Alexandria, VA;  Civil War service enl. Pvt., Co. E, 17th Va. Inf. 04/17/1861 at Alexandria, VA, age 35, occ. Blacksmith; detailed at Manassas as a Blacksmith 1861-1862; detached to QM Dept. 1862-1864; deserted 6/64, but postwar roster (c. 1880) shows him detached at Lynchburg, VA, now dead.[63]

VIRGINIA VOLUNTEERS IN MEXICO

Day, John Thomas, Pvt., Co. L; b. 05/21/1828, Calvert Co., MD son of Robert & Mary Day; enl. Mex. War service 03/01/1847 Fairfax C.H., VA, age 20; pres. 06/1847; pres. 08/1847; pres. 10/1847, pay stopped for: 1 forage cap-$.95, 1 pr. pants-$2.28; pres. 12/1847, pay stopped for: 1 jacket-$2.66, 1 pr. pants-$2.28, 2 flannel shirts-$1.80, 3 cotton shirts-$1.29, 1 blanket-$2.22, 1 pr. socks-$.24$^{1/2}$; pres. 02/1848; pres. 04/1848; on detached service as a ??? since 04/07/1848 by order of Major Early; BLW sent to John Day, Alexandria, VA; c. 1860 res. Fairfax Co., VA, age 30, occ. Physician, w. Elizabeth (29); [519] voted for Secession 04/23/1861 at Dranesville, Fairfax Co., VA[520] arrested 11/27/1861 and confined in Old Capitol Prison, Washington, D.C., charged with murdering Union pickets and persecuting Union men in Fairfax Co. Allegedly led a party to Big Falls on the Potomac River, where they killed four Union soldiers. Showed an 18 inch knife which he had made at the Blacksmith shop to cut out the hearts of Union men;[521] known in the community as "Dr. Jack;" c. 1892 charter member of the Fairfax County Med. Soc. Elected the first Treasurer; Founding member of St. Timothy's Episcopal Church, Herndon, VA; d. 07/20/1893, *Heart Disease*, Dranesville, Fairfax Co.; bur. Chestnut Grove Cem., Herndon, VA;[522] 08/11/1893 a stained glass window placed in St. Timothy's Church (Herndon, VA) in his memory.

Photo courtesy Fairfax City Regional Library, Fairfax, VA.

Dean, James T., Pvt., Co. L; b. c. 1825; enl. Mex. War service 03/06/1847 Fairfax C.H., VA, age 22; absent 06/1847 left sick in hospital at Point Isabel from 04/29/1847; pres. 08/1847 reduced from Drummer; sick 12/1847, pay stopped for: 1 cap-$.95$^{1/2}$, 1 pr. shoes-$1.22, 1 cotton shirt-$.43, 3 pr. drawers-$1.06$^{1/2}$, 1 pr. socks-$.24$^{1/2}$; desc., age 22, 5'6$^{1/2}$", fair complexion, blue eyes, light hair, occ. Shoemaker;[26] discharged 03/18/1848 at Buena Vista, Mex. as a minor.[72]

Deemer, Nicholas J., Co. A; Catherine Taylor 10/20/1847 Louisville, KY; enl. Mex. War service 11/25/1846 Richmond, VA, age 26; pres. until sick 04/1847, in Hosp. at Monterey, Mex. since 04/27/1847; discharged 06/18/1847 for disease by order Maj. Gen. Taylor; d. 01/26/1875 Louisville, KY; wid. Catherine, WC #2595, 06/15/1887, filed from 1008 16$^{th}$ St. Louisville, Jefferson Co., KY (CTD b. c. 1823 Steubenville, OH, d. 06/28/1912).[523]

Deneal, James C., Pvt., Co. L; b. 1825; pres. 06/1847; discharged 08/30/1847 at Saltillo, Mex. on Surgeon's Certificate of Disability;[72] m/1 Elizabeth McGranahan, date unknown (d. 05/01/1857, Lafayette, IN, while the family was moving from Fountain Co. to Tippecanoe Co., IN, bur. Lafayette Cem.), m/2 Harriet McGranahan (sister of Elizabeth) 12/15/1859, Vermilion Co., IL; c. 1880 res. Newell, Vermilion Co., IL, age 55, occ. Farmer, list as sick *"Billious,"* b. D.C., w. Harriet (39), b. MD, son David (18) son Samuel (16), son Walter (9), son Austin (6), son Harry (7/12);[524] SC #739, 02/04/1887, filed from State Line City, Warren Co., IN, d. 03/24/1906 *"Nephritis;"*[525] bur. Walnut Corner Cemetery, Vermilion Co., IL;[526] wid. Harriet, WC #14437, 04/11/1906, filed from Danville, IL; In a deposition, Harriet states that after her sisters death and subsequent marriage to James C. Deneal she raised her sisters two sons from infancy; (HMD d. 05/27/1917, Danville, IL).[527]

Diamond, John, Pvt., Co. M; enl. Mex. War service 07/07/1847 Lynchburg, VA, age 29; pres. 09/1847; pres. 11/1847; pres. 12/1847; confined 02/1848 since 02/26/1848, pay stopped for: 1 blanket-$2.22, 1 cotton shirt-$.43, 1 drum head-$.90; in confinement 04/1848; deserted

115

OFF TO WAR

07/05/1848 at the Mouth of the Rio Grande, pay stopped for: 1 musket & accoutrements complete-$16.22, 1 pr. shoes-$1.22; [a John Diamond, b. 04/17/1817, Giles Co., VA, son of William Clay & Malinda Diamond, m. Alicey Muncy, 01/03/1839, Giles Co., d. 08/01/1881, Lawrence Co., KY][528]

**Diddep, Archibald W.**, 3$^{rd}$ Cpl., Co. G; enl. Mex. War service 11/18/1846 Richmond, VA, age 36; pres. 06/1847; pres. 08/1847; pres. 10/1847, pay stopped for: 1 pr. overalls-$2.28, 1 cotton shirt-$.43, 1 pr. drawers-$.35$^{1/2}$, 1 shoes-$1.22, 3 pr. socks-$.73$^{1/2}$, 1 forage cap-$.95$^{1/2}$; pres. 12/1847, prom. 4$^{th}$ Cpl., pay stopped for: 2 cotton shirts-$.86, 2 flannel shirts-$1.80, 1 blanket-$2.22, 1 jacket-$2.66, 1 pr. socks-$.24$^{1/2}$; pres. 02/1848, prom. 3$^{rd}$ Cpl., pay stopped for: 1 brush & pick-$.12, overcharged for 1 jacket-$2.66 on 12/1847 muster roll; pres. 04/1848; pres. 08/1848, pay stopped for: 1 pr. shoes-$1.16, 1 cartridge box plate-$.10; BLW sent to Richmond, VA

**Didlake, Andrew J.**, Pvt., Co. G; enl. Mex. War service 11/28/1846 Richmond, VA, age 26; pres. 06/1847, reduced from 3$^{rd}$ Cpl.; absent 08/1847 on detached service as a Clerk in Adjt. office since 08/29/1847; absent 10/1847, on detached service as Clerk in Actg. Asst. Adjt. Office, pay stopped for: 1 pr. overalls-$2.28, 2 cotton shirts-$.86, 1 pr. drawers-$.35$^{1/2}$, 2 shoes-$2.44, 5 pr. socks-$1.22$^{1/2}$, 1 forage cap-$.95$^{1/2}$; pres. 12/1847, reduced to ranks at his own request, pay stopped for: 2 pr. shoes-$2.44, 2 pr. pants-$4.56, 1 overcoat-$6.93$^{1/2}$; pres. 02/1848, pay stopped for: 1 jacket-$2.66, overcharged for 1 overcoat-$6.93$^{1/2}$ on 12/1847 muster roll; pres. 04/1848; pres. 08/1848, pay stopped for: 1 cartridge box-$.60, 1 cartridge box belt plate-$.10; BLW sent to Richmond, VA; Civil War service conscript assigned as Pvt., Co. K, 8$^{th}$ Va. Inf. 03/13/1864; pres. 12/31/1864; captured 04/06/1865 Sandy Creek; released on oath from Pt. Lookout, MD 06/26/1865; desc. 5'11", brown hair, blue eyes.[529]

**Dillard, John Quincy Adams**, Pvt., Co. M; b. 04/03/1825, Amherst Co., VA;[530] enl. Mex. War service 08/10/1847 Stapleton, VA, age 25; pres. 09/1847; pres. 11/1847; deserted 12/07/1847 at Ft. Monroe, VA; I *"was taken very sick [fever] and returned home on furlough given by commanding officers and recommended by Hospital Physician. I returned before my furlough expired, but there had been a sudden call for the company and they had left before I got there. I then reported to the Governor. It was impossible to send me on alone, so I was honorably discharged;"*[531] *"Private J.Q.A. Dillard, of Capt. Talbot's Company of Virginia Volunteers, left behind at the departure of his company, is hereby discharged [from] the service of the United States in compliance with the request of his friends – R. Jones, Adjt. Genl.;"*[532] c. 1850 res. Amherst Co., VA, age 26, occ. Lawyer, w. Elizabeth H. (26), dau. Narcissa (3), son James L. (1);[533] m. Mary E. Turner, dau. of Wm. S. Turner, before 1851;[534] c. 1860 res. Stapleton, Amherst Co., VA, age 34, occ. Farmer, w. Mary E. (29), son William T., (7), son John F. (3/12);[535] Civil War service enl. Pvt., Co. G, 51$^{st}$ Va. Inf.; captured Waynesboro, VA 03/02/1865; sent to Harper's Ferry, to Winchester, to Ft. Delaware 03/12/1865; released 06/14/1865; desc. 5'101/2", light complex., light hair, blue eyes;[536] c. 1870 res. Stapleton, Amherst Co., VA, age 45, occ. Farmer, w. Mary E. (39), son Willie T. (17), son John F. (10), bro.? Samuel Dillard (51);[537] SC #16733, 02/28/1887, filed from Stapleton, Amherst Co., VA; phys. desc. 5'10", age 62 [1887], light complexion, blue eyes, auburn hair, occ. Farmer; c. 1893 res. 115 Cabell St., Lynchburg, VA;[530] c. 1902 res. 504 Amherst St., Lynchburg, VA;[530] d. 04/03/1908, Amherst Co., VA;[530] Granddaughter, D.McC. Weekly, of 1124 W. Grace St., Richmond, VA, inquired on August 15, 1949, as to pension for his *"needy widowed daughter."*[538]

**Dixon, Charles C.**, Pvt., Co. M; b. c. 1817; enl. Mex. War service 08/09/1847 Lynchburg, VA, age 33; pres. 09/1847; pres. 11/1847; pres. 12/1847; pres. 02/1848; pres. 04/1848, pay stopped for: 1 pr. shoes-$1.22; m. Sarah Ann Kirby, 08/10/1844, Lynchburg, VA; Civil War service enl. Sgt., Purcell Artillery 05/01/1861 at Richmond, VA; resigned as Sgt. 12/1/1861 and trans. to Dabney Arty;[539] enl. 4$^{th}$ Sgt., (Dabney's), 20$^{th}$ VA Btln. Hvy. Arty, 04/23/1862 in Stafford Co., VA; pres. thru 03/31/1864; nfr;[470] [a Charles C. Dixon res. James City Co., VA, c. 1870,

VIRGINIA VOLUNTEERS IN MEXICO

age 53, occ Deputy Clerk of Court, w. Rosanna H. (43), M.E. (22), Samuel J. (21);[540] d. 06/14/1887.][539]
**Dixon, Henry**, Pvt., Co. I; enl. Mex. War service 02/05/1847 Richmond, VA, age 25; pres. 02/1847; pres. 04/1847; pres. 06/1847; pres. 08/1847; absent 10/1847, pay stopped for: 1 cotton shirt-$.43, 1 pr. shoes-$1.22, 1 flannel shirt-$.90, 1 pr. socks-$.24$^{1/2}$; pres. 12/1847, pay stopped for: 1 pr. socks-$.24$^{1/2}$, 1 pr. pants-$2.28, 1 blanket-$2.22, 1 jacket-$2.66, 2 flannel shirts-$1.80, 1 pr. drawers-$.35$^{1/2}$; absent 02/1848, on detached service in QM Dept., pay stopped for: 1 pr. overalls-$2.28; pres. 04/1848, pay stopped for: 1 blanket; pres. 08/1848, BLW sent to Washington, D.C.
**Doble, Carlise**, Pvt., Co. H; enl. Mex. War service 01/06/1847, Berkeley, VA, age 23; pres. 04/1847; absent 06/1847 as Orderly to Col. Hammtrack & Attendant to public horses at HQ; absent 08/1847 on detached service as Orderly & Attendant to public horses at Brig. HQ; absent 1847, on detached service at Brig HQ, pay stopped for: 1 forage cap-$.95$^{1/2}$, 1 pr. pants-$2.28, 2 cotton shirts-$.86, 2 pr. socks-$.49; absent 12/1847 on detached service as Orderly & Attendant to public horses, pay stopped for: 1 forage cap-$.95$^{1/2}$, 1 jacket-$2.66, 1 pr. pants-$2.28, 2 pr. drawers-$.71, 1 pr. shoes-$1.22, 3 pr. socks-$.73$^{1/2}$, 1 blanket-$2.22; absent 02/1848, on detached service as Orderly & Attendant to public horses; absent 04/1848 on detached service as Orderly & Attendant to public horses; pres. 07/1848, BLW sent to Trenton, NJ.
**Dockerty, George W.**, Pvt., Co. A; enl. 12/05/1846 Richmond, VA, age 24; deserted 01/21/1847 at Old Point, VA
**Dodge, Richard**, Pvt., *Recruit Co.*, enl. Mex. War service 02/25/1848 Charlestown, VA, age 40; pres. 02/1848; pres. 04/1848; pres. 06/1848; BLW sent to Charlestown, Jefferson Co., VA
**Done, William D.**, Pvt., Co. H; b. c. 1828, Philadelphia, Pa.; enl. Mex. War service 01/06/1847, Berkeley, VA, age 19; absent 04/1847 left in Hosp. at Matamoros, Mex. 03/18/1847; pres. 06/1847, left sick in Hosp. at Matamoros, Mex. 03/18/1847; pres. 08/1847; pres. 10/1847, pay stopped for: 2 flannel shirts-$1.80, 1 pr. shoes-$1.22, 2 pr. socks-$.49, 1 greatcoat-$6.93$^{1/2}$; desc., age 19, 5'4", light complexion, blue eyes, dark hair, occ. Printer; discharged 11/28/1847 at Buena Vista, Mex. on Surgeon's Certificate of Disability.[26]
**Donevant, William E.**, Pvt., Co. M; enl. Mex. War service 08/01/1847 Richmond, VA, age 18; pres. 09/1847; pres. 11/1847; pres. 12/1847; pres. 02/1848, pay stopped for: 1 blanket-$2.22, 2 cotton shirts-$.86; pres. 04/1848; pres. 08/1848, pay stopped for: 1 screw driver-$.07, 1 wormer-$.20, 1 gun sling-$.16; BLW sent to Richmond, VA.
**Donnan, James Munroe**, Pvt., Co. E; b. 05/24/1824, Mill Quarter, Amelia Co., VA, son of David & Mary (Stewart) Donnan;[541, 542] enl. Mex. War service 11/30/1846 Petersburg, VA, age 24; pres. 04/1847; pres. 06/1847; pres. 08/1847; Civil War service Pvt. Co. B, 12$^{th}$ Btln. VA Lt. Arty.;[202] pres. 10/1847, pay stopped for: 1 pr. overalls-$2.28, 4 pr. stockings-$.98, 1 pr. drawers-$.71, 1 cap-$.95$^{1/2}$; pres. 12/1847, [illegible]; pres. 02/1848; pres. 04/1848; c. 1850 res. Petersburg, Dinwiddie Co., VA, age 26, occ. Law;[543] m/1 Virginia T. Hubbard date/place unknown c. 1860 res. Petersburg, Dinwiddie Co., VA, age 35, occ. None Listed, w. Virginia (25), son James M., Jr. (4), son C.G. (1), m-i-l Mary T. Hubbard (48);[544] (VTD d. 07/07/1869, Petersburg, VA);[542] c. 1870 res. Petersburg, Dinwiddie Co., VA, age 46, occ. Lawyer, son Charles G., (10), son James M., Jr. (14), son Edward H. (3);[545] m/2 Mary Harrison Williams 08/17/1870, Petersburg, VA, divorced *"adultery,"* 09/18/1879, Petersburg, VA;[542] m/3 Annie Thompson 04/07/1880, Stranraer, Scotland;[542] SC #692, 02/04/1887, filed from 23 Shafer Building Richmond, VA; phys. desc. Age 62, 5'8", fair complexion, blue eyes, brown hair, occ. Lawyer; David A. Weisiger and John Poe, Jr. gave affidavits in pension application; d. 01/14/1893, *Congestion of Lungs*, Richmond, VA, bur. Blandford Cem., Sq. 4, Sec. 1, Ward C, Petersburg, VA;[546] wid. Annie T., WC #11089, 01/26/1893, filed from 220 S. Belvidere St., Richmond, VA; (ATD b. 07/13/1844, Lancashire, England, d. 12/16/1910, Belfast, Ireland);[547] brother of 2$^{nd}$ Lt. Robert Commings Donnan; *"James Munroe Donnan was*

OFF TO WAR

*a prominent lawyer of Petersburg, VA, practicing law with his brother, Alexander Donnan, under the firm name of Alexander and James M. Donnan. He served in the Mexican War of 1846, being a volunteer in Captain F.H. Archer's Company of the Virginia Regiment commanded by Colonel Hamtramck. He was also a volunteer on the Confederate Army, being a member of Martin's Artillery Company of Virginia. He was appointed from the United States to be U.S. Consul at Belfast, Ireland, serving there from 1873 to 1880, when he returned to Virginia. Prior to the Civil War he was a Whig in his political affiliations, whose bitterest political foes were the Democrats, so after the war he would have nothing to do with the Democratic Party and allied himself strongly with the Republican party. He was an exceptionally upright man, strong in his convictions, unflinching in his position, and noted for his courage and firmness of character."* [548]

**Donnan, Robert Commings**, 2$^{nd}$ Lt., Co. A; b. 09/19/1826, Petersburg, VA, son of David & Mary (Stewart) Donnan;[541, 549] enl. Mex. War service 11/18/1848, Richmond, VA, age 20; pres. 12/1846 - 04/1847; pres. 06/1847; resigned 08/11/1847; m/1 Mary Martin; c. 1850 res. Petersburg, Dinwiddie Co., VA, age 24, occ. Merchant, w. Mary (19);[550] c. 1860 res. Petersburg, Dinwiddie Co., VA, age 33, occ. Dep. Sergeant, w. Mary A. (30), son George W. (9), son Reuben R. (5), son Walter C. (2), son James M. (6/12);[551] Civil War service Pegram's Co., VA Lt. Arty.;[202] c. 1870 res. Petersburg, Dinwiddie Co., VA, age 43, occ. Baliff, w. Mary (39), son Reuben R. (15), son Walter C. (12);[552] (MMD d. 05/01/1874, Petersburg, VA); m/2 Hattie Bishop; 11/11/1874, Petersburg, VA;[553] SC #17219, 09/27/1888, filed from Petersburg, Dinwiddie Co., VA; d. 03/12/1892, *cerebral apoplexy*, Petersburg, VA; bur. Blandford Cem., Petersburg, VA;[541] wid. Hattie, WC #8506, 04/19/1892, filed from Petersburg, Dinwiddie Co., VA; (HBD b. 1843 Prince George Co., VA, d. 04/16/1907, Petersburg, VA); brother of Pvt. James Munroe Donnan.

**Donnell, John S.**, Pvt., Co. F; enl. Mex. War service 12/28/1846, Portsmouth, VA, age 19; pres. 06/1847; pres. 08/1847; pres. 10/1847, pay stopped for: 1 pr. overalls-$2.28, 6 cotton shirts-$2.58, 1 forage cap-$.95$^{1/2}$, 4 pr. socks-$.98, 3 pr. shoes-$3.66, 2 pr. drawers-.71, 1 blanket-$2.22; pres. 12/1847; pres. 02/1848, pay stopped for: 1 pr. overalls-$2.28, 3 pr. drawers-$1.06$^{1/2}$, 1 flannel shirt-$.90, 1 blanket-$2.22, 1 bed sack-$1.07; pres. 04/1848; pres. 08/1848, pay stopped for: 1 pr. shoes-$1.16, 4 cotton shirts-$1.76, BLW sent to Portsmouth, VA c/o E.T. Blamire; [Civil War service a John S. Donnell served as a 2$^{nd}$ Lt., Co. D, 26$^{th}$ Pa. Inf. & Capt., Co. I, 91$^{st}$ Pa. Inf.][554] SC #18774, 12/12/1889, from PA.

**Dopleb, Reynold**, Pvt., Co. A; enl. Mex. War service 11/18/1846 Richmond, VA, age 20; pres. until sick 04/1847, in Hosp. at Camargo, Mex. since 04/04/1847; sick in quarters 06/1847; pres. 08/1847; deserted 10/06/1847 at Buena Vista, Mex.

**Dorsey, Benjamin**, Pvt., Co. B; enl. 12/19/1846, Alexandria, VA, age 39; pres. 06/1847; pres. 08/1847; pres. 10/1847, pay stopped for: 1 pr. overalls-$2.28, 5 pr. socks-$1.22$^{1/2}$, 2 cotton shirts-$.86, 2 pr. cotton drawers-$.71; pres. 12/1847, pay stopped for: 1 cap-$.95$^{1/2}$, 1 pr. shoes-$1.22, 1 blanket-$2.22; pres. 02/1848; sick 04/1848; pres. 08/1848, pay stopped for: 1 pick & brush-$.12, 1 screw driver-$.07, 1 wiper-$.20, 1 gun sling-$.16, BLW sent to Westminster, Carroll Co., MD

**Doudge, Soloman B.**, Pvt., Co. E; b. c. 1821, Princess Anne Co., VA, son of Samuel Doudge; m/1 c. 1845 Betsy Ann Robinson, Norfolk, VA; enl. Mex. War service 11/26/1846 Petersburg, VA, age 23; pres. 04/1847; pres. 06/1847; pres. 08/1847; pres. 10/1847, pay stopped for: 1 pr. overalls-$2.28, 1 pr. shoes-$1.22, 2pr. stockings-$.49, 2 cotton shirts-$.86, 2 pr. drawers-$.71, 1 cap-$.95$^{1/2}$; pres. 12/1847 [illegible]; pres. 02/1848, pay stopped for: 1 pr. shoes; pres. 04/1848; m/2 Mary Munden, 10/1848;[555] res. Gates Co., N.C.; Civil War service appointed Capt., Co. H, 5$^{th}$ NC Inf. 05/16/1861; [202] resigned 09/21/1862, by reason of incompetency.[556]

## VIRGINIA VOLUNTEERS IN MEXICO

**Douglas, James S.**, 2nd Lt., Co. B; enl. 11/20/1846, Alexandria, VA; pres. 06/1847; pres. 08/1847; pres. 10/1847; pres. 12/1847; pres. 02/1848; pres. 04/1848; pres. 08/1848; m. Harriet F. Whittington 12/7/1854[557] c. 1870 res. Alexandria, VA, age 45, occ. Clerk at R.R. Depot, w. Harriet L. (33), son Sidney (14).[558]

**Douglas, Thomas H.**, Drummer, Co. K; b. Edenton, NC;[559] enl. Mex. War service Norfolk, VA 01/02/1847, age 18; pres. 06/1847; absent 08/1847 on detached as musician at Saltillo, Mex. since 08/24/1847; absent 10/1847 on detached service as musician in Saltillo, Mex., pay stopped for: 2 pr. drawers-$.71, 4 pr. socks-$.98, 3 cotton shirts-$1.29, 1 pr. overalls-$2.28; pres. 12/1847; pres. 04/1848; pres. 07/1848; BLW sent to Winchester, Frederick Co., VA; m. Eliza Nichols 09/28/1860, Norfolk, Norfolk Co., VA;[559] Civil War service Pvt., Huger's Battery, Norfolk Light Artillery, enl. 04/29/1862 at Norfolk, phys. desc. 5'8", brown hair, brown eyes, fair complexion, absent 06/12/1862 Chimborazo Hosp. No. 2, Richmond "bronchitis & debility," trans. 07/1862 to CSA Gen. Hosp., Danville, VA, pres. 11/18/1862, absent 11/20/1862 Gen. Hosp. No. 7, Richmond, VA, "bronchitis," trans. 02/29/1863 to Camp Winder Gen. Hosp., absent 04/24/1863 Gen. Hosp. Danville, VA "rheumatism," discharged 07/11/1863 on Surgeon's Cert. of Disability "heart disease," surrendered 01/20/1864 at Suffolk, VA, took oath Ft. Monroe, VA, claimed he was a Seaman before the war;[560] c. 1870 res. Portsmouth, Norfolk Co., VA, age 42, occ. House Painter, b. NC, w. Eliza (51);[561] phys. desc. age 58 [1886], dark complexion, dark eyes, dark hair, occ. Painter;[559] d. 04/28/1856, Portsmouth, Norfolk Co., VA;[559] wid. Eliza, WC #73, 02/26/1887, filed from 921 Green St., Portsmouth, Norfolk Co., VA; since discharge res. Norfolk and Portsmouth, VA;[559] (END b. 07/07/1819, Norfolk, VA, d. 1890).[559]

**Doyle, John**, Pvt., Co. A; enl. Mex. War 11/18/1846 Richmond, VA, age 19; pres. 12/1846 – 04/1847; pres. 06/1847; pres. 08/1847; pres. 10/1847, pay stopped for clothing: 1 pr. wool overalls-$2.28, 1 cap-$.95[1/2], 2 pr. stockings-$.49, 2 pr. shoes-$2.44, 1 wool jacket-$2.66; absent sick 12/1847,pay stopped for clothing: 2 pr. socks-$.49, 2 pr. shoes-$2.44, 1 pr. drawers-$.35[1/2], 1 pr. wool overalls-$2.28, 1 blanket-$2.22; pres. 02/1848, pay stopped for: 1 pr. wool overalls-$2.28, 1 pick & brush-$.12; pres. 04/1848; 07/1848, pay stopped for: 1 waist belt plate-$.10, 1 bayonet-$1.44, 1 pr. shoes-$1.16; BLW sent to Richmond, VA

**Doyle, William**, Drummer, Co. B; enl. 12/20/46, Alexandria, VA, age 44; deserted 01/19/1847 Fort Monroe, VA

**Dreury, Jesse C.**, Pvt., Co. A; b. c. 1825; enl. Mex. War service 01/02/1847 Richmond, VA, age 22; pres. 12/1846 - 04/1847, not yet pd. for 6 mos. clothing; pres. 06/1847; sick 08/1847; sick 10/1847, pay stopped for clothing: 1 pr. wool overalls-$2.28, 1 cap-$.95[1/2], 2 pr. stockings-$.49, 2 flannel shirts-$1.80; absent sick 12/1847, pay stopped for clothing: 1 blanket-$2.22, 1 pr. shoes-$1.21; pres. 02/1848, pay stopped for: 1 pr. shoes-$1.22, 1 pr. wool overalls-$2.28; pres. 04/1848; 07/1848, pay stopped for: 1 gun sling-$.16, 1 pick & brush-$.12, 1 wiper-$.20, 1 screw driver-$.25; BLW sent to Norfolk, VA; res. Norfolk Co., VA c. 1850, occ. Painter, w. Mary B. (23), children Arthur (8/12);[562] Civil War service enl. Pvt., Co. G, 53rd Va. Inf. 04/17/1862 at Norfolk, VA, AWOL by 06/30/1862 until discharged under Conscription Act 10/31/1862.[132]

**Drinkard, Charles Beverly**, 3rd Sgt., Co. E; b. 02/23/1826, Petersburg, VA, son of Beverly & Elizabeth Ann Firth (Cosby) Drinkard;[563] enl. Mex. War service 12/01/1846 Petersburg, VA, age 20; pres. 04/1847; pres. 06/1847, prom. 4th Sgt. 06/07/1847; in confinement 08/1847, prom. 3rd Sgt.; absent 10/1847 sick, pay stopped for: 1 pr. overalls-$2.28, 2 pr. shoes-$2.44, 4 pr. stockings-$.98, 2 cotton shirts-$.86, 2 flannel shirts-$1.80, 2 pr. drawers-$.71, 1 cap-$.95[1/2]; pres. 12/1847, pay stopped for: 1 pr. pants-$2.28, 1 pr. shoes-$1.22, 2 flannel shirts-$1.80, 1 blanket-$2.22; pres. 02/1848; pres. 04/1848, pay stopped for: 1 jacket-$2.37[1/2], Civil War service a C.B. Drinkard served as a 2nd Lt., Co. B, Clarkson's Btln. of Independent Rangers.[202]

OFF TO WAR

**Driscoll, John A.**, Pvt., Co. G; enl. Mex. War service 11/18/1846 Richmond, VA, age 18; pres. 06/1847; sick 08/1847; d. 09/23/1847 in Hosp. at Saltillo, Mex.

**Dubecq, John**, Pvt., LIC; b. Penn.; m. Charlotte Thompson, 02/03/1825, Rockbridge Co., VA;[564] enl. Mex. War service 12/07/1846 Staunton, VA, age 44; pres. 08/1847; pres. 10/1847, pay stopped for: 1 forage cap-$.95$^{1/2}$, 1 wool jacket-$2.66, 2 pr. overalls-$4.56, 1 pr. shoes-$1.22, 4 pr. socks-$.98, 5 cotton shirts-$2.15, 1 pr. drawers-$.35$^{1/2}$; pres. 12/1847, pay stopped for: 1 blanket-$2.22, 1 pr. shoes-$1.22, 1 pr. overalls-$2.28, 1 flannel shirt-$.90; pres. 04/1848, pay stopped for: 1 cotton shirt-$.43, 1 flannel shirt-$.90, 1 pr. shoes-$1.22; pres. 07/1848, pay stopped for: 1 bed sack-$.60, 1 screw driver-$.07, 1 wiper-$.20; BLW sent to Staunton, VA; c. 1850 res. Lexington, Rockbridge Co., VA, age 51, occ. Hatter, w. Charlotte (40);[565] c. 1870 res. Lexington, Rockbridge Co., VA , age 76, occ. Hatter, w. Charlotte (60).[566]

**Duckwiler, Daniel**, Pvt., *Recruit Co.*, enl. Mex. War service 01/07/1848 Christiansburg, VA, age 23; pres. 02/1848 Ft. Monroe, VA; pres. 04/1848; pres. 06/1848 Ft. Monroe, VA; BLW sent to Christiansburg, VA; SC #8103, 02/26/1887, from IL; d. 05/06/1917.

**Dudley, George B.**, Pvt., *Preston's Co.*; enl. Mex. War service 12/06/1846 Montgomery Co., VA, age 26; pres. 04/1847; sick 06/1847; pres. 08/1847; pres. 10/1847, pay stopped for: 1 pr. overalls-$2.28, 3 pr. socks-$.49, 2 flannel shirts-$.90, 2 cotton shirts-$.86; absent 12/1847, on detached service as Waggoner in QM Dept. since 12/11/1847, pay stopped for: 1 jacket-$2.66, 1 pr. shoes-$1.22, 1 cap-$.95$^{1/2}$, 1 pr. drawers-$.35$^{1/2}$, 1 blankets-$2.22; pres. 02/1848; pres. 04/1848; pres. 07/1848, pay stopped for: 1 cap-$.95$^{1/2}$, 1 pr. shoes-$1.22, 1 screw driver-$.07; BLW sent to Christiansburg, VA c/o Fleming Gardner; m. Mary W. Barnett, 02/22/1849, Montgomery Co., VA;[567] c. 1850 res. Montgomery Co., VA, age 28, occ. Farmer, w. Mary W. (21), dau. Sarah A. (4/12).[568]

**Dudley, Winston Price**, Pvt., *Recruit Co.*, b. 10/31/1822, Amherst Co., VA, son of Jesse Perkins & Dolly Dudley;[569] enl. Mex. War service 01/31/1848 Christiansburg, VA, age 25; pres. 02/1848; pres. 04/1848; pres. 06/1848; BLW sent to Christiansburg, VA; m/1 Sarah Graham, 08/28/1849, Montgomery Co., VA;[570] m/2 Sarah Jane Barnett 02/11/1854, Montgomery Co., VA[571]

**Duffey, Andrew**, Pvt., Co. H; enl. Mex. War service 11/30/1846, Berkeley, VA, age 26; pres. 04/1847; absent 06/1847, left sick in Hosp. at Monterey, Mex. 06/22/1847; d. 07/10/1847, Monterey, Mex.

**Duke, James W.**, 2$^{nd}$ Sgt., Co. K; b. c. 1820, Jefferson Co., VA; enl. Mex. War service Jefferson Co., VA 12/01/1846, age 27; pres. 06/1847, prom. 4$^{th}$ Sgt. 05/31/1847; sick 08/1847, prom. 3$^{rd}$ Sgt.; pres. 10/1847, prom. 2$^{nd}$ Sgt., pay stopped for: 1 pr. overalls-$2.28, 1 pr. shoes-$1.22, 3 pr. socks-$.73$^{1/2}$, 2 pr. drawers-$.71, 2 cotton shirts-$.86; sick 12/1847; discharged 01/08/1848 on Surgeon's Certificate; desc., age 27, 5'6", fair complexion, grey eyes, sandy hair, occ. Plasterer.[26]

**Dulaney, James Heath**, 1$^{st}$ Lt., Co. L; b. c. 1819, Fairfax Co., VA, son of Benjamin Tasker & Elizabeth (French) Dulaney;[572] enl. Mex. War service 03/01/1847 Fairfax C.H., VA; pres. 06/1847; pres. 08/1847, prom. 1$^{st}$ Lt. from 2$^{nd}$ Lt.; pres. 12/1847; pres. 02/1848; pres. 04/1848; pres. 07/1848; d. c. 1858, William H. Dulaney appointed administrator.[573]

**Dulany, John S.**, 4$^{th}$ Cpl., Co. B; enl. 12/12/1846, Alexandria, VA, age 40; pres. 06/1847; pres. 08/1847; pres. 10/1847, apptd. 4$^{th}$ Cpl. 09/25/1847, pay stopped for: 2 pr. shoes-$2.44, 1 pr. overalls-$2.28, 1 flannel shirt-$.90, 1 cotton shirt-$.43, 2 pr. cotton drawers-$.71, 1 blanket-$2.22, 2 pr. socks-$.49; sick 12/1847, pay stopped for: 1 flannel shirt-$.90; sick 02/1848; discharged 03/15/1848 on Surgeon's Certificate of Disability; c. 1850 res. Fairfax Co., VA, age 45, occ. Hog Raiser, b. Ireland;[574] became a U.S. citizen 11/07/1851;[575] c. 1860 res. Fairfax Co., age 55, occ. Merchant, b. Ireland.[576]

**Duncan, George**, Pvt., Co. D; enl. Mex. War service 01/08/1847, Richmond, VA, age 28; pres. 02/1847; pres. 04/1847; pres. 06/1847; pres. 08/1847, pay stopped for: 1 pr. shoes-$1.22; pres.

# VIRGINIA VOLUNTEERS IN MEXICO

10/1847, fined ½ by order (No. 120) of genl. court-martial, pay stopped for: 1 jacket-$2.66, 1 pr. pants-$2.28, 2 flannel shirts-$1.80, 2 cotton shirts-$.86, 1 pr. drawers-$.35$^{1/2}$, 3 pr. socks-$.73$^{1/2}$, 1 pr. shoes-$1.22; pres. 12/1847, pay stopped for: 1 cap-$.95$^{1/2}$, 1 pr. pants-$2.28, 1 pr. socks-$.24$^{1/2}$, 1 pr. shoes-$1.22, 1 blanket-$2.22; pres. 04/1848, pay stopped for: 1 musket & bayonet-$13.00, 1 haversack-$.20$^{3/4}$; pres. 08/1847, BLW sent to Norfolk, VA

**Dunlap, William**, Pvt., LIC; enl. Mex. War service 12/07/1846 Staunton, VA, age 21; pres. 06/1847, reduced to ranks from 3$^{rd}$ Sgt.; pres. 08/1847; pres. 10/1847, pay stopped for: 1 forage cap-$.95$^{1/2}$, 1 wool jacket-$2.66, 2 pr. overalls-$4.56, 2 pr. shoes-$2.44, 3 pr. socks-$.73$^{1/2}$, 4 cotton shirts-$1.72, 1 pr. drawers-$.35$^{1/2}$; pres. 12/1847, pay stopped for: 1 blanket-$2.22, 1 pr. shoes-$1.22, 1 pr. overalls-$2.28, 1 flannel shirt-$.90; absent 04/1848, on detached service as Orderly at H.Q. 04/02/1848; pres. 07/1848, pay stopped for: 1 gun sling-$.16, 1 pick & brush-$.12; BLW sent to Staunton, VA; c. 1850 res. Augusta Co., VA, age 25, occ. Farmer, m. Melvina Curry, 11/11/1850, Staunton, Augusta Co., VA;[577] w. Melvina (24);[578] [Civil War service a William Dunlap served as a Pvt., Co. D, 27$^{th}$ Ark. Inf.];[202] phys. desc. 6'0", black hair, blue eyes, light complexion, age 50 [1876], d. 01/06/1876, Cog Hill, McMinn Co., TN;[492] wid. Melvina, WC #5548, 04/13/1888, filed from Wilson, Pike Co., AR; Lists sons William J. Dunlap and James S. Dunlap;[492] (MCD b. 08/15/1825, Augusta Co., VA, d. 03/24/1904).[492]

**Dunn, James A.**, Pvt., Co. E; b. 1823, Sussex Co., VA, son of Thomas & Susan Dunn;[579] enl. Mex. War service 11/30/1846 Petersburg, VA, age 24; discharged 03/29/1847 Camargo, Mex. on account of disability; c. 1850 res. Petersburg, age 27, occ. None;[580] c. 1853 mbr. and *Past Commander*, Knights Templar, Appomattox Encampment No. 6, Petersburg, VA 1854;[40] m. Sarah Elizabeth Hall, 05/20/1857, Petersburg, VA;[581, 582] Civil War service enl. Pvt., Co. K, 5$^{th}$ Va. Cav. at Petersburg, VA, age 38; appointed 2$^{nd}$ Lt. 05/07/1862; resigned 01/31/1863; sick w/typhoid fever in Petersburg Hosp. 03/12/1863; nfr;[131] d. 04/24/1884, *Hemorrhage Bowels*, Petersburg, VA, bur. Blandford Cem., Sq. 3, Sec. 7, Ward H, Petersburg, VA;[581, 583] wid. Sarah E., WC #1326, 03/12/1887, filed from 101 Bollingbrook St., Petersburg, Dinwiddie Co., VA; (SED b. 03/1836, d. 07/01/1915).[581]

**Dunn, Thomas H.**, Pvt., Co. G, enl. Mex. War service 11/28/1846 Richmond, VA, age 19; pres. 06/1847; pres. 08/1847; sick 1847, pay stopped for: 1 pr. overalls-$2.28, 2 shoes-$2.44, 2 pr. socks-$.49, 1 forage cap-$.95$^{1/2}$; sick 12/1847, pay stopped for: 1 pr. pants-$2.28, 1 blanket-$2.22, 1 pr. socks-$.24$^{1/2}$; pres. 02/1848, pay stopped for: 1 brush & pick-$.12; pres. 04/1848, prom. 2$^{nd}$ Lt. 03/17/1848; pres. 08/1848.

**Dunn, William Washington**, Pvt., Co. H; 05/06/1822, Washington Co., VA, *"six miles from King's Salt Works, Washington Co., VA;"*[11, 584] enl. Mex. War service 01/30/1847, Richmond, VA, age 24; pres. 04/1847, transportation & subsistence due from residence to place of rendezvous, 300 miles; pres. 06/1847; pres. 08/1847; pres. 10/1847, pay stopped for: 1 pr. pants-$2.28, 1cotton shirt-$.43, 2 flannel shirts-$1.80, 2 pr. drawers-$.71, 1 pr. shoes-$1.22, 1 pr. socks-$.24$^{1/2}$; pres. 12/1847, pay stopped for: 1 forage cap-$.95$^{1/2}$, 1 pr. shoes-$1.22, 3 pr. socks-$.73$^{1/2}$, 1 jacket-$2.66, 1 pr. pants-$2.28, 1 blanket-$2.22; absent 02/1848, sick in Hosp. at Saltillo, Mex. since 01/28/1848; absent 04/1848, sick in Hosp. at Saltillo, Mex.; pres. 07/1848, pay stopped for: 1 cartridge box plate-$.10, BLW sent to Abingdon, VA; m/1 Emily Gillespie 11/05/1851, Tazewell Co., VA;[11] (EGD d. 12/14/1853); m/2 Nancy Jane (Davis) Center, 12/30/1863, Smith Co., TX; (NCD d. 08/23/1866); m/3 Lina Parker Gant, 08/20/1867, near Ft. Worth, TX; *"William Taylor has sold his interest in the Ladies Ice Cream Parlor to*

---

[11] **King's Salt Works**, was established by William King at Saltville, Washington Co., Va., (now in Smyth Co.) c. 1782. During the Civil War salt was a vital economic resource to the Confederacy as salt was the only readily available preservative of meat at the time. On December 20-21, 1864 Federal forces captured and destroyed the saltworks in an action known as the Battle of Saltville, or, The Raid on King's Salt Works.

OFF TO WAR

W. W. Dunn;"[585] SC #2771, 03/21/1887, filed form 4th and Rusk Sts., *"Mansion Hotel,"* Ft. Worth, Tarrant Co., TX; since discharge res. Abingdon and Tazewell, C.H., VA, 10 yrs., moved to Texas in 1858, lived in Smith Co., TX, 5 yrs., in Ft. Worth, TX, since; phys. desc. 6'1", fair complexion, blue eyes, light hair, occ. Merchant; d. 02/10/1910, *"erysipelas,"* bur. Oakwood Cemetery, blk. FF, lot G space 6, Ft. Worth, TX; wid. Lina, WC #15551, 04/01/1910, filed from 4th and Rusk Sts., *"Mansion Hotel,"* Ft. Worth, Tarrant Co., TX; OW IA #22468, rejected; Lists children Emma Dunn Hartman, b. 12/13/1853, Bascom H. Dunn, b. 09/21/1864; (LGD b. 02/16/1837, widow of Lewis Boon Gant, who died 11/25/1863, Camden, AR, d. 12/19/1914).

**Dyer, Robert N.**, Pvt., Co. L; b. 02/22/1827, Fairfax Co., VA, son of John D. & Mary E.N. (Davis?) Dyer;[586] enl. Mex. War service 03/15/1847 Fairfax C.H., VA, age 23; pres. 06/1847; pres. 08/1847; pres. 10/1847, pay stopped for: 1 F. Cap .95, 1 pr. Socks .10; pres. 12/1847, pay stopped for: 1 jacket-$2.66, 1 pr. pants-$2.28, 1 pr. shoes-$1.22, 1 flannel shirt-$.90, 1 cotton shirt-$.43, 1 blanket-$2.22, 1 pr. socks-$.24[1/2]; pres. 02/1848, pay stopped for: 1 Brush & Fork .12; pres. 04/1848, pay stopped for: 1 Cotton Shirt $.44; pres. 07/1848; BLW sent to Capt. Thrift c/o Robert Dyer, Fairfax Court House, Fairfax Co., VA; m/1 Alice c. 1860 res. Alexandria, VA, age 32, occ. House Carpenter, w. Rebecca (27), dau. Elizabeth (8), dau. Alice (6), son William (3), dau. Virginia (3/12);[587] [Civil War service Pvt., McNeill's Rangers, C.S.A., a resident of Pendleton Co., VA, enl. 09/01/1862 in Pendleton Co., pres. thru 12/1863, recvd. 08/10/1864;][588] c. 1870 res. Arlington, Alexandria Co., VA, age 41, occ. House Carpenter, w. Rebecca (36), dau. Elizabeth (17), dau. Alice (15), son William (13), dau. Virginia (10), dau. Ida (5);[589] (AD d. 06/1887); m. Sarah Abbott, 09/26/1888, Alexandria, VA;[590] d. 12/23/1890;[588] SC #8084, 02/14/1887, affidavit of James W. West, a member of the same Co. state that Robert Dyer was about 6 feet high, blue eyes, light hair, light complexion, and had one crooked foot; wid. Sarah, WC #9987, 06/12/1895, both from VA(SAD d. 04/29/1907).

**Dyes, Alexander**, Pvt., Co. F; enl. Mex. War service 12/28/1846, Portsmouth, VA, age 23; d. 02/28/1847 at sea on board the barque *Exact*; his death, probably of small pox, and subsequent burial were recorded in the diary of Capt. James. L. Kemper.[591]

**Dyes, Nathaniel G.**, 2nd Cpl., Co. F; enl. Mex. War service 12/28/1846, Portsmouth, VA, age 30; absent 06/1847 sent to Hosp. Saltillo, Mex. 06/25/1847; absent 08/1847 sick; pres. 10/1847, pay stopped for: 1 pr. overalls-$2.28, 1 pr. shoes-$1.22; pres. 12/1847; pres. 02/1848, pay stopped for: 1 pr. overalls-$2.28, 1 blanket-$2.22, 1 pr. shoes-$1.22, 1 pr. socks-$.24[1/2]; pres. 04/1848, prom. 03/01/1848 2nd Cpl.; pres. 08/1848, pay stopped for: 2 cotton shirts-$.88, 1 forage cap-$.83, BLW sent to Portsmouth, VA c/o E.T. Blamire; wid. Thuresa, WA #9265, 08/28/1890, from AR; [see Civil War pension claims].

**Dykes, Joel R.**, Pvt., Co. L; b. 1827, Stafford Co., VA; enl. Mex. War service 04/03/1847 Cumberland, MD, age 20; pres. 06/1847; pres. 08/1847; pres. 10/1847, pay stopped for: 1 pr. Pants 2.28, 1 pr. Shoes 1.22, 1 F shirt .90, 1 F Cap .95; pres. 12/1847, pay stopped for: 1 jacket-$2.66, 1 pr. pants-$2.28, 1 pr. shoes-$1.22, 4 cotton shirts-$1.72, 1 overcoat-$6.93[1/2], 4 pr. drawers-$1.42, 1 pr. socks-$.24[1/2]; absent 02/1848, on detached service as Teamster in QM Dept.; absent 04/1848, on detached service as a Teamster QM Dept. since 02/01/1848 by order of Col. Hamtramck.; pres. 07/1848; BLW sent to Joel R. Dykes, White Ridge P.O., Stafford Co., VA; m. Clara F. Sizer, 11/28/1850 City of Richmond, VA;[592] c. 1860 res. Henrico Co., VA, age 32, occ. Carpenter, w. Clara F. (31), son Marquis D. (4);[593] SC #19091, 02/04/1887, res. 1305 Brambleton Ave., Norfolk, VA, phys. desc. 5'10, fair complexion, dark eyes, light hair, occ. Carpenter; wid. Clara F., WC #7101, 09/13/1889, filed from Norfolk, VA, (CFD b. 12/20/1825, Caroline Co., VA; d. 01.03/1888, *Bright's Disease*).

**Eagle, Robert N.**, Pvt., Co. E; enl. Mex. War service 12/02/1846 Petersburg, VA, age 27; pres. 04/1847; pres. 06/1847; pres. 08/1847; pres. 10/1847, pay stopped for: 1 pr. overalls-$2.28, 2 pr. shoes-$2.44, 2 pr. stockings-$.49, 2 cotton shirts-$.86, 2 flannel shirts-$1.80; pres.

# VIRGINIA VOLUNTEERS IN MEXICO

12/1847, [illegible]; transferred 01/01/1848 to Capt. Mears Co. of Arkansas Cavalry; [c. 1870, a Robert Eagle res. Amherst Co., VA age 50, occ. Farm Hand, w. Susan (45), son Frederic S. (16), dau. Bettie (18), dau. Susan (17), dau. Virginia (13), dau. Sallie (9).][594]

**Eanes, James C.**, Pvt., Co. E; enl. Mex. War service 12/04/1846 Petersburg, VA, age 20; pres. 04/1847; pres. 06/1847; pres. 08/1847; pres. 10/1847, pay stopped for: 1 pr. overalls-$2.28, 2 pr. shoes-$2.44, 2 pr. stockings-$.49, 2 cotton shirts-$.86, 1 cap-$.95$^{1/2}$, 1 overcoat-$6.93$^{1/2}$; pres. 12/1847, [illegible]; pres. 02/1848, pay stopped for: 1 jacket-$2.66; pres. 04/1848, pay stopped for: 3 cotton shirts-$.88.

**Early, Jubal Anderson**, Major, 1$^{st}$ VA Vol. Inf. Regt., b. 11/03/1816, Gill's Creek, Franklin Co., VA, son of Joab & Ruth (Hairston) Early; graduated U.S. Military Academy 1837 ranking 18$^{th}$ out of a class of 50; studied law in Franklin Co., VA; member Virginia House of Delegates 1841-1842; Commonwealth's Attorney, Franklin Co., VA 1842-1851; m. Mary Ross, 01/03/1848, Montgomery Co., VA; c. 1850 res. Franklin Co., VA, age 33, occ. Attorney-At-Law;[595] c. 1860 res. Rocky Mount, Franklin Co., VA, age 44, occ. Lawyer;[596] Delegate to the Virginia Secession Convention 1861; Civil War service Lt. Gen. Army of Northern Virginia, C.S.A.; m/2 Bettie Waldron, 02/15/1877, Montgomery Co., VA; d. 03/02/1894, Lynchburg, VA, bur. Spring Hill Cem., Lynchburg, VA.

Photo credit: Virginia Historical Society, Richmond, VA

**East, John**, Pvt., *Recruit Co.*, enl. Mex. War service 05/01/1848 Wytheville, VA; pres. 06/1848; BLW sent to Patrick C.H., VA; m. Mary B. Abington 06/15/1848 Patrick Co., VA;[597] wid. Lydia, WA #16525, 02/25/1902, from NC, *"served in a VA unit."*

**Eaton, Edmond Henry**, Pvt., Co. L; b. 1828; enl. Mex. War service 03/01/1847 Fairfax C.H., VA, age 19; absent 06/1847 sick in hospital at Saltillo, Mex.; discharged 08/30/1847 at Saltillo, Mex. on Surgeon's Certificate of Disability;[72] m. Georgiana Rhoderick, 09/11/1856, Alexandria Co., VA;[598] c. 1860 res. Alexandria, VA, age 32, occ. Bar Keeper, w. Georgiana (22);[599] c. 1870 res. Alexandria, VA, age 42, occ. Clerk, w. Georgiana (33), son John H. (14), dau. Ida Virginia (7), dau. Minnie (4), son William (1);[600] d. 08/01/1883, bur. Methodist Protestant Cem., Alexandria, VA[601]

**Eaves, James Harvey**, Pvt., Co. M; enl. Mex. War service 11/09/1847 Brunswick C.H., VA, age 19; pres. 11/1847; pres. 12/1847, *"apprehended 9$^{th}$ Dec. 1847: to pay $30 for apprehension;"* pres. 02/1848; pres. 04/1848, pay stopped for: 1 pr. shoes-$1.22, 2 cotton shirts-$.86; pres. 08/1848; BLW sent to Brunswick C.H., VA; m. Frances Ann Debnam, 08/08/1850, Franklin Co., NC;[602] SC #6050, 02/26/1887, filed from Hayesville, Franklin Co., NC; phys. desc. age 63 [1887], 5'6", fair complexion, dark eyes, dark hair, occ. Stage Driver;[602] d. 04/14/1889, near Pughs, Franklin Co., NC;[603] wid. Frances A., WC #6345, 05/16/1889, filed from Pughs, Franklin Co., NC; (FDE b. 05/06/1826, Franklin Co., NC, d. 1909).[603]

**Edmundson, Upton A.**, 2$^{nd}$ Cpl., Co. M; enl. Mex. War service 09/02/1847 McFarlands, VA, age 26; pres. 10/1847; pres. 11/1847; pres. 12/1847; pres. 02/1848, pay stopped for: 1 blanket$2.22; pres. 04/1848, pay stopped for: 1 pr. shoes-$1.22, 1 cotton shirt-$.86; pres.

OFF TO WAR

08/1848, prom. 2nd Cpl., pay stopped for: 1 musket-$13.00, 1 gun sling-$.16, 1 screw driver-$.07, 1 wormer-$.20; BLW sent to McFarlands, Lunenburg Co., VA

**Edwards, Henry K.**, Pvt., Co. F; enl. Mex. War service 11/23/1846, Portsmouth, VA, age 27; absent 06/1847 left sick Camargo, Mex. 04/04/1847, reduced to ranks from 2nd Cpl. 04/27/1847; pres. 08/1847; discharged 10/16/1847, Buena Vista, Mex. on Surgeon's Certificate of Disability; [A Henry Edward *"Pvt. Mexican War,"* d. 06/18/1890, Soldiers Home Hampton, VA, bur. Hampton National Cemetery, Plot: 6311, Hampton, VA]

**Ellett, Joseph E.**, Pvt., Co. I; enl. Mex. War service 01/10/1847 Lynchburg, VA, age 20; pres. 02/1847; pres. 04/1847; pres. 06/1847; pres. 08/1847; absent 10/1847, pay stopped for: 4 cotton shirts-$1.72, 2 pr. drawers-$.71, 1 flannel shirt-$.90, 1 pr. pants-$2.28, 1 blanket-$2.22, 1 cap-$.95$^{1/2}$, 1 jacket-$2.66; pres. 12/1847, pay stopped for: 1 pr. socks-$.24$^{1/2}$, 2 pr. drawers-$.35$^{1/2}$, 1 pr. pants-$2.28, 1 pr. shoes-$1.22, 1 blanket-$2.22, 2 cotton shirts-$.86; pres. 02/1848, pay stopped for: 2 pr. cotton shirts-$.86; absent 04/1848, on extra duty in QM Dept.; pres. 08/1848, BLW sent to Lynchburg, VA

**Elliott, Curtis**, Pvt., *Preston's Co.*; enl. Mex. War service 12/15/1846 Montgomery Co., VA, age 23; absent 04/1847 left sick in hosp. at Ft. Monroe, VA since 02/27/1847; absent 06/1847 left sick in Ft. Monroe, VA; discharged 04/03/1847 at Ft. Monroe, VA; m. Virginia Ann Price, 08/23/1849, Montgomery Co., VA;[604] d. 05/19/1856, Montgomery Co., VA;[605] wid. Virginia A., WC #156, 03/14/1887, filed from Christiansburg, Montgomery Co., VA; (VPE b. 06/05/1823, d. 12/19/1914).[605]

**Ellis, John William**, Pvt., Co. A; b. 11/15/1825, Henrico Co., VA; enl. Mex. War service 12/01/1846 Richmond, VA, age 21; pres. 12/1846 - 04/1847; pres. 06/1847; pres. 08/1847; pres. 10/1847, pay stopped for clothing: 1 cap-$.95$^{1/2}$, 2 pr. shoes-$2.44, 1 pr. wool overalls-$2.28, 2 pr. stockings-$.49; pres. 12/1847, pay stopped for clothing: 1 wool jacket-$2.66, 1 blanket-$2.22; pres. 02/1848, pay stopped for: 1 pr. shoes-$1.22; pres. 04/1848; BLW sent to Richmond, VA; m. Margaret Ann Nicholson 07/12/1854, Macon, Bibb Co., Ga.; SC #15569, 02/02/1888, filed from Macon, Bibb Co., GA; Since discharge res. in Richmond, VA North Carolina and Georgia; phys. desc. blue eyes, light hair, fair complexion, occ. Cabinet Maker; Pvt. John Poe of Richmond, VA and Pvt. James Stagg of Henrico Co., VA gave affidavit for pension claim; d. 07/09/1904, 251 Jeff Davis St., Macon, Bibb Co., Ga.; wid. Margaret A., WC #13790, 08/06/1904, filed from Macon, Bibb Co., GA. Children Francis Virginia b. 04/25/1855, William W. b. 08/29/1857, Ella Susan b. 06/11/1860, Emma L. b. 11/04/1864, George F. b. 08/19/1867, Joseph O. b. 08/17/1871, Harriet J. b. 07/07/1874, John C. b. 03/13/1877, Mary N. b. 05/07/1880; (MAE b. 10/03/1838, Alexandria, VA).[606]

**Ellis, Joseph**, Pvt., Co. G; enl. Mex. War service 11/25/1846 Richmond, VA, age 18; pres. 06/1847; pres. 08/1847; pres. 10/1847, pay stopped for: 1 pr. overalls-$2.28, 4 cotton shirts-$1.72, 1 pr. drawers-$.35$^{1/2}$, 2 shoes-$2.44, 2 pr. socks-$.49, 1 forage cap-$.95$^{1/2}$; deserted 12/11/1847 Buena Vista, Mex.

**Ellis, Obadiah**, Pvt., Co. I; enl. Mex. War service 01/01/1847 Richmond, VA, age 39; pres. 02/1847; pres. 04/1847; pres. 06/1847; pres. 08/1847; absent 10/1847, pay stopped for: 3 flannel shirts-$2.70, 2 cotton shirts-$.86, 2 pr. shoes-$2.44, 3 pr. drawers-$1.06$^{1/2}$, 1 pr. pants-$2.28, 1 pr. socks-$.24$^{1/2}$, 1 overcoat-$6.93$^{1/2}$, 1 cap-$.95$^{1/2}$, 1 blanket-$2.22; pres. 12/1847, pay stopped for: 1 blanket-$2.22, 1 flannel shirt-$.90; pres. 02/1848, pay stopped for: 1 cotton shirt-$.43, 1 pr. overalls-$2.28, 1 blanket-$2.22; pres. 04/1848; pres. 08/1848, pay stopped for: 1 wait belt-$.21, 1 waist belt plate-$.10, BLW sent to Richmond, VA; c. 1850 res. Penitentiary, Richmond, VA, age 43, occ. Spooler, sentenced 1848 for *"horse stealing."*[607]

VIRGINIA VOLUNTEERS IN MEXICO

**Ellis, Samuel**, Pvt., Co. K; b. Clarke Co., VA, c. 1822, son of Elijah and Sallie H. Ellis;[608] enl. Mex. War service Frederick Co., VA 12/20/1846, age 24; pres. 06/1847; sick 08/1847;

Certificate of DISABILITY and DISCHARGE, in case of a Volunteer soldier who may be discharged *before* the expiration of his term, in consequence of wounds received or sickness incurred in course of service.

I HEREBY CERTIFY, That *Samuel Ellis* a *private* of company, [*K*,] of the Regiment of *Virginia* Volunteers, is *incapable of performing* the duties of a Volunteer soldier, for the following reasons: to wit; *Deafness*.

AND I FURTHER CERTIFY, That in the opinion of the undersigned, the *public interest* requires that the said *Samuel Ellis* be discharged from the Volunteer service of the United States. GIVEN at *Buena Vista Mexico*, this *11th* day of *September* 1847.

*B. My. Boyne Asst.*, Surgeon.

I CERTIFY, ON HONOR, That *Samuel Ellis* a *Private* of Captain *John W. Rowans* Company ( *K* ) of the *First* Regiment of *Virginia* Volunteers, of the State of *Virginia* born in *Frederick County* State of *Virginia*, aged *21* years; *5* feet *10½* inches high; *fair* complexion, *blue* eyes, *dark* hair, and by occupation a *Laborer*, was mustered into service of the United States at *Richmond Virginia* on the *27th* day of *January* 184*7*, to serve ~~months,~~ or for during the war with Mexico.

*John W. Rowan*
*Capt.* Commanding Company [ *K* ]
*1st* Regiment of *Virginia* Volunteers.

HONORABLY DISCHARGED this *11th* day of *September* 1847, at *Buena Vista Mexico*
GIVEN at *Buena Vista Mexico* this *11th* day of *September* 184*7*. *By order of Gen. Wool.*
*J. H. Carlton*
*Capt. 1st Dragoons*
*Acting Asst. Gen.*
~~Commanding the Regiment.~~

NOTE.—A duplicate of this Certificate will be forwarded to the Adjutant General of the Army, Washington—endorsed, "*For the Commissioner of Pensions*, BOUNTY LAND BUREAU."
ADJUTANT GENERAL'S OFFICE,
*April* 22, 1847.

discharged 09/11/1847 at Buena Vista, Mex. on Surgeon's Certificate of Disability; m/1 Alice McSherry c. 1861, (AME d. 09/26/1866, Darksville, Berkeley Co., WV;)[609] SC #816, 02/04/1887, m/2 Sallie McSherry, 09/28/1898, Martinsburg, Berkeley Co., WV, occ. Stone Mason / Fence Builder;[608] phys. desc. age 64 [1884], 5'10", light complexion, blue eyes, dark

125

hair, occ. Laborer at enl.;[608] *"I lost my hearing at China, Mexico about the last of May 1847 in this manner: We were firing salutes and it was my duty to ram the cartridge and spring the cannon. The report of said cannon destroyed my hearing entirely for about a month and then my hearing, in part, returned. But not sufficiently for me to perform my duty.... I was treated by my regimental surgeon and discharged for deafness and chronic diarrhea;"*[608] [see attached discharge] d. 05/06/1899, *"gangrene of the foot,"* Martinsburg, Berkeley Co., WV, bur. Martinsburg, WV;[609] wid. Sallie, WC #11807, 06/10/1899, filed from Martinsburg, Berkeley Co., WV; *"In 1871 I commenced to live with my late husband as his wife, not being married to him but, but continued to live with him from that year until September 28 1898 when he married me. I bore him six children, all are living. The youngest one, Allie May born August 20, 1877. It was generally known of* [and] *believed by my surrounding neighbors that I was his wife during the years 1871 to September 28, 1898;"*[610] (SME b. 07/12/1845, d. 11/07/1903).[609]

**Emerson, John H.**, Pvt., LIC; enl. Mex. War service 12/07/1846 Staunton, VA, age 24; discharged 06/1847 at Buena Vista, Mex.; m. Susan Shickel, 01/31/1850, Bridgewater, Rockingham Co., VA;[611] c. 1880 res. Grant Dist., Harrison Co., WV, age 56, occ. Laborer, w. Susana (58) Keeps House, son Alex A. (26) Laborer, son Martin L. (22) Laborer, son George T. (19) Laborer, son David F. (17) Laborer, dau. Sarah M. (15), son Thomas (12);[612] SC #824, 03/01/1887, filed from Horn Creek, Gilmer Co., WV; d. 10/21/1894, *"at his res. near Cox's Mill, on Horn Creek,"* Gilmer Co., WV;[613] wid. Susan, WC #9431, 11/17/1894, filed from Cox's Mill, Gilmer Co., WV. (SSE b. 02/04/1822, d. 1902).[613]

**English, John M.**, 3$^{rd}$ Sgt., Co. K; b. 09/18/1808, Washington, DC;[614] enl. Mex. War service Jefferson Co., VA 12/20/1846, age 38; pres. 06/1847, prom. 3$^{rd}$ Sgt. 05/31/1847; discharged 07/29/1847 at Buena Vista, Mex. on Surgeon's Certificate of Disability; c. 1860 res. Wheeling P.O., Ohio Co., VA;[615] c. 1880 res. Richland Dist., Ohio Co., WV, age 75, occ. Farmer, w. Mary (69) Keeping House, dau. Anna (44) At Home, dau. Mary (24) School Teacher, son Morgan (36) Works on Farm;[616] d. 01/1850, *Festula, age 44*, bur. Methodist Graveyard, Charlestown, WV.[614, 617]

**English, John**, Pvt., Co. G; enl. Mex. War service 12/01/1846 Richmond, VA, age 25; absent 06/1847, left sick in Hosp. at Monterey, Mex. 06/28/1847; discharged 06/25/1847 Monterey, Mex. on Surgeon's Certificate of Disability.

**Erskine, Henry**, Capt., Regtl. Commissary, b. 1787, son of Michael & Sarah Margaret (Handley Paulee) Erskine; m. Agatha Estill[618] res. Greenbrier, VA;[619] c. 1829, owned a large house on Court St., Lewisburg, Greenbrier Co., VA;[620] mbr. Virginia General Assembly 1830-32, 1839-42;[621] d. 09/26/1847, *"Sir, I regret to inform you that Captain Henry Erskine, Commissary, 1$^{st}$ Regiment of Virginia Volunteers, died yesterday afternoon at 4 o'clock p.m. He will be buried with military honors at 5 o'clock p.m. this afternoon. His remains will be deposited in a vault in the cemetery at this place* [Monterey] *and the coffin can be readily recognized, whenever his friends in Virginia send for him. His disease was chronic diarrhea complicated with diabetes;"*[622] bur. Old Stone Church Cemetery, Lewisburg, VA;[623] c. 1850 Agatha Erskine res. Greenbrier Co., VA, (59), Alex Erskine (18) occ. Student, b. Alabama;[624] c. 1860 res. Lewisburg, Greenbrier Co., VA, Agatha Erskine, widowed (70), Benjamin Estill (54), Eliza Estill (20).[625]

**Erwin, Charles**, Pvt., Co. H; enl. Mex. War service 01/06/1847, Berkeley, VA, age 21; pres. 04/1847; pres. 06/1847; pres. 08/1847; pres. 10/1847, pay stopped for: 1 forage cap-$.95$^{1/2}$, 1 pr. pants-$2.28, 3 cotton shirts-$1.29, 1 pr. shoes-$1.22, 1 pr. socks-$.24$^{1/2}$; pres. 12/1847, pay stopped for: 1 pr. shoes-$1.22, 1 blanket-$2.22; pres. 02/1848, pay stopped for: 1 forage cap-$.95$^{1/2}$, 1 jacket-$2.66, 2 pr. drawers-$.71, 2 pr. socks-$.49; pres. 04/1848, pay stopped for: 1 pr. shoes-$1.22; pres. 07/1848, pay stopped for: 1 screw driver-.25, 1 wiper-$.20, BLW sent to Philadelphia, Pa.; [Civil War service a Charles Erwin served as a Pvt., Co. B, 28$^{th}$ Pa. Inf.][554]

## VIRGINIA VOLUNTEERS IN MEXICO

**Etheridge, Nelson C.**, Pvt., Co. M; enl. Mex. War service 11/25/1847 Norfolk, VA, age 28; pres. 11/1847; pres. 12/1847; pres. 02/1848, pay stopped for: $30 fee for desertion from Ft. Monroe; pres. 04/1848, pay stopped for: $9.00 for desertion $21.00 having been retained last muster; pres. 08/1848, pay stopped for: 1 gun sling-$.16; BLW sent to Norfolk, VA; c. 1850 res. Portsmouth, Norfolk Co., VA, age 34, occ. Tailor, w. Sarah F. (29), dau. Juliana V. (3), dau. Cataretta (1/12);[626] dead by 1870, c. 1870 res. Portsmouth, Norfolk Co., VA wid. Sarah F. (49), occ. Seamtress, dau. Indiana V. (23), occ. Seamtress.[627]

**Eustace, Dabney M.**, Pvt., Co. M; enl. Mex. War service 11/30/1847 Ft. Monroe, VA, age 27; pres. 11/1847; pres. 02/1848, on detached service as Hosp. Steward 12/11/1847 - 01/25/1848, pay stopped for: 1 blanket-$2.22; absent 04/1848 on detached service since 04/01/1848 as Hospital Steward for Battalion; pres. 08/1848, pay stopped for: 1 gunsling-$.16, 1 wormer-$.20; BLW sent to Richmond, VA

**Evans, Henry**, Pvt., Co. L; b. 1811; enl. Mex. War service 03/01/1847 Fairfax C.H., VA, age 36; pres. 06/1847; pres. 08/1847; pres. 10/1847, pay stopped for: 1 pr. Shoes 1.22; pres. 12/1847, pay stopped for: 1 pr. pants-$2.28, 1 cap-$.95$^{1/2}$, 1 pr. shoes-$1.22, 1 flannel shirt-$.90, 1 cotton shirt-$.43, 1 blanket-$2.22, 2 pr. drawers-$.71, 1 pr. socks-$.24$^{1/2}$; absent 02/1848, sick in Hospital, pay stopped for: 1 Jacket 2.66; pres. 04/1848, pay stopped for: 2 Cotton Shirts .88; pres. 07/1848, pay stopped for: 1 Brush & Pick .12; BLW sent to Alexandria, VA

**Evans, James**, Pvt., Co. H; enl. Mex. War service 12/09/1846, Berkeley, VA, age 31; pres. 04/1847; pres. 06/1847; pres. 08/1847; pres. 10/1847, pay stopped for: 1 pr. pants-$2.28, 2 cotton shirts-$.86, 1 flannel shirt-$.90, 1 pr. shoes-$1.22, 2 pr. socks-$.49; pres. 12/1847, pay stopped for: 1 cotton shirt-$.43, 1 blanket-$2.22, 2 pr. drawers-$.71; pres. 02/1848; pres. 04/1848; pres. 07/1848, BLW sent to Cumberland, ?.

**Evans, John G.**, Pvt., Co. I; enl. Mex. War service 01/20/1847 Richmond, VA, age 20; pres. 02/1847; pres. 04/1847; pres. 06/1847; pres. 08/1847 sick; discharged 10/17/1847 on Surgeon's Certificate of Disability, pay stopped for: 1 cotton shirt-$.43, 2 pr. drawers-$.71.

**Evans, John, P.**, Pvt., Co. L; b. 1823; enl. Mex. War service 03/01/1847 Fairfax C.H., VA, age 24; pres. 06/1847; pres. 08/1847; pres. 10/1847, pay stopped for: 1 pr. Pants 2.28, 1 F Cap .95; 1 pr. Shoes 1.22; pres. 12/1847, pay stopped for: 1 jacket-$2.66, 1 pr. pants-$2.28, 1 cap-$.95$^{1/2}$, 3 pr. shoes-$3.66, 1 flannel shirt-$.90, 3 cotton shirts-$1.29, 1 overcoat-$6.93$^{1/2}$, 1 blanket-$2.22, 1 pr. drawers-$.35$^{1/2}$, 1 pr. socks-$.24$^{1/2}$; pres. 02/1848, pay stopped for: 1 Brush & Pick .12; pres. 04/1848, pay stopped for: 1 Blanket 2.25, 1 Cotton Shirt .44; pres. 07/1848, to forfeit 1 mos. pay by sentence of general court-martial; BLW sent to John Evans, Alexandria, VA; m/1 widow Rowena E. (Drish) Castle 12/27/1866, Loudoun Co., VA;[628] (REE d. 08/24/1887, bur. Union Cem. Leesburg, Loudoun Co., VA); m/2 Mary M. Harper 05/08/1888, Alms House, Loudoun Co., VA;[629] SC #887, 02/16/1887, filed from Philomont, Loudoun Co. VA; phys. desc. 5'9", light complex., light hair, blue eyes; He states he received a gunshot wound to the right shine bone at Buena Vista, Mex., the bone being fractured. He further states that he did not vote for secession and lived in Baltimore during the late war; d. 11/20/1891, near Unison, Loudoun Co., VA; wid. Mary M., WC #8910, 09/21/1893, both from VA; OW Invalid App. #24638 rejected.

**Evans, Joseph L.**, Pvt., Co. K; enl. Mex. War service Jefferson Co., VA 12/11/1846, age 20; pres. 06/1847; pres. 08/1847; pres. 10/1847, pay stopped for: 1 pr. overalls-$2.28, 6 cotton shirts-$2.58, 4 pr. socks-$.98, 1 pr. shoes-$1.22, 2 pr. drawers-$.71, 4 flannel shirts-$3.60, 1 cap-$.95$^{1/2}$; pres. 12/1847, pay stopped for: 1 jacket-$2.66, 1 pr. overalls-$2.28, 1 pr. boots-$1.22, 1 pr. socks-$.24$^{1/2}$, 2 pr. drawers-$.71, 1 blanket-$2.22, 1 cotton shirt-$.43; pres. 04/1848, pay stopped for: 1 pick & brush-$.12, 1 gun sling-$.18; pres. 07/1848, pay stopped for: 1 screw driver-$.25; BLW sent to Charlestown, Jefferson Co., VA; m. Sarah Rice, 02/12/1854, Clay Co., Mo.;[630] d. 02/09/1886, Kearney, Clay Co., Mo.;[630] wid. Sarah, WC

OFF TO WAR

#482, 04/18/1887, filed from Kearney, Clay Co., MO; (SRE b. 07/25/1833, d. Kearney, Clay Co., Mo.).[630]

**Evans, Montgomery**, Pvt., *Recruit Co.*, enl. Mex. War service 09/07/1847 Charlotte C.H., VA, age 27; discharged 09/22/1847 by Surgeon; [Civil War service a Montgomery Evans served as a Pvt., Co. E, 30th Ala. Inf.]

**Everett, Joseph L.**, Pvt., Co. K; b. 04/20/1824, Camden, Camden Co., NJ;[631] enl. Mex. War service Jefferson Co., VA 12/11/1846, age 23; sick 06/1847; pres. 08/1847; pres. 10/1847, pay stopped for: 1 pr. overalls-$2.28, 5 cotton shirts-$2.15, 2 pr. socks-$.49, 2 flannel shirts-$1.80, 1 cap-$.95$^{1/2}$; pres. 12/1847, pay stopped for: 1 jacket-$2.66, 1 pr. overalls-$2.28, 2 pr. drawers-$.71, 1 blanket-$2.22, 1 cotton shirt-$.43, 1 flannel shirt-$.90; pres. 07/1848, pay stopped for: 1 screw driver-$.25, 1 gun sling-$.18; BLW sent to Charlestown, Jefferson Co., VA; c. 1850 res. Charlestown, Jefferson Co., VA, age 25;[632] Civil War service enl. Pvt., Co. A, 5[th] Pa. Cav., 09/04/1864, discharged 09/21/1865;[631] SC 19943, 09/26/1889, filed from Salem, Salem Co., NJ; phys. desc. 5'5$^{1/2}$", fair complexion, dark hair, brown eyes, occ. House Plasterer;[631] since discharge res. Charlestown, WV and Salem, NJ;[631] admitted National Soldiers Home, Hampton, Elizabeth City Co., VA;[631] d. 1893?[631]

**Ewald, Stephen**, Pvt., *Recruit Co.*, b. Austria, emigrated to Wythe Co., VA c. 1835;[633] m. Angeline Seagle, c. 1835;[634] enl. Mex. War service 03/20/1848 Wytheville, VA; pres. 06/1848; BLW sent to Wytheville, VA; c. 1850 res. Wythe Co., VA, age 38, occ. Harness Maker, b. Germany, w. Angeline (34), son Jacob (14), son Charles (11), dau. Lucinda (9), son James (6), dau. Mary;[635] c. 1870, res. Fort Chiswell, Wythe Co., VA, age 59, occ. Saddler, w. Angeline E. (55), son James E. (23), dau. Mariah, son Joseph W., son Thomas W. (16);[636] sons Jacob and James served during the Civil War in 51st Va. Inf., C.S.A.[536]

**Eyrse, James W.**, Pvt., LIC; enl. Mex. War service 12/07/1846 Staunton, VA, age 23; sick 08/1847; pres. 10/1847, pay stopped for: 1 forage cap-$.95$^{1/2}$, 1 wool jacket-$2.66, 1 pr. overalls-$2.28, 2 pr. shoes-$2.44, 3 pr. socks-$.73$^{1/2}$, 4 cotton shirts-$1.72; pres. 12/1847, pay stopped for: 1 pr. shoes-$1.22, 2 flannel shirts-$1.80; pres. 04/1848, pay stopped for: 1 pr. shoes-$1.22; pres. 04/1848, pay stopped for: 1 cotton shirt-$.43; pres. 07/1848; BLW sent to _____, VA; SC #2100, 03/26/1887, filed from Atwood, Piatt Co., IL; d. 1889, *"bone eryesylis."*[637]

**Eyrse, William G.**, Pvt., LIC; enl. Mex. War service 12/07/1846 Staunton, VA, age 19; discharged 06/1847 at Camargo, Mex.

**Fagunders, Jacob H.**, Pvt., Co. C; enl. Mex. War service 12/30/1846, Bowling Green, VA, age 22; d. 06/27/1847, Monterey, Mex.; a letter from the Regtl. Surgeon, T.C. Madison to Lt. Thomas P. August, Co. A related the news, *Private J.H. Fagunders, Co. C, died on the 25th* [of June] *of Epilepsy."* [638]

**Fairfax, George William**, Pvt., Co. K; enl. Mex. War service Jefferson Co., VA 12/10/1846, age 40; absent 06/1847, on detached service in the Asst. Adjt. Genl. office, reduced to ranks 05/31/1847 at his own request; absent 08/1847 on detached service as Clerk in Asst. Adjt. Genl. office; absent 10/1847 on detached service as Clerk in Asst. Adjt. Genl. office; absent 12/1847 on detached service as Clerk A.A.G.'s office; absent 04/1848 on detached service as Clerk in A.A.G.'s office, pay stopped for: 1 pr. pants-$2.28; pres. 07/1848; BLW sent to Charlestown, Jefferson Co., VA; c. 1850 res. Preston Co., VA, age 38, occ. Farmer, w. Margaret S. (30), son John M.G. (3);[639] c. 1880 res. Preston Co., WV, age 65, occ. Farmer, dau. A.C. (22).[640]

**Fairfax, Henry**, Capt., Co. L; b. 05/04/1804, *Ashgrove*, Fairfax Co., VA, son of Thomas Cary Fairfax (9th Lord Fairfax) & Margaret (Herbert) Fairfax;[641] attended U.S. Military Academy, West Point, NY 1824-1826; m. Ann Caroline Herbert, 10/09/1827, Vansville, MD;[642] enl. Mex. War service 03/01/1847 Fairfax C.H., VA; pres. 06/1847; d. 08/14/1847 Saltillo, Mex.;[72] bur. Falls Church Episcopal Cem., Falls Church, VA.[45] Henry Fairfax used his own funds to restore the historic Falls Church in the 1830's. A monument commemorating the restoration is

128

VIRGINIA VOLUNTEERS IN MEXICO

near the west end of the south walk. The inscription is copied from the text of a lost plaque reported by a Civil War correspondent in Harper's Weekly of August 31, 1861; son Herbert C. Fairfax was in Co. D, 17$^{th}$ Va. Inf. during the Civil War.$^{63}$

**Farley, Thomas A.**, Pvt., Co. E; enl. Mex. War service 11/30/1846 Petersburg, VA, age 22; pres. 04/1847; transferred 06/1847, prom. Regtl. Sgt. Major 06/04/1847; phys, desc. age 22, 5'7", blonde complexion, blue eyes, light hair; m. Elizabeth Ann Conway, of Dinwiddie Co., 11/30/1848, Petersburg, VA;$^{643, 644}$ c. 1850 res. Dinwiddie Co., VA, age 25, occ. Farmer, w. Elizabeth A. (24), m-i-l? Mary Conway (49), dau. Mary R. Farley (8/12);$^{645}$ c. 1860 res. San Marino, Dinwiddie Co., VA, age 35, occ. Farmer, w. Bettie E. (34), dau. Mary R. (11), dau. Vuella F. (10), dau. Anna T. (7), son Ernest R. (3);$^{646}$ [Civil War service a Thomas A. Farley enl. 07/22/1861 Co. B, 12$^{th}$ Va. Inf., appointed principle regimental musician 07/23/1861, 07/1862 in Petersburg hosp., 08/1862 deserted from regt. Camp at Falling Creek, Chesterfield Co., VA]$^{21}$ SC #1006, 03/12/1887, filed from LaGrange, Fayette Co., TN; *"My said farm*[of 100 acres] *is located in Fayette Co., Tennessee about 6 miles west from the Town of LaGrange;"* Lists children Mary Rebecca Farley b. 10/24/1849, Vuella Salin Farley Carter b. 10/22/1850, Annie T. Farley Pleasants b. 06/18/1853, Ernest Comway Farley b. 09/28/1859; Since discharge res. Dinwiddie Co., VA to 1866, then moved to Fayette Co., TN; d. 05/24/1905.$^{643}$

**Farris, Jeremiah**, Pvt., *Preston's Co.*; b. Roanoke Co., VA, son of William and Nancy Farris;$^{647}$ enl. Mex. War service 12/24/1846 Montgomery Co., VA, age 21; absent 04/1847 left sick in hosp. at Ft. Monroe, VA since 02/27/1847; absent 06/1847 left sick at Ft. Monroe, VA; discharged 03/25/1847 *"small pox,"*$^{647}$ at Ft. Monroe, VA; m. Fannie Clingenpeel, 07/03/1884, Roanoke Co., VA;$^{647}$ d. 05/09/1886, Roanoke Co., VA;$^{647}$ wid. Fannie, WC #2471, 07/18/1887, filed from Boones Mill, Franklin Co., VA; (FCF b. Franklin Co., VA, d. 1889).$^{647}$

**Faulkner, George E.**, Pvt., *Preston's Co.*, b. 01/06/1820, Rockingham Co., VA;$^{648}$ enl. Mex. War service 12/06/1846 Montgomery Co., VA, age 27; pres. 04/1847; pres. 06/1847; pres. 08/1847 on detached service with QM Dept., to receive an additional $25 in addition to pay as a soldier; absent 10/1847, on detached service in QM Dept., pay stopped for: 1 pr. shoes-$1.22, 2 pr. socks-$.49, 1 flannel shirt-$.90, 2 cotton shirts-$.86, 1 pr. drawers-$.35$^{1/2}$, 1 cap-$.95$^{1/2}$; absent 12/1847, on detached service as Principal Teamster in QM Dept. since 12/11/1847, pay stopped for: 1 pr. overalls-$2.28, 1 pr. drawers-$.35$^{1/2}$; pres. 02/1848; absent 04/1848 on detached service as Principal Teamster in QM Dept.; pres. 07/1848, pay stopped for: 1 gun sling-$.18, 1 bayonet scabbard-$.56; BLW sent to Christiansburg, VA c/o Fleming Gardner; m/1 Susan Kinger, 02/14/1849, Montgomery Co., VA, (SKF d. 03/30/1853, Blacksburg, Montgomery Co., VA);$^{648}$ m/2 Luemma Elizabeth Songer, 10/14/1856, Catlettsburg, Boyd Co., KY;$^{648}$ SC #918, filed from Kidderville, Hodgeman Co., KS; phys. desc. at enl. age 27, occ. Farmer, 6'2", black hair, blue eyes, fair complexion; since discharge res. Blacksburg, Montgomery Co., VA to 1856, Catlettsburg, Boyd Co., KS 6 mos., then Clay Co., Mo. to 1859, Richardson Co., NE to 1879, Kidderville, Hodgeman Co., KS since then;$^{648}$ d. 06/23/1893, *"heart trouble,"* Kidderville, Hodgeman Co., KS, bur. Kidderville Cemetery, Kidderville, KS;$^{649}$ wid. Emma A., WC #9398, 11/14/1893, filed from Kidderville, Hodgeman Co., KS.

**Faulkner, John Floyd**, Pvt., *Preston's Co.*, b. Montgomery Co., VA;$^{650}$ enl. Mex. War service 12/07/1846 Montgomery Co., VA, age 18; pres. 04/1847; sick 06/1847; absent 08/1847 on detached service as a Hospital Attendant since 08/22/1847; pres. 10/1847, on detached service as Hospital Attendant, pay stopped for: 1 cotton shirt-$.43; absent 12/1847 on detached service as Hospital Attendant in Saltillo, Mex.; pres. 02/1848; absent 04/1848 sick in hosp.; pres. 07/1848, pay stopped for: 1 brush & pick-$.12, 1 gun sling-$.18; BLW sent to Christiansburg, VA c/o Fleming Gardner; m. Catherine Page, 08/19/1877, Catlettsburg, Boyd Co., KY;$^{650}$ Civil War service enl. Capt., Co. A, 22$^{nd}$ Regt. KY Vols. 1864;$^{650}$ SC #15041,

OFF TO WAR

07/30/1887, filed from Catlettsburg, Boyd Co., KY; since discharge res. Blacksburg, Montgomery Co., VA until 1850 when he moved to Catlettsburg, KY; phys. desc. age 59 [1887], 5'11", fair complexion, blue eyes, dark hair, occ. Blacksmith;[650] John P. Smith gave affidavit in pension claim;[650] d. 10/02/1888, Catlettsburg, KY;[651] wid. Catherine, WC #7126, 02/04/1889, filed from Catlettsburg, Boyd Co., KY

**Faulkner, Josiah**, Pvt., Co. A; b. 06/15/1820, King William Co., VA; enl. Mex. War service 11/19/1848 Richmond, VA, age 26; pres. 12/1846 - 04/1847; pres. 06/1847; pres. 08/1847; sick 10/1847, pay stopped for clothing: 2 cotton shirts-$.86, 1 cap-$.95$^{1/2}$, 2 pr. shoes-$2.44, 2 pr. wool overalls-$4.56, 2 pr. drawers-$.71, 2 blankets-$4.44, 4 pr. stockings-$.98, 1 great coat-$6.93$^{1/2}$; pres. 12/1847, pay stopped for clothing: 2 pr. wool overalls-$4.56, 1 pr. shoes-$1.22, 2 flannel shirt-$1.80, 1 blanket-$2.22; pres. 02/1848, pay stopped for: 1 pr. shoes-$1.22; pres. 04/1848, pay stopped for 1 wool jacket; 07/1848, pay stopped for: 1 musket sling-$.16; BLW sent to Lynchburg, VA; c. 1850 res. Nelson Co., VA, age 30, occ. Plasterer, b. Hanover Co., VA, w. Mary Jane (23);[652] m. Mary T. Harris, 01/28/1852, Liberty Hall, Nelson Co., VA;[653] c. 1860 res. Lovingston, Nelson Co., VA, age 39, occ. Plasterer, w. Mary J. (35), dau. Bettie L. (13), dau. Katherine A. (8);[654] [Civil War service a Josiah Faulkner enl. 04/19/1861 as a Pvt., Co. D, 19$^{th}$ Va. Inf. at Howardsville, VA, mustered 05/10/1861 at Charlottesville, VA, age 40, occ. farmer, appointed Capt. 07/01/1861, under arrest by order of Genl. Winder 01/16/1862, under arrest by order of Gen. Longstreet 02/18/1862, re-elected Capt. 02/28/1862, wounded 05/05/1862 at Williamsburg, VA, resigned 01/30/1863, a resident of Nelson Co., VA;[655] c. 1870 res. Lovingston, Nelson Co., VA, age 46, occ. Farmer, w. Mary J. (44), dau. Maria C. (16);[656] Suffered a stroke while working as a plasterer in Buckingham Co., VA 06/1882;[657] SC #958, 02/28/1887, filed from Howardsville, Albemarle Co., VA; Since discharge res. Lynchburg, VA to 1850 since then Nelson and Albemarle Cos., VA; d. 05/06/1889 Howardsville, Albemarle Co., VA; wid. Mary Jane, WC #6471, 07/22/1889, filed from Howardsville, Albemarle Co., VA

**Featherston(e), John Randolph**, 3$^{rd}$ Cpl., Co. M; b. 12/24/1824, Amelia Co., VA, son of Joshua & Ann (Wilkinson) Featherston;[658] enl. Mex. War service 07/01/1847 Lynchburg, VA, age 21; pres. 09/1847; pres. 11/1847; pres. 12/1847; pres. 02/1848; pres. 04/1848; pres. 08/1848, prom. 3$^{rd}$ Cpl. 05/08/1848; BLW sent to Lynchburg, VA; c. 1850 res. Lunenburg Co., VA, age 25, occ. Farmer;[659] m. Jennie Winston, 01/1855, Hanover Co., VA;[658] (JWF d. 05/1855);[658] c. 1860, res. Pleasant Grove P.O., Lunenburg Co., VA, occ. Merchant, age 36;[660] Civil War service enl. as a Pvt., Co. G, 1$^{st}$ Va. Cav.05/09/1861 at Amelia C.H., pres. until discharged 08/10/1862 for being overage; organized Co. B, 3$^{rd}$ Regt. VA Arty., Local Defense Troops, enl. as Capt. 02/05/1862;[493, 441] SC #915, 02/04/1887, filed from Cleburne, Johnson Co., TX; phys. desc. 5'11', swarthy complexion, gray eyes, black hair, occ. Farmer; *"I have been a widower since the death of my wife in 1855 and will be until I go to heaven...there we will have a reunion forever;"*[658] d. 03/03/1910 *"senile debility,"* Cleburne, TX.,[658] bur. Cleburne Cem., Tex.?

**Fegan, Thomas**, Pvt., Co. B; enl. 12/21/1846, Richmond, VA, age 23; pres. 10/1847, pay stopped for: 1 pr. shoes-$1.22, 2 cotton shirts-$.86, 1 pr. overalls-$2.28, 2 pr. socks-$.49, 2 flannel shirts-$1.80, 1 cap-$.95$^{1/2}$; pres. 12/1847, pay stopped for: 1 blanket-$2.22; pres. 02/1848, pay stopped for: 1 pr. cotton drawers-$.35$^{1/2}$, 1 pr. shoes-$1.22; pres. 04/1848; pres. 08/1848, BLW sent to Washington City, DC.; m. Ann Toland 10/30/1858, Washington, DC; c. 1860 occ. Painter, res. B St. north, 1$^{st}$ St. west., Washington, D.C.;[661] [Civil War service enl. as Pvt., McDermott's Co., 5$^{th}$ Btln. DC Militia]

**Felts, John**, Pvt., Co. B; enl. Dec. 27, 1846, Richmond, VA, age 43; pres. 06/1847; sick 08/1847; d. 09/24/1847 Regimental Hosp., pay due from 08/31/1847, pay stopped for: 2 cotton shirts-$.86, 1 jacket-$2.66, 2 pr. socks-$.49, 1 ramrod-$.57, 1 pricker & brush-$.12, 1 canteen & strap-$.27, 1 haversack-$.20$^{3/4}$, 1 screw driver-$.07, 1 wiper-$.13, a pr. overalls-$2.28.

## VIRGINIA VOLUNTEERS IN MEXICO

**Fenwick, Benedict J.**, 4$^{th}$ Sgt., Co. B; enl. 11/20/1846, Alexandria, VA, age 23; court-martialed 01/18/1847 at Fort Monroe, VA, Charge #1: *Violation of the 9$^{th}$ Article of War*, Charge #2: *Conduct Prejudicial to Good Order and Military Discipline*, Specification: *" In this, that he, Corporal Benedict Fenwick of Capt. Corse's Co. of the VA Regiment of Volunteers was absent, with his arms, from the Garrison of Fort Monroe, without permission from the proper authority, and being ordered by Lieut. Garnett, of the regiment aforesaid, Officer of the Guard, to return to the Garrison, did refuse to obey said order, and did say to Lieut. Garnett aforesaid, when attempting to arrest Pvt. Dulany, 'I will be damned if you shall touch him,' or words to that effect, and did, with arms, resist and offer violence to the said Lieut. Garnett while in the execution of his duty;"* pled not guilty, court found him not guilty; pres. 06/1847; pres. 08/1847; pres. 08/1847; pres. 10/1847, pay stopped for: 1 pr. overalls-$2.28, 1 pr. shoes-$1.22, 2 pr. cotton drawers-$.71, 2 pr. socks-$.49, 1 blanket-$2.22; pres. 12/1847, pay stopped for: 1 pr. overalls-$2.28, 2 pr. cotton drawers-$.35$^{1/2}$, 1 blanket-$2.22, 1 dragoon overcoat-$8.75$^{1/2}$; pres. 02/1848, pay stopped for: 1 pr. shoes-$1.22; pres. 04/1848, prom. 4$^{th}$ Sgt. 04/18/1848; pres. 08/1848, pay stopped for: 1 pick & brush-$.12, 1 screw driver-$.07, BLW sent to Georgetown, D.C.

**Fenwick, Richard Maury Augustus**, Pvt., Co. L; b. 03/23/1826, Washington, D.C.;[662] enl. Mex. War service 03/01/1847 Fairfax C.H., VA, age 21; pres. 06/1847; pres. 08/1847; discharged 01/31/1848 at Saltillo, Mex. on Surgeon's Certificate of Disability;[72] m. Emeline L. 10/11/1849, Washington, D.C.; c. 1863-1907 res. H St., Washington, D.C.;[663] c. 1863 occ. Policeman, Washington, D.C.;[664] c. 1868 occ. Treasury Detective, res. H St. nr. 2$^{nd}$ St., NW;[665] served in Civil War (US), Pvt., Co. M, 2$^{nd}$ Btln. D.C. Vol. Inf.; IC #577274; 1874 occ. Painter, res. 634 H St., NW, house 208 H St., NW, Wash. D.C.;[666] SC #7838, 04/20/1887; phys. desc. b. D.C., hazel eyes, brown hair, occ. Painter; wid. Emeline Levinia, WC #14701, 04/19/1907, both0 from D.C.; d. 04/10/1907, *"senile debility;"*[667,668] bur. Congressional Cemetery, Wash., D.C.

**Ferguson, Robert**, Pvt., Co. B; enl. 11/20/1846, Alexandria, VA, age 31; pres. 06/1847; pres. 08/1847; pres. 10/1847, pay stopped for: 4 flannel shirts-$3.60, 1 pr. overalls-$2.28, 3 pr. socks-$.73$^{1/2}$, 1 pr. shoes-$1.22, 1 cap-$.95$^{1/2}$, 2 pr. cotton drawers-$.71; pres. 12/1847, pay stopped for: 1 blanket-$2.22, 1 pr. overalls-$2.28; pres. 02/1848, pay stopped for: 1 pr. shoes-$1.22; pres. 04/1848; pres. 08/1848, BLW sent to Alexandria, VA; c. 1850 res. Alexandria, VA, age 32, occ. Laborer, w. Ann E. (20), dau. Margaret (10/12);[669] c. 1860 res. Alexandria, VA, age 46, occ. Laborer, w. Ann (30), dau. Margaret (11), son William (9), son Robert (7), son Marcus (3);[670] d. 11/29/1878 Bluff Point, VA *a widower* on the farm of W.A. Smoot, body transported for interment.[671]

**Ferguson, William G.**, Pvt., LIC; b.09/11/1822, Augusta Co., VA;[672] enl. Mex. War service 12/19/1846 Staunton, VA, age 23; pres. 08/1847; absent 10/1847 sick in Hosp. at Saltillo, Mex., pay stopped for: 1 forage cap-$.95$^{1/2}$, 1 wool jacket-$2.66, 1 pr. overalls-$2.28, 2 pr. shoes-$2.44, 2 pr. socks-$.49, 1 cotton shirts-$.43; discharged 12/08/1847 on Surgeon's Certificate of Disability; m. Sarah Elizabeth Small, 06/26/1849, Norfolk, VA, (SSF d. 12/24/1884);[672] SC #904, 03/09/1887, filed from 1816 E. Broad St., Richmond, Henrico Co., VA; phys. desc. 5'8$^{1/2}$", 140 lbs., blue eyes, white hair, light complexion; since discharge res. in Norfolk & Richmond, VA;[672] Robert H. Vaden and Samuel Searl gave affidavits in pension claim;[672] lists children Ida Virginia Ferguson Jarvis b. 05/13/1870, Katie Lee Spott b. 07/26/1861;[672] d. 12/08/1909.[672]

## OFF TO WAR

**Ficklin, Benjamin Franklin,** 4th Cpl., Co. A; b. 12/18/1827 Albemarle Co., VA, son of Rev. Benjamin & Ellen (Slaughter) Ficklin; never married; entered the Virginia Military Institute (VMI) 1845, where he was a legendary prankster. In the fall of 1846 he was arrested and expelled for placing a bucket of water over the door of a superior officers room and smearing the door handle with *"a quantity of filth,"*[673,674] enl. Mex. War service 11/25/1846, age 19; pres. until sick 04/1847, in hosp. at Monterey, Mex., since 04/25/1847; discharged 04/30/1847 for disease by order of Maj. Gen. Taylor; was reinstated at VMI and grad. in 1849; early 1850's was employed with Russell, Majors & Waddell a express freight co.; c. 1854 originated the idea for the *Pony Express*, *"Ben Ficklin is the man who originated the Pony Express and carried it into operation.";*[675] c. 1860 was a Route Superintendent for the *Pony Express*; Civil War service apptd. Lt. Col., 45th Va. Inf. 06/17/1861, refused commission and dropped from roll;[676] apptd. Capt. Asst. Quartermaster 08/1862;[677] briefly commanded a Blockade Runner and is alleged to have served in the Confederate Secret Service;[678] was arrested for suspicion of complicity in Abraham Lincoln's assassination but was released a few months afterward; c. 1867 moved to Texas received a government contract for weekly mail service from Fort Smith, Ark. to San Antonio, Tex. with a branch line to El Paso. He established his headquarters in the community that came to bear his name - Ben Ficklin, Texas. The town is now flooded by a reservoir for the City of San Angelo, Tex.; d. 03/10/1871 Willard's Hotel, Washington, D.C. While dining a fishbone lodged in his throat. During an attempted excision the bone sliced an artery and he literally drowned in his on blood; bur. Maplewood Cem., Charlottesville, VA[679]

Photo credit: VMI Archives, Lexington, VA

**Fields, Richard,** Pvt., Co. C; enl. Mex. War service 12/30/1846, Bowling Green, VA, age 23; sick 06/1847; pres. 08/1847, pay stopped for: 1 cap-$.95[1/2], 2 pr. socks-$.49, 2 cotton shirts-$.86, 2 woolen shirts-$1.80; pres. 10/1847, pay stopped for: 1 pr. socks-$.24[1/2], 2 pr. drawers-$.71, 1 pr. pants-$2.28, 1 cotton shirt-$.43, 2 woolen shirt-$1.80; pres. 12/1847, pay stopped for: 2 pr. socks-$.49, 2 woolen shirts-$1.80, 1 pr. shoes-$1.22; pres. 04/1848, pay stopped for: 1 jacket-$2.66, 1 flannel shirt-$.90, 1 pr. shoes-$1.22, 1 india rubber canteen-$.27; pres. 08/1848, [Civil War service a Richard Fields served as a Pvt., 8th Pa. Cav.];[554] BLW sent to Philadelphia, Pa.; wid. Henrietta, WA #9355, 10/02/1890, from NJ; pension file missing 07/16/2001.

**Fielder, Martin D.,** Pvt., Co. G; enl. Mex. War service 11/28/1846 Richmond, VA, age 27; deserted 12/17/1846 Richmond, VA; m. Mary Frances Matthews, 10/05/1848, Albemarle Co., VA;[680] c. 1850 res. Albemarle Co., VA, age 30, occ. None Listed, w. Francis (22), son John (1);[681]

**Finnall, William,** Pvt., Co. C; enl. Mex. War service 12/10/1846, Fredericksburg, VA, age 23; sick 06/1847; pres. 08/1847, pay stopped for: 1 cap-$.95[1/2], 2 pr. socks-$.49, 2 cotton shirts-$.86, 2 woolen shirts-$1.80, 1 pr. shoes-$1.22, 1 knapsack & straps-$1.10; pres. 10/1847, pay stopped for: 2 pr. socks-$.49, 2 pr. drawers-$.71, 1 jacket-$2.66, 2 pr. pants-$4.56, 1 pr. shoes-$1.22, 1 great coat-$6.93[1/2]; pres. 12/1847, pay stopped for: 1 blanket-$2.22; pres. 04/1848, pay stopped for: 1 jacket-$2.66, 1 pr. shoes-$1.22; 1 india rubber canteen-$.27; pres. 08/1848, BLW sent to Fredericksburg, VA

**Fisher, Addison K.,** Bugler, LIC; b. Rockingham Co., VA;[682] m. Sarah A. Jennings, 02/27/1844, Augusta Co., VA;[683] enl. Mex. War service 11/27/1846 Staunton, VA, age 24;

## VIRGINIA VOLUNTEERS IN MEXICO

pres. 06/1847; pres. 08/1847; absent 10/1847 on detached service as Bugler at HQ's., pay stopped for: 1 forage cap-$.95$^{1/2}$, 1 wool jacket-$2.66, 2 pr. overalls-$4.56, 1 pr. shoes-$1.22, 2 pr. socks-$.49, 2 cotton shirts-$.86; absent 12/1847, on detached service as Bugler at HQ, pay stopped for: 1 blanket-$2.22, 1 pr. shoes-$1.22, 1 pr. overalls-$2.28, 1 pr. drawers-$.35$^{1/2}$; pres. 04/1848, reduced to ranks from Bugler; pres. 07/1848, pay stopped for: 1 bayonet scabbard-$.56, 1 waist belt-$.21, 1 waist belt plate-$.10, 1 gun sling-$.16, 1 pick & brush-$.12, 1 wiper-$.20; BLW sent to Staunton, VA; c. 1850 res. Augusta Co., VA, age 27, occ. (not listed), w. Sarah A. (25), son Edward (7), son Addison (3), dau. Elizabeth (5), dau. Lucinda (1);[684] c. 1860, res. Augusta Co., VA, age 38, occ. Miller;[685] Civil War service Pvt., Co. C, 52$^{nd}$ Va. Inf., enl. 07/16/1861 at Staunton, VA, on detached service 11/1861-04/1862 in QM Dept., d. Staunton before 03/1864.[686]

**Fisher, Amos Thomas**, Pvt., Co. B; b. 10/03/1825, Occoquan, Prince William Co., VA , son of Samuel Henry & Elizabeth (Mattingly) Fisher;[687] enl. 12/05/1846, Alexandria, VA, age 21; phys. desc. 5'4$^{1/2}$", fair complexion, gray eyes, black hair, occ. Carpenter; discharged 04/02/1847 Camargo, Mex. on Surgeon's Certificate of disability, *insanity*; rcvd. Invaild pension 1851; bro. Isaiah Fisher appointed guardian 09/01/1851;[687] 05/03/1853 invalid pension questioned under allegations insanity *"...did not originate in military service, but was the result of a fall from a building while he was an apprentice to the Carpenter's business in Alexandria...;"*[687] William McKnight and a Dr. Murphy both of Alexandria state in rebuttal that the fall, which occurred while constructing a house in Maryland, did not cause any type of brain damage. They further asserted that the damage resulted from a fever the claimant suffered while in Mexico. McKnight had employed Fisher and Murphy examined him after the fall;[688] m. Margaret Lyles, 03/08/1862, Brentsville, Prince William Co., VA;[689] During the Civil War was *"...employed in carrying written communications from and to the Ladies Association at Mount Vernon, he being permitted by the military on both sides to pass without interruption in consequence of his mental condition...;"*[687] Children Ellen Rebecca b. 12/20/1864, Henry Dogan b. 07/03/1867, Annie Wills b. 11/11/1869, Clara Matilda 08/04/1872; House burned down in 1866 along with all important papers including discharge;[690] SC #16675, 07/11/1888, from VA, OW IF #25087, Since discharge res. in Prince William and Alexandria, VA, except 1849 when in California; Occ. Stamping Clerk at Post Office, Alexandria, VA 1885-1889, Night Watchman at Citizens National Bank, Alexandria, VA, 1889-1892;[690] d. 3/11/1919 210 Prince St., Alex., VA; bur. Bethel Cem., Alex., VA;[45] (MLF d. 06/30/1888, Alexandria);[687] brother of Pvt. Isiah Fisher.

**Fisher, Isaiah**, Pvt., Co. B; b. 08/31/1828, Occoquan, Prince William Co., VA, son of Samuel Henry & Elizabeth (Mattingly) Fisher;[691] enl. 12/22/1846, Alexandria, VA, age 18; pres. 06/1847; pres. 08/1847; pres. 10/1847, pay stopped for: 2 flannel shirts-$1.80, 4 pr. socks-$.98, 1 pr. shoes-$1.22, 1 cotton shirt-$.43, 1 pr. overalls-$2.28, 1 overcoat-$ 6.93$^{1/2}$, 1 cap-$.95$^{1/2}$, 1 pr. cotton drawers-$.35$^{1/2}$; pres. 12/1847, pay stopped for: 1 pr. cotton drawers-$.35$^{1/2}$, 2 flannel shirts-$1.80, 1 pr. shoes-$1.22, 1 blanket-$2.22; pres. 02/1848; pres. 04/1848, pay stopped for: 1 jacket-$2.66, 2 flannel shirts-$1.82; pres. 08/1848, BLW sent to Occoquan, Prince Wm. Co., VA; m. Sallie Stevenson 06/20/1861, Savannah, Andrew Co., Mo.;[692] SC #15281, 10/24/1887, d. 03/13/1892, *Old Age, 64 yrs.*, pension indicates *Bright's Disease*, bur. First Presbyterian Cemetery, Alex., VA;[100] wid. Sallie A., WC #8287, 07/14/1892, Sallie Fisher (SSF b. Woodford Co., KY 10/01/1842, d. Alexandria, VA 04/29/1911), names sons John H. Fisher and Charles S. Fisher; both pension filed from Alexandria, VA; brother of Pvt. Amos T. Fisher.

**Fisher, John W.**, 1$^{st}$ Sgt., Co. D; enl. 01/04/1847, Petersburg, VA, age 24; pres. 02/1847; pres. 04/1847; pres. 06/1847, prom. 1$^{st}$ Sgt. 06/07/1847; pres. 08/1847, pay stopped for: 1 cap-$.95$^{1/2}$; pres. 10/1847, pay stopped for: 1 pr. pants-$2.28, 2 pr. socks-$.49, 1 pr. shoes-$1.22, 1 overcoat-$6.93$^{1/2}$; pres. 12/1847, pay stopped for 1 cap-$.95$^{1/2}$, 1 jacket-$2.66, 1 pr. pants-

OFF TO WAR

$2.28, 1 pr drawers-$.71, 2 pr. socks-$.49, 1 pr. shoes-$2.44, 1 blanket-$2.22; pres. 04/1848, pay stopped for: 1 pr. pants-$2.28, 1 overcoat-$6.93$^{1/2}$, error in charging for blanket last muster roll $2.22; pres. 08/1847, BLW sent to Hicks Ford, Greensville Co., VA; m. Sallie Bagwell, of Halifax Co., 06 or 07/1872.[693]

**Fitzgerald, Edward Ward**,[694] **"Ned,"** Pvt., Co. E; b. 08/03/1823 Nottoway Co., VA son of Benjamin W. & Elizabeth C. Fitzgerald;[694] enl. Mex. War service 11/30/1846 Petersburg, VA, age 22; pres. 04/1847; pres. 06/1847; pres. 08/1847; pres. 10/1847, pay stopped for: 1 pr. shoes-$1.22, 1 pr. stockings-$.24$^{1/2}$, 2 cotton shirts-$.86, 1 cap-$.95$^{1/2}$; pres. 12/1847, [illegible]; pres. 02/1848; pres. 04/1848, pay stopped for: 1 jacket-$2.66; m. Mary Ann Key 11/16/1854, Panola Co., MS;[695] SC #2104, 03/17/1887, filed from Senatobia, Tate Co., MS, phys. desc. 5'9", light complexion, light blue eyes, light hair, occ. Farmer, occ. at enlistment Clerk; d. 09/11/1903 *"heart disease,"* 1409 Liberty Avenue, Beaumont, TX, bur. Magnolia Cemetery, Beaumont, TX;[696] wid. Mary A., WC #13782, 11/14/1903, filed from 1409 Liberty Avenue, Beaumont, Jefferson Co., TX; Lists children Edgar Poe Fitzgerald b. 09/28/1855, Thomas Benjamin Fitzgerald b. 08/31/1859, d. 10/10/1889, James Key Fitzgerald b. 02/03/1861, Martha Lee Fitzgerald b. 04/16/1863, Edward Robert Fitzgerald b. 04/09/1871;[694] (MAF b. 07/12/1836 Ga., d. 04/15/1915, Beaumont, Jefferson Co., TX).[696]

**Fitzhugh, John H.**, Pvt., Co. G; b. 12/21/1821, King & Queen Co., VA;[697] enl. Mex. War service 12/07/1846 Richmond, VA, age 24; pres. 06/1847, prom. 1$^{st}$ Cpl.; pres. 08/1847; pres. 10/1847, pay stopped for: 1 pr. overalls-$2.28, 2 cotton shirts-$.86, 2 pr. drawers-$.71,2 pr. socks-$.49, 1 forage cap-$.95$^{1/2}$; pres. 12/1847, reduced to ranks, pay stopped for: 1 blanket-$2.22, 2 pr. pants-$4.56; pres. 02/1848; pres. 04/1848; pres. 08/1848; BLW sent to Gloucester Co. C.H., VA; m. Harriet Bullitt, 11/30/1854, Gloucester, VA; SC #3047, 05/02/1887, filed from Austin, Travis Co., TX; suffering *"asthma since 1848 and rupture;"* since discharge res. Covington, KY, 12 yrs., Travis and Hays Cos., TX, 27 yrs., then Austin, TX; bro. of Pvt. Lafayette H. Fitzhugh.

**Fitzhugh, Layfayette Henry**, 4$^{th}$ Sgt., Co. G; b. 05/09/1829, VA, son of Phillip & Mary Macon (Aylett) Fitzhugh; enl. Mex. War service 12/07/1846 Richmond, VA, age 18; pres. 06/1847, prom. 2$^{nd}$ Cpl.; pres. 08/1847; sick 10/1847, pay stopped for: 1 pr. overalls-$2.28, 1 cotton shirt-$.43, 1 pr. drawers-$.35$^{1/2}$, 2 shoes-$2.44, 3 pr. socks-$.73$^{1/2}$, 1 great coat-$6.95$^{1/2}$, 1 forage cap-$.95$^{1/2}$; sick 12/1847 in Hosp. at Saltillo, Mex., prom. to 4$^{th}$ Sgt., pay stopped for: 2 pr. drawers-$.71, 1 blanket-$2.22; pres. 02/1848, pay stopped for: 1 cap-$.95$^{1/2}$, 2 cotton shirts-$.86; pres. 04/1848, pay stopped for: 1 blanket-$2.22; pres. 08/1848, BLW sent to Middlesex Co. C.H.; m/1 Elizabeth Garlick Semple, 12/16/1849; m/2 Anna Eliza Bullitt, after 01/04/1851; Civil War service Capt., Co. H, 1$^{st}$ KY Inf.;[202] SC #19701, 07/30/1891, wid. Anna Eliza, WC #14242, 10/19/1905, both from TX.

**Flagg, Thomas, G., (Jr.)**, 4$^{th}$ Sgt., Co. M; b. 03/12/1825, Martinsburg, Berkeley Co., VA; son of Thomas G. & Margaret Flagg;[698] enl. Mex. War service 06/06/1847 Martinsburg, VA, age 22; pres. 09/1847; pres. 11/1847, reduced to 1$^{st}$ Cpl. from 3$^{rd}$ Sgt.; pres. 12/1847; pres. 02/1848, pay stopped for: 1 over coat-$6.93$^{1/2}$; pres. 04/1848; pres. 08/1848, prom. 4$^{th}$ Sgt., pay stopped for: 1 cartridge box belt plate-$.10; BLW sent to Martinsburg, VA; c. 1850 res. Martinsburg, Berkeley Co., VA, age 24, occ. Wheelwright;[699] m. his cousin Martha M. Flagg 06/09/1853, Montgomery Co., MD;[698] c. 1860 res. Berryville, Clarke Co., VA, age 33, occ. Painter, w. Martha N. (26), dau. Sarah B. (6), dau. Bertha (2);[700]c. 1870 res. Berryville, Clarke Co., VA, age 45, occ. House Painter, w. Martha (37), dau. Sallie B. (15), dau. Bertha W. (12), son Horatio (9);[701]Civil War service enl. Pvt., Co. H, 27$^{th}$ Va. Inf.04/19/1861 at Darksville; pres. until disbanded 06/10/1861;[702] enl. Co. A, 11$^{th}$ Va. Cav. 10/07/1861, promoted 2$^{nd}$ Lt.; paroled at Winchester, VA, 04/20/1865; desc. age 40, 5'8½", fair complex., dark hair, gray eyes; SC #7203, 04/12/1887, from VA; since discharge res. Martinsburg, VA to 1850, Berryville, VA to 1893, Shennandoah Junction to 1901, Martinsburg, WV since then;[698] phys. desc. 5'8$^{1/2}$",

## VIRGINIA VOLUNTEERS IN MEXICO

fair complexion, gray eyes, light brown hair, occ. House and Sign Painter;[698] Edward W. Maxwell gave affidavit in pension claim; d. 01/22/1910, *"Infirmation of old age, age 85,"* Martinsburg, WV; [698, 703] bur. Old Norbourne Ch. Cem., Berkeley Co., WV.[702]

**Flournoy, Peter Creed**,[704] 4$^{th}$ Sgt., Co. A; b. 09/15/1828, Chesterfield Co., VA, son of Daniel H. & Martha (Graves) Flournoy;[705] enl. Mex. War service 12/08/1846 Richmond, VA, age 18; pres. 12/1846 - 04/1847; pres. 06/1847, prom. 4$^{th}$ Cpl. 05/01/1847; pres. 08/1847, prom. 4$^{th}$ Sgt. 08/23/1847; pres. 10/1847, pay stopped for: 2 cotton shirts-$.86, 2pr. wool overalls-$4.56, 1 cap-$.95$^{1/2}$, 2 pr. shoes-$2.44, 2 pr. stockings-$.49, 2 flannel shirts-$1.80; pres.12/1847, pay stopped for clothing: 1 pr. drawers-$.35$^{1/2}$; pres. 02/1848, pay stopped for 1 pr. wool overalls-$2.28; pres. 04/1847, pay stopped for: 1 wool jacket; BLW sent to, Chesterfield C.H., VA; c. 1850 res. Chesterfield Co., VA, age 21, occ. None Listed;[706] m. Mary Daniel Jeter 01/06/1852, Amelia Co., VA;[707] listed as a Physician;[704] [Civil War service a Peter C. Flournoy served as a Col., 6$^{th}$ Mo. Inf.;] [202] SC # 23184, 11/11/1890, filed from Linneus, Linn Co., MO.; Since discharge lived near Richmond, VA, Arkansas for 10 years, and Linneus, Mo. for 26 years; d. 03/02/1891, Linneus, Linn Co., MO.;[707] wid. Mary D., WC #7405, 04/06/1891, filed from Linneus, Linn Co., MO.; (MDF b. 09/05/1831, d. 11/09/1907 Pine Bluff, AR).[704]

**Foley, James S., Jr.**, 4$^{th}$ Sgt., Co. E; enl. Mex. War service 11/30/1846 Petersburg, VA, age 22; pres. 04/1847; pres. 06/1847; pres. 08/1847, prom. 4$^{th}$ Sgt. 07/26/1847; pres. 10/1847, pay stopped for: 1 pr. overalls-$2.28, 2 pr. stockings-$.49; pres. 12/1847, pay stopped for: 2 pr. socks-$.49, 1 blanket-$2.22; pres. 02/1848.

**Folks, Algernon R.**, Pvt., Co. M; enl. Mex. War service 08/16/1847 Richmond, VA, age 28; pres. 09/1847; pres. 11/1847; pres. 12/1847; pres. 02/1848; pres. 04/1848, pay stopped for: 1 blanket-$2.22; pres. 08/1848, pay stopped for: 1 gun sling-$.16, 1 bayonet-$1.44, 1 pick & brush-$.12; BLW sent to City Point, Prince George Co., VA

**Folks, Robert W.**, 2$^{nd}$ Lt., Co. M; enl. Mex. War service 08/29/1847 Nottoway C.H., VA, age 21; pres. 10/1847; pres. 11/1847, reduced to 2$^{nd}$ Sgt. from 1$^{st}$ Sgt.; pres. 12/1847; in confinement 02/1848, reduced to ranks from 1$^{st}$ Sgt. 02/09/1848, pay stopped for: 1 blanket-$2.22, 2 flannel shirts-$1.80; in confinement 04/1848; pres. 08/1848, prom. 2$^{nd}$ Lt. 02/26/1848; BLW sent to Nottoway C.H., VA

**Forbes, John P.**, Pvt., Co. F; enl. Mex. War service 11/24/1846, Portsmouth, VA, age 35; pres. 06/1847; pres. 08/1847, reduced from Fifer 08/31/1847 by order of Actg. Insp. Genl; pres. 10/1847, pay stopped for: 1 pr. overalls-$2.28, 7 pr. socks-$1.71$^{1/2}$, 3 pr. drawers-1.06$^{1/2}$, 1 forage cap-$.95$^{1/2}$, 1 pr. shoes-$1.22, 2 flannel shirts-$1.80, 1 overcoat-$6.93$^{1/2}$, 1 blanket-$2.22, 2 cotton shirts-$.86; pres. 02/1848, pay stopped for: 1 pr. overalls-$2.28, 1 pr. shoes-$1.22; pres. 04/1848; pres. 08/1848, pay stopped for: 1 cartridge box belt plate-$.10, 1 gun sling-$.18, 1 jacket-$2.37, BLW sent to Portsmouth, VA c/o E.T. Blamire.

OFF TO WAR

Force, Charles Fairchild, 1st Corp., Co. B; b. 02/09/1827, Washington, D.C.; son of Gen. Peter (Mayor of Washington, D.C.) & Martha (Evans) Force; educated at Episcopal Seminary, Alexandria, VA and Columbia College, Washington, D.C.; enl. 11/30/1846, Alexandria, VA, age 19; pres. 06/1847; pres. 08/1847; pres. 08/1847; pres. 10/1847, pay stopped for: 1 pr. overalls-$2.28, 1 blanket-$2.22; pres. 02/1848, pay stopped for: 1 pr. shoes-$1.22; pres. 08/1848, pay stopped for: 1 screw driver-$.07, 1 ball screw-$.12, 1 spring vice-$.35, 1 pr. shoes-$1.16, BLW sent to Washington, DC; Civil War service Capt. Co. E, 51st Ala. Cav. (Partisan Rangers), cited for conspicuous gallantry 07/03/1864, captured at Murfreesboro and sent to Johnson's Island, OH; m. Mary E. Mathews of Tuscaloosa, AL, 06/15/1867; post war occ. Physician and Hardware Store Owner, Selma, AL; d. 08/04/1884 Selma, AL photograph;[708] bur. Sec. D, Lot 190, Live Oak Cemetery, Selma, AL; WC #7497 "Mary A." dated 4/18/1891 rcvd. from AL (d. 05/31/1923).

Photo credit: Confederate Veteran Magazine, © 1896

Ford, James B., Pvt., Recruit Co., enl. Mex. War service 09/07/1847 Charlotte C.H., VA, age 20; discharged 09/19/1847 by Surgeon; m. Sarah A. Garden, 02/20/1849, Charlotte Co., VA;[709] c. 1850 res. Charlotte Co., VA, age 23, occ. Plasterer, w. Sarah A. (23);[710] c. 1860 res. Charlotte C.H., Charlotte Co., VA, age 34, occ. Negro Trader, w. Sarah S. (34), dau. L. Ford (9), dau. O. Ford (4);[711] Civil War service Cpl., Co. B, 22nd Va. Inf. Btln., enl. 12/31/1861 Charlotte Co. for 12 mos., reduced to Pvt. 05/19/1862, pres. 07/1862 through 04/1864; NFR.[712]

Forde, Joseph W., [James W.]Fifer, Co. B; enl. 12/18/1846, Alexandria, VA, age 18; pres. 06/1847; pres. 08/1847; pres. 12/1847, fined 2 mos. pay by order (103 & 120) genl. Court-martial, pay stopped for: 2 cotton shirts-$.86, 1 pr. shoes-$1.22, 1 pr. overalls-$2.28, 1 blanket-$2.22; 1 cap-$.95$^{1/2}$; sick 02/1848, pay stopped for: overpymnt. of $1.47 on last pay roll; pres. 04/1848, pay stopped for: 1 jacket-$2.66; pres. 08/1848, pay stopped for 1 musket-$13.00, 1 pick & brush-$.12, BLW sent to Alexandria, VA

Forinash, Elmore, Smith's Co.; m. Margaret Mawyer 11/27/1851 Lewis Co., VA;[713] c. 1880 res. Lewis Co., WV, age 52, occ. Farm Laborer, w. Mariah (50) Keeping House, s-i-l Lucinda Reed (54);[714] SA #24087, 10/07/1892, from WV.

Foster, Elijah, Pvt., Co. M; b. 05/02/1825, Putnam Co., Ga.;[715] enl. Mex. War service 08/01/1847 Richmond, VA, age 19; pres. 09/1847; pres. 11/1847; pres. 12/1847; m. Mary Ann Howell, 12/13/1847, Old Point, Elizabeth City Co., VA;[715] pres. 02/1848, pay stopped for: 1 flannel shirt-$.90; pres. 04/1848, pay stopped for: 1 pr. shoes-$1.22, 1 cap-$.95$^{1/2}$; pres. 08/1848; BLW sent to Ft. Monroe, VA; [Civil War service an Elijah Foster served as a Pvt., Co. I, 32nd Va. Inf., enl. 05/27/1861 at Williamsburg, VA, phys. desc. age 33, 5'3", light complexion, dark eyes, red hair, occ. Sailor, illiterate, captured 09/12/1862 at Middletown, MD, sent to Ft. Delaware, exchanged 11/02/1862, in Chimborazo Hosp. 11/1862, detailed as Wagon Driver 01/22/1863, pres. 05/12/1863, absent 10/1864 sick, captured 06/06/1865 at Sayler's Creek, VA, sent to Pt. Lookout, MD, took oath of allegiance and released 06/26/1865, a res. of Elizabeth City Co., VA,[716] SC #6752, 03/05/1887, filed from Ft. Monroe, Elizabeth City Co., VA; phys. desc. 5'3", auburn hair, hazel eyes, occ. Laborer; d. 02/25/1889, Phoebus

# VIRGINIA VOLUNTEERS IN MEXICO

Station, Elizabeth City Co., VA;[717] wid. Mary Ann, WC #6204, 03/18/1889, filed from Phoebus, Elizabeth City Co., VA; (MHF b. 09/07/1824, Back River, VA, d. 07/15/1911).[717]

**Foster, Lewis H.**, Pvt., Co. D; b. 02/19/1824;[718] enl. Mex. War service 01/12/1846, Petersburg, VA, age 22; pres. 02/1847; pres. 04/1847; pres. but sick 06/1847; pres. 08/1847; pres. 10/1847, pay stopped for: 1 pr. pants-$2.28, 1 pr. drawers-$.35$^{1/2}$, 3 pr. socks-$.73$^{1/2}$, 1 pr. shoes-$1.22, 1 blanket-$2.22; pres. 12/1847, pay stopped for: 1 pr. pants-$2.28, 1 blanket-$2.22; pres. 04/1848, pay stopped for: 1 jacket-$2.66, error in charging for 1 pr. pants on last roll, $2.28; pres. 08/1847, BLW sent to Hicks Ford, Greensville Co., VA; c. 1870 res. Poplar Mount, Greensville Co., VA, age 47, occ. Farmer & School Teacher, w. Addie (26);[719] SC #968, 02/17/1887, filed from Skippers, Greensville Co., VA; phys. desc. 5'11", light complexion, blue eyes, dark hair, occ. School Teacher, since discharge res. Greensville Co., VA; c. 1900 res. Zion Dist., Greensville Co., VA, age 77, widower, occ. Farmer, enumerated w/niece, Emily Bailey (63), nephew, Willie Bailey (22); d. 02/22/1908.[718]

**Fowler, James Herbert**, Pvt., Co. B; b. 01/14/1808, Joinersville, Southampton Co., VA;[720] muster roll says b. c. 1825, Chesterfield Co., VA; enl. 12/14/1846, Richmond, VA, age 22; pres. 06/1847; pres. 08/1847; pres. 10/1847, pay stopped for: 4 pr. socks-$.98, 1 pr. shoes-$1.22, 2 cotton shirts-$.86, 2 flannel shirts-$1.80, 1 pr. overalls-$2.28, 2 pr. cotton drawers-$.71, 1 cap-$.95$^{1/2}$; sick 12/1847, pay stopped for: 1 pr. shoes-$1.22; phys. desc., 5'5", light complexion, blue eyes, light hair, occ. Shoemaker; discharged 01/07/848, Buena Vista, Mex. on Surgeon's Certificate;[26] SA #20672, 11/5/1888, from VA; In a deposition Fowler states he res. at Isaacs, VA was enlisted by Capt. Corse at Ettrick, Chesterfield Co., VA where he was then working;[721] Deposition indicates that Fowler is suffering from some mental impairment. He is forgetful and confused. He states: *"I have been crazy, a little, all my life;"* after discharge resided 4 yrs. in North Carolina have lived ever since in Southampton Co., VA, now lives in Alms House, Vicksville, VA 09/03/1892. Pension examiner, in a handwritten note, acknowledges Fowler's mental condition and believes he is not more than 65 to 70 years old.

**Fowlkes, Calvin B.**, Pvt., Co. D; b. 06/30/1825 Nottoway Co., VA;[722] enl. Mex. War service 08/09/1847 Lewistown, VA, age 22; pres. 04/1848, pay stopped for: 1 pr. pants-$2.28; pres. 08/1847, BLW sent to Rehoboth P.O., Lunenburg Co., VA; m. Permelia Price Russell, 09/07/1857, Lunenburg Co., VA;[723, 722] Civil War service enl. as Pvt., Co. K, 21$^{st}$ Va. Inf. 07/21/1861 in Richmond, VA, prom. Lt. 04/21/1861; resigned 04/21/1862;[724] conscripted Co. G, 9$^{th}$ Va. Cav. 07/06/1864, pres. thru 09/30/1864, captured 04/03/1865 at Aberdeen Run, sent to Pt. Lookout, MD, released from Pt. Lookout 06/12/1865;[725] SC #2288, 02/04/1887, filed from Union City, Obion Co., TN; phys. desc. 6'1", light complexion, blue eyes, gray hair, occ. Hotel Keeper, occ. at enl. Farmer; res. Lunenburg Co. 44 yrs., Charleston, Mo., 2 yrs., Ballan Co., KY 12 yrs. Union City, TN 4 yrs., Memphis, TN 21 yrs.; d. 01/26/1908 765 Saxon Street, Memphis, TN, bur. South Grove Sect., Lot 166, Elmwood Cemetery, Memphis, TN;[722, 726] wid. Parmelia P., WC #18924, 02/12/1908, filed from 765 Saxon St., Memphis, TN; lists children Ida Fowlkes Andrews b. 11/18/1859, Laura Fowlkes Johnson b. 08/11/1858, Nannie Bass Fowlkes Klein b. 02/01/1861; (PRF b. 06/24/1835 Lunenburg Co., VA, d. 04/10/1910, Memphis, TN, bur. Elmwood Cem., Memphis, TN).

**Fraizer, John D.**, Pvt., Co. M; enl. Mex. War service 08/28/1847 Richmond, VA, age 19; pres. 09/1847; pres. 11/1847; pres. 12/1847; pres. 02/1848, pay stopped for: 1 cotton shirt-$.43; pres. 04/1848, pay stopped for: 2 cotton shirts-$.86; pres. 08/1848, pay stopped for: 1 gun sling-$.16, 1 pick & brush-$.12, 1 wormer-$.20; BLW sent to Richmond, VA

**Francis, William**, Co. A; b. 01/25/1829, Darbytown, Richmond, VA, son of Peter and Agnes (Robertson) Francis;[727] enl. Mex. War service 11/18/1846 Richmond, VA, age 19; phys. desc. 5'6", black hair, dark brown eyes, dark complexion;[728] pres. 12/1846 - 04/1847; pres. 06/1847; pres. 08/1847; pres. 10/1847, pay stopped for clothing: 3 cotton shirts-$1.29, 2 pr. wool overalls-$4.56, 1 cap-$.95$^{1/2}$, 1 pr. shoes-$1.22, 2 pr. stockings-$.49, 1 wool jacket-$2.66, 1

OFF TO WAR

great coat-$6.93$^{1/2}$, 1 blanket-$2.22; pres. 12/1847, pay stopped for clothing: 2 pr. socks-$.49, 1 pr. drawers-$.35$^{1/2}$, 1 pr. wool overalls-$2.28, 1 pr. shoes-$1.22, 1 cotton shirt-$.46; pres. 02/1848, pay stopped for: 1 pr. shoes-$1.22; sick 04/1848, pay stopped for 1 wool jacket; 07/1848, pay stopped for: 1 cartridge box-$1.10, cart. Box belt plate-$.10, waist belt plate-$.10, 1 pick & brush-$.12, 1 pr. shoes-$1.16; BLW sent to Richmond, VA; m Mary Jane Sandifer 09/11/1852, Petersburg, Dinwiddie Co., VA;[728] SC #10910, 08/11/1887, filed from 34 Thorn St., Woburn, MA; States he was too old for the Civil War, but lived in Virginia during the war. His usual trade was a Leather Tanner. Never had children;[728] Since discharge res. in Pittsburgh, Pa., Boston and Woburn, Mass.; d. 12/19/1911 *acute intestinal obstruction*, bur. Cavalry Cem., Woburn, MA.

**Francis, William T.**, Pvt., Co. I; enl. Mex. War service 02/05/1847 Richmond, VA, age 21; pres. 02/1847; absent 04/1847, left sick at Point Isabel, Tex. 03/16/1847; discharged 06/17/1847 for disability at Monterey, Mex.; [Civil War service a William T. Francis served as a Pvt., Cos. A & D, 1$^{st}$ Btln. Loc. Def.;][202] c. 1870 res. Richmond, Henrico Co., VA, age 43, occ. Moulder, dau. Adaline C. (23), dau. Mary J. (16), son Walter J. (4), dau. Rosa B. (2).[729]

**Franklin, James Benjamin**, Pvt., Co. D; enl. Mex. War service 12/23/1846, Petersburg, VA, age 19; pres. 02/1847; pres. 04/1847; pres. 06/1847; pres. 08/1847, pay stopped for: 1 cap-$.95$^{1/2}$, 1 cotton shirt-$.43; pres. 10/1847, pay stopped for: 1 pr. pants-$2.28, 2 cotton shirts-$.86, 1 pr. drawers-$.35$^{1/2}$, 1 pr. socks-$.24$^{1/2}$; pres. 12/1847, pay stopped for: 1 jacket-$2.66, 1 pr. pants-$2.28, 1 cotton shirt-$.43; absent 04/1848, detailed as a Baker, pay stopped for: 1 pr. pants-$2.28, 1 pr. shoes-$1.22, 1 blanket-$2.22; pres. 08/1847, BLW sent to Petersburg, VA; m. Anna Jane Cheatham 02/16/1853, Petersburg, VA;[730] d. 10/05/1880, Charlotte, NC, bur. Elmwood Cemetery, Charlotte, NC; wid. Ann Jane, WC #6261, 04/03/1889, filed from Charlotte, Mecklenburg Co., NC. Lt. Aurelius R. Shands & Pvt. William H. Britt gave affidavits on pension claim; (AJF b. 02/16/1831 Surrey Co., VA, d. 05/31/1908, *"blood on the brain."*)[730]

**Franklin, Layfayette B.**, Pvt., Co. C; b. 09/22/1825, Rappahannock Co., VA, son of William & Agnes Franklin;[731] enl. Mex. War service 12/10/1846, Fredericksburg, VA, age 20; disabled by gunshot wound lost forefinger of right hand; discharged 05/15/1847 Monterey, Mex. on Surgeon's Certificate of Disability; pensioned $4 per mth. 04/29/1847 for loss of finger; c. 1850 res. Stafford Co., VA, age 23, occ. None Listed;[732] m/1 Mary Ellen Cowne 02/1853; (MEF d. 02/1861 Fredericksburg, VA); Civil War service Pvt., Fredericksburg Arty., enl. 04/03/1862, phys. desc. 5'9", auburn hair, black eyes, res. of Falmouth, Stafford Co., VA, deserted to enemy 08/06/1863, sent to Philadelphia, Pa. 09/24/1863, Went to Philadelphia, Pa., Ohio and *"oil regions of Pennsylvania"* during the war; SC #15883, 02/06/1888 filed from Stafford Co., VA; m/2 Minnie (Nash) Gallahan 03/19/1901, Stafford Co., VA; d. 04/16/1911 Mussleman's, Stafford Co., VA; wid. Minnie, WC #15691, 05/19/1911, filed from Mussleman's, Stafford Co., VA; lists children Anna M. Franklin b. 04/12/1854 and Virginia B. Franklin b. 08/16/1858; (MF b. 06/20/1855 South Carolina, d. 03/01/1926).

**Freer, Henry S.**, Pvt., Co. H; enl. Mex. War service 12/30/1846, Richmond, VA, age 27; pres. 04/1847, transportation & subsistence due from residence to place of rendezvous – 82 miles; pres. 06/1847; pres. 08/1847; Court-martialed 09/21/1847, Buena Vista, Mex. *Charge #1: Disobedience of Orders; Specification: In this that he, the said Pvt. Henry S. Freer, Co. H, Va. Regt. of Vols., having been detailed for Guard duty, positively refused to perform said duty. This at Buena Vista, Mex. on or about the 6$^{th}$ day of September 1847. Charge #2: Mutinous Conduct; Specification: In this that he, the said Pvt. Henry S. Freer, Co. H, Va. Regt. of Vols., having been detailed for Guard on the 6$^{th}$ of Sept. 1847, swore he would be damned if he would go on Guard and that he could not be forced, that all the officers in the Regiment could not compel him to perform Guard Duty, or words to that effect. This at Buena*

# VIRGINIA VOLUNTEERS IN MEXICO

*Vista, Mex., on or about the evening of the 6$^{th}$ and the morning of the 7$^{th}$ of Sept. 1847. Charge #3: Conduct Prejudicial to Good Order and Military Discipline; Specification: In this that he, the said Pvt. Henry S. Freer, Co. H, Va. Regt. of Vols., when detailed for guard declared in the presence of the assembled company, that he would not perform the duty for which he had been detailed, thereby attempting to excite a spirit of mutiny, insubordination and disobedience of order on the part of the members of the company. This at Buena Vista, Mex. on or about the night of the 6$^{th}$ and morning of the 7$^{th}$ of September 1847. To which charges and specification the prisoner plead Not Guilty. Capt. E.G. Alburtis, Va. Regt. of Vols., a witness for the prosecution being duly sworn, says: I know that the prisoner was detailed for guard on the evening of the 6$^{th}$ of September 1847. He persistently refused to do the duty. On the morning of the 7$^{th}$ Sept., I was sitting in front of my tent when I heard the prisoner, who was getting his breakfast, make use of the following language. He swore he would be damned if he would go on guard and that he could not be forced, that all the officers in the Regiment could not compel him to perform Guard Duty, or words to that effect. On the evening of the 6$^{th}$ the prisoner declared before the whole company that he would not perform the duty for which he had been detailed. He was under the influence of liquor at the time. Question by the Court: Was the prisoner detailed in his regular order or not? Answer: I do not know. I do not think he was. Question by the Court: Do you know if the there was any particular cause connected with the conduct of the prisoner which was the reason of his being detailed at this time? If so state the cause. Answer: I had given my Orderly Sergt. orders to detail men for an extra tour of Guard or other duty. Being absent from drills and roll calls without permission. The prisoner was detailed for an offence of this kind. Question by the Court: Was or was not the prisoner still under the influence of liquor in the morning subsequent to his being detailed, when the remarks were made by him while getting his breakfast? Answer: I do not think he was. Sergt. John O. Reid, Co. H, Va. Regt. of Vols., a witness for the prosecution, being duly sworn, says: I know that the prisoner was detailed for guard on or about the evening of the 6$^{th}$ of Sept. 1847. The prisoner said, 'dog my flippers' if I go on guard. Question by the prisoner: Did you not think my remarks were made in a fisting mood? Answer: He was laughing at the time. Sergt. Edward Maxfield, [Maxwell?]Co. H, Va. Regt. of Vols., a witness for the defense, being duly sworn, says: Question by the Prisoner: Was the tour of guard for which I was detailed on the evening of the 6$^{th}$ Sept. 1847, a regular or an extra tour? Answer: I am not positive, but think it was an extra tour. Question by the Prisoner: Had I not an understanding with you, before the detail was made, to the effect that I should not be detailed til the next day? Answer: No. Sergt. Jno. Jamison, Co. H, Va. Regt. of Vols., a witness for the defense being duly sworn says: Question by the Prisoner: Did I not march off Guard on the morning of the 6$^{th}$ Sept. 1847? Answer: Yes. Question by the Prisoner: What do you know of my character as regards attention to duty? Answer: The prisoner has always been very attentive to his duty. I have never known him to be detailed for any extra duty as a punishment previous to the 6$^{th}$ of Sept. 1847. He has always been orderly and stands high in the company. Pvt. William L. Shoemaker, Co. H, Va. Regt. of Vols., a witness for the defense was called and being duly sworn says: Question by the Prisoner: Were not the remarks that I made on the morning of the 7$^{th}$ of September 1847 made in a fisting manner? Answer: I thought the prisoners remarks were made in fist. After deliberation the Court found the prisoner Guilty of all charges and specifications. Sentenced him to be confined at hard labor in charge of the Provost Guard for two calendar months and to forfeit two months pay;*[733] in confinement 10/1847, fined 1 mos. pay by order of genl. court-martial 10/25/1847; pres. 12/1847, pay stopped for: 1 forage cap-$.95$^{1/2}$, 1 pr. shoes-$1.22, pay due from 08/1847 muster roll; pres. 02/1848, pay stopped for: 1 forage cap-$.95$^{1/2}$, 1 pr. pants-$2.28, 1 pr. socks-$.24$^{1/2}$; absent 04/1848, sick in Hosp. at Saltillo, Mex. since 04/04/1848; pres. 07/1848, pay stopped for: 2 gun slings-$.32, 1 cartridge box plate-$.20, 1 brush & pick-$.12, 1 screw driver-$.12, 1 wiper-$.20, BLW sent to Richmond, VA [Civil War service a Henry H. Frear served as a Hospital

OFF TO WAR

Steward in Co. D, 60th Va. Inf. enl. 06/26/1861 at Lewisburg, VA, detailed as a nurse at Salem, VA, pres. until close.]¹⁶⁹

**French, Charles**, Pvt., Co. K; b. 05/13/1821, Baltimore, Baltimore Co., MD;⁷³⁴ enl. Mex. War service Jefferson Co., VA 01/20/1847, age 25; discharged 03/30/1847 at Camargo, Mex. on Surgeon's Certificate of Disability; n. Margaret Lambert, 07/09/1850, Baltimore, MD;⁷³⁴ SC #2998, 03/29/1887, filed from 407 E. Lombard St., Baltimore, MD; since discharge res. Baltimore, MD, occ. Tailor, d. 1906.⁷³⁴

**Fry, John J.**, 2ⁿᵈ Lt., Co. A; b. 02/05/1824 Fredericksburg, VA;⁷³⁵ enl. Mex. War service 11/18/1846 Richmond, VA, age 23; pres. 12/1846 - 04/1847; pres. 06/1847; resigned 08/15/1847; [Treas., Hollywood Cem., Richmond, VA, 06/03/1849;⁷³⁶] m. Mary C. Lewis, 02/06/1850, Glencastle, near Keswick, Albemarle Co., VA;⁷³⁷,⁷³⁵ [Fire Chief, Richmond, VA, 10/25/1858;⁷³⁸] c. 1870 res. Lovingston, Nelson Co., VA age 48, occ. Farmer, w. Mary C. (37), son H. Lewis (20), occ. Civil Engr., son John W. (17), son Sam Gordon (14), dau. Sarah S. (7);⁷³⁹ SC #2787, 03/29/1887, filed from Keswick, Albemarle Co., VA; d. 06/04/1888, Keswick, Albemarle, VA;⁷⁴⁰ wid. Mary C., WC #5398, 07/12/1888, filed from Keswick, Albemarle Co., VA(MCF b. 10/06/1832 near Keswick, VA, d. 11/09/1907).⁷⁴⁰

**Fry, Joshua D.**, Pvt., Co. A; enl. Mex. War service 11/18/1846 Richmond, VA, age 27; pres. until sick 04/1847 - 06/1847, in Hosp. at Camargo, Mex. 04/04/1847; pres. 06/1847; pres. 08/1847; pres. 10/1847 pay stopped for clothing: 1 pr. wool overalls-$2.28, 1 cap-$.95¹/², 2 pr. shoes-$2.44, 1 wool jacket-$2.66, 2 pr. stockings-$.49; pres. 12/1847, pay stopped for clothing: 1 pr. wool overalls-$2.28, 2 flannel shirt-$1.80, 1 pr. shoes-$1.22; pres. 02/1848, pay stopped for: 1 pr. shoes-$1.22; BLW sent to Bath C.H., VA; constable 1857-58 Bath Co., VA⁷⁴¹

**Funkhouser, John N.**, Pvt., *Preston's Co.*; b. 01/18/1825; enl. Mex. War service 01/06/1847 Montgomery Co., VA, age 26; pres. 04/1847; pres. 06/1847; pres. 08/1847; pres. 10/1847, pay stopped for: 1 pr. overalls-$2.28, 1 pr. shoes-$1.22, 3 pr. socks-$.73¹/², 1 cotton shirt-$.43, 1 cap-$.95¹/²; absent 12/1847, on detached service with company clothing since 12/07/1847, pay stopped for: 1 jacket-$2.66, 1 pr. shoes-$1.22, 1 pr. socks-$.24¹/², 2 pr. drawers-$.71, 1 blankets-$2.22; pres. 02/1848; pres. 04/1848; pres. 07/1848, pay stopped for: 1 waist belt-$.25; BLW sent to Christiansburg, VA, c/o Fleming Gardner; m. Larinda L. Mitchell 09/26/1848, New Glasgow, Amherst Co., VA;⁷⁴² d. 10/10/1885, Nelson Co., VA; wid. Larinda L., WC #2536, 06/24/1887, filed from Lynchburg, Campbell Co., VA; (LMF b. 06/04/1825, Campbell Co., VA, d. 04/25/1904).⁷⁴²

**Fuqua, Robert F.**, Pvt., Co. E; b. Prince Geo. Co., VA, son of James & Martha Ann (Blackwell) Fuqua;⁷⁴³ enl. Mex. War service 11/30/1846 Petersburg, VA, age 21; pres. 04/1847; pres. 06/1847; pres. 08/1847; 10/1847 [illegible]; pres. 12/1847, [illegible]; absent 02/1848, on daily duty in Bakery since 01/30/1848; absent 04/1848 on daily duty in Bakery; c. 1850 res. Richmond, Henrico Co., VA, age 28, occ. Baker;⁷⁴⁴ c. 11/1856, *"Mexican Volunteer, who left this city for Kansas in Col. Rossar's party, sick and destitute in Missouri. Subcriptions raised to enable him to return home;"*⁷⁴⁵ Civil War service a Robert Fuqua served as a Pvt., Co. K, 12ᵗʰ Va. Inf., enl. 05/04/1861, occ. Baker, res. Grove Ave., Petersburg, VA, on detached service 04/1862 through 04/1864 to work on war contract presumably as a Baker, KIA 07/30/1864 at the Crater,²¹ bur. Blandford Cem., Sq. 4, Sec. 45, Ward D, Petersburg, VA⁷⁴⁶

**Fust, Richard, Jr.**, 4ᵗʰ Cpl., Co. E; b. c. 1822 son of Richard & E.M. Furt;⁷⁴⁷,⁷⁴⁸ enl. Mex. War service 11/30/1846 Petersburg, VA, age 25; pres. 04/1847; pres. 06/1847; pres. 08/1847; pres. 10/1847, pay stopped for: 1 pr. overalls-$2.28, 2 pr. shoes-$1.22, 2 pr. stockings-$.49, 2 cotton shirts-$.86, 2 pr. drawers-$.71, 1 cap-$.95¹/²; absent 12/1847, on detached service in Provost Guard, prom. 4ᵗʰ Cpl. 11/19/1847, pay stopped for: 1 pr. pants-$2.28, 1 pr. shoes-$1.22, 1 blanket-$2.22; absent 02/1848, on daily duty at Provost Guard since 12/21/1847, prom. 3ʳᵈ Cpl.; absent sick in quarters 04/1848; c. 1860 res. Petersburg, Dinwiddie Co., VA, age 37, occ. Book Keeper;⁷⁴⁹ c. 1870 res. Petersburg, Dinwiddie Co., VA, age 48, occ. Grocer, w.

140

## VIRGINIA VOLUNTEERS IN MEXICO

Mary J. (38);[750] SA #2216, 04/07/1887, from VA [pension file missing]; d. 06/10/1889, *Uremia*, bur. Blandford Cem., Sq. 5, Sec. 17, Ward F, Petersburg, VA[751]

**Gaines, Thomas W.**, Pvt., *Preston's Co.*, b. 03/25/1827, Botetourt Co., VA; [752] enl. Mex. War service 12/07/1846 Montgomery Co., VA, age 19; pres. 04/1847; sick 06/1847; pres. 08/1847; pres. 10/1847, pay stopped for: 1 pr. overalls-$2.28, 1 pr. shoes-$1.22, 2 pr. socks-$.49, 1 flannel shirt-$.90, 2 cotton shirts-$.86; pres. 12/1847, pay stopped for: 1 jacket-$2.66, 1 pr. overalls-$2.28, 1 pr. shoes-$1.22, 1 cap-$.95$^{1/2}$, 1 pr. drawers-$.35$^{1/2}$; pres. 02/1848; pres. 04/1848; pres. 07/1848, pay stopped for: 1 gun sling-$.18; BLW sent to Lafayette, VA; moved to Adams Co., Ill. C. 1855; m. Eliza Ann Fulton, 02/19/1857, Adams Co., Ill.; Civil War service enl. Capt., Co. D, 50$^{th}$ Ill. Inf., 09/12/1861, res. Payson, Ill., prom. Major 10/09/1862, prom. Lt. Col. 03/27/1863, furloughed 20 days 06/27/1863, apptd. Provost Marshall, Corinth, Miss. 09/1863, absent 12/1863, on recruiting service in Ill., apptd. Provost Marshall, Pulaski, TN date unknown, resigned 07/18/1864, due to blindness in one eye; elected Treasurer, Adams Co., Ill.; c. 1870 moved to Clarksville, Tex. apptd. Postmaster, Clarkesville, Tex. 1889-1894;[753] wid.

Photo credit: Library of Virginia, Richmond, VA

Eliza Ann, LW WO#609614; *photograph*.

**Gainor, Robert**, Pvt., Co. H; enl. Mex. War service 11/30/1846, Berkeley, VA, age 18; pres. 04/1847; pres. 06/1847; pres. 08/1847; pres. 10/1847, pay stopped for: 1 forage cap-$.95$^{1/2}$, 1 pr. pants-$2.28, 3 cotton shirts-$1.29, 3 flannel shirts-$2.70, 1 pr. drawers-$.35$^{1/2}$, 1 pr. shoes-$1.22, 4 pr. socks-$.98, 1 greatcoat-$6.93$^{1/2}$, 1 jacket-$2.66; pres. 12/1847, pay stopped for: 1 pr. pants-$2.28, 1 cotton shirt-$.43, 1 flannel shirt-$.90, 1 pr. shoes-$1.22, 1 blanket-$2.22; pres. 02/1848, pay stopped for: 2 pr. drawers-$.71; pres. 04/1848; pres. 07/1848, pay stopped for: 2 gun slings-$.32, 2 wipers-$.20, 1 screw driver-$.25, 1 pr. shoes-$1.16, BLW sent to Martinsburg, VA

**Gaither, Edward**, Pvt., Co. M; b. c. 1818; m. Mary Ann Kelly 12/18/1839;[754] enl. Mex. War service 06/30/1847 Richmond, VA, age 29; pres. 09/1847; pres. 11/1847; pres. 12/1847; pres. 02/1848; pres. 04/1848; pres. 08/1848, pay stopped for: 1 musket & accoutrements complete-$16.22; BLW sent to Washington City, D.C.; c. 1850 res. Elizabeth City Co., VA, age 32, occ. Soldier.[755]

**Gallager, John**, Pvt., *Recruit Co.*, enl. Mex. War service 12/29/1847 Alexandria, VA, age 32; pres. 02/1848; pres. 04/1848; pres. 06/1848; BLW sent to Alexandria, VA; *"John S. Gallagher, Co. A, Md. & DC Vols.,"* S #18682 03/03/1888, d. 10/03/1917, Brooklyn, NY.

**Gallaher, John S., Jr.** Pvt., Co. H; enl. Mex. War service 01/04/1847, Berkeley, VA, age 32; pres. 04/1847; pres. 06/1847; pres. 08/1847; pres. 10/1847, pay stopped for: 1 forage cap-$.95$^{1/2}$, 1 pr. pants-$2.28, 2 cotton shirts-$.86, 1 pr. shoes-$1.22, 2 pr. socks-$.49, 1 jacket-$2.66, 1 blanket-$2.22; pres. 12/1847, pay stopped for: 2 cotton shirts-$.86, 2 flannel shirts-$1.80; pres. 02/1848, pay stopped for: 2 cotton shirts-$.86, 1 flannel shirt-$.90, 1 pr. drawers-$.35$^{1/2}$, 1 pr. shoes-$1.22, 2 pr. socks-$.49; pres. 04/1848; pres. 07/1848, pay stopped for: 2 gun slings-$.32, BLW sent to Martinsburg, VA; c. 1850 res. Berkeley Co., VA, age 36, occ Tailor;[756] c. 1860 res. Evansville, Preston Co., VA, age 45, occ. Tailor, w. Elizabeth (30), [*remainder illegible;*][757] Civil War service Co. I, 17$^{th}$ W.Va. Vols.; IC #654211;[554] c. 1880 res. Grafton, Taylor Co. WV, age 65, occ. Tailor, w. Elisabeth (49) Keeping House, dau.

OFF TO WAR

Missouri (34), son John L. (18) Works for RR, dau. Maggie A. (14), son Charles K. (11);[758] SC #1637, 02/08/1887, from WV; [see Civil War pension claim].

**Gallaher, John W.**, 2nd Lt., Co. K; b. 03/02/1819, Martinsburg, Berkeley Co., VA, son of James & Hannah Gallaher;[759] m. Mary McKee, 08/27/1840, Hagerstown, Washington Co., MD;[759] enl. Mex. War service Jefferson Co., VA 12/01/1846, age 27; pres. 06/1847, prom. 1st Sgt. 05/31/1847; pres. 08/1847; pres. 10/1847, pay stopped for: 1 pr. overalls-$2.28, 2 pr. drawers-$.71; pres. 12/1847, pay stopped for: 1 pr. overalls-$2.28; pres. 04/1848 prom. 2[nd] Lt. 12/31/1847, pay stopped for: 1 flannel shirt-$.90, 1 cotton shirt-$.43, 1 cap-$.95$^{1/2}$, 1 bedsack-$1.07$^{1/2}$; pres. 07/1848; 1849-1850 *California 49er*, went overland from Jefferson Co., VA to Sacramento, Calif. with the Charles Town Mining Co.;[760] c. 1860 res. Charlestown, Jefferson Co., VA, age 42, occ. Plasterer, w. Mary (37), son Charles E. (18) Carpenter's Apprentice, dau. Ann (16), dau. Mary E., (14), dau. [*illegible*] (11);[761] (MMG d. 09/04/1868, Charlestown, WV); c. 1880 res. Charles Town, Jefferson Co., WV, age 62, occ. Plasterer;[762] SC #9509, 02/10/1887, filed from Charlestown, Jefferson Co., WV; phys. desc. 5'7$^{3/4}$", dark eyes, occ. Plasterer;[759] John Avis and George A. Porterfield gave affidavits in pension claim;[759] since discharge res. Charlestown, WV;[759] d. 05/06/1888, *"paralysis,"* Charlestown, Jefferson Co., WV.[763, 759]

**Gallenar, Henry**, Pvt., Co. K; enl. Mex. War service Richmond, VA 01/21/1847, age 30; d. 04/20/1847 on route between China & Camargo, Mex.

**Galloway, Joseph**, Pvt., Co. E; enl. Mex. War service 11/30/1846 Petersburg, VA, age 21; discharged 03/29/1847 Camargo, Mex. on account of disability; [Civil War service a Joseph E. Galloway b. c. 1821, enl. 06/27/1861 as a Pvt., Co. A, 50th Va. Inf., Wytheville, VA, wounded 02/15/1862 left leg below the knee at Ft. Donelson, TN, res. of Lee Co., VA in 1900, age 79.]

**Gardner, Fleming**, 1st Lt., *Preston's Co.*, b. 10/24/1815, Montgomery Co., VA;[764] enl. Mex. War service 11/24/1846 Montgomery Co., VA, age 20; pres. 04/1847; sick 06/1847; pres. 08/1847; absent 08/1847 on recruiting service in Virginia since 10/13/1847; absent 12/1847, on recruiting service in Virginia; absent 02/1848 on recruiting service in VA; absent 04/1848 on recruiting service in VA; pres. 07/1848; SC #10768, 07/01/1887, filed from Christiansburg, Montgomery Co., VA; occ. Civil Engineer;[764] Civil War service a Fleming Gardner served as a Capt., Adj. Genls. Dept., Aide to Gen. Earley, 1861, also as a Capt., C.S. Engrs., 1864;[765] d. 1899.[764]

**Gardner, James**, Pvt., Co. L; b. 1819; enl. Mex. War service 03/01/1847 Fairfax C.H., VA, age 28; deserted 04/22/1847 in New Orleans, La.[72]

**Gardner, Robert Davison**, Pvt., *Preston's Co.*, b. VA, 12/22/1829, Montgomery Co., VA, son of Alexander & Mary (Shanklin) Gardner;[766, 767] enl. Mex. War service 12/06/1846 Montgomery Co., VA, age 18; pres. 04/1847; pres. 06/1847; pres. 08/1847; absent 10/1847, on detached service in QM Dept., pay stopped for: 1 jacket-$2.66, 1 pr. overalls-$2.28, 1 pr. shoes-$1.22, 2 pr. socks-$.49, 1 cotton shirt-$.43, 1 pr. drawers-$.35$^{1/2}$, 1 cap-$.95$^{1/2}$; absent 12/1847, on detached service as Wagoneer in QM Dept. since 12/11/1847, pay stopped for: 1 pr. shoes-$1.22, 1 blankets-$2.22; pres. 02/1848; absent 04/1848 on detached service as Teamster in QM Dept.; pres. 07/1848, pay stopped for: 1 gun sling-$.18, 1 wipers-$.13; BLW sent to Christiansburg, VA c/o Fleming Gardner; m/1 Elizabeth J. Haney, 11/26/1856, Newbern, Pulaski Co., VA;[767] c. 1860 res. Newbern, Pulaski Co., VA, age 29, occ. Carpenter, w. Elizabeth J. (28);[768] Civil

Photo credit: H.E. Howard, Inc., Appomattox, VA

# VIRGINIA VOLUNTEERS IN MEXICO

War service enl. 04/17/1861, 1st Lt., Co. C, 14th Va. Cav.; elected Capt. 07/25/1861; prom. to Lt. Col. 04/22/1862; shot in face 12/13/1862 Fredericksburg, VA; retired from field service 04/09/1864; commanded Dublin Depot;[769] c. 1870 res. Newbern, Pulaski Co., VA, age 39, occ. County Clerk, w. Elizabeth J. (39), dau. Mary R. (1), son? Robert S. (14), Clerk in Store, dau.? Ginnie M. (11);[770] (EHG d. 11/26/1870, Newbern, Patrick Co., VA);[766] m/2 Belle M. Cook, 02/17/1876, Newbern, Pulaski Co., VA;[766, 771] elected Pulaski County Circuit Court Clerk 1870 - 1893; SC #20064, 05/27/1893; filed from Newbern, Patrick Co., VA; phys. desc. at enl. age 18, 6', blue eyes, dark hair, fair complexion, occ. Carpenter;[766] since discharge res. Christiansburg, Montgomery Co., VA to 1857, since then in Patrick Co., VA;[766] Alpheus W. Poage and Bird Roop gave affidavits in pension claim;[766] member Newbern Lodge No. 280 A.F & A.M.;[766] d. 07/12/1906, Dublin, VA; bur. Newbern Cemetery, Newbern, Pulaski Co., VA;[772, 773] wid. Belle M., WC #15191, 03/01/1909, filed from Dublin, Pulaski Co., VA; letter, *edged in black*, from widow to Pension Board requesting a pension application is located in pension file;[772] (BMG b. 03/28/1845, Wytheville, VA, m/1 George W. Woodson, 1865, divorced 12/05/1873, d. 03/27/1912, Dublin, Pulaski Co., VA).[772]

**Garnett, James J.**, Pvt., Co. A; enl. Mex. War service 12/01/1846 Richmond, VA, age 22; pres. 12/1846 - 04/1847; sick in quarters 06/1847; pres. 08/1847; pres. 10/1847, pay stopped for clothing: 2 cotton shirts-$.86, 1 pr. wool overalls-$2.28, 1 cap-$.95$^{1/2}$, 4 pr. stockings-$.98, 2 flannel shirts-$1.80, 1 great coat-$6.93$^{1/2}$, 1 knapsack and 2 long stea[illegible]; sick 12/1847, pay stopped for clothing: 1 blanket-$2.22, 1 pr. wool overalls-$2.28, 1 pr. shoes-$1.22, 1 pr. drawers-$.35$^{1/2}$; pres. 02/1848, pay stopped for: 1 pr. wool overalls-$2.28, 1 pr. shoes-$1.22; 1 pick & brush-$.12; pres. 04/1848, pay stopped for 1 wool jacket; 1 musket-$13.00, 1 bayonet sheath-$.56, cartridge box & belt-$1.70, [illegible], belt-$.25, plate-$.10, 1 wiper-$.20, screw driver-$.25; BLW sent to Bowling Green, Caroline Co., VA [m. Mary Chenault, 11/11/1845, Caroline Co., VA;[774] c. 1850 a James R. Garnett res. Caroline Co., VA, age 26, occ. Farmer, w. Mary (22);[775] c. 1860 res. Sparta, Caroline Co., VA, age 42, occ. Farmer, w. Mary (33), son Joseph (10), dau. Columbia (9), son Remmington (8), dau. Mary A. (6), dau. Ruwenia (2), son James R. (3/12);[776] c. 1870 res. Bowling Green, Caroline Co., VA, age 49, occ. Farmer, w. Mary A. (45), dau. Columbia (18), son Remmington (15), dau. Alice (12), dau. Rowena (10), James M. (8), dau. Sarah B. (5), son Willie T. (3), son Maccau (1).][777]

**Garnett, John**, Pvt., *Recruit Co.*, enl. Mex. War service 11/25/1847 Fincastle, VA, age 21; pres. 02/1848; absent 04/1848 on detached service as Hospital Attendant; pres. 06/1848; BLW sent to Washington City, D.C.

**Garnett, Thomas Stuart**, 1st Lt., Co. C; b. 04/19/1825, Westmoreland Co., VA; son of Henry Thomas & Eliza Stuart (Bankhead) Garnett; attended VMI 1840-41, resigned. Grad. from UVA, medicine, 1845; Lawyer, Caroline Co., VA, 1845-1846. enl. Mex. War service 12/18/1846, Bowling Green, VA, age 22; pres. 06/1847; Court-martialed 06/25/1847, Buena Vista, Mex. *Charge #1: Neglect of Duty; Specification: In this that 1st Lt. Thomas S. Garnett, of the Virginia Regt. of Volunteers being regularly mounted on guard as Officer of the Left Flank Guard on the 23rd of June 1847, did neglectingly permit members of his guard to absent themselves from the guard tents before being regularly relieved. This at Head Qtrs., Buena Vista, Mexico on or about the 23rd of June 1847. Specification #2: In this that the said 1st. Lt. Thomas S. Garnett, Virginia Regt. Volunteers, being regularly mounted on guard as Officer of the Left Flank Guard on the 23rd of June 1847 did neglectingly permit members of his guard to put off their accoutrements while on guard*

Photo credit: H.E. Howard, Inc., Appomattox, VA

## OFF TO WAR

duty, this at Head Quarters, Buena Vista, Mexico on or about the 23$^{rd}$ of June 1847. Specification #3: In this that the said 1$^{st}$ Lt. Thomas S. Garnett of the Va. Regt. of Vols. being regularly mounted on guard as Officer of the Left Flank Guard on the 23$^{rd}$ day of June 1847, did neglectingly fail to have a proper vigilance observed by the guard whilst on duty at the guard tents so as to challenge persons approaching the guard. This at Head Qtrs., Buena Vista, Mexico, at night on or about the 23$^{rd}$ of June 1847. Specification #4:In this that the said 1$^{st}$ Lt. Thomas S. Garnett, of the Virginia Regt. of Vols. being regularly mounted as Officer of the Left Flank Guard, on the 23$^{rd}$ of June 1847, did negligently fail to have an officer awake at the quarters of the guard and to have the guard kept under arms at the guard quarters whilst the relief was being posted and did whilst the relief was so being posted negligently suffer the guard to absent themselves from the guard quarters so that they could not be found. This at Head Quarters, Buena Vista, Mexico before reveille on or about the 24$^{th}$ of June 1847. To which charge and specifications the accused pled Not Guilty. Col. Robert T. Paine, of the North Carolina Regiment of Volunteers, a witness on the part of the prosecution duly sworn, says: I was Field Officer of the Day on the 23$^{rd}$ instant and commenced to visit the different guards about 10 o'clock A.M. I went to the quarters of the Left Flank Guard which Lt. Garnett was commanding as Officer of the Guard and saw some of the men, members of the guard, had taken off their accoutrements. Some of the guard were also absent from the tents. I told Lt. Garnett that it was against the orders of Genl. Wool, the commanding General, that the men should take off their accoutrements or clothing during the time that they were on guard, that the guard should be paraded and the roll called whenever a relief was to be posted and remain under arms 'til the relief returned. Either at this time or a subsequent one, a number of the guard, about five or six were absent. As I ascertained when the guard was paraded to receive me, and I asked Lt. Garnett where they were" He first answered that they had gone for water, and then, during the conversation, that they had gone to dinner, all but two and they had gone for water. [I] supposing from his reply that they had gone off without his permission. I directed him to make a report in writing of the names of the absentees and the cause of their absence which order he did not, nor has not complied with, having only reported one name to me in his report the next morning, as having gone to dinner. I think at this visit I saw one man without his accoutrements, who came out of the tent after the guard was paraded to receive me as Officer of the Day. I again cautioned Lt. Garnett to be more vigilant and to exact from the guard a strict performance of their duty. After 2 o'clock A.M. on the 24$^{th}$, I made another visit to the Left Flank Guard. Lt. Garnett was present and I obtained from him a Sergt. and file of men to go the guard rounds. I proceeded as far as the Provost Guard, some two hundred and fifty or three hundred yards, and ascertaining it was time, or about time, to post the relief, I returned with the escort to the guard of the left flank guard and went up to the tents with the escort, without challenges. Lt. Garnett was present, I think in his tent, and came out after I asked why I was not challenged? After the relief had been posted, I took the escort and proceeded to go the guard rounds. I took the escort back from the next guard that I visited, having finished the rounds. I returned to the quarters of the Left Flank Guard, between daylight and reveille. On approaching the guard tent I saw only one man. He was sitting, I think, by the side of the tent and when I came near he jumped up and took his arms. He neither challenged me nor called for the guard. I went up to the guard tents unopposed found the Corpl. Fast asleep in the guard tent and no other person or persons present except the man already mentioned. When I asked where the Officer of the Guard was, he told me he had gone out. I saw him across the lines some hundred and fifty yards from the guard tent. He was evidently <u>necessarily</u> absent from his guard. I do not think that any member of the guard appeared before the Sergt. returned with the relief, which he was posting when I first came up. The Officer of the Guard himself came up in the meantime. Question by the Judge Advocate: What number of officers, non-commissioned officers and privates composed the Left Flank Guard? Answer: One officer, one Sergt., one Corpl., and I think twelve privates. Question by

VIRGINIA VOLUNTEERS IN MEXICO

*the Judge Advocate: Did Lt. Garnett march on guard with the left flank guard at the usual hour of guard mounting on the 23rd instant? Answer: I cannot say. I found him in command of the guard on my first visit to it. Question by the Accused: Was there near them one man without his accoutrements on your first visit to the guard on the 23rd? Answer: There was more than one, and that fact led me to speak to Lt.. Garnett about the orders of Genl. Wool and the regulations. Question by the accused: Did I not state to you that I had ordered the guard not to take off their accoutrements? Answer: I do not think he did. At this time it was at a subsequent visit when I spoke more decided about this and asked him if he had forgotten the caution I had given him as to the men's taking off their accoutrements. This was at the time I saw the one man come out of the tent without his accoutrements.* Pvt. George Liscomb, Co. A, Miss. Regt., Cpl. Francis Benson, Co. F, Va. Regt., Capt. McMillan, Miss. Regt., all testified as witnesses. *After deliberation the court found the accused Not Guilty of the charge and specifications.*[778] detached 08/1847 as Actg. Adj. of the Regt. from 08/24/1847; detached 10/1847 Actg. Adjt. of the regt. since 08/24/1847; detached 12/1847 as Actg. Adjt. of the Regt.; pres. 04/1848 commanding the company; m. Emma L. Baber, 1848;[281] c. 1850 res. Westmoreland Co., VA, age 25, occ. Physician, w. Emma M. (23), dau. Emma B. (11/12); [779] c. 1860 res. Kinsale, Westmoreland Co., VA, age 36, occ. Physician, w. E.S. (30), dau. E.B. (11), son H.T. (9), son T. (7), son Unamed Infant (1/12);[780] Civil War service enl. Co. E, 9th Va. Cav., 1861;[725] Commissioned Lt. Col. 48th Va. Inf., C.S.A, 06/17/1861; prom. to Col. 04/03/1863; mortally wded. Chancellorsville, VA 05/03/1863, d. 05/04/63; bur. Hollywood Cem., Richmond, VA;[781] WC #1080, 04/14/1887, from VA; pension file missing 07/16/2001.

**Garrett, Wesley B.**, Pvt., Co. D; enl. Mex. War service 01/06/1847, Petersburg, VA, age 19; pres. 02/1847; absent 04/1847 sick, sent from Camargo, Mex. to Hosp. Matamoros, Mex. 03/29/1847; absent 06/1847 in Hosp. Matamoros, Mex.; absent 08/1847 sick Hosp. Matamoros, Mex.; absent sick 10/1847 Hosp. Matamoros, Mex.; absent sick 12/1847 Hosp. Matamoros, Mex.; discharged for *"inguinal hernia of the left side, general ill health with jaundice supposed induced by the bite of a trantula;"* m. Mary Ann Smith 01/01/1850, St. John's Chapel, Charleston, SC;[782] IC filed from Company Shop's, Alamance Co., NC, *"In the line of duty and unloading a government vessel at the wharf at Matadors, Mexico, detailed for such duty by and under the authority of his commanding officers, was ruptured in the groin and disabled by a hogshead of provisions rolling upon him. That himself and several others were to remove and break open a hogshead of bacon for the use of the troops;"*[783] phys. desc. at discharge, 5'10", 19 yrs., occ. Railroad Engineer; since discharge res. at Charleston, SC to 1854, Company Shop's, NC, since then, occ. Railroad Engineer; d. 07/08/1877, Graham, NC; wid. Mary Ann, WC #1021, 02/26/1887, filed from Burlington, Alamance Co., NC.[783]

**Garrison, William B.**, Pvt., Co. I; enl. Mex. War service 01/01/1847 Richmond, VA, age 32; absent 04/1847, left sick at Matamoros, Mex. 04/01/1847; discharged 06/1847 Matamoros, Mex. exact date unknown.

**Gately, Patrick**, Pvt., Co. L; b. 1815, Altlone, Ireland; m. Mary Demeree, 05/1844 *"in a hotel or tavern,"* Sanford, Broome Co., NY;[784] enl. Mex. War service 03/15/1847 Alexandria, VA, age 32; occ. Wool Spinner, enlisted because he was unable to find employment;[785] sick 06/1847; wrote a poem to his wife while in Mexico (*see next page*); sick 08/1847; pres. 10/1847; pres. 12/1847, to forfeit 1 mos. pay by sentence of general court-martial, pay stopped for: 1 pr. pants-$2.28, 1 pr. shoes-$1.22, 1 flannel shirt-$.90, 1 pr. drawers-$.35$^{1/2}$; pres. 02/1848, pay stopped for: 1 pr. Shoes 1.22, 1 Jacket 2.66; pres. 04/1848; pres. 07/1848; BLW sent to Capt. Thrift c/o Patrick Gately, Fairfax Court House, Fairfax Co., VA; enl. 12/06/1848 as a Pvt. in the U.S. Marines stationed on board the U.S. Frigate *Raritan.* The *Raritan* cruised

## OFF TO WAR

the West Indes. While on board Pvt. Gately was posted at the *"scuttle-butt."*[12] discharged 8/21/1851 after being thrown against a gun and injuring his back; recvd. a pension for U.S. Navy service, I #611, wid Mary, WC #7365 dated 3/26/1890, filed from Brooklyn, NY. *"My husband disappeared from his home 28 years ago while the late war was going on and I have never seen nor heard from him, either directly or indirectly, at anytime since. At the time of his disappearance we were living on what was called the Plank Road near the Orphan Asylum, just outside of the City of Albany. He had been on a terrible spree immediately previous for about two weeks. During this spree he slept on different nights and during the last night previous to his disappearance he slept in the open fields. The last time I saw him about 28 years ago, he came home about 9 o'clock in the morning and changed his clothes. He was still intoxicated and I endeavored to get him to eat some Breakfast, but he positively refused. Without saying anything about where he was going or intended to do, he left the house at the back door went across the fields and disappeared from view. ...When he left me his age was near 70 years. I do not know what his exact age was. His only occupation was to buy ginger snaps and peddle them from house to house and street to street in Albany on his own account. I bore him seven children only one of whom is living."* Daughter, Eleanor Zinova, of New York City;[786] last pension payment to Patrick Gately was 07/01/1862;[787] another child, Margaret Ann, was born 09/01/1859, baptized at Church of the Assumption, York & Jays Streets, Brooklyn, NY.[788]

To My Mary

I know my love you always loved, but never loved in vain
My only pet you must not fret, I may return again
So now my dear be of good cheer my words may yet come true
No earthly store would keep me from my lovely boy and you.

My only pet you must not fret with every breath you draw.
Your love would soon return if peace was proclaimed by law.
Tho, in a foreign country his journey he'd soon pursue
And leave the trifling foe behind to meet his Johnny dear & you.

Johnny dear and darling whatever shall you do.
Your mother is broken hearted, Boy, what shall become of you.
Your father is in the battlefield away in Mexico.
Where many a valiant heart has gone to face the daring foe.

My dear pay no attention to the base and slanderous crew.
Who first said I went away to be rid of you.
May God pour down his vengeance on the false and filthy crew.
Who try's to plague my faithful wife when I am far from you.

My dear have better courage and do not be afraid.

---

[12] **Scuttlebutt.** Scuttle is a fairly old term for a small rectangular hole cut into the deck or side of a ship for light, ventilation, and sometimes communication between decks. A butt was simple a wooden cask for provisions. Traditionally, a butt of water was to last for two days. The problem was, how to keep the crew from drinking the whole cask in one day. Eventually, someone thought to *scuttle a butt* (put a hole in it halfway up), attach it to the upper deck, and have the water ration poured in each day up to the hole. Before long, the place to get a drink became known as the *scuttled butt*, and eventually, the **scuttlebutt**. The term came to be applied to rumors passed around while waiting to get a drink.

VIRGINIA VOLUNTEERS IN MEXICO

For me to go and leave you it never shall be said.
Unless to the battlefield to answer my Country's call.
There like another hero for my Country's sake to fall.

From a letter to Mary Gately c/o Job A. Demarie, from Pvt. Patrick Gately, Co. L, 1st Va. Regt., near Saltillo, Mexico, July 31, 1847.[789]

**Gates, Vincent,** Pvt., Co. A; enl. Mex. War service 11/28/1846 Richmond, VA, age 25; deserted 01/21/1847 at Old Point, VA
**Gayle, Benjamin,** Pvt., Co. F; enl. Mex. War service 12/18/1846, Portsmouth, VA, age 19; pres. 06/1847; pres. 08/1847; pres. 10/1847, pay stopped for: 2 pr. overalls-$4.56, 2 pr. shoes-$2.44, 4 cotton shirts-$1.72, 3 pr. drawers-$1.06$^{1/2}$, 1 forage cap-$.95$^{1/2}$; 3 pr. socks-$.73$^{1/2}$, 1 blanket-$2.22; pres. 02/1848, pay stopped for: 1 infantry jacket-$2.66, 2 pr. shoes-$2.44, 1 pr. overalls-$2.28, 1pr. drawers-$.35$^{1/2}$, 1 brush & pick-$.12; pres. 04/1848; pres. 08/1848, pay stopped for: 1 wiper-$.20, 2 blankets-$4.50, 1 forage cap-$.83, 6 cotton shirts-$2.64, 1 pr. shoes-$1.16, BLW sent to Portsmouth, VA c/o E.T. Blamire; m Sarah Mariah Darden 01/05/1856, Hertford Co., NC;[790] Civil War service enl. Pvt., Co. G, 1st NC Inf.; 01/01/1864, phys. desc. age 46, 5'6", dark complexion, dark hair, blue eyes, trans. to Co. C, 2nd NC Inf., trans. Co. F, 2nd NC Inf., absent 04/30/1864 on detached service at Newbern, NC, discharged 06/27/1865;[790] c. 1880 res. Bethel Perquimans Co., NC, age 60, occ. Laborer, w. Sally (52), dau. Martha (17);[791] SC #7589, 02/24/1887, filed from Creswell, Washington Co., NC; wid. Sarah WC #10972, 10/08/1896, file from Belvidere, Perquimans Co., NC; d. 09/01/1896 Winfall, Perquimans Co., NC, bur. near Hertford, Perquiman's Co., NC;[792] CW IC #872858; (SMG b. 09/18/1827, Murfreesboro, Hertford Co., NC, d. 07/15/1901).[792]
**Geiger, Vincent Epley,** 2nd Lt., LIC; b. 05/24/1824 son of George Henry & Susannah (Tapp) Geiger; enl Mex. War service 11/27/1846 Staunton, VA; pres. 06/1847; sick 08/1847; pres. 10/1847; pres. 12/1847; pres. 04/1848; pres. 07/1848; 1849-1850 *California 49er*, went overland from Jefferson Co., VA to Sacramento, Calif. with the Charles Town Mining Co;[760] Agent for the Nome Lackee (Nomlaki) Indian Reservation (Calif.) c. 1859; accused of fraud, mismanagement, and indenturing Indians;[793] owned land in Tehama Co., Ca. 1861; m. Maggie Burwell, 08/01/1861, Tehama Co., Ca.;[794] in October 1863, Geiger, a Secessionist, got into an argument with Capt. Ashbel Shipley Wells, a Unionist, over the War. Geiger fatally stabbed Wells in front of the Magnolia Saloon in Red Bluff, Calif.[795, 796] He was reported to have escaped to Victoria, British Columbia.[797] However, leaving his wife and family he spent the remaining years of his life a fugitive; d. 09/06/1869, Valparaiso, Chile;[798, 799, 800] kept a journal which was published in 1945 *Trail To California. The Overland Journal of Vincent Geiger and Wakeman Bryarly;*[801]
**Gennett, Samuel,** Pvt., Co. I; enl. Mex. War service 01/15/1847 Richmond, VA, age 22; pres. 02/1847; pres. 04/1847; discharged 06/17/1847 for disability at Monterey, Mex.
**Gibbs, Joseph F.,** Co. D; enl. Mex. War service 01/17/1847, Petersburg, VA, age 25; absent 02/1847 left sick at Hosp. Fort Monroe, VA; absent 04/1847 left sick at Hosp. Fort Monroe, VA; absent 06/1847 left sick at Hosp. Fort Monroe VA 02/27/1847 *"and not since heard from;"* discharged 09/11/1847 Old Point, VA on Surgeon's Certificate of Disability; m. Rebecca H. Rawlings, 01/08/1849, Brunswick Co., VA;[802, 803] c. 1850 res. Brunswick Co., VA age 27, occ. Planter, w. Rebecca (18);[804] c. 1860 res. Sturgeonsville, Brunswick Co., VA, age 36, occ. Farmer, w. Rebecca H. (29), dau. Lucretia E. (6), dau. Virginia E. (5);[805] Civil War service *"Conscripted and sent out with the Reserves in the War of the Rebellion;"*[806] c. 1870 res. Sturgeonsville, Brunswick Co., VA, age 52, occ. Farmer, w. Rebecca H. (39), dau. Lucretia E. (16), dau. Virginia E. (14), dau. Adella R. (9), son Joseph E. (5), dau. Marsha V. (1);[807] SC filed from Thomasburg, Brunswick Co., VA; wid. Rebecca H., WA #10400,

OFF TO WAR

02/10/1892, filed from Smoky Ordinary, Brunswick Co., VA Pvt. Robert A. Goodwyn gave affidavit in pension claim. (RRG b. 03/28/1831).[806]

**Gibson, Carter**, Pvt., Co. K; enl. Mex. War service Richmond, VA 01/24/1847, age 19; pres. 06/1847; pres. 08/1847; pres. 10/1847, pay stopped for: 1 pr. overalls-$2.28, 2 pr. socks-$.49, 1 pr. shoes-$1.22, 2 flannel shirts-$1.80; pres. 12/1847; pres. 04/1848, pay stopped for: 1 pick & brush-$.12, 1 gun sling-$.18, 1 pr. shoes-$1.22; pres. 07/1848, pay stopped for: 1 screw driver-$.25, 1 wiper-$.20; BLW sent to Union, Loudoun Co., VA

**Gibson, John Moses**, Pvt., *Preston's Co.*, b. 08/03/1812, Franklin Co., VA;[808] enl. Mex. War service 12/06/1846 Montgomery Co., VA, age 33; pres. 04/1847; pres. 06/1847; sick 08/1847; pres. 10/1847, pay stopped for: 1 pr. overalls-$2.28, 2 pr. socks-$.49, 1 flannel shirt-$.90, 1 cotton shirt-$.43; pres. 12/1847, pay stopped for: 1 pr. overalls-$2.28, 1 pr. shoes-$1.22, 1 blanket-$2.22; pres. 02/1848; pres. 04/1848, pay stopped for: 1 pick & brush-$.12; pres. 07/1848, pay stopped for: 1 cap-$.95$^{1/2}$, 1 jacket-$2.37, 1 screw driver-$.07, 1 wiper-$.13; BLW sent to Floyd C.H., VA; Civil War service Pvt., Co. C, 12$^{th}$ Va. Cav., b. 1817?, 5'6", fair complex., blue eyes, dark hair, dark, whiskers, farmer, Frederick Co., VA; captured in Frederick Co., sent to Camp Chase, Oh. then Ft. Delaware; paroled 09/28/1864; nfr;[809] m. Harriet Hart, 10/04/1865, Wytheville, Wythe Co., VA;[808] SC #11546, 09/26/1887, filed from Wytheville, Wythe Co., VA; James H. Moyers and Alpheus W. Poage gave affidavits in pension claim;[808] d. 11/04/1891, Wytheville, bur. Bethel Cemetery, Wytheville, VA;[810] wid. Harriet, WC #7879, 11/30/1891, filed from Wytheville, Wythe Co., VA; (HHG b. 1836, Wythe Co., VA, d. 03/06/1916, *"cerebral hemorrhage and cancer of the eye,"* Max Meadows, Wythe Co., VA, bur. McGavock Cemetery, Max Meadows, VA).[810]

**Gibson, John W.**, Co. A; b. c. 1828, King William Co., VA, son of William and Judith Gibson;[811] enl. Mex. War service 11/19/1846 Richmond, VA, age 20; pres. 12/1846 - 04/1847; discharged 06/02/1847 for disease by order of Maj. Gen. Taylor; m/1 Mary Mountcastle c. 1850 (MMG d. c. 1850 *"scarlet fever,"* Richmond, VA); m/2 Matilda F. Barnard 10/24/1855 Danville, VA; c. 1870 res. Danville, Pittsylvania Co., VA age 44, occ. Tobacco Trader, w. Matilda (33), son Joseph W. (12) , son John E. (10), son Robert Lee (7), son George P. (5), son William A. (3), dau. Flora M. (1);[812] d. 06/22/1882 *"inflammation of the stomach and bowels,"* Henderson, Vance Co., N.C., bur. Elmwood Cemetery, Henderson, N.C.;[811] wid. Matilda F., WC #9582, 08/25/1890, filed from 60 Mariner St., Norfolk, VA; c. 1924 res. 174 Belford Ave., Rutherford, NJ; (MFG b. 11/03/1831, Danville, VA, d. 03/05/1924).[811]

**Giles, George N.**, 3$^{rd}$ Cpl., Co. G; enl. Mex. War service 11/25/1846 Richmond, VA, age 22; pres. 06/1847; pres. 08/1847; pres. 10/1847, pay stopped for: 1 pr. overalls-$2.28, 1 cotton shirt-$.43, 1 flannel shirt-$.90, 1 pr. drawers-$.35$^{1/2}$,2 shoes-$2.44, 2 pr. socks-$.49, 1 forage cap-$.95$^{1/2}$; pres. 12/1847, prom. 3$^{rd}$ Cpl., pay stopped for: 1 pr. shoes-$1.22, 2 blankets-$4.44, 1 pr. pants-$2.28, 1 jacket-$2.66, 1 pr. socks-$.24$^{1/2}$; pres. 02/1848, reduced to ranks 02/24/1848; pres. 04/1848; absent 08/1848 left in Monterey, Mex. QM Dept.; BLW sent to Manchester, VA

**Gilmore, Charles**, Pvt., Co. F; enl. Mex. War service 01/18/1847, Portsmouth, VA, age 21; d. 04/11/1847 *"lost when killed Pasa La Carta (Catta, Callo) while with the advance guard, supposed to have been killed by Mexicans."*

**Gilmore, Thomas**, Pvt., *Preston's Co.*, b. 04/15/1824, Montgomery Co., VA;[813] enl. Mex. War service 12/14/1846 Montgomery Co., VA, age 19; pres. 04/1847; pres. 06/1847; pres. 08/1847; pres. 10/1847, pay stopped for: 1 jacket-$2.66, 1 pr. overalls-$2.28, 2 pr. socks-$.49, 1 flannel shirt-$.90, 2 cotton shirts-$.86, 1 pr. drawers-$.35$^{1/2}$, 1 cap-$.95$^{1/2}$; pres. 12/1847, pay stopped for: 1 pr. shoes-$1.22, 1 cap-$.95$^{1/2}$, 2 pr. drawers-$.71, 1 blanket-$2.22; sick 02/1848; absent 04/1848, with leave since 04/11/1848; pres. 07/1848, pay stopped for: 1 cartridge box-$1.10, 1 cartridge box plate-$.10, 1 cartridge box belt & plate-$.80, 1 waist belt & plate-$.33, 1 brush & pick-$.12, 1 gun sling-$.18, 1 screw driver-$.07, 1 wiper-$.13; BLW sent to Christiansburg, VA c/o Fleming Gardner; m. Mary Taylor, 03/15/1850, Pulaski Co.,

## VIRGINIA VOLUNTEERS IN MEXICO

VA;[813]c. 1850 res. Pulaski Co., VA, age 22, occ. Day Laborer, w. Mary (29);[814] Civil War service Pvt., Co. C, 51st Va. Inf., enl. 04/01/1862, Wytheville, VA, Captured 03/02/1865 at Waynesboro, VA, sent to Harper's Ferry, WV, the to Winchester, VA then to Ft. Delaware, released on oath 06/20/1865, phys. desc. fair complexion, gray eyes, 5'5", ares. of Wytheville;[536] c. 1870 res. Rural Retreat, Wythe Co., VA, age 46, occ. Day Laborer, w. Mary (53), dau. Ellen (15), dau. Katy (13);[815] SC #3970, 03/07/1887, filed from Long's Shop, Montgomery Co., VA; Henry Collins and Wyatt Akers gave affidavits in pension claim;[813] d. 04/30/1894;[816] wid. Mary, WA #12173, 06/26/1894, filed from Long's Shop, Montgomery Co., VA; Lists children E.H. (Gilmore) Linkous and Virginia B. (Gilmore) Linkous;[816] (MTG b. 08/16/1814, Liberty, Bedford Co., VA, d. 07/28/1894).[816]

**Givens, James E.**, Pvt., Co. L; b. 1817; m. Isabella Dunn, 06/04/1840, Washington, D.C.;[817] enl. Mex. War service 03/01/1847 Fairfax C.H., VA, age 30; pres. 06/1847; pres. 08/1847; pres. 10/1847, pay stopped for: 1 pr. Pants 2.28, 1 F Cap .95; pres. 12/1847, to forfeit 1 mos. pay by sentence of general court-martial, pay stopped for: 1 jacket-$2.66, 3 pr. shoes-$3.66, 2 cotton shirts-$.86, 2 pr. drawers-$.71, 3 pr. socks-$.73$^{1/2}$; pres. 02/1848, pay stopped for: 1 Blanket 2.22, 1 Brush & Pick .12; pres. 04/1848, pay stopped for: 1 Blanket 2.22, 1 pr. Shoes 1.16, 2 Cotton Shirts .88;pres. 07/1848, pay stopped for: 1 pr. Shoes 1.16, 1 Bayonet Scabbard .56, 1 Brush & Pick .12; BLW sent to James E. Givens Washington City, D.C.; c. 1862-1863 occ. Clerk, boarder at 343 Mass. Ave., Wash., D.C.[818]

**Gladwell, Valentine**, Pvt., LIC; b. 01/14/1824;[819] enl. Mex. War service 12/07/1846 Staunton, VA, age 24; discharged 06/1847 at Camargo, Mex. on Surgeon's Certificate of Disability, *"chronic rheumatism;"*[819] m. Clemmentine Ballenger, 10/21/1855, Ripley, MO;[820] m/2 Mary E. Walker 08/14/1883, Union, MO;[819] SC #5304, 05/23/1887, file from Edge Hill, Reynolds Co., MO; admitted 10/10/1893 Southern Branch of National Soldiers Home, Elizabeth City, VA, *"chronic bronchitis and asthma, left hand useless from paralysis;"*[819] d. 03/15/1899, Western Branch National Soldiers Home, Leavenworth, KS,[819] bur. Leavenworth National Cemetery, Plot: 13 4 7, Leavenworth, KS; *Note:* the name *Valentine Gladwell* appears six times in the marriage indices of six different Missouri counties from 1855-1878.

**Glasscock, David Bludsoe**, 2nd Cpl., Co. K; b. 01/23/1823, Fleming Co., KY;[821] son of Asa & Mary (Penquite) Glasscock; enl. Mex. War service Alexandria, VA 01/21/1847, age 24; sick 06/1847; pres. 08/1847; pres. 10/1847, pay stopped for: 1 pr. overalls-$2.28, 2 cotton shirts-$.86, 2 pr. drawers-$.71, 1 blanket-$2.22, 2 flannel shirts-$1.80; pres.12/1847; pres. 04/1848, prom. 2nd Cpl. 04/01/1848, pay stopped for: 1 flannel shirt-$.90, 1 tick-$1.07$^{1/2}$; pres. 07/1848; BLW sent to Clarksville, Clinton Co., Ohio; m. Frances Ann Virginia Penquite, 04/05/1849, Washington, Warren Co., Ohio;[821, 822, 823] c. 1850 res. Salem, Warren Co., OH;[824] Civil War service Sgt., Co. K, 146th Ohio Inf. 05/02/1864 at Camp Dennison, discharged 09/07/1864, *Got overheated on march into Virginia, then rained on overnight. Developed rheumatism the following morning*;[823] c. 1881 Superintendent of the Warren County Infirmary, Lebanon, Ohio;[825] SC #8759, 02/26/1887 filed from Lebanon, Warren Co., OH; phys. desc. 5'6$^{1/2}$", dark complexion, hazel eyes, dark hair, occ. Carpenter;[823] lists children Mary E. (Glasscock) Scott, b. 01/27/1850, John Stephen Glasscock, b. 12/10/1853, Emma Alsina (Glasscock) Hawkins, b. 02/13/1862;[823] m/2 Ruth E. Jones 04/29/1902, Clinton Co., OH;[823] d. 10/02/1907, *"paralysis,"* Blanchester, Clinton Co., OH, bur. Blanchester I.O.O.F. Cemetery, Blanchester, Clinton Co., OH;[826, 827] wid. Ruth E., WC #15789, 12/15/1911, filed from Blanchester, Clinton Co., OH; (REG d. 10/02/1924).[827]

**Goens, James**, Pvt., LIC; b. Rockingham Co., VA;[828] enl. Mex. War service 12/03/1846 Staunton, VA, age 21; discharged 06/1847 at Camargo, Mex. on Surgeon's Certificate of Disability; m. Ellen Campbell, 05/09/1865, Fayette Co., OH;[828] d. 10/07/1881, *"chronic pleurisy,"* Leon, Decatur Co., IA, bur. Leon Cemetery, Leon, IA;[828] wid. Ellen, WC #4368, 05/04/1887, filed from Leon, Decatur Co., IA; Lists children Jennie Goens b. 02/04/1866,

OFF TO WAR

James Goens b. 09/01/1867, George Goens b. 04/14/1869;[828] (ECG b. 07/12/1834, near Washington C.H., Fayette Co., OH, m/1 Benjamin Glaize, Jr., ECG d. 12/25/1916).[828]

**Goens, William**, Pvt., LIC; b. at the *"Head of Middle River, Rockbridge Co., VA,"* son of John Goens;[829] enl. Mex., War service 12/03/1846 Staunton, VA, age 19; pres. 08/1847; pres. 10/1847, pay stopped for: 1 forage cap-$.95$^{1/2}$, 1 wool jacket-$2.66, 1 pr. overalls-$2.28, 1 pr. shoes-$1.22, 2 pr. socks-$.49, 3 cotton shirts-$.86, 1 overcoat-$6.93$^{1/2}$; pres. 12/1847, pay stopped for: 1 blanket-$2.22, 1 pr. shoes-$1.22, 1 pr. overalls-$2.28; pres. 04/1848, pay stopped for: 3 cotton shirts-$1.29; pres. 07/1848; BLW sent to Staunton, VA; c. 1850 res. Augusta Co., VA, age 23, occ. Cooper;[830] m/1 Nancy Ann Whetzel date/place unknown, (NWG d. 08/1859, Augusta Co., VA);[829] c. 1860, res. Augusta Co., VA, age 30, occ. Cooper;[831] Civil War service Pvt., Co. C, 5$^{th}$ Va. Inf., enl. 03/01/1862, at Staunton, VA, wded. 06/27/1862 severely in right hand at Gaines Mill, VA, absent wded. through 02/1864, NFR;[128] m/2 Sarah Ann Zeigler, 07/04/1865, Washington C.H., Fayette Co., OH;[829] SC #8624, 02/16/1887, filed from Parkersburg, Wood Co., WV; phys. desc. age 62 [1887], 5'5", fair complexion, light eyes, black hair, occ. Carpenter;[829] d. 09/06/1903;[832] wid. Sarah A., WC #13456, 09/25/1903, filed from Parkersburg, Wood Co., WV; Lists children Carrie Z. (Goens) King b. 06/28/1878, George William Goens b. 09/11/1867;[832] (SZG b. 09/12/1841, Wilmington, OH, d. 01/22/1911, d. Columbus, OH, bur. Parkersburg, WV).[832]

**Golden, George W.**, Pvt., Co. M; enl. Mex. War service 07/05/1847 Lynchburg, VA, age 25; pres. 09/1847; pres. 11/1847; pres. 12/1847; pres. 02/1848; pres. 04/1848; pres. 08/1848; BLW sent to Lynchburg, VA; c. 1860 res. Botetourt Co., VA, age 38, occ. Saddler, w. Margaret (30), dau. M.C. (3), son James C. (2), son Alex. Golden (3/12);[833] c. 1870 res. Daggers Springs, Botetourt Co., VA, age 45, occ. Works of a Farm, w. Margaret (40), Melissa M. (12), son James W. (10), son William (8), ??? Brown R. Goldwin (28);[834] SC #14807, 09/01/1887, filed from Rockbridge Co., VA; deemed insane by Rockbridge Co. Circuit Court and sent to Eastern State Hospital;[13, 835] *"He is disabled by reason of a blow received on his head while in the service. He is now in the Lunatic Asylum at Williamsburg, VA, helpless and without mind;"* d. 02/04/1890.[835]

**Good, Jonathan R.**, 2$^{nd}$ Sgt., Co. C; b. 10/13/1823, Lebanon Co., Pa.;[836] enl. Mex. War service 12/29/1846, Bowling Green, VA, age 23; pres. 06/1847, prom 3$^{rd}$ Sgt. 06/16/1847; pres. 08/1847, prom. 2$^{nd}$ Sgt., pay stopped for: 1 cap-.95$^{1/2}$, 2 pr. socks-$.49, 2 cotton shirts-$.86, 2 woolen shirts-$1.80, 1 knapsack & straps-$1.10; pres. 10/1847, pay stopped for: 3 pr. socks-$.73$^{1/2}$, 1 pr. pants-$2.28, 1 cotton shirt-$.43, 1 woolen shirt-$.90, 1 pr. shoes-$1.22; pres. 12/1847, pay stopped for: 1 pr. pants-$2.28, 1 pr. shoes-$1.22, 2 blankets-$4.44; pres. 04/1848, pay stopped for: 1 jacket-$2.66, 1 cotton shirt-$.43, 1 india rubber canteen-$.27, 1 pr. shoes-$1.22; pres. 08/1848, BLW sent to Lebanon, Lebanon County, Pa.; m. Mary P. Mahan 12/30/1849 Philadelphia, Pa.;[836] [Civil War service a Jonathan Good served as a Musician, Co. A, 77$^{th}$ Pa. Inf.;][554] SC #2108, 03/24/1887, filed from Philadelphia, Philadelphia Co., Pa.; Pvt. Thomas T. Mahan and John Roach gave affidavits on pension claim; Since discharge res. in Philadelphia and Lancaster, Pa.; d. 03/07/1894 *"pneumonia,"* Ridley Park, Delaware Co., Pa., bur. Odd Fellows Cemetery, 23rd & Diamond Sts.(removed to Mount Peace/Lawnview, Huntingdon Pike)Philadelphia, Pa.;[837] wid. Mary P., WC #9090, 03/21/1894, filed from Ridley Park, Deleware Co., PA.(MPG b. 09/19/1824 Chester Co., Pa.)

**Goodrich, John F.**, Pvt., Co. B; enl. 12/05/1846, Alexandria, VA, age 20; pres. 06/1847; pres. 08/1847; pres. 10/1847, pay stopped for: 2 pr. shoes-$2.44, 1 cotton shirt-$.43, 4 pr. socks-

---

[13] **Eastern State Hospital**, now part of the Virginia Department of Mental Health, Mental Retardation, and Substance Abuse Services system, was founded in 1773 with a well-intentioned emphasis on community-focused mental health care. The 24-bed facility located in Williamsburg, Virginia, was the first public psychiatric hospital in North America, and was originally designed to admit and treat only those who could return rapidly to their communities.

## VIRGINIA VOLUNTEERS IN MEXICO

$.98, 1 pr. overalls-$2.28, 3 pr. cotton drawers-$1.06$^{1/2}$, 2 flannel shirts-$1.80, 1 overcoat-$ 6.93$^{1/2}$, 1 cap-$.95$^{1/2}$, 1 blanket-$2.22; pres. 12/1847, pay stopped for: 1 pr. overalls-$2.28, 1 jacket-$2.66, 2 pr. socks-$.49, 1 blanket-$2.22; pres. 02/1848; pres. 04/1848, pay stopped for: 1 pr. shoes-$1.22; pres. 08/1848, pay stopped for: 1 wiper-$.20, 1 gun sling-$.16, BLW sent to Georgetown, DC.

**Goodwin, Archibald B.**, Pvt., Co. E; enl. Mex. War service 11/28/1846 Petersburg, VA, age 22; pres. 04/1847; absent 06/1847 sick Hosp. Saltillo, Mex. 06/27/1847; pres. 08/1847; 10/1847 [illegible]; pres. 12/1847, [illegible]; pres. 02/1848; pres. 04/1848; c. 1850 res. Dinwiddie Co., VA, age 25, occ. Bricklayer;[838] [Civil War service an Archibald B. Goodwin served as Capt., 2$^{nd}$ Co. H, 9$^{th}$ Va. Inf.; fair complex., light hair, blue eyes, 5'11"; captured 04/01/1865 at White Oak Road; paroled 06/18/1865 Johnson's Island, Oh.;[211] also listed as Capt. 1$^{st}$ Co. I, 12$^{th}$ Va. Inf.;[202] c. 1860 res. Dinwiddie Co., VA, age 40, occ. Bricklayer, w. Mary (28), dau. Bettie (9), dau. Ada B. (6);[839] c. 1870 res. Dinwiddie C.H., Dinwiddie Co., VA, age 45, occ. Farmer, w. Mary P. (36);[840] SC #5571, 04/23/1887, wid. Mary P., WC #9830, 09/12/1895, both from VA; [pension file missing].

**Goodwin, Arthur M.**, Pvt., Co. E; b. Alabama;[841] enl. Mex. War service 12/01/1846 Petersburg, VA, age 19; pres. 04/1847; pres. 06/1847; pres. 08/1847;10/1847 [illegible]; pres. 12/1847, [illegible]; pres. 02/1848 [illegible]; pres. 04/1848; c. 1860 res. San Marino, Dinwiddie Co., VA, age 33, occ. Farmer, w. Aline (25), son Edward B. (7), son James M. (5), son Arthur (3), dau. Aline E. (6/12), Ada B. (6/12) "twins;"[842] Civil War service enl. as 3$^{rd}$ Lt., 9$^{th}$ Va. Inf. 01/22/1863 at Norfolk, VA; comm. 02/22/1864; pres. 10/1864; recvd. Brevet as 2$^{nd}$ Lt. date not listed;[211] also listed as Capt., 1$^{st}$ Co. I, 12$^{th}$ Va. Inf.;[202] c. 1870 res. Dinwiddie C.H., Dinwiddie Co., VA, age 44, occ. Farmer, w. Aline (36), son Edward E. (16), son James M. (14), son Arthur W. (13), dau. Aline E. (11), dau. Addie B.S. (11), dau. Celia B. (9), son Archibald (5), son John H. (3);[843] wid. Aline, WC #3298, 01/20/1888, from VA; [pension file missing].

**Goodwin, Henry**, Pvt., Co. G; enl. Mex. War service 12/03/1846 Richmond, VA, age 21; pres. 06/1847; pres. 08/1847; pres. 10/1847, pay stopped for: 1 pr. overalls-$2.28, 1 pr. drawers-$.35$^{1/2}$, 2 shoes-$2.44, 2 pr. socks-$.49, 1 great coat-$6.95$^{1/2}$, 1 jacket- $2.66, 1 forage cap-$.95$^{1/2}$; pres. 12/1847, pay stopped for: 1 pr. shoes-$1.22, 2 cotton shirts-$.86, 2 flannel shirts-$1.80, 1 cap-$.95$^{1/2}$, 1 jacket-$2.66, 1 pr. drawers-$.35$^{1/2}$, 1 pr. pants-$2.28; sick 02/1848, pay stopped for: 1 brush & pick-$.12; pres. 04/1848, pay stopped for: 1 jacket-$2.66; pres. 08/1848; BLW sent to Powhattan Co. C.H., VA; served Co. C, 3$^{rd}$ US Arty. 1850-1871; Civil War service IC #302193; SC #9955, 04/29/1887, from CA; [see Regular Army pension claim].

**Goodwin, John L.**, Pvt., Co. M; enl. Mex. War service 10/04/1847, Ft. Monroe, VA, age 32; pres. 09/1847; pres. 11/1847; pres. 12/1847; pres. 02/1848; pres. 04/1848; pres. 08/1848; BLW sent to Lovingston, VA

**Goodwin, Robert A.**, Pvt., Co. D; b. c. 1824, Brunswick Co., VA, son of James & Mary Ann H. (Talley) Goodwin; enl. Mex. War service 01/05/1847, Petersburg, VA, age 22; absent 02/1847 left sick at Hosp. Fort Monroe, VA; absent 04/1847 left sick at Hosp. Fort Monroe, VA; absent 06/1847 left sick at Hosp. Fort Monroe, VA 02/27/1847 *"and not since heard from;"* discharged 03/17/1847 on Surgeon's Certificate of Disability; c. 1850 res. Brunswick Co., VA, age 30, occ. Carpenter;[844] m. Elizabeth J. Kirkland, 05/26/1852, Brunswick Co., VA;[845] c. 1860 res. Sturgeonsville, Brunswick Co., VA, age 33, 0cc. Farmer, w. Elizabeth J. (26), son James H. (7), dau. Mary J. (5), dau. Maria J. (2), son Nathaniel B. (1);[846] Civil War service Pvt., Co. D, 46$^{th}$ Va. Inf.; florid complex., hazel eyes, chestnut hair, 5'10";[847] sick 05/1862 - 6/1862; discharged for being overage 09/02/1862;[462] c. 1870 res. Sturgeonville, Brunswick Co., VA, age 50, occ. Farmer, son James A. (17), dau. Mary E. (15), son Nathaniel B. (12), son Robert A, Jr. (10), dau. Nannie W. (4);[848] SC #8200, 05/02/1887, from VA; [pension file not found].

OFF TO WAR

**Goodwin, Timoleon W.**, Pvt., *Archer's Co.*; SA #24417, 09/05/1893, from VA
**Goodwyn, Edward Washington**, Pvt., Co. M; b. 11/13/1824, Lunenburg Co., VA;[849] enl. Mex. War service 09/02/1847, Jonesborough, VA, age 21; pres. 10/1847; pres. 11/1847; pres. 12/1847; pres. 02/1848; sick 04/1848; pres. 08/1848, pay stopped for: 1 musket & accoutrements-$16.22; BLW sent to Jonesborough, Brunswick Co., VA; m. Virginia E. Tucker, 12/08/1857, Lunenburg Co., VA;[849, 850] Civil War service Pvt., Co. H, 9$^{th}$ Va. Inf., enl. 06/12/1861 at Fletcher's Chapel, Lunenburg Co., VA, trans. 05/08/1862 to 28$^{th}$ Va. Inf. Btln.;[211] c. 1870 res. Lunenburg C.H., Lunenburg Co., VA, age 45, occ. Farmer, w. Virginia (4), dau. Julia Ann (11), son George W. (9), son Edward C. (6), dau. Della (3), son Cammie (6/12);[851] SC #2585, 03/18/1887, from VA; John W. Overby and James H. Bishop gave affidavits in pension claim;[849] d. 12/04/1907.[849]
**Goolesby, Thomas**, Pvt., Co. G; enl. Mex. War service 11/28/1846 Richmond, VA, age 23; pres. 06/1847; pres. 08/1847; in confinement 10/1847, pay stopped for: 1 overalls-$2.28, 1 cotton shirt-$.43, 1 pr. drawers-$.35$^{1/2}$, 1 shoes-$1.22, 2 pr. socks-$.49, 1 great coat-$6.95$^{1/2}$, 1 forage cap-$.95$^{1/2}$; pres. 12/1847, pay stopped for: 1 pr. shoes-$1.22, 1 blanket-$2.22, 1 pr. pants-$2.28, 1 jacket-$2.66, 1 pr. socks-$.24$^{1/2}$, 2 flannel shirts-$1.80; pres. 02/1848, pay stopped for: 1 brush & pick-$.12; sick 04/1848; pres. 08/1848; BLW sent to Richmond, VA; [c. 1850 a Thomas N. Goolsby res. Nelson Co., VA, age 26, occ. Overseer;[852] c. 1860 a Thomas N. Goolsby res. Allen's Creek, Nelson Co., VA, age 36, occ. Overseer.][853]
**Gordon, Aaron K.**, Pvt., Co. H; enl. Mex. War service 11/21/1846, Berkeley, VA, age 35; pres. 04/1847; pres. 06/1847; pres. 08/1847; pres. 10/1847, pay stopped for: 1 forage cap-$.95$^{1/2}$, 1 pr. pants-$2.28, 2 cotton shirts-$.86, 2 flannel shirts-$1.80, 1 pr. shoes-$1.22, 2 pr. socks-$.49, 1 jacket-$2.66; sick 12/1847 in Hosp. at Saltillo, Mex., pay stopped for: 1 pr. pants-$2.28, 1 pr. shoes-$1.22, 1 blanket-$2.22, 2 pr. drawers-$.71; pres. 02/1848, pay stopped for: 2 cotton shirts-$.86, 1 flannel shirt-$.90, 2 pr. socks-$.49; pres. 04/1848; pres. 07/1848, pay stopped for: 1 screw driver-$.25, BLW sent to Hedgesville, VA
**Gordon, Archibald Alexander**, Pvt., LIC; b. 12/24/1827, Staunton, Augusta Co., VA;[854] enl. Mex. War service 12/27/1846 Staunton, VA, age 22; pres. 06/1847, reduced to ranks from Drummer; pres. 08/1847; pres. 10/1847, pay stopped for: 1 forage cap-$.95$^{1/2}$, 1 wool jacket-$2.66, 1 pr. overalls-$2.28, 1 pr. shoes-$1.22, 2 pr. socks-$.49, 2 cotton shirts-$.86; pres. 12/1847, pay stopped for: 1 pr. shoes-$1.22, 1 pr. overalls-$2.28; absent 04/1848, on detached service in QM Dept. since 12/11/1847, pay stopped for: 1 blanket-$2.22; pres. 07/1848, pay stopped for: 1 bayonet scabbard-$.56, 1 cartridge box belt plate-$.10, 1 gun sling-$.16, 1 screw driver-$.07, 1 wiper-$.20; BLW sent to Staunton, VA; c. 1850 res. Augusta Co., VA, age 25, occ. Painter, mo.? Sarah (64), dau.? Sarah A. (8);[855] m. Francis R. Gibbs, 07/26/1860, Lawrenceburg, Anderson Co., KY;[854] [Civil War service an Archibald Gordon served in Co. B, 62$^{nd}$ Mtd. Inf.][202] d. 01/09/1884, *"heart failure and dropsy,"* Frankfort, KY, wid. Frances R., WC #6306, 03/12/1889, filed from 319 Todd St., South Frankfort, KY; (FGG b. 1844, Staunton, VA, d. 07/1906, Louisville, KY)[854]
**Gordon, Henry**, Pvt., Co. B; enl. 12/19/1846, Alexandria, VA, age 21; pres. 06/1847; sick 08/1847; pres. 10/1847, pay stopped for: 2 pr. shoes-$2.44, 1 pr. overalls-$2.28, 4 cotton shirt-$.86, 2 pr. cotton drawers-$.71, 2 pr. socks-$.49; Court-martialed 11/05/1847 Buena Vista, Mex. *Charge #1: Desertion; Specification: In this that Pvt. Henry Gordon, Co. B, Va. Vols., did desert the service of the United States, and was apprehended on the Monclova Road ten (10) or twelve (12) miles from Saltillo. This at Camp Buena Vista, Mex. Oct. 31$^{st}$, 1847. To which charge and specification the prisoner pleaded Not Guilty. Lt. R.F. Coleman, Va. Regt., a witness for the prosecution being duly sworn says: I overtook the prisoner about eleven (11) miles below Saltillo, on the Monclova Road. He offered no resistance, but remarked that if he had arms he would not have been taken, and that he would not walk back. He was in company with two other men and I procured horses for them and brought them back. The prisoner also remarked that he would not remain in the Virginia Regt. but would transfer to the Rangers or*

VIRGINIA VOLUNTEERS IN MEXICO

some other Corps He left camp on the same day that I overtook him, the 31$^{st}$ of last month. I was ordered in pursuit of this prisoner and two other men of the Regt. He was sober when I met him but some one of the party said that they had been drinking. Question by the Court: Did you understand him to say when you overtook me 'that if I had had arms I would not have been taken by you or not?' Answer: I did understand him to say these words ' if they had had arms he would not have been taken." Lt. W.J. Minor, Va. Regt., a witness on the part of the prosecution being duly sworn says in answer to the following: Question by the Judge Advocate: What was the amount of money you paid for the expenses of apprehending the prisoner? Answer: The amount of the expenses was about six (6) or eight (8) dollars for the prisoner and the two other men. Question by the Court: Did the prisoner leave camp without permission? Answer: Yes., he did.. The prisoner stated to the court that the act of desertion was not premeditated. But that when they got to Saltillo they made up their minds to leave. That he did not mean the remark Lt. Coleman took to himself to apply to him, but to the Mexicans who they met on the road. The court deliberated and found the prisoner Guilty and sentenced him to be confined at hard labor with a ball an chain attached to his leg under the charge of the Provost Guard during the continuance of the war. To forfeit his pay proper and then to be _dishonorably discharged_ from the service;[856] Court-martialed 12/06/1847 Buena Vista, Mex. Charge #1 Desertion; Specification: "In that the said Private Henry Gordon, Co. B, Va. Regt. Vols., being in confinement in the Provost Guard under charges did break his arrest and desert the service of the United States on or about the night of the 26$^{th}$ of Nov. 1847, and did remain away from said Guard and service until the night of the 29$^{th}$ of the same month. This at Camp Buena Vista, Mexico....Lt. E.T. Blamire, Va. Regt. Vols. A witness for the prosecution being duly sworn says. The Prisoner Gordon left the Provost Guard on the night of the 26$^{th}$ of Nov. 1847 after tatto and remained away until the morning of the 29$^{th}$ when he was found in his bunk in the Provost Guard. Question of the Judge Advocate: Were there any arms taken from the Provost Guard on that night? Answer: The Sergt. of the Guard missed his musket the next morning and it seemed have been taken by some of the prisoners who escaped on that night. It has not been heard of since. Question by the Court: How many prisoners left the Provost Guard on that night, and how many returned or been brought back and how many are still absent? Answer: Eight left the Provost Guard on that night, of whom, four returned by themselves, one was apprehended in Saltillo and brought back, and three (3) are still absent." Sentenced: "To be made to stand on the head of a barrel two (2) hours each day for one month with a ball and chain weighing 18 pounds attached to his leg...to forfeit his pay proper, and afterward to be kept in confinement in the Provost Guard during the continuance of the war with Mexico. Then to be marked with the letter 'D', one and a half inch long, on the left hip, with india ink, and to be dishonorably discharged from the service;"[857] in confinement 12/1847, rejoined from deserter on 12/04/1847, pay stopped for: 1 pr. shoes-$1.22, 1 cap-$.95$^{1/2}$, 2 flannel shirts-$1.80, 1 jacket-$2.66, 1 overcoat-$6.93$^{1/2}$; in confinement 02/1848, this man's pay is stopped by order (No. 27), pay stopped for: 1 pr. shoes-$1.22, 1 cap-$.95$^{1/2}$, 2 flannel shirts-$1.80, 1 jacket-$2.66, 1 overcoat-$6.93$^{1/2}$,1 pr. overalls-$2.28; deserted from the Provost Guard at Saltillo, Mex. and murdered [no date given], pay stopped by order (No. 27) and to be dishonorably discharged.
**Gough, William**, Pvt., Co. I; enl. Mex. War service 01/10/1847 Richmond, VA, age 19; pres. 02/1847; pres. 04/1848, pay stopped for: 1 blanket, 2 cotton shirts; pres. 04/1847; absent 06/1847, left sick in Hosp. at Monterey, Mex. 06/22/1847; pres. 08/1847; absent 10/1847, pay stopped for: 3 flannel shirts-$2.70, 3 cotton shirts-$1.29, 2 pr. drawers-$.71, 2 pr. shoes-$2.44, 1 overcoat-$6.93$^{1/2}$, 1 cap-$.95$^{1/2}$, 1 jacket-$2.66, 2 pr. socks-$.49; pres. 12/1847, pay stopped for: 1 pr. socks-$.24$^{1/2}$, 1 pr. pants-$2.28, 1 pr. shoes-$1.22, 1 blanket-$2.22, 2 flannel shirts-$1.80, 1 cotton shirt-$.43, 2 pr. drawers-$.35$^{1/2}$; pres. 02/1848, pay stopped for: 1 pr. shoes-$1.22, 1 pr. overalls-$2.28; pres. 04/1848, pay stopped for: 1 blanket, 2 cotton shirts; pres. 08/1848, pay stopped for: 1 cartridge box-$1.10, 1 cartridge box plate-$.10, 1 cartridge box

OFF TO WAR

belt-$.60, 1 cartridge box belt plate-$.10, 1 pick & brush-$.12, 1 bayonet-$1.44; , BLW sent to Lynchburg, VA; m. Ann M.E. Beck, 09/11/1849, Campbell Co., VA;[858] c. 1850 res. Campbell Co., VA, age 22, occ. Farmer, w. Ann M. (20), son John W. (1/12).[859]

**Goulden, Henry L.**, Pvt., Co. I; enl. Mex. War service 01/10/1847 Richmond, VA, age 22; pres. 02/1847; absent 04/1847, left sick at Matamoros, Mex. 04/01/1847; pres. 06/1847; pres. 08/1847; absent 10/1847, pay stopped for: 3 pr. drawers-$1.06$^{1/2}$, 1 pr. shoes-$1.22, 1 flannel shirt-$.90, 1 pr. socks-$.24$^{1/2}$, 1 cap-$.95$^{1/2}$, 1 blanket-$2.22; pres. 12/1847, pay stopped for: 1 pr. shoes-$1.22, 1 pr. socks-$.24$^{1/2}$, 1 pr. pants-$2.28, 1 jacket-$2.66, 1 pr. pants-$2.28, 1 blanket-$2.22, 1 flannel shirt-$.90; pres. 02/1848, pay stopped for: 1 pr. shoes-$1.22, 2 cotton shirts-$.86; pres. 04/1848, pay stopped for: 1 blanket, 1 pr. shoes, 2 cotton shirts; pres. 08/1848, BLW sent to Lynchburg, VA; c. 1850 res. Lynchburg, Campbell Co., VA, age 25, occ. Laborer;[860] c. 1860 res. Castle Craig, Campbell Co., VA, age 36, occ. Laborer, w. Luvena (26), son Benjamin F. (4), son Henry C. (2);[861] Civil War service enl. Pvt., Co. H, 11$^{th}$ Va. Inf. 05/15/1861, age 36, farmer; absent sick 10/61–11/61; KIA 12/20/1861 at Dranesville, VA[121]

**Gover, William C.**, Pvt., Co. K; b. 04/23/1821, Leesburg, Loudoun Co., VA;[862] enl. Mex. War service Jefferson Co., VA 01/01/1847, age 25; pres. 06/1847; sick 08/1847, to forfeit 1 mos. pay by order of garrison court-martial; discharged 10/16/1847 at Buena Vista, Mex. on Surgeon's Certificate of Disability; m. Mary Maria Stone, 02/25/1869, Snickersville, Loudoun Co., VA;[863, 862] c. 1870 res. Snickersville, Loudoun Co., VA, age 44, occ. Shoemaker, w. Mary M., dau. Minnie (5/12);[864] SC #3390, 03/19/1887, filed from Snickersville, Loudoun Co., VA; since discharge res. Loudoun Co., VA; d. 03/05/1900, Bluemont, Loudoun Co., VA, bur. Ebenezer Baptist Church Cemetery, Bloomfield, Loudoun Co., VA;[865] wid. Mary M., WC #12442, 07/24/1900, filed from Snickersville, Loudoun Co., VA; c. 1901 widow res. Gore, Frederick Co., VA; (MSG b. 02/25/1840, d. 02/01/1913); dau. Katie Gover wrote letter from Rockville, MD to pension bureau in 1950 inquiring about a minor pension on her father's Mexican War service.[865]

**Graff, Felix H.**, Pvt., LIC; m. Lydia Jane Carroll, b. 01/21/1851, Louisville, Jefferson Co., KY;[866] c. 1860 res. Union Township, Clark Co., IN, age 32, w. Lydia J. (23), dau. Ella J. (7), Lila J. (4), dau. Mary B. (10/12); d. 02/08/1874, Jeffersonville, IN;[866] wid. Lydia Jane, WC #4542, 02/01/1887, filed from Court Avenue, Jeffersonville, Clark Co., IN; phys. desc. of soldier age 51 [1874], b. Zurich, Switzerland, 5'5", fair complexion, blue eyes, black hair, occ. Moulder;[866] since discharge res. Louisville, KY until 05/25/1860, moved to Sylvan Grove, IN until 11/03/1863, returned to Louisville, KY until 07/01/1866 when moved to Jeffersonville, IN;[866] (LCG b. 10/06/1833, Elizabethtown, Pa., d. 12/18/1916, 215 Watt St., Jeffersonville, IN).[866]

**Graham, Isaac T.**, Pvt., Co. E; b. 10/05/1820, Richmond, VA;[867] m Rosetta Larmand 03/07/1839, Richmond, VA;[867] enl. Mex. War service 11/30/1846 Petersburg, VA, age 25; pres. 04/1847; pres. 06/1847; pres. 08/1847; 10/1847 [illegible]; pres. 12/1847, [illegible]; pres. 02/1848, [illegible]; pres. 04/1848; c. 1850 res. Henrico Co., VA, age 30, occ. Tinner, w. Rosetta (27), dau. Catherine (11), dau. Josephine (8), son Robert (7), son John (5), son George (2);[868] c. 1860 res. Orange Co., VA, age 42, occ. Merchant, w. Rosetta (40), dau. Catherine (19), dau. Josephine (17), son John (14), son George (11), son William (8), son Issac (6), dau. Elizabeth (4),son Charles (2);[869] c. 1870 res. Orange C.H., Orange Co., VA, age 50, occ. Tinsmith & Merchant, w. Rosetta (48), dau. Catherine (31), son John T. (24), son George W. (20), dau. Elizabeth (16), son Charles (12), son Richard (10), son Oscar R. (5), son Marshall (2);[870] Civil War service enl. as a 3$^{rd}$ Lt., Co. A, 13$^{th}$ Va. Inf. 04/25/1861 at Harper's Ferry, VA; resigned 09/09/1861;[871] SC #4819, 05/14/1887, filed from 67 Defrees St., Washington, DC; lists children Kate Graham b. 1840, Josephine Graham b. 1842, William I. Graham b. 1851, Elizabeth Graham b. 1853, George Graham b. 1849, Charles Graham b. 1857, Richard Graham b. 1860, Robert Oscar b. 1865; listed in Boyd's Directories of Washington D.C. from

## VIRGINIA VOLUNTEERS IN MEXICO

1874 – 1905; (RLG d. 04/13/1892)[867] d. 02/20/1911 Chain Bridge Road, Alexandria Co., VA, bur. Congressional Cemetery, Washington, D.C.[867]
**Graham, James S.**, Pvt., LIC; enl. Mex. War service 12/07/1846 Staunton, VA, age 33; pres. 08/1847; pres. 10/1847, pay stopped for: 1 forage cap-$.95$^{1/2}$, 1 wool jacket-$2.66, 1 pr. overalls-$2.28, 5 pr. socks-$1.22$^{1/2}$, 2 pr. shoes-$2.44, 4 cotton shirts-$1.72, 1 flannel shirt-$.90, 1 blanket-$2.22; pres. 12/1847, pay stopped for: 1 pr. socks-$.24$^{1/2}$, 1 pr. shoes-$1.22, 1 pr. overalls-$2.28, 1 flannel shirt-$.90, 1 pr. drawers-$.35$^{1/2}$; pres. 04/1848; pres. 07/1848, pay stopped for: 1 pr. shoes-$1.16, 1 gun sling-$.16, 1 pick & brush-$.12, 1 screw driver-$.07, 1 wiper-$.20; BLW sent to Staunton, VA
**Graham, Thomas M.**, Pvt., Co. C; enl. Mex. War service 12/13/1846, Bowling Green, VA, age 40; pres. 06/1847; pres. 08/1847, pay stopped for: 1 cap-$.95$^{1/2}$, 2 pr. socks-$.49, 2 cotton shirts-$.86, 2 woolen shirts-$1.80; pres. 10/1847, pay stopped for: 2 pr. socks-$.49, 2 pr. drawers-$.71, 1 pr. pants-$2.28, 1 cotton shirt-$.43, 1 woolen shirt-$.90; pres. 12/1847, pay stopped for: 1 pr. pants-$2.28, 4 blanket-$8.88; pres. 04/1848, pay stopped for: 1 pr. pants-$2.28, 1 india rubber canteen-$.27; pres. 08/1848, BLW sent to Bowling Green, Caroline Co., VA
**Grandberry, John Gregory**, Pvt., Co. K; b. 08/27/1807, Norfolk Co., VA, son of Josiah & Elizabeth (Cowper) Granberry;[872] enl. Mex. War service Norfolk, VA 12/26/1846, age 38; pres. 06/1847; pres. 08/1847; pres. 10/1847, prom. 2$^{nd}$ Cpl. 09/06/1847; pres. 12/1847, pay stopped for: 1 jacket-$2.66, 1 pr. overalls-$2.28, 3 pr. boots-$3.66, 2 pr. drawers-$.71, 1 blanket-$2.22, 1 cap-$.95$^{1/2}$, 2 cotton shirts-$.86, 2 flannel shirts-$1.80; pres. 04/1848, reduced to ranks 04/01/1848, pay stopped for: 1 pr. pants-$2.28, 1 pr. shoes-$1.22, 1 flannel shirt-$.90; pres. 07/1848; BLW sent to Norfolk, VA; c. 1850 res. Norfolk, VA age 40, occ. Painter;[873]
**Grant, William**, Pvt., Co. G; enl. Mex. War service 12/15/1846 Richmond, VA, age 21; pres. 06/1847; pres. 08/1847; pres. 10/1847, pay stopped for: 1 pr. overalls-$2.28, 2 cotton shirts-$.86, 1 pr. drawers-$.35$^{1/2}$, 1 shoes-$1.22, 1 pr. socks-$.24$^{1/2}$, 1 great coat-$6.95$^{1/2}$, 1 jacket-$2.66, 1 forage cap-$.95$^{1/2}$; pres. 12/1847, pay stopped for: 1 jacket-$2.66, 1 blanket-$2.22, 1 pr. socks-$.24$^{1/2}$; pres. 02/1848; pres. 04/1848, pres. 08/1848, pay stopped for: 1 pr. shoes-$1.16, 1 gun sling-$.16, 1 wiper-$.20; BLW sent to Richmond, VA
**Gravatt, William Broaddus**, 2$^{nd}$ Lt., Co. A; b. 03/11/1826, son of John G. & Amanda (Broaddus) Gravatt;[874] enl. Mex. War service 11/25/1846, Richmond, VA, age 29?; pres. 12/1846 - 04/1847; pres. 06/1847; pres. 08/1847, prom. 2$^{nd}$ Lt. 08/20/1847; pres.12/1847 in command of company as Capt. Scott on furlough and 1$^{st}$ Lt. August under arrest; pres. 02/1848; pres. 04/1848; BLW sent to Port Royal, Caroline Co., VA; m. Mary Jane Chapman, 12/09/1850, Caroline Co., VA;[875] c. 1850 res. Caroline Co., VA, occ. Teacher;[876] c. 1860 res. Sparta, Caroline Co., VA , age 34, occ. Farmer, w. Mary J. (30), son Walter H. (6), dau. Lelia J. (2), m-i-l? Sophia Chapman (50);[877] Civil War service enl. as a Pvt., Co. H, 30$^{th}$ Va. Inf. 04/21/1861, absent 08/1861, discharged by 10/1861;[414] c. 1870 res. Bowling Green, Caroline Co., VA age 44, occ. Farmer, w. Mary J. (39), son Walter H. (16), dau. Lelia J. (11), son William J. (9), son George E. (6), son John B. (2), m-i-l? Sophia Champan;[878] d. 07/26/1872, Caroline Co., VA of consumption.[879]
**Graves, James**, Pvt., Co. G; Not on Muster Rolls, wid. Nancy C. , WA #14008, 06/18/1897, from FL.
**Graves, John R.**, Pvt., Co. G; enl. Mex. War service 11/18/1846 Richmond, VA, age 24; pres. 06/1847; pres. 08/1847; pres. 10/1847, pay stopped for: 1 pr. overalls-$2.28, 1 pr. shoes-$2.22, 5 pr. socks-$1.22$^{1/2}$, 1 forage cap-$.95$^{1/2}$; pres. 12/1847, pay stopped for: 1 pr. shoes-$1.22, 2 cotton shirts-$.86, 1 blanket-$2.22, 2 pr. pants-$4.56; pres. 02/1848, pay stopped for: 1 brush & pick-$.12; pres. 04/1848, pay stopped for: 1 jacket-$2.66; pres. 08/1848; BLW sent to Richmond, VA; [Civil War service a John R. Graves enl. Pvt., Co. D, 13$^{th}$ Va. Inf.

OFF TO WAR

04/17/1862 in Culpeper Co., VA; AWOL 04/1862-05/1862; absent sick 06/17/1862 through 08/02/1862; discharged as insane 10/25/1862.][871]

**Gray, Benjamin H.**, 3rd Cpl., Co. D; enl. Mex. War service 12/31/1846, Petersburg, VA, age 26; pres. 02/1847; pres. 04/1847; pres. 06/1847, prom. 3rd Cpl. 06/16/1847; d. 08/20/1847 Buena Vista, Mex.

**Gray, David W.**, 2nd Lt., Co. H; enl. Mex. War service 11/27/1846, Berkeley, VA; AWOL from 04/23/1847; resigned 05/1847.

**Gray, Layfayette W.**, 2nd Sgt., Co. G; enl. Mex. War service 11/18/1846 Richmond, VA, age 22; deserted 01/26/1847 Fort Monroe, VA

**Green, Henry G.**, Pvt., Co. I; b. 11/1819, Mecklenburg Co., VA;[880] enl. Mex. War service 01/01/1847 Richmond, VA, age 26; pres. 02/1847; pres. 04/1847; pres. 06/1847; pres. 08/1847; absent 10/1847, prom. 4th Cpl. 10/14/1847, pay stopped for: 3 flannel shirts-$2.70, 1 cap-$.95$^{1/2}$, 1 pr. pants-$2.28, 2 pr. shoes-$2.44, 2 cotton shirts-$.86, 1 pr. socks-$.24$^{1/2}$, 1 pr. drawers-$.35$^{1/2}$; pres. 12/1847, pay stopped for: 1 jacket-$2.66, 1 blanket-$2.22; pres. 02/1848; pres. 04/1848, reduced from 4th Cpl. 03/25/1848; pres. 08/1848, pay stopped for: 1 screw driver, 1 pr. shoes-$1.16, BLW sent to Boydton, Mecklenburg Co., VA; c. 1850 res. Mecklenberg Co., VA, age 29, occ. School Master;[881] c. 1870 res. Boydton, Mecklenberg Co., VA, age 49, occ. Teacher;[882] SC #5569, 05/18/1887, filed from St. Tammany, Mecklenburg Co., VA; David A. Weisiger and Augustus Stone gave affidavits in pension claim;[880] since discharge res. Mecklenburg Co., VA;[880] d. 12/24/1897.[880]

**Green, Jesse Carson**, Pvt., Co. B; enl. 12/03/1846, Alexandria, VA, age 20; sick 06/1847; pres. 08/1847; sick 10/1847, pay stopped for: 2 pr. shoes-$2.44, 3 pr. socks-$.73$^{1/2}$, 1 pr. cotton drawers-$.35$^{1/2}$, 1 cotton shirt-$.43; discharged 12/08/1847 on Surgeon's Certificate of Disability; J. Carson Green d. 11/17/1855, age 26, in a fire. Fireman?, Alexandria, VA [883]

**Green, John,** Pvt., *Recruit Co.*, enl. Mex. War service 01/20/1848 Christiansburg, VA, age 18; pres. 02/1848; pres. 04/1848; pres. 06/1848; BLW sent to Christiansburg, VA

**Greenhow, Thomas B.**, Pvt., Co. E; b. 06/17/1826, Chesterfield Co., VA;[884] enl. Mex. War service 11/30/1846 Petersburg, VA, age 20; pres. 04/1847; discharged 06/05/1847 Monterey, Mex. for disability; c. 1850 res. Petersburg, Dinwiddie Co., VA, age 24, occ. Coachmaker;[885] m/1 Elizabeth Bunkley 01/12/1854 Isle of Wight Co., VA;[884] (EBG d. 01/27/1857, Petersburg, VA);[884] c. 1860 res. Petersburg, Dinwiddie Co., VA, age 32, occ. Bricklayer;[886] Civil War service 2nd Lt., Co. B, 12th Va. Inf. enl. 04/19/1861, not reelected 05/01/1862 at reorganization;[21] m/2 Dora A. Judkins 08/12/1862, Petersburg, VA;[884] c. 1870 res. Petersburg, Dinwiddie Co., VA, age 42, occ. Brick Mason, w. Dora (28), son Thomas (4);[887] SC #16579, 06/30/1880, filed from 129 Old St.(now Grove Avenue), Petersburg, VA; Since discharge res. in Petersburg, VA last 28 years; Thomas J. McCaleb and David F. Shields gave affidavits in pension claim; d. 01/31/1899, bur. Blandford Cemetery, Petersburg, VA; wid. Dora A., WC #11820, 02/24/1899, filed from 129 Old St.(now Grove Ave.), Petersburg, VA; (DAG b. 07/18/1837, d. 07/18/1915).

**Gregory, Augustus Armstrong**, Pvt., LIC; enl. Mex. War service 12/05/1846 Staunton, VA, age 20; pres. 08/1847; pres. 10/1847, pay stopped for: 1 forage cap-$.95$^{1/2}$, 1 wool jacket-$2.66, 1 pr. overalls-$2.28, 3 pr. shoes-$3.66, 1 pr. socks-$.35$^{1/2}$, 1 flannel shirt-$.90; pres. 12/1847, pay stopped for: 1 pr. socks-$.24$^{1/2}$, 1 flannel shirt-$.90, 1 pr. drawers-$.35$^{1/2}$; pres. 04/1848, pay stopped for: 1 pr. shoes-$1.22; pres. 07/1848, pay stopped for: 1 pr. shoes-$1.16, 1 gun sling-$.16, 1 pick & brush-$.12, 1 wiper-$.20; BLW sent to Staunton, VA; m. Clara A. McIntyre, 03/06/1851, Layfayette, Tippecanoe, Ind.;[888] c. 1860 res. West Point P.O., Wayne Township, Tippecanoe Co., Ind., age 20, occ. Wagon Maker, w. Clara E. (32);[889] d. 12/16/1885, Covington, IN;[888] wid. Clara A., WC #2975, 10/20/1887, filed from Covington, Fountain Co., IN; (CAG b. 05/27/1824, Conneaut, Astabulah Co., OH).[888]

## VIRGINIA VOLUNTEERS IN MEXICO

**Griffin, Andrew M.**, Pvt., Co. H; enl. Mex. War service 01/04/1847, Richmond, VA, age 43; pres. 04/1847; discharged 05/17/1847 at camp near Monterey, Mex. on Surgeon's Certificate of Disability.
**Griffith, James**, Pvt., Co. L; b. 1809; [a James Griffith m. Mary Jane McGee, Washington, D.C.;][890] enl. Mex. War service 03/01/1847 Fairfax C.H., VA, age 38; absent 06/1847 left sick in hosp. at Pt. Isabel, Tex. 04/29/1847; absent 08/1847 in hosp. at Pt. Isabel, Tex.; pres. 10/1847; pres. 12/1847, pay stopped for: 2 pr. pants-$.4.56, 2 caps-$1.91, 1 pr. shoes-$1.22, 1 flannel shirt-$.90, 1 blanket-$2.22, 1 pr. socks-$.24$^{1/2}$; pres. 02/1848, pay stopped for: 1 pr. shoes-$1.22; pres. 04/1848, pay stopped for: 1 pr. Shoes 1.16, 2 Cotton Shirts .88; pres. 07/1848; BLW sent to James Griffith, Washington City, D.C.
**Grimes, James (W.)**, Pvt., Co. F; enl. Mex. War service 12/24/1846, Portsmouth, VA, age 23; pres. 06/1847; pres. 08/1847; pres. 10/1847, pay stopped for: 2 pr. overalls-$4.56, 2 pr. shoes-$2.44, 2 cotton shirts-$.86, 2 pr. drawers-$.71, 4 pr. socks-$.98, 3 flannel shirts-$2.70, 1 overcoat-$6.93$^{1/2}$, 1 forage cap-$.95$^{1/2}$; pres. 02/1848, pay stopped for: 2 cotton shirts-$.86, 1 flannel shirt-$.90, 1 pr. overalls-$2.28, 1 pr. shoes-$1.22, 1 blanket-$2.22, 1 pr. socks-$.24$^{1/2}$, 1 infantry jacket-$2.66; pres. 04/1848; pres. 08/1848, pay stopped for: 1 wiper-$.20, 1 pr. shoes-$1.16, 1 forage cap-$.83, 1 jacket-$2.37, 2 cotton shirts-$.88, 3 blankets-$6.75, BLW sent to Portsmouth, VA c/o E.T. Blamire; m. Deby Ann Manning 02/11/1849, Portsmouth, Norfolk Co., VA;[891] c. 1850 res. Portsmouth, Norfolk Co., VA, age 28, occ. Laborer, w. Debra A. (22);[892] [Civil War service a James Grimes, of Norfolk Co., VA, served as a Pvt., Co. D, 61$^{st}$ Va. Inf. enl. 04/03/1862 in Norfolk Co., VA, in Capt. Virginius O. Cassell's Co. of Heavy Arty. (co. trans. to 61$^{st}$ Va. Inf.) deserted 05/10/1862;][395] phys. desc. 5'8", light complexion, blue eyes, dark hair, occ. Laborer;[891] d. 07/27/1880, Portsmouth, Norfolk Co., VA; wid. Ann, WC #1961, 02/26/1887, filed from 511 Fayette St., Portsmouth, Norfolk Co., VA; since death of husband res. Portsmouth, VA;[891] Francis L. Benson, res. 920 Green St., Portsmouth, VA and William W. Manning res. Berkley, Norfolk Co., VA gave affidavits in pension claim;[891] (DAG b. 01/15/1825, d. 01/23/1899).[891]
**Grimes, Joshua**, Pvt., Co. F; enl. Mex. War service 12/24/1846, Portsmouth, VA, age 20; pres. 06/1847; pres. 08/1847; pres. 10/1847, pay stopped for: 2 pr. overalls-$4.56, 4 cotton shirts-$1.72, 1 forage cap-$.95$^{1/2}$, 4 pr. socks-$.98, 3 pr. drawers-$1.06$^{1/2}$, 1 pr. shoes-$1.22; pres. 02/1848, pay stopped for: 1 pr. overalls-$2.28, 1 pr. drawers-$.35$^{1/2}$, 2 flannel shirts-$1.80, 1 forage cap-$.95$^{1/2}$, 1 jacket-$2.66, 1 pr. socks-$.24$^{1/2}$, 1 pr. shoes-$1.22; pres. 04/1848; pres. 08/1848, pay stopped for: 1 wiper-$.20, 1 gun sling-$.18, 1 jacket-$2.37, 1 forage cap-$.83, BLW sent to Portsmouth, VA c/o E.T. Blamire; c. 1850 res. Portsmouth, Norfolk Co., VA, age 26, occ. Huckster, w. Rebecca (21);[893] c. 1860 a Rebecca Grimes res. Portsmouth, Norfolk Co., VA, age 29, son Joshua (7).[894]
**Grove, Alexander**, Pvt., LIC; enl. Mex. War service 11/27/1846 Staunton, VA, age 22; d. 06/23/1847 at Saltillo, Mex. of dropsy.
**Grove, Lewis Henry**, Pvt., Co. H; enl. Mex. War service 12/30/1846, Berkeley, VA, age 30; phys. desc. 5'3", dark complexion, dark hair, dark eyes; pres. 04/1847; pres. 06/1847; pres. 08/1847; pres. 10/1847, pay stopped for: 1 forage cap-$.95$^{1/2}$, 2 flannel shirts-$1.80, 1 pr. shoes-$1.22, 2 pr. socks-$.49, 1 jacket-$2.66; pres. 12/1847, pay stopped for: 1 forage cap-$.95$^{1/2}$, 1 jacket-$2.66, 2 pr. pants-$4.56, 2 cotton shirts-$.86, 2 flannel shirts-$1.80, 3 pr. shoes-$3.66, 2 pr. socks-$.49; pres. 02/1848, pay stopped for: 2 cotton shirts-$.86, 2 pr. drawers-$.71, 1 pr. shoes-$1.22, 1 blankets-$2.22; pres. 04/1848; pres. 07/1848, BLW sent to Sharpsburg, MD; m. Lavinia Himes 03/20/1851, Washington Co., MD; d. 06/28/1856 Sharpsburg, MD; wid. Levina, WC #2359, 02/03/1887, filed from West Fairview, Cumberland Co., PA; Since discharge res. Sharpsburg, MD Where soldier died. Since his death widow has res. w/ her brother William M. Himes, West Fairview, Cumberland Co., PA.
**Groves, John B.**, Pvt., LIC, enl. Mex. War service 01/06/1847 Staunton, VA, age 22; pres. 06/1847; sick 08/1847; pres. 10/1847, pay stopped for: 1 forage cap-$.95$^{1/2}$, 1 wool jacket-

OFF TO WAR

$2.66, 2 pr. overalls-$4.56, 1 pr. shoes-$1.22, 3 pr. socks-$.73$^{1/2}$, 2 cotton shirts-$.86, 1 pr. drawers-$.35$^{1/2}$; pres. 12/1847, pay stopped for: 1 pr. socks-$.24$^{1/2}$, 1 blanket-$2.22, 1 pr. shoes-$1.22; pres. 04/1848, pay stopped for: 1 pr. shoes-$1.22; pres. 07/1848, pay stopped for: 1 gun sling-$.16, 1 screw driver-$.12; BLW sent to _____, VA [see deposition of Greenberry B. Terrell].

**Grubb, Hiram**, Pvt., *Recruit Co.*, b. c. 1828; enl. Mex. War service 02/21/1848 Charlestown, VA, age 20; pres. 02/1848; pres. 04/1848; pres. 06/1848; BLW sent to Washington City, D.C.; Civil War service enl. as Pvt., Co. C, 13$^{th}$ Va. Inf., 04/17/1861 at Gordonsville, VA, prom. Sgt. by 03/1862, prom. Lt. 04/23/1862, mortally wded. 06/27/1862 at Gaines Mill, VA, d. 06/29 or 30/1862.[871]

**Grubb, James**, Pvt., *Recruit Co.*, enl. Mex. War service date unknown Wytheville, VA; pres. 06/1848; BLW sent to Wytheville, VA [Civil War service a James L. Grubb, b. 02/13/1831, enl. Co. A, 4$^{th}$ Va. Inf., d. 05/03/1863 in Chancellorsvile Hosp. of wds. received, bur. in Crockett Section of Wythe Co., VA[54]]

**Grymes, Benjamin Andrew**, 4$^{th}$ Cpl., Co. G; b. 1824; enl. Mex. War service 11/18/1846 Richmond, VA, age 22; pres. 06/1847; sick 08/1847; pres. 10/1847, pay stopped for: 1 pr. overalls-$2.28, 2 cotton shirts-$.86, 1 pr. drawers-$.35$^{1/2}$, 2 pr. shoes-$2.44, 3 pr. socks-$.73$^{1/2}$, 1 great coat-$6.95$^{1/2}$, 1 forage cap-$.95$^{1/2}$; pres. 12/1847, pay stopped for: 1 pr. shoes-$1.22, 1 jacket-$2.66, 1 blanket-$2.22, 1 pr. socks-$.24$^{1/2}$; pres. 02/1848, prom. 4$^{th}$ Cpl.; pres. 04/1848; pres. 08/1848, pay stopped for: 1 gun sling-$.16; discharged 08/01/1848, Ft. Monroe, VA; [see copy of discharge] phys. desc. b. Orange Co., VA, 22 yrs., 5'8", light complexion, light eyes, sandy hair, occ. Citizen;[895] BLW sent to Orange Co. C.H., VA; m. Harriet H. Beale, 01/05/1853, Orange Co., VA;[895] c. 1860 res. Orange Co., VA, age 34, occ. Farmer, w. Harriet H. (32), dau. Catherine (6), son Benjamin (3), dau. Alice G. (2);[896] Civil War service Pvt., Co. A, 13$^{th}$ Va. Inf., enl. 04/17/1861 at Orange C.H., VA, dropped from roll 05/1861;[871] c. 1870 res. Orange C.H., Orange Co., VA, age 45, occ. Farmer, w. Harriet H. (43), dau. Kate C. (17), son Benjamin (14), Alice (12), son. Eddie (10), son William (7), dau. Sarah (5), son John (1), fa.? Peyton (81);[897] d. 01/22/1884, *"Mountain Side,"* Orange Co., VA; bur. Graham Cem., Rt. 20, Orange, VA; [45, 895] wid. Harriet H., WC #1575, 03/10/1887, filed from Orange C.H, Orange Co., VA; lists daughter Eugenia Grymes; (HHG b. 11/19/1828, Culpeper Co., VA, d. 10/18/1912. Orange Co., VA, bur. Graham Cem., Orange, VA).[895]

**Gunnell, John Ratcliffe**, 2$^{nd}$ Cpl., Co. L; b. 08/23/1825, Fairfax Co., VA, son of George West & Locian (Ratcliffe) Gunnell;[898] enl. Mex. War service 03/01/1847 Fairfax C.H., VA, age 22; pres. 06/1847; sick 08/1847, prom. 2$^{nd}$ Cpl. from 3$^{rd}$ Cpl.; pres. 10/1847, reduced to ranks from Cpl. by sentence of garrison court-martial 10/22/1847, pay stopped for: 1 pr. Pants 2.28, 1 F Cap .95; pres. 12/1847, to forfeit 1 mos. pay by sentence of general court-martial, pay stopped for: 1 jacket-$2.66, 1 pr. pants-$2.28, 1 flannel shirt-$.90, 2 cotton shirts-$.86, 1 blanket-$2.22, 3 pr. drawers-$1.06$^{1/2}$, 1 pr. socks-$.24$^{1/2}$; pres. 02/1848, pay stopped for: 1 pr. Shoes 1.22, 1 Brush & Pick .12; pres. 04/1848, pay stopped for: 2 Cotton Shirts .88; pres. 07/1848, pay stopped for: 1 Brush & Pick .12, 1 B. Plate .10; BLW sent to James F. Waldron c/o John R. Gunnell, Dranesville P.O. Fairfax Co., VA; C. 1850 res. Fairfax Co., VA age 22, occ. Farmer;[899] c. 1860 res. Fairfax Co., VA, age 34, occ. Clerk;[900] m. Catherine Virginia Swink, 09/27/1868, Fairfax Co., VA;[901] c. 1870 res. Springvale, Fairfax Co., VA, age 45, occ. Farmer, w. Catherine V. (38), son George W. (15), son William T. (20);[902] Civil War service 2$^{nd}$ Lt., Co. G, 8$^{th}$ Va. Inf., wded. (stomach) at Hatcher's Run 03/31/1865, discharged on oath 06/29/1865 from Petersburg Hosp.;[529, 898] SC #15886, 03/05/1886, filed from Great Falls, Fairfax Co., VA; d. 05/20/1906, Fairfax Co., VA, obit. states *"last surviving member of Thrift's Co. Mexican War."*[903]

**Guthrow, William**, Pvt., Co. A; enl. Mex. War service 12/09/1846 Richmond, VA, age 32; pres. until sick 04/1847, in Hosp. at Camargo, Mex. since 04/04/1847; d. 04/12/1847 in Hosp. at Camargo, Mex.

VIRGINIA VOLUNTEERS IN MEXICO

**Hagan, Arthur**, Pvt., Co. H; enl. Mex. War service 01/06/1847, Berkeley, VA, age 18; pres. 04/1847; pres. 06/1847; pres. 08/1847; pres. 10/1847, pay stopped for: 1 forage cap-$.95$^{1/2}$, 1 pr. pants-$2.28, 4 cotton shirts-$1.72, 2 flannel shirts-$1.80, 1 pr. drawers-$.35$^{1/2}$, 2 pr. shoes-$2.44, 4 pr. socks-$.98, 1 greatcoat-$6.93$^{1/2}$, 1 jacket-$2.66; pres. 12/1847, pay stopped for: 1 pr. pants-$2.28, 2 flannel shirts-$1.80, 1 pr. shoes-$1.22, 1 pr. socks-$.24$^{1/2}$; pres. 02/1848, pay stopped for: 2 pr. drawers-$.71, 1 pr. shoes-$1.22; pres. 04/1848; pres. 07/1848, pay stopped for: 2 gun slings-$.32, BLW sent to Philadelphia, Pa.; [Civil War service an Arthur Hagan served as a Pvt., Co. B, 24$^{th}$ Pa. Inf. & Pvt., Co. B, 69$^{th}$ Pa. Inf.]$^{554}$

**Hagan, William**, Pvt., Co. L; b. 1820, Ireland;$^{904}$ enl. Mex. War service 03/01/1847 Fairfax C.H., VA, age 28; pres. 06/1847; absent 08/1847 on detached service in QM Dept. for 22 days from 08/22/1847, to receive $25 in addition to pay as a soldier; absent 10/1847, on detached service in QM Dept. as a Teamster; absent 12/1847, on detached service in QM Dept., pay stopped for: 1 pr. pants-$2.28, 1 cap-$.95$^{1/2}$, 1 pr. shoes-$1.22, 2 cotton shirts-$.86, 1 overcoat-$6.93$^{1/2}$, 1 blanket-$2.22, 3 pr. drawers-$1.06$^{1/2}$, 2 pr. socks-$.49; pres. 02/1848; pres. 04/1848; pres. 07/1848, pay stopped for: 1 Bayonet 1.44; BLW sent to Capt. Thrift c/o William Hagan, Fairfax Court House, Fairfax Co., VA; c. 1860 res. Fairfax Co., VA, age 40, occ. Laborer.$^{905}$

**Haines, Charles F., (Haynes)**, Pvt., Co. L; b. 11/23/1825, [pension records state 1818], Loudoun Co, VA, son of Joseph & Mary (Handy) Haines;$^{906}$ enl. Mex. War service 03/02/1847 Fairfax C.H., VA, age 25; pres. 06/1847; pres. 10/1847, absent 12/1847, on detached service as a Teamster in QM Dept., pay stopped for: 1 pr. pants-$2.28, 1 blanket-$2.22, 1 pr. drawers-$.71; absent 02/1848, on detached service as a Teamster in QM Dept.; absent 04/1848 on detached service as a Teamster in QM Dept. since 02/21/1848 by order of Col. Hamtramck, pay stopped for: 1 Knapsack .76; pres. 07/1848; Capt. Thrift c/o Charles F. Haines, Fairfax Court House, Fairfax Co., VA; m. Mary J. Ingram 11/06/1855, Loudoun Co. VA;$^{907}$ SA #2786, 02/04/1887, filed from Point of Rocks, Frederick Co., MD, SC #1198, (no date) phys. desc. 5'6", dark complexion, hazel eyes, black hair, occ. Farmer; d. 07/20/1887, Point of Rocks, Frederick Co. MD; wid. Mary J., WC #1407, 08/18/1887, filed from Point of Rocks, Frederick Co., MD (MJH b. 07/22/1833, Loudoun Co., VA; d. 01/18/1903).$^{908}$

**Haley, Woodson**, Pvt., Co. A; b. 1820 Campbell Co., VA, son of Edmund & Rachel Haley;$^{909}$ enl. Mex. War service 12/14/1846 Richmond, VA, age 23; pres. 12/1846 - 04/1847; pres. 06/1847; pres. 08/1847; pres. 10/1847, pay stopped for clothing: 4 cotton shirts-$1.72, 1 pr. wool overalls-$2.28, 1 cap-$.95$^{1/2}$, 2 pr. shoes-$2.44, 2 pr. stockings-$.49, 1 wool jacket-$2.66; absent sick 12/1847, pay stopped for clothing: 1 pr. socks-$.49, 1 pr. wool overalls-$2.28, 2 pr. drawers-$.71, 2 cotton shirts; pres. 02/1848, pay stopped for: 2 pr. shoes-$2.44; pres. 04/1848; BLW sent to Lynchburg, VA; c. 1850 res. Lynchburg, Campbell Co., VA, age 32, occ. Shoemaker;$^{910}$ c. 1860 res. Lynchburg, Campbell Co., VA, age 42, occ. Shoemaker, son John R. (6), dau Sarah A. (2);$^{911}$ m Frances Martin 08/08/1861 Lynchburg, VA;$^{909}$ d. 07/28/1886 near Lynchburg, VA; wid. Frances, WC #2725, 09/27/1887, filed from Lynchburg, Campbell Co., VA; (FMH b. c. 1836 Prince Edward Co., VA).$^{909}$

**Hall, Frederick**, Pvt., Co. A; enl. Mex. War service 12/08/1846 Richmond, VA, age 24; pres. 12/1846 - 04/1847; pres. 06/1847; pres. 08/1847; in confinement 10/1847, pay stopped for clothing: 4 cotton shirts-$1.72, 2 pr. wool overalls-$4.56, 1 cap-$.95$^{1/2}$, 2 pr. shoes-$2.44, 1 wool jacket-$2.66, 1 great coat-$6.93$^{1/2}$, 1 blanket-$2.22; pres. 12/1847, pay stopped for clothing: 2 pr. wool overalls-$4.56, 1 cotton shirt-$.43, 1 wool jacket-$2.11, 1 pr. shoes-$1.22; pres. 02/1848, pay stopped for: 1 pr. shoes-$1.22; 1 cartridge box belt-$.25, 1 pick & brush-$.12; pres. 04/1848; 07/1848, pay stopped for: 1 cartridge box belt-$.60, 1 musket sling-$.16, 1 cartridge box belt plate-$.10, 1 pick & brush-$.12; BLW sent to Portsmouth, VA c. 1850 res. Norfolk, VA, age 28, occ. School Teacher;$^{912}$ c. 1860 res. Norfolk, VA, age 38, occ. Farm Laborer, w. Cecilia? (24);$^{913}$ [Civil War service a Frederick A. Hall enl. as a Pvt., Co. A, 41$^{st}$

OFF TO WAR

Va. Inf., 06/20/1861 at Petersburg, VA, for 1 year, on 03/1862 he refused to reenlist and was drafted back into war; discharged 06/24/1862 on Surgeon's Cert. of Disability.][404]

**Hall, George**, Pvt., Co. C; enl. Mex. War service 12/30/1846, Bowling Green, VA, age 21; pres. 06/1847; pres. 08/1847, pay stopped for: 1 cap-$.95$^{1/2}$, 2 pr. socks-$.49, 2 cotton shirts-$.86, 2 woolen shirts-$1.80, 1 pr. shoes-$1.22; pres. 10/1847, pay stopped for: 2 pr. socks-$.49, 2 pr. drawers-$.71, 1 jacket-$2.66, 1 pr. pants-$2.28, 2 cotton shirts-$.86, 1 woolen shirt-$.90, 1 pr. shoes-$1.22, 1 great coat-$6.93$^{1/2}$; pres. 12/1847, pay stopped for:, 2 pr. pants-$4.56, 2 woolen shirts-$1.80, 1 pr. shoes-$1.22, 1 blanket-$2.22; pres. 04/1848, pay stopped for: 1 jacket-$2.66, 1 india rubber canteen-$.27; pres. 08/1848, BLW sent to Washington, DC.

**Hall, William**, Pvt., Co. B; enl. 12/01/1846, Alexandria, VA, age 24; pres. 06/1847; pres. 08/1847; pres. 10/1847, pay stopped for: 2 pr. shoes-$2.44, 2 flannel shirts-$1.80, 1 pr. overalls-$2.28, 4 pr. socks-$.98, 2 cotton shirts-$.86, 1 blanket-$2.22, 1 pr. cotton drawers-$.35$^{1/2}$, 1 overcoat-$ 6.93$^{1/2}$; pres. 12/1847, pay stopped for: 2 cotton shirts-$.86, 1 pr. overalls-$2.28, 2 pr. cotton drawers-$.71; pres. 02/1848; pres. 04/1848; pres. 08/1848, pay stopped for: 1 gun sling-$.16, 1 pr. shoes-$1.16, BLW sent Alexandria, VA; c. 1850 res. Alexandria, VA, age 26, occ. Shoemaker;[914] c. 1860 res. Fairfax Co., VA, age 35, occ. Shoemaker;[915] c. 1870 res. Fairfax C.H., Fairfax Co., VA, age 46, occ. Works on A Farm;[916] voted for secession at West End, Fairfax Co., VA 04/23/1861; Civil War service Pvt., Co. D, 17$^{th}$ Va. Inf., enl. 05/23/1861 at Fairfax Station, VA, wded. Sharpsburg, MD 09/17/1862, accidentally wded. 12/1862 (fore finger rt. hand), captured 04/16/1865 at Fairfax C.H., VA, took oath 05/19/1865 at Alexandria, VA;[63, 898] SC #7013, 02/21/1887, age 65, filed from Burke's Station, Fairfax Co., VA, phys. desc. at enlistment age 24, b. Fairfax Co., VA, 5'6", black hair, black eyes, occ. Shoemaker; requested a pension increase 02/08/1894, states he is totally blind, increase granted; d. 09/08/1901.[917]

**Hallman, Peter Fritz**, Pvt., Co. A; enl. Mex. War service 11/19/1846 Richmond, VA, age 21; pres. 12/1846 - 04/1847; pres. 06/1847; pres. 08/1847; pres. 10/1847, pay stopped for clothing: 2 cotton shirts-$.86, 1 pr. wool overalls-$2.28, 1 cap-$.95$^{1/2}$, 2 pr. stockings-$.49, 2 flannel shirts-$1.80, 1 pr. shoes-$1.22, 1 blanket-$2.22; pres. 12/1847, pay stopped for clothing: 1 pr. wool overalls-$2.28, 1 pr. shoes-$1.22, 2 flannel shirts-$1.80; pres. 02/1848, pay stopped for: 1 pick & brush-$.12; sick 04/1848; 07/1848, pay stopped for: 1 musket sling-$.16, 1 waist belt plate-$.10, 1 bayonet-$1.44; BLW sent to Philadelphia, Pa.; Civil War service Pvt., Co. A, 114$^{th}$ Pa. Inf., *Collis' Zouaves*.[554]

**Halsey, George W.**, Pvt., Co. M enl. Mex. War service 11/17/1847, Norfolk, VA, age 22; pres. 11/1847; pres. 12/1847; pres. 02/1848, pay stopped for: 1 over coat-$6.93$^{1/2}$; sick 04/1848; pres. 08/1848; BLW sent to Rochester, N.Y.

**Hamilton, Alfred A.**, Pvt., *Recruit Co.*, enl. Mex. War service ??/1848 Richmond, VA; pres. 06/1848; BLW sent to Richmond, VA

**Hamilton, Edward L.**, Pvt., Co. L; b. 1812; enl. Mex. War service 03/01/1847 Fairfax C.H., VA, age 35; pres. 06/1847; pres. 08/1847; pres. 10/1847, pay stopped for: 1 pr. Pants 2.28, 1 F Cap .95, 2 F Shirts 1.80; pres. 12/1847, pay stopped for: 1 jacket-$2.66, 1 cap-$.95$^{1/2}$, 1 flannel shirt-$.90, 2 cotton shirts-$.86, 1 blanket-$2.22, 4 pr. drawers-$1.42, 1 pr. socks-$.24$^{1/2}$; pres. 02/1848, pay stopped for: 1 pr. Shoes 1.22, 1 Brush & Pick .12; pres. 04/1848; pres. 07/1848, pay stopped for: 1 Brush & Pick .12, 1 Waist Belt Plate .10; E. L. Hamilton, Washington City, D.C.; c. 1850 res. King George Co., VA, age 35, occ. Carpenter;[918] c. 1860 res. Comorn, King George Co., VA, age 47, occ. Carpenter;[919] Civil War service 2$^{nd}$ Lt., Co. A, 25$^{th}$ VA Militia (King George Militia);[202] c. 1870 res. King George Co., VA, age 60, occ. Farmer, w. Martha (50), son Pierce (18), dau. Marion (14).[920]

**Ham(b)lin, Richard (H.)**, Pvt., Co. D; enl. Mex. War service 01/08/1847, Petersburg, VA, age 21; deserted 02/01/1847, not paid; As the first deserter from the Capt. Robinson placed the following ad in the Petersburg Republican: *"$30 Reward. Stop the deserter! The above reward will be paid to any person or persons, who will deliver up RICHARD HAMLIN, who deserted*

VIRGINIA VOLUNTEERS IN MEXICO

*from his company - The Petersburg Union Volunteers, on the 1st inst. He is about 5'9"in height, dark hair and eyes, complexion rather whitish, oval face, stout in person. He had on when he absconded a black dress coat, much worn, checked cassinet pantaloons, and a dark blue pilot cloth peajacket. His hat was a broad brimmed black hat without any nap. He is supposed to be lurking in the vicinity of Cabin Point, if not still in the neighborhood of Swift Creek Factory, where he worked. W.M. Robinson'*[921] c. 1850 res. Prince George Co., VA, age 23, occ. Laborer;[922] c. 1860 res. Cabin Point, Surry Co., VA, age 32, occ. Fisherman;[923] Civil War service Pvt., Co. D, 19th Btln. Hvy. Arty., enl. 05/10/1861 at Jamestown, VA, absent 02/21/1864 in Gen. Hosp. #13 w/ typhoid pneumonia, court-martialed 04/25/1864, pres. 05/14/1864; captured 09/1864 at Ft. Harrison, VA, sent to Pt. Lookout, MD, exchanged 02/18/1865, paroled 05/05/1865 Richmond, VA, a res. of Surry Co., VA[33]

**Hammock, Lewis Lambert**, Pvt., Co. M; enl. Mex. War service 00/02/1847, Nottoway, VA, age 34; pres. 10/1847; pres. 11/1847; pres. 12/1847; pres. 02/1848, pay stopped for: 1 pr. shoes-$1.22; sick 04/1848; pres. 08/1848, pay stopped for: 1 musket-$13.00, 1 waist belt-$.21, 1 waist belt plate-$.10, 1 bayonet-$1.44, 1 screw driver-$.07; BLW sent to Nottoway C.H., VA; m. Elizabeth S. Freeman, 10/15/1852, Lunenburg Co., VA;[924] c. 1860 res. Jonesboro, Brunswick Co., VA, age 45, occ. Farmer, w. Elizabeth (24), dau. Lucy E. (6), son James W. (4), dau. Elizabeth S. (1);[925] Civil War service Pvt., Co. I, 8th Va. Inf. enl. 08/1863, absent 03/1864 sick, pres. 08/30/1864, pres. 12/31/1864, captured 04/03/1865, Amelia C.H., VA, sent to Pt. Lookout, MD, d. 05/20/1865 "chronic diarrhea;"[529] wid. Elizabeth S., WC #2367, 06/18/1887, from VA; Edward W. Goodwyn and John W. Overby gave affidavits in pension claim;[924] (EFH b. 04/03/1822, Lunenburg Co., VA).[924]

**Hammon, Otis**, Pvt., Co. M; enl. Mex. War service 08/28/1847 Richmond, VA, age 29; discharged 09/09/1847 at Ft. Monroe, VA

**Hammond, Charles**, Pvt., Co. G; enl. Mex. War service 08/19/1847, Petersburg, VA, age 29; absent 02/1848, on furlough for 30 days, joined the co. 01/25/1848 from the regtl. depot; pres. 04/1848; pres. 08/1848, pay stopped for: 1 wiper-$.20.

**Hammond, Rodolphus**, Pvt., Co. D; enl. Mex. War service 01/22/1847, Petersburg, VA, age 25; pres. 02/1847; pres. 04/1847; pres. 06/1847; pres. 08/1847, pay stopped for: 2 cotton shirts-$.86, 1 pr. shoes-$1.22; pres. 10/1847, pay stopped for: 1 cap-$.95$^{1/2}$, 1 jacket-$2.66, 1 pr. pants-$2.28,1 pr. socks-$.24$^{1/2}$, 1 pr. shoes-$1.22; pres. 12/1847, pay stopped for: 1 cap-$.95$^{1/2}$, 1 jacket-$2.66, 1 pr. pants-$2.28, 1 pr drawers-$.35$^{1/2}$, 2 pr. socks-$.49, 1 pr. shoes-$1.22, 1 blanket-$2.22, 1 overcoat-$6.93$^{1/2}$; pres. 04/1848, fined 1 mos. pay by order of genl. court-martial, pay stopped for: 1 jacket-$2.66, 1 blanket-$2.22, 1 cap-$.95$^{1/2}$, 1 pr. shoes-$1.22; pres. 08/1847, BLW sent to Baltimore, MD; c. 1850 res. Nansemond Co., VA, age 23, occ. None.[926]

**Hammons, Henry**, Pvt., Co. I; enl. Mex. War service 01/25/1847 Richmond, VA, age 24; pres. 02/1847; pres. 04/1847; pres. 06/1847; pres. 08/1847; pres. 10/1847, pay stopped for: 2 flannel shirts-$1.80, 3 cotton shirts-$1.29, 3 pr. drawers-$1.06$^{1/2}$, 1 pr. socks-$.24$^{1/2}$, 1 cap- $.95$^{1/2}$, 1 jacket-$2.66, 1 pr. pants-$2.28, 1 pr. shoes-$1.22; pres. 12/1847, pay stopped for: 1 pr. socks-$.24$^{1/2}$, 1 pr. shoes-$1.22, 1 pr. pants-$2.28, 1 blanket-$2.22, 1 flannel shirt-$.90; pres. 02/1848, pay stopped for: 1 pr. overalls-$2.28; pres. 04/1848; pres. 08/1848, pay stopped for: 1 pr. shoes-$1.16, 1 screw driver-$.25, BLW sent to Abingdon, VA

**Hampton, Joseph L.**, Pvt., Co. K; enl. Mex. War service Jefferson Co., VA 12/29/1846, age 18; pres. 06/1847; pres. 08/1847; pres. 10/1847, pay stopped for: 1 pr. shoes-$1.22, 2 cotton shirts-$.86, 1 pr. overalls-$2.28, 2 pr. drawers-$.71, 2 pr. socks-$.49; pres. 12/1847, pay stopped for: 1 pr. socks-$.24$^{1/2}$, 1 blanket-$2.22, 1 cap-$.95$^{1/2}$, 1 flannel shirt-$.90; pres. 04/1848, pay stopped for: 1 pick & brush-$.12, 1 wiper-$.20, 1 screw driver-$.25 1 pr. shoes-$1.22, 1 gun sling-$.18; pres. 07/1848; BLW sent to Aldie, Loudoun Co., VA; [Civil War service a Joseph T. Hampton served in Co. C, 8th Va. Cav. from Mercer Co., VA].[450]

OFF TO WAR

**Hamtramck, John Francis**, Colonel, 1st VA Vol. Inf. Regt., b. 04/19/1798, Ft. Wayne, Indiana, son of John Francis & Rebecca (McKenzie) Hamtramck; graduated United States Military Academy 1819 15th out of a class of 29; m/1 Miss Williamson; m/2 Ellen Selby of Shepherdstown; m/2 Sarah Selby of Shepherdstown;[927] Mayor of Shepherdstown, VA 1850-1854, Judge, Jefferson Co. Circuit Court 1854-1858;[928] wid. Sarah E.; d. 04/21/1858, bur. Elmwood Cem., Shepherdstown, WV.[614]

**Hannah, Musty**, Pvt., Co. I; enl. Mex. War service 02/01/1847 Richmond, VA, age 40; pres. 02/1847; pres. 04/1847; pres. 06/1847; pres. 08/1847; pres. 10/1847, pay stopped for: 2 flannel shirts-$1.80, 2 cotton shirts-$.86, 3 pr. drawers-$1.06$^{1/2}$, 1 pr. shoes-$1.22, 1 pr. pants-$2.28, 1 cap- $.95$^{1/2}$, 1 pr. socks-$.24$^{1/2}$, 1 jacket-$2.66; pres. 12/1847, pay stopped for: 1 pr. shoes-$1.22, 1 pr. socks-$.24$^{1/2}$, 1 pr. pants-$2.28, 1 pr. shoes-$1.22, 1 cotton shirt-$.43, 1 pr. drawers-$.35$^{1/2}$; Court-martialed 02/04/1848 Buena Vista, Mex. *Charge #1: Drunkeness; Specification: In this that the said Private Musty Hannah, Co. I, Va. Regt. of Vols., has been drunk from the 17th day of January 1848 to this the 24th day of January 1848. This at Camp Buena Vista, Mexico. Charge #2: Disobedience of Orders; Specification: In this that he, Private Musty Hannah, Co. I, Va. Regt., did refuse to go upon Guard Duty when ordered. All this at Buena Vista, Mexico the 24th day of January 1848. Before taking the plea of the prisoner to these charges the Judge Advocate stated to the Court that specification of the 1st Charge was indefinite and vague. It would be impossible for the prosecution to sustain it. The Court there upon ordered it set aside. The prisoner the plead Not Guilty. Sergt. W.L. Taylor, Co. I, Va. Regt. of Vols., a witness for the prosecution being duly sworn, says: The prisoner, Hannah, was regularly detailed for Guard on the 23rd of January last and refused to go on, he did not go on, and another man had to be put on in his place. This was at the camp of the Va. Regt. at this place. Question by the Court: Was the prisoner in the Guard House or in his company at the time he was detailed for Guard? Answer: He was in his company when I detailed him for guard on the 23rd. Question by the Judge Advocate: Was the Prisoner detailed for Guard on the 23rd or 24th of January last? Answer: He was taken out of the Guard House on the 23rd in the morning and named for the Guard on the 23rd. Question by the Court: Was this the regular tour of Guard for the prisoner? Answer Yes. It was his regular tour of guard. After deliberation the Court found the prisoner Guilty of the Charge and Specification. Sentenced him to forfeit two (2) months pay.*[929] in confinement 02/1848; discharged 04/20/1848, on Surgeon's Certificate of Disability.

**Harding, John A.B.**, Pvt., Co. K; enl. Mex. War service Jefferson Co., VA 12/04/1846, age 45; sick 06/1847; on 06/27/1847 Pvt. Harding wrote to Col. Hamtramck complaining of *"being sorely afflicted with Hemorrhoids in the worst form."* As a consequence he requested he be assigned duties *"humble not menial that will exempt me from exposure and fatigues of a common sentinel;"*[930] sick 08/1847; discharged 09/13/1847 at Buena Vista, Mex. on Surgeon's Certificate of Disability.

**Hardy, Green**, *Archer's Co.*; *Not On Muster* Rolls, SA #19279, 05/04/1888.

**Harlan, George**, 4th Cpl., LIC; b. 11/26/1821 Petersburg, Dinwiddie Co., VA, son of George & Elizabeth (Dilworth) Harlan;[931] enl. Mex. War service 12/07/1846 Staunton, VA, age 25; pres. 08/1847; pres. 10/1847, pay stopped for: 1 forage cap-$.95$^{1/2}$, 1 wool jacket-$2.66, 1 pr. overalls-$2.28, 2 pr. shoes-$2.44, 4 pr. socks-$.98, 4 cotton shirts-$1.72, 1 pr. drawers-$.35$^{1/2}$; pres. 12/1847, pay stopped for: 1 pr. overalls-$2.28, 2 flannel shirts-$1.80; pres. 04/1848, prom. 4th Cpl., pay stopped for: 1 pr. shoes-$1.22; pres. 07/1848, pay stopped for: 1 gun sling-$.16; BLW sent to Staunton, VA; c. 1850 res. Staunton, Augusta Co., VA, age 28, occ. Printer;[932] m. Jane S. Ball, 06/05/1851, Staunton, VA;[931] c. 1860, res. Augusta Co., VA, age 39, occ. Printer;[933] [a George Boyd Harlan served in the Civil War as a Pvt., Co. C, 1st Va. Cav.; enl. 06/17/1861 at Martinsburg, VA, pres. thru 8/1862; detailed as QM Sgt. 08/1862-08/1864; paroled 04/28/1865 Winchester, VA; desc. age 35, 5'10", dark complexion, dark hair, dark eyes;] c. 1870 res. Staunton, Augusta Co., VA, age 48, occ. Jailor, w. Jane S. (52),

VIRGINIA VOLUNTEERS IN MEXICO

dau. Kate E. (13), son George T. (10);[934] SC #1344, 02/03/1887, filed from Staunton, Augusta Co., VA; phys. desc. 5'9", occ. Printer, light brown hair, gray blue eyes, fair complexion;[935] William E. Skeen & William O. Bickle gave affidavits in pension application;[935] d. 09/06/1889, Martinsburg, WV., age 60; bur. Harlan Cem., near Falling Waters, WV;][441]
**Harland, James**, Pvt., Co. I; enl. Mex. War service 01/30/1847 Richmond, VA, age 20; pres. 02/1847; pres. 04/1847; pres. 06/1847; pres. 08/1847; in confinement 10/1847, pay stopped for: 2 flannel shirts-$1.80, 4 cotton shirts-$1.72, 3 pr. drawers-$1.06$^{1/2}$, 1 overcoat-$6.93$^{1/2}$, 1 pr. socks-$.24$^{1/2}$, 1 cap- $.95$^{1/2}$, 1 jacket-$2.66, 1 pr. shoes-$1.22; pres. 12/1847, pay stopped for: 1 pr. socks-$.24$^{1/2}$, 1 pr. pants-$2.28, 1 pr. shoes-$1.22, 2 cotton shirts-$.86, 1 pr. drawers-$.35$^{1/2}$; in confinement 02/1848; pres. 04/1848; pres. 08/1848, BLW sent to Washington, D.C.
**Harless, Ballard**, Pvt., Co. A; *Not on Muster Rolls*; c. 1880 res. Roane Co., WV, age 54, occ. Farmer, w. Mary J. (52) Keeping House, son James (18) Works on Farm, son George (10) Works on Farm;[936] SA #21997, 08/26/1889, from WV.
**Harmon, Daniel**, Pvt., *Preston's Co.*; enl. Mex. War service 12/07/1846 Floyd Co., VA, age 30; pres. 04/1847; d. 05/26/1847 in hosp. at Monterey, Mex.
**Harmon, William Henry**, 2$^{nd}$ Lt., LIC; b. 02/17/1828, Waynesboro, VA, son of Sarah Harmon;

Photo credit: Virginia Grand Lodge AF&AM

enl. Mex. War service 11/27/1846 Staunton, VA; pres. 08/1847; pres. 10/1847; pres. 12/1847; pres. 04/1848, Actg. Adjt. of Parras Battalion since 02/25/1848; pres. 07/1848; m. Margaret S. Garber, 12/26/1848, Staunton, Augusta Co., VA;[937] c. 1850 res. Augusta Co., VA, age 23, occ. Lawyer;[938] c. 1860, res. Augusta Co., VA, age 33, occ. Attorney at Law, w. Margaret S. (29), son Arthur (6), Albert G. (4), dau. Ellen (3), dau. Augusta (1);[939] Commonwealth's Attorney, Augusta Co., VA, 1851 - 1861; Civil War service Commissioned Lt. Col., 5$^{th}$ Va. Inf.; prom. to Col. 09/11/1861 succeeding Kenton Harper who resigned; not re-elected 04/21/1862 after reorganization; vol. Aide-de-Camp, as Col., to Gen. Edward Johnson 05/17/1862; apptd. Asst. Adj. Gen, P.A.C.S. 02/19/1864; killed 03/02/1865 near his birthplace at Gallagher's Mill; Grand Master of Virginia A.F.& A.M. (Masons) 1864 - until his death; monument to his memory on West Main St., Waynesboro, VA; bur. Thornrose Cem., Staunton, VA;[128] wid. Margaret S., WC #2255, 06/15/1887, filed from 404 Lewis St., Staunton, Augusta Co., VA; (MGH b. 01/02/1829, d. 06/03/1895).[937]

**Harper, Kenton**, Capt., LIC; b. Pa., son of George Kenton Harper; moved to Staunton 1823; established the *Staunton Spectator* and edited it for 16 years; member of Virginia House of Delegates 1836-1837; resigned 1842 as Capt. of Staunton Light Inf.; enl. Mex. War service 12/07/1846 Staunton, VA; pres. 05/01 to 05/04/1847 commanding post at China, Mex., 05/28 to 06/12/1847 in command of detachment of VA and N.C. volunteers on march from Monterey to Buena Vista, Mex.; absent 08/1847 on detached service as Actg. Insp. Genl. since 08/29/1847; absent 10/1847 Actg. Insp. Genl.; absent 12/1847 Actg. Insp. Genl.; pres. 04/1848, in command of Parras Battalion since 02/25/1848; pres. 07/1848; Military Governor of New Mexico territory; c. 1850 res. Augusta Co., VA, age 49, occ. Farmer, w. Elinor (49), son Samuel (18), dau. Nancy (16), dau. Mary (14), served as agent of the Chickasaws 1851-1852; assistant to U. S. Secretary of Interior; returned to his farm, Glen Allen, Augusta Co., VA; Capt. in VA Militia 12-21-59; appointed Maj. Gen. in 5th Div. VA Militia 1860-1861; c. 1860 res. Burke's Mill, Augusta Co., VA, age 58, occ. Farmer, w. Ellen (59), son Samuel C.

(28), dau. Nancy (26), dau. Mary (24); [940]Col. of 5th Va. Inf., C.S.A. 05/07/1861; resigned 09/1861;[128] Lt. Col. of Augusta Home Guard 1863-1864; Col. 1864-1865; His career included also the offices of mayor and magistrate of Staunton, President of the Valley Bank, and publisher of the *Staunton Vindicator*; d. 12/25/1867, pneumonia, Glen Allen, VA; bur. Thornrose Cemetery, Staunton, VA[249]

**Harris, Hamlin Eppes**, Pvt., Co. E; b. 1829, Dinwiddie Co., VA, son of Benjamin & Joanna B. Harris;[941] enl. Mex. War service 12/01/1846 Petersburg, VA, age 18; pres. 04/1847; pres. 06/1847; pres. 08/1847; pres. 10/1847, pay stopped for: 1 pr. overalls-$2.28, 2 pr. shoes-$2.44, 2 pr. stockings-$.49, 1 pr. drawers-$.71, 1 cap-$.95$^{1/2}$, 1 blanket-$2.22; pres. 02/1848, [illegible]; pres. 04/1848, [illegible]; c. 1850 res. Petersburg, Dinwiddie Co., VA, age 21, occ. Clerk;[942] d. 06/15/1855, *"Pulmonary consumption. Volunteer Mexican War. Largest funeral procession ever seen in Petersburg;"*[943] bur. Blandford Cem., Sq. 8, Sec. 16, Ward C, Petersburg, VA[944]

**Harrison, George W.**, Pvt., Co. D; enl. Mex. War service 01/03/1847, Petersburg, VA, age 19; pres. 02/1847; pres. 04/1847; pres. 06/1847; pres. 08/1847, pay stopped for: 1 cap-$.95$^{1/2}$, 1 pr. pants-$2.28; pres. but sick 10/1847, pay stopped for: 1 pr. socks-$.24$^{1/2}$; absent 12/1847, on detached service as Hosp. Attendant Saltillo, Mex. since 11/01/1847; pay stopped for: 1 cap-$.95$^{1/2}$, 1 jacket-$2.66, 1 pr. pants-$2.28, 1 cotton shirt-$.43, 1 pr drawers-$.35$^{1/2}$, 2 pr. socks-$.49, 1 pr. shoes-$1.22, 1 blanket-$2.22; pres. 04/1848; pres. 08/1847, BLW sent to Templeton P.O, Prince George Co., VA; c. 1850 res. Prince George Co., VA, age 23, occ. Overseer; [945] c. 1860 res. Brandon Church, Prince George Co., VA, age 32, occ. Lighthouse Keeper, w. L.F. (24), dau. E.F. (6), son Tho. C. (1), dau. H.C. (3);[946] a George W. Harrison, d. 07/11/1862 *chronic diarrhea*, bur. Blandford Cem., Petersburg, VA[947] [Civil War service a George W. Harrison enl. as Pvt., Co. F, 12th Va. Inf., 06/06/1861 at Hicksford, VA, was discharged 09/01/1861 by furnishing a substitute, John W. Harrison, enl. again 02/22/1862 as a Pvt., Co. I, 12th Va. Inf., absent sick 04/1862-01/1863, detailed as nurse, Petersburg Hosp., 1/1863-8/31/1863, absent sick 11/1863-12/1863 at C.H., NFR.][21]

**Harrison, John N.**, Co. E; enl. Mex. War service 12/02/1846 Petersburg, VA, age 24; pres. 04/1847; discharged 05/01/1847 Monterey, Mex. for disability; d. 11/1857, *"of Henrico Co.;"*[948] wid. Margaret E.A., WC #783, 05/03/1887.

**Harrison, Otho H.**, 1st Lt., Co. H; enl. Mex. War service 11/21/1846, Martinsburg, VA; pres. 04/1847; absent sick 06/1847 in Saltillo, Mex. since 06/27/1847; absent 10/1847 Actg. Assr. Commissary since 08/01/1847; absent 02/1848 Actg. Adjt. of Va. Regt.; pres. 04/1848, commanding the company; pres. 07/1848. [an Otho Holland Harrison, b. Springfield, MD, c. 1812, m. Ann H. Burt ]

**Harrow, Morgan**, Fifer, LIC; b. 1822, Augusta Co., VA;[949] enl. Mex. War service 12/24/1846 Staunton, VA, age 18; pres. 08/1847, pay stopped for: 1 cartridge box-$1.10, 1 cartridge box belt-$.70, 1 bayonet scabbard & belt-$.56, eagle and U.S. plates-$.20; pres. 10/1847, pay stopped for: 1 forage cap-$.95$^{1/2}$, 1 wool jacket-$2.66, 2 pr. overalls-$4.56, 1 pr. shoes-$1.22, 3 pr. socks-$.73$^{1/2}$, 3 cotton shirts-$1.29; pres. 12/1847, pay stopped for: 1 pr. socks-$.24$^{1/2}$, 1 blanket-$2.22, 1 pr. shoes-$1.22, 1 flannel shirt-$.90, 1 pr. drawers-$.35$^{1/2}$; pres. 04/1848, pay stopped for: 1 pr. overalls-$2.28, 1 pr. shoes-$1.22; pres. 07/1848; BLW sent to Staunton, VA; c. 1850 res. Augusta Co., VA, age 20, occ. Laborer, *illiterate*;[950] c. 1860 res. McDowell, Highland Co., VA, age 34, occ. Farm Hand;[951] c. 1870 res. Monterey, Highland Co., VA, age 45, occ. None Listed;[952] m. Nancy Griffen date/place unknown;[953] SC #4664, 04/09/1887, filed from Hightown, Highland Co., VA; phys. desc. 5'6", dark hair, blue eyes, occ. laborer;[949] Christian G. Merritt gave affidavit in pension claim;[949] d. 02/28/1898, bur. Wade Family Cemetery, Mill Gap, Highland Co., VA[949, 954]

**Harry, James M.**, 3rd Cpl., Co. K; enl. Mex. War service Frederick Co., VA 12/26/1846, age 32; sick 06/1847; pres. 08/1847; pres. 10/1847, pay stopped for: 1 pr. overalls-$2.28, 2 pr. socks-$.49, 2 pr. drawers-$.71, 1 flannel shirt-$.90, 1 blanket-$2.22; pres. 12/1847, pay stopped for:

VIRGINIA VOLUNTEERS IN MEXICO

1 blanket-$2.22; pres. 04/1848, prom. 3rd Cpl. 04/01/1848, pay stopped for: 1 pr. shoes-$1.22, 1 gun sling-$.18; pres. 07/1848, pay stopped for: 1 waist belt-$.21, 1 bayonet scabbard & frog-$.56; BLW sent to Winchester, Frederick Co., VA;  c. 1850 res. Winchester, Frederick Co., VA, age 37, occ. Bricklayer;⁹⁵⁵  Civil War service Pvt., Co. A, 13th Va. Cav.; ²⁰² c. 1870 res. Covington, Alleghany Co., VA, age 49, occ. Brick Mason.⁹⁵⁶
**Hart, John R.**, Pvt., Co. D; enl. Mex. War service 08/16/1847 Lunenburg Co., VA, age 18; pres. 04/1848, pay stopped for: 1 blanket-$2.22; pres. 08/1847, BLW sent to [illegible].
**Hart, John L.**, Pvt., Co. C; m. Synia Mason. 06/09/1845, Caroline Co., VA;⁹⁵⁷ enl. Mex. War service 12/20/1846, Bowling Green, VA, age 25; pres. 06/1847; pres. 08/1847, pay stopped for: 1 cap-$.95^{1/2}, 2 pr. socks-$.49, 2 cotton shirts-$.86, 2 woolen shirts-$1.80, 1 pr. shoes-$1.22, 1 pr. drawers-$.35^{1/2}; pres. 10/1847, pay stopped for: 1 pr. socks-$.24^{1/2}, 1 pr. drawers-$.35^{1/2}, 1 jacket-$2.66, 1 pr. pants-$2.28; pres. 12/1847, pay stopped for: 2 pr. socks-$.49, 1 pr. pants-$2.28, 1 pr. shoes-$1.22, 1 blanket-$2.22; pres. 04/1848, pay stopped for: 1 blanket-$2.22, 1 haversack-$.20^{3/4}, 1 india rubber canteen-$.27; pres. 08/1848, BLW sent to Bowling Green, Caroline Co., VA
**Harwood, James D.**, Pvt., Co. H; enl. Mex. War service 12/16/1846, Richmond, VA, age 21; pres. 04/1847; pres. 06/1847; pres. 08/1847; absent 10/1847, on detached service as Commissary Sgt. 10/01/1847, pay stopped for: 1 forage cap-$.95^{1/2}, 1 pr. pants-$2.28, 4 cotton shirts-$1.72, 2 pr. shoes-$2.44, 4 pr. socks-$.98, 1 jacket-$2.66; pres. 12/1847, pay stopped for: 1 pr. pants-$2.28, 2 flannel shirts-$1.80, 2 pr. drawers-$.71, 1 overcoat-$6.93^{1/2}, 1 blanket-$2.22, 1 pr. shoes-$1.22; pres. 02/1848, pay stopped for: 1 pr. shoes-$1.22; pres. 04/1848; pres. 07/1848, pay stopped for: 1 bayonet-$1.44, 1 bayonet scabbard & frog-$.56, 1 screw driver-$.25, BLW sent to Norfolk, VA; SC #16204, 04/09/1888, from VA; [pension file located, but pension documents missing].
**Haslay, John W.**, Pvt., Co. F; enl. Mex. War service 01/06/1847, Portsmouth, VA, age 39; pres. 06/1847; absent 08/1847 sick; discharged 10/16/1847, Buena Vista, Mex.
**Hatcher, Edmund J.**, Pvt., Co. A; enl. Mex. War service 11/28/1846 Richmond, VA, age 27; pres. 12/1846 - 04/1847; pres. 06/1847; AWOL 08/1847, since the morning of 08/31/1847; pres. 10/1847, pay stopped for clothing: 1 cap-$.95^{1/2}, 2 pr. stockings-$.49, 1 pr. wool overalls-$2.28, 1 pr. shoes-$1.22; pres. 12/1847, pay stopped for clothing: 1 pr. drawers-$.35^{1/2}, 1 blanket-$2.22; pres. 02/1848, pay stopped for: 1 pr. wool overalls-$2.28, 1 pr. shoes-$1.22; BLW sent to Richmond, VA
**Hawkins, John J.**, Pvt., Co. I; 09/30/1827, Prince Edward Co., VA;⁹⁵⁸ enl. Mex. War service 08/09/1847 Fort Monroe, VA, age 18; pres. 02/1848, joined co. 01/26/1848; pres. 04/1848, pay stopped for: 1 blanket; pres. 08/1848, BLW sent to Lunenburg C.H., VA; m. Ella R. Lanier, 09/20/1854, Weldon, NC;⁹⁵⁸ SC #3405, 03/11/1887, filed from 105 Bollingbrook St., Petersburg, Dinwiddie Co., VA; since discharge res. in Petersburg, VA;⁹⁵⁸ David F. Shields and William E. Alley gave affidavits in pension claim;⁹⁵⁸ d. 01/06/1894, Petersburg, VA, bur. Blandford Cemetery, Petersburg, VA;⁹⁵⁹ wid. Ella R., WC #9172, 02/01/1894, ftled from 105 Bollingbrook St., Petersburg, Dinwiddie Co., VA; (ERH d. 11/12/1912, 525 Goodson St., Bristol, VA, the home of her daughter, Mrs. R.E.Hooper;.).⁹⁵⁹
**Hawkins, Nathaniel B.**, Pvt., Co. F; m. Elizabeth B. Andrews,  01/27/1841, Petersburg, VA;⁹⁶⁰ enl. Mex. War service 01/26/1847, Richmond, VA, age 28; pres. 06/1847; pres. 08/1847; pres. 10/1847, pay stopped for: 1 pr. overalls-$2.28, 2 cotton shirts-$.86, 2 pr. shoes-$2.44, 1 forage cap-$.95^{1/2}, 3 pr. socks-$.73^{1/2}; pres. 02/1848, pay stopped for: 1 pr. overalls-$2.28, 1 blanket-$2.22, 1 pr. shoes-$1.22, 1 flannel shirt-$.90, 1 infantry jacket-$2.66; pres. 04/1848; pres. 08/1848, pay stopped for: 1 screw driver-$.25, 2 pr. shoes-$2.32, 1 cotton shirt-$.44, BLW sent to Portsmouth, VA c/o E.T. Blamire.
**Hawkins, William R.**, Pvt., Co. A; b. 06/22/1821 Mathews Co., VA;⁹⁶¹ m. Harriet J. Jarvis 04/24/1842, Mathews Co., VA; enl. Mex. War service 12/08/1846, age 25; pres. 12/1846 - 04/1847; pres. 06/1847; pres. 08/1847; pres. 10/1847, pay stopped for clothing: 1 cap-$.95^{1/2},

165

OFF TO WAR

2 pr. shoes-$2.44, 2 pr. stockings-$.49, 2 flannel shirts-$1.80, 1 wool jacket-$2.66, 1 pr. wool overalls-$2.28, 2 cotton shirts-$.86; pres. 12/1847, pay stopped for clothing: 1 pr. shoes-$1.22, 1 blanket-$2.22; pres. 02/1848, pay stopped for: 1 pr. wool overalls-$2.28, 1 pr. shoes-$1.22; 07/1848, pay stopped for: musket sling-$.16; 07/1848, pay stopped for: 1 bayonet sheath-$.56, 1 cart. Box belt-$.60, 1 musket sling-$.16, 1 pick & brush-$.12; BLW sent to Mathews C.H., VA; c. 1850 res. Mathews Co., VA, age 30, occ. Jeweller, w. Harriet J. (30), dau. Amanda R. (7), son William R. (5), son Reginald (1);[962] Civil War service enl. Co. I, 14th Me. Inf. 06/1862 at New Orleans, La. wded. 08/17/1862 Baton Rouge, La. *lost right eye by the explosion of a percussion cap*, prom. Sgt. Major 09/1863, trans. Co. A 03/1865, discharged 08/17/1865 Savannah, Ga. enl. 04/22/1867 Co. G, 42nd U.S. Inf. at Bangor Me, age 36, b. Kingston, VA, 5'9[1/2]," dark complexion, hazel eyes, dark hair, occ. Clerk, discharged 03/12/1868 Madison Barracks, NY;[961] received Invalid Pension 1885 for loss of eye; SC #10657, 06/10/1887, filed from Soldiers Home, Washington, DC; phys. desc. 5'10[1/2]", dark complexion, dark hair, blue eyes; Pvt. James W. Spratt, Co. F, gave affidavit on behalf of pension claim; d. 10/20/1888 Soldiers Home, Washington D.C.; wid. Harriet J., WC #7068, 05/01/1890, filed from 57 Duke St., Norfolk, VA; (HJH b. 03/06/1819 Mathews Co., VA, d. c. 1903).[963]

**Hawthorn, Joel B.**, Pvt., Co. C; b. c. 1800 son of Peter & Nancy (Blackwell) Hawthorn, Jr. enl. Mex. War service 08/16/1847 Boydton, VA, age 45; pres. 04/1848, joined company 01/27/1848 from Regtl. Depot; c. 1850 res. Mecklenburg Co., VA, age 50, occ. Overseer;[964] c. 1860 res. Boydton, Mecklenburg Co., VA, age 60, occ. Farm Laborer;[965] moved to Louisiana.[966]

**Hayden, Franklin G.**, (Headen) Pvt., Co. I; enl. Mex. War service 01/10/1847 Lynchburg, VA, age 29; pres. 02/1847; pres. 04/1847; pres. 06/1847; pres. 08/1847; pres. 10/1847, pay stopped for: 2 pr. drawers-$.71, 2 flannel shirts-$1.80; Court-martialed 11/08/1847 Buena Vista, Mex., *Charge #1: Sleeping on Post; Specification: In this that the said Private Franklin Haden was found asleep on his post by the Officer of the Day on the night of the 20th of October 1847 thereby neglecting his duty as a sentinel and laying the camp liable to great exposure. This at Camp Buena Vista, Mexico. To which charge and specification the prisoner plead Guilty; The court deliberated and found the prisoner Guilty and sentenced him to forfeit one months pay and to be confined at hard labor with a ball and chain attached to his leg in the Provost Guard for the period of one month.*[967] in confinement 12/1847, pay stopped for: 1 pr. pants-$2.28, 1 blanket-$2.22; pres. 02/1848, pay stopped for: 1 pr. shoes-$1.22; pres. 04/1848; pres. 08/1848, BLW sent to The Meadows, Bedford Co., VA; m. Minerva Ann Hippenstall, 03/22/1841, Bedford, VA;[968] wid. Minerva A., WC #5343, 11/28/1887, from TN; [pension file missing].

**Hays, John**, Pvt., Co. C; enl. Mex. War service 12/18/1846, Fredericksburg, VA, age 27; d. Camargo, Mex. 03/31/1847.

**Haywood, Joseph**, Pvt., Co. C; enl. Mex. War service 12/13/1846, Fredericksburg, VA, age 39; pres. 06/1847; pres. 08/1847, pay stopped for: 1 cap-$.95[1/2], 2 pr. socks-$.49, 2 cotton shirts-$.86, 2 woolen shirts-$1.80, 1 pr. shoes-$1.22; 1 pr. drawers-$.35[1/2], 1 knapsack & straps-$1.10; pres. 10/1847, pay stopped for: 2 pr. socks-$.49, 1 pr. shoes-$1.22; pres. 12/1847, pay stopped for: 1 jacket-$2.66, 1 pr. pants-$2.28, 1 blanket-$2.22; pres. 04/1848, pay stopped for: 2 cotton shirts-$.86, 1 haversack-$.20[3/4], 1 india rubber canteen-$.27; pres. 08/1848, BLW sent to Boydton, Mecklenburg County, VA

**Heafer, Richard W.**, 1st Cpl., Co. K; b. 10/20/1821, Jefferson Co., VA;[969] enl. Mex. War service Jefferson Co., VA 12/13/1846, age 24; pres. 06/1847; pres. 08/1847; pres. 10/1847, pay stopped for: 1 pr. overalls-$2.28, 5 cotton shirts-$2.15, 1pr. overalls-$2.28, 3 pr. drawers-$1.06[1/2], 4 pr. socks-$.98, 2 flannel shirts-$1.80, 1 cap-$.95[1/2]; pres. 10/1847, pay stopped for: 4 cotton shirts-$1.72, 2 pr. drawers-$.71, 1 pr. shoes-$1.22, 1 flannel shirt-$.90, 1 pr. overalls-$2.28, 1 cap-$.95[1/2]; pres. 12/1847, pay stopped for: 1 jacket-$2.66, 2 pr. overalls-$4.56, 1 pr.

VIRGINIA VOLUNTEERS IN MEXICO

boots-$1.22, 1 pr. socks-$.24$^{1/2}$, 1 blanket-$2.22; pres. 04/1848, prom. 1$^{st}$ Cpl. 04/01/1848, pay stopped for: 1 pick & brush-$.12, 1 gun sling-$.18; pres. 07/1848, pay stopped for: 1 cartridge box belt-$.60, 1 screw driver-$.25, 1 wiper-$.20, 1 belt plate-$.10; BLW sent to Charlestown, Jefferson Co., VA; m. Mary Jane Roderick, 01/17/1850, Harper's Ferry, Jefferson Co., VA;[969] c. 1850 res. Harper's Ferry, Jefferson Co., VA, age 29, occ. Cooper, w. Mary J. (24);[970] c. 1880 res. Bolivar, Jefferson Co., WV, age 60, occ. Stone Mason, w. Mary J. (54) Keeping House, son George R. (26) Cooper, son John W. (21) Cooper, son Jesse B. (13), dau. Laura W. (9), grandson Charles W. Powers (8);[971] SC #5108, 02/24/1887, filed from Harper's Ferry, Jefferson Co., WV; phys. desc. age 25, 5'5$^{3/4}$", brown hair, blue eyes, occ. Stone Mason;[969] since discharge res. Harper's Ferry except the years 1856 & 1857 when he lived in Bloomington, McLean Co., IL;[969] lists children Amelia Heafer b. 01/25/1852, George Heafer b. 10/12/1854, John Heafer b. 08/09/1859, Jessia Heafer b. 07/17/1866, Laura Heafer b. 07/01/1870;[969] George W. Chambers gave affidavit in pension claim; d. 07/06/1906.[969]

**Heath, William**, Pvt., Co. D; b. Prince Geo. Co., VA, son of John & Sarah Heath;[972] enl. Mex. War service 01/17/1847, Petersburg, VA, age 35; pres. 02/1847; pres. 04/1847, pay stopped for 1 musket complete & 1 gun sling, *"lost by negligence;"* discharged 05/15/1847 Monterey, Mex. on Surgeon's Certificate of Disability; c. 1850 res. Petersburg, Dinwiddie Co., VA, age 38, occ. Huckster;[973] d. 07/11/1864, *malaria*?, bur. Blandford Cem., Petersburg, VA.[972]

**Heatwole, Gabriel T.**, Co. LIC; b. 08/15/1824, Rockingham Co., VA, son of David & Susannah (Helbert) Heatwole;[974, 975] enl. Mex. War service 09/13/1847 Petersburg, VA, age 23; pres. 04/1848, joined the co. from regtl. depot 01/28/1848, pay stopped for: 1 blanket-$2.22; pres. 07/1848, pay stopped for: 1 cartridge box-$1.10, 1 cartridge box belt plate-$.10; BLW sent to Harrisonburg, VA; SC #11407, 09/03/1887, filed from Philadelphia, Neshoba Co., MS; phys. desc. occ. Watchmaker, 5'4$^{1/2}$"or 5", light hair, gray eyes, 125 lbs.[974]

**Hecht, Frederick**, Pvt., Co. A; enl. Mex. War service 12/07/1846 Richmond, VA, age 29; pres. 12/1846 - 04/1847; sick in quarters 06/1847; pres. 08/1847; pres. 10/1847, prom. 10/12/1847 4$^{th}$ Cpl. by order #116, pay stopped for clothing: 1 cap-$.95$^{1/2}$, 2 pr. stockings-$.49; pres. 12/1847, pay stopped for: 1 pr. shoes-$1.22, 1 pr. drawers-$.35$^{1/2}$; pres. 02/1848; pres. 04/1848; BLW sent to, Richmond, VA

**Heck, David H.**, Pvt., Co. H; b. Boonsboro, MD;[976] enl. Mex. War service 01/06/1847, Berkeley, VA, age 18; pres. 04/1847; pres. 06/1847; pres. 08/1847; pres. 10/1847, pay stopped for: 1 forage cap-$.95$^{1/2}$, 1 pr. pants-$2.28, 2 cotton shirts-$.86, 1 flannel shirt-$.90, 1 pr. shoes-$1.22, 3 pr. socks-$.73$^{1/2}$; pres. 12/1847, pay stopped for: 1 jacket-$2.66, 1 pr. pants-$2.28, 2 flannel shirts-$1.80, 1 pr. drawers-$.35$^{1/2}$, 1 pr. shoes-$1.22, 1 pr. socks-$.24$^{1/2}$,1 blanket-$2.22; pres. 02/1848, pay stopped for: 1 pr. drawers-$.71, 2 pr. socks-$.49; pres. 04/1848; pres. 07/1848, BLW sent to Boonsboro, MD; c. 1850 res. Barbour Co., age 21, occ. Farmer;[977] m. Martha Ellen Sowders 01/05/1850, Harper's Ferry, VA;[976] c. 1880 res. Charles Town, Jefferson Co., WV, age 50, occ. Boot & Shoe Maker, w. Martha E. (48) Keeping House, dau. Sally A. (16), dau. Carrie L. (12), dau. Arlena (9);[978] phys. desc. age 54 [1883], 5'8", dark complexion, gray eyes, black hair, occ. Shoemaker;[976] d. 04/18/1883 Charlestown, WV;[976] wid. Martha E., WC #2039, 02/18/1887, filed from Charlestown, Jefferson Co., WV; since discharge res. Charlestown, WV and Boonsboro, MD;[976] (MEH b. 07/15/1829, d. 11/02/1901).[976]

**Heckel, George A.**; Co. not stated, *Not on Muster Rolls*, SA #19906, 07/18/1888, from OH.

**Heflin, John Marshall**, Pvt., Co. K; b. 11/29/1828, Strasburg, Shennandoah Co., VA, son of William and Elizabeth (Saffell) Heflin;[979] enl. Mex. War service Frederick Co., VA 01/20/1847, age 19; pres. 06/1847; pres. 08/1847; pres. 10/1847, pay stopped for: 2 pr. overalls-$4.56, 4 cotton shirts-$1.72, 3 pr. drawers-$1.06$^{1/2}$, 2 pr. socks-$.49, 2 pr. shoes-$2.44, 1 flannel shirt-$.90, 2 caps-$1.91; pres. 12/1847, pay stopped for: 1 jacket-$2.66, 1 pr. socks-$.24$^{1/2}$, 1 blanket-$2.22; pres. 04/1848, pay stopped for: 1 jacket-$2.66, 1 flannel shirt-$.90, 1 gun sling-$.18; pres. 07/1848, pay stopped for: 1 pick & brush-$.12, 1 wiper-$.20, 1

OFF TO WAR

screw driver-$.25; BLW sent to Winchester, Frederick Co., VA; m. Mary Ellen Bare, 02/05/1855, Staunton, Augusta Co., VA;⁹⁷⁹ Civil War service enl. Pvt., Co. B (2ⁿᵈ), 52ⁿᵈ Va. Inf. 09/24/1862, Bunker Hill, VA; pres. thru 01/1863; detailed in Hosp. Richmond and Staunton 02/1863 – 12/31/1864; paroled Appomattox C.H., VA 04/09/1865;⁶⁸⁶ c. 1870 res. Staunton, Augusta Co., VA, age 39, occ. Gardner, w. Mary E. (34), dau. Mary A. (15);⁹⁸⁰ SC #20058, 01/25/1892, filed from Staunton, Augusta Co., VA; phys. desc. 5'7", fair complexion, light hair, gray eyes, occ. Tailor; since discharge res. in Staunton and Augusta Co. except 2 yrs. in Front Royal, VA;⁹⁷⁹ wid. Mary Ellen, WC #13411, 06/06/1903, filed from 105 Locust Ave., Staunton, Augusta Co., VA; d. 02/24/1903, Augusta Co., VA; bur. Thornrose Cem., Staunton, VA ⁹⁷⁹, ⁹⁸¹ (MBH b. 10/07/1835, Augusta Co., VA, d. 02/18/1914).⁹⁸²

**Helfeistein, Jacob H.**, (Helferstay?) Pvt., Co. H; enl. Mex. War service 11/24/1846, Berkeley, VA, age 25; pres. 04/1847; discharged 05/09/1847 at camp near Monterey, Mex. on Surgeon's Certificate of Disability; 1848 mbr. Berkeley Section No. 8 *Cadets of Temperance*, Martinsburg VA⁹⁸³

**Heller, Josiah**, Pvt., Co. H; b. c. 1805 England;⁹⁸⁴ enl. Mex. War service 12/16/1846, Berkeley, VA, age 42; pres. 04/1847; pres. 06/1847; pres. 08/1847; pres. 10/1847, pay stopped for: 1 forage cap-$.95¹ᐟ², 1 pr. pants-$2.28, 2 cotton shirts-$.86, 1 pr. shoes-$1.22, 2 pr. socks-$.49; pres. 12/1847; pres. 02/1848, pay stopped for: 1 pr. pants-$2.28, 2 pr. drawers-$.71, 1 pr. shoes-$1.22, 1 blankets-$2.22; pres. 04/1848; pres. 07/1848, BLW sent to Little York, Pa.; c. 1880 a Joseph Heller b. England, res. Charlestown, Jefferson Co., WV, age 75, occ. Laborer;⁹⁸⁵ SC #3644, 02/04/1887, filed from Charlestown, Jefferson Co., WV; phys. desc. age 79 [1884], 5'7¹ᐟ²," dark complexion, dark eyes, dark hair, occ. Tanner; *"for many years a resident of the Little Sisters of the Poor"* Richmond, VA;⁹⁸⁴ d. 11/28/1895, National Soldiers Home, Elizabeth City Co., Hampton, VA, bur. Hampton National Cemetery, Plot 7172, Hampton, VA

**Helms, Samuel McCune**, Pvt., LIC; b. 02/06/1829, Long Meadows, Augusta Co., VA;⁹⁸⁶ enl. Mex. War service 12/07/1846 Staunton, VA, age 18; sick 08/1847; absent 10/1847, on detached service as Orderly to Col. Randolph since 10/25/1847, pay stopped for: 1 forage cap-$.95¹ᐟ², 2 pr. overalls-$4.56, 1pr. shoes-$1.22, 3 pr. socks-$.73¹ᐟ², 3 cotton shirts-$1.29; pres. 12/1847, pay stopped for: 2 blanket-$4.44, 1 pr. overalls-$2.28, 2 flannel shirts-$1.80; absent 04/1848, on detached service marker, pay stopped for: pres. 07/1848, pay stopped for: 1 cartridge box plate-$.10, 1 gun sling-$.16, 1 pick & brush-$.12, 1 screw driver-$.07, 1 wiper-$.20; BLW sent to Staunton, VA; c. 1850 res. Augusta Co., VA, age 18, occ. Cabinetmaker;⁹⁸⁷ m. Martha Eleanor Stover, 05/15/1851, Staunton, Augusta Co., VA;⁹⁸⁶ occ. Cabinetmaker;²⁴⁹ c. 1860 res. Staunton, Augusta Co., VA, age 29, occ. Cabinetmaker, w. Martha E. (28), dau Cara V. (7), son Lewis M. (5), dau. Elizabeth P. (3), son Thomas A. (4/12);⁹⁸⁸ Lt. in Southern Guard 1860; Civil War service enl. 04/17/1861 as 2ⁿᵈ Lt., Co. D, 5ᵗʰ Va. Inf.; capt. Battle of Spotsylvania C.H. 05/12/1862; sent to Ft. Delaware; exchanged 03/13/65;¹²⁸ SC #16503, 06/22/1888, filed from Middlebrook, Augusta Co., VA; Lists children Cora V. (Helms) Ervin b. 04/29/1852, Lewis H. Helms b. 10/30/1853, Bettie P. (Helms) Frenzer b. 04/18/1857, Minnie M. Helms b. 05/05/1862, Thomas A. Helms b. 05/01/1860, Alonzo S. Helms b. 09/07/1874; William E. Skeen and George Harlan gave affidavit in pension claim;⁹⁸⁶ d. 02/29/1911, Midway, VA; bur. Mt. Carmel Presbyterian Church, Steele's Tavern, VA;²⁴⁹ (MSH d. 10/02/1900).⁹⁸⁶

**Henderson, Alexander**, Pvt., Co. D; enl. Mex. War service 12/23/1846, Petersburg, VA, age 33; pres. 02/1847; pres. 04/1847; pres. but sick 06/1847; in confinement 08/1847; in confinement 10/1847, fined 1 mos. pay by order (No. 120) of genl. court-martial, pay stopped for: 1 pr. pants-$2.28, 2 flannel shirts-$1.80, 2 cotton shirts-$.86, 1 pr. drawers-$.35¹ᐟ², 2 pr. socks-$.49, 1 pr. shoes-$1.22, 1 overcoat-$6.93¹ᐟ²; in confinement 12/1847, pay stopped for: 1 cap-$.95¹ᐟ², 2 jackets-$5.32, 1 pr. pants-$2.28, 1 pr drawers-$.35¹ᐟ², 2 pr. socks-$.49, 1 pr. shoes-$1.22, 1

## VIRGINIA VOLUNTEERS IN MEXICO

blanket-$2.22, 1 overcoat-$6.93$^{1/2}$; pres. 04/1848, pay stopped for: 1 cap-$.95$^{1/2}$, 1 pr. shoes-$1.22, 1 pr. shoes-$2.00; pres. 08/1847, BLW sent to Norfolk, VA

**Henderson, Burton C.**, 3$^{rd}$ Sgt., Co. I; enl. Mex. War service 12/01/1847 Richmond, VA, age 23; pres. 02/1847; pres. 04/1847, prom. 4$^{th}$ Cpl. 04/10/1847; pres. 06/1847, prom. 4$^{th}$ Sgt. 06/21/1847; pres. 08/1847; pres. 10/1847, prom. 4$^{th}$ Sgt., pay stopped for: 2 pr. drawers-$.71, 1 pr. pants-$2.28, 1 pr. socks-$.24$^{1/2}$, 1 pr. shoes-$1.22, 1 cap- $.95$^{1/2}$, 1 flannel shirt-$.90; pres. 12/1847, pay stopped for: 1 pr. socks-$.24$^{1/2}$, 1 jacket-$2.66, 2 pr. pants-$4.56, 2 blankets-$4.44, 1 flannel shirt-$.90, 1 cotton shirt-$.43, 2 pr. drawers-$.71; pres. 02/1848; pres. 04/1848; pres. 08/1848, prom. 3$^{rd}$ Sgt., BLW sent to Drummond Town, Accomac Co., VA

**Henderson, John F.**, Pvt., Co. E; enl. Mex. War service 11/30/1846 Petersburg, VA, age 24; pres. 04/1847; pres. 06/1847; pres. 08/1847; 10/1847 [illegible]; pres. 02/1848, [illegible]; pres. 04/1848, [illegible]; phys. desc. 5'7", light complexion, blue eyes, fair hair – auburn or light brown, occ. Tailor;[989] m. Sophia A. Cowan 06/13/1855, North Carolina;[989] d. 04/09/1887, Durango, LaPlata Co., CO; wid. Sophia A., WC #4613, 11/16/1887, filed from Durango, LaPlata Co., CO; (SAH b. 07/18/1831, d. 12/20/1905, Durango, CO).[989]

**Henderson, Thomas D.**, Pvt., Co. I; b. 08/26/1820, Montgomery Co., VA, son of Thomas and Rhoda Henderson;[990] enl. Mex. War service 02/01/1847 Richmond, VA, age 32; pres. 02/1847; pres. 04/1847; pres. 06/1847; pres. 08/1847; pres. 10/1847, pay stopped for: 2 pr. drawers-$.71, 1 flannel shirt-$.90, 1 cap- $.95$^{1/2}$, 1 pr. socks-$.24$^{1/2}$, 1 pr. shoes-$1.22, 1 blanket-$2.22; pres. 12/1847, pay stopped for: 1 pr. socks-$.24$^{1/2}$, 1 pr. pants-$2.28, 1 blanket-$2.22, 2 flannel shirts-$1.80; pres. 02/1848; pres. 04/1848; pres. 08/1848, BLW sent to Belle Haven, Accomac Co., VA; m/1 Julia Ann Henderson, 04/06/1850, place unknown;[991] (JAH d. 12/13/1855); m/2 Renee Massey, 10/22/1857, Sand Lick or Trap Hill, Raleigh Co., VA;[990, 991] SC #7225, 02/24/1887, filed from Coal River Marshes, Raleigh Co., WV; phys. desc. black eyes, black hair, dark complexion, occ. Farmer;[990] *"About one month after my enlistment and at Point Comfort, VA, I contracted the Mumps which went down on me causing the loss of one of my testicles for which I claim a pension;"*[990] since discharge res. Montgomery Co., VA several years then Raleigh Co., WV;[990] William B. Tucker gave affidavit in pension claim;[990] d. 06/17/1897, *"cancer of the face;"*[991] wid. Renee, WC #11285, 09/02/1887, filed from Coal River Marshes, Raleigh Co., WV; Lists children: Harvey Green Henderson, b. 01/08/1851, Samuel Thomas Henderson, b. 02/06/1853, d. 12/12/1882, Ann Montgomery Henderson, b. 09/03/1855, d. 05/26/87, *"The above is the children of Thomas Henderson first wife."* Sarah Mariah Henderson, b. 10/18/1858, Mary Etty Henderson, b. 10/09/1860, Celia Bell Henderson, b. 07/25/1863, George Dixon Henderson, b. 05/19/1865, Geneva Celestria Henderson, b. 09/18/1867, Vandora Henderson, b. 11/01/1869, Ida Winchester Henderson, b. 08/26/1872;[991] (RMH b. 10/21/1834, Logan Co., VA, d. 03/01/1900).[991]

**Henderson, Thomas**, Pvt., *Preston's Co.*; enl. Mex. War service 12/06/1846 Montgomery Co., VA, age 27; pres. 04/1847; pres. 06/1847; pres. 08/1847; pres. 10/1847, pay stopped for: 1 pr. shoes-$1.22, 3 pr. socks-$.73$^{1/2}$, 1 flannel shirt-$.90; pres. 12/1847, pay stopped for: 1 jacket-$2.66, 1 pr. drawers-$.35$^{1/2}$, 1 blanket-$2.22; pres. 02/1848; pres. 04/1848; pres. 07/1848; BLW sent to Christiansburg, VA c/o Fleming Gardner; S #3006, 02/24/1887, wid. Renee, W #14140, 09/02/1897, both from WV.

**Henderson, William T.**, 3$^{rd}$ Cpl., *Preston's Co.*; b. 03/16/1825, near Blacksburg, Montgomery Co., VA;[992] enl. Mex. War service 12/06/1846 Montgomery Co., VA, age 21; pres. 04/1847; pres. 06/1847; pres. 08/1847; pres. 10/1847, pay stopped for: 1 pr. shoes-$1.22, 2 pr. socks-$.49; pres. 12/1847, prom. 4$^{th}$ Cpl. 11/30/1847, pay stopped for: 1 jacket-$2.66, 2 pr. overalls-$4.56, 1 pr. shoes-$1.22, 1 cap-$.95$^{1/2}$, 1 pr. drawers-$.35$^{1/2}$, 1 blanket-$2.22; pres. 02/1848; pres. 04/1848, prom. 3$^{rd}$ Cpl.; pres. 07/1848; BLW sent to Christiansburg, VA c/o Fleming Gardner; m. Elizabeth S. Luster, 09/20/1849, Fincastle, Botetourt Co., VA;[992] c. 1850 res. Montgomery Co., VA, age 24, occ. Farmer, w. Elizabeth (19);[993] c. 1860 res. Blacksburg,

OFF TO WAR

Montgomery, VA, age 35, w. Elizabeth (29), son Jonas (10), son James (8), dau. Lilly (6), dau. Mary T. (4), son Giles (6/12);[994] SC #1555, 03/31/1887, filed from Craig, Craig Co., VA; phys. desc. 6', light complexion, grey eyes, dark hair, occ. Farmer;[992] since discharge res. Montgomery Co., VA to 1850, since then in Fincastle, VA;[992] Charles S. Willis and Henry Collins gave affidavit in pension claim;[992] Lists children Jonas Henderson b. 09/28/1850, James L. Henderson b. 04/01/1852, Lillie V. Henderson b. 09/24/1854, Mollie S. Henderson b. 10/14/1855, Giles T. Henderson b. 11/27/1858, d. 01/19/1867, William B. Henderson b. 01/30/1862, Roberta L. Henderson b. 10/20/1864, Emma C. Henderson b. 05/01/1863;[992] d. 10/08/1909.[992]

**Heninger, John K.**, Pvt., Co. B; enl. 12/05/1846, Alexandria, VA, age 32; d. 01/04/1847; Fort Morris.

**Henning, Joseph (R.)**, Pvt., Co. K; enl. Mex. War service Frederick Co., VA 12/29/1846, age 23; sick 06/1847; pres. 08/1847; pres. 10/1847, pay stopped for: 2 pr. drawers-$.71, 1 flannel shirt-$.90, 1 pr. socks-$.24$^{1/2}$, 1 blanket-$2.22, 1 pr. overalls-$2.28; pres. 12/1847, pay stopped for: 1 jacket-$2.66, 1 pr. overalls-$2.28, 1 pr. boots-$1.22, 2 pr. drawers-$.71, 1 cotton shirt-$.43; pres. 04/1848, pay stopped for: 1 jacket-$2.66, 1 blanket-$2.22, 1 cap-$.95$^{1/2}$, 1 gun sling-$.18; pres. 07/1848, pay stopped for: 1 pick & brush-$.12, 1 wiper-$.20, 1 screw driver-$.25; BLW sent to Winchester, Frederick Co., VA; c. 1850 res. Frederick Co., VA, age 26, occ. Farmer, w. Mary M. (18), son Charles E. (1).[995]

**Hensley, John G.**, alias John Steel; Co. LIC; SA #24207, 01/21/1893, from IL.

**Herbert, Upton Heath**, 2$^{nd}$ Lt., Co. L; b. Shutter's Hill, Fairfax Co., VA 04 or 06/1820; enl. Mex. War service 03/01/1847 Fairfax C.H., VA, age 26; pres. 06/1847; pres. 08/1847; pres. 10/1847, pay stopped for: 1 W. Jacket-$2.66; pres. 12/1847, prom. 2$^{nd}$ Lt. from 1st Sgt. 11/04/1847; pres. 12/1847; Court-martialed 02/09/1848 Buena Vista, Mex. *Charge #1: Neglect of Duty; Specification: In this that he, 2$^{nd}$ Lt. Upton Herbert, Va. Regt. of Vols., did, when certain prisoners were ordered by Col. Paine, Military Governor and Commandant of Saltillo, to stand upon the heads of barrels as punishment for misdemeanors, neglect to have said punishment executed, He being Officer of the Guard. All this at Saltillo, Mexico, on or about the 8$^{th}$ of January 1848. Charge #2: Disobedience of Orders; Specification: In this that he, 2$^{nd}$ Lt. Upton Herbert, Va. Regt. of Vols., did when ordered to cause certain prisoners to stand upon the heads of barrels for a certain period of time as punishment inflicted on them for certain misdemeanors by Col. Paine, Military Governor and Commandant of Saltillo, disobey said order by allowing said prisoners, before the period of their sentence had expired, to sit down on the heads of barrels in his own presence and under his own observation. All this in Saltillo, Mexico, on or about the 8$^{th}$ of January 1848. To which charges and specification the accused pleaded Not Guilty. Lt. J.B. Whitaker, Adjutant, N.C. Regt. Vols, a witness for the prosecution being duly sworn, says: On the morning that Lt. Herbert, the accused, was last Officer of the Guard in Saltillo. I was crossing the main plaza which is in the front of the Guard House. I saw two or three prisoners who had been ordered to stand on the heads of barrels, sitting or squatting down on the barrels. I mentioned it to Colonel Paine, Governor and Commandant of Saltillo and by time was directed to order the Officer of the Day to arrest Lt. Herbert. I delivered the order to the Officer of the Day. Question by the Judge Advocate: State about what day of the month this was? Answer: I do not now remember the day of the month. It was perhaps four weeks ago. Question by the Judge Advocate: Are you or not the Adjutant of Col. Paine and was or was not this order conveyed by you to the Officer of the Day? Answer: I am the Adjutant of Colonel Paine, but the order for the punishment of these men was given by Colonel Paine himself to the Officer of the Day. Question by the Judge Advocate: Do you know whether the period of the sentences of these men had expired or not at the time you saw them sitting or squatting upon the barrels? And state also what time of day it was you saw them. Answer: It was between 9 and 10 o'clock A.M. I do not know whether their sentences had expired or not. Question by the Judge*

# VIRGINIA VOLUNTEERS IN MEXICO

*Advocate: At the time you saw these men sitting as you have described was or was not the Officer of the Guard present? Answer: He was. The accused was sitting in a chair in front of the Guard House near them. Question by the Accused: Did you stop anytime to know how long the prisoners remained in this sitting or squatting position? Answer: I did not stop, but continued on to the North Carolina Hospital. I was out of sight of the Guard House perhaps ten minutes and when I returned they were still sitting or squatting upon the barrels. Question by the Accused: Did you hear the order given by Colonel Paine to the Officer of the Day relative to the men? Answer: Yes. I heard the Colonel read the order to the Officer of the Day and in the presence of the prisoners themselves. Question by the Accused: Could you identify the men on the barrels as the men ordered to be punished by Colonel Paine. Answer: No. Question by the Accused: Do you know of your own knowledge whether the order of Col. Paine to the Officer of the Day was ever read or shown to the Officer of the Guard? Answer: No. I do not. Question by the Accused: Do you know whether or not the Officer of the Guard saw these prisoners whilst in the position you have described, and if he did, did he or did he not order them to stand up? Answer: He certainly saw them. Tho' I was not near enough to have heard any order he might have given. Question by the Accused: Can you say positively whether the men on the barrels were sitting or squatting? Answer: I can not. Question by the Accused: Was there a sentinel over the prisoners or not? Answer: I do not know. There was a sentinel in post of the Guard House door and the prisoners were immediately in front of the Guard House door. Question by the Court: What was the relative positions of the accused and the prisoners at the time you saw them sitting or squatting upon the barrels? Answer: The accused was sitting in a chair in front of the Guard House door with his face towards the prisoners. Question by the Court: Were these prisoners citizens or soldiers? Answer: One of them I know was a soldier the others I cannot say positively tho' they had on soldiers clothing. Question by the Court: Do you know whether the prisoners were punished for drunkeness or not? Answer: I do not know for what offence they were punished. Question by the Court: Do you know whether they were punished by command of Col. Paine or by sentence of a court-martial? Answer: By Col. Paine. Question by the Court: To what Regt. or Company did the soldiers whom you recognized belong? Answer: The soldiers belonged to one of the batteries in Saltillo. Major Webster's I think. The uniform of the others was light blue and gray perhaps. Question by the Court: Do you know whether the prisoners remained squatting during the interim of time from your first passing through the plaza and the time you saw them again? Answer: I do not. Question by the Court: Were any of the prisoners standing up on the barrels? Answer: One of them. The man belonging to the battery both times that I saw them. Question by the Court: How many prisoners were sentenced by the Governor to stand on barrels at that time? Answer: Three or four. I do not know positively which. Question by the Judge Advocate: Are or are not these orders of the Governor recorded in his office? Answer: They are not. Surgeon G.D. Cobb, U.S.A., a witness for the prosecution being duly sworn, says: One morning some three or four weeks ago I had been to the North Carolina Regimental Hospital and in passing by the Guard House on my return I saw one man standing on a barrel in front of the Guard House and two or three men sitting down on barrels. I saw the accused Lt. Herbert sitting in a chair near the door of the Guard House reading. Question by the Judge Advocate: At the time you saw these men were they sitting down fairly on the barrels or merely squatting? Answer: There were two men sitting down and one standing up. The reason I noticed them was because they were out beyond the pavement. Question by the Court: Was it or was it not a common practice for Col. Paine to order men to be put upon the heads of barrels? Answer: I have seen men frequently on barrels in front of the Guard House by order of Col. Paine. Question by the Accused: Do you know of your own knowledge whether Lt. Herbert was Officer of the Guard on the morning you allude to? Answer: I do not. Question by the Judge Advocate: He or had not Lt. Herbert his sword and sash on at the time you have stated you saw him sitting in front of the Guard House? Answer: I do not know whether he* had or not. *Question by the Judge Advocate: Do you or not know whether these men who you saw on the barrels in front of the Guard House were put there by order of Col. Paine? Answer: I do not?* The court adjourned until 10 o'clock A.M. tomorrow. Capt. P.M. Henry , N.C. Regt., a witness for the prosecution being duly sworn, was interrogated as follows: *Question by the Judge Advocate: Were you Officer of the Day in Saltillo, Mexico, on or about the $8^{th}$ of January last? If so state what orders you received from the Commandant and Governor of Saltillo in relation to the punishment of certain prisoners? Answer: I was Officer of the Day on the $8^{th}$ of January last in Saltillo, and received a written order from Col. Paine on that morning which I delivered the to Lt. Herbert, who was the Officer of the Guard, or to the Sergt. of the Guard. I do not remember which now. It ordered Pvts. Richards and Shells*[Sheckles?]*, I think to stand upon the head of a barrel for one or two hours, I am not positive which, for the offences of drunkeness and fighting. There was also another man whose name I do not know belonging to the Artillery who was ordered to undergo the same punishment. I do not remember the particular offence for which he was punished. I was ordered by Col. Paine to proceed to the Guard House some short time after they had been placed upon the barrels and arrest Lt. Herbert, the Officer of the Guard for allowing tow of three prisoners to sit down on the head of the barrels in his presence. I went to the Guard House but found in my arrival the prisoners all standing upon the heads of the barrels. I executed the order of Colonel Paine and arrested Lt. Herbert. Question by the Judge Advocate: State about what time of day it was when you made this visit to the Guard House and arrested Lt. Herbert? Answer: It was between 9 and 10 o'clock A.M. About one quarter of 10 o'clock I might say. Question by the Judge Advocate: At the time of this visit to the Guard House had the sentences of these men expired or not? Answer: They had not. Question by the Judge Advocate: Did you or did you not at the time you gave the order of Col. Paine to the Officer of the Guard or the Sergt. repeat to him, verbally, the substance of the order? Answer: I think I did tho' I am not positive. I left the order with him. My memory is indistinct on this point. Question by the Accused: Can you state positively whether Lt. Herbert ever saw or received the written order of Col. Paine in relation to the punishment of the prisoners? Answer: I can not. Question by the Accused: Were the prisoners soldiers and were they punished by order of Col. Paine or by the sentence of a court-martial? Answer: They were soldiers and were punished by order of Colonel Paine. Question by the Accused: At what time was the Guard mounted on the morning you allude to? Answer: 9 o'clock. Question by the Accused: At what time were the prisoners placed upon the heads of the barrels? Answer: some few minutes after, half an hour more probably. Question by the Accused: At what time did you visit the Guard for the purpose of arresting Lt. Herbert? Answer: Nearly ten o'clock a quarter of ten perhaps as near as I can recollect. Question by the Accused: What is the distance from the Guard House to the Governors quarters? Answer: Two or three hundred yards. Say two (2) hundred perhaps. Question by the Accused: Did the Governor send for you in relation to this business? Answer: No. having heard of it immediately after the prisoner had been sent down I reported to the Governor at once. Question by the Accused: Did you or not at the time of your first visit to the Guard give Lt. Herbert permission to be absent from the Guard? Answer: I think I did. Question by the Accused: Do you know of your own knowledge whether or not the prisoners stood upon the barrels all the time mentioned in the order. Answer: I do not. Question by the Judge Advocate: At the time you gave the accused permission to be absent from the Guard House, did you specify any length of time he might remain absent? Answer: Yes. A short time. He said he wished to make some purchases for a dinner to be given in town by the Officers of the Regt. that day which he had been specifically requested to make Question by the Court: Was it upon your second visit to the Guard House that you carried the order relative to the punishment of the men or was it not? Answer: Yes It was the second. Question by the Court: Was or was not a specified time in the order when the punishment should commence and end? Answer: No there was not. Question by the Court: Are you*

VIRGINIA VOLUNTEERS IN MEXICO

*positive Lt. Herbert was at the Guard House at the time you delivered this order or not? Answer: I am not positive whether he was there or not there. Question by the Court: To what Corps did these men belong? Answer: The two men I have alluded to by name belonged to Capt. Thrift's Co., Va. Regt. the regular soldier to one of the Arty companies in town. Question by the Court: Do you know whether the men were drunk or sober at the time they were punished that morning? Answer: They appeared to be perfectly sober. Question by the Court: Was the order signed by Col. Paine or not, if so in what capacity? Answer: It was signed by him in his own hand as military and Civil Governor and Commandant of Saltillo.* Sergt. Daniel Poisel, Co. H., Va. Regt. of Vols. testified as a witness for the prosecution corroborating the testimony previously given. *After deliberation the Court found the accused Not Guilty of all charges and specifications;*[996] in confinement 02/1848; pres. 04/1848; pres. 07/1848; c. 1850 res. Alexandria, VA, age 25, occ. None Listed;[997] was appointed Superintendent of Mount Vernon, President George Washington's former home, by the Ladies Mount Vernon Association in 1859; c. 1860 res. S. of the Orange & Alex. R.R., Fairfax Co., VA, age 39, occ. "Mine Host, Mt. Vernon," Farmer;[998] m. Sarah Cornelia Tracy, of Troy, NY, c. 1878, Philadelphia, Pa., (SCH d. 12/1896); SC #20531, 01/28/1902, from VA, Arthur Herbert listed as guardian; d. 04/17/1906; bur. Ivy Hill Cem., Alexandria, VA

**Herrington, Dennis**, Pvt., Co. K; b. New York; enl. Mex. War service Jefferson Co., VA 12/17/1846, age 22; pres. 06/1847; pres. 08/1847, to forfeit 1 mos. pay by order of garrison court-martial; pres. 10/1847, pay stopped for: 2 pr. drawers-$.71, 1 pr. overalls-$2.28, 1 pr. shoes-$1.22; pres. 12/1847, pay stopped for: 1 jacket-$2.66, 1 pr. socks-$.24$^{1/2}$, 1 blanket-$2.22; pres. 04/1848, pay stopped for: 1 pr. pants-$2.28, 1 gun sling-$.18; pres. 07/1848; BLW sent to Shepherdstown, Jefferson Co., VA; m. Margaret Ann _____, date/place unknown;[999] c. 1850 Shepherdstown, Jefferson Co., VA, age 25, occ. Bricklayer, w. Ann (20), son John S. (2/12);[1000] c. 1860 res. Martinsburg, VA, age 36, occ. Tailor, w. Margaret (31), son John (10), dau. Marg. (8), son Daniel (6), dau. Rose (5), dau. Ellen (3);[1001] (MAH d. 05/21/1868, Martinsburg, Berkeley Co., WV); m/2 Susan E. McDade, 03/03/1874, Martinsburg, Berkeley, WV;[999] c. 1880, res. Martinsburg, Berkeley Co., WV, age 53, occ. Boiler Maker, w. Susan (39) keeping house, son John D. (11), son James O. (10), dau. Burtha (3);[1002] SC #8181, 03/07/1887, filed from Martinsburg, Berkeley Co., WV; d. 05/11/1890, *"heart failure,"* Martinsburg, Berkeley Co., WV;[1003] bur. Green Hill Cem., Berkeley Co., WV;[45] wid. Susan E.,WC #9818, 12/13/1892, filed from Martinsburg, Berkeley Co., WV; lists children Bertha D. Herrington, b. 1877 and Ada V. Herrington, b. 1883, 2 dead children;[1003] (SHE b. 07/22/1840, m/1 David McDade abt. 1868, Frederick Co., MD, he died 12/28/1872, Martinsburg, Berkeley Co., WV; d. 09/22/1914).[1003]

**Hesser, Theodore**, 2$^{nd}$ Cpl., Co. C; enl. Mex. War service 12/29/1846, Bowling Green, VA, age 19; pres. 06/1847, prom. 4$^{th}$ Cpl. 06/16/1847; pres. 08/1847, prom. 3$^{rd}$ Cpl. 08/25/1847, pay stopped for: 1 pr. drawers-$.35$^{1/2}$, 1 cap-$.95$^{1/2}$, 2 pr. socks-$.49, 2 cotton shirts-$.86, 2 woolen shirts-$1.80, 1 pr. shoes-$1.22; pres. 10/1847, pay stopped for: 2 pr. socks-$.49, 1 jacket-$2.66, 1 pr. pants-$2.28, 1 pr. shoes-$1.22, 1 brush & picker-$.12; pres. 12/1847, prom. 2$^{nd}$ Cpl. 12/16/1847, pay stopped for: 2 cotton shirts-$.86, 1 pr. shoes-$1.22, 1 blanket-$2.22; pres. 04/1848, pay stopped for: 1 pr. pants-$2.28, 1 haversack-$.20$^{3/4}$, 1 india rubber canteen-$.27, 1 pr. shoes-$1.50; pres. 08/1848, BLW sent to Philadelphia, Pa.; m. Mary Ann Bird, 10/21/1852, Philadelphia, Pa.;[1004] [Civil War service a Theodore Hesser served as a Capt., Co. K, 18$^{th}$ Pa. Inf. & Lt. Col., 72$^{nd}$ Pa. Inf.,[554] was KIA 11/26/1863 at Robertson's Cross Roads, VA *(Mine Run Campaign)*][1005]

**Higdon, John H.**, 1$^{st}$ Lt., Co. B; enl. 11/20/1846, Alexandria, VA, age 25; pres. 06/1847; sick 08/1847; pres. 10/1847, pay stopped for: 2 pr. socks-$.49, 1 pr. shoes-$1.22, 1 pr. overalls-$2.28, 1 blanket-$2.22; pres. 12/1847, pay stopped for: 2 pr. socks-$.49, 1 pr. overalls-$2.28, 1 dragoon overcoat-$8.75$^{1/2}$; sick 02/1848, pay stopped for: 1 pr. shoes-$1.22; pres. 04/1848, prom. 1$^{st}$ Lt. by election; pres. 08/1848; m. Mary Ann Pickering, 12/13/1848, Alexandria,

173

OFF TO WAR

VA;[1006] d. 12/31/1859, Alexandria Co., VA, *"Bilious diarrhea,"* age 38 years, occ. Tailor, w. Mary Ann Higdon.[1007]

**Hill, John**, enl. Mex. War service 03/16/1847 Alexandria, VA, age 21.

**Hillard, Joseph**, Pvt., Co. C; enl. Mex. War service 12/18/1846, Fredericksburg, VA, age 21; deserted 01/02/1847 Richmond, VA

**Hillard, William**, Pvt., Co. K; enl. Mex. War service Jefferson Co., VA 12/29/1846, Age 28; pres. 06/1847; pres. 08/1847, to forfeit 1 mos. pay by order of garrison court-martial; pres. 10/1847, pay stopped for: 4 pr. socks-$.98, 2 pr. drawers-$.71, 4 flannel shirts-$3.60; pres. 12/1847, pay stopped for: 1 blanket-$2.22; pres. 04/1848, has received pay to the 29th of Feb. '48 in Saltillo, Mex.; pres. 07/1848; BLW sent to Leesburgh, Loudoun Co., VA

**Hilliard, Richard**, Pvt., Co. A; enl. Mex. War service 12/07/1846 Richmond, VA, age 34; pres. 12/1846 - 04/1847; pres. 06/1847; pres. 08/1847; pres. 10/1847, pay stopped for clothing: 1 pr. wool overalls-$2.28, 4 pr. stockings-$.98, 2 flannel shirts-$1.80, 1 pr. drawers-$.71, 1 pr. shoes-$1.22; pres. 12/1847, pay stopped for clothing: 1 blanket-$2.22, 1 pr. socks-$.24$^{1/2}$, 1 flannel shirt-$.90, 1 cap 95$^{1/2}$, 1 pr. shoes-$1.22; pres. 02/1848; pres. 04/1848; 07/1848, pay stopped for: 1 musket sling-$.16; BLW sent to Richmond, VA

**Hinchman, John E.**, Pvt., Co. F; enl. Mex. War service 12/23/1846, Portsmouth, VA, age 41; deserted 05/26/1847 from China, Mex.

**Hines, William S.**, Pvt., *Recruit Co.*, b. c. 1824 son of Robert & Sarah C. Hines;[1008] enl. Mex. War service 11/05/1847 Staunton, VA, age 23; pres. 02/1848; pres. 04/1848; pres. 06/1848; BLW sent to Fincastle, Botetourt Co., VA; c. 1850 res. Botetourt Co., VA, age 26, occ. Farmer;[1008] Civil War service Pvt., Co. C, 2$^{nd}$ Va. Cav., enl. 05/20/1861 at Lynchburg, VA, age 36, occ. Farmer, pres. 06/30/1861 – 10/1861, absent 02/17/1862 sick at home, AWOL 02/28/1862, discharged for being overage date not stated, reenlisted 05/25/1864 at Dublin, VA, supposed to have deserted to the enemy 05/1864;[1009] SC 11557, 04/09/1887, wid. Catherine, WC #13835, 02/16/1904, both from VA

**Hobgood, Edward**, Pvt., Co. D; enl. Mex. War service 01/05/1847, Petersburg, VA, age 26; absent 02/1847 left as Attendant at Hosp. Fort Monroe, VA; absent 04/1847 left as Attendant at Hosp. Fort Monroe, VA; absent 06/1847 left as Attendant at Hosp Fort Monroe, VA *"and not since heard from;"* discharged 03/31/1847 Old Point, VA on Surgeon's Certificate of Disability.

**Hobgood, John R.**, Pvt., Co. D; enl. Mex. War service 01/28/1847, Petersburg, VA, age 21; absent 02/1847 left sick at Hosp. Fort Monroe, VA; absent 02/1847 left sick at Hosp. Fort Monroe, VA; absent 06/1847 left sick at Hosp Fort Monroe, VA *"and not since heard from;"* discharged 03/31/1847 at Old Point, VA on Surgeon's Certificate of Disability; [Civil War service a John R. Hobgood served as a Pvt., Co. A, 24$^{th}$ NC Inf.][202]

**Hobson, Joseph M.**, 3$^{rd}$ Cpl., Co. I; b. Powhattan Co., VA; enl. Mex. War service 01/25/1847 Richmond, VA, age 22; pres. 02/1847, prom. 4$^{th}$ Cpl. 02/27/1847; pres. 04/1847, prom. 4$^{th}$ Sgt. 04/10/1847; pres. 06/1847, reduced to ranks from 4$^{th}$ Sgt. 06/16/1847; pres. 08/1847; pres. 10/1847, pay stopped for: 3 pr. drawers-$1.06$^{1/2}$, 2 pr. shoes-$2.44, 1 pr. pants-$2.28, 1 overcoat-$6.93$^{1/2}$, 2 pr. socks-$.49, 1 cap- $.95$^{1/2}$; pres. 12/1847, pay stopped for: 2 pr. socks-$.49, 3 pr. drawers-$1.06$^{1/2}$, 1 jacket-$2.66, 1 blanket-$2.22, 1 pr. shoes-$1.22, 4 flannel shirts-$3.60; pres. 02/1848, pay stopped for: 1 flannel shirt-$.90, 1 pr. overalls-$2.28, 1 blanket-$2.22; pres. 04/1848, prom. 3$^{rd}$ Cpl.; pres. 08/1848, pay stopped for 1 gun sling-$.16, 1 waist belt-$.21, 1 waist belt plate-$.10, 1 cartridge box-$1.10, 1 cartridge box plate-$.10, BLW sent to Richmond, VA; attended Hampden-Sydney College; Civil War service enl. Pvt., Co. E, 4$^{th}$ Va. Cav., 04/25/1861; absent sick 10/1861 w/typhoid fever; elected 2$^{nd}$ Lt. 04/25/1862; prom. 1$^{st}$ Lt. 04/28/1862, apptd. Capt. 10/14/1864;[1010] m. Katrina Vanpelt Schlaffenberger, of Rockingham Co., VA 12/1864;[1011] paroled 05/11/1865 Manchester, VA (opposite Richmond, VA); d. 04/19/1919, Powhattan, VA[1010]

VIRGINIA VOLUNTEERS IN MEXICO

Hodgden, Ivory P., Pvt., Co. I; enl. Mex. War service 02/22/1847 Richmond, VA, age 40; pres. 02/1847; pres. 04/1847, prom. 3$^{rd}$ Sgt.; pres. 06/1847, prom 1$^{st}$ Sgt. 06/21/1847; pres. 08/1847; pres. 10/1847, pay stopped for: 2 pr. drawers-$.71, 2 flannel shirts-$1.80, 1 pr. socks-$.24$^{1/2}$, 1 pr. pants-$2.28, 1 pr. shoes-$1.22, 1 blanket-$2.22; pres. 12/1847, pay stopped for: 1 pr. socks-$.24$^{1/2}$, 1 cap-$.95$^{1/2}$, 1 jacket-$2.66, 1 blanket-$2.22, 1 pr. pants-$2.28, 1 pr. shoes-$1.22, 2 pr. drawers-$.71, 2 cotton shirts-$.86; pres. 02/1848, Court-martialed 11/16/1847 Buena Vista, Mex. *Charge #1 Neglect of Duty; Specification: "In that the said Sergt. I.P. Hodgden, Co. I, Va. Regt. Vols., having permission to visit Saltillo on the 11$^{th}$ of November and return by evening parade did remain in Saltillo until the morning of the 12$^{th}$, knowing that his permission had expired on the evening before, thereby neglecting his duty as First Sergt. of his company. This on or about the 11$^{th}$ day of Nov. 1847. Charge #2: Drunkenness; Specification: In this that he the said Sergt. I.P. Hodgden having permission to visit Saltillo on the 11$^{th}$ day of Nov. did while in Saltillo become intoxicated and neglect his duty towards men who were under his charge and allow them to get drunk also; and did remain away from the camp of his regiment all the night of the 11$^{th}$ of Nov. '47. This to the prejudice of good order and military discipline on or about the 11$^{th}$ of November 1847. Pleaded Guilty to Charge #1 and Not Guilty to Charge #2. Lt. Otho Harrison, Va. Regt. Vols. A witness for the prosecution being duly sworn says: I was in town on the 11$^{th}$ of Nov. and in passing down the main street I saw the accused, Sergt. Hodgden in a groggery and I thought he was drinking and in a state of intoxication. Question by the Judge Advocate: What time of day was this? Answer: I think about two or three o'clock P.M. Lt. L.M. Shumaker a witness for the prosecution being duly sworn says: The prisoner came to me on the 11$^{th}$ of November with a permit for Sergt. Taylor, himself and Pvt. Barnett to go to town. I told him, knowing Barnett as I do to be an intemperate man that I was afraid to allow him to go for fear he should get into some difficulty. The Sergt. then remarked that his being with him he would keep him out of difficulty and that he would be able to manage him. Upon that I gave permission to be absent until dress parade on that evening. The prisoner did not return until the next morning. This man Barnett who was with him did not come back until the next morning either. Question by the Court: Did you consider this man Barnett to be particularly under the charge of the Sergt? Answer: I considered both Barnett and the other Sergt. under his charge. Barnett particularly in knowing him as I did to be an intemperate man. I only gave him permission to go with the Sergt. thinking that he would be able to restrain him. Question by the Court: Was Barnett drunk or sober when you saw him the next day? Answer: In reflection now, I do not think I saw him until the morning of the day after he came to camp with the Sergt. Sergt. J.P. Taylor a witness for the defense being duly sworn says: Myself and Sergt. Hodgden left Saltillo on the evening of the 11$^{th}$ of Nov. to return to Camp about 3 o'clock in the afternoon. Pvt. Barnett had started on before us. When we got part of the way up the street we saw Barnett come running out of a Mexican house and three Mexicans after him. He ran and got away from the Mexicans and we followed after him and found him in the General Hospital. I left Sergt. Hodgden then with him and I came out to camp and reported this to my company officer. I thought at the time Barnett was very much drunk, more so then he really was. We thought him too much so to bring out to camp that evening. Question by the Prisoner: Do you or not know of Barnett's difficulty was the sole cause of detaining me in town that night? Answer: I think if Barnett had not got into this difficulty we would all have been out at camp in time for parade that evening. Question by the Judge Advocate: Did the prisoner tell you that the reason for his remaining in town was on account of Barnett's difficulty? Answer: No. I did not hear him say anything about staying with him after he got to the hospital. I heard him say in the town of the day he wished Barnett to come out when he came. Question by Judge Advocate: Did he send any word to his company officer by you for the reason of his remaining in town? Answer: No. He did not. Question by the Court: Was the prisoner drunk or sober when you started for camp? Answer: He was neither very much drunk or very sober he had been drinking!*

## OFF TO WAR

*Question by the Court: How long before you started for Camp did Barnett start? Answer: He was just a little ahead of us, he was within sight. Question by the Court: Was the prisoner drunk when you left him at the hospital? Answer: I could not say he was drunk. He had been drinking! Question by the Court: Had he been drunk during the course of the day? Answer: Not more so than he was then. Question by the Court: Did he consider Barnett under his charge? Answer: Yes. He said he was going to take care of him. Question by the Court: Was Barnett drunk during the day in town.? Answer: Yes! He was right tight! Question by the Court: Was this man Barnett the same man for whom the prisoner got permission to go to town on that day? Answer: Yes. He was. Lt. Robert H. Keeling, Va. Regt. Of Vols., a witness for the defense being duly sworn says in answer to the following: Question by the prisoner: What has been my character as a soldier in the company heretofore? Answer: He has always been very obedient and attentive to duty as far as I know. He has borne the character of the Regt. of being a very rigid non-commissioned officer. I was on guard when the prisoner came out to camp with Barnett on the morning after the difficulty in town, and they had to pass the Guard. I saw those men both sober then. To the Charge #1: Guilty; To the Charge #2: Not Guilty. Sentenced to be reprimanded by his company officer;[1012]* reduced ranks from 1st Sgt. 01/26/1848, pay stopped for: 1 blanket-$2.22; pres. 04/1848; pres. 08/1848, BLW sent to Richmond, VA

**Hodges, George**, Pvt., Co. H; b. 08/09/1824, New York, NY;[1013] enl. Mex. War service 01/06/1847, Berkeley, VA, age 22; pres. 04/1847; pres. 06/1847; pres. 08/1847; pres. 10/1847, pay stopped for: 1 forage cap-$.95$^{1/2}$, 1 pr. pants-$2.28, 1 cotton shirt-$.43, 1 flannel shirt-$.90, 1 pr. drawers-$.35$^{1/2}$, 1 pr. shoes-$1.22, 2 pr. socks-$.49; pres. 12/1847, pay stopped for: 1 pr. shoes-$1.22, 1 pr. socks-$.24$^{1/2}$, 1 blanket-$2.22; pres. 02/1848, pay stopped for: 1 jacket-$2.66; pres. 04/1848; pres. 07/1848, BLW sent to Philadelphia, Pa. m. Esther G. McDowell, 11/10/1850, Wilmington, DE; Civil War service enl. Cpl., Co. E, 5th Del. Inf. 10/25/1862, age 38, discharged 08/10/1863;[1013, 554] SC #1195, 02/04/1887, filed from 915 W. 9th St., Wilmington, New Castle Co., DE; phys. desc. age 61 [1885], 5'6", dark complexion, blue eyes, dark hair, occ. Cooper;[1013] since discharge a res. of Wilmington. DE;[1013] d. 07/28/1893, Wilmington, DE, bur. Wilmington and Brandywine Cemetery, Wilmington, DE;[1014] wid. Esther G., WC #8839, 09/08/1893, filed from 915 W. 9th St., Wilmington, New Castle, DE; (b. 10/14/1833, d. 07/13/1913, bur. Wilmington and Brandywine Cemetery, Wilmington, DE).[1014]

**Hoffmaer, Frederick**, Pvt., Co. B; enl. 12/22/1846, Richmond, VA, age 29; deserted 01/02/1847 Richmond, VA

**Hoffman, Carrington**, Pvt., LIC; b. 02/14/1825, Lexington, Rockbridge Co., VA;[1015] enl. Mex. War service 12/07/1846 Staunton, VA, age 21; discharged 04/28/1847 at China, Mex. on Surgeon's Certificate of Disability; m. Margaret Eads, 01/28/1848, Irving, Estel Co., KY;[1015] SC #3802, 04/25/1887, filed from Versailes, Brown Co., IL; *"I am commonly known as Jackson Hoffman. The way I came by the name was General Jackson.[He] was the first President I ever saw and I was a great admirer of him because he came to me and shook hands with me as a small boy. The people gave me the name Jackson and it has followed me all my life. But, my proper name is Carrington Hoffman;"*[1015] d. 12/04/1905.[1015]

**Hogan, John F.**, Pvt., Co. K; enl. Mex. War service Jefferson Co., VA 12/20/1846, age 29; sick 06/1847; pres. 08/1847; pres. 10/1847, pay stopped for: 4 cotton shirts-$1.72, 2 pr. shoes-$2.44, 2 pr. drawers-$.71, 2 pr. socks-$.49, 2 flannel shirts-$1.80, 1 blanket-$2.22; pres. 12/1847, pay stopped for: 1 jacket-$2.66, 1 pr. boots-$1.22, 1 blanket-$2.22; pres. 04/1848, pay stopped for: 1 pick & brush-$.12, 1 gun sling-$.16; pres. 07/1848, pay stopped for: 1 cartridge box plate-$.10; BLW sent to Charlestown, Jefferson Co., VA

**Hogg, William C.**, Pvt., Co. A; enl. Mex. War service 12/01/1846, age 28; pres. until sick 04/1847, in hosp. at Matamoros sent there from Camargo, Mex. 04/02/1847; discharged 06/18/1847 for disease by order Maj. Gen. Taylor; [Civil War service a William Hogg, age

## VIRGINIA VOLUNTEERS IN MEXICO

41, occ. Farmer, enl. as a Pvt., Co. G, 26<sup>th</sup> Va. Inf. 06/02/1861 at Little Plymouth, King & Queen Co., VA, discharged 09/05/1862 at Chaffin's Farm, VA expiration of service and being over 35 years of age;[1016] c. 1870 res. Little Plymouth, King & Queen Co., VA, age 55, occ. Farmer, w. Juliet A. (43), dau. Virginia M. (18), son James W. (16), dau. Antoinette (10), dau. Sarah A. (7), son John R. (5), son William T. (3).][1017]

**Hohn, John**, Pvt., Co. A; enl. Mex. War service 12/13/1846 Richmond, VA, age 30; pres. 12/1846 - 04/1847; pres. 06/1847; pres. 08/1847, fined $7.00 by order (#72) of regtl. court-martial 08/1847; pres. 10/1847, fined $7.00 by order (#103) of regtl. court-martial, pay stopped for clothing: 1 pr. wool overalls-$2.28, 1 cap-$.95$^{1/2}$, 2 pr. stockings-$.49, 1 pr. shoes-$1.22; Court-Martialed 12/02/1847 Charge #1 *Drunkeness on Duty;* Specification: *"in that Pvt. John Hohn, Co. A, Va. Regt. Vols., being a member of the Provost Guard was found drunk upon his guard...at Camp Buena Vista November 28<sup>th</sup>, 1847;"* Pleading *Guilty;* Sentenced *"to forfeit one (1) months pay and to be kept on extra police duty in his company for the period of one month;"*[1018] absent 12/1847 in confinement, pay stopped for clothing: 1 cotton shirt-$.43; pres. 02/1848, pay stopped for: 1 pr. shoes-$1.22, fined $7.00 by order (#27) of genl. court-martial; pres. 04/1848; 07/1848, pay stopped for: [illegible]; BLW sent to Richmond, VA

**Holland, Thomas A.**, Pvt., Co. I; enl. Mex. War service 02/19/1847 Norfolk, VA, age 18; pres. 02/1847; absent 04/1847, left sick at Matamoros, Mex. 04/01/1847; discharged 05/15/1847 for disability at camp near Monterey, Mex.

**Holloway, Cornelius**, Pvt., Co. D; enl. Mex. War service 01/12/1847, Petersburg, VA, age 20; pres. 02/1847; d. 03/22/1847 at Hosp. Port Isabel, Tex.

**Hood, Benjamin**, Pvt., Co. C; enl. Mex. War service 12/30/1846, Bowling Green, VA, age 41; pres. 06/1847; pres. 08/1847, pay stopped for: 1 cap-$.95$^{1/2}$, 2 pr. socks-$.49, 2 cotton shirts-$.86, 2 woolen shirts-$1.80, 1 pr. drawers-$.35$^{1/2}$; pres. 10/1847, pay stopped for: 1 pr. drawers-$.35$^{1/2}$, 1 jacket-$2.66, 1 pr. pants-$2.28, 2 woolen shirt-$1.80; pres. 12/1847, pay stopped for: 2 pr. socks-$.49, 2 pr. shoes-$2.44, 1 blanket-$2.22; pres. 04/1848, pay stopped for: 1 haversack-$.20$^{3/4}$, 1 india rubber canteen-$.27; pres. 08/1848, BLW sent to Philadelphia, Pa.

**Hood, John W.**, Pvt., Co. H; enl. Mex. War service 12/01/1846, Berkeley, VA, age 22; pres. 04/1847; pres. 06/1847; pres. 08/1847; pres. 10/1847, pay stopped for: 1 forage cap-$.95$^{1/2}$, 3 cotton shirts-$1.29, 2 flannel shirts-$1.80, 2 pr. socks-$.49, 1 jacket-$2.66; pres. 12/1847, pay stopped for: 1 jacket-$2.66, 1 pr. pants-$2.28, 1 pr. shoes-$1.22, 3 pr. socks-$.73$^{1/2}$, 2 pr. drawers-$.71; pres. 02/1848; pres. 04/1848; pres. 07/1848, BLW sent to Little York, Pa.; m. Hannah Schibner, 04/23/1848, Mechanicsburg, Pa.;[1019] Civil War service enl. Pvt., Co. 31<sup>st</sup>, 2<sup>nd</sup> Btln. Veteran Reserve Corps 05/08/1861, discharged 07/29/1864 at Ft. Monroe, VA;[1019] d. 07/17/1870, near Shiremanstown, Pa.;[1019] wid. Hannah, WC #6067, 12/13/1888, from PA; ( HSH b. 10/21/1828, d. 02/29/1908).[1019]

**Hooser, Francis W.M.**, Pvt., Co. H; enl. Mex. War service 01/28/1847, Richmond, VA, age 19; pres. 04/1847, transportation & subsistence due from residence to place of rendezvous, 300 miles; pres. 06/1847; pres. 08/1847; pres. 10/1847, pay stopped for: 1 forage cap-$.95$^{1/2}$, 1 pr. pants-$2.28, 4 cotton shirts-$1.72, 1 flannel shirt-$.90, 1 pr. shoes-$1.22, 4 pr. socks-$.98, 1 greatcoat-$6.93$^{1/2}$, 1 jacket-$2.66; pres. 12/1847, pay stopped for: 1 pr. shoes-$1.22, 1 pr. socks-$.24$^{1/2}$; pres. 02/1848, pay stopped for: 1 pr. shoes-$1.22; pres. 04/1848; pres. 07/1848, pay stopped for: 1 gun sling-$.16, 1 waist jacket-$2.37$^{1/2}$, BLW sent to Marion C.H., Smyth Co., VA; m. Saphronia A.H. Brumfield 01/11/1849, Symth Co., VA[1020]

**Hoover, William**, Pvt., Co. H; enl. Mex. War service 01/06/1847, Berkeley, VA, age 33; pres. 04/1847; pres. 06/1847; pres. 08/1847; pres. 10/1847, pay stopped for: 1 pr. pants-$2.28, 1 cotton shirt-$.43, 2 pr. drawers-$.71, 1 pr. shoes-$1.22, 2 pr. socks-$.49; in confinement 12/1847, pay stopped for: 1 jacket-$2.66, 2 pr. shoes-$2.44, 1 blanket-$2.22; pres. 02/1848, 1 drum rim; pres. 04/1848.

OFF TO WAR

**Horne, Nicholas R.**, Pvt., Co. I; enl. Mex. War service 01/01/1847 Richmond, VA, age 21; pres. 02/1847; pres. 04/1847; pres. 06/1847; absent 08/1847 sick; discharged 10/17/1847 on Surgeon's Certificate of Disability, pay stopped for: 2 pr. drawers-$.71.

**Hoskins, Joseph**, Pvt., Co. G; b. c. 1828 son of Sarah Hoskins;[1021] enl. Mex. War service 11/28/1846 Richmond, VA, age 18; pres. 06/1847; pres. 08/1847; pres. 10/1847, pay stopped for: 1 pr. overalls-$2.28, 2 flannel shirts-$1.80, 1 pr. drawers-$.35$^{1/2}$, 3 pr. shoes-$3.66, 4 pr. socks-$.98, 1 forage cap-$.95$^{1/2}$; pres. 12/1847, pay stopped for: 1 pr. shoes-$1.22, 2 cotton shirts-$.86, 2 pr. drawers-$.71, 1 blanket-$2.22, 1 pr. pants-$2.28, 1 cap-$.95$^{1/2}$, 1 jacket-$2.66; pres. 02/1848, pay stopped for: 1 brush & pick-$.12, 1 pr. shoes-$1.22; pres. 04/1848; pres. 08/1848; BLW sent to Hanover Co. C.H., VA; c. 1850 res. Hanover Co., VA, age 22, occ. Laborer;[1021] Civil War service enl. Pvt., Co. A, Ashland Arty., 11/1861, pd a $50 bounty, pres., wded. slightly 12/13/1862 at Fredericksburg, VA, absent 03/1864 – 07/1864 on detached service as a teamster and driver in QM Dept., under arrest 09/30/1864; surrendered at Appomattox C.H., VA 04/10/1865, from Hanover Co., VA, signed name with an X.[1022]

**Hoskins, William A.**, Pvt., Co. G; enl. Mex. War service 11/28/1846 Richmond, VA, age 22; pres. 06/1847; pres. 08/1847; pres. 10/1847, pay stopped for: 1 blanket-$2.22, 1 pr. overalls-$2.28, 2 cotton shirts-$.86, 2 flannel shirts-$1.80, 1 pr. drawers-$.35$^{1/2}$, 2 shoes-$2.44, 3 pr. socks-$.73$^{1/2}$, 1 forage cap-$.95$^{1/2}$; pres. 12/1847, pay stopped for: 1 pr. shoes-$1.22, 2 pr. socks-$.49, 1 cap-$.95$^{1/2}$, 1 jacket-$2.66; pres. 02/1848; pres. 04/1848; pres. 08/1848; BLW sent to Hanover Co. C.H., VA

**Houston, Thomas H.**, Pvt., Co. C; enl. Mex. War service 12/30/1846, Bowling Green, VA, age 21; pres. 06/1847; pres. 08/1847, pay stopped for: 1 cap-$.95$^{1/2}$, 2 pr. socks-$.49, 2 cotton shirts-$.86, 2 woolen shirts-$1.80, 1 pr. shoes-$1.22, 1 pr. drawers-$.35$^{1/2}$; pres. 10/1847, pay stopped for: 2 pr. socks-$.49, 1 pr. pants-$2.28, 2 woolen shirts-$1.80, 1 pr. shoes-$1.22; pres. 12/1847, pay stopped for: 1 pr. pants-$2.28; pres. 04/1848, pay stopped for: 1 jacket-$2.66, 1 india rubber canteen-$.27; pres. 08/1848, BLW sent to Lap P.O., Lancaster County, Pa.

**Howard, Alexander**, Pvt., Co. A; enl. Mex. War 01/02/1847 Richmond, VA, age 18; discharged 01/23/1847 at Old Point, VA under a writ of habeas corpus, no payment made in money for 6 mos. clothing.

**Howard, Jacob**, Pvt., Co. B; enl. 12/10/1846, Alexandria, VA, age 23; deserted 01/02/1847 Richmond, VA

**Howard, Tazewell M.**, Pvt., *Preston's Co.*; enl. Mex. War service 12/08/1846 Montgomery Co., VA, age 18; pres. 04/1847; absent 06/1847 left sick in hosp. at Monterey, Mex. since 06/22/1847; absent 08/1847 sick at Monterey, Mex. since 06/22/1847; pres. 10/1847, pay stopped for: 1 pr. overalls-$2.28, 1 pr. socks-$.24$^{1/2}$, 1 pr. drawers-$.35$^{1/2}$; pres. 12/1847, pay stopped for: 1 pr. shoes-$1.22, 1 pr. socks-$.24$^{1/2}$, 1 blanket-$2.22; pres. 02/1848; absent 04/1848 on detached service as a Teamster in QM Dept.; pres. 07/1848, pay stopped for: 1 cap-$.95$^{1/2}$, 1 jacket-$2.37, 1 gun sling-$.18; BLW sent to Floyd C.H., VA; m. Virginia A. Latham, 03/05/1857, Campbell Co., Ga.[1023]

**Howell, John V.**, Pvt., Co. K; enl. Mex. War service Jefferson Co., VA 12/24/1846, age 26; pres. 06/1847; pres. 08/1847; pres. 10/1847, pay stopped for: 2 pr. shoes-$2.44, 1 greatcoat-$6.93$^{1/2}$, 1 pr. overalls-$2.28, 3 cotton shirts-$1.29, 3 pr. drawers-$1.06$^{1/2}$, 3 pr. socks-$.73$^{1/2}$, 2 flannel shirts-$1.80; pres. 12/1847, pay stopped for: 1 jacket-$2.66, 1 pr. overalls-$2.28, 1 pr. drawers-$.35$^{1/2}$, 1 blanket-$2.22; pres. 04/1848, pay stopped for: 1 gun sling-$.18, 1 pick & brush-$.12; BLW sent to Charlestown, Jefferson Co., VA; c. 1850 res. Jefferson Co., VA, age 30, occ. Laborer.[1024]

**Howell, Lorenzo D.**, Pvt., *Preston's Co.*; enl. Mex. War service 12/07/1846 Montgomery Co., VA, age 21; phys. desc. at enl. b. Floyd Co., VA;[1025] occ. Carpenter, 5'10", light eyes, light hair, light complexion; pres. 04/1847; pres. 06/1847; pres. 08/1847; pres. 10/1847, pay stopped for: 1 jacket-$2.66, 1 pr. overalls-$2.28, 1 pr. shoes-$1.22, 3 pr. socks-$.73$^{1/2}$, 3 flannel shirts-$1.80, 3 cotton shirts-$1.29, 1 cap-$.95$^{1/2}$, 1 blanket-$2.22; pres. 12/1847, pay

## VIRGINIA VOLUNTEERS IN MEXICO

stopped for: 1 pr. overalls-$2.28, 2 pr. drawers-$.71; pres. 02/1848; pres. 04/1848, pay stopped for: 1 bayonet scabbard & frog-$.56; pres. 07/1848, pay stopped for: 1 pr. shoes-$1.16; BLW sent to Christiansburg, VA c/o Fleming Gardner; m. Mary McDonald, 02/08/1849, Elliott's Creek, Montgomery Co., VA; [1025, 1026] c. 1860, res. Newbern, Pulaski Co., VA, age 33, occ. Carpenter, w. Mary (33), dau. Melinda (10), dau. Victoria (7), dau. Francine (5), dau. Caroline (2);[1027] Civil War service enl. as Pvt., Co. C, 4$^{th}$ Va. Inf.03/13/1862; captured 05/05/1864 at Wilderness; sent to Pt. Lookout Prison, MD; d. 08/21/1864, Pt. Lookout, MD;[54, 1025] wid. Mary, WC #1034; 02/17/1887, filed from Newbern, Pulaski Co., VA; (MMH b. 02/18/1824).[1025]

**Howell, Morriss B.**, Pvt., Co. K; enl. Mex. War service Jefferson Co., VA 12/17/1846, age 25; pres. 06/1847; pres. 08/1847; in confinement 10/1847, pay stopped for: 1 pr. overalls-$2.28, 1 cotton shirt-$.43; absent 12/1847 on detached service as Clerk A.A.G.'s since 12/26/1847; pres. 04/1848, pay stopped for: 1 jacket-$2.66, 1 gun sling-$.18; pres. 07/1848; BLW sent to Charlestown, Jefferson Co., VA; c. 1850 res. Jefferson Co., VA, age 28, occ. None.[1028]

**Howell, Richard S.**, Pvt., Co. F; enl. Mex. War service 12/23/1846, Portsmouth, VA, age 24; pres. 06/1847; pres. 08/1847; pres. 10/1847, pay stopped for: 1 pr. overalls-$2.28, 2 cotton shirts-$.86, 1 forage cap-$.95$^{1/2}$; 3 pr. socks-$.73$^{1/2}$, 1 pr. shoes-$1.22, 1 flannel shirt-$.90; pres. 02/1848, pay stopped for: 1 pr. overalls-$2.28, 1 blanket-$2.22, 1 bed sack-$1.07; pres. 04/1848, pres. 08/1848, pay stopped for: 1 gun sling-$.18, 1 wiper-$.20, BLW sent to Portsmouth, VA c/o E.T. Blamire; c. 1850 res. Norfolk Co., VA, age 28, occ. Laborer, b. New York, w. Emma Jane (21) b. Virginia.[1029]

**Howle, James**, Pvt., Co. I; enl. Mex. War service 02/09/1847 Richmond, VA, age 28; pres. 02/1847; pres. 04/1847; discharged 06/17/1847 for disability at camp near Monterey, Mex.; c. 1850 res. New Kent Co., VA, age 32, occ. None.[1030]

**Howle, William T.**, Pvt., Co. D; enl. Mex. War service 01/29/1847, Petersburg, VA, age 18; pres. 02/1847; pres. 04/1847; pres. 06/1847; pres. 08/1847, pay stopped for: 1 cap-$.95$^{1/2}$, 2 cotton shirts-$.86, 2 flannel shirts-$1.80, 1 pr. shoes-$1.22; pres. but sick 10/1847, pay stopped for: 1 jacket-$2.66, 1 pr. pants-$2.28, 1 pr. drawers-$.35$^{1/2}$, 2 pr. socks-$.49, 1 pr. shoes-$1.22, 1 overcoat-$6.93$^{1/2}$; pres. 12/1847, pay stopped for: 2 cotton shirt-$.86, 1 pr drawers-$.35$^{1/2}$, 1 pr. socks-$.24$^{1/2}$, 1 blanket-$2.22; pres. 04/1848, pay stopped for: 1 set of picks & brushes-$.12, 1 pr. pants-$2.28, 2 pr. shoes-$2.44, 1 pr. shoes-$1.30; pres. 1847, BLW sent to Jarratt's Depot, Sussex Co., VA; c. 1850 res. Amelia Co., VA, age 22, occ. Overseer.[1031]

**Hoy, Francis**, Pvt., Co. E; enl. Mex. War service 12/02/1846 Petersburg, VA, age 21; discharged 01/1847 Fort Monroe, VA by order of Col. Watreck.

**Hubbard, George W.**, Pvt., Co. G; b. c. 1825 New Kent Co., VA;[1032] enl. Mex. War service 11/28/1846 Richmond, VA; phys. desc. age 21, 5'11", fair complexion, blue eyes, auburn hair, occ. soldier;[1032] pres. 06/1847; Court-martialed 07/22/1847, Buena Vista, Mexico, *Charge #1: Sleeping On Post; Specification: In this that Pvt. George W. Hubbard, Co. G, Va. Regt. Vols. having been duly posted as a Sentinel at the Camp at Buena Vista, Mexico on the 4$^{th}$ of July 1847, did go to sleep on his post before being regularly relieved. To which charge and specification the prisoner pled Guilty. Offering no defense the Court confirmed the plea of the prisoner and sentenced him to forfeit one months pay and to stand on the head of a barrel on the parade ground of his Regiment for two successive hours, from 5 o'clock to 7 P.M., for two successive days, under the charge of the Provost Guard;*[1033] pres. 08/1847; pres. 10/1847, pay stopped for: 2 pr. overalls-$2.28, 1 cotton shirt-$.43, 2 flannel shirts-$1.80, 1 pr. drawers-$.35$^{1/2}$, 2 shoes-$2.44, 4 pr. socks-$.98, 1 forage cap-$.95$^{1/2}$; pres. 12/1847, pay stopped for: 1 pr. shoes-$1.22, 1 pr. socks-$.24$^{1/2}$; pres. 02/1848; pres. 04/1848; pres. 08/1848; BLW sent to Richmond, VA; c. 1850 res. Richmond, Henrico Co., VA, age 25, occ. Public Guard;[1034] m. Sarah A. McGraw 12/17/1851, Richmond, Henrico Co., VA;[1032] d. 06/29/1873, Richmond,

OFF TO WAR

VA, bur. Oakwood Cem., Richmond, VA; wid. Sarah A., WC #1514, 02/15/1887, filed from 2005 Broad St., Richmond, Henrico Co., VA; (SAH d. 12/18/1895).[1032]

**Hudgins, John W.**, Pvt., Co. D; enl. Mex. War service 01/06/1847, Petersburg, VA, age 32; pres. 02/1847; absent 04/1847, left sick in Hosp. China, Mex. 04/16/1847; absent 06/1847, left sick in Hosp. China, Mex. since 04/16/1847 *"and not since heard from;"* deserted about 06/08/1847 China, Mex.

**Hudnall, William Gower**, Pvt., Co. G; b. 09/04/1818, Richmond, VA, son of Daniel Gower & Martha T. (Ball) Hudnall;[1035] enl. Mex. War service 12/01/1846 Richmond, VA, age 25; pres. 06/1847; pres. 08/1847; pres. 10/1847, pay stopped for: 1 pr. overalls-$2.28, 1 cotton shirt-$.43, 1 pr. drawers-$.35$^{1/2}$, 3 shoes-$3.66, 3 pr. socks-$.73$^{1/2}$, 1 great coat-$6.95$^{1/2}$, 1 forage cap-$.95$^{1/2}$; absent 12/1847, on extra duty in QM Dept., pay stopped for: 2 pr. shoes-$2.44, 1 blanket-$2.22, 1 pr. pants-$2.28, 1 jacket-$2.66; absent 02/1848, on extra duty in QM Dept.; absent 04/1848 on extra duty in QM Dept.; absent 08/1848, left in Monterey, Mex. in QM Dept.; BLW sent to Richmond, VA; m. Louise Elizabeth Page 08/16/1849, *"Bethel,"* Amherst Co., VA;[1037] c. 1850 res. Amherst Co., VA, age 29, occ. Carpenter, w. Louisa (25), dau. Elizabeth (1);[1036] Civil War enl. Sgt., Co. D, 19$^{th}$ Btln. Hvy. Arty.; 03/24/1862 in Amherst Co., VA; paid $50 Bounty 04/24/1862; pres. 08/1862 – 04/1863; pres. 08/1864; absent on 15 day furlough 12/27/1864; pres. 02/28/1865; SC #14402, 09/24/1887, filed from Coffee, Bedford Co., VA; since discharge res. Richmond, VA, 1 yr., Amherst Co., 32 yrs., Bedford Co., 10 yrs., Lynchburg, VA 4 yrs.; d. 12/24/1895, 510 Franklin St., Lynchburg, VA, funeral from Trinity M.E. Church. Lynchburg, VA;[1037, 33] wid. Louisa W., WC #10013, 01/24/1896, both from VA; (LEH b. near Amherst, Amherst Co., VA, d. 01/23/1899).[1037]

**Hudson, Daniel**, Pvt., Co. M; enl. Mex. War service 09/15/1847, Lunenburg, VA, age 21; pres. 10/1847; pres. 11/1847; pres. 12/1847; pres. 02/1848, pay stopped for: 2 flannel shirts-$1.80; sick 04/1848, pay stopped for: 1 blanket-$2.22, 1 pr. shoes-$1.22, 2 cotton shirts-$.86; pres. 08/1848, pay stopped for: 1 waist belt plate-$.10; BLW sent to Lunenburg C.H., VA

**Hughes, Hezekiah**, Pvt., Co. E; enl. Mex. War service 12/03/1846 Petersburg, VA, age 23; pres. 04/1847; pres. 06/1847; pres. 08/1847; 10/1847 [illegible]; pres. 02/1848 [illegible]; pres. 04/1848, [illegible]; a Hezekiah V. Hughes m. Saluda A. Wilson 12/1848;[1038] c. 1850 res. Petersburg, Dinwiddie Co., VA, age 28, occ. Painter, b. Maryland, w. Saluda (23), son Anderson (9/12).[1039]

**Hull, John**, Pvt., Co. L; b. 1826; discharged 03/24/1847 by order of Adj. Genl.[72]

**Hull, William H.**, Pvt., LIC; enl. Mex. War service 12/15/1846 Staunton, VA, age 20; absent 08/1847 on detached service as Hospital Attendant since 08/22/1847; pres. 10/1847, pay stopped for: 1 forage cap-$.95$^{1/2}$, 1 wool jacket-$2.66, 1 pr. overalls-$2.28, 1 pr. shoes-$1.22, 1 pr. socks-$.35$^{1/2}$, 1 cotton shirts-$.43; pres. 12/1847, pay stopped for: 1 pr. socks-$.24$^{1/2}$, 1 pr. shoes-$1.22, 1 pr. overalls-$2.28, 1 pr. drawers-$.35$^{1/2}$; pres. 04/1848; pres. 07/1848, 1 wiper-$.20; BLW sent to Staunton, VA

**Hulvey, Guy H.** Pvt., LIC; b. near New Market, Shennandoah Co., VA;[1040] enl. Mex. War service 12/10/1846 Staunton, VA, age 24; pres. 08/1847; pres. 10/1847, pay stopped for: 1 forage cap-$.95$^{1/2}$, 1 wool jacket-$2.66, 1 pr. overalls-$2.28, 1 pr. shoes-$1.22, 1 pr. socks-$.35$^{1/2}$, 1 cotton shirts-$.43; pres. 12/1847, pay stopped for: 1 pr. shoes-$1.22, 1 pr. overalls-$2.28, 1 pr. drawers-$.35$^{1/2}$; pres. 04/1848, pay stopped for: 1 pr. shoes-$1.22; pres. 07/1848, pay stopped for: 1 pr. shoes-$1.16; BLW sent to Staunton, VA; c. 1850 res. Augusta Co., VA, age 31, occ. Farmer;[1041] c. 1860 res. Augusta Co., VA, age 41, occ. Farmer, w. E.A. (32), son P.J. (12), son W.H. (11), son J.C. (9), son E.S. (8), dau. V.A. (6), son G.M. (4), son B.F. (2);[1042] Civil War service Co. E, 10$^{th}$ IA Inf., m/1 Ellen Munson 08/11/1867, Fulton Co., IL;[1043] divorced 09/01/1869, Fulton Co., IL [*Ellen filed for divorce on the grounds of adultery, alleging that Guy was frequenting women of illrepute*];[1040] m/2 Mary Lois Taylor 05/11/1871, Newton Co., Mo.;[1040] LW MO #670509; SC #2461, 02/23/1887, filed from Granby, Newton Co., MO; phys. desc. age 66 [1887] 6', dark complexion, blue eyes, dark hair, occ. Farmer;[1040]

180

## VIRGINIA VOLUNTEERS IN MEXICO

since discharge res. in Virginia to 1854, then Iowa to 1861 then to Missouri;[1040] d. 10/29/1892, *"general debility and old age,"* Blendville, Jasper Co., Mo.;[1040] (MTH d. 04/28/1893, Galena, Cherokee Co., KS);[1040] Lists children William Albert Hulvey b. 05/08/1879, Thomas Hulvey b. 03/15/1881, George Hulvey b. 04/10/1884, Guy Edward Hulvey b. 10/24/1886.[1040]

**Humphreys, John R.**, Pvt., Co. M; enl. Mex. War service 09/20/1847, Richmond, VA, age 18; pres. 10/1847; pres. 11/1847, reduced to ranks from musician; pres. 12/1847; pres. 02/1848, pay stopped for: 1 cotton shirt-$.43; pres. 04/1848, pay stopped for: 1 blanket-$2.22, 1 pr. shoes-$1.22, 2 cotton shirts-$.86; pres. 08/1848, pay stopped for: 1 gun sling-$1.16; BLW sent to Richmond, VA; [Civil War service a John R. Humphries enl. as 1st Lt. in Richmond Fayette Arty., date unknown, resigned 1862, NFR.]

**Hunter, John Harrison.**, Pvt., Co. H; b. 03/29/1829, Martinsburg, Berkeley Co., VA;[1044] 1845 Chairman of the Martinsburg Literary Society, organized *"for improvement in History, Debate and Composition;"*[1045] enl. Mex. War service 12/26/1846, Berkeley, VA, age 18; pres. 04/1847; pres. 06/1847; pres. 08/1847; absent 10/1847, on detached service as Commissary Sgt. since 09/06/1847, pay stopped for: 1 pr. pants-$2.28, 1 pr. shoes-$1.22; absent 12/1847 on extra duty in Commissary Dept. as Sgt., pay stopped for: 3 pr. socks-$.49, 2 blankets-$4.44, 1 pr. pants-$2.28; transferred 02/25/1848 to QM Dept. as Sgt.; pres. 07/1848, pay stopped for: 1 bayonet-$1.44, 1 cartridge box plate-$.10, 1 brush & pick-$.12, 1 screw driver-$.25, BLW sent to Martinsburg, VA; res. Calif.; m. Sophie B. Summers 04/23/1857, Martinsburg, VA; practiced medicine Kanawha Co., (W.) VA; served 3rd Ark. Inf., in Smithville, Ark. 06/05/1861; appointed Asst. Surg. P.A.C.S., 07/19/1861 and ordered to Richmond, VA; Vol. Surg. w/ 2nd Va. Inf. at Manassas, 07/21/1861; ordered to Huntersville, VA 08/27/1861; Surg.-in-charge, Warm Springs Hosp. 09/03/1861 – 12/1861; appointed Asst. Surg. 42nd Va. Inf. by 01/1862 when ordered to est. hosp. at Romney, VA, to receive sick of B.G. W.W. Loring's Div.; pres. 03/1862; prom. Surg. 04/26/1862; wded. left foot, Cedar Run, 08/09/1862; absent sick leave thru 08/03/1863; Surg., Montgomery White Sulphur Springs, 03/1864 – 04/1864; captured Bristol, TN, 12/27/1864; NFR;[1046] c. 1880 res. Martinsburg, Berkeley Co., WV, age 50, occ. Physician, w. Sophia F. (45) keeping house, dau. Susan (20) at home, son Summers (18) clerk in store, dau. Nannie S. (16), dau. Mary (11), son Otho (9), dau. Marian (7), son Berkley (3);[1047] SC #16022, 05/23/1887, filed from Berkeley Springs, Morgan Co., WV; phys. desc. age 57 [1885], 5'8 1/2", fair complexion, blue eyes, brown hair, occ. Physician; d. 09/26/1905, *"aged 76 yrs., 6 mos., 3 days;"*[1048] wid. Sophie Forrest, WC #14205, 10/20/1905, filed from Berkeley Springs, Morgan Co., WV; Lists children Mrs. Susan S. Hunter Saltonstall, b. 05/1860, C.S. Hunter, b. 01/1862, Nannie H. Hunter, b. 11/1863, Mercy Hunter Sherwood, b. 02/1868, Otho H. Hunter, b. 10/1870, John B. Hunter, b. 01/1877, Minnie C. Hunter, b. 12.1873;[1048] (SFH b. 05/03/1834 Rockville, MD, d. 06/26/1907).[1048]

**Hunter, Zachariah P.**, Pvt., Co. B; m. Julia Edumnds, 02/24/1834, Washington, D.C.;[1049] enl. 12/01/1846, Alexandria, VA, age 35; pres. 06/1847, served as Fifer from 12/30/1846 – 04/30/1847, excess pay over Pvt. due for four mos.; pres. 08/1847; in confinement 10/1847, pay stopped for: 1 pr. shoes-$1.22, 2 pr. overalls-$4.56, 2 pr. socks-$.49, 2 cotton shirts-$.86; pres. 12/1847, fined 1 mos. pay by order (129) of genl. court-martial, pay stopped for: 1 blanket-$2.22; pres. 02/1848; pres. 04/1848; pres. 08/1848, pay stopped for 1 pr. shoes-$1.16, 1 wiper-$.20, BLW sent to Alexandria, VA; c. 1850 res. Alexandria Co., VA, age 36, occ. Shoemaker, w. Julia (38), dau. Julia A. (15), dau. Maria A. (7), son William H.W. (1).[1050]

**Hurst, Rhoten**, Pvt., Co. I; b. 08/18/1827, Salem, Roanoke Co., VA;[1051] enl. Mex. War service 01/10/1847 Lynchburg, VA, age 19; pres. 02/1847; pres. 04/1847; pres. sick 06/1847 in Hosp. at Saltillo, Mex.; pres. 08/1847; pres. 10/1847, pay stopped for: 1 flannel shirt-$.90, 3 pr. drawers-$1.06 1/2, 1 pr. socks-$.24 1/2, 1 pr. pants-$2.28, 1 cap- $.95 1/2; pres. 12/1847, pay stopped for: 1 pr. socks-$.24 1/2, 1 jacket-$2.66, 1 pr. shoes-$1.22, 1 blanket-$2.22, 1 cotton shirt-$.43; pres. 02/1848, pay stopped for: 1 pr. shoes-$1.22, 1 pr. overalls-$2.28; pres.

OFF TO WAR

04/1848; pres. 08/1848, pay stopped for: 1 pick & brush-$.12, BLW sent to Salem, Roanoke Co., VA; m/1 Mary Barnhardt, 08/30/1849, Roanoke, VA;[1051] Civil War service Co. M, 8th Ind. Cav.; m/2 Sarah Ann Clevenger 04/13/1873, Randolph, Ind.; IO #827039 bur. Delaware Co., Ind., & WC #659806; SC #11432, 08/29/1887, from IN; d. 06/06/1908, *Bright's Disease*, Muncie, Delaware Co., IN; bur. Beech Grove Cem., Sect. A, Lot 87, Muncie IN;[1052, 1053] [see Civil War pension claim].

**Hurst, Stephen D.**, Pvt., Co. K; b. 02/11/1825, son of William & Mary (Shirley) Hurst; enl. Mex. War service Jefferson Co., VA 12/07/1846, age 22; pres. 06/1847; pres. 08/1847; pres. 10/1847, pay stopped for: 1 pr. overalls-$2.28, 1 cap-$.95$^{1/2}$, 2 pr. shoes-$2.44, 4 cotton shirts-$1.72, 4 pr. socks-$.98, 3 pr. drawers-$1.06$^{1/2}$, 4 flannel shirts-$3.60; pres. 12/1847, pay stopped for: 1 pr. overalls-$2.28, 1 pr. boots-$1.22, 2 pr. drawers-$.71, 1 blanket-$2.22; pres. 04/1848, pay stopped for: 1 pick & brush-$.12, 1 gun sling-$.18, 1 blanket-$2.22, 1 cap-$.95$^{1/2}$; pres. 07/1848, pay stopped for: 1 bayonet-$1.44, 1 bayonet scabbard & frog-$.56, 1 waist belt-$.21, 1 waist belt plate-$.10, 1 screw driver-$.25, 1 wiper-$.20, 1 pick & brush-$.12; BLW sent to Charlestown, Jefferson Co., VA; c. 1850 res. Jefferson Co., VA, age 25, occ. None;[1054] d. 03/17/1860; bur. Edge Hill Cem., Charlestown, WV.

**Hurt, Moses**, Pvt., LIC, enl. Mex. war service 08/09/1847 Staunton, VA, age 18; joined the co. 01/26/1848 from the regtl. depot; d. 03/17/1848 near Parras, Mex. *"assassinated by Mexicans,"* pay stopped for: 1 blanket-$2.22, 1 pr. shoes-$1.22.

**Hutchings, George W.**, Pvt., Co. B; enl. 11/10/1847, Alexandria, VA, age 22; pres. 02/1848, 6 mos. clothing pd. in advance; pres. 04/1848, pay stopped for: 1 jacket-$2.66; pres. 08/1848, pay stopped for 1 gun sling-$.16, BLW sent to Alexandria, VA; m. Diana Dyer 04/24/1850, Washington, DC;[1055] c. 1850 res. Alexandria, VA, age 25, occ. Painter & Varnisher, w. Diannah (21);[1056] c. 1860 res. Alexandria, VA, occ. Chair Painter, age 33;[1057] d. 05/05/1865, *"Funeral from his late residence on Wolfe St."*[1058]

**I'Anson, William H.**, Pvt., Co. E; b. 1817, Petersburg, VA; grad. Univ. of Maryland College of Medicine 1846, wrote a Doctoral Thesis on *Puerperal Fever* or *Childbed Fever*;[1059] enl. Mex. War service 11/30/1846 Petersburg, VA, age 27; discharged 04/1847, prom. Regtl. Surgeon 02/03/1847; Editor of *The Press*, Petersburg, VA; Civil War service apptd. Maj., QM Dept., Florida, 12/24/1861;[202,1060] Physician, d. Lake City, FL 12/1875.[1061]

**Illick, Jacob**, Pvt., LIC; enl. Mex. War service 12/05/1846 Staunton, VA, age 40; pres. 08/1847; pres. 10/1847, pay stopped for: 1 forage cap-$.95$^{1/2}$, 1 wool jacket-$2.66, 1 pr. overalls-$2.28, 2 pr. shoes-$2.44, 2 pr. socks-$.49, 2 cotton shirts-$.86; pres. 12/1847, pay stopped for: 1 blanket-$2.22, 1 pr. shoes-$1.22, 1 pr. overalls-$2.28, 1 flannel shirt-$.90; pres. 04/1848; pres. 07/1848; BLW sent to Staunton, VA; c. 1850 res. Augusta Co., VA, age 46, occ. Miller;[1062] wid. Mary M. WC #395, 02/11/1887, filed from near Staunton, Augusta Co., VA; m. Mary M. Ochleman, 05/08/1851, Augusta Co., VA; phys. desc. at enl. age 43, occ. Butcher, b. Germany, 5'1", black hair, gray eyes, dark complexion; George Harlan and William O. Bickle; (MOI b. 07/24/1824, Augusta Co., VA, m/1 John Ochleman 02/07/1841, he died 01/28/1851, MOI d. 1891); d. 12/13/1876, Staunton, VA

**Imboden, Benjamin F.**, 3rd Cpl., LIC; b. 12/01/1828, Augusta Co., VA, son of George & Isabella (Wunderlich) Imboden;[1063] enl. Mex. War service 12/07/1846 Staunton, VA, age 19; pres. 06/1847; pres. 08/1847, prom. 3rd Cpl.; d. 09/19/1847 at Saltillo, Mex., pay stopped for: 1 forage cap-$.95$^{1/2}$, 1 wool jacket-$2.66, 1 pr. overalls-$2.28, 1 pr. shoes-$1.22, 2 pr. socks-$.49, 1 cotton shirts-$.43; his body was allegedly bur. 10/27/1847 in Augusta Co, VA Augusta Historical Bulletin read, *"'Camp Buena Vista, September 19, 1847...Corporal Benjamin F. Imboden is no more...He breathed his last today...Typhus fever...remains will be interred tomorrow with military honors (27 Oct. 1847).' None of the three sources of his death indicate where Benjamin was buried. Because of the article above and the length of time between his death and interment, it believed his body was shipped home to Virginia;"*[1064] bro. of Confederate Gen. John Daniel Imboden.

## VIRGINIA VOLUNTEERS IN MEXICO

**Jackson, Andrew**, 1st Cpl., Co. E; b. 07/01/1828, Petersburg, VA, son of John B. & Elizabeth Jackson;[1065] possibly attended VMI Class of 1847;[281] enl. Mex. War service 11/27/1846 Petersburg, VA, age 18; absent 04/1847 on detached service as Clerk to Col. Hamtramck in Monterey, was acting Sgt. Major of the 1st Detachment from 03/02/1847 – 03/23/1847; absent 06/1847 on detached service with Col. Hamtramck; absent 08/1847 on detached service with Col. Hamtramck; pres. 10/1847, pay stopped for: 1 pr. overalls-$2.28, 2 pr. stockings-$.49, 1 cap-$.95$^{1/2}$; pres. 12/1847, pay stopped for: 1 jacket-$2.66, 1 pr. pants-$2.28, 2 pr. socks-$.49, 1 cotton shirt-$.43, 2 flannel shirts-$1.80, 2 pr. drawers-$.71; prom. Lt., 3rd Regt. Inf., U.S.A.; possibly the same as Lt. Andrew Jackson, of Petersburg, VA, appointed Assistant Tutor of Spanish at the U.S. Military Academy, West Point, NY, in 1858;[1066] d. 11/17/1863, *Consumption*, bur. Blandford Cem., Sq. 1, Sec. 21, Ward D, Petersburg, VA[1065]

**Jackson, Charles**, Pvt., *Preston's Co.*, b. c. 11/16/1821, Fairfax Co., VA, son of Richard & Jane (Donaldson) Jackson; enl. Mex. War service 12/06/1846, Floyd Co., VA, age 24; pres. 04/1847; pres. 06/1847 reduced to ranks from 4th Sgt.; sick 08/1847; pres. 10/1847, pay stopped for: 1 pr. shoes-$1.22, 1 pr. socks-$.24$^{1/2}$, 1 cap-$.95$^{1/2}$; pres. 12/1847, pay stopped for: 1 pr. socks-$.24$^{1/2}$, 1 pr. drawers-$.35$^{1/2}$, 2 blankets-$4.44; pres. 02/1848, pay stopped for: 1 pr. shoes-$1.22; pres. 04/1848; pres. 07/1848, pay stopped for: 1 cartridge box belt-$.10, 1 bayonet scabbard & frog-$.56, 1 brush & pick-$.12, 1 screw driver-$.07, 1 gun sling-$.18; BLW sent to Prospect Hill, VA; Civil War service Pvt. , Co. B, 2nd S.C. Inf., enl. as a Pvt., Co. D, 17th Va. Inf., 05/06/1861 at Fairfax C.H., VA, trans. 11/27/1861, discharged 07/16/1862, phys. desc. age 40, farmer, 5'11", dark complexion, hazel eyes, dark hair;[63] m. widow Mary Ann (East) Finney 10/11/1868 Blackberry, Henry Co., VA; Charles Jackson was then a resident of Patrick Co., VA; SC #10885, 07/01/1887, filed from Pilot, Montgomery Co., VA; phys. desc. 6', gray eyes, light hair, fair complexion, occ. School Teacher;[1067] *"I studied medicine with Charles Jackson and was with him from discharge until about 1880"* - affidavit of Dr. C.M. Stiglman,Floyd C.H., VA;[1068]res. Blackberry, VA 1868-1903; d. 08/01/1903, Blackberry, Henry Co., VA, bur. Finney Cemetery, Rt. 718, off Rt. 698, s.w. of Blackberry Church, Henry Co., VA;[1069] wid. Mary A., WC #13675, 10/08/1903, filed from Bassett, Henry Co., VA;[1070] (MAJ b. 09/23/1834, Patrick Co., VA, d. 02/04/1908, Henry Co., VA; m/1 Marshall Finney, 09/04/1855, he d. 04/17/1864; m/2 Charles Jackson); Charles Jackson was the bro. of James W. Jackson, Proprietor of the Marshall House, Alexandria, VA *first civilian causality of the Civil War*;[1071]

**Jackson, Nathaniel**, Pvt., Co. C; enl. Mex. War service 12/30/1846, Bowling Green, VA, age 44; discharged 05/15/1847 Matamoros, Mex. on Surgeon's Certificate of Disability.

**Jackson, Robert**, Pvt., *Recruit Co.*, enl. Mex. War service 08/27/1847 Petersburg, VA, age 18; NFR.

**James, Joseph H.**, 2nd Sgt., Co. F; m. Mary C. Gaskins 12/22/1846, Portsmouth, Norfolk Co., VA;[1072] enl. Mex. War service 11/23/1846, Portsmouth, VA, age 22; prom. 4th Sgt. date unknown; pres. 06/1847; pres. 08/1847; pres. 10/1847, pay stopped for: 1 pr. overalls-$2.28, 2 pr. shoes-$2.44, 3 pr. drawers-$1.06$^{1/2}$, 1 blanket-$2.22, 2 pr. socks-$.49, 1 cotton shirt-$.43, 1 flannel shirt-$.90; pres. 12/1847; pres. 02/1848 sick, pay stopped for: 1 pr. overalls-$2.28, 1 flannel shirt-$.90, 1 cotton shirt-$.43, 1 infantry jacket-$2.66, 1 blanket-$2.22, 2 pr. socks-$.49; pres. 04/1848, prom. 2nd Sgt. 04/27/1848; pres. 08/1848, pay stopped for: 1 gun sling-$.18, 1 wiper-$.20, 1 blankets-$2.25, 2 cotton shirts-$.88, BLW sent to Portsmouth, VA c/o E.T. Blamire; [c. 1850 a Joseph H. James res. Richmond, Henrico Co., VA, age 27, occ. Jeweler, w. Sarah (26), son Henry F. (1);][1073] d. 02/20/1862 Wilmington, NC; wid. Mary C., WC #2636, 08/01/1887, filed from 610 Dinwiddie St., Portsmouth, Norfolk Co., VA; (MCJ b. 09/29/1827 Portsmouth, Norfolk Co., VA, d. 01/15/1894).[1072]

**James, William D.**, Pvt., Co. F; enl. Mex. War service 12/24/1846, Portsmouth, VA, age 18; pres. 06/1847; pres. 08/1847; pres. 10/1847, pay stopped for: 1 pr. overalls-$2.28, 4 pr. socks-$.98, 1 pr. shoes-$1.22; pres. 02/1848; pres. 04/1848; pres. 08/1848, pay stopped for: 1 pr.

OFF TO WAR

shoes-$1.16, BLW sent to Portsmouth, VA c/o E.T. Blamire; m. Emily H. Gaskins, 05/06/1852, Portsmouth, Norfolk Co., VA;[1074] wid. Emily W., WC #2638, 08/01/1887, filed from 305 Loudoun St., Portsmouth, Norfolk Co., VA; Francis L. Benson and George W. Richardson gave affidavits in pension claim;[1074] (EHJ b. 09/29/1829, Portsmouth, Norfolk Co., VA, d. 01/23/1894).[1074]

**James, William H.**, Pvt., Co. D; enl. Mex. War service 01/04/1847, Petersburg, VA, age 26; pres. 02/1847; pres. 04/1847; pres. 06/1847; pres. 08/1847, pay stopped for: 1 cap-$.95$^{1/2}$, 2 cotton shirts-$.86, 2 flannel shirts-$1.80, 1 pr. shoes-$1.22; pres. 10/1847, pay stopped for: 1 jacket-$2.66, 1 pr. pants-$2.28, 1 pr. drawers-$.35$^{1/2}$, 2 pr. socks-$.49, 1 pr. shoes-$1.22; pres. 12/1847, pay stopped for: 1 pr. pants-$2.28, 1 pr drawers-$.35$^{1/2}$, 1 pr. socks-$.24$^{1/2}$; pres. 04/1848; pres. 08/1847, BLW sent to Hicks Ford, Greensville Co., VA; m. Louisa Elizabeth Jarratt 12/22/1853, Greensville Co., VA;[1075] (LEJ d. 1886); SC #2821, 02/17/1887, filed from Rural Bower, Greensville Co., VA; phys. desc. at enlistment age 26, occ. Farmer, 5'11", fair complexion, blue eyes. Lists children William T. James b. 06/12/1859, Richard H. James b. 08/20/1861; d. 01/11/1907.[1075]

**James, William M.**, Co. A; *Not on Muster Rolls*, WC #3875, 06/14/1887, from MO.

**Jamison, John**, Pvt., Co. H; enl. Mex. War service 11/27/1846, Berkeley, VA, age 22; pres. 04/1847; pres. 06/1847, prom. 3$^{rd}$ Sgt.; pres. 08/1847; in confinement 10/1847, pay stopped for: 1 forage cap-$.95$^{1/2}$, 1 pr. pants-$2.28, 2 sgts. cotton shirts-$.86, 2 pr. drawers-$.71, 3 pr. socks-$.73$^{1/2}$; sick 12/1847, pay stopped for: 2 pr. pants-$4.56, 1 pr. shoes-$1.22, 2 pr. socks-$.24$^{1/2}$, 1 blanket-$2.22; pres. 02/1848, pay stopped for: 2 forage caps-$1.91, 1 jacket-$2.66, 2 pr. drawers-$.71, 1 pr. shoes-$1.22; pres. 04/1848, reduced to ranks by order of genl. court-martial 04/12/1848; pres. 07/1848, BLW sent to Martinsburg, VA; c. 1850 res. Martinsburg, Berkeley Co., VA, age 23, occ. None;[1076] [Civil War service a John Jamison enl. 08/22/1863, Pvt., Co. G, 21$^{St}$ Va. Cav.; captured at Moorefield, WV 08/07/1864; desc. age 45, 5'9", dark hair, blue eyes, occ. Farmer from Franklin Co.; sent to Camp Chase; d. 04/16/1865, pneumonia; bur. grave #1878.][1077]

**Jarrett, John**, Co. G; *Not on Muster Rolls*; SC #8154, 04/09/1887, from VA

**Jenkins, John**, Pvt., Co. M; enl. Mex. War service 07/05/1847, Richmond, VA, age 19; pres. 09/1847; pres. 11/1847; pres. 12/1847; pres. 02/1848, pay stopped for: 1 blanket-$2.22, 1 cotton shirt-$.43; pres. 04/1848; pres. 08/1847, pay stopped for: 1 ram rod-$.63, 1 pick & brush-$.12; pres. 10/1847, pay stopped for: 1 F Cap .95; BLW sent to Richmond, VA

**Jenkins, William**, 2$^{nd}$ Sgt., Co. B; b. c. 1825; enl. 11/30/1846, Alexandria, VA, age 22; pres. 06/1847; absent 08/1847 on detached service as Provost Sgt. from 08/14/1847; pres. 08/1847; pres. 10/1847, pay stopped for: 2 pr. socks-$.49, 1 pr. shoes-$1.22, 1 pr. overalls-$2.28, 4 pr. cotton drawers-$1.42, 1 blanket-$2.22; absent 10/1847 on detached service as Provost Sgt., pay stopped for: 1 pr. shoes-$1.22, 1 pr. overalls-$2.28, 2 pr. drawers-$.71, 1 cap-$.95$^{1/2}$; pres. 12/1847, pay stopped for: 6 pr. socks-$1.47; 1 pr. shoes-$1.22, 1 blanket-$2.22; pres. 02/1848; pres. 04/1848, prom. 2$^{nd}$ Sgt., pay stopped for: 1 jacket-$2.66; pres. 08/1848, pay stopped for: 1 screw driver-$.07, 1 spring vice-$.35, BLW sent to Alexandria, VA; c. 1850 res. Alexandria, VA, age 25, occ. Carpenter, w. Martha E.;[1078] mbr. Sun Fire Engine Co., Alexandria, VA; 1$^{st}$ Sgt., Alexandria Artillery, 1859; c. 1860 res. Alexandria, VA, age 35, occ. Carpenter, w. Martha (31);[1079] Civil War service enl. Pvt., Co. E, 17$^{th}$ Va. Inf., Manassas Junction, VA 05/30/1861; det. to Div. Scouts 06/1862;[63] d. 2/17/1872, Alexandria, VA, age 47, "Funeral from St. Mary's Church;"[1080] wid. Martha m. B.F. Jenkins, Alexandria, VA 12/13/1874;[1081] listed as a member of Co. B, 1$^{st}$ Virginia Volunteers in *Alexandria Gazette*.[1082]

**Jenkins, William H.**, Pvt., Co. L; b. 1824; m. Elizabeth Dove;[1083] enl. Mex. War service 03/01/1847 Fairfax C.H., VA, age 23; absent 06/1847 on detached service in QM Dept.; pres. 12/1847, pay stopped for: 1 pr. pants-$2.28, 1 cotton shirt-$.43, 1 blanket-$2.22, 2 pr. socks-$.49; pres. 02/1848; pres. 04/1848, pay stopped for: 2 Cotton Shirts .88; pres. 07/1848; BLW sent to William Jenkins, Springvale P.O., Fairfax Co., VA; c. 1850 res. Fairfax Co., VA, age

184

VIRGINIA VOLUNTEERS IN MEXICO

43, occ. Farmer, w. Elizabeth (36), son Washington (18), dau. Lydia A. (17), dau. Elizabeth (15), son Samuel (12), son Gilson (7), son John (5), dau. Caroline (1).[1084] c. 1860 res. Fairfax Co., VA, age 53, w. Elizabeth (48), son Washington (28), son Samuel (20), son Gilson (19), dau. Elizabeth (21), son John W. (15), son Charles W. (12), dau. Mary (10);[1085] voted for Secession 04/23/1861 at Dranesville, Fairfax Co., VA[1086]

**Jennings, James**, Pvt., Co. I; enl. Mex. War service 02/05/1847 Richmond, VA, age 19; pres. 02/1847; pres. 04/1847; pres. 06/1847, pay stopped for loss of bayonet scabbard belt-$.56; pres. 08/1847; pres. 10/1847, pay stopped for: 2 pr. drawers-$.71, 1 cotton shirt-$.43, 1 pr. shoes-$1.22, 1 pr. socks-$.24$^{1/2}$, 1 flannel shirt-$.90; pres. 12/1847, pay stopped for: 1 pr. shoes-$1.22, 1 pr. socks-$.24$^{1/2}$, 1 jacket-$2.66, 1 pr. pants-$2.28, 1 cotton shirt-$.43, 1 flannel shirt-$.90, 1 pr. drawers-$.35$^{1/2}$; pres. 02/1848; pres. 04/1848; pres. 08/1848, pay stopped for: 1 bayonet-$1.44; BLW sent to Spotsylvania C.H., VA

**Jennings, William**, Fifer, Co. C; enl. Mex. War service 12/18/1846, Fredericksburg, VA, age 23; pres. 06/1847; pres. 08/1847, pay stopped for: 1 cap-$.95$^{1/2}$, 2 pr. socks-$.49, 2 cotton shirts-$.86, 2 woolen shirts-$1.80, 1 pr. shoes-$1.22; pres. 10/1847, pay stopped for: 1 pr. socks-$.24$^{1/2}$, 1 jacket-$2.66, 1 pr. pants-$2.28; pres. 12/1847, pay stopped for: 2 pr. socks-$.49, 1 pr. pants-$2.28, 1 woolen shirt-$.90, 1 pr. shoes-$1.22; pres. 04/1848, pay stopped for: [illegible], 1 india rubber canteen-$.27, 1 flannel shirt-$.90; pres. 08/1848, BLW sent to Fredericksburg, VA

**Jewett, Noah**, Pvt., Co. A; enl. Mex. War service 12/01/1846 Richmond, VA, age 30; pres. 12/1846 - 04/1847; pres. 06/1847; pres. 08/1847; pres.10/1847, pay stopped for clothing: 1 pr. wool overalls-$2.28; pres. 12/1847, pay stopped for clothing: 1 pr. drawers-$.71, 1 blanket-$2.22; pres. 02/1848; pres. 04/1848; pres. 07/1848, pay stopped for: 1 musket sling-$.16; BLW sent to Richmond, VA

**Johns, Elhanan**, Pvt., Co. C; enl. Mex. War service 12/30/1846, Bowling Green, VA, age 36; d. 06/27/1847 Monterey, Mex., a letter from Asst. Surgeon, T.C. Madison to Lt. Thomas P. August, Co. A related the news.[1087]

**Johnson, Almon**, Pvt., Co. A; enl. Mex. War service 12/07/1846 Richmond, VA, age 31; pres. 12/1846 - 04/1847; pres. 06/1847; pres. 08/1847; sick 10/1847, pay stopped for clothing: 1 cap-$.95$^{1/2}$, 2 pr. stockings-$.49, 2 pr. shoes-$2.44, 1 pr. wool overalls-$2.28; pres. 12/1847, pay stopped for clothing: 2 pr. socks-$.49, 1 blanket-$2.22; pres. 02/1848; pres. 04/1848; BLW sent to Richmond, VA

**Johnson, Charles Y.**, Pvt., *Preston's Co.*; enl. Mex. War service 12/06/1846 Lynchburg, VA, age 28; pres. 04/1847; pres. 06/1847; absent 08/1847 on detached service in Regimental Band since 07/30/1847; pres. 10/1847, prom. Musician *"Drummer"*[1088] 10/01/1847, pay stopped for: 1 jacket-$2.66, 1 pr. overalls-$2.28, 2 pr. socks-$.49, 1 cap-$.95$^{1/2}$, 1 wiper-$.15, 1 pick & brush-$.12, 1 gun sling-$.08; pres. 12/1847, pay stopped for: 1 pr. socks-$.24$^{1/2}$, 1 blanket-$2.22; pres. 02/1848; pres. 04/1848; pres. 07/1848, pay stopped for: 1 pr. shoes-$1.16; BLW sent to Lynchburg, VA; m. Parthenia Oliver, 06/19/1856, Lynchburg, Campbell Co., VA;[1088] c. 1850 res. Lynchburg, Campbell Co., VA, age 32, occ. Musician & Shoemaker, w. Parthenia Oliver (2);[1089] d. 01/06/1867, Madison [Heights], Amherst Co., VA;[1088] wid. Parthenia, WC #1007, 04/08/1887, filed from Madison Amherst Co., VA; (POJ b. 02/14/1815, Lynchburg, VA).[1088]

**Johnson, Francis A.**, Pvt., Co. M; enl. Mex. War service 07/05/1847, Richmond, VA, age 24; pres. 09/1847; pres. 11/1847; pres. 12/1847; sick 02/1848; pres. 04/1848; pres. 08/1848, pay stopped for: 1 gun sling-$.16, 1 cartridge box belt plate-$.10, 1 bayonet scabbard-$.56; BLW sent to Richmond, VA

**Johnson, Isaac W.**, Pvt., LIC; enl. Mex. War service 12/07/1846 Staunton, VA, age 25; pres. 08/1847; pres. 10/1847, pay stopped for: 1 forage cap-$.95$^{1/2}$, 1 wool jacket-$2.66, 1 pr. overalls-$2.28, 2 pr. shoes-$2.44, 2 pr. socks-$.49, 2 cotton shirts-$.86; pres. 12/1847, pay

OFF TO WAR

stopped for: 1 blanket-$2.22, 1 pr. overalls-$2.28, 2 flannel shirts-$1.80; pres. 07/1848, pay stopped for: 1 screw driver-$.07; BLW sent to Staunton, VA

**Johnson, John**, Pvt., *Recruit Co.*, enl. Mex. War service ??/1848 Christiansburg, VA, age 25; pres. 02/1848; pres. 04/1848; pres. 06/1848; BLW sent to Washington City, D.C.

**Johnson, John Albert**, Pvt., Co. M; enl. Mex. War service 05/28/1847, Richmond, VA, age 26; pres. 09/1847; pres. 11/1847; pres. 12/1847; sick 02/1848; sick 04/1848; pres. 08/1848, pay stopped for: 1 waist belt plate-$.10, 1 gun sling-$.16; BLW sent to Richmond, VA; m/1 Catherine Kelly, date/place unknown, divorced 1862;[1090] m/2 Mary Ann Booker, 09/14/1865, Richmond, VA;[1090] d. 09/27/1884, 1300 N. 1st St., Richmond, VA;[1090] wid. Mary A., WC #4095, 06/07/1887, filed from 1300 N. 1st St., Richmond, VA; (MBJ d. 01/02/1907).[1090]

**Johnson, Joseph A.**, 2nd Sgt., Co. M; b. 03/27/1827, Richmond, Henrico Co., VA;[1091] enl. Mex. War service 07/15/1847, Richmond, VA, age 20; pres. 09/1847; pres. 11/1847, reduced to 3rd Sgt. from 2nd Sgt.; pres. 12/1847; pres. 02/1848, pay stopped for: 1 over coat-$6.93$^{1/2}$, 1 blanket-$2.22, 1 flannel shirt-$.90; pres. 04/1848, pay stopped for: 1 pr. shoes-$1.22, 2 cotton shirts-$.86; pres. 08/1848, prom. 2nd Sgt., pay stopped for: 1 thumb vise-$.35, 1 wormer-$.20, 1 sword belt plate-$.10; BLW sent to Richmond, VA; m. Ann E. Garrett, 08/1850, Richmond, Henrico Co., VA;[1091] SC #8801, 03/21/1887, filed from Atlanta, Fulton Co., GA, phys. desc. 5'6", dark eyes, brown hair, rather dark complexed, occ. Cabinet Maker; since discharge res. Richmond, VA until 1865 when he moved to Atlanta, Ga.;[1091] d. 07/22/1913, 202 Luckie St., Atlanta, GA; abstract of obituary states: *"Joseph A. Johnson – 86, 302 Luckie St., A pioneer Atlantan, having come here 47 years ago from Richmond, VA Was connected with the manufacturing interests of the city. He was a veteran of the Mexican War, having fought under General Scott as a Sgt. was Capt. of the National Grays of Richmond. His wife, to whom he had been married 55 yrs. died a few years ago. Leaves 3 sons: George E, Orie, & W.L. Johnson and two nephews in Richmond, George & Charlie Crawford. Oakland Cemetery;"*[1091, 1092] bur. Oakland Cemetery, Atlanta, GA; (AGJ d. 09/24/1906).[1091]

**Johnson, Joseph**, Pvt., Co. H; enl. Mex. War service 01/06/1847, Berkeley, VA, age 23; pres. 04/1847; pres. 06/1847; pres. 08/1847; pres. 10/1847, pay stopped for: 1 forage cap-$.95$^{1/2}$, 1 pr. pants-$2.28, 4 cotton shirts-$1.72, 1 pr. shoes-$1.22, 2 pr. socks-$.49, 1 jacket-$2.66; pres. 12/1847; pres. 02/1848, pay stopped for: 1 jacket-$2.66, 2 pr. drawers-$.71, 1 blanket-$2.22; pres. 04/1848; pres. 07/1848, pay stopped for: 1 gun sling-$.16, 1 wiper-$.20, 1 screw driver-$.25, BLW sent to Philadelphia, Pa. SC #3268, 03/14/1887, from KS; [see Civil War pension claim].

**Johnson, Richard E.**, Pvt., Co. F; enl. Mex. War service 01/12/1847, Portsmouth, VA, age 18; pres. 06/1847; pres. 08/1847; pres. 10/1847, pay stopped for: 1 pr. overalls-$2.28, 2 cotton shirts-$.86, 1 forage cap-$.95$^{1/2}$, 1 pr. shoes-$1.22, 2 pr. socks-$.49; pres. 02/1848, pay stopped for: 1 pr. shoes-$1.22, 1 blanket-$2.22, 1 pr. overalls-$2.28; pres. 04/1848; pres. 08/1848, pay stopped for: 1 bayonet-$1.44, 1 cartridge box belt & plate-$1.90, 1 brush & pick-$.12, 1 gun sling-$.18, 2 pr. shoes-$2.32, 1 blanket-$2.25, 1 forage cap-$.83, BLW sent to Portsmouth, VA c/o E.T. Blamire.

**Johnson, Richard**, Pvt., LIC; enl. Mex. War service 12/07/1846 Staunton, VA, age 30; pres. 08/1847; sick 10/1847, pay stopped for: 1 forage cap-$.95$^{1/2}$, 1 wool jacket-$2.66, 2 pr. overalls-$4.56, 1 pr. shoes-$1.22, 4 pr. socks-$.98, 1 overcoat-$6.93$^{1/2}$; pres. 12/1847, pay stopped for: 1 pr. socks-$.24$^{1/2}$, 1 blanket-$2.22, 1 pr. shoes-$1.22, 1 pr. overalls-$2.28, 1 flannel shirt-$.90, 1 pr. drawers-$.35$^{1/2}$; pres. 04/1848; pres. 07/1848, pay stopped for: 1 pr. shoes-$1.16; BLW sent to Staunton, VA

**Johnson, Samuel**, Pvt., LIC; b. Ireland; enl. Mex. War service 12/07/1846 Staunton, VA, age 22; sick 08/1847; pres. 10/1847, pay stopped for: 1 forage cap-$.95$^{1/2}$, 1 wool jacket-$2.66, 1 pr. overalls-$2.28, 2 pr. shoes-$2.44, 3 pr. socks-$.73$^{1/2}$, 4 cotton shirts-$1.72, 1 pr. drawers-$.35$^{1/2}$; pres. 12/1847, pay stopped for: 1 pr. shoes-$1.22, 1 pr. overalls-$2.28; pres. 04/1848;

# VIRGINIA VOLUNTEERS IN MEXICO

pres. 07/1848, pay stopped for: 1 wiper-$.20; BLW sent to Staunton, VA; c. 1860 res. Augusta Co., VA, age 34, occ. Gardner at Western Lunatic Asylum.[1093]

**Johnson, Vincent**, Pvt., *Recruit Co.*; b. 03/18/1830, son of Jonathan & Margaret Johnson; enl. Mex. War service 03/??/1848 Wytheville, VA; pres. 06/1848; BLW sent to Wytheville, VA; Civil War service enl. as Pvt., Co. I, 8$^{th}$ Va. Cav. 05/27/1861 Kanawha Falls, Fayette Co., VA, paroled 06/26/1865 at Charleston, WV, age 33;[450] c. 1850 res. Fayette Co., VA, age 20;[1094] c. 1860 res. Fayetteville, Fayette Co., WV;[1095] d. 08/02/1902, bur. Johnson Family Cem., Oak Hill, Fayette Co., WV.][1096]

**Johnson, William H.**, Pvt., Co. M; enl. Mex. War service 11/17/1847, Norfolk, VA, age 18; pres. 11/1847; pres. 12/1847; pres. 02/1848; sick 04/1848; d. 05/09/1848 at Saltillo, Mex.

**Johnson, William R.**, Pvt., *Preston's Co.*; enl. Mex. War service 01/04/1847 Montgomery Co., VA, age 22; pres. 04/1847, pay stopped for: 1 gun sling; pres. 06/1847; absent 08/1847 on detached service in the QM Dept., to receive an additional $25 in addition to his pay as a soldier; absent 10/1847, on detached service in QM Dept., pay stopped for: 1 blanket-$2.22, 1 cap-$.95$^{1/2}$; absent 12/1847, on detached service as Wagoneer in QM Dept. since 12/11/1847, pay stopped for: 1 pr. overalls-$2.28, 1 pr. shoes-$1.22; pres. 02/1848; in confinement 04/1848; pres. 07/1848, pay stopped for: 1 waist belt-$.25, 1 waist belt plate-$.08, 1 brush & pick-$.12, 1 jacket-$2.37, 1 gun sling-$.18; BLW sent to Rocky Mount, VA

**Johnstone, James Henry**, Pvt., Co. D; b. 03/1830, Washington, D.C.;[1097] enl. Mex. War service 01/06/1847, Petersburg, VA, age 18; pres. 02/1847; pres. 04/1847; pres. 06/1847, pay stopped for: 1 bayonet scabbard w/ frog, white waist belt & plate complete, *"lost through negligence"* 03/17/1847; pres. 08/1847, pay stopped for: 1 pr. shoes-$1.22; pres. 10/1847, pay stopped for: 1 cap-$.95$^{1/2}$, 1 jacket-$2.66, 1 pr. pants-$2.28, 1 pr. drawers-$.35$^{1/2}$, 2 pr. socks-$.49, 1 pr. shoes-$1.22, 1 blanket-$2.22; Court-martialed 11/10/1847 Buena Vista, Mex. *Charge Sleeping on Post: Specification: That he the said Private James H. Johnson, Co. D, Va. Regt., did on the night of the 4$^{th}$ of November 1847, lay down and go to sleep on his post, he the said Private James H. Johnson, then and there being a sentinel and on the line of sentinels of the Virginia Regt. of Volunteers at Buena Vista, Mexico, and stationed on post No. 6. To which charge the prisoner plead Guilty. Sentenced to two months police in his company. The court was lenient in consideration of his extreme youth and delicate health.*[1098] in confinement 12/1847, pay stopped for: 1 blanket-$2.22; pres. 04/1848, pay stopped for: 1 set of picks & brushes-$.12, 1 cap-$.95$^{1/2}$, 1 pr. pants-$2.28; pres. 08/1847, BLW sent to Petersburg, VA; d. 05/10/1856, *"member associated volunteers of Petersburg, body accompanied to cemetery Petersburg by volunteers;"* bur. Blandford Cem., Sq. 8, Sec. 13, Ward I, Petersburg, VA[1099]

**Joiner, William M.**, [aka Joyner, William M.] Pvt., Co. F; enl. Mex. War service 12/24/1846, Portsmouth, VA, age 18; d. 02/16/1847 Fort Monroe, VA; wid. Eliza, WA #7778, 03/11/1889, from VA; [pension file not found].

**Jones, Benson W.**, Pvt., *Preston's Co.*; enl. Mex. War service 01/12/1847 Lynchburg, VA, age 25; pres. 04/1847; absent 06/1847 sick in hosp. at Saltillo, Mex. since 06/27/1847; pres. 08/1847; pres. 10/1847, pay stopped for: 1 pr. socks-$.24$^{1/2}$, 1 cotton shirt-$.43; pres. 12/1847, pay stopped for: 1 jacket-$2.66, 1 pr. overalls-$2.28, 1 pr. shoes-$1.22, 2 pr. socks-$.49, 1 cap-$.95$^{1/2}$, 1 pr. drawers-$.35$^{1/2}$, 1 blankets-$2.22; pres. 02/1848; pres. 04/1848, pay stopped for: 1 pick & brush-$.12; pres. 07/1848, pay stopped for: 1 brush & pick-$.12, 1 gun sling-$.18, 1 screw driver-$.07, 1 wiper-$.13; BLW sent to Lynchburg, VA

**Jones, Charles R.**, Pvt., Co. I; b. Campbell Co., VA;[1100] enl. Mex. War service 01/10/1847 Lynchburg, VA, age 20; phys. desc. 5'10", blue eyes, brown hair, sallow complexion, occ. Sexton;[1100] pres. 02/1847; absent 04/1847, left sick at China, Mex. 04/17/1847; pres. 06/1847; pres. 08/1847; pres. 10/1847, pay stopped for: 3 flannel shirts-$2.70, 2 cotton shirts-$.86, 3 pr. drawers-$1.06$^{1/2}$, 2 pr. shoes-$2.44, 1 pr. socks-$.24$^{1/2}$, 1 pr. pants-$2.28, 1 cap- $.95$^{1/2}$, 1 overcoat-$6.93$^{1/2}$, 1 jacket-$2.66; pres. 12/1847, pay stopped for: 1 pr. socks-$.24$^{1/2}$, 1 blanket-$2.22, 1 flannel shirt-$.90; pres. 02/1848; pres. 04/1848; pres. 08/1848, BLW sent to

## OFF TO WAR

Lynchburg, VA; enl. Pvt., Co. F, U.S. Mounted Rifles, 09/10/1850 Richmond, VA, trans. 10/24/1851 Carlisle Barracks, Pa., discharged 09/10/1855, Ft. Merrill, TX;[1100] m/1 Bettie F. Anderson, 01/29/1865, Lynchburg, Campbell Co., VA, (BAJ d. 12/11/1890, 1217 W. Marshall St., Richmond, VA, bur. Hollywood Cemetery, Richmond, VA);[1100] SC #8917, 02/24/1887, filed from 1217 W. Marshall St., Richmond, Henrico Co., VA; m/2 Virginia "Jennie" Harper, 03/13/1895, Richmond, Henrico Co., VA;[1100] d. 12/22/1899;[1101] wid. Jennie V., WC #12246, 05/31/1900, filed from 1100 W. Marshall St., Richmond, Henrico Co., VA; (JHJ b. 01/10/1868, King William Co., VA, d. 06/27/1911, Richmond, Henrico Co., VA, bur. Riverview Cemetery, Richmond, VA).[1101]

**Jones, Edward W.**, Pvt., Co. M; enl. Mex. War service 08/29/1847, Forksville, VA, age 34; pres. 10/1847; pres. 11/1847; pres. 12/1847; pres. 02/1848, pay stopped for: 1 pr. shoes-$1.22; pres. 04/1848; pres. 08/1848, pay stopped for: 1 cartridge box-$1.10, 1 cartridge box belt plate-$.10; BLW sent to Walsborow, Newnanburg, VA; wid. Lucy A., WA #19016, 05/06/1908, from KY; [pension file not found].

**Jones, George**, Pvt., Co. C; enl. Mex. War service 12/30/1846, Bowling Green, VA, age 19; deserted 01/12/1847 Fort Monroe, VA

**Jones, John A.**, Co. A; enl. Mex. War service 12/07/1846 Richmond, VA, age 25; pres. 12/1846 - 04/1847; deserted 06/20/1847 at Monterey, Mex.; returned to company at Buena Vista 07/01/1847; pres. 08/1847; 10/1847 pres. pay stopped for clothing: 2 cotton shirts-$.86, 1 pr. wool overalls-$2.28, 4 pr. stockings-$.98, 1 wool jacket-$2.66, 1 cap-$.95$^{1/2}$, 2 pr. drawers-$.71, 1 pr. shoes-$1.22, 1 great coat-$6.93$^{1/2}$; AWOL since morning of December 31, 1847; pres. 02/1848, pay stopped for: 1 pr. shoes-$1.22; 1 pr. wool overalls-$2.28, 2 flannel shirts-$1.80, 1 cotton shirt-$.43, 1 pr. drawers-$.35$^{1/2}$, 1 blanket-$2.22, 1 pr. socks-$.24$^{1/2}$; pres. 04/1848; BLW sent to Hampton, VA; SC #12800, 10/14/1887, from GA; [see Civil War pension claim].

**Jones, John J.**, Fifer, Co. B; enl. 12/21/1846, Richmond, VA, age 21; pres. 06/1847; pres. 08/1847; pres. 10/1847, pay stopped for: 1 pr. overalls-$2.28, 3 flannel shirts-$2.70, 3 pr. socks-$.73$^{1/2}$, 2 pr. cotton drawers-$.71, 1 pr. shoes-$1.22, 1 blanket-$2.22; pres. 12/1847, fined 1 mos. pay by order (129) of genl. court-martial, pay stopped for: 1 pr. shoes-$1.22, 2 pr. socks-$.49; pres. 02/1848; pres. 04/1848 pres. 08/1848, pay stopped for 1 gun sling-$.16, 1 pr. shoes-$1.16, BLW sent to Alexandria, VA c/o Capt. Corse.

**Jones, John**, Pvt., Co. H; enl. Mex. War service 01/06/1847, Berkeley, VA, age 18; pres. 04/1847; pres. 06/1847; discharged 08/09/1847 Buena Vista, Mex. by order of Sec. of War.

**Jones, Joseph N.**, Pvt., Co. K; b. 01/20/1821, Washington Co., MD;[1102] enl. Mex. War service Jefferson Co., VA 12/12/1846, age 25; pres. 06/1847, reduced to ranks from 3$^{rd}$ Cpl.; pres. 06/1847; pres. 08/1847, to forfeit 1 mos. pay by order of garrison court-martial; pres. 10/1847, pay stopped for: 2 pr. drawers-$.71, 3 cotton shirts-$1.29, 1 pr. shoes-$1.22, 2 flannel shirts-$1.80, 1 pr. overalls-$2.28, 1 cap-$.95$^{1/2}$; pres. 12/1847, pay stopped for: 1 jacket-$2.66, 1 pr. overalls-$2.28, 2 pr. boots-$2.44, 2 pr. drawers-$.71, 1 blanket-$2.22; pres. 04/1848, pay stopped for: 1 pick & brush-$.12, 1 gun sling-$.18; pres. 07/1848, pay stopped for: 1 screw driver-$.25; BLW sent to Shepherdstown, Jefferson Co., VA; m/1 Harriet _____, date/place unknown;[1102] c. 1850 a Joseph Jones, age 27, res. Shepherdstown, Jefferson Co., VA, w. Harriet Jones (23);[1103] m/2 Mary Black 11/14/1856, West Alexandria, Preble Co., OH;[1102] SC #2848, 01/28/1887, filed from West Florence, Preble Co., OH; phys. desc. age 64 [1886], 5'9$^{3/4}$", light complexion, auburn hair, blue eyes, occ. Tailor;[1102] since discharge res. Jefferson Co., VA until the spring of 1856 when he moved to Preble Co., OH;[1102] m/3 Elizabeth _____, 09/26/1895, Eaton, Preble Co., OH;[1102] d. 03/11/1900, Eaton, Preble Co., OH, at the home of his dau. Mrs. Ellia Ruppy.[1102]

**Jones, Richard**, Pvt., Co. B; enl. 12/01/1846, Alexandria, VA, age 37; pres. 06/1847; pres. 08/1847; pres. 10/1847, pay stopped for: 1 pr. overalls-$2.28, 2 pr. shoes-$2.44, 2 pr. socks-$.49, 2 cotton shirts-$.86, 1 overcoat-$ 6.93$^{1/2}$; sick 12/1847, pay stopped for: 2 pr. cotton

VIRGINIA VOLUNTEERS IN MEXICO

drawers-$.71, 1 pr. shoes-$1.22, 1 blanket-$2.22; 1 pr. socks-$.24$^{1/2}$; pres. 02/1848; pres. 04/1848, pres. 08/1848, pay stopped for: 1 wiper-$.20, 1 gun sling-$.16, BLW sent to Norfolk, VA; [c. 1850 a Richard Jones res. Norfolk Co., VA, age 37, occ. Laborer, w. Jane (21).][1104]
**Jones, Richard**, Pvt., Co. I; enl. Mex. War service 01/10/1847 Lynchburg, VA, age 18; pres. 02/1847; pres. 04/1847; pres. 06/1847; pres. 08/1847; pres. 10/1847, pay stopped for: 3 cotton shirts-$1.29, 3 pr. drawers-$1.06$^{1/2}$, 1 cap- $.95$^{1/2}$, 1 pr. socks-$.24$^{1/2}$, 1 pr. shoes-$1.22, 1 pr. pants-$2.28; pres. 12/1847, pay stopped for: 1 jacket-$2.66, 1 pr. pants-$2.28, 1 blanket-$2.22, 1 cotton shirt-$.43; pres. 02/1848; pres. 04/1848; pres. 08/1848, pay stopped for: 1 wiper-$.20, BLW sent to Liberty, VA
**Jones, Sparrell**, 4$^{th}$ Cpl., Co. F; enl. Mex. War service 12/13/1846, Portsmouth, VA, age 20; pres. 06/1847; pres. 08/1847; pres. 10/1847, pay stopped for:1 pr. overalls-$2.28, 2 pr. drawers-$.71, 1 cotton shirt-$.43, 2 pr. socks-$.49, 1 pr. shoes-$1.22; pres. 02/1848, pay stopped for: 1 blanket-$2.22; pres. 04/1848, prom. 04/01/1848 4$^{th}$ Cpl.; pres. 08/1848, pay stopped for: 1 forage cap-$.83, 1 pr. shoes-$1.16, BLW sent to Portsmouth, VA c/o E.T. Blamire.
**Jones, Thomas R.**, Pvt., Co. M; m/1 Parthenia Woody, (PWJ d. 1842, Richmond, VA);[1105] enl. Mex. War service 08/01/1847, Richmond, VA, age 27; pres. 09/1847; pres. 11/1847; pres. 12/1847; pres. 02/1848; pres. 04/1848, pay stopped for: 1 pr. shoes-$1.22; pres. 08/1848, pay stopped for: 1 gun sling-$.16; BLW sent to Richmond, VA; m/2 Mary Ann Franklin, 11/25/1849, Richmond, Henrico Co., VA;[1105] d. 04/23/1874, *"heart disease,"* Richmond, VA;[1105] *"Died suddenly of heart disease at his residence, Union Hill, corner twenty-seventh and P streets, Mr. Thomas R. Jones aged fifty five years. He leaves a wife and five children and many friends to mourn their loss. His funeral will take place from St. John's Church today (Friday) at 4 o'clock P.M. Philadelphia and St. Louis papers please copy;"*[1105] wid. Mary A., WC #3355, 03/12/1887, filed from 920 27$^{th}$ St., cor. of P, Richmond, Henrico Co., VA; (MFJ b. 07/03/1825, Henrico Co., VA, d. 09/06/1904).[1105]
**Jones, William A.**, *"Cottonhead Billy,"* Co. G; b. c. 1831, Amherst Co., VA;[1106] enl. Mex. War service 09/27/1847 Petersburg, VA, age 18; pres. 02/1848, pay stopped for: 1 pr. pants-$2.22; pres. 04/1848; c. 1850 res. Lunenburg Co., VA, age 25, occ. Shoemaker, enumerated with Mathias Boyd;[1107]m. Rebecca Johnson, Lunenburg Co., VA; c. 1860 res. Pleasant Grove, Lunenburg Co., VA, age 35, occ. Shoemaker, w. R.S (24), Mary F. (7);[1108] (SA #25371, 11/06/1903, filed from Trix, Lunenburg Co., VA; since discharge res. Brunswick and Lunenburg Cos., VA; *"I, William A. Jones, a private in the 1$^{st}$ Regiment Virginia Volunteers in the Mexican War, do make the following affidavit, that I was generally called by the nick name 'Cottonhead Bill Jones' by the soldiers in the Mexican War;"*[1106] before enlistment res. Charlottesville, Albemarle Co., VA, occ. Shoemaker; phys. desc. 5'7", 150 lbs., fair complexion, grayish blue eyes, black hair when young, now gray;[1106] William T. Clark and Parks E. Ashworth gave affidavits in pension claim;[1106] d. 12/1910, Lunenburg Co., VA *before* pension claim was approved.[1106]
**Jordan, Alexander**, Pvt., Co. D; enl. Mex. War service 12/30/1846, Petersburg, VA, age 30; pres. 02/1847; pres. 04/1847; absent 06/1847 left sick in Hosp. Monterey, Mex. 06/22/1847; discharged 07/28/1847 Buena Vista, Mex. on Surgeon's Certificate of Disability; an Alexander G. Jordan, of Prince George Co., m. Euginia B.C. Hatch, of Prince George Co., 12/1856.[1109]
**Judkins, William N.B.**, 4$^{th}$ Cpl., Co. E; b. c. 1823; enl. Mex. War service 12/01/1846 Petersburg, VA, age 23; pres. 04/1847; pres. 06/1847; pres. 08/1847; pres. 10/1847, pay stopped for: 1 pr. overalls-$2.28, 2 pr. shoes-$2.44, 2 pr. stockings-$.49, 2 cotton shirts-$.86, 1 cap-$.95$^{1/2}$; absent sick 12/1847, pay stopped for: 2 pr. socks-$.49, 2 pr. drawers-$.71, 1 blanket-$2.22; pres. 02/1848, prom. 4$^{th}$ Cpl. 02/24/1848, pay stopped for: 1 pr. pants-$2.28, 1 pr. shoes-$1.22, 1 jacket-$2.66; pres. 04/1848; m. Mary A. Watson, 03/26/1851, Petersburg, VA;[1110] Civil War service enl. 1$^{st}$ Sgt., Co. D, 18$^{th}$ Va. Inf., 04/24/1861; desc. age 38, occ. Clerk, 5'10", grey eyes, brown hair, sallow complex.; discharged 12/14/1861, because of *"stricture*

189

OFF TO WAR

*of urethra;"*[1111] enl. Pvt., Co. E, 25th Btln. Va. Inf. 11/01/1863 for war at Richmond, VA, substitute for T.T. Adams of Pittsylvania Co., VA, admitted Camp Jackson Hosp., Richmond, 03/20/1864, *"stricture of urethra,"* absent sick 04/01/1864 at Camp Jackson Hosp. trans. 04/07/1864 Chimborazo Hosp., trans. 05/05/1864 Hosp. Farmville, VA, returned to duty 08/16/1864, admitted Chimborazo Hosp. #3, *"stricture of urethra,"* pres. 10/31/1864, listed as deserter 11/21/1864;[1110] *"Our regiment was stationed at Chaffin's Farm in front of Ft. Harrison. W.N.B. Judkins was on picket previous to his disappearance. Whether he was captured or deserted I know not;"*[1112] wid. Mary A., WC #5675, 05/21/1888, filed from Hickory, Catawba Co., NC; pension brief states William Judkins *"missing since 1864, death presumed."*[1110]

**Karp, Peter**, Pvt., LIC; enl. Mex. War service 01/19/1847 Ft. Monroe, VA, age 19; pres. 08/1847; deserted 09/05/1847 from provost guard, pay stopped for: 1 forage cap-$.95$^{1/2}$, 1 wool jacket-$2.66, 1 pr. overalls-$2.28, 1 pr. shoes-$1.22, 2 pr. socks-$.49, 2 cotton shirts-$.86; to forfeit 1 mos. pay by sentence of court-martial; Court-martialed 11/23/1847 Buena Vista, Mex. *Charge #1 Desertion; Specification: In this that he, Private Peter Karp, of the Lt. Infty. Co., Va. Regt. of Vols. Being in confinement in the Provost Guard and under sentence of a Genl. Court-martial, did desert the service of the United States, on or about the 5$^{th}$ day of October 1847, and did remain away until he was brought back under guard from some place beyond Monterey on or about the 13$^{th}$ day of November 1847. This at the camp near Buena Vista, Mexico. Charge #2: Conduct to the Prejudice of Good Order and Military Discipline. Specification: In this that he, Private Peter Karp, of Co. and Regt. aforesaid whilst a prisoner in the Provost Guard at the camp Buena Vista, did break his arrest and desert the service of the United States, on or about the 5$^{th}$ day of October 1847. To which the prisoner pleaded: Not Guilty to the first charge and specification and Guilty to the second charge and specification. Sentenced: To forfeit his pay proper and to be confined in charge of the Provost Guard with a ball and chain attached to his leg and be kept at hard labor during the continuance of the war with Mexico and then to be dishonorably discharged from the service;"*[1113] pres. 12/1847 in confinement, pay stopped for: 2 forage caps-$1.91, 1 wool jacket-$2.66, 2 pr. overalls-$4.56, 2 pr. shoes-$2.44, 2 pr. socks-$.49, 2 cotton shirts-$.86, 2 flannel shirts-$1.80; absent 04/1848 confined in the provost guard in Buena Vista, Mex.; pres. 07/1848, to be dishonorably discharged; BLW sent to Staunton, VA; c. 1850 res. Old Point Comfort, Elizabeth City Co., VA, age 25, occ. Ordnance, b. Germany, w. Elizabeth (23), son John (2).[1114]

**Keefe, John William**, 1$^{St}$ Cpl., Co. H; b. 07/06/1828, Berkeley Co., VA;[1115] enl. Mex. War service 11/21/1846, Berkeley, VA, age 18; pres. 04/1847, reduced to ranks from drummer 01/27/1847; pres. 06/1847, prom. 3$^{rd}$ Cpl.; pres. 08/1847; pres. 10/1847, pay stopped for: 1 forage cap-$.95$^{1/2}$, 1 pr. pants-$2.28, 2 flannel shirts-$1.80, 1 pr. drawers-$.35$^{1/2}$, 1 pr. shoes-$1.22, 3 pr. socks-$.73$^{1/2}$, 1 jacket-$2.66; pres. 12/1847, pay stopped for: 1 pr. shoes-$1.22, 1 pr. pants-$2.28, 1 flannel shirt-$.90, 1 pr. drawers-$.35$^{1/2}$; pres. 02/1848; pres. 04/1848, prom. 1$^{st}$ Cpl.; pres. 07/1848, pay stopped for: 1 wiper-$.20, BLW sent to Martinsburg, VA; m. Sarah Frances Leathers 03/29/1852 Berkeley Co., VA;[1116, 1117] Civil War service Pvt., Co. D, 2$^{nd}$ Va. Inf., 11/01/1862, Winchester, VA; desc. 5'8$^{1/2}$", muddy complex., blue eyes, dark hair, res. Berkeley Co.; wded. Chancellorsville, VA, 05/03/1863; pres. again 07/1863; charged $12.86 for lost ordinance 12/1863; captured 05/12/1864 Spotsylvania C.H.; sent to Pt. Lookout, MD then to Elmira, N.Y.; took oath 02/20/1865;[387] c. 1880, res. Martinsburg, Berkeley Co., WV, age 52, occ. none listed, w. Sarah (46) keeping house, son Hugh (28) Brakeman on RR, son George (26) Brakeman on RR, dau. Maggie (18), son Artie (13), dau. Annie (10), son Charles (8), dau. Martha (3);[1118] SC #19614, 04/16/1890, filed from Martinsburg, Berkeley Co., WV; states disability occurred *"while in the service of the Baltimore & Ohio R.R. Company by being squeezed between Locomotive tenders;"*[1115] Lists children Hugh Keefe, b. 04/22/1852, Margaret Keefe, b. 04/14/1860, Artie Keefe, b. 02/28/1866, John Keefe, b. 06/09/1858, Charles Keefe, b. 11/15/1871, Martha Keefe, b.

## VIRGINIA VOLUNTEERS IN MEXICO

11/10/1877;[1115] Edward W. Maxwell gave affidavit in pension claim;[1115] *"Mr. John W. Keef* [sic] *is and has been a sober, worthy and industrious man."*[1119] d. 07/21/1903, *"diarrhea & paralysis, age 77, at his house on John St., Martinsburg, W.VA;"*[1116, 1120] bur. Greenhill Cem., Martinsburg, WV;[1121] wid. Sarah F., WC #13660, 10/24/1903, filed from 301 S. Maple Avenue, Martinsburg, Berkeley Co., WV; (SLK b. 07/11/1832, Middleway, Jefferson Co., VA, d. 02/12/1914).[1116]

**Keeling, Robert Henry,** 2$^{nd}$ Lt., Co. I; b. 1823, Richmond, VA, son of Rev. Henry Keeling; VMI graduate Class of 1846; enl. Mex. War service 11/15/1846 Richmond, VA, age 27; pres. 02/1847; pres. 04/1847, commanding the co. since 04/29/1847; pres. 06/1847; pres. 08/1847; pres. 10/1847; pres. 12/1847; absent 02/1848 on detached service in QM Dept.; absent 04/1848 on duty as Provost Marshal; pres. 08/1848; helped organize approx. 80 men in the Charles Town Mining Co. in the Spring of 1849 and served as their commander on the overland journey from Jefferson Co., VA to Sacramento, Calif. 1849-1850.;[760] educator in Tuskeegee, AL; m. Caroline Salmons, 10/24/1848, Goochland Co., VA;[1122] Civil War service Capt., 13th Ala Inf.; d. 1862 in battle at Seven Pines.

***Keilholtz, John,*** Pvt., Co. B; enl. 12/19/1846, Richmond, VA, age 36; discharged 04/02/1847 Camargo, Mex. on Surgeon's Certificate of Disability.

**Keister, George A.,[Alva?]** 1$^{st}$ Cpl., *Preston's Co.,* b. 02/06/1825, Montgomery Co., VA;[1123] [son of Jacob & Margaret (Bolton) Keister of Giles Co., VA?]; enl. Mex. War service 11/24/1846 Montgomery Co., VA, age 21; pres. 04/1847; pres. 06/1847; pres. 08/1847, prom. 1$^{st}$ Cpl. from 2$^{nd}$ Cpl.; pres. 10/1847, pay stopped for: 1 pr. overalls-$2.28, 1 pr. shoes-$1.22, 2 pr. socks-$.49, 2 cotton shirts-$.86, 1 cap-$.95$^{1/2}$; sick 12/1847, pay stopped for: 1 blanket-$2.22; pres. 02/1848, pay stopped for: 1 pr. shoes-$1.22, 1 pr. overalls-$2.28; pres. 04/1848; pres. 07/1848; BLW sent to Christiansburg, VA c/o Fleming Gardner; c. 1850 res. Montgomery Co., VA, age 23, occ. Peddlar;[1124] m. Sarah Jane Virginia Stewart, 11/20/1852, Montgomery Co., VA;[1123, 1125] [Civil War service a George Keister enl. Pvt., Co. C, 19$^{th}$ Va. Cav., 03/15/1863, Frankfort, Greenbrier Co., VA; NFR;] SC #17775, 01/21/1889, filed from Wichita, Sedgwick Co., KS; phys. desc. at enl. age 22, 5'7", fair complexion, light hair, blue eyes;[1123] Michael Kipps gave affidavit in pension claim;[1123] d. 12/22/1891, *"bronchitis,"* Wichita, KS; wid. Sarah J.V., WC #7935, 02/02/1892, filed from Wichita, Sedgwick Co., KS;[1126] OW W #24608; (SSJ b. 08/27/1831, Roanoke Co., VA, d. 04/19/1904, Wichita, KS, bur. Highland Cem., Blk. 2, Lot 162, #9, Wichita, KS).[1126]

**Keiter, Isaac,** Pvt., Co. C; enl. Mex. War service 12/30/1846, Bowling Green, VA, age 21; pres. 06/1847, prom. 1$^{st}$ Cpl. 06/16/1847; pres. 08/1847, prom. 4$^{th}$ Sgt. 08/25/1847, pay stopped for: 1 cap-$.95$^{1/2}$, 2 pr. socks-$.49, 2 cotton shirts-$.86, 2 woolen shirts-$1.80, 1 pr. overalls-$2.28, 1 knapsack & straps-$1.10; pres. 10/1847, pay stopped for: 4 pr. socks-$.98, 2 pr. drawers-$.71, 1 cotton shirt-$.43, 1 woolen shirt-$.90, 1 pr. shoes-$1.22, 1 blanket-$2.22; pres. 12/1847, reduced to ranks from 4$^{th}$ Sgt. 12/16/1847, pay stopped for: 1 cap-$.95$^{1/2}$, 1 pr. pants-$2.28, 1 blanket-$2.22; pres. 04/1848, pay stopped for: [illegible], 1 india rubber canteen-$.27; pres. 08/1848, BLW sent to Philadelphia, Pa.

**Kellam, James S.,** 2$^{nd}$ Lt., Co. I; b. 03/26/1824, Downing's Wharf, Northampton Co., VA; enl. Mex. War service 01/01/1847 Richmond, VA, age 22; pres. 02/1847; pres. 04/1847; pres. 06/1847, prom. 1$^{st}$ Cpl.; pres. 08/1847, reduced from Cpl. 07/10/1847 (regtl. order #62); pres. 10/1847, pay stopped for: 1 flannel shirt-$.90, 2 pr. drawers-$.71,3 cotton shirts-$1.29, 1 pr. pants-$2.28, 1 pr. shoes-$1.22, 1 cap- $.95$^{1/2}$; pres. 04/1848, prom. 2$^{nd}$ Lt. from 3$^{rd}$ Cpl.; pres. 12/1847, prom. 2$^{nd}$ Lt. 11/22/1847; pres. 02/1848; pres. 04/1848; pres. 08/1848, BLW sent to Drummond Town, Accomac Co., VA; c. 1860, res. Northampton Co., VA, age 36; [Civil War service a James S. Kellam served as Capt., 39$^{th}$ Va. Inf. until Regt. was disbanded served as 1$^{st}$ Lt., Co. B/E3, 19$^{th}$ VA Heavy Arty.]; m/1 09/12/1862; m/2 Sarah Doughty, 12/14/1885, Downing's Wharf, Northampton Co., VA;[1127] SC #11412, 09/06/1887, filed Exmore, Northampton Co., VA; occ. Public School Teacher [1887]; since discharge res. in Accomac

191

OFF TO WAR

and Northampton Cos., *"having visited Australia and California during said time;"* d. 07/20/1887, *"acute dysentery,"* near Hadlock, Northampton Co., VA,[1128] *"aged 69 yrs.,"*[1129] bur. Old. Downing Graveyard, Northampton Co., VA; wid. Sarah E., WC #6940, 05/11/1889, filed from Exmore, Northampton Co., VA; Lists one daughter; (SDK b. 08/19/1868, Hog Island, Northampton Co., VA).[1128]

**Kelly, William**, Pvt., Co. L; b. 1817; enl. Mex. War service 03/16/1847 Alexandria, VA, age 30; pres. 06/1847, *"this man reported upon the last muster roll as a deserter has since joined the company having been left by accident at New Orleans;"* pres. 08/1847; pres. 10/1847, pay stopped for: 1 pr. Pants 2.28, 1 F Shirt .90, 1 W Jacket 2.66; sick 12/1847, pay stopped for: 1 cap-$.95$^{1/2}$, 1 pr. shoes-$1.22, 1 flannel shirt-$.90, 1 overcoat-$6.93$^{1/2}$, 1 blanket-$2.22, 2 pr. drawers-$.86, 1 pr. socks-$.24$^{1/2}$; absent 02/1848, sick in Hospital; discharged 04/21/1848 at Saltillo, Mex. on Surgeon's Certificate of Disability.[72]

**Kemper, James Lawson**, Captain, Quartermaster, 1$^{st}$ VA Vol. Inf. Regt., b. 06/11/1823, Madison Co., VA, son of William & Maria E. (Allison) Kemper; grad. Washington College 1852; m. Cremora Conway Cave, 07/04/1853, Madison County, VA; mbr. Board of Visitors, Virginia Military Institute 1856-1858; Pres. VMI 1858; mbr. VA House of Delegates, 1853 - 1862, elected Speaker of the House 1858-1861; Civil War service Col. 7$^{th}$ Va. Inf., 05/02/1861, prom. Brig. Gen. 06/02/1862, led his brigade in "Pickett's Charge" 07/03/1863 and was wded.; Governor of Virginia, 1874-1878; d. 04/07/1895, Orange Co., VA[1130]

**Kendall, William**, 3$^{rd}$ Sgt., Co. K; b. 11/29/1823, Loudoun Co., VA;[1131] enl. Mex. War service Alexandria, VA 12/20/1846, age 23; pres. 06/1847, prom. 4$^{th}$ Cpl. 05/31/1847; pres. 08/1847, prom. 3$^{rd}$ Cpl.; pres. 10/1847, on detached service in provost guard since 09/17/1847, prom. 4$^{th}$ Sgt.; pres. 12/1847, pay stopped for: 1 jacket-$2.66, 2 pr. overalls-$4.56, 1 pr. boots-$1.22, 2 pr. socks-$.49, 2 pr. drawers-$.71, 1 blanket-$2.22, 1 cotton shirt-$.43, 2 flannel shirts-$1.80; pres. 04/1848, prom. 3$^{rd}$ Sgt., pay stopped for: 1 pr. pants-$2.28, 1 pr. shoes-$1.22, 1 pr. drawers-$.35$^{1/2}$, 1 pick & brush-$.12, 1 gun sling-$.18; pres. 07/1848, pay stopped for: 1 bayonet-$1.44, 1 pick & brush-$.12, 1 belt plate-$.10, 1 wiper-$.20; BLW sent to Upperville, Fauquier Co., VA; m. Sarah Catherine Hooper, 03/24/1851, Upperville, Fauquier Co., VA;[1131,] [1132] SC #9258, 02/18/1888, filed from Paris Fauquier Co., VA; phys. desc. age 63 [1887], 5'9", light complexion, blue eyes, grey hair, occ. tanner;[1131] since discharge res. Upperville, VA when he moved to Paris, VA;[1131] lists children John F. Kendall b. 11/14/1854, Mary E. Kendall b. 04/11/1857, Edison L. Kendall b. 07/13/1865;[1131] John W. Gallaher and George A. Porterfield gave affidavits in pension claim;[1131] d. 09/23/1915; bur. Ivy Hill Cemetery, Upperville, VA[45, 1131]

**Kennedy, Charles**, Pvt., Co. L; b. 1819; enl. Mex. War service 04/24/1847 New Orleans, La., age 21; pres. 06/1847; pres. 08/1847; discharged 10/16/1847 at Saltillo, Mex. on Surgeon's Certificate of Disability.[72]

**Kennon, James**, Pvt., Co. I; enl. Mex. War service 02/05/1847 Richmond, VA, age 28; pres. 02/1847; pres. 04/1847; pres. 06/1847; pres. 08/1847; pres. 10/1847, pay stopped for: 2 flannel shirts-$1.80, 3 pr. drawers-$1.06$^{1/2}$, 2 cotton shirts-$.86, 1 pr. socks-$.24$^{1/2}$, 1 pr. pants-$2.28, 1 overcoat-$6.93$^{1/2}$, 1 cap- $.95$^{1/2}$; pres. 12/1847, pay stopped for: 1 pr. pants-$2.28, 1 blanket-$2.22, 1 jacket-$2.66; pres. 02/1848; pres. 04/1848; pres. 08/1848, BLW sent to Richmond, VA

**Kerr, George**, Pvt., Co. L; b. 1823; enl. Mex. War service 03/01/1847 Fairfax C.H., VA, age 24; sick 06/1847; pres. 10/1847, pay stopped for: 1 pr. pants-$2.28; pres. 12/1847, pay stopped for: 1 jacket-$2.66, 1 cap-$.95$^{1/2}$, 2 pr. shoes-$2.44, 2 cotton shirts-$.86, 1 blanket-$2.22, 2 pr. drawers-$.71, 1 pr. socks-$.24$^{1/2}$; pres. 02/1848, pay stopped for: 1 Brush & Pick .12; pres. 04/1848, pay stopped for: 1 pr. Shoes 1.16; pres. 07/1848; BLW sent to George Kerr, Washington City, D.C.

# VIRGINIA VOLUNTEERS IN MEXICO

**Kidd, William E.**, Pvt., Co. G; enl. Mex. War service 12/05/1846 Richmond, VA, age 32; pres. 06/1847; pres. 08/1847; pres. 10/1847, pay stopped for: 1 pr. overalls-$2.28, 2 flannel shirts-$1.90, 3 pr. shoes-$3.66, 3 pr. socks-$.73$^{1/2}$, 1 forage cap-$.95$^{1/2}$; pres. 12/1847, pay stopped for: 1 pr. pants-$2.28, 1 dragoon overcoat-$8.72; pres. 02/1848; pres. 04/1848; pres. 08/1848, pay stopped for: 1 gun sling-$.16, 1 wiper-$.20; BLW sent to Richmond, VA
**Kidd, William**, Pvt., Co. I; enl. Mex. War service 02/05/1847 Richmond, VA, age 28; pres. 02/1847; absent 04/1847, left sick at Camargo, Mex. 04/04/1847; pres. 06/1847; pres. 08/1847; pres. 10/1847, pay stopped for: 2 flannel shirts-$1.80, 3 cotton shirts-$1.29, 1 pr. socks-$.24$^{1/2}$, 1 blanket-$2.22, 1 cap- $.95$^{1/2}$, 1 pr. pants-$2.28, 1 jacket-$2.66; pres. 12/1847, pay stopped for: 1 pr. socks-$.24$^{1/2}$, 1 pr. shoes-$1.22, 1 pr. drawers-$.35$^{1/2}$; pres. 02/1848, pay stopped for: 1 pr. overalls-$2.28; pres. 08/1848, BLW sent to Richmond, VA
**Kile, George W.**, Pvt., Co. K; b. 03/14/1827; enl. Mex. War service Jefferson Co., VA 01/02/1847, age 24; pres. 06/1847; pres. 08/1847; pres. 10/1847, pay stopped for: 2 pr. overalls-$4.56, 2 cotton shirts-$.86, 3 pr. socks-$.73$^{1/2}$, 2 pr. drawers-$.71, 1 pr. shoes-$1.22, 2 flannel shirts-$1.80, 1 cap-$.95$^{1/2}$; pres. 12/1847, pay stopped for: 1 jacket-$2.66, 1 pr. overalls-$2.28, 1 pr. boots-$1.22, 2 pr. socks-$.49, 2 pr. drawers-$.71; pres. 04/1848, pay stopped for: 1 pr. shoes-$1.22, 1 pr. shoes-$1.50; pres. 07/1848, pay stopped for: 1 screw driver-$.25, 1 wiper-$.20; BLW sent to Charlestown, Jefferson Co., VA; c. 1850 res. Doddridge Co., VA, age 23, occ. Farmer, w. Sarah (20), dau. Elizabeth;[1133] Civil War service Pvt., Co. C, 46th Regt. VA Militia (Pendleton County), C.S.A., enl. 11/14/1861;[202] d. 06/11/1913, bur. Underwood Cem., Ashley, Doddridge Co., WV (5 of their children are buried here as well).[45]
**Kindley, William**, Pvt., Co. H; enl. Mex. War service 01/08/1847, Berkeley, VA, age 22; pres. 04/1847; pres. 06/1847; pres. 08/1847; pres. 10/1847, pay stopped for: 2 flannel shirts-$1.80, 1 pr. drawers-$.35$^{1/2}$; pres. 12/1847, pay stopped for: 1 pr. shoes-$1.22, 1 pr. pants-$2.28, 1 pr. socks-$.24$^{1/2}$; pres. 02/1848, pay stopped for: 1 jacket-$2.66, 1 pr. socks-$.24$^{1/2}$; pres. 04/1848; pres. 07/1848, pay stopped for: 1 wiper-$.20, BLW sent to Philadelphia, Pa.
**King, John**, Pvt., *Recruit Co.*, enl. Mex. War service 02/13/1848 Charlestown, VA; pres. 06/1848; BLW sent to Charlestown, Jefferson Co., VA [the name John King appears on the Confederate Monument in Elmwood Cem., Charles Town, WV as having served in Co. H, 2nd Va. Inf., no other record].
**King, John H.**, Pvt., Co. A; enl. Mex. War service 11/18/1846 Richmond, VA, age 20; pres. until sick 04/1847, in hosp. at Matamoros sent there from Camargo, Mex. 04/02/1847; discharged 06/02/1847 for disease by order of Maj. Gen. Taylor; wid. Mary A., WC #3641, 04/22/1887, from MS; **Pension File Not Found.**
**King, Thomas F.**, Pvt., Co. G; enl. Mex. War service 12/11/1846 Richmond, VA, age 18; pres. 06/1847; dishonorably discharged 08/16/1847 Buena Vista, Mex., Brig. Gen. C. Cushing made the following remarks, *"My Dear Colonel, It is the desire of the General Commanding that Private Thomas King, of your Regiment, should be required to leave the Camp immediately so as to incur no danger of his being a subject of disorderly sympathy this night."*[1134]
**Kinney, Robert Henry**, 1st Lt., LIC; m. Rebecca R. Wayland, 05/20/1841, Augusta Co., VA;[1135] enl. Mex. War service 11/27/1846 Staunton, VA; rejoined co. 05/07/1847 having been detached as military engineer; suffered a hernia injury on the march for China to Buena Vista, Mexico. As a consequence of which he wrote to Col. Hamtramck on 06/10/1847 requesting he be reassigned to recruiting duty in order *"...to get myself all right again, in two or three months;"*[1136] absent 06/1847, on recruiting service in US, absent 08/1847 on recruiting service; absent 10/1847 on recruiting service; absent 12/1847 on recruiting service; absent 04/1848 on recruiting service; pres. 07/1848, returned to company 07/23/1848; c. 1850 res. Augusta Co., VA, age 30, occ. Engineer, w. Rebecca R. (25), dau. Elizabeth C. (7), son Lewis N. (5), dau. Mary A. (3), son Charles P. (1).[1137]

## OFF TO WAR

**Kisner, Ashford**, Pvt., *Recruit Co.*, b. 01/12/1828 enl. Mex. War service 04/01/1848 Charlestown, VA; pres. 06/1848; BLW sent to Yellow Spring, Hampshire Co., VA; c. 1850 res. Mineral Co., VA, age 22, occ. Laborer;[1138] m. Calista Ann Reasoner, 05/08/1856, Blackford, Ind.; c. 1860 res. Pettis Co. Mo.; c. 1880 res. Missouri, son Lorenzo (22) born Ind., son William (21) born Ind., son Charles (20) born Mo., John M. (18) born Mo., son Francis A. (16) born Mo., son Robert A. (14) born Mo., dau. Evelena (10) born Mo., son Benoma (8) born Mo., dau. Roda A. (6) born Mo., son Eddie L. (5) born Mo., dau. Minnie M. (2) born Mo.; d. 10/7/1896, Butler, Bates Co., Mo.

**Kipps, Michael**, Pvt., *Preston's Co.*, b. 05/25/1825, Montgomery Co., VA, son of John & Mary Kipps;[1139, 1140] enl. Mex. War service 12/06/1846 Montgomery Co., VA, age 21; pres. 04/1847; pres. 06/1847; pres. 08/1847; pres. 10/1847, pay stopped for: 1 pr. overalls-$2.28, 1 pr. shoes-$1.22, 3 pr. socks-$.73$^{1/2}$, 1 flannel shirt-$.90, 1 cotton shirt-$.43, 1 pr. drawers-$.35$^{1/2}$, 1 cap-$.95$^{1/2}$; absent 12/1847, on detached service as Wagoneer in QM Dept. since 12/11/1847, pay stopped for: 1 jacket-$2.66, 1 pr. shoes-$1.22, 2 pr. socks-$.49, 1 blanket-$2.22; absent 02/1848 on detached service as a Teamster in QM Dept., pay stopped for: 1 pr. shoes-$1.22, 1 pr. overalls-$2.28; pres. 04/1848; pres. 07/1848, pay stopped for: 1 screw driver-$.07; BLW sent to Christiansburg, VA c/o Fleming Gardner; m. Mary Elizabeth Linkous, 01/09/1856, Montgomery Co., VA;[1140] c. 1860 res. Matamoras, Montgomery Co., VA, age 35, w. Mary E. (29), son Henry B. (3), Loretta F. (1), mo.? Mary Kipps (62);[1141] SC #10920, 06/03/1887, filed from Blacksburg, Montgomery Co., VA; Charles A. Ronald and John H. Minnick gave affidavits in pension claim;[1139] d. 10/16/1903.[1139]

**Kirk, William**, Pvt., Co. K; enl. Mex. War service Jefferson Co., VA 12/11/1846, age 20; d. 02/14/1847 at Ft. Monroe, VA

**Kisinger, Otho**, Pvt., Co. H; b. c. 1811, Berkeley Co., VA, son of John & Susanna Kisinger; enl. Mex. War service 12/17/1846, Berkeley, VA, age 36; m. Elizabeth Speck 02/24/1831, Berkeley Co., VA;[1142] discharged 02/20/1847 at Ft. Monroe, VA on Surgeon's Certificate of Disability.

**Kitchen, Caleb**, Pvt., Co. L; b. 11/11/1829 Rockville, Montgomery Co., MD;[1143, 1144] enl. Mex. War service 03/15/1847 Fairfax C.H., VA, age 18; pres. 06/1847; pres. 08/1847; absent 10/1847, on detached service in QM Dept. as a Teamster; absent 12/1847, on detached service in QM Dept., pay stopped for: 1 pr. pants-$2.28, 2 flannel shirts-$1.80, 3 cotton shirts-$1.29, 1 overcoat-$6.93$^{1/2}$, 1 blanket-$2.22, 2 pr. drawers-$.71, 2 pr. socks-$.49; absent 02/1848, on detached service as a Teamster in QM Dept.; absent 04/1848 on detached service as a Teamster in Qtr. Mast. Dept. since Dec. 31st 1847 by order of Col. Hamtramck; pres. 07/1848, pay stopped for: 1 Bayonet 1.44, 1 Bayonet Scabbard .56, 1 Brush & Pick .12, 1 S. Driver .25, 1 Wiper .20; BLW sent to Fairfax Court House, Fairfax Co., VA; m/1 Elizabeth Kidwell 11/17/1849;[1145] c. 1850 res. Fairfax Co., VA, age 21, occ. Laborer, w. Mary E. (19);[1146] m/2 Sarah Ann Mills 01/21/1853, Georgetown, D.C.; Civil War service Pvt. Co. D, 40$^{th}$ Mo. Inf. Regt., wded. 04/1865 *gunshot wd. Right hand*, index finger shot off, Spanish Fort, Ala,; SC #9850, 04/07/1887, filed from St. Louis, MO, Since discharge have resided St. Louis, Mo. and National Soldiers Home, Ft. Leavenworth, Kan.; d. 04/01/1888, St. Louis, Mo., bur. Bellfountaine Cem., St. Louis, Mo.; wid. Sarah Ann, WC #6104, 06/11/1888, filed from Dranesville, Fairfax Co., VA (SAK b. 12/08/1834, d. 04/27/1926, bur. Cedar Hill Cemetery, Prince George Co., MD).[1147]

**Klein, Charles H.**, Pvt., Co. H; enl. Mex. War service 01/06/1847, Berkeley, VA, age 21; pres. 04/1847; absent 06/1847, left as Attendant in Hosp. at Monterey, Mex. 06/23/1847; d. 07/15/1847 in Hosp. Monterey, Mex.

**Knowles, John**, Pvt., LIC; enl. Mex. War service 12/15/1846 Staunton, VA, age 44; absent 08/1847 for 30 days on detached service as a Teamster in QM Dept., to receive $25 in addition to pay as a soldier; absent 10/1847, on detached service for 30 days as a Teamster in the QM Dept., to receive $25 in addition to pay as a soldier, pay stopped for: 1 forage cap-$.95$^{1/2}$, 1

## VIRGINIA VOLUNTEERS IN MEXICO

wool jacket-$2.66, 1 pr. overalls-$2.28, 1 pr. shoes-$1.22, 3 pr. socks-$.73$^{1/2}$, 3 cotton shirts-$1.29; absent 12/1847, on detached service in QM Dept., pay stopped for: 2 pr. socks-$.49, 1 blanket-$2.22, 1 pr. shoes-$1.22, 1 pr. overalls-$2.28, 1 pr. drawers-$.35$^{1/2}$; pres. 04/1848; pres. 07/1848, pay stopped for: 1 bayonet scabbard-$.56, 1 waist belt-$.21, 1 waist belt plate-$.10, 1 gun sling-$.16, 1 pick & brush-$.12, 1 screw driver-$.07; BLW sent to Staunton, VA; c. 1860 res. Augusta Co., VA, age 58, occ. Laborer. [1148]

**Knox, Samuel T.**, 3$^{rd}$ Cpl., Co. E; enl. Mex. War service 12/04/1846 Petersburg, VA, age 38; absent 04/1847 detailed to wait on Lt. Pegram sick in Monterey, Mex.; prom. 4$^{th}$ Cpl. 06/07/1847, detailed as Staff Sgt. 06/09/1847; absent 08/1847 on detached service as Clerk Brig. HQ, prom. 3$^{rd}$ Cpl.; absent10/1847, on detached service as Clerk Brig. HQ, pay stopped for: 1 pr. overalls-$2.28, 2 pr. stockings-$.49; absent 12/1847, on duty in Subsistence Dept. from 12/11/1847, reduced to ranks at his own request by order of Capt. Preston commanding Regt., pay stopped for: 1 pr. drawers-$.35$^{1/2}$, 1 blanket-$2.22; prom. Regtl. Sgt. Major 01/11/1848; drowned 07/1848.[1149]

**Kolp, Henry**, Pvt., Co. G; enl. Mex. War service 12/03/1846 Richmond, VA, age 32; pres. 06/1847; pres. 08/1847; pres. 10/1847, pay stopped for: 1 pr. overalls-$2.28, 1 flannel shirt-$.90, 2 shoes-$2.44, 3 pr. socks-$.73$^{1/2}$, 1 forage cap-$.95$^{1/2}$; pres. 12/1847, pay stopped for: 1 pr. shoes-$1.22, 1 flannel shirt-$.90, 1 pr. drawers-$.35$^{1/2}$, 1 blanket-$2.22, 1 pr. pants-$2.28; pres. 02/1848, overcharged 1 pr. shoes-$1.22, 1 flannel shirt-$.90; pres. 04/1848; pres. 08/1848; BLW sent to Richmond, VA

**Krishmann, Anthony**, Pvt., Co. A; enl. Mex. War service 11/18/1846 Richmond, VA, age 19; pres. until detached 04/1847 - 06/1847 as Hosp. Steward at China, Mex. w/ 2$^{nd}$ Battalion; detached service 08/1847 as Hosp. Steward at Saltillo, Mex. since 08/01/1847; in confinement 10/1847, pay stopped for clothing: 1 pr. wool overalls-$2.28, 1 pr. drawers-$.35$^{1/2}$, 1 pr. shoes-$1.22, 2 cotton shirts-$.86, 2 pr. socks-$.49, 2 flannel shirts-$1.80, 1 blanket-$2.22; pres. 02/1848, pay stopped for: 1 pr. shoes-$1.22, 1 pick & brush-$.12; pres. 04/1848, pay stopped for 1 wool jacket; 07/1848, pay stopped for: 1 musket sling-$.16, 1 pr. shoes-$1.16; BLW sent to Richmond, VA

**Krumbein, Henry**, Pvt., *Recruit Co.*, enl. Mex. War service 12/18/1847 Ft. Monroe, VA; d. 02/17/1848 in hosp. at Ft. Monroe, VA

**Kurt, John**, 1$^{st}$ Sgt., Co. G; enl. Mex. War service 11/28/1846 Richmond, VA, age 33; pres. 06/1847, prom. 1$^{st}$ Sgt. 05/26/1847; pres. 08/1847; pres. 10/1847, pay stopped for: 1 pr. overalls_$2.28, 2 flannel shirts-$1.80, 1 pr. drawers-$.35$^{1/2}$, 1 shoes-$1.22, 2 pr. socks-$.49, 1 forage cap-$.95$^{1/2}$; deserted 12/11/1847 Buena Vista, Mex.

**Kurtz, Isaac**, Pvt., LIC; enl. Mex. War service 12/07/1846 Staunton, VA, age 23; pres. 08/1847; pres. 10/1847, prom. 4$^{th}$ Cpl. 09/20/1847, pay stopped for: 1 forage cap-$.95$^{1/2}$, 1 wool jacket-$2.66, 1 pr. overalls-$2.28, 2 pr. shoes-$2.44, 4 pr. socks-$.98, 4 cotton shirts-$1.72, 1 flannel shirt-$.90, 1 pr. drawers-$.35$^{1/2}$; pres. 12/1847, prom. 3$^{rd}$ Cpl., pay stopped for: 2 pr. socks-$.49, 1 blanket-$2.22, 2 pr. shoes-$2.44, 1 pr. overalls-$2.28, 1 pr. drawers-$.35$^{1/2}$; pres. 04/1848, reduced to ranks 02/23/1848; pres. 07/1848, pay stopped for: 1 pr. shoes-$1.16, 1 pick & brush-$.12, 1 screw driver-$.07, 1 wiper-$.20; BLW sent to Staunton, VA; c. 1850 res. Augusta Co., VA, age 28, occ. Carriage Maker;[1150] [a Robert Isaac Kurtz, b. 01/28/1823, Winchester, VA; Civil War service enl. 03/22/62 Winchester, VA, Pvt., Co. A, 5$^{th}$ Va. Inf.; wded. 03/23/1862 at Kernstown, VA in the head;[128] enl. 03/01/1864 Sgt., Co. K, 23$^{rd}$ Va. Cav.; wded. 09/19/1864. Jailor and Deputy Sheriff in Frederick Co.; member of Gen. Turner Ashby Camp C. V.; removed to Florida 1885; d. 02/09/1900, Deland, Fla., bur. Mt. Hebron Cem., Winchester, VA][249]

**Lahmeyer, John Henry**, Pvt., Co. E; b. 02/02/1824, Hanover, Germany;[45] enl. Mex. War service 12/01/1846 Petersburg, VA, age 21; phys. desc. age 21, 5'10", fair complexion, light hair, blue eyes; pres. 04/1847; pres. 06/1847; pres. 08/1847; pres. 10/1847, pay stopped for: 1 pr. overalls-$2.28, 2 pr. shoes-$2.44, 4 pr. stockings-$.98, 2 cotton shirts-$.86, 1 cap-$.95$^{1/2}$;

pres. 12/1847, pay stopped for: 1 pr. pants-$2.28, 1 pr. shoes-$1.22, 2 pr. socks-$.49, 2 pr. drawers-$.71, 1 blanket-$2.22; pres. 02/1848, pay stopped for: 1 pr. pants-$2.28, 1 jacket-$2.66, 1. pr. shoes-$1.22, 1 cotton shirt-$.43; pres. 04/1848; m. Virginia Morrison 05/10/1849;[45,1151] c. 1850 res. Petersburg, Dinwiddie Co., VA, age 26, occ. Saddler, w. Virginia (25), m-i-l? Mary Harrison;[1152] c. 1860 res. Petersburg, Dinwiddie Co., VA, age 34, occ. Harness Maker, w. Virginia (34), son William F. (8), dau. Elizabeth (2);[1153] d. 05/25/1880, *Paralysis*, bur. Blandford Cem., Sq. 1, Sec. 14, Ward B, Petersburg, VA;[76] wid. Virginia, WC #5234, 06/11/1888, filed from 226 Sycamore St., Petersburg, VA; (VML b. 05/20/1826, Prince George Co., VA, d. 01/22/1906).[1151]

**Lakeman, Abner Jesse**, Pvt., Co. L; b. 10/19/1826, Paris, Fauquier Co., VA;[1154] enl. Mex. War service 03/01/1847 Fairfax C.H., VA, age 21; pres. 06/1847; pres. 08/1847; pres. 10/1847, pay stopped for: 1 pr. Shoes 1.22; pres. 12/1847, pay stopped for: 1 jacket-$2.66, 1 pr. pants-$2.28, 1 cap-$.95$^{1/2}$, 1 pr. shoes-$1.22, 4 cotton shirts-$1.72, 1 blanket-$2.22, 2 pr. drawers-$.71, 1 pr. socks-$.24$^{1/2}$; pres. 02/1848, pay stopped for: 1 pr. Shoes 1.22, 1 Jacket 2.66, 1 Bayonet Scabbard .50, 1 Brush & Pick .12; absent 04/1848, sick in Qtrs., pay stopped for: 1 Blanket 2.25, 4 Cotton Shirts 1.76; pres. 07/1848, pay stopped for: 1 pr. Shoes 1.16, 1 Screw Driver .25, 1 Wiper .20; BLW sent to A.J. Lakeman, Washington City, D.C.; m. Malinda C. Hall 02/20/1851 Lockhardt's, Gore, Frederick Co., VA;[1154]c. 1870 res. Hayfield, Frederick Co., VA, age 46, occ. Farm Hand, w. Malinda (41), Jacob (21), Elizabeth (14), John D. (12), Abner J. (10), Mary F. (7), Josiah (4), Margaret A. (1);[1155] SC #14536, 02/01/1888, filed from Frederick Co., VA; d. 01/13/1892; wid. Malinda C., WC #9083, 04/06/1892, filed from Rosenberger, Frederick Co., VA (MCL b. 03/15/1830).[1156]

**Lamb, Samuel**, Pvt., Co. F; enl. Mex. War service 01/20/1847, Portsmouth, VA, age 23; pres. 06/1847; pres. 08/1847; pres. 10/1847, pay stopped for: 1 pr. overalls-$2.28, 2 pr. shoes-$2.44, 2 cotton shirts-$.86, 3 pr. socks-$.73$^{1/2}$, 1 pr. drawers-$.35$^{1/2}$, 1 forage cap-$.95$^{1/2}$, 1 overcoat-$6.93$^{1/2}$, 2 flannel shirts-$1.80; pres. 02/1848, pay stopped for: 2 pr. overalls-$4.56, 1 pr. shoes-$1.22, 1 blanket-$2.22, 2 pr. socks-$.49, 1 infantry jacket-$2.66, 1 bed sack-$1.07; pres. 04/1848; pres. 08/1848, pay stopped for: 1 brush & pick-$.12, 1 pr. shoes-$1.16, 2 shirts-$.88, BLW sent to Portsmouth, VA c/o E.T. Blamire.

**Lambert, Henry**, Pvt., LIC; enl. Mex. War service 12/07/1846 Staunton, VA, age 18; d. 08/16/1847 at Saltillo, Mex. of fever.

**Lancaster, Beverley W.**, Pvt., Co. K; enl. Mex. War service Jefferson Co., VA 12/06/1846, age 22; sick 06/1847; pres. 08/1847; pres. 10/1847, pay stopped for: 2 pr. socks-$.49, 2 pr. drawers-$.71, 1 pr. overalls-$2.28, 1 pr. shoes-$1.22, 1 cap-$.95$^{1/2}$; pres. 12/1847, pay stopped for: 1 pr. overalls-$2.28, 1 pr. boots-$1.22, 1 pr. socks-$.24$^{1/2}$, 1 blanket-$2.22; pres. 04/1848, pay stopped for: 1 jacket-$2.66, 1 flannel shirt-$.90, 1 cap-$.95$^{1/2}$; pres. 07/1848, pay stopped for: 1 pick & brush-$.12, 1 wiper-$.20; BLW sent to Charlestown, Jefferson Co., VA

**Lambert, Sterling L.**, 1$^{st}$ Lt., Co. M, enl. Mex. War service 09/08/1847 Nottoway C.H., VA, age 20; NFR; Civil War service Pvt., Co. D, 3$^{rd}$ VA Arty. (Local Defense); [a Sterling Lambert d. 01/25/1908, Leona, Brown Co., KS, *old age, age 81, widower, farmer*.][1157]

**Landes, Samuel**, Pvt., Co. E; b. 06/14/1818, Lancaster, Fairfield Co., OH, son of Joseph & Catherine Landes;[1158] enl. Mex. War service 11/28/1846 Petersburg, VA, age 28; pres. 04/1847; pres. 06/1847; absent 08/1847 furloughed 30 days from 08/08/1847; absent 10/1847 furloughed 30 days from 10/1847, pay stopped for: 1 pr. overalls-$2.28, 2 pr. shoes-$2.44, 2 pr. stockings-$.49, 1 cap-$.95$^{1/2}$; absent 12/1847 on detached service as a Clerk to Col. Hamtramck; absent 02/1848 on furlough since 12/08/1847; absent 04/1848 on furlough; m. Lucinda G. McKeag, 06/10/1851, Cincinnati, Hamilton Co., OH;[1158] Civil War service enl. Co. A, 39$^{th}$ NJ Inf., 09/23/1864, phys. desc. 5'4$^{1/2}$", light complexion, blue eyes, black hair, occ. Hatter, pres. 10/31/1864, wded. Petersburg, VA 11/24/1864 in face by exploding shell received *"contusions"* and *"burns,"* admitted Hosp. City Point, VA 12/01/1864, returned to

## VIRGINIA VOLUNTEERS IN MEXICO

duty 01/03/1865; wded. *"...while scaling a fence, which broke and caused him to fall while on the march from Petersburg, Va. to Farmville, Va...in pursuit of the rebel forces on the day of their evacuation of Richmond. He said the fall injured him in the groin and temporarily disabled him...;"*[1159] pres. 04/30/1865, discharged 06/17/1865 at Alexandria, VA; d. 05/20/1881, 880 Mt. Prospect Avenue, Newark, Essex Co., NJ, bur. Bloomfield Cemetery, Lot 134, Bloomfield, Essex Co., NJ;[1158] WO #307578; wid. Lucinda G., WC #2328, 06/07/1887, filed from 880 Mt. Prospect Ave., Newark, Essex Co., NJ; lists children Mary Landes b. 07/27/1866, Cadie Landes b. 12/21/1869;[1158] (LGL b. 02/27/1830 Cincinnati, OH, d. 09/18/1911).[1158]

**Landrum, John**, Pvt., Co. C; enl. Mex. War service 12/25/1846, Fredericksburg, VA, age 32; discharged 04/14/1847 Camargo, Mex. on Surgeon's Certificate of Disability.

**Lane, John G.**, Co. A; *Not on Muster Rolls*; wid. Elizabeth A., WA #5400, 11/11/1887, from MO.

**Langford, William**, Pvt., Co. G; enl. Mex. War service 12/14/1846 Richmond, VA, age 29; discharged on Habeas Corpus for insanity 01/07/1847.

**Lanier, John T.**, 3rd Sgt., Co. D; son of Robert & Frances (Pegram) Lanier;[1160] enl. Mex. War service 12/22/1846, Petersburg, VA, age 35; pres. 02/1847; pres. 04/1847, prom. 2nd Cpl. 03/25/1847; pres. but sick 06/1847, prom. 4th Sgt. 06/21/1847; pres. 08/1847, pay stopped for: 1 bayonet-$1.44, 1 cap-$.95$^{1/2}$, 1 pr. shoes-$1.22; pres. 10/1847, prom. 3rd Sgt., pay stopped for: 1 jacket-$2.66, 2 pr. pants-$4.56, 2 cotton shirts-$.86, 1 pr. drawers-$.35$^{1/2}$, 3 pr. socks-$.73$^{1/2}$, 1 pr. shoes-$1.22, 1 overcoat-$6.93$^{1/2}$; absent 12/1847, detailed as Provost Sgt. 12/20/1847, pay stopped for: 1 pr. pants-$2.28, 1 pr drawers-$.35$^{1/2}$, 2 flannel shirts-$1.80, 1 blanket-$2.22; pres. 04/1848; pres. 08/1847, BLW sent to Dinwiddie C.H., VA; c. 1850 res. Petersburg, Dinwiddie Co., VA, age 50, occ. Clerk, w. Martha L. (29), son Norbourne F. (9), dau. Martha E.H. (6), son John R. (3);[1161] 2nd cousin of Lt. Franklin Pegram.[1160]

**Lavell, Owen C.**, Pvt., LIC; enl. Mex. War service 11/27/1846 Staunton, VA, age 23; pres. 06/1847; pres. 08/1847, prom. 2nd Cpl.; pres. 10/1847, pay stopped for: 1 forage cap-$.95$^{1/2}$, 1 wool jacket-$2.66, 2 pr. overalls-$4.56, 2 pr. shoes-$2.44, 4 pr. socks-$.98, 3 cotton shirts-$1.29; absent 12/1847, on detached service in QM Dept., pay stopped for: 1 pr. socks-$.24$^{1/2}$, 1 blanket-$2.22, 1 cotton shirt-$.43, 1 pr. drawers-$.35$^{1/2}$; pres. 04/1848, reduced to ranks from 2nd Cpl., pay stopped for: 1 cotton shirt-$.43, 1 pr. shoes-$1.22; pres. 07/1848, pay stopped for: 1 gun sling-$.16, 1 screw driver-$.07, 1 wiper-$.20; BLW sent to Staunton, VA; d. 06/27/1887, bur. Hampton National Cemetery, Plot: 5891, Hampton, VA

**Lappin, John**, 1st Sgt., Co. F; enl. Mex. War service 11/23/1846, Portsmouth, VA, age 30; pres. 06/1847; pres. 08/1847; pres. 10/1847, pay stopped for: 1 pr. overall-$2.28, 1 forage cap-$.95$^{1/2}$; 2 pr. shoes-$2.44, 3 cotton shirts-$1.29, 2 pr. drawers-.71; pres. 12/1847; pres. 02/1848, pay stopped for: 1 pr. overalls-$2.28, 1 overcoat-$6.93$^{1/2}$, 1 pr. shoes-$1.22, 1 cotton shirt-$.43, 2 flannel shirts-$1.80, 2 pr. drawers-$.71, 1 blanket-$2.22, 1 bed sack-$1.07; pres. 04/1848, prom. 04/01/1848 1st Sgt.; pres. 08/1848, pay stopped for: 3 blankets-$6.75, 2 cotton shirts-$.88, BLW sent to Portsmouth, VA c/o E.T. Blamire.

**Lawrence, Christopher**, Drummer, Co. F; enl. Mex. War service 11/24/1846, Portsmouth, VA, age 30; pres. 06/1847; pres. 08/1847, reduced to ranks 08/31/1847 by order of Actg. Insp. Genl.; pres. 10/1847, pay stopped for: 1 pr. overalls-$2.28, 2 cotton shirts-$.86, 2 pr. socks-$.49, 1 pr. shoes-$1.22; pres. 02/1848, pay stopped for: 1 pr. shoes-$1.22, 1 forage cap-$.95$^{1/2}$, 1 pr. drawers-$.35$^{1/2}$, 1 blanket-$2.22; pres. 04/1848; pres. 08/1848, BLW sent to Portsmouth, VA c/o E.T. Blamire.

**Laurence, John E.**, Pvt., *Preston's Co.*; b. 03/16/1823;[1162] enl. Mex. War service 12/04/1846 Montgomery Co., VA, age 20; pres. 04/1847; discharged 05/05/1847 at Monterey, Mex., on Surgeon's Certificate of Disability; c. 1850 res. Montgomery Co., VA, age 24, occ. Farmer;[1163] m. Celinda A. Barnett, 03/15/1854, Alleghany Springs, Montgomery Co., VA;[1162] [Civil War service a John C.E. Lawrence enl. as a Pvt., Co. B, 13th Va. Inf. at Culpeper, VA

OFF TO WAR

04/17/1861, b. 1826, pres. through 01/17/1862 when mustered out;[871] enl. Pvt., Sturdivants Battery, at Culpeper, VA 03/13/1862, prom. Sgt. 03/28/1862, prom. 1st Sgt. 05/16/1863, furloughed 03/25/1863 – 04/07/1863, pres 08/02/1864, NFR;][1164] SC #10813, 07/01/1887, filed from Lafayette, Montgomery Co., VA; Lists children Theresa M.J. Laurence b. 08/22/1855, James R. Laurence b. 01/18/1859, Willia A. Laurence b. 03/24/1862, Charles E. Laurence b. 03/26/1868, Celinda V.L. Laurence b. 05/24/1873;[1162] d. 06/16/1906.[1162]

**Lawson, Lewis**, Pvt., Co. C; m. Betsy Carnall, 08/21/1845, Caroline Co., VA;[1165] enl. Mex. War service 12/15/1846, Bowling Green, VA, age 18; pres. 06/1847; pres. 08/1847, pay stopped for: 1 cap-$.95$^{1/2}$, 2 pr. socks-$.49, 2 cotton shirts-$.86, 2 woolen shirts-$1.80; pres. 10/1847, pay stopped for: 2 pr. socks-$.49, 2 pr. drawers-$.71, 1 pr. pants-$2.28, 2 cotton shirts-$.86, 2 pr. shoes-$2.44, 1 blanket-$2.22; pres. 12/1847, pay stopped for: 1 jacket-$2.66; pres. 04/1848, pay stopped for: 1 pr. pants-$2.28, 1 pr. shoes-$1.22; 1 pr. shoes-$2.25, 1 haversack-$.20$^{3/4}$, 1 india rubber canteen-$.27; pres. 08/1848, BLW sent to Bowling Green, Caroline Co., VA; [a Lewis Lawson c. 1850 res. Richmond, Henrico Co., age 23, occ. Public Guard, w. Lucy (26), son John H. (11/12).][1166]

**Leard, Samuel**, Pvt., Co. G; enl. Mex. War service 12/20/1847 Richmond, VA, age 27; pres. 06/1847; d. 08/12/1847 Saltillo, Mex.

**Leckie, John**, Pvt., Co. C; enl. Mex. War service 12/30/1846, Bowling Green, VA, age 30; pres. 06/1847; pres. 08/1847, pay stopped for: 1 cap-$.95$^{1/2}$, 2 pr. socks-$.49, 2 cotton shirts-$.86, 2 woolen shirts-$1.80, 1 pr. shoes-$1.22; in confinement 10/1847 in provost guard, fined 1 mos. pay by order of genl. court-martial, pay stopped for: 2 pr. socks-$.49, 2 pr. drawers-$.71, 1 pr. pants-$2.28, 1 pr. shoes-$1.22; pres. 12/1847, pay stopped for: 1 jacket-$2.66, 2 woolen shirts-$1.80, 1 pr. shoes-$1.22, 1 blanket-$2.22; pres. 04/1848, pay stopped for: 1 pr. shoes-$1.22; 1 haversack-$.20$^{3/4}$, 1 india rubber canteen-$.27; pres. 08/1848, BLW sent to Providence, Rhode Island.

**Lee, Charles**, Pvt., *Preston's Co.*, b. 09/1822, Kanawha Co., VA;[1167] enl. Mex. War service 12/06/1846 Montgomery Co., VA, age 23; absent 04/1847 left sick at Pt. Isabel, Tex. since 03/15/1847; pres. 06/1847; sick 08/1847; pres. 10/1847, pay stopped for: 2 pr. socks-$.49, 1 cotton shirt-$.43; pres. 12/1847, pay stopped for: 1 pr. overalls-$2.28, 1 pr. shoes-$1.22; pres. 02/1848; pres. 04/1848; pres. 07/1848, pay stopped for: 1 pr. shoes-$1.16; BLW sent to Christiansburg, VA c/o Fleming Gardner; m. 12/19/1848, Elizabeth Collins, Montgomery Co., VA;[1168] c. 1850 res. Montgomery Co., VA, age 28, occ. Farmer, w. Elizabeth (21), son James F.P. (8/12);[1169] c. 1860 res. Christiansburg, Montgomery Co., VA, age 37, occ. Laborer, w. Elizabeth (31), son James P. (10), son William D. (6), dau. Araminta (3), son Hamilton M. (1);[1170] SC #5636, 05/02/1887, filed from Elmo, Nodaway Co., MO; phys. desc. 5'4", fair complexion, blue eyes, dark hair, occ. Farmer; since discharge res. VA to 1887, since then to Nodaway Co., Mo.; Henry Collins (b-i-l) and Michael Kipps gave affidavit; d. 01/02/1915, *"old age and senility,"* Nodaway Co., Mo., bur. High Prarie Cemetery, Elmo, Nodaway Co., Mo.; (ECL d. 11/30/1896).

**Lee, James**, Pvt., *Preston's Co.*; enl. Mex. War service 12/06/1846 Montgomery Co., VA, age 24; absent 04/1847 left sick at Ft. Monroe, VA since 02/27/1847; absent 06/1847 left sick in hosp. at Ft. Monroe, VA; discharged 03/23/1847 at Ft. Monroe, VA

**Lee, Robert W.**, 4th Cpl., Co. M; enl. Mex. War service 07/17/1847, Lynchburg, VA, age 23; pres. 09/1847; pres. 11/1847, reduced to ranks from 4th Cpl.; pres. 12/1847; pres. 02/1848; pres. 04/1848; pres. 08/1848, prom. 4th Cpl 05/08/1848, pay stopped for: 1 gun sling-$.16, 1 wormer-$.20; BLW sent to Lynchburg, VA.

**Lennox, John**, Pvt., Co. G; b. 12/29/1825, Richmond, VA;[1171] *"Bound to John Pearce and Son to learn the business of Harness Maker, John Smith, a poor boy aged ten years, until he attain the age of twenty one years. His parents are incapable of supporting him and bringing him up in honest courses;"*[1172] *"In the Hustings Court of the City of Richmond, December 10th 1838, Ordered that John Pearce and Jonathan Pearce be summoned to appear here on the first day*

198

## VIRGINIA VOLUNTEERS IN MEXICO

*of the next term to answer the complaint of their apprentice John Lennox, who was bound to them by the name of John Smith, this day made against them, for insufficient food, clothing, etc., and that they suffer him the said John Lennox to come here at the next Court to make good his complaint aforesaid, and do not presume to beat or misuse him on this account;"*[1172] enl. Mex. War service 11/18/1846 Richmond, VA, age 19; phys. desc. 5'11", light complexion, blue eyes, sandy hair, occ. Harness Maker;[1171] pres. 06/1847; pres. 08/1847; pres. 10/1847, pay stopped for: 1 pr. overalls-$2.28, 2 pr. shoes-$2.44, 2 pr. socks-$.49, 1 forage cap-$.95$^{1/2}$; pres. 12/1847, pay stopped for: 1 pr. shoes-$1.22, 1 pr. drawers-$.35$^{1/2}$, 1 blanket-$2.22; pres. 02/1848, pay stopped for: 1 jacket-$2.66; pres. 04/1848; pres. 08/1848, pay stopped for: 1 gun sling-$.16; BLW sent to Richmond, VA; SC #20163, 01/04/1889, filed from Redlands, San Bernadino Co., CA; since discharge res. Virginia, Louisiana, Pennsylvania, Missouri, and since 1851 in California; Theoderick Nunnally and Augustus Stone gave affidavits on pension claim; d. 03/12/1915.[1171]

**Levy, William Mallory**, 2$^{nd}$ Lt., Co. F; b. 10/31/1827, Isle of Wight, VA; grad. William & Mary College, Williamsburg, VA 1844;[1173] enl. Mex. War service 11/23/1846, Portsmouth, VA; pres. 06/1847; Court-martialed 06/29/1847 Buena Vista, Mex. *Charge: Neglect of Duty; Specification #1: In that 2$^{nd}$ Lt. W.M. Levy, of the Va. Regt. of Vols., being regularly mounted on guard, as Officer of the Provost Guard, on the 23$^{rd}$ of June 1847, did absent himself repeatedly from the guard quarters before being regularly relieved. This at Head Quarters, Buena Vista, Mexico on or about the 23$^{rd}$ of June 1847. Specification #2: In that 2$^{nd}$ Lt. W.M. Levy, of the Va. Regt. of Vols., being regularly mounted on guard, as Officer of the Provost Guard, on the 23$^{rd}$ of June 1847, did neglectly fail to instruct the non-commissioned officers and men of his guard in their guard duties. This at Head Quarters, Buena Vista, Mexico on or about the 23$^{rd}$ of June 1847. Specification #3: In that 2$^{nd}$ Lt. W.M. Levy, of the Va. Regt. of Vols., being regularly mounted on guard, as Officer of the Provost Guard, on the 23$^{rd}$ of June 1847, negligently fail to have the light extinguished in the common tent at the western corner of the limits of the line of sentinels of his guard, and did negligently suffer the prisoner to play at cards and gamble in said tent whilst the light was thence burning. This after 10 o'clock at night at Head Quarters, Buena Vista, Mexico on or about the 23$^{rd}$ of June 1847. Specification #4: In that 2$^{nd}$ Lt. W.M. Levy, of the Va. Regt. of Vols., being regularly mounted on guard, as Officer of the Provost Guard, on the 23$^{rd}$ of June 1847, carelessly go to sleep in his tent at the guard quarters and negligently fail to have a proper vigilance observed at the quarters of his guard so as to prevent persons coming up to the guard without being challenged. This at Head Quarters, Buena Vista, Mexico on or about the 23$^{rd}$ of June 1847. To which charge and specification the accused pleaded Not Guilty.* Col. Robert T. Paine, N.C. Volunteers, Sergt. W.N. Peoples, Co. H, N.C. Regt., 1$^{st}$ Lt. J.K. Cooke, Va. Regt. testified as witnesses. *After deliberation the court found the accused Not Guilty of the charge and specifications.*[1174] pres. 08/1847; pres. 10/1847; pres. 12/1847; pres. 02/1848; absent 04/1848 acting adjutant; pres. 08/1848; studied law; was admitted to the bar in 1851 and commenced practice in Norfolk, VA, moved to Natchitoches, LA, in 1852 and continued the practice of law; elected as a Delegate to the State House of Representatives 1859-1861; published the *Natchitoches Chronicle* in the 1850's; Civil War service Capt., Co. A, 2$^{nd}$ La. Inf., *The Lecompte Guards, Louisiana Zouaves* prom. Colonel 08/1861, surrendered at Appomattox C.H, VA 04/09/1865; Presidential elector Northwest Louisiana 1860; elected as a Democrat to the U.S. Congress 1875-1877; unsuccessful candidate for renomination in 1876; member of the State constitutional convention in 1879; appointed associate justice of the State Supreme Court in 1879 and served until his death, d. 08/14/1882, Saratoga, N.Y bur. American Cemetery, Natchitoches, La.;[1175] wid. Catherine E., WC #1506, 04/14/1887, from LA.

**Lewellen, John Richard**, 2$^{nd}$ Lt., Co. G; b. c. 1822, Campbell Co., VA; enl. Mex. War service 11/18/1846 Richmond, VA, age 25; prom. 2$^{nd}$ Lt. 05/25/1847 on the death of Lt. Munford; pres. 06/1847; pres. 08/1847; pres. 10/1847; pres. 12/1847; absent 02/1848 on furlough since

## OFF TO WAR

01/29/1848; resigned 02/29/1848; c. 1850 res. Henrico Co., VA, age 27, occ. Printer, mo? Sarah (62);[1176] m. c. 1850, Virginia Louisa Morris; editor, *The Conductor*, a religious newspaper; roomed on High St., Petersburg, VA; Civil War service enl. 1$^{st}$ Lt., Co. K, 12$^{th}$ Va. Inf., 05/04/1861, Petersburg, VA; prom. Capt. 07/01/1861; wded. severely 09/14/1862 Crampton's Gap, MD; in Hosp. 09/1862-11/1862; prom. Major 10/03/1862; detached 11/1862–01/1864 as Conscript Officer; prom. Lt. Col. 02/23/1865 to rank from 07/1864; in Hosp. 02/1865; postwar occ. Farmer, politician, newspaper editor, *Danville Register*; d. 12/04/1886, Danville, VA; desc. in 1886 as over 6 ft. tall, fine personal appearance, made venerable by white hair and beard; bur. Blandford Cem., Petersburg, VA[21]

**Lewis, Charles**, Pvt., Co. C; enl. Mex. War service 12/27/1846, Bowling Green, VA, age 20; pres. 06/1847; pres. 08/1847, pay stopped for: 1 cap-$.95$^{1/2}$, 2 pr. socks-$.49, 2 cotton shirts-$.86, 2 woolen shirts-$1.80, 1 pr. shoes-$1.22; 1 pr. drawers-$.35$^{1/2}$, 1 pr. overalls-$2.28; pres. 10/1847, pay stopped for: 2 pr. drawers-$.71, 1 jacket-$2.66, 1 pr. pants-$2.28, 2 woolen shirts-$1.80, 1 pr. shoes-$1.22, 1 great coat-$6.93$^{1/2}$; pres. 12/1847, pay stopped for: 2 pr. socks-$.49, 1 pr. pants-$2.28, 1 pr. shoes-$1.22, 1 blanket-$2.22; pres. 04/1848, pay stopped for: 1 pr. shoes-$1.22; 1 haversack-$.20$^{3/4}$, 1 india rubber canteen-$.27; pres. 08/1848, BLW sent to Washington City, DC.

**Lewis, James**, Pvt., Co. H; enl. Mex. War service 11/22/1846, Berkeley, VA, age 24; pres. 04/1847; pres. 06/1847; pres. 08/1847; pres. 10/1847, pay stopped for: 1 forage cap-$.95$^{1/2}$, 1 pr. pants-$2.28, 1 cotton shirt-$.43, 1 pr. drawers-$.35$^{1/2}$, 2 pr. socks-$.49; pres. 12/1847, pay stopped for: 1 pr. pants-$2.28, 2 cotton shirts-$.86, 1 pr. drawers-$.71, 1 pr. shoes-$1.22, 1 pr. socks-$.24$^{1/2}$, 1 blanket-$2.22; pres. 02/1848, pay stopped for: 1 jacket-$2.66; pres. 04/1848; pres. 07/1848, pay stopped for: 1 gun sling-$.16, 1 wiper-$.20, BLW sent to Hedgesville, VA

**Lewis, Joseph**, Pvt., Co. C; enl. Mex. War service 12/29/1846, Bowling Green, VA, age 35; pres. 06/1847; pres. 08/1847, pay stopped for: 1 cap-$.95$^{1/2}$, 2 pr. socks-$.49, 2 cotton shirts-$.86, 2 woolen shirts-$1.80, 1 pr. shoes-$1.22; 1 knapsack & straps-$1.10; pres. 10/1847, pay stopped for: 2 pr. socks-$.49, 1 jacket-$2.66, 1 pr. pants-$2.28, 2 cotton shirts-$.86, 1 pr. shoes-$1.22; pres. 12/1847, fined 1 mos. pay by order of regtl. court-martial, pay stopped for: 3 cotton shirts-$1.29; pres. 04/1848, pay stopped for: 3 pr. socks-$.73$^{1/2}$, 1 pr. shoes-$1.22; 1 pr. shoes-$1.50, 1 haversack-$.20$^{3/4}$, 1 india rubber canteen-$.27; pres. 08/1848, BLW sent to Philadelphia, Pa.

**Lightfoot, William T.**, Pvt., Co. E; enl. Mex. War service 12/01/1846 Petersburg, VA, age 22; pres. 04/1847; pres. 06/1847; pres. 08/1847; pres. 10/1847, pay stopped for: 1 pr. overalls-$2.28, 2 pr. shoes-$2.44, 2 pr. stockings-$.49, 2 pr. drawers-$.71, 1 cap-$.95$^{1/2}$; pres. 12/1847, pay stopped for: 1 pr. pants-$2.28, 2 pr. socks-$.49, 2 flannel shirts-$1.80; pres. 02/1848, [illegible]; pres. 04/1848;

**Lindsay, (Hiram) Opie**, Pvt., Co. L; b. 1825; enl. Mex. War service 03/16/1847 Alexandria, VA, age 22; pres. 06/1847; sick 08/1847; pres. 12/1847, pay stopped for: 1 jacket-$2.66, 1 pr. pants-$2.28, 2 flannel shirts-$1.80, 1 cotton shirt-$.43, 1 blanket-$2.22, 2 pr. drawers-$.71$^{1/2}$, 2 pr. socks-$.49; pres. 02/1848; pres. 04/1848, pay stopped for: 1 Flannel Shirt .77; pres. 07/1848, pay stopped for: 1 Brush & Pick .12; BLW sent to Capt. Thrift c/o Opie Lindsay, Fairfax Court House, Fairfax Co., VA; c. 1850 res. Fairfax Co., VA, age 24, occ. Laborer;[1177] m. Mary Gorum, 02/04/1851, Washington, D.C.;[1178] c. 1860 res. Fairfax Co., VA, age 34, occ. Laborer, w. Mary S. (31), son George H. (7), dau. Mary T. (6), dau. Ann E. (5), son John R. (3), son William Thomas (2), dau. Martha J. (5/12);[1179] SC #1241, 02/23/1887, filed from Burnt Mills, Montgomery Co., MD; d. 07/27/1899.[1180]

**Lindsey, Stephen**, Pvt., *Preston's Co.*; enl. Mex. War service 01/04/1847 Montgomery Co., VA, age 21; absent 04/1847 left sick at Ft. Monroe, VA since 02/17/1847; absent 06/1847 left sick at Ft. Monroe, VA; pres. 10/1847, pay stopped for: 1 pr. Pants 2.28; d. 02/28/1847 at Ft. Monroe, VA, *"died of small pox."*[243]

VIRGINIA VOLUNTEERS IN MEXICO

**Linkous, Benjamin R.**, 3$^{rd}$ Sgt., *Preston's Co.*; b. 04/25/1825, Raleigh Co., VA, son of Henry and Fanny Linkous;[1181, 1182] enl. Mex. War service 12/06/1846 Montgomery Co., VA, age 21; pres. 04/1847; pres. 06/1847 prom. 3$^{rd}$ Sgt.; sick 08/1847; pres. 10/1847, pay stopped for: 1 pr. overalls-$2.28, 1 pr. shoes-$1.22, 2 flannel shirts-$1.80, 1 pr. drawers-$.35$^{1/2}$; pres. 12/1847, pay stopped for: 1 pr. overalls-$2.28, 1 pr. shoes-$1.22, 1 cap-$.95$^{1/2}$, 1 blankets-$2.22; pres. 02/1848; pres. 04/1848; pres. 07/1848, pay stopped for: 1 cartridge box plate-$.10, 1 brush & pick-$.12, 1 gun sling-$.18, 1 screw driver-$.07, 1 non-comm. Officers sword-$4.50; BLW sent to Christiansburg, VA c/o Fleming Gardner; m/1 c. 1852 Susan F. Beckley, date/place unknown; c. 1860 res. Beckley, Raleigh Co., VA also c. 1860 res. Matamoras, Montgomery Co., VA, age 32, occ. Trader;[1183] Civil War service enl. Capt., Co. C, 36$^{th}$ Va. Inf., 04/16/1862, age 37; pres. until 06/1862 when on leave; pres. until sick 12/1862; prom. Lt. Col. 05/15/1862; resigned 03/30/1864 to serve in Virginia Legislature; wded. 05/09/1864 Cloyd's Mountain; paroled 04/1864 Blacksburg, VA; m/2 Margaret Augusta Browning, 04/08/1886, Botetourt Co., VA;[1182] d. 04/03/1887, Montgomery Co., bur. Municipal Cem., Christiansburg, Va;[390, 1182] wid. Margaret A., WC #2598, 07/01/1887, from VA; Michael Kipps and Henry Collins gave affidavits in pension claim;[1182] (MBL b. 12/19/1847, Highland Co., OH, attended Hillsborough Female College, Highland Co., OH, in 1857, d. 02/15/1822, Fincastle, Botetourt Co., VA);[1182] 1$^{st}$ cousin of Pvt. Crockett Linkous and Pvt. William B. Linkous.
**Linkous, Crockett**, Pvt., *Preston's Co.*; b. 07/27/1818, New River, Montgomery Co., VA;[1184] son of Jacob & Mary (Kipps) Linkous;[1185] enl. Mex. War service 12/06/1846 Montgomery Co., VA, age 26; absent 04/1847 left sick in hosp at Ft. Monroe, VA since 02/27/1847; absent 06/1847 sick at Ft. Monroe, VA; discharged 03/31/1847 with *"smallpox"*[1184] at Ft. Monroe, VA; m. Mary C. Kipps, 07/18/1855, Blacksburg, Montgomery Co., VA;[1184, 1185] SC #12681, 03/17/1887, filed from Christiansburg, Montgomery Co., VA; since discharge res. Montgomery Co., VA to 1860, Wythe Co., VA to 1861, Montgomery Co., VA since then;[1184] Robert G. Newlee and Henry Collins gave affidavits in pension claim;[1184] d. 09/28/1889, Matamoras, Montgomery Co., VA;[1186] wid. Mary C., WC #6690, 11/16/1889, filed from Price's Fork, Montgomery Co., VA; (MKL b. 08/12/1831, Blacksburg, Montgomery Co., VA, d. 05/10/1915);[1186] brother of Pvt. William B. Linkous; 1$^{st}$ cousin of Pvt. Benjamin R. Linkous.
**Linkous, William B.**, Pvt., *Preston's Co.*, son of Jacob & Mary (Kipps) Linkous; enl. Mex. War service 12/06/1846 Montgomery Co., VA, age 19; absent 04/1847 left sick in hosp. at China, Mex. since 04/16/1847; d. 04/22/1847 in hosp. at China, Mex., *"of disease;"*[243] brother of Pvt. Crockett Linkous; 1$^{st}$ cousin of Pvt. Benjamin R. Linkous.
**Lipscomb, George B.**, Pvt., Co. E; enl. Mex. War service 11/28/1846 Petersburg, VA, age 20; discharged 12/30/1846 Petersburg, VA by writ of habeas corpus signed by Judge Gholson; m. Sarah B. Hargrave, 12/1849.[1187]
**Little, Moses A.**, 3$^{rd}$ Sgt., Co. C; enl. Mex. War service 12/18/1846, Fredericksburg, VA, age 40; pres. 06/1847, prom. 4$^{th}$ Sgt. 06/16/1847; pres. 08/1847, prom. 3$^{rd}$ Sgt. 08/25/1847, pay stopped for: 1 pr. drawers-$.35$^{1/2}$, 1 cap-$.95$^{1/2}$, 2 pr. socks-$.49, 2 cotton shirts-$.86, 2 woolen shirts-$1.80; pres. 10/1847, pay stopped for: 3 pr. socks-$.73$^{1/2}$, 2 pr. drawers-$.71, 1 pr. pants-$2.28, 1 pr. shoes-$1.22; pres. 12/1847, pay stopped for: 2 pr. socks-$.49, 1 pr. pants-$2.28, 2 cotton shirts-$.86, 1 pr. shoes-$1.22, 1 blanket-$2.22; pres. 04/1848, pay stopped for: 1 jacket-$2.66, 1 pr. shoes-$1.22; 1 blanket-$2.22, 1 pr. shoes-$1.50, 1 haversack-$.20$^{3/4}$, 1 india rubber canteen-$.27; pres. 08/1848, BLW sent to Fort Monroe, VA
**Loftin, Charles**, Pvt., Co. H; b. 08/05/1827, Medford, Burlington Co., NJ;[1188] enl. Mex. War service 01/06/1847, Berkeley, VA, age 19; pres. 04/1847; pres. 06/1847; pres. 08/1847; pres. 10/1847, pay stopped for: 1 forage cap-$.95$^{1/2}$, 1 pr. pants-$2.28, 4 cotton shirts-$1.72, 3 flannel shirts-$2.70, 3 pr. shoes-$3.66, 2 pr. socks-$.49, 1 jacket-$2. 66; pres. 12/1847, pay stopped for: 1 jacket-$2.66, 1 pr. pants-$2.28, 1 flannel shirt-$.90, 2 pr. drawers-$.71, 1 pr. shoes-$1.22, 1 pr. socks-$.24$^{1/2}$; pres. 02/1848, pay stopped for: 1 pr. drawers-$.35$^{1/2}$, 1 pr.

shoes-$1.22, 2 pr. socks-$.49, 1 blanket-$2.22; pres. 04/1848; pres. 07/1848, pay stopped for: 2 gun slings-$.32, 1 bayonet-$1.44, 1 screw driver-$.25, 1 wiper-$.20, BLW sent to Philadelphia, Pa.; m. Margaret Louge c. 1851, Philadelphia, Pa.; enl. U.S. Navy at Norfolk, VA 04/19/1853 as a Landsman on U.S.S. Pennsylvania, trans. 08/09/1853 to U.S.S. Savannah, discharged 12/16/1856; Civil War service enl. Sgt., Co. H, 29$^{th}$ NJ Inf., 08/31/1862, discharged 08/02/1863, Camp Monmouth, NJ; #1084587; SC #20290, 07/03/1891, filed National Military Home, Dayton, Montgomery Co., OH; since discharge res. Philadelphia, Pa. and Vicksburg, MS; phys. desc. age 63 [1891], 5'4$^{3/4}$", dark complexion, dark hair, dark eyes, occ. Tailor; Lists dau. Margaret Loftin; admitted 08/30/1891, National Military Home, Marion, Grant Co., Ind., discharged 09/29/1892; admitted 06/16/1893, National Military Home, Hampton, Elizabeth City Co., VA, dropped from roll 12/26/1894; c. 1895 a res. West Point, Troupe Co., Ga., *"I will bee heare fore some time. I am trieng to start a shop heare and will bee heare some time I hope;"*[1189] admitted 07/17/1895, National Military Home, Marion, Grant Co., Ind., discharged 02/27/1898; admitted 07/31/1900, National Military Home, Dayton, Montgomery Co., OH; *"treated for malaria,"* discharged 08/13/1900; readmitted 10/16/1900, *"acute alcoholism,"* discharged 10/26/1900; d. 06/01/1904, National Military Home, Dayton, Montgomery Co., OH, bur. Dayton National Cemetery, Plot: N 16 22, Dayton, OH.

**Logan, John J.**, Pvt., LIC; enl. Mex. War service 12/07/1846 Staunton, VA, age 28; pres. 08/1847; pres. 10/1847, pay stopped for: 1 forage cap-$.95$^{1/2}$, 1 wool jacket-$2.66, 1 pr. overalls-$2.28, 2 pr. shoes-$2.44, 3 pr. socks-$.73$^{1/2}$, 4 cotton shirts-$1.72, 1 flannel shirt-$.90, 1 pr. drawers-$.35$^{1/2}$, 1 blanket-$2.22; pres. 12/1847, pay stopped for: 1 pr. socks-$.24$^{1/2}$, 1 pr. overalls-$2.28; pres. 04/1848, pay stopped for: 1 pr. overalls-$2.28; pres. 07/1848, pay stopped for: 1 gun sling-$.16, 1 pick & brush-$.12, 1 screw driver-$.07, 1 wiper-$.20; BLW sent to Lexington, VA; m. Margaret Elizabeth Armstrong,[1190] 05/03/1860, Collierstown, Rockbridge Co., VA; d. 11/14/1875, Collierstown, Rockbridge Co., VA;[1190] wid. Margaret E., WA #1317, 03/29/1887, from VA; (MAL b. 01/06/1831, d. 09/15/1923).[1190]

**Logwood, Valentine S.**, Pvt., Co. I; son of Burwell & Prudence (Peyton) Logwood;[1191] enl. Mex. War service 01/10/1847 Lynchburg, VA, age 37; pres. 02/1847; pres. 04/1847; discharged 06/15/1847 for disability at camp near Monterey, Mex.; c. 1850 res. Bedford Co., VA, age 30, occ. Farmer;[1192] SC #10523, 03/14/1887, filed from Curtis, Bedford Co., VA *"never married;"* phys. desc. age 75 [1887], 5'4", dark complexion, blue eyes, black hair, occ. Farmer; James Neighbors gave affidavit in pension claim; d. 1892.

**Long, Charles C.**, *Not on Muster Rolls*; wid. Mary, WA #15294, 09/23/1899, from AL.

**Long, Jacob**, Pvt., LIC; enl. Mex. War service 12/07/1846 Staunton, VA, age 21; d. 03/29/1847 at Monterey, Mex. of diarrhea.

**Long, Napoleon B.**, Pvt., Co. E; b. 01/06/1821, Northampton, NC, son of Frederick & Rebecca Long;[1193] enl. Mex. War service 12/01/1846 Petersburg, VA, age 25; pres. 04/1847; discharged 06/05/1847 Monterey, Mex. for disability; c. 1850 Chesterfield Co., VA, age 30, occ. Clerk;[1194] d. 06/29/1855, *"Mr. N.B. Long accidentally drowned while bathing in the Appomattox River;"*[1195] bur. Blandford Cem., Sq. 314, Ward A, Petersburg, VA

**Long, William**, Pvt., LIC; b. c. 1830; enl. Mex. War service 12/22/1846 Staunton, VA, age 19; absent 06/1847 sick in quarters; pres. 08/1847; pres. 10/1847, pay stopped for: 1 forage cap-$.95$^{1/2}$, 1 wool jacket-$2.66, 2 pr. overalls-$4.56, 1 pr. shoes-$.22, 5 pr. socks-$1.22$^{1/2}$, 1 pr. drawers-$.35$^{1/2}$, 1 blanket-$2.22; pres. 12/1847, pay stopped for: 1 pr. socks-$.24$^{1/2}$, 1 blanket-$2.22, 1 pr. overalls-$2.28, 2 flannel shirts-$1.80, 1 pr. drawers-$.35$^{1/2}$; pres. 04/1848, on detached service as a Hospital Attendant since 03/09/1848, pay stopped for: 1 flannel shirt-$.90, 1 pr. shoes-$1.22; pres. 07/1848, pay stopped for: 1 ramrod-$.63, 1 waist belt-$.21, 1 gun sling-$.16, 1 screw driver-$.07, 1 wiper-$.20; BLW sent to Waynesborough, VA; c. 1860 res. Augusta Co., VA, age 30, occ. Saddler;[1196] 2$^{nd}$ Lt., Waynesboro Greys VA Militia; Civil War service enl. 07/15/61 at Waynesboro, VA Capt., Co. B, 52$^{nd}$ Va. Inf.; elected Capt.

## VIRGINIA VOLUNTEERS IN MEXICO

05/01/1862; wded. 05/08/1862 Battle of McDowell, in the head; d. 05/12/1862; bur. Riverview Cemetery, Waynesboro, VA; [249,686] [see deposition of Greenbury B. Terrell].

**Loomis, Charles T.**, Pvt., Co. E; son of Charles & Sarah (McIntyre) Loomis;[1197] enl. Mex. War service 12/08/1846 Petersburg, VA, age 18; discharged 01/1847 by writ of habeas corpus; SA #23772, 12/29/1891, filed from Laguna, San Diego Co., CA; Pension claim rejected *"did not serve 60 days."*[1198]

**Loomis, Ralph J.**, Pvt., Co. D; transferred 05/27/1847 from Co. E, 1st Va. Regt., Buena Vista, Mex., age 35; pres. 04/1848, pay stopped for: 1 jacket-$2.66, 1 pr. pants-$2.28, 2 cotton shirts-$.86, 1 flannel shirt-$.80, 1 blanket-$2.22; pres. 08/1847, BLW sent to [illegible].

**Lorton, Robert**, Pvt., *Preston's Co.*; b. 06/01/1814, Montgomery Co., VA;[1199] enl. Mex. War service 01/04/1846 Montgomery Co., VA, age 33; absent 04/1847 left sick in hosp. at Ft. Monroe, VA since 02/27/1847; absent 06/1847 sick at Ft. Monroe, VA; discharged 03/25/1847 at Ft. Monroe, VA; m. Susanna Ritter, 07/18/1836, Montgomery Co., VA;[1200] Civil War service enl. Pvt., Co. C, 4th Va. Inf., 04/17/1861, age 48, detailed 09/17/1861 as a wagoneer, discharged 04/1862;[54] SC #8446, 02/15/1887, filed from Newbern, Pulaski Co., VA; phys. desc. age 41 [1887], 6'2", auburn hair, blue eyes, occ. Farmer;[1199] since discharge res. Pulaski Co., VA;[1199] d. 06/1893.[1199]

**Lottier, Lewis**, Pvt., Co. A; enl. Mex. War service 12/01/1846 Richmond, VA, age 20; pres. 12/1846 - 04/1847; sick in quarters 06/1847; pres. 08/1847; pres. 10/1847, pay stopped for clothing: 2 cotton shirts-$.86, 2 pr. wool overalls-$4.56, 1 cap-$.95^{1/2}, 2 pr. shoes-$2.44, 4 pr. socks-$.98, 2 flannel shirts-$1.80, 2 pr. drawers-$.71, 1 great coat-$6.93^{1/2}; pres. 12/1847, pay stopped for clothing: 1 pr. shoes-$1.22, 1 blanket-$2.22, 1 pr. socks-$.49; pres. 02/1848, pay stopped for: 1 pr. shoes-$1.22; 1 pick & brush-$.12; pres. 04/1848, pay stopped for 1 wool jacket; pres. 07/1848, pay stopped for: 1 musket sling-$.16, 1 cart. Box belt plate-$.10; BLW sent to Richmond, VA; c. 1850 res. Henrico Co., VA, occ. Tobbaconist, age 23;[1201] d. 09/1_/1853, age 27, bur. Hollywood Cem., Richmond, VA, Sect. D, Lot 209.[119]

**Lotts, John**, Pvt., Co. B; enl. 12/01/1846, Alexandria, VA, age 37; pres. 06/1847; sick 08/1847, pay stopped for 1 musket complete-$14.00; in confinement 10/1847, pay stopped for: 1 pr. shoes-$1.22, 1 pr. overalls-$2.28, 4 pr. socks-$.98, 4 flannel shirts-$3.60; sick 12/1847, forfeit 1 mos. pay by order (120) genl. court-martial, pay stopped for: 1 pr. overalls-$2.28, 1 pr. shoes-$1.22; pres. 02/1848, *"this man is to be paid for a bayonet which was wrongly charged to him with 'a musket complete,' not having been lost with the musket on pay roll of 08/1847;"* sick 04/1848. pres. 08/1848, pay stopped for 1 pick &$ brush-$.12, 1 wiper-$.20, 1 cartridge box plate-$.10, BLW sent to Alexandria, VA

**Love, Hugh**, Pvt., Co. C; enl. Mex. War service 09/26/1847, Petersburg, VA, age 24; pres. 04/1848, joined the company 01/27/1848 from the Regtl. Depot; pres. 04/1848, pay stopped for: 1 india rubber canteen-$.27; d. Monterey, Mex.

**Love, James**, Pvt., Co. A; enl. Mex. War service 11/25/1846 Richmond, VA, age 23; deserted 01/21/1847 at Old Point, VA

**Lucado, Edwin T.**, Pvt., Co. M; b. 01/09/1826, Lynchburg, VA; son of Isaac & Sally (Noell) Lucado; enl. Mex. War service 06/22/1847, Lynchburg, VA, age 22; pres. 09/1847; pres. 11/1847; pres. 12/1847; sick 02/1848; pres. 04/1848, 1 blanket-$2.22, 1 pr. shoes$1.22, 1 cap-$.95^{1/2}; pres. 08/1848, pay stopped for: 1 pr. shoes-$1.22; BLW sent to Lynchburg, VA; m. Sarah Agnes Wright, 04/19/1853, Bedford Co., VA; SC #9686, 02/26/1887, filed from 736 S. Main St., South Bend, IN; phys. desc. age 61 [1887], 5'9", dark complexion, dark gray eyes, black hair, occ. Tailor;[1202] d. 07/02/1896, South Bend, Ind.

OFF TO WAR

*"stomach trouble,"* bur., South Bend City Cem., South Bend, Ind. [1203]

**Lundie, Thomas Y.**, Pvt., Co. D; enl. Mex. War service 08/29/1847, Petersburg, VA, age 18; d. 04/20/1848, Parras, Mex.; wid. Mary, WA #12442, 12/03/1894, from VA; [pension file not found].
**Lunsford, James**, Pvt., Co. E; b. Chesterfield Co., VA;[1204] enl. Mex. War service 12/01/1846 Petersburg, VA, age 18; pres. 04/1847; pres. 06/1847; pres. 08/1847; absent 10/1847 sick, pay stopped for: 2 pr. overalls-$4.56, 2 pr. shoes-$2.44, 2 pr. stockings-$.49, 2 cotton shirts-$.86, 1 cap-$.95$^{1/2}$; pres. 12/1847, pay stopped for: 1 pr. pants-$2.28, 2 pr. socks-$.49, 1 blanket-$2.22; pres. 02/1848; pres. 04/1848, pay stopped for: 1 jacket-$2.37$^{1/2}$; m. Elizabeth Sarah Porch12/22/1852, Petersburg, VA;[1205] Civil War service Pvt., Co. C 18$^{th}$ Btln. VA Arty. 06/01/1861 at Petersburg, VA for 1 yr., pres. 08/31/1861, absent 09/1861, discharged 09/28/1861 to work on Government work, occ. Govt. Blacksmith;[20, 1206] SC #17924, 12/28/1888; filed from 545 Sheppard St., Petersburg, VA; d. 02/22/1894, *Typhoid Fever*, bur. Blandford Cem., Sec. 1, Ward L, Petersburg, VA;[1207] wid. Elizabeth S., WC #9101, 03/08/1894, both from VA; (ESL d. 11/19/1914).[1206]
**Lynch, Joseph N.**, Pvt., Co. G; enl. Mex. War service 11/18/1846 Richmond, VA, age 20; pres. 06/1847; pres. 08/1847; sick 10/1847, pay stopped for: 1 pr. overalls-$2.28, 2 shoes-$2.44, 3 pr. socks-$.73$^{1/2}$, 1 forage cap-$.95$^{1/2}$; absent 12/1847 on extra duty as Hospital Attendant at Saltillo, Mex.; pres. 02/1848, pay stopped for: 1 pr. pants-$2.28; pres. 04/1848; pres. 08/1848, pay stopped for: 1 pr. shoes-$1.16; BLW sent to Richmond, VA
**Mack, George W.**, Pvt., Co. K; enl. Mex. War service Richmond, VA 12/26/1846, age 20; pres. 06/1847; pres. 08/1847; pres. 10/1847, pay stopped for: 2 pr. overalls-$4.56, 4 cotton shirts-$1.72, 4 pr. drawers-$1.42, 4 pr. socks-$.98, 2 pr. shoes-$2.44, 2 flannel shirts-$1.80, 1 greatcoat-$.95$^{1/2}$; pres. 12/1847, pay stopped for: 1 blanket-$2.22; pres. 04/1848, pay stopped for: 1 jacket-$2.66, 1 pr. socks-$.25$^{1/2}$, 1 flannel shirt-$.90, 1 cap-$.95$^{1/2}$, 1 pick & brush-$.12, 1 gun sling-$.18; pres. 07/1848, pay stopped for: 1 gun sling-$.18, 1 wiper-$.20; BLW sent to Richmond, VA
**Magee, Bernard D.**, Pvt., Co. H; b. Ireland;[1208] enl. Mex. War service 01/06/1847, Berkeley, VA, age 18; occ. Hatter;[1208] pres. 04/1847; pres. 06/1847; pres. 08/1847; pres. 10/1847, pay stopped for: 1 forage cap-$.95$^{1/2}$, 1 pr. pants-$2.28, 4 cotton shirts-$1.72, 2 pr. drawers-$.71, 2 pr. shoes-$2.44, 3 pr. socks-$.73$^{1/2}$, 1 blanket-$2.22, 1 jacket-$2.66; pres. 12/1847, pay stopped for: 1 forage cap-$.95$^{1/2}$, 2 flannel shirts-$1.80, 1 pr. shoes-$1.22, 1 pr. pants-$2.28; pres. 02/1848, pay stopped for: 1 jacket-$2.66, 1 cotton shirt-$.43, 1 pr. drawers-$.35$^{1/2}$, 1 pr. shoes-$1.22, 2 pr. socks-$.49; pres. 04/1848; pres. 07/1848, pay stopped for: 1 gun sling-$.16, 2 wipers-$.40, 1 screw driver-$.25, BLW sent to Philadelphia, Pa. m. Ann Corley, 08/10/1851, St. Mary's Catholic Church, Philadelphia, Pa.;[1208] was *"president of the Mexican War Veteran League of Brooklyn, NY;"*[1209] d. 06/07/1885, *"nephritis,"* 750 Myrtle Avenue, Brooklyn, Kings Co., NY;[1210] wid. Ann, WC #37, 03/14/1887, filed from 107 Roger Avenue, Brooklyn, Kings Co., NY; (ACM b. 06/06/1828, Glassworth, Moneghan Co., Ireland).[1211]
**Major, Henry**, [aka Maygar, Magger] Pvt., Co. C; enl. 12/29/1846, Bowling Green, VA, age 22; deserted 01/02/1847 Richmond, VA
**Mahan, Thomas T.**, Pvt., Co. C; enl. Mex. War service 12/30/1846, Bowling Green, VA, age 24; pres. 06/1847; pres. 08/1847, pay stopped for: 1 cap-$.95$^{1/2}$, 2 pr. socks-$.49, 1 pr. drawers-$.35$^{1/2}$; sick 12/1847, pay stopped for: 1 jacket-$2.66, 1 pr. pants-$2.28, 1 blanket-$2.22; pres. 04/1848, pay stopped for: 1 haversack-$.20$^{3/4}$, 1 india rubber canteen-$.27; pres.

204

# VIRGINIA VOLUNTEERS IN MEXICO

08/1848, BLW sent to Philadelphia, Pa.; [Civil War service a Thomas Mahan served as a Pvt., Co. D, 97$^{th}$ Pa. Inf. & as a Sgt., Co. E, 175$^{th}$ Inf. (Draft Militia)]; SC #3296, 03/15/1887, from PA; *"Listed as a photographist in Philadelphia, Pa., 1853-1858. In 1853 he was listed at 312 Market Street, and lived on Olive Street. was listed at the same address in 1854 and 1855, in as Swift (Henry B.) and Mahan. From 1856 to 1858 he was listed at the same address in partnership as Mahan and Good (J.). One source noted him in Baltimore, MD in 1860. An identified image exists from the partnership of Swift and Mahan; one case is embossed on the front, another is gilded on the back. He died in Atlantic City in 1899."*[1212]

**Mahan, Washington L.**, 2$^{nd}$ Lt., Co. C; son of Francis Mahan; law student of Hon. Robert M. Lee of Philadelphia, Pa.; m. w/2 children; enl. Mex. War service Bowling Green, VA, 12/29/1846, age 22; d. 06/01/1847 China, Mex. in a duel, *"I was present on the ground as a friend of Lt. Mahan and a more honorable meeting never took place. They fought with muskets advancing as they chose. They fired when within thirty yards of each other, both falling seriously wounded."*[1213]

**Malone, Marshall**, Pvt., Co. A; enl. Mex. War service 12/01/1846 Richmond, VA, age 25; pres. 12/1846 - 04/1847; under guard 06/1847 by order of Capt. Kemper; *"...confined under guard for theft in which he was detected. The officers of his company report him to be an exceedingly bad man - mutinous - thieving - and difficult to command. His example it is thought by them has been prejudicial to the discipline and good order of the company, and they have reported his case to me with the view to my requesting you order him to be drummed out of camp. They think that such a course would have a happy influence upon the company and lead to the reformation of those who have been under the influence of the prisoner whilst the example of so disgraceful an expulsion from the Army would prove advantageous to the regiment...;"*[1214] discharged 07/11/1847 *"with disgrace and drummed out of camp at Buena Vista."*

**Manning, William W.**, Pvt., Co. F; enl. Mex. War service 11/23/1846, Portsmouth, VA, age 23; absent 06/1847 sick in camp; pres. 08/1847; pres. 10/1847, pay stopped for: 1 pr. overalls-$2.28, 2 cotton shirts-$.86, 4 pr. socks-$.98, 2 pr. drawers-$.71, 2 pr. shoes-$2.44; in confinement 02/1848, pay stopped for: 1 pr. overalls-$2.28, 1 forage cap-$.95$^{1/2}$, 1 cotton shirt-$.43, 1 pr. drawers-$.35$^{1/2}$, 1 blanket-$2.22, 1 flannel shirt-$.90, 1 pr. socks-$.24$^{1/2}$; Court-Martialed 02/18/1848 Buena Vista, Mex. *Charge #1: Absence Without Leave; Specification: In this that Pvt. Wm. W. Manning Co. F, Va. Regt of Vols., did on the 11$^{th}$ of February 1848, get from Lt. J.K. Cooke, Co. F, permission to visit Saltillo to return by Battalion Drill of that day, which he the said Pvt. Wm. W. Manning failed to do. This at Buena Vista, Mexico on or about the 11$^{th}$ of February 1848. Charge #2: Disobedience of Orders; Specification: In this that he, Pvt. Wm. W. Manning, Co. F, Va. Regt., having been detailed for guard on the morning of the 12$^{th}$ instant, positively refused to obey said order, This at Buena Vista, Mexico on or about the 12$^{th}$ of February 1848. To which charges and specification the prisoner pleaded Guilty. 1$^{st}$ Lt. J.A. Cooke, Va. Regt., a witness for the defense being duly sworn, says in answer to the following: Question by the accused: What has been my character as a soldier previous to the offence? Answer: I have been a good deal away from the company, but while I have been on duty with the company I have always found him attentive to his duty and have never known him to miss a time of guard duty previous to this offence. After deliberation the court found the prisoner Guilty of all Charges and Specifications. Sentenced him to forfeit two (2) months pay and to be kept on Police Duty in his company for the period of one month."*[1215] pres. 04/1848, fined 2 mos. pay by order of regtl. court-martial; pres. 08/1848, pay stopped for: 1 waist belt & plate-$.31, 1 bayonet scabbard-$.56, 1 gun sling-$.18, 2 pr. shoes-$2.32, 2 cotton shirts-$.88, 1 blanket-$2.25, BLW sent to Portsmouth, VA c/o E.T. Blamire; SC #2366, 02/26/1887, from VA; OW IA #24216, rejected.

**Mansell, James J.**, Pvt., Co. L; enl. Mex. War service 04/05/1847 Brownsville, Pa., age 19; pres. 06/1847; pres. 08/1847; pres. 10/1847, pay stopped for: 1 pr. pants $2.28, 2 pr. shoes, 1 F Cap.95; pres. 12/1847, pay stopped for: 1 jacket-$2.66, 1 pr. pants-$2.28, 2 pr. shoes-$2.22, 2

OFF TO WAR

cotton shirts-$.86, 1 blanket-$2.22, 3 pr. drawers-$1.06$^{1/2}$, 2 pr. socks-$.49; pres. 02/1848, pay stopped for: 1 pr. Shoes-$1.22, 1 blanket-$2.22, 1 Jacket-$2.66; pres. 04/1848, pay stopped for: 1 Blanket-$2.22, 1 pr. Shoes-$1.22, 4 Cotton Shirts-$1.76; pres. 07/1848; BLW sent to Cumberland, MD; Civil War service 4$^{th}$ W.Va. Vols., IC #712682; SC #8824, 02/23/1887, from OH.

**Mansford, Robert**, Pvt., Co. H; enl. Mex. War service 12/28/1846, Berkeley, VA, age 31; pres. 04/1847; pres. 06/1847; pres. 08/1847; discharged 10/16/1847 Buena Vista, Mex. on Surgeon's Certificate of Disability.

**Manson, John L.**, Pvt., *Preston's Co.*; attended Washington College, Lexington, VA, a classmate of James L. Kemper;[1216] enl. Mex. War service 12/06/1846 Lynchburg, VA, age 21; pres. 04/1847; pres. 06/1847; pres. 08/1847; pres. 10/1847, pay stopped for: 1 jacket-$2.66, 1 pr. overalls-$2.28, 2 pr. socks-$.49, 1 flannel shirt-$.90, 1 cotton shirt-$.43, 1 pr. drawers-$.35$^{1/2}$, 1 cap-$.95$^{1/2}$; pres. 12/1847, pay stopped for: 1 pr. overalls-$2.28, 2 pr. shoes-$2.44, 1 pr. socks-$.24$^{1/2}$; d. 02/24/1848 at Buena Vista, Mex., *"of disease."*[243]

**Manson, Josiah**, Pvt., Co. M; enl. Mex. War service 09/02/1847, Jonesborough, VA, age 20; pres. 10/1847; pres. 11/1847; pres. 12/1847; sick 02/1848; pres. 08/1848, pay stopped for: 1 cartridge box-$1.10, 1 waist belt plate-$.10, 1 bayonet scabbard-$.56, 1 bayonet-$1.44; BLW sent to Jonesborough, Brunswick Co., VA

**Marable, Thomas F.**, Pvt., Co. M; b. Henrico Co., VA;[1217] enl. Mex. War service 06/01/1847, Richmond, VA, phys. desc. of soldier at enl. age 30, 5'8", gray blue eyes, dark hair, fair complexion, occ. Farmer;[1217] pres. 09/1847; pres. 11/1847; pres. 12/1847; pres. 02/1848, pay stopped for: 1 pr. shoes-$1.22; sick 04/1848; pres. 08/1848; BLW sent to Richmond, VA; c. 1850 res. Henrico Co., VA, age 35, occ. None;[1218] m/1 Mary Sharp date/place unknown;[1217] m/2 Robert Ann Throckmorton, 12/15/1853, Richmond, Henrico Co., VA;[1217] d. 11/07/1881;[1217] wid. Roberta A., WC #10486, 10/15/1892, filed from Richmond, Henrico Co., VA; (RTM b. 03/15/1831, Henrico Co., VA, d. 11/11/1903).[1217]

**Marmon, Washington**, 2$^{nd}$ Cpl., Co. B; enl. 11/27/1846, Alexandria, VA, age 23; pres. 06/1847, trans. and subsistence for traveling to rendezvous (114 miles) due; pres. 08/1847; pres. 10/1847, reduced from Cpl. 09/01/1847 by order (103) of genl. court-martial, pay stopped for: 1 pr. shoes-$1.22, 1 cap-$.95$^{1/2}$, 2 pr. socks-$.49, 2 flannel shirts-$1.80; Court-martialed 11/05/1847 Buena Vista, Mex. *Charge #1: Desertion; Specification: In this that Pvt. Washington Marmon, Co. B, Va. Vols., did desert the service of the United States, and was apprehended on the Monclova Road ten (10) or twelve (12) miles from Saltillo. This at Camp Buena Vista, Mex. Oct. 31$^{st}$, 1847.* To which charge and specification the prisoner pleaded *Not Guilty. Lt. R.F. Coleman, Va. Regt., a witness for the prosecution being duly sworn says: I overtook the prisoner about eleven (11) miles from Saltillo, on the Monclova Road in company with two other men of the Regt. on the 31$^{st}$ of last month. He gave himself up and offered no resistance but made some complaints with reference to his Captain and he also remarked that he would leave the country. He had he a large knife, no other weapon. I was ordered in pursuit of him and the two other men of the Regt. He was in the same condition as the other men, sober, but had been drinking apparently. The prisoner also remarked to me at this time of his apprehension, that he could make a living in the country and beat the Mexicans at their own game. That he would not serve with Capt. Corse. He would not stay in the Virginia Regt., but would transfer to some other Corps or words to that effect. Lt. W.J. Minor, Va. Regt., a witness for the prosecution, being duly sworn says in answer to the following question by the Judge Advocate: What was the amount of money you paid for the expenses attending to the apprehension of the prisoner? Answer: The amount of the expenses was about six (6) or eight (8) dollars. I know the prisoner left cap without permission on 31$^{st}$ of Oct. 1847. The court deliberated and found the prisoner Guilty and sentenced him to forfeit two (2) months pay and to be kept at hard labor in the Provost Guard with a ball and chain attached to his leg for the period of two (2) months, and to forfeit five (5) dollars to reimburse,*

# VIRGINIA VOLUNTEERS IN MEXICO

Lt. Minor, for the expenses attending his apprehension;[1219] Court-martialed 12/04/1847 Buena Vista, Mex. *Charge #1 Desertion; Specification: "In that the said Pvt. Washington Morman, Co. B, Va. Regt. Vols., being in confinement in the Provost Guard under charges did break his arrest and desert the service of the United States on or about the night of the 26th of November 1847, and remain away from said Guard and service until the night of the 29th of the same month. This at Camp Buena Vista, Mexico." Lt. E.T. Blamire, Va. Regt. Vols. A witness for the prosecution being duly sworn says. The Prisoner Morman and several others left the Provost Guard on the night of the 26th of November 1847 after tatto call. The Prisoner and Gordon came back on the night of the 29th of Nov. 1847. I do not know how they got out or in.. Question of the Judge Advocate: Did the Prisoner take away with him any of his clothes or things? Answer: I do not know. Question by the Court: Were there any arms missing from the Guard?" Answer: The Sergt. Of the Guard's musket was missing the next morning and it was supposed that some of them men who left took it with them. It has not been heard of since. Question by the Court: How many prisoners of the Provost Guard on the night of the 25th and how many have been brought back? Answer: Eight left, four of them returned of themselves. One was brought back from Saltillo and 3 of them are still absent." Sentenced: "To be made to stand on the head of a barrel two (2) hours each day for one month with a ball and chain weighing 18 pounds attached to his leg...to forfeit his pay proper, and afterward to be kept in confinement in the Provost Guard during the continuance of the war with Mexico. Then to be marked with the letter 'D', one and a half inch long, on the left hip, with india ink, and to be dishonorably discharged from the service;"*[1220] in confinement 12/1847, rejoined company 12/04/1847 from desertion, pay stopped for: 2 pr. cotton drawers-$.71, 1 pr. overalls-$2.28, 1 overcoat-$6.93$^{1/2}$, 1 pr. shoes-$1.22, 2 flannel shirts-$1.80, 1 cap-$.95$^{1/2}$, 2 pr. socks-$.49, 1 blanket-$2.22; 4 cotton shirts-$1.72, 1 jacket-$2.66, 2 blanket-$4.44, in confinement 02/1848, pay stopped by order (No. 27) genl. court-martial, pay stopped for: 2 pr. cotton drawers-$.71, 1 pr. overalls-$2.28, 1 overcoat-$6.93$^{1/2}$, 2 pr. shoes-$2.44, 4 flannel shirts-$3.60, 1 cap-$.95$^{1/2}$, 2 pr. socks-$.49; Court-martialed 04/03/1848 Buena Vista, Mexico, *Charge #1: Desertion; Specification: In this that Pvt. Washington Marmon, Co. B, Va. Regt. Vols., being a prisoner under sentence in the Provost Guard, did break his Guard and remain away from the service of the United States until brought back by a party of mounted men under Corpl. Parke, of Capt. Mears Company, sent in pursuit by order of the Colonel Commanding. This at Buena Vista, Mexico on or about the night of the 17th of January 1848. To which charge and specification the prisoner pleads Not Guilty and Guilty respectively. Lt. P.A. Peterson, Va. Regt. Vols., a witness for the Prosecution, being duly sworn, says: The prisoner left the Provost Guard between 8 and 9 o'clock on the night alluded to in the charge and was brought back between 9 and 10 o'clock the same night by Corpl. Parker. It may have been between 10 and 11, but I am not positive. He was brought back with Pvts. Bibb of the Miss. Regt. and Hurt of the Va. Regt. and they left about the same time. Private John Vine, Capt Mears Cavalry, a witness for the defense, being duly sworn, says: I saw the prisoner, Mormon, in our camp at the Alamo Ranch with Pvt. Bibb of the Miss. Regt. the same night that Corpl. Parker took them back to the Provost Guard. He had been then about half an hour before the Corpl. Took them. After deliberation the Court found the prisoner Not Guilty of the charge but Guilty of Absence Without Leave and Guilty of the specification. He was sentenced to forfeit one months pay;*[1221] in confinement 04/1848, pay stopped by order of genl. court-martial, pay stopped for: 2 pr. cotton drawers-$.71, 1 pr. overalls-$2.28, 1 overcoat-$6.93$^{1/2}$, 2 pr. shoes-$2.44, 4 flannel shirts-$3.60, 1 cap-$.93$^{1/2}$, 2 pr. socks-$.49; dishonorably discharged 08/1848 at the close of the war by order (No. 27) of genl. court-martial; [a Washington Marmon m. Elizabeth Lowe, 09/28/1852, German Reformed Church, Frederick, MD][1222]

**Marshall, Andrew J.**, Pvt., Co. I, enl. Mex. War service 01/01/1847 Richmond, VA, age 24; absent 02/1847, left sick in Hosp. at Ft. Monroe; absent 04/1847 sick at Ft. Monroe, VA;

OFF TO WAR

absent 06/1847 sick at Ft. Monroe, VA; deserted 03/10/1847 Richmond, VA; [an Andrew J. Marshall c. 1850 res. Richmond, Henrico Co., VA, age 30, occ. None, *"Poor House."*[1223]

**Marshall, Charles H.**, Pvt., Co. I; enl. Mex. War service 02/04/1847 Richmond, VA, age 30; pres. 02/1847; pres. 04/1847; pres. 06/1847; d. 08/10/1847 in Hosp. at Saltillo, Mex.

**Martin, James, Jr.**, Pvt., Co. E; enl. Mex. War service 12/04/1846 Petersburg, VA, age 19; pres. 04/1847; pres. 06/1847; pres. 08/1847; pres. 10/1847, pay stopped for: 1 pr. overalls-$2.28, 2 pr. shoes-$2.44, 4 pr. stockings-$.98, 1 cap-$.95$^{1/2}$; pres. 12/1847, pay stopped for: 1 pr. pants-$2.28, 1 pr. shoes-$1.22, 1 cotton shirt-$.43, 1 flannel shirt-$.90, 2 pr. drawers-$.71, 1 blanket-$2.22; pres. 02/1848, pay stopped for: 1 jacket-$2.66, 1 pr. shoes-$1.22, 1 cotton shirt-$.43; pres. 04/1848.

**Martin, John Peter**, Pvt., Co. B; b. c. 1816, Rhine Germany; occ. Butcher; m/1 Sarah Ann Johnson c. 1841;enl. 12/18/1846, Alexandria, VA, age 30; pres. 06/1847; pres. 08/1847; Court-martialed 10/18/1847, Buena Vista, Mex. *Charge #1: Disorderly Conduct; Specification: In this that he, the said Private Peter Martin, Co. B, Va. Regt., did behave in a very riotous and disorderly manner in the streets of Saltillo, Mexico, cursing, fighting and throwing stones. This at Saltillo on or about the 5$^{th}$ of October 1847. Charge #2: Resisting Lawful Authority; Specification: In this that he, the said Private Peter Martin, Co. B, Va. Regt., after being confined in the Guard House and ordered to remain there by the Officer of the Guard, did break open one of the doors of said Guard House and escape there from and remain away until retaken by the guard. This at Saltillo, Mex. on or about the 5$^{th}$ of October 1847. To which charges and specification the prisoner pled Guilty. The prisoner having no defense to make confirmed his plea and sentenced him to be confined at hard labor with a ball and chain attached to his leg in the charge of the Provost Guard for one month. To stand upon the head of a barrel for four hours each day from 7 to 9 o'clock A.M. and from 3 to 5 o'clock P.M. for five days with the ball swung over his shoulder, and to forfeit one months pay;*[1224] in confinement 10/1847, pay stopped for: 2 pr. shoes-$2.44, 1 pr. overalls-$2.28, 4 cotton shirts-$1.72, 2 flannel shirts-$1.80, 1 pr. socks-$.24$^{1/2}$; in confinement 12/1847, forfeit 1 mos. pay by order (No. 117) of genl. court-martial, pay stopped for: 1 pr. overalls-$2.28, 1 pr. shoes-$1.22, 1 cap-$.95$^{1/2}$, 2 cotton shirts-$.86, 1 blanket-$2.22, 1 overcoat-$6.93$^{1/2}$; pres. 02/1848, pay stopped for: being overpaid on last pay roll $.47, 1 pr. shoes-$1.22; pres. 04/1848, pay stopped for: 1 jacket-$2.66; pres. 08/1848, pay stopped for 1 bayonet-$1.44, 1 bayonet scabbard-$.56, 1 waist belt-$.21, 1 waist belt plate-$.10, 1 wiper-$.20, 1 gun sling-$.16, 1 pr. shoes-$1.16, BLW sent to Washington City, DC; (SAM d. 12/14/1869, bur. Congressional Cem., Wash., D.C.); m/2 Nancy (Syncox) Clark 02/22/1871. Washington, D.C. d. 04/03/1883 *consumption*, Leigh St., Richmond, VA, bur. Occoquan, Prince William Co., VA;[1225] wid. Nancy, WA #19135, 09/16/1908, filed from 1813 Guilford Avenue, Baltimore, MD; (NSM b. 11/1833 *"the year the stars fell."*)[14] Soldiers daughter, Mary A. Davis, is only living relative.[1225]

**Martin, William**, Co. E; *Not on Muster Rolls*; wid. Mary C., WC #6341, 03/11/1889, from MO.

**Martin, William A.**, Pvt., Co. I; enl. Mex. War service 01/10/1847 Lynchburg, VA, age 19; pres. 02/1847; pres. 04/1847; pres. 06/1847; absent 08/1847 sick; discharged 10/17/1847 on Surgeon's Certificate of Disability, pay stopped for: 2 cotton shirts-$.86, 1 pr. drawers-$.35$^{1/2}$.

---

[14] The night of November 12-13, 1833, marks the discovery of the Leonid meteor shower and the birth of meteor astronomy. During the hours following sunset on November 12, some astronomers noted an unusual number of meteors in the sky, but it was the early morning hours of the 13th that left the greatest impression on the people of eastern North America. During the 4 hours which preceded dawn, the skies were lit up by meteors. Reactions to the 1833 display are varied from the hysterics of the superstitious claiming Judgement Day was at hand, to the just plain excitement of the scientific, who estimated that a thousand meteors a minute emanated from the region of Leo. Newspapers of the time reveal that almost no one was left unaware of the spectacle, for if they were not awakened by the cries of excited neighbors, they were usually awakened by flashes of light cast into normally dark bedrooms by the fireballs

VIRGINIA VOLUNTEERS IN MEXICO

**Martin, William D.**, Pvt., Co. D; enl. Mex. War service 01/06/1847, Petersburg, VA, age 20; pres. 02/1847; pres. 04/1847; pres. 06/1847; pres. 08/1847, pay stopped for: 1 cap-$.95$^{1/2}$, 2 cotton shirts-$.86, 1 pr. shoes-$1.22; pres. but sick 10/1847, pay stopped for: 1 jacket-$2.66, 1 pr. pants-$2.28, 2 flannel shirts-$1.80, 2 cotton shirts-$.86, 1 pr. drawers-$.35$^{1/2}$, 2 pr. socks-$.49, 1 pr. shoes-$1.22, 1 overcoat-$6.93$^{1/2}$; pres. 12/1847, pay stopped for: 1 cap-$.95$^{1/2}$, 1 pr. pants-$2.28, 1 pr drawers-$.35$^{1/2}$, 2 pr. shoes-$2.44, 2 pr. socks-$.49, 2 blankets-$4.44, 2 flannel shirts-$1.80; pres. 04/1848, pay stopped for: 1 pr. pants-$2.28, 2 cotton shirts-$.86, 1 blanket-$2.22, 1 haversack-$.20$^{3/4}$; pres. 08/1847, BLW sent to [illegible] Dinwiddie Co., VA

**Marye, John B.P.**, Pvt., Co. E; enl. Mex. War service 11/30/1846 Petersburg, VA, age 27; absent 04/1847 on detached service as Hosp. Steward since 02/28/1847; absent 06/1847 on detached service as Hosp. Steward; absent 08/1847 on detached service as Hosp. Steward; absent 10/1847 on detached service as Hosp. Steward; discharged 11/24/1847 Monterey, Mex.

**Mason, Thomas S.**, 2$^{nd}$ Lt., Co. C; enl. Mex. War service 12/29/1846, Bowling Green, VA, age 28; pres. 06/1847, prom. 1$^{st}$ Sgt. 06/13/1847; pres. 08/1847, prom. 2$^{nd}$ Lt. 08/25/1847, pay stopped for: 1 pr. drawers-$.35$^{1/2}$, 2 pr. socks-$.49, 2 woolen shirts-$1.80; pres. 10/1847; discharged 12/31/1847 Buena Vista, Mex., by order of Genl. Wool.

**Mason, Thompson**, Pvt., Co. H; b. c. 1819, Washington Co., MD; enl. Mex. War service 12/21/1846, Berkeley, VA, age 29; pres. 04/1847; absent 06/1847 left sick in Hosp. at Monterey, Mex. 06/23/1847; pres. 08/1847; pres. 10/1847, pay stopped for: 1 forage cap-$.95$^{1/2}$, 1 pr. pants-$2.28, 3 cotton shirts-$1.29, 2 flannel shirts-$1.80, 2 pr. shoes-$2.44, 3 pr. socks-$.73$^{1/2}$, 1 greatcoat-$6.93$^{1/2}$, 1 blanket-$2.22, 1 jacket-$2.66; discharged 12/21/1847 Saltillo, Mex. by order of Sec. of War; desc., age 29, 5'10$^{1/2}$", light complexion, light hair, hazel eyes, occ. Lawyer.[26]

**Matthews, Robert**, 3$^{rd}$ Cpl., Co. B; enl. 12/18/1846, Alexandria, VA, age 30; pres. 06/1847; sick 08/1847; discharged 02/17/1847 Buena Vista, Mex. on Surgeon's Certificate of Disability.

**Maule, Lewis**, Pvt., Co. A; enl. Mex. War service Richmond, VA, age 22; pres. 12/1846 – 04/1847; pres. 06/1847; pres. 08/1847; Court-martialed 09/20/1847, Buena Vista, Mex. Charge #1: *Laying Down and Sleeping On Post; Specification: In this that he, the said Pvt. Lewis Maul, Co. A, Va. Regt. of Vols., being regularly detailed and duly posted as a sentinel on post No. 6 Quarter Guard, was found by the Officer of the Day, laying down on his post and believed to be asleep. This at Buena Vista, Mexico on or about the morning of the 4$^{th}$ day of September 1847.* To which charges and specifications the prisoner pleaded Not Guilty. Captain E.G. Alburtis, Va. Regt. of Vols., a witness for the prosecution, being duly sworn, says: *I was Officer of the Day at the time specified. I visited the Guards between one and two o'clock A.M. of the 4$^{th}$ Sept,. 1847. When I came to the post of the prisoner I found him laying down. I approached within a few feet of him before he attempted to rise. I think he was laying on his side with his musket near him and his blanket drawn over him and had the appearance of being asleep. I asked him: Why he had laid down? He replied that he was very sick and had been so during the night. He also stated to me that before going on his post he had taken some oil. I asked him why he had not reported himself as sick? He replied that he did not think to do it. Thus he thought he could stand out his tour of duty. I passed on to the Guard tents and found upon inquiry that the prisoner had complained of being sick and had taken medicine before going on post.* Question by the Judge Advocate: Did the prisoner rise and hail to you before you addressed him? Answer: No. Question by the Judge Advocate: Did you have to make exertions to rouse him by shaking him or speaking in a loud voice? Answer: No. Pvt. William Radikin, Co. A, Va. Regt. of Vols., a witness for the defense, being duly sworn, says: *I was posted on post No.5 at the time specified. The prisoner complained of being sick. I spoke to the prisoner who was standing on his post and walked from him to post No. 4 when I saw the Officer of the Day approaching. It could not have been more than five minutes from the time that I left the prisoner till he was found laying down by the Officer of the Day.* Col. J. F. Hamtramck, Va. Regt., a witness for the defense, being duly sworn, says: *The character of the*

## OFF TO WAR

*prisoner is good. There are few privates in his company who are better for attention to duty. The prisoner addressed the court in his own defense stating: I was sick before marching on guard, but did not wish to get excused from duty as complaints had been made by members of the company of men getting excused when detailed for duty. I did not rise when the officer of the day approached by reason of being confused at being found lying down on post. After deliberation the Court found the prisoner Not Guilty of the Charge and Guilty of the specification of lying down on his post. Sentenced him to be confined at hard labor in the Provost Guard for two weeks;"*[1226] in confinement 10/1847; pay stopped for clothing: 2 pr. stockings-$.49, 1 cap-$.95$^{1/2}$, 1 cotton shirts-$.43; pres. 12/1847, pay stopped for clothing: 1 pr. shoes-$1.22, 1 pr. wool overalls-$2.28, 1 blanket-$2.22, 2 pr. socks-$.49, 1 flannel shirt-$.90; pres. 02/1848, pay stopped for: 1 pick & brush-$.12; pres. 04/1848; BLW sent to Richmond, VA; c. 1850 res. City of Richmond, VA, occ. Painter, age 25;[1227] c. 1860 res. City of Richmond, occ. Painter, age 35, m. Pheobe;[1228] d. 1861[1229]

**Maxwell, Edward W.**, 1$^{st}$ Sgt., Co. H; b. 07/23/1818, Martinsburg, VA; son of James & Emily Maxwell;[1230, 1231] Wrote in to the Martinsburg Gazette: *"Patrick Henry – A name ever dear to this country. In the hour of gloom he hovered over her dark fortunes, like the spirit of hope upon the verge of despair;"*[1232] enl. Mex. War service 11/21/1846, Berkeley, VA, age 28; pres. 04/1847; pres. 06/1847; pres. 08/1847; pres. 10/1847, pay stopped for: 1 pr. pants-$2.28, 4 pr. drawers-$1.42, 2 pr. shoes-$2.44, 9 pr. socks-$2.20$^{1/2}$, 1 greatcoat-$6.93$^{1/2}$; pres. 12/1847, pay stopped for: 1 forage cap-$.95$^{1/2}$, 2 pr. pants-$4.56, 2 flannel shirts-$1.80, 2 pr. socks-$.49, 1 blanket-$2.22; pres. 02/1848, pay stopped for: 1 jacket-$2.66, 1 pr. pants-$2.28, 1 pr. shoes-$1.22; pres. 04/1848; pres. 07/1848, BLW sent to Martinsburg, Berkeley Co., VA; m. Rosa Alburtis, 05/20/1850, Hagerstown, Washington Co., MD;[1230] c. 1860 res. Charles Town, Jefferson Co., VA;[1233] w. Dianna; SC #7940, 03/11/1887, filed from Martinsburg, Berkeley Co., WV; since discharge res. Virginia, Iowa, *"and now* [1887] *West Virginia;"*[1230] John W. Keef gave affidavit in pension claim; d. 05/221891, Martinsburg, WV, *General Debility, age 73;"*[1234] bur. Old Norbourne Cem., Berkeley Co., WV.[45]

**Maxwell, William B.**, 3$^{rd}$ Cpl., Co. B; enl. 12/13/1846, Alexandria, VA, age 22; pres. 06/1847; pres. 08/1847; pres. 10/1847, apptd. 3$^{rd}$ Cpl. From Pvt. 09/25/1847 by regt. order #110, pay stopped for: 3 pr. socks-$.73$^{1/2}$, 3 pr. cotton drawers-$1.06, 1 cotton shirts-$1.86, 1 flannel shirt-$.90, 1 pr. shoes-$1.22; pres. 12/1847, pay stopped for: 1 pr. overalls-$2.28, 1 pr. shoes-$1.22, 1 pr. cotton drawers-$.35$^{1/2}$, 2 blanket-$4.44, 1 overcoat-$6.93$^{1/2}$, 2 flannel shirts-$1.80, 1 blanket-$2.22; pres. 02/1848; pres. 04/1848, prom. 2$^{nd}$ Cpl.; pres. 08/1848, pay stopped for: 1 bayonet scabbard-$.56, 1 wiper-$.20, 1 screw driver-$.07, 1 pr. shoes-$1.16, BLW sent to Washington, DC; SC #16689, 03/27/1888, wid. Sarah E., WC #2795, 12/20/1887, from NM; Navy WA #2147, rejected.

**Maygar, Henry**, [aka Magger, Major] 3$^{rd}$ Cpl., Co. C; enl. Mex. War service 12/29/1846, Bowling Green, VA, age 22; deserted 01/02/1847 Richmond, VA

**Maynard, Mendoza B.**, *"Dose"* Co. D; b. 04/07/1825 Surry Co., VA;[1235] enl. Mex. War service 12/11/1847, Petersburg, VA, age 22; pres. 02/1847; pres. 04/1847; pres. 06/1847; pres. 08/1847, pay stopped for: 1 cap-$.95$^{1/2}$, 1 pr. shoes-$1.22; pres. 10/1847, pay stopped for: 2 cotton shirts-$.86, 2 pr. socks-$.49, 1 pr. shoes-$1.22; pres. 12/1847, pay stopped for: 1 jacket-$2.66, 1 pr. pants-$2.28, 1 blanket-$2.22; pres. 04/1848, pay stopped for: 1 set of picks & brushes-$.12, 2 cotton shirts-$.86, 1 pr. shoes-$1.22, 1 haversack-$.20$^{3/4}$; pres. 08/1847, BLW sent to Richmond, VA; Civil War service Co. C, 33$^{rd}$ Tx. Cav.; m/1 Guadalupe Co., TX? c. 1862 Illione Mary Catherine Hector; m/2 Sallie E. Hillyear 10/06/1871 Bastrop, TX;[1235] Announces himself an independent candidate for Treasurer, Bastrop County, TX 1873, actually runs on the Republican ticket;[1236] loses election 1097 votes to 1128 votes;[1237] Candidate for Alderman Bastrop, TX 1875;[1238] (SEM d.10/06/1882, Leachville, Milam Co., TX);[1235] SC #7284, 05/25/1887, filed from Bastrop, Bastrop Co., TX; d. 02/27/1899, bur. Fairview Cemetery, Bastrop, TX.[1235]

VIRGINIA VOLUNTEERS IN MEXICO

**Mays, Mortimer N.**, Pvt., *Recruit Co.*, enl. Mex. War service 03/01/1848 Lynchburg, VA; pres. 06/1848; BLW sent to Lynchburg, VA; Civil War service 2nd Lt., Co. H, 49th Va. Inf.[1239]

**McAllister, William T.**, Pvt., Co. G; enl. Mex. War service 11/28/1846 Richmond, VA, age 30; absent 06/1847, left sick in Hosp. at Camargo, Mex. 05/21/1847; d. 06/12/1847 in Hosp. Camargo, Mex.

**McArthur, John D.**, Pvt., Co. A; enl. Mex. War service 12/14/1846 Richmond, VA, age 25; deserted 12/25/1846 at Richmond, VA; [a John D. McArthur d. 01/__/1854; bur. Hollywood Cem., Richmond, VA, Sect., Lot 134.][119]

**McCaleb, Thomas J.**, Pvt., Co. E; b. Manchester, VA;[1240] enl. Mex. War service 12/03/1846 Petersburg, VA, age 26; pres. 04/1847; pres. 06/1847; pres. 08/1847; pres. 10/1847, pay stopped for: 1 pr. overalls-$2.28, 2 pr. shoes-$2.44, 2 pr. stockings-$.49, 1 cap-$.95$^{1/2}$, 1 blanket-$2.22; pres. 12/1847, pay stopped for: 1 pr. pants-$2.28, 1 pr. shoes-$1.22, 2 pr. drawers-$.71; pres. 02/1848, pay stopped for: 1 jacket-$2.66, 1 pr. shoes-$1.22, 1 cap-$.95$^{1/2}$; pres. 04/1848, pay stopped for: 1 jacket-$2.37$^{1/2}$; Civil War service Sgt., Co. D, 3rd Btln. VA Reserves (Archer's);[202] Asst. Assessor, U.S. Revenue Dept., Petersburg, VA 1870;[1241] SC #2492, 03/05/1887; d. 11/28/1899, *Paralysis*, bur. Blandford Cem., Sq. 4, Sect. 7, Ward G, Petersburg, VA;[1242] wid. Ella, WC #11917, 12/08/1899, both from VA; [pension file not found].

**McCarthy, Dennis**, Pvt., Co. D; b. c. 1819; enl. Mex. War service 12/11/1846, Petersburg, VA, age 28; pres. 02/1847; pres. 04/1847; pres. but sick 06/1847; absent 08/1847, on detached service as Hosp. Attendant, pay stopped for: 1 cap-$.95$^{1/2}$; absent 10/1847 on detached service as Hosp. Attendant since 07/15/1847; pres. but sick 12/1847; discharged 11/19/1847 on Surgeon's Certificate, *"fistula in ano;"*[1244] discharge desc., b. Washington Co., TN, age 28, 5'9", fair complexion, blue eyes, brown hair, occ. Tanner;[26] m. Sarah E. Wilson 10/28/1855 Caldwell Co. or Wautauga Co., NC (pension files also suggests m. 12/19/1856, Taylorsville TN);[1243] OW IC #134490, file #45913, 11/13/1874, filed from Cherokee Station, Crawford Co., KS; *"I was detailed to wait on the sick at Buena Vista and there where I was ruptured by one Samuel Pleasants falling on me when I was moving him from one bed to another. We had strewn on the floor some mint and I got my feet tangled in it as I was turning around and fell and he fell on me and caused the rupture..."*[1244] since discharge res. North Carolina 13 yrs., Cherokee, KS 13 yrs., Joplin MS 10 yrs;[1244] admitted 12/13/1885 Soldier's Home, Washington, D.C.;[1244] d. 01/27/1893, Joplin, Jasper Co., Mo.;[1243] wid. Sarah, WC #12169, 04/22/1893, filed from Joplin, Jasper Co., Mo.; letter lists four children *"2 boys & 2 girls;"*[1245] (SEM b. 04/25/1838, NC, d. 12/30/1906, Dearing, KS).[1243]

**McClure, William C.**, Pvt., Co. K; enl. Mex. War service Jefferson Co., VA 01/04/1847, age 18; pres. 06/1847, prom. 2nd Cpl. from 4th Cpl. 05/31/1847; pres. 08/1847, prom. 1st Cpl.; pres. 10/1847, reduced to ranks from 1st Cpl. 09/18/1847, pay stopped for: 3 pr. socks-$.73$^{1/2}$, 2 pr. shoes-$2.44, 2 pr. overalls-$4.56, 1 cap-$.95$^{1/2}$, 1 pr. drawers-$.35$^{1/2}$, 2 flannel shirts-$1.80, 4 cotton shirts-$1.72; pres. 12/1847, pay stopped for: 1 jacket-$2.66, 1 pr. boots-$1.22, 2 pr. socks-$.49, 1 blanket-$2.22, 1 flannel shirt-$.90; pres. 04/1848, pay stopped for: 1 pr. shoes-$1.22, 1 gun sling-$.18; pres. 07/1848, pay stopped for: 1 screw driver-$.25, 1 wiper-$.20, 1 cartridge box plate-$.10; BLW sent to Upperville, Fauquier Co., VA; SC #17109, 08/30/1888, from VA

**McCollum, Daniel**, Pvt., Co. D; enl. Mex. War service 01/08/1847, Richmond, VA, age 28; pres. 02/1847; absent 04/1847 sick sent from Camargo, Mex. to Hosp. Matamoros, Mex. 03/29/1847; absent 06/1847, sick in Hosp. Matamoros, Mex.; deserted about 05/01/1847 near Camargo, Mex.; pres. 12/1847, rejoined the company *"accounts satisfactorily for his long absence, continued sickness at Matamoros-Camargo, Mex. being the cause,"* pay stopped for: 1 cap-$.95$^{1/2}$, 1 jacket-$2.66, 2 pr. pants-$4.56, 2 cotton shirts-$.86, 1 flannel shirts-$1.80, 1 pr

OFF TO WAR

drawers-$.35$^{1/2}$, 1 pr. shoes-$1.22, 1 blanket-$2.22, 1 overcoat-$6.93$^{1/2}$; pres. 04/1848, pay stopped for: 1 haversack-$.20$^{3/4}$; pres. 08/1847, BLW sent to New Orleans, La.

**McCorkle, Alexander C.**, Pvt., Co. H; b. 1823, Rockbridge Co., VA, son of John & Sarah Etchison (Cunningham) McCorkle; enl. Mex. War service 01/28/1847, Richmond, VA, age 23; pres. 04/1847, transportation & subsistence due from place of residence to rendezvous, 300 miles; d. 06/091847 Monterey, Mex.; attended VMI (non-graduate); never married.

**McCormack, William**, Pvt., Co. H; enl. Mex. War service 01/06/1847, Berkeley, VA, age 19; pres. 04/1847; pres. 06/1847; pres. 08/1847; pres. 10/1847, pay stopped for: 1 forage cap-$.95$^{1/2}$, 1 pr. pants-$2.28, 2 cotton shirts-$.86, 2 flannel shirts-$1.80, 1 pr. drawers-$.35$^{1/2}$, 2 pr. shoes-$2.44, 3 pr. socks-$.73$^{1/2}$, 1 blanket-$2.22, 1 jacket-$2.66; pres. 12/1847, pay stopped for: 1 pr. socks-$.24$^{1/2}$, 1 blanket-$2.22; pres. 02/1848, pay stopped for: 2 pr. drawers-$.71, 1 pr. shoes-$1.22; pres. 04/1848; pres. 07/1848, pay stopped for: 1 gun sling-$.16, 1 brush & pick-$.12, 1 screw driver-$.25, 1 wiper-$.20, BLW sent to Philadelphia, Pa.

**McCormick, William**, 2$^{nd}$ Lt., Co. K; enl. Mex. War service Jefferson Co., VA 12/12/1846; pres. 06/1847; pres. 08/1847; pres. 10/1847; sick 12/1847 on leave of absence in Saltillo, Mex., resigned 12/31/1847.

**McCoy, George M.**, Pvt., Co. L; b. 1823; enl. Mex. War service 03/02/1847 Fairfax C.H., VA, age 24; sick 06/1847; discharged 08/30/1847 at Saltillo, Mex. on Surgeon's Certificate of Disability.[72]

**McCready, Jeremiah**, Pvt., Co. F; enl. Mex. War service 01/22/1847, Portsmouth, VA, age 18; pres. 06/1847; court-martialed 06/17/1847, Buena Vista, Mex. *Charge #1: Conduct Prejudicial to Good Order and Military Discipline; Specification: "In this that Pvt. Jeremiah McCready, Co. F, 1$^{st}$ Virginia Regiment, did on the morning of the 11$^{th}$ of June 1847 strike, Pvt. John Shilling of said company without provocation; To which charge and specification the prisoner pled Not Guilty. Pvt. John Shilling, of Co. F, Virginia Regt. of Volunteers a witness for the prosecution being duly sworn, says: n the camp of the Virginia Regt. about a week ago I accused the prisoner of giving me lice and found some upon me and never had any before he came to the tent. He called me a 'God damned son of a bitch,' and said 'I'll take a musket and shoot your brains out.' I then took hold of him by the collar when he stooped down and picked up a rock (the witness here exhibited a large stone weighing seven or eight pounds) and hit me along side of the head with it. About three minutes afterwards I fell down from the effects of the blow wich I believe has broken my ear. Private John Connor, of Co. F, Va. Regt., of Volunteers, a witness for the prosecution being duly sworn says: I was standing in the camp of the Va. Regt. on the parade ground of Co. F, about six, seven or eight days ago, when I heard language somewhat excited. I saw two men, one had the other by the throat with his left hand, and with threats and by the motion of his arm I heard him threaten to knock off his head or words to that effect. I heard him to let go he did so for a short time but then caught hold of him again. When McCready, who was the man held by the other, caught up a rock or stone and hit the man in the side of the head. I am not certain whether this is the stone(referring to exhibit) thrown by McCready or not. I think the one thrown was not so large or so dark a color. The man who held the prisoner by the throat was Pvt. John Shillings, of Co. F. Other witnesses who corroborated this version were: Pvt. Henry Webster, of Co. F, Pvt. Christopher Lawrence, of Co. F; The prisoner then stated to the court: "On the morning referred to I cooked breakfast myself and we ate together. Afterwards Shilling went away. When he came back he commenced rising? And swearing and said he had got lice on him and that he got them from me. He came out of the tent and said he would search me. He came towards me and caught me by the throat and choked me. I told him to let go, he did so, but ran at me again and caught hold of me. I caught up a stone and as he grabbed at my arm it fell out of my hand and hit him on the head. He then stripped me up and choked me on the ground, struck me with his fists swore at me and abused me some time; the court found him not guilty and dismissed the charges;"*[1246] pres. 08/1847; pres. 10/1847, pay stopped for: 1 pr. overalls-

VIRGINIA VOLUNTEERS IN MEXICO

$2.28, 2 cotton shirts-$.86, 1 forage cap-$.95$^{1/2}$, 1 pr. shoes-$1.22, 1 pr. socks-$.24$^{1/2}$; pres. 02/1848, pay stopped for: 1 pr. overalls-$2.28, 1 cotton shirt-$.43, 1 pr. shoes-$1.22, 1 blanket-$2.22, 1 infantry jacket-$2.66; pres. 04/1848; pres. 08/1848, pay stopped for: 1 waist belt plate-$.10, 1 wiper-$.20, 1 brush & pick-$.12, 1 screw driver-$.25, 1 forage cap-$.83, BLW sent to Philadelphia, Pa.; Civil War service 2$^{nd}$ Lt., Co. G, 51$^{st}$ Pa. Inf.; XC #2660564; SC #16504, 02/16/1904, wid. Annie J., WC #16380, 10/08/1908, both from PA; d. 08/01/1908, Philadelphia, PA; [pension file in custody of Department of Verterans Affairs].
**McCrory, Thomas**, Pvt., Co. K; enl. Mex. War service Frederick Co., VA 01/20/1847, age 39; pres. 06/1847; pres. 08/1847, to forfeit 1 mos. pay by order of garrison court-martial; pres. 10/1847, pay stopped for: 1 pr. overalls-$2.28, 1 cap-$.95$^{1/2}$, 2 pr. drawers-$.71, 2 pr. socks-$.49, 2 pr. shoes-$2.44; pres. 12/1847, pay stopped for: 1 jacket-$2.66, 1 pr. overalls-$2.28, 1 blanket-$2.22; d. 03/04/1848 at Parras, Mex. *"was assassinated by a Mexican."*
**McDaniel, Reuben**, Pvt., *Preston's Co.*; b. 02/07/1825 Floyd Co., VA;[1247] enl. Mex. War service 12/09/1846 Montgomery Co., VA, age 21; absent 04/1847 left sick in hosp. at Ft. Monroe, VA from 02/27/1847; absent 06/1847 sick at Ft. Monroe, VA; discharged 03/25/1847 at Ft. Monroe, VA; BLW sent to Washington City, D.C. m. Mary F. Rogers, 10/11/1848, Mt. Airy, Surry Co., NC;[1247] [see Recruit Co. muster rolls]; Civil War service Pvt., Co. H, 54$^{th}$ Va. Inf. enl. 10/01/1861 at Jacksonville, pres. 01/01/1862, deserted from Emory & Henry College Hosp. 12/01/1863;[192] c. 1870 res. Big Spring, Montgomery Co., VA, age 46, occ. Works at Steam Saw Mill, w. Mary (42), son Osborne (19), Alfred (17), son William (14), Edward (12), Samuel (4), Elizabeth G. (4), Laura (1);[1248] SC #5736, 05/02/1887, filed from Big Spring, Montgomery Co., VA; phys. desc. at enl. age 27, 5'10", dark hair, fair complexion, blue eyes, occ. Hatter;[1247] since discharge res. Floyd Co. and Montgomery Co., VA;[1247] Henry Collins, John E. Laurence and John H. Minnick gave affidavits in pension claim;[1247] d. 05/14/1897, near Elliston, Montgomery Co., VA;[1249] wid. Mary F., WC #10986, 05/28/1897, filed from Elliston, Montgomery Co., VA; (MRM b. 12/25/1829, Floyd Co., VA, d. 08/16/1908).[1249]
**McDonald, John A.**, Pvt., Co. L; b. 1828; enl. Mex. War service 04/02/1847 Rely House, VA, age 19; pres. 06/1847; pres. 08/1847; pres. 10/1847, to forfeit $7 sent. of garrison court-martial. pay stopped for: 1 pr. Pants 2.28, 1 pr. Shoes 1.22; Court-martialed 11/15/1847 at Buena Vista, Mex. *Charge #1: Unsoldierlike and Disorderly Conduct: Specification: In this that the said John McDonald, a Private of the 13$^{th}$ Co., Va. Regt. of Vols., did on the night of the 6$^{th}$ of November 1847 in the streets of Saltillo behave in a riotous and disorderly manner swearing in a loud tone that he 'did not care a damn for anybody' or words to that effect; Charge #2: Abusive Language to His Superior Officer; Specification: In this that he, Pvt. John McDonald, 13$^{th}$ Co., Va. Regt., did on the 8$^{th}$ day of November 1847 curse and abuse Sergt. Phillips the Sergeant of the Guard on that day, swearing 'that he would be a match for him, 'a damned old son of a bitch, that he would kill him,' or words to that effect; Charge #3: Mutinous Conduct; Specification #1: In this that he, Pvt. John McDonald, did resist the Guard on the 8$^{th}$ day of November 1847 using threatening and abusive language, refusing to obey orders and swearing that he would kill any man that would touch him. All this at Saltillo, Mexico. Specification #2: In this that he, Pvt. John McDonald, 13$^{th}$ Co., Va. Regt., said on the 8$^{th}$ day of November 1847 that he would do no more duty in the company but would desert or words to that effect, and that he used similar language on the 6$^{th}$ day of November and on several occassions. At Saltillo, Mexico. Charge #4: Resisting Lawful Authority; Specification: In this that the said Private John McDonald, being confined in the Guard House in Saltillo on the 8$^{th}$ day of November 1847, did make an effort to force his way by the guard swearing that he 'would kill any man who would touch him.' All this at Saltillo, Mexico. To Charge #1, #2, #4 and all specifications the prisoner plead Not Guilty. To Charge #3 and specifications the prisoner plead Guilty. Sergt. Charles Bishop, 13$^{th}$ Co., Va. Regt. Vols., a witness for the prosecution, being duly sworn says: On the night the prisoner was confined the 6$^{th}$ instant, I was in the Captains room in Saltillo. The prisoner came into his quarters, drunk and making a*

OFF TO WAR

*good deal of noise, cursing and swearing in a loud tone. The Captain warned him to stop making noise. He did not stop and the Captain then ordered me to go for a file of the Guard and take him to the Guard House. I started but came back and took him down myself. The prisoner was cursing and swearing and made a good deal of noise this was at Saltillo, Mexico on or about the 6$^{th}$ of Nov. Question by the Judge Advocate: Did the prisoner use the words that he didn't care a damn for anything or words of like import? Answer I can not say positively as to those words but he used some of similar import. I took them to be the boast of a drunken man than anything else. Question by the Judge Advocate: Did the prisoner make any noise in the street before he came into the quarters? Answer: He was drunk and noisy in the street just before the guardhouse. Sergt. Lewis B. Phillips, Co., G, N.C. Regt., a witness for the prosecution, being duly sworn, says: I was Sergt. of the Guard in Saltillo on that day about the 8$^{th}$ of Nov. I think. The prisoner was confined in the Guard Room and attempted to come out. I met him at the door and told him that he should not come out. He asked why? I told him he was a prisoner and had not the right to come out when he pleased. He then swore that he would come out and attempted to do so. I pushed him back perhaps as often as twice before I had an opportunity to shut the door. He then commenced with abusive language. Cursing and calling me a 'damned old rascal,' and making threats as to what he would do and that he would see me at another time. Lt. Mastin was Officer of the Guard but was absent just at this time. He cam back in a short time however and I reported to him immediately the conduct of the prisoner. He the went into the room to confine him. The prisoner got hold of a black bottle and swore that he would kill the first man that would venture to touch him. Then some four or five of the guard came into the room to assist in taking him and it was for some time before they could succeed in getting hold of him and he threw the bottle as it was shaken out of his hand in the scuffle. They then succeeded in throwing him down and tying him. He untied himself and Lt. Mastin had him bound, his abuse after this was if anything more scurrilous than before. After deliberation the court found him Guilty of all charges and specifications and sentenced him to forfeit one months pay and to be kept at hard labor with a ball and chain attached to his leg with charge of the Provost Guard for the period of two months.*[1250] in confinement 12/1847, pay stopped for: 1 jacket-$2.66, 2 pr. pants-$4.56, 1 cap-$.95$^{1/2}$, 3 pr. shoes-$3.66, 3 cotton shirts-$1.29, 1 overcoat-$6.93$^{1/2}$, 2 pr. drawers-$.71, 1 pr. socks-$.24$^{1/2}$; pres. 02/1848, pay stopped for: 1 Blanket 2.22, 1 Brush & Pick .12; absent 04/1848 sick in hospital, to forfeit 1 mos. pay by sentence of general court-martial; pres. 07/1848, pay stopped for: 1 pr. Shoes 1.16, 1 Screw Driver, 1 Wiper .20; BLW sent to Washington City, D.C.

**McFarland, Samuel**, Pvt., Co. C; enl. Mex. War service 12/30/1846, Bowling Green, VA, age 25; d. 06/04/1847 China, Mex.

**McGathey, Levi**, Pvt., Co. C; enl. Mex. War service 12/29/1846, Bowling Green, VA, age 44; pres. 06/1847; pres. 08/1847, pay stopped for: 1 cap-$.95$^{1/2}$, 2 pr. socks-$.49, 2 cotton shirts-$.86, 2 woolen shirts-$1.80, 1 pr. shoes-$1.22; pres. 10/1847, pay stopped for: 2 pr. drawers-$.71, 1 jacket-$2.66, 1 pr. pants-$2.28, 1 pr. shoes-$1.22; pres. 12/1847, pay stopped for: 1 cap-$.95$^{1/2}$, 1 woolen shirt-$.90, 1 blanket-$2.22; pres. 04/1848, fined 1 mos. pay by order of genl. court-martial, pay stopped for: 1 pr. shoes-$1.50, 1 india rubber canteen-$.27; pres. 08/1848, BLW sent to Philadelphia, Pa.

**McGee, Fleming C.**, Pvt., Co. E; b. 04/04/1822 Sussex Co., VA;[1251] enl. Mex. War service 12/14/1846 Petersburg, VA, age 24; pres. 04/1847; pres. 06/1847; pres. 08/1847; pres. 10/1847, pay stopped for: 1 pr. overalls-$2.28, 2 pr. shoes-$2.44, 2 pr. stockings-$.49, 2 cotton shirts-$.86, 2 pr. drawers-$.71, 1 cap-$.95$^{1/2}$, 1 overcoat-$6.93$^{1/2}$; pres. 12/1847, pay stopped for: 1 pr. pants-$2.28, 2 pr. socks-$.49, 2 flannel shirt-$1.80, 1 blanket-$2.22; pres. 02/1848, pay stopped for: 1 blanket-$2.22; absent 04/1848 sick in Hosp.; m. Martha A.S. Wilbourne, 02/1849;[1252] Civil War service Pvt., 2$^{nd}$ Co. A, 9$^{th}$ Va. Inf. enl. 03/14/1862, detailed for duty by special order 04/05/1864;[211] SC #3988, 04/07/1881, filed from Petersburg, Dinwiddie Co.,

## VIRGINIA VOLUNTEERS IN MEXICO

VA; Thomas J. McCaleb gave affidavit in pension claim;[1251] d. 1888, bur. Blandford Cem., Petersburg, VA[1251, 76]

**McGowan, William G.**, 2nd Lt., Co. D; enl. Mex. War service 12/24/1846, Petersburg, VA; *"Lt. William J. McCowan received from old schoolmates sword, sash and epaulettes;"*[1253] absent 02/1847 sailed from Fort Monroe, VA 02/22/1847 on board the Barque *Exact* for Port Isabel, Tex.; under arrest 04/1847, rejoined company at Camargo, Mex. 03/27/1847, AWOL from camp near Monterey, Mex. from 4:00 04/27/1847 until 04/29/1847 arrested by order of Maj. Early; pres. 06/1847, released from arrest 05/09/1847; pres. 08/1847; pres. 10/1847; pres. 12/1847; pres. 04/1848; pres. 08/1848; d. 08/24/1874, *"Maj. Wm. J. McGowan, of Prince George Co., Mexican War veteran;"*[1254] tribute by the Hibernian Society and Mexican volunteers;"[1255] d. of *Apoplexy*, bur. Blandford Cem., Sq. 139, Ward A, Petersburg, VA[1256]

**McGuire, Patrick**, Pvt., Co. H; enl. Mex. War service 01/06/1847, Berkeley, VA, age 19; deserted 01/22/1847 Richmond, VA, *"nothing paid before desertion."*

**McIntosh, Joseph**, Pvt., Co. E; enl. Mex. War service 12/01/1846 Petersburg, VA, age 22; pres. 04/1847; pres. 06/1847; pres. 08/1847; pres. 10/1847, pay stopped for: 1 pr. overalls-$2.28, 3 pr. shoes-$3.66, 2 pr. stockings-$.49, 4 cotton shirts-$1.72, 2 flannel shirts-$1.80, 1 cap-$.95$^{1/2}$, 1 overcoat-$6.93$^{1/2}$, 1 blanket-$2.22; pres. 12/1847, pay stopped for: 1 jacket-$2.66, 1 pr. pants-$2.28, 1 pr. shoes-$1.22, 1 cotton shirt-$.43, 1 flannel shirt-$.90; pres. 02/1848; pres. 04/1848, pay stopped for: 1 jacket-$2.37$^{1/2}$, 2 cotton shirts-$.88.

**McKay, Pilate**, Pvt., Co. K; enl. Mex. War service Jefferson Co., VA 12/11/1846, age 18; sick 06/1847; pres. 08/1847; pres. 10/1847, pay stopped for: 1 pr. overalls-$2.28, 1 cap-$.95$^{1/2}$, 2 pr. drawers-$.71, 2 flannel shirts-$1.80; pres. 12/1847, pay stopped for: 1 pr. boots-$1.22; pres. 04/1848, to forfeit 1 mos. pay by sentence of garrison court-martial, pay stopped for: 1 pr. pants-$2.28, 1 pr. shoes-$1.22, 1 cotton shirt-$.43, 1 flannel shirt-$.90, 1 gun sling-$.18; pres. 07/1848, pay stopped for: 1 gun sling-$.18, 1 screw driver-$.25; BLW sent to Charlestown, Jefferson Co., VA

**McKinney, James W.**, Pvt., Co. K; enl. Mex. War service Jefferson Co., VA 12/25/1846, age 25; pres. 06/1847; sick 08/1847, to forfeit 1 mos. pay by order of garrison court-martial; pres. 10/1847, pay stopped for: 1 pr. shoes-$1.22, 2 cotton shirts-$.86, 2 pr. socks-$.49, 4 flannel shirts-$3.60, 1 greatcoat-$6.93$^{1/2}$, 1 pr. overalls-$2.28; pres. 12/1847, pay stopped for: 1 jacket-$2.66, 1 pr. overalls-$2.28, 1 pr. boots-$1.22, 1 pr. socks-$.24$^{1/2}$; pres. 04/1848, to forfeit 1 mos. pay by sentence of garrison court-martial, pay stopped for: 1 pr. shoes-$1.22, 1 pick & brush-$.12, 1 gun sling-$.18; pres. 07/1848, pay stopped for: 1 gun sling-$.18, 1 screw driver-$.25, 1 wiper-$.20; BLW sent to Hillsborough, Loudoun Co., VA

**McKinney, Meridith C.**, Pvt., Co. A; enl. Mex. War service 11/18/1846 Richmond, VA, age 26; pres. 12/1846 - 04/1847; pres. 06/1847; pres. 08/1847; pres. 10/1847, pay stopped for clothing: 1 cotton shirts-$.43, 1 pr. wool overalls-$2.28, 1 cap-$.95$^{1/2}$, 1 pr. shoes-$1.22, 2 pr. stockings-$.49, 1 flannel shirts-$.90, 2 pr. drawers-$.71; pres. 12/1847, pay stopped for clothing: 1 pr. wool overalls-$2.28, 1 dragoon overcoat-$8.75$^{1/2}$; pres. 02/1848; pres. 04/1848; 07/1848, pay stopped for: 1 screw driver-$.25; BLW sent to Chesterfield C.H., VA

**McLondon, James A.**, Pvt. LIC, enl. Mex. War service 09/20/1847 Staunton, VA, age 21; pres. 04/1848, joined co. 01/26/1848 form regtl. depot, pay stopped for: 1 pr. overalls-$2.28, 1 blanket-$2.22, 1 pr. shoes-$1.50; pres. 07/1848, pay stopped for: 1 bayonet scabbard-$.56, 1 gun sling-$.16, 1 pick & brush-$.12; BLW sent to Crossville, Bledsoe Co., VA?

**McMann, John**, Pvt., Co. A; enl. Mex. War service 11/18/1846 Richmond, VA, age 23; pres. until detached 04/1847 detailed as *Ostler*[one who takes care of horses or mules] for Col. Hamtramck 03/28/1847 - 10/1847 by order of Col. Hamtramck; 10/1847, pay stopped for clothing: 1 pr. wool overalls-$2.28, 1 cap-$.95$^{1/2}$, 1 pr. shoes-$1.22, 2 pr. stockings-$.49, 1 wool jacket-$2.66, 2 cotton shirts-$.86; on detached service as Ostler 12/1847, pay stopped for clothing: 1 pr. wool overalls-$2.28, 1 pr. shoes-$1.22, 1 blanket-$2.22; on detached service as Ostler 02/1848; on detached service as Ostler 04/1848; BLW sent to Richmond, VA

OFF TO WAR

**McMinn, Joseph**, Pvt., Co. H; b. 03/21/1825; m/1 Catherine Morse, date/place unknown; enl. Mex. War service 12/15/1846, Berkeley, VA, age 22; pres. 04/1847; pres. 06/1847; pres. 08/1847; pres. 10/1847, pay stopped for: 1 forage cap-$.95$^{1/2}$, 1 pr. pants-$2.28, 2 cotton shirts-$.86, 2 flannel shirts-$1.80, 2 pr. shoes-$2.44, 3 pr. socks-$.73$^{1/2}$; absent 12/1847, sick in Hosp., pay stopped for: 1 jacket-$2.66, 1 pr. pants-$2.28, 2 pr. drawers-$.71 , 3 pr. socks-$.73$^{1/2}$; absent 02/1848, sick in Hosp. at Saltillo, Mex. since 12/23/1847; pres. 04/1848; pres. 07/1848, BLW sent to Sharpsburg, MD; (CMM d. 09/02/1859, Sharpsburg, MD); m/2 Emily Barteto, 05/27/1861, Muttontown, Pa.; moved from Sharpsburg, MD to Lebanon, Pa. about 1862; SC #10926, 08/05/1887, filed from Lebanon, Lebanon Co., Pa.; phys. desc. age 62 [1886], 5'4$^{1/2}$", dark complexion, dark hair, dark eyes; occ. *"tends fire in a public school building for a few dollars a month;"* d. 05/13/1899, Lebanon, Pa.; wid. Emma, WC #11773, 06/12/1899, filed from Lebanon, Lebanon Co., PA; List children Mary Hellen McMinn, b. 09/23/1847, Charles Henry McMinn, b. 11/04/1851, George William McMinn, b. 06/30/1854, Barbara Ann McMinn, b. 12/02/1856; (EBM d. 08/09/1911).

**McNulty, Arthur**, Pvt., Co. G; enl. Mex. War service 11/28/1846 Richmond, VA, age 26; d. 01/03/1847, *"drowned."*

**McNorton, Taylor**, *Preston's Co.*; *Not on Muster* Rolls, SA #9449, 03/09/1887, from VA

**McPhail, Dougald**, 1$^{st}$ Cpl., Co. B; enl. 12/18/1846, Richmond, VA, age 37; pres. 06/1847, appointed 4$^{th}$ Cpl. 06/30/1847 upon the death of Silas Moore; absent 08/1847, on detached service as a clerk in the adjutant's office, Va. Regt., since 07/09/1847; on extra duty 10/1847 as clerk adj. office, pay stopped for: 1 pr. socks-$.24$^{1/2}$; on extra duty 12/1847 as clerk adj. office, prom. 2$^{nd}$ Cpl., pay stopped for: 1 pr. overalls-$2.28, 1 jacket-$2.66, 1 pr. cotton drawers-$.35$^{1/2}$, 2 blanket-$4.44; on extra duty 02/1848 as clerk in Adj. Genl. office Va. Regt.; pres. 04/1848, prom. 1$^{st}$ Cpl.; pres. 08/1848, BLW sent to Norfolk, VA

**McPhelin, Peter alias Patrick**, Pvt., Co. C; b. Canada; enl. Mex. War service 12/18/1846, Bowling Green, VA, phys. desc. age 35, 5'8", dark hair, dark eyes, dark complexion; discharged 05/20/1847 Monterey, Mex. on Surgeon's Certificate of Disability; *"diarrhea;"* res. Cumberland, MD C. 1878; m. Mary E. Hose 02/06/1881, Cumberland, MD, d. 09/16/1885, Cumberland, MD; wid. Mary E., WC #589, 04/19/1887, filed from Little Orleans, Alleghany Co., MD; OW IA #16384, rejected; (MCM b. 01/23/1853 Hancock, MD, d. c. 1890).[1257]

**Meador, Albert**, Pvt., Co. M; m. Sarah Sally Talley, 11/23/1840, VA;[1258] enl. Mex. War service 08/29/1847, Amelia C.H., VA, age 27; pres. 10/1847; pres. 11/1847; pres. 12/1847; pres. 02/1848; pres. 04/1848; pres. 08/1848, pay stopped for: 1 gun sling-$.16; BLW sent to Amelia C.H., VA; c. 1850 res. Cumberland Co., VA, age 35, occ. Farmer, w. Sally (34), dau. Martha (7) , son Richard (5), dau. Emily (2).[1259]

**Mellon, Alexander C.**, Pvt., LIC; enl. Mex. War service 12/07/1846 Staunton, VA, age 24; pres. 08/1847; pres. 10/1847, pay stopped for: 1 forage cap-$.95$^{1/2}$, 1 wool jacket-$2.66, 1 pr. overalls-$2.28, 1 pr. shoes-$1.22, 4 pr. socks-$.98, 2 cotton shirts-$.86, 1 pr. drawers-$.35$^{1/2}$, 1 blanket-$2.22; pres. 12/1847, pay stopped for: 1 blanket-$2.22, 1 pr. shoes-$1.22, 1 pr. overalls-$2.28, 1 flannel shirt-$.90, 1 pr. drawers-$.35$^{1/2}$; pres. 04/1848; pres. 07/1848, pay stopped for: 1 bayonet scabbard-$.56, 1 waist belt-$.21, 1 waist belt plate-$.10, 1 gun sling-$.16; BLW sent to Staunton, VA

**Mendenall, Elijah L.**, Pvt., Co. K; b. VA c. 1814, son of Jacob & Mary Mendenhall;[1260] enl. Mex. War service Frederick Co., VA 12/20/1846, age 31; pres. 06/1847; pres. 08/1847; pres. 10/1847, pay stopped for: 1 pr. overalls-$2.28, 2 pr. drawers-$.71, 2 pr. shoes-$2.44, 1 cap-$.95$^{1/2}$; Court-martialed 11/27/1847 Buena Vista, Mex. *Charge #1: Drunkness on Duty; Specification: In this that said Pvt. Elijah Mendenhall, Co. K, Va. Regt. of Vols. Being regularly posted as a sentinel was found drunk on his post by the officer of the day. This at Camp Buena Vista, Mexico Nov. 27$^{th}$, 1847. To which charge and specification the prisoner pleaded Not Guilty. Capt M.D. Corse, Va. Regt. Vols., a witness for the prosecution being*

## VIRGINIA VOLUNTEERS IN MEXICO

*duly sworn says: I was officer of the day on the 17th of Nov. last in the Va. Regt. As I was passing across the parade ground of the Regiment going towards Headquarters, the prisoner was posted on the left flank of the line of sentinels of the Regt. as I approached his post I noticed his staggering on his post and that he presented something of the appearance of a drunken man. I crossed his post without his hailing me. It was just before tatto between 7 an 8 o'clock I think. After I had passed he made use of some exclamation such as "Hello! Who's That?" or something of that kind but he did not hail me as a sentinel should do. I stopped and he approached me, I asked him if he was posted there as a sentinel. He said he was. At the same time the Sergt. came up with the relief. I ordered him to relieve the prisoner and take him to the Provost Guard. Question by the Judge Advocate: Did you have the prisoner relieved off post because he was too drunk to perform his duties as a sentinel properly? Answer: Yes. I did. Question by the Court: Did the prisoner hail the relief when it came up? Answer: He did Not. Corporal J. Miller, Co. H, Va. Regt. of Vols. A witness for the defense being duly sworn says in answer to the following: Question by the Prisoner: What time was I posted on the night of the 17th of Nov. last? Answer: I am not positive, but I think it was about 5 o'clock P.M. Question by the Prisoner: Was I fit to perform the duties of a sentinel? Answer: At the time the prisoner was posted I thought that he was, but when I relieved him I did not think he was. After deliberation the Court found a verdict of Guilty. Sentenced: To stand on the head of a barrel in the Provost Guard two successive two each day for fourteen successive days, and afterwards to be confined at hard labor with a ball and chain attached to his leg in charge of the Provost Guard for sixteen days;*[1261] pres. 12/1847, pay stopped for: 1 jacket-$2.66, 1 pr. overalls-$2.28, 1 pr. socks-$.24$^{1/2}$, 1 blanket-$2.22; pres. 04/1848, pay stopped for: 1 pr. pants-$2.28; pres. 07/1848, pay stopped for: 1 pick & brush-$.12, 1 screw driver-$.25, 1 wiper-$.20; BLW sent to Winchester, Frederick Co., VA; c. 1850 res. Frederick Co., VA, age 36, occ. Plasterer.[1262] d. 03/25/1885.[1263]

**Merrick, John W.**, Pvt., *Recruit Co.*, enl. Mex. War service 04/10/1848 Richmond, VA; pres. 06/1848; BLW sent to Richmond, VA

**Merritt, Christian Garber**, 4th Sgt., LIC; b. 12/23/1821, Augusta Co., VA, son of John & Elizabeth (Forbes) Merritt;[1264] enl. Mex. War service 11/27/1846 Staunton, VA, age 24; pres. 06/1847, prom. 4th Sgt.; pres. 08/1847, pay stopped for 1 Sergeants sword, belt and belt plate-$4.50; pres. 10/1847, pay stopped for: 1 forage cap-$.95$^{1/2}$, 1 wool jacket-$2.66, 2 pr. overalls-$4.56, 2 pr. socks-$.49; pres. 12/1847, pay stopped for: 1 pr. socks-$.24$^{1/2}$, 1 blanket-$2.22, 1 flannel shirt-$.90, 2 pr. drawers-$.71; pres. 04/1848; pres. 07/1848, pay stopped for: 1 screw driver-$.07; BLW sent to Staunton, VA; 49'er in Calif.; c. 1860 res. Augusta Co., VA, age 37, occ. Farmer;[1265] Civil War service Capt. Regtl. QM, 25th Va. Inf., pres. 7/61 - 8/61; pres. 1/63 - 2/63; absent 1/64 buying leather; absent 5/64 - 10/64 assigned to Gen. Gordon's supply train;[249, 1266] m. Elizabeth Ellen Wilson, 12/19/1866, near Greenville, Augusta Co., VA;[1264] c. 1870 res. Fishersville, Augusta Co., VA, age 48, occ. Farmer, w. Elizabeth E. (33), son Edwin A. (1), dau. Mary L. (2/12);[1267] SC #2918, 03/04/1887, filed from Greenville, Augusta Co., VA; since discharge res. Virginia 1848-1850, California 1850-1856, Virginia since 1856;[1264] phys. desc. 5'10", light complexion, grey eyes, light hair, occ. Farmer;[1264] George Harlan and William E. Skeen gave affidavits in pension claim;[1264] d. 11/15/1907, Greenville, VA, bur. Bethel Presb. Cem.;[249, 1268] wid. Elizabeth M., WC #14900, 01/03/1908, filed from Greenville, Augusta Co., VA; (EWM b. 10/20/1835, d. 03/18/1908).[1268]

**Merritt, Edwin B.**, Pvt., Co. C; enl. Mex. War service 12/10/1846, Bowling Green, VA, age 22; pres. 06/1847; pres. 08/1847, pay stopped for: 1 cap-$.95$^{1/2}$, 2 pr. socks-$.49, 1 knapsack & straps-$1.10; pres. 10/1847, pay stopped for: 2 pr. drawers-$.71, 1 pr. pants-$2.28, 4 cotton shirts-$1.72, 2 woolen shirts-$1.80; pres. 12/1847, pay stopped for: 2 pr. socks-$.49, 1 jacket-$2.66, 1 pr. pants-$2.28, 2 pr. shoes-$2.44, 1 blanket-$2.22; pres. 04/1848, pay stopped for: 1 pr. shoes-$1.50, 1 haversack-$.20$^{3/4}$, 1 india rubber canteen-$.27; m. Sarah V. Highwood 03/16/1856, South Charleston, Clark Co., OH;[1269] d. 04/13/1886 Clyde, Cloud Co., Kan.; wid.

OFF TO WAR

Sarah V., WC #4600, 04/09/1887, filed from Clyde, Cloud Co., KS. Since discharge res. Chester, Pa. 2 yrs., Clark Co., OH 1 yr., St. Louis, Mo. $1^{1/2}$ yrs., LaSalle Co., Ill., 26 yrs., Clyde, Kan. 4 yrs.; Claim lists children Caleb E., William H., John H., Josephine Cusac, Mary E. Page, Clarence M. Merritt; (SVM b. 01/28/1832, Darby, Pa., d. 03/07/1907 near Clyde, Cloud Co., KS.).[1269]

**Merryman, Pulaski P.**, Co. A; b. 06/23/1823 Cumberland Co., VA;[1270] enl. Mex. War service 12/01/1846 Richmond, VA, age 21; phys. desc. 5'10", fair complexion, grey eyes, auburn hair, occ. Farmer; pres. 12/1846 - 04/1847; pres. 06/1847; pres. 08/1847; Court-martialed 09/20/1847, Buena Vista, Mex. *Charge #1: Gross and Willful Neglect of Duty; Specification: In this that he, the said Pvt. Pulaski P. Merryman, Co. A, Va. Regt. of Vols. being regularly posted as a sentinel on post No. 4 Quarter Guard, was found by the Officer of the Day, when visiting the sentinels, sitting down on his post, and did fail to hail the officer as he approached his post. This at Camp Buena Vista, Mexico about 2 o'clock on or about the morning of the $4^{th}$ of September 1847. To which charge and specification the prisoner pleaded Not Guilty. Captain E.G. Alburtis, Va. Regt. of Vols., a witness for the prosecution being duly sworn, says: I was Officer of the Day at the time specified. When visiting the Guards between one and two o'clock A.M. on the $4^{th}$ Sept. 1847, I approached within ten or fifteen paces of the prisoner when I saw him rise. I asked him why he was sitting down and not walking his post! He replied that he was tired and that he was not himself. Question by the Judge Advocate: Did the prisoner hail you as you approached his post? Answer: He might have done so. After deliberation the Court found the prisoner Guilty of the charge and specification, except to the specification that he 'did fail to hail the officer as he approached his post.' Sentenced to be kept at hard labor in charge of the Provost Guard for the period of one calendar month;*[1271] in confinement 10/1847, pay stopped for clothing: 2 cotton shirts-$.86, 1 cap-$.95$^{1/2}$, 1 pr. shoes-$1.22.; sick 12/1847, pay stopped for clothing: 1 pr. wool overalls-$2.28, 1 pr. drawers-$.35$^{1/2}$, 1 blanket-$2.22; pres. 02/1848, pay stopped for: 1 pr. shoes-$1.22; pres. 04/1848; BLW sent to Cartersville, VA; c. 1850 res. Cumberland Co., VA, age 22, occ. Clerk;[1272] SC #18489, 08/27/1889, filed from Cartersville, Cumberland Co., VA; Since discharge lived in California thirty two years returned 05/1890; 1902 res. near Bush Park, Cumberland Co., VA;  d. 10/23/1910 Cumberland Co., VA[1273]

**Merton, Cornelius W.**, Va. Vols.; Not on Muster Rolls; wid. Eliza J. WA #5348, 11/18/1887, from VA

**Mesley, John**, $1^{st}$ Cpl., Co. F; enl. Mex. War service 12/22/1846, Portsmouth, VA, age 27; pres. 06/1847; pres. 08/1847; pres. 10/1847, pay stopped for: 1 pr. overalls-$2.28, 3 pr. socks-$.73$^{1/2}$, 1 forage cap-$.95$^{1/2}$, 1 blanket-$2.22; pres. 02/1848, pay stopped for: 1 blanket-$2.22, 1 pr. shoes-$1.22; pres. 04/1848, prom. 03/01/1848 $1^{st}$ Cpl.; pres. 08/1848, pay stopped for: 1 bayonet-$1.44, BLW sent to Portsmouth, VA  c/o E.T. Blamire; c. 1850 res. Richmond, Henrico Co., VA, age 30, b. New York, occ. Builder, w. Mary (21), son John A. (1).[1274]

**Meyer, Joseph**, Pvt., Co. K; enl. Mex. War service Frederick Co., VA 01/20/1847, age 27; sick 08/1847; discharged 09/11/1847 at Buena Vista, Mex. on Surgeon's Certificate of Disability.

**Michael, Carl**, Pvt., Co. A; enl. Mex. War service 12/01/1846 Richmond, VA, age 40; pres. until detailed 04/1847 for service at Hosp. in Monterey, Mex. 04/28/1847; detached service as Hosp. Steward Saltillo, Mex. 08/01/1847 - 10/30/1847; absent 10/1847, on furlough from December 20 for two mos.; discharged 02/26/1848 at Buena Vista, Mex.  on Surgeon's Certificate.

**Millholland, John**, $3^{rd}$ Cpl., Co. C; enl. Mex. War service 12/29/1846, Bowling Green, VA, age 21; pres. 06/1847; pres. 08/1847, prom. $4^{th}$ Cpl. 08/25/1847, pay stopped for: 1 pr. drawers-$.35$^{1/2}$, 1 cap-$.95$^{1/2}$, 2 pr. socks-$.49, 2 cotton shirts-$.86, 2 woolen shirts-$1.80, 1 pr. shoes-$1.22, 1 pr. overalls-$2.28; pres. 10/1847, pay stopped for: 1 pr. socks-$.24$^{1/2}$, 1 jacket-$2.66, 4 cotton shirt-$1.72, 2 pr. shoes-$2.44; pres. 12/1847, prom. $3^{rd}$ Cpl., pay stopped for: 3 pr. socks-$.73$^{1/2}$, 2 pr. pants-$4.56, 1 pr. shoes-$1.22, 1 blanket-$2.22; pres. 04/1848, pay stopped

## VIRGINIA VOLUNTEERS IN MEXICO

for: 1 jacket-$2.66, 1 cotton shirt-$.43, 1 pr. shoes-$1.50, 1 haversack-$.20³/⁴, 1 india rubber canteen-$.27; pres. 08/1848, BLW sent to Philadelphia, Pa.

**Millan, James R.**, Pvt., Co. L; b. 02/06/1816 son of George & Ann (DeBell) Millan; enl. Mex. War service 03/18/1847 Ft. Washington, MD, age 30; pres. 08/1847; pres. 10/1847, pay stopped for: 1 W Jacket 2.66, 1 pr. Shoes 1.22; pres. 12/1847, pay stopped for: 1 pr. pants-$2.28, 1 cap-$.95$^{1/2}$, 1 pr. shoes-$1.22, 2 flannel shirts-$1.80, 5 cotton shirts-$2.15, 3 pr. drawers-$1.06$^{1/2}$, 2 pr. socks-$.49; pres. 02/1848, pay stopped for: 1 Blanket 2.22, 1 Bayonet Scabbard .50, 1 Bayonet Belt .56, 1 Bayonet Plate .10; pres. 04/1848, pay stopped for: 1 Blanket 2.22, 2 Cotton Shirts .88; pres. 07/1848, pay stopped for: 1 pr. Shoes 1.16; BLW sent to James R. Millan, Fairfax Court House, Fairfax Co., VA; m. Eliza Minerva Draper;[1275] c. 1850 res. Fairfax Co., VA, age 33, occ. None, w. Eliza M. (28), son George L. (8).[1276]

**Miller, Jacob G.**, Pvt., Co. M; b. 01/28/1826, Hagerstown, Washington Co., MD;[1277] enl. Mex. War service 06/16/1847, Richmond, VA, age 21; pres. 09/1847; pres. 11/1847, reduced to ranks from 2$^{nd}$ Cpl.; pres. 12/1847; pres. 02/1848; sick 04/1848; pres. 08/1848; BLW sent to Martinsburg, VA; m. Margaret E. Sigler, 12/22/1858, Shepherdstown, Jefferson Co., VA;[1277] c. 1860 res. Shepardstown, Jefferson Co., VA;[1278] d. 07/10/1871, *"bronchial consumption,"* bur. Elmwood Cem., Charles Town, WV;[45, 1277] wid. Margaret E., WC #7630, 03/11/1890, from WV; lists son C.S. Miller; phys. desc. at enl. age 21, 5'6", dark complexion, black hair, dark eyes, occ. Confectioner;[1277] (MSM b. 08/08/1830, d. 02/06/1911).[1277]

**Miller, John**, Pvt., Co. C; enl. Mex. War service 08/19/1848, Orange C.H., VA, age 26; pres. 04/1848, joined company 01/27/1848 from Regtl. Depot; pres. 08/1848, BLW sent to Lunenburg C.H., VA

**Miller, James**, Pvt., Co. F; date and place of enlistment unknown; pres. 06/1847, *"denies that he is a volunteer and refuses pay &c;"* deserted 04/27/1847 Buena Vista, Mex.; may have been a San Patricio; In a letter to Capt. Irwin McDowell, Asst. Adjt. Genl., Col. Hamtramck refutes Pvt. Miller's claim, *"Captain, Herewith I have the honor to transmit the reports of Captain Young and Lt. Cooke, Co. F, in relation to the enlistment of Pvt. Miller of their company, in the service of the U.S., which matter had been submitted to me for investigation, Upon the reading of the reports I can but express my astonishment that any question should arise in the mind of Miller as to the legality of his enrollment, and feel confident that his perseverance in declaring himself illegally held to service, proceed rather from a mutinous spirit and a disposition to harass his officers than anything else. Capt. Young and Lt. Cooke are both Gentlemen of Worth and integrity, they never would descend to misrepresent facts and implicit reliance may be confidently placed upon any report they make;"*[1279] On Tuesday, 02/26/1847 at Ft. Monroe, VA Capt. James L. Kemper recorded in his diary that he *"Saw a member of Capt. Young's Company forced off to Richmond to be mustered into service, and forced to volunteer;"*[1280] Court-martialed 07/21/1847, Buena Vista, Mexico, Charge #1: *Disobedience of Orders; Specification: In this that Pvt. James Miller, Co. F, Va. Regt. Vols. has repeatedly refused to attend drills and parade of his company and more particularly on the 8$^{th}$ and 9$^{th}$ of July 1847, at Camp Buena Vista, when being ordered by Lt. Blamire, Va. Regt., to go to company drill, positively refused to do so, in the presence of the whole company, alleging that he was a private man, and could not be compelled to do duty. To which charge and specification the prisoner pleaded Guilty. Lt. E.F. Blamire, Va. Regt., a witness on behalf of the prosecution, duly sworn, says: On the 8$^{th}$ of July when the company was going to drill. I observed the prisoner standing by. I told him to get his musket and accoutrements and go to drill. He replied that he did not consider himself a soldier, and that Capt. Young, said he would go with him to Col. Hamtramck and have the matter investigated. I said nothing more to him at this time, but the next morning when the company was going to drill that same thing occurred. I ordered the prisoner to go to drill. He replied that he did not intend to do duty. That he was not a soldier. I told him that I considered him as much a soldier as any other man in the company and that if he did not go to drill I would send him to the Guard House. He*

## OFF TO WAR

*replied I might do so, but that he would not do duty and would not put on any uniform. I therefore had him confined. After deliberation the Court found the prisoner Guilty and sentenced him to one months police duty in his company, attending to all his duties.*[1281]

**Miller, John Alexander** Pvt., Co. M; b. 12/23/1828, Ireland;[1282] enl. Mex. War service 11/17/1847, Norfolk, VA, age 21; pres. 11/1847; pres. 12/1847; pres. 02/1848; in confinement 04/1848, pay stopped for: 1 pr. shoes-$1.22; pres. 08/1848, pay stopped for: 1 gun sling-$.16, 1 cartridge box belt plate-$.10, 1 wormer-$.20, 1 pr. shoes-$1.16; BLW sent to Norfolk, VA; Civil War service enl. 2nd Lt., 4th U.S. Inf. 07/18/1862, prom. 1st Lt. 10/19/1863, prom Capt. 07/18/1866, prom. Major date unknown, retired 03/20/1879;[1282] m/1 Josephine Joyce date/place unknown;[1282] (JJM phys. desc. 6'2", fair complexion, blue eyes, light brown hair; d. 03/12/1888, *"heart failure,"* 1002 11th St., N.W., Washington, D.C., bur. Oak Hill Cemetery, Washington, D.C.);[1282] Civil War service 4th US Inf.; m. Clara Josephine Dante, 11/08/1898 place unknown;[1282] d. 04/11/1907, *"Bright's Disease,"* The Westover Apartment House, cor. 16th & U Sts., Washington, D.C., bur. Arlington National Cemetery, Arlington, VA;[1282] wid. Clara D., WC #14974, 04/25/1907, from DC; (CDM b. 09/13/1858, Washington, D.C., d. 06/25/1940, *"ovarian cancer,"* Walter Reed Army Hosp., Washington, D.C.).[1282]

**Miller, John McClelland**, 2nd Cpl, Co. H; enl. Mex. War service 12/15/1846, Berkeley, VA, age 21; pres. 04/1847; pres. 06/1847, prom. 4th Cpl. 06/05/1847; pres. 08/1847; in confinement 10/1847, stopped for: 1 forage cap-$.95$^{1/2}$, 1 pr. pants-$2.28, 2 cotton shirts-$.86, 2 flannel shirts-$1.80, 1 pr. shoes-$1.22, 6 pr. socks-$1.47; pres. 12/1847, pay stopped for: 1 jacket-$2.66, 1 pr. pants-$2.28, 1 flannel shirt-$.90, 2 pr. drawers-$.71, 2 pr. shoes-$2.44; pres. 02/1848, 1 pr. shoes-$1.22, 1 pr. socks-$.24$^{1/2}$, 2 blankets-$4.44; pres. 04/1848, prom. 2nd Cpl.; pres. 04/1848; pres. 07/1848, BLW sent to Boonsboro, MD

**Miller, Joseph**, Pvt., *Preston's Co.*; enl. Mex. War service 12/06/1846 Pulaski Co., VA, age 22; pres. 04/1847; pres. 06/1847; pres. 08/1847; pres. 10/1847, pay stopped for: 3 pr. socks-$.73$^{1/2}$, 1 flannel shirt-$.90, 2 cotton shirts-$.86, 1 pr. drawers-$.35$^{1/2}$, 1 blanket-$2.22; pres. 12/1847, pay stopped for: 1 jacket-$2.66, 2 pr. overalls-$4.56, 1 pr. shoes-$1.22, 2 pr. socks-$.49; sick 02/1848; pres. 04/1848, reduced to ranks from 2nd Cpl. 04/14/1848 (regtl. order #54); pres. 07/1848, pay stopped for: 1 pr. shoes-$1.16, 1 brush & pick-$.12; BLW sent to Newbern, VA

**Miller, Peter**, Pvt., Co. K; b. 06/1826, Bartersville, Frederick Co., VA;[1283] enl. Mex. War service Frederick Co., VA 12/24/1846, age 20; pres. 06/1847; pres. 08/1847; pres. 10/1847, pay stopped for: 2 pr. overalls-$4.56, 4 cotton shirts-$1.72, 2 pr. shoes-$2.44, 2 pr. drawers-$.71, 2 pr. socks-$.49, 1 cap-$.95$^{1/2}$; pres. 12/1847, pay stopped for: 1 jacket-$2.66, 1 pr. overalls-$2.28, 2 pr. boots-$2.44, 1 pr. socks-$.24$^{1/2}$, 1 blanket-$2.22; pres. 04/1848, to forfeit 1 mos. pay by sentence of garrison court-martial;, pay stopped for: 1 cotton shirt-$.43, 1 gun sling-$.18; pres. 07/1848; BLW sent to Winchester, Frederick Co., VA; m/1 Julia A. Sebright, c. 1850;[1283] c. 1860 Romney, Hampshire Co., VA age 34, occ. House Painter, w. Julia A. (25), dau. Ann E. (8), son Lewis N. (6), dau. Laura (4), dau. Virginia (2);[1284] (JSM b. 10/07/1833, d. ??/30/1870, Moorefield, Hardy Co., WV, bur. Indian Mound Cemetery near Romney, Hampshire Co., WV);[1283] m/2 Margaret J. Shelton, 11/30/1871, Romney Hampshire Co., WV;[1283] (MSM d. 05/29/1889, Petersburg, Grant Co., WV, bur. Indian Mound Cemetery, Romney, WV);[1283] m/3 Hoppie Jacobs Cooper, 04/28/1892, Hampshire Co., WV; SC #10037, 02/04/1887, filed from Maysville, Grant Co., WV; phys. desc. age 59 [1885], 5'8", dark complexion, gray eyes, black hair, occ. House Painter; lists children: *"I have ten living and 2 dead, Ann E., Louis N., Laurah C., Virginia B., Emanuel, Charles W., Mary E., Turner A., Claudie T., these were by the first wife, but she, the last – Claudie T. she was by the 2nd wife;"*[1283] d. 10/28/1908, bur. Indian Mound Cemetery, Romney, WV;[1285] wid. Hoppie J., WC #15160, 12/04/1908, filed from Romney, Hampshire Co., WV. (HCM b. 12/22/1871, Romney, WV, d. 05/02/1921, bur. Indian Mound Cemetery, Romney, WV).[1285]

# VIRGINIA VOLUNTEERS IN MEXICO

**Miller, Samuel W.**, Pvt., Co. F; enl. Mex. War service 01/20/1847, Portsmouth, VA, age 22; pres. 06/1847; pres. 08/1847; pres. 10/1847, pay stopped for: 2 pr. overalls-$4.56, 2 pr. socks-$.49, 1 pr. shoes-$1.22, 1 blanket-$2.22; in confinement 02/1848, pay stopped for: 1 infantry jacket-$2.66; Court-martialed 02/15/1848 at Buena Vista, Mex. *Charge #1: Absence Without Leave; Specification: In this that he, Pvt. Samuel W. Miller, of Co. F, Va. Regt. of Vols., did on the 11$^{th}$ of February 1848 get from Lt. John K. Cooke, Commanding Co. F, permission to visit Saltillo. To return by Battalion Drill of that day, which he the said Pvt. Samuel W. Miller failed to do. Charge #2: Disobedience of Orders; Specification: In this that he, Pvt. Samuel W. Miller, of Co. F, Va. Regt. of Vols., having been detailed for Guard on the morning of the 12$^{th}$ of February 1848, positively refused to obey said order. This at Camp Buena Vista, Mexico. To which the prisoner plead Guilty to Charge #1 and Not Guilty to Charge #2. Sergt. J.W. Butt, Co. F, Va. Regt. Vols., a witness for the prosecution being duly sworn, says: I had orders from Lt. Cooke, to put the accused on guard and I detailed him for guard on the 12$^{th}$ of January 1848. He refused to go on. He said he would not go on unless the other men were put on, alluding to two men who had been absent before without leave, when there was no drill. Question by the prisoner: Were there or not three men who missed drill on that same afternoon? Answer: In have no recollection of it now. Question by the Court: Was this the prisoners regular tour of guard? Answer: It was not. 1$^{st}$ Lt. J.K. Cooke, Va. Regt. Vols., a witness for the defense being duly sworn, says in answer to the following: Question by the prisoner: What has been my character as a soldier since I have been in service? Answer: I have been a good deal absent from the company, but since I have been with it I have known the prisoner to be generally attentive to his duty and I have never known him to miss a tour of Guard Duty previous to this offence. After deliberation the Court found the prisoner Guilty of all Charges and Specifications. Sentenced him to forfeit two (2) months pay and be kept on Police Duty in his company for the period of one month.*[1286] pres. 04/1848, fined 2 mos. pay by order of regtl. court-martial; pres. 08/1848, pay stopped for: 1 pr. shoes-$1.16, 1 blanket-$2.25, 2 cotton shirts-$.88, BLW sent to Portsmouth, VA c/o E.T. Blamire.

**Miller, William A.**, Pvt., LIC; b. Fauquier Co., VA; enl. Mex. War service 12/07/1846 Staunton, VA, age 20; discharged 06/1847 at Monterey, Mex. 06/1847 on Surgeon's Certificate of Disability; m. Charlotte Boone, 08/02/1848, Staunton, Augusta Co., VA;[1287] c. 1860 res. Augusta Co., VA, age 34, occ. Master Shoemaker, w. Charlotte (40);[1288] wid. Charlotte, WC #261, 02/15/1887, filed from Staunton, Augusta Co., VA; since discharge res. Rockbridge and Augusta Cos., VA;[1287] d. 05/20/1876, bur. Thornrose Cemetery, Lot 43, B St., Staunton, VA; (CBM d. 08/20/1898).[1287]

**Mills, Farmstead T.**, Pvt., Co. L; b. 07/22/1822, son of Peter Mills;[1289] enl. Mex. War service 03/15/1847 Alexandria, VA, age 25; pres. 06/1847; pres. 08/1847; pres. 10/1847, pay stopped for: 1 F Cap .95; pres. 12/1847, pay stopped for: 1 jacket-$2.66, 1 pr. pants-$2.28, 2 cotton shirts-$.86, 1 blanket-$2.22, 2 pr. drawers-$.71, 2 pr. socks-$.49; pres. 02/1848 sick in Qtrs.; absent 04/1848 on detached service as Hospital Attendant since 04/25/1848 by order Col. Hamtramck; pres. 07/1848; BLW sent to Capt. Thrift c/o Armistead T. Mills, Fairfax Court House, Fairfax Co., VA; c. 1850 res. Fairfax Co., VA, age 28, occ. Carpenter;[1290] m/1 Elizabeth E. Jerman, 12/28/1854, Washington, D.C.;[1291] divorced/separated? by 1860; c. 1860 res. Fairfax Co., VA, age 36, occ. Carpenter, w. Virginia (30);[1292] voted for Secession 04/23/1861 at Fairfax C.H., Fairfax Co., VA;[1293] c. 1870 res. Fairfax C.H., VA, age 45, occ. Wagon Maker;[1294] m/2 Cornelia Frances Gheen, 09/06/1870, Washington, D.C.;[1295] c. 1880 res. Fairfax Co., VA, age 60, occ. Wheelwright, w. Cornelia F. (30), son Robert F. (6), son Armistead M. (1), s-i-l. Annie E. Gheen (21);[1296] SC #2490, 02/12/1887, phys. desc. 5'11$^{1/2}$", black hair, grey eyes, occ. Carpenter;[1297] d. 07/23/1892, *"consumption,"* Fairfax Co., VA;[1298] bur. Fairfax Cem. in an unmarked grave;[1299] wid. Cornelia, WA #11206, 03/11/1893, both from D.C.

## OFF TO WAR

**Mills, Henry**, Pvt., Co. L; b. 1818; enl. Mex. War service 03/15/1847 Alexandria, VA, age 29; pres. 06/1847; pres. 08/1847; pres. 10/1847; pres. 12/1847, pay stopped for: 1 pr. pants-$2.28, 1 pr. shoes-$1.22, 1 cotton shirt-$.43, 1 blanket-$2.22, 2 pr. drawers-$.71, 2 pr. socks-$.49; pres. 02/1848, pay stopped for: 1 Jacket 2.66; pres. 04/1848, pay stopped for: 1 Cotton Shirt .44; pres. 07/1848; BLW sent to Capt. Thrift c/o Henry Mills, Fairfax Court House, Fairfax Co., VA; c. 1860 res. Fairfax Co., VA, age 42, occ. Laborer, son George (24).[1300]

**Mills, Mahlon**, Pvt., Co. L; b. 1824; enl. Mex. War service 03/15/1847 Alexandria, VA, age 23; sick 06/1847; d. 08/19/1847 Buena Vista, Mex.[72]

**Mills, Robert**, Pvt., Co. L; b. 1824; enl. Mex. War service 03/18/1847 Ft. Washington, MD, age 23; pres. 06/1847; d. 08/23/1847 Buena Vista, Mex.[72]

**Mills, William J.**, Pvt., Co. I; enl. Mex. War service 02/06/1847 Richmond, VA, age 22; pres. 02/1847; absent 04/1847, left as Hospital Attendant at Point Isabel, Tex. 03/16/1847; pres. 06/1847; pres. 08/1847; pres. 10/1847, pay stopped for: 3 flannel shirts-$2.70, 1 cotton shirts-$.43, 3 pr. drawers-$1.06$^{1/2}$, 1 pr. pants-$2.28, 1 blanket-$2.22, 1 pr. socks-$.24$^{1/2}$, 1 cap-$.95$^{1/2}$, 1 overcoat-$6.93$^{1/2}$; pres. 12/1847, pay stopped for: 1 pr. shoes-$1.22, 1 pr. socks-$.24$^{1/2}$, 1 jacket-$2.66, 1 pr. shoes-$1.22, 1 blanket-$2.22, 2 cotton shirts-$.86; pres. 02/1848, pay stopped for: 1 cotton shirt-$.43, 1 pr. overalls-$2.28; pres. 04/1848; pres. 08/1848, pay stopped for: 1 pr. shoes, BLW sent to New York City.

**Millspaugh, Charles**, 2$^{nd}$ Lt., Co. M; b. 08/26/1822, Orange Co., NY, son of Charles & Mehitable (Van Tassel) Millspaugh; enl. Mex. VA service 09/03/1847, Richmond, VA, age 25; NFR; m. Henrietta Virginia Talbott, c. 1849, Richmond, VA; c. 1850 res. Henrico Co., VA, age 28, occ. Druggist, b. New York, w. Henrietta (18), dau. Emma (9/12);[1301] d. 11/08/1857, Richmond, VA[1302]

**Minnick, John H.**, Pvt., *Preston's Co.*; b. 12/11/1823, Botetourt Co., VA;[1303] enl. Mex. War service 12/07/1846 Montgomery Co., VA, age 21; pres. 04/1847; absent 06/1847 on detached service as Hospital Attendant in Monterey, Mex. since 06/22/1847; absent 08/1847 on detached service as Hospital Attendant in Monterey, Mex.; pres. 10/1847, pay stopped for: 1 pr. socks-$.24$^{1/2}$, 1 cotton shirt-$.43; pres. 12/1847, pay stopped for: 1 pr. overalls-$2.28, 1 blanket-$2.22; sick 02/1848; pres. 04/1848; pres. 07/1848, pay stopped for: 1 pr. shoes-$1.16; BLW sent to Christiansburg, VA c/o Fleming Gardner; c. 1850 a Henry Minnick res. Montgomery Co., VA, age 26, occ. Laborer;[1304] m. Susan Bradley, 01/1852, Roanoke Co., VA;[1303] c. 1860 res. Layfayette, Montgomery Co., VA, age 35, occ. Wagon Maker, w. Susan A. (27), dau. Amy M. (5), Mary S.F. (3), Charles A. (1);[1305] Civil war service Capt. Bowers Co. of Militia, Co. B, 157$^{th}$ VA Militia; CSA;[1303] SC #7619, 05/26/1887, filed from Lafayette, Montgomery Co., VA; phys. desc. 5'5", light complexion, light hair, grey eyes, occ Wheelwright;[1303] Charles A. Ronald and Michael Kipps gave affidavit in pension claim; d. 05/26/1913.[1303]

**Minor, Albert G.**, Pvt., Co. B; b. 07/31/1823, Alexandria, D.C.,[1306] son of Daniel & Mary (Ross) Minor; enl. 11/20/1846, Alexandria, VA, age 24; pres. 06/1847; pres. 08/1847; pres. 10/1847, pay stopped for: 1 pr. socks-$.24$^{1/2}$, 1 flannel shirts-$.90, 1 blanket-$2.22; pres. 12/1847, pay stopped for: 2 pr. overalls-$4.56, 2 pr. socks-$.49, 2 pr. shoes-$2.44, 1 cotton shirt-$.43; pres. 02/1848, pay stopped for: 1 pr. shoes-$1.22,1 pr. overalls-$2.28; pres. 04/1848; pres. 08/1848, pay stopped for: 1 musket-$13.00, 1 waist belt plate-$.10, 1 pick & brush-$.12, 1 screw driver-$.07, 1 wiper-$.20, 1 pr. shoes-$1.16, BLW sent to Alexandria, VA; c. 1850 res. Fairfax Co., VA, age 37, occ. Gentleman;[1307] 1859 ordered to serve on a patrol against slave illegal slave gatherings in Fairfax Co., VA;[1308] Civil War service Pvt., Co. F, 6$^{th}$ Va. Cav. enl. 05/24/1861, pres. through 07/26/1862 when discharged, enl. Pvt., Co. A, 43$^{rd}$ Btln. Va. Cav., 07/03/1863 at Richmond, VA, pres. 07/1863 through 12/1863, paroled 05/15/1865 at Fairfax C.H., VA, phys. desc. 5'8", light complexion, brown hair, hazel eyes; m. Lucelia (Shackleford) Carlin, 06/11/1895, Fairfax Co., VA; d. 01/06/1896, Fairfax Co., VA, bur. Christ Church Cem., Alex., VA;[324, 898, 1309, 1310] wid. Luclia, WC #10988, 05/05/1896, from VA *"We lived*

## VIRGINIA VOLUNTEERS IN MEXICO

together and I was his common law wife for about thirty years. I had nine children by him. The reason we were not married sooner was because he would be liable to lose his property if he married against the wishes of his father's family and also he did not want to marry me until he was satisfied that my first husband was dead. Albert and I had been engaged before the war broke out and he went into the Confederate Army. While he was away I married George W. Carlin, a sutler in the Union Army. I was but 17 years old then and had never been previously married. ...I had been acquainted with Carlin, my first husband, about five months before our marriage. We were married 02/29/1864 in Alexandria, Va at a private house. ...He came from Carrolton, Greene Co., Ill. where he said he was born and raised. ...Carlin was about 45 years of age when I married him. ...Carlin left me in August of 1865, saying he was going to Ft. Leavenworth, Kan. with the Reno expedition. I received one letter from him, posted at Annapolis, MD, about three or four weeks after his departure. About a month or so after I received a second letter posted at Indianapolis, Ind. ...I have written to William Carlin [a brother] and to the editor of the paper there. I wrote for the purpose of ascertaining whether they knew what had become of my husband. I never received an answer and none of my letters was returned to me. ...When Carlin left here he wanted me to go with him, but my mother would not let me go as I was then within six weeks of giving birth to a child, the only one I ever had by Carlin. Her name is Emma. She is now the wife Fred Leary who lives on Diamond Farm, 45 miles from Dover, N.H. ...He told me that if I didn't go West with him he would never come back.[1311] During the last year of the Civil War George W. Carlin was employed as a "Wood Watcher,"[15] in the 4th Regt. Quartmaster Vols. He and Lucelia were living in a tent at **Edsall's Hill**, Fairfax Co. on the Orange and Alexandria R.R.[1312] According to one family source in Carrollton, Ill., George W. Carlin died in 1867 or 1868 in Carrollton, Ill. after eating a radish.[1313]

**Minor, Philip B.**, Pvt., Co. G; enl. Mex. War service 12/08/1846 Richmond, VA, age 20; pres. 06/1847; pres. 08/1847; pres. 10/1847, pay stopped for: 1 pr. overalls-$2.28, 3 cotton shirts-$1.29, 1 flannel shirt-$.90, 1 pr. drawers-$.35$^{1/2}$, 4 shoes-$4.88, 3 pr. socks-$.73$^{1/2}$, 1 great coat-$6.95$^{1/2}$, 1 forage cap-$.95$^{1/2}$; pres. 12/1847, pay stopped for: 1 pr. shoes-$1.22, 1 cotton shirt-$.43, 1 flannel shirt-$.90, 1 blanket-$2.22, 1 cap-$.95$^{1/2}$, 1 jacket-$2.66,1 pr. pants-$2.28; pres. 02/1848, pay stopped for: 1 jacket-$2.66, 1 pr. pants-$2.28; pres. 04/1848; pres. 08/1848, pay stopped for: 1 pr. shoes-$1.16; BLW sent to Richmond, VA

**Minor, William G. (J.)**, 2$^{nd}$ Lt., Co. B; b. c. 1820, son of William & Catherine Minor;[1314] enl. 11/20/1846, Alexandria, VA; pres. 06/1847; pres. 08/1847; pres. 10/1847; pres. 12/1847; pres. 02/1848; pres. 04/1848; pres. 08/1848, BLW sent to Alexandria, VA; c. 1850 res. Alexandria Co., VA, age 30, occ. None;[1315] c. 1860 res. Alexandria Co., VA, age 40, occ. Farmer, mo. Catherine (72);[1316] d. 03/15/1880, "near Saegmuller's," Alexandria Co., VA, of Bright's Disease, age 65 years, single.[1317]

**Mitchell, Robert F.**, 4$^{th}$ Cpl., Co. B; b. 01/09/1823 Fairfax Co.; enl. 12/19/1846, Alexandria, VA, age 25; pres. 06/1847; pres. 08/1847; pres. 10/1847, pay stopped for: 2 pr. shoes-$2.44, 2 pr. socks-$.49, 1 pr. cotton drawers-$.35$^{1/2}$, 1 cotton shirt-$.43, 1 flannel shirt-$.90; pres. 12/1847, pay stopped for: 1 pr. socks-$.24$^{1/2}$, 1 pr. overalls-$2.28, 1 pr. cotton drawers-$.35$^{1/2}$, 1 blanket-$2.22; pres. 02/1848, pay stopped for: 1 pr. shoes-$1.22; pres. 04/1848, prom 4$^{th}$ Cpl. 04/18/1848; pres. 08/1848, pay stopped for: 1 screw driver-$.07, 1 wiper-$.12, BLW sent to Centreville, Fairfax Co., VA; phys. desc. 5'10", dark florid complexion, black hair, dark hazel eyes, occ. Accountant or Bookkeeper; m. Josephine Miller 06/10/1856, Henderson, Rusk Co., TX; d. 07/09/1874, Winneboro, Wood Co., TX; wid. Josephine, WC #4144, 10/25/1887, filed from Overton, Rusk Co., TX; (JMM b. 03/25/1836 Cassville, Cass Co., Ga., d. 08/09/1918 510 N. Cheyenne St., Tulsa, OK).[1318]

---

[15] Vast quantities of wood were cut in Fairfax Co., Va. for use by the Union Army. Evidently George W. Carlin was employed for a time to guard or "watch" this stockpile.

OFF TO WAR

**Montague, Richard T.**, 1st Cpl., Co. F; b. 1813, Middlesex Co., VA, son of John Currie & Nancy Ann (Lee) Montague;[1319] enl. Mex. War service 11/23/1846, Portsmouth, VA, age 33; absent 06/1847 left sick in Hosp. Monterey, Mex. 05/26/1847; discharged 08/20/1847 Monterey, Mex. on Surgeon's Certificate if Disability.

**Monterio, Andrew A.**, Co. A; b. c. 1827; enl. Mex. War service 11/18/1846 Richmond, VA, age 20; pres. 12/1846 - 04/1847; pres. 06/1847; pres. 08/1847; sick 10/1847, pay stopped for clothing: 1 pr. wool overalls-$2.28, 1 cap-$.95$^{1/2}$, 2 pr. stockings-$.49, 1 wool jacket-$2.66, 1 pr. shoes-$1.22, 1 great coat-$6.93$^{1/2}$; pres. 12/1847, pay stopped for clothing: 1 blanket-$2.22; pres. 02/1848, pay stopped for: 1 pr. wool overalls-$2.28, 1 pr. shoes-$1.22; 1 cross belt & plate-$.80; pres. 04/1848; 07/1848, pay stopped for: 1 cartridge box & belt-$1.70, waist belt-$.27, 1 musket sling-$.16, 1 belt plate.10, 1 waist belt plate-$.10; BLW sent to Richmond, VA; m. Pocahontas C. Woodson 11/18/1856, Goochland Co., VA; d. 06/29/1875, Richmond, VA;[1320] wid. Pocahontas C., WC #492, 03/09/1887, filed from Greenville, Pitt Co., NC. (PCM b. 05/03/1833, d. 05/29/1914).

**Montgomery, Benjamin**, Pvt., Co. G; enl. Mex. War service 12/16/1846 Richmond, VA, age 20; pres. 06/1847; pres. 08/1847, reduced from musician; pres. 10/1847, pay stopped for: 1 pr. overalls-$2.28, 1 pr. drawers-$.35$^{1/2}$, 1 shoes-$1.22, 3 pr. socks-$.73$^{1/2}$, 1 forage cap-$.95$^{1/2}$; absent 12/1847, on extra duty as Hospital Attendant, pay stopped for: 1 blanket-$2.22, 1 pr. pants-$2.28; pres. 02/1848, pay stopped for: 1 pr. shoes-$1.22; pres. 04/1848; pres. 08/1848, pay stopped for: 1 pr. shoes-$1.16, 1 brush & pick-$.12, 1 gun sling-$.16; BLW sent to Richmond, VA

**Montgomery, Charles H.**, Pvt., Co. G; b. c. 1819, Mecklenburg Co., VA; enl. Mex. War service 12/14/1846 Richmond, VA, age 28; pres. 06/1847; pres. 08/1847; pres. 10/1847, pay stopped for: 1 blanket-$2.221 pr. overalls-$2.28, 2 cotton shirts-$.86, 1 pr. shoes-$1.22, 4 pr. socks-$.98, 1 forage cap-$.95$^{1/2}$; sick 12/1847, pay stopped for: 1 pr. shoes-$1.22, 2 pr. drawers-$.71, 1 pr. pants-$2.28; desc., age 28, 5'6", occ. Painter; discharged 01/31/1848 on Surgeon's Certificate;[26] wid. Anastasia, WC #1100, 03/22/1887, from KY [pension file missing].

**Moody, George A.**, Pvt., Co. B; enl. 12/01/1846, Alexandria, VA, age 18; pres. 06/1847; sick 08/1847; sick 10/1847, pay stopped for: 1 pr. shoes-$1.22, 1 pr. socks-$.49, 1 jacket-$2.66; pres. 12/1847, pay stopped for: 1 pr. overalls-$2.28, 1 blanket-$2.22; pres. 02/1848; pres. 04/1848, pay stopped for: 1 jacket-$2.66; pres. 08/1848, pay stopped for: 1 jacket-$2.37$^{1/2}$, BLW sent to Alexandria, VA; m/1 Sinah A. DeVaughn 10/4/1849, Washington, D.C.;[1321] m/2 Laura Ann Ellis 04/01/1863, Washington, D.C.; d. 09/12/1868, Washington, D.C., burial by Joseph Birch, Undertaker;[1322] wid. Laura Ann, WC #717, 04/29/1887, from D.C.

**Mooney, George S.**, Co. B; b. 10/31/1828, Fauquier Co., VA; enl. 08/19/1847, Warrenton, VA, age 19; pres. 02/1848, pay stopped for 1 pr. overalls-$2.22; pres. 04/1848; pres. 08/1848, pay stopped for: 1 pick & brush, BLW sent to Warrenton, Fauquier County, VA; m. Martha B. Harp 01/07/1858 Clinton, DeWitt Co., Ill.; Civil War service Pvt., Co. K, 6th Kansas State Militia, enl. 1864;[1323] SC #19440, 11/10/1890, filed from Galena, Cherokee Co., KS; phys. desc. 5'8$^{1/2}$", light complexion, light hazel eyes, black hair; d. 01/31/1903 Maysville, AR, bur. Maysville Cemetery, *"1 mile n. of Maysville,"* Benton Co., AR;[1324] wid. Martha B., WC #13241, 03/02/1903, filed from Maysville, Benton Co., AR.; (MBM b. 04/11/1840, Clinton, DeWitt Co., Ill.); res. Galena, Kan. 11/03/1916. Children Alice b. 10/16/1861, Burrilda Jane b. 10/08/1861, James R. b. 10/13/1863, George S. b. 10/08/1865, Edward H. b. 08/03/1863.

**Moore, James E.**, Pvt., Co. F; enl. Mex. War service 12/21/1846, Portsmouth, VA, age 29; d. 06/18/1847 Hosp. Saltillo, Mex.

**Moore, James M.**, Pvt., Co. D; enl. Mex. War service 01/04/1847, Petersburg, VA, age 21; pres. 02/1847; pres. 04/1847; pres. 06/1847; pres. 08/1847, pay stopped for: 1 cap-$.95$^{1/2}$, 2 cotton shirts-$.86, 2 flannel shirts-$1.80, 1 pr. shoes-$1.22; pres. 10/1847, pay stopped for: 1 pr. drawers-$.35$^{1/2}$, 2 pr. socks-$.49, 1 pr. shoes-$1.22; pres. 12/1847, pay stopped for: 1 pr.

# VIRGINIA VOLUNTEERS IN MEXICO

pants-$2.28, 1 jacket-$2.66, 1 pr drawers-$.35$^{1/2}$, 1 pr. shoes-$1.22; pres. 04/1848; pres. 08/1847, BLW sent to Gholsonville, Brunswick Co., VA; m. Nancy E.T. Harrison 08/23/1848, Northampton, NC;[1325] d. 01/10/1860; wid. Nancy E., WC #2290, 06/03/1887, filed from Powellton, Brunswick Co., VA (NEM d. 01/12/1901 Greensville Co., VA)[1325]

**Moore, John**, Pvt., Co. G; enl. Mex. War service 11/18/1846 Richmond, VA, age 35; pres. 06/1847; pres. 08/1847; discharged 10/16/1847 on Surgeon's Certificate of Disability.

**Moore, John L.**, 3$^{rd}$ Cpl., Co. L; b. 1827, son of William H. & Mary A. (Blackburn) Moore;[1326,1327] enl. Mex. War service 03/01/1847 Fairfax C.H., VA, age 20; pres. 06/1847; pres. 08/1847; pres. 10/1847, pay stopped for: 1 F Cap .95; pres. 12/1847, pay stopped for: 1 jacket-$2.66, 1 pr. pants-$2.28, 1 pr. shoes-$1.22, 1 overcoat-$6.93$^{1/2}$, 1 blanket-$2.22, 2 pr. drawers-$.71, 3 pr. socks-$.73$^{1/2}$; pres. 02/1848, pay stopped for: 1 pr. Shoes 1.22; pres. 04/1848, pay stopped for: 1 Cotton Shirts .88; pres. 07/1848; BLW sent to W.A. Moore c/o John L. Moore, Fairfax Court House, Fairfax Co., VA; m. Elvira Finch 7/2/1853, Washington, D.C.;[1328] c. 1860 res. Fairfax Co., VA, age 32, occ. Farmer, w. Elvira (33), son Lewis E. (5), dau. S.E. (1/12);[1329] c. 1870 res. Vienna, Fairfax Co., VA, age 42, occ. Farmer, w. Elvira (43) b. N.Y., son Lewis E. (15), dau. Lillian E. (10), son Millard J. (9);[1330] voted against Secession 04/23/1861 at Lydecker's, Fairfax Co., VA; WC #723, 4/22/1887, from D.C.; Elvira res. with her son Millard J. Moore in Washington, D.C. after John L. Moore's death.[1331]

**Moore, Philip A.**, Pvt., *Preston's Co.*; b. 08/27/1826, Rockingham Co., VA; enl. Mex. War service 12/07/1846 Montgomery Co., VA, age 19; absent 04/1847 left sick in hosp at China, Mex. since 04/16/1847; pres. 06/1847; pres. 08/1847; pres. 10/1847, pay stopped for: 1 jacket-$2.66, 1 pr. overalls-$2.28, 1 pr. shoes-$1.22, 3 pr. socks-$.73$^{1/2}$, 1 flannel shirt-$.90, 1 cotton shirt-$.43, 1 pr. drawers-$.35$^{1/2}$, 1 cap-$.95$^{1/2}$; pres. 12/1847, pay stopped for: 1 pr. overalls-$2.28, 1 pr. drawers-$.35$^{1/2}$, 1 blanket-$2.22; pres. 02/1848; pres. 04/1848; pres. 07/1848, pay stopped for: 1 pr. shoes-$1.16, 1 gun sling-$.18; BLW sent to Big Lick, VA; SC #18691, 12/05/1889, filed from Roanoke, Woodford Co., IL; George A. Keister gave affidavit in pension claim; d. 03/08/1907, Inglewood, Los Angeles Co., Ca.

**Moore, Richard G.**, Pvt., Co. H; enl. Mex. War service 01/06/1847, Berkeley, VA, age 21; pres. 04/1847, appointed Drummer 01/27/1847; sick 06/1847; pres. 08/1847 reduced to ranks 08/31/1847; pres. 10/1847, pay stopped for: 1 forage cap-$.95$^{1/2}$, 2 cotton shirts-$.86, 2 flannel shirts-$1.80, 2 pr. shoes-$2.44, 1 greatcoat-$6.93$^{1/2}$, 1 jacket-$2.66; pres. 12/1847, pay stopped for: 2 pr. pants-$4.56, 2 pr. shoes-$2.44, 1 pr. socks-$.24$^{1/2}$, 1 blanket-$2.22; pres. 02/1848, pay stopped for: 1 forage cap-$.95$^{1/2}$, 1 jacket-$2.66, 2 pr. drawers-$.71, 2 pr. shoes-$2.44; pres. 04/1848; pres. 07/1848, pay stopped for: 2 brush & picks-$.24,1 gun sling-$.16, 1 cartridge box plate-$.10, BLW sent to Philadelphia, Pa.

**Moore, Silas**, 2$^{nd}$ Cpl., Co. B; enl. 11/20/1846, Alexandria, VA, age 41; d. 05/31/1847 China, Mex.

**Moore, Thomas M.**, 2$^{nd}$ Lt., Co. L; b. 7/8/1819, son of Ammishaddai & Susan (Lindsey) Moore;

enl. Fairfax C.H. 3/1/1847; absent 06/1847 on detached service in QM Dept.; absent 08/1847 on detached service in QM Dept.; absent 10/1847 on detached service in QM Dept. as clerk; absent 12/1847 on detached service as a Clerk in the QM Dept., pay stopped for: 1 Jacket 2.66, 1 pr. Pants 2.28, 1 Cap .95, 2 prs. Shoes 2.44, 2 F shirts 1.80, 4 Ct. Shirts 1.72, 7 blankets, 15.47; pres. 02/1848, pay stopped for: 1 Jacket 2.66; pres. 04/1848, prom. 2$^{nd}$ Lt. from Sgt. 01/17/1848; pres. 07/1848; c. 1850 res. Fairfax Co., VA, age 31, occ. Teacher;[1332] m/1 Priscilla Haviland date unknown;[1333] Civil War Service (CS), Capt. QM Dept. Army HQ, m/2

OFF TO WAR

Hannah Morris Moore, Ostego Co., NY 05/05/58 (HMM b. 05/25/1835); c. 1860 res. Fairfax Co., VA, age 40, occ. Attorney;[1334] SC #7286, 01/29/1887, d. 06/17/1899, bur. Fairfax City Cem., Fairfax VA;[45] wid. Hannah M., WC #11717, 07/01/1899 both from VA; Thomas Moore was the grandson of early Baptist preacher Jeremiah Moore(1746-1815) & Lydia Reno Moore.

**Moore, William**, Pvt., *Recruit Co.*, enl. Mex. War service 04/17/1848 Wytheville, VA; pres. 06/1848; BLW sent to Wytheville, VA

**Moore, William H.**, Pvt., Co. E; b. 05/04/1823, Dinwiddie Co., VA, son of Morse & Rebecca Moore;[1335] m. Mary Ann White 03/1845, Lunenburg Co., VA;[1336] enl. Mex. War service 12/01/1846 Petersburg, VA, age 23; pres. 04/1847; pres. 06/1847; pres. 08/1847; pres. 10/1847, pay stopped for: 1 pr. overalls-$2.28, 2 pr. shoes-$1.22, 2 pr. stockings-$.49, 2 flannel shirts-$1.80, 1 pr. drawers-$.35$^{1/2}$, 1 cap-$.95$^{1/2}$; pres. 12/1847, pay stopped for: 1 pr. pants-$2.28, 1 blanket-$2.22; pres. 02/1848; pres. 04/1848; d. 08/12/1883, *Lung Disease*, Petersburg, VA, bur. Blandford Cem., Sec. 7, Ward F.S.G., Petersburg, VA;[1336, 1337] wid. Mary Ann, WC #201, 03/14/1887, filed from 609 Washington St., Petersburg, VA; (MAM b. 09/29/1824, Lunenburg Co., VA, d. 1903).[1336]

**Morgan, David W.**, Pvt., Co. C; enl. Mex. War service 12/30/1846, Bowling Green, VA, age 19; pres. 06/1847; pres. 08/1847, pay stopped for: 1 cap-$.95$^{1/2}$, 2 pr. socks-$.49, 2 cotton shirts-$.86, 2 woolen shirts-$1.80; discharged 09/13/1847 Buena Vista, Mex. on Surgeon's Certificate of Disability.

**Morlick, Michael**, Pvt., Co. B; enl. 12/01/1846, Alexandria, VA, age 40; pres. 06/1847; pres. 08/1847; pres. 10/1847, pay stopped for: 1 pr. cotton drawers-$.35$^{1/2}$; pres. 12/1847, pay stopped for: 2 flannel shirts-$1.80, 1 pr. overalls-$2.28, 1 cap-$.95$^{1/2}$, 3 pr. socks-$.73$^{1/2}$, 1 pr. shoes-$1.22; pres. 02/1848; pres. 04/1848, pay stopped for: 1 jacket-$2.66; pres. 08/1848, pay stopped for: 1 screw driver-$.07, 1 pr. shoes-$1.16, BLW sent to Alexandria, VA

**Morse, Daniel**, Pvt., Co. F; enl. Mex. War service 01/20/1847, Portsmouth, VA, age 33; pres. 06/1847; pres. 08/1847; pres. 10/1847, pay stopped for: 1 pr. overalls-$2.28, 2 cotton shirts-$.86, 2 pr. socks-$.49, 1 pr. shoes-$1.22, 2 pr. drawers-$.71; pres. 02/1848, pay stopped for: 1 pr. overalls-$2.28, 1 pr. shoes-$1.22, 1 forage cap-$.95$^{1/2}$, 1 infantry jacket-$2.66, 1 blanket-$2.22; pres. 04/1848; pres. 08/1848, pay stopped for: 1 screw driver-$.25, 1 wiper-$.20, 1 pr. shoes-$1.16, 1 cotton shirt-$.44, BLW sent to Portsmouth, VA c/o E.T. Blamire.

**Moss, James O.**, Pvt., Co. M; b. 09/02/1818, Brunswick Co., VA;[1338] m. Mary A. Bowers, 08/12/1838, Mecklenburg Co., VA;[1338, 1339] enl. Mex. War service 08/29/1847, Forksville, VA, age 35; pres. 10/1847; pres. 11/1847; pres. 12/1847; pres. 02/1848; sick 04/1848; pres. 08/1848, pay stopped for: 1 gun sling-$.16; BLW sent to Boydton, VA; c. 1850 a Mary A. Moss, age 35, res. Mecklenburg Co., VA, dau. Emily (6);[1340] Civil War service Pvt., Branch Arty., enl. 03/28/1862 in Petersburg, VA, pres. through 10/1864, issued clothing 11/30/1864, NFR.[77] (MBM d. 06/19/1865, Brunswick Co., VA);[1338] SC #6114, 02/04/1887, filed from Crichton, Brunswick Co., VA; phys. desc. 5'9", light complexion, blue eyes, black hair, occ. Farmer;[1338] since discharge res. Brunswick Co., VA[1338]

**Moss, James**, Pvt., Co. F; enl. Mex. War service 12/06/1846, Portsmouth, VA, age 18; d. 03/02/1847 at sea on board the barque *Exact*; his death, probably of small pox, and subsequent burial were recorded in the diary of Capt. James. L. Kemper.[1341]

**Moss, John J.**, Pvt., Co. D; enl. Mex. War service 01/06/1847, Petersburg, VA, age 22; pres. 02/1847; pres. 04/1847; pres. 06/1847, pay stopped for: 1 canteen; pres. 08/1847, pay stopped for: 1 cap-$.95$^{1/2}$, 2 cotton shirts-$.86, 2 flannel shirts-$1.80, 1 pr. shoes-$1.22; pres. but sick 10/1847, pay stopped for: 1 pr. socks-$.24$^{1/2}$; pres. 12/1847, pay stopped for: 1 jacket-$2.66, 1 pr. pants-$2.28, 1 pr drawers-$.35$^{1/2}$, 1 pr. socks-$.24$^{1/2}$, 1 pr. shoes-$1.22, 1 blanket-$2.22; pres. 04/1848, pay stopped for: 1 set of picks & brushes-$.12, 1 pr. pants-$2.28, 1 flannel shirt-$.90, 1 pr. socks-$.24$^{1/2}$, 1 haversack-$.20$^{3/4}$; pres. 08/1847, BLW sent to Hicks Ford, Greensville Co., VA; [c. 1850 a John Moss res. Buckingham Co., VA, age 28, w. Jamima

## VIRGINIA VOLUNTEERS IN MEXICO

(24), dau. Mary C. (5), dau. Ann (1);[1342] Civil War service Pvt., Co. F, 18th Va. Inf. enl. 03/13/1862 Buckingham Co., occ. Carpenter, phys. desc. 5'10", brown eyes, gray hair, fair complexion, hosp. rheumatism 03/1862 through 06/1862, discharged 02/01/1864 with chronic rheumatism;[1111] c. 1870 res. Curdsville, Buckingham Co., VA, age 49, occ. Carpenter, dau. Ann Eliza (19), son William E. (18).][1343]

**Moyer, John**, Pvt., Co. F; enl. Mex. War service 01/20/1847, Portsmouth, VA, age 24; absent 06/1847 left sick at Fort Monroe 02/20/1847 and not since heard from; absent 08/1847 sick at Fort Monroe; absent 10/1847 sick at Fort Monroe; discharged date unknown at Old Point Comfort, VA

**Moyers, James Harvey**, 2nd Sgt., *Preston's Co.*; b. 03/17/1822, Wytheville, Wythe Co., VA;[1344] enl. Mex. War service 12/24/1846 Wythe Co., VA, age 24; pres. 04/1847; pres. 06/1847; pres. 08/1847; pres. 10/1847, pay stopped for: 2 pr. socks-$.49, 1 cotton shirt-$.43, 1 pr. drawers-$.35$^{1/2}$; pres. 12/1847, pay stopped for: 1 pr. overalls-$2.28, 1 pr. shoes-$1.22, 1 cap-$.95$^{1/2}$, 1 pr. drawers-$.35$^{1/2}$, 2 blankets-$4.44; pres. 02/1848; pres. 04/1848, pay stopped for: 1 pick & brush-$.12; pres. 07/1848; BLW sent to Wytheville, VA; c. 1870 res. Fort Chiswell, Wythe Co., VA, age 46, occ. Cabinet Maker, w. Margaret (42), dau. Mary E. (14), dau. Margaret M. (12), son James P. (9), dau. Susan J. (7), dau. Florence B. (6);[1345] c. 1880 res. Wythe Co., VA, age 64, occ. Carpenter, w. Margaret (46), dau. Margaret (23), son James P. (19), dau. Susan J. (16), dau. Florence B. (14);[1346] SC #3009, 03/03/1887, filed from Wytheville, Wythe Co., VA; d. 1889.[1344]

**Moyler, John**, 3rd Cpl., Co. D; *"sues David Neves for slander";*[1347] enl. Mex. War service 01/05/1847, Petersburg, VA, age 26; pres. 02/1847; pres. 04/1847; pres. 06/1847; absent sick 08/1847, prom. 4th Cpl. 08/30/1847, pay stopped for: 1 cap-$.95$^{1/2}$, 1 pr. pants-$2.28, 2 cotton shirts-$.86, 1 pr. shoes-$1.22; pres. 10/1847, prom. 3rd Cpl., pay stopped for: 1 pr drawers-$.35$^{1/2}$, 2 pr. socks-$.73$^{1/2}$, 1 overcoat-$6.93$^{1/2}$; pres. 12/1847, pay stopped for: 1 cap-$.95$^{1/2}$, 1 jacket-$2.66, 1 pr. pants-$2.28, 2 cotton shirts-$.86, 1 blanket-$2.22; pres. 04/1848, pay stopped for: 1 pr. shoes-$1.22, 1 haversack-$.20$^{3/4}$, overpaid $4.00 on 08/1847 pay roll; pres. 08/1847, BLW sent to Petersburg, VA

**Muirhead, James W.**, Pvt., *Preston's Co.*; enl. Mex. War service 01/04/1847 Montgomery Co., VA, age 36; pres. 04/1847; absent 06/1847 in hosp. at Saltillo, Mex. since 06/27/1847; d. 08/17/1847 at Buena Vista, Mex.," *of consumption,"*[243] pay stopped for: 1 canteen-$.27, 1 haversack-$.20$^{3/4}$.

**Mullen, Charles**, Pvt., Co. B; enl. 12/05/1846, Alexandria, VA, age 18; pres. 06/1847; pres. 08/1847; pres. 10/1847, pay stopped for: 2 pr. cotton drawers-$.71, 1 pr. overalls-$2.28, 1 blanket-$2.22; sick 12/1847, pay stopped for: 3 pr. shoes-$3.66, 3 cotton shirts-$1.29, 1 pr. overalls-$2.28, 4 pr. wool socks-$.98; pres. 02/1848; pres. 04/1848, pay stopped for: 1 jacket-$2.66; pres. 04/1848, pay stopped for: 1 jacket-$2.66; pres. 08/1848, pay stopped for: 1 wiper-$.20, 1 gun sling-$.16, 1 screw driver-$.07, 1 pr. shoes-$1.16, BLW sent to Alexandria, VA

**Mullen, Robert**, Pvt., Co. B; enl. Mex. War service 12/20/1846, Richmond, VA, age 21; deserted 01/02/1847, Richmond, VA

**Muloy, Francis P.**, Pvt., Co. M; enl. Mex. War service 10/07/1847, Ft. Monroe, VA, age 29; pres. 09/1847; pres. 11/1847; pres. 12/1847; sick 02/1848, pay stopped for: 1 blanket-$2.22; discharged 03/16/1848 at Saltillo, Mex. on Surgeon's Certificate of Disability.

**Munford, Carlton Radford**, 2nd Lt., Co. G; b. 1824 Richmond, VA; son of William & Sarah (Radford) Munford; attended VMI Class of 1844 (non-graduate);[281] enl. Mex. War service 11/18/1846 Richmond, VA, age 23; d. 1847 Mexico from wound received in a duel; On the morning of the 18th of May 1847, while a portion of the Va. Regt. was stationed at China. Mexico, Lt. Mahan reported Capt. John P. Young, in his quarters that he had seen a body of forty mounted armed Mexicans one to two miles from China. This was in the presence of several other officers, including Lt. Munford. Lt. Munford then stated that he did not believe Lt. Mahan and *"believed him to be a damned liar."* That he had previously caught Mahan

OFF TO WAR

telling lies. The story Lt. Mahan told, of his having seen this armed force, created a considerable excitement. Shortly afterward, on the morning of the 20th of May 1847, the two men met again in the tent of Capt. Young with several other officers present. Lt. Mahan came in with his sword in his hand. He complimented Lt. Munford on his sword. Lt. Munford replied to Lt. Mahan that he was not fit to carry a sword and that he would disgrace any sword that could be placed in his hands and that he did not consider him a fit associate for the officers of the detachment. Capt. Young suggested to Lt. Mahan that he had been *"grossly insulted"* and that he *"could no longer appreciate him as an Officer or a Gentleman, unless he resented"* how Lt. Munford had insulted him. Lt. Mahan then went to speak with Capt. Bankhead on the matter. Bankhead advised him not to escalate the trouble and Mahan agreed he would not. At about this time Lt. Munford came into the room and again insulted Lt. Mahan in the presence of Capt. Bankhead, Lts. Garnett and Coleman. Lt. Mahan then challenged Lt. Munford to fight him with weapons. To which challenge Lt. Munford agreed. All efforts of Capt. Bankhead, Capt. Young and Lt. Garnett to induce Lt. Munford to retract the offensive language and to settle the matter peaceably proved futile. The duel took place on the evening of the 20th of May 1847 with muskets. Lt. Mahan was struck with *"slug"* in his chest and a *"ball"* in the left axilla, which came out, left of the spinal column; he died on the 1st of June 1847. Lt. Munford was struck with eight buckshot and died some thirty hours later. A letter of petition from several *"concerned citizens"* in Philadelphia was sent to President James K. Polk, charging that Capt. Bankhead, Young and Lt. Thomas S. Garnett were *"guilty of a manifest violation of military duty, in aiding abetting and countenancing by their presence, the fatal meeting between Lts. Mahan & Munford."* The Pres. evidently agreed and a Court of Inquiry was held at Buena Vista, Mexico 01/03/1848.[1348] The Court of Inquiry subsequently found no evidence of wrongdoing or complicity in the deaths of Lts. Mahan and Munford. 1st cousin of Dr. John Blair Radford founder of the Town of Radford, VA[1349]

**Munn, Daniel**, Pvt., Co. G; b. c. 1823, son of Willett Munn;[1350] enl. Mex. War service 12/20/1846, Richmond, VA, age 23; in confinement 10/1847, pay stopped for: 1 pr. overalls-$2.28, 2 cotton shirts-$.86, 1 pr. shoes-$1.22, 1 pr. socks-$.24^{1/2}, 1 great coat-$6.95^{1/2}; pres. 12/1847, pay stopped for: 1 pr. shoes-$1.22, 2 cotton shirts-$.86, 2 flannel shirts-$1.80, 2 pr. drawers-$.71, 1 pr. pants-$2.28, 1 cap-$.95^{1/2}; pres. 02/1848, pay stopped for: 1 brush & pick-$.12; pres. 04/1848; pres. 08/1848; BLW sent to Richmond, VA; c. 1850 res. Richmond, Henrico Co., VA, age 27, occ. Finisher.[1350]

**Muny, John**, Pvt., Co. H; enl. Mex. War service 01/06/1847, Berkeley, VA, age 24; pres. 04/1847; discharged 05/17/1847 at Monterey, Mex. on Surgeon's Certificate of Disability.

**Murdaugh, John W.**, Pvt., Co. D; b. 10/1823, Bertie, NC, son of James & Mary Murdaugh;[1351] enl. Mex. War service 01/09/1847, Petersburg, VA, age 23; pres. 02/1847; pres. 04/1847; pres. but sick 06/1847; pres. 08/1847, pay stopped for: 1 cap-$.95^{1/2}; discharged 09/13/1847 Buena Vista, Mex. on Surgeon's Certificate of Disability; d. 01/23/1849, *Intemperance*, bur. Blandford Cem., Sq. 225, Ward A, Petersburg, VA.[1351]

**Murphy, Daniel**, Pvt., Co. B; b. 02/05/1830 City of Cork, Ireland;[1352] enl. 12/18/1846, Alexandria, VA, age 18; pres. 06/1847; pres. 08/1847; pres. 10/1847, forfeit 1 mos. pay by order (No. 162) of genl. court-martial, pay stopped for: 2 pr. overalls-$4.56, 1 pr. shoes-$1.22, 2 pr. cotton drawers-$.71, 1 cotton shirt-$.43, 2 pr. socks-$.49, 1 blanket-$2.22; pres. 12/1847, pay stopped for: 2 pr. shoes-$2.44, 3 pr. socks-$.73^{1/2}, 4 cotton shirts-$1.72, 1 pr. overalls-$2.28, 1 cap-$.95^{1/2}, 1 bayonet-$1.49; pres. 02/1848, pay stopped for: 1 pr. shoes-$1.22; pres. 04/1848; pres. 08/1848, pay stopped for: 1 musket lock-$3.04, 1cartridge box plate-$.10, 1 pick & brush-$.12, 1 screw driver-$.07, 1 wiper-$.20, BLW sent to Baltimore, MD; m/1 Sarah Hinfey 08/20/1852, San Antonio, Bexar Co., Tex. (Sarah Murphy d. 10/05/1865 San Antonio, Bexar Co., Tex.); m/2 Susan Hinfey 09/1867, San Antonio, Bexar Co., TX, (Susan Murphy d. 08/4/1896) sister of Sarah Hinfey; Texas Delegate to Mexican War Veterans Assoc. 1881; SC #19868, 04/03/1891, from Ft. Davis, Jeff Davis Co., TX; phys. desc. 5'10", fair complexion, light black hair, gray eyes, occ. Farmer; listed children Thomas O. Murphy b. 07/01/1853, Ellen I. b. 12/1854, Mary b. 1856, Sarah b. 08/1858, Cathren b. *summer* 1860, Susan b. 1862; d. 11/15/1902.[1352]

**Murphy, William W.**, 2nd Sgt., Co. G; enl. Mex. War service 11/18/1846 Richmond, VA, age 30; pres. 06/1847; pres. 08/1847; pres. 10/1847, pay stopped for: 1 pr. overalls $2.28, 1 shoes-$1.22, 2 pr. socks-$.49, 1 forage cap-$.95$^{1/2}$; pres. 12/1847, pay stopped for: 1 blanket-$2.22, 1 jacket-$2.66, 1 pr. socks-$.24$^{1/2}$; pres. 02/1848; pres. 04/1848; pres. 08/1848, pay stopped for: 1 bayonet-$1.44, 1 waist belt-$.21, 1 waist belt plate-$.10, 1 scabbard & frog-$.56; BLW sent to Richmond, VA

**Murray, James**, Pvt., Co. I; enl. Mex. War service 08/19/1847 Ft. Monroe, VA, age 21; pres. 02/1848, joined co. 01/26/1848; pres. 04/1848; d. 07/03/1848, drowned at the mouth of the Rio Grande River.

**Murray, Lewis**, Pvt., *Preston's Co.*; enl. Mex. War service 12/06/1846 Montgomery Co., VA, age 18; pres. 04/1847; pres. 06/1847; pres. 08/1847; pres. 10/1847, pay stopped for: 1 jacket-$2.66, 1 pr. overalls-$2.28, 1 pr. shoes-$1.22, 4 pr. socks-$.98, 1 flannel shirt-$.90, 2 cotton shirt-$.86, 1 cap-$.95$^{1/2}$; pres. 12/1847, pay stopped for: 1 pr. shoes-$1.22, 1 pr. drawers-$.35$^{1/2}$; pres. 02/1848; pres. 04/1848; pres. 07/1848, pay stopped for: 1 pr. shoes-$1.16; BLW sent to Salem, VA

**Naugle, William H.**, Drummer, Co. B; enl. 11/20/1846, Alexandria, VA, age 22; pres. 06/1847; sick 08/1847, pay stopped for 1 musket complete-$14.00, 1 cartridge box-$1.28, belt-$.70, plate-$.10, 1 bayonet scabbard with frog-$.50, 1 waist belt-$.25 and plate-$.10, 1 pricker and brush-$.12, 1 gun sling-$.18; discharged 09/17/1847 Buena Vista, Mex. on Surgeon's Certificate of Disability.

**Nees, John M.**, Pvt., Co. G; enl. Mex. War service 11/26/1846 Richmond, VA, age 27; pres. 06/1847; pres. 08/1847; pres. 10/1847, pay stopped for: 1 pr. overalls-$2.28, 1 flannel shirt-$.90, 1 pr. shoes-$1.22, 3 pr. socks-$.73$^{1/2}$, 1 forage cap-$.95$^{1/2}$; pres. 12/1847, pay stopped for: 1 pr. shoes-$1.22, 1 pr. pants-$2.28, 1 pr. socks-$.24$^{1/2}$; absent 02/1848 on furlough for 30 days; pres. 04/1848; pres. 08/1848, pay stopped for: 1 pr. shoes-$1.16; BLW sent to Norfolk, VA

**Neighbors, Christopher**, Co. K; *Not on Muster Rolls*, SC #14823, 12/10/1887, from TX.

**Neighbors, James**, Pvt., Co. I; 01/23/1818, Bedford Co., VA;[1353] enl. Mex. War service 01/10/1847 Lynchburg, VA, age 22; pres. 02/1847; absent 04/1847, left sick at Point Isabel, Tex., 03/16/1847; pres. 06/1847 sick; pres. 08/1847; pres. 10/1847, pay stopped for: 3 cotton shirts-$1.29, 2 pr. drawers-$.71, 1 pr. shoes-$1.22, 1 cap- $.95$^{1/2}$, 1 pr. socks-$.24$^{1/2}$, 1 jacket-$2.66; pres. 12/1847, pay stopped for: 1 pr. socks-$.24$^{1/2}$, 1 pr. pants-$2.28, 1 pr. shoes-$1.22, 1 pr. pants-$2.28, 1 blanket-$2.22, 2 flannel shirts-$1.80, 1 pr. drawers-$.35$^{1/2}$; pres. 02/1848, pay stopped for: 1 pr. shoes-$1.22, 1 pr. overalls-$2.28; 04/1848, pay stopped for: 2 blankets, 2 cotton shirts; pres. 08/1848, BLW sent to Liberty, VA; m. Mary Ann Ganoe, c. 1868, Greenville?, WV;[1353] SC #6844, 03/14/1887, filed from Indian Mills, Summers Co., WV [Indian Mills is just across the Monroe County line]; phys. desc. age 74 [1887], 5'11$^{3/4}$", light complexion, light hair, blue eyes;[1353] *"Was taken with small pox* [on board ship, enroute to Mexico] *from which I lost my right eye;"*[1353] since discharge res. Washington Co., VA and Red Sulphur Springs, WV, occ. Laborer;[1353] d. 04/15/1888, Monroe Co., WV;[1354] wid. Mary Ann, WA #7130, 09/11/1888, filed from Union, Monroe Co., WV; Lists son A.R. Neighbors;[1354] (MGN b. 1848, Monroe Co., VA).[1354]

**Neill, William V.**, 2nd Lt., Co. L; enl. Mex. War service 03/01/1847 Fairfax C.H., VA; sick 06/1847; 07/1847 relieved of duty and confined to his tent to await court-martial for disobeying a direct order to return to camp;[1355] pres. 08/1847; pres. 12/1847; in confinement 02/1848; resigned 04/15/1848.[72]

OFF TO WAR

**Newall, James**, Pvt., Co. L; b. 1828; enl. Mex. War service 03/01/1847 Fairfax C.H., VA, age 19; pres. 06/1847; deserted 04/22/1847 in New Orleans, La.[72]

**Newell, Benjamin C.**, Pvt., Co. D; enl. Mex. War service 12/25/1846, Petersburg, VA, age 25; pres. 02/1847; pres. 04/1847; discharged 05/01/1847, Monterey, Mex. on Surgeon's Certificate of Disability; c. 1850 res. Prince George Co., age 29, occ. Overseer.[1356]

**Newhall, Charles G.**, Pvt., Co. G; b. c. 1821, Essex Co., VA, son of Amos & Vetoria (Montague) Newhall;[1357] enl. Mex. War service 12/14/1846 Richmond, VA, age 25; pres. 06/1847; pres. 08/1847; in confinement 10/1847, pay stopped for: 1 pr. overalls-$2.28, 2 flannel shirts-$1.80, 2 shoes-$2.44, 3 pr. socks-$.73$^{1/2}$, 1 forage cap-$.95$^{1/2}$; pres. 12/1847, pay stopped for: 1 pr. shoes-$1.22, 2 pr. drawers-$.71, 1 blanket-$2.22, 1 pr. pants-$2.28; sick 02/1848; pres. 04/1848; pres. 08/1848; BLW sent to Essex Co. C.H., VA; c. 1850 res. Essex Co., VA, age 23, occ. Carpenter. [1358]

**Newlee, Robert G.**, 1$^{st}$ Sgt., *Preston's Co.*; b. 03/14/1819, Christiansburg, Montgomery Co., VA, son of William & Mary Davis (Glenn) Newlee;[1359, 54] enl. Mex. War service 12/06/1846 Montgomery Co., VA, age 27; pres. 04/1847; pres. 06/1847; pres. 08/1847; pres. 10/1847, pay stopped for: 1 pr. overalls-$2.28, 7 pr. socks-$1.71$^{1/2}$, 3 flannel shirts-$2.70; pres. 12/1847, pay stopped for: 3 pr. overalls-$6.84, 1 pr. socks-$.24$^{1/2}$, 1 cap-$.95$^{1/2}$, 2 blankets-$4.44, 1 overcoat-$6.93$^{1/2}$; pres. 02/1848, pay stopped for: 1 pr. shoes-$1.22; pres. 04/1848; pres. 07/1848, pay stopped for: 1 pr. shoes-$1.16, 1 cartridge box belt plate-$.10, 1 spring vise-$.35, 1 brush & pick-$.12; BLW sent to Christiansburg, VA c/o Fleming Gardner; c. 1850 res. Montgomery Co., VA, age 31, occ. Tailor;[1360]m. Martha Bennett, 03/22/1859, Montgomery Co., VA;[1361] c. 1860 res. Blacksburg, Montgomery Co., VA, age 40, occ. Farmer, w. Martha J. (27), dau. Malinda (4/12);[1362] Civil War service Capt., Co. L, 4$^{th}$ Va. Inf., 07/16/1861, resigned 04/21/1862 at reorganization;[54] SC #3314, 03/14/1887, from VA; Henry Collins and Crockett Linkous gave affidavits in pension claim;[1359] d. 05/14/1904, bur. Blacksburg, VA

**Nicholson, David W.**, Pvt., Co. D; enl. Mex. War service 01/06/1847, Petersburg, VA, age 24; pres. 02/1847; pres. 04/1847; pres. 06/1847; pres. 08/1847, pay stopped for: 1 cap-$.95$^{1/2}$, 1 pr. shoes-$1.22; pres. but sick 10/1847, pay stopped for: 1 jacket-$2.66, 1 pr. pants-$2.28, 1 flannel shirt-$.90, 1 pr. drawers-$.35$^{1/2}$, 2 pr. socks-$.49, 1 pr. shoes-$1.22, 1 overcoat-$6.93$^{1/2}$; absent 12/1847 on extra duty obtaining uniforms, pay stopped for: 1 pr. pants-$2.28, 1 pr. socks-$.24$^{1/2}$, 1 blanket-$2.22; pres. 04/1848, pay stopped for: 2 cotton shirts-$.86; pres. 08/1847, BLW sent to Jerusalem, Southampton Co., VA; c. 1850 res. Southampton Co., VA, age 28, occ. Farmer, w. Caroline (26);[1363] Civil War service Cpl., Co. H, 5$^{th}$ Va. Cav. & Pvt., Co. B, 13$^{th}$ Va. Cav.;[131] d. 03/1872, *'David W. Nicholson, of Southampton Co., served in Mexican War and in the C.S.A.'*[1364]

**Nicholson, John W.**, Pvt., Co. M; enl. Mex. War service 11/11/1847, Brunswick, VA, age 25; pres. 11/1847; pres. 12/1847; sick 02/1848; sick 04/1848; pres. 08/1848, pay stopped for: 1 pick & brush-$.12, 1 screw driver-$.07, 1 wormer-$.20; BLW sent to Brunswick C.H., VA; c. 1850 res. Brunswick Co., VA, age 26, occ. Farmer.[1365]

**Nicholson, Lemuel**, Pvt., Co. C; enl. Mex. War service 12/09/1847, Alexandria, VA, age 39; pres. 04/1848, joined company 01/27/1848 from Regtl. Depot, pay due from enlistment; pres. 08/1848, BLW sent to Alexandria, VA [c. 1850, a Lemuel P. Nicholson, age 48, occ. Physician, res. Southampton Co., VA[1366]]

**Noble, Moses Greer**, 1$^{st}$ Cpl., Co. I; b. 04/27/1829, Rocky Mount, Franklin Co., VA, son of Daniel & Nancy (Greer) Noble;[1367] enl. Mex. War service 01/10/1847 Lynchburg, VA, age 18; pres. 02/1847; pres. 04/1847; pres. 06/1847, prom. 3$^{rd}$ Cpl.; pres. 08/1847; pres. 10/1847, prom. 1$^{st}$ Cpl., pay stopped for: 2 cotton shirts-$.86, 3 pr. drawers-$1.06$^{1/2}$, 1 pr. pants-$2.28, 1 pr. shoes-$1.22, 1 cap- $.95$^{1/2}$, 1 pr. socks-$.24$^{1/2}$; pres. 10/1847, pay stopped for: 1 pr. socks-$.24$^{1/2}$, 2 pr. drawers-$.71, 1 jacket-$2.66, 1 pr. pants-$2.28, 1 pr. shoes-$1.22, 1 blanket-$2.22; pres. 02/1848; pres. 04/1848; pres. 08/1848, pay stopped for: 1 wiper-$.20, BLW sent to Gogginsville, Franklin Co., VA; m. Cornelia Maria Woods, 09/13/1857, Rocky Mount,

## VIRGINIA VOLUNTEERS IN MEXICO

Franklin Co., VA;[1367] Civil War service enl. Cpl., Co. A, 36th Tex. Cav.; SC #18702, 12/07/1889, filed from Lorena, McLennan Co., TX; phys. desc. 5'10", light complexion, blue eyes, light hair, occ. Farmer;[1367] since discharge res. in California 1849-1861, since then in Texas;[1367] Lists children Robert W. Noble, b. 11/03/1863, Alpha E. Noble, b. 01/20/1878;[1367] d. 10/11/1912, 17 N 2nd St., Temple, Bell Co., TX,[1367] bur. Georgetown, Williamson Co., TX.[1367]

**Noel, Landon**, Pvt., Co. D; enl. Mex. War service 01/03/1847, Petersburg, VA, age 24; pres. 02/1847; pres. 04/1847; pres. 06/1847; pres. 08/1847, pay stopped for: 1 cap-$.95[1/2], 2 cotton shirts-$.86; pres. 10/1847, pay stopped for: 1 jacket-$2.66, 1 pr. pants-$2.28, 1 cotton shirts-$.43, 2 pr. drawers-$.71, 1 pr. socks-$.24[1/2], 1 pr. shoes-$1.22; pres. but sick 12/1847, fined 1 mos. pay by order (No. 162) of genl. court-martial 12/14/1847, pay stopped for: 1 pr. pants-$2.28, 1 pr. socks-$.24[1/2], 1 pr. shoes-$1.22, 1 blanket-$2.22; pres. 04/1848; pres. 08/1847, BLW sent to Prince George C.H., VA

**Noon, Hugh D.**, Pvt., LIC; b. Ireland c. 1819; enl. Mex. War service 12/20/1846 Staunton, VA, age 27; absent 06/1847 sick; discharged 08/1847at Monterey, Mex. on Surgeon's Certificate of Disability; m. Mary Adeline Bickle; c. 1850 res. Augusta Co., VA, age 30, occ. Laborer, son Michael (4), son John (5), w. Mary A. (24), dau. Margaret (2);[1368] c. 1860 res. Augusta Co., VA, age 41, occ. Laborer;[1369] Civil War service enl. 03/17/1862 at Staunton, VA as Pvt., Staunton Artillery; pres. through 12/31/1862; pres. as a Hosp. Steward 1/63 - 2/63; detailed to get horses 3/63 - 4/63; pres. 5/63 - 12/63; absent on leave 1/64 - 2/64; pres. 3/64 - 10/64; absent sick "diarrhea" in hosp. 6/15/64 - 6/22/64; absent detailed to make Neatsfoot Oil 2/28/1865; c. 1870 res. Staunton, Augusta Co., VA, age 51, occ. Drayman, w. Mary A. (45), son John A. (20), dau. Annie H. (17), dau. Susan B. (15), dau. Euphema (11), dau. Caroline (9), son Robert (6);[1370] d. 09/20/1876, Argenta, Ark.

**Nopie, William**, Pvt., Co. H; enl. Mex. War service 01/06/1847, Berkeley, VA, age 28; pres. 04/1847; absent 06/1847 left sick in Hosp. at Monterey, Mex. 06/22/1847; discharged 08/20/1847 Monterey, Mex. on Surgeon's Certificate of Disability.[Civil War service a William Nopie served as a Pvt., Co. A, 7th La. Inf.][202]

**Norfleet, Christopher**, Pvt., Co. F; b. 09/10/1824, Nansemond Co., VA son of Christopher and Letitia (Duke) Norfleet;[1371] enl. Mex. War service 01/22/1846, Suffolk, VA, age 18; pres. 06/1847; pres. 08/1847; pres. 10/1847, pay stopped for: 1 pr. overalls-$2.28, 2 cotton shirts-$.86, 5 pr. socks-$1.22[1/2], 1 forage cap-$.95[1/2], 2 pr. drawers-$.71, 1 blanket-$2.22; pres. 02/1848, pay stopped for: 2 pr. drawers-$.71, 1 pr. overalls-$2.28, 1 pr. shoes-$1.22, 1 cotton shirt-$.43, 1 infantry jacket-$2.66; pres. 04/1848; pres. 08/1848, pay stopped for: 2 cotton shirts-$.88, 2 blankets-$4.50, 1 pr. shoes-$1.16, BLW sent to Portsmouth, VA c/o E.T. Blamire; m/1 Louisa Rabby 03/13/1856, Suffolk, Nansemond Co., VA; Civil War service enl. Pvt., Co. A, 16th Va. Inf., occ. carpenter and shingle inspector, phys. desc. 5'10[1/2]", swallow complexion, yellowish-grey eyes, black hair;[77] states he assisted Dr. Powell, Regtl. Surgeon with amputations after the Battle of Malvern Hill in 1862 and that he was discharged at his own request *"because I was over age;"*[1371] (LRN d. 1867); m/2 Mary Frances Smith 03/13/1870, Nansemond Co., VA;[1371] SC #16338, 02/18/1888, filed from Suffolk, Nansemond Co., VA; phys. desc. 5'7", light complexion, gray eyes, white hair, scar between first and second fingers of left hand said to be a pistol shot before enlistment;[1371] lists children: Luella C. b. 06/01/1860, Hadley C. b. 08/21/1865, Elizabeth b. 01/26/1871, Annie L. b. 12/30/1874; Daisy b. 04/25/1878, Linwood b. 06/26/1884, Fannie J. b. 09/26/1887,[1371] (MSN d. 03/02/1902, Suffolk, VA);[1371] *"I am 77 years old [1902], P.O. and residence Suffolk, VA I am a Painter (House) by trade. I was born 6 miles south of Suffolk, VA September 10th 1824. My father was named Christopher Norfleet. I have lived in Suffolk, VA and nearby all my life. I enlisted in Dr. Young's Company, Co. F, 1st Virginia Vols. In the fall of the year 1847 at Suffolk, Va....;"*[1371] d. 11/09/1906, bur. Cedar Hill Cem., Block B, Lot 39, Suffolk, VA;[1372]

## OFF TO WAR

**Norville, George W.**, Pvt., Co. A; m. Nancy A. Bailey 12/18/1835 Nelson Co., VA; enl. Mex. War service 11/18/1846 Richmond, VA, age 36; pres. until sick 04/1847, in Hosp. at Matamoros sent there from Camargo, Mex. 04/02/1847 - 06/1847, discharged 05/15/1847 on Surgeon's Certificate; d. 07/28/1847 *"diarrhea,"* Baltimore, MD;[1373] wid. Nancy, WC #2876, 06/09/1887, filed from Fabers Mills, Nelson Co., VA; c. 1874 res. Elmington, Nelson Co., VA; OW W #16793, rejected. (NAN b. 02/17/1817).[1373]

**Nottingham, William Thomas**, Pvt., Co. F; b. 06/23/1821 Northampton Co., VA, son of Jacob & Sarah Jarvis (Bell) Nottingham; m/1 Margaret Sarah Williams, 11/19/1844, Northampton Co., VA; enl. Mex. War service 12/22/1846, Portsmouth, VA, age 18?; discharged 03/26/1847 Camargo, Mex. on Surgeon's Certificate of Disability; m/2 Lucy Ann Carpenter,09/01/1852, Northampton Co., VA; m/3 Laurett V. Carpenter, 01/25/1859, Northampton Co., VA; d. 02/22/1859; phys. desc. age 65 [1885], 5'6", light complexion, blue eyes, light hair, occ. at enlistment Blacksmith; SC #2651, 02/04/1887, filed from Santa Rosa, Sonoma Co., CA; since discharge went to California mining camps then to San Francisco; res. with Mary N. McLaughlin since 1878 or 1879; m/4 Annie Finley Harrington 11/02/1889, Santa Rosa, Sonoma Co., CA; d. 08/02/1908, Merced, Merced Co., CA; wid. Anna, WC #15617, 09/02/1908, filed from Merced, Merced Co., CA; also served as Pvt., Co. H, 7$^{th}$ US Inf.; (AFN b. 10/13/1837, Dromara, Ireland, d. 07/26/1916, St. John's Hosp., Springfield, Mo., bur. St. Mary's Cemetery, Springfield, Mo.).

**Nunnally, Theoderick**, Co. G; enl. Mex. War service 12/20/1846 Richmond, VA, age 20; pres. 06/1847; pres. 08/1847; pres. 10/1847, pay stopped for: 1 pr. overalls-$2.28, 2 pr. shoes-$2.44, 3 pr. socks-$.73$^{1/2}$, 1 forage cap-$.95$^{1/2}$; pres. 12/1847, pay stopped for: 2 pr. shoes-$2.44, 2 flannel shirts-$1.80, 1 pr. drawers-$.35$^{1/2}$, 1 jacket-$2.66, 1 pr. pants-$2.28, 1 overcoat-$6.93$^{1/2}$, 1 cap-$.95$^{1/2}$; pres. 02/1848, pay stopped for: 1 pr. pants-$2.28; pres. 04/1848; pres. 08/1848, pay stopped for: 1 gun sling-$.16; BLW sent to Richmond, VA; SC #7326, 03/09/1887, wid. Mary A., WC #9948, 12/11/1895, both from VA [pension file missing].

**O'Bannon, Dagobert B.**, Pvt., Co. L; b. 1828; enl. Mex. War service 03/01/1847 Fairfax C.H., VA, age 19; pres. 06/1847; pres. 08/1847; pres. 10/1847, pay stopped for: 1 pr. Pants 2.28; pres. 12/1847, pay stopped for: 1 jacket-$2.66, 1 cap-$.95$^{1/2}$, 1 pr. shoes-$1.22, 2 flannel shirts-$1.80, 1 cotton shirt-$.43, 1 blanket-$2.22, 1 pr. drawers-$.35, 2 pr. socks-$.49; pres. 02/1848, pay stopped for: 1 Brush & Pick .12; pres. 04/1848, pay stopped for: 2 Cotton Shirts .88; pres. 07/1848, pay stopped for: 1 Bayonet Scabbard .56, 1 Waist Belt .21; BLW sent to Capt. Thrift c/o Dagobert B. O'Bannon, Fairfax Court House, Fairfax Co., VA; m. Sarah Ann Wilson 3/21/1853, Washington, D.C.;[1374] Civil War service enl. Pvt., Co. H, 6$^{th}$ Va. Cav. "Black Horse Troop," Warrenton, VA Promoted to 1$^{st}$ Lt. 7/1/1861. Absent recruiting 1 - 2/1862. Captured 7/21/1863 at Chester Gap, VA sent to Old Capitol Prison and Johnson's Island 10/20/1863; exchanged 3/14/1865 from Pt. Lookout Prison, MD[324] C. 1870 res. Greenville, Washington Co., MS, age 37, occ. Planter, had a sizable estate valued at *$10,000* for land and *$4,000* for personal property;[1375] m. Mary P. Heard, 10/13/1870, Washington, Mississippi;[1376] SC #19482, 04/03/1891, from MS.

**Obitz, Danial L.**, *Not on Muster Rolls*; wid. Rebecca, WA #8866, 04/02/1890, from PA.

**Olcott, Henry B.**, Pvt., Co. M; enl. Mex. War service 11/26/1847, Ft. Monroe, VA, age 26; pres. 11/1847; pres. 12/1847; pres. 02/1848, prom. 2$^{nd}$ Sgt. 02/09/1848; pres. 04/1848; res. 08/1848, reduced to ranks by sentence of court-martial, pay stopped for: 1 musket-$13.00; BLW sent to Norfolk, VA

**O'Neil, Felix**, Pvt., Co. G; enl. Mex. War service 12/14/1846 Richmond, VA, age 28; pres. 06/1847; pres. 08/1847; pres. 10/1847, pay stopped for: 1 pr. overalls-$2.28, 1 shoes-$1.22, 2 pr. socks-$.49, 1 forage cap-$.95$^{1/2}$; pres. 12/1847, pay stopped for: 1 pr. shoes-$1.22, 2 cotton shirts-$.86, 1 pr. pants-$2.28, 1 blanket-$2.22; pres. 02/1848; pres. 04/1848; pres. 08/1848; BLW sent to Richmond, VA

## VIRGINIA VOLUNTEERS IN MEXICO

**Onion, John R.**; alias John R. Williams; Pvt., Co. H; b. 03/21/1827, *"on farm Hartford Co., MD;"* Apprenticed to Benjamin Upton, Cabinet Maker, Hartford Ave. near Madison St., Baltimore, MD; enl. Mex. War service 01/06/1847, Berkeley, VA, age 21; pres. 04/1847; pres. 06/1847 left sick in Hosp. at Monterey, Mex. 06/22/1847; absent 08/1847 sick at Monterey, Mex. since 06/22/1847; absent sick 10/1847 in Hosp. at Monterey, Mex.; absent 12/1847 sick in Hosp. at Monterey, Mex.; absent 02/1848, sick in Hosp. at Monterey, Mex.; absent 04/1848, sick in Hosp. at Monterey, Mex.; pres. 07/1848, BLW sent to Baltimore, MD m/1 Sarah A. (SAO d. 09/12/1861, Baltimore, MD); m/2 Sarah C. Smyser, 12/26/1866, Baltimore, MD; SC 13449, 08/26/1887, filed from 1226 Chew St., Baltimore, MD; d. 05/26/1910.

**Organ, John T.**, Pvt., Co. M; enl. Mex. War service 11/26/1847, Lynchburg, VA, age 19; pres. 09/1847; pres. 11/1847; pres. 12/1847; pres. 02/1848, pay stopped for: 1 flannel shirt-$.90; sick 04/1848, pay stopped for: 1 cap-$.95$^{1/2}$; pres. 08/1848, pay stopped for: 1 pick & brush-$.12; BLW sent to New London, Bedford Co., VA

**Orrison, Albert W.**, Pvt., Co. B; enl. 12/16/1846, Alexandria, VA, age 28; pres. 06/1847; sick 08/1847; discharged 10/11/1847 Buena Vista, Mex. on Surgeon's Certificate of Disability.

**Orton, George W.**, Pvt., Co. F; enl. Mex. War service 12/24/1846, Portsmouth, VA, age 26; pres. 06/1847; pres. 08/1847; pres. 10/1847, pay stopped for: 1 pr. overalls-$2.28, 2 cotton shirts-$.86, 3 pr. socks-$.73$^{1/2}$; pres. 02/1848, pay stopped for: 1 blanket-$2.22, 1 forage cap-$.95$^{1/2}$, 2 pr. drawers-$.71, 1 pr. overalls-$2.28, 1 pr. socks-$.24$^{1/2}$; pres. 04/1848; pres. 08/1848, pay stopped for: 1 cartridge box belt plate-$.10, 1 brush & pick-$.12, 4 cotton shirts-$1.76, 3 blankets-$6.75, BLW sent to Portsmouth, VA c/o E.T. Blamire; [c. 1850 res. Portsmouth, Norfolk Co., VA, age 38, occ. None.][1377]

**Ott, John H.**, Pvt., Co. H; m. Ellen R. Poisal, 01/09/1845, Berkeley Co., VA;[1378] 05/1844 established himself as a Saddler on Queen St., Martinsburg, VA;[1379] 03/1846 with Samuel L. Stewart, established *Stewart & Ott* a Saddle, Harness and Trunk Manufactory in Hedgesville, Berkeley Co., VA;[1380] partnership dissolved 04/09/1846 by mutual consent;[1381] enl. Mex. War service 11/21/1846, Berkeley, VA, age 26; pres. 04/1847; pres. 06/1847; pres. 08/1847; pres. 10/1847, pay stopped for: 1 forage cap-$.95$^{1/2}$, 1 pr. pants-$2.28, 3 cotton shirts-$1.29, 2 pr. drawers-$.71, 1 pr. shoes-$1.22, 2 pr. socks-$.49, 1 blanket-$2.22; in confinement 12/1847, pay stopped for: 1 pr. shoes-$1.22, 2 pr. socks-$.49; pres. 02/1848; pres. 04/1848, prom. 3$^{rd}$ Cpl.; pres. 07/1848, reduced to Pvt., pay stopped for: 1 cartridge box plate-$.10, 1 brush & pick-$.12, 1 screw driver-$.25, 1 wiper-$.20, BLW sent to Martinsburg, VA

**Otter, William**, Pvt., Co. C; enl. Mex. War service 12/30/1846, Bowling Green, VA, age 18; deserted 01/12/1847 Fort Monroe, VA

**Otey, Van Renselar**, 1$^{st}$ Cpl., Co. G; b. 04/25/1827, Lynchburg, VA, son of John M. & Lucy Wilhelmenia (Norvell) Otey;[1382] enl. Mex. War service 12/01/1846 Richmond, VA, age 19; NFR; c. 1860 res. Castle Craig, Campbell Co., VA, age 33, occ. Farmer, w. Lucy R. (31), dau. Lucy D. (6), dau. Ann D. (3).[1383] enl. Civil War service 3$^{rd}$ Sgt., Co. B, 2$^{nd}$ Va. Cav. 05/13/1861 Lynchburg, VA, age 34, occ. Farmer; apptd. 2$^{nd}$ Lt. 08/27/1861; absent 10/1861-01/1862 on detached service w/ Gen. Stuart; retired and apptd. Commander of Lynchburg Public Guard 03/22/1862; Provost Marshall, Lynchburg, VA; d. 09/13/1864 of disease, bur. Spring Hill Cem., Lynchburg, VA;[1009]

**Ourey, Robert V.**, Pvt., *Recruit Co.*, enl. Mex. War service 03/27/1848 Wytheville, VA; pres. 06/1848; BLW sent to Wytheville, VA; m. Sally Smith, 07/13/1852, Wythe Co., VA[1384]

**Outland, Richard W.**, Pvt., Co. M; m. Susan A. Richardson, 08/10/1839, Mecklenburg Co., VA;[1385] enl. Mex. War service 09/04/1847, Richmond, VA, age 28; pres. 09/1847; pres. 11/1847; pres. 12/1847; pres. 02/1848; pres. 04/1848, pay stopped for: 1 blanket-$2.22, 1 pr. shoes-$1.22, 1 cap-$.95$^{1/2}$; pres. 08/1848, pay stopped for: 1 gun sling-$.16; BLW sent to Mecklenburg, VA; c. 1850 res. Mecklenburg Co., VA, age 34, occ. Shoemaker, w. Susan (30), dau. Mary (10), dau. Sarah (8), son Calvin (7), dau. Eliza (4), dau. Malinda (1/12);[1386] c. 1860 res. Manchester, Chesterfield Co., VA, age 44, occ. Boot & Shoemaker, w. Susan

OFF TO WAR

(40), dau. Mary (21), dau. Sarah (18), son C.S. (16), dau. Jane (14), dau. Isabella (8);[1387] Civil War service Cpl., Marion Arty., disbanded 02/14/1862; [202, 493] Pvt., Lechter Arty. enl. 02/17/1862 at Richmond, VA, killed 04/10/1862 when *"run over by a caisson at Camp Lee;"*[539] bur. Hollywood Cem., Richmond, VA

**Overby, John W.**, Pvt., Co. F; enl. Mex. War service 08/09/1847 Lunenburg, VA, age 18; pres. 02/1848; pres. 04/1848, 1 mo. and 3 days clothing money due him; pres. 08/1848, pay stopped for: 1 blankets-$2.25, 1 cotton shirt-$.44, BLW sent to Portsmouth, VA c/o E.T. Blamire; m. Minerva P. Bishop, 03/12/1849, Lunenburg Co., VA;[1388] c. 1850, res. Lunenburg Co., VA, age 21, occ. Farmer, w. Minerva (21).[1389] C. 1860 res. Pleasant Grove, Lunenburg Co., VA, age 31, occ. Farmer, w. Manerva P. (32), son Thomas A. (7), son John S.; (4).[1390]

**Owens, William W.**, Pvt., Co. B; enl. 12/01/1846, Alexandria, VA, age 22; pres. 06/1847; pres. 08/1847; pres. 10/1847, pay stopped for: 2 pr. cotton drawers-$.71, 1 pr. overalls-$2.28, 1 pr. shoes-$1.22, 1 blanket-$2.22, 1 pr. socks-$.24$^{1/2}$; pres. 12/1847, pay stopped for: 1 pr. overalls-$2.28, 3 pr. socks-$.73$^{1/2}$, 2 cotton shirts-$.86, 2 flannel shirts-$2.70, 1 jacket-$2.66, 1 cap-$.95$^{1/2}$, 1 pr. shoes-$1.22; pres. 02/1848; pres. 04/1848; pres. 08/1848, pay stopped for: 1 pr. shoes-$1.16, BLW sent to Alexandria, VA c/o Capt. Corse.

**Padgett, Reuben B.**, aka Reuben B. Wilkes, Fifer, Co. M; b. c. 1828, Lynchburg, VA;[1391] enl. Mex. War service 07/03/1847, Lynchburg, VA, age 19; pres. 09/1847; pres. 11/1847; pres. 12/1847; pres. 02/1848; pres. 04/1848, pay stopped for: 1 pr. shoes-$1.22; pres. 08/1848; BLW sent to Lynchburg, VA; c. 1850 res. Lynchburg, Campbell Co., VA, age 20, occ. Grocer;[1392] m. Sophia Schminke, 09/29/1853, Baltimore, MD;[1391] c. 1860 res. Lynchburg, Campbell Co., VA, age 30, occ. Clothier, w. Sophia (26);[1393] phys. desc. 5'7" or 8", dark complexion, dark hair, dark blue eyes;[1391] *"We were married Sept. 29, 1853 at Balt., MD and lived together until the year 1860 when he lost his mind and was carried to the Asylum at Staunton, VA where he remained until his death July 20, '65;"*[1391] d. 07/20/1865, *"cerebral lesion,"* Western State Hospital, Staunton, Augusta Co., VA;[1391] wid. Sophia, WC #10362, 03/02/1896, filed from 649 W. German St., Baltimore, MD; (SSP b. 06/05/1834, d. 12/20/1906).[1391]

**Page, William H.**, 2$^{nd}$ Cpl., Co. H; 1846 mbr. of *Gratitude Lodge No. 24*, International Order of Odd Fellows, I.O.O.F., Martinsburg, VA;[1394] enl. Mex. War service 12/26/1846, Berkeley, VA, age 23; pres. 04/1847; discharged 06/09/1847 at Monterey, Mex. on Surgeon's Certificate of Disability.

**Painter, James C.**, Pvt., *Recruit Co.*; enl. Mex. War service 04/17/1848 Wytheville, VA; pres. 06/1848; BLW sent to Wytheville, VA; c. 1850 res. Wythe Co., VA, age 30, occ. Plasterer, w. Eliza (22), dau. Jane (4), dau. Margaret (2);[1395] c. 1860 res. Wythe Co., VA, age 39, occ. Bricklayer, w. Eliza (36), dau. Martha (14), dau. Margaret (12), son Wythe (7), son George (5);[1396] Civil War service Pvt., Co. C, 51$^{st}$ Va. Inf. enl. 05/01/1862 at Wytheville, captured 03/02/1865 at Waynesboro, VA, sent to Ft. Delaware 03/12/1865, released 06/20/1865;[536] SC #13351, 03/21/1887, wid. Eliza, WA #13656, 11/30/1896, both from VA

**Painter, Stewart Dabney**, Pvt., *Recruit Co.*; b. Wythe Co., VA 05/15/1828, son of Debney Painter enl. Mex. War service 04/18/1848 Wytheville, VA; pres. 06/1848; BLW sent to Wytheville, VA; m. Sophia Leedy, 05/24/1849, Wythe Co., VA;[1397] c. 1850 res. Wythe Co., VA, age 22, occ. Laborer, w. Sophia (24);[1398] Civil War service Pvt., Co. B, 45$^{th}$ Va. Inf. enl. 05/29/1861 at Wytheville, VA, wded. Hawk's Nest (Fayette Co., VA) 08/20/1861 *"left lung,"* captured at Waynesboro 03/02/1865, sent to Ft. Delaware, released 06/20/1865, phys. desc. 5'7", blue eyes, dark hair, res. Wythe Co.,[676] c. 1880 res. Wythe Co., VA, age 52, occ. Miller, w. Sophia (53), son Jefferson Davis (18), dau. Alice (16), dau. Cynthia P. (13), dau. Sophia M. (10);[1399] SA #22742, d. date unknown, bur. St. John's Church, Wythe Co., VA, wid. Virginia L., WA #9912, 06/06/1891, both from VA

# VIRGINIA VOLUNTEERS IN MEXICO

**Palmer, William L.**, Co. C; enl. Mex. War service 09/06/1847, Charlotte C.H., VA, age 20; pres. 04/1848, pay stopped for: 1 haversack-$.20$^{3/4}$; pres. 08/1848, BLW sent to Charlotte C.H., VA; SC #14261, 06/10/1887, from DC; [pension file not found].

**Parent, John S.**, Pvt., LIC; b. Lexington, Rockbridge Co., VA, son of Eli H. and Elizabeth (Fuller), Parent;[1400] enl. Mex. War service 11/27/1846 Staunton, VA, age 28; sick 08/1847; discharged 10/19/1847 on Surgeon's Certificate of Disability; c. 1850 res. Augusta Co., VA, age 30, occ. Cabinetmaker;[1401] m/1 Louise Wiley date/place unknown, (LWP d. 1868);[1400] c. 1860 res. Augusta Co., VA, age 41, occ. Master Cabinet Maker, w. Louisa (31);[1402] m/2 Margaret L. (Bickle) Birtnett, 08/02/1870, Staunton, Augusta Co., VA;[1400] d. 12/15/1886, *"consumption,"* Staunton, Augusta Co., VA, bur. Thornrose Cem., Staunton, VA;[1400] wid. Margaret L., WC #1604, 02/24/1887, filed from Staunton, Augusta Co., VA; (MBP b. 04/27/1828, Staunton, VA, m/1 _____ Birtnett, 07/16/1861, he died 06/16/1864, MBP d. 03/28/1901).[1400]

**Parker, Francis W.**, Pvt., Co. F; enl. Mex. War service 11/23/1846, Portsmouth, VA, age 18; pres. 06/1847; pres. 08/1847, prom. 1$^{st}$ Cpl.; pres. 10/1847, pay stopped for: 1 pr. overalls-$2.28, 1 forage cap-$.95$^{1/2}$, 4 cotton shirts-$1.72, 5 pr. socks-$1.22$^{1/2}$, 2 pr. shoes-$2.44, 2 pr. drawers-.71, 1 overcoat-$6.93$^{1/2}$; pres. 12/1847; pres. 02/1848, pay stopped for: I infantry jacket-$2.66, 1 pr. overalls-$2.28, 2 flannel shirts-$1.80, 1 pr. socks-$.24$^{1/2}$; pres. 04/1848, reduced to ranks from 1$^{st}$ Cpl. 03/01/1848 at his own request; pres. 08/1848, pay stopped for: 1 gun sling-$.18, 5 cotton shirts-$2.20, 1 pr. shoes-$1.16, BLW sent to Portsmouth, VA c/o E.T. Blamire.

**Parr, George Berham**, Pvt., Co. E; b. c. 1822; enl. Mex. War service 12/05/1846 Petersburg, VA, age 22; pres. 04/1847; pres. 06/1847; pres. 08/1847; pres. 10/1847, pay stopped for: 1 pr. overalls-$2.28, 1 pr. shoes-$1.22, 4 pr. stockings-$.98, 2 pr. drawers-$.71; pres. 12/1847, pay stopped for: 1 pr. pants-$2.28, 2 pr. socks-$.49, 2 flannel shirts-$1.80, 2 pr. drawers-$.71, 1 blanket-$2.22; pres. 02/1848; pres. 04/1848, on daily duty in Actg. Asst. Genl's. office since 03/13/1848; m. Sarah Pamela (Givens) Parr; elected Clerk of Live Oak County Court date unknown; d. c. 1860; wid. Sarah P., WC #6762, 10/25/1887, from TX[pension file missing]; father of Texas State Senator Archer Parr and grandfather of George B. Parr the father and son duo that established the most notorious of all the South Texas political machines. Archer and George Parr controlled politics in Duval County from 1908 until the death of the younger Parr in 1975. The rule of the Parr family weathered public outcries over apparent political murders, repeated state and federal investigations into blatant acts of graft and election fraud, and even the imprisonment of George Parr in 1936 for income-tax evasion. The Parr machine gained nationwide attention 1948 when late and allegedly fraudulent election returns from Duval County and neighboring Jim Wells County gave Lyndon B. Johnson a narrow primary victory over Coke R. Stevenson in the United States Senate race. Johnson allegedly called George Parr who arranged for the ballots in Duval County to be "corrected."[1403, 1404, 1405]

**Parrish, William N.**, Pvt., Co. M; enl. Mex. War service 09/05/1847, Brickland, VA, age 26; pres. 10/1847; pres. 11/1847; pres. 12/1847; sick 02/1848; pres. 04/1848; pres. 08/1848, pay stopped for: 1 waist belt plate-$.10, 1 wormer-$.20; BLW sent to Brickland, Lunenburg Co., VA; c. 1850 res. Lunenburg Co., VA, age 27, occ. Carpenter.[1406]

**Partin, Andrew Jackson**, Pvt., Co. E; enl. Mex. War service 12/01/1846 Petersburg, VA, age 20; absent 04/1847, sick Matamoros, Mex. since 03/29/1847; pres. 06/1847; pres. 08/1847; pres. 10/1847, pay stopped for: 1 pr. overalls-$2.28, 1 pr. shoes-$1.22, 2 pr. stockings-$.49, 1 cap-$.95$^{1/2}$; pres. 12/1847, pay stopped for: 1 pr. pants-$2.28, 2 pr. socks-$.24$^{1/2}$, 2 flannel shirts-$1.80, 2 pr. drawers-$.71; pres. 02/1848; pres. 04/1848; m. Elizabeth F. Bain, 05/15/1855, Raleigh Wake Co., NC;[1407] c. 1860 res. Petersburg, Dinwiddie Co., VA, age 30, occ. Clerk, w. Elizabeth (26), dau. Alice (4), son Thomas (1);[1408] [Civil War service an Andrew J. Partin served as a 2$^{nd}$ Lt., Co. B, 39$^{th}$ VA Militia (City of Petersburg);][202] c. res. Raleigh, Wake Co., age 52, occ. Clerk State Dept., w. E.F. Partin (45), dau. Alice Partin,

## OFF TO WAR

School Teacher (23), son Thomas A. Partin, Clerk (21), dau. Mattie E. Partin (18), Julia B. Partin (8), Donald B. Partin (3), S-I-L Julia G. Bain (34);[1407] d. 10/05/1880, Raleigh, Wake Co., NC;[1407] wid. Elizabeth F., WC #1621, 03/05/1887, filed from Raleigh, Wake Co., NC. (EFP b. 08/15/1834, Pittsboro, NC, d. 07/10/1907).[1407]

**Partin, Edward G.**, Pvt., Co. E

**Patterson, Charles**, Pvt., Co. L; b. 1813; enl. Mex. War service 03/26/1847 Ft. Washington, MD, age 34; pres. 06/1847; pres. 08/1847; pres. 10/1847, pay stopped for: 1 pr. Pants 2.28, 1 pr. Shoes 1.22, 1 F Cap .95; pres. 12/1847, pay stopped for: 1 jacket-$2.66, 1 pr. shoes-$1.22, 2 flannel shirts-$1.80, 1 cotton shirt-$.43, 1 blanket-$2.22, 2 pr. drawers-$.71, 1 pr. socks-$.24$^{1/2}$; pres. 02/1848, pay stopped for: 1 Brush & Pick .12; pres. 04/1848, pay stopped for: 2 Flannel Shirts 1.55; pres. 07/1848; BLW sent to Capt. Thrift, c/o Charles Patterson, Fairfax Court House, Fairfax Co., VA

**Pavo, John**, Pvt., Co. G; enl. Mex. War service 11/28/1846, Petersburg, VA, age 43; pres. 06/1847; pres. 08/1847; pres. 10/1847, pay stopped for: 1 blanket-$2.22, 1 pr. overalls-$2.28, 1 pr. shoes-$1.22, 3 pr. socks-$.73$^{1/2}$, 1 forage cap-$.95$^{1/2}$; pres. 12/1847, pay stopped for: 1 pr. pants-$2.28; pres. 02/1848; pres. 04/1848; pres. 08/1848, 1 gun sling-$.16; BLW sent to Richmond, VA

**Payne, Edwin F.**, Pvt., Co. D; b. Petersburg, VA, son of Littleton & Minerva Payne;[1409] enl. Mex. War service 12/29/1846, Petersburg, VA, age 19; pres. 02/1847; pres. 04/1847; pres. 06/1847; pres. 08/1847, pay stopped for: 1 cap-$.95$^{1/2}$, 1 pr. shoes-$1.22; pres. 10/1847, pay stopped for: 1 jacket-$2.66, 1 pr. pants-$2.28, 2 cotton shirts-$.86, 1 pr. drawers-$.35$^{1/2}$; pres. 12/1847, pay stopped for: 2 pr. socks-$.49, 1 pr. shoes-$1.22, 1 blanket-$2.22; pres. 04/1848, pay stopped for: 1 set of picks & brushes-$.12, 1 pr. pants-$2.28, 2 cotton shirts-$.86; pres. 08/1847, BLW sent to Petersburg, VA; [Civil War service an E.F. Payne served as a Pvt., Co. B, 39$^{th}$ VA Militia (City of Petersburg);[202] d. 01/03/1863, *Typhoid Pneumonia*, bur. Blandford Cem., Petersburg, VA[1409]

**Payne, Robert F.**, Pvt., Co. D; enl. Mex. War service 12/30/1846, Petersburg, VA, age 18; pres. 02/1847; pres. 04/1847; pres. 06/1847; pres. 08/1847, pay stopped for: 1 cap-$.95$^{1/2}$, 1 pr. pants-$2.28, 2 cotton shirts-$.86, 1 pr. shoes-$1.22; pres. 10/1847, pay stopped for: 1 pr. pants-$2.28, 1 flannel shirt-$.90, 1 pr. drawers-$.35$^{1/2}$, 1 pr. socks-$.24$^{1/2}$, 1 pr. shoes-$1.22; pres. 12/1847, pay stopped for: 1 jacket-$2.66, 1 cotton shirt-$.43, 2 pr. socks-$.49; pres. 04/1848, pay stopped for: 1 cap-$.95$^{1/2}$, 1 cotton shirt-$.43, 1 pr. shoes-$1.22, 1 haversack-$.20$^{3/4}$; [illegible] Montgomery Co., Ala.

**Payne, William T.**, Pvt., Co. D; enl. Mex. War service 12/28/1846, Petersburg, VA, age 21; pres. 02/1847; pres. 04/1847; pres. 06/1847; pres. 08/1847, pay stopped for: 1 cap-$.95$^{1/2}$, 2 cotton shirts-$.86, 1 pr. shoes-$1.22; pres. 10/1847, pay stopped for: 1 cap-$.95$^{1/2}$, 1 jacket-$2.66, 1 pr. pants-$2.28, 2 flannel shirts-$1.80, 1 pr. drawers-$.35$^{1/2}$, 2 pr. socks-$.49, 1 pr. shoes-$1.22; pres. 12/1847, fined 1 mos. pay by order (No. 162) of genl. court-martial, pay stopped for: 1 pr. pants-$2.28, 2 cotton shirts-$.86, 1 blanket-$2.22; pres. 04/1848, pay stopped for: 1 cap-$.95$^{1/2}$, 1 pr. shoes-$1.22; pres. 08/1847, BLW sent to Jarratt's Depot, Sussex Co., VA; c. 1860 res. Sussex C.H., Sussex Co., VA, age 34, occ. Merchant, w. Virginia A. (32), son ____ U. (7), dau. ____ W. (4), son John B. (2);[1410] Civil War service 2$^{nd}$ Lt., Co. E, 16$^{th}$ Va. Inf., enl. as 1$^{st}$ Sgt. 04/27/12861 at Suffolk, VA, age 34, elected 2$^{nd}$ Lt. 05/01/1862, det on conscription duty, in hosp. 06/06/1862 Richmond, VA, returned to duty 07/16/1864, admitted to hosp. 08/01/1864 w/ diarrhea, d. 08/18/1864, bur. Hollywood Cem., Richmond, VA[77]

**Peare, James**, Pvt., Co. H; enl. Mex. War service 12/14/1846, Berkeley, VA, age 29; pres. 06/1847; pres. 08/1847; pres. 10/1847, pay stopped for: 1 forage cap-$.95$^{1/2}$, 1 pr. pants-$2.28, 2 cotton shirts-$.86, 1 flannel shirt-$.90, 3 pr. socks-$.73$^{1/2}$, 1 jacket-$2.66; pres. 12/1847, pay stopped for: 1 pr. pants-$2.28, 1 cotton shirt-$.43, 1 pr. shoes-$1.22, 1 blanket-$2.22; pres.

## VIRGINIA VOLUNTEERS IN MEXICO

02/1848, pay stopped for: 1 cotton shirt-$.43, 1 pr. drawers-$.35$^{1/2}$, 3 pr. socks-$.73$^{1/2}$; pres. 04/1848; pres. 07/1848, pay stopped for: 2 brush & picks-$.24, 1 waist belt plate-$.10, 1 screw driver-$.25, 1 wiper-$.20, 1 bayonet-$1.44, BLW sent to Hedgesville, VA

**Peare, John**, Pvt., Co. H; b. 06/27/1817, Berkeley Co., VA;[1411] enl. Mex. War service 12/12/1847, Berkeley, VA, age 29; discharged 05/17/1847 at camp near Monterey, Mex. on Surgeon's Certificate of Disability; SC #4453, 04/13/1887, filed from Spring Mills, Berkeley Co., WV; Edward W. Maxwell and John W. Keef gave affidavits in pension claim;[1411] d. 03/1891.[1411]

**Pebworth, Nathaniel**, 4$^{th}$ Sgt., Co. D; b. 11/02/1801, Norfolk Co., VA, son of William & Mary Pebworth;[1412] m. Mary Hill, 11/25/1828, Cumberland Co., VA;[1413] enl. Mex. War service 12/10/1846, Petersburg, VA, age 39; pres. 02/1847; pres. 04/1847; pres. 06/1847; pres. 08/1847, pay stopped for: 1 cap-$.95$^{1/2}$, 1 pr. pants-$2.28; pres. 10/1847, prom. 4$^{th}$ Sgt. 09/16/1847, pay stopped for: 1 cotton shirt-$.43, 1 pr. drawers-$.35$^{1/2}$, 1 pr. shoes-$1.22, 1 pr. pants-$2.28, 2 pr. socks-$.49; pres. 12/1847, pay stopped for: 1 jacket-$2.66, 1 cotton shirt-$.50$^{1/2}$, 1 pr. socks-$.24$^{1/2}$, 1 blanket-$2.22, 1 flannel shirt-$.90; pres. 04/1848; pres. 08/1847, BLW sent to Petersburg, VA; d.. 12/04/1852, *Delirium Tremens*, bur. Blandford Cem., Sq. 214, Ward A, Petersburg, VA[1412]

**Peck, Israel**, Pvt., LIC; enl. Mex. War service 12/26/1846 Staunton, VA, age 18; pres. 08/1847; pres. 10/1847, pay stopped for: 1 forage cap-$.95$^{1/2}$, 1 wool jacket-$2.66, 2 pr. overalls-$4.56, 2 pr. shoes-$2.44, 4 pr. socks-$.98, 4 cotton shirts-$1.72, 1 overcoat-$6.93$^{1/2}$; pres. 12/1847, pay stopped for: 1 pr. socks-$.24$^{1/2}$, 1 blanket-$2.22, 1 pr. shoes-$2.44, 1 flannel shirt-$.90, 1 pr. drawers-$.35$^{1/2}$; d. 03/17/1848 near Parras, Mex. *"assassinated by Mexicans,"* pay stopped for: 1 musket & bayonet-$14.00, 2 flannel shirts-$1.80.

**Peck, William F.**, 1$^{st}$ Sgt., Co. G; enl. Mex. War service 03/30/1847, Buffalo Grove, Ill., Pvt., Co. A, 16$^{th}$ U.S. Inf., age 30; transferred 11/07/1847 to Co. G, 1$^{st}$ Va. Regt., pay stopped for: 1 pr. socks-$.24$^{1/2}$; pres. 02/1848; pres. 04/1848, pay stopped for: 1 jacket-$2.66; pres. 08/1848, pay stopped for: 1 sword belt-$.52, 1 sword belt plate-$.10; BLW sent to Bantam Falls, Conn.

**Peed, James W.**, Pvt., Co. F; enl. Mex. War service 12/22/1846, Portsmouth, VA, age 42; discharged date unknown at Fort Monroe, VA on Surgeon's Certificate of Disability; [c. 1850 res. Portsmouth, Norfolk Co., VA, age 55, occ. Timber Inspector, w. Margaret (48).][1414]

**Peel, Richard**, Pvt., Co. F; enl. Mex. War service 12/18/1846, Nansemond, VA, age 23; d. 02/07/1847 Fort Monroe, VA.

**Peer, John**, Pvt., LIC; b. Augusta Co., VA 10/10/1819;[1415] enl. Mex. War service 12/29/1846 Staunton, VA, age 24; discharged 04/1847 at Monterey, Mex. on Surgeon's Certificate of Disability; c. 1850 res. Augusta Co., VA, age 29, occ. Blacksmith, fa.? David (55), bro.? Claudius (15), son Alonzo O. (1), mo.? Nancy (53), sis.? Emily A. (13), w.? Margaret S. (22);[1416] c. 1860 res. Augusta Co., VA, age 35, occ. Master Blacksmith;[1417] Civil War service; enl. Capt. John H. McClanahan's Co., VA Horse Arty.; absent sick in camp 6/62; c. 1870 res. Staunton, Augusta Co., VA, age 51, occ. Blacksmith, w. Margaret J. (40), son Alonzo (21), dau. Della Ann (19);[1418] mbr. of Stonewall Jackson Camp No. 25 U.C.V. Staunton; SC #5412, 02/09/1887, filed from West Augusta, Augusta Co., VA; d. 03/16/1907 Staunton, VA, bur. Thornrose Cem.[249]

**Pegram, Franklin**, 1$^{st}$ Lt., Co. E; b. 09/27/1822, Dinwiddie Co., VA, son of Hon. John & Martha Ward (Gregory) Pegram;[1160] (father John Pegram was a member of the Virginia State house of delegates 1797-1801; served in the Virginia State Senate 1804-1808; Maj. Gen. of the Virginia State militia in the War of 1812; again a member of the Virginia State house of delegates 1813-1815; U.S. Congressman 1818-1819); enl. Mex. War service 11/30/1846 Petersburg, VA, age 24; absent 04/1847 sick in Monterey, Mex. since 04/21/1847; absent 06/04/1847 returned to United States on 60 day furlough; AWOL 08/1847 since 08/04/1847,

## OFF TO WAR

*"I have further the disagreeable duty of again reporting Capt. W.B. Archer, Co. I, Va. Regt. Vols., Lieut. Pegram, Co. E, Va. Regt. Vols., Lieut. L. Washington, Co. K, Va. Regt. Vols. Absent without leave;"*[1419] AWOL 10/1847; a letter from Lt. Pegram states he is stationed at Fort Monroe, VA *"in charge of some forty men"* whom he is drilling daily. He further states that he hopes to return to the regiment;[1420] AWOL 12/1847; pres. 02/1848; pres. 04/1848; c. 1850 res. Petersburg, Dinwiddie Co., VA, age 26, occ. None Listed;[1421] d. 09/05/1852, Petersburg, VA; 2$^{nd}$ cousin of Pvt. John T. Lanier.

**Pelter, James T.**, Pvt., LIC; b. c. 1825; enl. Mex. War service 01/06/1847 Staunton, VA, age 22; sick 06/1847 in quarters; pres. 08/1847; pres. 10/1847, pay stopped for: 1 forage cap-$.95$^{1/2}$, 1 wool jacket-$2.66, 2 pr. overalls-$4.56, 1 pr. shoes-$1.22, 2 pr. socks-$.49, 2 cotton shirts-$.86, 1 flannel shirt-$.90, 1 blanket-$2.22; pres. 12/1847, pay stopped for: 1 pr. socks-$.24$^{1/2}$, 1 cotton shirt-$.43; pres. 04/1848, pay stopped for: 1 pr. shoes-$1.22; pres. 07/1848, pay stopped for: 1 screw driver-$.07, 1 wiper-$.20, 1 spring vise-$.35; BLW sent to Waynesborough, VA; c. 1850 res. Augusta Co., VA, age 24, occ. Laborer;[1422] m. Virginia Jane Cook 10/1855 Harper's Ferry, Jefferson Co., VA; d. 1861, *"reportedly killed by Indians while crossing the plains to California;"*[1423] wid. Jane, WA #12000, 04/09/1894, filed from Basic City (Augusta Springs), Augusta Co., VA; *"I, Greenberry B. Terrell, do certify to the following: On or about Dec. 25$^{th}$ 1846 Capt. Canton [sic] Harper's company (which I think was known as Co. "C" of 1$^{st}$ VA Regiment of Light Infantry, John C. Hamtramck being Colonel) passed through Waynesborough, VA on its way to Richmond, VA About ten days afterwards I, in company with <u>James Pelter</u> (in whose behalf this statement is made), Wm. Long & John Grove (all of this vicinity) followed going by stage to Gordonsville and rail from there to Richmond. We reached Richmond on January 6$^{th}$ 1847 (to the best of my recollection) and were all mustered into service the same evening. We joined Capt. Harper's Company (Robt. Kinney 1$^{st}$ Lieut., Vincent E. Geiger, 2$^{nd}$ Lieut. & Wm. H. Harman 3$^{rd}$ Lieut.) & volunteered for the war. On the next day we were sent on boat to Fortress Monroe & about two weeks afterwards were put aboard the "Mayflower" & sent to Mexico. We were 33 days on the voyage & were landed at the mouth of the Rio Grande River. We were in service as long as the war lasted (same known as the Mexican War) & were sent back to Fortress Monroe & disbanded & honorably discharged about the latter part of July 1848. The said James Pelter being with us the whole time & returning with us to Waynesboro, VA Written in my hand this 20$^{th}$ day of March 1894. Greenberry B. Terrell. Subscribed & sworn before the undersigned Notary Public this the 20$^{th}$ day of March 1894. W.S. Fishburne, N.P."*[1424](VJP b. 04/29/1839 near Waynesboro, Augusta Co., VA); lists one child Bettie (Pelter) Humphreys.[1425]

**Pendergrass, Sylvester G.**, Pvt., *Preston's Co.*; enl. Mex. War service 12/25/1846 Wythe Co., VA, age 21; pres. 04/1847; pres. 06/1847; pres. 08/1847; pres. 10/1847, pay stopped for: 2 pr. socks-$.49; pres. 12/1847, pay stopped for: 1 jacket-$2.66, 1 pr. overalls-$2.28, 1 cap-$.95$^{1/2}$, 1 pr. drawers-$.35$^{1/2}$, 1 blanket-$2.22; pres. 02/1848; pres. 04/1848, pay stopped for: 1 cartridge box-$1.10, 1 cartridge box belt & plate-$.80, 1 pick & brush-$.12, 1 wiper-$.13, 1 screw driver-$.07, 1 cartridge box plate-$.10; pres. 07/1848, pay stopped for: 1 brush & pick-$.12; BLW sent to Christiansburg, VA c/o Fleming Gardner; c. 1850 res. Lee Co., VA[1426]

**Pentony, James**, Pvt., Co. H; enl. Mex. War service 12/14/1846, Morgan, VA, age 21; pres. 04/1847; pres. 06/1847; pres. 08/1847; pres. 10/1847, pay stopped for: 1 forage cap-$.95$^{1/2}$, 3 cotton shirts-$1.29, 1 pr. drawers-$.35$^{1/2}$, 2 pr. shoes-$2.44, 2 pr. socks-$.49, 1 jacket-$2.66; pres. 12/1847, pay stopped for: 1 pr. pants-$2.28, 1 cotton shirt-$.43, 1 pr. shoes-$1.22, 2 pr. socks-$.49; pres. 02/1848, pay stopped for: 1 pr. shoes-$1.22; pres. 04/1848; pres. 07/1848, pay stopped for: 2 gun slings-$.32, 1 pr. shoes-$1.16, BLW sent to Beckely Springs, VA; Civil War service Cpl., Co. F, P.H.B. Md. Inf., IC #518153; SC #3476, wid. Meresa, WC #14684, 03/06/1906, both from OH; [pension file missing].

VIRGINIA VOLUNTEERS IN MEXICO

**Perkinson, George W.**, Pvt., Co. D; enl. Mex. War service 01/11/1847, Petersburg, VA, age 26; pres. 02/1847; pres. 04/1847; absent 06/1847 left as Attendant in Hosp. Monterey, Mex., 06/22/1847 absent 08/1847, on detached service as Hosp. Attendant, pay stopped for: 1 cap-$.95$^{1/2}$, a pr. pants-$2.28; absent 10/1847 on detached service as Hosp. Attendant since 08/01/1847; absent 12/1847 on detached service as Hosp. Attendant Saltillo, Mex., pay stopped for: 1 jacket-$4.56; 2 pr. pants-$4.56; absent 04/1848, on detached service as Hosp. Attendant, pay stopped for: 1 pr. shoes-$1.22, 1 cotton shirt-$.43, 1 haversack-$.20$^{3/4}$; pres. 08/1847, BLW sent to Petersburg, VA.

**Peterson, Peter Archibald**, 2$^{nd}$ Lt., Co. E; b. 09/28/1828, Dinwiddie, VA, son of William McKendree & Martha Ann Peterson;[21] enl. Mex. War service 11/26/1846 Petersburg, VA, age

Photo credit: *Sketches and Portraits*..., Richmond, VA

18; pres. 04/1847; pres. 06/1847; pres. 08/1847; pres. 10/1847; absent 12/1847 on daily duty as Provost Marshall since 12/20/1847; absent 02/1848 on daily duty as Provost Marshall; pres. 04/1848; m. Lucy Ann Williamson12/28/1848, Petersburg, VA;[1427] c. 1850 res. Petersburg, Dinwiddie Co., VA, age 22, occ. Carpenter, w. L.A. (20), dau. C.M. (3/12);[1428] c. 1852 Methodist Church Deacon, Minister and Circuit Rider for forty-one years until his death; c. 1860 res. Amherst C.H., Amherst Co., VA, age 31, occ. M.E. Preacher, w. Lucy A. (28), dau. C.A. (11), son Frank (8), dau. Minnesota (6);[1429] Civil War service Chaplin, 12$^{th}$ Va. Inf., appointed 05/25/1862, absent sick 07/1862, resigned 11/01/1862;[21] c. 1870 res. City of Norfolk, Norfolk Co., VA, age 42, occ. Minister, w. Lucy A. (40), dau. Cornelia M. (20), son Frank (18), dau. Minnie (15), son George P. (11/12);[1430] Trustee of Randolph Macon College 1877, author *The Handbook of the M.E. Church, South* and *The History of the Revisions of the* Discipline;[1431] SC #19304, 10/15/1890 filed from 209 N 19$^{th}$ St., Richmond, VA; Thomas J. McCaleb and William E. Alley gave affidavits in pension claim; d. 10/06/1893, *Ischisrectal Celluitis*, Richmond, VA, bur. Blandford Cem., Sq. 8, Sec. 5, Ward H, Petersburg, VA;[1432, 1433] wid. Lucy Ann, WC #9092, 11/02/1893, filed from 14 Dartmouth St., Norfolk, VA; (LAP b. 02/19/1830, d. 09/24/1898).[1432]

**Peterson, William T.**, Pvt., Co. E; b. Petersburg, VA, son of William & Martha Peterson;[1434]enl. Mex. War service 11/26/1846 Petersburg, VA, age 19; pres. 04/1847; pres. 06/1847; pres. 08/1847; pres. 10/1847, pay stopped for: 1 pr. overalls-$2.28, 1 pr. shoes-$1.22, 1 pr. stockings-$.24$^{1/2}$, 1 cap-$.95$^{1/2}$; pres. 12/1847, pay stopped for: 1 pr. pants-$2.28, 1 pr. socks-$.24$^{1/2}$, 2 pr. drawers-$.71; pres. 02/1848, pay stopped for: 1 pr. shoes-$1.22; pres. 04/1848, pay stopped for: 1 jacket-$2.37$^{1/2}$; c. 1860 res. Petersburg, Dinwiddie Co., VA, age 32, occ. Bailiff, w. Amelia A. (26), dau. Anna (7), son William H. (2);[1435] a Capt. William T. Peterson d. 04/03/1866, *Consumption*, bur. Blandford Cem., Sq. 4, Sec. 14, Ward D, Petersburg, VA[1436, 1437]

**Peverelly, Anthony**, Pvt., Co. M; b. c. 1824, Boston, Ma.;[1438] enl. Mex. War service 11/17/1847, Norfolk, VA, age 23; pres. 11/1847; pres. 12/1847; absent 02/1848, on detached service in Bakery since 01/26/1848, pay stopped for: 1 flannel shirt-$.90; absent 04/1848 on detached service in Bakery in Saltillo, Mex.; pres. 08/1848, pay stopped for: 1 musket & accoutrements complete-$16.22; BLW sent to New York, N.Y.; m/1 Mary Bross, date/place unknown (MBP d. c. 1859);[1438] m/2 Margaret Leary 04/23/1865, St. Peter's Church, Poughkeepsie, Dutchess Co., NY;[1438] phys. desc. at enl. age 19, fair complexion, light hair, blue eyes, occ. Confectioner;[1438] since discharge res. Bleecker St., New York City, then Detroit, MI, then

239

OFF TO WAR

back to NYC, then to Newburg and Poughkeepsie, NY;[1438] d. 04/11/1878, 300 W. 29th St., New York, NY;[1438] wid. Margaret, WC #3593, 10/17/1887, filed from 134 Water St., Newburg, Orange Co., NY; (MLP m/1 Micheal Leary date/place unknown, he died 01/14/1857).[1438]

**Philips, Alfred**, Pvt., *Recruit Co.*, enl. Mex. War service 11/27/1847 Clarksburg, VA, age 21; pres. 02/1848; pres. 04/1848; pres. 06/1848; BLW sent to Westerford, Randolph Co., VA; m. Sarah K. Robinson, 09/18/1848;[1439] c. 1850, res. Barbour Co., VA, age 24, occ. farmer, w. Sarah;[1440] c. 1860 res. Horseshoe Run, Tucker Co., VA, age 29, occ. Farm Laborer, w. Sarah (25), dau. Susan (10), son Washington (8), dau. Martha (6), son Jonathan W. (4), son George H. (1);[1441] c. 1870 res. Barbour Co., WV, age 44, occ. Farmer, w. Sarah C. (38), son William W. (18), dau Caroline E. (16), son Jonathan W. (14), son George M. (12), dau. Emma May (11), dau. Hannah A. (9), dau. Minnie L. (2).[1442] d. 04/13/1876; wid. Sarah K., WC #5529, 03/11/1887, filed from Pleasant Creek, Barbour Co., WV; (SRP b. 05/19/1832, m/2 John Robinson, 03/16/1891, Pleasant Creek, WV, he died 08/09/1907).[1439]

**Philips, Robert H.**, Pvt., Co. G; enl. Mex. War service 11/18/1846 Richmond, VA, age 20; deserted 05/26/1847 at China, Mex.; may have been a San Patricio, a Henry Phillips enl. 11/1847 at Queretaro, Mex.

**Phillips, Alexander**, Pvt., *Preston's Co.*; enl. Mex. War service 12/06/1846 Montgomery Co., VA, age 19; pres. 04/1847; pres. 06/1847; pres. 08/1847, pay stopped for 1 spring vise-$.35; pres. 10/1847, pay stopped for: 1 jacket-$2.66, 1 pr. overalls-$2.28, 2 pr. socks-$.49, 3 flannel shirts-$2.70, 2 cotton shirts-$.86, 1 pr. drawers-$.35$^{1/2}$, 1 cap-$.95$^{1/2}$; pres. 12/1847, pay stopped for: 1 pr. overalls-$2.28, 1 pr. socks-$.24$^{1/2}$, 1 blankets-$2.22; pres. 02/1848; pres. 04/1848; pres. 07/1848, pay stopped for: 1 gun sling-$.18, 1 wiper-$.13; BLW sent to Christiansburg, VA c/o Fleming Gardner; c. 1850 res. Montgomery Co., VA, age 22, occ. Sawyer;[1443] [Civil War service an Alexander Phillips enlisted Co. G, 6th Va. Inf. 10/23/1863 at Christiansburg, VA, MWIA at the Crater (Petersburg, VA), gunshot wd. right knee, d. Chimborazo Hosp. #3, bur. Hollywood Cem., Richmond, VA][465]

**Phillips, Robert H.**, Pvt., Co. M; enl. Mex. War service 08/29/1847, Forksville, VA, age 18; pres. 10/1847; pres. 11/1847; pres. 12/1847; pres. 02/1848, pay stopped for: 1 pr. shoes-$1.22, 1 flannel shirt-$.90; pres. 04/1848, pay stopped for: 1 blanket-$2.22, 1 pr. shoes-$1.22, 1 cotton shirt-$.95$^{1/2}$; pres. 08/1848, pay stopped for: 1 gun sling-$.16, 1 pick & brush-$.12; BLW sent to Forksville, Mecklenburg Co., VA

**Phipps, Robert H.**, Pvt., Co. D; enl. Mex. War service 12/30/1846, Petersburg, VA, age 19; pres. 02/1847; pres. 04/1847; pres. but sick 06/1847; d. 07/21/1847 Buena Vista, Mex.

**Pickett, Rufus**, Pvt., *Recruit Co.*, enl. Mex. War service 05/13/1848 Bowling Green, VA; pres. 06/1848; BLW sent to Bowling Green, Caroline Co., VA; c. 1850 res. Caroline Co., VA, age 23, occ. Ditcher;[1444] wid. Margaret, WA #6203, 03/29/1888, from VA

**Pierce, Dorastus**, Pvt., Co. A; m. Martha Ann Childress, 06/30/1844, Henrico Co., VA;[1445] enl. Mex. War service 12/14/1846 Richmond, VA, age 30; pres. 12/1846 - 04/1847; pres. 06/1847; pres. 08/1847; sick 10/1847, pay stopped for clothing: 1 pr. wool overalls-$2.28, 1 cap-$.95$^{1/2}$, 2 pr. stockings-$.49; pres. 12/1847, pay stopped for clothing: 2 flannel shirt-$1.80, 2 pr. shoes-$2.44, 1 pr. drawers-$.35$^{1/2}$, 1 blanket-$2.22; pres. 02/1848; pres. 04/1848; BLW sent to Richmond, VA; c. 1850 res. Henrico Co., VA, age 35, occ. Farmer, w. Martha A. (27), son Adolphus (11), dau. Lenora C. (6), dau. Rachel (2);[1446] c. 1860 res. Richmond, Henrico Co., VA, age 46, occ. Farmer, w. Martha Ann (43), son Adolphus (20F), dau. Lenora C. (14), dau. Rachel M. (11), dau. Virginia K. (9), son William M. (5), son Augustus N. (3), son Oscar R. (1).[1447]

**Pinnell, Joseph J.W.**, Pvt., Co. M; b. 02/19/1821, Buckingham Co., VA;[1448] enl. Mex. War service 08/10/1847, Stapleton, VA, age 26; pres. 09/1847; pres. 11/1847; pres. 12/1847; pres. 02/1848, pay stopped for: 1 over coat-$6.93$^{1/2}$; sick 04/1848, pay stopped for: 1 blanket-$2.22; pres. 08/1848, pay stopped for: 1 bayonet-$1.44, 1 wormer-$.20; BLW sent to Stapleton,

VIRGINIA VOLUNTEERS IN MEXICO

Amherst Co., VA; SC #9418, 04/14/1887, filed from near Stonewall Ferry, Appomattox Co., VA; since discharge res. near Stapleton Mills, Appomattox Co., VA;[1448] phys. desc. 5'11", blue eyes, light hair, occ. Farmer, *"was never married;"*[1448] d. 10/31/1904.[1448]

**Piper, Joseph F.**, Pvt., Co. C; enl. Mex. War service 12/24/1846, Westmoreland Co., VA, age 27; pres. 06/1847; pres. 08/1847, pay stopped for: 1 cap-$.95$^{1/2}$, 2 pr. socks-$.49, 2 cotton shirts-$.86, 2 woolen shirts-$1.80, 1 pr. shoes-$1.22; pres. 10/1847, pay stopped for: 2 pr. socks-$.49, 1 jacket-$2.66, 1 pr. pants-$2.28, 2 cotton shirts-$.86, 1 great coat-$6.93$^{1/2}$; pres. 12/1847, pay stopped for: 1 pr. socks-$.24$^{1/2}$, 1 jacket-$2.66, 4 cotton shirts-$1.72, 1 blanket-$2.22; pres. 04/1848, pay stopped for: 2 cotton shirt-$.86, 1 flannel shirt-$.90, 1 pr. shoes-$1.22; 1 haversack-$.20$^{3/4}$, 1 india rubber canteen-$.27; pres. 08/1848, BLW sent to Washington, DC.

**Pitts, Virginius L.**, Pvt., Co. F; b. 03/09/1828, Blackwater, Princess Anne Co., VA;[1449, 1450] enl. Mex. War service 01/3/1847, Portsmouth, VA, age 19; pres. 06/1847; pres. 08/1847; pres. 10/1847, pay stopped for: 1 pr. overalls-$2.28, 3 cotton shirts-$1.29, 3 pr. socks-$.73$^{1/2}$, 1 forage cap-$.95$^{1/2}$, 2 pr. shoes-$2.44, 1 flannel shirt-$.90, 1 overcoat-$6.93$^{1/2}$; pres. 02/1848, pay stopped for: 1 pr. overalls-$2.28, 2 pr. drawers-$.71, 1 blanket-$2.22, 1 infantry jacket-$2.66; pres. 04/1848; pres. 08/1848, pay stopped for: 1 cartridge box belt plate-$.10, 1 gun sling-$.18, 1 pr. shoes-$1.16, 1 blanket-$2.25, BLW sent to Portsmouth, VA c/o E.T. Blamire; m. Mary Jane Bell, 01/10/1850, Currituck C.H., Currituck Co., NC;[1450, 1451] c. 1850 res. Currituck Co., NC age 22, occ. Farmer, w. Mary (20);[1452] c. 1860 res. London Bridge, Princess Anne Co., VA, age 30, occ. Tutor, w. Emma J. (30), dau. Sarah Frances (8);[1453] Civil War service enl. Pvt., Co. I, 5$^{th}$ Va. Cav. 04/20/1861 at Cape Henry, VA, paroled 07/21/1861 as 2$^{nd}$ Lt., trans. to Co. A, 08/06/1861, age 33, occ. farmer, pres. thru 02/1862, trans. Co. K, 15$^{th}$ Va. Cav. 03/27/1862, prom. Capt. 10/25/1862, paroled Eastern VA Dist. 04/25/1865, a res. of Currituck Co., NC.[131] near Grandy, NC? c. 1870 res. Powell's Point, Currituck Co., NC, age 48, occ. School Teacher, w. Mary (39), b. NC, dau. Fanny (15), b. NC;[1454] *"...Physician, Educator, Superintendent of Currituck County Public Schools,...;"*[1455] SC #15230, 11/21/1887, filed from Poplar Branch, Currituck Co., NC; states in pension application that he returned to Virginia from Mexico by way of ship *"Herman;"* since discharge res. Princess Anne Co., Norfolk Co., VA and Currituck Co., NC; Charles J. Creekmur and Francis L. Benson gave affidavits in pension claim; d. 07/15/1898, Poplar Branch, Currituck Co., NC; bur. Woodhouse Cem., Grandy, Currituck Co., NC; wid. Mary Jane, WC #11528, 08/13/1898, filed from Poplar Branch, Currituck Co., NC; (MJP b. 02/24/1825 Currituck Store, NC, d. 08/07/1900).

**Pleasants, Samuel S.**, 2$^{nd}$ Cpl., Co. G; enl. Mex. War service 12/05/1846 Richmond, VA, age 20; pres. 06/1847; Court-martialed 07/22/1847, Buena Vista, Mexico, *Charge #1: Sleeping On Post; Specification: In this that Pvt. Samuel S. Pleasants, Co. G, Va. Regt. Vols. having been duly posted as a Sentinel at the Camp at Buena Vista, Mexico on the 4$^{th}$ of July 1847, did go to sleep on his post before he was regularly relieved. To which charge and specification the prisoner pled Guilty. Offering no defense the Court confirmed the plea of the prisoner and sentenced him to forfeit one months pay and to stand on the head of a barrel on the parade ground of his Regiment for two successive hours, commencing at Guard Mounting, for successive days, under the charge of the Provost Guard*;[1456] pres. 08/1847; sick 10/1847, pay stopped for: 1 pr. overalls-$2.28, 2 pr. shoes-$2.44, 3 pr. socks-$.73$^{1/2}$, 1 forage cap-$.95$^{1/2}$, sick 12/1847 in Hosp. at Saltillo, Mex.; sick 02/1848, pay stopped for: 1 pr. pants-$2.28; discharged 03/1848, Saltillo, Mex. for disability; c. 1850 res. Petersburg, Dinwiddie Co., VA, age 24, occ. Carpenter;[1457] c. 1860 res. Petersburg, Dinwiddie Co., VA, age 32, occ. Carpenter;[1458] Civil War service Pvt., Co. K, 12$^{th}$ Va. Inf. enl. date unknown, paroled 04/17/1865 at Richmond, VA, res. stated as High St., Petersburg, VA[21]

**Pleasants, William H.**, 2$^{nd}$ Lt., Co. M; enl. Mex. War service 05/15/1847, Richmond, VA, age 28; pres. 09/1847; pres. 11/1847; pres. 12/1847; pres. 02/1848; pres. 04/1848; pres. 08/1848;

OFF TO WAR

m. Julia Page West, 02/07/1860, Springfield, Henrico Co., VA;[1459] c. 1860 res. Richmond, Henrico Co., VA, age 30?, w. Julia (28);[1460] c. 1870 res. Richmond, Henrico Co., VA, age 52, occ. Commission Merchant, w. Julia (38), son William (7), dau. Ellen (5), dau. Mary (3), son Jefferson (6/12);[1461] d. 04/22/1887 in Richmond, VA;[1459] wid. Julia P., WC #2387, 08/22/1887, from VA (JPP b. 10/21/1831, d. 05/21/1923, bur. Hollywood Cem., Richmond, VA, Sect. 15, Lot 22); [1459, 119]

**Plumb, William**, Pvt., Co. A; enl. Mex. War service 11/28/1846 Richmond, VA, age 35; deserted 01/21/1847 at Old Point, VA, 6 mos. pd. in advance.

**Poage, Alpheus Wilson**, 1st Cpl., LIC; b. 07/04/1818, near Staunton, Augusta Co., VA, son of William & Margaret Poage;[1462, 1463] enl. Mex. War service 11/27/1846 Staunton, VA, age 26; pres. 06/1847; pres. 08/1847, prom. 4th Cpl. 07/02/1847; pres. 10/1847, pay stopped for: 1 forage cap-$.95$^{1/2}$, 1 wool jacket-$2.66, 1 pr. overalls-$2.28, 1 pr. shoes-$1.22, 2 pr. socks-$.49, 1 flannel shirt-$.90; pres. 12/1847, pay stopped for: 1 blanket-$2.22, 1 flannel shirt-$.90, 2 pr. drawers-$.71, 1 forage cap-$.95$^{1/2}$; pres. 04/1848, prom. 1st Cpl.; pres. 07/1848, pay stopped for: 1 pr. shoes-$1.16; BLW sent to Staunton, VA; c. 1850 res. Augusta Co., VA, age 29, occ. Farmer;[1464] c. 1860 res. Newbern, Pulaski Co., VA, age 40, occ. Deputy Clerk;[1465] Civil War service Pvt., Co. F, 54th Va. Inf., enl. 09/09/1861 at Newbern, VA, det. as a Nurse 01/01/1862 at Piketon, KY, NFR, enl. as Capt., Co. K, 4th VA Reserves, 04/20/1864 at Pulaski, VA, pres. 04/1864 through 08/1864, elected Major 08/27/1864, furloughed 15 days 01/1865; NFR; SC #3488, 02/21/1887, filed from Wytheville, Wythe Co., VA; since discharge res. Augusta Co., VA from 1848- 1857, Pulaski Co., VA from 1857-1879, and Wythe Co., VA since 1879;[1462] phys. desc. age 69 [1887], 6'$^{1/2}$", rather dark complexion, hazel eyes, gray hair, occ. Clerk;[1462] d. 05/02/1902;[1462] b-i-l of Gen J.A. Walker;[192] bro. of Col. Thomas Poague, 50th Va. Inf.

Photo credit: Virginia Fire & Police Museum, Richmond, VA.

**Poe, John, Jr.**, Co. A; b. 07/31/1827; enl. Mex. War service 12/05/1846 Richmond, VA, phys. desc. at enl. age 19, 6', light hair, gray eyes, occ. Clerk; pres. 06/1847; pres. 08/1847; pres. 10/1847, pay stopped for clothing: 1 pr. wool overalls-$2.28, 1 cap-$.95$^{1/2}$, 2 pr. stockings-$.49, 1 pr. drawers-$.35$^{1/2}$, 1 pr. shoes-$1.22, 1 great coat-$6.93$^{1/2}$; pres. 12/1847, pay stopped for clothing: 1 pr. wool overalls-$2.28, 2 pr. drawers-$.71, 2 pr. socks-$.49; pres. 02/1848, pay stopped for: 1 pick & brush-$.12; on detached service 04/1848 as Ward Master in hosp. at Saltillo, Mex. since 04/25/1848; 07/1848, pay stopped for: 1 cart. Box & belt-$1.70, waist belt-$.21, 1 bayonet sheath-$.56, 1 gun sling-$.16, 1 pick & brush-$.12, 1 wiper-$.20, 1 screw driver-$.25; BLW sent to Richmond, VA; m. C. Cornelia Williams, 11/1849(d. 05/1869, bur. Hollywood Cem., Sect. K, Lot 29);[1466, 119] c. 1850 res. Henrico Co., VA, age 23, occ. Merchant, w. Pamelia (21), mo? Rebecca (55), sis? Virginia (25);[1467] Civil War service 2nd Lt., Co. A, 25th Btln. Va. Inf., enl. 07/08/1862, age 35, pres. 07/1862 through 11/1863, resigned 11/13/1863, due to *"defective sight;"*[116] SC #6850, 02/24/1887, filed from 503 W. Grace St., Richmond, Henrico Co., VA; Capt. Robert G. Scott, 406 E. Grace St., Richmond, VA and James M. Donnan, 300 S. Pine St., Richmond, VA gave affidavits for pension claim; Major John Poe, Chief of Police, d. 06/10/1895, Richmond, VA;[1468] bur. Hollywood Cem., Richmond, VA, Sect. 16, Lot 87.[119]

## VIRGINIA VOLUNTEERS IN MEXICO

**Poe, Thomas**, Pvt., Co. A, enl. Mex. War service 12/14/1846 Richmond, VA, age 28; pres. 12/1846 – 04/1847; sick in quarters 06/1847, detailed as Commissary Sgt. 06/28/1847; pres. 08/1847, fined $7.00 by order (#86) of regtl. court-martial, in confinement, 08/1847; sick 10/1847, pay stopped for clothing: 1 pr. wool overalls-$2.28, 1 cap-$.95$^{1/2}$, 4 pr. socks-$.98, 2 flannel shirts-$1.80, 1 great coat-$6.93$^{1/2}$; pres. 12/1847, pay stopped for clothing: 1 pr. wool overalls-$2.28, 1 blanket-$2.22; pres. 02/1848; AWOL 04/1848 since the morning of 04/29/1848; BLW sent to Richmond, VA

**Poisal, Daniel**, 2$^{nd}$ Lt., Co. H; enl. Mex. War service 11/21/1846, Berkeley, VA, age 27; pres. 04/1847; pres. 06/1847, prom. 4$^{th}$ Sgt. 05/06/1847; pres. 08/1847; pres. 10/1847, pay stopped for: 1 forage cap-$.95$^{1/2}$, 1 pr. pants-$2.28, 1 cotton shirt-$.43, 2 pr. drawers-$.71, 1 pr. shoes-$1.22, 2 pr. socks-$.49; pres. 12/1847, pay stopped for: 1 pr. pants-$2.28, 2 flannel shirts-$1.80, 2 pr. socks-$.49, 1 blanket-$2.22; pres. 02/1848, pay stopped for: 1 pr. drawers-$.35$^{1/2}$; pres. 04/1848, prom. 2$^{nd}$ Lt. 03/01/1848; pres. 07/1848, BLW sent to Martinsburg, VA

**Poland, John F.**, 4$^{th}$ Sgt., Co. K; b. 02/27/1818, Loudoun Co., VA;[1469] enl. Mex. War service Richmond, VA 01/20/1847, age 28; pres. 06/1847; pres. 08/1847; pres. 10/1847, pay stopped for: 1 pr. overalls-$2.28, 2 cotton shirts-$.86, 2 pr. socks-$.49, 1 pr. drawers-$.35$^{1/2}$, 2 flannel shirts-$1.80, 1 greatcoat-$6.93$^{1/2}$; pres. 12/1847, pay stopped for: 1 jacket-$2.66, 2 pr. overalls-$4.56, 1 blanket-$2.22; pres. 04/1848, prom. 4$^{th}$ Sgt. 01/07/1848, pay stopped for: 2 flannel shirts-$1.80, 1 cotton shirt-$.43; pres. 07/1848; BLW sent to Charlestown, Jefferson Co., VA; SC #13355, 12/01/1887, filed from Reno, Washoe Co., NV; *"not married, never married;"*[1469] d. 1902.[1469]

**Pollard, James D.**, Pvt., Co. F; enl. Mex. War service 01/20/1847, Portsmouth, VA, age 31; pres. 06/1847; pres. 08/1847; pres. 10/1847, pay stopped for: 1 pr. overalls-$2.28, 1 forage cap-$.95$^{1/2}$, 3 pr. shoes-$3.66, 2 cotton shirts-$.86, 3 pr. socks-$.73$^{1/2}$, 2 pr. drawers-$.71; pres. 02/1848, pay stopped for: 1 musket-$14.00, 1 blanket-$2.22; transferred 03/01/1848 to Co. H, NC Regt.

**Pollard, Peyton**, 1$^{St}$ Sgt., Co. E; son of Capt. John & Mary Ann Pollard, enl. Mex. War service 11/28/1846 Petersburg, VA, age 28; pres. 04/1847; pres. but sick 06/1847; discharged 07/26/1847 on Surgeon's Certificate of Disability; d. New Orleans, La. 09/1847, bur. Petersburg, VA;[1470] d. 08/31/184(7)? *Mexican Diarrhea*, bur. Blandford Cem., Sq. 3, Sec. 9, Ward B, Petersburg, VA[1471]

**Pollock, Robert**, 2$^{nd}$ Lt., Co. H; b. 09/17/1819, Philadelphia, Pa.;[1472] enl. Mex. War service 01/01/1847, Berkeley, VA, phys. desc. age 28, 5'9$^{1/2}$", light brown hair, blue eyes, occ. Carpenter; pres. 04/1847; pres. sick 06/1847, prom. 2$^{nd}$ Lt. 05/06/1847; pres. 08/1847; pres. 10/1847; pres. 12/1847; pres. 02/1848; pres. 04/1848; pres. 07/1848, BLW sent to Philadelphia, Pa. Civil War service enl. Major 3$^{rd}$ Calif. Inf. 09/04/1861, prom. Lt. Col. 12/12/1861, on detached service since 09/07/1862, in command of troops stationed at Stockton, Calif., on detached service 12/31/1862 in command of troops stationed at Camp Union, Sacramento, Calif., prom. Col., 03/29/1863, discharged 11/14/1864; enl. Lt. Col. 2$^{nd}$ Calif. Inf. 01/07/1865, discharged 06/23/1866; enl. 1$^{st}$ Lt. 32$^{nd}$ U.S. Inf. 07/28/1866, trans. 21$^{st}$ U.S. Inf., prom. Capt. 02/19/1873, commanded Ft. Goodwin, Arizona territory, did duty in California, Arizona Territory, Washington and Oregon, retired 09/17/1883;[1472] WO #4998; SC #17865, 01/19/1899, filed from Cornelius, Washington Co., OR; d. 02/24/1901, Cornelius, OR.[1472]

**Porterfield, George Alexander**, 1$^{st}$ Lt., Co. G; b. 11/24/1822, Berkeley C., VA;[1473, 1474] son of George & Mary (Tabb) Porterfield; VMI graduate, Class of 1844; enl. Mex. War service 11/18/1846 Richmond, VA, age 24; pres. 06/1847 in command of company; apptd. Regimental Adjutant 07/10/1847, by order of Col. J.F. Hamtramck;[1475] absent 08/1847 on detached service as Actg. Asst. Adjt. Genl since 08/28/1847; absent 10/1847 on detached service as Actg. Asst. Adjt.; absent 12/1847 on detached service; absent 02/1848 on detached service; absent 04/1848, on detached service; discharged 07/20/1848; m. Emily C. Terrill,

243

OFF TO WAR

07/10/1849, Warm Springs, Bath Co., VA;[1473, 281] c. 1850 res. Martinsburg, VA, age 37, occ. Editor, w. Emily (19);[1476] c. 1860 res. Charles Town, VA, age 36, occ. Farmer, w. Emily C., (27), son William F. (9), dau. Elizabeth M. (7), son John A. (6), son George (4), dau. Mary (1);[1477] Civil War service Col. 25th Va. Inf., Relieved of command 06/14/1861, Court of Inquiry ordered for actions at Phillippi, VA, on staff of Gen. W.W. Loring 08/09/1861 through 01/12/1862, Chief of Ordnance, Assigned to command what is left of 25th Va. Inf. & 9th Btln. Va. Inf., retired 05/01/1862 not reelected Col.; postwar occ. banker;[1266] c. 1880 res. Harper's Ferry, Jefferson Co., WV, age 53, occ. Cashier in Bank, w. Emily C. (45) Keeping House, dau. Mary J. (21), son Charles (18), dau. Serena (17), dau. Kate S. (10);[1478] SC #3732, 02/04/1887, filed from Charles Town, Jefferson Co., WV., phys. desc. age 62 [1884], 5'9", dark complexion, dark eyes, dark hair;[1473] lists children: William Terrill Porterfield, b. 12/07/1850, (now dead), Elizabeth Morton Porterfield Cooke, b. 1853, John Porterfield, b. 03/15/1855, George Porterfield b. 08/03/1857, Mary (Porterfield) Morton, b. 1859, Charles Porterfield, b. 01/03/1861, E. Serena (Porterfield) Washington, b. 05/03/1863, Katherine S. Porterfield Mackey, b. 1870;[1473] d. 02/271919 *Pneumonia, age 96 yrs., 21 days*, Charlestown, WV; bur. Green Hill Cem., Martinsburg, WV.[1479]

Photo credit: H.E. Howard, Inc., Lynchburg, VA

**Poston, John F.**, Pvt., Co. B; b. 10/12/1821, son of Leonard & Ann (Waters) Poston; m. Mary McAtee, 05/30/1843, Loudoun Co., VA;[1480] enl. 11/20/1846, Alexandria, VA, age 26; discharged 01/02/1847, left at Richmond, VA, disabled by wound in hand; c. 1850 a John Poston res. Loudoun Co., VA, age 30, occ. Farmer, w. Nancy (28), dau. Jane (5), dau. Sally (3), son Peter (1);[1481] c. 1860 res. Clarke Co., VA, age 37, occ. Farmer, w. Mary (37), dau. Jane A. (14), dau. Susan C. (13), son Joseph B. (11), son John T. (9), son Frank (7), dau. Catherine (4), dau. Mary T. (3), son Randolph (1);[1482] c. 1870 res. Battletown, Clarke Co., VA, age 48, occ. Shoemaker, w?. Ann E. (25), dau. Catherine (15), son Randolph (10), son Robert (4), dau. Lydia (2), son John (8/12);[1483] SC #8165, 04/22/1887, from MD, [Pension file not found]; d. 02/01/1901, Loudoun Co. VA, bur. Ebenezer Cem., Round Hill, Loudoun Co., VA[1484]

**Potts, John H.**, Pvt., Co. A; b. 1827; enl. Mex. War service 12/09/1846 Richmond, VA, age 19; pres. 12/1846 - 04/1847; pres. 06/1847; pres. 08/1847; pres.10/1847 pay stopped for clothing: 3 pr. shoes-$3.66, 4 pr. stockings-$.98, 2 cotton shirts-$.86, 1 wool jacket-$2.66, 1 pr. wool overalls-$2.28, 1 cap-$.95$^{1/2}$, 2 flannel shirts-$1.80, 1 great coat-$6.93$^{1/2}$; pres. 12/1847, pay stopped for clothing: 1 pr. wool overalls-$2.28, 1 pr. shoes-$1.22; pres. 02/1848, pay stopped for: 1 pr. wool overalls-$2.28, 1 pr. shoes-$1.22; 1 pick & brush-$.12; pres. 04/1848, pay stopped for: 1 bayonet; BLW sent to Louisa C.H., VA; Civil War service Pvt., Co. E, 4th KY Inf., enl. 08/07/1861, mustered out 08/17/1865; SC #15959, 05/17/1888, from KY; d. 07/23/1917, Natl. Military Home in Ohio; bur. Plot 1, 19, 3, Dayton Natl. Cem., Dayton, OH, *"res. New Albany, Ind.;"*[1485] [see Civil War pension claim].

## VIRGINIA VOLUNTEERS IN MEXICO

**Powell, Edward**, Pvt., Co. G; enl. Mex. War service 11/26/1846 Richmond, VA, age 31; pres. 06/1847; pres. 08/1847; pres. 10/1847, pay stopped for: 1 pr. overalls-$2.28, 2 cotton shirts-$.86, 1 flannel shirt-$.90, 2 shoes-$2.44, 4 pr. socks-$.98, 1 forage cap-$.95$^{1/2}$; pres. 12/1847, pay stopped for: 1 pr. pants-$2.28; pres. 02/1848; pres. 04/1848; pres. 08/1848, pay stopped for: 1 pr. shoes-$1.16, 1 bayonet-$1.44; BLW sent to Richmond, VA; c. 1850 res. Richmond, Henrico Co., VA, age 35, occ. Cooper, w. Mary (27).[1486]

**Powell, Robert**, 2$^{nd}$ Cpl., Co. G; enl. Mex. War service 12/08/1846 Richmond, VA, age 22; pres. 06/1847; pres. 08/1847; pres. 10/1847, pay stopped for: 2 pr. overalls-$4.56, 1 flannel shirt-$.90, 2 shoes-$2.44, 3 pr. socks-$.73$^{1/2}$, 1 forage cap-$.95$^{1/2}$; pres. 12/1847, prom. 2$^{nd}$ Cpl., pay stopped for: 1 pr. shoes-$1.22, 3 pr. drawers-$1.06$^{1/2}$, 1 blanket-$2.22, 1 pr. pants-$2.28, 1 cap-$.95$^{1/2}$, 2 pr. socks-$.49; pres. 02/1848; pres. 04/1848; absent 08/1848, left in Monterey, Mex. QM Dept., not discharged at Ft. Monroe, VA; BLW sent to Richmond, VA

**Powers, James**, Pvt., LIC; enl. Mex. War service 12/07/1846 Staunton, VA, age 32; sick 06/1847 in quarters; pres. 08/1847; discharged 10/19/1847 on Surgeon's Certificate of Disability.

**Powers, Walter**, Pvt., Co. M; enl. Mex. War service 11/04/1847, Norfolk, VA, age 36; pres. 11/1847; pres. 12/1847; pres. 02/1848; pres. 04/1848, pay stopped for: 1 blanket-$2.22, 1 pr. shoes-$1.22, 1 cotton shirt-$.43, 1 cap-$.95$^{1/2}$; pres. 08/1848, pay stopped for: 1 musket & accoutrements complete-$16.22, 1 pr. shoes-$1.16; BLW sent to Norfolk, VA

**Poynts, James W.**, Pvt., Co. D; enl. Mex. War service 01/03/1847, Petersburg, VA, age 20; pres. 02/1847; pres. 04/1847; discharged 06/06/1847 Monterey, Mex. on Surgeon's Certificate of Disability;[a James W. Points served as a Pvt., Co C, 8$^{th}$ Ga. Inf. during the Civil War].[202]

**Prather, Socrates**, Pvt., Co. H; enl. Mex. War service 12/04/1846, Hampshire, VA, age 22; 02/1847 Socrates Prather, of Hampshire Co., VA, is listed as being sick in *Martinsburg Gazette*;[1487] absent 04/1847 left in Hosp. at Ft. Monroe, VA 02/20/1847; absent 06/1847 left sick in Hosp. at Ft. Monroe, VA; d. 04/19/1847 at Ft. Monroe, VA; bur. *"on the shores of the Chesapeake Bay."*[1488]

**Preston, James Francis**, Capt., *Preston's Co.*; b. 11/08/1813, son of James Patton and Nancy (Taylor) Preston,[16, 45, 1489] Cadet United States Military Academy, 1833 (non-graduate); Delegate to the Virginia General Assembly 1852; enl. Mex. War service 11/24/1846 Montgomery Co., VA; pres. 04/1847; pres. 06/1847; pres. 08/1847; pres. 10/1847; pres. 12/1847; pres. 02/1848; pres. 04/1848; pres. 07/1848; c. 1850 res. Montgomery Co., VA, age 35, occ. Lawyer;[1490] m. Sarah Ann Caperton, 01/18/1855, Union, Monroe Co., VA;[1491] c. 1860 res. Christiansburg, Montgomery Co., VA, age 46, occ. Farmer, w. Sarah A. (30), son Hugh C. (4), son William B. (3), son James (1/12);[1492] Civil War service Col. of the 4$^{th}$ Va.. Inf. at muster, wounded 07/21/1861 at 1$^{st}$ Manassas, d. at home 01/20/1862 reputedly from wounds, bur. "Smithfield," Montgomery Co., VA;[54] a United Confederate Veterans Camp (U.C.V.) in Christiansburg, VA, was named in his honor;[1493] wid. Sarah A., WC 6086, 12/08/1888, filed from Blacksburg, Montgomery Co., VA;[1491] Charles A. Ronald and Michael Kipps gave affidavit in pension claim;[1491] OW W #23457, rejected; (SCP b. 06/29/1826, Union Co., VA).[1491]

**Preston, John F.**, Pvt., Co. B; a John F. Preston, Washington Co., VA d. 01/1875.[1494]

**Price, Edward T.**, Pvt., Co. E; enl. Mex. War service 11/26/1846 Petersburg, VA, age 19; pres. 04/1847; pres. 06/1847; pres. 08/1847; pres. 10/1847, pay stopped for: 1 pr. overalls-$2.28, 2 pr. shoes-$2.44, 3 pr. stockings-$.73$^{1/2}$, 2 cotton shirts-$.86, 2 flannel shirts-$1.80, 1 cap-$.95$^{1/2}$, 1 overcoat-$6.93$^{1/2}$, 1 blanket-$2.22; pres. 10/1847, pay stopped for: 2 pr. stockings-$.49; pres. 12/1847, pay stopped for: 1 pr. pants-$2.28, 1 blanket-$2.22; pres. 02/1848, pay

---

[16] James Patton Preston was Governor of Virginia 1816-1819.

OFF TO WAR

stopped for: 1 pr. shoes-$1.22; pres. 04/1848; d. 11/1875, *'Edward T. Price, formerly of Dinwiddie Co., who served in the Mexican War, died in Halifax Co., N.C.'*[1495]

**Price, Williamson C.**, Pvt., Co. G; enl. Mex. War service 11/28/1846 Richmond, VA, age 23; pres. 06/1847; pres. 08/1847; pres. 10/1847, pay stopped for: 1 blanket-$2.22, 2 pr. overalls-$4.56, 4 cotton shirts-$1.72, 2 pr. shoes-$2.44, 3 pr. socks-$.73$^{1/2}$, 1 forage cap-$.95$^{1/2}$; pres. 12/1847, pay stopped for: 1 pr. shoes-$1.22, 1 blanket-$2.22, 1 pr. pants-$2.28, 1 jacket-$2.66, 1 pr. socks-$.24$^{1/2}$; pres. 02/1848, pay stopped for: 1 brush & pick-$.12; pres. 04/1848; pres. 08/1848, pay stopped for: 1 pr. shoes-$1.16, 1 cartridge box plate-$.10, 1 gun sling-$.16; BLW sent to Campbell Co. C.H., VA

**Prichard, Samuel H.**, Pvt., Co. E; enl. Mex. War service 12/02/1846 Petersburg, VA, age 21; pres. 04/1847; absent 06/1847 detailed as Commissary Sgt. 06/18/1847; absent 08/1847 on detached service in Subsistence Dept.; pres. 10/1847, pay stopped for: 1 pr. shoes-$1.22, 1 pr. stockings-$.49, 2 cotton shirts-$.86, 1 cap-$.95$^{1/?}$; absent 12/1847, on daily duty in Commissary Dept. since 12/20/1847, pay stopped for: 2 pr. pants-$4.56, 2 pr. socks-$.49, 1 pr. shoes-$1.22, 2 cotton shirts-$.86, 2 flannel shirts-$1.80; absent 02/1848, on daily duty in Commissary Dept.; pres. 04/1848, on daily duty in Commissary Dept.

**Prichett, William Lewis**, Pvt., Co. E; enl. Mex. War service 12/01/1846 Petersburg, VA, age 22; pres. 04/1847; pres. 06/1847; pres. 08/1847; pres. 10/1847, pay stopped for: 1 pr. overalls-$2.28, 2 pr. shoes-$2.44, 2 pr. stockings-$.49, 3 cotton shirts-$1.29, 1 cap-$.95$^{1/2}$; pres. 12/1847, pay stopped for: 1 pr. pants-$2.28, 1 pr. socks-$.24$^{1/2}$, 1 pr. shoes-$1.22, 2 cotton shirts-$.86, 2 pr. drawers-$.35$^{1/2}$; pres. 02/1848; pres. 04/1848, pay stopped for: 1 jacket-$2.37$^{1/2}$, 2 cotton shirts-$.88; c. 1850 res. Richmond, Henrico Co., VA, age 26, occ. Public Guard;[1496] c. 1860 res. Richmond, VA, age 25?, occ. Member of the State Guard.[1497]

**Procise, Joseph D.**, Pvt., Co. D; enl. Mex. War service 12/26/1846, Petersburg, VA, age 18; pres. 02/1847; pres. 04/1847; pres. 06/1847; pres. 08/1847, reduced to ranks 08/31/1847 by order of Capt. Carleton Actg. Insp. Genl., pay stopped for: 1 cap-$.95$^{1/2}$, 1 pr. pants-$2.28, 2 flannel shirts-$1.80; pres. 10/1847, pay stopped for: 1 jacket-$2.66, 2 flannel shirts-$1.80, 1 pr. drawers-$.35$^{1/2}$, 1 pr. socks-$.24$^{1/2}$, 1 pr. shoes-$1.22, 1 blanket-$2.22; pres. 12/1847, pay stopped for: 1 cap-$.95$^{1/2}$, 1 pr. pants-$2.28, 1 blanket-$2.22; sick 04/1848, pay stopped for: 1 pr. pants-$2.28, 1 cotton shirt-$.43, 1 pr. shoes-$1.22, 1 blanket-$2.22; pres. 08/1847, BLW sent to Hicks Ford, Greensville Co., VA; c. 1860 res. Petersburg, Dinwiddie Co., VA, age 30, occ. None Listed, w. Mary (25), son John (1).[1498]

**Procise, Thomas**, Pvt., Co. D; enl. Mex. War service 01/03/1847, Petersburg, VA, age 20; pres. 02/1847; pres. 04/1847; pres. 06/1847; pres. 08/1847, pay stopped for: 1 cap-$.95$^{1/2}$, 2 cotton shirts-$.86; pres. 10/1847, pay stopped for: 1 jacket-$2.66, 1 pr. pants-$2.28, 2 flannel shirts-$1.80, 1 pr. drawers-$.35$^{1/2}$, 2 pr. socks-$.49, 1 pr. shoes-$1.22, 1 blanket-$2.22; pres. 12/1847, pay stopped for: 1 pr. socks-$.24$^{1/2}$, 2 pr. shoes-$2.44; pres. 04/1848, pay stopped for: 1 pr. pants-$2.28, 1 haversack-$.20$^{3/4}$; pres. 08/1847, BLW sent to Petersburg, VA; c. 1860 res. San Marino, Dinwiddie Co., VA, age 28, occ. Blacksmith, w. Mary A. (22), son Thomas J. (1).[1499]

**Provost, James**, Pvt., Co. A; enl. Mex. War service 11/22/1846 Richmond, VA, age 39; pres. 12/1846 - 04/1847; pres. 06/1847; pres. 08/1847; in confinement 10/1847, pay stopped for clothing: 1 cap-$.95$^{1/2}$, 2 pr. stockings-$.49, 1 pr. wool overalls-$2.28, 1 pr. drawers-$.35$^{1/2}$, 1 pr. shoes-$1.22; deserted 11/27/1847 at Buena Vista, Mex.

**Pullen, Romulus F.**, Pvt., Co. G; enl. Mex. War service 11/18/1846 Richmond, VA, age 19; pres. 06/1847; pres. 08/1847; pres. 10/1847, pay stopped for: 1 blanket-$2.22, 1 pr. overalls-$2.28, 3 cotton shirts-$1.29, 1 flannel shirt-$.90, 2 shoes-$2.44, 3 pr. socks-$.73$^{1/2}$, 1 forage cap-$.95$^{1/2}$; pres. 12/1847, pay stopped for: 1 pr. shoes-$1.22, 1 overcoat-$6.93$^{1/2}$, 1 pr. pants-$2.28, 1 cotton shirt-$.43, 2 flannel shirts-$1.80, 2 pr. drawers-$.71, 1 blanket-$2.22, 1 cap-$.95$^{1/2}$; pres. 02/1848, pay stopped for: 1 brush & pick-$.12, 1 pr. shoes-$1.22; sick 04/1848, pay stopped for: 1 pr. shoes-$1.22; pres. 08/1848, pay stopped for: 1 gun sling-$.16, 1

# VIRGINIA VOLUNTEERS IN MEXICO

bayonet-$1.44; BLW sent to Richmond, VA; c. 1850 res. Richmond, Henrico Co., VA, age 22, occ. Clerk;[1500] [a Romulus Pullen m. Mary Willman, 02/28/1858, St. Louis, Mo.][1501]
**Pulman, William**, Pvt., *Recruit Co.*, enl. Mex. War service 09/20/1847 Charlotte, VA, age 20; NFR.
**Quinn, Martin**, Pvt., Co. A; enl. Mex. War service 11/18/1846 Richmond, VA, age 41; pres. 06/1847; pres. 08/1847; pres. 10/1847, pay stopped for clothing: 1 pr. wool overalls-$2.28, 1 cap-$.95$^{1/2}$, 2 pr. stockings-$.49, 1 pr. drawers-$.35$^{1/2}$, 1 pr. shoes-$1.22; pres. 12/1847, pay stopped for clothing: 1 pr. wool overalls-$2.28, 1 pr. drawers-$.35$^{1/2}$, 2 flannel shirts-$1.80, 1 blanket-$2.22; pres. 02/1848; pres. 04/1848; 07/1848, pay stopped for: 1 musket sling-$.16, 1 pick & brush-$.12, 1 wiper-$.20; BLW sent to Philadelphia, Pa.; Civil War service Pvt., Co. C, 26$^{th}$ Pa. Inf.
**Ralls, George Norton**, Pvt., Co. D; b. 10/23/1823, Washington, Rappahannock Co., VA;[1502] enl. Mex. War service 09/01/1847, Petersburg, VA, age 23; pres. 04/1848, pay due from 12/01/1847 - 01/28/1848 as Sgt. of Recruits; pres. 08/1847, BLW sent to Keysville, Charlotte Co., VA; m. Martha Jane Clarke, 05/20/1850, Lunenburg Co., VA;[1502] c. 1860 res. Keysville, Charlotte Co., VA, age 36, occ. Farmer, w. Martha J. (36), son Thomas O. (7), dau. Maria L. (5), son George E. (3), son John W. (5/12);[1503] Civil War service 1$^{st}$ Lt., Co. B, 22$^{nd}$ Btln Va. Inf., enl. 12/31/1861 for 1 year, resigned 05/19/1862, reenlisted as a Pvt. date/place unknown, admitted to Gen. Hosp. #9, 10/05/1864, paroled 04/25/1865 at Burkeville, VA;[712] c. 1870 res. Walton, Charlotte Co., VA, age 46, occ. Farmer, w. Martha (46), son Thomas (17), dau. Maria (14), son George (11), dau. Marina (9), dau. Flora (6);[1504] c. 1884 moved to Greensboro, NC then to Richmond, VA;[1505] SC #4854, 04/01/1887, filed from Richmond, Henrico Co., VA; *"Mr. & Mrs Ralls have a family of five children;"* d. 8/17/1892, 805 N 26$^{th}$ St., Richmond, VA;[1506] wid. Martha J., WC #8359, 10/04/1892, filed from 805 26$^{th}$ St., Richmond Henrico Co., VA; (MJR b. 03/24/1823).[1506]
**Randolph, Thomas Beverly**, Lt. Colonel, 1$^{st}$ VA Vol. Inf. Regt.; b. 05/31/1792, Chiloe, Cumberland Co., VA, son of William & Lucy (Bolling) Randolph; graduated 1812 U.S.M.A. at West Point, NY, commissioned a 2$^{nd}$ Lt., Light Artillery 1811;[1507] served in the War of 1812, prom. 1$^{st}$ Lt., Light Artillery, 01/13/1813;[1508] m. Maria Barbara Mayer, 05/31/1814, Lancaster, Pa.; resigned 1815 as a Capt.; Officer VA Militia 1822-34; elected Sergeant-At-Arms, U.S. House of Representatives, 1832-1833;[1509] c. 1850 res. Warren Co., VA, age 57. occ. Farmer, w. Maria B. (56), dau. Susan B. (28), son Thomas M. (21), son Christopher M. (19), dau. Ann C. (14); *"Last Saturday, Aug. 17 was the 60th anniversary of the battle of Churnbusco, Mexico, in which a Warren County boy, Corporal Peyton Randolph, gave up his life for his country. He was a son of Gen. Thomas B. Randolph, then Col., but was not in his father's regiment and the latter knew nothing of his death until after the war. Old settlers remember the great reception and banquet given Col. Randolph here by the militia and citizens of Front Royal on his return from Mexico. He was the grandfather of Sam'l Rolfe Millar and of Mrs. Ernest A. Jones;"*[1510] d. 11/12/1867, near Cascade, Dubuque Co., Iowa.; bur. Zion Reform Church, Clarence Martin Farm, Cascade, IA.[1511]
**Ratcliffe, Thomas**, Pvt., Co. L; b. 1828; enl. Mex. War service 03/24/1847 Ft. Washington, MD, age 19; pres. 06/1847; pres. 08/1847; pres. 10/1847, to forfeit $3.50 by sentence of garrison court-martial, pay stopped for: 1 pr. Pants 2.28, 1 pr. Shoes 1.22, 1 F Cap .95; pres. 12/1847, pay stopped for: 4 cotton shirts-$1.72, 2 pr. drawers-$.71, 2 pr. socks-$.49; pres. 02/1848, pay stopped for: 1 Jacket 2.66; pres. 04/1848, pay stopped for: 1 pr. Shoes 1.16; pres. 07/1848, pay stopped for: pr. Shoes 1.16; BLW sent to Washington City, D.C.
**Raux, Emile**, 3$^{rd}$ Sgt., Co. A; enl. 11/18/1846, Richmond, VA, age 28; pres. until left sick 04/04/1847 in hosp. at Camargo, Mex.; pres. 06/1847; pres. 08/1847, prom. 3$^{rd}$ Sgt. 08/23/1847; pres. 10/1847 pay stopped for: 2 pr. wool overalls-$4.56, 8 pr. stockings-$1.96, 3 caps-$2.86$^{1/2}$, 4 flannel shirts-$3.60, 1 cotton shirt-$.43$^{1/2}$, 2 pr. shoes-$2.44; pres.12/1847, pay stopped for clothing: 1 wool overalls-$2.28, 1 pr. drawers-$.35$^{1/2}$, 2 pr. socks-$.49, 2 pr.

OFF TO WAR

shoes-$2.44, 2 blankets-$4.44; pres. 02/1848, pay stopped for: 1 pr. shoes-$1.22; absent 04/1848, on furlough since 03/25/1848 for two months; 07/1848 pay stopped for: pick, brush and screw driver-$.25; BLW sent to, Richmond, VA

**Rawlins, Edward Albin** Pvt., Co. F; b. 04/09/1822;[45] enl. Mex. War service 08/16/1847 Boydton, VA; pres. 02/1848 joined company from regtl. depot; pres. 04/1848, 1 mos. and 3 days clothing allowance due him; pres. 08/1848, pay stopped for: 2 cotton shirts-$.88, 1 forage cap-$.83, BLW sent to Elhanon Grove, Mecklenburg, VA; c. 1850 res. Mecklenburg Co., VA, age 30, occ. Manager of Farm;[1512] m. Anna Terry Guy; c. 1860 res. Townsville, Mecklenburg Co., VA, age 37, occ. Farmer, w. Ann F. (37), dau. Mary G. (12), son Edward F. (4), son Edward A. (2);[1513] Civil War service Sgt., Co. D, 22nd Btln. Va. Inf., enl. as Pvt. 01/28/1862 at Lombardy Grove (Mecklenburg Co.), VA, pres. until 07/02/1862 when admitted to Gen Hosp. #7 with contusion, RTD 07/18/1862, prom. 5th Sgt. 12/1862, prom. 4th Sgt. 04/1863, absent sick 06/14/1863 through 12/1863, wded. 05/03/1864, admitted Chimborazo Hosp. #5 05/25/1864 and furloughed for 60 days on 06/21/1864, admitted to Wayside Hosp., Farmville, VA 08/26/1864, transferred 09/27/1864, retired to the Invalid Corps. 11/10/1864;[712] Director, Roanoke Land and Colonization Company;[1514] d. 11/03/1871, bur. Old St. Luke's Church Cemetery, Hwy. 718, Mecklenburg Co., VA.[45]

**Rawls, Elisha**, Pvt., Co. F, *Not on Muster Rolls*, SA #23457, 04/16/1891, from VA

**Reamy, John T.**, Pvt., Co. H; enl. Mex. War service 01/01/1847, Richmond, VA, age 20; pres. 04/1847; absent 06/1847 left sick in Hosp. at Monterey, Mex. 06/22/1847; a letter from T.C. Madison, Asst. Surgeon notes *"Please say to Capt. Alburtis that Reamy is little better and wishes him to send him the balance of his money $11.24 cts. I gave him $10;"* [1515] d. 07/12/1847 Monterey, Mex.

**Reed, John C.**, 2nd Sgt., Co. H; enl. Mex. War service 11/27/1846, Morgan, VA, age 30; pres. 04/1847; pres. 06/1847; pres. 08/1847; pres. 10/1847, pay stopped for: 2 forage cap-$1.91, 1 pr. pants-$2.28, 3 flannel shirts-$2.70, 1 pr. shoes-$1.22, 6 pr. socks-$1.47; pres. 12/1847, pay stopped for: 1 blanket-$2.22, 2 pr. socks-$.49; pres. 02/1848, pay stopped for: 1 jacket-$2.66, 1 pr. shoes-$1.22; pres. 04/1848; pres. 07/1848, BLW sent to Baltimore, MD

**Reed, John D.**, Pvt., *Recruit Co.*, enl. Mex. War service 08/17/1848 Staunton, VA age 25; pres. 02/1848; absent 04/1848 on recruiting service; pres. 06/1848; BLW sent to Waynesborough, Augusta Co., VA; c. 1880 res. Greenbrier, Summers Co., WV, age 53, occ. Taylor, w. Mary A. (43) House Wifery, dau. Sarah E. (21), dau. Sivena Ann (20), son John W. (18), son Thomas F. (16), son Samuel P. (15), son Joseph F. (13), dau. Mary E. (11), dau. Eliza C. (5), dau. Dazetta (3);[1516] SC #11925, 07/03/1887, wid. Mary Ann, WC #13813, 08/09/1904, both from WV.

**Reed, William**, Pvt., Co. F; enl. Mex. War service 12/11/1846, Portsmouth, VA, age 18; absent 06/1847 sick in camp; pres. 08/1847; pres. 10/1847, pay stopped for: 1 pr. overalls-$2.28, 1 forage cap-$.95$^{1/2}$, 1 pr. shoes-$1.22, 3 pr. socks-$.73$^{1/2}$, 2 pr. drawers-$.71, 2 cotton shirts-$.86, 2 flannel shirts-$1.80; pres. 02/1848, pay stopped for: 1 pr. overalls-$2.28, 1 pr. shoes-$1.22, 1 infantry jacket-$2.66, 1 pr. socks-$.24$^{1/2}$, 2 cotton shirts-$.86; pres. 04/1848; pres. 08/1848, pay stopped for: 1 gun sling-$.18, 2 pr. shoes-$2.32, 1 forage cap-$.83, BLW sent to Portsmouth, VA c/o E.T. Blamire.

**Reed, William H.**, Pvt., LIC, enl. Mex. War service 09/23/1847 Stanton, VA, age 20; joined co. 01/26/1848 from regtl. depot; pres. 04/1848, pay stopped for: 1 pr. overalls-$2.28, 1 blanket-$2.22; pres. 07/1848; BLW sent to Staunton, VA; m. Mary Jane Staunton, 09/06/49, near Waynesboro, Augusta Co., VA;[1517] c. 1850 res. Augusta Co., VA, age 25, occ. Laborer, w. Mary (24);[1518] c. 1860 res. Augusta Co., VA, age 30, w. Mary (30);[1519] d. *"Spring"* 1864, Spotsylvania, VA;[1517] wid. Mary I, WC #2371, 06/22/1887, filed from Fishersville, Augusta Co., VA; William O. Bickle and William E. Skeen gave affidavit; (MSR b. Mossy Creek, Augusta Co., VA, d. 05/26/1901).[1517]

248

## VIRGINIA VOLUNTEERS IN MEXICO

**Reese, Jeremiah R.**, Pvt., Co. H; b. 11/08/1824, Adams Co., Pa.;[1520] enl. Mex. War service 11/27/1847, Berkeley, VA, age 22; pres. 04/1847; pres. 06/1847; pres. 08/1847; pres. 10/1847, pay stopped for: 1 pr. pants-$2.28, 2 cotton shirts-$.86, 2 flannel shirts-$1.80, 2 pr. socks-$.49; pres. 12/1847, pay stopped for: 1 forage cap-$.95$^{1/2}$, 1 jacket-$2.66, 1 pr. pants-$2.28, 1 pr. shoes-$1.22, 1 pr. socks-$.24$^{1/2}$; pres. 02/1848, pay stopped for: 1 cotton shirts-$.43, 2 pr. drawers-$.71; pres. 04/1848; pres. 07/1848, pay stopped for: 1 cartridge box plate-$.10, 1 cartridge box belt plate-$.10, 2 screw drivers-$.50, 2 wipers-$.40, 2 brush & picks-$.24, BLW sent to Martinsburg, VA; c. 1850 a Jeremiah Reece res. Berkeley Co., VA, age 22, occ. Farmer;[1521] m. Roxanna Moorman, 10/04/1854, Wilmington, Clinton, OH;[1520] moved to Union Co., IA in 1856;[1520] In 1887 filed for a pension from Creston, Union Co., IA; phys. desc. age 63 [1887], 6', florid complexion, blue eyes, light gray hair, occ. Miller, died before pension approved;[1520] d. 02/24/1889, *"congestion of the lungs,"* Platte Township, Union Co., IA;[1520] wid. Roxanna, WC #6874, 10/28/1889, filed from Creston, Union Co., IA; (RMR b. 05/18/1822, Highland Co., OH).[1520]

**Reinhart, Michael**, Pvt., Co. B; enl. 12/01/1846, Alexandria, VA, age 39; pres. 06/1847; sick 08/1847; sick 10/1847; pres. 12/1847, pay stopped for: 1 pr. overalls-$2.28, 1 pr. socks-$.24$^{1/2}$, 1 cotton shirt-$.43, 1 blanket-$2.22; pres. 02/1848; pres. 04/1848; pres. 08/1848, BLW sent to Washington City, DC.

**Reisinger, Daniel C.**, Pvt., Co. B; enl. 12/18/1846, Alexandria, VA, age 21; pres. 06/1847; pres. 08/1847; pres. 10/1847, pay stopped for: 1 pr. overalls-$2.28, 2 pr. socks-$.49, 1 pr. shoes-$1.22, 1 blanket-$2.22; pres. 12/1847, pay stopped for: 2 pr. shoes-$2.44, 3 pr. socks-$.73$^{1/2}$; pres. 02/1848, pay stopped for: 1 pr. overalls-$2.28; sick 04/1848; pres. 08/1848, pay stopped for: 1 pick & brush-$.12, 1 ramrod-$.63, BLW sent to Baltimore, MD; m. Rebecca Alice Baldwin, 02/15/1859, Rockingham, Pottawatomie Co., KS;[1522] c. 1870 res. Mt. Pleasant, Atchison Co., KS, age 45, occ. Dry Goods Merchant, w. Rebecca (34), son Lee (8), son Otis (6), son Clay (4), dau. Lydia (1);[1523] d. 12/27/1879, Mt. Pleasant, Atchison Co., KS;[1522] wid. Rebecca Alice, WC #4060, 06/07/1887, filed from Mt. Pleasant, Atchison Co., KS. (RAR b. 01/03/1838 Batavia, OH, d. 02/16/1917 Stroud, OK).

**Reynolds, Samuel**, Pvt., Co. F; enl. Mex. War service 01/05/1847, Portsmouth, VA, age 34; pres. 06/1847; pres. 08/1847; pres. 10/1847, pay stopped for: 1 pr. overalls-$2.28, 3 pr. socks-$.73$^{1/2}$, 2 cotton shirts-$.86, 1 pr. shoes-$1.22, 1 pr. drawers-$.35$^{1/2}$, 1 blanket-$2.22; pres. 02/1848, pay stopped for: 1 pr. shoes-$1.22, 1 pr. drawers-$.35$^{1/2}$; pres. 04/1848; pres. 08/1848, pay stopped for: 1 jacket-$2.37, 1 blanket-$2.25, 1 pr. shoes-$1.16, 1 forage cap-$.83, 1 cartridge box belt & plate-$1.90, 1 bayonet scabbard-$.56, 1 brush & pick-$.12, 1 gun sling-$.18, 1 screw driver-$.25, BLW sent to Portsmouth, VA c/o E.T. Blamire.

**Ricard, Benjamin R.**, Pvt., Co. E; enl. Mex. War service 12/02/1846 Petersburg, VA, age 31; pres. 04/1847; pres. 06/1847; pres. 08/1847; pres. 10/1847, pay stopped for: 1 pr. shoes-$1.22, 2 pr. stockings-$.49, 1 flannel shirts-$.90, 1 cap-$.95$^{1/2}$; pres. 12/1847, pay stopped for: 1 pr. pants-$2.28, 1 pr. shoes-$1.22, 2 pr. drawers-$.71, 1 blanket-$2.22; pres. 02/1848, pay stopped for: 1 jacket-$2.66, 2 cotton shirts-$.86, 1 flannel shirt-$.90; pres. 04/1848, pay stopped for: 1 jacket-$2.37$^{1/2}$; SC #2511, 02/26/1887, from MD

**Richards, George Frederick**,[1524] Pvt., Co. L; b. 08/23/1823, Leesburg, Loudoun Co., VA; son of George F. & Anna Beall (Rose) Saunders Richards; right hand badly crippled by accidental discharge of a shotgun at Jonathan McGarity's house 12/1845 or 1846; enl. Mex. War service 03/01/1847 Fairfax C.H., VA, age 22; pres. 06/1847; pres. 08/1847; pres. 10/1847, to forfeit $3.50 by sentence of garrison court-martial, pay stopped for: 1 Pr. Shoes 1.22, 1 pr. Pants 2.28, 1 F Cap .95; pres. 12/1847, pay stopped for: 2 pr. shoes-$2.44, 2 cotton shirts-$.86, 2 pr. drawers-$.71, 1 pr. socks-$.24$^{1/2}$; pres. 02/1848, pay stopped for: 1 jacket-$2.66, 1 bayonet scabbard belt-$.56; pres. 04/1848; pres. 07/1848, pay stopped for: 1 Wiper .20; BLW sent to G. F. Richards, Washington City, D.C.; m. Catherine Horseman 12/29/1859, Georgetown, D.C.; (CHR d. 09/15/1863) SC #11831, 10/13/1887, from Indian Territory (now OK); since

OFF TO WAR

discharge res. Fairfax Co., VA until 1880, Chariton Co., Mo. 1880-1882, Cherokee Nation, Indian Territory, 1883-1887 w/ Avery Edward Terrett [s-i-l]; c. 1893 res. Brandenburg, Custer Co., Montana, w/daughter Anna Beall (Richards) Terrett *for last ten years*; d. 06/05/1904, near Miles City, Custer Co., MT. bro. of Pvt. John R. Richards.

**Richards, Henry Claggett**, Pvt., Co. L; b. 1828; enl. Mex. War service 03/01/1847 Fairfax C.H., VA, age 19; pres. 06/1847; sick 08/1847; pres. 10/1847; pres. 12/1847, pay stopped for: 1 pr. pants-$2.28, 3 pr. shoes-$3.66, 1 flannel shirt-$.90, 1 blanket-$2.22, 1 pr. socks-$.24$^{1/2}$; pres. 02/1848, pay stopped for: 1 Jacket 2.66; pres. 04/1848, pay stopped for: 1 pr. Shoes 1.16; pres. 07/1848, pay stopped for: 1 pr. Shoes 1.16; BLW sent to Washington City, D.C.; enl. U.S. Navy 1850 at Norfolk, VA served on board Frigate *U.S.S. Raritan* for about 9 mos. Afterwards went on Amazon Exploring Expedition for about 18 mos. He was known in these services as Henry C. Richards. Enl. U.S. Navy 1857 as Henry Clagett. Served as Ordinary Seaman and Seaman on Sloop of War *U.S.S. Saratoga*, transferred to Ironclad *U.S.S. Sangamon*. Discharged 09/1863 from the Naval Hospital, Norfolk, VA Enl. 11/1863 Pvt., Co. C, 43$^{rd}$ Btln., Va. Cav. (Mosby's Rangers). Captured 12/1863 set to Ft. Warren, Boston, Mass. and held until close of war;[1309, 1525] SC #11904, 02/07/1887, filed from 225 N. 12$^{th}$ St., Philadelphia, PA, phys. desc. 5'6", light complexion, brown eyes, gray hair, b. Leesburg, Loudoun Co., VA

**Richards, John Rose**,[1526] Pvt., Co. L; b. 1819, Leesburg, Loudoun Co.; George F. & Anna Beall (Rose) Saunders Richards; m. Mary Eleanor Gantt, 02/10/1844;[1527] enl. Mex. War service 04/01/1847 Fairfax C.H., VA, age 27; pres. 06/1847 *"the name of this man was inadvertently omitted on the last muster roll;"* sick 08/1847; pres. 10/1847, pay stopped for: 1 F Cap .95, 1 pr. Pants 2.28, 1 pr. Socks .10; pres. 12/1847, pay stopped for: 1 cap-$.95$^{1/2}$, 1 pr. shoes-$1.22, 2 cotton shirts-$.86, 1 overcoat-$6.93$^{1/2}$, 1 blanket-$2.22, 1 pr. drawers-$.35$^{1/2}$, 1 pr. socks-$.24$^{1/2}$; pres. 02/1848, pay stopped for: 1 Jacket 2.66, 1 pr. Shoes 1.22, 1 Brush & Pick .12; pres. 04/1848, pay stopped for: 1 Blanket 2.22, 1 Cotton Shirts .44; pres. 07/1848; BLW sent to J.R. Richards, Washington City, D.C.; c. 1850 res. Fairfax Co., VA, age 31, occ. Farmer, w. Mary A. (31), son Dulany M. (5), dau. Priscilla (3);[1528] bro. of Pvt. George F. Richards.

**Richardson, George W.**, Pvt., Co. F; b. 08/22/1824; enl. Mex. War service 01/19/1847 Wilmington, NC, Co. H, 1$^{st}$ NC Vols., trans. 03/01/1848 to Co. F, 1$^{st}$ Va. Vols.; pres. 04/1848; pres. 08/1848, pay stopped for: 1 pr. shoes-$1.16, 3 cotton shirts-$1.32, BLW sent to Portsmouth, VA c/o E.T. Blamire; Civil War service enl. U.S. Navy 2$^{nd}$ Class Fireman USS Fulton, 08/19/1859 to 11/03/1859, U.S.S. Pensacola 01/31/1860 to 05/01/1860, U.S.S. Dacotah 12/31/1861 to 02/25/1862, U.S.S. North Carolina 02/25/1862 to 07/08/1862 when discharged; SC #2277, 02/18/1887, filed from 1155 Crawford St., Portsmouth, Norfolk Co., VA; phys. desc. age 62 [1887], 5'7", light complexion, blue eyes, gray hair, occ. Cooper; Francis L. Benson gave affidavit in pension claim; c. 1894 res. National Military Home, Hampton, Elizabeth City Co., VA; BLW #30459-160-47; d. 08/19/1899, National Military Home, Hampton, VA, bur. Hampton National Cemetery, Hampton, VA

**Richardson, John**, 2$^{nd}$ Cpl., Co. I; enl. Mex. War service 01/20/1847 Richmond, VA, age 35; pres. 02/1847; pres. 04/1847; pres. 06/1847, prom. 4$^{th}$ Cpl. 06/21/1847; pres. 08/1847, prom. 3$^{rd}$ Cpl.; pres. 10/1847, prom. 2$^{nd}$ Cpl., pay stopped for: 2 pr. drawers-$.71, 2 pr. socks-$.49; pres. 12/1847, pay stopped for: 1 cap-$.95$^{1/2}$, 1 pr. pants-$2.28, 1 jacket-$2.66, 1 blanket-$2.22; sick 02/1848; pres. 04/1848; pres. 08/1848, pay stopped for: 1 cartridge box-$1.10, 1 cartridge box plate-$.10, 1 cartridge box belt-$.60, 1 cartridge box belt plate-$.10, 1 pick & brush-$.12, BLW sent to Lynchburg, VA

**Riddle, Alexander**, Pvt., Co. C; enl. Mex. War service 12/30/1846, Bowling Green, VA, age 33; pres. 06/1847; discharged 08/03/1847 Saltillo, Mex. on Surgeon's Certificate of Disability; [c. 1850 an Alexander Riddle res. Ohio Co., VA, age 35, occ. Laborer, w. Ann (37), son William J. (17), son James (10), dau. Mary Ann (5);[1529] Civil War service an Alexander Riddle served as a Pvt., Co. I, 6$^{th}$ W.Va. Inf.]$^{554}$

250

## VIRGINIA VOLUNTEERS IN MEXICO

**Riggins, John J.**, 4th Cpl., Co. I; enl. Mex. War service 08/10/1847 Ft. Monroe, VA, age 20; pres. 02/1848 joined co. 01/26/1848; pres. 04/1848, prom. 4th Cpl. 04/20/1848, pay stopped for: 1 blanket, 2 cotton shirts; pres. 08/1848, BLW sent to Oakey, Mecklenberg Co., VA; c. 1850 res. Mecklenburg Co., VA, age 25, occ. Store Keeper;[1530] Civil War service Pvt., Co. F, 18th Va. Inf., conscripted 02/26/1861, phys. desc. 5'5", hazel eyes, brown hair, dark complexion, captured 07/03/1863 at Gettysburg, Pa., paroled at Fort Delaware Prison 05/05/1864, returned to co. 11/1864, captured 04/06/1865 at Sayler's Creek, VA, sent to Pt. Lookout Prison, paroled there 06/17/1865;[1111] c. 1870 res. Farmville, Prince Edward Co., VA, age 44, occ. Farmer, w. Martha (53), dau. Mary A. (18).[1531]

**Riley, David**, Pvt., *Recruit Co.*, enl. Mex. War service 02/??/1848 Charlestown, VA; pres. 04/1848; pres. 06/1848; BLW sent to Charlestown, Jefferson Co., VA

**Riley, William**, Pvt., Co. G; enl. Mex. War service 12/01/1846 Richmond, VA, age 31; deserted 12/18/1846 Richmond, VA

**Rinor, Jacob**, Pvt., Co. H; enl. Mex. War service 11/23/1846, Berkeley, VA, age 18; pres. 04/1847; pres. 06/1847; pres. 08/1847; pres. 10/1847, pay stopped for: 1 forage cap-$.95$^{1/2}$, 1 pr. pants-$2.28, 2 cotton shirts-$.86, 2 pr. drawers-$.71, 2 pr. shoes-$2.44, 2 pr. socks-$.49; pres. 12/1847, pay stopped for: 1 pr. pants-$2.28, 1 pr. shoes-$1.22; pres. 02/1848, pay stopped for: 2 jackets-$5.32, 2 pr. shoes-$2.44; pres. 04/1848; pres. 07/1848, BLW sent to Martinsburg, VA

**Rittenburg, Alfred**, Pvt., Co. D; enl. Mex. War service 01/05/1847, Petersburg, VA, age 18; pres. 02/1847; pres. 04/1847; pres. but sick 06/1847; discharged 07/29/1847 Buena Vista, Mex. on Surgeon's Certificate of Disability;

**Rivers, James W.**, Pvt., Co. D; enl. Mex. War service 12/22/1846, Petersburg, VA, age 22; pres. 02/1847; pres. 04/1847, resigned as 4th Sgt. 03/25/1847 and reduced to ranks; pres. 06/1847, pay stopped for: 1 cartridge box, belt & plate complete, *"lost through negligence;"* pres. 08/1847, pay stopped for: 1 cap-$.95$^{1/2}$, 2 cotton shirts-$.86, 2 flannel shirts-$1.80; pres. 10/1847, pay stopped for: 1 jacket-$2.66, 1 pr. pants-$2.28, 2 cotton shirts-$.86, 1 pr. drawers-$.35$^{1/2}$, 2 pr. socks-$.49, 1 pr. shoes-$1.22; pres. 12/1847, pay stopped for: 1 pr drawers-$.35$^{1/2}$, 2 pr. socks-$.49, 1 pr. shoes-$1.22, 1 blanket-$2.22, 2 flannel shirts-$1.80; pres. 04/1848, pay stopped for: 1 pr. pants-$2.28, 1 musket & bayonet-$13.00, 1 haversack-$.20$^{3/4}$; pres. 08/1847, BLW sent to Jarratt's Depot, Sussex Co., VA; c. 1850 res. Sussex Co., VA, age 26, occ. Farmer, w. Mary E. (19), son Robert L. (2/12); Civil War service Pvt., Co. G, 61st Va. Inf., enl. 10/23/1861 at Sussex C.H., VA, age 37, prom. 4th Sgt. 02/11/1862, reduced to ranks 05/22/1862, wded. in right hip 07/30/1864 at The Crater (Petersburg, VA), in hosp. 08/1864, furloughed 60 days 09/01/1864 to Sussex Co., paroled 05/18/1865 in Sussex Co.[395]

**Rives, William F.**, 2nd Sgt., Co. D; enl. Mex. War service 12/31/1846, Petersburg, VA, age 23; pres. 02/1847; pres. 04/1847, prom. 4th Sgt. 03/25/1847; pres. 06/1847, prom. 2nd Sgt.; pres. 08/1847, pay stopped for: 1 cap-$.95$^{1/2}$, 2 pr. wool pants-$4.56; discharged 09/16/1847 on account of promotion to Lt., 13th Infantry, U.S. Army.

**Roach, John**, Pvt., Co. C; b. 05/30/1828 Bristol, England;[1532] enl. Mex. War service 12/30/1846, Bowling Green, VA, age 19; pres. 06/1847; pres. 08/1847, pay stopped for: 1 cap-$.95$^{1/2}$, 2 pr. socks-$.49, 2 cotton shirts-$.86, 2 woolen shirts-$1.80; pres. 10/1847, pay stopped for: 1 pr. socks-$.24$^{1/2}$, 4 pr. drawers-$1.06$^{1/2}$, 1 jacket-$2.66, 1 pr. pants-$2.28, 2 cotton shirts-$.86, 1 woolen shirt-$.90; pres. 12/1847, pay stopped for: 1 pr. socks-$.24$^{1/2}$, 1 pr. pants-$2.28, 1 pr. shoes-$1.22, 1 blanket-$2.22; pres. 04/1848, pay stopped for: 1 pr. shoes-$1.22; 1 pr. shoes-$1.50; pres. 08/1848, BLW sent to Philadelphia, Pa.; m. Catherine Loane 07/15/1849, Church of the Redemption, Philadelphia, Pa.;[1533] Civil War service Sgt., Co. F, 118th Pa. Inf. enl. 08/08/1862, phys. desc. age 34, 5'7", dark complexion, blue eyes, brown hair, b. Bristol, Eng., occ. Shoemaker; discharged 06/01/1865 near Washington, D.C.; W0 #813563 & WC #390010. *"We were encamped at Stoneman Switch, near Falmouth, VA The place had been a strip of pines and when cut down left a lot of stumps. On the evening of the 2md of January*

## OFF TO WAR

*1863 I was running down the hill where our quarters was, I was tripped by one of the stumps and fell when 2 or 3 men came on top of me. In this way I sprained my ankle;"*[1534] SC #11923, 03/14/1887, filed from 2212 Hare St., Philadelphia, Pa.; Pvts. Jonathan Good and Thomas T. Mahan gave affidavits in pension claim; d. 09/08/1904 *"tuberculosis, occ. Janitor,"* Philadelphia, Pa., bur. Mt. Moriah Cemetery, Philadelphia, Pa.;[1535] wid. Catherine, WC #14176, 08/09/1905, filed from 812 Judson St., Philadelphia, PA;(CLR b. 02/04/1829, d. 12/04/1909).

**Roadcap, George Robert**, Pvt., LIC; b. Rockingham Co., VA, son of Christian & Elizabeth Roadcap; m. Eliza Jane Graham, 10/03/1842, Rockbridge Co., VA;[1536] enl. Mex. War service 11/06/1846, age 25; joined the co. from the regtl depot 01/26/1848; pres. 04/1848, to forfeit 1 mos. pay by sentence of garrison court-martial, pay stopped for: 1 blanket-$2.22; pres. 07/1848, pay stopped for: 1 musket-$13.00, 1 bayonet scabbard-$.56, 1 cartridge box-$1.10, 1 cartridge box plate-$.10, 1 cartridge box belt & plate-$.70, 1 waist belt & plate-$19, 1 gun sling-$.16, 1 pick & brush-$.12, 1 screw driver-$.07, 1 wiper-$.20; BLW sent to Harrisonburg, VA; c. 1850 res. Rockbridge Co., VA, age 35, occ. None Listed, w. Eliza J., (22), dau. Elizabeth N. (7), son John W. (5), dau. Virginia C. (3);[1537] d. 12/18/1859 of *"typhoid fever, aged 40 years,"* Rockbridge Co., VA[1538]

**Roane, William A.**, Pvt., Co. A; enl. Mex. War service 11/20/1846 Richmond, VA, age 20; pres. 12/1846 - 04/1847; pres. 06/1847; pres. 08/1847; pres. 10/1847, pay stopped for clothing: 2 cotton shirts-$.86, 2 pr. wool overalls-$4.56, 1 cap-$.95$^{1/2}$, 2 pr. stockings-$.49, 1 pr. shoes-$1.22, 1 blanket-$2.22; pres. 12/1847, pay stopped for clothing: 1 pr. shoes-$1.22, 2 pr. drawers-$.71, 2 flannel shirts-$1.80, 1 pr. socks-$.49; pres. 02/1848; pres. 04/1848; BLW sent to Richmond, VA

**Robbins, George T.**, Pvt., Co. H; enl. Mex. War service 01/06/1847, Berkeley, VA, age 20; pres. 04/1847; pres. 06/1847; pres. 08/1847; pres. 10/1847, pay stopped for: 1 forage cap-$.95$^{1/2}$, 2 pr. pants-$4.56, 1 cotton shirt-$.43, 2 pr. drawers-$.71, 2 pr. shoes-$2.44, 3 pr. socks-$.73$^{1/2}$, 1 jacket-$2.66; pres. 12/1847, pay stopped for: 1 pr. pants-$2.28, 2 pr. drawers-$.71, 2 flannel shirts-$1.80, 3 pr. socks-$.73$^{1/2}$, 1 blanket-$2.22; pres. 02/1848, pay stopped for: 1 jacket-$2.66, 2 pr. shoes-$2.44, 2 pr. socks-$.49; pres. 04/1848; pres. 07/1848, pay stopped for: 1 waist belt plate-$.10, BLW sent to Philadelphia, Pa.

**Robertson, David S.**, Pvt., Co. M; b. 09/11/1811, Lunenburg Co., VA;[1539] enl. U.S. Navy date/place unknown, Master of Arms, on U.S.S. Constitution;[17] *"...anchored in the harbor of Mazatlan, on the Pacific Ocean coast of Mexico when the war commenced and although bound home Capt. Percival[18] commanding, decided to remain and fight the enemy and did so till he received orders from the Commodore to sail...;"*[1540] discharged 10/26/1846, Boston, MA; enl. Mex. War service 11/18/1847, Norfolk, VA, age 35; pres. 11/1847; pres. 12/1847; pres. 02/1848; pres. 04/1848; pres. 08/1848, pay stopped for: 1 bayonet scabbard-$.56, 1 pick & brush-$.12, 1 screw driver-$.07, 1 wiper-$.20; BLW sent to Norfolk, VA; c. 1850 res. Portsmouth, Norfolk Co., VA, age 27, occ. Clerk, w. Martha A. (22);[1541] c. 1860 res. Portsmouth, Norfolk Co., VA, age 46, occ. Clerk, w. Martha A. (41);[1542] Civil War service Sgt., Co. F, 16$^{th}$ Pa. Cav.;[554] SC #3848, 03/29/1887, filed from U.S. Naval Asylum, Philadelphia, PA; since discharge res. at my birth place and at the U.S. Naval Asylum; James H. Bishop gave affidavit in pension claim.

---

[17] The frigate U.S.S. Constitution is the oldest commissioned vessel in the U.S. Navy. First launched in 1797 she has served numerous wars and circumnavigated the globe. Her mission today is one of education as a representative of the Navy's great days of fighting sail, and symbol of the courage and patriotic service of generations of Americans at sea. She is moored in Boston Harbor, Massachusetts.

[18] Captain John "Mad Jack" Percival (1779-1862). An early hero of the U.S. Navy. Circumnavigated the world aboard the U.S.S. Constitution 1844-1846 arriving on the coast of Mexico just as the war started.

VIRGINIA VOLUNTEERS IN MEXICO

**Robertson, James Berkeley**, Pvt., Co. E; enl. Mex. War service 11/28/1846 Petersburg, VA, age 23; absent 04/1847 sick in Matamoros, Mex. since 03/29/1847; discharged Camargo, Mex. date unknown; d. 05/20/1847, age 23, at Camargo, Mexico.[1543]

**Robertson, William C.**, Pvt., LIC; enl. Mex. War service 12/07/1846 Staunton, VA, age 44; pres. 08/1847; pres. 10/1847, pay stopped for: 1 forage cap-$.95$^{1/2}$, 1 wool jacket-$2.66, 1 pr. overalls-$2.28, 2 pr. socks-$.49, 1 cotton shirts-$.43; pres. 12/1847; pres. 04/1848, pay stopped for: 1 cotton shirt-$.43, 1 pr. shoes-$1.22; pres. 07/1848; BLW sent to Staunton, VA

**Robey, William**, Pvt., Co. L; b. 1825; enl. Mex. War service 03/16/1847 Alexandria, VA, age 22; pres. 06/1847; pres. 08/1847; pres. 10/1847; pres. 12/1847, pay stopped for: 1 pr. pants-$2.28, 1 cap-$.95$^{1/2}$, 1 pr. shoes-$1.22, 2 flannel shirts-$1.80, 4 cotton shirts-$1.72, 1 blanket-$2.22, 1 pr. socks-$.24$^{1/2}$; pres. 02/1848, pay stopped for: 1 Jacket 2.66, 1 pr. Shoes 1.22; pres. 04/1848, pay stopped for: 1 pr. Shoes 1.16, 3 Cotton Shirts 1.32; pres. 07/1848; BLW sent to Alexandria, VA

**Robinson, James Arthur**, Pvt., Co. E; b. c. 1822 Fulani Co., VA;[1544] m. Ann M. Vaden 01/29/1846, Petersburg, VA;[1544] enl. Mex. War service 12/01/1846 Petersburg, VA, age 24, occ. Saloon Keeper at enlistment;[1544] absent 04/1847 sick Camargo, Mex. since 04/30/1847; pres. 06/1847; pres. 08/1847; pres. 10/1847, pay stopped for: 1 pr. overalls-$2.28, 2 pr. shoes-$2.44, 3 pr. stockings-$.73$^{1/2}$, 2 cotton shirts-$.86, 1 pr. drawers-$.35$^{1/2}$; pres. 12/1847, pay stopped for: 1 pr. pants-$2.28, 1 pr. shoes-$1.22, 2 flannel shirts-$1.80, 1 blanket-$2.22; pres. 02/1848, pay stopped for: 1 jacket-$2.66; pres. 04/1848; c. 1850 res. Chesterfield Co., VA, age 21, occ. Laborer, w. Ann (20);[1545] c. 1860 res. Manchester, Chesterfield Co., VA, age 38, occ. None Listed, w. Ann M. (33), dau. Anetta E. (9);[1546] c. 1870 res. Chester, Chesterfield Co., VA, age 47, occ. Works in a Cotton Factory, w. Ann M. (43);[1547] d. 07/02/1886 Manchester, Chesterfield Co., VA;[1544] wid. Ann M., WC #1035, 03/03/1887, filed from Manchester, Chesterfield Co., VA; (AMR d. 1910).[1544]

**Robinson, William Murray**, Capt., Co. D; b. 1807, son of Dr. Thomas & Anne (Murray) Robinson; m. Sarah Ann Mills 05/03/1832, Richmond, VA;[1548] was a friend of Poet, Edgar Allan Poe, who is alleged to have regarded Robinson as among the few good conversationalists he had known;[1549] enl. Mex. War service 12/10/1846, Petersburg, VA; pres. 02/1847; pres. 04/1847; pres. 06/1847; absent sick 08/1847; absent sick 10/1847; pres. 12/1847, Aid-de-Camp to Col. Hamtramck; pres. 04/1848, Aide-de-Camp to Col. Hamtramck; pres. 08/1848; *"When Capt. Robinson was mustered out of the Army he came directly to Richmond, VA and lived with me as my husband up to 1861. He then went to New York and never returned to Richmond, VA but he was always looked upon as my husband;"*[1548] divorced 05/15/1867, Richmond, VA; d. 02/09/1878, New York City; wid. Sarah A., WC #2498, 07/05/1887, filed from 104 N. 7$^{th}$ St., Richmond, VA; Children listed Andrew R. Robinson, Rev. Thomas V. Robinson; Pvt. James M. Donnan gave affidavit in claim; Widow's Claim rejected *"not the legal wife of the soldier at the time of his death;"*[1548] (SAR b. 10/21/1810 Manchester, Chesterfield Co.); brother of Capt. Powhatan Robinson C.S. Engineers.

**Rodecker, William**, Pvt., Co. A; enl. 12/06/1846 Richmond, VA, age 28; pres. until sick 04/1847 in Hosp. at Matamoros sent there from Camargo, Mex. 04/02/1847; sick in quarters 06/1847; pres. 08/1847; deserted 10/06/1847 at Buena Vista, Mex.; c. 1850, res. Marshall Co., VA, age 27, occ. farmer, b. Pa., w. Hannah J. (23);[1550] Civil War service enl. as a Pvt., Co. G, 17$^{th}$ W.Va. Inf., 02/18/1865, age 42, discharged 06/03/1865 for disability.[1551]

**Rodgers, Nathaniel G.**, 4$^{th}$ Sgt., Co. F; enl. Mex. War service 11/23/1846, Portsmouth, VA, age 28; d. 04/20/1847, Camargo, Mex.

**Rollberg, Henry G.**, (aka. **Rollberg, Henrich Gottlieb**), Co. A; b. 06/26/1829 Germany, son of Johann Gottlob & Catherine (Cramer) Rollberg; enl. Mex. War service 12/01/1846 Richmond, VA, age 20; pres. 12/1846 - 04/1847; sick in quarters 06/1847; pres. 08/1847; pres. 10/1847, pay stopped for clothing: 1 cap-$.95$^{1/2}$, 2 flannel shirts-$1.80, 1 pr. wool overalls-$2.28, 1 pr. shoes-$1.22; sick 02/1848, pay stopped for: 1 blanket-$2.22, 1 jacket-$2.66; pres. 04/1848,

OFF TO WAR

pay stopped for: 1 wool jacket; BLW sent to Richmond, VA; m. Friderika Carolina Louisa Bergman 11/27/1870, St. George's Church, Tanusbruck, Germany; SC #20612, 03/25/1893, filed from Tanusbruck, Bad Lagensalza, Germany; Since discharge res. Richmond, VA, Portland, OR, Colusa Co., CA *1849 – 04/05/1869*, Tanusbruck, Bad Lagensalza Germany *06/24/1869*; children Henrich Wilhelm b. 05/08/1873, Dorothea Louise Selma b. 04/30/1876; d.10/16/1914. (FCLR b. 09/30/1845, d. unknown).

**Ronald, Charles Augustus**, Pvt., *Preston's Co.*; b. 01/18/1825, Roanoke, Roanoke Co., VA, son of William G. & Mary (Crow) Ronald;[1552, 54] pres. 04/1847; enl. Mex. War service 01/06/1847 Montgomery Co., VA, age 21; pres. 04/1847; pres. 06/1847; absent 08/1847 on detached service in QM Dept. since 07/28/1847; absent 10/1847, on detached service as Hospital Steward, pay stopped for: 1 pr. overalls-$.2.28; absent 12/1847, on detached service as Regimental Steward since 11/24/1847, pay stopped for: 1 pr. drawers-$.35$^{1/2}$; absent 02/1848 on detached service as Regimental Hospital Steward Parras, Mex. since 02/25/1848; pres. 04/1848 as Hosp. Steward in Parras Battalion; pres. 07/1848, pay stopped for: 1 brush & pick-$.12, 1 screw driver-$.07, 1 wiper-$.13; BLW sent to Blacksburg, VA; c. 1850 res. Blacksburg, Montgomery Co., VA, age 23, occ. None Listed;[1553] elected 1853 Commonwealth's Attorney, Montgomery Co., VA elected 1855 Virginia House of Delegates; m. Sally A. McCullough, 06/01/1859, near Abingdon, Washington Co., VA;[1552] c. 1860 res. Blacksburg, VA, occ. Lawyer, w. Sally A. (23);[1554] Civil War service enl. as Capt., Co. E, 4$^{th}$ Va. Inf.,04/18/1861, prom. Lt. Col. 02/20/1862, prom. Col. 04/23/1862, wded. 10/16/1862 at Kearneysville, VA in left thigh, resigned 09/11/1863 due to wd.;[54] elected 1874 Virginia House of Delegates; SC #15663, 04/28/1888, filed from Christiansburg, Montgomery Co., VA; phys. desc. at enl. age 21, 6'1", blue eyes, light brown hair, fair complexion, since discharge, res. Blacksburg, VA, age 46 yrs., Roanoke , VA 6 yrs.;[1552] Michael Kipps and Charles Jackson gave affidavits in pension claim; d. 07/01/1898 in Roanoke, VA, bur. Blacksburg, VA;[1555, 54] wid. Sallie A., WC #11442, 08/22/1898, filed from 111 7$^{th}$ Ave., Roanoke, Roanoke Co., VA; (SMR b. 04/07/1836, d. 09/08/1906).[1555]

**Roop, Byrd**, Pvt., *Preston's Co.*; b. 07/28/1821, near Childress Store, Montgomery Co., VA;[1556] enl. Mex. War service 12/02/1846 Montgomery Co., VA, age 19; pres. 04/1847; pres. 06/1847; pres. 08/1847; pres. 10/1847, pay stopped for: 1 jacket-$2.66, 1 pr. overalls-$2.28, 1 pr. shoes-$1.22, 3 pr. socks-$.73$^{1/2}$, 2 flannel shirts-$1.80, 1 cotton shirt-$.43, 1 cap-$.95$^{1/2}$; pres. 12/1847, pay stopped for: 1 pr. overalls-$2.28, 2 pr. shoes-$2.44, 1 pr. socks-$.24$^{1/2}$, 1 pr. drawers-$.35$^{1/2}$, 1 blanket-$2.22; pres. 02/1848; pres. 04/1848; pres. 07/1848, pay stopped for: 1 pr. shoes-$1.16, 1 jacket-$2.37, 1 cartridge box belt plate-$.10, 1 brush & pick-$.12, 1 gun sling-$.18, 1 screw driver-$.07; BLW sent to Christiansburg, VA c/o Fleming Gardner; m. his 1$^{st}$ cousin Rachel Roop, 04/17/1849, Montgomery Co., VA;[1557] c. 1850 res. Montgomery Co., VA, age 23, occ. None Listed, w. Rachel (30);[1558] c. 1860 res. Childress Store, Montgomery Co., VA, age 32, occ. Laborer, w. Rachel (36), son James P. (10), dau. Nancy (7), dau. Harriet (6), dau. Jane (5), son William (3);[1559] SC #14396, 05/16/1887, filed from Snowville, Pulaski Co., VA; phys. desc. at enl. age 27, 5'11", blue eyes, black hair, light complexion, occ. Farmer, since discharge res. Montgomery Co., VA 26 yrs. and Pulaski Co., VA 22 yrs.;[1556] d. 01/12/1897, Dublin, Pulaski Co., VA, bur. Christiansburg, VA;[1560] wid. Rachel, WC #10771, 04/10/1897, filed from Newbern, Pulaski Co., VA; (RR b. 04/09/1821, near Childress' Store, Montgomery Co., VA, d. 10/1909).[1560]

**Roop, Crockett**, Pvt., *Preston's Co.*; enl. Mex. War service 12/06/1846 Montgomery Co., VA, age 24; absent 04/1847 left sick at Ft. Monroe, VA since 02/27/1847; absent 06/1847 sick at Ft. Monroe, VA; pres. 08/1847; discharged 03/25/1847 at Ft. Monroe, VA; a Crockett Roop m. Paratha McAlexander, 03/29/1853, Patrick Co., VA;[1561] c. 1860 res. Christiansburg, Montgomery Co., VA, age 37, occ. Farmer, w. Paratha (24), son Washington (6), dau. Isabella (4), dau. Laura A. (2), son Reed C.P. (1);[1562] Paratha Roop d. 01/31/1887, Albany, Shackleford Co., Tex., bur. Albany Cem., Albany, Tex.

## VIRGINIA VOLUNTEERS IN MEXICO

**Rose, Uriah Jackson**, Pvt., *Preston's Co.*; b. c. 1828 son of Uriah and Susanna (Taylor) Rose; enl. Mex. War service 01/09/1847 Bedford Co., VA, age 18; pres. 04/1847; sick 06/1847; pres. 08/1847; pres. 10/1847, pay stopped for: 1 jacket-$2.66, 1 pr. overalls-$2.28, 1 pr. shoes-$1.22, 4 pr. socks-$.98, 2 flannel shirts-$1.80; pres. 12/1847, pay stopped for: 1 pr. overalls-$2.28, 1 pr. shoes-$1.22, 1 cap-$.95$^{1/2}$, 1 blanket-$2.22; sick 02/1848; discharged 03/15/1848 on Surgeon's Certificate of Disability; m. Sarah A. Carter, 12/09/1850;[1563] c. 1860 res. Peaks of Otter, Bedford Co., VA, age 32, occ. Sawyer, w. Sarah Ann (28), son James P. (9), dau. Nancy L. (6), dau. Susan F. (4), son William L. (4/12);[1564] SC #12551, 03/29/1887, from VA; Civil War service Pvt., Co. A, 4$^{th}$ Va. Inf.03/10/1862, wded. severely 07/03/1863 at Gettysburg, Pa., in arm; captured 05/23/1864 at North Anna River, VA, sent to Elmira, NY, paroled 06/30/1865, phys. Desc. 5'7", gray eyes, dark hair, florid complexion;[54] c. 1870 res. Wytheville, Wythe Co., VA, age 41, occ. Sawyer, w. Sarah A. (37), son James P. (19), dau. Nancy J. (16), dau. Susan (14), son William F. (12), son Uriah J. (8), son Robert L. (4),son George W. (2/12);[1565] d. 01/18/1926, Thaxton, VA

**Rowan, John William**, Capt., Co. K; b. 08/03/1810; enl. Mex. War service Jefferson Co., VA 12/01/1846; pres. 06/1847; Court-martialed 07/10/1847, *Charge #1: Disobedience of Orders; Specification: In this that Captain John W. Rowan, Co. K, Virginia Regiment, Virginia Volunteers, on the 4$^{th}$ day of July at Camp Buena Vista, Mexico, absent himself from camp and visit Saltillo without leave, and continue so absent until after tatto. Charge #2: Neglect of Duty; Specification: In this that the said Captain John W. Rowan, having contrary to orders, absented himself from camp and visited Saltillo without leave on the 4$^{th}$ of July 1847 at Camp at Buena Vista, Mexico, thereby neglected to attend to the retreat roll-call and tatto and other important duties of his company. To which charges and specifications the accused pleaded Not Guilty. Sergeant John W. Gallaher, Co. K, Virginia Regiment, a witness for the prosecution, being duly sworn, says: The accused was absent from Camp at the time and place specified. That is I did not see him on that afternoon nor until next morning at breakfast. I do not know where he was during that time. Question by the Accused: Was there not a commissioned officer present at both retreat and tatto roll calls? Answer: There was. There might have been two. Question: Has it been the custom in the Regiment for all company officers to be present at all the roll calls? Answer: It has not been the practice in our battalion nor in our company. Question: Have any orders to that effect been issued? Answer: Not that I have heard of. Question: Did you ever know the accused to be negligent in the discharge of his duties? Answer: Never, and I have been with the company ever since it was raised. Colonel J.F. Hamtramck, Virginia Regiment of Volunteers, a witness for the prosecution, being duly sworn, says: I went to the accused's company at the time and place specified, called at the officers tents and enquired where they were, as they were all absent from their tents. The reply was that Captain Rowan had gone to town. Having been a good deal importuned during the day, I had retired for the purpose of avoiding giving permission to officers to be absent and to men to buy liquor. My orderly told those who inquired for me that I was alseep. Among those so enquiring, I recognized the voice of the accused. The accused is a good officer and has always tried to do his duty, and I have no doubt had not examined the question in all its bearings when he went off without leave. I arrested the accused because he is the only officer who has committed the like offence, and thought it important to take notice of the first case. I saw him the next morning and asked him where he had been the evening previous. He replied that he had been to town. He had not permission from me. Question by the accused: Did you on the day specified, give permission to any officers to go to town? Answer: I do not think that I did, though, I may have done so. Lt. John Avis, Virginia Regiment, a witness for the defense, was duly sworn: Question by the accused: Did you hear the order given by Colonel Hamtramck on the day specified, and what was it? Answer: Yes. I understood him to state by order of General Wool, That there would be no further drilling that day and that the officers and soldiers would be allowed to enjoy themselves in a rational*

OFF TO WAR

manner. *Question by the Accused: At the time you missed the accused in camp, was everything quiet in the company? Answer: No, for I did not miss him until a row occurred in the company.* After deliberation the accused found Guilty of all charges and specifications and sentenced to be privately reprimanded. pres. 08/1847; Court-martialed 09/20/1847 (record not found); pres. 10/1847; pres. 12/1847; pres. 04/1848; pres. 07/1848; m. Ellen N. Henson, date unknown;[1566] c. 1850 res. Charles Town, Jefferson Co., VA, age 39, occ. Stonemason, w. Ellen (29), dau. Ann (11), son John D. (6), dau. Sarah (3), son William W. (8/12);[1567] (wife Ellen N. d. 03/08/1855, Charlestown, VA);[1566] c. 1860 res. Charles Town, Jefferson Co., VA, age 50, occ. Stonemason, w. Ann C. (40), son John (15), dau. Sarah (13), son William (11);[1568] Civil War service Capt., Co. A, $2^{nd}$ Va. Inf., phys. desc. 5'10", dark complexion, blue eyes, black hair, A.F. & A.M., wded. (ankle) 07/21/1861 First Manassas, absent at home through 04/26/1862, pres. 02/1863, retired to Invalid Corps 04/26/1864 because of wound, Provost Marshall, Staunton, VA; d. 12/24/1872, bur. Edge Hill Cemetery, Charles Town, WV.[387]

**Rucks, Stephen C.**, Pvt., Co. A; enl. Mex. War service 12/01/1846 Richmond, VA, age 21; pres. until sick 04/1847 - 06/1847, in hosp. at Matamoros sent there from Camargo, Mex.; sick 08/1847; discharged 10/16/1847 at Buena Vista, Mex. on Surgeon's Certificate; c. Civil War service enl. Pvt., H, $28^{th}$ Btln. Va. Inf. 05/20/1862 at Summit Sta., Caroline Co., VA, co. reorganized as $3^{rd}$ Co. I, $59^{th}$ Va. Inf. pres. throughout war, lost bayonet 12/1863, under arrest 08/31/1864, detached 10/1864 on Color Guard, paroled 04/13/1865 Lynchburg, VA[267]

**Russell, Ellerson**, Pvt., Co. I; enl. Mex. War service 02/05/1847 Richmond, VA, age 30; pres. 02/1847; pres. 04/1847; pres. 06/1847, reduced to ranks from $1^{st}$ Cpl. 06/21/1847; pres. 08/1847; pres. 10/1847, pay stopped for: 2 pr. drawers-$.71, 2 cotton shirts-$.86, 1 pr. shoes-$1.22, 1 cap- $.95$^{1/2}$; pres. 12/1847, pay stopped for: 1 pr. pants-$2.28, 1 jacket-$2.66, 1 blanket-$2.22, 2 flannel shirts-$1.80; pres. 02/1848; pres. 04/1848; pres. 08/1848, pay stopped for: 1 wiper-$.20, BLW sent to Richmond, VA; c. 1850 res. Richmond, Henrico Co., VA, age 34, occ. Shoemaker, w. Elizabeth (28), son Wiley (2).[1569]

**Saddler, Frederick Augustus**, Co. C; enl. Mex. War service 11/06/1847, Fayette C.H., age 22; pres. 04/1848, joined company 01/27/1848 from Regtl. Depot, pay stopped for: 1 pr. shoes-$1.50; pres. 08/1848, m. c. 1849, Harriett Parker; BLW sent to Washington, DC; SC #16534, 06/20/1888, filed from Stewartsville, Contra Costa Co., CA; Since discharge *"came to California in 1849 in Benicid & Stewartsville;"*[1570] d. 10/23/1898, Black Diamond, WA.

**Salmon, Charles G.**, Pvt., Co. I; enl. Mex. War service 12/01/1846 Richmond, VA, age 19; pres. 02/1847; pres. 04/1847; pres. 06/1847; d. 08/15/1847 Saltillo, Mex.

**Sampson, William**, Pvt., Co. C; enl. Mex. War service 12/31/1846, Richmond, VA, age 36; d. 06/1847, Matamoros, Mex.

**Sanders, Robert H.**, Pvt., *Recruit Co.*, enl. Mex. War service 10/16/1847 Alexandria, VA, age 18; pres. 02/1848; pres. 04/1848; pres. 06/1848; BLW sent to Alexandria, VA; SA #18717, wid. Priscilla C., WA #20576, 07/23/1920, both from MD, BLW #14850-160-47; d. 07/13/1907, Doncaster, MD

**Sandifer, James**, Pvt., Co. G; enl. Mex. War service 08/29/1847, Petersburg, VA, age 18; pres. 02/1848, joined co. 01/25/1848 from regtl. depot, pay stopped for: 1 pr. pants-$2.28; pres. 04/1848, pay stopped for: 1 jacket-$2.66, 1 blanket-$2.22, 1 pr. shoes-$1.22; pres. 08/1848, pay stopped for: 1 gun sling-$.16; BLW sent to Petersburg, VA

**Sandidge, Joseph E.**, $1^{st}$ Sgt., Co. I; enl. Mex. War service 02/25/1847 Richmond, VA, age 27; pres. 02/1847; pres. 04/1847; discharged 06/20/1847 for disability at Monterey, Mex.; c. 1860 res. Fredericks Hall, Louisa Co., VA, age 40, occ. Clerk;[1571] Civil War service $2^{nd}$ Lt., Co. G, $23^{rd}$ Va. Inf., enl. as Pvt. 04/24/1861 at Fredericks Hall for 1 yr., appointed $2^{nd}$ Lt. 06/01/1861, resigned 06/16/1861, NFR;[107] d. 1862.[1572]

VIRGINIA VOLUNTEERS IN MEXICO

Satterfield, Thomas Robinson, Pvt., Co. K; b. 04/11/1828, Berkeley Co., VA, son of Thomas Jefferson & Lydia (Robinson) Satterfield; enl. Mex. War service Jefferson Co., VA 12/20/1846, age 19; deserted 02/15/1847 at Ft.

Monroe, VA; attended Cassnova Seminary, Huntington, VA; m/1 c. 1850 Susanna Manspeeker; ordained a Methodist Minister 1854; m/2 c. 1855 Sarah Matilda Tate, of Clearfield, Pa.; Civil War service Chaplain, 95th Ill. Inf. 1862 to 1864; retired from the Ministry 1895; d. 08/25/1909, Hollywood, CA, bur. Sect. 6, Lot 265, Hollywood Memorial Park, Hollywood, CA.[1573, 1574]

Photo credit: First United Methodist Church, DeKalb, IL

Saunders, Stephen P., *Preston's Co.*; *Not on Muster Rolls;* SA #21802, 06/20/1889, from WV; Civil War service Pvt., 57th Va. Inf. enl. 04/17/1862 at Norfolk, VA, age 35, b. Bedford Co., VA, phys. desc. 5'6", dark complexion, light hair, grey eyes, discharged 05/25/1862.[1575]

Savage, Paul L., Pvt., Co. M; b. 07/29/1824, near Variety Mills, Nelson Co., VA;[1576] enl. Mex. War service 07/05/1847, Lynchburg, VA, age 22; pres. 09/1847; pres. 11/1847; pres. 12/1847; pres. 02/1848; sick 04/1848; pres. 08/1848, pay stopped for: 1 wormer-$.20; BLW sent to Lynchburg, VA; Civil War service Pvt., Co. B, 51st Va. Inf. enl. 07/01/1861 at Lovingston, VA, b. Nelson Co., age 37, phys. desc. 6'0", light complexion, dark hair, blue eyes, discharged 03/28/1862 due to a tumor in the abdomen.[536] SC #3514, 03/17/1887, filed from Arrington, Nelson Co., VA; *"not married;"*[1576] d. 05/09/1896.[1576]

Schwitzer, Joseph Stephen, Pvt., Co. G; b. 12/09/1814, Karlsruhe, Germany;[1577] enl. Mex. War service 11/28/1846 Richmond, VA, age 31; phys. desc. 5'9", dark complexion, black curly hair, grey eyes, occ. Butcher;[1577] pres. 06/1847; pres. 08/1847; pres. 10/1847, pay stopped for: 1 blanket-$2.22, 3 pr. overalls-$6.84, 2 flannel shirts-$1.80, 2 pr. drawers-$.71, 1 pr. shoes-$1.22, 4 pr. socks-$.98, 1 forage cap-$.95$^{1/2}$; pres. 12/1847, pay stopped for: 1 pr. shoes-$1.22; pres. 02/1848, pay stopped for: 1 waist belt plate-$.10; pres. 04/1848, pay stopped for: 1 jacket-$2.66; pres. 08/1848, pay stopped for: 1 pr. shoes-$1.16; BLW sent to Norfolk, VA; m. Mary A. Becker, 10/29/1854, Weston, Mo.; c. 1870 res. Liberty, Clay Co., Mo., age 54, occ.

257

OFF TO WAR

Saloon Keeper, w. Anna (19) b. Pa., dau. Lydia (13), dau. Emily (11), dau. Minnie (9), son John (2);[1578] d. 05/25/1876, Liberty, Clay Co., Mo.; *"Joseph Switzer, aged about 60, an old and kind-hearted and inoffensive man;"*[1579] wid. Mary A., WC #8337, 07/09/1891, filed from Liberty, Clay Co., MO; (MAB b. 09/29/1829, Karlsruhe, Germany, m/1 Valentine Becker, who died 1854 at St. Paul MN, *"Cholera,"* two children w/ VB: Joseph Becker, Annie Becker Costello; d. 08/19/1907); Will lists heirs Joseph Becker, Charles Schweitzer, Annie Becker Costello, John Schweitzer, Mollie Schweitzer Kinney, Minnie Schweitzer Patrick, Thomas A. Brown, John "Jack" Brown, Mary A. Brown, children of deceased daughter Lettie Schweitzer Brown, Flora Becker, and Bessie Becker grandchildren.[1580]

**Scott, James A.**, 1$^{st}$ Sgt., Co. I; 01/10/1823;[1581] enl. Mex. War service 08/20/1847 Ft. Monroe, VA, age 24; pres. 02/1848, prom. 1$^{st}$ Sgt. 01/26/1848, pay stopped for: 1 jacket-$2.66; pres. 04/1848, pay stopped for: 1 cap, 1 blanket; pres. 08/1848, BLW sent to Washington, D.C.; m/1 Pheobe Scott date/place unknown, (PS d. 04/04/1880, Butler, Harrison Co., Mo.);[1581] m/2 Julia Ann Bell, 08/19/1880, Harrison Co., Mo.;[1581] SC #2701, filed Bellwood, Butler Co., NE; *"SCOTT--August 13, of dropsy, after an illness of one year, James A. Scott. Mr. Scott came here from Butler county. Although he was seventy years old, lame, and very hard of hearing, he seemed to enjoy life well until he was stricken with the disease which closed his earthly career. He leaves a widow and several grown-up children, who will cherish the memory of a loving husband and indulgent father. It had been almost a half century since he served his country as a soldier in the war with Mexico, but his patriotism grew with the passing years, and the flag was to him the emblem of our national liberty and prosperity. "Brave, tender and true" may fitly be written on the monument under which shall rest his mortal remains. The body was embalmed and will be taken today to Missouri for burial;"*[1582] wid. Julia A., WC #11964, 11/10/1897, filed from Columbus, Platte Co. NE; (JAS b. 01/27/1822, Raytown, Union Co., TN, m/1 John A. Bell who d. c. 1852 near Sacramento, CA, d. 04/10/1904).[1581]

**Scott, John K.**, Pvt., Co. A; son of Capt. Robert G. & Annie T. Scott; enl. Mex. War service 11/18/1846 Richmond, VA, age 24; pres. 12/1846 - 04/1847, but a letter to Col Hamtramck from R. Jones, Adjutant General of Virginia suggests he was AWOL when the regiment sailed for Mexico, *"...Under the peculiar circumstances of the case, the subject is referred to you, and it may be that in view of the fact that the company to which this soldier belongs has already sailed for Mexico, and on account of his unsettled state of mind and irregular habits, the interests of the public service would be promoted be his discharge, which you are hereby authorized to grant upon his furnishing a substitute;"*[1583] several days latter Col. Hamtramck wrote to Capt. Scott, *"Sir, orders have been received from the Adjutant General of U.S.A. by todays mail, authorizing the discharge of your son John K. Scott, upon his furnishing a substitute, and I deem it proper to give you the information with the view of enabling you to engage the substitute and sending him to his post, before the troops embark. Before the reception of the order I had released your son from confinement and attached him to Capt. Rowan's company for drill &c. until he reached Point Isabel, when he would be returned to Capt. Scott's company to which he belongs;"*[1584] pres. 06/1847; pres. 08/1847; pres. 10/1847, pay stopped for clothing: 2 cotton shirts-$.86, 2 pr. wool overalls-$4.56, 1 cap-$.95$^{1/2}$, 3 pr. stockings-$.73$^{1/2}$, 1 wool jacket-$2.66, 2 flannel shirts-$1.80, 1 pr. shoes-$1.22, 1 great coat-$6.93$^{1/2}$; sick 12/1847, pay stopped for clothing: 1 pr. drawers-$.35$^{1/2}$, 1 pr. socks-$.24$^{1/2}$, 1 pr. shoes-$1.22, 1 cap-$.95$^{1/2}$, 2 flannel shirts-$1.80; pres. 02/1848, pay stopped for: 1 pick & brush-$.12; pres. 04/1848, pay stopped for: 1 wool jacket; BLW sent to Richmond, VA

**Scott, Joseph P.**, Pvt., Co. G; enl. Mex. War service 11/28/1846 Richmond, VA, age 20; pres. 06/1847; pres. 08/1847; in confinement 10/1847, pay stopped for: 1 pr. overalls-$2.28, 1 cotton shirt-$.43, 2 pr. socks-$.49, 1 forage cap-$.95$^{1/2}$; pres. 12/1847, pay stopped for: 2 pr. shoes-$2.44, 1 cotton shirt-$.43, 2 flannel shirts-$1.80, 1 pr. drawers-$.35$^{1/2}$, 1 blanket-$2.22, 1 pr. pants-$2.28, 1 overcoat-$6.93$^{1/2}$, 1 jacket-$2.66; sick 02/1848; pres. 04/1848; pres.

VIRGINIA VOLUNTEERS IN MEXICO

08/1848, pay stopped for: 1 gun sling-$.16; BLW sent to Richmond, VA; c. 1850 res. Richmond, Henrico Co., VA, age 24, occ. Confectioner.[1585]

**Scott, Robert Gourmain, Jr.**, Capt., Co. A; b. 01/04/1820, son of Robert G. Scott; grad. William & Mary 1839;[1586] enl. Mex. War service 11/18/1846 Richmond, VA, age 27; phys. desc. 6', grey or blue eyes, dark hair, fair complexion, occ. Lawyer;[1587] pres. 12/1846 - 04/1847; pres. 06/1847 under arrest; Court-martialed 07/06/1847, Buena Vista, Mexico, *Charge #1: Gross Neglect and Violation of Duty; Specification: In this that the said Captain R.G. Scott, of the 1$^{st}$ Regiment of Virginia Volunteers, in the service of the United States, having been ordered by his commanding officer Major J. A. Early, 1$^{st}$ Regiment Virginia Volunteers, to occupy on the 17$^{th}$ day of May 1847 the fort near Monterey known as the Black Fort, with his company of Virginia Volunteers and to take the necessary steps for the protection of the public property in the said fort and for the preservation of good order, and having marched into said fort with his company on the said 17$^{th}$ day of May 1847, did, without taking the necessary steps to carry into effect the instructions given to him, in a very short time after his arrival at the said fort and on the said 17$^{th}$ day of May 1847 leave the said fort and the company under his command in charge of a subaltern of his company and did go into the town of Monterey without having any business or sufficient cause to do so, and did remain absent from the said fort until a late hour of the night of the said 17$^{th}$ day of May 1847. Charge #2: Conduct Prejudicial to Good Order and Military Discipline; Specification#1: In this that the said Captain R. G. Scott, being in command of the fort near Monterey, Mexico, known as the Black Fort, and having absented himself from the said fort on the 17$^{th}$ day of May 1847, did, at or about 11 o'clock at night of that day, return to said fort in a state of intoxication, and did conduct himself in a very disorderly manner, and was so noisy and obstreperous as to awaken and disturb the whole garrison. Specification #2: In this that the said Captain R.G. Scott, being in command of the fort near Monterey, Mexico known as the Black Fort, and having absented himself from the said fort on the 18$^{th}$ day of May 1847, did, at or about 10 o'clock on the night of that day return to said fort very much intoxicated, and with a quantity of intoxicating liquor in his possession, and did conduct himself in a very disorderly manner and did assemble the sergeants of his company and make them drink and converse with him until he was in such a state of intoxication as to be unable to get to his tent without assistance and did induce or force the sergeant of the guard of said fort to drink until he was so drunk as to be unable to perform his duties. Charge#3: Conduct Unbecoming an Officer and a Gentleman; Specification: In this that the said Captain R.G. Scott, being in command of the fort near Monterey, Mexico, known as the Black Fort, was very much intoxicated at the said fort on or about the night of the 18$^{th}$ of May 1847, and in such condition did exhibit himself before his company and then and there did conduct himself in a very disorderly and ungentlemanly manner, and did assemble the Sergeants of his company and make them drink and converse with him until he was so much intoxicated as to be unable to get to his tent without assistance, and did force or induce the sergeant of the guard of the said fort to drink until he was so drunk as to be unable to attend to his duties. To which charges and specifications the accused pleaded Not Guilty. Major J.A. Early, 1$^{st}$ Regiment Virginia Volunteers, a witness for the prosecution, being duly sworn says: I was in command of a battalion of the Virginia Regiment of six companies, one of which was commanded by the accused, which was encamped near the Walnut Springs, near Monterey. Two or three days before the 17$^{th}$ May, I received an order from General Taylor to relieve the 1$^{st}$ Ohio Regiment and to occupy Monterey and the Black Fort with my command. I designated Captain Scott's company as the one to occupy the Black Fort and on the 17$^{th}$ I gave him orders in relation to his duties. I directed him to take possession of and make arrangements for the protection of the public property in the fort and for the preservation of good order and to have a guard detailed to relieve that of the Ohio Regiment. I ordered that an officer was always to remain with the company and that no officer was to be absent from the fort after 9 o'clock P.M. without my permission. On the afternoon of*

## OFF TO WAR

*the 17th May, somewhere between two and three o'clock P.M. Captain Scott marched from the camp to occupy the Black Fort. I remained behind with the other five companies composing my command waiting for transportation. In an hour or two after the accused marched with the rest of the command into Monterey. I arrived there a little after 4 P.M., formed my command in the Main Plaza, and immediately after my arrival there I saw the accused in the plaza. The Black Fort, at which he should have been at the time was from a half a mile to a mile from the plaza. Question by the Accused: Did I or did I not ask permission of you to march my company to the Black Fort, and did you not tell me that I was to relieve the Ohio Companies, that I was to mount a guard of nine men (three relief's) to take care of the public property and at no time to permit more than five men to be absent at once and they to have permission in writing, and further did you not state that you would give me written instructions in regard to my separate command of the fort? Answer: I had given an order on parade the evening of the 16th May designating the company to occupy the fort and those to occupy Monterey. I had also informed the accused verbally that his company was to garrison the fort, that one officer was always to be with the company and that no officer was to be out of the fort after 9 o'clock P.M. without my permission. I told him at the same time that I would draw up more fully in writing, instructions relative to his command, which however, I did not furnish him with, as a short time afterwards he was detailed on a court martial, was taken ill, and was not afterwards on duty with his company. I did not intend at any time that he was to have a separate command, but that he was always to be under my orders. Question by the Accused: Was not the conversation between us at the Walnut Springs a hurried one? Answer: It was not a hurried one. I had time to give him all the instructions I desired, though they were given to him a very short time before he marched. Question: Why did you not give me the instructions in writing that you contemplated? Answer: I have already stated that a very short time after his occupation of the Black Fort, the accused was put on court-martial, was taken ill and was not on duty with his company afterwards. I also had some regulations printed relating to the government of Monterey of which I furnished the accused with a copy, informing him that they were to apply to his command as far as they were applicable. Question: Were you not very much engaged on the afternoon of the 17th, and could I have procured the written instructions alluded to if I had applied to you for them? Answer: I was engaged on the afternoon alluded to. I had not fully made out the instructions, and the accused could not therefore have procured them out afterwards. Question: At what time was the accused arrested? Answer: I think it was some time in June. Question: At whose instance? Answer: A complaint had been made to me by men of his company in relation to other matters besides those charged, who appealed to me to do them justice. I went over to the Black Fort, to enquire into the matter, and upon information received there, I sometime afterwards, arrested Captain Scott. Question: Were these complaints made in writing? Answer: They were. Question: Have you the written complaint alluded to in your possession? Answer: It may be among my papers. It was among them at Monterey. 07/07/1847 Was not the written complaint before alluded to made by a private or privates of my company, and did you not know of your own knowledge that some of the charges were false? Answer: The paper was handed to me one evening in Monterey, by a man whom I did not notice at the time. I took it to my quarters, thinking it to be upon some ordinary matter of business, opened it there, and ascertained its contents. I went to the Black Fort the next morning and got an officer of the accused's company such information as induced me to make out the charges against him. Question: From what officer of the company did you get the information you allude to? Answer: From Lt. Fry. Question: Was this before or after your interview with the accused in Monterey on the 25th May? Answer: It was before I had any interview with him relating to the matter, but I do not recollect the date of any of our interviews. Question: Did you have more than one interview with the accused relating to the matter? Answer: I only recollect one relating to the matter, in which he asked me to have it investigated. There might have been others, there might have been half a dozen. I*

## VIRGINIA VOLUNTEERS IN MEXICO

*do not recollect. Question: Did I or not, on the 25$^{th}$ May, ask you to see the officers of my company with a view to the investigation of the matter, and what was your reply? Answer: I do not recollect the dates of any interviews I had with the accused there might have been one on the 25$^{th}$ May. I told him I intended to have it investigated. Question: Did you not at that interview leave me under the impression that you had not up to that time made any investigation in regard to this matter? Answer: I can not say under what impression I left the accused, I only know it was not my intention to leave him under that impression. It was my purpose and wish to have as little communication as possible in relation to the matter with him. I had already made up my mind as to the course I should pursue. Question: Was I at the Black Fort on the morning you went then to see Lt. Fry? Answer: I believe not. The accused was on a court-martial and I think was present with the court at the time or working at Monterey for the meeting of the Court. Question: How long after your enquiries of Lt. Fry was the accused arrested? Answer: It was some days. It may have been two weeks perhaps. Question: How long after he was arrested, were charges preferred against the accused? Answer: Not long, a few days after. Question: When did you send the charges to the accused? Answer: I do not recollect. It was some days before we left Monterey. We left there on the 22$^{nd}$ June. Question: Who was in command of the fort after the arrest of the accused, and did you give to him the written instructions you have before alluded to? Answer: Lt. Fry was in command before the arrest of the accused in consequence of his illness, and remained in until we left Monterey. I did not give him the instructions, though I gave him, at his request, an order in relation to the men leaving the fort? Question: Did the accused ever violate any order or command you gave him, or had you any reason to suppose he would do so prior to the time spoken of? Answer: The accused had on some occasions not complied with my orders and had not carried out others in the spirit I desired and I therefore had intended to give him written instructions in order that there should be no caviling about them. Question: You say the accused was not at the fort where he should have been the evening you arrived at Monterey. Do you know that he had no sufficient reason to be in town on that day? Answer: I do not know what reason he had to be there. I mean that he had no right to be there. If he had had any good reason, he should have communicated it to me at the time I gave him his instructions. Lt. John J. Fry, Co. A, Virginia Regiment, a witness for the prosecution, being duly sworn, says: We arrived at the Black Fort about 3$^{1/2}$ o'clock P.M. on the 17$^{th}$ May. Immediately after our arrival the accused said he wanted to get something to eat and see Col. Weller*[John B. Weller, 1$^{st}$ Ohio Regt. of Vols., of Butler Co., Ohio] *and some friends at Monterey who were about to leave there, and shortly after the wagons were unloaded, he went to town, leaving with me directions to see what guard was necessary and to post them. He returned about 10$^{1/2}$ o'clock P.M. When he returned some of the tents were pitched farther apart than they should have been. The sentinel stopped him at the gate and he sent to me to pass him in. When he came in he noticed the tents and asked me the cause of it and went over to see about it. I saw that he had been drinking a little but he was not intoxicated. He went to his tent soon afterwards I went to bed and heard nothing more of him till morning. On the morning of the 18$^{th}$ he stated to me that he was detailed for some duty in town and he left the fort very early in the morning. He returned a little after 9 o'clock P.M. When the sentinel challenged him the sergeant of the guard went and let him in. I saw that he had been drinking a good deal and was under the influence of liquor. He came to my tent, where the Orderly Sergeant was talking with me, and asked for the other Sergeants. He sent after them by the Orderly Sergeant and said he wanted them to take a drink with him. They did not come for some time, and the Sergeant of the Guard, coming up to my tent, the Captain sent him also for the other Sergeants. In about five or ten minutes they came to the tent and he asked them to take a drink with him and pulled a bottle of liquor from his pocket. After they had taken a one drink round, the Captain and the 2$^{nd}$ Sergeant got into a conversation about the company. They spoke very loud but I don't know what they said. He asked them to take another drink*

# OFF TO WAR

*and still continued the conversation. After they had taken three drinks round, the Captain asked the Sergeant of the Guard to take another. The Sergeant replied that as he had to sit up all night he did not think it would hurt him much. While the Captain and 2$^{nd}$ Sergeant were talking very loud, a good many of the men were listening to their conversation. After they had taken four drinks round, the Sergeants went to their tents. The Captain then sat down and asked me for a pipe to smoke. After smoking a few minutes he complained of being sick and I thought he had better be put to bed and went off and got a man to take him to his tent. After that I went to bed and in half an hour or so I heard quarrelling in the guard tent. I got up to see what it was and found the Sergeant of the Guard and a man of the company quarrelling. It was with great difficulty that I could separate them. After I had done so the Sergeant attempted to draw his sword. I rushed to him, took the sword out of his hands and threw it upon the ground. I then put him in arrest and sent him to his tent and told the Corporal to take charge of the guard till morning. I released the Sergeant in the morning and he went to his duties. Question by the Judge Advocate: Was the accused able to get to his tent without assistance on the night of the 18$^{th}$? Answer: I judged not from what he said. Question: What was his manner after he returned to the fort that night? Answer: He spoke very loud and I thought it very wrong to set such an example to the men. Question: Did the accused use any inducements to the Sergeants to drink, besides inviting them to do so? Answer: He only insisted on their drinking. They did not decline drinking when he invited them. Question by the Accused: Did not the accused take all the necessary steps as Captain of the Company before he left the fort on the 17$^{th}$ and give you all the orders necessary to be observed during his absence? Answer: Yes, he did. Question: Did he conduct himself in the manner described in the specification to the second charge? Answer: He was talking there till all the liquor was gone, after which, when the Sergeants returned to their tents, the conversation was in a very loud tone. Question: Was there any thing else disorderly in his conduct except talking in a loud tone of voice. Answer: No, they were discussing some matter relating to the company. Question: Did you receive from the accused any order prohibiting officers from being absent from the fort after 9 o'clock P.M.? Answer: Not to my recollection. Question: At what time did you have an interview with Major Early in relation to this matter? Answer: I do not recollect the date. It was while the accused was all in town. Question: How long was the accused in command of the fort? Answer: I think about a week. Question: How long was he sick at the fort before he went to town? Answer: I believe two days. Question: Did not Major Early, when you had the interview with him, say that he did not wish the subject mentioned to any one? Answer: Yes, he did. Question: Have I previously to the time referred to exhibited any laxity of discipline, or been familiar with the non-commissioned officers or privates of my company? Answer: No you have not. Question: While I was on the court-martial alluded to, did I not attend to my duties as Captain of the Company? Answer: Yes you did. Lt. R.C. Donnan, Co. A, Virginia Regiment, a witness for the prosecution, being duly sworn, says: The accused came into the Black Fort about ten or half past ten on the night we arrived there. He was slightly intoxicated, but made no noise or disturbance that I know of. On the night after I was asleep in my tent when the accused arrived between 10 and 11 o'clock P.M. I think I was awakened by my servant. The accused came to the tent and took a seat, but made no noise to disturb me, and I went to sleep again. Question by the Court: Are you not a very sound sleeper? Answer: Yes, I am very hard to wake when I get asleep. Question by the Accused: Did I not tell you that the Corporals of the company were to command the guard at the fort? Answer: You did after you went to town. Were you aware of the existence of any order prohibiting officers being absent from the fort after 9 o'clock P.M. Answer: I never heard of any such order. Question: Has the accused ever exhibited undue familiarity with the non-commissioned officers or men of his company before the time referred to? Answer: He has not to my knowledge, but rather the reverse. Question: Was it or not after the written complaint had been handed to Major Early that I left the fort to live in town? Answer it was*

# VIRGINIA VOLUNTEERS IN MEXICO

*after. Private Andrew A. Montero, Co. A, Virginia regiment, A witness for the prosecution, being duly sworn, says:* On the 18$^{th}$ May after guard mounting the accused left the fort. I saw him again between 10 and 12 o'clock P.M. that night. I was in my tent when he entered the fort and recognized his voice at the Lieutenant's tent, which was directly opposite mine. I approached to within ten or fifteen paces of the Lieutenant's tent where I discovered two persons standing, whom I recognized as the 2$^{nd}$ and 3$^{rd}$ Sergeants. The accused was sitting near the tent, they were standing in front of him. He was conversing with the Sergeants and I very distinctly heard him say that he had two of the best Lieutenants and the best non-commissioned officers in the Regiment. I heard him also say that he was very much attached to his company and was very sorry, but did not know why they were not attached to him. I heard him say that he was a Democrat and a Republican, that he had never imposed upon his men, had never gagged and never intended to have them treated in the way that some other Captains treated their men. I heard on of the Sergeants say, 'Captain, there [is] no doubt that the men have treated you badly.' After this I turned to go to my tent and heard the accused say to the Sergeant that he had made his Captain drunk. The Captain spoke very loud, but not much more so than he usually does, and I observed no disorderly conduct in him. *Private James Prevost, Co. A, Virginia Regiment, a witness for the prosecution, being duly sworn, says:* I was asleep in my tent at the Black Fort on the night of the 18$^{th}$ of May, and was awoke by loud talking. I recognized the voice of the accused and of two of the Sergeants and got up and approached to within twenty yards of where they were. They all appeared to be very merry and were boisterous in their talking. I was near enough to observe them and thought that they all appeared to be what you may call pretty drunk. There were a good many of the men out when I came out of my tent, and a good many came out afterwards. I remained there for about an hour, until the accused was taken to his tent. *Question by the Court:* What induced you to go out of your tent? *Answer:* I thought when I first awoke that there was a spree or fight of some kind, until I recognized Captain Scott's voice. *Question:* Was it necessary to help the accused to his tent? *Answer:* He had hold of a man's arm, who walked with him to his tent. *07/08/1847 – First Sergeant William Gravatt, Co. A, Virginia Regiment, a witness for the defense, being duly sworn, says:* I was at the Black Fort on the 17$^{th}$ and 18$^{th}$ May. On the 17$^{th}$, the accused left the fort shortly after we arrived there, while we were pitching our tents. On the 18$^{th}$, in the night, I was standing in front of the Lieutenant's tent when the accused returned to the fort. He had with him a bottle of liquor, and asked me to take a drink with him. I declined and he asked me the second time, when I again declined. He then asked me where Sergeants Watkins and Tillson were. I told him they were in their tents. He asked me to go for them and tell them he wanted to see them. I did so and remained in my tent during the rest of the night. I went to sleep and heard no disturbance during the night. My tent was about 60 yards from that of the Lts. There was no inducement used, other than asking me twice, to drink. *Question by the Accused:* Has the accused ever on any other occasion offered liquor to the non-commissioned officers or men of his company or drank with them? *Answer:* I don't know that he has drunk with any of the men. He drank with me in Havana, but never since we have been in Mexico. *Question by the Court:* Was the accused intoxicated on the night of the 18$^{th}$ May when you saw him? *Answer:* Yes, he was under the influence of liquor, but I saw him for a very short time. *Thomas E. Watkins, 3$^{rd}$ Sergeant, Co. A, Virginia Regiment, a witness for the defense, being duly sworn, says:* I was in the Black Fort on the evening of the 17$^{th}$ May and saw the accused there. I did not think he was sober. I also saw him on the evening of the 18$^{th}$. I was in my tent when he arrived. He sent for me and I went to him after he had sent the second time. He asked us to take a drink with him. He had been drinking a little, but was not there so drunk as he was before he got through. I was with him fifteen minutes, perhaps more. He used no inducement to drink except inviting us to do so. He was not disorderly in his behavior while I was with him, nor did I hear of any disorder. I saw the Sergeant of the Guard on that night. He came from the Lieutenant's tent to mine with a

## OFF TO WAR

*message from the Captain and went back with me to the Lieutenant's tent. I did not think he was sober then I saw him afterwards, about 12 or 1 o'clock, he was then very intoxicated. Private M.C. McKinney, Co. A, Virginia Regiment, a witness for the defense, being duly sworn, says: I saw the accused in the Black Fort on the evening of the $17^{th}$ and $18^{th}$ May, he was not guilty of any disorderly conduct as I considered. He did not speak in a louder tone than usual. I could hear from my tent a common conversation at the Lieutenant's. I saw the Sergeant of the Guard just before night on the $18^{th}$. He was a little under the influence of liquor. I had drunk with him about 3 o'clock. Being well acquainted with him I could tell if he were slightly under the influence of liquor. I thought him so when I first drank with him. He had about a pint of liquor with him at that time. Sergeant William Gravatt was recalled. Question by the accused: Did you think the Sergeant of the Guard intoxicated when the accused offered him liquor on the night of the $18^{th}$ May? Answer: No, I did not. I had seen him frequently during the day and evening. Lieutenant Fry was recalled by the accused. Question by the accused: Was the Sergeant of the Guard, on the night of the $18^{th}$ May, drunk when he left your tent, or incapacitated from performing his duty? Answer: No, he was not when he first left the tent. He left before the Captain and returned a few minutes after the Captain left. I thought then that he was a little lively. When he first came to my tent he did not appear to be at all intoxicated. Question by the Court: Was Major Early in the habit of visiting the Black Fort? Answer: I never saw him there except once upon the occasion before alluded to and I do not think that he gave any orders at that time in relation to the command of the fort. I understood the accused to say that the Black Fort was a separate command. He told me so several times. I never made any report to Major Early while in command of the fort. I did not consider it necessary to obtain permission to go to town. Captain E.G. Alburtis, Virginia Regiment, a witness for the defense, was duly sworn: Question by the Accused: Do you know what was the impression of the accused in regard to the command of the Black Fort, and what was your own impression? Answer: I had a conversation with the accused on the subject. He appeared displeased at being ordered there, and I remarked to him that I conceived it to be what he was entitled to and that if he had not been ordered there he would have been dissatisfied. I remarked at the same time that I would have been pleased to receive the order, as I looked upon the command of the fort, being detached, as agreeable. I was under the impression that the fort was under the orders of Major Early. Lt. Thomas P. August, Virginia Regiment, a witness for the defense, was duly sworn: Question by the Accused: Did you know what was the impression of the accused in regard to the command of the Black Fort, and what was your impression? Answer: I can only judge of the impression of the accused from what he said both before and after he took command of the Black Fort. He stated that it was a separate command and spoke of it as such in my presence on several occasions. It was my impression that it was a separate command and I told him so when he expressed dissatisfaction at the order. I did not profess to know much about the Army Regulations and it was an impression founded upon my ignorance of them. Lt. Otho H. Harrison, Virginia regiment, a witness for the defense, was duly sworn. Question: Did you know what was the impression of the accused in regard to the command of the Black Fort, and what was your impression? Answer: I heard the accused say on one or two occasions, that his was a separate command. I had no distinct impression on the subject, except from what he said. The accused introduced before the Court the printed regulations for the government of Monterey, referred to in the testimony of Major Early, dated May $18^{th}$ 1847, the fourth of which is as follows: 'Non-commissioned officer and privates of any troops stationed out of Monterey, will not be allowed to come into town unless on public business, or by leave in writing from the commanding officer of their regiment, battalion, or corps, or by permission from the Commanding General.' 07/09/1847 – The accused presented and read a written defense [9 pages]. After deliberation the Court found the accused Not Guilty on the $1^{st}$ Charge and Specification; Guilty of the $2^{nd}$ Charge and $2^{nd}$ Specification all before the words 'and with a quantity...,' but Not Guilty of the $1^{st}$*

VIRGINIA VOLUNTEERS IN MEXICO

*Specification; Not Guilty of the 3$^{rd}$ Charge, but Guilty of the Specification of all before the words 'and in such condition...' He was sentenced to be privately reprimanded;*[1588] sick 08/1847; absent 10/1847, furloughed 60 days from 08/25/1847 by order of Genl. Taylor; absent 12/1847, furlough extended on Surgeon's Certificate; pres. 02/1848, ret. to duty 01/27/1848; pres. 04/1848; c. 1850 res. Richmond, Henrico Co., VA, age 29, occ. None Listed, w? Susan E. (25);[1589] Consul to Rio De Janerio 1855 - 1861; m. Annie K. Thompson, 04/04/1859, U.S. Legature, Rio de Janerio, Brazil;[1590] Lawyer in Richmond, VA;[1591] SC #5702, 03/09/1887, filed from Richmond, VA; Since discharge res. Brazil, Alabama, 406 E. Grace St., Richmond, VA; d. 11/24/1894, Binfords, Brunswick Co., VA;[1592] obit. *"Died suddenly on November 24$^{th}$, at the residence of Mrs. M.F. Baker, in Brunswick County, VA, Captain ROBERT G. SCOTT, in the 75$^{th}$ year of his age. Funeral will take place from the Church of the Holy Trinity (Moore-Memorial) TUESDAY, November 27$^{th}$, at 12 o'clock. Pallbearers are requested to meet at No. 909 Park Avenue at 11:30 A.M. Friends of the family are respectfully invited to attend."* A copy of the obituary accompanies a letter *edged in black* to Sidney L. Wilson [Pension Board] dated 1/01/1894;[1593] bur. Hollywood Cem., Richmond, VA, Sect. 15, Lot 92;[119] wid. Annie T.(b. Mt. Dessert, Maine, d. 05/13/1915, bur. Hollywood Cem. Richmond, VA, Sect. 15, Lot 92), [119] WC #12622, 03/25/1895, filed from 909 Park Ave., Richmond, Henrico Co., VA; from VA; c. 1870 res. Richmond, Henrico Co., VA, age 50, occ. Attorney;[1594] bro of Pvt. John K. Scott.

**Scott, Thomas**, 1$^{st}$ Sgt., Co. E; b. 10/24/1824, Petersburg, VA;[1595] enl. Mex. War service 11/30/1846 Petersburg, VA, age 22; pres. 04/1847; pres. 06/1847; pres. 08/1847 prom. 1$^{st}$ Sgt. 07/26/1847; pres. 10/1847, pay stopped for: 1 pr. overalls-$2.28, 2 pr. shoes-$2.44, 3 pr. stockings-$.73$^{1/2}$, 1 cap-$.95$^{1/2}$; pres. 12/1847, pay stopped for: 1 pr. pants-$2.28, 2 pr. socks-$.49, 2 pr. drawers-$.71, 2 blankets-$4.44; pres. 02/1848, pay stopped for: 1 jacket-$2.66, 1 cotton shirt-$.43; pres. 04/1848; SC #12780, 10/29/1887, filed from Jamestown, Tuolumne Co., CA; Since discharged res. in Virginia until 03/1849 since then res. in California; d. 12/11/1898.[1595]

**Scott, William Arthur**, 1$^{st}$ Lt., Co. M; b. c. 1825, Dinwiddie Co., VA, son of William Baker & Elizabeth (Torborne) Scott; attended VMI 1846 (non-graduate); enl. Mex. War service 08/27/1847, Amelia C.H., VA, age 22; pres. 10/1847; pres. 11/1847, reduced to 2$^{nd}$ Lt.; pres. 12/1847; pres. 02/1848; pres. 04/1848; pres. 08/1848; *California 49er*, d. 1849 in California.[1160]

**Scott, William H.**, Pvt., Co. M; enl. Mex. War service 11/10/1847, Ft. Monroe, VA, age 25; pres. 11/1847; pres. 12/1847; pres. 02/1848; pres. 04/1848, pay stopped for: 1 blanket-$2.22, 1 cap-$.95$^{1/2}$; pres. 08/1848, pay stopped for 1 wormer-$.20; BLW sent to Washington, D.C.

**Seabright, James C.**, Pvt., Co. K; enl. Mex. War service Frederick Co., VA 12/28/1846, age 27; sick 06/1847; pres. 08/1847, to forfeit 1 mos. pay by order of garrison court-martial; pres. 10/1847, prom. 4$^{th}$ Cpl. 09/17/1847; pres. 12/1847, pay stopped for: 2 pr. overalls-$4.56, 3 pr. socks-$.73$^{1/2}$, 2 pr. drawers-$.71, 1 blanket-$2.22, 1 cap-$.95$^{1/2}$, 2 cotton shirt-$.86; pres. 04/1848, reduced to ranks 04/23/1848, pay stopped for: 1 jacket-$2.66, 1 gun sling-$.18, 1 pr. shoes-$1.22; pres. 07/1848, pay stopped for: 1 gun sling-$.18; BLW sent to Charlestown, VA

**Searl, Samuel**, Pvt., LIC; b. 07/09/1818, Philadelphia, Pa.;[1596] enl. Mex. War service 01/06/1847 Richmond, VA, age 32; sick 08/1847; pres. 10/1847, pay stopped for: 1 forage cap-$.95$^{1/2}$, 1 wool jacket-$2.66, 1 pr. overalls-$2.28, 1 pr. shoes-$1.22, 3 pr. socks-$.73$^{1/2}$, 3 cotton shirts-$1.29, 1 blanket-$2.22, 1 overcoat-$6.93$^{1/2}$; pres. 12/1847, pay stopped for: 1 pr. socks-$.24$^{1/2}$, 1 blanket-$2.22, 2 pr. shoes-$2.44, 1 pr. overalls-$2.28, 1 flannel shirt-$.90, 1 pr. drawers-$.35$^{1/2}$; absent 04/1848, on detached service as Baker to the Battalion since 03/09/1848; pres. 07/1848, pay stopped for: 1 bayonet scabbard-$.56, 1 waist belt-$.21, 1 waist belt plate-$.10, 1 gun sling-$.16, 1 pick & brush-$.12, 1 screw driver-$.07, 1 wiper-$.20; BLW sent to Richmond, VA; c. 1850 res. Richmond, Henrico Co., VA, age 33, occ. Baker, b. Pa.;[1597] Civil

OFF TO WAR

War service Pvt., Co. F, 21st Va. Inf., enl. 02/28/1863 in Richmond, VA, absent sick 09/1864 through 12/1864, paroled 04/15/1865 at Lynchburg, VA, admitted to R.E. Lee Camp No. 1 Soldiers Home, Richmond VA 05/13/1886, deserted; NFR;[724] m. Isabella D. (Covar) Legg, 01/13/1867, Edgefield, Edgefield Co., SC;[1596] SC #9452, 03/09/1887, filed from Richmond, Henrico Co., VA; William G. Ferguson and Robert G. Scott gave affidavits in pension claim;[1596] d. 05/16/1892;[1598] wid. Isabella D., WA #10710, 06/17/1892, from SC; (ICS b. 03/04/1832, Edgefield, SC, m/1 William E. Legg, 07/03/1855, he died 01/23/1863).[1598]
**Seigler, William**, Pvt., Co. H; enl. Mex. War service 12/27/1846, Berkeley, VA, age 19; pres. 04/1847; pres. 06/1847; pres. 08/1847; pres. 10/1847, pay stopped for: 1 forage cap-$.95$^{1/2}$, 1 pr. pants-$2.28, 3 cotton shirts-$1.29, 2 pr. shoes-$2.44, 2 pr. socks-$.49, 1 greatcoat-$6.93$^{1/2}$, 1 jacket-$2.66; Court-Martialed 12/02/1847 Buena Vista, Mex. Charge #1 *Drunkeness on Duty,* Specification *"in that Pvt. William Zeigler...being regularly posted as a Sentinel of the Provost Guard, was found drunk on his post...Nov. 27$^{th}$, 1847;"* Pleading: *Guilty;* Sentenced *"to forfeit two months pay and to be made to stand on the head of a barrel two hours a day for two week on the parade ground of his Regiment;"* [1599] in confinement 12/1847, pay stopped for: 1 pr. pants-$2.28, 2 flannel shirts-$1.80, 1 pr. shoes-$1.22, 3 pr. socks-$.73$^{1/2}$, 1 blanket-$2.22; pres. 02/1848, pay stopped for: 2 cotton shirts-$.86, 2 pr. drawers-$.71, 1 pr. shoes-$1.22; pres. 04/1848; pres. 07/1848, pay stopped for: 1 gun sling-$.16, 1 waist belt plate-$.10, 1 screw driver-$.25, BLW sent to Boonsboro, MD; SC #18736, 01/07/1889, from VA; [pension file missing].
**Self, Thomas**, Pvt., Co. B; enl. 12/01/1846, Alexandria, VA, age 19; deserted 01/02/1847, Richmond, VA
**Seymore, Richard H.**, Pvt., Co. E; b. 03/01/1826, Dinwiddie Co., VA, son of Zack & Mary Seymore;[1600, 1601] enl. Mex. War service 11/28/1846 Petersburg, VA, age 20, 5'9", light blue eyes, light hair, light complexion, occ. Blacksmith; sick Matamoros, Mex. since 03/29/1847; absent 04/1847; pres. 06/1847; pres. 08/1847; pres. 10/1847, pay stopped for: 1 pr. overalls-$2.28, 2 flannel shirts-$1.80, pres. 12/1847, pay stopped for: 1 pr. socks-$.24$^{1/2}$, 1 pr. shoes-$1.22, 1 cap-$.95$^{1/2}$, 1 blanket-$2.22; pres. 02/1848; pres. 04/1848, pay stopped for: 1 cotton shirt-$.44; m/1 Lucy Bishop 06/01/1849, Petersburg, VA, (LB d. 07/12/1879 Dinwiddie Co., VA);[1600] c. 1850 res. Petersburg, Dinwiddie Co., VA, age 24, occ. Laborer, w. Lucy (23), son Walter (3/12);[1602] c. 1860 res. Petersburg, Dinwiddie Co., VA, age 32, occ. Carpenter, w. Lucy H. (29), son Walter (10), dau. Laura (7);[1603] Civil War service Pvt., Co. K, 12$^{th}$ Va. Inf., enl. 05/04/1861 at Petersburg, VA, b. 1828, discharged 05/08/1862 claiming to have been born in 1824;[21] c. 1870 res. Petersburg, Dinwiddie Co., VA, age 45, occ. Blacksmith, w. Lucy A. (40), dau. Laura (16);[1604] m/2 Sarah Frances Griffin 02/03/1881, Petersburg, VA;[1605] SC #15576, 04/27/1888, filed from 29 Old Street,(now Grove Ave.) Petersburg, VA; David F. Shields and Joseph L. Carter gave affidavits in pension claim; d. 08/10/1900 *Marasmus, aged 75 years, 11 mos., 6 days*, Petersburg, VA, bur. Blandford Cemetery, Sq. 1, Sec. 8, Ward G, Petersburg, VA;[1606] wid. Sarah F., WA #15778, 08/28/1900, filed from Windsor, Isle of Wight Co., VA; Claim rejected *"not the legal widow of the soldier, she having been previously married to a man who was still alive subsequent to her marriage with the soldier, divorce of said former husband is neither shown or alleged;"* (SFG b.12/31/1844 Southampton Co., VA, m/1 Charles J. Phillips, aka Dixon Phillips, George W. Dixon 11/11/1869, Isle of Wight Co., VA Charles J. Phillips ran away from home, Hookerton, NC, in 1865 at age 13. Changed his name to George W. Dixon to keep his father, Richard Phillips, from finding him. After marrying Sarah F. Griffin ran off with a widow named Mrs. Britt in the Spring of 1871. He left her. As of 1886 Charles J. Phillips was living in Williamston, NC, had a 2$^{nd}$ wife, Sarah B., and child in Hoboken, NJ whom he had also left).
**Shackelford, Andrew Jackson**, Pvt., LIC; b. near Standardsville, Green Co., VA;[1607] enl. Mex. War service 12/07/1846 Staunton, VA, age 18; sick 06/1847 in quarters; pres. 08/1847; pres. 10/1847, pay stopped for: 1 pr. overalls-$2.28, 2 pr. shoes-$2.44, 3 pr. socks-$.73$^{1/2}$, 4 cotton

VIRGINIA VOLUNTEERS IN MEXICO

shirts-$1.72, 1 pr. drawers-$.35$^{1/2}$; pres. 12/1847, pay stopped for: 2 pr. socks-$.49, 1 pr. shoes-$1.22, 1 flannel shirt-$.90, 1 pr. drawers-$.35$^{1/2}$; pres. 04/1848, pay stopped for: 1 pr. shoes-$1.22; pres. 07/1848, pay stopped for: 1 gun sling-$.16, 1 screw driver-$.07; BLW sent to Charlottesville, VA; m. Virginia Smith, 08/25/1852, Charlottesville, VA;[1607] SC #8139, 02/28/1887, filed from Charlottesville, Albemarle Co., VA; phys. desc. 5'9", light complexion, blue eyes, gray hair, occ. Wheelwright;[1607] d. 07/15/1889, Charlottesville, VA;[1608] wid. Virginia, WC #6686, 10/10/1889, filed from Charlottesville, Albemarle Co., VA; (VSS b. 03/25/1825, Milton, VA, d. 04/11/1900).[1608]

**Shands, Aurelius Rives**, 2$^{nd}$ Lt., Co. D; b. 03/11/1822, Blandford, Prince George Co., VA, son of William & Sarah McGee (Rives) Shands;[1609] enl. Mex. War service 12/26/1846, Petersburg, VA; absent 02/1847 sailed from Fort Monroe, VA 02/22/1847 on board the Barque *Exact* for Port Isabel, Tex.; absent 04/1847 sick at Hosp. Matamoros, Mex. since 04/09/1847; resigned 05/31/1847 on account of ill health, honorably discharged; c. 1850 res. Prince George Co., VA, age 28, occ. Physician;[1610] m. Martha Carter Wood, 04/27/1852, City Point, Prince George Co., VA;[1611] c. 1860 res. City Point, Prince George Co., VA, age 38, occ. Farmer, w. M.C. (30), dau. P.E. (4), son W.R. (1);[1612] Civil War service Pvt., Co. F, 5$^{th}$ Va. Cav., enl. 04/20/1861 at Prince George C.H., VA, pres. 06/1861 through 12/1861, discharged 01/15/1862 for disability caused by kick from horse below the knee fracturing the leg, phys. desc. age 39, florid complexion, light hair, blue eyes, Farmer, res. Prince George Co., VA;[131] Pvt., VA Mtd. Guards, enl. 05/01/1864 at Powhattan, VA for war, pres. 10/1864, assigned to light duty;[1613] c. 1870 res. Garysville, Prince George Co., VA, age 48, occ. Farmer, dau. Martha C. (40), son A.R., Jr. (9), dau. Anna Jane (1), m-i-l Anna C. Wood (74);[1614] SC #4035, 03/26/1887, filed from Westover, Charles City Co., VA;[1611] Thomas H. Bond gave affidavit for pension claim: *"I was present when the officers of Capt. Wm. Robinson's Co. were publically presented with swords and know that he was one of them;"*[1615] d. 03/30/1891, neat Westover, Charles City, VA, *Paralysis*, bur. Blandford Cem., Sq. 7, Sec. 59, Ward D, Petersburg, VA;[76, 1616, 1617] wid. Martha C., WA #9959, 06/30/1891, filed from Westover, Charles City Co., VA; (MCS b. 12/26/1829 City Point, VA).[1617]

**Shank, Jacob**, Pvt., Co. H; b. 05/15/1815;[1618] enl. Mex. War service 11/27/1846, Morgan, VA, phys. desc. age 30, 6', dark complexion, dark hair, dark eyes; 02/1847 Jacob Shanks, of Morgan Co., VA is listed as being sick in *Martinsburg Gazette*;[1619] pres. 04/1847; pres. 06/1847; pres. 08/1847; pres. 10/1847, pay stopped for: 1 pr. pants-$2.28, 2 cotton shirts-$.86, 1 pr. shoes-$1.22; pres. 12/1847, pay stopped for: 1 forage cap-$.95$^{1/2}$, 1 jacket-$2.66, 1 pr. pants-$2.28, 2 cotton shirts-$.86, 1 pr. shoes-$1.22, 1 pr. socks-$.24$^{1/2}$; pres. 02/1848; pres. 04/1848; pres. 07/1848, BLW sent to Berkeley Springs, VA; m. Susan Gall, 11/15/1849, Barbour Co., VA;[1620] c. 1850 res. Barbour Co., VA, age 33, occ. Merchant, w. Susan (23);[1621] c. 1860 res. Philippi, Barbour Co., VA;[1622] c. 1880 res. Philippi, Barbour Co., WV, age 65, occ. Farmer, w. Susan (53) Keeping House, son John W. (28) Farmer;[1623] SC #11932, 02/11/1887, filed from Philippi, Barbour Co., WV; res. Barbour Co. since discharge; Lists children John W. and Margaret J. Shank, b. 05/21/1851, Sarah E. Shank, b. 11/22/1852, Virginia Alcinda Shank, b. 02/12/1855, Rosa Lee Shank, b. 10/13/1861, *"Two girls living in Kan., one in Colorad, and one girl and one boy living in West Virginia;"*[1618] d. 05/25/1908, bur. Mt. Vernon Cemetery, Barbour Co., WV;[1620] wid. Susan, WC #15083, 09/02/1908, filed from Volga, Barbour Co., WV; (SGS b. 09/22/1827, Crabbottom, VA, d. 03/20/1925).[1620]

**Shaw, Elias**, Pvt., Co. B; enl. 12/14/1846, Alexandria, VA, age 25; pres. 06/1847; sick 08/1847; d. 09/05/1847 in hosp. Saltillo, Mex., pay due from 08/31/1847, pay stopped for 1 pick & brush-$.12. 1 haversack-$.20$^{3/4}$, 1 screw driver-$.07, 1 wiper-$.15, 1 pr. pants-$2.28, 1 flannel shirt-$.90, 1 pr. socks-$.49, 2 pr. socks-$.49, 1 canteen and strap-$.27.

**Sheaf, George W.**, Drummer, *Preston's Co.*; enl. Mex. War service 12/06/1846 Montgomery Co., VA, age 31; pres. 04/1847, prom. Drummer 01/17/1847; pres. 06/1847; pres. 08/1847; pres. 10/1847, pay stopped for: 1 jacket-$2.66, 1 pr. overalls-$2.28; pres. 12/1847; pres.

267

OFF TO WAR

02/1848; pres. 04/1848; pres. 07/1848; BLW sent to Christiansburg, VA c/o Fleming Gardner; m. Malinda Barton, 11/14/1849, Montgomery Co., VA;[1624] c. 1850, res. Blacksburg, Montgomery Co., VA, age 35, occ. Shoemaker, w. Malinda (22), Mary (3);[1625] Civil War service enl. as Pvt., Co. E, 4$^{th}$ Va. Inf. 08/27/1861, detailed as a Drummer 11/29/1861, discharged 03/03/1862 for disability, desc. 5'5", hazel eyes, auburn hair, fair complex, also served in Wade's Regt. of Local Defense;[54] c. 1870 res. Blacksburg, Montgomery Co., VA, age 54, occ. Shoemaker, b. Pa., w. Malinda (41), dau. Ellen M. (22), son Amos B. (20), son William W. (16), son John T. (14), son Robert (11), son Henry L. (6), dau. Olivia (1).[1626]

**Sheckles, Samuel**, Pvt., Co. L; b. 1828; enl. Mex. War service 03/01/1847 Fairfax C.H., VA, age 19; pres. 06/1847; pres. 08/1847; pres. 10/1847, pay stopped for: 1 pr. Pants 2.28, 1 pr. Shoes 1.22, 1 F Cap .95; pres. 12/1847, pay stopped for: 1 jacket-$2.66, 1 pr. pants-$2.28, 2 pr. shoes-$2.44, 1 flannel shirt-$.90, 3 cotton shirts-$1.29, 1 blanket-$2.22, 1 pr. socks-$.24$^{1/2}$; pres. 02/1848, to forfeit 1 mos. pay per sent. genl. court-martial, pay stopped for: 1 pr. Shoes 1.22, 1 Brush & Pick .12; pres. 04/1848, pay stopped for: 1 Blanket 2.25, 1 Flannel Shirt .77, 1 Cotton Shirt .44; pres. 07/1848, pay stopped for: 1 Wiper .20, 1 Screw Driver .25; BLW sent to Levi Sheckles c/o Samuel Sheckles, Washington City, D.C.; admitted 07/10/1874 to National Soldiers Home, Elizabeth City (Hampton), VA by reason of *rheumatism and age* [49 years]; SC #9752 dated 2/19/1887 filed from National Soldiers Home, Elizabeth City, Co., VA; transferred 07/05/1898 to Government Insane Aslyum, Washington, D.C., sister listed as Mrs. William Brooks, Washington, D.C.; d. 05/14/1900, Government Insane Aslyum, Wash. D.C.[1627]

**Sheets, John William**, Pvt., Co. K; b. c. 1827 Charlestown, Jefferson Co., VA, son of Samuel & Elizabeth Sheetz;[1628, 1629] enl. Mex. War service Jefferson Co., VA 12/01/1846, age 19; pres. 06/1847; pres. 08/1847; sick 10/1847, pay stopped for: 1 pr. overalls-$2.28, 2 pr. socks-$.49, 2 pr. drawers-$.71, 2 flannel shirts-$1.80, 2 pr. shoes-$2.44; pres. 12/1847, pay stopped for: 1 jacket-$2.66; pres. 04/1848, to forfeit 1 mos. pay by sentence of garrison court-martial, pay stopped for: 1 pick & brush-$.12, 1 gun sling-$.18, 1 pr. shoes-$1.22; pres. 07/1848; BLW sent to Charlestown, Jefferson Co., VA; c. 1850 res. Charlestown, Jefferson Co., VA, age 23, occ. None Listed;[1630] m. Pheobe Ann Wade 03/10/1854, Charlestown, Jefferson Co., VA;[1628, 1631] c. 1860 res. Charles Town, Jefferson Co., VA;[1632] d. 10/20/1881, Charlestown, bur. Zion Episcopal Church Graveyard, Charlestown, WV;[45, 1628] wid. Pheobe, WC #441, 02/17/1887, filed from Charlestown, Jefferson Co., WV; phys. desc. of soldier age 56 [1881], 6'1"or 2", light complexion, blue eyes, light hair, occ. laborer;[1628] John W. Gallaher gave affidavit in pension claim; d. 01/01/1902.[1628]

**Shell, Henry B.**, Pvt., *Preston's Co.*; b. 07/28/1821, Christiansburg, Montgomery Co., VA;[1633] enl. Mex. War service 12/06/1846 Montgomery Co., VA, age 25; absent 04/1847 left sick in hosp. at Pt. Isabel, Tex. since 03/11/1847; pres. 06/1847; pres. 08/1847, prom. 4$^{th}$ Sgt. 07/08/1847; pres. 10/1847, pay stopped for: 1 pr. overalls-$2.28, 3 pr. socks-$.73$^{1/2}$, 1 flannel shirt-$.90, 3 cotton shirts-$1.29, 1 pr. drawers-$.35$^{1/2}$, 1 cap-$.95$^{1/2}$; absent 12/1847, on detached service as Teamster in the QM Dept. since 12/11/1847, reduced to ranks from 4$^{th}$ Cpl. at his own request, pay stopped for: 1 jacket-$2.66, 1 pr. overalls-$2.28, 1 pr. shoes-$1.22; absent 02/1848 on detached service; pres. 04/1848; pres. 07/1848, pay stopped for: 1 gun sling-$.18, 1 screw driver-$.07; BLW sent to Christiansburg, VA c/o Fleming Gardner; m. Sarah Jane Sawyer, 11/26/1851, Montgomery Co., VA;[1634] c. 1860 res. Matamoras, Montgomery Co., VA, age 39, occ. Blacksmith, w. Sarah J. (36), dau. Laura E. (6), son Armando V. (4), son Stan (2), dau. Laura G.F. (1);[1635] Civil War service Pvt., Co. D, 4$^{th}$ VA Reserves (Preston's Regt.), enl. 12/03/1864, at Dublin, VA, pres. 01/1865, phys. desc. age 25, 5'9", fair complexion, blue eyes, light hair, occ. Blacksmith, NFR;[1636] c. 1870, res. Newbern, Pulaski Co., VA, age 49, occ. Blacksmith, w. Sarazon (46), dau. Octara (16), son Amakus (14), son Starwith (13), dau. Sora (11), dau. Sector H. (9), dau. Orlena (6), son Mason W. (3).[1637] SC #12253, 03/29/1887, filed from Pearisburg Giles Co., VA; phys. desc. at enl. age

# VIRGINIA VOLUNTEERS IN MEXICO

25, blue eyes, light hair, fair complexion, occ. Blacksmith, since discharge res. Montgomery Co., VA 17 yrs., Pulaski Co., VA from 1866-1874, Giles Co., VA until death;[1633] c. 1900 res. Pearisburg, Giles Co., VA; d. 12/22/1900;[1638] wid. Sarah J., WC #12623, 04/11/1901, filed from Pearisburg, Giles Co., VA; Lists children Octavia Ellen Shell b. 06/27/1854, Americus Vaspucis Shell b. 09/10/1856, Staritt A. Shell b. 04/27/1857, Laura Frances Shell b. 09/18/1858, Aolena Kansas Shell b. 04/04/1863, Mason Newton Shell b. 02/22/1867;[1638] (SSS d. 03/10/1913, Elwood, Madison Co., Ind., bur. Pearisburg, Giles Co., VA)[1638]

**Shell, John H.**, Pvt., Co. G; enl. Mex. War service 11/28/1846 Richmond, VA, age 32; absent 06/1847, left sick in Hosp. at Camargo, Mex. 05/21/1846; discharged 08/11/1847 Monterey, Mex. on Surgeon's Certificate of Disability.

**Shelling, Barnhardt**, Pvt., Co. K; enl. Mex. War service Richmond, VA 12/25/1846, age 27; pres. 06/1847; pres. 08/1847; pres. 10/1847, pay stopped for: 1 pr. overalls-$2.28, 1 cap-$.95$^{1/2}$, 2 cotton shirts-$.86, 2 pr. drawers-$.71, 1 pr. socks-$.24$^{1/2}$, 1 flannel shirt-$.90, 1 greatcoat-$6.93$^{1/2}$, 1 blanket-$2.22; pres. 12/1847, pay stopped for: 1 jacket-$2.66, 1 pr. overalls-$2.28, 1 pr. boots-$1.22, 1 blanket-$2.22; pres. 04/1848, pay stopped for: 1 gun sling-$.18; pres. 07/1848, pay stopped for: 1 gun sling-$.18, 1 screw driver-$.25, 1 wiper-$.20; BLW sent to Richmond, VA; m. Elizabeth Fowler, date/place unknown; SC #19729, 01/20/1891, wid. Elizabeth, WA #4877, 09/20/1887, both from VA; (EFS d. 03/23/1888, Alms House, Richmond, VA).[1639]

**Shelling, John**, Pvt., Co. F; enl. Mex. War service 11/26/1846, Portsmouth, VA, age 25; pres. 06/1847; Court-martialed 07/16/1847, Buena Vista, Mex., *Charge #1: Unsoldierlike Conduct and Disobedience of Orders; Specification: In this that Private John Shelling, Co. F, Va. Regt. Vols., was on the 5$^{th}$ day of July 1847 in a state of intoxication, and when ordered by the Captain of his company to his tent, did obstinately and imprudently refuse to obey, this in defiance to the orders of his commanding officer, and giving an example of insubordination to the men of his company there and then present. This at camp at Buena Vista. Charge #2: Violation of the 9$^{th}$ Article of War; Specification: In this that when Capt. John P. Young, Va. Regt., called upon a non-commissioned officer to arrest Private John Shelling, aforesaid, he, the said John Shelling, most violently resisted and made several efforts to get the hand of the said Capt. John P. Young, in his mouth and bite him. This on the 5$^{th}$ of July 1847 at Camp at Buena Vista. Capt. Young, Va. Regt., a member of the Court having preferred the charges, and being an unimportant witness for the prosecution was excused by the court from sitting as a member during the trial of this case. The prisoner pled Not Guilty to the charges and specifications. Capt. J.P. Young, a witness for the prosecution, was duly sworn: Question by the Judge Advocate: Was Private Shelling drunk on the 5$^{th}$ instant? Answer: On my return from dinner on the 5$^{th}$ instant Shelling came up and said he was going back to the Rancho. I turned round, saw he was drunk, and ordered him to his tent. He refused to go, and I ordered him again. When he swore he would not, but would go back to the Rancho for some cups. I then called the Sergt. to send him to the Guard House, and before he came, Shelling swore so much that I walked up to him and took him by the collar, and he seized me at the same time, swearing that no one should carry him to the Guard House. A scuffle ensued between us, and I found that he was trying to get my hand in his mouth. By the interference of Lt. Coleman and Lt. Collier, I extricated my hand. I am certain that he knew it was my hand at the time. When sober, Sheling is an orderly, quiet man. Lt. Coleman, Va. Regt., a witness for the prosecution was duly sworn. Question by the Judge Advocate: was the accused drunk on the 5$^{th}$ instant? Answer: I judge that he was from his conduct. I was passing by at the time, and saw Capt. Young attempt to take hold of him. He resisted and attempted to bite the Captain's finger, but I succeeded in releasing him almost immediately with the assistance of four or five men. Private F.A. Cunningham, Va. Regt., a witness for the defense was duly sworn. Question by the Judge Advocate: Did you see the accused on the 5$^{th}$ instant, and was he drunk? Answer: I did see him and he was drunk. The Captain ordered the Sergeant to arrest Shelling and the Sergeant*

OFF TO WAR

*ordered me to help him. He resisted and several officers and men rushed in to help, among others Capt. Young and Lt. Coleman. I heard Capt. Young exclaim do not strike him, and saw the accused attempt to get his hand in his mouth. He is quiet and respectful generally. I never saw him drunk before since he has been in the service. He is not quarrelsome. Private N.B. Hawkins, Va. Regt., a witness for the defense was duly sworn: Question by the Judge Advocate: Was Shelling drunk on the $5^{th}$ instant? Answer: He was. Question by the Judge Advocate: Did you see him resist Capt. Young's order to go to the Guard House? Answer: I saw some resistance when the Capt. Ordered him to the Guard House, but I did not see the Capt's finger in his mouth. He is quiet and respectful when sober. I have never seen him drunk before. He is not quarrelsome. After deliberation the prisoner was found Guilty of all charges and specifications and sentenced to forfeit one months pay and to perform police duty for one month, in addition to his regular duty;*[1640] absent 08/1847 sick; in confinement 10/1847, pay stopped for: 1 pr. overalls-$2.28, 1 forage cap-$.95$^{1/2}$, 4 cotton shirts-$1.72, 4 pr. socks-$.98, 1 overcoat-$6.93$^{1/2}$; Court-martialed 11/11/1847 at Buena Vista, Mex. *Charge: Conduct Prejudicial to Good Order and Military Discipline; Specification: In that the said Pvt. John Shilling, Co. F, Va. Regt., did steal a pair of dueling pistols the property of Lt. August of the same Regt. which pistols were found in the knapsack of said John Shilling on or about the $29^{th}$ of September 1847. A search having been made by order of Lt. Col. Randolph. This at the Camp of the Va. Regt. near Buena Vista, Mexico. To which charge and specification the prisoner plead Not Guilty. Capt. J.P. Young, Va. Regt. Vols., a witness for the prosecution, being duly sworn, says: On the morning of the $29^{th}$ of September '47 Col. Randolph came to my tent and stated to me that he had reason to believe that his and Lt. August's pistols were in possession of this man Shilling and ordered me to have his tent searched. I did so. His knapsack was produced and a pair of dueling pistols found in the knapsack, which proved to be the property of Lt. August. Question by the Judge Advocate: Was the prisoner present when this search was made, and what was his manner? Answer: He was present shortly after the pistols were found and being charged with having stolen them his manner evinced guilt. Question by the Judge Advocate: At that time did he attempt to explain how the pistols came into his possession? Answer: No. He did not. Question by the Court: How long after the pistols were found as you have stated was the prisoner sent to the Provost Guard? Answer: Immediately after discovery. The prisoner stated to the court that the pistols were given to him by a man who has since deserted. After deliberation the court found him Not Guilty.*[1641] in confinement 12/1847; pres. 02/1848, pay stopped for: 1 pr. overalls-$2.28, 2 blanket-$4.44, 1 pr. shoes-$3.66, 2 pr. drawers-$.71, 4 cotton shirts-$1.72, 1 overcoat-$6.93$^{1/2}$, 1 forage cap-$.95$^{1/2}$; pres. 04/1848, overpaid $1.98 on 02/1848 muster roll; pres. 08/1848, pay stopped for: 2 pr. shoes-$2.32, 1 jacket-$2.37, 1 forage cap-$.83, 2 cotton shirts-$.88, 1 blanket-$2.25, BLW sent to Portsmouth, VA c/o E.T. Blamire.

**Shelton, John F.**, Pvt., Co. C; b. c. 1825 Stafford Co., VA;[1642] enl. Mex. War service 12/22/1846, Bowling Green, VA, age 20; pres. 06/1847; pres. 08/1847, pay stopped for: 1 cap-$.95$^{1/2}$, 2 pr. socks-$.49, 2 cotton shirts-$.86, 2 woolen shirts-$1.80, 1 pr. drawers-$.35$^{1/2}$; pres. 10/1847, pay stopped for: 2 pr. socks-$.49, 1 jacket-$2.66, 1 pr. pants-$2.28, 1 blanket-$2.22; pres. 12/1847, pay stopped for: 1 pr. shoes-$1.22; pres. 04/1848, pay stopped for: 1 pr. shoes-$1.22, 1 india rubber canteen-$.27; pres. 08/1848, BLW sent to Fredericksburg, VA; m. Hester Ann Robinson 02/02/1854 Stafford Co. VA; c. 1870 res. Fredericksburg, Spotsylvania Co., VA, age 44, occ. Farmer, w. Ann H. (36), dau. Ann E. (15), dau. Elmira (14), dau. Margaretta (12), son Luther (9), son William (7), son Wesley (4), son Joseph (2);[1643] SC #9794, 02/18/1887, phys. desc. age 61, 5'10", dark complexion, black eyes, gray hair, occ. Farmer; since discharge res. *"Stafford Co. until the year 1859 when I removed to Spotsylvania County, VA where I have resided to this time."*[1887] Owned 33 acres of land one mile N.E. of Spotsylvania C.H.;[1642] Pvt. Lafayette Franklin *"of Fredericksburg, VA"* gave affidavit in pension claim; d. 01/06/1906 near Spotsylvania C.H., Spotsylvania Co., VA;[1642] wid. Hester

## VIRGINIA VOLUNTEERS IN MEXICO

A., WC #14336, 02/02/1906, both filed from Spotsylvania C.H., Spotsylvania Co., VA; (HAS b. 03/07/1834, d. 08/14/1913 near Spotsylvania C.H., Spotsylvania Co., VA, bur. Baca? Cemetery, Spotsylvania).

**Shelton, Stephen**, Pvt., Co. I; enl. Mex. War service 08/18/1847, Ft. Monroe, VA, age 19; pres. 02/1848 joined co. 01/26/1848; pres. 04/1848, pay stopped for: 1 jacket, 1 blanket; pres. 08/1848, BLW sent to Pleasant Grove, Lunenburg Co., VA; c. 1850 res. Lunenburg Co., VA, age 23, occ. Laborer.[1644]

**Shepherd, John Newton**, Pvt., *Recruit Co.*; b. 01/24/1829;[45] enl. Mex. War service 02/25/1848 Charlestown, VA, age 19; pres. 02/1848; pres. 04/1848; pres. 06/1848; BLW sent to Berryville, Clarke Co., VA; c. 1860 res. Mill Creek, Berkeley Co., VA, age 31, occ. Farmer, w. Mary S. (21), son Washington (5/12);[1645] Civil War service enl. Pvt., Co. C, 12$^{th}$ Va. Cav., 03/11/1862 at Winchester, VA, phys. desc. 6'1", light complexion, hazel eyes, auburn hair, res. Berkeley Co., VA, wded. 06/09/1863 at Brandy Sta., VA "gunshot wd. through head fracturing mastoral process," furloughed 07/20/1863 for 60 days, absent wded. through 08/1864, paroled 04/21/1865 at Winchester, VA;[809] SC #12843, 08/11/1887, from VA; d. 01/06/1896, bur. Greenhill Cem., Berryville, VA.[45]

**Shepherdson, William N.**, Pvt., Co. D; enl. Mex. War service 01/02/1847, Petersburg, VA, age 23; pres. 02/1847; pres. 04/1847; discharged 05/15/1847 Monterey, Mex. on Surgeon's Certificate of Disability; a William Shepherdson m. Susan Rebecca Rainey, 01/1847;[1646] c. 1870 res. Petersburg, Chesterfield Co., VA, age 45, occ. Laborer, w. Rebecca (44), dau. Lucy (21), dau. Emma J. (18), dau. Sallie A. (16), dau. Susannah (14);[1647] [Civil War service a William Shepperson served as a Pvt., Co. B, 40$^{th}$ Btln. Va. Cav., trans. to 10$^{th}$ Va. Cav.;][202, 312] SC #5703, 05/09/1887, from TN; [pension file not found].

**Shepperson, George C.P.**, Pvt., *Recruit Co.*, b. c. 1828, Black Lick, Wythe Co., VA; enl. Mex. War service 08/09/1847 Lunenburg C.H., VA, age 22; discharged 12/28/1847 at Ft. Monroe, VA on Surgeon's Certificate of Disability; m. Elizabeth Rhoda Ward 03/08/1854, Wythe Co., VA[1648]

**Sherard, Benjamin W.**, *Not on Muster Rolls*; wid. Ann, WC #4891, 05/22/1888, from MS, OW W #19747, rejected.

**Sherrard, William**, 4$^{th}$ Sgt., Co. H; b. 09/08/1820, Berkeley Co., VA;[1649] enl. Mex. War service 11/27/1846, Berkeley, VA, age 26; pres. 04/1847; pres. 06/1847, prom. 2$^{nd}$ Cpl.; pres. 08/1847; pres. 10/1847, pay stopped for: 1 forage cap-$.95$^{1/2}$, 1 pr. pants-$2.28, 2 cotton shirts-$.86, 2 pr. drawers-$.71, 2 pr. socks-$.49; pres. 12/1847, pay stopped for: 1 forage cap-$.95$^{1/2}$, 1 jacket-$2.66, 3 pr. socks-$.73$^{1/2}$, 1 pr. pants-$2.28; pres. 02/1848; pres. 04/1848, prom. 4$^{th}$ Sgt. 04/12/1848; pres. 07/1848, BLW sent to Martinsburg, VA; m. Harriet E. Daniel, 09/24/1849, Hagerstown, Washington Co., MD;[1649] c. 1850 res. Berkeley Co., VA, age 30, occ. Farmer, w. Harriet (20);[1650] c. 1860 res. Mill Creek, Berkeley Co., VA, age 40, occ. Farmer, w. Harriet (30), son Joseph (9), dau. Mary (3), son William (1);[1651] Civil War service enl. Capt., Co. H, 27$^{th}$ Va. Inf. 04/191861 Darkesville, VA, pres. until AWOL 06/04/1861, resigned 06/05/1861;[702] enl. Pvt., Co. I, 12$^{th}$ Va. Cav. (no date), at Bartonsville, VA, res. Berkeley Co., phys. desc. 5'9", light complex., gray eyes, light hair, AWOL since 06/12/1863, captured 09/10/1863 at Winchester, VA sent to Ft. McHenry 09/12/1863 and Pt. Lookout 09/16/1863, exchanged 12/25/1863, AWOL 02/20/1864 – 03/1864, pres. 04/30/1864, paroled at Winchester 05/08/1865;[809] SC #13164, 12/09/1887, filed from Eagle Pass, Maverick Co., TX; phys. desc. 5'8", grey eyes, dark hair, rather fair complexion, occ. Farmer and Miller; since discharge res. Gerrardstown, VA, 16 yrs. and Texas 33 yrs.;[1649] d. 08/06/1898, *"Bright's Disease, age 82, farmer,"*[1652] Martinsburg, Berkeley Co., bur. Lutheran Cem.,? Berkeley Co., WV;[1653] wid. Harriet E., WC #11676, 02/25/1899, from WV; (HDS b. 04/09/1829, Gerrardstown, Berkeley Co., VA, d. 08/08/1901).[1653]

OFF TO WAR

**Shields, David F.**, Pvt., Co. E; b. c. 1827, New Kent Co., VA;[1654] enl. Mex. War service 12/05/1846 Petersburg, VA, age 21; pres. 04/1847; pres. 06/1847; pres. 08/1847; pres. 10/1847, pay stopped for: 1 pr. overalls-$2.28, 3 pr. shoes-$3.66, 4 pr. stockings-$.98, 2 cotton shirts-$.86, 1 cap-$.95$^{1/2}$; pres. 12/1847, pay stopped for: 2 pr. socks-$.49, 2 flannel shirt-$1.80, 2 pr. drawers-$.71, 1 blanket-$2.22; pres. 02/1848, pay stopped for: 1 pr. pants-$2.28, 1 pr. shoes-$1.22; pres. 04/1848, pay stopped for: 1 jacket-$2.37$^{1/2}$; m/1 Rebecca Ann Davis 12/13/1849; c. 1860 res. Petersburg, Dinwiddie Co., VA, age 33, occ. Carpenter, w. Rebecca T. (27), dau. Mary E. (10), son Wm. T. Shields (6), son D.H. Shields (30), dau. Emma (5/12);[1655] c. 1870 res. Petersburg, Dinwiddie Co., VA, age 43, occ. Carpenter, w. Rebecca (38), dau. Mary (20) son William (17), son Hamlin (14), dau. Alice (9);[1656] m/2 Angelina P. Farley, 04/23/1879, widow of Peter Farley; SC #15352, 01/05/1888, filed from 18 Lombard St., Petersburg, VA; lists children Mary E. Shields b. 11/25/1850, David Hamlin Shields b. 10/08/1857, Almeria E. Shields b. 12/24/1859; (APS d. 07/14/1896); d. 09/20/1906, *Endocarditis, aged 79 yrs., 11 mos. 12 days*, bur. Blandford Cemetery, Sq. 2, Sec. 4, Ward E, Petersburg, VA, aged 79;[1654, 1657] [pension file not found].
**Shinault, James**, Co. K; *Not on Muster Rolls*; wid. Susan E., WA #9980, 07/14/1891, from VA
**Shinn, Thomas A.**, Pvt., Co. F; enl. Mex. War service 01/20/1847, Portsmouth, VA, age 31; absent 06/1847 sent to Hosp. at Camargo, Mex. 04/04/1847; absent 08/1847 sick at Camargo, Mex. 4/04/1847; absent 10/1847 sick; absent 12/1847 sick; discharged date unknown Matamoros, Mex.
**Shipman, William P.**, Pvt., Co. K; b. 02/14/1823, New Market, Frederick Co., MD;[1658] enl. Mex. War service Jefferson Co., VA 12/28/1846, age 23; pres. 06/1847, prom. Fifer from Pvt. 05/28/1847; pres. 08/1847; pres. 10/1847; pres. 12/1847, pay stopped for: 1 pr. overalls-$2.28, 1 pr. socks-$.24$^{1/2}$, 1 pr. drawers-$.35$^{1/2}$, 1 blanket-$2.22, 1 cotton shirt-$.43; pres. 04/1848, pay stopped for: 1 overcoat-$6.93$^{1/2}$, 1 jacket-$2.66, 2 pr. pants-$4.56, 2 pr. socks-$.49, 1 cap-$.95$^{1/2}$, 1 pr. drawers-$.35$^{1/2}$, 1 pr. shoes-$1.22; pres. 07/1848, pay stopped for: 1 screw driver-$.25, 1 wiper-$.20, 1 cartridge box plate-$.10, 1 pick & brush-$.12, 1 waist belt plate-$.10; BLW sent to Charlestown, Jefferson Co., VA; c. 1860 res. Hanging Rock, Hampshire Co., VA;[1659] c. 1880 res. Capon, Hardy Co., WV, age 56, occ. Shoemaker, w. Eliza Ann (42) Keeping House, dau. Laura V. (19), son Wm. C. (16), son Charles (14), son Benjamin M. (10);[1660] SC #12993, 02/26/1887, filed from Wardensville, Hardy Co., WV; phys. desc. age 64 [1887], 5'6$^{1/2}$", light complexion, gray eyes, dark hair, occ. shoemaker;[1658] d. 06/24/1897.[1658]
**Shoemaker, William L.**, Pvt., Co. H; enl. Mex. War service 01/06/1847, Berkeley, VA, age 34; pres. 04/1847; pres. 06/1847; pres. 08/1847; pres. 10/1847, pay stopped for: 1 pr. pants-$2.28, 2 cotton shirts-$.86, 1 pr. drawers-$.35$^{1/2}$, 2 pr. shoes-$2.44, 1flannel-$.90; Court-martialed 12/02/1847 Buena Vista, Mex. *"Charge #1 Drunkeness on Duty; Specification: In that Pvt. W.L. Shoemaker, Co. H, Va. Regt. Vols., being posted as a Sentinel of the Provost Guard was found drunk on his post...at Buena Vista, Mexico Nov. 27$^{th}$, 1847; Charge #2 Selling Liquor to the Provost Prisoners; Specification: In that said Pvt. W.L. Shoemaker was seen in the act of selling liquor to a prisoner of the provost guard...at Buena Vista, Mexico Nov. 27$^{th}$, 1847; Pleaded Guilty to Charge #1 and Not Guilty to Charge #2; Sentenced...to forfeit one (1) months pay and to be kept on extra police duty in his company for the period of one month;"*[1661] in confinement 12/1847, pay stopped for: 1 blanket-$2.22; pres. 02/1848, pay stopped for: 1 forage cap-$.95$^{1/2}$, 1 pr. drawers-$.35$^{1/2}$, 2 pr. shoes-$2.44; pres. 04/1848; pres. 07/1848, pay stopped for: 2 gun slings-$.32, 1 screw driver-$.25, BLW sent to Pottsville, Pa.
**Short, Calvin R.**, Pvt., *Preston's Co.*; b. c. 1803, Floyd Co., VA, son of Reuben & Lydia (Clarke) Short;[1662, 1663] m. Sarah Janney 05/05/1834 Franklin Co., VA;[1664] enl. Mex. War service 12/09/1846 Montgomery Co., VA, age 43; pres. 04/1847; discharged 05/05/1847 on Surgeon's Certificate of Disability; c. 1850 res. Wythe Co., VA, age 48, occ. Laborer, w?. Sarah (25), dau. Americus (12), son Benjamin (10), son Albert (7);[1665] c. 1860 res. Wythe Co., VA, age 56, occ. Laborer, w. Sarah (48), dau. Mary (6);[1666] Civil War service Pvt., Co. E, 36$^{th}$

## VIRGINIA VOLUNTEERS IN MEXICO

Va. Inf., enl. 01/27/1863 at Princeton, WV, pres. until sick, 05/13/1864, NFR;[390] (SJS d. 09/25/1865);[1662] m/1 Elizabeth A. (Castle) Ahlt, 08/18/1867, Wythe Co., VA;[1662] phys. desc. 5'6" or 7", dark complexion, dark hair, dark eyes, occ. Laborer;[1662] d. 07/18/1877, Wythe Co., VA;[1662] *"Died at his home, in this county, on Wednesday, 18th July, 1877, Calvin R. Shortt, aged about 70 years. The deceased was an honest man. He served his country faithfully as a soldier in the Mexican and Confederate Wars...He leaves a wife, sons and daughters to mourn the demise of a kind father. Peace to his ashes. A FRIEND;"* [1662, 1667] wid. Elizabeth A., WC #8624, 03/24/1893, from VA; Lists living children Chancellor G. Short and Henrietta Short Pattison;[1662] (ECS b. 10/21/1831 Wythe Co., VA, m/1 Thomas A. Ahlt, he d. 09/19/1862, ECS d. 02/18/1915).[1662]

**Shriver, William**, Pvt., *Recruit Co.*, enl. Mex. War service 02/15/1848 Charlestown, VA; pres. 02/1848; absent 04/1848 sick in hosp.; pres. 02/1848; pres. 06/1848; BLW sent to Washington City, D.C.

**Shryock, James F.**, Pvt., Co. K; enl. Mex. War service Frederick Co., VA 12/20/1846, age 24; pres. 06/1847; pres. 08/1847; pres. 10/1847, pay stopped for: 2 pr. drawers-$.71, 3 pr. socks-$.73$^{1/2}$, 1 pr. shoes-$1.22, 1 pr. overalls-$2.28, 1 cap-$.95$^{1/2}$; pres. 12/1847; pres. 04/1848, pay stopped for: 1 jacket-$2.66, 1 pr. pants-$2.28; pres. 07/1848, pay stopped for: 1 gun sling-$.18; BLW sent to Winchester, Frederick Co., VA; m. Caroline Kerns, 02/06/1849, Frederick Co., VA;[1668, 1669] c. 1850 res. Frederick Co., VA, age 27, occ. Carpenter, w. Caroline (26), dau. Ann A. (1);[1670] c. 1860 res. Winchester, Frederick Co., VA, w. Caroline (37), dau. Ann A. (10), son Theodore (8), son Frederick (6), dau. Billie (4);[1671] Civil War service Pvt., Jackson Arty., enl. 09/23/1862, absent 10/1862 through 04/1863 conveying broken down horses to S.C., absent 04/1862 through 06/1863 sick in Staunton, VA, deserted 07/31/1863; rejoined battery at unknown date, KIA 09/19/1864 at Winchester, VA;[180] [a James Frederick Shryock is also reported as a Pvt., Co. A, 1st Va. Cav., enl. 07/10/1863 at Newtown, VA, AWOL through 02/1864, court-martialed and confined in C.S. Military Prison, Lynchburg, VA, 07/1864, RTD, transferred to 1st Md. Cav. 01/10/1865? NFR.;][441] wid. Caroline, WC #603, 04/11/1887, filed from Kernstown, Frederick Co., VA; phys. desc. of soldier b. near Newtown, Stephensburg, over 5', dark hair, gray eyes, dark complexion;[1668] A.J. Copenhaver gave affidavit in pension claim;[1668] (CKS b. 08/15/1822, Frederick Co., VA).[1668]

**Shumaker, Lindsay Mayo**, 1st Lt., Co. I; b. c. 1825, son of Lindsey & Elizabeth Shoemaker;[1672] enl. Mex. War service 01/10/1847 Richmond, VA; pres. 02/1847; in confinement 04/1847, for AWOL from 4 o'clock on 04/27/1847 until 04/29/1847 and disobedience of orders; pres. 06/1847, released from arrest 05/09/1847, in command of company; pres. 08/1847; pres. 10/1847; pres. 12/1847 in command of the co.; pres. 02/1848 in command of the co.; pres. 04/1848; pres. 08/1848; c. 1850 res. Bedford Co., VA, age 25, occ. Attorney at Law;[1673] m. Ella W. Tunstall, 02/05/1857, Pittsylvania Co., VA;[1674] c. 1860 res. Danville, Pittsylvania Co., VA, age 34, occ. Lawyer, w. Ella E. (22), son Tunstall (1);[1675] Civil War service Maj., Gen. Staff, Artly., C.S.A., raised a company of Artillery and appointed Captain 04/22/1861, wded. slightly 10/03/1861 at Greenbriar River, absent recruiting 12/1861, absent sick 1/1862 through 02/1862, not reelected, appointed Major of Artillery, commanding Taliafero's Division, 07/05/1862, relieved of duty 10/10/1862, reported to Adjt. & Insp. Genls. Office in N.C., NFR, postwar military appointee Superior Court, Pittsylvania Co., VA, 1869, Circuit Court Judge, Pittsy. Co. 1869-1870, Editor of the *Danville Register*, c. 1870 res. Danville, Pittsylvania Co., VA, age 45, occ. Lawyer, w. Ella W. (31), son Tunstall (11), dau. Anna (8), dau. Ella Lee (3), son Lindsay (11/12);[1676] d. 10/28/1884?, bur. Masonic Section, Greenhill Cemetery, Danville, VA[1677]

**Silvers, William**, Pvt., *Preston's Co.*; son of Abram & Delila Silvers;[1678] enl. Mex. War service 12/06/1846 Montgomery Co., VA, age 19; pres. 04/1847; discharged 05/05/1847 on Surgeon's Certificate of Disability; m/1 Ruth Akers, 09/15/1849, Montgomery Co., VA;[1679] c. 1850 res. Montgomery Co., VA, age 24, occ. Farmer, w. Ruth (22);[1680] (RAS d. 01/21/1862);

OFF TO WAR

m/2 Narcissa Akers, 04/09/1863, Montgomery Co., VA;[1678] d. 07/06/1869, Montgomery Co., VA;[1681] c. 1870 res. Christiansburg, Montgomery Co., VA, w. Narcissa (48), son Charles T. (18), dau. Octavia A. (16), dau. Mary M. (13), Susan F. (12), Virginia C. (10), dau. Emaline M. (4);[1682] wid. Narcissa, WC #2756, 07/06/1887, filed from Snowville, Pulaski Co., VA; Henry Collins and Michael Kipps gave affidavit in pension claim;[1681] (NAS b. 09/22/1821, d. 04/09/1898).[1681]

**Simes, Miles**, Pvt., LIC; m. Martha Blair, 07/13/1826, Augusta Co., VA;[1683] enl. Mex. War service 01/06/1846 Staunton, VA, age 42; d. 06/28/1847 at Saltillo, Mex.; c. 1850 res. Augusta Co., VA, wid. Martha (55), son James L. (28), Plasterer, dau. Eliza A. (21), dau. Louisa J. (19), son William L. (16), Farmer, son Samuel M. (15), dau. Isabella F. (11).[1684]

**Simmons, James F.**, Pvt., Co. C; enl. Mex. War service 12/30/1846, Bowling Green, VA, age 37; pres. 06/1847; pres. 08/1847, pay stopped for: 1 cap-$.95$^{1/2}$, 2 pr. socks-$.49, 2 cotton shirts-$.86, 2 woolen shirts-$1.80; Court-martialed 10/15/1847 Buena Vista, Mex. *Charge #1: Conduct Unbecoming a Soldier; Specification: In this that he, the said Private James Simmons, Co. C, Va. Regt., did steal from the trunk of Captain Smith P. Bankhead, ninety-seven dollars and fifty cents in gold and from ten to fifteen dollars in silver, and did feloniously and fraudulently expend a large portion of said money. This at Saltillo, Mex. on or about the 2$^{nd}$ day of October 1847. To which charge the prisoner plead Guilty and Not Guilty to the specification. Capt. W.M. Robinson, Va. Regt., a witness for the prosecution, being duly sworn, says: Before the prisoner was charged with taking the money, he tried to throw suspicion upon another person. And when charged with the theft he denied positively having taken the money. Afterwards he confessed that he had taken $80.50, but denied having taken more. The amount of $80.50 was returned to Captain Bankhead. This occurred in Saltillo, Mex. on or about the 2$^{nd}$ of October 1847. After deliberation the Court found the prisoner Guilty of the Charge and Specification. He was sentenced to forfeit all pay and allowances due him. To be confined in irons in the Provost Guard for one week. To be "bucked" two hours each day of said week from 3 to 5 o'clock P.M. To stand on the head of a barrel each day of said week from 7 to 9 o'clock A.M. To have one side of his head shaved, his face blacked, the letter "T" branded on his right hip. And at the end of the week to be drummed out of service;*[1685] in confinement 10/1847, in provost guard, all pay and allowances stopped by order of genl. court-martial; b. Pa. c. 1810; desc., age 37, 5'11", dark complexion, dark hair, dark eyes; discharged 11/09/1847 by sentence of general court-martial, *"drummed out of camp."*[26]

**Simmons, Wesley C.**, Pvt., Co. G; b. c. 1822; enl. Mex. War service 12/08/1846 Richmond, VA, age 26; discharged at Fort Monroe, VA no date or explanation; m. Lucy Jane Blaylock, 03/16/1848, Richmond, Henrico Co., VA;[1686] c. 1860 res. Richmond, Henrico Co., VA, age 40, occ. Shoemaker, b. Maryland, w. Lucy (32), dau. Ann (11), dau. Augusta (8), son John (4), son William (9/12);[1687] Civil War service Pvt., Co. C, 10$^{th}$ Btln. VA Hvy. Arty., enl. 03/10/1862 at Richmond, VA, age 41, detailed to Manchester Cotton Factory by order of Gen. G.W. Smith, trans. to C.S. Shoe Dept., Richmond, never rejoined the btln., paroled 04/12/1865 at Richmond, VA, res. Oregon Hill, Richmond, VA, occ. Farmer;[33] c. 1870 res. Richmond, Henrico Co., VA, age 50, occ. Laborer, w. Lucy (42), dau. Augusta (17), son John (13);[1688] d. 01/01/1885, Richmond, VA;[1686] wid. Lucy Jane, WC #4380, 03/14/1887, filed from 626 High St., Richmond, Henrico Co., VA

**Simpkins, William D.**, Pvt., *Preston's Co.*; enl. Mex. War service 12/06/1846 Montgomery Co., VA, age 32; absent 04/1847 left sick in hosp at Pt. Isabel, Tex. since 03/11/1847; pres. 06/1847; pres. 08/1847; pres. 10/1847, pay stopped for: 1 jacket-$2.66, 1 cotton shirt-$.43, 1 pr. drawers-$.35$^{1/2}$; absent 12/1847, on detached service as Wagoneer in QM Dept. since 12/11/1847; absent 02/1848 on detached service; pres. 04/1848; pres. 07/1848, pay stopped for: 1 pr. shoes-$1.16, 1 gun sling-$.18; BLW sent to Christiansburg, VA c/o Fleming Gardner; m. Eliza Jane Woodall, 1849, Pulaski Co., VA;[1689] d. 09/12/1883, near Moorehead,

VIRGINIA VOLUNTEERS IN MEXICO

Rowan Co., KY;[1689] wid. Eliza A., WC #3768, 07/20/1887, filed from Percal, Elliot Co. KY; (EWS b. 1826, North Carolina).[1689]

**Simpson, James R.**, Pvt., *Preston's Co.*; b. 09/13/1823, near Fincastle, Botetourt Co., VA, son of Thomas and Susan Simpson;[1690] enl. Mex. War service 01/05/1847 Montgomery Co., VA, age 23; absent 04/1847 left sick at Ft. Monroe, VA since 02/27/1847; absent 06/1847 sick at Ft. Monroe, VA; pres. 08/1847; sick 10/1847, pay stopped for: 1 pr. overalls-$2.28, 1 pr. shoes-$1.22, 4 pr. socks-$.98, 2 cotton shirts-$.98, 1 pr. drawers-$.35$^{1/2}$; pres. 12/1847, pay stopped for: 1 pr. overalls-$2.28; sick 02/1848, pay stopped for: 1 cap-$.95$^{1/2}$; pres. 04/1848; pres. 07/1848, pay stopped for: 1 brush & pick-$.12, 1 jacket-$2.37, 1 cap-$.95$^{1/2}$, 1 bayonet scabbard-$.56, 1 waist belt-$.25, 1 waist belt plate-$.08, 1 screw driver-$.12; BLW sent to Christiansburg, VA c/o Fleming Gardner; m/1 Sarepta A. Hudson, 12/27/1854, New Albany, Floyd Co., Ind.;[1690] (SHS d. 04/16/1868, Nicholas Co., WV);[1690] m/2 Elizabeth Hess, 03/14/1870, Open Fork, Bell Creek, WV;[1690] c. 1880 res. Jefferson Dist., Nicholas Co., WV, age 56, occ. Farmer, w. Elizabeth (44) Keeping House, son Oscar J. (17) Works on Farm, son John G. (14) Works on Farm, dau. Mary C. (6), dau. Susan (3), stepson James W. Hess (12) Works on Farm;[1691] SC #4195, 03/18/1887, filed from Dixie, Nicholas Co., WV; phys. desc. age 63 [1887], 5'9", dark complexion, hazel eyes, dark hair, occ. Farmer, since discharge res. Montgomery Co., VA until 12/25/1853, Clarke Co., Ind. until 09/17/1857, Nicholas and Fayette Cos., WV since then;[1690] d. 10/21/1889, Bell Creek, Fayette Co., WV, *"...and was buried in sight of his house in Nicholas Co., WV;"*[1692] wid. Elizabeth, WC #7526, 10/25/1890, filed from Dixie, Nicholas Co., WV; (EHS b. 02/03/1841, Fayette Co., VA, d. 02/04/1921, Vaughan, Nicholas Co., WV, bur. Vaughan, WV).[1692]

**Simpson, Robert**, Pvt., Co. E; enl. Mex. War service 11/30/1846 Petersburg, VA, age 20; pres. 04/1847; absent 06/1847 on furlough 6 mos. from 06/07/1847 as Clerk in Commissary Dept. Monterey, Mex.; absent 08/1847 on furlough; absent 10/1847 on furlough; absent 12/1847 on furlough for 1 mo. from 12/07/1847; absent 02/1848, in Actg. Asst. Adj. Genl.'s office since 01/21/1848, pay stopped for: 1 knapsack-$1.10, 2 pr. socks-$.49; pres. 04/1848, on daily duty in Actg. Asst. Genl's. office.

**Sinclair, James H.**, Pvt., *Recruit Co.*, enl. Mex. War service 12/30/1847 Christiansburg, VA, age 24; pres. 02/1848; pres. 04/1848; pres. 06/1848; BLW sent to Christiansburg, VA

**Sine, Lorenzo Dow**, Pvt., *Recruit Co.*, b. 11/10/1829, Hampshire Co., VA, son of Rev. Christy & Margaret (Kackley) Sine;[1693] enl. Mex. War service 01/21/1848 Charleston, VA, age 18; pres. 02/1848; pres. 04/1848; pres. 06/1848; BLW sent to Charlestown, Jefferson Co., VA; d. 06/10/1876.[1694]

**Sira, Nicholas**, Pvt., *Recruit Co.*, enl. Mex. War service 01/07/1848 Christiansburg, VA, age 21; pres. 02/1848; pres. 04/1848; pres. 06/1848; BLW sent to Christiansburg, VA

**Skeen, William E.**, Pvt., LIC; b. 03/21/1828, Ripley Co., IN;[1695] enl. Mex. War service 12/07/1846 Staunton, VA, age 18; pres. 08/1847; pres. 10/1847, pay stopped for: 1 forage cap-$.95$^{1/2}$, 1 wool jacket-$2.66, 2 pr. overalls-$4.56, 1 pr. shoes-$1.22, 2 pr. socks-$.49, 1 cotton shirts-$.43; pres. 12/1847, pay stopped for: 1 blanket-$2.22, 1 pr. shoes-$1.22, 1 pr. overalls-$2.28; pres. 04/1848, pay stopped for: 4 cotton shirts-$1.72; pres. 07/1848; BLW sent to Staunton, VA; SC #6171, 02/02/1887, filed from Staunton, Augusta Co., VA; *"I reside at Staunton, Virginia. My age is 66 years* [1893]. *I have suffered for more than 30 years past, and am still afflicted in that way, with hernia of the bowels. Received a pistol shot in left groin whilst in service in the Mexican War from which I have never recovered and never will...;"*[1695] phys. desc. at enl. age 19, 5'10", light hair, blue eyes, occ. Tanner;[1695] d. 11/22/1902.[1695]

**Skiles, William**, *Ruffner's Co.*; Not on Muster Rolls; c. 1850 res. Kanawha Co., VA, age 22, occ. Cooper, Frances (17);[1696] c. 1860 res. Kanawha C.H., Kanawha Co., VA, age 32, occ. Cooper, w. Frances (27), dau. Mary C. (7), dau. Margaret A. (3), son William H. (1);[1697] SA #24890, 12/19/1896, from WV.

OFF TO WAR

**Slack, Daton A.**, 2nd Lt., *Ruffin's Co.*; *Not on Muster Rolls;* c. 1850 res. Kanawha Co., VA, age 28, occ. Laborer, w. Elizabeth (23), dau. Mary C. (3), dau. Caroline (1/12);[1698] c. 1860 res. Kanawha Salines, Kanawha Co., VA, age 39, occ. Boatman, w. Elizabeth (38), dau. Mary C. (10), dau. Caroline (9), dau. Louella (6), son William A. (5), son James L. (2);[1699] wid. Elizabeth A., WA #13774, 02/12/1887, from WV.

**Sly, William M.**, Pvt., LIC; b. c. 1827, son of Henry V. & Rachel (Tankersly) Sly; enl. Mex. War service 12/22/1846 Staunton, VA, age 19; NFR; c. 1850 res. Rockbridge Co., VA, age 23, occ. Millwright;[1700] c. 1860 res. Lexington, Rockbridge Co., VA, age 33, occ. Farmer, w. Mary (25), dau. Malory (5), dau. Luella (10/12);[1701] m. Mary Jane Gregory, 07/03/1854, Rockbridge Co., VA[1702]

**Smiley, Theodore B.**, Pvt., Co. D; enl. Mex. War service 01/01/1847, Petersburg, VA, age 29; pres. 02/1847; pres. 04/1847; pres. but sick 06/1847; pres. 08/1847, pay stopped for: 1 pr. shoes-$1.22; pres. but sick 1847, pay stopped for: 1 cap-$.95$^{1/2}$, 1 pr. pants-$2.28, 2 flannel shirts-$1.80, 2 cotton shirts-$.86, 2 pr. drawers-$.71, 2 pr. socks-$.49; pres. 12/1847, fined 1 mos. pay by order (No. 162) of genl. court-martial 12/14/1847, pay stopped for: 1 jacket-$2.66, 2 pr. socks-$.49, 1 blanket-$2.22; pres. 04/1848, pay stopped for: 1 flannel shirt-$.90, 1 pr. shoes-$1.22, 1 haversack-$.20$^{3/4}$; pres. 08/1847, BLW sent to Petersburg, VA; Civil War service Pvt., Co. A, 24th NC Inf.[202]

**Smith, Abijah B.**, Pvt., Co. L; b. 1827; enl. Mex. War service 03/30/1847 Ft. Washington, MD, age 20; pres. 06/1847; pres. 08/1847; pres. 10/1847, pay stopped for: 1 pr. Pants 2.28, 1 pr. Shoes 1.22, 1 F Cap .95; pres. 12/1847, pay stopped for: 1 jacket-$2.66, 1 pr. pants-$2.28, 2 flannel shirts-$1.80, 1 cotton shirts-$.43, 1 blanket-$2.22, 2 pr. drawers-$.71, 1 pr. socks-$.24$^{1/2}$; pres. 02/1848, pay stopped for: 1 pr. Shoes 1.22, 1 Brush & Pick .12; pres. 04/1848, pay stopped for: 1 Blanket 2.25, 1 Cotton Shirt .44; pres. 07/1848, pay stopped for: 1 Wiper .20; BLW sent to Washington City, D.C.

**Smith, Albert A. (T.)**, Pvt., Co. D; b. c. 1825; enl. Mex. War service 01/05/1847, Petersburg, VA, age 21; pres. 02/1847; absent 04/1847 sick in Hosp. Monterey, Mex. since 04/1847; pres. 06/1847; pres. 08/1847, pay stopped for: 1 cap-$.95$^{1/2}$, 2 cotton shirts-$.86, 1 pr. shoes-$1.22; pres. 10/1847, pay stopped for: 1 jacket-$2.66, 1 pr. pants-$2.28, 2 flannel shirts-$1.80, 1 cotton shirt-$.43, 1 pr. drawers-$.35$^{1/2}$, 2 pr. socks-$.49; pres. 12/1847, pay stopped for: 1 pr. pants-$2.28, 2 cotton shirts-$.86, 1 pr drawers-$.35$^{1/2}$, 1 pr. shoes-$1.22, 1 blanket-$2.22; pres. 04/1848; pres. 08/1847, BLW sent to Dinwiddie C.H., VA; c. 1850 res. Dinwiddie Co., VA, age 25, w. Martha P. (16), bro.? John W. (12);[1703] c. 1860 res. Petersburg, Dinwiddie Co., VA, age 35, occ. Farmer, son? John E. (8);[1704] Civil War service Pvt., Co. C, 3rd Va. Inf., enl. 05/23/1861 at Dinwiddie C.H., VA, age 32, occ. Overseer, pres. 05/1861 through 06/1862 when hosp. at Farmville with the Mumps, deserted from Winder, Div. No. 5 Hosp. 09/23/1862;[1705] m. Martha A. Wells, 08/19/1878, Dinwiddie Co., VA;[1706] SC #4538, 04/01/1887, filed from Rowanta, Dinwiddie Co., VA; phys. desc. at enlistment age 22, 5'8", dark hair, blue eyes, occ. Farmer;[1706] d. 02/11/1889, Dinwiddie Co., VA;[1707] wid. Martha A., WC #6213, 03/21/1889, filed from Ream's Station, Dinwiddie Co., VA (MAS b. 03/11/1838 Dinwiddie Co., VA, d. 11/03/1902).[1707]

**Smith, Calvin N.**, Pvt., Co. D; enl. Mex. War service 01/07/1847, Petersburg, VA, age 22; pres. 02/1847; pres. 04/1847; pres. 06/1847; pres. 08/1847, pay stopped for: 1 pr. pants-$2.28; pres. 10/1847, pay stopped for: 1 cap-$.95$^{1/2}$, 1 pr. pants-$2.28, 1 pr. drawers-$.35$^{1/2}$; pres. 12/1847, pay stopped for: 1 jacket-$2.66, 2 pr drawers-$.71; pres. 04/1848; pres. 08/1847, BLW sent to Harrisonburg, Rockingham Co., VA; SC #17277, 10/27/1888, from VA; d. Providence, R.I., 1897, was the brother of 2nd Cpl. William B. Smith[1708]

**Smith, Edmond P.**, Pvt., *Recruit Co.*, enl. Mex. War service 01/05/1848 Christiansburg, VA, age 20; pres. 02/1848; pres. 04/1848; pres. 06/1848; BLW sent to Taylorsville, Patrick Co., VA

**Smith, Jerome B.**, Pvt., Co. D; enl. Mex. War service 08/16/1847 Boydton, VA, age 19; pres. 04/1848, pay stopped for: 1 overcoat-$6.93$^{1/2}$; pres. 08/1847, BLW sent to [illegible]

276

VIRGINIA VOLUNTEERS IN MEXICO

Mecklenburg Co., VA; [Civil War service a Jerome B. Smith served Pvt., Co. D, 16$^{th}$ Tenn. Inf. and also Pvt., Co. F, 2$^{nd}$ Miss. Inf.] [202]

**Smith, James L.**, Pvt., Co. L; b. 1827; enl. Mex. War service 04/03/1847 Cumberland, MD, age 20; pres. 06/1847; pres. 08/1847; pres. 10/1847, pay stopped for: 1 F Cap .95; pres. 12/1847, pay stopped for: 1 pr. pants-$2.28, 1 pr. shoes-$3.66, 4 cotton shirts-$1.72, 1 blanket-$2.22, 1 pr. drawers-$.35$^{1/2}$, 2 pr. socks-$.49; pres. 02/1848, pay stopped for: 1 Jacket 2.66; pres. 04/1848, pay stopped for: 1 Blanket 2.25, 1 pr. Shoes 1.16, 2 Cotton Shirt .88; pres. 07/1848; BLW sent to Washington City, D.C.

**Smith, James**, Pvt., Co. M; enl. Mex. War service 11/04/1847, Norfolk, VA, age 34; pres. 11/1847; pres. 12/1847; pres. 02/1848; pres. 04/1848, pay stopped for: 1 blanket-$2.22, 1 pr. shoes-$1.22, 2 cotton shirts-$.86; pres. 08/1848, pay stopped for: 1 musket & accoutrements complete-$16.22, 1 pr, shoes-$1.16; BLW sent to Norfolk, VA [a James E. Smith *"Pvt., Mex. War,"* d. 09/01/1889, at National Soldiers Home, Hampton, VA, bur. Hampton National Cemetery, Plot: 6194, Hampton, VA]

**Smith, James**, Pvt., Co. E; enl. Mex. War service 11/30/1846 Petersburg, VA, age 24; absent 04/1847 on detached service Monterey, Mex. with Col. Hamtramck; AWOL 06/1847 since 06/22/1847; pres. 08/1847; in confinement 10/1847, pay stopped for: 1 pr. shoes-$1.22, 4 pr. stockings-$.98, 1 cotton shirt-$.43, 1 cap-$.95$^{1/2}$; Court-martialed 10/14/1847, Buena Vista, Mex. *Charge #1: Sleeping On Post; Specification: In this that he, the said Private James Smith, Co. E, Va. Regt., being regularly mounted on guard and posted as a Sentinel, did sit down and fall asleep on his post. This at Saltillo, Mex. on or about the 4$^{th}$ of October 1847. To which charge and specification the prisoner pleaded Guilty. Private James L. White, Co. E, Va. Regt. Vols., a witness for the defense, being duly sworn, says: Question by the Prisoner: In what manner was I posted at 11 o'clock P.M. before I was found asleep? Answer: It has been usual for the Corporal of the Guard to go a short distance with the Sentinels and then allow them to go and take post. I think the prisoner was not regularly posted at the time specified but sent to take post himself. Question by the Court: How long has this practice existed?: Answer: Since I have been in town. About two months. Capt. F.H. Archer, Va. Regt., a witness for the defense, being duly sworn, says: Question by the Prisoner: What is my General Character? Answer: The prisoner is one of the most obedient and respectful men I ever saw. Occasionally, however, he will indulge too freely in ardent spirits. Question by the Court: Has the prisoner been frequently confined for misconduct? Answer: He has been confined, but three or four times within my recollection. After deliberation the Court confirmed the plea of the prisoner and sentenced him to be confined at hard labor in the charge of the Provost Guard for two months and to stand upon the head of a barrel for ten successive days for four hours each day, from 7 to 9 o'clock A.M. and from 3 to 5 o'clock P.M.;*[1709] in confinement 12/1847, pay stopped for: 4 pr. socks-$.98, 1 pr. shoes-$1.22, 1 cap-$.95$^{1/2}$, 1 cotton shirt-$.43, 1 blanket-$2.22; absent sick 02/1848, pay stopped for: 1 pr. pants-$2.28, 1 pr. shoes-$1.22, 1 blanket-$2.22; pres. 04/1848.

**Smith, Jonathan**, Pvt., LIC; enl. Mex. War service 12/22/1846 Staunton, VA, age 18; sick 08/1847; pres. 10/1847, pay stopped for: 1 forage cap-$.95$^{1/2}$, 1 wool jacket-$2.66, 1 pr. overalls-$2.28, 2 pr. socks-$.49, 1 pr. drawers-$.35$^{1/2}$; pres. 12/1847, pay stopped for: 1 pr. socks-$.24$^{1/2}$, 1 blanket-$2.22, 1 pr. overalls-$2.28, 1 flannel shirt-$.90, 1 pr. drawers-$.35$^{1/2}$, 1 pr. shoes-$1.22; pres. 04/1848; pres. 07/1848; BLW sent to Brooksville, Albemarle Co., VA

**Smith, Samuel**, Pvt., Co. E; enl. Mex. War service 11/29/1846 Petersburg, VA, age 31; pres. 04/1847; pres. 06/1847; pres. 08/1847; pres. 10/1847, pay stopped for: 1 pr. overalls-$2.28, 2 pr. shoes-$2.44, 1 pr. stockings-$.24$^{1/2}$, 1 cotton shirt-$.43, 2 flannel shirts-$1.80, 1 pr. drawers-$.35$^{1/2}$, 1 cap-$.95$^{1/2}$; absent sick 12/1847, pay stopped for: 1 pr. pants-$2.28, 2 pr. socks-$.24$^{1/2}$, 1 pr. shoes-$1.22, 3 flannel shirts-$2.70, 1 blanket-$2.22; absent sick 02/1848,

OFF TO WAR

pay stopped for: 1 pr. pants-$2.28; absent sick 04/1848 in Hosp.; wid. Susan A., WC #212, 03/11/1887, from VA

**Smith, Samuel**, Pvt., Co. LIC; b. c. 1825 Rockbridge Co., VA;[1710] enl. Mex. War service 01/06/1847 Staunton, VA, age 21; pres. 04/1848, pay stopped for: 1 pr. shoes-$1.22; pres. 07/1848; BLW sent to Brownsburg, Rockbridge Co., VA; m/1 Potina Estel, date unknown, Lexington, Rockbridge Co., VA;[1710] (PES d. 10/09/1873, Greenbrier Co., WV); [1710] m/2 Isabella Susan Keyes, 02/02/1874, place unknown;[1710] c. 1880 res. Kentucky Dist., Nicholas Co., WV, age 62, occ. Farm Laborer, w. Isabel S. (46) Keeping House;[1711] SC #15718, 06/28/1887, filed from Snowhill, Nicholas Co., WV; phys. desc. 5'11$^{1/2}$", florid or red complexion, dark hair, dark eyes;[1710] d. 08/31/1900, *"heart disease coupled with old age and senility;"*[1712] wid. Isabella S., WC #12662, 10/09/1900, filed from Donald, Nicholas Co., WV; In 1905 her son-in-law Henry W. Bryant indicted for pension fraud in Charleston, WV. Bryant had been intercepting her mail, forging her name and cashing her pension checks of $8 per month. He would keep half and only give her half;[1712] (ISS b. 05/23/1833, m/1 11/15/1859, Monroe Co., VA, he died 11/1862, Monroe Co., VA; d. 01/22/1913).[1712]

**Smith, William B.**, 2$^{nd}$ Cpl., Co. D; enl. Mex. War service 01/07/1847, Petersburg, VA, age 21; pres. 02/1847; pres. 04/1847; pres. 06/1847; absent 08/1847 sick, prom. 3$^{rd}$ Cpl.; pres. 10/1847, prom. 2$^{nd}$ Cpl., pay stopped for: 1 pr. pants-$2.28, 1 pr. drawers-$.35$^{1/2}$, 1 pr. socks-$.24$^{1/2}$, 1 blanket-$2.22; pres. 12/1847, pay stopped for: 1 jacket-$2.66, 2 pr. socks-$.49; pres. 04/1848; pres. 08/1847, BLW sent to Harrisonburg, Rockingham Co., VA, was brother of Pvt. Calvin N. Smith.[1713]

**Snead, Jesse L.**, Pvt., Co. I; b. Elba, Henrico Co., VA;[1714] enl. Mex. War service 01/01/1847 Richmond, VA, age 23; pres. 02/1847; pres. 04/1847; discharged 05/15/1847 for disability at camp near Monterey, Mex.; m. Adaline Hilman Ellis,02/03/1848, Goochland Co., VA;[1714, 1715] c. 1850 res. Goochland Co., VA, age 25, occ. Overseer, w. Adeline (21), dau. Emma (7/12);[1716] c. 1860 res. Richmond, Henrico Co., VA, age 37, occ. Engineer, w. Adaline (28), dau. Louisa (7), dau. Georgianna (5), dau. Jesse Anna (4), son Eugene (4/12);[1717] Civil War service enl. as Pvt., Co. C, 38$^{th}$ Btln. VA Arty.05/11/1861, AWOL 08/15/1862; c. 1870 res. Tuckahoe, Henrico Co., VA, age 46, occ. Engineer, w. Adeline H. (42), dau. Louisa (17), dau. Georgianna (15), dau. Jesse Ann (13), son Eugene (11);[1718] entered Lee Camp Soldiers Home 02/03/1885, age 60; [1719] SC #3022, 02/24/1887, filed from Lee Camp Soldiers Home, Richmond, Henrico Co., VA; phys. desc. age 62$^{11/12}$ [02/1887], 5'5$^{1/2}$", dark complexion, grey eyes, dark hair, occ. at enl. Farmer; res. discharge res. Goochland Co., VA, 3 yrs., Henrico Co., VA, 40 yrs.; d. 12/02/1890, Lee Camp Soldiers Home, Richmond, VA, bur. Hollywood Cemetery, Richmond, VA;[1720] wid. Adaline H., WC #10005, 01/30/1896, both filed from 627 Church St., Richmond, Henrico Co., VA; (AES b. 08/05/1828, Henrico Co., near Goochland Co. line).[1720]

**Snead, Robert L.**, Pvt., LIC; enl. Mex. War service 12/07/1846 Staunton, VA, age 22; pres. 08/1847; pres. 10/1847, pay stopped for: 1 forage cap-$.95$^{1/2}$, 1 wool jacket-$2.66, 2 pr. overalls-$4.56, 2 pr. shoes-$2.44, 4 pr. socks-$.98, 5 cotton shirts-$2.15, 1 pr. drawers-$.35$^{1/2}$; pres. 12/1847, pay stopped for: 2 pr. socks-$.49, 1 blanket-$2.22, 1 pr. shoes-$1.22, 2 flannel shirts-$1.80, 1 pr. drawers-$.35$^{1/2}$; pres. 04/1848; pres. 07/1848, pay stopped for: 1 pr. shoes-$1.16; BLW sent to Lynchburg, VA; c. 1850 res. Lynchburg, Campbell Co., VA, age 25, occ. Carpenter; c. 1860 res. Lynchburg, Campbell Co., VA, age 33, occ. Cabinetmaker, w. Margaret E. (19);[1721] c. 1870 res. Lynchburg, Campbell Co., VA, age 45, occ. Carpenter, w. Margaret E. (30), son Samuel W. (15), son Robert J. (8), son Edward (6).[1722]

**Snead, Samuel M.**, Pvt., Co. G; enl. Mex. War service 11/28/1846 Richmond, VA, age 22; pres. 06/1847; absent 08/1847 on detached service as Orderly for Col. Hamtramck; absent 10/1847 on detached service as Orderly, pay stopped for: 1 pr. overalls-$2.22; absent 12/1847, on extra duty in QM Dept., pay stopped for: 1 pr. pants-$2.28; absent 02/1848 on extra duty in QM Dept.; absent 04/1948 on extra duty in QM Dept.; pres. 08/1848, pay

## VIRGINIA VOLUNTEERS IN MEXICO

stopped for: 1 gun sling-$.16, 1 screw driver-$.07, 1 wiper-$.20; BLW sent to Lynchburg, VA

**Snyder, George R.**, Pvt., Co. B; enl. 12/20/1846, Alexandria, VA, age 38; pres. 06/1847; pres. 08/1847; pres. 10/1847, pay stopped for: 2 pr. cotton drawers-$.71, 2 pr. socks-$.49, 1 blanket-$2.22; pres. 12/1847, pay stopped for: 2 pr. shoes-$2.44, 1 jacket-$2.66, 1 pr. overalls-$2.28, 1 cap-$.95$^{1/2}$, 2 pr. socks-$.49; pres. 02/1848; pres. 04/1848; pres. 08/1848, BLW sent to Alexandria, VA c/o Capt. Corse; c. 1850 res. Alexandria Co., VA, age 38, occ. Coopersmith, w. Ann E. (36).[1723]

**Snyder, William**, *Va. Vols.*; *Not on Muster Rolls*, m. Frances Jones, WA #10007, 08/03/1891, from TN.

**Sorbor, William B.**, Pvt., Co. H; b. 01/01/1827, Philadelphia, Pa.;[1724] enl. Mex. War service 01/06/1847, Berkeley, VA, age 21; pres. 04/1847; pres. 06/1847; pres. 08/1847; pres. 10/1847, pay stopped for: 1 forage cap-$.95$^{1/2}$, 1 pr. pants-$2.28, 3 cotton shirts-$1.29, 1 pr. drawers-$.35$^{1/2}$, 1 pr. shoes-$1.22, 4 pr. socks-$.98; pres. 12/1847, pay stopped for: 1 forage cap-$.95$^{1/2}$, 1 jacket-$2.66, 1 pr. pants-$2.28, 2 flannel shirts-$1.80, 2 pr. drawers-$.71, 1 pr. shoes-$1.22, 1 blanket-$2.22; pres. 02/1848, pay stopped for: 1 jacket-$5.32, 2 pr. shoes-$2.44, 1 pr. socks-$.24$^{1/2}$; pres. 04/1848; pres. 07/1848, pay stopped for: 1 bayonet-$1.44, 1 cartridge box-$1.10, 1 cartridge box belt plate-$.10, 1 cartridge box plate-.10, 1 cartridge box belt-$.60, 1 brush & pick-$.12, 1 screw driver-$.25, 1 wiper-$.20, BLW sent to Philadelphia, Pa.; m/1 c. 1850 (Unknown wife d. 03/25/1863);[1724] m/2 Eliza Wilson, 11/05/1864, Philadelphia, Pa., (EWS d. 03/21/1890);[1724] SC #19139, 02/14/1890, filed from Philadelphia, PA; William Kindley gave affidavit in pension claim;[1724] Lists children William L. Sorbor, b. 06/18/1854, Anna M. Sorbor, b. 01/03/1858, Eliza May Sorbor, b. 05/03/1861;[1724] d. c. 1900.[1724]

**Sorrell, Harrison**, Pvt., Co. C; enl. Mex. War service 12/25/1846, Bowling Green, VA, age 36; sick 06/1847; pres. 08/1847, pay stopped for: 1 cap-$.95$^{1/2}$, 2 pr. socks-$.49, 2 cotton shirts-$.86, 2 woolen shirts-$1.80, 1 pr. drawers-$.35$^{1/2}$; pres. 10/1847, pay stopped for: 4 pr. socks-$.98, 2 cotton shirts-$.86; pres. 12/1847, pay stopped for: 2 pr. drawers-$.71, 2 pr. socks-$.49, 2 pr. pants-$4.56, 2 cotton shirta-$.86, 1 pr. shoes-$1.22, 1 blanket-$2.22; pres. 04/1848, pay stopped for: 1 flannel shirt-$.90, 1 pr. shoes-$1.22; 1 jacket-$2.66, 1 pr. shoes-$1.50, 1 haversack-$.20$^{3/4}$; pres. 08/1848, BLW sent to Bowling Green, Caroline County, VA; c. 1850 res. Caroline Co., VA, age 42, occ. None;[1725] c. 1860 res. Bowling Green, Caroline Co., VA, age 40, occ. None, *"Pauper;"* c. 1870 res. Ruther Glen, Caroline Co., VA, age 55, occ. Pauper, *can not vote*.[1726]

**Spaulding, James J.**, Pvt., Co. D; enl. Mex. War service 01/01/1847, Petersburg, VA, age 22; pres. 02/1847; pres. 04/1847; pres. 06/1847; pres. 08/1847, pay stopped for: 2 cotton shirts-$.86, 1 pr. shoes-$1.22; pres. 10/1847, pay stopped for: 1 cap-$.95$^{1/2}$, 1 jacket-$2.66, 1 pr. pants-$2.28, 1 cotton shirt-$.43, 1 pr. drawers-$.35$^{1/2}$, 2 pr. socks-$.49; pres. 12/1847, pay stopped for: 1 pr. pants-$2.28, 1 pr drawers-$.35$^{1/2}$, 1 pr. socks-$.24$^{1/2}$, 1 pr. shoes-$1.22, 1 blanket-$2.22; pres. 04/1848, pay stopped for: 1 set of picks & brushes-$.12, 1 pr. shoes-$1.22; pres. 08/1847, BLW sent to Petersburg, VA; c. 1850 res. Petersburg, Dinwiddie Co., VA, age 26, occ. Bar Keeper;[1727] c. 1860 res. Petersburg, Dinwiddie Co., VA, age 36, occ. None Listed, w. Mary (26), dau. Ella (7), dau. Sarah (3), dau. Lucy C. (2);[1728] Civil War service Pvt., Co. K, 12$^{th}$ Va. Inf., enl. 04/30/1862 at Craney Island (Norfolk, VA), b. Charlotte Co., VA, 1823, absent 11/1862 in hosp. asthma/emphysema, discharged date unknown, oyster dealer, Grove Avenue, Petersburg, VA;[21] m. Martha A. Gates, of Petersburg, 12/1865;[1729] c. 1870 res. Petersburg, Dinwiddie Co., VA, age 46, occ. Keeps Public House, w. Martha (42), dau. Ella F. (17), dau. Sarah E. (13), dau. Lucy J. (11), son Thomas B. (1).[1730]

**Spencer, John**, Pvt., Co. F; enl. Mex. War service 11/23/1846, Portsmouth, VA, age 28; pres. 06/1847; pres. 08/1847; pres. 10/1847, pay stopped for: 1 pr. overalls-$2.28, 1 forage cap-$.95$^{1/2}$, 5 pr. socks-$1.22$^{1/2}$, 2 pr. shoes-$2.44, 2 flannel shirts-$1.80; pres. 12/1847; pres.

OFF TO WAR

02/1848, pay stopped for: 1 blanket-$2.22, 1 pr. shoes-$1.22; pres. 04/1848; pres. 08/1848, pay stopped for: 3 pr. shoes-$3.48, 2 cotton shirts-$.88, 2 blankets-$4.50, BLW sent to Portsmouth, VA c/o E.T. Blamire; m/1 Nancy Dillon, date unknown, Henry Co., VA;[1731] moved to Missouri shortly afterward where Nancy Spencer died, returned to VA;[1731] m/2 Susan Echols 1852, Henry Co., VA;[1731] d. 12/1876, Kapp's Mill (Judesville), Surry Co., NC;[1731] wid. Susan, WC #443, 03/31/1887, file from White Plains, Surry Co., NC. (SES b. 04/15/1805).[1731]

**Spencer, John S.**, Pvt., Co. I; enl. Mex. War service 01/10/1847 Lynchburg, VA, age 40; pres. 02/1847; pres. 04/1847; pres. 06/1847; pres. 08/1847; pres. 10/1847, pay stopped for: 2 flannel shirts-$2.70, 5 cotton shirts-$2.15, 3 pr. drawers-$1.06$^{1/2}$, 1 overcoat-$6.93$^{1/2}$, 1 jacket-$2.66; pres. 12/1847, pay stopped for: 2 pr. shoes-$2.44, 1 cap-$.95$^{1/2}$, 1 pr. pants-$2.28, 1 blanket-$2.22, 2 flannel shirts-$1.80, 1 pr. drawers-$.35$^{1/2}$; pres. 02/1848, pay stopped for: 1 flannel shirt-$.90, 1 pr. overalls-$2.28; pres. 04/1848; pres. 08/1848, pay stopped for: 1 musket complete & accoutrements complete-$16.15, BLW sent to Penn's Store, Patrick Co., VA; c. 1860 res. Mayo Forge, Patrick Co., VA, age 53, occ. Miller, w. Susan (55).[1732]

**Spillman, James W.**, QM Sgt., Co. A; enl. Mex. War service 12/08/1846 Richmond, VA, age 31; pres. until sick 04/1847, in Hosp. at Matamoros sent there from Camargo, Mex. 04/02/1847; sick in quarters 06/1847; pres. 08/1847, prom. 3$^{rd}$ Cpl. 08/23/1847; prom. 10/03/1847 Regt. QM Sgt.; pres. 10/1847, pay stopped for clothing: 2 cotton shirts-$.86, 1 cap-$.95$^{1/2}$, 2 pr. shoes-$2.44, 3 pr. stockings-$.73$^{1/2}$; pres. 02/1848; on detached service 04/1848 as Clerk in QM Dept. since 01/25/1848; BLW sent to Fredericksburg, VA; c. 1850 res. King George Co., VA, age 35, occ. Farmer, w. Elizabeth (19);[1733] [Civil War service a James Spillman, age 42, enl. as a Pvt., Co. I, 9$^{th}$ Va. Cav. 10/12/1861, illiterate, captured 04/30/1863 near Fredericksburg, VA, paroled 05/23/1863 from Ft. Delaware, absent sick 05/1863 until d. 11/04/1863 in King George Co., VA of scurvy, diarrhea, and debility.][725]

**Spooner, Charles Coburn**, Pvt., Co. D; b. 05/20/1826, Halifax, NC, son of Abner & Louisiana (Marcy) Spooner;[1734] enl. Mex. War service 01/08/1847, Petersburg, VA, age 40; pres. 02/1847; pres. 04/1847; pres. 06/1847; pres. 08/1847, pay stopped for: 1 cap-$.95$^{1/2}$, 2 cotton shirts-$.86, 2 flannel shirts-$1.80; pres. 10/1847, pay stopped for: 1 pr. pants-$2.28, 2 cotton shirts-$.86, 1 pr. drawers-$.35$^{1/2}$, 2 pr. socks-$.49, 1 pr. shoes-$1.22; pres. 12/1847, pay stopped for: 1 pr. pants-$2.28, 1 jacket-$2.66, 2 pr drawers-$.71, 1 pr. socks-$.24$^{1/2}$, 1 pr. shoes-$1.22, 1 blanket-$2.22; pres. 04/1848, pay stopped for: 1 pr. shoes-$1.22, 1 haversack-$.20$^{3/4}$; pres. 08/1847, BLW sent to Guston, Northampton Co., NC; m. Eliza Ann Collins, 03/22/1853, Halifax, NC.[1734]

**Spooner, Samuel J.**, Pvt., Co. A; enl. Mex. War service 12/01/1846 Richmond, VA, age 22; pres. until sick 04/1847 in hosp. at Matamoros, sent there 04/02/1847 from Camargo; d. 05/06/1847 in Hosp. at Matamoros.

**Spotswood, Edward J.**, alias Joseph E., Pvt., Co. E; enl. Mex. War service 11/30/1846 Petersburg, VA, age 18; pres. 04/1847; pres. 06/1847; pres. 08/1847; pres. 10/1847, pay stopped for: 1 pr. shoes-$1.22, 2 pr. stockings-$.49, 1 cap-$.95$^{1/2}$; pres. 12/1847, pay stopped for: 1 pr. pants-$2.28, 1 pr. shoes-$1.22, 1 blanket-$2.22; pres. 02/1848, pay stopped for: 1 jacket-$2.66; pres. 04/1848; m. Lucy S. Cooper, 04/1872;[1735] SC #20174, 01/12/1894, wid. Lucy S., WC #14888, 01/23/1908, both from VA; see mother's O #689152 as mother of Joseph C. Spotswood who served in Co. K, 4$^{th}$ Va. Inf. In the Spanish American War; [pension file in custody of Department of Veterans Affairs].

**Spratt, James W.**, Pvt., Co. F; b. 01/07/1824 Deep Creek, Norfolk Co., VA;[1736] enl. Mex. War service 12/21/1846, Portsmouth, VA, age 22; pres. 06/1847; pres. 08/1847; pres. 10/1847, pay stopped for: 1 pr. overalls-$2.28, 1 forage cap-$.95$^{1/2}$, 2 pr. socks-$.49, 1 pr. shoes-$1.22, 1 pr. drawers-$.35$^{1/2}$, 1 blanket-$2.22; pres. 12/1847; pres. 02/1848, pay stopped for: 1 blanket-$2.22, 1 white cotton shirt-$.43; pres. 04/1848; pres. 08/1848, pay stopped for: 2 pr. shoes-$2.32, BLW sent to Portsmouth, VA c/o E.T. Blamire; c. 1850 res. Norfolk Co., VA, age 24,

# VIRGINIA VOLUNTEERS IN MEXICO

occ. None;[1737] SC #6195, 05/11/1887, filed from Pacific Branch National Soldiers Home, Los Angeles Co., Los Angeles, CA;[1736] disability *"double hernia"* incurred *"on Mex. Central R.R. in Old Mexico 27th Dec. 1882 by jumping of the cars in a Railway accident;"*[1736] Francis L. Benson gave affidavit in pension claim;[1736] spent remaining years of his life residing in various National Soldiers Homes across the country; c. 1897 res. National Soldiers Home, Washington Co., TN, phys. desc. 5'11", light complexion, gray eyes, gray hair, occ. Railroader; d. 05/06/1911.[1736]

**Spratt, John T.**, Pvt., Co. F; enl. Mex. War service 11/23/1846, Portsmouth, VA, age 21; d. 04/06/1847 Point Isabel, Tex.

**St. Clair, Francis**, Pvt., Co. C; enl. Mex. War service 12/30/1846, Bowling Green, VA, age 21; pres. 06/1847, reduced to ranks from 4th Cpl. 06/07/1847; pres. 08/1847, pay stopped for: 1 cap-$.95$^{1/2}$, 2 pr. socks-$.49, 2 cotton shirts-$.86, 2 woolen shirts-$1.80, 1 pr. shoes-$1.22; 1 pr. drawers-$.35$^{1/2}$; pres. 10/1847, pay stopped for: 2 pr. socks-$.49, 2 pr. drawers-$.71, 1 pr. pants-$2.28, 1 cotton shirt-$.43, 1 woolen shirt-$.90, 1 great coat-$6.93$^{1/2}$; pres. 12/1847, pay stopped for: 1 pr. drawers-$.35$^{1/2}$, 1 pr. shoes-$1.22, 1 blanket-$2.22; pres. 04/1848, pay stopped for: 1 pr. pants-$2.28, 1 pr. shoes-$1.22, 1 pr. shoes-$1.50, 1 india rubber canteen-$.27.

**Stafford, William H.**, Pvt., Co. M; enl. Mex. War service 11/18/1847, Norfolk, VA, age 26; pres. 11/1847; pres. 12/1847, *"apprehended 27th Nov. 1847, to pay $30 for apprehension;"* pres. 02/1848, pay stopped for: $30 for desertion from Ft. Monroe, VA, 1 blanket-$2.22, 2 cotton shirts-$.86; pres. 04/1848, pay stopped for: 1 blanket-$2.22, 1 pr. shoes-$1.22, 2 cotton shirts-$.86; pres. 08/1848, pay stopped for: 1 musket & accoutrements complete-$16.22, 1 pr. shoes-$1.16; BLW sent to Norfolk, VA; Civil War service Pvt., Co. A, 6th Va. Inf., enl. 04/22/1861 at Norfolk, VA for 1 yr., b. 1829, occ. Huckster, enl. extended 04/30/1862, deserted 05/08/1862 in the evacuation of Norfolk, VA[465] [a W.H. Stafford, age 60, d. 11/22/1887 @ 413 Queen St., Norfolk, bur. Elmwood Cemetery, Norfolk, VA][1738]

**Stagg, James**, Pvt., Co. A; enl. Mex. War 01/02/1847 Richmond, VA, age 19; pres. 12/1846 – 04/1847 not yet pd. for 6mos. clothing or 20 mile subsidy; pres. 06/1847; pres. 08/1847; pres. 10/1847, pay stopped for clothing: 2 cotton shirts-$.86, 1 pr. wool overalls-$2.28, 1 cap-$.95$^{1/2}$, 2 pr. shoes-$2.44, 2 pr. stockings-$.49, 1 wool jacket-$2.66, 1 great coat-$6.93$^{1/2}$; pres. 12/1847, pay stopped for clothing: 1 pr. wool overalls-$2.28, 1 pr. drawers-$.35$^{1/2}$, 1 pr. shoes-$1.22; pres. 04/1848; BLW sent to Richmond, VA; SC #13364, 10/13/1887, filed from Henrico Co., VA; John Poe, Jr. and Robert G. Scott of Richmond, VA gave affidavits on behalf of pension claim;[1739] d. 01/03/1892, bur. Hollywood Cem., Richmond, VA, Sect. R, Lot 46][119]

**Stagg, John F.**, 1st Sgt., Co. M; enl. Mex. War service 05/15/1847, Richmond, VA, age 21; pres. 09/1847; pres. 11/1847; pres. 12/1847; pres. 02/1848; pres. 04/1848, pay stopped for: 1 blanket-$2.22; pres. 08/1848, pay stopped for: 1 wormer-$.20, 1 gun sling-$.16; BLW sent to Richmond, VA; c. 1850 res. Brunswick Co., VA, age 23, occ. Clerk;[1740] c. 1860 res. Richmond, Henrico Co., VA, age 34, occ. Salesman, Sarah A. (27), son John J. (8), son Joseph B. (5), dau. Elizabeth A. (2);[1741] Civil War service Capt., Co. A, 2nd VA Reserves, enl. 07/02/1863, pres. 07/1864, pd. $260, 01/23/1865 for 2 mos., NFR;[1742] d. 02/__/1865 bur. Hollywood Cem., Richmond, VA, Sect. P, Lot 1.[119]

**Stanfield, Henderson**, Pvt., Co. I; enl. Mex. War service 01/10/1847 Lynchburg, VA, age 39; absent 02/1847, left sick in Richmond, VA; absent 04/1847 sick in Richmond, VA; absent 06/1847 left sick in Richmond, VA; deserted 03/10/1847 Richmond, VA; [a Henderson Stanfield m. Mary Ann Winn, 12/27/1853, Harrison, TX.][1743]

**Stanger, Henry S.**, 2nd Lt., *Preston's Co.*; b. 1819 KY, son of Jacob & Elizabeth (Linkous) Stanger;[1744] enl. Mex. War service 12/06/1846 Montgomery Co., VA; pres. 04/1847; pres. 06/1847; pres. 08/1847; pres. 10/1847; pres. 12/1847; pres. 02/1848; absent 04/1848 on sick leave since 04/11/1848; pres. 07/1848; m. Ellen J. Webb, 09/17/1850, Montgomery Co.,

# OFF TO WAR

VA;[1745] c. 1860 res. Blacksburg, Montgomery Co., VA, age 41, Farmer, w. Ellen (34), dau. Mary (7), dau. William (6), son Nicholas (3);[1746] Civil War service enl. Co. E, James E. Wade's Regt. of Local Defense of Montgomery Co., VA; [202, 493] d. 1867; 1st cousin of Pvt. Crockett Linkous, Pvt. William B. Linkous, and 3rd Sgt. Benjamin R. Linkous.

**Stark, Ebenezer E.**, Pvt., Co. L; b. 1828; enl. Mex. War service 03/01/1847 Fairfax C.H., VA, age 38; pres. 06/1847; pres. 08/1847; 10/1847, 1 pr. Pants 2.28, 1 F Cap .95, 1 pr. Shoes 1.22; pres. 12/1847, pay stopped for: 1 pr. pants-$2.28, 1 pr. shoes-$1.22, 2 flannel shirts-$1.80, 2 cotton shirts-$.86, 1 blanket-$2.22, 2 pr. drawers-$.71; pres. 02/1848, pay stopped for: 1 Jacket 2.66; pres. 04/1848; pres. 07/1848, pay stopped for: 2 Cotton Shirts .88; BLW sent to Washington City, D.C.

**Starke, Henry**, Drummer, Co. G; enl. Mex. War service 11/28/1846 Richmond, VA, age 22; pres. 06/1847; pres. 08/1847; pres. 10/1847, pay stopped for: 2 pr. overalls-$4.56, 2 shoes-$2.44, 2 pr. socks-$.98, 1 jacket- $2.66, 2 forage caps-$1.91; in confinement 12/1847, pay stopped for: 2 pr. shoes-$2.44, 1 flannel shirt-$.90, 1 blanket-$2.22, 1 pr. pants-$2.28, 1 jacket-$2.66; Court-Martialed 12/29/1847, Buena Vista, Mex. *Charge #1: Assault and Battery; Specification: In this that he, the said Drummer Henry Starke, Co. G, Va. Regt., did strike and otherwise maltreat Thomas Garcia, a Mexican citizen at Saltillo, Mexico on or about the 22$^{nd}$ day of December 1847. To which charge and specification the prisoner pleaded Not Guilty. Pablo Castinada, a Mexican and a witness for the prosecution, being duly sworn, says: The prisoner was eating in the market plaza at Saltillo, Mex. on or about the 22$^{nd}$ day of December 1847 and after he had finished eating he charged a Mexican standing by with having taken his money. This one Casimiro Castinada ran off and the prisoner followed him and shortly afterwards returned leading Thomas Garcia by the collar and asked the woman from where he had procured his meal if that was not the man that he had accused of taking his money. In receiving a reply in the negative, he let the man go after kicking and striking him. The blows and kicks were given after the prisoner was told that Garcia was not the man whom he had accused of taking his money. I did not see the prisoner give money to any one. Question by the Court: What did Garcia say when the prisoner brought him up by the collar? Answer: Not a word. Casimiro Castinada, a Mexican and witness for the prosecution, being duly sworn, says: I was eating at the same table with the prisoner in the market plaza at Saltillo, Mexico on or about the 22$^{nd}$ of Dec. 1847. I took a dollar from my pocket to pay for my meal and the prisoner took it. He did not charge me with taking any money that I know of. I said nothing to him, but he took hold of me and tore my garments. I ran off as fast as possible and the prisoner followed me. I do not know how far. I did not get the money back again neither did I make any complaint of the matter. I do not know Thomas Garcia. The prisoner then stated that he wished to find a witness belonging to the Va. Regt. which saw the transaction, but he did not know his name although this person was familiar. The Court took a recess of a half hour to allow the prisoner an opportunity to find the witness. At the end of that time the commission was assembled and the prisoner stated that the person he wished to find was not in camp and desired that he might be allowed till tomorrow to find him. His request was granted and the Court adjourned until 11 o'clock on Thursday the 30$^{th}$ of December 1847, in Saltillo, Mex. 12/3-/1847 – The prisoner was called and having no further testimony to give the Court found him Guilty of the charge and specification and sentenced him to forfeit five dollars from his monthly pay and to be confined at hard labor in charge of the Provost Guard for ten days*[1747] pres. 02/1848, pay stopped for: 1 waist belt-$.25, 1 blanket-$2.22; pres. 04/1848, pay stopped for: 1 pr. shoes-$1.22; pres. 08/1848, pay stopped for: 1 pr. shoes-$1.16; BLW sent to Richmond, VA

**Starke, Richard**, 1st Cpl., Co. G; enl. Mex. War service 11/29/1846 Richmond, VA, age 44; pres. 06/1847; pres. 08/1847; pres. 10/1847, pay stopped for: 2 pr. overalls-$4.56, 1 flannel shirt-$.90, 2 shoes-$2.44, 3 pr. socks-$.73$^{1/2}$, 1 great coat-$6.95$^{1/2}$, 1 jacket- $2.66, 1 forage cap-$.95$^{1/2}$; pres. 12/1847, prom. 1st Cpl., pay stopped for 1 pr. pants-$2.28, 1 jacket-$2.66, 1 pr.

VIRGINIA VOLUNTEERS IN MEXICO

socks-.24$^{1/2}$; pres. 02/1848, 1 blanket-$2.22; pres. 04/1848; pres. 08/1848, pay stopped for: 1 pr. shoes-$1.22, 1 gun sling-$.16; BLW sent to Richmond, VA
**Starr, John W.**, Pvt., *Preston's Co.*; enl. Mex. War service 01/05/1847 Montgomery Co., VA, age 20; absent 04/1847 on detached service as Hospital Attendant at Pt. Isabel, Tex. since 02/27/1847; pres. 06/1847; d. 05/04/1847 in hosp. at Ft. Monroe, VA, *"Congestion of the brain."*[243]
**Steel, John H.**, alias John G. Hensley, Pvt., LIC; b. 04/15/1813, Rockbridge Co., VA, son of Samuel & Frances (Hunter) Steele;[1748] enl. Mex. War service 11/27/1846 Staunton, VA, age 33; pres. 08/1847; pres. 10/1847, pay stopped for: 1 forage cap-$.95$^{1/2}$, 1 wool jacket-$2.66, 1 pr. overalls-$2.28, 2 pr. shoes-$2.44, 2 pr. socks-$.49, 2 cotton shirts-$.86, 1 flannel shirt-$.90, 1 pr. drawers-$.35$^{1/2}$; pres. 12/1847, pay stopped for: 1 blanket-$2.22; pres. 04/1848, pay stopped for: 1 pr. shoes-$1.22, 1 pr. shoes-$2.25; pres. 07/1848, pay stopped for: 1 wiper-$.20; BLW sent to Waynesborough, VA; c. 1850 res. Augusta Co., VA, age 37, occ. Farmer;[1749] d. 10/16/1880, *"heart disease,"* Fisherville, near Waynesboro, Augusta Co., VA, *"unmarried;"*[1748] SA #24207, 01/21/1893, filed from Saybrook, McLean Co., IL. *"Claimant is an impostor...The claimant, John G. Hensley, was born and reared near Barterbrook, Augusta Co., VA, in about six miles of the birthplace and home of the solider, John H. Steele. He has a brother, Robert Hensley, living at the old house and his, William D. Hensley, a nephew of the claimant was the undertaker that buried the soldier, John H. Steele;"*[1748] John G. Hensley pled guilty *"to charge of presenting a fraudulent claim for pension"* in federal court, 10/22/1897, Cairo, IL.[1748]
**Stephens, Richard H.**, Pvt., Co. H; enl. Mex. War service 12/29/1846, Berkeley, VA, age 26; d. 03/03/1847 at Ft. Monroe, VA bur. *"on the shores of the Chesapeake Bay."*[1750]
**Stephenson, James E.**, Pvt., Co. B; enl. 12/14/1846, Alexandria, VA, age 21; pres. 06/1847; sick 08/1847; pres. 10/1847, pay stopped for: 1 pr. overalls-$2.28, 2 pr. cotton drawers-$.71, 1 cap-$.95$^{1/2}$, 2 pr. socks-$.49, 1 blanket-$2.22; pres. 12/1847, pay stopped for: 2 pr. socks-$.49; pres. 02/1848; pres. 04/1848; pres. 08/1848, BLW sent to Barnesville, Montgomery Co., MD
**Stevens, Crawford B.**, Pvt., *Preston's Co.*; enl. Mex. War service 12/06/1846 Montgomery Co., VA, age 22; absent 04/1847 left sick in hosp. at Camargo, Mex. since 04/06/1847; sick 06/1847; pres. 08/1847; pres. 10/1847, pay stopped for: 1 pr. overalls-$2.28, 1 pr. socks-$.24$^{1/2}$, 2 cotton shirts-$.86; pres. 12/1847, pay stopped for: 1 pr. shoes-$1.22, 1 blankets-$2.22; pres. 02/1848, pay stopped for: 1 pr. of shoes-$1.22, 1 jacket-$2.66, 1 cap-$.95$^{1/2}$; pres. 04/1848, pay stopped for: 1 pick & brush-$.12; pres. 07/1848; BLW sent to Christiansburg, VA c/o Fleming Gardner; m. Lucinda Collins, 12/19/1848, Montgomery Co., VA;[1751] c. 1850 res. Montgomery Co., age 29, occ. Farmer, w. Lucinda (26), dau. Lydia (5/12);[1752] c. 1860 res. Christiansburg, Montgomery Co., VA, age 39, occ. Laborer, w. Lucinda (39), dau Lydia A. S. (10), dau. Jane F. (6), son James C. (5), son Robert N. (1);[1753] Civil War service Pvt., Co. G, 4$^{th}$ Va. Inf., enl. 04/17/1861, age 40, occ. Laborer, trans. 05/17/1862 to 54$^{th}$ Va. Inf.; NFR;[54,] [192] Pvt., Co. K, 25$^{th}$ Va. Cav., enl. 09/01/1862 at Montgomery Co., VA, dismounted and detached to Battalion HQ 12/01/1862, on leave 04/25/1863 in Montgomery Co., trans. 04/01/1864 to Co. E, discharged 05/19/1864 as overage, age 46, and term expired, phys. desc. brown hair, grey eyes, b. Bedford Co., VA, 6'1/2", was charged for the spurs he lost prior to separation;[1754] c. 1870 res. Christiansburg, Montgomery Co., VA, age 50, occ. Works on R.R., w. Lucinda (48), dau. Jane F. (18), son James C. (14);[1755] d. 01/09/1885, Montgomery Co., VA;[1756] wid. Lucinda, WC #282, 03/07/1887, filed from Christiansburg, Montgomery Co., VA; Henry Collins gave affidavit in pension claim;[1756] (LCS b. 12/23/1848, Montgomery Co., VA, d. 11/06/1894).[1756]
**Stevens, Harvey B.**, Pvt., *Preston's Co.*; b. Bedford Co., VA;[1757] enl. Mex. War service 01/05/1847 Montgomery Co., VA, age 21; pres. 04/1847; absent 06/1847 sick in hosp. at Monterey, Mex. since 06/22/1847; sick 08/1847; pres. 10/1847, pay stopped for: 1 pr. overalls-$2.28, 1 pr. shoes-$1.22, 3 pr. socks-$.73$^{1/2}$, 1 flannel shirt-$.90, 2 cotton shirts-$.86,

OFF TO WAR

1 pr. drawers-$.35$^{1/2}$; pres. 12/1847, pay stopped for: 1 jacket-$2.66, 1 pr. overalls-$2.28, 1 pr. shoes-$1.22, 2 pr. socks-$.49, 1 cap-$.95$^{1/2}$, 1 blankets-$2.22; pres. 02/1848, pay stopped for: 1 pr. shoes-$1.22; pres. 04/1848, pay stopped for: 1 pick & brush-$.12; pres. 07/1848, m. Sarah Jane Hewlett, 1848, Berkeley Co., VA;[1757] 1860 res. Oak Hill, Fayette Co., VA, age 33, occ. Day Laborer, w. Jane (30), son John T. (10), dau. Malinda M. (8), dau. Cynthia A. (1), f-i-l John Hewlett (80);[1758] Civil War service Pvt., Co. F, 59$^{th}$ Va. Inf., enl. 06/26/1861 at Gauley Bridge (Fayette Co.), VA age 34, pres. 08/1861, NFR;[267] Pvt., Co. C, 60$^{th}$ Va. Inf., pres. until discharged for an enlarged heart 02/14/1863, age 35, 6'0", blue eyes, black hair, res. Bedford Co., Va;[169] c. 1880 res. Clear Fork, Raleigh Co., WV, age 53, occ. Farmer, w. Jane (48) Keeping House, dau. Cynthia (20), son Harvey P. (17) Works on Farm, dau. Rebecca Jane (15), dau. Elizabeth (13);[1759] SC #8544, 02/26/1887, filed from Clear Creek, Raleigh Co., WV; phys. desc. at enl. age 18, 6', black eyes, black hair, dark complexion, occ. Farmer, since discharge res. Fayette and Raleigh Cos., WV;[1757] d. 05/08/1903, Roseville, Willis Branch, Fayette Co., WV;[1760] wid. Sarah J., WC #14029, 06/23/1903, filed from Roseville, Fayette Co., WV; (SHS b. 05/28/1828, d. 1905).[1760]

**Steward, James**, Pvt., Co. L; b. 1828; enl. Mex. War service 03/01/1847 Fairfax C.H., VA, age 19; pres. 06/1847; pres. 08/1847; pres. 10/1847; pres. 12/1847, pay stopped for: 1 jacket-$2.66, 1 cap-$.95$^{1/2}$, 2 pr. shoes-$2.44, 1 flannel shirt-$.90, 3 cotton shirts-$1.29, 1 blanket-$2.22, 3 pr. drawers-$1.06$^{1/2}$; pres. 02/1848, sick in Qtrs., pay stopped for: 1 Bayonet Scabbard .50, 1 Brush & Pick .12; discharged 03/17/1848 at Saltillo, Mex. on Surgeon's Certificate of Disability.[72]

**Stewart, Edward G.**, Pvt., Co. F; enl. Mex. War service 01/07/1847, Portsmouth, VA, age 40; pres. 06/1847; absent 08/1847 sick; absent 10/1847 sick, pay stopped for: 1 pr. overalls-$2.28, 1 forage cap-$.95$^{1/2}$, 2 cotton shirts-$.86, 2 pr. socks-$.49; discharged 12/1847 Buena Vista, Mex. on Surgeon's Certificate of Disability;

**Stewart, John P.**, Pvt., Co. H; c. 1842 Postmaster of Martinsburg, VA;[1761] 1843 mbr. *Maffitt Lodge*, International Order of Odd Fellows;[1762] enl. Mex. War service 11/23/1846, Berkeley, VA, age 36; absent 04/1847 on duty in QM Dept. at China, Mex. since 04/16/1847; absent 08/1847 on detached service in Commissary Dept. since 08/15/ 1847; pres. 10/1847, pay stopped for: 1 pr. shoes-$1.22, 1 pr. socks-$.24$^{1/2}$; absent 12/1847, on extra duty in Adjt. Genls. Office since 11/08/1847, pay stopped for: 1 pr. pants-$2.28, 2 pr. drawers-$.71, 1 pr. shoes-$1.22; absent 02/1848, on extra duty in Asst. Adjt. Genl. office at HQ; pres. 04/1848; pres. 07/1848, BLW sent to Martinsburg, VA; [a John W. Stewart, son of R & Mary Stewart, age 65 yrs., 4 mos., 13 days, d. 09/26/1876, Kidney Disease, Mill Creek, Berkeley Co., WV.][1763]

**Stith, Drury B.**, Fifer, Co. D; [son of Robert and Mary (Goodwyn) Stith]; enl. service Mex. War 12/10/1846, Petersburg, VA, age 21; absent 02/1847 left sick in hosp. Fort Monroe, VA; absent 04/1847 left sick in Hosp. Fort Monroe, VA; absent 06/1847 left sick in Hosp. Fort Monroe, VA *"and not since heard from;"* discharged 03/17/1847 Old Point, VA on Surgeon's Certificate of Disability; c. 1850 res. Brunswick Co., VA age 23, enumerated w/ Robert (60) and Mary (62) Stith.[1764]

**Stoffer, Daniel A.**, Pvt., LIC; b. 05/05/1821, Middlebrook, VA;[1765] enl. Mex. War service 11/30/1846 Staunton, VA, age 28; absent 06/1847 on detached service as Actg. Sgt, Major; pres. 08/1847; pres. 10/1847, pay stopped for: 1 forage cap-$.95$^{1/2}$, 1 pr. overalls-$2.28, 4 pr. socks-$.98; absent 12/1847, on detached service as Clerk in Actg. Insp. Genls. office since 11/01/1847, pay stopped for: 1 blanket-$2.22, 1 pr. drawers-$.35$^{1/2}$; absent 04/1848, on detached service as Clerk in Actg. Insp. Genls. office; pres. 07/1848, pay stopped for: 1 cartridge box plate-$.10, 1 gun sling-$.16, 1 pick & brush-$.12, 1 screw driver-$.07, 1 wiper-$.20; BLW sent to Lewisburg, VA; c. 1850 res. Pocahontas Co., VA, age 30, occ. Lawyer[1766] also Greenbrier Co., age 30, occ. Lawyer;[1767] c. 1860 res. Huntersville, Pocahontas Co., VA, age 38, occ. Lawyer;[1768] Civil War service Capt., 127$^{th}$ VA Militia (Pocahontas Reserves); [202]

# VIRGINIA VOLUNTEERS IN MEXICO

c. 1880 res. Huntersville, Pocahontas Co., WV, single, age 60, occ. Lawyer;[1769] SC #1770, 02/15/1887, filed from Huntersville, Pocahontas Co., WV; since discharge res. Lewisburg, WV, 6 years and Huntersville, WV 34 years, never married;[1765] d. c. 1891.[1765]

**Stone, Augustus**, Pvt., Co. I; b. 12/21/1822, Fluvanna Co., son of John A. and Susan Stone;[1770] enl. Mex. War service 12/10/1846 Richmond, VA, age 23; pres. 02/1847; pres. 04/1847; pres. 06/1847; pres. 08/1847; pres. 10/1847, pay stopped for: 2 pr. drawers-$.71, 1 cotton shirt-$.43, 1 pr. pants-$2.28, 1 pr. shoes-$1.22, 1 cap- $.95$^{1/2}$, 1 jacket-$2.66; pres. 12/1847, pay stopped for: 1 pr. shoes-$1.22, 1 pr. socks-$.24$^{1/2}$, 1 pr. pants-$2.28, 2 cotton shirts-$.86 1 flannel shirt-$.90; 1pr. drawers-$.35$^{1/2}$; pres. 02/1848; pres. 04/1848; pres. 08/1848, BLW sent to Columbia P.O., Goochland Co., VA; m/1 Mary Jane Thurston (MTS d. 07/30/1855, Waller Gold Mine, Goochland Co., VA);[1770] m/2 Matilda Ann Brooks 09/15/1859, Manchester, Chesterfield Co., VA;[1770] c. 1870 res. Edinburg, Shennandoah Co., VA, age 50, occ. Carpenter, w. Matilda A. (36), dau. Josephine A. (10), son John D. (5), dau. Florence (1);[1771] SC #1834, 03/12/1887, filed from Richmond, Henrico Co., VA; since discharge res. Fluvanna Co. and City of Richmond, VA, occ. Carpenter;[1770] Theoderick Nunnally and John Moore gave affidavits in pension claim;[1770] d. 05/12/1903, *"exhaustion,"* 609 High St., Richmond, VA, bur. Riverview Cemetery, Richmond, VA;[1772] wid. Matilda A., WC #13440, 11/12/1903, filed from 609 High St., Richmond, Henrico Co., VA; Lists children John Daniel Stone, b. 06/11/1853, George Washington Stone, b. 03/05/1874, granddaughter Katie Reid;[1772] (MBS d. 08/28/1821, bur. Riverview Cemetery, Richmond, VA).[1772]

**Stottlemyre, James M.**, *Willson's Co.*; *Not on Muster Rolls*; SA #21007, 01/09/1889, from WV.

**Stout, William**, Pvt., *Recruit Co.*, enl. Mex. War service 01/30/1848 Christiansburg, VA; pres. 02/1848; pres. 04/1848; pres. 06/1848; BLW sent to Washington City, D.C.

**Stow, Lemuel C.**, Pvt., *Preston's Co.*; b.11/04/1820, Pittsylvania Co., VA;[1773] enl. Mex. War service 12/07/1846 Montgomery Co., VA, age 25; absent 04/1847 left sick in hosp. at Ft. Monroe, VA since 02/27/1847; absent 06/1847 sick at Ft. Monroe, VA; discharged at Monterey, Mex. 07/31/1847 on Surgeon's Certificate of Disability; SC #1961, 03/12/1887, filed from Gleason, Weakley Co., TN; since discharge res. Weakley Co., TN;[1773] phys. desc. at enl. age 27, 5'10$^{1/2}$", dark hair, blue eyes, occ. Farmer.[1773]

**Strong, Tarlton**, *Swiney's Co.*; *Not on Muster Rolls*, SA #25308, 10/21/1902, from TX.

**Stuart, John H.**, Pvt., *Preston's Co.*; b. 12/20/1823, Newport, Cocke Co., TN;[1774] enl. Mex. War service 12/25/1846 Wythe Co., VA, age 23; pres. 04/1847; pres. 06/1847; pres. 08/1847; pres. 10/1847, pay stopped for: 1 pr. overalls-$2.28, 3 pr. socks-$.73$^{1/2}$, 2 flannel shirts-$1.80, 1 cotton shirt-$.43, 2 pr. drawers-$.71, 1 cap-$.95$^{1/2}$; pres. 12/1847, pay stopped for: 1 pr. shoes-$1.22, 1 pr. socks-$.24$^{1/2}$, 1 pr. drawers-$.35$^{1/2}$, 1 blanket-$2.22; pres. 02/1848; pres. 04/1848, pay stopped for: 1 pick & brush-$.12; pres. 07/1848, pay stopped for: 1 pr. shoes-$1.16, 1 bayonet scabbard-$.56, 1 waist belt-$.25, 1 waist belt plate-$.08, 1 gun sling-$.18, 1 screw driver-$.07, 1 wiper-$.13; BLW sent to Christiansburg, VA c/o Fleming Gardner; m. Nannie C. Hanson, 09/16/1858, Wytheville, Wythe Co., VA;[1774] SC #6427, 05/23/1887, filed from Crockett, Houston Co., TX; James H. Moyers gave affidavit in pension claim;[1774] since discharge res. in Virginia and Texas;[1774] d. 1895.[1774]

**Stuart, William W.**, Pvt., Co. D; enl. Mex. War service 01/04/1847, Petersburg, VA, age 23; d. 02/25/1847 at Fort Monroe, VA

**Sullivan, Andrew**, Pvt., Co. B; enl. 11/20/1846, Alexandria, VA, age 38; pres. 06/1847; pres. 08/1847; pres. 10/1847, pay stopped for: 1 pr. overalls-$2.28, 2 pr. cotton drawers-$.71; pres. 12/1847, pay stopped for: 2 pr. shoes-$2.44, 2 pr. socks-$.49, 1 cap-$.95$^{1/2}$; pres. 02/1848; pres. 04/1848; pres. 08/1848, pay stopped for: 1 gun sling-$.16, BLW sent to Alexandria, VA; c. 1850 res. Alexandria Co., VA, age 45, occ. Coach/Harness Maker, w. Maria (41), son Edward (8), dau. Maria (10), son George (6), son Andrew (14);[1775] d. 07/26/1857, *"after a painful illness... in the fiftieth year of his age... He was a volunteer in the Mexican war, in the Alexandria Volunteers...,"*[1776] bur.? Christ Church Episcopal Cemetery, Alexandria, VA;[1777] c.

OFF TO WAR

1860 res. Alexandria Co., VA, wid. Maria (50), son John (25), son Andrew (20), son George (12);[1778] wid. Maria, WC #898, 2/8/1887, from VA

**Swann, Benjamin**, Pvt., Co. B; enl. 11/20/1846, Alexandria, VA, age 20; pres. 06/1847; sick 08/1847; pres. 10/1847, pay stopped for: 1 pr. shoes-$1.22, 1 overcoat-$6.93$^{1/2}$; sick 12/1847, pay stopped for: 1 pr. shoes-$1.22, 3 cotton shirts-$1.29, 1 jacket-$2.66, 1 pr. overalls-$2.28, 2 pr. socks-$.49, 2 pr. cotton drawers-$.71; pres. 02/1848; sick 04/1848; pres. 08/1848, pay stopped for: 1 pr. shoes-$1.16, 1 bayonet scabbard-$.56, 1 waist belt-$.20, 1 waist belt plate-$.10, 1 gun sling-$.16, 1 wiper-$.20, 1 screw driver-$.07, BLW sent to Alexandria, VA c/o Capt. Corse; [a Benjamin Swann m. Susanna Benter, 08/17/1848, Alexandria, VA;[1779] c. 1850 a Benjamin Swann res. Alexandria, VA, age 28, occ. Plasterer, w. Susanna (25) her "twin sister" Catherine Benter (25), b-i-l John Benter (23).][1780]

**Sweeney, William B.**, Pvt., Co. I; enl. Mex. War service 01/10/1847 Richmond, VA, age 28; pres. 02/1847; pres. 04/1847; d. 05/28/1847 in Hosp. at Monterey, Mex.

**Sykes, James W.**, *Gray's Co.*; *Not on Muster Rolls*; Civil War service Pvt., Co. F, 41$^{St}$ Va. Inf.;[404] SA #14591, 06/24/1887, from VA

**Tabb, Augustus G.**, Pvt., Co. F; b. c. 1826, son of Maurice Langhorne & Lovey (Tatum) Tabb;[1781] enl. Mex. War service 11/23/1846, Portsmouth, VA, age 19; pres. 06/1847, on daily duty as Provost Sgt. since 06/10/1847; pres. 08/1847; absent 10/1847 on detached service as Provost Sgt. since 10/29/1847, pay stopped for: 2 pr. overalls-$4.56, 3 pr. shoes-$3.66, 7 pr. socks-$1.71$^{1/2}$, 4 pr. drawers-1.42, 1 forage cap-$.95$^{1/2}$, 1 blanket-$2.22; absent 12/1847 sick, returned to company 12/20/1847; pres. 02/1848, pay stopped for: 3 pr. drawers-$1.06$^{1/2}$, 2 flannel shirts-$1.80, 1 pr. overalls-$2.28, 1 blanket-$2.22, 1 pr. shoes-$1.22; pres. 04/1848, reduced to ranks from 3$^{rd}$ Sgt. 03/01/1848; pres. 08/1848, pay stopped for: 1 gun sling-$.18, 2 pr. shoes-$2.32, 1 cotton shirt-$.44, BLW sent to Portsmouth, VA c/o E.T. Blamire.

**Talbott, William A.**, Capt., Co. M; b. 1814; enl. Mex. War service 06/21/1847, Lynchburg, VA, age 30; pres. 09/1847; pres. 11/1847; pres. 12/1847; pres. 02/1848; pres. 04/1848; pres. 08/1848; c. 1850 res. Lynchburg, Campbell Co., VA, age 36, occ. Constable, w. Sarah C. (29), son Melville S. (5);[1782] d. 1855, bur. Old City Cemetery, Lynchburg, VA

**Talbot, William R.**, Sgt., *Recruit Co.*, enl. Mex. War service 01/03/1848 Alexandria, VA, age 33; pres. 02/1848; pres. 04/1848; pres. 06/1848, prom. Sgt.; BLW sent to Alexandria, VA; c. 1850, res. Fort Lincoln of the Seco Creek, Medina Co., Tex., Pvt., Co. G, 2$^{nd}$ U.S. Dragoons;[1783] d. 05/21/1851 at Ft. Lincoln, Tex., *"William R. Talbert...d. of chronic diarrhea, son of Thomas Talbert of Fairfax County, VA The deceased was connected with the Army in Texas..."*[1784]

**Taliaferro, John R.**, Pvt., Co. C; enl. Mex. War service 12/24/1846, Bowling Green, VA, age 20; pres. 06/1847; d. 08/15/1847 hosp. Saltillo, Mex., pay stopped for: 1 cap-$.95$^{1/2}$, 2 pr. socks-$.49, 2 cotton shirts-$.86, 2 woolen shirts-$1.80.

**Talley, Crawford A.**, Pvt., *Preston's Co.*, enl. Mex. War service 04/07/1848 Wytheville, VA; pres. 06/1848; BLW sent to Wytheville, VA; c. 1850 res. Smyth Co., VA, age 23, occ. Painter, w. Nancy (23);[1785] c. 1860 res. Wythe Co., VA, age 32, occ. Painter, w. Wesley? (33), dau. Lucy (10);[1786] Civil War service Pvt., Co. C, 4$^{th}$ Va. Inf., enl. 06/05/1862 as a substitute for J.R.K. Bentley, captured 06/06/1862 at Harrisonburg, VA, exchanged 08/05/1862, listed as a deserter 12/1862;[54] m. Matilda V. Beck, 12/29/1865, Shelbyville, Bedford Co., TN;[1787] d. 05/24/1886, Lewisburgh, Marshall Co. TN;[1787] wid. Matilda V., WC #1721, 03/14/1887, filed from Tullahoma, Coffee Co., TN; (MBT b. 11/06/1822, Bedford Co. TN, d. 02/21/1901).[1787]

**Talley, Miles**, Pvt., Co. I; enl. Mex. War service 01/30/1847 Richmond, VA, age 18; pres. 02/1847; pres. 04/1847; pres. 06/1847; Court-martialed 07/22/1847, Buena Vista, Mex. *Charge #1 Sleeping On Post; Specification: In this that Private Miles Talley, Co. I, Va. Regt. Vols., being regularly posted as a Sentinel in the town of Saltillo, Mex. on the night of the 16$^{th}$ and 17$^{th}$ of July 1847, was found asleep upon his post between the hours of 3 & 5 o'clock in the morning of the 17$^{th}$. To which charge and specification the prisoner pled Guilty. Corp.*

## VIRGINIA VOLUNTEERS IN MEXICO

*Clarke, Co. I, Va. Regt., a witness for the defense, being duly sworn, says in answer to the following: Question by the Prisoner: Do you know if I was on guard the night of the 15$^{th}$ of July 1847 and again put on guard on the morning of the 16$^{th}$ of July? Answer: A man on guard the day before was taken sick. The prisoner was Supernumerary and next on guard in place of this man without letting the Orderly Sgt. Know anything about it. He stood that night about 4 hours. The next morning, the 16$^{th}$ of July '47, the Orderly Sergt. put him on guard again and he stood the 24 hours out. It was on this last morning that I found him asleep on Post, about 5 o'clock. Question by the Prisoner: What has been the character of the accused with reference to attention to duty generally? Answer: He has always been perfectly attentive to duty and I believe has done more duty than any three men in the company. Question by the Court: Where did this occur? Answer: At Saltillo, Mexico. After deliberation the Court confirmed the plea of the prisoner and sentenced him to be kept at hard labor in his company, attending to all his duties, for the period of one week;*[1788] pres. 08/1847; pres. 10/1847, pay stopped for: 2 pr. drawers-$.71, 5 cotton shirts-$2.15, 1 pr. pants-$2.28, 1 pr. shoes-$1.22, 1 cap- $.95$^{1/2}$, 1 pr. socks-$.24$^{1/2}$, 1 jacket-$2.66; pres. 12/1847, pay stopped for: 1 pr. socks-$.24$^{1/2}$, 2 blankets-$4.44, 1 pr. pants-$2.28, 1 cotton shirt-$.43, 1 flannel shirt-$.90, 2 pr. drawers-$.71; pres. 04/1848, 1 cap, 4 cotton shirts; pres. 02/1848, pay stopped for: 1 pr. shoes-$1.22, 1 pr. overalls-$2.28, 1 jacket-$2.66, 1 blanket-$2.22; pres. 04/1848, pay stopped for: 1 cap, 4 cotton shirts; pres. 08/1848, pay stopped for: 1 cartridge box-$1.10, 1 cartridge box plate-$.10, 1 gunsling-$.16, 1 pr. shoes, BLW sent to Richmond, VA; Civil War service Pvt., Coffin's Btry., VA Hvy. Arty., enl. 03/27/1862, Richmond, VA, for 3 yrs., pres. until wded. (slightly in leg) and captured 07/09/1863 at Port Hudson, La., paroled as of 08/1863 "at his home in Richmond, VA," signs by X mark, listed as a deserter 03/14/1864, in hosp. 05/16/1864 Richmond, VA, w/ "nyctalopia," NFR.[1789]

**Tankersley, George W.**, Pvt., *Preston's Co.*; m. Juda A. Faulkner, 06/22/1838, Halifax Co., VA;[1790] enl. Mex. War service 12/09/1846 Floyd Co., VA, age 27; pres. 04/1847; sick 06/1847; pres. 08/1847; pres. 10/1847, pay stopped for: 1 jacket-$2.66, 1 pr. overalls-$2.28, 1 pr. shoes-$1.22, 2 pr. socks-$.49, 1 cotton shirt-$.43; pres. 12/1847, pay stopped for: 1 jacket-$2.66, 1 pr. overalls-$2.28, 1 pr. shoes-$1.22, 1 cap-$.95$^{1/2}$, 1 blanket-$2.22; pres. 02/1848; pres. 04/1848; pres. 07/1848, pay stopped for: 1 pr. shoes-$1.16, 1 cartridge box-$1.10, 1 cartridge box belt & plate-$.80, 1 bayonet scabbard-$.56, 1 waist belt-$.25, 1 waist belt plate-$.08, 1 brush & pick-$.12, 1 gun sling-$.18, 1 wiper-$.13; BLW sent to Christiansburg, VA c/o Fleming Gardner; c. 1850 res. Pittsylvania Co., age 35, occ. Farmer, w. Julia (age 24);[1791] c. 1860, res. Lee Co., VA, age 48, b. Dinwiddie Co., VA, occ. Carpenter, w. Judith (age 38);[1792] Civil War service Pvt., Co. A, 9$^{th}$ Va. Inf. 05/14/1861 enl. at Salem, Roanoke Co., VA, age 43?, occ. laborer, light complexion, light brown hair, blue eyes, 5'7 1/2", discharged 08/22/1862 due to rheumatism;[211] c. 1870 res. Jonesville, Lee Co., VA, age 60, occ. Farmer, w. Judith (49), son William L. (27), son George W. (24), dau. Ellen (18), son Henry (15), dau. Mariah J. (13), dau. Mary E. (10), dau. Francis R. (7).[1793]

**Tare, Abram V.**, 3$^{rd}$ Cpl., LIC; b. 01/10/1825, Headwaters of Mossy Creek, Augusta Co., VA;[1794] enl. Mex. War service 12/07/1846 Staunton, VA, age 20; pres. 08/1847; pres. 10/1847, pay stopped for: 1 forage cap-$.95$^{1/2}$, 1 wool jacket-$2.66, 1 pr. overalls-$2.28, 1 pr. shoes-$1.22, 2 pr. socks-$.49, 2 cotton shirts-$.86, 1 pr. drawers-$.35$^{1/2}$; pres. 12/1847, pay stopped for: 1 blanket-$2.22, 1 pr. shoes-$1.22, 1 pr. overalls-$2.28, 1 pr. drawers-$.35$^{1/2}$; pres. 04/1848, prom. 3$^{rd}$ Cpl. 02/23/1848, pay stopped for: 1 pr. shoes-$1.50; pres. 07/1848, pay stopped for: 1 screw driver-$.07; BLW sent to Staunton, VA; m. Susan Jane Thomasson, 05/30/1850, Spring Hill, Augusta Co., VA;[1794] c. 1850 res. Augusta Co., VA, age 23, occ. Cooper, w. Susan (18);[1795] c. 1860 res. Augusta Co., VA, age 34, occ. Cooper, w. S.J. (22), dau. E.A. (9), son J.S. (5), dau. M.E. (3);[1796] Civil War service enl. 04/17/1861 Staunton, VA as 1$^{st}$ Lt., Co. C, 5$^{th}$ Va. Inf.; dropped 04/17/62 declined reelection; enl. Pvt., Co A, 28$^{th}$ Va. Inf.;08/08/1863 Augusta, pres. thru 12/1864, nfr, claims he was with Lee at the surrender;[128]

OFF TO WAR

[168, 249, 1794] c. 1880 res. Parkersburg, Wood Co., WV, age 50, occ. Cooper, w. Thomason (43) Keeping House, dau. Elizabeth (25), son John S. (22), d-i-l Fannie (25), dau. Maud (20), s-i-l Sylvester Ditman (37) Butcher;[1797] SC #13551, 10/06/1887, filed from 1030 Lynn St., Parkersburg, Wood Co., WV; phys. desc. age 62 [1887], 5'5$^{1/2}$", light complexion, bluish-grey eyes, dark hair, occ. cooper;[1794] since discharge res. Staunton, Augusta Co., VA until 04/04/1866, to Parkersburg, WV until 05/1867, to Hockingport, Meigs Co., OH until 05/01/1876, to Parkersburg, WV to present;[1794] Lists children Emma Maude Tare b. 06/06/1860, Charles Robert Tare b. 06/23/1867, Ann Vinson Tare;[1794] d. 03/071908;[1794] last known address [1908] 5012 Pennsylvania Ave., Pittsburgh, Allegheny Co., Pa.[1794]

**Taylor, George**, Pvt., Co. I; enl. Mex. War service 01/25/1847 Richmond, VA, age 29; pres. 02/1847; pres. 04/1847; pres. 06/1847; pres. 08/1847; pres. 10/1847, pay stopped for: 3 cotton shirts-$1.29, 1 flannel shirt-$.90, 2 pr. drawers-$.71, 2 pr. shoes-$2.44, 1 pr. socks-$.24$^{1/2}$, 1 blanket-$2.22, 1 cap- $.95$^{1/2}$, 1 jacket-$2.66; pres. 12/1847, pay stopped for: 1 pr. socks-$.24$^{1/2}$, 1 pr. pants-$2.28, 2 cotton shirts-$.86, 1 pr. pants-$2.28; pres. 02/1848, pay stopped for: 1 pr. overalls-$2.28; pres. 04/1848; pres. 08/1848, pay stopped for: 1 screw driver-$.25, BLW sent to Richmond, VA

**Taylor, George William**, Pvt., *Preston's Co.*; enl. Mex. War service 12/06/1846 Montgomery Co., VA, age 21; pres. 04/1847; sick 06/1847; sick 08/1847; pres. 10/1847, pay stopped for: 1 pr. overalls-$2.28, 3 pr. socks-$.73$^{1/2}$, 1 flannel shirt-$.90, 1 cotton shirt-$.43, 1 pr. drawers-$.35$^{1/2}$, 1 cap-$.95$^{1/2}$; pres. 12/1847, pay stopped for: 1 jacket-$2.66, 1 pr. overalls-$2.28, 1 pr. shoes-$1.22, 1 pr. drawers-$.35$^{1/2}$; pres. 02/1848; pres. 04/1848; pres. 07/1848, pay stopped for: 1 gun sling-$.18; BLW sent to Christiansburg, VA

**Taylor, Isaiah**, *Va. Vols.*; *Not on Muster Rolls*; wid. Sarah, WA #5071, 10/10/1887, from KY

**Taylor, James**, *Preston's Co.*; *Not on Muster Rolls*; wid. Sarah J., WA #10972, 11/03/1892, from PA.

**Taylor, James Craig**, Pvt., *Preston's Co.*; b. 09/23/1826, Montgomery Co., VA son of Creed Taylor;[1798] enl. Mex. War service 12/06/1846 Montgomery Co., VA, age 20; pres. 04/1847; pres. 06/1847; discharged 03/31/1847 at Ft. Monroe, VA; c. 1850 res. Montgomery Co., VA, age 24, occ. Student-At-Law;[1799] m. Catherine R. Wade,12/23/1851, Christiansburg, Montgomery Co., VA;[1800] c. 1860 res. Christiansburg, Montgomery Co., VA, age 32, occ. Lawyer, w. Catherine R. (27), son Wade (5), dau Mary E. (2), Margaret V. (6/12), bro.? John L. Taylor (36);[1801] Civil War service Major, 54$^{th}$ Va. Inf., raised Co. C, 54$^{th}$ Va. Inf., 09/10/1861 was its first Capt., pres. 01/01/1862, elected Major 05/13/1862, resigned 09/20/1862 due to ill health, Surgeon' Certificate cites *"chronic disease spermerhorrhea,"* elected to the Virginia Senate 1863-1865; mbr. VA General Assembly, VA Attorney General 1870-1874;[192] c. 1870 res. Christiansburg, Montgomery Co., VA, age 44, occ. Lawyer, w. Kate R. (38), son Wade (15), dau. Mary E. (12), dau. Maggie C. (10), dau. Bettie M. (7), son Robert C. (3);[1802] d. Christiansburg, Montgomery Co., 10/25/1887; SC #11052, 08/08/1887, filed from Christiansburg, Montgomery Co.; Henry Collins, Charles Jackson and Thomas Gilmore gave affidavit in pension claim;[1798] d. 10/25/1887, Christiansburg, Montgomery Co., VA;[1803] wid. Kate, WC #2233, 12/19/1887, filed from Christiansburg, Montgomery Co., VA; (CWT b. 02/29/1832, Christiansburg, Montgomery Co., VA, d. 05/28/1893).[1803]

**Taylor, John**, Pvt., Co. M; enl. Mex. War service 11/18/1847, Norfolk, VA, age 24; pres. 11/1847; deserted 12/07/1847 at Ft. Monroe, VA

**Taylor, John**, Pvt., Co. C; enl. Mex. War service 12/29/1846, Bowling Green, VA, age 26; pres. 06/1847; pres. 08/1847, pay stopped for: 1 cap-$.95$^{1/2}$, 2 pr. socks-$.49, 2 cotton shirts-$.86, 2 woolen shirts-$1.80, 1 pr. shoes-$1.22; 1 pr. overalls-$2.28, 1 knapsack & straps-$1.10; pres. 10/1847, pay stopped for: 2 pr. socks-$.49, 2 pr. drawers-$.71, 1 jacket-$2.66, 3 cotton shirt-$1.29, 2 woolen shirts-$1.80, 1 pr. shoes-$1.22; pres. 12/1847, pay stopped for: 2 pr. socks-$.49, 1 pr. pants-$2.28, 2 cotton shirts-$.86, 1 pr. shoes-$1.22, 1 great coat-$6.93$^{1/2}$, 1 blanket-$2.22; pres. 04/1848, pay stopped for: 5 cotton shirts-$2.15, 2 flannel shirts-$1.80, 1 pr. shoes-

## VIRGINIA VOLUNTEERS IN MEXICO

$1.50, 1 india rubber canteen-$.27; pres. 08/1848, BLW sent to Bowling Green, Caroline County, VA; [c. 1850 a John C. Taylor res. Caroline Co., VA, age 30, occ. Carpenter, w. Lucy M. (21), son Burton L. (3), dau. Laura A. (6/12); c. 1860 res. Sparta, Caroline Co., VA, age 44, occ. Carpenter, w. Lucy A. (26), son Burton L. (11), dau. Laura A. (10), son James L. (9), dau. Virginia R. (6), dau. Alberta Y. (5), son John L. (1).][1804]

**Taylor, Jordon**, Pvt., *Recruit Co.*, enl. Mex. War service 05/13/1848 Bowling Green, VA; pres. 06/1848; BLW sent to Bowling Green, Caroline Co., VA; m. Catherine Martin, 02/27/1851, Caroline Co., VA;[1805] Civil War service Pvt., Caroline Artillery, enl. 07/23/1861 at Bowling Green, VA, pres. for war, paroled 05/01/1865 at Ashland, VA;[1806] c. 1870 res. Millers Tavern, Essex Co., VA, age 50, occ. Farm Laborer, w. Kitty (40);[1807] wid. Kitty, WA #5568, 12/17/1887, from VA

**Taylor, Thomas**, Pvt., Co. C; enl. Mex. War service 12/29/1846, Bowling Green, VA, age 38; pres. 06/1847; pres. 08/1847, pay stopped for: 1 cap-$.95$^{1/2}$, 2 pr. socks-$.49, 2 cotton shirts-$.86, 2 woolen shirts-$1.80, 1 pr. drawers-$.35$^{1/2}$; sick 10/1847, pay stopped for: 3 pr. socks-$.73$^{1/2}$, 1 pr. drawers-$.35$^{1/2}$, 1 jacket-$2.66, 1 pr. pants-$2.28, 1 cotton shirt-$.43, 2 woolen shirts-$1.80, 1 pr. shoes-$1.22, 1 blanket-$2.22; pres. 12/1847, pay stopped for: 1 pr. pants-$2.28, 1 pr. shoes-$1.22; pres. 04/1848, pay stopped for: 1 cotton shirt-$.43, 1 flannel shirt-$.43, 1 blanket-$2.22, 1 haversack-$.20$^{3/4}$, 1 india rubber canteen-$.27; pres. 08/1848, BLW sent to Bowling Green, Caroline County, VA

**Taylor, William G.**, Pvt., LIC; enl. Mex. War service 12/10/1846 Staunton, VA, age 31; pres. 08/1847; pres. 10/1847, pay stopped for: 1 forage cap-$.95$^{1/2}$, 1 wool jacket-$2.66, 1 pr. overalls-$2.28, 1 pr. shoes-$1.22, 4 pr. socks-$.98, 4 cotton shirts-$1.72, 1 pr. drawers-$.35$^{1/2}$; absent 12/1847, on detached service in QM Dept. since 12/17/1847, pay stopped for: 1 pr. socks-$.24$^{1/2}$, 1 pr. shoes-$1.22, 1 pr. drawers-$.35$^{1/2}$; pres. 04/1848, pay stopped for: 1 pr. shoes-$1.22; pres. 07/1848; BLW sent to Mt. Carmel, Fleming Co., KY

**Taylor, William L.**, Pvt., Co. I; enl. Mex. War service 02/05/1847 Richmond, VA, age 25; pres. 02/1847; pres. 04/1847; pres. 06/1847; pres. 08/1847; pres. 10/1847, pay stopped for: 2 pr. drawers-$.71, 1 flannel shirt-$.90, 1 pr. pants-$2.28, 1 pr. socks-$.24$^{1/2}$; pres. 12/1847, pay stopped for: 1 pr. shoes-$1.22, 1 pr. socks-$.24$^{1/2}$, 2 pr. drawers-$.71, 1 cap-.95$^{1/2}$, 1 jacket-$2.66, 1 blanket-$2.22, 1 pr. pants-$2.28, 1 overcoat-$6.93$^{1/2}$; pres. 02/1848; pres. 04/1848; pres. 08/1848, reduced to ranks from 2$^{nd}$ Sgt., BLW sent to Richmond, VA; m. Elizabeth Saunders 12/19/1850 place unknown;[1808] occ. Shoemaker; d. 11/25/1876, Alms House, Richmond, Henrico Co., VA;[1808] wid. Elizabeth, WC #4357, 02/03/1888, from VA; (EST b. 06/16/1832, Caroline Co., VA, d. 06/19/1904).[1808]

**Tellson, Henry H.**, Co. A; *Not on Muster Rolls*, SA #10419, 03/23/1887, from MD

**Templeton, James**, Fifer, Co. A; enl. 12/01/1846 Richmond, VA, age 28; pres. 12/1846 – 04/1847; pres. 06/1847; detached service 08/1847, with Regtl. Band since 05/01/1847; detached service 08/1847 with Regt. Band; pres. 10/1847, pay stopped for clothing: 2 flannel shirts-$1.80, 1 wool jacket-$2.66, 1 pr. wool overalls-$2.28, 1 cap-$.95$^{1/2}$, 2 pr. stockings-$.49, 1 pr. shoes-$1.22; on detached service 02/1848–04/1848 at Parras, Mex. since 02/25/1848; 07/1848, pay stopped for: 1 pr. shoes-$1.16; BLW sent to, Chesterfield Co., VA c/o Robert Blair, Wheelwright.

**Tenain, John E.**, Pvt., Co. E; enl. Mex. War service 11/26/1846 Petersburg, VA, age 19; pres. 04/1847; absent 06/1847 sick in Monterey, Mex. since 06/22/1847; pres. 08/1847; pres. 10/1847; pres. 12/1847, pay stopped for: 1 pr. pants-$2.28, 2 pr. socks-$.49, 1 pr. shoes-$1.22, 2 cotton shirts-$.86, 2 flannel shirts-$1.80, 2 pr. drawers-$.71, 1 cap-$.95 $^{1/2}$, 1 blanket-$2.22; pres. 02/1848, pay stopped for: 1 pr. pants-$2.28, 1 jacket-$2.66; pres. 04/1848.

**Terrell, Greenberry B.**, Pvt., LIC; b. c. 1821, VA; enl. Mex. War service 01/06/1847 Staunton, VA, age 25; sick 06/1847 in quarters; pres. 08/1847; pres. 10/1847, pay stopped for: 1 forage cap-$.95$^{1/2}$, 1 wool jacket-$2.66, 1 pr. overalls-$2.28, 2 pr. socks-$.49, 1 pr. drawers-$.35$^{1/2}$; absent 12/1847, sick in quarters, pay stopped for: 1 pr. socks-$.24$^{1/2}$, 1 blanket-$2.22, 1 pr.

## OFF TO WAR

drawers-$.35$^{1/2}$; pres. 04/1848, pay stopped for: 1 pr. shoes-$1.22; pres. 07/1848, pay stopped for: 1 pr. shoes-$1.16, 1 gun sling-$.16, 1 pick & brush-$.12, 1 screw driver-$.07, 1 wiper-$.20; BLW sent to Waynesborough, VA; m. Sarah Margaret Edgar, 10/25/1849, Rockingham Co., VA;[1809] c. 1850 res. Rockingham Co., VA, age 29, occ. Laborer, w. Sarah M. (17);[1810] c. 1860 res. Augusta Co., VA, age 39, occ. Laborer;[1811] Civil War service enl. 07/22/1864 in Augusta Co., VA as Pvt., 6$^{th}$ Va. Inf.; desc. 5'8", grey eyes, brown hair; capt. 10/27/64 Burgess Mill; sent Pt. Lookout, MD; released 06/19/1865;[249, 465] SC #3889, 02/15/1887, filed from Waynesboro, Augusta Co., VA; res. *"in a small house and lot near Blue Ridge Tunnel at the foot of the Blue Ridge Mountains, 2$^{1/2}$ miles from Waynesboro;"*[1812] since discharge res. Waynesboro, Augusta Co., VA;[1812] phys. desc. at enl. age 25, b. Waynesboro, occ. Blacksmith, 5'8$^{3/4}$", brown hair, gray eyes, fair complexion;[1812] d. 06/16/0901;[1812] *"I, Greenberry B. Terrell, do certify to the following: On or about Dec. 25$^{th}$ 1846 Capt. Canton [sic] Harper's company (which I think was known as Co. "C" of 1$^{st}$ VA Regiment of Light Infantry, John C. Hamtramck being Colonel) passed through Waynesborough, VA on its way to Richmond, VA About ten days afterwards I, in company with <u>James Pelter</u> (in whose behalf this statement is made), Wm. Long & John Grove (all of this vicinity) followed going by stage to Gordonsville and rail from there to Richmond. We reached Richmond on January 6$^{th}$ 1847 (to the best of my recollection) and were all mustered into service the same evening. We joined Capt. Harper's Company (Robt. Kinney 1$^{st}$ Lieut., Vincent E. Geiger, 2$^{nd}$ Lieut. & Wm. H. Harman 3$^{rd}$ Lieut.) & volunteered for the war. On the next day we were sent on boat to Fortress Monroe & about two weeks afterwards were put aboard the "Mayflower" & sent to Mexico. We were 33 days on the voyage & were landed at the mouth of the Rio Grande River. We were in service as long as the war lasted (same known as the Mexican War) & were sent back to Fortress Monroe & disbanded & honorably discharged about the latter part of July 1848. The said James Pelter being with us the whole time & returning with us to Waynesboro, VA Written in my hand this 20$^{th}$ day of March 1894. Greenberry B. Terrell. Subscribed & sworn before the undersigned Notary Public this the 20$^{th}$ day of March 1894. W.S. Fishburne, N.P.;"*[1813]

**Terrell, John J.**, Pvt., *Recruit Co.*, enl. Mex. War service 12/26/1847 Christiansburg, VA, age 19; pres. 02/1848; discharged 03/13/1848 by order of Sec. of War; SA #24144, 11/11/1892, from VA

**Terrell, Lewis K.**, Pvt., LIC; enl. Mex. War service 12/20/1846 Staunton, VA, age 31; absent 06/1847 sick in quarters; d. 08/20/1847 at Saltillo, Mex.

**Thompson, Charles M.**, Regt. Qtr. Mstr. Sgt., Co. K; b. 10/12/1830, Harper's Ferry, Jefferson Co., VA;[1814] enl. Mex. War service 12/20/1846 Frederick Co., VA, age 18; pres. 06/1847; pres. 08/1847; Pvt. Thompson evidently wrote home giving an inaccurate picture of his condition while in Mexico in the hopes of securing a early discharge. Col. Hamtramck wrote of the matter, *"He has grown a good deal since he left Richmond. Appears strong, healthy and able to do duty...I must therefore report against their procuring their discharge."*[1815] pres. 10/1847, pay stopped for: 2 pr. overalls-$4.56, 4 pr. drawers-$1.42, 2 pr. shoes-$2.44, 2 flannel shirts-$1.80, 1pr. socks-$.24$^{1/2}$, 1 greatcoat-$6.93$^{1/2}$; pres. 12/1847, 1 blanket-$2.22; discharged 02/24/1848 by order of Sec. of War; desc. age 18, 5'8", dark complexion, dark eyes, dark hair, occ. Printer;[26] m. Jane Lyon, 05/08/1851, place unknown;[1814] SC #19985, 01/18/1893, filed from St. Joseph, Buchanan Co., MO; since discharge res. Charlestown, Jefferson Co., VA until 10/1849 when he moved to St. Joseph, Mo. In 1856 he moved to Doniphan Co., KS lived there 2 yrs.. Returned to St. Joseph in 1858. Moved to Hastings, NE in 1878 for 1 yr. Then returned to St. Joseph, Mo.;[1814] phys. desc. age 62 [1892], 5'10", dark complexion, gray eyes, gray hair, occ. Clerk at enl. occ. Printer;[1814] c. 1899 res. Encinitas, San Diego Co., Calif.;[1814] d. 06/23/1903.[1814]

**Thomson, James**, Pvt., *Recruit Co.*, enl. Mex. War service 01/03/1848 Christiansburg, VA, age 19; pres. 02/1848; pres. 04/1848; pres. 06/1848; BLW sent to Christiansburg, VA

VIRGINIA VOLUNTEERS IN MEXICO

**Thompson, James**, Pvt., Co. K; b. 05/27/1829, Floyd Co., VA;[1816] enl. Mex. War service Jefferson Co., VA 12/26/1846, age 40; pres. 06/1847; pres. 08/1847; pres. 10/1847, pay stopped for: 1 cap-$.95$^{1/2}$, 1 pr. drawers-$.35$^{1/2}$, 2 flannel shirts-$1.80; pres. 12/1847, pay stopped for: 1 pr. overalls-$2.28, 1 blanket-$2.22; pres. 04/1848, pay stopped for: 1 bedsack-$1.07$^{1/2}$; pres. 07/1848, pay stopped for: 1 cartridge box-$1.10, 1 cartridge box belt-$.60, 1 cartridge box belt plate-$.10, 1 bayonet scabbard & frog-$.56, 1 waist belt-$.21, 1 waist belt plate-$.10, 1 pick & brush-$.12; BLW sent to Winchester, Frederick Co., VA; m. Mary Ellen Elswick 11/01/1850, Montgomery Co., VA;[1816] SC #8674, 05/03/1887, filed from Christiansburg, Montgomery Co., VA; d. 10/28/1894 *"Bright's Disease,"* at home, Floyd Co., VA *"near the Montgomery Co. line;"*[1817] wid. Mary E., WC #10734, 12/12/1894, filed from Childress Store, Montgomery Co., VA; Lists son R.K. Thompson, dau. Etta Thompson and Cynthia Thompson;[1816] (MET b. 1830, d. 10/07/1909).[1817]

**Thompson, John W.**, Pvt., Co. E; enl. Mex. War service 12/01/1846 Petersburg, VA, age 18, 5'5", stout, black hair, grey eyes, dark complexion, occ. Hardware & Tinware, b. Dinwiddie Co., VA; pres. 04/1847; pres. 06/1847; pres. 08/1847; pres. 10/1847, pay stopped for: 1 pr. overalls-$2.28, 2 pr. shoes-$2.44, 2 pr. stockings-$.49, 1 cap-$.95$^{1/2}$; pres. 12/1847, pay stopped for: 1 pr. pants-$2.28, 2 cotton shirts-$.86, 2 flannel shirts-$1.80, 2 pr. drawers-$.71, 1 blanket-$2.22; pres. 02/1848, pay stopped for: 1 pr. shoes-$1.22; pres. 04/1848; m. Annie E. Williams 11/14/1850, Petersburg, VA;[1818] d. 08/02/1869 *"cholera,"* Kansas City, Jackson Co., Mo.;[1818] wid. Annie E., WC #5033, 03/14/1888, filed from 113 W. 13$^{th}$ St., Kansas City, Jackson Co., MO; since discharge res. in Petersburg about 3 years since then in Kansas City, Mo; (AET d. 1897).

**Thompson, William**, Pvt., Co. B; b. 05/12/1812, Patrick Co., VA; m. Mary Pike, 04/20/1842, Patrick Co., VA;[1819] enl. 12/10/1846, Alexandria, VA, age 30; pres. 06/1847; pres. 08/1847; pres. 10/1847, pay stopped for: 1 jacket-$2.66, 1 pr. overalls-$2.28, 2 pr. cotton drawers-$.71, 1 blanket-$2.22; sick 12/1847, pay stopped for: 3 pr. socks-$.73$^{1/2}$, 2 pr. shoes-$2.44, 2 cotton shirts-$.86; pres. 02/1848, pay stopped for: 2 cotton shirts-$.86; in confinement 04/1848; pres. 08/1848, pay stopped for: 1 musket-$13.00, 1 bayonet scabbard-$.56, 1 cartridge box belt plate-$10, 1 waist belt-$.21, 1 waist belt plate-$.10, 1 pick & brush-$.12, 1 screw driver-$.07, 1 wiper-$.20, 1 gun sling-$.16, BLW sent to Alexandria, VA c/o Capt. Corse; SC #13299, 11/22/1887, file from Grayson Co., KY; d. 01/01/1899 Grayson Co., KY; wid. Mary, WC #11860, 04/18/1899, filed from 2820 W. Madison St., Louisville, KY (MPT b. 04/28/1823, Patrick Co., VA, d. 02/06/1915 the result of a fall and broken hip, Louisville, KY, bur. Eastern Cemetery, Louisville, KY).[1819]

**Thornton, Henry F.**, Pvt., *Recruit Co.*, 07/24/1824, Petersburg, VA, son of Anthony & Ann (Rose) Thornton;[1820] enl. Mex. War service 12/02/1847 Bowling Green, VA, age 23; pres. 02/1848; pres. 04/1848; discharged 05/17/1848 at his own request; c. 1850 res. Richmond, Henrico Co., VA, age 23?, occ. College Steward;[1821] c. 1860 res. Richmond, Henrico Co., VA, age 29?, occ. Salesman;[1822] Civil War service Pvt., Co. F, 30$^{th}$ Va. Inf., enl. 05/20/1861, age 36, manager at Guiney's, absent sick 11/1861 through 02/1862, RTD, absent sick 09/1862 in hosp. at Warrenton, VA, captured there on 09/30/1862 and paroled, detached as a Teamster and Ambulance Driver for Corse's Brigade 03/1863 through 01/1865;[414] SC #9623, 02/25/1887, wid. Meta, WC #12066, 01/14/1899, both from KY

**Thorpe, Henry**, Pvt., Co. M; enl. Mex. War service 08/01/1847, Richmond, VA, age 25; pres. 09/1847; pres. 11/1847, deserted 11/22/1847 at Ft. Monroe, VA

**Thrift, Benjamin Franklin**, 3$^{rd}$ Sgt., Co. L; b. 04/25/1827 Fairfax Co., VA, son of James and Sinah (Ball) Thrift;[1823] enl. Mex. War service 03/22/1847 Fairfax C.H., VA, age 20; pres. 06/1847; pres. 08/1847; pres. 10/1847, prom. 2$^{nd}$ Cpl. from Pvt. 09/01/1847, pay stopped for: 1 pr. pants-$2.28; pres. 12/1847, prom. 4$^{th}$ Sgt. from 3$^{rd}$ Cpl. 11/04/1847, pay stopped for: 2 pr. Pants 4.56, 1 pr. Shoes 1.22, 6 F. Shirts 5.40, 7 Ct. Shirts 3.01, 1 Blanket 2.22, 2 pr. Drawers 1.42, 4 pr. Socks; pres. 02/1848, pay stopped for: 1 pr. Shoes 1.22; pres. 04/1848, pay stopped for: 5 prs. Drawers 1.75; pres. 07/1848; BLW sent to Capt. Thrift c/o Benjamin F. Thrift, Fairfax Court House, Fairfax Co., VA; drew a BLW in the vicinity of Putnam Co., OH on which he settled;[1824] m/1 Columbia Caroline Black 11/1852, Kalida, Putnam Co., OH (CCT d. 08/25/1861 Buffalo, Wright Co., MN); 1 dau. Linda M. Thrift b. 05/10/1857 was adopted by her Aunt, Sarah Duvall, and subsequently known as Linda M. Duvall, res. Delaware, OH; Civil War service, Pvt., Arty. Co., 43$^{rd}$ Btln. Va. Cav.;[1309] m/2 Mary A. Eckley 03/29/1873, Hartsburg, Putnam Co., OH; mbr. Washington Camp U.C.V.;[1825] SC #999, 03/22/1887, filed from Ozark, Webster Co., MO; since discharge has resided Kalida & Hartsburg, Putnam Co., OH, some years at Buffalo, Wright Co., MN, moved to Marshfield, Webster Co., OH c. 1886; pension contains the affidavit of a niece *"on wifes side,"* Rosa Vail, wife of J.P. Vail, of Lima, Allen Co. OH; c. 1898 res. Marshfield, Webster Co., MO;[1824] c. 1900 res. Ozark, Webster Co., Mo., age 73, occ. Farmer, b. VA, w. Mary A. (44) b. Ohio, no children;[1826] d. 04/04/1904 *"General debility from old age, enlarged liver and obstruction of billery duct,"* Conway Springs, Sumner Co., Kan.; bro. of Capt. James H. Thrift;[1823] wid. Mary A., WC #13911, 04/28/1904, filed from Webster Co., MO. (MAT b. 03/28/1856 near Hartsburg, Putnam Co., OH, d. 01.25/1913 Conway Springs, Sumner Co. KS).[1827]

**Thrift, James Harvey**, Capt., Co. L; b. c. 1817, son of James & Sinah (Ball) Thrift;[1823] enl. Mex. War service 03/01/1847 Fairfax C.H., VA; pres. 06/1847; pres. 08/1847, prom. Capt. upon the death of Henry Fairfax; pres. 12/1847; pres. 02/1848; pres. 04/1848; pres. 07/1848; m. Lucretia N. Reid 10/31/1848, Fairfax Co., VA;[1828] 1849-1850 *California 49er*; c. 1850 res. Fairfax Co., VA, age 33, occ. Engineer, w. Lucretia M. (25), dau. Mary R. (1);[1829] member Virginia House of Delegates 1855-1856; vtd. for Secession at Fairfax C.H., VA, 04/23/1861; Civil War service Capt., Co. G, 8$^{th}$ Va. Inf., prom. Major 04/26/1862 at Yorktown, VA; mortally wded. 05/31/1862 at Seven Pines, VA, d. 06/03/1862 at Richmond, VA;[529, 898] bro. of Sgt. Benjamin F. Thrift.[1823]

**Tibbets, Charles D.**, Co. B; b. 08/28/1830, Rectortown, Fauquier Co., VA; enl. 08/15/1847, Warrenton, VA, age 17; pres. 02/1848; pres. 04/1848; pres. 08/1848, pay stopped for: 1 pick & brush-$.12, 1 wiper-$.20, 1 gun sling-$.16, BLW sent to Rectortown, Fauquier Co., VA; SC #11450, 05/26/1887, filed from 1320 Prince St., St. Louis, MO. phys. desc. 5'10", blue eyes, dark hair, light complexion, occ. Merchant; Since discharge res. Fauquier Co., 3yrs., Desoto Parish, La., 3 yrs., California, 3 yrs., DeSoto Parish, La., 15 yrs., St. Louis, Mo., 18 yrs., National Soldiers home; admitted to National Soldiers Home 09/26/1889 seriously injured when struck by an automobile while crossing Main St. & 12$^{th}$ St., Lynchburg, VA; transferred to National Soldiers Home, Hampton, VA from Mt. Branch 1920; d. 04/12/1924 *"General arterior-sclerosis,"* National Soldiers Home, Hampton, VA, bur. Hampton National Cemetery, Plot: 603-A, Hampton, VA;[1830] Never married.[1831]

**Tiffin, Joseph**, Pvt., Co. M; enl. Mex. War service 08/01/1847, Richmond, VA, age 30; pres. 09/1847; pres. 11/1847; pres. 12/1847; pres. 02/1848, *"having enrolled on board barque 11$^{th}$ Dec. 1847 and no opportunity offering to be mustered into the U.S. service Col. Hamtramck has ordered payment from date of enrollment and six months commutation for clothing,"* pay stopped for: 1 blanket-$2.22, 2 cotton shirts-$.86; pres. 04/1848, pay stopped for: 2 cotton shirts-$.86; pres. 08/1848, pay stopped for: 1 gun sling-$.16; BLW sent to Richmond, VA

**Tillson, Henry H.**, 1$^{st}$ Sgt., Co. A; b. 10/04/1820 London, England;[1832] m/1 Elizabeth Phillips, 10/30/1845, Richmond, VA; (EHT d. 04/16/1846)[1833] enl. 11/25/1846, Richmond, VA; pres. 12/1846 - 04/1847; pres. 06/1847; pres. 08/1847, prom. 1$^{st}$ Sgt. 08/23/1847; pres. 10/1847, pay stopped for clothing: 2 wool overalls-$4.56, 4 pr. Stockings-$.98, 2 cotton shirts-$.86, 1 cap-$.95, 2 sergt.(chevrons?), 6 shirts, 2 flannel shirts $1.80, 2 pr. Drawers-$.71, 1 great coat-$6.93, 1 blanket-$2.22; pres. 12/1847, pay stopped for clothing: 2 blanket-$4.44, 2 wool overalls-$4.56, 1 pr. Drawers-$.35$^{1/2}$, 2 cotton shirts-$.86, 1 pr. shoes-$1.22, 1 pr. Socks-$.24$^{1/2}$, 2 flannel shirts $1.80; pres. 02/1848, pay stopped for: 1 pr. wool overalls-$2.28, 1

## VIRGINIA VOLUNTEERS IN MEXICO

blanket-$2.22, 1 pr. shoes-$1.22; pres. 04/1848; BLW sent to, Richmond, VA; m. Harriet H. Mull 12/19/1848, Richmond, Henrico Co., VA;[1834] c. 1860 res. Richmond, Henrico Co., VA, age 37, occ. Tailor, w. Harriet H. (31), son Henry H. (10), Alice C. (9), Hattie L. (6);[1835] Civil War service Pvt., Co. D, 26$^{th}$ Va. Inf., enl. 04/06/1862 at Yorktown, VA, discharged 07/30/1862 due to chronic rheumatism;[1016] moved to Baltimore, MD C. 1869;[1836] SC #4234, 03/23/1887 filed from 418 S. Sharp St., Baltimore, MD; phys. desc. age 66 yrs., 5'7", florid complexion, brown eyes, brown hair, occ. Clothing Cutter; Since discharge res. in Richmond, VA 21 years, and Baltimore 37 years; d. 11/01/1906, *"chronic nephritis, cardiac failure,"* Baltimore, MD;[1837] obit. and *photograph* in *Baltimore Sun* newspaper *"The funeral of Mr. Henry Tillson, the Mexican War veteran who died Thursday at his home 1500 West Mulberry Street, will take place today. Mr. Tillson served in both the conflict with Mexico and the Civil War in which he fought for the Confederacy;"*[1838] bur. Loudoun Park Cem., Baltimore, MD; wid. Harriet H., WC #14598, 11/14/1906. (HHT b. 09/25/1828 New York, NY, d. 02/21/1908)

Photo credit: Baltimore Sun, Balt., MD

**Totten, Samuel,** Pvt., Co. F; enl. Mex. War service 01/18/1847, Portsmouth, VA, age 20; pres. 06/1847; pres. 08/1847; pres. 10/1847, pay stopped for: 1 pr. overalls-$2.28, 1 forage cap-$.95$^{1/2}$, 3 cotton shirts-$1.29, 4 pr. socks-$.98, 2 pr. shoes-$2.44, 4 pr. drawers-$1.42, 3 flannel shirts-$2.70, 1 infantry jacket-$2.66; pres. 12/1847; pres. 02/1848, pay stopped for: 1 pr. overalls-$2.28, 1 pr. drawers-$.35$^{1/2}$, 1 blanket-$2.22, 2 pr. socks-$.49, 1 infantry jacket-$2.66, 2 pr. shoes-$2.44, 1 bed sack-$1.07; pres. 04/1848; pres. 08/1848, pay stopped for: 1 gun sling-$.18, 2 pr. shoes-$2.32, 1 forage cap-$.83, 2 cotton shirts-$.88, 1 blanket-$2.25, BLW sent to Portsmouth, VA c/o E.T. Blamire; m. Sarah Snail 07/1853, Norfolk, Norfolk Co., VA;[1839] Civil War service Pvt., Co. B, 18$^{th}$ Btln. VA Hvy. Arty., enl. 02/27/1861 in Norfolk, VA, detached service 09/1862 as a guard at Redoubts C & D, charged $1.50 for screw driver lost, 08/31/1864, deserted to enemy 11/02/1864, sent to Bermuda Hundred and took oath, trans. furnished to Norfolk, VA;[20] d. 11/25/1868 Norfolk, Va;[1839] wid. Sarah, WA #4207, 07/16/1887, filed from Norfolk, VA; (SST b. 1831).[1839]

**Totty, John,** Pvt., Co. D; b. 07/05/1813, Chesterfield Co., VA;[1840] m. Mary Watts Jamison 07/02/1834, Petersburg, VA;1840 enl. Mex. War service 12/31/1846, Petersburg, VA, age 34; pres. 02/1847; pres. 04/1847; pres. 06/1847, pay stopped for: 1 musket & gun sling lost at Rinconada on 06/23/1847 through negligence; pres. 08/1847, on 06/1847 muster roll pay stopped for musket & gunsling by mistake; pres. 10/1847, pay stopped for: 1 cap-$.95$^{1/2}$, 1 pr. pants-$2.28, 1 pr. drawers-$.35$^{1/2}$, 2 pr. socks-$.49, 1 pr. shoes-$1.22, 1overcoat-$6.93$^{1/2}$, 1 blanket-$2.22; pres. 12/1847, fined 1 mos. pay by order (No. 162) of genl. court-martial, pay stopped for: 1 jacket-$2.66, 1 pr. pants-$2.28, 2 cotton shirts-$.86, 1 pr. shoes-$1.22, 1 blanket-$2.22; pres. 04/1848, pay stopped for: 1 cap-$.95$^{1/2}$; pres. 08/1847, BLW sent to

OFF TO WAR

Petersburg, VA; SC #1847, 02/24/1887, filed from 516 Commerce St., Petersburg, VA; Since discharge res. Petersburg, VA; d. 07/26/1889, *Overdose of Laudanum*, bur. Blandford Cemetery, Sec. 1, Ward L; Petersburg, VA; wid. Mary D., WC #6546, 08/17/1889, filed from 516 Commerce St., Petersburg, VA; (MWT d. 07/1893).

**Towner, Thomas Harris**, 4th Cpl., Co. D; b. 1822, Jefferson Co., VA, son of Benjamin F. and Elizabeth Towner;[1841] enl. Mex. War service 01/08/1847, Richmond, VA, age 25; prom. QM Sgt. 01/1847; absent 02/1847, sailed on board the *Exact* 02/22/1847 for Port Isabel, Tex.; pres. 10/1847, reduced to ranks 09/13/1847, pay stopped for: 1 cotton shirt-$.43; pres. 12/1847, prom. 4th Cpl. 12/31/1847, pay stopped for: 1 cap-$.95$^{1/2}$, 1 jacket-$2.66, 1 blanket-$2.22; pres. 04/1848, 1 haversack-$.20$^{3/4}$, 1 pr. shoes-$1.22; pres. 08/1847, BLW sent to Shepherdstown, VA; c. 1850 res. Shepherdstown, Jefferson Co., VA, age 28, occ. Lawyer;[1841] Civil War service 1st Sgt., Co. B, 2nd Va. Inf., mortally wded. in action 03/23/1862 at Kernstown, VA, d. 03/26/1862 at Winchester, VA;[387] bur. Methodist Graveyard, Shepherdstown, VA.[45]

**Traylor, Richard B.**, Pvt., Co. E; enl. Mex. War service 12/01/1846 Petersburg, VA, age 19; absent 04/1847 sick Camargo, Mex. since 04/03/1847; pres. 06/1847; pres. 08/1847; pres. 10/1847, pay stopped for: 1 pr. overalls-$2.28, 2 pr. shoes-$2.44, 2 pr. stockings-$.49, 1 cotton shirt-$.43, 1 cap-$.95$^{1/2}$; absent sick 12/1847, pay stopped for: 1 pr. pants-$2.28, 1 pr. shoes-$1.22, 3 flannel shirts-$2.70, 1 blanket-$2.22; pres. 02/1848, pay stopped for: 1 pr. shoes-$1.22; d. 03/30/1848 Saltillo, Mex.

**Tridle, John T.**, Pvt., Co. B; b. c. 1825, Alexandria, VA; enl. 12/01/1846, Alexandria, VA, age 18; pres. 06/1847; pres. 08/1847; pres. 10/1847, pay stopped for: 1 pr. overalls-$2.28, 2 pr. cotton drawers-$.71, 2 flannel shirts-$1.80, 1 pr. shoes-$1.22, 1 blanket-$2.22; pres. 12/1847, pay stopped for: 2 pr. shoes-$2.44, 1 pr. overalls-$2.28, 4 cotton shirts-$1.72, 2 pr. socks-$.49, 2 pr. cotton drawers-$.71, 1 overcoat-$6.93$^{1/2}$, 1 cap-$.95$^{1/2}$, 2 flannel shirts-$1.80, 1 jacket-$2.66; pres. 02/1848; pres. 04/1848; pres. 08/1848, BLW sent to Alexandria, VA c/o Capt. Corse; c. 1850 res. Fairfax Co., VA, age 24, occ. Butcher;[1842] c. 1860 res. Fairfax Co., VA, age 30, occ. Butcher, illiterate;[1843] m. Bridget Agnes Nevill 12/26/1860, St. Aloysius Catholic Church, Washington, D.C.;[1844] Civil War service Pvt., Co. D, 17th Va. Inf.;[63, 898] on census of ex-confederate soldiers in Fairfax Co., VA 1898, age 73;[72] SC #13006, 10/26/1887, phys. desc. 5'6", dark hair, blue eyes, occ. Butcher; d. 01/14/1899, *"aged 74,"* Burke's Station, Fairfax Co., VA, bur. St. Mary's Cem., Fairfax Station, VA;[45] wid. Bridget Agnes, WC #11605, 02/23/1899, both from VA (BAT d. 08/06 or 07/1916, Swetnam, Fairfax Co., VA).

**Trott, Samuel**, Pvt., Co. L; b. 1827, possibly the son of Rev. Samuel & Elizabeth Jane (Williams) Trott of Fairfax Station, VA; enl. Mex. War service 03/15/1847 Fairfax C.H., VA, age 20; pres. 06/1847; d. 08/17/1847 Buena Vista, Mex.[72]

**Trump, James N.**, Pvt., *Preston's Co.*; b. c. 1827, Montgomery Co., VA, son of William & Malinda (Hawkins) Trump;[1845] enl. Mex. War service 01/03/1847 Montgomery Co., VA, age 20; absent 04/1847 on detached service as a Hospital Steward at Ft. Monroe, VA since 02/27/1847; absent 06/1847 on detached service as Hospital Steward at Ft. Monroe, VA; d. 03/17/1847 at Ft. Monroe, VA, *"of smallpox."*[243]

**Tucker, Armsted O.**, *Preston's Co.*; *Not on Muster Rolls*; wid. Elizabeth, WA #7416, 11/27/1888, from WV.

**Tucker, George W.**, 4th Cpl., *Preston's Co.*, enl. Mex. War service 01/04/1847 Montgomery Co., VA, age 23; pres. 10/1847, pay stopped for: 1 pr. overalls-$2.28, 1 pr. shoes-$1.22, 2 pr. socks-$.49, 2 flannel shirts-$1.80, 2 cotton shirts-$.86, 1 pr. drawers-$.35$^{1/2}$, 1 blanket-$2.22, 1 cap-$.95$^{1/2}$; pres. 12/1847, pay stopped for: 1 jacket-$2.66, 1 pr. socks-$.24$^{1/2}$; pres. 02/1848, pay stopped for: 1 pr. shoes-$1.22; pres. 04/1848, prom. 4th Cpl.; pres. 07/1848, pay stopped for: 1 pr. shoes-$1.16, 1 screw driver-$.07; BLW sent to Blacksburg, VA c/o Harvey Black.

## VIRGINIA VOLUNTEERS IN MEXICO

Tucker, William B., Pvt., *Preston's Co.*; b. 08/04/1826, Randolph Co., NC;[1846] enl. Mex. War service 12/06/1846 Montgomery Co., VA, age 18; absent 04/1847 left sick in hosp. at Pt. Isabel, Tex. since 03/16/1847, reduced to ranks from Fifer 04/01/1847; pres. 06/1847; pres. 08/1847; pres. 10/1847, pay stopped for: 1 pr. shoes-$1.22, 2 pr. socks-$.49, 1 flannel shirt-$.90, 2 cotton shirts-$.86; pres. 12/1847, pay stopped for: 1 pr. overalls-$2.28, 1 cap-$.95$^{1/2}$; pres. 02/1848, pay stopped for: 1 pr. shoes-$1.22; pres. 04/1848; pres. 07/1848; BLW sent to Christiansburg, VA c/o Fleming Gardner; m. Catherine Kilmer, 02/18/1850, Montgomery Co., VA;[1847] Civil War service Cpl., Co. G, 4$^{th}$ Va. Inf., 04/17/1861, age 33, occ. Laborer, discharged 04/30/1861 at Richmond, VA due to disability;[54] SC #17458, 11/09/1888, filed from Price's Fork, Montgomery Co., VA; phys. desc. 5'7";[1846] James H. Moyers gave affidavit in pension claim;[1846] [*About 1890 William Tucker is alleged to have run off with a "lewd" woman and her three illegitimate children to Vinton, Gallia Co., OH. He subsequently attempted to file for divorce from Catherine. The divorce suit failed. In the meantime, Catherine filed for, and received, half of William's Mexican War pension as a "deserted wife"*];[1846] d. 08/13/1920 "*chronic nephritis,*" at Soldiers Home, Johnson City, TN;[1848] wid. Catherine, WC 16312, 10/12/1920, filed from 107 Reese St., Bluefield, Mercer Co., WV; (CKT b. 04/14/1832, d. 01/13/1925).[1848]

Tudor, Richard, Pvt., Co. D; enl. Mex. War service 12/28/1846, Petersburg, VA, age 24; pres. 02/1847; pres. 04/1847; pres. 06/1847; pres. 08/1847, pay stopped for: 1 cap-$.95$^{1/2}$, 2 cotton shirts-$.86, 2 flannel shirts-$1.80, 1 pr. shoes-$1.22; pres. 10/1847, pay stopped for: 1 jacket-$2.66, 1 pr. pants-$2.28, 1 pr. drawers-$.35$^{1/2}$, 2 pr. socks-$.49, 1 pr. shoes-$1.22, 1 blanket-$2.22; pres. 12/1847, pay stopped for: 1 jacket-$2.66, 2 pr drawers-$.71; pres. 04/1848, pay stopped for: 1 pr. pants-$2.28; pres. 08/1847, BLW sent to Sussex C.H., VA; c. 1850 res. Sussex Co., VA, age 29, occ. Carpenter, w. Mary E. (16);[1849] c. 1860 res. Petersburg, Dinwiddie Co., VA, age 38, occ. Carpenter, w. Mary (24);[1850] Civil War service Pvt., Co. K, 12$^{th}$ Va. Inf., enl. 05/04/1861 as a Sgt., b. Sussex Co., reduced to Pvt., 08/21/1861, discharged 08/08/1862 as overage;[21] Pvt., Co. F, 32$^{nd}$ Va. Inf., conscripted 12/23/1863 in Petersburg, VA, assigned to regt. 05/05/1864, absent sick 07/30/1864, furloughed 30 days 08/10/1864, AWOL 09/1864 through 12/1864, paroled 04/09/1865 at Appomattox C.H., VA, NFR.[716]

Turner, Francis L., Pvt., Co. C; enl. Mex. War service 12/30/1846, Bowling Green, VA, age 34; pres. 06/1847; d. 07/15/1847, supposed to have been killed by the Mexicans in Saltillo, Mex., pay stopped for: 1 cap-$.95$^{1/2}$, 2 pr. socks-$.49, 2 cotton shirts-$.86, 2 woolen shirts-$1.80.

Turner, Henry Thomas, Pvt., Co. F; b. 03/1821, Southampton Co., VA;[1851] enl. Mex. War service 11/23/1846, Portsmouth, VA, age 21; pres. 06/1847; pres. 08/1847; pres. 10/1847, pay stopped for: 2 pr. overalls-$4.56, 2 cotton shirts-$.86, 3 pr. socks-$.73$^{1/2}$, 1 blanket-$2.22, 1 forage cap-$.95$^{1/2}$, 1 pr. shoes-$1.22, 1 overcoat-$6.93$^{1/2}$; pres. 12/1847; pres. 02/1848, pay stopped for: 1 pr. overalls-$2.28, 2 flannel shirts-$1.80, 1 pr. socks-$.24$^{1/2}$, 1 infantry jacket-$2.66, 1 pr. shoes-$1.22; pres. 04/1848; pres. 08/1848, pay stopped for: 1 gun sling-$.18, 2 cotton shirts-$.88, 2 blankets-$4.50, BLW sent to Portsmouth, VA c/o E.T. Blamire; SC #11744, 07/16/1887, filed from Jerusalem, Southampton Co., VA; phys. desc. at enlistment, age 25 yrs., 5'11", red hair, blue eyes, occ. Farmer;[1851] since discharge res. Southampton Co., VA;[1851] "*He resides on a small parcel of poor and unimproved land for which he has contracted to pay One Hundred and Fifty dollars but for which he has paid nothing. He is allowed to occupy the premises, in all only fifteen acres, through the charity of the original owner. The land is located about three miles from Courtland, VA, of the character commonly described as 'poor old fields.' The pensioner lives in an old decayed log cabin, barely protecting his family from the storms of the seasons and the winter cold;*"[1851] d. 10/05/1902.

Tuttle, Joseph, Pvt., Co. L; b. 1823; enl. Mex. War service 03/01/1847 Fairfax C.H., VA, age 24; absent 06/1847 left sick at Ft. Washington, MD since 04/01/1847; absent 08/1847 sick at Ft. Washington, MD; discharged 08/30/1847 at Saltillo, Mex. on Surgeon's Certificate of Disability.[72]

OFF TO WAR

**Tymeson, J.P.**, 1st Cpl., *Recruit Co.*, enl. Mex. War service 12/22/1847 Bowling Green, VA, age 25; pres. 02/1848; pres. 04/1848; pres. 06/1848, prom. 1st Cpl.; BLW sent to Baltimore, MD; c. 1850 an Isaac P. Tymeson res. Elizabeth City Co., VA, age 30, occ. Teacher, b. New York.[1852]

**Vaden, Paskil**, Pvt., Co. H; b. c. 1812, Richmond, VA; enl. Mex. War service 01/15/1847, Richmond, VA, age 35; pres. 04/1847, left in Hosp. at Matamoros, Mex. 03/18/1847; absent 06/1847 left sick in Hosp. at Matamoros, Mex.; pres. 08/1847; pres. 10/1847, pay stopped for: 2 cotton shirts-$.86, 2 flannel shirts-$1.80, 2 pr. socks-$.49; desc., age 35, 5'8", light complexion, blue eyes, light hair, occ. Shoemaker; discharged 01/30/1848, Buena Vista, Mexico, on Surgeon's Certificate;[26] c. 1850 res. Chesterfield Co., VA, age 45, occ. None;[1853] c. 1870 res. Manchester, Chesterfield Co., VA, age 61, occ. Inmate of the County Poor House.[1854]

**Vaden, Robert H.**, Pvt., Co. D; b. 09/20/1820, Chesterfield Co., VA;[1855] enl. Mex. War service 01/09/1847, Petersburg, VA, age 18; pres. 02/1847; pres. 04/1847; pres. 06/1847; pres. 08/1847, pay stopped for: 1 pr. pants-$2.28, 2 cotton shirts-$.86, 1 pr. shoes-$1.22; pres. 10/1847, pay stopped for: 1 cap-$.95$^{1/2}$, 1 pr. pants-$2.28, 1 pr. drawers-$.35$^{1/2}$, 3 pr. socks-$.73$^{1/2}$, 1 pr. shoes-$1.22, 1 flannel shirt-$.90; pres. 12/1847, pay stopped for: 1 pr drawers-$.35$^{1/2}$, 1 pr. socks-$.24$^{1/2}$, 1 pr. shoes-$1.22; pres. 04/1848, pay stopped for: 1 pr. shoes-$1.22, 1 pr. socks-$.24$^{1/2}$; pres. 08/1847, BLW sent to Petersburg, VA; m. Elizabeth Fealty 09/17/1853, Richmond, VA; SC #1976, 03/09/1887, filed 16 30$^{th}$ St., Richmond, Henrico Co., VA; since discharge res. Baltimore, MD & Richmond, VA; Robert G. Scott & William Ferguson gave affidavit in pension claim; c. 1893 inmate of City Hospital, Petersburg, VA; d. 01/09/1897;[1855] (EFV d. 06/01/1886).[1855]

**Vaiden, Mordecia**, Pvt., Co. E; b. Chesterfield Co., son of Phebe Vaiden;[1856] enl. Mex. War service 12/03/1846 Petersburg, VA, age 28; pres. 04/1847; pres. 06/1847; pres. 08/1847; absent 10/1847 furloughed 30 days from 10/06/1847, pay stopped for: 1 pr. overalls-$2.28, 2 pr. shoes-$2.44, 2 pr. stockings-$.49, 1 cap-$.95$^{1/2}$; pres. 12/1847, pay stopped for: 1 pr. pants-$2.28, 2 pr. socks-$.49, 1 pr. shoes-$1.22, 1 cotton shirt-$.43, 2 flannel shirts-$1.80, 2 pr. drawers-$.71, 1 blanket-$2.22; pres. 02/1848, pay stopped for: 1 pr. pants-$2.28; absent 04/1848 sick in quarters; c. 1850 res. Petersburg, Dinwiddie Co. VA, age 28, occ. None, w. Elizabeth (28), dau. Mary (11), son John (6), son Lucius (4), son Thomas (2);[1857] d. 06/19/1856, *Consumption, age 39,* bur. Blandford Cem., Petersburg, VA[1856]

**Vallett, Francis**, Musician, Co. M; enl. Mex. War service 07/25/1847, Richmond, VA, age 30; pres. 09/1847; pres. 11/1847; pres. 12/1847; pres. 02/1848; pres. 04/1848, pay stopped for: 1 pr. shoes-$1.22; pres. 08/1848; BLW sent to Portsmouth, VA; c. 1850 res. Norfolk Co., VA, age 24, occ. None Listed, b. France, w. Columbia (23).[1858]

**Vanhorn, John C.**, Pvt., Co. H; enl. Mex. War service 01/06/1847, Berkeley, VA, age 20; pres. 04/1847; absent 06/1847 left as Attendant in Hosp. at Monterey, Mex. 06/22/1847; absent 08/1847 on detached service as Attendant in Hosp. at Monterey, Mex.; absent 10/1847 on detached service as Hosp. Attendant at Monterey, Mex.; absent 12/1847 on detached service as Hosp. Attendant at Monterey, Mex.; absent 02/1848 on detached service as Hosp. Attendant at Monterey, Mex.; absent 04/1848 on detached service as Hosp. Attendant at Monterey, Mex.; pres. 07/1848, BLW sent to Philadelphia, Pa.

**Van Leer, John**, 3$^{rd}$ Cpl., Co. H; enl. Mex. War service 01/06/1847, Berkeley, VA, age 22; pres. 04/1847; pres. 06/1847; pres. 08/1847; pres. 10/1847, pay stopped for: 1 pr. shoes-$1.22, 2 pr. socks-$.49; pres. 12/1847, pay stopped for: 1 pr. pants-$2.28 1 jacket-$2.66; pres. 02/1848, pay stopped for: 1 forage cap-$.95$^{1/2}$, 2 pr. drawers-$.71, 1 pr. pants$2.28; pres. 04/1848, prom. 4$^{th}$ Cpl.; pres. 07/1848, prom. 3$^{rd}$ Cpl., pay stopped for: 1 gun sling-$.16, BLW sent to Peoli P.O., Pa.

# VIRGINIA VOLUNTEERS IN MEXICO

**Vanmetre, Abram G.**, Pvt., Co. H; b. c. 1827; enl. Mex. War service 11/26/1846, Berkeley, VA, age 19; phys. desc. 5'8" or 9", chestnut hair, blue eyes;[1859] pres. 04/1847; pres. 06/1847; pres. 08/1847; pres. 10/1847, pay stopped for: 1 forage cap-$.95$^{1/2}$, 1 pr. pants-$2.28, 2 cotton shirts-$.86, 1 pr. shoes-$1.22, 3 pr. socks-$.73$^{1/2}$; pres. 12/1847, pay stopped for: 1 pr. pants-$2.28, 2 pr. drawers-$.71, 1 pr. shoes-$1.22, 2 pr. socks-$.49; absent 02/1848, on extra duty as a Teamster in QM Dept., pay stopped for: 1 blanket-$2.22; absent 04/1848 on extra duty as a Teamster in QM Dept.; pres. 07/1848, pay stopped for: 1 axe-$.75, 2 bayonets-$2.44, 1 bayonet scabbard & frog-$.56, 1 brush & pick-$.12, 1 gun sling-$.16, 1 belt plate-$.10, 1 wiper-$.20, BLW sent to Martinsburg, VA; m. Malvina Roberts 11/30/1869 Lafayette Co., Mo.;[1859] wid. Malvina, d. 04/13/1872, Lafayette Co., Mo.;[1859] WC #3937, 05/13/1884, file from Corden, Lafayette Co., MO; Edward W. Maxwell gave affidavit in pension claim; (MRV b. 09/29/1837, Elizabethtown, Hardin Co., KY; res. Dalzell, South Dakota by 09/19/1916; d. 05/12/1918).[1859]

**Vanzant, James Robert**, Pvt., Co. B; b. 04/12/1828, son of James & Elizabeth (Abercrombie) Vansant;[45] enl. 12/10/1846, Alexandria, VA, age 18; pres. 06/1847; pres. 08/1847; in confinement 10/1847, rejoined company from desertion 11/02/1847, pay stopped for: 1 pr. overalls-$2.28, 1 blanket-$2.22; Court-martialed 11/04/1847 Buena Vista, Mex. *Charge #1: Desertion; Specification: In this that Private James R. Vansant, of Co. B, VA. Regt. of Vols. did desert the service of the United States and was apprehended ten or twelve miles from Saltillo on the Monclova Road. This at Camp Buena Vista, Mexico October 31$^{st}$, 1847. To the Charge and specification the prisoner plead Not Guilty. Lt. W.I. Minor, Va. Regt. of Vols., a witness for the prosecution, being duly sworn says: I met the prisoner on his way back some ten (10) or twelve (12) miles from Saltillo on the Monclova Road. He had been apprehended by Lt. Coleman and Corp. Maxwell of the Va. Regt. together with two other men of the Regt. The prisoner left camp without permission on Sunday last and I was ordered in pursuit of him and the other men of my company. Question of the Court: How long was the prisoner absent? Answer: He left Camp on Saturday morning and I met him on Sunday evening. Question by the Court: Did you have to pay anything for the apprehension and bringing back of the prisoner? Answer: I paid five dollars for horses for the three men to bring them back to camp. Question by the Court: Was the prisoner at the time you met him sober or intoxicated? Answer: He was sober but from his appearance had evidently been drinking. Corp. W. Maxwell, Co. B, Va. Regt., a witness for the prosecution being duly sworn says: I was one of the party that left Saltillo in pursuit of the prisoner and two other men of the Regt. I fell behind on the road and when I came up Lt. Coleman had the prisoner and the other men in custody. This was on Sunday last on the Monclova Road about twelve (12) or fifteen (15) miles from Saltillo. Lt. R.F. Coleman, Va. Regt. Vols., a witness for the prosecution, being duly sworn says: I overtook the prisoner in company with two other men of the Va. Regt. about 11 miles from Saltillo on the Monclova Road on Sunday last (the 31$^{st}$ of Oct.). I took him in custody and brought him back, he offered no resistance. Question by the Court: Was the prisoner drunk? Answer: He was perfectly sober. Question by the Court: Did the prisoner say anything to you at the time of his apprehension? Answer: He acknowledge his intention to desert without any threat or menace. Question by the Court: Was the prisoner in possession of any clothing or provisions for such a trip? Answer: None, nor had he any arms. Question by the Prisoner: Did you understand me to admit that I had intended to desert when I left Camp? Answer: I did not know whether he meant it was his intention to desert then or afterwards. Lt. W.J. Minor, Va. Regt of Vols. was recalled on the part of the defense and says in answer to the following: Question by the Prisoner: What has been my character as a soldier previous to this offense? Answer: He has borne a good character in the company previously. Had been attentive to duty and a good soldier. The prisoner stated to the court in his defense that he had no intention to desert when he left camp. He merely intended to go to Saltillo. When he got there he made the resolve suddenly to go off and was at the time under the influence of*

OFF TO WAR

*liquors. The court found the prisoner Guilty and sentenced him to be confined at hard labor in the Provost Guard, with a ball and chain attached to his leg for the period of one month, and to forfeit five ($5) dollars of his pay to reimburse Lt. Minor for the expenses of his apprehension;*[1860] pres. 12/1847, pay stopped for: 4 cotton shirts-$1.72, 2 flannel shirts-$1.80, 2 pr. socks-$.49, 1 pr. shoes-$1.22, 1 pr. overalls-$2.28; pres. 02/1848, pay stopped for: 1 pr. overalls-$2.28, 1 blanket-$2.22; pres. 04/1848; pres. 08/1848, pay stopped for: 1 bayonet scabbard-$.56, 1 pick & brush-$.12, 1 screw driver-$.07, 1 wiper-$.20, 1 gun sling-$.16, 1 pr. shoes-$1.16, BLW sent to Alexandria, VA; d. 02/18/1863, bur. Ivy Hill Cemetery, Alexandria, VA.[45]

**Vaughan, Alfred J.**, Pvt., Co. D; enl. Mex. War service 12/21/1846, Petersburg, VA, age 23; absent 02/1847 left as Attendant at Hosp. Fort Monroe, VA; absent 04/1847 left as Attendant at Hosp. Fort Monroe, VA since 02/27/1847; absent 06/1847 left as Attendant at Hosp. Fort Monroe, VA since 02/27/1847, *"not since heard from;"* discharged 03/17/1847 Old Point, VA on Surgeon's Certificate of Disability; c. 1850 res. Warren Co., VA, age 26, occ. Blacksmith, c. Catherine (26), son Gary H. (2), dau. Mary E. (5/12), Gary (21);[1861] c. 1860 res. Linden, Warren Co., VA, age 37, occ. Blacksmith, w. Catherine (37), son Gary H. (11), dau. Mary (10), son John (7);[1862] c. 1870 res. Warrenton, Fauquier Co., VA, age 46, occ. Blacksmith, w. Mildred (35), dau. Mary E. (17), son John A. (16), son George (7), son J. William (5), dau. Maria C. (2).[1863]

**Velines, Charles H.**, Pvt., Co. A; enl. Mex. War service 11/21/1846 Richmond, VA, age 26; pres. 12/1846 - 04/1847; sick in quarters 06/1847; pres. 08/1847; pres. 10/1847, pay stopped for clothing: 1 pr. wool overalls-$2.28, 1 cap-$.95$^{1/2}$, 2 cotton shirts-$.86, 1 flannel shirts-$.90, 4 pr. socks-$.98, 1 great coat-$6.93$^{1/2}$; pres. 12/1847, pay stopped for clothing: 1 pr. drawers-$.35$^{1/2}$, 2 pr. shoes-$2.44, 2 pr. socks-$.49; pres. 02/1848; pres. 04/1848, pay stopped for: 1 wool jacket; BLW sent to Richmond, VA

**Vernon, William A.C.**, Pvt., Co. E; enl. Mex. War service 12/03/1846 Petersburg, VA, age 19; discharged 04/1847.

**Vonreason, Henry G.**, Pvt., Co. K; enl. Mex. War service Frederick Co., VA 12/20/1847, age 22; pres. 06/1847; pres. 08/1847; sick 10/1847, pay stopped for: 1 pr. overalls-$2.28, 2 cotton shirts-$.86, 3 pr. socks-$.73$^{1/2}$, 1 pr. shoes-$1.22; pres. 12/1847, pay stopped for: 1 jacket-$2.66, 1 pr. overalls-$2.28, 1 pr. socks-$.24$^{1/2}$, 1 blanket-$2.22, 2 flannel shirts-$1.80; pres. 04/1848, pay stopped for: 1 flannel shirt-$.90, 1 cotton shirt-$.43, 1 pick & brush-$.12; pres. 07/1848; BLW sent to Charlestown, VA; c. 1850 res. Winchester, Frederick Co., VA, age 26, occ. Tobacconist;[1864] c. 1860 res. Gainsborough, Frederick Co., VA, age 35, occ. Glove Maker, w. Sarah F. (26), dau. Susan G. (2), son Samuel (1/12).[1865]

**Waddell, Charles**, Pvt., Co. K; enl. Mex. War service Frederick Co., VA 12/23/1846, age 28; pres. 06/1847; pres. 08/1847, to forfeit 1 mos. pay by order of garrison court-martial; pres. 10/1847, pay stopped for: 2 pr. shoes-`$2.44, 2 pr. overalls-$4.56, 2 pr. drawers-$.71, 2 flannel shirts-$1.80; pres. 12/1847, pay stopped for: 1 jacket-$2.66, 1 pr. socks-$.24$^{1/2}$, 1 blanket-$2.22; discharged 04/1848 on Surgeon's Certificate of Disability.

**Wade, James Montague**, 2$^{nd}$ Lt., *Preston's Co.*; b. 02/19/1824, son of William & Emily Wade;[54,1866] enl. Mex. War service 11/24/1846 Montgomery Co., VA, age 20; pres. 04/1847; pres. 06/1847; pres. 08/1847; pres. 10/1847; pres. 12/1847; sick 02/1848; pres. 04/1848; pres. 07/1848; c. 1850 res. Montgomery Co., VA, age 26, occ. Clerk;[1867] m. Margaret C. Ingles, 08/04/1852, Montgomery Co., VA;[1868] c. 1860 res. Christiansburg, Montgomery Co., VA, age 36, occ. Clerk of Co. Circuit Court, w. Margaret C. (26), son Charles J. (6), McClanhan (4), son Frank M. (3), Thomas L. (1);[1869] Civil War service 1$^{st}$ Lt., Co. G, 4$^{th}$ Va. Inf., 04/17/1861, apptd. Regtl Adjt., resigned 11/1863 due to poor health;[54] c. 1870 res. Christiansburg, Montgomery Co., VA, age 46, occ. County Clerk, w. Margaret C. (36), son Charles J. (16), son McClanhan (14), son Frank M. (12), son Thomas L. (10), son James S. (9), son Harry M. (7), son John J. (5), dau. Agnes M. (3), dau. Mary (1);[1870] d. 11/01/1873, bur. Christiansburg,

## VIRGINIA VOLUNTEERS IN MEXICO

VA;[1871] wid. Margaret C., WC #833, 05/03/1887, filed from Christiansburg, Montgomery Co., VA; Charles A. Ronald and Robert G. Newlee gave affidavits in pension claim; (MIW b. 05/18/1834, Montgomery Co., VA, d. 09/03/1917).[1871]

**Wade, John**, Pvt., Co. G; enl. Mex. War service 11/28/1846 Richmond, VA, age 27; deserted at Richmond, VA, date not known, apprehended and $30 paid for his apprehension; deserted 05/26/1847 China, Mex.; dishonorably discharged 06/1848.

**Wade, Reuben Alexander**, Pvt., *Recruit Co.*, b. 09/01/1827, Highland Co., VA, son of John & Matilda (Slaven) Wade;[1872] enl. Mex. War service 12/16/1847 Staunton, VA, age 20; pres. 02/1848; absent 04/1848 on detached service as Hospital Attendant; pres. 06/1848; BLW sent to Washington City, D.C.

**Wade, Samuel P.**, Pvt., LIC; enl. Mex. War service 12/22/1846 Staunton, VA, age 27; in confinement 06/1847; court-martialed 06/16/1847, Buena Vista, Mex., *Charge #1: Sleeping on Post; Specification: In this that Private Samuel Wade, of the Light Infantry Comp., Virginia Regt of Volunteers having been duly posted as a sentinel was found sleeping upon his post between the hours of one and three o'clock am on the 8th of June 1847 at the Hacindal[sic] Guard near Buena Vista, Mex. To which charge and specification the prisoner pled Guilty. Pvt. William Kendle, of Co. K, Virginia Regt. of Volunteers, a witness for the prosecution, being duly sworn, says: I was acting Sergt. of the Guard about seven or eight days ago at the Hacienda Guard, and during the night I think between three and five o'clock, I was called out by a sentinel on the post next to the prisoners. When I approached his post I found him lying down. I lifted him up and let him down again and then took his musket away without waking him. I do not know whether he was asleep or in a fit. I went back to the Officer of the Guard. He brought the men of the Guard with him, who merely touched the prisoner when he woke up. Question by the Court: Was the prisoner on his post or had he retired from his post? Answer: His post was on the road and he was lying down by the side of it. Question by the Court: What induced you to suppose the prisoner might have been in a fit, and what was his department after being aroused? Answer: From his not waking when I raised his head and shoulders up and then letting then fall I thought there must be something more the matter with him than merely being asleep. I did not notice anything strange in his department when he aroused. Capt. Kenton Harper, Virginia Regt, of Volunteers, a witness for the defense was duly sworn. Question by the prisoner: What has been my character, as regards attendance to duty and obedience to orders previous to this time? Answer: Since I have been in Mexico and while we were away from the facilities of getting liquor, no soldier could perform his duties better. Indeed he was exemplary as a soldier. But in regard to liquor he has an appetite which it is difficult to control. Question by the prisoner: Have I ever been reported to you as having neglected my duty previous to this instance? Answer: I do not remember an instance. After deliberation the court found him Guilty. Sentenced him to forfeit 2 mos. Pay and to be kept at hard labor under charge of the Provost Guard for the period of one month;*[1873] pres. 08/1847, pay stopped for two mos. by sentence of general court-martial 07/02/1847; pres. 10/1847, two mos. pay previously forfeited by sentence of court-martial restored by order of Maj. Gen. Taylor, pay stopped for: 1 forage cap-$.95$^{1/2}$, 1 wool jacket-$2.66, 2 pr. overalls-$4.56, 2 pr. shoes-$2.44, 5 pr. socks-$1.22$^{1/2}$, 4 cotton shirts-$1.72, 1 flannel shirt-$.90, 1 pr. drawers-$.35$^{1/2}$, 1 blanket-$2.22; pres. 12/1847, pay stopped for: 1 pr. socks-$.24$^{1/2}$, 1 blanket-$2.22, 1 pr. shoes-$1.22, 2 pr. drawers-$.71; pres. 04/1848, pay stopped for: 1 flannel shirt-$.43, 1 cotton shirt-$.43, 1 pr. shoes-$1.22; pres. 07/1848, pay stopped for: 1 bayonet-$1.44, 1 cartridge box plate-$.10, 1 pick & brush-$.12, 1 screw driver-$.07, 1 wiper-$.20; BLW sent to Louisa C.H., VA; c. 1850 res. Louisa Co., VA, age 31, occ. Carpenter.[1874]

**Waldon, James F.**, 2nd Sgt., Co. L; b. 1804; enl. Mex. War service 03/01/1847 Fairfax C.H., VA, age 43; sick 06/1847; pres. 08/1847; pres. 10/1847, prom. 4th Sgt. from 1st Cpl. 09/01/1847, pay stopped for: 1 forage cap-$.95; 1 pr. socks-$.10; pres. 12/1847, pay stopped for: 1 Jacket 2.66, 1 pr. Pants 2.28, 2 pr. Shoes 2.44, 1 F. shirt .90, 1 Blanket 2.21, 2 pr. Drawers .71, 1 pr.

OFF TO WAR

Socks; pres. 02/1848, pay stopped for: 1 pr. Shoes 1.22; absent 04/1848 on detached service as Provost Sergeant since 04/24/1848 by order of Col. Hamtramck; pres. 07/1848; BLW sent to Dranesville P.O., Fairfax Co., VA

**Walker, Benjamin Joseph**, Pvt., Co. I; enl. Mex. War service 01/10/1847 Lynchburg, VA, age 21; pres. 02/1847; pres. 04/1847; pres. 06/1847; pres. 08/1847, prom. 4$^{th}$ Cpl. 08/26/1847 (regtl. order #93); pres. 10/1847, pay stopped for: 3 flannel shirts-$2.70, 2 pr. drawers-$.71, 1 pr. shoes-$1.22, 1 cap- $.95$^{1/2}$, 2 pr. socks-$.49; pres. 12/1847, pay stopped for: 1 pr. socks-$.24$^{1/2}$, 1 pr. pants-$2.28, 1 jacket-$2.66, 1 blanket-$2.22, 2 cotton shirts-$.86, 1 pr. drawers-$.35$^{1/2}$, 1 pr. pants-$2.28; pres. 02/1848, pay stopped for: 1 pr. shoes-$1.22; pres. 04/1848, reduced from 3$^{rd}$ Cpl. 03/25/1848; pres. 08/1848, BLW sent to Liberty, VA; m. Joannah A. Bailey, 02/15/1849, Howard Ville, Albemarle Co., VA;[1875, 1876] c. 1850 res. Albemarle Co., VA age 24, occ. Carpenter, w. Joanna (16), son William (1);[1877] Civil War service Pvt. Co. C, 19$^{th}$ Va. Inf., enl. 04/17/1861 Scottsville, VA, age 41, occ. Mechanic, pres. until detailed as a Baggage Guard 04/1862, in guard house 06/1862, absent under arrest 08/1862, discharged 05/13/1863, paroled 04/28/1865 Farmville, VA;[655] d. 08/16/1866, near Buckingham C.H., Buckingham Co., VA;[1876] wid. Joanah A., WC #6192, 03/06/1889, filed from Lynchburg, Campbell Co., VA; Jubal A. Earley gave affidavit in pension claim;[1876] List children William A. Walker, b. 08/04/1851, Vanessa D. Walker, b. 01/30/1853, Lula E. Walker, b. 01/28/1855, Maggie M. Walker, b. 11/15/1856, Joseph A. Walker, b. 02/15/1860, John L. Walker, b. 07/05/1864, *"4 dead children;"*[1876] (JBW b. 05/31/1833, d. 03/1908).[1876]

**Wall, Alexander A.**, Pvt., Co. C; enl. Mex. War service 08/16/1847, Boydton, VA, age 22; pres. 04/1848, joined company 01/27/1848 from Regtl. Depot, pay stopped for: 1 pr. shoes-$1.22, 1 jacket-$2.66; pres. 08/1848, BLW sent to Boydton, Mecklenburg Co., VA

**Wall, Harvey**, Pvt., *Preston's Co.*; enl. Mex. War service 01/02/1847 Montgomery Co., VA, age 30; discharged 04/04/1847 at Camargo, Mex. on Surgeon's Certificate of Disability; c. 1850, res. Montgomery Co., VA, age 31, occ. Teacher.[1878]

**Wall, James L.**, Pvt., Co. C; enl. Mex. War service 08/16/1847, Boydton, VA, age 18; pres. 04/1848, joined company 01/27/1848 from Regtl. Depot; pres. 08/1848, BLW sent to Boydton, Mecklenburg Co., VA

**Wall, Treadwell S.**, Pvt., Co. K; enl. Mex. War service Frederick Co., VA 12/23/1846, age 24; pres. 06/1847; pres. 08/1847; pres. 10/1847, pay stopped for: 1 pr. overalls-$2.28, 2 pr. drawers-$.71, 2 cotton shirts-$.86, 2 pr. shoes-$2.44; pres. 12/1847, pay stopped for: 1 pr. boots-$1.22; pres. 04/1848, pay stopped for: 1 jacket-$2.66; pres. 07/1848, pay stopped for: 1 screw driver-$.25, 1 wiper-$.20; BLW sent to Winchester, Frederick Co., VA; c. 1870 res. Winchester, Frederick Co., VA, age 44, occ. R.R. Hand, w. Alberta (30).[1879]

**Wallace, Gustavus A.** Pvt., *Pleasant's Co.*; *Not on Muster Rolls*, SA #25324, 02/07/1903, from VA

**Wallace, Robert**, Pvt., Co. C; b. c. 11/1828 Ireland;[1880] enl. Mex. War service 12/29/1846, Bowling Green, VA, age 19; pres. 06/1847; pres. 08/1847, pay stopped for: 1 cap-$.95$^{1/2}$, 2 pr. socks-$.49, 2 cotton shirts-$.86, 2 woolen shirts-$1.80, 1 pr. shoes-$1.22; pres. 10/1847, pay stopped for: 1 jacket-$2.66, 1 pr. pants-$2.28, 2 cotton shirts-$.86, 4 woolen shirts-$3.60, 1 pr. shoes-$1.22, 1 great coat-$6.93$^{1/2}$, 1 pr. socks-$.24$^{1/2}$; sick 12/1847, pay stopped for: 2 pr. socks-$.49, 2 pr. pants-$4.56, 3 woolen shirts-$2.70, 1 blanket-$2.22; pres. 04/1848, pay stopped for: 1 pr. shoes-$1.22, 1 pr. shoes-$1.50, 1 india rubber canteen-$.27; pres. 08/1848, BLW sent to Philadelphia, Pa.; m. Eliza Jane Patterson 03/06/1851, Philadelphia, Pa.;[1880] Civil War service Musician. Co. D, 22$^{nd}$ Pa. Inf., enl. 04/23/1861, discharged 08/07/1861, enl. 08/19/1861 Sgt. Co. K, 3$^{rd}$ Pa. Cav., discharged 11/18/1862, enl. 11/19/1862 Pvt. Co. A, 2$^{nd}$ U.S. Cav., reenl. 02/27/1864, discharged 02/27/1864 at Ft. McPhearson, Neb.; in 1874 applied for disability pension for Civil War service claiming *"that at Wayne's Station, VA August 30, 1864 his horse was shot in action and fell on his right foot crushing it,"* claim rejected;[1881] SC #14245, 06/21/1887, filed from 806 N. 23$^{rd}$ St., Philadelphia, Pa.; phys. desc.

## VIRGINIA VOLUNTEERS IN MEXICO

age 58 $^{8/12}$ yrs. of age, 5'11', light complexion, grey eyes, brown hair, occ. Blacksmith at time of enlistment now Watchman; Pvts. John Roach and Robert Chase gave affidavits in pension claim; d. 10/30/1890, *"consumption, age 62,"* 806 N 23$^{rd}$ St., Philadelphia, Pa., bur. Woodlands Cemetery, Philadelphia, Pa.;[1880] wid. Eliza Jane, WA #11143, 02/18/1893, filed from 806 N. 23$^{rd}$ St., Philadelphia, Pa.

**Wallace, Robert**, Pvt., Co. I; enl. Mex. War service 02/06/1847 Richmond, VA, age 28; pres. 02/1847; deserted Brasos Island 03/18/1847.

**Wallace, Sterling L.**, 3$^{rd}$ Cpl., Co. M; enl. Mex. War service 09/13/1847, Nottoway, VA, age 20; pres. 10/1847; pres. 11/1847, reduced to 3$^{rd}$ Cpl. from 1$^{st}$ Cpl.; pres. 12/1847; sick 02/1848; discharged 04/21/1848 on Surgeon's Certificate of Disability; c. 1850 res. Lunenburg Co., VA, age 22, occ. Farmer;[1882] c. 1870 res. Sturgeonville, Brunswick Co., VA, age 42, occ. Farmer, w. Mary M. (40), son Sterling J. (14), dau. Eliza S. (9), son Thomas I. (7), son William (5), dau. Lucy G. (3).[1883]

**Wallace, William W.**, Pvt., Co. C; enl. Mex. War service 12/29/1846, Bowling Green, VA, age 23; pres. 06/1847, reduced to ranks from 1$^{st}$ Sgt. 01/12/1847; pres. 08/1847, pay stopped for: 1 cap-$.95$^{1/2}$, 2 pr. socks-$.49, 2 cotton shirts-$.86, 2 woolen shirts-$1.80; pres. 10/1847, pay stopped for: 2 pr. drawers-$.71, 1 pr. pants-$2.28, 2 cotton shirts-$.86, 4 woolen shirts-$3.60, 1 pr. shoes-$1.22; sick 12/1847, pay stopped for: 1 jacket-$2.66, 1 pr. pants-$2.28, 1 blanket-$2.22; pres. 04/1848, pay stopped for: 1 india rubber canteen-$.27; pres. 08/1848, BLW sent to Philadelphia, Pa.

**Waller, John P.**, Pvt., Co. G; enl. Mex. War service 12/20/1847 Richmond, VA, age 21; pres. 06/1847; pres. 08/1847; discharged 10/16/1847 on Surgeon's Certificate of Disability.

**Waller, Thomas B.**, Pvt., Co. G; b. 05/25/1825, Hanover Co., VA;[1884] enl. Mex. War service 11/30/1846 Richmond, VA, age 19; pres. 06/1847; pres. 08/1847; pres. 10/1847, pay stopped for: 1 blanket-$2.22, 1 pr. overalls-$2.28, 3 cotton shirts-$1.29, 1 pr. drawers-$.35$^{1/2}$, 3 pr. shoes-$3.66, 3 pr. socks-$.73$^{1/2}$, 1 great coat-$6.95$^{1/2}$, 1 forage cap-$.95$^{1/2}$; pres. 12/1847, pay stopped for: 2 pr. shoes-$2.44, 1 pr. pants-$2.28, 2 pr. socks-$.49, 1 pr. drawers-$.35$^{1/2}$; sick 02/1848, pay stopped for: 1 pr. pants-$2.28; pres. 04/1848, pay stopped for: 1 pr. shoes-$1.22; absent 08/1848 left in Monterey, Mex. QM Dept.; BLW sent to Gloucester Co. C.H., VA; m. Margaret Deliah Connor, 01/18/1860, Mobile, Mobile Co., AL;[1884] SC #15925, 05/16/1888, filed from 108 20$^{th}$ St., Birmingham, Jefferson Co., AL; since discharge res. Mobile, Selma, Richmond, and Tuscaloosa, AL; d. 07/12/1897, Jackson Co., FL; wid. Margaret D., WC #10905, 07/22/1897, filed from Marianna, Jackson Co., FL; c. 1898 MDW res. 108 20$^{th}$ St., Birmingham, Jefferson Co., AL; (MDW b. 01/03/1847 Pickens Co., AL, d. 07/13/1906).[1884]

**Walls, William I.**, *Not on Muster Rolls*, SC #13947, (no date), wid. Martha A., WC #11387, 06/24/1898, both from VA

**Waples, Isaac**, Pvt., Co. F; enl. Mex. War service 01/15/1846, Portsmouth, VA, age 22; d. 06/17/1847 Hosp. Saltillo, Mex.

**Ward, Nicholas**, Pvt., Co. G; enl. Mex. War service 12/16/1846 Richmond, VA, age 20; pres. 06/1847; sick 08/1847; pres. 10/1847, pay stopped for: 1 pr. overalls-$2.28, 1 flannel shirt-$.90, 2 shoes-$2.44, 3 pr. socks-$.73$^{1/2}$, 1 forage cap-$.95$^{1/2}$; pres. 12/1847, pay stopped for: 1 pr. shoes-$1.22, 2 cotton shirt-$.86, 2 pr. drawers-$.71, 1 blanket-$2.22, 1 pr. pants-$2.28, 1 cap-$.95$^{1/2}$; pres. 02/1848; pres. 04/1848; pres. 08/1848, pay stopped for: 1 pr. shoes-$1.16, 1 cartridge box-$1.00, 1 cartridge box belt-$.60, 1 cartridge box plate-$.10, 1 cartridge box belt plate-$.10, 1 brush & pick$.12, 1 screw driver-$.07; BLW sent to Washington City, D.C.

**Warden, James**, Pvt., Co. M; enl. Mex. War service 07/01/1847, Lynchburg, VA, age 33; pres. 09/1847; pres. 11/1847; pres. 12/1847; pres. 02/1848; pres. 04/1848; pres. 08/1848, pay stopped for: 1 gun sling-$.16, 1 pr. shoes-$1.16; BLW sent to Lynchburg, VA

**Warden, John M.**, Pvt., *Recruit Co.*; enl. Mex. War service 04/07/1848 Wytheville, VA; pres. 06/1848; BLW sent to Wytheville, VA; wid. Rachel, WC #4681, 04/20/1888, from VA; brother of Johnson B. Warden.

OFF TO WAR

**Warden, Johnson B.**, Pvt., *Recruit Co.*, b. c. 1828, son of Thomas & Rebecca (Bateman) Warden;[1885] enl. Mex. War service 04/??/1848 Wytheville, VA; pres. 06/1848; BLW sent to Wytheville, VA; c. 1860, res. Wythe Co., VA, age 35, occ. Farmer, w. Sarah; Civil War service Sgt., Co. I, 50th Va. Inf.;[202] brother of John M. Warden.

**Washington, Lawrence Berry**, 2nd Lt., Co. K; b. 11/26/1811, *Berry Hill* (aka Cedar Lawn), Jefferson Co., VA, son of John Thornton Augustine & Elizabeth Conrad (Bedinger) Washington; Great-great nephew of President George Washington;[1886] studied law, author and poet;[1887] enl. Mex. War service Jefferson Co., VA 12/06/1846; absent 06/1847 on 60 day furlough since 06/08/1847; Lt. Washington wrote to Col. Hamtramck, *"Sir, The eighth of this month being the completion of the first month of my furlough, I should have reported at the time agreeable to orders, but was sick on the Steam Boat. My health is still bad, and my recovery has doubtless been retarded by the protracted voyage which it was my bad luck to undergo."*[1888] absent 08/1847 sick in Charlestown, VA; *I have further the disagreeable duty of again reporting Capt. W.B. Archer, Co. I, Va. Regt. Vols., Lieut. Pegram, Co. E, Va. Regt. Vols., Lieut. L. Washington, Co. K, Va. Regt. Vols. absent without leave;"*[1889] AWOL 10/1847; AWOL 12/1847; absent 04/1848 in the States on recruiting service; pres. 07/1848; 1849-1850 *California 49er*, went overland from Jefferson Co., VA to Sacramento, Calif. with the Charles Town Mining Co.;[760] moved to Missouri in the 1850's, d. 09/21/1856 near Rocheport, Boone Co., Mo. after falling off a steamboat into the Missouri River.[1890, 1891]

**Waterman, James A.**, Pvt., Co. M; enl. Mex. War service 09/01/1847, Petersburg, VA, age 21; d. 09/09/1847 at Ft. Monroe, VA

**Waters, Benjamin Garretson**, 2nd Lt., Co. B; b. Alexandria, VA, 08/10/1820, son of Benjamin & Dorothy (Edmundstone) Waters; m. Lucy Berkeley, c. 1843; enl. 12/20/1846, Alexandria, VA; d. 04/15/1847 China, Mex.; subsequent to his son's death Benjamin Waters, Sr. wrote to Thomas S. Jessup, Quarter Master General, U.S.A. in Washington, D.C. to request that his son's effects be returned to him;[1892] on the order of Capt. Corse, Lt. Waters sword was forwarded to his father.[1893]

**Watkins, Edward**, Pvt., Co. E; enl. Mex. War service as a Fifer 12/10/1846 Petersburg, VA, age 23; pres. 04/1847, reduced to ranks from Fifer 12/20/1846; pres. but sick 06/1847; pres. 08/1847; pres. 10/1847, pay stopped for: 1 pr. overalls-$2.28, 1 pr. shoes-$1.22, 4 pr. stockings-$.98, 1 cotton shirt-$.43, 2 flannel shirts-$1.80, 2 pr. drawers-$.71, 1 cap-$.95$^{1/2}$, 1 blanket-$2.22; pres. 12/1847, pay stopped for: 1 pr. pants-$2.28, 2 pr. socks-$.49; absent sick 02/1848, pay stopped for: 1 pr. shoes-$1.22, 1 jacket-$2.66, 1 cotton shirt-$.43; absent 04/1848, sick in quarters; [c. 1850 an Edward Watkins res. Dinwiddie Co., VA, age 24, occ. Farmer, w. Julia A. (22);[1894] c. 1860 res. San Marino, Dinwiddie Co., VA, age 36, occ. Farmer, w. Julia A. (34), son William A. (9), dau. Julia P. (7), son James E. (4), dau. Hattie (2);[1895] Civil war service Pvt., 9th Va. Inf., res. Dinwiddie Co., paroled 1865;[211] c. 1870 res. Dinwiddie C.H., Dinwiddie Co., VA, age 43, occ. Farmer, w. Ann F. (38), son William (20), dau. Julia (18), son James (15), dau. Hetty (12), son Franklin (9), son illegible (6), dau. Susan (2).][1896]

**Watkins, Thomas E.**, 3rd Sgt., Co. A; enl. 11/25/1846 Richmond, VA, age 26; pres. 12/1846 – 04/1847; pres. 06/1847; pres. 08/1847, prom. 2nd Sgt. 08/23/1847; pres. 10/1847, pay stopped for: 2 pr. wool overalls-$4.56; 4 pr. stockings-$.98, 2 flannel shirts-$1.80, 2 pr. drawers-$.71, 1 blanket-$2.22; absent sick 12/1847, pay stopped for clothing: 1 blanket-$2.22; sick 02/1848; pres. 04/1848, detailed acting Sgt. Maj. since 04/05/1848, pay stopped for 1 wool jacket; BLW sent to, Richmond, VA [appears to have been lined out]; c. 1850, res. Chesterfield Co., VA, age 28, occ. Mechanic;[1897] c. 1860, res. Chesterfield Co., VA, age 35, occ. Wheelwright;[1898] Civil War service Pvt., Co. I, 14th Va. Inf., enl. 05/11/1861 at Chester, VA, age 38, occ. wheelwright, pres. 07/1861 until 05/1862 when sick in camp, AWOL for 5 days in 07/1862, AWOL for 12 days in 08/1862, AWOL for 24 days in 09/1862, pres. 11/1862 until

## VIRGINIA VOLUNTEERS IN MEXICO

AWOL from 08/04/1863 – 09/16/1863, pres. 11/1863 until 05/13/1864 when AWOL, discharged 08/13/1864 at the end of 3 yr. enlistment, did not reenlist as over age 45.[1899]

**Watson, David H.**, Pvt., Co. K; enl. Mex. War service Frederick Co., VA 01/20/1847, age 22; pres. 06/1847, prom. 3$^{rd}$ Cpl. 05/31/1847; pres. 08/1847, prom. 2$^{nd}$ Cpl.; pres. 10/1847, pay stopped for: 1 pr. overalls-$2.28, 2 cotton shirts-$.86, 3 pr. socks-$.73$^{1/2}$, 3 pr. drawers-$.71, 1 cap-$.95$^{1/2}$; pres. 12/1847, pay stopped for: 1 pr. overalls-$2.28, 1 pr. boots-$1.22, 1 pr. socks-$.24$^{1/2}$, 1 pr. drawers-$.35$^{1/2}$, 2 cotton shirts-$.86; pres. 04/1848, reduced to ranks 01/07/1848, pay stopped for: 1 cotton shirt-$.43; pres. 07/1848, pay stopped for: 1 gun sling-$.18, 1 screw driver-$.25, 1 wiper-$.20; BLW sent to Winchester, Frederick Co., VA; c. 1850 res. Winchester, Frederick Co., VA, age 25, occ. Waggonmaker, w. Susan (34), dau. Elizabeth (15).[1900]

**Watson, John**, Pvt., Co. I; enl. Mex. War service 02/25/1847 Richmond, VA, age 24; pres. 02/1847; pres. 04/1847; pres. 06/1847; pres. 08/1847; pres. 10/1847, pay stopped for: 1 pr. shoes-$1.22; pres. 12/1847, pay stopped for: 1 cap-$.95$^{1/2}$, 1 pr. pants-$2.28, 1 jacket-$2.66, 1 blanket-$2.22, 2 cotton shirts-$.86, 1 flannel shirts-$.90; 2 pr. drawers-$.71; absent 02/1848 on detached service in QM Dept.; absent 04/1848, on extra duty in QM Dept.; pres. 08/1848, BLW sent to Lynchburg, VA

**Watson, John T.**, Pvt., Co. G; b. 12/28/1813 Stafford Co., VA;[1901] enl. Mex. War service 07/16/1847 Warrenton, VA; occ. Stage Driver;[1901] pres. 02/1848, joined co. from regtl. depot 01/25/1848, pay stopped for: 1 pr. pants-$2.28, 1 blanket-$2.22; pres. 04/1848; pres. 08/1848; BLW sent to Mt. Crawford, Rockingham Co., VA; m. Susan English, 12/19/1849, Stafford Co., VA;[1901] SC #1601, 02/04/1887, filed from Comorn, King George Co., VA; phys. desc. age 72 [1886], 5'7$^{1/2}$", florid complexion, gray eyes, white hair, occ. Farmer;[1901] (SEW d. 08/12/1871, Stafford Co., VA).

**Waugh, Frederick**, Drummer, Co. C; enl. Mex. War service 12/30/1846, Bowling Green, VA, age 38; on detached service 06/1847 as Drum Major; pres. 08/1847, pay stopped for: 1 pr. drawers-$.35$^{1/2}$, 1 cap-$.95$^{1/2}$, 2 pr. socks-$.49, 2 cotton shirts-$.86, 2 woolen shirts-$1.80, 1 pr. shoes-$1.22, 1 woolen jacket-$2.66, 1 pr. overalls-$2.28; in confinement 10/1847 in provost guard, pay stopped one mo. by order of genl. court-martial; pres. 12/1847; pres. 04/1848, pay stopped for: [illegible] 2 pr. shoes-$2.44; 1 india rubber canteen-$.27.

**Waugh, John**, Pvt., Co. L; b. 1821; res. Noland's Ferry, Loudoun Co., VA and White's Ferry, Montgomery Co., MD; enl. Mex. War service 03/08/1847 Fairfax C.H., VA, age 26; phys. desc. at enl. 5'7$^{1/2}$", brown hair, black eyes, dark complexion, age 26, occ. Ferryman;[1902]pres. 06/1847; pres. 08/1847; pres. 10/1847, pay stopped for: 1 forage cap-$.95, 1 pr. Pants 2.28; pres. 12/1847, pay stopped for: 1 jacket-$2.66, 1 pr. pants-$2.28, 1 pr. shoes-$1.22, 3 cotton shirts-$1.29, 1 blanket-$2.22, 2 pr. socks-$.49; pres. 02/1848, pay stopped for: 1 Jacket 2.66, 1 Brush & Pick .12; pres. 04/1848, pay stopped for: 1 Cotton Shirt .44; pres. 07/1848, pay stopped for: 1 pr. Shoes 1.16, 1 Screw Driver .25; BLW sent to Washington City, D.C.; m/1 Emily Ponder c. 1855 (EPW d. c. 1859); res. w/ widow Miranda Lowe until her death in 1879; m/2 Ellen V. Lowe 09/18/1884, Montgomery Co., MD; SC #5724, 03/23/1887, filed from Montgomery Co., MD; Since discharge res. Montgomery Co., MD 1848-1851, Frederick Co., MD 1851-1853, Montgomery Co., MD 1853-1887; c. 1893 res. between Hunting Hill and Travilah, Montgomery Co., MD; d. 08/22/1893, bur. Presbyterian Cem., Darnestown, MD;[1903] wid. Ellen V., WC #9458, 12/11/1893, both from MD, OW Invalid Cert. #21727 rejected.(EVW b. 07/29/1858, d. 02/19/1931).[1904]

**Weast, George L.**, Pvt., Co. H; enl. Mex. War service 12/18/1846, Berkeley, VA, age 19; pres. 04/1847; pres. 06/1847; pres. 08/1847; pres. 10/1847, pay stopped for: 1 forage cap-$.95$^{1/2}$, 1 pr. pants-$2.28, 3 cotton shirts-$1.29, 4 flannel shirts-$3.60, 2 pr. shoes-$2.44, 3 pr. socks-$.73$^{1/2}$; pres. 12/1847, pay stopped for: 1 jacket-$2.66, 1 pr. pants-$2.28, 2pr. drawers-$.71, 1 pr. shoes-$1.22, 1 pr. socks-$.24$^{1/2}$, 1 blanket-$2.22; pres. 02/1848, pay stopped for: 2 pr. shoes-$2.44, 2 pr. socks-$.49; pres. 04/1848; pres. 07/1848, pay stopped for: 1 cartridge box

belt plate-$.10, 1 bayonet scabbard & frog-$.56, 1 waist belt-$.21, 1 waist belt plate-$.10, 1 screw driver-$.25, 1 wiper-$.20, BLW sent to Boonsboro, MD
**Weaver, Isaac**, Pvt., *Recruit Co.*; enl. Mex. War service 01/13/1848 Christiansburg, VA, age 26; pres. 02/1848; pres. 04/1848; pres. 06/1848; BLW sent to Floyd C.H., VA; wid. Sarah V., WC #3724, 03/07/1887, from VA
**Webb, Joel H.**, *Preston's Co.*; *Not on Muster Rolls;* SC #11747, 10/13/1887, from AR.
**Webster, Archibald**, Pvt., Co. G; enl. Mex. War service 12/20/1847, Richmond, VA, age 23; pres. 06/1847; pres. 08/1847; pres. 10/1847, pay stopped for: 1 pr. overalls-$2.28, 1 cotton shirt-$.43, 1 pr. drawers-$.35$^{1/2}$, 2 shoes-$2.44, 3 pr. socks-$.73$^{1/2}$, 1 forage cap-$.95$^{1/2}$; pres. 12/1847, pay stopped for: 1 pr. drawers-$.35$^{1/2}$, 1 blanket-$2.22, 1 pr. pants-$2.28, 1 cap-$.95$^{1/2}$, 2 pr. socks-$.49; pres. 02/1848; pres. 04/1848; pres. 08/1848, pay stopped for: 1 musket-$13.00; BLW sent to Gloucester Co. C.H., VA; [Civil War service an Archibald Webster enl. as a Pvt., Co. D, 9$^{th}$ Va. Inf., 08/01/1861 at Craney Island (Norfolk), VA, occ. Cabinetmaker, phys. desc. 5'6$^{1/2}$", light complexion, light hair grey eyes, discharged 08/11/1862 as overage;[211] enl. Pvt., Co. G, 25$^{th}$ Btln. Va. Inf., 12/31/1862 at Richmond, VA, pres. 12/1862 through 04/1863, NFR, Pvt., Co. B, 15$^{th}$ Va. Inf., conscripted 01/21/1864 at Richmond, VA, assigned to co. 02/29/1864, KIA 05/16/1864 at Drewry's Bluff, VA][116]
**Webster, Henry**, 3$^{rd}$ Cpl., Co. F; enl. Mex. War service 01/20/1847, Portsmouth, VA, age 20; pres. 06/1847; pres. 08/1847; pres. 10/1847, pay stopped for: 1 pr. overalls-$2.28, 2 cotton shirts-$.86, 1 forage cap-$.95$^{1/2}$, 3 pr. socks-$.73$^{1/2}$, 1 pr. shoes-$1.22; pres. 12/1847; pres. 02/1848, pay stopped for: 1 pr. overalls-$2.28, 1 pr. shoes-$1.22, 1 forage cap-$.95$^{1/2}$, 1 infantry jacket-$2.66, 1 blanket-$2.22; pres. 04/1848, prom. 04/01/1848 3$^{rd}$ Cpl.; pres. 08/1848, pay stopped for: 1 cartridge box & belt complete-$1.00, 2 blankets-$4.50, 2 shirts-$.88, 1 forage cap-$.83, BLW sent to Portsmouth, VA c/o E.T. Blamire.
**Weeks, James**, Pvt., *Preston's Co.*; enl. Mex. War service 12/14/1846 Montgomery Co., VA, age 25; d. 02/21/1847 in hosp. at Ft. Monroe, VA
**Weeks, John**, Pvt., Co. B; enl. 12/22/1846, Richmond, VA, age 22; deserted 01/19/1847 Fort Monroe, VA
**Weisiger, David Addison**, 2$^{nd}$ Lt., Co. E; b. 12/23/1818, at "The Grove," Chesterfield Co., VA, son of Daniel & Seginora Tabb (Smith) Weisiger; enl. Mex. War service 11/30/1846

Photo credit: Alabama Archives, Montgomery, AL

Petersburg, VA, age 28; m/1 Rebecca D. McIndoe, 10/1843, Petersburg, VA;[1905] (RDW d. 05/27/1847);[1906] absent 04/1847 on detached service w/ 1$^{st}$ Ohio Regt. since 03/24/1847; pres. 06/1847; pres. 08/1847; pres. 10/1847; pres. 12/1847; absent 02/1848 in command of Co. G, 1$^{st}$ Va. Regt.; absent 04/1848, Actg. Regtl. Adj.; mbr. and *Generalissimo*, Knights Templar, Appomattox Encampment No. 6, Petersburg, VA 1854;[40] m/2 Alice Sydnor Barksdale05/02/1855, Halifax Co., VA; (ASW d. 07/08/1856); Civil War service Col. Va. Inf.; m/3 Louise Christine Bland 04/29/1862, Petersburg, VA; wded. at 2nd Manassas; absent wded. until 7/63; prom. Brig. Gen. after Battle of the Wilderness 5/64; led his Brigade in counterattack at the Battle of the Crater, 07/30/1864, where he was wded.; paroled 04/09/1865 at Appomattox C.H., VA; Post War occ. banker and businessman; c. 1870 res. Petersburg, Dinwiddie Co., VA, age 53, occ. Cashier at Bank, w. Louisa (41);[1907] SC #1986, 02/05/1887, filed from Manchester, Chesterfield Co., VA; phys. desc. 5'8$^{3/4}$", florid complexion, dark brown eyes, gray hair; since discharge res. Manchester and Richmond, VA; d. 02/23/1899, *La Grippe*, bur.

# VIRGINIA VOLUNTEERS IN MEXICO

Blandford Cemetery, Sq. 2, Sec. 10, Ward C, Petersburg, VA;[76, 1908] wid. Louise C., WC #11954, 04/03/1899, filed from 209 East Grace St., Richmond, VA; (LCW b. 08/13/1827 Nottoway Co., VA, d. 03/03/1911).

**Weisiger, James L.**, Pvt., Co. I; enl. Mex. War service 11/16/1846 Richmond, VA, age 35; pres. 02/1847; pres. 04/1847; discharged 06/17/1847 for disability at Monterey, Mex.; Civil War service Pvt., Co. C, 9th Va. Inf., enl. 05/23/1861 at Chesterfield C.H., occ. Bricklayer, phys. desc. 6'4", fair complexion, blue eyes, discharged 06/18/1862 due to physical disability and being age 49.[211]

**Wells, Alexander**, Pvt., Co. M; enl. 09/10/1847, Petersburg, VA, age 40; NFR.

**Wells, John H.**, Pvt., Co. D; b. 04/25/1825, Dinwiddie Co., VA;[1909] enl. Mex. War service 01/12/1847, Petersburg, VA, age 19; pres. 02/1847; pres. 04/1847; pres. but sick 06/1847, pay stopped for: 1 bayonet scabbard & frog, 1 waist belt & plate complete, *"lost through negligence;"* absent sick 08/1847, pay stopped for: 1 cap-$.95$^{1/2}$; discharged 09/13/1847 Buena Vista, Mex. on Surgeon's Certificate of Disability; m/1 Anna Eliza Summerson 03/01/1855, Charlottesville, Albemarle Co., VA;[1910] Civil War service enl. Lt., Co. F, 19th Va. Inf. Charlottesville, VA, age 37, occ. gunsmith, pres. till detailed as Baggage Guard 10/02/1861, not re-elected and dropped from roll 04/28/1862;[655, 1911] moved to Texas in 1872;[1912] (AEW b. 05/27/1837, NC, d. 12/11/1877, *"puerpuerel fever,"* [childbirth] Austin, Travis Co., TX);[1909] m/2 Mary H. Robertson 02/10/1879, Round Rock, Williamson Co. TX; moved to Arkansas in 1879;[1912] SC #12134, 08/08/1887, filed from Newport, Jackson Co., AR; d. 08/29/1904, "80 years old...formerly Mayor of the town [Newark, Ark.], "[1912] Newark, Independence Co., AR, bur. Macedonia Cemetery, Newark, AR;[45, 1913, 1914] wid. Mary H., WA # 17780, 10/03/1904, filed from Newark, Independence Co., AR; Lists children Hattie L Woodward, Los Angeles, CA.[1913] (MHW b. 08/13/1852, d. 08/08/1905, bur. Macedonia Cemetery, Newark, AR).[45Error! Bookmark not defined.]

**Wells, William H.**, Pvt., Co. G; enl. Mex. War service 12/20/1847, age 29; discharged 06/08/1847 Monterey, Mex. on Surgeon's Certificate of Disability; c. 1860 res. Petersburg, Dinwiddie Co., VA, age 35, occ. Laborer, w. Martha (25);[1915] c. 1870 res. Petersburg, Dinwiddie Co., VA, age 50, occ. Works in Flour Mill, w. Martha (37);[1916] SC #13947, 03/12/1887, wid. Martha J., WC #11387, 06/24/1898, both from VA; BLW #49320-160-47; d. 05/29/1893; wid. d. 12/01/1900.

**Wells, William J.**, Pvt., Co. E; enl. Mex. War service 11/30/1846 Petersburg, VA, age 20; pres. 04/1847; pres. 06/1847; absent 08/1847 on detached service as Hosp. Attendant since 07/01/1847 absent 10/1847 on detached service as Hosp. Attendant, pay stopped for: 1 cap-$.95$^{1/2}$; absent 12/1847 on detached service as Hosp. Attendant; absent 02/1848, on detached service as Hosp. Attendant; absent 04/1848, on daily duty as Hosp. Attendant; c. 1870 res. Dinwiddie C.H., Dinwiddie Co., VA, age 47, occ. Farmer, w. Elizabeth (45).[1917]

**Wells, William O.**, Archer's Co.; *Not on Muster Rolls*; wid. Martha J., WC #1858, 03/12/1887, from VA

**West, Charles**, Pvt., Co. L; b. 1815; enl. Mex. War service 03/01/1847 Fairfax C.H., VA, age 32; pres. 06/1847; d. 08/06/1847 Buena Vista, Mex.[72]

**West, Covington O.**, Pvt., Co. B; enl. 12/18/1846, Alexandria, VA, age 26; pres. 06/1847; pres. 08/1847; pres. 10/1847, pay stopped for: 2 pr. socks-$.49, 2 blanket-$4.44; sick 12/1847, pay stopped for: 1 pr. shoes-$1.22, 1 flannel shirts-$1.80, 2 pr. socks-$.49, 2 cotton shirts-$.86, 1 pr. overalls-$2.28; sick 02/1848, pay stopped for: 1 pr. overalls-$2.22; pres. 04/1848, pay stopped for: 1 pr. shoes-$1.22; pres. 08/1848, BLW sent to Rockville, Montgomery Co., MD; m. Atheriah Barker 1/2/1851, Washington, D.C.[1918]

**West, James W.**, Pvt., Co. L; b. 11/02/1827, Fairfax Co., VA; enl. Mex. War service 03/15/1847 Alexandria, VA, age 19; phys. desc. 5'6", fair complexion, blue eyes, brown hair, occ. Farmer, age 19;[1919] absent 06/1847 sick in hosp. at Saltillo, Mex.; discharged 10/16/1847 at

OFF TO WAR

Saltillo, Mex. on Surgeon's Certificate of Disability;[72] c. 1850 res. Fairfax Co., VA, age 22, occ. Laborer, w. Eliza M. (22); [1920] Civil War service Sgt., Co. B, 5th DC Inf. enl. 04/22/1861, discharged 06/11/1861; Quartermaster Dept., Alexandria, VA 1861-1863; c. 1870 res. Falls Church, Fairfax Co., VA, age 40, occ. Works on the Highway, w. Catherine (34), son Frank (4/12);[1921] SC #11683, 09/24/1887, filed from Fairfax Co., VA; res. w/Samuel Dove 1885-1887 and Meade Battaile 1887; d. 12/30/1898, bur. Oakwood Cemetery, Falls Church, VA.[45]

**Westbrook, James H.**, Pvt., Co. I; enl. Mex. War service 08/25/1847 Ft. Monroe, VA, age 28; pres. 02/1848 joined co. 01/26/1848; pres. 04/1848, pay stopped for: 1 jacket, 1 blanket; pres. 08/1848, BLW sent to White Plains; d. 11/1848, *"Mexican Volunteer."*[1922]

**Westmore, Richard Henry**, Pvt., Co. E; b. 05/12/1825, Dublin, Ireland;[76] enl. Mex. War service 12/03/1846 Petersburg, VA, age 22; pres. 04/1847; pres. 06/1847; pres. 08/1847; pres. 10/1847, pay stopped for: 1 pr. overalls-$2.28, 2 pr. shoes-$2.44, 4 pr. stockings-$.98, 1 cap-$.95$^{1/2}$, 1 blanket-$2.22; pres. 12/1847, pay stopped for: 1 pr. pants-$2.28, 2 pr. socks-$.49, 2 pr. drawers-$.71; pres. 02/1848, pay stopped for: 1 pr. pants-$2.28; pres. 04/1848, on daily duty in Adjt's. office since 04/24/1848; c. 1850 res. Petersburg, Dinwiddie Co., VA, age 35?, occ. Clerk;[1923] m. Mary Ann Brown 11/18/1851, Petersburg, VA;[1924] c. 1860 res. Petersburg, Dinwiddie Co., VA, age 35, occ. Bookkeeper, w. Mary (28);[1925] c. 1870 res. Petersburg, Dinwiddie Co., VA, age 45, occ. Bookkeeper, w. Mary A. (38);[1926] SC #6226, 04/08/1902, filed from 175 Old St.(now Grove Ave.), Petersburg, VA; Fletcher H. Archer, Thomas J. McCaleb and William E. Alley gave affidavits in pension claim; d. 09/30/1902, *Apoplexy, aged 77 yrs., 4 mos.*, bur. Blandford Cem., Sq. 146, Ward A, Petersburg, VA;[76, 1927] wid. Mary A., WC #13134, 11/19/1902, filed from 175 Old St., Petersburg, VA; (MAW b. 03/03/1832, Petersburg, VA, d. 07/25/1913, Petersburg, VA).[1928]

**Wharton, Benjamin T.**, 4th Sgt., Co. G; enl. Mex. War service 1/18/1846 Richmond, VA, age 22; pres. 06/1847, prom. 4th Sgt.; pres. 08/1847; in confinement 10/1847, reduced from 4th Sgt. by resignation 09/23/1847, pay stopped for: 1 pr. overalls-$2.28, 1 flannel shirt-$.90, 3 pr. shoes-$3.66, 3 pr. socks-$.73$^{1/2}$, 1 great coat-$6.95$^{1/2}$, 1 forage cap-$.95$^{1/2}$; deserted 12/11/1847 Buena Vista, Mex.

**White, Cyrus C.**, Pvt., LIC; b. 04/13/1824, near Waynesboro, Augusta Co., VA;[1929] enl. Mex. War service 12/07/1846 Staunton, VA, age 22; discharged 06/1847 at Camargo, Mex. on Surgeon's Certificate of Disability; c. 1850 res. Nelson Co., VA, age 25, occ. Miller;[1930] m. Harriet P. Hill, 05/01/1850, Massies Mill, Nelson Co., VA;[1929] (HHW d. 08/19/1857, Massies Mill, VA);[1929] c. 1860 res. Roseland, Nelson Co., VA, age 36, occ. Miller, dau. Susan J. (8), dau. Mary E. (6);[1931] Civil War service Pvt. Co. E, 2nd Va. Cav., enl. 02/15/1863 at Amherst Co., VA, pres. 03/1863 through 04/1863, detailed as a Courier 08/24/1863 through 08/31/1863, pres. 11/1863 through 03/1864, absent on horse detail 04/21/1864 through 06/30/1864, NFR;[1009] c. 1870 res. Massies Mill, Nelson Co., VA, age 46, occ. Miller, dau. Susan J. (18), dau. Mary E. (16);[1932] SC #5470, 05/05/1887, filed from Sandiges, Amherst Co., VA; since discharge res. Bedford Co., Nelson Co. and Amherst Co., VA;[1929] d. c. 1890.[1929]

**White, David M.**, Pvt., Co. M; b. 02/06/1822, Lunenburg Co., VA;[1933] m/1 Roanna Farlow, 08/15/1844, Brunswick Co., VA;[1933] enl. Mex. War service 10/20/1847, Lunenburg, VA, age 25; pres. 11/1847; pres. 12/1847; *"While there[Buena Vista, Mexico] myself and a man by the name of Bowin were detailed to cut wood (10) miles above Buena Vista. On our return to camp we were on a wagon when the wagon was turned over. I had my axe in my right hand and cut the two first fingers on my left hand so near off that the surgeon deemed it necessary and did take them off. At the same time my right hand was badly hurt but the Dr. said he thought it would get well and that I would not be inconvenienced by it...I then returned to my home and after getting home my right hand commenced to braking out, or rising, and continued in this way until I lost the bones from all four fingers on said hand;"*[1934] sick 02/1848; discharged 04/21/1848 at Saltillo, Mex. on Surgeon's Certificate of Disability; c.

## VIRGINIA VOLUNTEERS IN MEXICO

1850 res. Lunenburg Co., VA, age 28, occ. Bricklayer, w. Rauna M. (23), son Harry J. (6), son Demarcus (3), son Charles E. (1), sis. Elvira A. (18);[1935] received an "invalid pension" in 1851; c. 1860 res. Pleasant Grove, Lunenburg Co., VA, age 37, occ. Stone Mason, w. Roana (31), son Henry (15), son Fountain (12), son Edward (10), son William (7), son Patrick (5), dau. Mary (2);[1936] (RFW d. 07/26/1862, near Pleasant Grove, Lunenburg Co., VA);[1933] m/2 Mary Jane Hudson, 05/06/1867, near Red Oak Grove, Charlotte, Co., VA;[1933] c. 1870 res. Plantersville, Lunenburg Co., VA, age 48, occ. Rock & Brick Mason, w. Mary B. (28), son Patrick (15), son John T. (10), son Henry (1);[1937] SC #7653, 04/04/1887, filed from Rehoboth, Lunenburg Co., VA; phys. desc. 6'6", dark complexion, dark eyes, black hair;[1933] lists son Walter White;[1933] since discharge res. in Lunenburg Co., VA; d. 11/06/1895;[1938] wid. Mary J., WC #10096, 01/28/1896, filed from Plantersville, Lunenburg Co., VA; (MHW b. 09/16/1847, Charlotte Co., VA, d. 11/04/1919, *"paralysis"*).[1938]

**White, George W.**, 2nd Corp., Co. L; b. 1827;[72] enl. Mex. War service 04/03/1847 Cumberland, MD, age 20; pres. 06/1847; pres. 10/1847; pres. 12/1847, prom. 4th Cpl. from Pvt. 11/04/1847 by regtl. order No. 131, pay stopped for: 1 pr. Pants 2.28, 1 Blanket 2.22, 2 pr. Drawers .71, 1 pr. Socks .24; pres. 02/1848, pay stopped for: 1 Jacket 2.66; pres. 04/1848, pay stopped for: 2 Flannel Shirts 1.55, 1 pr. Shoes 1.16; pres. 07/1848, pay stopped for: 1 Wiper .20; BLW sent to Baltimore, MD.

**White, James E.**, Pvt., Co. C; enl. Mex. War service 12/30/1846, Bowling Green, VA, age 25; pres. 06/1847; pres. 08/1847, pay stopped for: 1 cap-$.95$^{1/2}$, 2 pr. socks-$.49, 2 cotton shirts-$.86, 2 woolen shirts-$1.80, 1 pr. overalls-$2.28; pres. 10/1847, pay stopped for: 2 pr. socks-$.49, 2 pr. drawers-$.71, 1 jacket-$2.66; pres. 12/1847, pay stopped for: 1 pr. pants-$2.28, 1 blanket-$2.22; pres. 04/1848, 1 haversack-$.20$^{3/4}$, 1 india rubber canteen-$.27; pres. 08/1848, BLW sent to Philadelphia, Pa.

**White, Joseph L.**, Pvt., Co. E; b. 03/30/1825, Bertie Co., NC;[1939] enl. Mex. War service 11/30/1846 Petersburg, VA, age 21; pres. 04/1847; pres. 06/1847; pres. 08/1847; pres. 10/1847, pay stopped for: 1 pr. overalls-$2.28, 2 pr. stockings-$.49, 1 cap-$.95$^{1/2}$; pres. 12/1847, pay stopped for: 1 pr. pants-$2.28, 1 pr. shoes-$1.22, 1 blanket-$2.22; pres. 02/1848; pres. 04/1848; m. Elizabeth P. Ferguson, 10/14/1852, Petersburg, VA;[1939] c. 1860 res. San Marino, Dinwiddie Co., VA, age 35, occ. Farmer, w. Elizabeth P. (27), dau. Emily M. (6), son Richard D. (4), son Benjamin L. (2), dau. Mary (1/12);[1940] Civil War service Capt., Co. B, 5th Btln. Va. Inf., enl. 05/16/1861 at Crimea, for 1 yr., pres. until furloughed 07/20/1861 for seven days, pres. until 05/1862 when elected Major, declined election due to ill health and resigned, 08/08/1863 requested reinstatement from Sec. of War to the rank of Major, was not reassigned, NFR;[116] SC #10286, 03/19/1887, filed from Harper's Home, Brunswick Co., VA; phys. desc. 5'7", fair complexion, brown eyes, brown hair, occ. Clerk; since discharge res. Petersburg, VA to 1854 then Harper's Home, Brunswick Co., VA;[1939] lists children Richard D. White b. 1855, Benjamin L. White b. 1857, Stephen G. White b. 1862, L.C. Harrison b. 1865, Annie E. White b. 1868, J.W. White b. 1871, L.G. Jones b. 1875, W.T. White b. 1878;[1939] (EPW d. 07/14/82);[1939] d. 02/09/1910, bur. Harper's Home, VA [19, 1939]

**White, Philip**, Pvt., Co. B; enl. 11/20/1846, Alexandria, VA, age 29; pres. 06/1847; pres. 08/1847; pres. 10/1847, pay stopped for: 2 pr. socks-$.49, 2 pr. cotton drawers-$.71, 1 blanket-$2.22; pres. 12/1847, pay stopped for: 1 pr. shoes-$1.22, 2 pr. socks-$.49, 2 pr. cotton drawers-$.71, 5 cotton shirts-$2.15, 1 pr. overalls-$2.28, 1 cap-$.95$^{1/2}$; pres. 02/1848, pay stopped for: 1 pr. shoes-$1.22; pres. 04/1848, pay stopped for: 2 flannel shirts-$1.80; pres. 08/1848, pay stopped for: 1 musket-$13.00, 1 gun sling-$.16, BLW sent to Alexandria, VA

---

[19] Harper's Home was a postal village located along the Nottoway River, the boundary between Brunswick and Dinwiddie Cos, in the vicinity of Rawlings, VA. The location is recorded as the home of Colonel J.W. Harper a nephew of General Winfield Scott.

OFF TO WAR

**White, William**, Pvt., Co. F; enl. Mex. War service 01/20/1847, Portsmouth, VA, age 20; absent 06/1847 sick in camp; pres. 08/1847, prom. 4th Cpl. 08/20/1847; pres. 10/1847, pay stopped for: 1 pr. overalls-$2.28, 1 forage cap-$.95$^{1/2}$; 5 pr. socks-$1.22, 1 pr. shoes-$1.22, 1 flannel shirt-$.90, 1 pr. drawers-.35$^{1/2}$; pres. 12/1847; pres. 02/1848, pay stopped for: 1 pr. overalls-$2.28, 1 pr. drawers-$.35$^{1/2}$, 1 flannel shirt-$.90, 1 blanket-$2.22, 1 pr. shoes-$1.22; pres. 04/1848, reduced to ranks from 4th Sgt. 04/01/1848; pres. 08/1848, pay stopped for: 1 forage cap-$.83, 1 jacket-$2.37, 1 pr. shoes-$1.16, BLW sent to Portsmouth, VA c/o E.T. Blamire.

**Whiteman, Charles**, Pvt., Co. H; enl. Mex. War service 01/06/1847, Berkeley, VA, age 18; absent 04/1847, left in Hosp. at Ft. Monroe, VA; absent 06/1847 left sick in Hosp. at Ft. Monroe, VA; discharged 04/21/1847 at Ft. Monroe, VA by order of Sec. of War.

**Whiting, John B.**, Pvt., Co. K; b. 12/25/1818, Prince William Co., VA;[1941] enl. Mex. War service Frederick Co., VA 12/09/1846, age 28; pres. 06/1847; pres. 08/1847; pres. 10/1847, pay stopped for: 1 pr. overalls-$2.28, 2 pr. drawers-$.71, 2 pr. socks-$.49, 2 flannel shirts-$1.80, 1 pr. shoes-$1.22, 1 blanket-$2.22, 1 cotton shirt-$.43; pres. 12/1847, pay stopped for: 1 pr. overalls-$2.28, 1 pr. boots-$1.22, 1 pr. socks-$.24$^{1/2}$; pres. 04/1848, pay stopped for: 3 cotton shirts-$1.29, 1 pick & brush-$.12, 1 gun sling-$.18; pres. 07/1848, pay stopped for: 1 cartridge box-$.60, 1 cartridge box plate-$.10, 1 cartridge box belt plate-$.10, 1 bayonet scabbard & frog-$.56, 1 waist belt-$.21, 1 waist belt plate-$.10, 1 pick & brush-$.12; BLW sent to Winchester, Frederick Co., VA; committed to Western State Lunatic Asylum [Western State Hospital], Staunton, VA 05/06/1850;[1941] c. 1860 res. Staunton, Augusta Co., VA, age 43, occ. Clerk;[1942] c. 1870 res. Staunton, Augusta Co., VA, age 52, occ. Patient Lunatic Asylum;[1943] SC #5979, 04/27/1887, from VA; d. 11/10/1898.[1941]

**Whitlock, Robert A.**, Pvt., Co. M; enl. Mex. War service 08/26/1847, Richmond, VA, age 35; pres. 09/1847; pres. 11/1847; pres. 12/1847; pres. 02/1848, pay stopped for: 1 over coat-$6.93$^{1/2}$; pres. 04/1848; pres. 08/1848, pay stopped for: 1 musket & accoutrements complete-$16.22; BLW sent to Richmond, VA

**Whitlock, William W.**, Pvt., Co. A; enl. Mex. War service 12/03/1846 Richmond, VA, age 25; deserted 01/21/1847 at Old Point, VA, 6 mos. pd. in advance.

**Whitlow, James L.**, Pvt., Co. A; b. 07/20/1825 Richmond, VA; enl. Mex. War service 11/18/1846 Richmond, VA, age 22; pres. 12/1846 - 04/1847; pres. 06/1847; pres. 08/1847; pres. 10/1847, pay stopped for clothing: 2 cotton shirts-$.86, 2 pr. wool overalls-$4.56, 1 cap-$.95$^{1/2}$, 2 pr. stockings-$.49, 4 flannel shirts-$3.60, 1 pr. shoes-$1.22, 1 great coat-$6.93$^{1/2}$; pres. 12/1847, pay stopped for clothing: 1 blanket-$2.22; pres. 02/1848, pay stopped for: 1 pick & brush-$.12; pres. 04/1848; BLW sent to Richmond, VA; m/1 Martha Yoakley of Sullivan Co., TN date unknown; Civil War service Confederate Army; (MYW d. 09/1868 Washington Co., TN); m/2 Deborah A. Harrison, 12/14/1871, Buffalo Ridge, Washington Co., TN;[1944] SC #15924, 02/07/1887, filed from Johnson City, Washington Co., TN; *"... a resident of Carter county,*[Tennessee] *and receives his mail at Johnson City, Tennessee. Owns a small house, 4 rooms, and about 4 acres of land situated on the east bank of Sinking Creek, Carter Co.;"*[1945] d. 04/15/1902 Johnson City, Washington Co., TN; wid. Deborah A., WC #12861, 04/22/1902, filed from Johnson City, Washington Co., TN; *"This claimant is a very fleshy woman, and is unable on account of her flesh and her age from earning a support by her daily labor;"*[1946] 1916 res. 515 Myrtle Ave., Johnson City, Washington Co., TN; (DAW b. 06/19/1840, d. 11/25/1916).

**Whitson, James M.**, Pvt., Co. F; b. c. 1824, Poplar Branch, Currituck Co., NC;[1947] enl. Mex. War service 12/16/1846, Portsmouth, VA, age 22; absent 06/1847 sick in camp; pres. 08/1847; pres. 10/1847, pay stopped for: 1 pr. overalls-$2.28, 1 forage cap-$.95$^{1/2}$, 2 pr. socks-$.49, 2 cotton shirts-$.86, 1 pr. drawers-$.35$^{1/2}$, 1 pr. shoes-$1.22; pres. 12/1847; pres. 02/1848, pay stopped for: 1 pr. overalls-$2.28, 1 forage cap-$.95$^{1/2}$, 1 blanket-$2.22, 1 infantry jacket-$2.66, 1 pr. shoes-$1.22; pres. 04/1848; pres. 08/1848, pay stopped for: 1 gun sling-$.18, 1 forage cap-$.83, 1 pr. shoes-$1.16, BLW sent to Portsmouth, VA c/o E.T. Blamire; n/1 Elvira Dowdy

# VIRGINIA VOLUNTEERS IN MEXICO

12/14/1848, Poplar Branch, Currituck Co., NC;[1947] Civil War service Col. 8th NC Inf.;[1947] (EDW d. 02/12/1874); m/2 Sarah Matilda Blivens, widow of Alfred Blivens, 04/17/1875, Stumpy Point, Dare Co., NC;[1947] c. 1880 res. Stumpy Point, Dare Co., NC, age 52, occ. Public and Private School Teacher, w. Sarah M. (33), dau. Sarah E. (4), son Vernon W. (1), s-i-l Charles A. Bliven (9);[1948] SC #1804, 03/08/1887, filed from Manteo, Dare Co., NC; since discharge res. in NC to 1848, Norfolk Co., VA to 1871, Deep Creek, Norfolk City, VA 1873-1874, Dare Co., NC since that time; phys. desc. 5'9", light complexion, blue eyes, red hair, occ. Farmer;[1947] d. 03/08/1899 *"cancer of the eye,"* Elizabeth City, NC;[1947] wid. Sarah M., WC #11924, 04/15/1899, filed from Manteo, Dare Co., NC; lists her children in order of age Vida Whitson Harris, Abraham Shelton Whitson, Alethea H. Whitson Seigel, Lennie C. Whitson, Emma Whitson Woodhouse; children of JMW and EDW J.B. Whitson and P.H. Whitson Gregory;[1949] (SMW b. 02/12/1847, Roanoke Island, Dare Co., NC, d. 11/21/1931, *"cancer of the face and ear,"* Norfolk, Norfolk Co., VA, bur. Elizabeth City, NC);[1949] 04/09/1935 dau. Emma Whitson Woodhouse requested her *"minor pension"* for the dates 1899 - 1909 - rejected.[1949]

**Whittington, George F.**, *Va. Vols.*; *Not on Muster Rolls;* SA #21159, 02/01/1889, from VA

**Widdifield, George Wooley**, Pvt., Co. C; b. 07/29/1827, Philadelphia, Pa., son of George & Abigail (Thomas) Widdifield; enl. Mex. War service 12/29/1846, Bowling Green, VA, age 19; discharged 01/03/1847 Richmond, VA by act of habeas corpus.[1950]

**Wigden, Thomas G.**, 4th Cpl., Co. D; enl. Mex. War service 12/31/1846, Petersburg, VA, age 44; pres. 02/1847; pres. 04/1847; pres. 06/1847 sick sent from Camargo, Mex. to Hosp. Matamoros, Mex. 03/29/1847 - 05/1847; pres. 08/1847; pres. 10/1847, prom. 4th Cpl. 09/16/1847, pay stopped for: 1 cap-$.95$^{1/2}$, 1 jacket-$2.66, 1 pr. pants-$2.28, 1 flannel shirt-$.90, 1 pr. drawers-.35$^{1/2}$, 2 pr. socks-$.49, 1 pr. shoes-$1.22; pres. 12/1847, reduced to ranks & fined 1 mos. pay by order (No. 162) of genl. court-martial 12/14/1847, pay stopped for: 1 pr drawers-$.35$^{1/2}$, 1 pr. shoes-$1.22, 1 blanket-$2.22; pres. 04/1848, pay stopped for: 1 haversack-$.20$^{3/4}$; pres. 08/1847, BLW sent to Richmond, VA

**Wiglesworth, Ed L.**, Pvt., Co. M; enl. Mex. War service 09/26/1847, Ft. Monroe, VA, age 18; discharged 10/06/1847 by writ of habeus corpus *"he being under the age of 18 years."*

**Wilbourn, William Robert**, Pvt., *Recruit Co.*, enl. Mex. War service 04/??/1848 Wytheville, VA; pres. 06/1848; BLW sent to Wytheville, VA; c. 1860 res. Lexington, Rockbridge Co., VA, age 30, occ. Saddler, w. Edna (26), son Thomas (7), son illegible (5), son Samuel (4), son William (2), dau. Cornelia (4/12);[1951] Civil War service Pvt., Co. I, 4th Va. Inf., enl. 10/23/1864, captured 03/25/1865 at Ft. Steadman, VA, confined at Pt. Lookout, MD, paroled there 06/19/1865 phys. desc. 5'5", grey eyes, black hair, dark complexion;[54] c. 1870 res. Lexington, Rockbridge Co., VA, age 39, occ. Saddler, w. Edmonia (35), son Thomas W. (17), son Henry (16), son Samuel (14), dau. Cornelia (10), son Emery (8), dau. Fannie (5), dau. Dorah (1);[1952] SC #16626, 02/21/1887, d. 08/25/1905, bur. Lexington, VA;[54] wid. Edna J., WC #14243, 04/28/1905, both from VA

**Wilhelm, Henry**, Pvt., Co. H; enl. Mex. War service 12/26/1846, Berkeley, VA, age 20; pres. 04/1847; discharged 06/09/1847 at Monterey, Mex. on Surgeon's Certificate of Disability.

**Wilkes, Benjamin W.**, Pvt., Co. M; enl. Mex. War service 09/02/1847, Jonesborough, VA, age 32; pres. 10/1847; pres. 11/1847; pres. 12/1847; pres. 02/1848; pres. 04/1848; pres. 08/1848, pay stopped for: 1 musket-$13.00, 1 bayonet-$1.44, 1 cartridge box-$1.10, 1 cartridge box belt-$.21, 1 cartridge box belt plate-$.10, 1 screw driver-$.07, 1 wormer-$.20; BLW sent to Jonesborough, VA; c. 1850 res. Lunenburg Co., VA, age 35, occ. Laborer, w. Catherine (34), son William R. (11), dau. Mary C. (5), dau. Susan J. (3);[1953] c. 1860 res. Pleasant Grove, Lunenburg Co., VA, age 46, occ. Carpenter, w. Catherine (42), dau. Mary C. (16), dau. Susan J. (13), dau. Sarah H. 10), son Edward A. (6);[1954] Civil War service Pvt., Co. B, 20th Va. Inf., enl. 05/21/1861 at Lewiston, VA, captured 07/11/1861 at Rich Mountain, VA, paroled 07/17/1861 in Randolph Co., VA, age 44, occ. Carpenter, res. of Lunenburg Co., VA, phys.

OFF TO WAR

desc. 5'6", dark complexion, brown hair, hazel eyes, discharged 11/23/1861, on roll of exchanged prisoners 09/02/1862, age 46, occ. Carpenter.[1955]

**Wilkes, Reuben B.**, aka Reuben B. Padgett, Musician, Co. M; enl. Mex. War service 07/03/1847, Lynchburg, VA, age 18.

**Wilkins, Berryman**, Pvt., Co. D; b. 11/15/1821 Halifax Co., VA;[1956] enl. Mex. War service 01/19/1847, Petersburg, VA, age 24; pres. 02/1847; pres. 04/1847; pres. 06/1847, pay stopped for: 1 cartridge box & belt, 1 bayonet scabbard & frog, 1 waist belt & plate, *"lost through negligence;"* pres. 08/1847, pay stopped for: 1 cap-$.95$^{1/2}$, 1 pr. pants-$2.28, 2 cotton shirts-$.86; pres. 10/1847, pay stopped for: 1 jacket-$2.66, 2 flannel shirts-$1.80, 2 cotton shirts-$.86, 1 pr. drawers-$.35$^{1/2}$, 2 pr. socks-$.49, 1 pr. shoes-$1.22; pres. but sick 12/1847, pay stopped for: 1 pr. pants-$2.28, 2 pr drawers-$.71, 1 pr. socks-$.24$^{1/2}$, 1 pr. shoes-$1.22, 2 blankets-$4.44; pres. 04/1848, pay stopped for: 1 haversack-$.20$^{3/4}$; pres. 08/1847, BLW sent to Filehouse, Mecklenburg Co., VA; m. July A.E.M. Tuck, 11/20/1850, Red Bank, Halifax Co., VA; Civil War service Pvt., Co. I, 10$^{th}$ Mo. Cav.;[202] SC #1720, 02/26/1887, filed from Supply, Randolph Co., AR; phys. desc. 6'1", fair complexion, gray eyes, gray hair; since discharge res. Halifax Co., VA to 1856, Franklin Co., MO, 1857 – 1862, Gasconade Co., MO 1862 – 1869, No permanent place of res. 1869 – 1880, Ripley Co., MO 1880 – 1884, Randolph Co., AR, 1884 – 1887; c. 1893 filed for pension increase from Maynard, Randolph Co., AR; d. 07/16/1896, Middlebrook, AR;[1957] wid. Elizabeth, WC #10659, 08/14/1896, filed from Middlebrook, Randolph Co., AR. (ETW b. 02/16/1834, Halifax Co., VA, d. 08/13/1896).[1957]

**Wilkinson, Joseph**, Pvt., Co. E; enl. Mex. War service 12/01/1846 Petersburg, VA, age 23; pres. 04/1847; pres. 06/1847; absent 08/1847 sick; absent 10/1847 sick, pay stopped for: 1 pr. overalls-$2.28, 2 pr. shoes-$2.44, 2 pr. stockings-$.49, 2 cotton shirts-$.86, 1 cap-$.95$^{1/2}$; pres. 12/1847, pay stopped for: 1 pr. pants-$2.28, 2 pr. socks-$.49, 1 pr. shoes-$1.22, 2 cotton shirts-$.86, 4 flannel shirts-$3.60, 2 pr. drawers-$.71, 1 overcoat-$6.93$^{1/2}$, 1 blanket-$2.22; pres. 02/1848, pay stopped for: 1 jacket-$2.66, 1 blanket-$2.22; pres. 04/1848, pay stopped for: 1 cotton shirt-$.44, 2 flannel shirts-$1.55, 1 jacket-$2.37$^{1/2}$;

**Willey, Ira**, Pvt., Co. M; enl. Mex. War service 11/25/1847, Norfolk, VA, age 40; pres. 11/1847; pres. 12/1847; pres. 02/1848; pres. 04/1848, pay stopped for: 1 blanket-$2.22; pres. 08/1848, pay stopped for: 1 musket & accoutrements complete-$16.22; BLW sent to Norfolk, VA

**Williams, Edward**, Pvt., Co. E; b. 08/09/1824 Sussex Co. VA, son of Heartwell Y. and Martha Williams;[1958] enl. Mex. War service 11/30/1846 Petersburg, VA; phys. desc. age 23, 6'0", blue eyes, dark hair, light complexion, occ. farmer; pres. 04/1847; discharged 06/05/1847 Monterey, Mex. for disability; res. Dinwiddie Co., VA; m/1 Cordelia F. Williams date/place unknown, separated 12/06/1860; m/2 Adelaide Rebecca Simmons, 04/08/1874, Prince George Co., VA;[1958, 1959] SC #1801, 03/10/1887, filed from Hebron, Amelia Co., VA; since discharge *"I have lived in Texas, California & Virginia. I now live at Hebron, Amelia Co., VA;"*[1958] d. 08/23/1895; wid. Addie R., WA #12924, 09/10/1895, filed from Macer, Dinwiddie Co., VA; Claim rejected *"on grounds that claimant is not the legal widow of soldier, a former undivorced wife still living."*[1960] (ARW b. 04/19/1840 Prince George Co., VA)

**Williams, George Washington**, Pvt., Co. E; b. 10/28/1822, Mecklenburg Co., VA, son of Richard C. & Elizabeth Williams;[1961] enl. Mex. War service as Drummer 12/05/1846 Petersburg, VA, age 25; pres. 04/1847; pres. but sick 06/1847, reduced to ranks from Drummer 04/30/1847; pres. 08/1847; pres. 10/1847, pay stopped for: 1 pr. overalls-$2.28, 2 pr. shoes-$2.44, 4 pr. stockings-$.98, 1 cap-$.95$^{1/2}$; pres. 12/1847, pay stopped for: 1 pr. socks-$.24$^{1/2}$, 1 blanket-$2.22; pres. 02/1848, pay stopped for: 1 pr. pants-$2.28, 1 blanket-$2.22; pres. 04/1848, pay stopped for: 1 jacket-$2.37$^{1/2}$; d. 03/28/1854, *Consumption, "a member of Capt. Archer's company of Mexican volunteers,"* bur. Blandford Cem., Sq. 222, Ward A, Petersburg, VA[1962,1963]

VIRGINIA VOLUNTEERS IN MEXICO

**Williams, Isaac D.**, Pvt., *Recruit Co.*, enl. Mex. War service 01/03/1848 Christiansburg, VA, age 31; pres. 02/1848; discharged 04/19/1848 at his own request; Civil War service Pvt., Beckett's Co., 36th Va. Inf., enl. 05/16/1861 at Hurricane (Putnam Co.), VA, age 35?, NFR;[390] c. 1880 res. Curry, Putnam Co. WV, age 64, occ. Carpenter/Farmer, w. Eliza J. (54) Keeping House, son Fernando (14), dau. Sarah A. (11), son Charles W. (9), son Willeford W. (1);[1964] SC #15869, 11/07/1887, wid. Eliza J., WA #14859, 12/28/1898, both from WV.
**Williams, John R.**, see alias John R. Onion,
**Williams, John W.**, Pvt., Co. G; enl. Mex. War service 11/18/1846 Richmond, VA, age 18; NFR.
**Williams, Richard F.**, *Archer's Co.*; Not on Muster Rolls; wid. Cordelia, WA #9626, 02/31/1887, from IL.
**Williams, Thomas R.**, Pvt., Co. M; enl. Mex. War service 08/08/1847, Forksville, VA, age 25; pres. 10/1847; pres. 11/1847; pres. 12/1847; sick 02/1848; absent 04/1848 on detached service since 04/22/1848 as Hospital Attendant, pay stopped for: 1 blanket-$2.22, 1 pr. shoes-$1.22; pres. 08/1848, pay stopped for: 1 wormer-$.20; BLW sent to Forksville, VA; m. Mary V.H. King, 05/01/1850, Brunswick Co., VA;[1965] d. c. 1866, *"consumption,"* in Georgia?;[1965] wid. Mary V.H., WC #6006, 11/18/1887, filed from Crane Eater, Gordon Co., GA;[20] lists children Safronia Elizabeth Williams b. 03/05/1852, John James Williams b. 12/24/1854, William Henry Williams b. 12/11/1856, Hugh Lorenzo Williams b. 10/09/1858, Andrew Jackson Williams b. 10/27/1861, Justice Wright Williams b. 11/25/1863;[1965] (MKW b. 12/16/1822).[1965]
**Williams, William H.H.**, Pvt., Co. G; enl. Mex. War service 08/16/1847 Boydton, VA, age 31; pres. 02/1848, joined co. 01/25/1848 from regtl. depot; pres. 04/1848; pres. 08/1848; BLW sent to Boydton, VA; c. 1860 res. Pleasant Grove, Lunenburg Co., VA, age 44, occ. Farmer, w. Mary A. (30), son R.E. (9), dau. Harriet L. (5), dau. Virginia (1);[1966] Civil War service Sgt., 2nd Co. H, 38th Tenn. Inf.;[202] c. 1870 res. Keysville, Lunenburg Co., VA, age 54, occ. Farmer, w. Mary A. (41), son Richard E. (19), dau. Harriet L. (14), dau. Sarah P. (9), dau. Anna R. (5), dau. No Name (2);[1967] SC #6902, 03/28/1887, from VA
**Williamson, Andrew**, Pvt., Co. F; enl. Mex. War service 12/28/1846, Portsmouth, VA, age 32; pres. 06/1847; pres. 08/1847; transferred 09/07/1847 to Capt. Prentis Co. of Arty., pay stopped for: 1 pr. overalls-$2.28, 2 cotton shirts-$.86, 2 pr. drawers-$.71.
**Williamson, Henry Watson**, 2nd Lt., Co. G; b. 09/23/1823 Norfolk VA, son of Thomas & Anne (Walker) Williamson;[1968] VMI graduate Class of 1845; enl. Mex. War service 11/24/1846 Richmond, VA, age 23; pres. 06/1847; pres. 08/1847, presumably commanding the Co.; pres. 10/1847; pres. 12/1847; in confinement 02/1848; pres. 04/1848, commanding co.; pres. 08/1848 commanding co.; c. 1860 res. National Hotel, Norfolk Co., VA, age 37, occ. Clerk;[1969] m. Patty S. Green in 1861; Civil War service 6th Va. Inf., CSA;[465] c. 1870 res. Norfolk, Norfolk Co., VA, age 47, occ. Civil Engineer;[1970] VMI Librarian 1876-1884; d. 1884, Lexington, VA[281]
**Willis, Charles S.**, 2nd Cpl., *Preston's Co.*; b. 09/02/1825, Alleghany Springs, Montgomery Co., VA, son of William & E. Willis;[1971, 1972] enl. Mex. War service 12/06/1846 Montgomery Co., VA, age 21; pres. 04/1847; pres. 06/1847; pres. 08/1847; pres. 10/1847, pay stopped for: 1 pr. overalls-$2.28, 2 pr. socks-$.49, 1 pr. drawers-$.35$^{1/2}$; pres. 12/1847, prom. 3rd Cpl. 11/30/1847, pay stopped for: 1 pr. shoes-$1.22, 1 cap-$.95$^{1/2}$, 1 pr. drawers-$.35$^{1/2}$; pres. 02/1848; absent 04/1848, on detached service as Provost Cpl. since 03/25/1848; pres. 07/1848, pay stopped for: 1 pr. shoes-$1.16; BLW sent to Christiansburg, VA c/o Fleming Gardner; c. 1850 res. Montgomery Co., VA, age 25, occ. Farmer;[1973] m. 03/31/1880, Victoria E. Shively,

---

[20] Crane Eater, Georgia is an unincorporated place named for a Cherokee Indian chief of the same name. Chief Crane Eater and his family were forced out of Georgia in 1838 to present day Oklahoma along the infamous *Trail of Tears*. The community of Crane Eater is located along Red Bud Road just outside of Calhoun, Gordon Co., Georgia.

## OFF TO WAR

Montgomery Co., VA;[1974] SC #13553, 12/19/1887, filed form Alleghany Springs, Montgomery Co., VA; phys. desc. at enl. age 19, 6', blue eyes, dark hair, ruddy complexion, occ. Farmer;[1971] Since discharge res. in Atlanta, Ga. 1849-1878, in Richmond, VA 1880-1883, in Warrenton, NC 1883-1886, since then in Montgomery Co., VA;[1971] Henry Collins and Charles Jackson gave affidavits in pension claim;[1971] d. 10/07/1896, Salem, Roanoke Co., VA, bur. "...*Montgomery County in the family burying ground of his father's family about two miles west of Alleghany Springs...;*"[1975] wid. Victoria, WC #10714, 11/27/1896, filed from Alleghany Springs, Montgomery Co., VA; (VSW b. 07/01/1862, Hillsville, Carroll Co., VA).[1975]

**Willis, John H.**, Pvt., Co. I; enl. Mex. War service 01/02/1847 Richmond, VA, age 18; pres. 02/1847; absent 04/1847, left sick at Camargo, Mex., reduced to ranks from Drummer; in confinement 06/1847; pres. 08/1847; pres. 10/1847, pay stopped for: 3 pr. drawers-$1.06$^{1/2}$, 1 flannel shirt-$.90, 2 cotton shirts-$.86, 2 pr. socks-$.49, 1 cap- $.95$^{1/2}$; pres. 12/1847, pay stopped for: 2 pr. shoes-$2.44, 1 pr. socks-$.24$^{1/2}$, 1 pr. pants-$2.28, 4 cotton shirts-$1.72, 1 blanket-$2.22, 1 jacket-$2.66; pres. 02/1848; pres. 04/1848; pres. 08/1848, pay stopped for: 1 pr. shoes, BLW sent to Richmond, VA

**Wills, Richard D.**, 3rd Sgt., Co. M; b. 04/16/1826, Amelia Co., VA;[1976] enl. Mex. War service 08/29/1847, Nottoway C.H., VA, age 21; pres. 11/1847; pres. 12/1847; pres. 02/1848, pay stopped for: 1 over coat-$6.93$^{1/2}$, 2 cotton shirts-$.86, 2 flannel shirts-$1.80; sick 04/1848, pay stopped for: 1 blanket-$2.22; pres. 08/1848, pay stopped for: 1 musket-$13.00, 1 cartridge box-$1.10, 1 cartridge box belt plate-$.10, 1 bayonet scabbard-$.56, 1 pick & brush-$.12, 1 screw driver-$.07, 1 wormer-$.20, 1 thumb vise-$.35; BLW sent to Nottoway C.H., VA; m. Christie E. Lewis, 12/12/1854, Staunton, Augusta Co., VA;[1976] SC #15815, 05/07/1887, filed from Amelia Co., VA; d. 03/06/1895, Amelia Co., VA;[1977] wid. Christie E., WC #10078, 05/04/1895, filed from Hebron, Dinwiddie Co., VA; (CLW b. 10/06/1836, Dinwiddie Co., VA, d. 04/02/1904).[1977]

**Wills, Armistead B.**, Pvt., Co. D; b. c. 1815 Amelia Co., VA;[1978] enl. Mex. War service 01/12/1847, Petersburg, VA, age 28; pres. 02/1847; absent 04/1847 sick in Hosp. Monterey, Mex.; discharged 05/09/1847 Monterey, Mex. on Surgeon's Certificate of Disability; Civil War service Pvt., Co. H, 44th Va. Inf., enl. 03/13/1862 at Crab Bottom, b. 1815, illiterate, pres. 04/1862, absent sick 05/1862 through 07/20/1862 when listed as AWOL, pres. 03/1863, admitted 07/22/1863 Chimborazo Hosp., trans. 07/28/1863 to Petersburg, VA deserted 09/25/1863 from Petersburg Hosp., captured 05/12/1864 at Spotsylvania, VA, sent to Pt. Lookout, MD from Belle Plain 05/18/1864, trans. 07/30/1864 to Elmira, NY, exchanged 10/29/1864, pres. 11/1864 through 12/1864 when transferred to Co. I, NFR,[175] c. 1870 res. Petersburg, Dinwiddie Co., VA, age 56, occ. Farmer, w. Anne C. (50), son Robert S. (19), son William D. (12);[1979] admitted 08/18/1886 to Confederate Soldiers Home, Richmond, VA; d. 12/10/1887, bur. Hollywood Cemetery, Richmond, VA

**Wills, William**, Pvt., Co. M; enl. Mex. War service 09/10/1847, Petersburg, VA, age 20; pres. 10/1847; pres. 11/1847; pres. 12/1847; pres. 02/1848; pres. 04/1848, 1 pr. shoes-$1.22, 2 cotton shirts-$.86; pres. 08/1848, pay stopped for: 1 gun sling-$.16, 1 wormer-$.20; BLW sent to Petersburg, VA

**Wilson, Frances S.**, Pvt., Co. L; b. 1805; enl. Mex. War service 03/31/1847 Ft. Washington, MD, age 42; pres. 06/1847; pres. 10/1847, pay stopped for: 1 pr. Pants 2.28; pres. 12/1847, to forfeit 1 mos. pay by sentence of garrison court-martial, pay stopped for: 1 jacket-$2.66, 1 cap-$.95$^{1/2}$, 2 pr. shoes-$2.44, 3 flannel shirts-$2.70, 1 blanket-$2.22, 2 pr. drawers-$.71, 2 pr. socks-$.49; pres. 02/1848 to forfeit half mos. pay by sentence of garrison court-martial; pres. 04/1848, pay stopped for: 1 Blanket 2.25; pres. 07/1848, pay stopped for: 1 Screw Driver .25; BLW sent to Capt. Thrift c/o Frances S. Wilson, Fairfax Court House, Fairfax Co., VA

**Wilson, Francis S.**, Pvt., Co. F; enl. Mex. War service 12/15/1846, Portsmouth, VA, age 42; discharged, date & place unknown, by order of Sec. of War;

## VIRGINIA VOLUNTEERS IN MEXICO

**Wilson, Peter H.**, Pvt., Co. M; enl. Mex. War service 09/02/1847, Petersburg, VA, age 29; pres. 09/1847; pres. 11/1847; pres. 12/1847; pres. 02/1848; pres. 04/1848; pres. 08/1848; BLW sent to Lynchburg, VA

**Wilson, Samuel G.**, 2$^{nd}$ Sgt., Co. E; enl. Mex. War service 11/30/1846 Petersburg, VA, age 22; pres. 04/1847; pres. 06/1847; pres. 08/1847, prom. 2$^{nd}$ Sgt.; pres. 10/1847, pay stopped for: 1 pr. overalls-$4.56, 2 pr. shoes-$1.22, 3 pr. stockings-$.49, 1 cap-$.95$^{1/2}$; absent sick 12/1847, pay stopped for: 1 pr. shoes-$1.22, 2 flannel shirts-$1.80; in confinement 02/1848; pres. 04/1848.

**Wilson, Samuel W.**, Pvt., LIC; enl. Mex. War service 12/07/1846 Staunton, VA, age 23; pres. 08/1847; absent 10/1847, in Hosp. at Saltillo, Mex., pay stopped for: 1 forage cap-$.95$^{1/2}$, 1 wool jacket-$2.66, 2 pr. overalls-$4.56, 3 pr. shoes-$3.66, 4 pr. socks-$.98, 4 cotton shirts-$1.72, 1 pr. drawers-$.35$^{1/2}$; absent 12/1847, sick in quarters, pay stopped for: 1 cotton shirt-$.43, 1 pr. drawers-$.35$^{1/2}$, 1 blanket-$2.22; pres. 04/1848; pres. 07/1848, pay stopped for: 1 gun sling-$.16, 1 pick & brush-$.12, 1 screw driver-$.07, 1 wiper-$.20; BLW sent to Staunton, VA

**Winfree, Thomas**, Pvt., Co. G; enl. Mex. War service 11/18/1846 Richmond, VA, age 34; discharged 04/06/1847 Monterey, Mex.

**Wingfield, Albert G.**, Pvt., Co. M; enl. Mex. War service 08/01/1847, Lovingston, VA, age 20; pres. 09/1847; pres. 11/1847; pres. 12/1847; pres. 02/1848; pres. 04/1848; pres. 08/1848, pay stopped for: 1 gun sling-$.16; BLW sent to Lovingston, VA

**Winfield, Benjamin Franklin**, Pvt., Co. D; b. 03/31/1823, Sussex Co., VA;[1980] enl. Mex. War service 12/10/1846, Petersburg, VA, age 23; pres. 02/1847; pres. 04/1847, on detached service in charge of the sick at Port Isabel, Tex. from 03/17/1847 - 04/26/1847; pres. 06/1847, reduced to ranks at his own request 06/21/1847; Court-martialed 07/27/1847, *Charge #1: Disobedience of Orders; Specification 1$^{st}$: In this that the said Benjamin F. Winfield, Private in Capt. William M. Robinson's company 1$^{st}$ Regt. VA Volunteers, did refuse to attend Reveille Roll Call, although warned to do so, and all this at the Camp at Buena Vista, Mexico on or about the 17$^{th}$ July 1847; Specification 2$^{nd}$: In this, that the said Benj. F. Winfield, private of Capt. W.M. Robinson's company 1$^{st}$ Regt. Va. Vols. Did not answer to his name in the ranks at Reveille Roll Call although repeatedly warned of the necessity of doing so and all this at the Camp at Buena Vista, Mexico on or about the 18$^{th}$ of July 1847; Charge #2: Insubordinate Conduct; Specification 1$^{st}$ in this that the said Benjamin F. Winfield, a private in Captain Wm. M. Robinson's company (D) 1$^{st}$ Regiment Virginia Volunteers, when ordered to go on company police duty at the regular hour, did refuse to do so, until after he had concluded his morning nap, and when ordered a second time by Captain Robinson did send back an answer in these words to this effect viz that "he would not leave his morning nap for him or any other man." All this at the Camp at Buena Vista, Mexico on or about the 18$^{th}$ of July 1847; Charge #3 Disrespect to His Superior Officer; Specification 1$^{st}$: In this that the said Benj. F. Winfield, a Private in Capt. Wm. Robinson's company (D) 1$^{st}$ Regt. VA Volunteers when ordered a second time to go on company police duty by Capt Robinson, did send back an answer in these words to this effect viz that "he would not leave his morning nap for him or any other man." All this in the Camp at Buena Vista, Mexico on or about the 18$^{th}$ of July 1847. To the charges and specification the Prisoner pleaded "Not Guilty" except to the 2$^{nd}$ Specification in the 1$^{st}$ charge, to which he pleaded "Guilty." The Court after mature deliberation on the testimony adduced find the prisoner "Not Guilty" of the Charge 1$^{st}$ Specification 1$^{st}$ under the same charge, and "Guilty" of Specification 2$^{nd}$ under same charge. "Not Guilty" of Charge 2$^{nd}$ but guilty of the Specification...; The Court after mature deliberation finds the Prisoner Guilty of the Charges and Specifications and sentences him to be sent under the direction of the Provost Sergeant to the Creek and thoroughly scrubbed and to labor for Four Hours each day, from 8 until 12 o'clock for 15 days - and marched backward and forward for Three Hours each day, from 2 to 5 o'clock with shouldered arms in front of the Provost Guard;* pres. 08/1847, pay

OFF TO WAR

stopped for: 1 pr. pants-$2.28; Court-martialed 10/04/1847, Buena Vista, Mex. *Charge#1: Disobedience of Orders; Specification: In this that he, the said Private Benj. S. Winfield, of Co. D, Va. Regt. Vols., did refuse to go on guard after being regularly detailed by the VA Sergt. and after being repeatedly warned by said Sergt. and his commanding officer to go on guard. This at Buena Vista, Mexico on the 20$^{th}$ of Sept. 1847. Charge #2: Neglect of Duty; Specification: In this that he, the said Private Benj. S. Winfield, of Co. D, Va. Regt. Vols., failed to go on guard after being regularly detailed and after being repeatedly warned by the 1$^{st}$ Sergt. and by his commanding officer to go on guard. Charge #3: Using Improper Language to his Commanding Officer; Specification: In this that he, the said Private Benj. S. Winfield, of Co. D, Va. Regt. Vols., when asked to go on guard by his commanding officer, did refuse saying, 'he would not go on guard.' And when ordered by his commanding officer to the Quarter Guard said, 'You have made your point, now I must obey. I had rather be under guard all of the time than under your command,' or words to that effect. This at Buena Vista, Mex. on the 20$^{th}$ September 1847. To which charges and specifications the prisoner plead Guilty. Lt. Col. T.B. Randolph, a witness for the defense, being duly sworn, says: I am in command of the Virginia Regt. The prisoner came to me to get excused from guard as he was nearly bare footed before the 20$^{th}$ Sept. 1847. I excused him at the time and released him from confinement. But he came a second time to get released from confinement having been confined for refusing to go on guard. I refused to release him. Lt. Benj. W. Collier, Va. Regt. Vols., a witness for the defense, being duly sworn, says: The prisoner had, when he refused to go on guard, a pair of old boots, which I had given him a few days previous and which were serviceable when I gave them to him. I do not know how the boots were on that day. Question by the Court: Has the prisoner a great coat, jacket or forage cap? Answer: I do not know. Question by the Court: Do you know whether the prisoner is careful or careless with his clothing? Answer: I think he is disposed to be careless. Question by the Court: Was the prisoner a non-commissioned officer of his company and relieved at his own request? Answer: Yes. Sergeant Jno. W. Fisher, Co. D, Va. Regt. Vols., a witness for the defense, being duly sworn, says: The prisoner had, when he refused to go on guard, a pair of shoes or boots as good as other men in the company had who were performing duty. The prisoner then addressed the Court in his own defense: I did not consider my shoes good enough to go on guard with. Lt. Bryan said that he thought I had thrown my shoes away to avoid doing guard duty. Which irritated me and I answered him in the words of the specification. I considered too, that I was still excused by Col. Randolph. After deliberation the Court found the prisoner Guilty and sentenced him to march four hours each day for thirty days from 7 to 9 o'clock A.M. and from 1 to 3 o'clock P.M. with his musket and accoutrements in rear of the Main Regimental Guard of his Regiment and to attend daily company police and all other duty except that of guard;.*[1981] pres. 10/1847, pay stopped for: 1 cap-$.95$^{1/2}$, 1 jacket-$2.66, 1 pr. pants-$2.28, 1 cotton shirt-$.43, 1 pr. socks-$.24$^{1/2}$, 1 pr. shoes-$1.22; absent 12/1847, appointed Ward Master Hosp. Saltillo, Mex. 12/15/1847, pay stopped for: 1 jacket-$2.66, 1 pr. pants-$2.28, 2 pr drawers-$.71, 1 blanket-$2.22; pres. 04/1848, pay stopped for: 1 haversack-$.20$^{3/4}$; pres. 08/1847, BLW sent to Stony Creek, Sussex Co., VA; c. 1860 res. Sussex Co., Benjamin F. Winfield, age 37, occ. Physician;[1982] Civil War service Capt., Co. D, 13$^{th}$ Va. Cav., enl. 03/09/1862 at Sussex C.H., VA, pres. 09/1862 through 01/01/1863, when furloughed for 30 days, pres. 07/1863 through 07/1864, prom. to Major 04/1864, effective 12/19/1863, absent sick 09/1864 through 10/1864, resigned 10/1864, admitted date unknown R.E. Lee Camp Soldiers Home, Richmond, VA, SC #6487, 03/17/1887, filed from Confederate Soldiers Home, Richmond, Henrico Co., VA; Since discharge res. Sussex Co., Petersburg, & Henrico Co., VA; David A. Weisiger & James M. Donnan gave affidavits on pension claim; d. 05/06/1888, Lee Camp Soldiers Home, age 65.[1983]

**Wingfield, Charles,** *Frye's Co.; Not on Muster Rolls;* SA #13764, wid. Melvina, WA #11623, 09/23/1893, both from MO.

## VIRGINIA VOLUNTEERS IN MEXICO

**Winn, James**, 2$^{nd}$ Cpl., Co. A; enl. Mex. War 11/28/1846, age 25; pres. 12/1846 - 04/1847; sick in quarters 06/1847; pres. 08/1847, prom. 2$^{nd}$ Cpl. 08/23/1847; pres. 10/1847, pay stopped for clothing: 1 cap-$.95$^{1/2}$, 1 pr. shoes-$1.22, 2 pr. stockings-$.49; pres.12/1847, pay stopped for clothing: 1 pr. shoes-$2.44, 1 pr. drawers-$.35$^{1/2}$; sick 02/1848; pres. 04/1848; BLW sent to, Richmond, VA;  m. Mary Anne Douglas 10/24/1848, Richmond, VA; d. 07/21/1866 Portsmouth, VA;[1984] wid. Mary Ann, WC #3347, 12/23/1887, filed from Portsmouth, Norfolk Co., VA (MAW b. 04/13/1829, d. 1894).[1984]

**Winston, Thomas B.**, Pvt., Co. A; enl. Mex. War service 12/01/1846 Richmond, VA, age 30; pres. 12/1846 - 04/1847; pres. 06/1847; pres. 08/1847; pres. 10/1847, pay stopped for clothing: 1 pr. wool overalls-$2.28, 1 cap-$.95$^{1/2}$, 2 pr. stockings-$.49, 1 pr. shoes-$1.22; pres. 12/1847; pres. 02/1848, pay stopped for: 1 pr. shoes-$1.22; pres. 04/1848; BLW sent to Richmond, VA

**Winston, William J.[James]**, Pvt., Co. A; son of William S. & Ann L. (Poindexter) Winston;[1985] enl. Mex. War service 12/2/1846 Richmond, VA, age 21; pres. until sick 04/1847, in Hosp. at Camargo, Mex. since 03/20/1847; pres. 06/1847; sick 08/1847; discharged 10/16/1847 at Buena Vista, Mex. on Surgeon's Certificate; c. 1850, res. Louisa Co., VA, age 25, occ. Farmer; [1986] c. 1860, res. Trevellians Depot, Louisa Co., VA, age 35, occ. Farmer, w. Mary P.;[1987] Civil War service 1$^{st}$ Lt., Co. D, 23$^{rd}$ Va. Inf., enl. 05/23/1861 at Trevillians Sta., VA for 1 yr., resigned 07/21/1861;[107] c. 1870 res. Trevillians, Louisa Co., VA, age 45, occ. Farmer, w. Mary (40).[1988]

**Winter, Richard**, Pvt., Co. H; enl. Mex. War service 01/06/1847, Berkeley, VA, age 26; pres. 04/1847; pres. 06/1847; pres. 08/1847; pres. 10/1847, pay stopped for: 2 cotton shirts-$.86, 1 pr. shoes-$1.22, 2 pr. socks-$.49; pres. 12/1847, pay stopped for: 1 jacket-$2.66, 3 pr. socks-$.73$^{1/2}$, 1 forage caps-$.95$^{1/2}$, 1 pr. shoes-$1.22; pres. 02/1848, pay stopped for: 1 flannel shirt-$.90, 1 pr. shoes-$1.22; pres. 04/1848; pres. 07/1848, pay stopped for: 1 bayonet scabbard & frog-$.56, 1 gun sling-$.16, BLW sent to Philadelphia, Pa.

**Wolford, William R.**, Pvt., *Recruit Co.*, enl. Mex. War service 03/19/1848 Wytheville, VA; pres. 06/1848; BLW sent to Wytheville, VA

**Womack, Abram N.**, 3$^{rd}$ Sgt., Co. G; enl. Mex. War service 12/10/1846 Richmond, VA, age 29; pres. 06/1847, reduced to 3$^{rd}$ Sgt.; pres. 08/1847; pres. 10/1847, pay stopped for: 1 pr. overalls_$2.28, 3 pr. socks-$.73$^{1/2}$, 1 jacket- $2.66, 1 forage cap-$.95$^{1/2}$; pres. 12/1847, reduced to ranks at his own request 12/01/1847, pay stopped for: 1 pr. shoes-$1.22, 2 cotton shirts-$.86, 2 pr. drawers-$.71, 1 blanket-$2.22, 1 pr. pants-$2.28; pres. 02/1848, pay stopped for: 1 pr. socks-$.24$^{1/2}$; pres. 04/1848, pay stopped for: 1 jacket-$2.66; pres. 08/1848, pay stopped for: 1 pr. shoes-$1.22, 1 gun sling-$.16; BLW sent to Richmond, VA; c. 1850 res. Amelia Co., VA, age 31, occ. Superintendent on R.R.;[1989] Civil War service Pvt., Co. F, 18$^{th}$ Va. Inf. enl. 04/23/1861, age 47, occ. Farmer, phys desc. 5'10, gray eyes, brown hair, dark complexion, detailed 10/1861 through 12/1861 as a baggage agent for Regt., AWOL 01/1862, discharged 07/23/1862;[1111] res. Prince George Co., VA, d. 11/1869.[1990]

**Womack, James**, Pvt., Co. D; enl. Mex. War service 01/01/1847, Petersburg, VA, age 41; deserted 02/24/1847 at Fort Monroe, VA

**Wood, Andrew J.**, Pvt., Co. K; enl. Mex. War service Jefferson Co., VA 12/29/1846, age 20; pres. 06/1847; absent 08/1847, on detached service altering clothing for Regtl. Band since 08/20/1847; pres. 10/1847, pay stopped for: 2 pr. shoes-$2.44, 2 pr. overalls-$4.56, 3 cotton shirts-$1.29, 3 pr. socks-$.73$^{1/2}$, 2 flannel shirts-$1.80; pres. 12/1847, pay stopped for: 1 jacket-$2.66, 1 pr. overalls-$2.28, 1 pr. socks-$.24$^{1/2}$, 1 blanket-$2.22, 1 cap-$.95$^{1/2}$; pres. 04/1848, pay stopped for: 1 pr. shoes-$1.22, 1 gun sling-$.18; pres. 07/1848, pay stopped for: 1 wiper-$.20; BLW sent to Harper's Ferry, Jefferson Co., VA

**Woodrow, Joseph J.**, Pvt., Co. I; enl. Mex. War service 01/10/1847 Lynchburg, VA, age 31; pres. 02/1847; pres. 04/1847; pres. 06/1847; pres. 08/1847; pres. 10/1847, pay stopped for: 3 flannel shirts-$2.70, 3 cotton shirts-$1.29, 3 pr. drawers-$1.06$^{1/2}$, 2 pr. shoes-$2.44, 1 pr.

OFF TO WAR

socks-$.24$^{1/2}$, 1 cap- $.95$^{1/2}$; pres. 12/1847, pay stopped for: 1 pr. socks-$.24$^{1/2}$, 1 pr. pants-$2.28, 1 jacket-$2.66, 1 overcoat-$6.93$^{1/2}$, 2 blankets-$4.44, 1 cotton shirts-$.43, 2 flannel shirts-$1.80; 1 pr. drawers-$.35$^{1/2}$; pres. 02/1848; pres. 04/1848, on extra duty in QM Dept., pay stopped for: 1 blanket; pres. 08/1848, pay stopped for: 1 musket complete & accoutrements complete-$16.15, BLW sent to Richmond, VA

**Woodruff, Hiram**, Pvt., Co. G; b. abt. 1818, Amherst Co., VA, son of Jesse & Elizabeth Woodroof;[1991] enl. Mex. War service 12/16/1846 Richmond, VA, age 30; pres. 06/1847; d. 07/29/1847 in Hosp. Buena Vista, Mex.

**Woodson, Martin R.**, Pvt., Co. A; enl. Mex. War service 12/02/1846 Richmond, VA, age 19; pres. 12/1846 - 04/1847; discharged 06/02/1847 for disease by order of Maj. Gen. Taylor.

**Wren, Charles B.**, Pvt., Co. L; b. 03/25/1818, Fairfax Co., VA;[1992] enl. Mex. War service 03/16/1847 Alexandria, VA, age 28; in confinement 06/1847; court-martialed 06/16/1847, Buena Vista, Mex. *Charge #1: Drunkeness on Duty; Specification: "In this that Private Charles B. Wren, of the 13th Company , Virginia Regiment of Volunteers, was found drunk on his Guard at the Hacinda, near Buena Vista, Mex. On the 8th day of June 1847. To which charge and specification the prisoner pled Guilty. Capt. H. Fairfax, Virginia Regt. of Volunteers, a witness for the defense was duly sworn. Question by the prisoner: What has been my character as regards to sobriety previous to this offence. Answer: The prisoner knowing his infirmity, avoids liquor, and has never sought it. But when brought to him by others, I have twice known him to drink to excess. After deliberation the court found him guilty and sentenced him "to be confined at hard labor under the charge of the Provost Guard for a period of one month*;[1993] pres. 08/1847; pres. 10/1847, to forfeit $3.50 by sentence of garrison court-martial; pres. 12/1847, pay stopped for: 1 pr. pants-$2.28, 2 caps-$1.91, 1 pr. shoes-$1.22, 1 flannel shirt-$.90, 3 cotton shirts-$1.29, 1 blanket-$2.22, 1 pr. socks-$.24$^{1/2}$; pres. 02/1848, pay stopped for: 1 Jacket 2.66, 1 Brush & Pick .12; pres. 04/1848; pres. 07/1848; BLW sent to Capt. Thrift c/o Charles B. Wren, Fairfax Court House, Fairfax Co., VA; m. Catherine Lindsay 11/28/1839, Washington, D.C.;[1994] c. 1860 res. Fairfax Co., VA, age 40, occ. Laborer, w. Catherine (39), mo. Frances (65), son Albert (20), son William H. (18), dau. Sarah C. (16), dau Frances J. (10), dau Mary V. (8), son Caldwell (2);[1995] Civil War service Pvt., Co. F, 6th Va. Cav. Enl. 05/25/1861, discharged 07/26/1862;[324] SC #1693, 02/12/1887, filed from Dunn-Loring, Fairfax Co., VA;[1992] phys. desc. 5'8", dark hair, blue eyes, occ. Farmer.

**Wrenn, Lewis W.**, Pvt., Co. A; b. Fredericksburg, Spotsylvania Co., VA; enl. Mex. War service 11/21/1846 Richmond, VA, age 26; phys. desc. 5'10$^{1/2}$", fair complexion, black eyes, black hair, occ. Saddler & Harness Maker; pres. until sick 04/1847, in Hosp. at Matamoros since 02/26/1847; sick in quarters 06/1847; pres. 08/1847; pres. 10/1847, pay stopped for clothing: 1 pr. wool overalls-$2.28, 1 cap-$.95$^{1/2}$, 1 pr. stockings-$.24$^{1/2}$, 4 flannel shirts-$3.60, 2 pr. drawers-$.71, 1 pr. shoes-$1.22; pres. 12/1847, pay stopped for clothing: 2 pr. socks-$.49, 1 pr. shoes-$1.22, 1 blanket-$2.22; pres. 02/1848; pres. 04/1848; c. 1850 res. Lynchburg, Campbell Co., VA, age 28, occ. Saddler;[1996] m. Martha J. Jennings, 09/05/1850, Lynchburg, VA;[1997] c. 1860 res. Lynchburg, Campbell Co., VA, age 38, occ. Saddler, w. Martha J. (25), dau. Rozella N. (8), son William N. (6), dau. Olivia (4), dau. Leotha (2), m-i-l? Mary Jennings (67);[1998] Civil War service Pvt., Co. C, 3rd VA Reserves, only record is an undated parole at Lynchburg, VA;[116] c. 1870 res. Lynchburg, Campbell Co., VA, age 48, Saddler, w. Martha (37), dau. Rosella (18), son William M. (16), dau. Lillie (14), son L.O. (10), dau. Annie B. (5),son John A. (4);[1999] SC #10798, 07/18/1887, filed from 717 Main St., Lynchburg, Campbell Co., VA; d. 07/10/1899, Lynchburg, VA, bur. Spring Hill Cem., Lynchburg, VA; wid. Martha J., WC #11996, 08/21/1899, filed from 819 Main St., Lynchburg, Campbell Co., VA (MJW b. 08/23/1833, Lynchburg, VA, d. 06/21/1918).

**Wrenn, Roberson Boswell**, Pvt., Co. A; b. 01/21/1825, Fredericksburg, Spotsylvania Co., VA, son of Lewis & Elizabeth (Mills) Wren;[2000] enl. Mex. War service 02/02/1847 Richmond, VA,

VIRGINIA VOLUNTEERS IN MEXICO

age 19; pres. 04/1847, not yet pd. for 6 mos. clothing; pres. 06/1847; pres. 08/1847; pres. 10/1847, pay stopped for clothing: 3 cotton shirts-$1.29, 2 pr. wool overalls-$4.56, 2 caps-$1.91, 2 pr. shoes-$2.44, 4 pr. stockings-$.98, 2 flannel shirts-$1.80; pres. 12/1847, pay stopped for clothing: 2 pr. shoes-$2.44, 1 pr. wool overalls-$2.28, 1 blanket-$2.22; pres. 02/1848, pay stopped for: 1 pr. shoes-$1.22; sick 04/1848; BLW sent to Richmond, VA; m/1 Susan C. Wrenn, 04/12/1852, Fredericksburg, VA;[2001] (SCW d. 02/1853 *"in childbirth at Lewis Wrenn's House,"* near Culpeper C.H., VA; m/2 Martha Ella Hudson, 11/10/1856, Alexandria Co., VA;[2002] c. 1870 res. Alexandria Co., VA, age 42, occ. Carpenter, w. Martha (32), son Norman (12), dau. Ada (11), dau. Georgia (9), son Stonewall (8), son Robert Lee (6), son Herbert (3), son Augustine (1);[2003] 1881 occ. Carpenter, res. 3418 O St, NW, Wash., D.C.;[2004] 1890 occ. Carpenter, res. 1461 S St., NW, Wash., DC;[2005] SC #12136, filed from Washington, D.C.; d. 10/12/1899, *"typhoid fever & exhaustion,"* bur. Alexandria, VA;[2006] wid. Martha E., WC #12024, 11/13/1899, filed from 225 E St., N.W., Washington, DC. Had 12 children; (MEW b. 09/19/1835, near Culpeper C.H., d. 01/24/1912).

**Wright, John T.**, Pvt., Co. L; b. 1815; enl. Mex. War service 03/16/1847 Alexandria, VA, age 32; pres. 06/1847; pres. 10/1847; absent 12/1847, on furlough for 1 mo. w/ Col. March, Beef Contractor, from 12/21/1847, pay stopped for: 1 pr. pants-$2.28, 1 pr. shoes-$1.22, 2 flannel shirts-$1.80, 1 pr. drawers-$.35$^{1/2}$, 1 pr. socks-$.24$^{1/2}$; absent 02/1048 on furlough for in employ of Col. March Beef Contractor; absent 04/1848 on furlough for 1 mo. from 02/21/1848 in employ of Col. March, Beef Contractor, by order Col. Hamtramck; pres. 07/1848, pay stopped for: 1 Brush & Pick .12; BLW sent to Washington City, D.C.

**Wyatt, John N.**, Pvt., Co. D; enl. Mex. War service 01/01/1847, Petersburg, VA, age 18; pres. 02/1847; pres. 04/1847; pres. 06/1847; pres. 08/1847, pay stopped for: 1 cap-$.95$^{1/2}$, 1 pr. pants-$2.28, 2 cotton shirts-$.86, 2 flannel shirts-$1.80, 1 pr. shoes-$1.22; pres. 10/1847, pay stopped for: 1 jacket-$2.66, 1 flannel shirt-$.90, 2 cotton shirts-$.86, 1 pr. drawers-$.35$^{1/2}$, 1 pr. socks-$.24$^{1/2}$, 1 pr. shoes-$1.22, 1 overcoat-$6.93$^{1/2}$; pres. 12/1847, pay stopped for: 1 pr. pants-$2.28, 1 pr. socks-$.24$^{1/2}$, 1 pr. shoes-$1.22, 1 blanket-$2.22; pres. 04/1848, pay stopped for: 1 jacket-$2.66, 1 cap-$.95$^{1/2}$, 1 pr. pants-$2.28, 1 haversack-$.20$^{3/4}$; pres. 08/1847, BLW sent to Petersburg, VA; m. Elizabeth Allen 1850;[2007] a John Wyatt, *"of Richmond, formerly of Petersburg,"* d. 12/14/1875, bur. Oakwood Cemetery, Richmond, VA;[2008, 2007] wid. Elizabeth, WC #4116, 01/16/1888, filed from Petersburg, Dinwiddie Co., VA; (EAW d. 10/10/1900).

**Wyatt, William C.**, Pvt., Co. I; b. 04/02/1828, Accomac Co., VA;[2009] enl. Mex. War service 12/01/1846 Richmond, VA, age 18; pres. 02/1847; pres. 04/1847; pres. 06/1847; Court-martialed 07/22/1847, Buena Vista, Mex. *Charge #1 Sleeping On Post; Specification: In this that Private William Wyatt, Co. I, Va. Regt. Vols., being regularly posted as a Sentinel in the town of Saltillo, Mex. on the night of the 16$^{th}$ and 17$^{th}$ of July 1847, was found asleep upon his post between the hours of 3 & 5 o'clock in the morning of the 17$^{th}$. To which charge and specification the prisoner pled Guilty. Offering no defense the Court confirmed the plea of the prisoner and sentenced him to forfeit one months pay and be kept at hard labor in his company, attending to all his duties, for the period of one month;*[2010] pres. 08/1847 sick; pres. 10/1847, pay stopped for: 1 pr. drawers-$.35$^{1/2}$, 1 pr. socks-$.24$^{1/2}$; pres. 12/1847, pay stopped for: 1 pr. shoes-$1.22, 1 pr. socks-$.24$^{1/2}$, 1 pr. pants-$2.28, 1 flannel shirts-$.90, 1 blanket-$2.22; pres. 02/1848; pres. 04/1848; pres. 08/1848, BLW sent to Drummond Town, Accomac Co., VA; SC #15582, 04/05/1888, filed from Charlestown, Jefferson Co., WV; c. 1888 res. Soldiers Temperance Home, 329 Missouri Avenue, N.W., Washington, D.C.; c. 1893 res. Lambert's Point, Norfolk Co., VA;[2009] d. c. 1894.[2009]

**Yates, William M.**, Pvt., Co. M; enl. Mex. War service 08/27/1847, Yatesville, VA, age 30; pres. 10/1847; pres. 11/1847; pres. 12/1847; pres. 02/1848, pay stopped for: 1 blanket-$2.22; sick 04/1848, pay stopped for: 1 pr. shoes-$1.22, 1 cotton shirt-$.43; pres. 08/1848, pay stopped for: 1 gun sling-$.16; BLW sent to Yatesville, VA; SC #11454, 08/22/1887, wid. Frances L., WC #10386, 07/13/1896, both from VA; [pension file not found].

OFF TO WAR

**Yopp, William**, Pvt., *Preston's Co.*: enl. Mex. War service 11/24/1846 Montgomery Co., VA; d. 03/10/1847 on board transport ship *Sophia Walker*, *"off the Island of Cuba."*[243]

**Young, Christopher Clarke**, Pvt., *Recruit Co.*, enl. Mex. War service 02/24/1848 Charlestown, VA, age 21; pres. 02/1848; pres. 04/1848; pres. 06/1848; BLW sent to Charlestown, Jefferson Co., VA; Civil War service Co. D, 186$^{th}$ Ohio Inf., IC #842623 & WO #892760; SC #8462, 02/05/1887, from OH, wid. Mary E., WC #15243, 11/14/1908, from IA.

**Young, George W.**, Pvt., *Recruit Co.*, enl. Mex. War service 12/06/1847 Alexandria, VA, age 22; pres. 02/1848; pres. 04/1848; pres. 06/1848; BLW sent to Alexandria, VA

**Young, John L.**, Pvt., *Preston's Co.*; b. 09/22/1824, Blacksburg, Montgomery Co., VA;[2011] enl. Mex. War service 01/03/1847 Montgomery Co., VA, age 20; pres. 04/1847; pres. 06/1847; absent 08/1847 on detached service in QM Dept., to receive $25 in addition to pay as a soldier; pres. 10/1847, pay stopped for: 1 jacket-$2.66, 1 pr. overalls-$2.28, 3 pr. socks-$.73$^{1/2}$, 1 flannel shirt-$.90, 3 cotton shirts-$1.29, 1 pr. drawers-$.35$^{1/2}$, 1 cap-$.95$^{1/2}$; pres. 12/1847, pay stopped for: 2 pr. overalls-$4.56, 1 pr. socks-$.24$^{1/2}$, 1 blanket-$2.22; pres. 02/1848, pay stopped for: 1 pr. shoes-$1.22; pres. 04/1848, pay stopped for: 1 pick & brush-$.12; pres. 07/1848, pay stopped for: 1 pr. shoes-$1.16, 1 cartridge box & plate-$1.20, 1 cartridge box belt & plate-$.80, 1 bayonet & scabbard-$.56, 1 waist belt-$.25, 1 waist belt plate-$.08, 1 brush & pick-$.12, 1 gun sling-$.18, 1 wiper-$.13; BLW sent to Christiansburg, VA c/o Fleming Gardner; m. Catherine A. Berley 12/18/1855, Russellville, Hawkins Co., TN;[2011] Civil War service Pvt., Co. C, 8$^{th}$ Tenn. Cav.,[2011] IC #673900; SC # 16682, 07/10/1888, filed from Sheridan, Yamhill Co., OR; phys. desc. at enl. age 21, 5'11", dark eyes, dark hair, occ. Carpenter;[2011] d. 12/16/1893, *"Pneumonia,"* Portland, Oregon;[2012] wid. Catherine A., WC #9263, 02/10/1894, filed from Sheridan, Yamhill Co., OR; states she has two daughters;[2012] (ABY b. 03/10/1836, d. 04/1906).[2012]

**Young, John P.**, Capt., Co. F; enl. Mex. War service 11/23/1846 Portsmouth, VA; pres. 06/1847, resumed command of the company 06/28/1847; pres. 08/1847; pres. 10/1847; pres. 12/1847; absent with leave 02/1848 since 01/1848; AWOL 04/1848 since 04/01/1848; discharged 07/20/1848 by order of the War Dept.; c. 1850 res. Portsmouth, Norfolk Co., VA, age 46, occ. M.D., w. Huldah (42), son John W. (16) Student, dau. Constance (14).[2013]

**Young, John T.**, 1$^{st}$ Sgt., Co. B; enl. 11/30/1847, Alexandria, VA, age 29; pres. 06/1847, on extra duty in Commissary Dept.; pres. 08/1847; pres. 10/1847, pay stopped for: 2 pr. socks-$.49, 1 pr. shoes-$1.22, 1 pr. overalls-$2.28, 4 pr. cotton drawers-$1.42, 1 blanket-$2.22; pres. 12/1847, pay stopped for: 1 pr. shoes-$1.22, 1 pr. overalls-$2.28, 1 cap-$.95$^{1/2}$; pres. 02/1848; pres. 04/1848, prom. 04/18/1848 to1$^{st}$ Sgt.; pres. 08/1848, pay stopped for: 1 ball screw-$.12, 1 spring vice-$.35, 1 screw driver $.07, 2 pr. shoes-$2.32.

**Young, Richard**, 2$^{nd}$ Lt., Co. L; b. 1818; enl. Mex. War service 03/01/1847 Fairfax C.H., VA, age 29; absent 06/1847 on detached service in QM Dept.; pres. 08/1847 2$^{nd}$ Lt. from 3$^{rd}$ Sgt.; absent 10/1847 on leave; resigned 10/31/1847;[72] d. *"at his mothers"* 7/9/1850, age 33, bur. Bethel Regular Baptist Church, Great Falls, VA.[45]

# VIRGINIA VOLUNTEERS IN MEXICO

## Deaths in Service

**Adams, Joseph C.**, Pvt., Co. D; d. 07/20/1847, Buena Vista, Mex.
**Archer, Edwin C.**, Pvt., Co. D; d. 03/16/1847 *"off Brasos Island."*
**Barker, William**, Pvt., Co. G; d. 06/12/1847, Monterey, Mex.
**Belt, John C.**, Pvt., Co. B; d. 07/01/1847, Monterey, Mex.
**Black, William A.**, Pvt., *Preston's Co.*; d. 02/04/1847 at Ft. Monroe, VA; *"congestion of the brain."*[243]
**Blondell, Benjamin W.**, Fifer, Co. H; d. 02/28/1847 Ft. Monroe, VA
**Booker, Peter**, Pvt., Co. K; d. 02/12/1847 Ft. Monroe, VA
**Boatright, Merrett W.**, Pvt., Co. I; d. 03/08/1847 at sea on board the transport ship *Sophia Walker*.
**Bowen, Jesse P.**, Pvt., Co. M; d. 04/28/1848 in Hosp. at Saltillo, Mex.
**Bowles, John**, Pvt., LIC; d. 05/03/1847 at China, Mex. of dysentery.
**Boykin, Joseph**, Pvt., Co. F; d. date unknown Matamoros, Mex.
**Brichett, Alexander E.**, Pvt., Co. E; d. 01/18/1847 Fort Monroe, VA
**Brown, James B.**, Pvt., LIC; d. 06/24/1847 at Monterey, Mex. of fever;
**Bryant, William**, Pvt., Co. K; d. 02/14/1847 at Ft. Monroe, VA
**Bush, Vance W.**, Pvt., Co. K; d. 09/20/1847 at Buena Vista, Mex.
**Choate, Jesse C.**, Pvt., Co. E; d. 04/05/1847, Matamoros, Mexico Hospital of diarrhea.
**Clifton, Andrew J.**, Pvt., *Preston's Co.*; . 08/21/1847 at Buena Vista, Mex., *"of Consumption."*
**Clingenpeel, Pleasant H.**, Pvt., *Preston's Co.*; d. 09/08/1847 in hosp. at Buena Vista, Mex.,
**Conrad, Henry K.**, Pvt., *Recruit Co.*, d. 05/22/1848 at Mill Creek Branch near Ft. Monroe, VA, *"whilst bathing. Was found two days after and buried."*
**Davis, James P.**, 3rd Cpl., *Preston's Co.*; d. 03/03/1847 at Ft. Monroe, VA, *"of smallpox."*
**Driscoll, John A.**, Pvt., Co. G; d. 09/23/1847 in Hosp. at Saltillo, Mex.
**Duffey, Andrew**, Pvt., Co. H; d. 07/10/1847, Monterey, Mex.
**Dyes, Alexander**, Pvt., Co. F; d. 02/28/1847 at sea on board the barque *Exact*.
**Erskine, Henry**, Capt., Regtl. Commissary, d. 09/26/1847, *"chronic diarrhea complicated with diabetes."*
**Fagunders, Jacob H.**, Pvt., Co. C; enl. Mex. War service 12/30/1846, Bowling Green, VA, age 22; d. 06/27/1847, Monterey, Mex., *"of Epilepsy."*
**Fairfax, Henry**, Capt., Co. L; d. 08/14/1847 Saltillo, Mex.
**Felts, John**, Pvt., Co. B; d. 09/24/1847 Regimental Hosp.
**Gallenar, Henry**, Pvt., Co. K; d. 04/20/1847 on route between China & Camargo, Mex.
**Gilmore, Charles**, Pvt., Co. F; d. 04/11/1847 *"lost when killed Pasa La Carta (Catta, Callo) while with the advance guard, supposed to have been killed by Mexicans."*
**Gray, Benjamin H.**, 3rd Cpl., Co. D; d. 08/20/1847 Buena Vista, Mex.
**Grove, Alexander**, Pvt., LIC; d. 06/23/1847 at Saltillo, Mex. of dropsy.
**Guthrow, William**, Pvt., Co. A; d. 04/12/1847 in Hosp. at Camargo, Mex.
**Harmon, Daniel**, Pvt., *Preston's Co.*; d. 05/26/1847 in hosp. at Monterey, Mex.
**Hays, John**, Pvt., Co. C; d. Camargo, Mex. 03/31/1847.
**Heninger, John K.**, Pvt., Co. B; d. 01/04/1847; Fort Morris.
**Holloway, Cornelius**, Pvt., Co. D; d. 03/22/1847 at Hosp. Port Isabel, Tex.
**Hurt, Moses**, Pvt., LIC, d. 03/17/1847 near Parras, Mex. *"assassinated by Mexicans."*
**Imboden, Benjamin F.**, 3rd Cpl., LIC; d. 09/19/1847 at Saltillo, Mex.
**Johns, Elhanan**, Pvt., Co. C; enl. Mex. War service 12/30/1846, Bowling Green, VA, age 36; d. 06/27/1847 Monterey, Mex., *"of Epilepsy."*

## OFF TO WAR

**Johnson, William H.**, Pvt., Co. M; d. 05/09/1848 at Saltillo, Mex.
**Joiner, William M.**, Pvt., Co. F;; d. 02/16/1847 Fort Monroe, VA;
**Kirk, William**, Pvt., Co. K; d. 02/14/1847 at Ft. Monroe, VA
**Klein, Charles H.**, Pvt., Co. H; d. 07/15/1847 in Hosp. Monterey, Mex.
**Krumbein, Henry**, Pvt., *Recruit Co.*, d. 02/17/1848 in hosp. at Ft. Monroe, VA
**Lambert, Henry**, Pvt., LIC; d. 08/16/1847 at Saltillo, Mex. of fever.
**Leard, Samuel**, Pvt., Co. G; d. 08/12/1847 Saltillo, Mex.
**Lindsey, Stephen**, Pvt., *Preston's Co.*; d. 02/28/1847 at Ft. Monroe, VA, *"died of small pox."*
**Linkous, William B.**, Pvt., *Preston's Co.*, d. 04/22/1847 in hosp. at China, Mex., *"of disease."*
**Long, Jacob**, Pvt., LIC; d. 03/29/1847 at Monterey, Mex. of diarrhea.
**Love, Hugh**, Pvt., Co. C; d. Monterey, Mex.
**Lundie, Thomas Y.**, Pvt., Co. D; d. 04/20/1848, Parras, Mex.
**Mahan, Washington L.**, 2$^{nd}$ Lt., Co. C; d. 06/01/1847 China, Mex. in a duel.
**Manson, John L.**, Pvt., *Preston's Co.*; d. 02/24/1848 at Buena Vista, Mex., *"of disease."*
**Marshall, Charles H.**, Pvt., Co. I; d. 08/10/1847 in Hosp. at Saltillo, Mex.
**McAllister, William T.**, Pvt., Co. G; d. 06/12/1847 in Hosp. Camargo, Mex.
**McCorkle, Alexander C.**, Pvt., Co. H; d. 06/091847 Monterey, Mex.
**McCrory, Thomas**, Pvt., Co. K; *"was assassinated by a Mexican."*
**McFarland, Samuel**, Pvt., Co. C; d. 06/04/1847 China. Mex.
**McNulty, Arthur**, Pvt., Co. G; d. 01/03/1847, *"drowned."*
**Mills, Mahlon**, Pvt., Co. L; d. 08/19/1847 Buena Vista, Mex.
**Mills, Robert**, Pvt., Co. L, d. 08/23/1847 Buena Vista, Mex.
**Moore, James E.**, Pvt., Co. F; d. 06/18/1847 Hosp. Saltillo, Mex.
**Moore, Silas**, 2$^{nd}$ Cpl., Co. B; d. 05/31/1847 China, Mex.
**Moss, James**, Pvt., Co. F; d. 03/02/1847 at sea on board the barque *Exact*.
**Muirhead, James W.**, Pvt., *Preston's Co.*; d. 08/17/1847 at Buena Vista, Mex., *"of consumption."*
**Munford, Carlton Radford**, 2$^{nd}$ Lt., Co. G; d. 1847 Mexico from wound received in a duel.
**Murray, James**, Pvt., Co. I; d. 07/03/1848, drowned at the mouth of the Rio Grande River.
**Peck, Israel**, Pvt., LIC; d. 03/17/1848 near Parras, Mex. *"assassinated by Mexicans."*
**Peel, Richard**, Pvt., Co. F; d. 02/07/1847 Fort Monroe, VA
**Phipps, Robert H.**, Pvt., Co. D; d. 07/21/1847 Buena Vista, Mex.
**Pollard, Peyton**, 1$^{st}$ Sgt., Co. E; d. New Orleans, La. 09/1847, bur. Petesrburg, VA
**Prather, Socrates**, Pvt., Co. H; d. 04/19/1847 at Ft. Monroe, VA
**Reamy, John T.**, Pvt., Co. H; d. 07/12/1847 Monterey, Mex.
**Robertson, James Berkeley**, Pvt., Co. E; d. 05/20/1847, Camargo, Mexico
**Rodgers, Nathaniel G.**, 4$^{th}$ Sgt., Co. F; d. 04/20/1847, Camargo, Mex.
**Salmon, Charles G.**, Pvt., Co. I; d. 08/15/1847 Saltillo, Mex.
**Sampson, William**, Pvt., Co. C; d. 06/1847, Matamoros, Mex.
**Shaw, Elias**, Pvt., Co. B; d. 09/05/1847 in hosp. Saltillo, Mex.,
**Simes, Miles**, Pvt., LIC; d. 06/28/1847 at Saltillo, Mex.;
**Spooner, Samuel J.**, Pvt., Co. A; d. 05/06/1847 in Hosp. at Matamoros, Mex.
**Spratt, John T.**, Pvt., Co. F; d. 04/06/1847 Point Isabel, Tex.
**Starr, John W.**, Pvt., *Preston's Co.*; d. 05/04/1847 in hosp. at Ft. Monroe, VA, *"Congestion of the brain."*
**Stephens, Richard H.**, Pvt., Co. H; d. 03/03/1847 at Ft. Monroe, VA
**Stuart, William W.**, Pvt., Co. D; d. 02/25/1847 at Fort Monroe, VA
**Sweeney, William B.**, Pvt., Co. I; d. 05/28/1847 in Hosp. at Monterey, Mex.
**Taliaferro, John R.**, Pvt., Co. C; d. 08/15/1847 hosp. Saltillo, Mex.,
**Terrell, Lewis K.**, Pvt., LIC; d. 08/20/1847 at Saltillo, Mex.
**Traylor, Richard B.**, Pvt., Co. E; d. 03/30/1848 Saltillo, Mex.

VIRGINIA VOLUNTEERS IN MEXICO

**Trott, Samuel**, Pvt., Co. L; d. 08/17/1847 Buena Vista, Mex.
**Trump, James N.**, Pvt., *Preston's Co.*; d. 03/17/1847 at Ft. Monroe, VA, *"of smallpox."*
**Turner, Francis L.**, Pvt., Co. C; d. 07/15/1847, supposed to have been killed by the Mexicans in Saltillo, Mex.,
**Waples, Isaac**, Pvt., Co. F; d. 06/17/1847 Hosp. Saltillo, Mex.
**Waterman, James A.**, Pvt., Co. M; d. 09/09/1847 at Ft. Monroe, VA
**Waters, Benjamin Garretson**, 2nd Lt., Co. B; d. 04/15/1847 China, Mex.;
**Weeks, James**, Pvt., *Preston's Co.*; d. 02/21/1847 in hosp. at Ft. Monroe, VA
**West, Charles**, Pvt., Co. L; d. 08/06/1847 Buena Vista, Mex.
**Woodruff, Hiram**, Pvt., Co. G; d. 07/29/1847 in Hosp. Buena Vista, Mex.
**Yopp, William**, Pvt., *Preston's Co.*; d. 03/10/1847 on board transport ship *Sophia Walker*, *"off the Island of Cuba.*

# Index

## A

**Abbott**
Sarah .................................................. 122
**Abercrombie**
Elizabeth ............................................ 297
**Abington**
Mary B. .............................................. 123
**Acree**
Edward H. ........................................... 50
**Acton**
John ..................................................... 50
**Adams**
Alice ..................................................... 50
Alice J. ................................................. 50
Bartlett P. ............................................. 50
David .................................................... 50
Elizabeth .............................................. 50
Harriet .................................................. 50
Hyphasia .............................................. 50
Joseph C. .............................................. 50
Mary A. ................................................ 50
Mollie ................................................... 50
Sarah E. ................................................ 50
St. Lawrence ........................................ 50
William T. ............................................ 82
**Ahlt**
Elizabeth A. ....................................... 273
Thomas A. ......................................... 273
**Aiken**
James H. .............................................. 50
Josepha A. ............................................ 51
Josepha Allevia .................................... 51

**Akers**
Aicha Lu ............................................. 51
Bailey R. .............................................. 51
David G. .............................................. 51
Eliza ..................................................... 51
Furley Mary ........................................ 51
General Wade ..................................... 51
H.W. .................................................... 51
Harry .................................................... 51
James .................................................... 51
Julia ..................................................... 51
Julia Ann ............................................. 51
Laura J. ................................................ 51
Liza ...................................................... 51
Lou Emma ........................................... 51
Narcissa ............................................. 274
Ruth ................................................... 274
Wyatt ..................... 51, 52, 104, 149
**Akin**
Edward ................................................ 51
**Alabama** .................................. 151, 202
Etowah Co., Gadsden ....................... 104
Jefferson Co., Birmingham ............... 301
Madison Co., Huntsville .................. 104
Mobile .................................................. 85
Mobile Co., Mobile .......................... 301
Montgomery Co. ............................... 237
Pickens Co. ....................................... 301
Richmond ......................................... 301
Selma ......................................... 136, 301
Tuscaloosa ................................. 136, 301
Tuskeege ........................................... 191
**Alabama - Cavalry**

321

51st Regt., Co. E .............................. 136
**Alabama - Infantry**
   13th Regt. ...................................... 191
   30th Regt., Co. E ............................ 128
**Albertson**
   Harvey............................................... 51
**Alburtis**
   Alburtis.............................................. 52
   Amelia............................................... 52
   Ephraim G. ....................... 97, 139, 209
   Ephraim Gaither ............................... 52
   Ephraim Gathier .............................. 264
   James L. ............................................ 52
   Jane R................................................ 52
   Josina ................................................ 52
   Mary C. .............................................. 52
   Mary L. .............................................. 52
   Nancy ................................................ 52
   Rosa .......................................... 52, 210
**Aldridge**
   Asa H. ............................................... 52
   Ballis ................................................. 52
   Gertrude ........................................... 52
   Isaac M. ............................................ 52
   Joanna .............................................. 52
   John H.C. .......................................... 52
   Laura ................................................. 52
   Letitia A. ........................................... 52
   Lucy J. .............................................. 52
   Mary C. .............................................. 52
   Octavia .............................................. 52
   William M. ........................................ 52
**Alexander**
   Elizabeth........................................... 53
   Florence K. ....................................... 52
   George .............................................. 52
   George A. .......................................... 53
   George W. ......................................... 52
   James................................................ 53
   Margaret ........................................... 52
   Virginia ............................................. 53
**Allen**
   Alcinda .............................................. 55
   Eliza .................................................. 55
   Eliza Ann Eppes ............................... 57
   Eliza M. ............................................. 55
   Elizabeth......................................... 317

Elizabeth V. ....................................... 55
Frances ............................................. 55
George H. ......................................... 55
George W. ......................................... 55
James W. .......................................... 55
Lucy .................................................. 55
Lucy Ann (Coyner)............................ 55
Margaret E. ....................................... 55
Martha Jane ..................................... 55
Mary J. .............................................. 55
Mary Jane ........................................ 55
Richard Farrar .................................. 55
Sarah J. ............................................ 55
William.............................................. 56
William A. ......................................... 55
**Alley**
   E.J. .................................................... 56
   L.E. ................................................... 56
   Mary B. ............................................. 56
   Nancy ............................................... 56
   Thomas............................................. 56
   William E. ................ 56, 165, 239, 306
**Allison**
   Maria E.......................................... 192
**Anderton**
   Eliza V. ............................................. 56
   Isaac A. ............................................ 56
   W.A. .................................................. 56
**Andrews**
   Elizabeth B. ................................... 165
   Ida Fowlkes ................................... 137
   John W. ............................................ 56
**Arbogast**
   Ann E. ............................................... 57
   Francis.............................................. 57
   George .............................................. 57
   John .................................................. 57
   Margaret ........................................... 57
   Michael............................................. 57
   Nicodemus....................................... 56
   Shiloerah .......................................... 57
   Thomas J. ........................................ 57
   Watson ............................................. 57
**Archer**
   Allen ................................................. 57
   Edwin C. ........................................... 57
   Eliza Ann Eppes ............................... 57

## VIRGINIA VOLUNTEERS IN MEXICO

Fletcher H. ........................................ 306
Fletcher Harris ..................... 57, 58, 277
Marietta ............................................. 59
Martha Georgiana Morton .................. 57
Mary (Marshall) ................................ 57
Prudence (Whitworth) ........................ 57
William B. .................. 57, 59, 238, 302
**Argabright**
John ............................................ 56, 98
**Arizona**
Fort Mojave ..................................... 104
**Arkansas** ........................... 122, 135, 304
    Argenta ............................................ 231
    Benton Co., Maysville ..................... 225
    Fort Smith ....................................... 132
    Independence Co., Newark .............. 305
    Jackson Co., Newport ..................... 305
    Oachita Co., Camden ...................... 122
    Pike Co., Wilson ............................. 121
    Randolph Co., Maynard .................. 310
    Randolph Co., Middlebrook ............ 310
    Randolph Co., Pocahontas ................. 86
    Randolph Co., Supply ..................... 310
    Smithville ....................................... 181
**Arkansas - Cavalry**
    Capt. Mears Co. .............................. 122
**Arkansas - Infantry**
    27th Regt., Co. D ............................ 121
    3rd Regt. .......................................... 181
**Armstrong**
    Margaret Elizabeth .......................... 202
    Richard ............................................. 60
**Ashby**
    Ann (Menefee) .................................. 60
    Elizabeth Smith (Gregory) ................ 60
    General Turner .................................. 60
    Thomson ........................................... 60
    Turner Wade ..................................... 60
**Ashley**
    Elizabeth A. ...................................... 78
**Ashton**
    Gurdon C. ......................................... 60
    Helen A. (Harrison) .......................... 60
**Ashworth**
    Anderson .......................................... 60
    Ann E. .............................................. 60
    Ann S. .............................................. 61

Ann Udora ......................................... 60
Charlie Sim ........................................ 60
Dura S. ............................................... 61
Eddie Lee ........................................... 60
Ellen ................................................... 61
Ellie May ........................................... 60
Eula Spergeon .................................... 60
George Gordon ................................... 60
Ida Jackson ........................................ 60
Isabella B. .......................................... 61
John P. ............................................... 60
Laura Wooten .................................... 60
Louisa ................................................ 60
Marshall Pegram ................................ 60
Martha A. ........................................... 60
Martha Ann ........................................ 60
Mavis F. ............................................. 61
Parker Anderson ................................. 60
Parks E. ...................................... 61, 189
Parks Edward ..................................... 60
Permelia A. ........................................ 60
Susan .................................................. 60
William A. ......................................... 60
William W. ........................................ 61
**Astrop**
    Robert F. ........................................... 61
**Atherton**
    John .................................................. 61
**August**
    Thomas P. ................. 85, 128, 185, 264
    Thomas Pearson .................. 61, 96, 270
**Austin**
    Alexander ......................................... 61
    Augustus L. ....................................... 61
    Charlotte ......................................... 109
    Elizabeth ........................................... 61
    Gemima ............................................ 62
    James P. ............................................ 62
    Mary E. ............................................. 62
    Nancy Elizabeth ............................... 62
    Permelia J. ........................................ 62
    Qctavia Ann ..................................... 62
    Robert ............................................... 62
    Sarah A. ............................................ 62
    William T. ........................................ 62
**Australia** ............................................ 192
**Austria** ............................................... 128

**Avis**
Ardelia ............................................... 62
Braxton D. ......................................... 62
Clegit ................................................. 62
Imogene ............................................. 62
James L. ............................................. 62
John ................................... 62, 142, 256
John L. ............................................... 62
Maggie ............................................... 62
Mary .................................................. 62
Walter ................................................ 62
**Ayers**
William .............................................. 62
**Aylett**
Mary Macon .................................... 134

# B

**Baber**
Emma L. .......................................... 145
**Bacon**
Gillee M. ........................................... 62
Inez .................................................... 62
Mary A. ............................................. 62
Waddy S. ........................................... 62
**Bagwell**
Sallie ................................................ 134
**Bailey**
Ann E. ................................................ 68
Eliza Jane .......................................... 63
Elizabeth J. ........................................ 63
Emily ............................................... 137
Joanna A. ......................................... 300
John G. .............................................. 63
John H. .............................................. 63
Nancy A. ......................................... 232
Permelia A. ....................................... 60
Richard A. ......................................... 63
Richard B.H. ..................................... 63
Willie ............................................... 137
**Bain**
Anna W. ............................................. 64
Charles ............................................... 64
Edward G. .......................................... 64
Elizabeth F. ...................................... 236
Frances M. ......................................... 64
George ............................................... 64
George A. (Rev.) ............................... 64

George Spillman ............................... 64
James H.H. ........................................ 64
Julia G. ............................................ 236
Thomas .............................................. 64
**Baker**
Ann F. ................................................ 64
Charles A. .......................................... 64
George W. .......................................... 64
Jackson .............................................. 64
James H. ............................................ 64
Mattie ................................................ 64
William A. ......................................... 65
**Baldwin**
James B. ............................................ 65
Rebecca Alice ................................. 249
**Ball**
Charles H. .......................................... 65
George C. ........................................... 65
Harriet ............................................... 65
James B. ............................................ 65
Jane S. ............................................. 162
Kate N. .............................................. 65
Lewis D. ............................................ 65
Malvania ............................................ 65
Martha T. ......................................... 180
Mary E. .............................................. 65
Sinah ........................................ 291, 292
Thomas C. ......................................... 66
**Ballenger**
Clemmentine ................................... 149
**Ballinger**
Ann .................................................... 66
Ann E. (Gregg) .................................. 66
James W. ........................................... 66
John ................................................... 66
Sarah A. ............................................. 66
**Ballow**
Isabella .............................................. 66
James T. ............................................. 66
Lavinia ............................................... 66
Mary A. ............................................. 66
Othello ............................................... 66
Victoria .............................................. 66
**Baltimore**
Baltimore Co., Baltimore ................ 140
**Bangs**
Adelphia ............................................ 66

## VIRGINIA VOLUNTEERS IN MEXICO

John W. ............................................... 66
**Bankhead**
   Adeline ............................................... 66
   Anne (Pyne) ........................................ 66
   Henry Clay .......................................... 66
   James Monroe .................................... 66
   John Pyne ............................................ 66
   Mary Stuart ....................................... 143
   Smith Pyne ................................. 66, 274
**Banks**
   Albert A. ............................................. 66
   Emma .................................................. 67
**Bare**
   Mary Ellen ........................................ 168
**Barker**
   Atheriah ............................................ 305
   James W. ............................................. 67
   William ................................................ 67
**Barksdale**
   Alice Sydnor .................................... 304
   Martha Georgiana Morton ................. 57
**Barnard**
   Abby S. ............................................... 68
   Caroline M.F. ..................................... 67
   George S. ............................................ 67
   John B.F. ............................................. 67
   Matilda F. .......................................... 148
**Barnes**
   Ann E. ................................................. 68
   Henrietta ............................................. 68
   James H. ............................................. 68
   John .................................................... 68
**Barnett**
   Anderson M. ..................... 68, 175, 176
   Ann ..................................................... 68
   Betty ................................................... 69
   Celinda A. ......................................... 198
   Eliz (Linkinhoker) .............................. 68
   Elizabeth ............................................. 68
   Emma J. .............................................. 68
   George E. ........................................... 69
   James F. .............................................. 69
   Joseph ................................................. 69
   Mary .................................................... 68
   Mary W. ........................................... 120
   Olivia .................................................. 68
   Robert ................................................. 68

Thomas R. ........................................... 68
William ................................................ 69
**Barnhardt**
   Mary ................................................. 182
**Barr**
   Araminta B. ........................................ 69
   Bettie .................................................. 69
   Charles ................................................ 69
   Cornelius B. ........................................ 69
   Henry .................................................. 69
   Ida ....................................................... 69
   John W. ............................................... 69
   Kate ..................................................... 69
   Mary Frances ..................................... 69
   Minnie ................................................ 69
   Robert ................................................. 69
**Barrett**
   George F. ............................................ 69
**Barringer**
   Anna Laura ........................................ 69
   Araminta ............................................ 69
   Arbilla ................................................ 69
   Dorthea M. ......................................... 69
   Jacob ................................................... 69
   John A. ............................................... 69
   Mary .................................................... 69
   Morilla Green (Jett) ........................... 69
   Sabra Ann ........................................... 69
   Sarah A. .............................................. 69
   Triphena ............................................. 69
   Virginia .............................................. 69
   William ............................................... 69
**Barrott**
   Belinda ............................................. 101
**Barry**
   Robert ................................................. 69
**Barteto**
   Emily ................................................ 216
**Barton**
   Malinda ........................................... 268
**Barziza**
   Edgar A. ............................................. 70
**Bateman**
   Ann ..................................................... 70
   James .................................................. 70
   James W. ............................................ 70
   Julian .................................................. 70

Stephen ............... 70
**Bates**
   Emma ............... 98
**Battaile**
   Lawrence ............... 70
   Meade ............... 306
**Beadles**
   Lewis J. ............... 70
**Beale**
   Harriet H. ............... 158
**Beales**
   John A. ............... 70
**Beam**
   Emanuel ............... 70
**Beatty**
   Ann Frances (Furrow) ............... 70
   Samuel J. ............... 70
**Beazley**
   Bettie A. ............... 102
**Beck**
   Alexander ............... 71
   Andrew D.S. ............... 71
   Ann M.E. ............... 154
   Anna A.V. ............... 71
   Elizabeth ............... 70, 71
   Jacob ............... 70
   John S.B. ............... 71
   Lilley ............... 71
   Matilda V. ............... 286
   Rose ............... 71
   Sarah (Summers) ............... 70
   William ............... 71
**Becker**
   Annie ............... 258
   Bessie ............... 258
   Flora ............... 258
   Joseph ............... 258
   Mary A. ............... 258
   Valentine ............... 258
**Bell**
   Bethany Jane ............... 111
   Julia Ann ............... 258
   Mary Jane ............... 241
   Sarah Jarvis ............... 232
**Belt**
   John C. ............... 71
**Bennett**
   Anderson ............... 71
   David M. ............... 71
   Edward ............... 71
   George McD. ............... 71
   John A. ............... 71
   Martha ............... 230
   Martha J. ............... 71
   Nancy Ann (McDonald) ............... 71
   Prudence ............... 71
   William G. ............... 71
   William H. ............... 71
**Benson**
   Francis L. ... 71, 110, 145, 184, 241, 250
   James ............... 71
   Mary A. ............... 71
**Benter**
   John ............... 286
   Susanna ............... 286
**Bentley**
   Hartwell ............... 72
   J.R.K. ............... 286
**Benton**
   Jesse ............... 72
**Bergman**
   Friderika Carolina Louisa ............... 254
**Berkeley**
   Edmund ............... 55
**Berry**
   Elizabeth ............... 72
   Elizabeth (Silmone) ............... 72
   Margaret ............... 72
   Thomas ............... 72
**Beverage**
   Susan ............... 83
**Beverley**
   Elizabeth ............... 107
**Bewley**
   Catherine A. ............... 318
**Bibb**
   Private ............... 207
**Bibey**
   James B. ............... 72
   Mary ............... 72
**Bickle**
   Margaret L. ............... 235
   Mary Adeline ............... 231
   William O. ............... 72, 163, 182, 249
**Bilson**
   Andrew J. ............... 72

Lucy Jane............................................ 72
Virginia M. ........................................ 72
**Bilvens**
Charles A........................................ 309
**Binford**
Hettie................................................ 73
John G. ............................................ 72
Kate.................................................. 73
Lucy W............................................. 73
Nettie................................................ 73
Thomas............................................ 72
Thomas H. ....................................... 73
**Bird**
Mary Ann ...................................... 173
**Birkitt**
Margaret Ann................................... 73
William............................................ 73
**Birtnett**
_____.......................................... 235
Margaret L..................................... 235
**Bishop**
Anna G. ........................................... 73
Charles ............................. 73, 86, 214
Fanny (McGoath) ............................ 73
Hattie.............................................. 118
Isabella ............................................ 73
James A. .......................................... 73
James H. ........................ 73, 152, 253
Joseph.............................................. 73
Joseph M., Jr.................................... 73
Minerva P. ..................................... 234
Peter B............................................. 73
Sarah B. ........................................... 73
Sarah F.T. ........................................ 73
Shedrack .......................................... 73
Thomas F......................................... 73
William............................................ 73
**Black**
Alexander ........................................ 74
Charles W........................................ 74
Columbia Caroline......................... 292
Elizabeth.......................................... 74
Elizabeth (McDonald)...................... 74
Harvey ....................................... 74, 80
Kent ................................................. 74
Mary.............................................. 188
Mary J. (Kent).................................. 74

Thomas C. ....................................... 74
William A. ....................................... 74
**Blackaby**
John.................................................. 74
**Blackard**
Joel................................................... 74
**Blackburn**
Albert B........................................... 75
Alice V. ........................................... 75
Augusta ........................................... 75
John H. ............................................ 75
Mary A. ................................... 75, 225
Mary E............................................. 75
Thomas............................................ 75
Thomas R. ....................................... 75
William Allen .................................. 75
**Blackwell**
Nancy............................................ 166
**Blair**
Martha .......................................... 274
Robert............................................ 289
**Blake**
Callie................................................ 98
**Blakney**
George W. ....................................... 75
**Blamire**
Edward ............................................ 75
Edward Thurston ....... 75, 153, 207, 220
Elizabeth.......................................... 75
Jarvis................................................ 75
Kate.................................................. 75
Lucretia F. (Browne) ....................... 75
**Bland**
Louise Christine ............................ 304
**Blaylock**
Lucy Jane...................................... 274
**Blessing**
John H. ............................................ 75
Susan................................................ 75
**Bliss**
William Wallace Smith Bliss........... 59
**Blivens**
Alfred ............................................ 308
Sarah Matilda................................. 308
**Blondell**
Abner ............................................... 76
Benjamin W..................................... 75
Ezra ................................................. 76

Freeman W. .................................. 76
Josephine ..................................... 76
Mary E. ......................................... 76
Sarah ............................................ 76
Theodore A. .................................. 75
**Bloxham**
Georgia B. (Veitch) ..................... 76
Mary ............................................. 76
Polly .............................................. 76
William Preston ............................ 76
**Boatright**
Merrett W. ..................................... 79
**Bodeker**
Ann ............................................... 78
Augustus ....................................... 78
Charles .................................... 76, 78
Pearl .............................................. 78
Ruby .............................................. 78
**Bohannan**
Abner J. ......................................... 78
George ........................................... 78
Mary .............................................. 78
**Bolling**
Lucy ............................................ 247
**Bolton**
Margaret ..................................... 191
**Bonner**
Elizabeth A. .................................. 78
James C.N. .................................... 78
**Booker**
Mary Ann .................................. 186
Peter .............................................. 78
William T. ..................................... 79
**Boone**
Charlotte .................................... 221
**Booth**
Capt. J.C. ...................................... 69
**Boothe**
Zerah ............................................ 79
**Boswell**
Chaney .......................................... 79
Henry Harrison ............................. 79
John Louis .................................... 79
Lucy Seawell ................................ 79
Mary Armistead ........................... 79
Nancy Ravenscroft ....................... 79
Thomas Taylor ............................. 79

William .......................................... 79
William C. ..................................... 79
**Bowen**
Abraham ....................................... 79
Agnes B. ....................................... 79
Benjamin W. ................................. 79
Harriet L. ...................................... 79
Hester ........................................... 79
Jesse P. ......................................... 79
John T. .......................................... 79
Mary C. ........................................ 79
Noah D. ........................................ 79
Sarah F. ........................................ 79
William C. .................................... 79
**Bowers**
Elizabeth M. ................................. 79
Mary A. ...................................... 227
Moriah L. ..................................... 79
Patterson ...................................... 79
Samuel .......................................... 80
Sarah F.T.) .................................... 73
**Bowles**
Caleb ............................................ 80
John .............................................. 80
Judy A. ......................................... 80
Martha A. ..................................... 80
Mary Elizabeth (Burkett) ............. 81
Nancy ........................................... 80
Peter ............................................. 80
Robert ........................................... 80
William Thomas ........................... 80
**Bowyer**
John P. .......................................... 81
Michael ........................................ 81
**Boyd**
Mathias ...................................... 189
**Boyer**
Silas ............................................. 81
William H. ................................... 54
**Boykin**
Joseph .......................................... 81
**Bozel**
Emily P. ..................................... 103
**Bradford**
Benjamin Hellenius ..................... 81
Col. Benjamin R. ......................... 81
Hellen W. (Edmonds) .................. 81

## VIRGINIA VOLUNTEERS IN MEXICO

**Bradley**
  Elizabeth F. (Clay).............................. 81
  Jesse P. .............................................. 81
  Michael............................................... 81
  Philip A. ............................................. 81
  Susan A. ........................................... 222
**Bragg**
  William F............................................ 82
**Bramblett**
  McHenry ............................................ 82
**Brazil**
  Rio de Janerio ................................. 265
**Breeden**
  Bartlett............................................... 82
  Catherine A........................................ 82
**Brevitt**
  Joseph P............................................ 82
**Brichett**
  Alexander E. ...................................... 83
**Bridges**
  Morgan M........................................... 83
  Susan................................................. 83
  Susannah .......................................... 83
**Bridgewater**
  Charles .............................................. 83
**Brigedine**
  John................................................... 83
**Briggs**
  Charlotte Ashmore (Keith) ................ 83
  James McDonald ............................... 83
  William Sheridan................................ 83
**Brigham**
  James S.A. ........................................ 83
**Britt**
  Elizabeth Ann .................................... 83
  George W. ......................................... 83
  James................................................. 83
  John................................................... 83
  Martha .......................................... 83, 84
  Mary................................................... 83
  Rebecca ............................................ 84
  Sally................................................... 83
  Sarah ................................................. 83
  William H. .................................. 83, 138
**Brittle**
  William............................................... 84
**Broaddus**
  Amanda ........................................... 155

**Brock**
  Abraham Edwin ................................. 84
  Amanda ............................................. 84
  Archibald............................................ 84
  Arezona F.V....................................... 84
  Caroline............................................. 84
  Caroline Amanda............................... 84
  Carrie L.............................................. 84
  Charles .............................................. 84
  Charles A........................................... 84
  Edna Dakota ..................................... 84
  Hugh Willie Lincoln ........................... 84
  John................................................... 84
  John P................................................ 84
  Rebecca ............................................ 84
  Rebecca A.C. .................................... 84
  Sallie Ariminta Nannie....................... 84
  Sally................................................... 84
  Sarah ................................................. 84
**Brooks**
  John................................................... 84
**Bross**
  Mary................................................. 240
**Brown**
  Abigail C. (Rash)............................... 84
  Alexander L. ...................................... 84
  Andrew............................................... 84
  Anna................................................... 86
  Anna J. .............................................. 84
  Blanche.............................................. 86
  Charles B........................................... 85
  Charles H........................................... 85
  Charles J............................................ 85
  Clarinda............................................. 85
  Edward .............................................. 86
  Emma I. ............................................. 84
  Hortense ............................................ 85
  James B............................................. 85
  James W. ........................................... 85
  Jane E.L. (Jackson)........................... 85
  John............................................. 62, 86
  John................................................. 258
  John G. .............................................. 86
  Joseph............................................... 86
  Lettie ................................................ 258
  Mary A. ............................................ 258
  Mary Ann ......................................... 306

Mary E. .............................................. 84
Mary H. (Rash) ................................ 84
Mary J. .............................................. 85
Matilda C. ......................................... 106
Peter A. ............................................. 86
Philip ................................................. 85
Preston .............................................. 86
Richard ............................................. 85
Robert A. .......................................... 84
Sallie A. ............................................ 84
Samuel .............................................. 86
Sarah H. ............................................ 85
Thomas A. ........................................ 258
Tudor ................................................. 85
William C. ........................................ 86
William J. ......................................... 86
William W. ....................................... 85
**Browne**
Lucretia F. ........................................ 75
**Browning**
Margaret Augusta ............................ 201
**Bruce**
Artemecia (Fox) ............................... 87
Landon H. ......................................... 87
Mariah ............................................... 87
Martha ............................................... 87
Reuben .............................................. 87
Winfied Scott ................................... 87
**Brumfield**
Saphronia A.H. ................................ 177
**Bryan**
Anne Aurelia .................................... 87
D'Arcy Pattison ................................ 87
Emily ................................................. 87
Emily Sherwood ............................... 87
Frank Otis ......................................... 87
Guy Lee ............................................ 87
James ................................................. 87
James Lawrenson ..................... 87, 314
Julian L. ............................................ 87
Lay .................................................... 87
Mary Virginia .................................. 87
Nora ................................................... 87
William Lewis Herndon .................. 87
**Bryant**
Henry W. .......................................... 278
Richard ............................................. 87

William ............................................. 88
**Buchannan**
Milo ........................................... 88, 96
**Bullard**
Ellen .................................................. 88
James ................................................. 88
Lucy .................................................. 88
Lucy L. ............................................. 88
Mary ................................................. 88
Reuben .............................................. 88
**Bullitt**
Anna Eliza ....................................... 134
Harriet .............................................. 134
**Bunkley**
Elizabeth ........................................... 156
**Burdine**
Francisco .......................................... 88
John ................................................... 88
**Burke**
\_\_\_\_ (Lee) ....................................... 88
Abdon Lee ........................................ 88
Adolohus T. ...................................... 88
Anna Eliza (Shrader) ....................... 88
Ethelbert ............................................ 88
Jane (Crafton) ................................... 88
William H. ........................................ 88
**Burkett**
Lulu North ........................................ 81
Mary Elizabeth ................................. 81
**Burks**
William A. .................................. 63, 88
**Burnett**
Richard C. ......................................... 89
**Burns**
Harman T. ......................................... 89
**Burruss**
John S. .............................................. 89
**Burt**
Ann H. .............................................. 164
**Burton**
William ............................................. 89
**Burwell**
Mary Armistead ............................... 79
**Bush**
Vance W. .......................................... 89
**Butcher,** ............................................ 50
**Butt**
James W. .................................... 89, 221

**Butts**
　Harriet A.M. .................................... 106
**Byrnes**
　John ................................................. 89

## C

**Cabell**
　Annie W. ........................................... 89
　Charles G. ......................................... 89
　Ellen C. ............................................. 89
　Henry L. ............................................ 89
　Sallie ................................................. 89
　Samuel J. .......................................... 89
**Caddis**
　Henry ................................................ 89
　Mary (Putt) ....................................... 89
**Cain**
　Benjamin .......................................... 90
　Frances A. ......................................... 90
　Jane Maria ........................................ 90
　Nathaniel D. ...................................... 90
　Nicholas R. ....................................... 90
　Virginia Sarah ................................... 90
　William Coulson ............................... 90
**Calhoun**
　John .................................................. 90
**California** ... 63, 151, 181, 192, 231, 232, 265
　California 49er ... 66, 94, 107, 142, 147, 191, 265, 292, 302
　Contra Costa Co., Stewartsville ........ 256
　Los Angeles ..................................... 305
　Los Angeles Co., Inglewood ............ 225
　Los Angeles Co., Los Angeles, National Soldiers Home ............................. 281
　Los Angeles Co., National Soldiers Home ................................................. 105
　Los Angeles Co., Santa Ana ............... 79
　Merced Co., Merced ........................ 232
　Sacramento ........................................ 51
　San Benito Co., Hollister .................... 99
　San Benito Co., Paicines .................... 99
　San Bernadino Co., Redlands ........... 199
　San Bernadino Co., San Bernadino ... 104
　San Diego Co., Encinitas .................. 290
　San Diego Co., Laguna .................... 203
　San Francisco .................................. 232
　Sonoma Co., Santa Rosa .................. 232
　Tuolumne Co., Jamestown ............... 265
**California - Infantry**
　3rd Regt. .......................................... 244
　4th Regt., Co. I ................................ 104
　8$^{th}$ Regt., Co. B ................................. 65
**Callaghan**
　Thomas .............................................. 90
**Callis**
　Bailey ................................................ 90
**Campbell**
　Ellen ................................................ 149
　George .............................................. 90
　Hannah M. ........................................ 91
　Lewis ................................................. 90
**Canada** ......................................... 60, 216
**Cantor**
　Sydney S. .......................................... 91
**Caperton**
　Sarah Ann ....................................... 245
**Cardwell**
　Cetia .................................................. 92
　Charles .............................................. 92
　James ................................................ 91
　James H. ........................................... 91
　John W. ............................................. 91
　Julia L. .............................................. 91
　Lucy A. ............................................. 91
　Marcellus .......................................... 92
　Mary L. ............................................. 92
　Robert Lee ........................................ 92
　Thomas W. ....................................... 91
**Cargill**
　Nathaniel E. ...................................... 92
**Carlin**
　Cornelius ........................................... 92
　Lucelia ............................................ 223
**Carmichael**
　Andrew ............................................. 92
**Carney**
　George W. ......................................... 92
　Noah .................................................. 92
**Carpenter** ......................................... 50
　Fayette D. ......................................... 92
　Laurett V. ........................................ 232
　Lucy Ann ........................................ 232
**Carr**

Hampton ............................................. 92
**Carrington**
   Edward C. ........................................ 92
   Edward Codrington, Jr. ..................... 92
   Eliza Henry (Preston) ........................ 92
   James McDowell .............................. 92
   Maria Antoinette (Swope) ................. 92
**Carroll**
   Franklin ............................................ 92
   Lydia Jane ...................................... 154
   Melvina ............................................ 93
   William K ......................................... 93
**Carter**
   Alexander ........................................ 93
   Catherine A. ..................................... 93
   Charles E. ......................................... 94
   Eliza ................................................. 94
   Emma L. ........................................... 94
   James J. ........................................... 93
   John E .............................................. 93
   John W. ............................................ 93
   Joseph LaFayette ............................. 93
   Margaret .......................................... 93
   Mary ................................................. 94
   Richard ............................................ 93
   Richard A. ........................................ 94
   Sarah A. ......................................... 255
   William J. ......................................... 94
   Zachariah ......................................... 94
**Cary**
   Elizabeth ........................................ 128
**Cassaday**
   John N. ............................................ 94
**Castinada**
   Casimiro ........................................ 282
   Pablo ............................................. 282
**Castle**
   Elizabeth A. ................................... 273
**Castleman**
   Alfred ............................................... 94
   Lucinda (Milton) ............................... 94
   Nathaniel Green ............................... 94
**Caterson**
   James ............................................. 94
**Cave**
   Cremora Conway .......................... 192
**Cawood**

Charles H. .......................................... 94
**Cemeteries - Alabama**
   Live Oak Cemetery, Selma .............. 136
**Cemeteries - Arkansas**
   Macedonia Cemetery, Newark ......... 305
   Maysville, Benton Co. ..................... 225
**Cemeteries - California**
   Fairhaven Memorial Park, Santa Ana .. 80
   Hollywood Memorial Park Cemetery,
      Hollywood .................................... 257
**Cemeteries - Delaware**
   Riverview Cemetery, Wilmington ....... 69
**Cemeteries – Delaware**
   Wilmington and Brandywine Cemetery,
      Wilmington .................................. 176
**Cemeteries - Georgia**
   Oakland Cemetery, Atlanta .............. 186
**Cemeteries – Illinois**
   Walnut Corner Cemetery, Vermilion. 115
**Cemeteries - Indiana**
   Beech Grove Cemetery, Muncie ....... 182
   Crown Hill Cemetery, Indianapolis ..... 50
   Green Lawn Cemetery, Indianapolis ... 50
   South Bend City Cemetery, South Bend
      .................................................... 204
**Cemeteries - Iowa**
   Leon Cemetery, Leon ...................... 149
   Zion Reform Church Cemetery, Cascade
      .................................................... 247
**Cemeteries - Kansas**
   Leavenworth National Cemetery,
      Leavenworth ............................... 149
**Cemeteries – Kentucky**
   Eastern Cemetery, Louisville ............ 291
**Cemeteries - Louisiana**
   American Cemetery, Natchitoches .... 200
**Cemeteries - Maryland**
   Cedar Hill, Prince Georges Co. ......... 194
   Green Mount Cemetery, Baltimore ..... 72
   Loudoun Park Cemetery, Baltimore .. 293
   Presbyterian Cemetery, Darnestown . 303
   Woodlawn Cemetery, Baltimore ......... 79
**Cemeteries - Massachusetts**
   Cavalry Cemetery, Woburn .............. 138
**Cemeteries - Missouri**
   Bellfountaine, St. Louis ................... 194
   High Prarie Cemetery, Elmo ............. 198
   St. Matthew's Cemetery, St. Louis ...... 86

St. Peter's Cemetery, St. Louis ........... 85
**Cemeteries - New Jersey**
   Bloomfield Cemetery, Bloomfield .... 197
**Cemeteries - New York**
   Greenbush Cemetery,Rensselaer ......... 68
**Cemeteries - North Carolina**
   Woodhouse Cemetery, Grandy, Currituck Co. ............................................. 241
**Cemeteries – North Carolina**
   Elmwood Cemetery, Charlotte .......... 138
   Elmwood Cemetery, Henderson ....... 148
**Cemeteries - Ohio**
   Blanchester I.O.O.F, Blanchester ...... 149
   Camp Chase Cemetery, Columbus .... 184
   Dayton National Cemetery .................. 99
   Dayton National Cemetery, Dayton ... 82, 202, 245
**Cemeteries - Oklahoma**
   Rose Hill Cemetery, Ardmore ............. 98
**Cemeteries - Pennsylvania**
   Mt. Moriah Cemetery, Philadelphia .. 252
   Odd Fellow Cemetery, Philadelphia .. 150
   Woodlands Cemetery, Philadelphia .. 301
**Cemeteries - Tennessee**
   Elmwood Cemetery, Memphis ... 66, 137
**Cemeteries - Texas**
   Albany Cemetery, Albany ................. 255
   Cleburne Cemetery, Cleburne ............ 130
   Fairview Cemetery, Bastrop .............. 211
   Long View Cemetery, Big Foot .......... 82
   Magnolia Cemetery, Beaumont ........ 134
**Cemeteries - Virginia**
   Arlington National Cemetery, Arlington ................................................. 220
   Austin Family, Campbell Co. .............. 62
   Baca? Cemetery, Spotsylvania Co. ... 271
   Bacon Family, Giles Co. ..................... 63
   Barringer Cemetery, Burk's Fork, Floyd Co. ............................................... 69
   Bethel Bapt. Ch. Cemetery, Great Falls ................................................. 318
   Bethel Cemetery, Wytheville ............ 148
   Bethel Presb. Ch. Cemetery, Staunton 218
   Bethlem Lutheren Church Cemetery ... 75
   Blandford Cemetery, Petersburg .. 50, 56, 57, 64, 90, 94, 102, 117, 118, 121, 140, 156, 164, 165, 167, 183, 187, 196, 200, 202, 204, 211, 215, 226,
229, 236, 237, 239, 240, 243, 266, 267, 272, 293, 296, 304, 306, 310
   Cedar Grove Cemetery, Portsmouth ... 71, 75, 110
   Cedar Hill Cemetery, Suffolk ........... 232
   Christ Church Cemetery, Alexandria. 223
   Crockett Section, Wythe Co. ............. 158
   Ebenezer Baptist Church Cemetery, Bloomfield ................................. 154
   Ebenezer Cemetery, Round Hill ....... 245
   Elmwood Cemetery, Norfolk ............ 281
   Falls Church Epis. Cemetery, Falls Church ........................................ 128
   Finney Cemetery, Blackberry ........... 183
   First Presbyterian Cemetery, Alexandria ................................................... 133
   Graham Cemetery, Orange ............... 158
   Greenhill Cemetery, Berryville ......... 271
   Greenhill Cemetery, Danville ........... 273
   hampton National Cemetery, Hampton ................................................... 124
   Hampton National Cemetery, Hampton .................................... 168, 250, 277
   Hampton National Cemetery., Hampton ................................................... 197
   Hollywood Cemetery Richmond 61, 100, 108, 145, 203, 234, 237, 240, 242, 243, 265, 281, 312
   Hollywood Cemetery, Richmond ..... 188, 278
   Ivy Hill Cemetery, Alexandria ... 60, 173, 298
   Ivy Hill Cemetery, Upperville .......... 192
   Ketoctin Baptist Church Cemetery, Round Hill .................................. 106
   Lincoln Cemetery, Edom ................... 84
   Maplewood Cemetery, Gordonsville. 132
   Methodist Protestant Cemetery, Alexandria ........................... 76, 123
   Mt. Carmel Presb. Ch. Cemetery, Steele's Tavern ........................................ 168
   Mt. Hebron Cemetery, Winchester .... 195
   Municipal Cemetery, Christiansburg. 201
   Newbern Cemetery ........................... 143
   Oak Grove Cemetery, Portsmouth ....... 73
   Oakwood Cemetery, Falls Church .... 306
   Oakwood cemetery, Richmond ......... 180

Oakwood, Richmond .......................... 78
Old City Cemetery, Lynchburg ......... 286
Old Downing Cemetery, Northampton Co. .............................................. 192
Old St. Luke's Ch. Cemetery, Boydton .................................................... 248
Riverview Cemetery, Richmond 188, 285
Riverview Cemetery, Waynesboro .... 203
Salem Church Cemetery, Floyd Co. .... 52
Shockoe Hill Cemetery, Richmond ..... 50
Smithfield Cemetery, Montgomery Co. .................................................... 246
Spring Hill Cemetery, Lynchburg .... 123, 234, 316
St John's Church Cemetery, Wytheville .................................................... 235
St. Mary's Cemetery, Fairfax Station 294
St. Paul's Episcopal Cemetery, Alexandria .................................... 107
Thornrose Cemetery, Staunton .... 52, 98, 163, 164, 168, 222, 235, 238
Wade Family Cemetery, Mill Gap .... 164
Westview Cemetery, Blacksmith ........ 74
**Cemeteries - Washington**
Congressional Cemetery ................... 155
Congressional Cemetery, DC ........... 208
Rock Creek Cemetery, DC ................. 92
**Cemeteries – Washington, D.C.**
Congressional .................................. 131
**Cemeteries - West Virginia**
Edge Hill Cemetery, Charlestown .... 182, 256
Edge Hill, Charlestown ...................... 62
Elmwood Cemetery, Charlestown .... 193, 219
Elmwood Cemetery, Shepherdstown 106, 162
Green Hill Cemetery, Martinsburg ..... 52, 173, 191, 244
Harlan Cemetery, Falling Waters ...... 163
Harper's Cemetery, Harper's Ferry ..... 97
Indian Mound Cemetery, Romney .... 221
Jefferson County, Charles Town ....... 244
Johnson Family Cemetery, Oak Hill . 187
Lutheran Cemetery, Berkeley Co. ..... 272
Methodist Cemetery, Shepherdstown 294
Methodist Graveyard, Charlestown ... 126
Old Norbourne Cemetery, Berkeley Co. ............................................ 135, 210
Old Stone Presbyterian Church Cemetery, Lewisburg .................................... 126
St. Joseph's Catholic Cemetery, Berkeley Co. ................................................ 75
Underwood Cemetery, Ashley .......... 193
Zion Episcopal Church Cemetery, Charlestown ................................. 268
**Cemeteries – West Virginia**
Green Hill Cemetery, Martinsburg ...... 52
Mt. Vernon Cemetery, Barbour Co. ... 267
**Center**
Nancy Jane ....................................... 121
**Central America** .................................. 63
**Chaille**
John .................................................... 94
**Chambers**
Fannie ................................................. 97
Frances A. ........................................... 97
George W. ........................................... 97
George W. ................................. 97, 167
Meta .................................................... 97
**Chandler**
Elizabeth (Fisher) ............................... 98
Elizabeth (Hodges) ............................. 97
Greenbery .......................................... 97
Moses .................................................. 97
**Chapman**
Mary Jane ......................................... 155
Sophia ............................................... 155
**Charles Town Mining Company** 147, 191, 302
**Charlton**
Walter D. ............................................ 98
**Chase**
Abel Dustin ........................................ 98
Callie .................................................. 98
Emma ................................................. 98
George E. ............................................ 98
Mary ................................................... 98
Nancy ................................................. 98
Robert ............................... 98, 100, 300
Ruth .................................................... 98
**Cheatham**
Anna Jane ........................................ 138
**Cheatzom**
Joseph D. ............................................ 98

**Chenault**
Mary .............................................. 143
**Cherry**
Caroline ........................................... 99
Chloe ............................................... 99
David ............................................... 99
William ............................................ 99
**Chichester**
Thompson M. .................................. 99
**Chick**
Frances E. ........................................ 99
George Washington .......................... 99
Lottie M. .......................................... 99
Mary ................................................ 99
Veda L. ............................................. 99
William ............................................ 99
**Choate**
Jesse C. ............................................ 99
**Christ**
Henry ............................................... 54
**Christian**
Anna W. ........................................... 64
**Churchill**
James ............................................... 99
**Clanton**
Sally ............................................... 100
Williamson S. ................................ 100
**Clark**
John ............................................... 100
John A. .......................................... 100
William T. ..................................... 189
**Clarke**
Belinda .......................................... 101
James L. ........................................ 100
Julia V. .......................................... 101
Lewis H. ................................ 100, 287
Lydia ............................................. 272
Martha Jane ................................... 247
William T. ..................................... 100
**Clay**
Elizabeth F. ..................................... 81
**Clayton**
Ann ............................................... 101
Clevie K. ....................................... 101
George B. ...................................... 101
Jasper S. ........................................ 101
Maria ............................................. 101
Rowena ......................................... 101

**Clemments**
Archibald D. ................................. 102
Francis D. ..................................... 101
James H. ....................................... 101
Margaret C. ................................... 101
Margaret Catherine ....................... 101
Marjorie ........................................ 102
Mary Ann ..................................... 101
Thomas H. .................................... 101
**Clerk,** ............................................. 50
**Clifton**
Andrew J. ..................................... 102
**Clingenpeel**
Fannie ........................................... 129
Pleasant H. ................................... 102
**Cobb**
G.D. .............................................. 171
**Cock**
Harrison C. ................................... 102
Walter ........................................... 102
**Coghill**
Bettie A. (Beazley) ....................... 102
Nancy ........................................... 102
Thomas Benjamin ......................... 102
William ........................................ 102
**Cohen**
Dora .............................................. 102
Lewis ............................................ 102
**Cole**
Corey W. ...................................... 103
Edward V. ..................................... 103
Fayette .......................................... 102
Jacob ............................................. 102
Richard ......................................... 102
Sarah Jane ..................................... 103
Susan Jane .................................... 102
Thomas ......................................... 102
**Coleman**
Addison ........................................ 103
Ellen D. ........................................ 103
John H. ......................................... 103
Robert F. .. 103, 152, 153, 206, 269, 297
**Colin**
William ........................................ 103
**Colleges & Universities**
Columbia College (DC) ................ 136
Emory & Henry ............................ 213

Hampden-Sydney .............................. 174
United States Military Academy ...... 128, 162, 245, 247
University of Virginia ................. 57, 143
Virginia Agricultural & Mechanical College .......................................... 74
Virginia Military Institute ..... 81, 87, 92, 132, 143, 183, 191, 192, 212, 228, 244, 265, 311
Washington College ................. 192, 206
William & Mary .............................. 259

**Collier**
Anna Maria ...................................... 103
Benjamin W. .................... 103, 269, 314
John ................................................. 103
Mary E. ............................................ 103

**Collins**
Albert G. .......................................... 103
Amy J. ............................................. 104
Charles T. ........................................ 104
Eliza Ann ........................................ 280
Eliza Jane ........................................ 104
Elizabeth ......................................... 198
Emily P. (Bozel) .............................. 103
Henry .... 103, 149, 170, 198, 201, 213, 230, 274, 283, 288, 312
Henry R. .......................................... 104
James M. ......................................... 104
John ................................................. 104
John A. ............................................ 104
John W. ........................................... 104
Joseph ............................................. 104
Lucinda ........................................... 283
Malinda .......................................... 104
Malinda C. ...................................... 104
Mary F. ............................................ 104
Rebecca A. ...................................... 104
Robert H. ......................................... 104

**Colorado**
LaPlata Co., Durango ...................... 169

**Colton**
John ................................................. 104

**Comann**
Fitzwilliam J. .................................. 104

**Comerford**
John ................................................. 104
Mary Ann ....................................... 104

**Compton**
James ............................................... 105

**Connecticut**
Bantam Falls ................................... 237

**Conner**
John ................................................. 105

**Conrad**
Henry K. .......................................... 105

**Conroy**
James J. ........................................... 105

**Converse**
Farmer ............................................. 105

**Conway**
Elizabeth Ann ................................. 129
Mary ................................................ 129

**Cook**
Belle M. .......................................... 143
Charles J. ........................................ 105
Hyphasia ........................................... 50
Lucy ................................................ 105
Virginia Jane ................................... 238

**Cooke**
John K. ............. 71, 105, 199, 205, 221

**Coontz**
Thornton ......................................... 106

**Cooper**
Albert .............................................. 107
Hoppie Jacobs ................................. 221
Lucy S. ............................................ 280

**Copeland**
Ann E. ............................................. 106
David H. .......................................... 106
Elizabeth A. .................................... 106
George E. ........................................ 106
Harriet A.M. (Butts) ........................ 106
James D. .......................................... 106
James R. .......................................... 106
Lydia Ann ....................................... 106
Mary ................................................ 106
Nancy .............................................. 106
Nancy Ann ...................................... 106
Rosanna L. ...................................... 106
Thomas ........................................... 106

**Copenhafer**
Matilda C. ....................................... 106

**Copenhaver**
Andrew J. .......................................... 89
Andrew Jackson ..................... 106, 273

Matilda C. .......................................... 106
**Coppedge**
   Martha A. ........................................ 107
   Marthy (Mourning) .......................... 107
   Thomas L. ........................................ 107
**Corbin**
   Catherine ......................................... 107
   Catherine S.M. ................................ 107
   Ella Amelia ..................................... 107
   Jameson ........................................... 107
   Lafayette .......................................... 107
   Lafayette Montague ......................... 107
   Mary F. ............................................ 107
   Mary Fannie .................................... 107
   Mary Nelson (Mason) ...................... 107
   Randall B. ........................................ 107
   Richard L. ........................................ 107
   Richard, Major ................................ 107
   Thomas B. ....................................... 107
**Corder**
   Elijah ............................................... 107
**Corley**
   Ann ................................................. 205
**Cornwell**
   William ........................................... 107
**Corrie**
   William W. ...................................... 107
**Corse**
   Elizabeth .......................................... 107
   John ................................................. 107
   Julia ................................................. 107
   Montgomery Dent ........... 107, 207, 217
**Cosby**
   Elizabeth Ann Firth ......................... 119
**Costello**
   Annie ............................................... 258
**Council**
   Joseph Goodwin .............................. 107
   Judith Yates (McClenney) ................ 107
**Councill**
   Eugene Deans ................................. 107
**Court-Martialed** ... 54, 61, 72, 73, 79, 89, 90, 91, 93, 97, 100, 101, 105, 112, 113, 114, 120, 127, 136, 139, 145, 149, 153, 154, 158, 161, 166, 168, 173, 174, 177, 181, 184, 188, 190, 198, 200, 203, 206, 208, 213, 215, 221, 229, 230, 231, 233, 237, 243, 248, 250, 252, 265, 268, 273, 274, 276, 293, 298, 299, 303, 309, 312, 313, 316

Absence Without Leave 57, 67, 205, 221
Abusive Language to a Superior Officer ..................................................... 213
Assualt and Battery .......................... 282
Conduct Prejudicial to Good Order and Military Discipline 57, 63, 76, 91, 94, 131, 138, 190, 212, 259, 270
Conduct Unbecoming a Soldier .. 79, 274
Conduct Unbecoming an Officer and a Gentleman .................................. 259
Desertion . 91, 100, 152, 153, 190, 206, 207, 297
Disobedience of Orders 80, 97, 113, 138, 162, 170, 205, 220, 221, 313
Disorderly Conduct ................... 80, 208
Disrespectful Conduct Towards his Commanding Officer ...................... 57
Drunkeness ....................... 76, 162, 175
Drunkeness on Duty ..... 177, 217, 266, 272, 316
Fross Neglect of Duty ...................... 259
Gross and Willful Neglect of Duty .... 218
Gross Neglect and Violation of Duty .. 58
Gross Neglect of Duty ....................... 53
Insubordinant Conduct ....................... 57
Laying Down and Sleeping on Post .. 209
Mutinous Conduct ................... 138, 214
Neglect of Duty 67, 113, 143, 170, 175, 199, 314
Resisting Lawful Authority ...... 208, 214
Riotous And Disorderly Conduct ........ 76
Selling Liquor to the Provost Prisoners ..................................................... 272
Sleeping on Post .............. 166, 187, 299
Sleeping On Post ...... 99, 179, 242, 277, 286, 317
Ungentlemanly and Unofficerlike Conduct ....................................... 76
Unsoldierlike and Disorderly Conduct ..................................................... 213
Unsoldierlike Conduct and Disobedience of Orders ..................................... 269

Using Improper Language to his Commanding Officer .................. 314
Using Insulting and Disrespectful Language to his Commanding Officer ..................................................... 97
Violation of the 42$^{nd}$ Article of War .... 58
Violation of the 9$^{th}$ Arctice of War .... 113
Violation of the 9$^{th}$ Article of War ..... 79, 131, 269
Violent and Disorderly Conduct ......... 54

**Covar**
Isabella D. ........................................ 266
**Cowan**
Sophia A. ......................................... 169
**Cowen**
Elizabeth .......................................... 108
George S. .......................................... 108
James M. .......................................... 108
Monnote ........................................... 108
Nancy ............................................... 108
Sarah R. ............................................ 108
William M. ....................................... 108
**Cowens**
George W. ........................................ 108
**Cowne**
Mary Ellen ....................................... 138
**Cowper**
Elizabeth .......................................... 155
**Cox**
Anna ................................................. 108
Cynthia ............................................. 108
James T. ........................................... 108
John W. ............................................ 108
Keziah H. .......................................... 108
Ross .................................................. 108
**Coyner**
Lucy Ann ........................................... 55
**Craft**
John C. ............................................. 108
**Crafton**
George Washington .......................... 109
James E. ........................................... 109
Jane .................................................... 88
**Cramer**
Catherine .......................................... 254
John J. .............................................. 109
Sarah A. ........................................... 109
**Crane**

John H. ............................................. 109
**Crawford**
Charlie .............................................. 186
Charlotte .......................................... 109
George .............................................. 186
Hattie ................................................ 109
Mary A. ............................................ 109
Samuel G. ........................................ 109
Samuel Leake .................................. 109
William ............................................. 109
**Creamer**
Jacob Q. ........................................... 109
John Q. ............................................. 109
**Creekmur**
Anna F. ............................................. 110
Charles J. ................................. 110, 241
Elizabeth J. ...................................... 110
Rose ................................................. 110
**Crist**
Andrew H. ....................................... 110
Elizabeth J. ...................................... 110
Herbert ............................................. 110
Lucy ................................................. 110
Robert M. ........................................ 110
**Crockett**
Mary ................................................ 110
William S. ....................................... 110
**Cropp**
Alexander J. .................................... 110
**Crossley**
John .................................................. 111
**Crow**
Mary ................................................ 254
**Crowder**
Armstead Mann ............................... 111
Bethany Jane (Bell) ......................... 111
James B. .......................................... 111
**Crowl**
Emily (Daylong) .............................. 111
Jacob ................................................ 111
**Crump**
Andrew C. ....................................... 111
**Cuba**
Havana ............................................. 263
**Cunningham**
Frederick A. ............................. 111, 270
John .................................................. 111
Josepha Allevia ................................. 51

    Sarah Etchinson............................... 212
**Curry**
    Maria E. (Mullen)............................ 111
    Melvina ........................................... 121
    Stephen C. ................................ 95, 111
**Cusac**
    Josephine ......................................... 218
**Cushing**
    Brigadier General C......................... 193
**Custer**
    Henry .............................................. 111
**Cutshaw**
    Frances A........................................... 97

## D

**Daniel**
    Harriet E. ......................................... 271
    John E.W. ........................................ 112
    Laura E............................................. 112
    Mabry............................................... 112
    Martha S. ......................................... 112
    Rebecca ........................................... 112
    Susan (Robinson) ............................ 112
    Theophilus ....................................... 112
**Dante**
    Clara Josephine ............................... 220
**Dantt**
    Sarah E. (Watson)............................ 112
    William L. ....................................... 112
    William T. ....................................... 112
**Danzy**
    Eliza J.............................................. 112
    Robert.............................................. 112
**Darden**
    Sarah Mariah................................... 147
**Davey**
    Henry .............................................. 112
**Davis**
    Augustus.......................................... 112
    Benjamin L. ..................................... 113
    Charles P. ........................................ 112
    Eliza J. (Thompson)......................... 113
    Fannie A. ......................................... 113
    Frances A. ............................... 112, 113
    James H. .......................................... 112
    James L. .......................................... 113
    James P............................................ 114
    Jane ................................................. 122

    Jehu................................................. 114
    Louis ............................................... 114
    Mary A. (Stanley)............................ 112
    Nancy Jane...................................... 121
    Rebecca Ann.................................... 272
    Sarah M. .......................................... 113
    Thomas............................................ 114
    William K. ....................................... 114
**Day**
    Elizabeth.......................................... 115
    James............................................... 114
    John Thomas................................... 115
    Mary................................................ 115
    Robert.............................................. 115
**Daylong**
    Emily............................................... 111
**Dean**
    James T. .......................................... 115
**DeBell**
    Ann ................................................. 219
**Debnam**
    Frances Ann.................................... 123
**Deemer**
    Catherine ......................................... 115
    Nicholas J. ....................................... 115
**Delaware**
    New Castle, Wilmington ................... 69
**Delaware - Infantry**
    5th Regt., Co. E............................... 176
**Deleware**
    New Castle, Wilmington ................. 176
**Demeree**
    Mary................................................ 145
**Deneal**
    Austin.............................................. 115
    David............................................... 115
    Elizabeth.......................................... 115
    Harriet ............................................. 115
    Harry ............................................... 115
    James C. .......................................... 115
    Samuel............................................. 115
    Walter.............................................. 115
**DeVaughn**
    Sinah A............................................ 225
**Deyerle**
    Emma ............................................... 67
**Diamond**
    Alicey (Muncy)............................... 116

John .................................................. 115
Malinda ............................................ 116
William Clay .................................... 116
**Diary**
Mexican War ..................................... 74
**Diddep**
Archibald W ..................................... 116
**Didlake**
Andrew J. ................................. 67, 116
**Dillard**
Elizabeth H. ..................................... 116
James L. ........................................... 116
John F ............................................... 116
John Quincy Adams ......................... 116
Mary E .............................................. 116
Narcissa ............................................ 116
William T. ........................................ 116
Willie T. ........................................... 116
**Dillon**
Nancy ............................................... 280
**Dilworth**
Elizabeth .......................................... 162
**District of Columbia**
Soldiers Temperance Home .............. 317
**District of Columbia - Cavalry**
Owen's Co ........................................ 112
**District of Columbia - Infantry**
2nd Btln.., Co. M .............................. 131
5th Btln., McDermott's Co ................ 130
$5^{th}$ D.C. Inf., Co. B ............................ 306
D.C. Vols., Co. A ............................... 92
**Ditman**
Sylvester ........................................... 288
**Dixon**
Charles C. ........................................ 116
George W. ........................................ 266
Henry ................................................ 117
M.E. .................................................. 116
Rosanna H. ....................................... 116
Samuel J. .......................................... 116
Sarah Ann (Kirby) ............................ 116
**Doble**
Carlise .............................................. 117
**Dockerty**
George W. ........................................ 117
**Dodge**
Richard ............................................. 117
**Donaldson**

Jane .................................................. 183
**Done**
William D. ....................................... 117
**Donevant**
William E. ........................................ 117
**Donnan**
Annie T. ........................................... 117
C.G .................................................... 117
David ........................................ 117, 118
George W. ........................................ 118
Hattie ................................................ 118
James A. ........................................... 314
James M. ............. 68, 84, 118, 243, 253
James M., Jr. ..................................... 117
James Monroe .................................. 117
James Munroe .................................. 118
Mary ................................................. 118
Mary (Martin) .................................. 118
Mary (Stewart) ......................... 117, 118
Mary A. ............................................ 118
Mary Harrison .................................. 117
Reuben R. ......................................... 118
Robert Commings .................... 118, 262
Virginia ............................................ 117
Virginia T. ........................................ 117
Walter C. .......................................... 118
**Donnell**
John S ............................................... 118
**Dopleb**
Reynold ............................................ 118
**Dorsey**
Benjamin .......................................... 118
**Doudge**
Betsy Ann (Robinson) ...................... 118
Mary (Munden) ................................ 118
Soloman B. ....................................... 118
**Doughty**
Sarah E. ............................................ 192
**Douglas**
Harriet F. (Whittington) ................... 119
James S ...................................... 77, 118
Mary Anne ....................................... 315
Sidney .............................................. 119
Thomas H. ........................................ 119
**Douglass**
Thomas H. ........................................ 119
**Dove**

Elizabeth............................................ 184
Samuel............................................. 306
**Dowers**
Francisco ......................................... 88
**Doyle**
John................................................. 119
William............................................ 119
**Draper**
Eliza Minerva................................. 219
**Dreury**
Arthur.............................................. 119
Jesse C............................................. 119
Mary B. .......................................... 119
**Drinkard**
Beverly............................................ 119
Charles Beverly.............................. 119
Elizabeth Ann Firth (Cosby)............. 119
**Driscoll**
John A............................................. 119
**Drummed Out of Camp**..................... 205
**Dubecq**
Charlotte (Thompson)....................... 120
John................................................. 120
**Duckwiler**
Daniel.............................................. 120
**Dudley**
Dolly ............................................... 120
George B. ........................................ 120
Jesse Perkins ................................... 120
Sarah (Graham) ............................... 120
Sarah A............................................ 120
Sarah Jane (Barnett)......................... 120
Winston Price.................................. 120
**Duffey**
Andrew............................................ 120
**Duke**
James W. ........................................ 120
Letitia .............................................. 232
**Dulaney**
Benjamin Tasker ............................. 120
Elizabeth (French) ........................... 120
James Heath.................................... 120
William H. ...................................... 120
**Dulany**
John S...................................... 120, 131
**Duncan**
George............................................. 120
**Dunlap**

James S............................................ 121
Melvina ........................................... 121
William............................................ 121
William J. ....................................... 121
**Dunn**
Bascom............................................ 122
Emily............................................... 121
Emma ............................................. 122
Isabella ........................................... 149
James A. ......................................... 121
Lina................................................. 121
Nancy Jane...................................... 121
Sarah Elizabeth .............................. 121
Susan............................................... 121
Thomas............................................ 121
Thomas H. ...................................... 121
William Washington........................ 121
**Duvall**
Linda M........................................... 292
Sarah............................................... 292
**Dyer**
Alice................................................ 122
Elizabeth......................................... 122
Jane (Davis) .................................... 122
John................................................. 122
Rebecca .......................................... 122
Robert N. ........................................ 122
Sarah (Abbott)................................. 122
Virginia ........................................... 122
William............................................ 122
**Dyes**
Alexander ....................................... 122
Nathaniel G..................................... 122
Thuresa ........................................... 122
**Dykes**
Clara F............................................. 122
Joel R. ............................................. 122
Marquis D. ...................................... 122

*E*

**Eads**
Margaret ......................................... 176
**Eagle**
Bettie............................................... 123
Frederic S. ...................................... 123
Robert.............................................. 123
Robert N. ........................................ 122

Sallie ............................................... 123
Susan .............................................. 123
Virginia .......................................... 123
**Eanes**
James C. ........................................ 123
**Early**
Betty (Waldron) ............................. 123
Joab Anderson ................................ 123
Jubal A. .......................................... 300
Jubal Anderson ........... 58, 123, 259, 262
Major ..................................... 115, 215
Mary (Ross) ................................... 123
Ruth (Hairston) .............................. 123
**East**
John ................................................ 123
Lydia .............................................. 123
Mary Ann ....................................... 183
Mary B. (Abington) ........................ 123
**Eaton**
Edmond Henry ............................... 123
Georgiana (Rhoderick) .................... 123
Ida Virginia .................................... 123
John H. ........................................... 123
Minnie ............................................ 123
William ........................................... 123
**Eaves**
Frances Ann ................................... 123
James Harvey ................................. 123
**Echols**
Susan .............................................. 280
**Eckley**
Mary A. .......................................... 292
**Edgar**
Sarah Margaret ............................... 290
**Editor** .................................................. 52
**Edmonds**
Hellen W. ........................................ 81
**Edmondson**
Lulu North ....................................... 81
**Edmundson**
Upton A. ......................................... 123
**Edumnds**
Julia ................................................ 181
**Edwards**
Eliza V. ............................................ 56
Henry K. ......................................... 124
**Elected Officials**
, Virginia, House of Delegates .......... 254

, Virginia, Montgomery Co.,
   Commonwealth's Attorney .......... 254
, Virginia, State Senate ..................... 288
Board of Supervisors, Amelia Co., Va. 68
Circuit Court Clerk, Berkeley Co. ........ 52
Circuit Court Clerk, Montgomery Co. 298
Circuit Court Clerk, Pulaski Co., Va. 143
Commonwealth's Attorney, Augusta Co.
   ....................................................... 163
Commonwealth's Attorney, Franklin Co.,
   Virginia ......................................... 123
Govenor, Virginia ............................ 192
Louisiana, House of Representatives. 199
Louisiana, U.S. Congress ................. 199
Mayor of Petersburg .......................... 57
Mayor, Harper's Ferry ........................ 97
Mayor, Newark, Arkansas ................ 305
Mayor, Staunton .............................. 164
Speaker of the House (Va.) ............... 192
Texas, Clerk of the Court, Live Oak
   County ......................................... 235
Treasurer, Adams Co., Illinois .......... 141
Virginia House of Delegates ....... 74, 123,
   126, 163, 192, 245, 292
Virginia, Attorney General ............... 288
Virginia, House of Delegates ............ 288
Virginia, House of Delegates .... 201, 254
**Ellett**
Joseph E. ........................................ 124
**Elliott**
Curtis .............................................. 124
Joseph .............................................. 63
Virginia Ann ................................... 124
**Ellis**
Adaline Hilman ............................... 278
Alice ............................................... 125
Allie May ........................................ 126
Elijah .............................................. 125
Ella Susan ....................................... 124
Emma L. ......................................... 124
Francis Virginia .............................. 124
George F. ........................................ 124
Harriet J. ......................................... 124
John C. ........................................... 124
John William .................................. 124
Joseph ............................................. 124
Joseph O. ........................................ 124

## VIRGINIA VOLUNTEERS IN MEXICO

Laura Ann .......................................... 225
Margaret Ann ..................................... 124
Mary N. ............................................. 124
Obadiah ............................................. 124
Sallie ................................................. 125
Sallie H. ............................................. 125
Samuel ............................................... 125
William W. ........................................ 124
**Elswick**
   Mary Ellen ..................................... 291
**Elvira**
   Dowdy ............................................ 308
**Emerson**
   Alex A. ........................................... 126
   David F. .......................................... 126
   George T. ........................................ 126
   John H. ........................................... 126
   Martin L. ........................................ 126
   Sarah M. ......................................... 126
   Susan .............................................. 126
   Thomas ........................................... 126
**England** ........................................... 168
   Bristol ............................................. 251
   London ........................................... 292
   Yorkshire .......................................... 55
**English**
   Anna ............................................... 126
   John ................................................ 126
   John M. ........................................... 126
   Mary ............................................... 126
   Morgan ........................................... 126
   Susan .............................................. 303
**Erskine**
   Agatha ............................................ 126
   Henry .............................................. 126
   Michael ........................................... 126
   Sarah Margaret ............................... 126
**Ervin**
   Cora V. ........................................... 168
**Erwin**
   Charles ............................................ 126
**Estill**
   Agatha ............................................ 126
**Etheridge**
   Cataretta ......................................... 127
   Indiana V. ....................................... 127
   Juliana V. ........................................ 127

   Nelson C. ........................................ 127
   Sarah F. .......................................... 127
**Eustace**
   Dabney M. ...................................... 127
**Evans**
   Henry .............................................. 127
   James .............................................. 127
   John G. ........................................... 127
   John P. ............................................ 127
   Joseph L. ........................................ 127
   Martha ............................................ 136
   Mary M. .......................................... 127
   Montgomery ................................... 128
   Sarah .............................................. 127
**Everett**
   Joseph L. ........................................ 128
**Ewald**
   Angeline ......................................... 128
   Charles ............................................ 128
   Jacob .............................................. 128
   James .............................................. 128
   Joseph W. ....................................... 128
   Lucinda ........................................... 128
   Mariah ............................................ 128
   Mary ............................................... 128
   Stephen ........................................... 128
   Thomas W. ..................................... 128
**Eyrse**
   James W. ........................................ 128
   William G. ...................................... 128

## F

**Fagunders**
   Jacob H. ......................................... 128
**Fairfax**
   A.C. ................................................ 128
   Elizabeth (Cary) .............................. 128
   George William ............................... 128
   Henry ........................... 128, 292, 316
   Herbert C. ....................................... 129
   John M.G. ....................................... 128
   Margaret S. ..................................... 128
   Thomas ........................................... 128
   Thomas 9th Lord ........................... 128
**Falconer**
   George .............................................. 80
**Farley**

Angelina P. ............................................ 272
Anna T. ................................................. 129
Bettie E. ................................................ 129
Elizabeth A. .......................................... 129
Elizabeth Ann ...................................... 129
Ernest R. ............................................... 129
Mary R. ................................................ 129
Peter ..................................................... 272
Thomas A. ............................................ 129
Virginia Sarah ........................................ 90
Vuella F. ............................................... 129
**Farlow**
    Roanna ................................................. 306
**Farris**
    Fannie ................................................... 129
    Jeremiah ............................................... 129
    Nancy ................................................... 129
    William ................................................. 129
**Faulkner**
    Bettie L. ................................................ 130
    Catherine .............................................. 129
    George E. .............................................. 129
    John F. .................................................. 129
    Josiah ................................................... 130
    Katherine A. ......................................... 130
    Luemma Elizabeth ............................... 129
    Maria C. ............................................... 130
    Mary J. ................................................. 130
    Mary Jane ............................................. 130
    Mary T. (Harris) ................................... 130
    Susan .................................................... 129
**Fealty**
    Elizabeth .............................................. 296
**Featherstone**
    Ann (Wilkinson) ................................... 130
    Jennie ................................................... 130
    John Randolph ..................................... 130
    Joshua .................................................. 130
**Fegan**
    Ann (Toland) ....................................... 130
    Thomas ................................................ 130
**Felts**
    John ...................................................... 130
**Fenwick**
    Benedick J. ........................................... 131
    Emeline Levinia ................................... 131
    Richard Maury Augustus ..................... 131

**Ferguson**
    Ann E. .................................................. 131
    Ida Virginia .......................................... 131
    Katie Lee .............................................. 131
    Marcus ................................................. 131
    Margaret .............................................. 131
    Robert .................................................. 131
    Sarah Elizabeth ................................... 131
    William ........................................ 131, 296
    William G. .................................. 131, 266
**Ficklin**
    Benjamin ............................................. 132
    Benjamin Franklin .............................. 132
    Ellen ..................................................... 132
**Fielder**
    Francis ................................................. 132
    John ..................................................... 132
    Martin .................................................. 132
    Mary Frances (Matthews) ................... 132
**Fields**
    Henrietta .............................................. 132
    Richard ................................................ 132
**Finch**
    Elvira ................................................... 225
**Finley**
    Anne .................................................... 232
**Finnall**
    William ................................................ 132
**Finney**
    Mary Ann ............................................ 183
**Fishburne**
    W.S. ..................................................... 239
**Fisher**
    Addison ............................................... 133
    Addison K. ........................................... 132
    Amos T. ............................................... 133
    Amos Thomas ..................................... 133
    Annie Wills .......................................... 133
    Charles S. ............................................. 133
    Clara Matilda ...................................... 133
    Edward ................................................ 133
    Elizabeth ....................................... 98, 133
    Elizabeth (Mattingly) .......................... 133
    Ellen Rebecca ..................................... 133
    Henry Dogan ....................................... 133
    Isaiah ................................................... 133
    John H. ................................................ 133

## VIRGINIA VOLUNTEERS IN MEXICO

John W. .................................. 133, 314
Lucinda............................................ 133
Margaret ......................................... 133
Sallie (Bagwell).............................. 134
Sallie A............................................ 133
Samuel Henry ................................ 133
Sarah A............................................ 133
**Fitzgerald**
   Benjamin W. .................................. 134
   Edgar Poe ....................................... 134
   Edward Robert ............................... 134
   Edward Ward ................................. 134
   Elizabeth C. .................................... 134
   James K. .......................................... 134
   Martha Lee...................................... 134
   Mary A. ........................................... 134
   Thomas Benjamin............................ 134
**Fitzhugh**
   Anna Eliza (Bullitt) ........................ 134
   Elizabeth Garlick (Semple) .............. 134
   Harriet ............................................. 134
   John H. ............................................ 134
   Layfayette Henry............................. 134
   Mary Macon (Aylett)....................... 134
   Phillip.............................................. 134
**Flagg**
   Bertha.............................................. 134
   Horatio ............................................ 134
   Margaret ......................................... 134
   Martha N. ........................................ 134
   Sarah B............................................ 134
   Thomas G. ....................................... 134
   Thomas G., Jr.................................. 134
**Florida**.................................................. 155
   Deland............................................. 195
   Jackson Co., Marianna .................... 301
   Lake City ......................................... 182
   Pensacola ........................................... 51
   Pensacola ........................................... 88
**Flournoy**
   Daniel H. ......................................... 135
   Martha (Graves) ............................. 135
   Mary D. ........................................... 135
   Peter C............................................. 135
**Folds**
   Amy J.............................................. 104
**Foley**

James S., Jr. ..................................... 135
**Folks**
   Algernon R. .................................... 135
   Robert W. ....................................... 135
**Forbes**
   Elizabeth.......................................... 217
   John P.............................................. 135
**Force**
   Charles Fairchild ............................ 136
   Martha (Evans)................................ 136
   Mary E. (Mathews)......................... 136
   Peter ................................................ 136
Ford
   James B. .......................................... 136
   Joseph W. ........................................ 136
   L. 136
   O. 136
   Sarah A. (Garden)........................... 136
   Sarah S. ........................................... 136
**Forinash**
   Elmore............................................. 136
   Margaret (Mawyer)......................... 136
   Mariah ............................................. 136
**Foster**
   Addie............................................... 137
   Elijah............................................... 136
   Lewis H. .................................. 113, 137
   Mary Ann ....................................... 136
**Fowler**
   Elizabeth.......................................... 269
   James Herbert ................................. 137
**Fowlkes**
   Calvin B. ......................................... 137
   Ida ................................................... 137
   Laura............................................... 137
   Nannie Bass .................................... 137
   Permelia Price ................................ 137
**Fox**
   Artemecia ......................................... 87
**Fraizer**
   John D............................................. 137
**France**................................................... 296
**Francis**
   Adaline C........................................ 138
   Agnes .............................................. 137
   Mary J. ............................................ 138
   Mary Jane ....................................... 138

Peter .................................................. 137
Rosa B. .............................................. 138
Walter J. ............................................ 138
William............................................... 137
William T. .......................................... 138
**Franklin**
Anna Jane ......................................... 138
Anna M. ............................................ 138
James B. ............................................ 138
Layfayette.......................................... 271
Layfayette B...................................... 138
Mary Ann .......................................... 189
Mary Ellen ........................................ 138
Minnie................................................ 138
Virginia B. ......................................... 138
**Freeman**
Elizabeth S........................................ 161
Sarah .................................................. 83
**Freer**
Henry S. ............................................ 138
**French**
Charles .............................................. 140
Elizabeth............................................ 120
**Fritz**
Margaret Ann ..................................... 73
**Fry**
H. Lewis ........................................... 140
John J. ........................... 140, 260, 261
John W. ............................................. 140
Joshua D. .......................................... 140
Mary C. ............................................. 140
Mary C. (Lewis)................................ 140
Sam Gordon ...................................... 140
Sarah S. ............................................. 140
**Fuller**
Elizabeth............................................ 235
**Fulton**
Eliza Ann .......................................... 141
**Funkhouser**
John N. .............................................. 140
Larinda L. ......................................... 140
**Fuqua**
James................................................. 140
Martha Ann ....................................... 140
Robert F. ........................................... 140
**Furrow**
Ann Frances ....................................... 70

**Fust**
E.M. .................................................. 140
Mary J. .............................................. 140
Richard .............................................. 140
Richard, Jr......................................... 140

***G***

**Gaines**
Eliza Ann (Fulton)............................ 141
Thomas W. ....................................... 141
**Gainor**
Robert................................................ 141
**Gaither**
Edward .............................................. 141
Mary Ann (Kelly).............................. 141
**Gall**
Susan................................................. 267
**Gallager**
John................................................... 141
**Gallahan**
Minnie............................................... 138
**Gallaher**
Ann .................................................... 142
Charles E. ......................................... 142
Charles K. ......................................... 141
Elizabeth............................................ 141
Hannah .............................................. 142
James................................................. 142
John L................................................ 141
John S................................................ 141
John W. ............... 62, 65, 142, 192, 255
Maggie A........................................... 141
Mary.................................................. 142
Mary E............................................... 142
Missouri ............................................ 141
**Gallenar**
Henry................................................. 142
**Galloway**
Joseph................................................ 142
**Ganoe**
Mary Ann ......................................... 230
**Gant**
Lewis Boon....................................... 122
Lina ................................................... 121
**Gantt**
Mary Eleanor .................................... 250
**Garber**
Margaret S. ....................................... 163

**Garcia**
Thomas .......................................... 282
**Garden**
Sarah A. ........................................ 136
**Gardner**
Alexander ..................................... 142
Belle M. ......................................... 143
Elizabeth J. ............................ 142, 143
Fleming .................................. 59, 142
Ginnie ........................................... 143
James ............................................ 142
Mary ............................................. 142
Mary R. ......................................... 143
Robert Davison ............................. 142
Robert S. ....................................... 143
**Garnett**
Columbia ...................................... 143
E.B. ............................................... 145
E.S. ............................................... 145
Emma B. (Baber) ........................... 145
Emma L. (Baber) ........................... 145
Emma M. (Baber) .......................... 145
H.T. ............................................... 145
James J. ........................................ 143
James M. ....................................... 143
James R. ........................................ 143
John .............................................. 143
Joseph ........................................... 143
Maccau ......................................... 143
Mary ............................................. 143
Mary (Chenault) ............................ 143
Mary A. ........................................ 143
Mary Stuart (Bankhead) ................. 143
Remmington ................................. 143
Rowena ......................................... 143
Sarah B. ........................................ 143
T. 145
Thomas ......................................... 143
Thomas S. ..................................... 144
Thomas Stuart ........................ 131, 143
Willie T. ........................................ 143
**Garrett**
Ann E. .......................................... 186
Mary Ann ..................................... 145
Wesley B. ..................................... 145
**Garrison**
William B. .................................... 145

**Garth**
Adeline ........................................... 66
**Gaskins**
Emily H. ....................................... 184
Mary C. ........................................ 183
**Gately**
Eleanor ......................................... 146
Margaret Ann ................................ 146
Mary (Demeree) ............................ 145
Patrick .......................................... 145
**Gates**
martha A. ...................................... 279
Vincent ......................................... 147
**Gay**
Keziah H. ..................................... 108
**Gayle**
Benjamin ...................................... 147
Sarah Mariah ................................. 147
**Geiger**
Vincent E. ..................................... 238
Vincent Epley ............................... 147
**Gennett**
Samuel .......................................... 147
**Gentry**
Hannah ......................................... 102
Mary ............................................. 102
Susan Jane .................................... 102
William ......................................... 102
**Georgia** ............................................. 188
Atlanta .......................................... 311
Bibb Co., Macon ........................... 124
Campbell Co. ................................ 178
Fulton Co., Atlanta ........................ 186
Gordon Co., Crane Eater ................ 311
Putnam Co. ................................... 136
Savannah ...................................... 166
Troupe Co., West Point .................. 202
**Georgia - Infantry**
8th Regt., Co. C ............................. 245
**Germany** ................................... 128, 190
Bad Lagensalza, Tanusbruck .......... 254
Hanover ................................. 78, 195
Karlsruhe ...................................... 257
**Gheen**
Annie ............................................ 222
Cornelia Frances ............................ 222
**Gibbs**

Adella R. .................. 147
Frances R. ................ 152
Joseph E. .................. 147
Joseph F. .................. 147
Lucretia E. ................ 147
Marsha V. ................. 147
Rebecca H. ............... 147
Virginia E. ................ 147
**Gibson**
Carter ...................... 148
Flora M. ................... 148
George P. .................. 148
Harriet ..................... 148
John E. ..................... 148
John Moses .............. 148
John W. .................... 148
Joseph W.. ................ 148
Judith....................... 148
Mary ........................ 148
Matilda F. ................. 148
Robert Lee ............... 148
William..................... 148
William A. ................ 148
**Giles**
George N. ................. 148
**Gill**
Rebecca .................... 84
**Gillespie**
Emily ....................... 121
**Gilmore**
Charles .................... 148
E.H. ......................... 149
Ellen ........................ 149
Katy ......................... 149
Mary ........................ 148
Thomas ............. 148, 288
Virginia B. ................ 149
**Givens**
Isabella (Dunn).......... 149
James E. ................... 149
Sarah Pamela ........... 235
**Gladwell**
Clemmentine (Ballenger) ........ 149
Mary E. .................... 149
Valentine .................. 149
**Glaize**
Benjamin .................. 150

**Glasscock**
Asa........................... 149
David B. ................... 149
Emma Alsina ............ 149
Frances Ann .............. 149
John Stephen ............. 149
Mary ........................ 149
Mary E. .................... 149
Ruth E. ..................... 149
**Glenn**
Catherine A. .............. 82
Mary Davis ............... 230
**Goens**
Carrie Z. ................... 150
Ellen ........................ 149
George ..................... 150
George William ......... 150
James ................ 149, 150
Jennie ...................... 149
Sarah Ann ................ 150
William..................... 150
**Golden**
Alex. ........................ 150
George W. ................ 150
James C. ................... 150
James W. .................. 150
M.C. ........................ 150
Margaret ................... 150
Melissa M. ................ 150
William..................... 150
**Good**
Jonathan ................... 252
Jonathan R. .......... 91, 150
Mary P. .................... 150
**Goodrich**
John F. ..................... 150
**Goodwin**
Ada .......................... 151
Ada B. ..................... 151
Addie B.S. ................ 151
Aline ........................ 151
Aline E. .................... 151
Araminta................... 69
Archibald B. .............. 151
Archibald.................. 151
Arthur ...................... 151
Arthur M. ................. 151

## VIRGINIA VOLUNTEERS IN MEXICO

Arthur W. ......... 151
Bettie ......... 151
Celia B. ......... 151
Edward B. ......... 151
Edward E. ......... 151
Elizabeth J. (Kirkland) ......... 151
Henry ......... 151
James ......... 151
James H. ......... 151
James M. ......... 151
John H. ......... 151
John L. ......... 151
Maria J. ......... 151
Marry J. ......... 151
Mary ......... 151
Mary Ann H. (Talley) ......... 151
Mary P. ......... 151
Nannie W. ......... 151
Nathaniel B. ......... 151
Robert A. ......... 151
Robert A., Jr. ......... 151
Timoleon W. ......... 152

**Goodwyn**
Cammie ......... 152
Della ......... 152
Edward C. ......... 152
Edward W. ......... 73, 161
Edward Washington ......... 152
George W. ......... 152
Julia Ann ......... 152
Robert A. ......... 148
Virginia ......... 152
Virginia E. ......... 152

**Goolesby**
Thomas ......... 152

**Gordon**
Aaron K. ......... 152
Archibald Alexander ......... 152
Frances R. ......... 152
Henry ......... 152, 207
Sarah ......... 152
Sarah A. ......... 152

**Gorum**
Mary ......... 200

**Gough**
Ann M. ......... 154
Ann M.E. (Beck) ......... 154

John W. ......... 154
William ......... 153

**Goulden**
Benjamin F. ......... 154
Henry C. ......... 154
Henry L. ......... 154
Luvena ......... 154

**Gover**
Katie ......... 154
Mary Maria ......... 154
Minnie ......... 154
William C. ......... 154

**Graff**
Felix H. ......... 154
Lydia Jane ......... 154

**Graham**
Catherine ......... 154
Charles ......... 154
Eliza Jane ......... 252
Elizabeth ......... 154
George ......... 154
Isaac T. ......... 154
Issac ......... 154
James S. ......... 155
John ......... 154
Josephine ......... 154
Marshall ......... 154
Oscar Robert ......... 154
Richard ......... 154
Robert ......... 154
Rosetta ......... 154
Sarah ......... 120
Thomas M. ......... 155

**Grandberry**
Elizabeth (Cowper) ......... 155
John Gregory ......... 155
Josiah ......... 155

**Grant**
William ......... 155

**Granville**
Julia ......... 107

**Gravatt**
Amanda (Broaddus) ......... 155
George E. ......... 155
John B. ......... 155
John G. ......... 155
Lelia J. ......... 155

Mary J. .............................................. 155
Mary Jane (Chapman)...................... 155
Walter H. ........................................... 155
William Broaddus..... 113, 155, 263, 264
William J. .......................................... 155
**Graves**
Elizabeth M....................................... 79
James................................................. 155
John R. .............................................. 155
Martha............................................... 135
Nancy C............................................. 155
**Gray**
Benjamin H....................................... 156
David W. ........................................... 156
Lafayette W...................................... 156
**Green**
Henry G. ............................................ 156
Jesse Carson..................................... 156
John................................................... 156
Patty S. .............................................. 311
**Greenhow**
Bunkley ............................................. 156
Dora A. .............................................. 156
Thomas.............................................. 156
Thomas B. ......................................... 156
**Greer**
Nancy................................................ 231
**Gregg**
Ann E. ................................................ 66
**Gregory**
Augustus Armstrong........................ 156
Clara A. ............................................. 156
Elizabeth Smith ................................ 60
Martha Ward.................................... 238
Mary Jane ......................................... 276
P.H. .................................................... 309
**Griffen**
Nancy................................................ 164
**Griffin**
Andrew M. ........................................ 157
James................................................. 157
Mary Jane (McGee) ......................... 157
Sarah Frances .................................. 266
**Grimes**
Debra Ann ........................................ 157
James W. ........................................... 157
Joshua............................................... 157

Rebecca ............................................ 157
**Grimm**
Mary Frances ................................... 69
**Grove**
Alexander ......................................... 157
John................................................... 238
Lavinia .............................................. 157
Lewis Henry ..................................... 157
**Groves**
John B. .............................................. 157
**Grubb**
Hiram ................................................ 158
James................................................. 158
**Grymes**
Alice................................................... 158
Alice G. ............................................. 158
Benjamin .......................................... 158
Benjamin Andrew............................. 158
Catherine ......................................... 158
Eddie ................................................. 158
Eugenia............................................. 158
Harriet H. ......................................... 158
John................................................... 158
Kate C. .............................................. 158
Peyton ............................................... 158
Sarah ................................................. 158
William.............................................. 158
**Gunnell**
Catherine V. ..................................... 158
Catherine Virginia ........................... 158
George W. ......................................... 158
George West .................................... 158
John Ratcliffe................................... 158
Locian (Ratcliffe) ............................. 158
William T. ......................................... 158
**Guthrow**
William.............................................. 158
**Guy**
Anna Terry....................................... 248

# *H*

**Habeas Corpus**
Insanity............................................. 197
Writ of......... 64, 75, 178, 201, 203, 309
**Habeus Corpus**
Writ of............................................... 309
**Hagan**
Arthur............................................... 159

## VIRGINIA VOLUNTEERS IN MEXICO

William............................................. 159
**Haines**
  Mary J. ............................................ 159
  *See Haynes*..................................... 159
**Hairston**
  Ruth ................................................. 123
**Hale**
  Nancy................................................. 80
**Haley**
  Frances ............................................ 159
  John R. ............................................ 159
  Sarah A............................................ 159
  Woodson .......................................... 159
**Hall**
  Cecilia .............................................. 160
  Frederick ......................................... 159
  George.............................................. 160
  Malinda C. ....................................... 196
  Sarah Elizabeth .............................. 121
  William............................................. 160
**Hallman**
  Peter Fritz ....................................... 160
**Halsey**
  George W. ........................................ 160
**Hamblin**
  Richard L.......................................... 160
**Hamilton**
  Alfred A. .......................................... 160
  Edward L. ........................................ 160
  Marion.............................................. 160
  Martha ............................................. 160
  Pierce ............................................... 160
**Hammock**
  Elizabeth S....................................... 161
  James W. .......................................... 161
  Lewis Lambert ............................... 161
  Lucy E. ............................................. 161
**Hammon**
  Otis .................................................. 161
**Hammond**
  Charles ............................................ 161
  Rodolphus........................................ 161
**Hammons**
  Henry ............................................... 161
**Hampton**
  Joseph L. .......................................... 161
**Hamtramck**
  Col. . 50, 59, 61, 64, 65, 159, 183, 193, 216, 219, 222, 244, 277, 278, 290, 299, 302
  Ellen................................................. 162
  Jean Francois .................................. 162
  John Francis 57, 59, 162, 210, 220, 255
  Rebecca (McKenzie) ...................... 162
  Sarah E............................................. 162
**Hancock**
  John................................................... 51
**Handley**
  Sarah Margaret............................... 126
**Handy**
  Mary................................................. 159
**Haney**
  Elizabeth J. ...................................... 142
**Hannah**
  Musty ............................................... 162
**Hanson**
  Nannie C.......................................... 285
**Harding**
  John A.B........................................... 162
**Hardy**
  Elizabeth............................................ 66
  Green................................................ 162
**Hargrave**
  Sarah B............................................. 201
**Harlan**
  Elizabeth (Dilworth) ...................... 162
  George.................... 162, 168, 182, 218
  George Boyd ................................... 162
  George T........................................... 163
  Jane S. .............................................. 162
  Jane S. (Ball).................................... 162
  Kate E............................................... 163
**Harland**
  James............................................... 163
**Harless**
  Ballard.............................................. 163
  George.............................................. 163
  James............................................... 163
  Mary J. ............................................. 163
**Harman**
  William H. ....................................... 238
**Harmon**
  Albert G............................................ 163
  Arthur.............................................. 163
  Augusta ........................................... 163

Daniel .................................. 163
Ellen .................................... 163
Margaret S. ........................ 163
William Henry ................... 163
**Harp**
Martha B. ........................... 225
**Harper**
Capt. ..................................... 89
Elinor ................................. 163
Ellen .................................... 163
George Kenton ................... 163
Kenton ...................... 163, 299
Mary ................................... 163
Nancy ................................. 163
Samuel ................................ 163
Samuel C. .......................... 164
Virginia .............................. 188
**Harrington**
Anne Finley ....................... 232
**Harris**
Benjamin ........................... 164
Hamlin Eppes .................... 164
Joanna B. ........................... 164
Mary T. .............................. 130
Vida .................................... 309
Virginia ................................ 53
**Harrison**
Ann H. (Burt) .................... 164
Deborah A. ........................ 308
E.F. ..................................... 164
George W. .......................... 164
H.C. .................................... 164
Helen A. ............................... 60
John N. ............................... 164
John W. .............................. 164
L.F. ..................................... 164
Margaret E.A. .................... 164
Mary ................................... 196
Nancy E.T. ......................... 225
Otho H. ................. 80, 164, 175
Otho Holland .................... 164
Otho Howell ..................... 264
Thomas C. ......................... 164
Virginia .............................. 196
**Harrow**
Morgan .............................. 164
Nancy ................................. 164

**Harry**
James M. ............................ 164
**Hart**
Harriet ............................... 148
John L. ............................... 165
John R. ............................... 165
**Hartman**
Emma ................................. 122
**Harwood**
James D. ............................ 165
**Haslay**
John W. .............................. 165
**Hatch**
Euginia B.C. ...................... 189
**Hatcher**
Edmund J. .......................... 165
**Hawkins**
Amanda R. ......................... 166
Elizabeth B. (Andrews) ..... 165
Ella R. ................................ 165
Emma Alsina ..................... 149
Harriet J. .................... 165, 166
John J. ................................ 165
Malinda ............................. 294
Nathaniel B. ............. 165, 270
Reginald ............................ 166
William R. ................. 165, 166
**Hawthorn**
Joel B. ................................ 166
Nancy ................................. 166
Peter, Jr. ............................. 166
**Hayden**
Franklin G. ........................ 166
Minerva Ann (Hippenstall) ... 166
**Haynes**
Charles F. .......................... 159
Joseph ................................ 159
Mary ................................... 159
**Hays**
John .................................... 166
**Haywood**
Joseph ................................ 166
**Heafer**
Amelia ............................... 167
George R. .......................... 167
Jesse B. .............................. 167
John W. .............................. 167
Laura W. ............................ 167

## VIRGINIA VOLUNTEERS IN MEXICO

Mary Jane ............................................ 167
Richard W. ................................. 65, 166
**Heard**
Mary P. ................................................ 233
**Heath**
John ..................................................... 167
Sarah ................................................... 167
William ................................................ 167
**Heatwole**
David ................................................... 167
Gabriel T. ............................................ 167
Susannah ............................................ 167
**Hecht**
Frederick ............................................ 167
**Heck**
Arlena ................................................. 167
Carrie L. .............................................. 167
David H. .............................................. 167
Martha E. ............................................ 167
Sally A. ................................................ 167
**Heckel**
George A. ............................................ 167
**Hector**
Illione Mary Catherine ..................... 211
**Heflin**
Elizabeth ............................................. 167
John Marshall .................................... 167
Mary A. ............................................... 168
Mary Ellen .......................................... 168
William ............................................... 167
**Helbert**
Susannah ............................................ 167
**Helfeistien**
Jacob H. .............................................. 168
**Heller**
Joseph ................................................. 168
Josiah .................................................. 168
**Helms**
Alonzo S. ............................................ 168
Cara V. ................................................ 168
Elizabeth P. ........................................ 168
Lewis M. ............................................. 168
Martha E. ............................................ 168
Martha Eleanor .................................. 168
Minnie M. ........................................... 168
Samuel McCune ................................. 168
Thomas A. .......................................... 168
**Henderson**

Alexander ........................................... 168
Ann Montgomery .............................. 169
Burton C. ............................................ 169
Celia Bell ............................................. 169
Charles E. ........................................... 170
Elizabeth ............................................. 170
Emma C. ............................................. 170
Geneva Celestria ............................... 169
George Dixon ..................................... 169
Giles .................................................... 170
Giles T. ................................................ 170
Harvey Green ..................................... 169
Ida Winchester ................................... 169
James ................................................... 170
James L. .............................................. 170
John F. ................................................. 169
Jonas ................................................... 170
Joseph R. ............................................ 170
Julia Ann ............................................ 169
Lillie V. ............................................... 170
Lilly ..................................................... 170
Mary Etty ........................................... 169
Mary M. .............................................. 170
Mary T. ............................................... 170
Mollie S. ............................................. 170
Renee ................................................... 169
Roberta L. ........................................... 170
Samuel Thomas .................................. 169
Sarah Mariah ..................................... 169
Sophia A. ............................................ 169
Thomas ............................................... 169
Thomas D. .......................................... 169
Vandora .............................................. 169
William B. .......................................... 170
William T. ........................................... 169
**Heninger**
John K ................................................. 170
**Henry**
P.M. ..................................................... 172
**Hensley**
John G. ..................................... 170, 283
Robert .................................................. 283
William D. .......................................... 283
**Henson**
Ellen N. ............................................... 256
**Herbert**
Ann Caroline ..................................... 128

Arthur .............................................. 173
Sarah Cornelia (Tracy) ..................... 173
Upton Heath .................................... 170
**Herrington**
Ada V. ............................................. 173
Burtha ............................................. 173
Daniel .............................................. 173
Dennis ............................................. 173
Ellen ................................................ 173
James O. ......................................... 173
John ................................................. 173
John D. ............................................ 173
John S. ............................................. 173
Margaret .......................................... 173
Margaret Ann .................................. 173
Rose ................................................ 173
Susan E. ........................................... 173
**Hess**
Elizabeth ......................................... 275
James W. ........................................ 275
**Hesser**
Mary Ann (Bird) ............................. 173
Theodore ......................................... 173
**Hewlett**
John ................................................. 284
**Higdon**
John H. ............................................ 173
Mary Ann (Pickering) ..................... 173
**Highwood**
Sarah V. .......................................... 218
**Hill**
Harriet P. ........................................ 306
John ................................................. 174
**Hillard**
Joseph ............................................. 174
William ........................................... 174
**Hilliard**
Richard ........................................... 174
**Himes**
Lavinia ............................................ 157
William M. ..................................... 157
**Hinchman**
John ................................................. 174
**Hines**
Catherine ........................................ 174
Robert ............................................. 174
Sarah C. .......................................... 174

William S. ....................................... 174
**Hippenstall**
Minerva Ann ................................... 166
**Hobgood**
Edward ........................................... 174
John R. ........................................... 174
**Hobson**
Joseph M. ....................................... 174
Katrina VanPelt (Schlaffenberger) .... 174
**Hodgden**
Ivory P. ........................................... 175
**Hodges**
Elizabeth ........................................... 97
Esther G. ......................................... 176
George ............................................ 176
**Hoffmaer**
Frederick ........................................ 176
**Hoffman**
Carrington ...................................... 176
Margaret ......................................... 176
**Hogan**
John F. ............................................ 176
**Hogg**
Antoniette ....................................... 177
James W. ........................................ 177
John R. ........................................... 177
Juliet A. .......................................... 177
Sarah A. .......................................... 177
Virginia M. ..................................... 177
William C. ...................................... 176
William T. ...................................... 177
**Hohn**
John ................................................. 177
**Holland**
Thomas A. ...................................... 177
**Holloway**
Cornelius ........................................ 177
**Hood**
Benjamin ........................................ 177
Hannah ........................................... 177
John W. .......................................... 177
**Hooper**
Sarah Catherine .............................. 192
**Hooser**
Francis W.M. ................................. 177
Saphronia A.H. (Brumfield) ............ 177
**Hoover**
William ........................................... 177

VIRGINIA VOLUNTEERS IN MEXICO

**Horne**
Nicholas R. ................................. 178
**Horseman**
Catherine ...................................... 250
**Hose**
Mary E. .......................................... 216
**Hoskins**
Joseph ........................................... 178
Sarah ............................................. 178
William A. ..................................... 178
**Houston**
Thomas H. ..................................... 178
**Howard**
Alexander ...................................... 178
Jacob ............................................. 178
Tazewell M. ................................... 178
Virginia A. (Latham) ...................... 178
**Howell**
Caroline ......................................... 179
Emma Jane ..................................... 179
Francine ......................................... 179
John V. .......................................... 178
Lorenzo D. ..................................... 178
Mary .............................................. 179
Mary Ann ...................................... 136
Melinda ......................................... 179
Morriss B. ...................................... 179
Richard S. ...................................... 179
Victoria ......................................... 179
**Howle**
James ............................................. 179
William T. ..................................... 179
**Hoy**
Francis .......................................... 179
**Hubbard**
George W. ..................................... 179
Mary T. .......................................... 117
Sarah A. ........................................ 180
Virginia T. ..................................... 117
**Hudgins**
John W. ......................................... 180
**Hudnall**
Daniel Gower ................................ 180
Louisa W. ...................................... 180
Louise Elizabeth ............................ 180
Martha T. ...................................... 180
William Gower .............................. 180

**Hudson**
Daniel ............................................ 180
Letitia A. ......................................... 52
Martha Ella ................................... 317
Mary Jane ..................................... 307
Sarepta A. ..................................... 275
**Hughes**
Anderson ...................................... 180
Hezekiah ....................................... 180
Hezekiah V. .................................. 180
R.D. ................................................ 81
Saluda A. ...................................... 180
Saluda A. (Wilson) ........................ 180
**Hull**
John ............................................... 180
William H. .................................... 180
**Hulvey**
B.F. ............................................... 180
E.S. ............................................... 180
Ellen ............................................. 180
G.M. ............................................. 180
George .......................................... 181
Guy Edward ................................. 181
Guy H. .......................................... 180
J.C. ............................................... 180
Mary Lois ..................................... 180
P.J. ................................................ 180
Thomas ......................................... 181
V.A. .............................................. 180
W.H. ............................................. 180
William Albert ............................. 181
**Humphreys**
Bettie ............................................ 239
John R. ......................................... 181
**Hunter**
C.S. ............................................... 181
Frances ......................................... 283
John Berkeley .............................. 181
John Harrison .............................. 181
Julia .............................................. 181
Julia (Edmunds) ........................... 181
Julia A. ......................................... 181
Maria A. ....................................... 181
Marian .......................................... 181
Mary ............................................. 181
Mercy ........................................... 181
Minnie C. ..................................... 181

Nannie S. ... 181
Otho H. ... 181
Sophia Forrest ... 181
Summers ... 181
Susan ... 181
William H.W. ... 181
Zachariah P. ... 181
**Hurst**
   Mary (Barnhardt) ... 182
   Mary (Shirley) ... 182
   Rhoten ... 181
   Sarah Ann (Clevenger) ... 182
   Stephen D. ... 182
   William ... 182
**Hurt**
   Moses ... 182, 207
**Hutchings**
   Diannah ... 182
   George W. ... 182

# I

**I'Anson**
   William H. ... 182
**Illick**
   George W. ... 182
   Mary M. ... 182
**Illinois** ... 120, 170, 311
   Adams Co. ... 141
   Brown Co., Versailles ... 176
   Buffalo ... 237
   Cairo ... 283
   Carroll Co., Mt. Carroll ... 75
   DeWitt Co., Clinton ... 225
   Fulton Co. ... 180
   LaSalle Co. ... 218
   McLean Co. ... 101
   McLean Co., Bloomington ... 167
   McLean Co., Saybrook ... 283
   Payson ... 141
   Piatt Co., Atwood ... 128
   Vermilion Co., Danville ... 115
   Woodford Co., Roanoke ... 225
**Illinois - Infantry**
   50th Regt., Co. D ... 141
   68th Regt., Co. E ... 112
   95th Regt. ... 257
**Imboden**
   Benjamin F. ... 182
   Blanche ... 86
   Gen. John Daniel ... 183
   George ... 182
   Isabella (Wunderlich) ... 182
**Indian Territory** ... 250
   Chagris ... 98
   Choctaw Nation, Doaksville ... 98
   Jefferson Co., Cornish ... 98
   Love Co., Marietta ... 98
   Pickens Co., Healdton, Chickasaw Nation
   ... 98
   Robbers Roost ... 98
   Virginia Hill, Old Fort Washita ... 98
**Indiana**
   Clark Co., Jeffersonville ... 154
   Clarke Co. ... 275
   Decatur Co., New Point ... 103
   Floyd Co., New Albany ... 275
   Fountain Co. ... 115
   Fountain Co., Covington ... 156
   Ft. Wayne ... 162
   Grant Co., Marion, National Military Home ... 202
   Indianapolis ... 50
   Madison Co., Elwood ... 269
   Ripley Co. ... 275
   Ripley Co., Batesville ... 103
   St. Joseph Co., South Bend ... 204
   Sylvan Grove ... 154
   Tippecanoe Co. ... 115
   Tippecanoe Co., Lafayette Co. ... 115
   Tippecanoe Co., Wayne ... 156
   Tippecanoe Co., West Point ... 156
   Warren Co., State Line City ... 115
**Indiana - Cavalry**
   8th Regt., Co. M ... 182
**Induiana**
   Randolph ... 182
**Ingles**
   Margaret C. ... 298
**Ingram**
   Mary J. ... 159
**Iowa** ... 210, 318
   Decatur Co., Leon ... 149
   Dubuque Co., Cascade ... 247
   Union Co., Creston ... 249

## Iowa - Infantry
10th Regt., Co. E .............................. 180
**Ireland** ................. 80, 104, 120, 220, 231
   Altlone............................................ 145
   Dromara ......................................... 232
   Dublin ............................................. 306
   Moneghan Co., Glassworth .............. 205
**Isaacs**
   Rose C............................................. 110

## J

**Jackson**
   Andrew............................................ 183
   Charles ................... 183, 254, 288, 312
   Elizabeth.......................................... 183
   Gen. Stonewall .................................. 74
   James W. ......................................... 183
   Jane .................................................. 183
   Jane E,L............................................. 85
   John B. ............................................. 183
   Mary Ann ............................... 104, 183
   Nathaniel ......................................... 183
   Richard ............................................ 183
   Robert.............................................. 183
**James**
   Emily H. ........................................... 184
   Henry F. ........................................... 183
   Joseph H. ......................................... 183
   Louisa Elizabeth............................... 184
   Mary C. ........................................... 183
   Sarah ............................................... 183
   William D. ....................................... 184
   William H. ....................................... 184
   William M. ...................................... 184
**Jamison**
   John...................................95, 139, 184
   Mary Watts ..................................... 293
**Janney**
   Sarah ............................................... 272
**Jarratt**
   Louisa Elizabeth............................... 184
**Jarrett**
   John................................................ 184
**Jarvis**
   Harriet J. .......................................... 165
   Ida Virginia...................................... 131
   Margaret Catherine ......................... 101

**Jenkins**
   Adelphia ........................................... 66
   B.F. .................................................. 184
   Caroline........................................... 185
   Elizabeth.......................................... 185
   Elizabeth (Dove) .............................. 184
   Gilson.............................................. 185
   John......................................... 184, 185
   Lydia A. ........................................... 185
   Martha E. ......................................... 184
   Samuel............................................. 185
   Washington..................................... 185
   William .................................... 184, 185
   William H. ....................................... 184
**Jennings**
   James............................................... 185
   Martha J. ......................................... 316
   Mary ............................................... 316
   Sarah A. ........................................... 132
   William ........................................... 185
**Jerman**
   Elizabeth E. ...................................... 222
**Jessup**
   Thomas S. ........................................ 302
**Jett**
   Morilla Green.................................... 69
**Jewett**
   Noah........................................ 96, 185
**Johns**
   Elhanan........................................... 185
**Johnson**
   Almon ............................................. 185
   Ann E. ............................................. 186
   Catherine ........................................ 186
   Charles Y. ........................................ 185
   Francis A. ........................................ 185
   George E. ........................................ 186
   Isaac W. .......................................... 186
   John................................................ 186
   John Albert ..................................... 186
   Joseph............................................. 186
   Joseph A. ........................................ 186
   Laura Fowlkes................................. 137
   Lyndon B. ........................................ 236
   Mary Ann ....................................... 186
   Orie ................................................. 186
   Parthenia......................................... 185

Rebecca ............................................. 189
Richard ............................................. 186
Richard E. ......................................... 186
Samuel .............................................. 186
Vincent ............................................. 187
W.L. .................................................. 186
William H. ........................................ 187
William R. ........................ 80, 108, 187
**Johnston**
Alice Adams ..................................... 50
**Johnstone**
James Henry ................................... 187
**Joiner**
William M. ...................................... 187
**Jones**
Benson W. ....................................... 187
Charles ............................................. 187
Elizabeth .......................................... 188
Ellia .................................................. 188
Eugina B.C. (Hatch) ........................ 189
Frances ............................................. 279
George .............................................. 188
Harriet .............................................. 188
Jane .................................................. 189
John .................................................. 188
John A. ............................................. 188
John J. .............................................. 188
Joseph N. ......................................... 188
Mary ................................................. 188
Mary Ann ........................................ 189
Mrs. Ernest A. ................................. 247
Rebecca ........................................... 189
Richard ............................................ 189
Roger, Adj. Gen., U.S. Army ............ 64
Ruth E. ............................................. 149
Sparrell ............................................ 189
Thomas R. ....................................... 189
Virginia ........................................... 188
William A. ....................................... 189
**Jordan**
Alexander ........................................ 189
**Joy**
Elizabeth ........................................... 53
**Joyce**
Josephine ......................................... 220
**Judkins**
Dora A. ............................................ 156

Mary A. ............................................ 190
William N.B. ................................... 189

# *K*

**Kackley**
Margaret .......................................... 275
**Kansas** ............................................... 186
Atchison, Mt. Pleasant .................... 249
Cherokee Co., Galena .............. 181, 225
Cloud Co., Clyde ............................. 218
Crawford Co., Cherokee ................. 211
Doniphan Co. ................................... 290
Douglas Co., Bond ............................ 81
Douglas Co., Lone Star ..................... 81
Ft. Leavenworth, National Soldiers Home
........................................................ 194
Hodgeman Co., Kidderville ............. 129
Leavenworth County, Leavenworth .. 149
Ness Co., Bazine ............................. 102
Pottawatomie Co., Rockingham ....... 249
Sedgwick Co., Wichita .................... 191
Sumner Co., Conway Springs .......... 292
Wyandotte Co. ................................... 51
**Kansas - Cemeteries**
Kidderville Cemetery, Kidderville .... 129
**Kansas - Infantry**
6th Regt., Co. K ................................ 225
**Kansas Territory**
Ft. Leavenworth ................................ 85
**Karp**
Elizabeth .......................................... 190
John .................................................. 190
Peter ................................................. 190
**Keef**
John W. ..................................... 52, 237
**Keefe**
Annie ................................................ 190
Artie ................................................. 190
Charles ............................................. 190
George .............................................. 190
Hugh ................................................ 190
John W. ............................................ 210
John William ................................... 190
Maggie ............................................. 190
Martha ............................................. 190
Sarah ................................................ 190
Sarah F. ............................................ 191

## VIRGINIA VOLUNTEERS IN MEXICO

**Keeling**
   Caroline (Salmons) .......................... 191
   Rev. Henry ...................................... 191
   Robert Henry ..................... 59, 176, 191
**Keilholtz**
   John ................................................ 191
**Keister**
   George A. ............................... 191, 225
   Jacob ............................................... 191
   Margaret .......................................... 191
   Sarah Jane Virginia ......................... 191
**Keiter**
   Isaac ............................................... 191
**Keith**
   Charlotte Ashmore ............................ 83
**Kellam**
   James S ........................................... 191
   Sarah E. .......................................... 192
**Kelly**
   Catherine ........................................ 186
   Mary Ann ....................................... 141
   William ........................................... 192
**Kemper**
   Capt. James L .................................. 122
   Cremora Conway (Cave) .................. 192
   James L. .......................... 206, 220, 227
   James Lawson ................................. 192
   Maria E. (Allison) ........................... 192
   William ........................................... 192
**Kendall**
   Edison L. ........................................ 192
   John F. ............................................ 192
   Mary E. ........................................... 192
   Sarah Catherine .............................. 192
   William .................................. 192, 299
**Kennard**
   Sarah Jane ...................................... 103
**Kennedy**
   Charles ........................................... 192
**Kennon**
   James .............................................. 192
**Kent**
   Mary J. ............................................. 74
**Kentucky** .... 93, 107, 112, 188, 224, 245, 288, 291
   Anderson Co., Lawrenceburg ........... 152
   Ballan Co. ....................................... 137
   Boyd Co., Catlettsburg .................... 129

   Elliot Co., Percal ............................. 275
   Estel Co., Irving .............................. 176
   Fayette Co., Louisville .................... 152
   Fleming Co. .................................... 149
   Fleming Co., Mt. Carmel ................. 289
   Franklin Co., South Frankfort .......... 152
   Grayson Co. .................................... 291
   Hardin Co., Elizabethtown ............... 297
   Jefferson Co., Louisville ......... 115, 154
   Kenton Co., Covington ................... 134
   Lawrence Co. .................................. 116
   Leitchfield, Grayson Co. .................... 93
   Louisville ........................................ 291
   Pendleton Co., Doudton .................. 110
   Rowan Co., Moorehead .................. 275
**Kentucky - Infantry**
   1st Regt., Co. H .............................. 134
   22$^{nd}$ Regt., Co. A ............................ 129
   4$^{th}$ Regt., Co. E (U.S.) ..................... 245
**Kerns**
   Carolin ........................................... 273
**Kerr**
   George ............................................ 192
**Key**
   Mary A. .......................................... 134
**Keyes**
   Isabella Susan ................................. 278
**Kidd**
   William ........................................... 193
   William E. ...................................... 193
**Kidwell**
   Elizabeth ......................................... 194
**Kile**
   Elizabeth ......................................... 193
   George W. ...................................... 193
**Killed**
   *Assassinated by Mexicans* ........ 213, 237
   *Assassinated by Mexicans* ............. 148
   By Indians ....................................... 238
   By Mexicans ................................... 182
**Killed In Action**
   Brandy Station ................................. 85
   Dranesville, Va. ............................... 154
   Drewry's Bluff ................................ 304
   Frayser's Farm .................................. 75
   Gaines Mill ..................................... 158
   Gallagher's Mill .............................. 163

McDowell .................................... 203
Robertson's Cross Roads ................. 173
The Crater .................................... 240
**Kilmer**
Catherine ..................................... 295
**Kindley**
William ................................ 193, 279
**King**
Carrie Z. ...................................... 150
John ............................................ 193
John H. ........................................ 193
Mary A. ....................................... 193
Mary V.H. .................................... 311
Thomas F. .................................... 193
**Kinger**
Susan ........................................... 129
**Kinney**
Charles P. .................................... 194
Elizabeth C. ................................. 194
Lewis N. ...................................... 194
Lt. ................................................. 85
Mary A. ....................................... 194
Mollie .......................................... 258
Rebecca R. ................................... 194
Rebecca R. (Wayland) .................... 193
Robert .......................................... 238
Robert Henry ................................ 193
**Kipps**
Elizabeth ...................................... 198
Henry B. ...................................... 194
John ............................................. 194
Loretta F. ..................................... 194
Mary .................................... 194, 201
Mary C. ....................................... 201
Mary Elizabeth ............................. 194
Michael .... 71, 191, 194, 201, 223, 246, 254, 274
**Kirby**
Sarah Ann .................................... 116
**Kirk**
William ....................................... 194
**Kirkland**
Elizabeth J. .................................. 151
**Kisinger**
John ............................................ 194
Otho ............................................ 194
Susanna ....................................... 194

**Kisner**
Ashford ....................................... 194
Calista Ann (Reasoner) .................. 194
**Kitchen**
Caleb ........................................... 194
Elizabeth ...................................... 194
Mary E. ....................................... 194
Sarah Ann .................................... 194
**Klein**
Charles H. .................................... 194
Nannie Bass Fowlkes ..................... 137
**Knight**
Clevie K. ..................................... 101
**Knowles**
John ............................................ 194
**Knox**
Samuel T. .................................... 195
**Kolp**
Henry .......................................... 195
**Krishmann**
Anthony ...................................... 195
**Krumbein**
henry ........................................... 195
**Kurt**
John ............................................ 195
**Kurtz**
Isaac ............................................ 195
Robert Isaac ................................. 195

# *L*

**Laborer** ........................................ 61
**Lahmeyer**
Elizabeth ...................................... 196
John Henry ................................... 195
Virginia (Harrison) ........................ 196
William F. .................................... 196
**Lakeman**
Abner Jesse .................................. 196
Elizabeth ...................................... 196
Jacob ........................................... 196
John D. ........................................ 196
Josiah .......................................... 196
Malinda C. ................................... 196
Margaret ...................................... 196
Mary F. ........................................ 196
**LaLock**
William .......................................... 53
**Lamb**

Samuel ............................................. 196
**Lambert**
  Henry ............................................. 196
  Lucy A. ............................................. 91
  Sterling L. ....................................... 196
**Lancaster**
  Beverley W. .................................... 196
**Landes**
  Catherine ....................................... 196
  Joseph ............................................ 196
  Lucinda G. ..................................... 196
  Samuel ........................................... 196
**Landrum**
  John ................................................ 197
**Lane**
  Elizabeth A. ................................... 197
  John G. ........................................... 197
**Langford**
  William .......................................... 197
**Lanier**
  Ella R. ............................................. 165
  Frances (Pegram) .......................... 197
  John R. ........................................... 197
  John T. ................................... 197, 238
  Martha E.H. ................................... 197
  Martha L. ....................................... 197
  Norbourne F. ................................. 197
  Robert ............................................ 197
**Lappin**
  John ................................................ 197
**Larmand**
  Rosetta ........................................... 154
**Latham**
  Virginia A. ..................................... 178
**Laurence**
  Celinda A. ...................................... 198
  Celinda V.L. .................................. 198
  Charles E. ....................................... 198
  James R. ......................................... 198
  John E. .................................. 198, 213
  Theresa M.J. .................................. 198
  Willia A. ......................................... 198
**Lavall**
  Owen C. ......................................... 197
**Lawrence**
  Christopher ................................... 197
**Lawson**
  John H. ........................................... 198

Lewis ............................................... 198
Lucy ................................................ 198
**Leard**
  Samuel ........................................... 198
**Leary**
  Margaret ........................................ 240
  Michael .......................................... 240
**Leckie**
  John ................................................ 198
**LeCompte**
  Emily ................................................ 87
**Lee**
  Arminta .......................................... 198
  Charles ........................................... 198
  Elizabeth ........................................ 198
  Hamilton M. .................................. 198
  James .............................................. 198
  James F.P. ...................................... 198
  James P. .......................................... 198
  Nancy Ann ..................................... 224
  Robert M. ....................................... 205
  Robert W. ....................................... 198
  William D. ..................................... 198
**Legg**
  Isabella D. ..................................... 266
  William E. ..................................... 266
**Lennox**
  John ................................................ 199
**Lester**
  Cynthia .......................................... 108
  Jacob .............................................. 108
**Levy**
  Catherine E. .................................. 200
  William M. ...................................... 79
  William Mallory ........................... 199
**Lewellen**
  John Richard ................................. 200
  Virginia Louisa (Morris) .............. 200
**Lewis**
  Charles ........................................... 200
  Chloe ................................................ 99
  Christie E. ...................................... 312
  James .............................................. 200
  Joseph ............................................ 200
  Mary C. .......................................... 140
**Lightfoot**
  William T. ...................................... 200
**Lincoln**

Caroline Amanda .............................. 84
**Lindsay**
  Ann E. ........................................... 200
  Catherine ...................................... 316
  George H. ..................................... 200
  Hiram Opie ................................... 200
  John R. ......................................... 200
  Martha J. ....................................... 200
  Mary (Gorum) ............................... 200
  Mary S. ......................................... 200
  Mary T. ......................................... 200
  Stephen ......................................... 201
  William Thomas ............................ 200
**Lindsey**
  Susan ............................................ 226
**Linkinhoker**
  Eliz. ................................................ 68
**Linkous**
  Benjamin R. .......................... 201, 282
  Crockett ......................... 201, 230, 282
  E.H. ............................................... 149
  Elixzabeth ..................................... 281
  Fanny ............................................ 201
  Henry ............................................ 201
  Jacob ............................................ 201
  Margaret Augusta .......................... 201
  Mary .............................................. 201
  Mary C. ......................................... 201
  Mary Elizabeth .............................. 194
  Virginia B. ..................................... 149
  William B. .............................. 201, 282
**Lipscomb**
  George B. ..................................... 201
  Sarah B. (Hargrave) ...................... 201
**Liscomb**
  George .......................................... 145
**Little**
  Imogene .......................................... 62
  Moses A. ...................................... 201
**Loftin**
  Charles ......................................... 202
  Margaret ....................................... 202
**Logan**
  John J. .......................................... 202
  Margaret Elizabeth ........................ 202
**Logwood**
  Burwell ......................................... 202

Prudence ....................................... 202
Valentine S. .................................. 202
**Long**
  Charles C. ..................................... 202
  Frederick ...................................... 202
  Jacob ............................................ 202
  Mary ............................................. 202
  Napoleon B. .................................. 202
  Rebecca ........................................ 202
  William ................................. 202, 238
**Loomis**
  Charles T. ..................................... 203
  Ralph J. ........................................ 203
**Lorton**
  Robert ........................................... 203
**Lottier**
  Lewis ............................................ 203
**Lotts**
  John .............................................. 203
**Louge**
  Margaret ....................................... 202
**Louisana - Infantry**
  7th Regt., Co. A ............................ 231
**Louisiana** ...................................... 200
  Baton Rouge ................................. 166
  DeSoto Parish ............................... 292
  New Orleans ... 142, 166, 212, 230, 243
  West Baton Rouge., Brusly Landing ... 82
**Louisiana - Infantry**
  2$^{nd}$ Regt., Co. A ............................ 199
**Love**
  Hugh ............................................. 203
  James ............................................ 203
**Lowe**
  Elizabeth ....................................... 208
  Miranda ........................................ 303
**Lucado**
  Edwin T. ....................................... 204
  Isaac ............................................. 204
  Sally (Noell) ................................. 204
  Sarah Agnes (Wright) .................... 204
**Lukens**
  Hannah M. ..................................... 91
**Lundie**
  Mary ............................................. 204
  Thomas Y. .................................... 204
**Lunsford**
  Elizabeth Sarah ............................. 204

James .............................................. 204
**Lyles**
　Margaret ........................................ 133
**Lynch**
　Joseph N. ....................................... 204
**Lyon**
　Jane ................................................ 290

## M

**Mack**
　George W. ..................................... 204
**Mackey**
　Katherine S. ................................... 244
**Madison**
　Doctor T.C. .............................. 57, 59
　T.C. .................................. 85, 128, 185
**Magee**
　Ann ................................................ 205
　Bernard D. ..................................... 204
**Mahan**
　Mary P. .......................................... 150
　Thomas S. ........................................ 51
　Thomas T. ...................... 150, 205, 252
　Washington L. ................................ 205
**Maine**
　Bangor ............................................ 166
**Maine - Infantry**
　14th Regt., Co. A ............................ 166
**Major**
　Henry ............................................. 205
**Malcom**
　Melvina ............................................ 93
**Malone**
　Marshall ......................................... 205
**Manning**
　Debra Ann ..................................... 157
　William W. .................................... 205
**Mansell**
　James J. ......................................... 206
**Mansford**
　Robert ............................................ 206
**Manson**
　John L. ........................................... 206
　Josiah ............................................. 206
**Manspeeker**
　Susanna ......................................... 257
**Marable**
　Mary .............................................. 206

Roberta A. ...................................... 206
Roberta Ann ................................... 206
Thomas F. ....................................... 206
**Marcey**
　William L., Sec. of War ..................... 64
**March**
　Col., Beef Contractor ....................... 317
**Marcy**
　Louisiana ....................................... 280
**Marmon**
　Elizabeth (Lowe) ............................ 208
　Washington .................................... 206
**Marshall**
　Andrew J. ...................................... 208
　Charles H. ...................................... 208
　Mary ................................................ 57
　Thomas ............................................ 57
**Martin**
　Catherine ....................................... 289
　James, Jr. ....................................... 208
　John Peter ...................................... 208
　Mary .............................................. 118
　Mary C. .......................................... 209
　Nancy ............................................ 208
　William .......................................... 209
　William A. ..................................... 209
　William D. ..................................... 209
**Marye**
　John B.P. ....................................... 209
**Maryland** ... 140, 180, 234, 245, 289, 303
　Alleghany Co., Little Orleans ........... 216
　Baltimore 61, 63, 79, 85, 161, 209, 229,
　　232, 233, 248, 249, 295, 307
　Baltimore Co., Baltimore ...... 82, 97, 98,
　　233, 234
　Boonsboro ................ 75, 220, 266, 303
　Cambridge ....................................... 87
　Carroll Co., Westminster ................. 118
　Cumberland ............ 206, 216, 277, 307
　Doncaster ....................................... 257
　Dorchester Co., Cambridge ............... 87
　Dorchester Co., Taylor's Island ......... 87
　Fort Washington ............................. 295
　Frederick Co. .................... 97, 173, 303
　Frederick Co., Frederick .................... 62
　Frederick Co., New Market ............. 272
　Frederick Co., Point of Rocks ........... 159

Ft. McHenry.......................................... 85
Montgomery Co. .............................. 134
Montgomery Co., Barnesville............ 283
Montgomery Co., Burnt Mills ........... 200
Montgomery Co., Hunting Hill.......... 303
Montgomery Co., Rockville .... 154, 181, 194, 305
Montgomery Co., Travilah ................ 303
Montgomery Co., White's Ferry ....... 303
Prince George's Co., Piscataway ......... 94
Relay House, Howard Co. ................. 101
Sharpsburg........................................ 216
Springfield ....................................... 164
Vansville .......................................... 128
Washington Co. ................. 70, 157, 209
Washington Co., Boonsboro............. 167
Washington Co., Hagerstown .. 142, 210, 219, 271
Washington Co., Keep Tryst .............. 65
**Washington Co., Sharpsburg............ 157**
Washington Co., Williamsport ........... 52
**Maryland - Cavalry**
2nd Regt., Co. A (US)........................ 82
**Maryland - Infantry**
13th Regt., Co. F ............................... 75
**Mason**
Mary Nelson ..................................... 107
Thomas S. ......................................... 209
Thompson......................................... 209
**Massachusetts**
Boston ..................................... 138, 240
Middlesex Co., Woburn .................... 138
**Massey**
Renee ................................................ 169
**Mathews**
Mary E.............................................. 136
**Mathie**
Alcinda ............................................... 55
**Matthews**
Mary Frances ................................... 132
Robert................................................ 209
**Mattingly**
Elizabeth........................................... 133
John.................................................... 52
Marie.................................................. 52
**Maule**
Lewis................................................. 209

Pheobe .............................................. 210
**Maxwell**
Dianna .............................................. 210
Edward ............................................. 139
Edward W......... 52, 135, 210, 237, 297
Rosa ................................................. 210
Sarah E. ............................................ 211
William B. .............................. 210, 297
William G. ....................................... 297
**Mayer**
Maria Barbara ................................. 247
**Maygar**
Henry ............................................... 211
**Maynard**
Illione Mary Catherine .................... 211
Mendoza B....................................... 211
**Mays**
Mortimer N. ..................................... 211
**McAlexander**
Paratha............................................. 255
**McAllister**
William T. ....................................... 211
**McArthur**
John D. ............................................. 211
**McCaleb**
Ella................................................... 211
Thomas J. ....... 156, 211, 215, 239, 306
**McCarthy**
Dennis .............................................. 211
Sarah E. ............................................ 211
**McClenney**
Judith Yates ..................................... 107
**McClintic**
Elizabeth Jane ................................. 110
**McClure**
William C. ....................................... 212
**McCollum**
Daniel............................................... 212
**McCorkle**
Alexander C..................................... 212
John.................................................. 212
Sarah Etchinson (Cunningham) ........ 212
**McCormack**
William............................................ 212
**McCormick**
William............................................ 212
**McCoy**
George M. ........................................ 212

# VIRGINIA VOLUNTEERS IN MEXICO

Nancy .................................................. 98
**McCrady**
   Annie J. ........................................ 213
   Jeremiah ...................................... 212
**McCrarey**
   Ada B. .......................................... 101
**McCrory**
   Thomas ........................................ 213
**McCullough**
   Sally A. ......................................... 254
**McDade**
   David ........................................... 173
   Susan E. ....................................... 173
**McDaniel**
   Alfred ........................................... 213
   Edward ........................................ 213
   Elizabeth G. .................................. 213
   Laura ............................................ 213
   Mary F. ......................................... 213
   Osborne ....................................... 213
   Reuben ........................................ 213
   Samuel ......................................... 213
   William ......................................... 213
**McDonald**
   Elizabeth) ..................................... 74
   John A. ......................................... 213
   Mary ............................................. 179
   Nancy Ann ................................... 71
**McDowell**
   Esther G. ...................................... 176
   Irwin ............................................. 219
**McFarland**
   Samuel ......................................... 215
**McGarity**
   Jonathan ...................................... 250
**McGathey**
   Levi .............................................. 215
**McGee**
   Fleming C. .................................... 215
   Martha A.S. Wilbourne ................. 215
   Mary Jane .................................... 157
**McGoath**
   Fanny) .......................................... 73
**McGowan**
   William G. .................................... 215
**McGranahan**
   Elizabeth ...................................... 115
   Harriet .......................................... 115

**McGraw**
   Sarah A. ....................................... 180
**McGuire**
   Patrick .......................................... 215
**McIndoe**
   Rebecca D. ................................... 304
**McIntosh**
   Joseph .......................................... 215
**McIntyre**
   Clara A. ........................................ 156
**McKay**
   Pilate ............................................ 215
**McKeag**
   Lucinda G. ................................... 196
**McKee**
   Mary ............................................. 142
**McKenzie**
   Rebecca ....................................... 162
**McKinney**
   James W. ..................................... 215
   Meridith C. .......................... 216, 264
**McLaughlin**
   Mary N. ........................................ 232
**McLondon**
   James A. ...................................... 216
**McMann**
   John ............................................. 216
**McMinn**
   Barbara Ann ................................ 216
   Catherine ..................................... 216
   Charles Henry ............................. 216
   Emily ............................................ 216
   Emma .......................................... 216
   George William ............................ 216
   Joseph ......................................... 216
   Mary Hellen ................................. 216
**McNorton**
   Taylor ........................................... 216
**McNulty**
   Arthur ........................................... 216
**McPhail**
   Dougald ....................................... 216
**McPhelin**
   Mary E. ........................................ 216
   Patrick .......................................... 216
   Peter ............................................ 216
**McSherry**
   Alice ............................................. 125

Sallie .............................................. 125
**Meador**
  Albert ............................................ 216
  Alexander C. ................................... 217
  Emily .............................................. 217
  Martha ........................................... 217
  Richard .......................................... 217
  Sally ............................................... 217
  Sarah Sally (Talley) ........................ 216
**Mears**
  Captain .......................................... 207
**Mendenall**
  Elijah L. .......................................... 217
  Jacob ............................................. 217
  Mary ............................................... 217
**Menefee**
  Ann .................................................. 60
**Merrick**
  John W. .......................................... 217
**Merritt**
  Caleb E. ......................................... 218
  Christian Garber ............................. 217
  Clarence M. ................................... 218
  Edwin A. ......................................... 218
  Edwin B. ......................................... 218
  Elizabeth ........................................ 217
  Elizabeth E. .................................... 218
  Elizabeth Ellen ............................... 218
  Elizabeth M. ................................... 218
  John ............................................... 217
  John H. ........................................... 218
  Josephine ...................................... 218
  Mary E. ........................................... 218
  Mary L. ........................................... 218
  Sarah V. ......................................... 218
  William H. ....................................... 218
**Merryman**
  Pulaski P. ....................................... 218
**Merton**
  Cornelius W. .................................. 218
  Eliza J. ............................................ 218
**Mesley**
  John ............................................... 219
  John A. ........................................... 219
  Mary ............................................... 219
**Mexico**
  Auga Nueva ................................... 113

Black Fort ............................... 259, 261
Buena Vista . 50, 53, 56, 60, 70, 79, 81, 84, 87, 89, 91, 92, 99, 102, 113, 115, 117, 118, 124, 125, 126, 137, 154, 156, 162, 163, 165, 188, 189, 190, 193, 195, 203, 205, 206, 209, 219, 222, 226, 228, 229, 233, 241, 247, 251, 254, 255, 256, 284, 294, 296, 299, 305, 306, 315, 316
Camargo 50, 69, 72, 78, 104, 113, 121, 124, 128, 133, 140, 142, 145, 149, 158, 166, 176, 191, 193, 197, 211, 212, 215, 232, 248, 253, 254, 256, 269, 272, 280, 283, 294, 300, 306, 309, 312, 315
China 26, 28, 64, 80, 86, 126, 142, 163, 174, 176, 180, 187, 193, 195, 201, 205, 215, 225, 226, 240, 284, 299, 302
Matamoros 50, 81, 82, 89, 99, 100, 113, 117, 145, 177, 183, 193, 212, 253, 256, 272, 280, 309, 316
Monclova Road ............... 152, 206, 297
Monterey 50, 51, 57, 63, 64, 66, 70, 71, 72, 81, 84, 85, 86, 88, 90, 94, 100, 111, 115, 120, 126, 128, 132, 138, 147, 148, 153, 156, 157, 163, 164, 167, 168, 177, 178, 179, 180, 183, 185, 188, 189, 194, 195, 198, 202, 203, 209, 212, 215, 216, 219, 221, 222, 224, 229, 230, 231, 233, 235, 237, 238, 239, 245, 248, 257, 259, 260, 269, 271, 275, 276, 277, 278, 283, 285, 286, 289, 296, 301, 305, 309, 310, 312, 313
Parras ...................... 89, 204, 213, 237
Queretaro ........................................ 240
Rinconada ....................................... 293
Rinconada Pass ................................ 91
Saltillo ... 72, 76, 79, 83, 84, 86, 89, 93, 100, 105, 107, 109, 114, 115, 119, 121, 122, 123, 125, 128, 129, 131, 134, 139, 151, 152, 153, 157, 164, 170, 174, 175, 181, 182, 187, 192, 195, 196, 198, 204, 205, 206, 207, 208, 209, 212, 213, 214, 216, 219, 221,

## VIRGINIA VOLUNTEERS IN MEXICO

225, 228, 239, 240, 242, 251, 255, 256, 267, 274, 277, 282, 284, 286, 290, 294, 295, 297, 301, 305, 306, 313, 314, 317
Walnut Springs .................. 58, 259, 260
**Meyer**
Joseph ............................................. 219
**Michael**
Carl ................................................. 219
**Michigan**
Detroit ............................................ 240
**Millan**
Ann ................................................. 219
Eliza M. .......................................... 219
Eliza Minerva (Draper) .................... 219
George ............................................ 219
George L. ........................................ 219
James R. ......................................... 219
**Millar**
Samuel Rolfe ................................. 247
**Miller**
Ann E. ............................................ 221
C.S. ................................................. 219
Charles W. ...................................... 221
Charlotte ......................................... 221
Clara Josephine .............................. 220
Claudie T. ....................................... 221
Emanuel .......................................... 221
Hoppie J. ........................................ 221
Hoppie Jacobs ................................ 221
Jacob G. .......................................... 219
James .............................................. 219
John ................................................ 219
John Alexander .............................. 220
John M. .......................................... 217
John McCelland ............................. 220
Joseph ............................................. 220
Josephine ........................................ 220
Julia A. ........................................... 221
Laura C. .......................................... 221
Lewis N. ......................................... 221
Margaret E. ..................................... 219
Margaret J. ..................................... 221
Mary E. ........................................... 221
Peter ............................................... 220
Samuel W. ...................................... 221
Turner A. ........................................ 221

Virginia B. ...................................... 221
William ........................................... 221
**Millholland**
John ................................................ 219
**Mills**
Armistead M. ................................. 222
Armistead T. .................................. 222
Cornelia .......................................... 222
Elizabeth ........................................ 316
Elizabeth E. .................................... 222
Elizabeth J. ..................................... 110
George ............................................ 222
Henry .............................................. 222
Mahlon ........................................... 222
Nancy Elizabeth ............................... 62
Peter ............................................... 222
Robert ............................................. 222
Robert F. ........................................ 222
Sarah Ann .............................. 194, 253
Virginia .......................................... 222
William J. ....................................... 222
**Millspaugh**
Charles ........................................... 222
Emma ............................................. 222
Henrietta Virginia (Talbott) ............. 222
Mehitable ....................................... 222
**Milton**
Lucinda ............................................ 94
**Minnesota**
Wright Co., Buffalo ........................ 292
**Minnick**
Amy M. .......................................... 222
Charles A. ...................................... 222
John H. .................... 194, 213, 222
Mary S.F. ....................................... 222
Susan A. ......................................... 222
**Minor**
Albert G. ........................................ 223
Catherine ........................................ 224
Daniel ............................................. 223
Lucelia Carlin ................................. 223
Mary (Ross) .................................... 223
Philip B. ......................................... 223
William ........................................... 224
William G. ............. 153, 207, 224, 297
**Mississippi** ................... 193, 271
Layfayette Co., Oxford ................... 103

Natchez, Adams Co. ......................... 101
Neshoba Co., Philadelphia ............... 167
Panola Co. ....................................... 134
Panola Co., Wallace......................... 113
Senatobia, Tate Co. .......................... 134
Vicksburg ........................................ 202
Washington ..................................... 233
**Mississippi - Infantry**
10th Regt., Co. G............................... 88
2nd Regt., Co. F .............................. 277
**Missouri** ............... 75, 184, 209, 292, 314
Andrew Co., Savannah.................... 133
Boone Co. Rocheport....................... 302
Buchanan Co., St. Joseph ................ 290
Chariton Co. .................................... 250
Charleston ....................................... 137
Clay Co., Kearney ........................... 128
Clay Co., Liberty ............................. 258
Franklin Co. .................................... 310
Gasconade Co. ................................ 310
Gasconade Co., Hermann ................. 63
Harrison Co., Butler ........................ 258
Jackson Co. ..................................... 102
Jackson Co., Kansas City ................ 291
Jasper Co., Joplin ............................ 212
Lafayette Co. ............................ 81, 102
Layfayette Co., Corden ................... 297
Linclon ............................................ 107
Linn Co., Linneus ........................... 135
Marion Co. ........................................ 51
Miller Co. .......................................... 81
Montgomery Co., Montgomery City ... 51
Newton Co., Granby ....................... 181
Nodaway Co., Elmo ........................ 198
Platte Co., Weston ........................... 258
Reynolds Co., Edge Hill .................. 149
Ripley Co. ....................................... 149
Scotland Co. ..................................... 99
Springfield ...................................... 232
St. Charles Co., St. Charles ............... 51
St. Louis ......................................... 194
St. Louis .............................. 85, 86, 292
St. Louis, St. Anthony's Hospital ........ 86
Warren Co. ....................................... 51
Webster Co., Marshfield ................. 292
Webster Co., Ozark ......................... 292
**Missouri - Cavalry**
10th Regt., Co. I .............................. 310
**Missouri - Infantry**
40th Regt., Co. D ............................. 194
6th Regt. ......................................... 135
**Mitchell**
Colonel ............................................. 59
Josephine ........................................ 224
Larinda L. ....................................... 140
Robert ............................................. 224
**Montague**
John Currie ..................................... 224
Nancy Ann (Lee) ............................ 224
Richard T. ....................................... 224
Vetoria ............................................ 230
**Montana**
Custer Co., Brandenburg ................. 250
Custer Co., Miles City .................... 250
**Monterio**
Pocahontas C. ................................. 224
**Montero**
Andre A. ......................................... 263
Andrew A. ................... 53, 94, 96, 224
**Montgomery**
Anastasia ........................................ 224
Benjamin ........................................ 224
Charles H. ....................................... 224
**Moody**
George A. ....................................... 224
Laura Ann ....................................... 225
Sinah A. (DeVaughn) ..................... 225
**Mooney**
Alice ............................................... 225
Burrilda Jane .................................. 225
Edward H. ...................................... 225
George S. ........................................ 225
James R. ......................................... 225
Martha B. ........................................ 225
**Moore**
Ammishaddai ................................. 226
Elvira .............................................. 225
Elvira (Finch) ................................. 225
Hannah (Morris) ............................. 226
James E. ......................................... 225
James M. ........................................ 225
Jeremiah ......................................... 226
John ........................................ 225, 285
John L. ............................................ 225

Lewis E. .......................................... 225
Lewis Elcon ................................... 225
Lillian E. ........................................ 225
Lydia Reno .................................... 226
Mary A. ......................................... 225
Mary Ann ...................................... 226
Milliard J. ...................................... 225
Morse ............................................. 226
Nancy E.T. ..................................... 225
Philip A. ........................................ 225
Rebecca ......................................... 226
Richard G. ..................................... 225
S. E. ............................................... 225
Silas ............................................... 226
Susan ............................................. 226
Thomas M. ..................................... 226
William .......................................... 226
William H. ............................ 225, 226

**Moorman**
Roxanna ........................................ 249
**Morgan**
David W. ....................................... 226
**Morlick**
Michael .......................................... 226
**Morris**
Hannah .......................................... 226
Virginia Louisa .............................. 200
**Morse**
Catherine ....................................... 216
Daniel ............................................ 226
**Morton**
Martha Georgiana ............................ 57
**Moss**
Ann ................................................ 227
Ann Eliza ....................................... 227
Emily .............................................. 227
James ............................................. 227
James O. ........................................ 227
Jamima ........................................... 227
John J. ............................................ 227
Mary A. .......................................... 227
Mary C. .......................................... 227
William E. ...................................... 227
**Mountcastle**
Mary .............................................. 148
**Mourning**
Marthy ........................................... 107

**Moyer**
John ............................................... 227
Sarah ............................................... 84
**Moyers**
Florence B. .................................... 227
James H. ........................ 148, 285, 295
James Harvey ................................ 227
James P. ......................................... 227
Margaret ........................................ 227
Margaret M. ................................... 227
Mary E. .......................................... 227
Susan J. .......................................... 227
**Moyler**
John ............................................... 227
**Muirhead**
James W. ....................................... 228
**Mullen**
Charles .......................................... 228
Maria E. ......................................... 111
Robert ............................................ 228
**Muloy**
Francis P. ....................................... 228
**Muncy**
Alicey ............................................ 116
Julia Ann ......................................... 51
**Munford**
Carlton Radford ............................. 228
Sarah (Radford) ............................. 228
William .......................................... 228
**Munn**
Daniel ............................................ 228
**Munson**
Ellen .............................................. 180
**Muny**
John ............................................... 229
**Murdaugh**
John W. ......................................... 229
**Murphy**
Daniel ............................................ 229
William W. .................................... 229
**Murray**
Anne .............................................. 253
James ............................................. 229
Lewis ............................................. 229

*N*

**Nash**
Minnie ........................................... 138

**Naugle**
  William H. ..................................... 229
**Nebraska** .............................................. 88
  Adams Co., Hastings ..................... 290
  Butler Co., Bellwood ..................... 258
  Ft. McPhearson .............................. 300
  Platte Co., Columbus ..................... 258
  Richardson Co. ................................ 129
**Nees**
  John M. ........................................... 229
**Neighbors**
  A.R. .................................................. 230
  Christopher ..................................... 230
  James ................................................ 230
  Mary Ann ........................................ 230
**Neill**
  William V. ....................................... 230
**Nevada**
  Washoe Co., Reno .......................... 243
**Neves**
  David ................................................ 227
**New Jersey** ........................................... 132
  Burlington, Medford ...................... 202
  Camden Co., Camden ..................... 128
  Essex Co., Bloomfield ................... 197
  Essex Co., Hoboken ....................... 266
  Essex Co., Newark ......................... 197
  Gloucester ........................................ 98
  Rutherford ....................................... 148
  Salem Co., Salem ........................... 128
  Trenton ............................................ 117
**New Jersey - Infantry**
  29th Regt., Co. H ............................ 202
  39th Regt., Co. A ............................ 196
**New Mexico** ......................................... 211
  Bernalillo Co., Albuquerque ............ 93
**New York** ..... 68, 173, 179, 219, 222, 295
  Broadway ......................................... 51
  Brooklyn ................................. 141, 146
  Dutchess Co., Poughkeepsie ........... 240
  Erie Co., Buffalo ............................. 51
  Hart's Island, NY Harbor ................ 56
  Kings Co., Brooklyn ....................... 205
  Long Island, Greenport ................... 100
  Madison Barracks ........................... 166
  New York ............... 222, 240, 253, 293
  Oneida Co., Uttica ........................... 88
  Orange Co. ....................................... 222
  Orange Co., Newburg ..................... 240
  Ostego Co. ....................................... 226
  Rochester ......................................... 160
**Newall**
  James ................................................ 230
**Newell**
  Benjamin C. .................................... 230
**Newhall**
  Amos ................................................ 230
  Charles G. ........................................ 230
  Vetoria .............................................. 230
**Newlee**
  Malinda ............................................ 230
  Martha .............................................. 230
  Martha J. .......................................... 230
  Mary Davis ...................................... 230
  Robert G. .......................... 201, 230, 298
  William ............................................. 230
**Newspaper**
  *Alexandria Gazette* ....................... 184
  *Baltimore Sun* ................................ 293
  *Danville Register* .................... 200, 273
  *Martinsburg Gazette* .. 52, 210, 245, 267
  *Natchitoches Chronicle* ................. 199
  *Staunton Spectator* ........................ 163
  *Staunton Vindicator* ....................... 164
  *The Conductor* ............................... 200
  *Valley Democrat* ............................ 97
**Newton**
  Ruth .................................................. 98
**Nicholson**
  Caroline ........................................... 231
  David W. ......................................... 230
  John W. ........................................... 231
  Lemuel ............................................. 231
  Lemuel P. ........................................ 231
  Margaret Ann .................................. 124
**Noble**
  Alpha E. .......................................... 231
  Cornelia Maria ................................ 231
  Daniel .............................................. 231
  Moses Greer .................................... 231
  Nancy .............................................. 231
  Robert W. ........................................ 231
**Noel**
  Landon ............................................ 231

**Noell**
  Sally .............................................. 204
**Noon**
  Annie H. ........................................ 231
  Caroline ........................................ 231
  Euphema ...................................... 231
  Hugh D. ........................................ 231
  John A. ......................................... 231
  Mary A. ........................................ 231
  Robert ........................................... 231
  Susan B. ....................................... 231
**Nopie**
  William ......................................... 231
**Norfleet**
  Annie L. ........................................ 232
  Christopher .................................. 232
  Daisy ............................................ 232
  Elizabeth ...................................... 232
  Fannie J. ....................................... 232
  Hadley C. ..................................... 232
  Letitia ........................................... 232
  Linwood ....................................... 232
  Louisa ........................................... 232
  Luella C. ....................................... 232
  Mary Frances ............................... 232
**North Carolina** ................................ 190
  Alamance Co., Burlington .............. 145
  Alamance Co., Company Shop's ...... 145
  Alamance Co., Graham .................... 145
  Asheville ......................................... 67
  Caldwell Co. .................................. 211
  Camden Co., Camden ....................... 99
  Catawba Co., Newton ....................... 67
  Chatham Co. Pittsboro .................... 236
  Craven Co., Newbern........................ 64
  Currituck Co. .................................. 241
  Currituck Co., Grandy ..................... 241
  Currituck Co., Poplar Branch ... 241, 308
  Currituck Co., Powell's Point ........... 241
  Dare Co., Manteo ............................ 309
  Dare Co., Roanoke Island ................ 309
  Dare Co., Stumpy Point ................... 309
  Elizabeth City ................................. 309
  Fayetteville ....................................... 69
  Franklin Co., Hayesville ................. 123
  Franklin Co., Pughs ........................ 123
  Gates Co. ........................................ 118
  Granville Co. .................................... 60
  Greene Co., Hookerton .................... 266
  Halifax ............................................ 280
  Halifax Co. .............................. 105, 246
  Halifax Co., Weldon ........................ 165
  Hatteras ............................................ 66
  Hendersonville .................................. 67
  Hertford Co. ................................... 147
  Hertford Co., Murfreesboro ............. 147
  Kinston ........................................... 112
  Martin Co., Williamston ................. 266
  Mecklenburg Co., Charlotte ............ 138
  Newbern ........................................... 85
  Northampton .................................. 202
  Northampton Co. ............................ 112
  Northampton Co., Garysburg ............ 50
  Northampton Co., Guston ............... 280
  Perquimans Co., Belvidere .............. 147
  Perquimans Co., Hertford ................ 147
  Perquimans Co., Winfall ................. 147
  Pitt Co., Greenville ......................... 224
  Raleigh ............................................. 53
  Randolph Co. .................................. 294
  Surry Co., Kapp's Mill ..................... 280
  Surry Co., Mt. Airy ......................... 213
  Surry Co., White Plains ................... 280
  Vance Co., Henderson ..................... 148
  Wake Co. Raleigh ........................... 236
  Wake Co., Raleigh ................... 78, 236
  Warrenton ....................................... 312
  Washington Co., Creswell ............... 147
  Wautauga Co. .................................. 211
  Western North Carolina Insane Asylum
  ......................................................... 67
**North Carolina - Infantry**
  1st Regt., Co. G .............................. 147
  1st Regt., Co. H .............................. 243
  24th Regt., Co. A ..................... 174, 276
  5th Regt., Co. H .............................. 118
  8th Regt. ......................................... 308
**Norville**
  George W. ...................................... 232
  Nancy A. ........................................ 232
**Nottingham**
  Anna ............................................... 232
  Anne Finley ................................... 232
  Jacob .............................................. 232

Laurett V. .................................. 232
Lucy Ann ................................... 232
Margaret Sarah .......................... 232
Sarah Jarvis ............................... 232
William Thomas ........................ 232
**Nunally**
Theoderick ................................. 199
**Nunnally**
Mary A. ..................................... 232
Theoderick ......................... 232, 285

## O

**O'Bannon**
Dagobert B. ................................ 232
Mary P. (Heard) ........................ 233
Sarah Ann (Wilson) ................... 233
**O'Neal**
Felix .......................................... 233
**Obitz**
Danial L. .................................... 233
Rebecca ..................................... 233
**Occupations** ............................. 88, 101
Assistant Tutor of Spanish ............... 183
Bailiff ........................................... 240
Baker ....................... 138, 140, 266
Baliff ........................................... 118
Bank Cashier .............................. 304
Banker ........................................ 244
Bar Keeper ......................... 123, 279
Blacksmith. 63, 68, 106, 114, 130, 232, 238, 246, 266, 268, 269, 298, 300
Boatman ..................................... 276
Boiler Maker .............................. 173
Bookkeeper .................. 64, 140, 306
Boot & Shoemaker ............. 167, 234
Brick Mason .................. 99, 156, 165
Bricklayer 69, 151, 156, 165, 173, 235, 305, 306
Builder ....................................... 219
Butcher ................ 98, 257, 288, 294
Cabinet Maker.. 79, 124, 168, 186, 227, 235, 278, 304
Carpenter 56, 61, 66, 75, 84, 87, 91, 94, 98, 105, 106, 122, 133, 142, 151, 160, 179, 180, 184, 222, 227, 230, 236, 239, 242, 266, 272, 273, 278, 285, 287, 289, 295, 299, 300, 309, 311, 317
Carpenter & Shingle Inspector .......... 232
Carriage Maker .................. 72, 76, 195
Cashier In Bank .............................. 244
Cattle Dealer .................................... 84
Chair Painter .................................. 182
Circuit Court Clerk ............ 52, 143, 298
Circus Man ..................................... 105
Civil Engineer ......................... 142, 311
Clerk 81, 100, 107, 110, 119, 123, 134, 158, 164, 190, 197, 202, 218, 236, 247, 253, 257, 281, 298, 306, 308, 311
Clothier .......................................... 234
Coach Maker ........................... 156, 285
College Steward ............................. 291
Commission Merchant .................... 242
Commonwelath's Attorney .............. 163
Confectioner ............. 65, 219, 240, 259
Constable ......................... 85, 140, 286
Cooper 72, 75, 110, 150, 167, 176, 245, 250, 275, 279, 287, 288
Customs Inspector ............................ 75
Day Laborer ........................... 149, 284
Dentist ............................................. 65
Deputy Clerk of Court ............. 116, 242
Deputy Sergeant ............................. 118
Deputy Sheriff ......................... 62, 195
Ditcher ........................................... 241
Druggist .................................. 78, 222
Editor .............................................. 97
Engineer ......................... 194, 278, 292
Engineer on Steamship ..................... 76
Espicopal Clergyman ........................ 87
Farm Hand ............................. 123, 164
Farm Laborer .................. 136, 240, 289
farmer ............................................. 56
Farmer ... 50, 51, 53, 55, 56, 60, 62, 68, 69, 71, 72, 73, 78, 79, 83, 84, 88, 101, 102, 104, 108, 109, 110, 113, 116, 120, 121, 126, 128, 129, 130, 137, 140, 143, 147, 148, 151, 152, 154, 155, 158, 160, 161, 163, 167, 169, 170, 173, 174, 177, 180, 183, 184, 185, 193, 198, 200, 202, 217,

218, 224, 225, 230, 231, 234, 240, 241, 242, 244, 245, 247, 248, 249, 250, 251, 254, 255, 267, 270, 271, 274, 275, 276, 280, 282, 283, 284, 287, 301, 302, 305, 307, 310, 311, 312, 315
Farmer & School Teacher ................ 137
Fencer................................................. 55
Ferryman ......................................... 303
Finisher............................................ 229
Fire Chief........................................ 140
Gardener.......................................... 187
Gardner............................................ 168
Glove Maker ................................... 298
Grocer ............................................. 140
Hardware Store ............................... 136
Harness Maker ... 56, 81, 128, 196, 199, 285
Hatter ...................................... 120, 197
Hog Raiser....................................... 120
Hotel Keeper..................................... 64
House Painter .................. 119, 134, 221
Huckster .................................. 157, 281
Jailor ................................ 62, 162, 195
Jeweller .................................... 166, 183
Keeps Public House......................... 279
Laborer ...... 56, 63, 64, 70, 81, 83, 102, 106, 111, 112, 126, 131, 149, 154, 157, 160, 161, 164, 166, 168, 178, 179, 189, 194, 195, 198, 200, 222, 231, 235, 238, 249, 251, 255, 266, 271, 272, 273, 274, 276, 278, 283, 287, 290, 295, 305, 306, 309, 316
Lawyer .. 57, 61, 66, 92, 116, 117, 123, 143, 163, 209, 226, 245, 254, 265, 273, 284, 288, 294
Librarian, Virginia Military Institute. 311
Lighthouse Keeper........................... 164
Machinist........................................... 91
Manager of Farm............................. 248
Manager on Rail Road ...................... 73
Master Carpenter............................... 76
Mayor ................................................ 97
Mechanic ......................................... 302
Medical Student ................................ 87

Merchant . 97, 118, 120, 130, 154, 237, 243, 267
Miller .. 69, 83, 91, 133, 182, 235, 280, 306
Millwright................................. 83, 276
Minister .......................................... 239
Moulder........................................... 138
Musician......................................... 185
Negro Trader................................... 136
Newspaper Editor ............................. 92
Ordnance ........................................ 190
Overseer .. 73, 152, 164, 166, 179, 230, 276, 278
Overseer on R.R. ............................... 90
Painter . 52, 66, 69, 105, 119, 134, 152, 155, 180, 210, 224, 286
Painter & Varnisher ........................ 182
Patient in Lunatic Asylum ................ 308
Pauper ............................................ 279
Physician ..... 74, 87, 89, 136, 145, 181, 182, 231, 267, 314
Plasterer... 71, 108, 120, 128, 130, 142, 217, 235, 274, 286
Postmaster ...................................... 141
Printer....... 97, 111, 117, 162, 200, 290
Public Guard ..... 82, 180, 198, 234, 246
Pump Borer....................................... 74
Pump Maker ..................................... 74
Quarrier ............................................ 93
Railroad Engineer ........................... 145
Retail Dealer ................................... 102
Saddler ....... 56, 65, 128, 150, 196, 203, 309, 316
Sailor......................................... 51, 136
Salesman ................................. 281, 291
Saloon Keeper................................. 253
Sawyer..................................... 240, 255
Sexton ............................................ 187
Ship's Carpenter ............................... 72
Shoemaker 62, 115, 137, 154, 159, 160, 181, 185, 189, 221, 234, 244, 252, 256, 268, 272, 274, 289, 296
Slave Dealer..................................... 62
Soldier............................................ 141
Spooler ........................................... 124
Stage Driver ................................... 123

Stone Mason ............. 55, 167, 256, 307
Stone Mason/Fence Builder.............. 125
Stonecutter......................................... 56
Store Keeper ................................... 251
Student ............................................. 55
Superintendent Poor House ................ 62
Tailor..... 70, 73, 78, 85, 104, 110, 112, 127, 141, 168, 169, 173, 174, 188, 230, 293
Tanner ...................... 79, 192, 211, 275
Teacher...... 67, 81, 126, 155, 156, 159, 226, 295, 300
Timber Inspector ............................. 237
Tinner............................................. 154
Tinsmith ......................................... 154
Tobacco Trader ............................... 148
Tobacconist..................................... 298
Tobbaconist .................................... 203
Trucker............................................. 94
Tutor ........................................ 62, 241
Waggonmaker................................. 303
Wagon Maker ......................... 156, 222
Wheelwright ................... 134, 289, 302
Whiskey Inspector............................. 83
Works In A Cotton Factory .............. 253
Works in Flour Mill......................... 305
Works on a Farm..................... 150, 160
Works on the Highway .................... 306

**Ochleman**
   John............................................... 182
   Mary M. ......................................... 182

**Ohio**................................ 66, 167, 239
   Allen Co., Lima.............................. 292
   Astabulah Co., Conneaut.................. 156
   Batavia .......................................... 249
   Butler Co., Melville ........................ 103
   Champaign Co., Urbana................... 101
   Clark Co., South Charleston ............. 218
   Clinton Co., Blanchester .................. 149
   Clinton Co., Clarksville ................... 149
   Clinton Co., Wilmington.................. 249
   Columbus ....................................... 150
   Dayton, Montgomery Co.................... 99
   Delaware Co., Delaware ................. 101
   Elizabeth City Co., Hampton............ 202
   Fairfield Co., Lancaster................... 196
   Fayette Co....................................... 149
   Fayette Co., Washington C.H. .......... 150
   Gallia Co., Gallipolis ....................... 107
   Grant Co., Marion ........................... 202
   Hamilton Co., Cincinnati ................. 196
   Highland Co............................ 201, 249
   Meigs Co., Hockingport................... 288
   Montgomery Co., Dayton........... 82, 202
   Montgomery Co., Dayton, National Military Home.............................. 202
   Montgomery Co., Dayton, National Soldiers Home............................... 90
   National Military Home ................... 245
   Preble Co., West Alexandria ............ 188
   Preble Co., West Florence................ 188
   Putnam Co., Hartsburg..................... 292
   Putnam Co., Kalida.......................... 292
   Starke Co. ........................................ 89
   Warren Co., Lebanon....................... 149
   Warren Co., Salem .......................... 149
   Warren Co., Washington.................. 149
   Wilmington..................................... 150

**Ohio - Infantry**
   146th Regt., Co. K........................... 149
   167$^{th}$ Regt., Co. I .............................. 103
   186th Regt., Co. D........................... 318

**Oklahoma**
   Carter Co., Ardmore ......................... 98
   Stroud............................................ 249

**Olcott**
   Henry B. ......................................... 233

**Oliver**
   Parthenia......................................... 185

**O'Neill**
   Mary................................................ 62

**Onion**
   John R. ................................... 233, 311

**Oregon**
   Multnomah Co., Portland................. 318
   Washington Co., Cornelius............... 244
   Yamhill, Sheridan............................ 318

**Organ**
   John T............................................. 233

**Orrison**
   Albert W. ........................................ 233

**Orton**
   George W. ....................................... 233

**Otey**
   Ann D. ............................................ 234

Lucy D. ............................................. 234
Lucy R. ............................................. 234
Van Renselar .................................... 234
**Ott**
   John H. ........................................... 233
**Otter**
   William ........................................... 234
**Ourey**
   Robert V. ......................................... 234
   Sally (Smith) ................................... 234
**Outland**
   Calvin .............................................. 234
   Eliza ................................................. 234
   Isabella ............................................ 234
   Jane .................................................. 234
   Malinda ........................................... 234
   Mary ................................................ 234
   Richard W. ...................................... 234
   Sarah ............................................... 234
   Susan ............................................... 234
   Susan A. (Richardson) .................... 234
**Overby**
   John S. ............................................. 234
   John W. ..................... 73, 152, 161, 234
   Minerva ........................................... 234
   Minerva P. (Bishop) ........................ 234
   Thomas A. ....................................... 234
**Owens**
   William W. ...................................... 234

# P

**Padgett**
   Reuben B. ................................ 234, 310
   Sophia .............................................. 234
**Pagan**
   Mary Ann ........................................ 101
**Page**
   Catherine ................................. 129, 130
   Louise Elizabeth .............................. 180
   Mary E. ............................................ 218
   William H. ....................................... 234
**Paine**
   Robert T. ......................... 144, 171, 199
**Painter**
   Alice ................................................ 235
   Cynthia P. ........................................ 235
   Debney ............................................. 235
   Eliza ................................................. 235

   George ............................................. 235
   James C. ........................................... 235
   Jane .................................................. 235
   Jefferson Davis ................................ 235
   Margaret ........................................... 235
   Martha ............................................. 235
   Sophia .............................................. 235
   Sophia M. ......................................... 235
   Stewart Dabney ............................... 235
   Virginia L. ....................................... 235
   Wythe ............................................... 235
**Palmer**
   William L. ....................................... 235
**Parent**
   Eli H. ............................................... 235
   Elizabeth .......................................... 235
   John S. ............................................. 235
   Louise .............................................. 235
   Margaret L. ...................................... 235
**Parker**
   Corporal ........................................... 207
   Francis W. ....................................... 235
   Lina ................................................. 121
**Parr**
   Archer .............................................. 235
   George Berham ............................... 235
   Sarah Pamela ................................... 235
**Parrish**
   William N. ....................................... 236
**Partin**
   Alice ................................................ 236
   Andrew Jackson .............................. 236
   Donald B. ......................................... 236
   Edward G. ........................................ 236
   Elizabeth .......................................... 236
   Elizabeth F. ...................................... 236
   Julia B. ............................................. 236
   Mattie E. .......................................... 236
   Thomas A. ....................................... 236
**Patrick**
   Minnie ............................................. 258
**Patterson**
   Charles ............................................ 236
   Eliza Jane ......................................... 300
**Pattison**
   Anne Aurelia ..................................... 87
   Henrietta .......................................... 273

**Paulee**
Sarah Margaret .................................. 126
**Pavo**
John ................................................... 236
**Payne**
Edwin F. ............................................ 236
John B. ............................................... 237
Littleton ............................................. 236
Minerva ............................................. 236
Robert F. ............................................ 236
Virginia A. ......................................... 237
William T. ......................................... 237
**Pearce**
John ................................................... 199
Jonathan ............................................ 199
**Peare**
James ................................................. 237
John ................................................... 237
**Pebworth**
Mary .................................................. 237
Mary (Hill) ........................................ 237
Nathaniel ........................................... 237
William ............................................. 237
**Peck**
Israel ................................................. 237
William F. .................................. 67, 237
**Peed**
James W. ........................................... 237
Margaret ............................................ 237
**Peel**
Richard .............................................. 238
**Peer**
Alonzo ............................................... 238
Alonzo O. .......................................... 238
Claudius ............................................ 238
David ................................................. 238
Della Ann .......................................... 238
Emily A. ............................................ 238
John ................................................... 238
Margaret J. ........................................ 238
Margaret S. ....................................... 238
Nancy ................................................ 238
**Pegram**
Franklin .............. 59, 195, 197, 238, 302
John ................................................... 238
Martha Ward (Gregory) .................... 238
**Pelter**
Bettie ................................................. 239
James T. ............................................ 238
Virginia Jane ..................................... 238
**Pendergrass**
Sylvester G. ...................................... 239
**Pennsylvania** ..... 109, 118, 120, 205, 213, 233, 250, 254, 266, 274, 288
Adams Co. ........................................ 249
Allegheny Co., Pittsburg .................. 288
Bradford ............................................. 65
Bucks Co., Bristol ............................. 98
Carlisle Barracks .............................. 188
Clearfield .......................................... 257
Cumberland Co., Mechanicsburg ..... 177
Cumberland Co., Shiremanstown ..... 177
Cumberland Co., West Fairview ...... 157
Darby ................................................ 218
Deleware Co., Ridley Park ............... 150
Elizabethtown ................................... 154
Franklin Co., Greencastle .................. 75
Franklin Co., Mays ............................ 70
Lancaster .......................................... 247
Lancaster Co., Lap P.O. .............. 90, 178
Lebanon .............................................. 62
Lebanon Co., Lebanon ............. 150, 216
Little York ................................. 168, 177
Montrose, Susquehanna Co. .............. 65
Muttontown ...................................... 216
Peoli P.O. .......................................... 296
Philadelphia ....................................... 51
Philadelphia . 51, 56, 67, 71, 74, 81, 86, 87, 90, 91, 98, 105, 110, 117, 126, 132, 159, 160, 173, 176, 177, 186, 191, 193, 200, 202, 205, 212, 213, 215, 219, 226, 244, 247, 252, 279, 296, 300, 301, 307, 309, 315
Philadelphia Co., Philadelphia .. 150, 265
Philadelphia Co., Philadelphia, U.S.
    Naval Asylum ............................. 253
Philadelphia, St. Mary's Catholic Church
    ..................................................... 205
Pittsburg ............................. 51, 99, 138
Pottsville ........................................... 272
**Pennsylvania - Cavalry**
16th Regt., Co. F .............................. 253
6th Regt., Co. C .................................. 91
8th Regt. ........................................... 132

## VIRGINIA VOLUNTEERS IN MEXICO

Co. K, 3rd Regt. ............................... 300
**Pennsylvania - Infantry**
114th Regt., Co. A ........................... 160
118th Regt., Co. F ........................... 252
175th Regt., Co. E, (Militia) ............. 205
18th Regt., Co. K .............................. 173
24th Regt., Co. B .............................. 159
26th Regt., Co. C .............................. 247
26th Regt., Co. D ............................. 118
28th Regt., Co. B .............................. 126
51st Regt., Co. G .............................. 213
69th Regt., Co. B .............................. 159
72nd Regt. ........................................ 173
76th Regt., Co. H ............................... 71
77th Regt., Co. A .............................. 150
91st Regt., Co. I ............................... 118
97th Regt., Co. D ............................. 205
Co. D, 22nd Regt. ............................. 300
Co. H, 31st Regt. ................................ 98
**Penquite**
Frances Ann .................................... 149
Mary ................................................ 149
**Pensylvania - Cavalry**
5th Regt., Co., A .............................. 128
**Pentony**
James .............................................. 239
Meresa ............................................ 239
**Peoples**
W.N. ................................................ 199
**Percival**
John ................................................ 253
**Perkins**
Martha ............................................ 109
**Perkinson**
George W. ...................................... 239
**Peterson**
Amelia A. ....................................... 240
Anna ............................................... 240
C.M. ................................................ 239
Cornelia M. .................................... 239
Frank .............................................. 239
George P. ........................................ 239
L.A. ................................................. 239
Lucy A. ........................................... 239
Lucy Ann (Williamson) .................. 239
Martha ............................................ 240
Martha Ann .................................... 239

Minnesota ....................................... 239
Minnie ............................................ 239
Peter Archibald ....................... 207, 239
William ........................................... 240
William H. ...................................... 240
William McKendree ....................... 239
William T. ....................................... 240
**Peverelly**
Anthony .......................................... 240
Margaret ......................................... 240
Mary ............................................... 240
**Peyton**
Prudence ........................................ 202
**Philips**
Alfred ............................................. 240
Caroline E. ..................................... 240
Emma May ..................................... 240
George H. ....................................... 240
George M. ...................................... 240
Hannah A. ...................................... 240
Jonathan W. ................................... 240
Martha ............................................ 240
Minnie L. ....................................... 240
Robert H. ........................................ 240
Sarah .............................................. 240
Sarah C. .......................................... 240
Sarah K. .......................................... 240
Susan .............................................. 240
Washington .................................... 240
William W. ..................................... 240
**Phillips**
Alexander ....................................... 240
Charles J. ....................................... 266
Dixon ............................................. 266
Elizabeth ........................................ 292
Lewis B. ......................................... 214
Robert H. ........................................ 240
**Phipps**
Robert H. ........................................ 241
**Pickering**
Mary Ann ....................................... 173
**Pickett**
Margaret ......................................... 241
Rufus .............................................. 241
**Pierce**
Adolphus ........................................ 241
Augustus N. ................................... 241

Dorastus ............................................ 241
Lenora C. .......................................... 241
Martha A. ......................................... 241
Martha Ann ...................................... 241
Oscar R. ............................................ 241
Rachel ............................................... 241
Rachel M. ......................................... 241
Virginia K. ........................................ 241
William M. ....................................... 241
**Pike**
Mary ................................................. 291
**Pinnell**
Joseph J.W. ....................................... 241
**Piper**
Joseph F. ........................................... 241
**Pitts**
Emma J. ............................................ 241
Mary Jane ......................................... 241
Sarah Frances ................................... 241
Virginius L. ............................ 110, 241
**Pleasants**
Ellen .................................................. 242
Jefferson ........................................... 242
Julia .................................................. 242
Julia P. .............................................. 242
Mary ................................................. 242
Samuel S. .......................................... 242
William ............................................. 242
William H. ........................................ 242
**Plumb**
William ............................................. 242
**Poage**
Alpheus W. .............................. 143, 148
Alpheus Wilson ................................ 242
Margaret ........................................... 242
Thomas, Col. .................................... 242
William ............................................. 242
**Poe**
C. Cornelia ....................................... 243
Edgar Allan ...................................... 253
Elizabeth Ann .................................... 83
John .................................................. 124
John, Jr. ................... 96, 117, 242, 281
Pamelia ............................................. 243
Rebecca ............................................ 243
Thomas ............................................. 243
Virginia ............................................. 243

**Poindexter**
Ann L. .............................................. 315
**Poisal**
Daniel .................................... 173, 243
**Poland**
John F. .............................................. 243
**Pollard**
James D. ........................................... 243
John (Capt.) ..................................... 243
Mary Ann ......................................... 243
Peyton .............................................. 243
**Pollock**
Robert ...................................... 97, 243
**Ponder**
Emily ................................................ 303
**Porch**
Elizabeth Sarah ............................... 204
**Porterfield**
Charles ............................................. 244
Elizabeth M. ..................................... 244
Emily C. ........................................... 244
George .............................................. 244
George A. ................................ 142, 192
George Alexander ............................ 244
John A. ............................................. 244
Kate S. .............................................. 244
Katherine S. ..................................... 244
Mary ................................................. 244
Mary (Tabb) ..................................... 244
Mary J. ............................................. 244
Serena ............................................... 244
William F. ........................................ 244
**Poston**
Ann E. .............................................. 244
Catherine ......................................... 244
Frank ................................................ 244
Jane .................................................. 244
Jane A. ............................................. 244
John .................................................. 244
John F. .............................................. 244
John T. ............................................. 244
Joseph B. .......................................... 244
Lydia ................................................ 244
Mary T. ............................................ 244
Nancy ............................................... 244
Randolph ......................................... 244
Robert .............................................. 244

## VIRGINIA VOLUNTEERS IN MEXICO

Sally .............................................. 244
Susan C. ........................................ 244
**Potts**
John H. .......................................... 245
**Powell**
Edward .......................................... 245
mary .............................................. 245
Robert ............................................ 245
**Powers**
Charles W. ..................................... 167
james ............................................. 245
Walter ............................................ 245
**Poynts**
James W. ....................................... 245
**Prather**
Socrates ......................................... 245
**Prentis**
Capt. ............................................... 311
**Preston**
Eliza Henry ..................................... 92
Hugh C. ......................................... 245
James ............................................. 245
James Francis ................................. 245
James Patton .................................. 245
John F. ........................................... 246
Nancy ............................................. 245
Nancy Ann ..................................... 106
Sarah A. ......................................... 245
Sarah Ann ...................................... 245
William B. ..................................... 245
**Price**
Edward T. ...................................... 246
Virginia Ann .................................. 124
William C. ..................................... 246
**Prichard**
Samuel H. ...................................... 246
**Prichett**
William Lewis ................................ 246
**Procise**
John ............................................... 246
Joseph D. ....................................... 246
Mary .............................................. 246
Mary A. .......................................... 246
Thomas .......................................... 246
Thomas J. ...................................... 246
**Provost**
James ..................................... 247, 263

**Prussia** ............................................. 102
**Pullen**
Mary (Willman) ............................. 247
Romulus F. .................................... 247
**Pulman**
William .......................................... 247
**Punishment**
Blackened With India Ink... 27, 153, 207
Blackened, Face .............................. 274
Bucked Two Hours a Day for a Week 274
Confined for Balance of War ..... 27, 153, 190, 207
Confined In Irons ............................ 274
Dishonorably Discharged 114, 153, 190, 207
Drummed Out of Service ................. 274
Executed ......................................... 112
Forfeit Pay ..... 67, 80, 91, 97, 100, 113, 139, 162, 166, 177, 179, 190, 206, 207, 208, 214, 221, 266, 270, 272, 282, 297, 299, 317
Hard Labor. 64, 97, 139, 210, 218, 277, 287, 299, 316, 317
Hard Labor for the Balance of War ... 114
Hard Labor with a Ball-and-Chain ... 190, 297
Hard Labor With a Ball-and-Chain .. 166, 208, 214, 217
Hard Labor With A Ball-and-Chain .. 100
Hatd Labor ..................................... 282
Head Shaved .................................. 274
Letter .............................................. 274
March Four Hours Each Day for 30 Days ............................................................ 314
Marked with Letter ............ 27, 153, 207
Police Duty 67, 91, 100, 177, 187, 206, 220, 221, 270, 272
Police Parade Ground and Sinks ....... 113
Public Reprimand ................. 78, 97, 176
Stand on the Head of a Barrell. 170, 179, 208, 217, 242, 266, 274, 277
Suspended From Rank & Pay ............. 97
**Putt**
Mary ................................................ 89
**Pyne**
Anne ................................................ 66

## Q
**Quinn**
  Martin.................................... 247

## R
**Rabby**
  Louisa.................................... 232
**Radford**
  Dr. John Blair...................... 228
  Sarah.................................... 228
**Radikin**
  William................................. 210
**Rainey**
  Susan Rebecca ................... 271
**Ralls**
  Flora..................................... 247
  George E............................. 247
  George Norton .................... 247
  John W................................. 247
  Maria L................................. 247
  Marina.................................. 247
  Martha J............................... 247
  Martha Jane ........................ 247
  Thomas O............................ 247
**Randolph**
  Ann C................................... 247
  Christopher M. .................... 247
  Col. ...................................... 168
  Lucy (Bolling)...................... 247
  Maria.................................... 247
  Maria Barbara (Mayer) ...... 247
  Peyton ................................. 247
  Susan B............................... 247
  Thomas................................ 270
  Thomas Beverly ......... 247, 314
  Thomas M............................ 247
  William................................. 247
**Rash**
  Abigail C................................ 84
  Mary H................................... 84
**Ratcliffe**
  Locian .................................. 158
  Thomas................................ 248
**Raux**
  Emile.................................... 248
**Rawlings**
  Rebecca H........................... 147

**Rawlins**
  Ann F.................................... 248
  Anna Terry........................... 248
  Edward A.............................. 248
  Edward Albin....................... 248
  Edward F.............................. 248
  Mary G.................................. 248
**Rawls**
  Elisha ................................... 248
**Reamy**
  John T................................... 248
**Reasoner**
  Calista Ann ......................... 194
**Reed**
  Dazetta ................................ 248
  Eliza C.................................. 248
  John C.................................. 248
  John D.................................. 248
  John W................................. 248
  Joseph F.............................. 248
  Lucinda................................ 136
  Mary A.................................. 248
  Mary Ann ............................. 248
  Mary E.................................. 248
  Mary Jane ........................... 249
  Samuel P.............................. 248
  Sarah E................................ 248
  Sivena Ann .......................... 248
  Thomas F............................. 248
  William................................. 248
  William H. ............................ 249
**Reese**
  Jeremiah R........................... 249
  Roxanna .............................. 249
**Reid**
  John C.................................. 139
  Katie..................................... 285
  Lucretia N............................ 292
**Reinhart**
  Michael................................ 249
**Reno**
  Lydia..................................... 226
**Resinger**
  Clay...................................... 249
  Daniel C............................... 249
  Lee....................................... 249
  Lydia..................................... 249

# VIRGINIA VOLUNTEERS IN MEXICO

Otis ................................................. 249
Rebecca Alice ................................ 249
**Reynolds**
Samuel........................................... 249
**Rhode Island**
Providence ............................. 198, 276
**Rhoderick**
Georgiana ..................................... 123
**Ricard**
Benjamin R. .................................. 249
**Rice**
Sarah ............................................. 127
**Richards**
Anna B. ......................................... 250
Anna Beall ..................................... 250
Catherine ...................................... 250
Dulany M. ..................................... 250
George F. ...................................... 250
George Frederick........................... 250
Henry ............................................ 250
Henry C. ....................................... 250
John R. ................................. 172, 250
Mary A. ......................................... 250
Mary Eleanor (Gantt)..................... 250
Priscilla.......................................... 250
**Richardson**
George W. ............................ 184, 250
John............................................... 250
Susan A. ........................................ 234
**Riddle**
Alexander ..................................... 251
Ann ............................................... 251
James............................................. 251
Mary Ann ...................................... 251
William J. ...................................... 251
**Riggins**
John J. ........................................... 251
Martha .......................................... 251
Mary.............................................. 251
**Riley**
David............................................. 251
William.......................................... 251
**Rinor**
Jacob ............................................. 251
**Rittenburg**
Alfred............................................ 251
**River**
Rio Grande.................................... 229

**Rivers**
James W. ....................................... 251
**Rives**
Sarah Gee ...................................... 267
William F....................................... 251
**Roach**
Catherine ...................................... 252
John......................... 51, 150, 251, 300
**Roadcap**
Christian ....................................... 252
Eliza J............................................ 252
Eliza Jane (Graham) ...................... 252
Elizabeth....................................... 252
Elizabeth N. .................................. 252
George Robert............................... 252
John W. ......................................... 252
Virginia C. ..................................... 252
**Roane**
William A. ..................................... 252
**Robbins**
George T........................................ 252
**Roberts**
Malvina ......................................... 297
**Robertson**
Agnes ............................................ 137
David S.......................................... 252
James Berkeley ............................. 253
Martha A. ...................................... 253
Mary H. ......................................... 305
William C. ..................................... 253
**Robey**
William.......................................... 253
**Robinson**
Andrew R. Thomas........................ 253
Anetta E. ....................................... 253
Ann M. .......................................... 253
Anne.............................................. 253
Betsy Ann ..................................... 118
Capt............................................... 160
Dr. Thomas ................................... 253
Hester Ann.................................... 270
James Arthur................................. 253
Lydia ............................................. 257
Rev. Thomas V. ............................. 253
Sarah Ann...................................... 253
Sarah K.......................................... 240
Susan............................................. 112

William Murray ........................ 253, 274
**Rodecker**
  Hannah J. ............................................ 254
  William ................................................ 254
**Roderick**
  Mary Jane ........................................... 167
**Rodgers**
  Nathaniel G. ....................................... 254
**Rogers**
  Mary F. ............................................... 213
**Rollberg**
  Catherine ........................................... 254
  Dorothea Louise Selma .................... 254
  Friderika Carolina Louisa ................. 254
  Henrich Gottlieb ................................ 254
  Henrich Wilhelm ............................... 254
  Henry .................................................. 254
  Johann Gottlob .................................. 254
**Ronald**
  Charles A. .......... 69, 194, 223, 246, 298
  Charles Augustus ............................... 254
  Mary .................................................... 254
  Sally A. ............................................... 254
  William S. ........................................... 254
**Roop**
  Bird ..................................................... 143
  Byrd .................................................... 254
  Crockett .............................................. 255
  Harriet ................................................ 255
  Isabella ............................................... 255
  James P. .............................................. 255
  Jane ..................................................... 255
  Laura A. .............................................. 255
  Nancy .................................................. 255
  Paratha (McAlexander) ..................... 255
  Rachel ................................................. 254
  Reed C.P. ............................................ 255
  Washington ........................................ 255
  William ............................................... 255
**Rose**
  Ann ..................................................... 291
  Anna B. ............................................... 250
  George W. .......................................... 255
  James P. .............................................. 255
  Nancy L. ............................................. 255
  Robert L. ............................................. 255
  Sarah A. (Carter) ............................... 255

Sarah Ann ........................................... 255
Susan F. .............................................. 255
Uriah J. ............................................... 255
Uriah Jackson .................................... 255
William L. .......................................... 255
**Ross**
  Mary ........................................... 123, 223
**Rowan**
  Ann ..................................................... 256
  Ellen ................................................... 256
  Ellen N. .............................................. 256
  John D. ............................................... 256
  John W. ................................................ 62
  John William ..................................... 255
  Sarah .................................................. 256
  William W. ......................................... 256
**Rucks**
  Stephen C. ......................................... 256
**Ruppy**
  Ellia .................................................... 188
**Russell**
  Elizabeth ............................................ 256
  Ellerson .............................................. 256
  Permelia Price ................................... 137
  Wiley .................................................. 256

# S

**Saddler**
  Frederick A. ....................................... 256
**Saffell**
  Elizabeth ............................................ 167
**Salmon**
  Charles G. .......................................... 256
**Salmons**
  Caroline ............................................. 191
**Saltonstall**
  Susan S. .............................................. 181
**Sampson**
  William .............................................. 256
**Samuel**
  Nancy ................................................. 102
**San Patricio** ..................................... 240
**Sanders**
  Priscilla C. ......................................... 257
  Robert H. ........................................... 257
**Sandidge**
  Joseph E. ............................................ 257
**Sandifer**

## VIRGINIA VOLUNTEERS IN MEXICO

James.............................................. 257
Mary Jane ....................................... 138
**Satterfield**
   Lydia (Robinson)............................ 257
   Sarah Matilda................................. 257
   Susanna .......................................... 257
   Thomas Robinson........................... 257
**Saunders**
   Elizabeth........................................ 289
   Stephen P. ...................................... 257
**Savage**
   Paul L............................................. 257
**Sawyer**
   Sarah Jane...................................... 268
**Schibner**
   Hannah........................................... 177
**Schlaffenberger**
   Katrina VanPelt.............................. 174
**Schminke**
   Sophia ............................................ 234
**Schwartz**
   Mrs.................................................. 55
**Schwitzer**
   Charles .......................................... 258
   John................................................ 258
   Joseph Stephen .............................. 257
   Lettie.............................................. 258
   Mary A. ......................................... 258
   Minnie............................................ 258
   Mollie............................................. 258
**Scotland**
   Stranraer........................................ 117
**Scott**
   Annie T. .................................. 258, 265
   Elizabeth (Torborne)...................... 265
   J. H.................................................. 95
   James A. ........................................ 258
   John K. .................................... 258, 265
   Joseph P.......................................... 258
   Julia Ann ....................................... 258
   Mary E............................................ 149
   Pheobe............................................ 258
   Robert G. ......... 243, 258, 266, 281, 296
   Robert Gourmain, Jr. ...................... 259
   Robert Gourmain, Sr....................... 259
   Susan E........................................... 265
   Thomas........................................... 265

William A. ...................................... 76
William Arthur............................... 265
William Baker................................ 265
William H. ..................................... 265
**Seabright**
   James C. ........................................ 265
**Searl**
   Isabella D....................................... 266
   Samuel........................................... 265
**Sebright**
   Julia A. .......................................... 221
**Secretary of War** 188, 209, 290, 307, 308
**Seigel**
   Alethea H....................................... 309
**Seigler**
   William.......................................... 266
**Selby**
   Ellen............................................... 162
   Sarah E. .......................................... 162
**Self**
   Thomas........................................... 266
**Semple**
   Elizabeth Garlick............................ 134
**Seymore**
   Laura.............................................. 266
   Lucy A. .......................................... 266
   Mary.............................................. 266
   Richard H. ..................................... 266
   Sarah Frances................................. 266
   Walter............................................ 266
   Zack ............................................... 266
**Shackelford**
   Andrew J. ...................................... 267
   Virginia ......................................... 267
**Shackleford**
   Lucelia........................................... 223
**Shands**
   A.R., Jr. .......................................... 267
   Anna Jane ...................................... 267
   Aurelius R...................................... 138
   Aurelius Rives................................ 267
   M.C. ............................................... 267
   Martha C........................................ 267
   P.E. ................................................ 267
   Sarah Gee ...................................... 267
   W.R. ............................................... 267
   William.......................................... 267
**Shank**

Jacob .................................................. 267
John W. ............................................... 267
Margaret J. .......................................... 267
Rosa Lee ............................................. 267
Sarah E. ............................................... 267
Susan .................................................. 267
Virginia Alcinda ................................. 267
**Sharp**
Mary .................................................... 206
**Shaw**
Elias .................................................... 267
**Sheaf**
Amos B. .............................................. 268
Ellen M. .............................................. 268
George W. ........................................... 268
Henry L. .............................................. 268
John T. ................................................. 268
Malinda ............................................... 268
Malinda (Barton) ................................ 268
Mary .................................................... 268
Olivia .................................................. 268
Robert .................................................. 268
William W. .......................................... 268
**Sheckles**
Levi ..................................................... 268
Samuel ......................................... 172, 268
**Sheets**
Elizabeth ............................................. 268
John William ....................................... 268
Pheobe ................................................. 268
Pheobe Ann ........................................ 268
Samuel ................................................ 268
**Shell**
Amakus ............................................... 269
Americus Vaspucis ............................. 269
Aolena Kansas .................................... 269
Armando V. ......................................... 268
Henry B. .............................................. 268
John H. ................................................ 269
Laura E. ............................................... 268
Laura Frances ..................................... 269
Laura G.F. ........................................... 268
Mason Newton ................................... 269
Mason W. ............................................ 269
Octara .................................................. 269
Octavia Ellen ...................................... 269
Orlena .................................................. 269

Sarah J. ......................................... 268, 269
Sarah Jane .......................................... 268
Sarazon ............................................... 269
Sector H. ............................................. 269
Sora ..................................................... 269
Stan ..................................................... 268
Staritt A. ............................................. 269
Starwith .............................................. 269
**Shelling**
Barnhardt ............................................ 269
Elizabeth ............................................. 269
John ............................................. 212, 269
John F. ................................................ 270
**Shelton**
Ann E. ................................................. 270
Ann H. ................................................. 270
Elmira .................................................. 270
Hester Ann .......................................... 270
Joseph ................................................. 270
Luther .................................................. 270
Margaret J. .......................................... 221
Margaretta .......................................... 270
Stephen ............................................... 271
Wesley ................................................ 270
William ............................................... 270
**Shepherd**
John Newton ...................................... 271
Mary S. ................................................ 271
Washington ........................................ 271
**Shepherdson**
Emma J. ............................................... 271
Lucy .................................................... 271
Rebecca .............................................. 271
Sallie A. .............................................. 271
Susan Rebecca (Rainey) .................... 271
Susannah ............................................ 271
William N. .......................................... 271
**Shepperson**
Elizabeth Rhoda (Ward) ................... 271
George C.P. ........................................ 271
**Sherrard**
Ann ..................................................... 271
Benjamin W. ....................................... 271
Harriet ................................................. 271
Harriet E. ..................................... 271, 272
Joseph ................................................. 271
Mary .................................................... 271

## VIRGINIA VOLUNTEERS IN MEXICO

William............................................. 271
**Sherwood**
　Mercy Hunter.................................. 181
**Shickel**
　Susan............................................. 126
**Shields**
　Alice............................................... 272
　Almeria E. ..................................... 272
　Angelina P. .................................... 272
　D.H. ............................................... 272
　David F.......................... 156, 165, 272
　David Hamlin................................. 272
　Emma............................................. 272
　Hamlin............................................ 272
　Mary E............................................ 272
　Rebecca Ann.................................. 272
　Susan E........................................... 272
　William T. ..................................... 272
**Shinn**
　Thomas A. ..................................... 272
**Shipman**
　Benjamin M. .................................. 272
　Charles ........................................... 272
　Eliza Ann....................................... 272
　Laura V. ......................................... 272
　William C. ..................................... 272
　William P....................................... 272
**Shively**
　Victoria E. ..................................... 311
**Shoemaker**
　William L. .............................. 139, 272
**Short**
　Albert ............................................. 273
　Americus ....................................... 273
　Benjamin ....................................... 273
　Calvin R. ....................................... 272
　Chancellor G. ................................. 273
　Elizabeth A. ................................... 273
　Henrietta........................................ 273
　Lydia.............................................. 272
　Reuben .......................................... 272
　Sarah ............................................. 272
**Shrader**
　Anna Eliza ....................................... 88
**Shriver**
　William........................................... 273
**Shryock**
　Ann A............................................. 273
　Billie .............................................. 273
　Caroline ......................................... 273
　Frederick ....................................... 273
　James F.......................................... 273
　James Frederick............................. 273
　Theodore ....................................... 273
**Shue**
　Mary................................................ 72
**Shumaker**
　Anna............................................... 273
　Elizabeth........................................ 273
　Ella Lee ......................................... 273
　Ella W. .......................................... 273
　Ella W. (Tunstall) ........................... 273
　Lindsay.......................................... 273
　Lindsay Mayo ......................... 175, 273
　Tunstall.......................................... 273
**Sibley**
　Abby ............................................... 67
**Sigler**
　Margaret E. .................................... 219
**Silmone**
　Elizabeth.......................................... 72
**Silvers**
　Abram ............................................ 273
　Charles T. ...................................... 274
　Delila............................................. 273
　Emaline ......................................... 274
　Mary M. ........................................ 274
　Narcissa......................................... 274
　Octavia A....................................... 274
　Ruth ............................................... 274
　Susan F.......................................... 274
　Virginia C. ..................................... 274
　William.......................................... 273
**Simes**
　Eliza A........................................... 274
　Isabella F. ...................................... 274
　James L. ........................................ 274
　Louisa J. ........................................ 274
　Martha (Blair) ................................ 274
　Miles.............................................. 274
　Samuel M. ..................................... 274
　William L. ..................................... 274
**Simmons**
　Adelaide Rebecca........................... 310

385

| | | | |
|---|---|---|---|
| Ann | 274 | Mary C. | 276 |
| Augusta | 274 | William A. | 276 |
| James F. | 274 | **Slaughter** | |
| John | 274 | Ellen | 132 |
| Lucy Jane (Blaylock) | 274 | **Slaven** | |
| Wesley C. | 274 | Matilda | 299 |
| William | 274 | **Sly** | |

**Simpkins**
- Eliza Jane .................. 275
- William D. .................. 274

**Simpson**
- Elizabeth .................. 275
- James R. .................. 275
- John G. .................. 275
- Mary C. .................. 275
- Oscar J. .................. 275
- Robert .................. 275
- Sarepta A. .................. 275
- Susan .................. 275
- Thomas .................. 275

**Sinclair**
- James H. .................. 275

**Sine**
- Lorenzo Dow .................. 275
- Margaret (Kackley) .................. 275
- Rev. Christy .................. 275

**Sira**
- Nicholas .................. 275

**Sizer**
- Clara F. .................. 122

**Skeen**
- William E. .................. 168, 218, 249, 275
- William E. .................. 163

**Skiles**
- Frances .................. 275
- Margaret A. .................. 276
- Mary C. .................. 276
- William H. .................. 276

**Skine**
- William .................. 275

**Slack**
- Caroline .................. 276
- Daton A. .................. 276
- Elizabeth .................. 276
- Elizabeth A. .................. 276
- James L. .................. 276
- Louella .................. 276

**Sly**
- Luella .................. 276
- Malory .................. 276
- Mary .................. 276
- Mary Jane (Gregory) .................. 276
- William M. .................. 276

**Small**
- Sarah Elizabeth .................. 131

**Smiley**
- Theodore B. .................. 276

**Smith**
- Abijah B. .................. 276
- Albert T. .................. 276
- Calvin N. .................. 276, 278
- Edmond P. .................. 276
- Isabella Susan .................. 278
- James .................. 277
- James L. .................. 277
- Jerome B. .................. 277
- John .................. 199
- John E. .................. 276
- John P. .................. 130
- John W. .................. 276
- Jonathan .................. 277
- Martha A. .................. 276
- Mary Ann .................. 145
- Mary Frances .................. 232
- Sally .................. 234
- Samuel .................. 277, 278
- Seginora Tabb .................. 304
- Susan A. .................. 278
- Virginia .................. 267
- William B. .................. 276, 278

**Smoot**
- W.A. .................. 131

**Snail**
- Sarah .................. 293

**Snead**
- Adaline .................. 278
- Adaline Hilman .................. 278
- Adeline .................. 278

Adeline H. ............................................ 278
Edmond P. ............................................ 278
Edward ................................................. 278
Emma ................................................... 278
Eugene .................................................. 278
Frances A. ............................................. 112
Georgianna ........................................... 278
Jesse L. ................................................. 278
Louisa ................................................... 278
Margaret E. ........................................... 278
Robert J. ............................................... 278
Robert L. ............................................... 278
Samuel M. ............................................ 278
Samuel W. ............................................ 278
**Snyder**
Ann E. .................................................. 279
Frances (Jones) ..................................... 279
George R. ............................................. 279
William ................................................ 279
**Songer**
Luemma Elizabeth ............................... 129
**Sorbor**
Ann M. ................................................. 279
Eliza ..................................................... 279
Eliza May ............................................. 279
William B. ............................................ 279
William L. ............................................ 279
**Sorrell**
Harrison ............................................... 279
**South Carolina** .................................... 111
Edgefield Co., Edgefield .................. 266
Ft. Moultrie ...................................... 66
**South Carolina - Infantry**
2nd Regt., Co. B .............................. 183
**South Dakota**
Dalzell ............................................ 297
**Southard**
Margaret .............................................. 52
**Sowers**
Elizabeth A. ......................................... 106
Triphena .............................................. 69
William B. ........................................... 106
**Spain**
Villa Carlos .......................................... 88
**Spaulding**
Ella ...................................................... 279
Ella F. .................................................. 279

James J. ................................................ 279
Lucy C. ................................................ 279
Lucy J. ................................................. 279
Martha A. (Gates) ................................ 279
Mary .................................................... 279
Sarah ................................................... 279
Sarah E. ............................................... 279
Susan ................................................... 280
Thomas B. ........................................... 279
**Speck**
Elizabeth .............................................. 194
**Spencer**
John .................................................... 279
John S. ................................................ 280
Nancy .................................................. 280
Susan ................................................... 280
**Spillman**
James W. ............................................. 280
**Spooner**
Abner ................................................... 280
Charles Coburn .................................... 280
Eliza Ann (Collins) .............................. 280
Louisiana (Marcy) ................................ 280
Samuel J. ............................................. 280
**Spotswood**
Edward J. ............................................. 280
Joseph C. ............................................. 280
Lucy S. (Cooper) .................................. 280
**Spott**
Katie Lee ............................................. 131
**Spratt**
James W. ............................................. 280
John T. ................................................ 281
**St. Clair**
Francis ................................................ 281
**Stafford**
William H. ........................................... 281
**Stagg**
Elizabeth A. ......................................... 281
James ........................................... 124, 281
John F. ................................................ 281
John J. ................................................ 281
Joseph B. ............................................. 281
Sarah A. .............................................. 281
**Stanfield**
Henderson ........................................... 281
Mary Ann (Winn) ................................ 281

**Stanger**
 Elizabeth .................................. 281
 Ellen ........................................ 282
 Ellen J. (Webb) ........................ 282
 Henry S. .................................. 281
 Jacob ....................................... 281
 Mary ........................................ 282
 Nicholas .................................. 282
 William .................................... 282
**Stanley**
 Mary A. ................................... 112
**Stark**
 Ebenezer E. .............................. 282
**Starke**
 Henry ...................................... 282
 Richard .................................... 282
**Starr**
 John W. ................................... 283
**Staunton**
 Mary Jane ................................ 249
**Steel**
 Frances .................................... 283
 John ......................................... 170
 John H. .................................... 283
 Samuel ..................................... 283
**Stephens**
 Richard H. ............................... 283
**Stephenson**
 James E. .................................. 283
**Stevens**
 Crawford B. ............................. 283
 Cynthia A. ............................... 284
 Elizabeth ................................. 284
 Harvey B. ................................ 283
 Harvey P. ................................ 284
 James C. .................................. 283
 Jane ......................................... 284
 Jane F. ..................................... 283
 John T. .................................... 284
 Lucinda (Collins) ..................... 283
 Lydia ....................................... 283
 Lydia A.S. ............................... 283
 Malinda M. .............................. 284
 Rebecca Jane ........................... 284
 Robert N. ................................. 283
 Sarah J. .................................... 284
**Stevenson**
 Coke R. ................................... 236
 Sallie A. .................................. 133
**Steward**
 James ...................................... 284
**Stewart**
 Edward G. ............................... 284
 John P. .................................... 284
 Mary ............................... 117, 118
 Sarah Jane Virginia .................. 191
**Stiglman**
 C.M. ....................................... 183
**Stith**
 Drury B. .................................. 284
**Stockard**
 Anna Maria ............................. 103
**Stoffer**
 Daniel A. ................................. 284
**Stone**
 Augustus .................. 156, 199, 285
 Florence .................................. 285
 George Washington ................. 285
 John A. .................................... 285
 John D. .................................... 285
 John Daniel ............................. 285
 Josephine A. ............................ 285
 Mary Maria ............................. 154
 Matilda A. ............................... 285
 Susan ...................................... 285
**Stottlemyre**
 James M. ................................. 285
**Stout**
 William ................................... 285
**Stover**
 Martha Eleanor ....................... 168
**Stow**
 Lemuel C. ............................... 285
**Stratton**
 Mary ......................................... 98
**Street**
 Inez .......................................... 62
 Mary A. .................................... 62
**Strong**
 Tarlton .................................... 285
**Stuart**
 John H. ................................... 285
 Nannie C. ................................ 285
 William W. .............................. 285
**Sullivan**

Andrew ............................................. 285
Edward ............................................. 285
George ............................................. 285
Maria ............................................... 285
**Summers**
Sarah ................................................. 70
**Summerson**
Anna Eliza ...................................... 305
**Swann**
Benjamin ........................................ 286
Catherine ........................................ 286
Susanna (Benter) ............................ 286
**Swartz**
Mary C. ............................................ 52
**Sweeney**
William B. ...................................... 286
**Swink**
Catherine Virginia .......................... 158
**Switzerland**
Zurich ............................................. 154
**Swively**
John C. ............................................. 53
**Swope**
Maria Antoinettte ............................. 92
Mary ................................................. 99
Washington ...................................... 92
**Sykes**
James W. ........................................ 286

# T

**Tabb**
Augustus G. .................................... 286
Mary ............................................... 244
**Talbot**
Thomas ........................................... 286
William A. ........................................ 76
William R. ...................................... 286
**Talbott**
Henrietta Virginia ........................... 222
Melville S. ..................................... 286
Sarah C. .......................................... 286
William A. ...................................... 286
**Taliaferro**
John R. ........................................... 286
**Talley**
Crawford A. ................................... 286
Mary Ann H. .................................. 151
Matilda V. ...................................... 286

Miles .............................................. 286
Sarah Sally ..................................... 216
**Tankersley**
Ellen ............................................... 287
Francis R. ...................................... 287
George W. ...................................... 287
Henry ............................................. 287
Judith ............................................. 287
Mariah J. ........................................ 287
Mary E. .......................................... 287
William L. ..................................... 287
**Tare**
Abram V. ........................................ 287
Anna Vinson .................................. 288
Charles Robert .............................. 288
E.A. ................................................ 287
Elizabeth ........................................ 288
Emma Maude ................................ 288
Fannie ............................................ 288
J.S. .................................................. 287
John S. ........................................... 288
Maud .............................................. 288
Susan ............................................. 287
Susan Jane ..................................... 287
Thomason ...................................... 288
**Tate**
Sarah Matilda ................................ 257
**Taylor**
Alberta Y. ...................................... 289
Bettie M. ........................................ 288
Burton L. ....................................... 289
Catherine ....................................... 115
Catherine (Martin) ......................... 289
Catherine R. .................................. 288
Creed ............................................. 288
Elizabeth ....................................... 289
General .......................................... 265
George ........................................... 288
George William ............................. 288
Isaiah ............................................. 288
James ............................................. 288
James Craig ................................... 288
James L. ........................................ 289
John ............................................... 288
John C. .......................................... 289
John L. ................................... 288, 289
Jordan ............................................ 289

Julia V. ............................................. 101
Kate R. ............................................. 288
Kitty ................................................. 289
Laura A. ........................................... 289
Lucy A. ............................................ 289
Lucy M. ........................................... 289
Maggie C. ........................................ 288
Major General .. 89, 111, 115, 132, 148, 176, 193, 316
Margaret Ann .................................. 73
Margaret V. ..................................... 288
Mary ................................................ 148
Mary E. ............................................ 288
Mary Lois ........................................ 180
Nancy ............................................... 245
Robert C. ......................................... 288
Sarah ................................................ 288
Sarah J. ............................................ 288
Thomas ............................................ 289
Virginia R. ....................................... 289
Wade ................................................ 288
William ............................................ 121
William G. ....................................... 289
William L. ............................... 162, 289
**Tellson**
Henry H. .......................................... 289
**Templeton**
James ............................................... 289
**Tenain**
John E. ............................................. 289
**Tennesse**
Washington Co., National Military Home ................................................. 281
**Tennessee** ........................ 166, 271, 279
Anderson Co., Andersonville ............ 111
Anderson Co., Clinton ..................... 111
Bedford Co., Shelbyville .................. 286
Bledsoe Co., Crossville .................... 216
Cocke Co., Newport ........................ 285
Coffee Co., Tullahoma ..................... 286
Fayette Co., LaGrange ..................... 129
Ft. Donelson ..................................... 50
Green Co. ......................................... 93
Hawkins Co., Russellville ................ 318
Johnson City .................................... 295
Knox Co. .......................................... 111
Marshall Co., Lewisburgh ................ 286

McMinn Co., Cog Hill ..................... 121
Obion Co., Union City .................... 137
Sullivan Co. ..................................... 308
Taylorsville ...................................... 211
Union Co., Raytown ........................ 258
Washington Co. ............................... 211
Washington Co., Buffalo Ridge ........ 308
Washington Co., Johnson City .......... 308
Weakley Co., Gleason ...................... 285
**Tennessee - Artillery**
Bankhead's Battery ............................ 66
**Tennessee - Cavalry**
8th Regt., Co. C ............................... 318
**Tennessee - Infantry**
16th Regt., Co. D ............................. 277
38th Regt., Co. H ............................. 311
7th Regt., Co. A ............................... 108
**Terrell**
Greenberry B. .......................... 158, 289
Greenbury B. ................................... 238
John J. .............................................. 290
Lewis K. .......................................... 290
Sarah Margaret ................................ 290
**Terrett**
Anna Beall ....................................... 250
Avery Edward ................................. 250
**Texas** ... 82, 134, 224, 229, 230, 235, 285
Bastrop Co., Bastrop ....................... 211
Bell Co., Temple ............................. 231
Ben Ficklin ...................................... 132
Brasos Island ...................... 57, 85, 301
Camp Verde ...................................... 85
Clarksville ....................................... 141
Clay Co., Bellevue ............................ 83
Cleburne .......................................... 130
Duvall County ................................. 236
El Paso ............................................ 132
Harrison .......................................... 281
Hays Co. .......................................... 134
Houston Co., Crockett ..................... 285
Jefferson Co., Beaumont ................. 134
Maverick Co., Eagle Pass ................ 271
McLennan Co., Lorena .................... 231
Medina Co., Fort Lincoln ................ 286
Milam Co., Leachville ..................... 211

## VIRGINIA VOLUNTEERS IN MEXICO

Point Iasbel ...... 98, 115, 138, 157, 177, 198, 215, 222, 230, 258, 267, 268, 281, 283, 294, 313
Point Isabel ..................................... 274
San Angelo ..................................... 132
San Antonio ..................................... 132
Shackleford Co., Albany .................. 255
Smith Co. ........................................ 121
Smith Co., Tyler ................................ 80
Tarrant Co., Ft. Worth...................... 121
Travis Co., Austin ................... 134, 305
Williamson Co., Georgetown ........... 231
Williamson Co., Round Rock ........... 305

**Texas - Cavalry**
36th Regt., Co. A ............................. 231
Co. C, 33rd Regt. .............................. 211
Ragsdale's Btln., Co. D ...................... 82

**Thomas**
Abigail ............................................ 309

**Thomasson**
Susan Jane ..................................... 287

**Thompson**
Ann (Rose) ..................................... 291
Annie ..................................... 117, 291
Annie K. ......................................... 265
Charles M. ...................................... 290
Charlotte ........................................ 120
Cynthia ........................................... 291
Eliza ................................................. 51
Eliza J. ............................................ 113
Etta ................................................ 291
James ............................................. 291
Jane ............................................... 290
John S. ........................................... 113
John W. .......................................... 291
Mary ............................................... 291
Mary E. ........................................... 291
Mary Ellen ...................................... 291
R.K. ................................................ 291
William ........................................... 291

**Thomson**
James ............................................. 291

**Thornton**
Anthony .......................................... 291
Henry F. ......................................... 291
Meta ............................................... 291

**Thorpe**

Henry ............................................. 291

**Thrift**
Benjamin F. .................................... 292
Benjamin Franklin ........................... 291
Columbia Caroline ........................... 292
James ....................... 77, 91, 291, 292
James H. ........................................ 292
Linda M. ......................................... 292
Lucretia M. ..................................... 292
Lucretia N. (Reid) ............................ 292
Mary A. .......................................... 292
Mary R. .......................................... 292
Sinah ...................................... 291, 292

**Throckmorton**
Roberta Ann ................................... 206

**Tibbets**
Charles D. ...................................... 292

**Tiffin**
Joseph ............................................ 292

**Tillson**
Alice C. .......................................... 293
Elizabeth ........................................ 292
Harriet H. ....................................... 293
Hattie L. ......................................... 293
Henry H. .................. 76, 77, 292, 293

**Tisdale**
Martha Jane .................................... 55

**Toland**
Ann ................................................ 130

**Torborne**
Elizabeth ........................................ 265

**Totten**
Samuel ........................................... 293
Sarah ............................................. 293

**Totty**
John ........................................ 84, 293
Mary Watts ..................................... 293

**Towner**
Benjamin F. .................................... 294
Elizabeth ........................................ 294
Thomas Harris ................................ 294

**Tracy**
Sarah Cornelia ................................ 173

**Traylor**
Richard B. ...................................... 294

**Trott**
Elizabeth Jane (Williams) ................ 294
Rev. Samuel ................................... 294

Samuel ............................................. 294
**Trump**
   James N. ........................................ 294
   Malinda (Hawkins) ......................... 294
   William ........................................... 294
**Tuck**
   July A.E.M. .................................... 310
**Tucker**
   Armsted O. ..................................... 294
   Catherine ........................................ 295
   Elizabeth ......................................... 294
   George W. ....................................... 294
   Virginia E. ...................................... 152
   William B. .............................. 169, 294
**Tudor**
   Richard ........................................... 295
**Tunstall**
   Ella W. ............................................ 273
**Turner**
   Francis L. ........................................ 295
   Henry Thomas ................................ 295
   Mary E. ........................................... 116
   William S. ....................................... 116
**Tuttle**
   Joseph ............................................. 295
**Tymeson**
   Isaac P. ........................................... 295
   J.P. .................................................. 295

## U

**U.S.S.**
   *Baring Brothers* .............................. 101
   *Constitution* ................................... 252
   *Dacotah* ......................................... 250
   *Exact* .............. 122, 215, 227, 267, 294
   *Fulton* ............................................ 250
   *Herman* ................................. 110, 241
   *Missouri* ......................................... 51
   *Monitor* .......................................... 66
   *North Carolina* ....................... 51, 250
   *Ohio* .............................................. 51
   *Pennsylvania* ................................. 202
   *Pensacola* ...................................... 250
   *Plymouth* ....................................... 51
   *Raritan* .................................. 145, 250
   *Sangamon* ..................................... 250
   *Saratoga* ............................... 104, 250

*Savannah* ....................................... 202
*Sophia Walker* .................... 79, 87, 317
**United States**
   13th Regt. ....................................... 251
   16th Regt., Co. A ............................ 237
   3rd Regt. ......................................... 183
   7th Regt., Co. H .............................. 232
   Military Academy .................. 128, 162
**United States - Artillery**
   3rd Regt., Co. C ............................. 151
   Battery A ........................................ 85
   Battery F ......................................... 85
   Battery K ........................................ 85
**United States - Cavalry** .................... 188
   2nd Regt., Co. D ............................. 85
   Co. A, 2nd Regt. ............................. 300
**United States - Infantry**
   25th Regt. U.S.C.T. ........................ 88
   2nd Btln. Vet. Res. Corps, 31st Co. ..... 177
   42nd Regt., Co. G ........................... 166
   4th Regt. ......................................... 220
**United States Army**
   Quartermaster Department .............. 306

## V

**Vaden**
   Ann M. ........................................... 253
   Elizabeth ......................................... 296
   Paskil .............................................. 296
   Robert H. ........................................ 296
**Vaiden**
   Elizabeth ......................................... 296
   John ................................................ 296
   Lucius ............................................. 296
   Mary ............................................... 296
   Mordecia ........................................ 296
   Phebe .............................................. 296
   Thomas ........................................... 296
**Vail**
   J.P. .................................................. 292
   Rosa ............................................... 292
**Vallett**
   Columbia ........................................ 296
   Francis ............................................ 296
**Van Leer**
   John ................................................ 296
**Van Sickel**

## VIRGINIA VOLUNTEERS IN MEXICO

Jane Maria ......................................... 90
**Van Tassel**
  Mehitable........................................ 222
**Vanhorn**
  John C. ........................................... 296
**Vanmetre**
  Abram G. ........................................ 296
  Malvina .......................................... 297
**Vanzant**
  Elizabeth (Abercrombie).................. 297
  James.............................................. 297
  James Robert................................... 297
**Vaughan**
  Alfred J........................................... 298
  Catherine ........................................ 298
  Gary ............................................... 298
  Gary H............................................ 298
  George............................................ 298
  J. William ....................................... 298
  John................................................ 298
  John A. ........................................... 298
  Maria C. ......................................... 298
  Mary E............................................ 298
  Mildred........................................... 298
**Veitch**
  Georgia B. ........................................ 76
**Velines**
  Charles H........................................ 298
**Vernon**
  William A.C.................................... 298
**Vine**
  John................................................ 208
**Virgina**
  Norfolk........................................... 105
**Virginia**
  Monroe Co...................................... 278
**Virginia**
  Accomac Co., Belle Haven............... 169
  Accomac Co., Drummond Town ..... 169, 191, 317
  Albemarle Co. .......................... 132, 140
  Albemarle Co., Brooksville .............. 277
  Albemarle Co., Charlottesville..... 65, 73, 78, 189, 267, 305
  Albemarle Co., Howardsville ... 130, 300
  Albemarle Co., Milton ..................... 267
  Albemarle Co., Scottsville.... 73, 86, 300

Alexandria ....................................... 124
Alexandria Co., Alexandria ... 50, 64, 72, 76, 86, 99, 105, 111, 112, 114, 115, 119, 122, 123, 127, 131, 133, 136, 141, 156, 160, 173, 174, 181, 182, 184, 188, 203, 223, 224, 225, 226, 228, 231, 234, 253, 257, 279, 285, 286, 291, 294, 298, 307, 317, 318
Alleghany Co., Covington.......... 73, 165
Amelia Co......... 81, 130, 179, 312, 315
Amelia Co., Amelia C.H. ........... 68, 217
Amelia Co., Hebron......................... 310
Amelia Co., Lodore ........................... 68
Amelia Co., Mill Quarter ................. 117
Amelia Co., Morven ......................... 68
Amherst Co..... 116, 120, 123, 180, 316
Amherst Co.,................................... 180
Amherst Co., Amherst C.H. ....... 81, 239
Amherst Co., Madison Heights......... 185
Amherst Co., New Glasgow ............. 140
Amherst Co., Sandiges..................... 306
Amherst Co., Stapleton ............ 116, 241
Appomattox Co., Stapleton Mills...... 241
Augusta Co. .................................... 163
Augusta Co., Augusta Springs .......... 238
Augusta Co., Barterbrook................. 283
Augusta Co., Basic City ................... 238
Augusta Co., Burke's Mill................ 163
Augusta Co., Craigsville ............. 71, 73
Augusta Co., Fishersville ................. 249
Augusta Co., Fisherville........... 218, 283
Augusta Co., Glen Allen .................. 163
Augusta Co., Greenville................... 218
Augusta Co., Long Meadows ........... 168
Augusta Co., Middle River................. 72
Augusta Co., Middlebrook ............... 284
Augusta Co., Mossy Creek....... 249, 287
Augusta Co., Mt. Sidney .................... 83
Augusta Co., Spring Hill............ 83, 287
Augusta Co., Staunton .... 52, 63, 65, 71, 72, 75, 93, 98, 120, 121, 133, 150, 152, 155, 156, 162, 163, 164, 168, 180, 182, 186, 187, 190, 195, 197, 217, 221, 231, 235, 238, 242, 249, 253, 256, 275, 287, 308, 312, 313
Augusta Co., Staunton, Western State Hospital ............................. 234, 308

Augusta Co., Staunton, Western State Lunatic Asylum............................ 308
Augusta Co., Waynesboro... 52, 55, 100, 163, 238, 248, 249, 283, 290, 306
Barbour Co. ..................... 167, 240, 267
Barbour Co., Philippi ....................... 267
Bath Co., Bath C.H. .......................... 140
Bath Co., Warm Springs .................. 244
Bedford Co. ... 166, 204, 257, 273, 283, 284
Bedford Co., Chambersburg ................ 82
Bedford Co., Coffee.......................... 180
Bedford Co., Curtis........................... 202
Bedford Co., Liberty. 80, 149, 189, 230, 300
Bedford Co., New London ................ 233
Bedford Co., Peaks of Otter.............. 255
Bedford Co., Peaksville ...................... 80
Bedford Co., Thaxton ....................... 255
Bedford Co., The Meadows.............. 166
Berkekey Co., Martinsburg 52, 110, 111, 141, 173, 181, 184, 190, 210, 219, 234, 243, 244, 249, 251, 271, 284, 297
Berkekey Co., Vancleavesville ......... 106
Berkeley Co. ............................ 237, 284
Berkeley Co., Gerrardstown ............. 272
Berkeley Co., Hedgesville........ 152, 237
Berkeley Co., Martinsburg ....... 134, 181
Berkeley Co., Mill Creek ................. 271
Berkeley Co., Spring Mills................ 237
Bluff Point ........................................ 131
Botetourt Co....... 55, 92, 109, 141, 150, 201, 222
Botetourt Co., Dagger's Springs........ 150
Botetourt Co., Fincastle .. 169, 174, 201, 275
Brigadier General ..................... 107, 304
Brunswick Co. 112, 151, 189, 190, 281, 306, 311
Brunswick Co., Binfords.................. 265
Brunswick Co., Brunswick C.H. ....... 107, 123, 231
Brunswick Co., Crichton.................. 227
Brunswick Co., Gholsonville............ 225
Brunswick Co., Harper's Home ........ 307

Brunswick Co., Jonesborough . 152, 161, 206
Brunswick Co., Powelton................. 225
Brunswick Co., Smokey Ordinary.... 104, 148
Brunswick Co., Sturgeonsville. 147, 151, 301
Brunswick Co., Thomasburg ............ 147
Buckingham Co............... 130, 227, 241
Buckingham Co., Buckingham C.H. . . 300
Buckingham Co., Curdsville............. 227
Campbell Co. ................................... 200
Campbell Co., Castle Craig ...... 154, 234
Campbell Co., Lynchburg 64, 67, 89, 99, 112, 124, 130, 140, 150, 154, 159, 180, 185, 187, 188, 198, 204, 211, 234, 246, 251, 256, 257, 266, 273, 278, 279, 286, 300, 301, 303, 312, 316
Campbell Co., New London ....... 62, 109
Caroline Co............. 108, 165, 198, 289
Caroline Co., Bowling Green 76, 85, 93, 94, 101, 143, 155, 165, 198, 241, 279, 289
Caroline Co., Flippo's Store.............. 102
Caroline Co., Port Royal .................. 155
Caroline Co., Ruther Glen................ 279
Caroline Co., Sparta......... 143, 155, 289
Caroline Co., Summit Station ........... 256
Carroll Co., Hillsville....................... 312
Charles City Co. ................................. 84
Charles City Co., Roxbury ................. 84
Charles City Co., Westover .............. 267
Charlotte Co...................... 57, 136, 279
Charlotte Co., Charlotte C.H. ... 136, 235
Charlotte Co., Keysville................... 247
Charlotte Co., Ontario........................ 60
Charlotte Co., Red Oak Grove .......... 307
Charlotte Co., Walton ...................... 247
Charlotte Co., Wylliesburg................. 60
Chesterfield Co. ..... 137, 156, 202, 204, 289, 293, 296, 302
Chesterfield Co., Chester ......... 101, 253
Chesterfield Co., Chesterfield C.H. ... 135, 216
Chesterfield Co., Falling Creek......... 129

## VIRGINIA VOLUNTEERS IN MEXICO

Chesterfield Co., Manchester... 101, 148, 234, 253, 254, 285, 296, 304
Chesterfield Co., Petersburg............. 271
Chesterfield Co., The Grove.............. 304
Clarke Co........................... 66, 125, 244
Clarke Co., Battletown...................... 244
Clarke Co., Berryville......... 94, 134, 271
Clarke Co., Bethel ............................ 106
Craig Co., Craig ................................ 170
Culpeper Co., Culpeper C.H.............. 317
Culpeper Co., Griffinsburg.................. 70
Cumberland Co. ....... 113, 217, 237, 247
Cumberland Co., Bush Park .............. 218
Cumberland Co., Cartersville ............ 218
Cumberland Co., Cumberland C.H. .. 103
Cumberland Co., Oak Forest ............. 102
Danville............................................... 79
Dinwiddie Co. 151, 164, 209, 226, 238, 239, 265, 287, 302, 305, 310
Dinwiddie Co., Dinwiddie C.H.151, 197, 276, 302, 305
Dinwiddie Co., Hebron ..................... 312
Dinwiddie Co., Macer........................ 310
Dinwiddie Co., Petersburg .... 50, 56, 63, 65, 66, 94, 110, 117, 118, 138, 140, 156, 162, 164, 165, 167, 180, 187, 196, 197, 227, 236, 237, 238, 239, 240, 242, 246, 257, 266, 272, 276, 279, 293, 295, 296, 304, 305, 306, 312, 317
Dinwiddie Co., *Rail Road Shanty* ....... 90
Dinwiddie Co., Ream's Station.......... 276
Dinwiddie Co., Rowanta ................... 276
Dinwiddie Co., San Marino62, 129, 151, 246, 302, 307
Elizabeth City Co. ..... 82, 136, 141, 295
Elizabeth City Co., Back River.......... 136
Elizabeth City Co., Ft. Monroe ......... 136
Elizabeth City Co., Hampton, National Military Home...................... 202, 250
Elizabeth City Co., Hampton, National Soldiers Home. 65, 90, 124, 128, 168
Elizabeth City Co., National Military Home.................................. 268, 292
Elizabeth City Co., Old Point ........... 136

Elizabeth City Co., Old Point Comfort .. 147, 174, 178, 190, 203, 227, 242, 284, 298, 308
Elizabeth City Co., Phoebus ............. 136
Elizabeth City Co., Phoebus Station.. 136
Essex Co........................................ 230
Essex Co., Dunsville.......................... 83
Essex Co., Essex C.H....................... 230
Essex Co., Miller's Tavern ....... 108, 289
Essex Co., Montague's Tavern............ 78
Fairfax Co...... 158, 183, 226, 250, 286, 292
Fairfax Co., Ashgrove...................... 128
Fairfax Co., Centreville.............. 55, 224
Fairfax Co., Dranesville ... 158, 194, 299
Fairfax Co., Dunn-Loring................. 316
Fairfax Co., Fairfax C.H...... 88, 89, 122, 145, 159, 160, 194, 200, 219, 222, 225, 233, 236, 292, 312, 316
Fairfax Co., Falls Church ... 76, 128, 306
Fairfax Co., Great Falls............ 158, 318
Fairfax Co., Springvale ............ 158, 185
Fairfax Co., West End...................... 160
Farersville........................................ 110
Fauquier Co. ................... 107, 221, 225
Fauquier Co., Farrowsville................. 81
Fauquier Co., Front Royal.................. 85
Fauquier Co., Markham ..................... 81
Fauquier Co., Paris .................. 192, 196
Fauquier Co., Rectortown ................ 292
Fauquier Co., Upperville..... 55, 92, 107, 192, 212
Fauquier Co., Warrenton..... 55, 87, 225, 298
Fayette Co., Fayetteville .................. 187
Fayette Co., Oak Hill ....................... 284
Fayette Co., Roseville ...................... 284
Fincastle Co. ...................................... 81
Floyd Co......................... 178, 213, 272
Floyd Co., Basham ............................ 51
Floyd Co., Burk's Fork ...................... 69
Floyd Co., Copper Hill................. 52, 62
Floyd Co., Floyd C.H.. 62, 69, 148, 178, 183, 304
Floyd Co., Graysville......................... 62
Floyd Co., Greasy Creek.................... 69
Floyd Co., Posey .............................. 108

Floyd Co., Salem Church ................... 52
Floyd Co., Simpson's ......................... 52
Floyd Co., Tindall ............................ 51
Fluvanna Co. .................................... 253
Fort Monroe. 83, 86, 88, 105, 114, 116, 119, 120, 124, 129, 136, 147, 151, 156, 161, 174, 179, 187, 188, 194, 195, 198, 201, 203, 213, 220, 227, 234, 237, 238, 245, 255, 257, 271, 274, 281, 283, 285, 288, 291, 294, 302, 304, 308, 315
Franklin ............................................ 97
Franklin Co. ..................... 148, 184, 272
Franklin Co., Boones Mill ................ 129
Franklin Co., Franklin C.H. ................ 52
Franklin Co., Gill's Creek ................. 123
Franklin Co., Gogginsville ............... 231
Franklin Co., Rocky Mount ..... 108, 111, 123, 187, 231
Frederick Co. .................................. 148
Frederick Co. .................................. 208
Frederick Co., Bartersville ............... 220
Frederick Co., Gainsborough ........... 298
Frederick Co., Gore ................ 154, 196
Frederick Co., Kernstown ................ 273
Frederick Co., Rosenberger .............. 196
Frederick Co., Winchester 64, 69, 70, 89, 106, 119, 165, 168, 170, 195, 217, 221, 273, 291, 298, 300, 303, 308
Giles Co. ........................ 56, 74, 98, 115
Giles Co., Pearisburg ....................... 269
Giles Co., Shumate ............................ 63
Gloucester Co., Gloucester C.H. ....... 134, 301, 304
Goochland Co. ......... 106, 191, 224, 278
Goochland Co., Columbia ................ 285
Goochland Co., Goochland C.H. ........ 73
Goochland Co., Waller Gold Mine .... 285
Grayson Co., Grayson C.H. ................ 68
Grayson Co., Hampton Cross Roads ... 68
Green Co., Standardsville ................ 267
Greenbrier Co. ......................... 102, 126
Greenbrier Co., Falling Spring .......... 103
Greenbrier Co., Frankfort ................. 191
Greenbrier Co., Lewisburg ....... 110, 284
Greensville Co. ................................ 225

Greensville Co., Brink ....................... 56
Greensville Co., Emporia .................. 56
Greensville Co., Hicks Ford .... 101, 134, 227, 246
Greensville Co., Hicksford ............... 103
Greensville Co., Hicksford 56, 112, 137, 184
Greensville Co., Poplar Mount ......... 137
Greensville Co., Rural Bower ........... 184
Greensville Co., Skippers ................. 137
Halifax Co. ............. 113, 134, 304, 310
Halifax Co., Red Bank ..................... 310
Hampshire Co., Hanging Rock ......... 272
Hampshire Co., Romney .................. 221
Hampshire Co., Yellow Spring ......... 194
Hampton ......................................... 188
Hanover Co. 59, 91, 101, 130, 178, 301
Hanover Co., Ashland ........................ 50
Hanover Co., Hanover C.H. ............. 178
Hanover Co., Hewlett's ...................... 91
Hanover Co., Negrofoot ..................... 91
Hanover Co., Old Church ................... 89
Henrico Co. ........ 67, 122, 124, 154, 200
Henrico Co., Darbytown ................. 137
Henrico Co., Elba ............................ 278
Henrico Co., Richmond .. 50, 53, 55, 70, 78, 79, 81, 82, 83, 86, 88, 93, 97, 109, 114, 116, 117, 119, 124, 127, 131, 137, 138, 139, 140, 145, 152, 155, 160, 165, 167, 174, 176, 177, 178, 180, 181, 183, 184, 185, 186, 188, 189, 192, 193, 195, 198, 199, 203, 204, 205, 206, 208, 210, 211, 215, 216, 217, 219, 222, 224, 228, 229, 232, 233, 234, 236, 237, 240, 241, 242, 243, 244, 245, 246, 247, 248, 251, 252, 254, 256, 258, 259, 265, 266, 269, 274, 278, 281, 282, 283, 285, 287, 288, 289, 291, 292, 293, 298, 299, 302, 308, 309, 312, 314, 315, 316, 317
Henrico Co., Richmond, Alms House
............................................. 269, 289
Henrico Co., Richmond, Lee Camp Soldiers Home ............................ 278
Henrico Co., Springfield .................. 242
Henrico Co., Tuckahoe .................... 278

Henrico Co., VA .............................. 64
Henry Co. ......................................... 79
Henry Co., Blackberry ..................... 183
Highland Co., Crabbottom ............... 267
Highland Co., Hightown .................. 164
Highland Co., McDowell ........... 93, 164
Highland Co., Meadow Dale .............. 93
Highland Co., Mill Gap..................... 164
Highland Co., Monterey.................... 164
Howardsville....................................... 89
Huntington........................................ 257
Isle of Wight Co. .............................. 156
Isle of Wight Co., Carrsville............. 107
Isle of Wight Co., Windsor............... 266
James City Co. ................................. 116
James City Co., Williamsburg 64, 70, 72
James City Co., Williamsburg, Eastern
 State Hospital................................ 73
James River and Kanawha Canal Co... 55
Jefferson Co., Charlestown...... 106, 109,
 111, 112, 117, 126, 127, 128, 142,
 167, 176, 178, 179, 182, 193, 196,
 210, 215, 243, 244, 251, 256, 265,
 268, 272, 275, 298, 318
Jefferson Co., Harper's Ferry .. 106, 238,
 290, 315
Jefferson Co., Harper's Ferry ...... 97, 167
Jefferson Co., Shepherdstown.. 106, 162,
 173, 188, 219, 294
Jonesborough ................................... 309
Kanawha Co..................................... 198
Kanawha Co., Kanawha C.H. ........... 275
Kanawha Co., Kanawha Salines ....... 276
King & Queen Co............................. 134
King & Queen Co., Little Plymouth.. 177
King George Co. ...................... 160, 280
King George Co., Clifton ................... 88
King George Co., Comorn........ 160, 303
King George Co., Passabytanzy.......... 88
King William Co. ............. 130, 148, 188
Kingston .......................................... 166
Lee Co............................. 142, 239, 287
Lee Co., Crawfordsville ................... 287
Lewis Co. ........................................ 136
Lewis Co. , Weston ............................ 79
Loudoun Co. ............ 112, 154, 243, 244
Loudoun Co., Aldie ......................... 161

Loudoun Co., Alms House ............... 127
Loudoun Co., Bloomfield................. 154
Loudoun Co., Bluemont................... 154
Loudoun Co., Daysville ..................... 66
Loudoun Co., Goresville .................... 66
Loudoun Co., Hillborough ................. 73
Loudoun Co., Hillsboro ............. 65, 106
Loudoun Co., Hillsborough.............. 215
Loudoun Co., Leesburg............ 174, 250
Loudoun Co., Middleburg................ 114
Loudoun Co., Noland's Ferry .......... 303
Loudoun Co., Philomont .................. 127
Loudoun Co., Purcellville .................. 65
Loudoun Co., Snickersville ...... 106, 154
Loudoun Co., Union ........................ 148
Loudoun Co., Unison....................... 127
Louisa Co. ....................................... 315
Louisa Co., Fredericks Hall.............. 257
Louisa Co., Gordonsville ......... 238, 290
Louisa Co., Green Springs................ 109
Louisa Co., Louisa C.H............ 245, 299
Louisa Co., Trevillians............. 109, 315
Louisa Co.Louisa C.H........................ 60
Lunenburg Co. 103, 152, 161, 247, 301
Lunenburg Co., Brickland.......... 80, 236
Lunenburg Co., Brown's Store............ 84
Lunenburg Co., Eubon ....................... 61
Lunenburg Co., Fletcher's Chapel ..... 152
Lunenburg Co., Keysville ................ 311
Lunenburg Co., Lunenburg C,H,....... 109
Lunenburg Co., Lunenburg C.H... 62, 84,
 152, 165, 180, 219
Lunenburg Co., McFarlands ............. 123
Lunenburg Co., Non-Intervention ....... 73
Lunenburg Co., Plantersville 60, 61, 307
Lunenburg Co., Pleasant Grove ... 60, 61,
 73, 88, 100, 130, 234, 271, 307,
 309, 311
Lunenburg Co., Rehoboth .. 60, 137, 307
Lunenburg Co., Trix ........................ 189
Lunenburg Co., Yatesville.......... 79, 317
Lynchburg ....................................... 292
Lynchburg, Trinity Methodist Episcopal
 Church........................................ 180
Madison Co...................................... 192
Manchester ...................................... 211
Marshall Co. .................................... 254

Mathews Co. ...................................... 78
Mathews Co., Mathews C.H. ............ 166
Mecklenburg Co. ....... 79, 224, 227, 234, 251, 277
Mecklenburg Co., Boydton ..... 105, 156, 166, 227, 300, 311
Mecklenburg Co., Elhanon Grove ..... 248
Mecklenburg Co., Filehouse ............. 310
Mecklenburg Co., Forksville ..... 61, 240, 311
Mecklenburg Co., Lombardy Grove .. 248
Mecklenburg Co., Oakey ................. 251
Mecklenburg Co., Townsville ........... 248
Mecklenburg, Clarksville ................... 66
Middlesex Co. .................................. 224
Middlesex Co., Middlesex C.H. ......... 134
Mill Creek Branch ........................... 105
Mineral Co. ...................................... 194
Monroe Co. ........................................ 93
Monroe Co., Union .......................... 245
Montgomery Co. ............... 70, 169, 203
Montgomery Co., Alleghany Springs . 68, 198, 311
Montgomery Co., Big Spring ........... 213
Montgomery Co., Blacksburg ...... 74, 81, 129, 169, 170, 194, 230, 246, 254, 268, 282, 294, 318
Montgomery Co., Childress Store .... 255, 291
Montgomery Co., Childress' Store .... 254
Montgomery Co., Christiansburg . 51, 56, 68, 71, 79, 90, 93, 98, 104, 114, 120, 124, 129, 140, 142, 149, 156, 169, 179, 186, 191, 194, 198, 201, 222, 230, 239, 240, 245, 246, 254, 255, 268, 274, 275, 283, 285, 287, 288, 291, 295, 298, 311, 318
Montgomery Co., Elliott's Creek ...... 179
Montgomery Co., Elliston ................ 213
Montgomery Co., Lafayette ...... 141, 222
Montgomery Co., Layfayette ............ 198
Montgomery Co., Long's Shop ......... 149
Montgomery Co., Matamoras ........... 201
Montgomery Co., Matamoros .. 194, 201, 268
Montgomery Co., McDonald's Mills ... 71

Montgomery Co., New River ........... 201
Montgomery Co., Pilot .................... 183
Montgomery Co., Price's Fork ......... 201
Montgomery Co., Price's Fork .......... 295
Montgomery Co., Radford ............... 228
Morgan Co., Berkeley Springs .......... 267
Nansemond Co. ................ 110, 161, 232
Nansemond Co., Suffolk .................. 232
National Military Homes, Hampton .. 292
Nelson Co. .............. 130, 140, 152, 232
Nelson Co., Allen's Creek ................ 152
Nelson Co., Arrington ...................... 257
Nelson Co., Elmington ..................... 232
Nelson Co., Fabers Mills .................. 232
Nelson Co., Liberty Hall .................. 130
Nelson Co., Lovingston .. 130, 140, 151, 313
Nelson Co., Massies Mill ................. 306
Nelson Co., Roseland ....................... 306
Nelson Co., Tye River Warehouse ...... 89
Nelson Co., Variety Mills ................. 257
New Kent Co. .................... 52, 179, 272
Norfolk ................................... 166, 237
Norfolk Co. ...................................... 241
Norfolk Co., Bell's Mill .................... 110
Norfolk Co., Deep Creek ............ 99, 309
Norfolk Co., Lambert's Point ........... 317
Norfolk Co., Norfolk .... 71, 92, 99, 100, 104, 110, 118, 119, 121, 155, 165, 169, 189, 216, 220, 230, 233, 239, 245, 258, 277, 281, 293, 309, 310, 311
Norfolk Co., Pinner's Pt. .................. 110
Norfolk Co., Portsmouth . 52, 68, 71, 73, 75, 83, 89, 90, 94, 99, 102, 104, 107, 108, 110, 111, 118, 119, 122, 127, 135, 147, 157, 159, 165, 179, 183, 184, 186, 189, 196, 197, 206, 219, 221, 227, 232, 233, 234, 235, 237, 241, 249, 250, 253, 270, 280, 281, 286, 293, 295, 296, 304, 308, 315
Northampton Co. ............. 191, 225, 232
Northampton Co., Downing's Wharf . 191
Northampton Co., Exmore ............... 192
Northampton Co., Hadlock ............... 192

## VIRGINIA VOLUNTEERS IN MEXICO

Northampton Co., Hog Island........... 192
Nottoway Co...................... 90, 134, 137
Nottoway Co., Blackstone.................. 84
Nottoway Co., Nottoway C.H.. 111, 135, 161, 312
Ohio Co. ......................................... 251
Ohio Co., Wheeling......................... 126
Old Point Comfort ........................... 117
Orange Co......................... 85, 154, 192
Orange Co., Orange C.H. .......... 154, 158
Page Co., Cedar Point ........................ 70
Page Co., Milford ............................... 70
Patrick Co. ...................... 183, 255, 291
Patrick Co., Mayo Forge .................. 280
Patrick Co., Patrick C.H. .................. 123
Patrick Co., Penn's Store .................. 280
Patrick Co., Taylorsville ................... 276
Pendelton Co..................................... 93
Penitentiary, Richmond.................... 124
Petersburg....................... 183, 236, 240
Petersburg, City Hospital ................. 296
Pittsylvania Co.................. 79, 285, 287
Pittsylvania Co., Danville......... 148, 273
Point Comfort ................................. 169
Powhattan Co................................... 174
Powhattan Co., Powhattan C.H......... 151
Preston Co. ..................................... 128
Preston Co., Evansville .................... 141
Prince Edward Co............................ 165
Prince Edward Co., Farmville........... 251
Prince Edward Co., Felden................. 55
Prince Edward Co., Prince Edward C.H. ........................................................ 55
Prince Edward Co., Worsham............. 55
Prince George Co. .. 102, 140, 161, 167, 189, 215, 230, 267, 310, 315
Prince George Co., Blandford........... 267
Prince George Co., Brandon Church . 164
Prince George Co., City Point... 135, 267
Prince George Co., Garysville .......... 267
Prince George Co., Prince George C.H. ...................................................... 231
Prince George Co., Templeton.... 56, 164
Prince William Co. .......................... 308
Prince William Co., Brentsville ........ 133
Prince William Co., Dumfries ............ 55
Prince William Co., Gainesville.......... 55

Prince William Co., Occoquan ......... 133
Prince William Co., Thoroughfare ...... 55
Prince William Co., Waterfall ............ 55
Prince William, Occoquan................. 92
Princes George Co. .......................... 189
Princess Anne Co. .................... 118, 241
Princess Anne Co., Blackwater......... 241
Princess Anne Co., London Bridge ... 241
Prospect Hill ................................... 183
Pulaski Co........................................ 149
Pulaski Co., Dublin.................. 143, 255
Pulaski Co., Newbern ..... 108, 142, 143, 179, 203, 220, 242, 255, 269
Pulaski Co., Snowville............. 255, 274
Raleigh Co., Beckley Springs ........... 239
Raleigh Co., Clear Creek.................. 284
Randolph Co. .................................... 79
Randolph Co., Westerford................ 240
Rappahannock Co., Sperryville .......... 87
Rappahannock Co., Washington ....... 247
Roanoke Co. ........... 129, 191, 222, 254
Roanoke Co., Big Lick(Roanoke) ..... 225
Roanoke Co., Roanoke..................... 254
Roanoke Co., Salem ... 62, 67, 181, 229, 287, 312
Rockbridge Co. ......... 83, 150, 212, 283
Rockbridge Co., Brownsburg ........... 278
Rockbridge Co., Collierstown........... 202
Rockbridge Co., Lexington 68, 120, 176, 202, 206, 235, 276, 278, 309, 311
Rockingham Co............... 129, 132, 225
Rockingham Co., Bridgewater.......... 126
Rockingham Co., Edom ..................... 84
Rockingham Co., Harrisonburg . 84, 167, 252, 276, 278
Rockingham Co., Lacy Spring.... 70, 102
Rockingham Co., Linville .................. 84
Rockingham Co., Mt. Crawford.. 70, 303
Rockingham Co., Smith's Creek? ....... 84
Rockingham Co., Sparta .................... 70
Rockingham Co., Spartapolis ..... 84, 102
Shennandoah Co................................ 97
Shennandoah Co., Edinburg ............. 285
Shennandoah Co., New Market ... 84, 97, 180
Shennandoah Co., Strasburg............. 167

Smyth Co. .................................. 74, 286
Smyth Co., Marion .................. 106, 177
Southampton Co. ............. 231, 266, 295
Southampton Co., Courtland ............ 295
Southampton Co., Isaacs .................. 137
Southampton Co., Jerusalem ..... 81, 231, 295
Southampton Co., Joinersville .......... 137
Southampton Co., Vicksvılle ............ 137
Spotsylvania..................................... 249
Spotsylvania Co. ............................... 75
Spotsylvania Co., Fredericksburg .... 103, 111, 132, 185, 270, 280, 316
Spotsylvania Co., Spotsylvania C.H. 185, 271
Stafford Co. ............. 107, 122, 138, 303
Stafford Co., Falmouth....... 83, 107, 138
Stafford Co., Mussleman.................. 138
Stafford Co., Stafford C.H.................. 93
Stafford Co., White Ridge ................ 122
*Stoney Hill* ........................................ 83
Surry Co. .................................. 83, 211
Surry Co., Cabin Point..................... 161
Surry Co., Jarratt's Depot................. 179
Sussex Co. ......... 93, 121, 215, 310, 313
Sussex Co., Henry P.O..................... 100
Sussex Co., Jarratt's Depot....... 237, 251
Sussex Co., Jarratt's Depot ................ 83
Sussex Co., Stoney Creek................. 314
Sussex Co., Sussex C.H. .. 100, 251, 295
Tazewell Co..................... 104, 106, 121
Tazewell Co., Tazewell C.H............. 104
Tazwell Co....................................... 121
Tucker Co., Horseshoe Run.............. 240
Warren Co. ............................. 247, 298
Warren Co., Front Royal ............ 66, 168
Warren Co., Linden .......................... 298
Washington Co....................... 230, 246
Washington Co., Abingdon . 69, 76, 121, 161
Washington Co., Bristol................... 165
Washington Co., King's Salt Works.. 121
Wayne's Station .............................. 300
West Augusta, Augusta.................... 238
Westmoreland Co. ........................... 145
Westmoreland Co., Kinsale ............. 145

Wise Co., Appalachia ........................ 76
Wise Co., Gladesville ........................ 76
Wythe Co......................... 79, 201, 272
Wythe Co., Black Lick..................... 271
Wythe Co., Fort Chiswell......... 128, 227
Wythe Co., Max Meadows............... 148
Wythe Co., Rural Retreat ................. 149
Wythe Co., Wythcville 67, 73, 108, 128, 148, 149, 158, 187, 226, 227, 234, 235, 255, 285, 286, 301, 302, 309, 315

**Virginia - Artillery**
10th Btln., Co. C ............................. 274
12th Btln., Co. B ............................. 117
18th Btln., Co. B ............................. 293
18th Btln., Co. C ............................... 50
19th Btln., Co. B ...................... 51, 192
19th Btln., Co. D ..................... 161, 180
1st Regt., Co. C ................................. 82
20th Btln., Co. C ............................. 109
20th Btln., Dabney's Co. .................. 116
38th Btln., Co. C ............................. 278
3rd Regt., Co. B .............................. 130
3rd Regt., Co. D .............................. 196
Ashland Atrillery, Co. A .................. 178
Branch's Field ..................... 56, 94, 227
Capt. A.E. Reed's Co. ........................ 51
Caroline Artillery ............................ 289
Charlottesville Artillery ..................... 92
Coffin's Battery ............................... 287
Curtis' Battery ................................. 111
Fredericksburg Artillery................... 138
French's Battery, Giles Artillery ......... 68
Jackson Artillery ............................. 273
Lechter Artillery.............................. 234
Marion Artillery .............................. 234
Norfolk Light Artillery, Huger's Battery ................................................... 119
Peagram's Co. ................................. 118
Purcell Artillery............................... 116
Richmond Fayette Artillery.............. 181
Staunton Artillery............................ 231
Staunton Hill Artillery ....................... 84
Stuart's Horse Artillery, McClanahan's Co. ................................................. 238
Sturdivant's Battery ......................... 198
Wise's, Co. B.................................... 52

## VIRGINIA VOLUNTEERS IN MEXICO

**Virginia -** Brigadier General ................ 192
**Virginia - Cavalry**
10th Regt. ...................................... 271
11th Regt., Co. A............................... 75
12th Regt., Co. C..................... 148, 271
13th Regt., Co. A............................. 165
13th Regt., Co. B............................. 231
13th Regt., Co. D............................. 314
14th Regt., Co. C............................. 143
14th Regt., Co. K............................. 110
15th Regt., Co. K............................. 241
16th Regt., Co. I .............................. 104
19th Regt., Co. C............................. 191
1st Regt., Co. C ............................... 162
1st Regt., Co. F ............................... 106
1st Regt., Co. G............................... 130
21st Regt., Co. G............................. 184
23rd Regt., Co. K ............................ 195
2nd Regt., Co. B.............................. 234
2nd Regt., Co. C.............................. 174
2nd Regt., Co. E .............................. 306
35th Regt., Co. C............................. 106
40th Btln., Co. B ............................. 271
43rd Btln., Arty. Co. ........................ 292
47th Btln., Aldredge's Co. ................ 111
4th Regt., Co. E ............................... 174
5th Regt., Co. C............................... 109
5th Regt., Co. F ............................... 267
5th Regt., Co. H .............................. 231
5th Regt., Co. I ................................ 241
5th Regt., Co. K ........................ 62, 121
62nd Regt., Co. B ............................ 152
6th Regt., Co. B................................ 87
6th Regt., Co. F ....................... 223, 316
6th Regt., Co. H .............................. 233
6th Regt., Co. I................................. 85
8th Regt., Co. A .............................. 106
8th Regt., Co. C............................... 161
8th Regt., Co. I ................................ 187
9th Regt., Co. E ............................... 145
9th Regt., Co. G............................... 137
9th Regt., Co. I ................................ 280
Clarkson's Btln. Independent Rangers 119
McNeill's Rangers ........................... 122
**Virginia - Infantry**
11th Regt., Co. B............................... 62
11th Regt., Co. H............................. 154

127 Regt., (Militia) .......................... 285
12th Regt., ...................................... 239
12th Regt., Co. B..................... 129, 156
12th Regt., Co. D............................... 50
12th Regt., Co. F ..................... 112, 164
12th Regt., Co. I ...................... 151, 271
12th Regt., Co. I .............................. 164
12th Regt., Co. K 57, 94, 140, 200, 242, 266, 279, 295
135th Regt., Co. C ........................... 110
13th Regt., Co. A..................... 154, 158
13th Regt., Co. B............................. 198
13th Regt., Co. C............................. 158
13th Regt., Co. D............................. 155
14th Regt., Co. I .............................. 302
157th Regt., Co. B ........................... 223
15th Regt. ......................................... 61
15th Regt., Co. C............................... 91
16th Regt., Co. C............................... 75
16th Regt., Co. D............................. 232
16th Regt., Co. E ............................. 237
16th Regt., Co. K............................... 56
17th Regt., Co. D..... 129, 160, 183, 294
17th Regt., Co. E ..................... 114, 184
18th Regt., Co. D............................. 190
18th Regt., Co. F ............. 227, 251, 315
19th Regt., Co. C............................. 300
19th Regt., Co. D..................... 130, 305
1st Btln., Co. A ................................. 83
1st Btln., Co. A, (Local Defense) ....... 138
1st Btln., Co. D, (Local Defense) ....... 138
1st Regt., Co. E ................................. 69
20th Regt., Co. B ............................. 309
21st Regt., Co. F.............................. 266
21st Regt., Co. K ............................. 137
22nd Btln., Co. B ............. 136, 247, 248
23rd Regt., Co. D ............................ 315
23rd Regt., Co. G ............................ 257
23rd Regt., Co. K ........................ 60, 61
25th Btln., Co. A ............................. 243
25th Regt. ....................................... 244
25th Regt., Co. A, (Militia) .............. 160
26th Regt., Co. D............................. 293
26th Regt., Co. G............................. 177
27th Regt., Co. H..................... 134, 271
28th Btln., Co. H ............................. 256

28th Regt., Co. A............................... 288
2nd Regt. ......................................... 181
2nd Regt., Co. A............................... 256
2nd Regt., Co. A, (Reserves) ............ 281
2nd Regt., Co. B............................... 294
2nd Regt., Co. D............................... 190
2nd Regt., Co. H............................... 193
2nd Regt., Co. K................................. 97
30th Regt., Co. F .............................. 291
30th Regt., Co. G.............................. 102
30th Regt., Co. H.............................. 155
32nd Regt., Co. F .............................. 295
32nd Regt., Co. I .............................. 136
36th Regt., Beckett's Co. ................... 310
36th Regt., Co. C.............................. 201
36th Regt., Co. E .............................. 273
36th Regt., Co. H................................ 98
37th Regt., Co. C.............................. 104
38th Regt., Co. F .............................. 113
39th Regt. ........................................ 191
39th Regt., Co. B, (Militia)................ 236
3rd Btln. Reserves .............................. 57
3rd Btln., Co. D................................ 211
3rd Regt., Co. C ............................... 276
3rd Regt., Co. C, (Reserves) ............. 316
41st Regt., Co. A ..................... 100, 160
41st Regt., Co. F ............................... 286
43rd Btln., Co. A .............................. 223
44th Regt., Co. H........................ 68, 312
45th Regt., Co. B .............................. 235
46th Regt., Co. A .............................. 108
46th Regt., Co. C, (Militia)................ 193
46th Regt., Co. D.............................. 151
48th Regt. ........................................ 145
49th Regt., Co. H.............................. 211
4th Regt. .................................... 74, 245
4th Regt., Co. A ................. 52, 158, 255
4th Regt., Co. C............... 179, 203, 286
4th Regt., Co. C, (Reserves) .............. 242
4th Regt., Co. D, (Reserves) .............. 268
4th Regt., Co. E................. 71, 254, 268
4th Regt., Co. G ............. 283, 295, 298
4th Regt., Co. I................................. 309
4th Regt., Co. L............................ 81, 230
50th Regt., Co. A .............................. 142
50th Regt., Co. I ............................... 302

51st Regt......................................... 128
51st Regt., Co. B .............................. 257
51st Regt., Co. C ..................... 149, 235
52nd Regt., Co. B ................... 168, 203
52nd Regt., Co. C ............................ 133
53rd Regt., Co. F ................................ 62
53rd Regt., Co. G ............................ 119
54th Regt., Co. C.............................. 288
54th Regt., Co. D................................ 69
54th Regt., Co. F .............................. 242
54th Regt., Co. H.............................. 213
56th Regt., Co. K................................ 50
57th Regt. ........................................ 257
59th Regt., Co. C................................ 78
59th Regt., Co. F .............................. 284
5th Btln............................................. 57
5th Btln., Co. B ................................ 307
5th Btln., Co. H .................................. 71
5th Regt. .......................................... 163
5th Regt., Co. A ........................ 69, 195
5th Regt., Co. C....................... 150, 287
5th Regt., Co. D ............................... 168
5th Regt., Co. L .................................. 75
60th Regt., Co. D.............................. 139
60th Regt., Co. K................................ 67
61st Regt., Co. D .............................. 157
61st Regt., Co. G .............................. 251
61st Regt., Co. H................................ 99
67th Regt., Co. B (Militia)................... 75
6th Regt. ................................. 290, 311
6th Regt., Co. A ............................... 281
6th Regt., Co. F ................................ 108
6th Regt., Co. G ............................... 240
7th Regt. .......................................... 192
7th Regt., Co. D ................................. 75
8th Regt., Co. G ....................... 158, 292
8th Regt., Co. I................................. 161
8th Regt., Co. K ............................... 116
9th Btln. Reserves, Co. D ................. 102
9th Regt. ................................. 151, 302
9th Regt., Co. A ....................... 215, 287
9th Regt., Co. C................................ 305
9th Regt., Co. D ............................... 304
9th Regt., Co. H ....................... 151, 152
9th Regt., Co. K ......................... 71, 110
Co. K, 17th Regt................................ 55

VIRGINIA VOLUNTEERS IN MEXICO

Lieutenant General ......................... 123
**Vonreason**
   Henry G. ......................................... 298
   Samuel. ........................................... 298
   Sarah F. .......................................... 298
   Susan G. .......................................... 298

# W

**Waddell**
   Charles ........................................... 298
**Waddle**
   Margaret J. ....................................... 93
**Wade**
   Agnes M. ......................................... 298
   Anna ................................................ 108
   Catherine R. .................................... 288
   Charles J. ....................................... 298
   Emily ............................................... 298
   Frank M. .......................................... 298
   Harry M. .......................................... 298
   James Montague ............................. 298
   James S. ......................................... 298
   John ................................................. 299
   John J. ............................................. 298
   Margaret C. ..................................... 298
   Mary ................................................ 298
   Matilda (Slaven) .............................. 299
   McClanahan .................................... 298
   McClanhan ..................................... 298
   Pheobe Ann .................................... 268
   Reuben Alexander .......................... 299
   Samuel P. ........................................ 299
   Thomas L. ....................................... 298
   William ............................................ 298
**Waldon**
   James F. .......................................... 299
**Waldron**
   Betty ............................................... 123
**Walker**
   Anne ............................................... 311
   Benjamin Joseph ............................ 300
   Joanna ............................................ 300
   Joanna A. ........................................ 300
   John L. ............................................ 300
   Joseph A. ........................................ 300
   Lula E. ............................................ 300
   Maggie M. ....................................... 300

   Mary E. ............................................ 149
   Vanessa D. ...................................... 300
   William ............................................ 300
   William A. ....................................... 300
**Wall**
   Alberta ............................................ 300
   Alexander A. ................................... 300
   Harvey ............................................ 300
   James L. ......................................... 300
   Treadwell S. .................................... 300
**Wallace**
   Eliza Jane ....................................... 300
   Eliza S. ........................................... 301
   Gustavus A. .................................... 300
   Lucy G. ........................................... 301
   Mary M. .......................................... 301
   Nettie ............................................... 73
   Robert ..................................... 300, 301
   Sterling J. ....................................... 301
   Sterling L. ....................................... 301
   Thomas I. ....................................... 301
   William ............................................ 301
   William W. ...................................... 301
**Waller**
   John P. ............................................ 301
   Margaret D. ..................................... 301
   Thomas B. ...................................... 301
**Walls**
   Martha A. ........................................ 301
   William I. ........................................ 301
**Waples**
   Isaac ............................................... 301
**Ward**
   Elizabeth Rhoda ............................. 271
   Nicholas ......................................... 301
**Warden**
   James .............................................. 301
   John M. ........................................... 301
   Johnson B. ...................................... 301
   Rebecca (Bateman) ......................... 301
   Sarah .............................................. 302
**Washington**
   Black Diamond .............................. 256
   D.C.. 60, 65, 66, 69, 73, 74, 85, 86, 89,
      91, 103, 107, 111, 112, 117, 126,
      130, 131, 132, 136, 141, 143, 149,
      155, 157, 158, 160, 163, 181, 182,

186, 193, 196, 200, 208, 211, 213, 214, 220, 222, 225, 233, 235, 241, 248, 249, 250, 256, 258, 265, 268, 273, 276, 277, 282, 285, 299, 301, 302, 303, 305, 316, 317
- D.C., Alms House .................................. 88
- D.C., Washington Asylum .................. 88
- D.C., Willard's Hotel ........................ 132
- District of Columbia .......................... 187
- District of Columbia, Georgetown .... 194
- Georgetown ............................. 131, 151
- Georgetown, D.C. ............................. 250
- Lawrence .......................... 59, 238, 302
- Lawrence B. ..................................... 302
- Soldiers Home, D.C. ......................... 166

**Waterman**
- James A. ........................................... 302

**Waters**
- Benjamin Garretson, Jr. ................... 302
- Benjamin Garretson, Sr. ................... 302

**Watkins**
- Ann F. ............................................... 302
- Edward ............................................ 302
- Franklin ........................................... 302
- Hattie .............................................. 302
- James E. .......................................... 302
- Julia A. ............................................ 302
- Julia P. ............................................. 302
- Susan ............................................... 302
- Thomas E. ............................... 263, 302
- William ............................................ 302
- William A. ....................................... 302

**Watson**
- David H. .......................................... 303
- Elizabeth ......................................... 303
- John ................................................. 303
- John T. ............................................. 303
- Sarah E. ........................................... 112
- Susan ............................................... 303

**Waugh**
- Ellen V. ............................................ 303
- Emily ............................................... 303
- Frederick ......................................... 303
- John ................................................. 303

**Wayland**
- Rebecca R. ....................................... 193

**Weast**
- George L. ......................................... 303

**Weaver**
- Isaac ................................................ 304
- Sarah V. ........................................... 304

**Webb**
- Ellen J. ............................................. 282
- Joel H. ............................................. 304

**Webster**
- Archibald ........................................ 304
- Henry .............................................. 304

**Weddle**
- Susan ................................................. 75

**Weeks**
- James .............................................. 304
- John ................................................. 304

**Weisiger**
- Alice Sydnor ................................... 304
- Daniel .............................................. 304
- David A. ................... 68, 117, 156, 314
- David Addison ................................ 304
- James L. .......................................... 305
- Louisa .............................................. 304
- Louise Christine .............................. 304
- Rebecca D. (McIndoe) ..................... 304
- Seginora (Tabb) ............................... 304

**Weller**
- John B. ............................................ 261

**Wells**
- Alexander ....................................... 305
- Anna Eliza ...................................... 305
- Elizabeth ......................................... 305
- Hattie L. .......................................... 305
- John H. ............................................ 305
- Martha ............................................. 305
- Martha A. ........................................ 276
- Martha J. ......................................... 305
- Mary H. ........................................... 305
- William H. ...................................... 305
- William J. ........................................ 305
- William O. ...................................... 305

**Welsh**
- Lucy Jane .......................................... 72

**West**
- Atheriah (Barker) ............................ 305
- Catherine ........................................ 306
- Charles ............................................ 305
- Covington O. ................................... 305

## VIRGINIA VOLUNTEERS IN MEXICO

Eliza M. ............................................. 306
Frank ................................................ 306
James ............................................... 122
James W. ......................................... 305
**West Virginia** ....................... 79, 248, 294
   Barbour Co. ..................................... 240
   Barbour Co., Philippi ....................... 267
   Barbour Co., Pleasant Creek............. 240
   Barbour Co., Volga.......................... 267
   Berkekey Co., Martinsburg 52, 163, 173, 181, 190
   Berkeley Co., Darksville ................... 125
   Berkeley Co., Hedgesville................. 200
   Berkeley Co., Martinsburg ....... 125, 142
   Cabell Co. .......................................... 53
   Cabell Co., Milton .............................. 53
   Clay Co. ............................................. 56
   Fayette Co., Bell Creek ..................... 275
   Gilmer Co., Cox's Mill ..................... 126
   Gilmer Co., Horn Creek ................... 126
   Grant Co., Maysville......................... 221
   Grant Co., Petersburg....................... 221
   Greenbrier Co................................... 278
   Greenbrier Co., Lewisburg ............... 110
   Hampshire Co., Romney ................... 221
   Hardy Co., Capon ............................ 272
   Hardy Co., Moorefield ..................... 221
   Hardy Co., Wardensville................... 272
   Harrison Co...................................... 126
   Harrison Co., Clarksburg ................. 107
   Jefferson Co., Bolivar .......... 70, 97, 167
   Jefferson Co., Charlestown.... 62, 65, 70, 82, 142, 167, 168, 244, 317
   Jefferson Co., Harper's Ferry ..... 70, 244
   Jefferson Co., Middleway ................ 191
   Jeffersonville.................................... 108
   Lewis Co. ......................................... 136
   Logan Co. ......................................... 169
   Mercer Co., Bluefield ....................... 295
   Monroe Co........................................ 110
   Monroe Co., Greenville ................... 230
   Monroe Co., Red Sulphur Springs .... 230
   Monroe Co., Union.......................... 230
   Morgan Co....................................... 267
   Morgan Co., Berkeley Springs.......... 181
   Nicholas Co. ............................. 275, 278
   Nicholas Co., Dixie ......................... 275
   Nicholas Co., Donald....................... 278
   Nicholas Co., Snowhill .................... 278
   Nicholas Co., Vaughan .................... 275
   Ohio Co. .......................................... 126
   Pocahontas Co.................................... 83
   Pocahontas Co., Huntersville............ 284
   Preston Co. ...................................... 128
   Putnam Co., Curry........................... 311
   Raleigh Co., Clear Fork ................... 284
   Raleigh Co., Coal River Marshes...... 169
   Raleigh Co., Sand Lick .................... 169
   Raleigh Co., Trap Hill...................... 169
   Roane Co. ........................................ 163
   Summers Co., Hinton....................... 110
   Summers Co., Indian Mills............... 230
   Taylor Co., Grafton ......................... 141
   Upshur Co., Buckhannon ................... 89
   Wood Co., Parkersburg............ 150, 288
**West Virginia - Infantry**
   17th Regt., Co. G............................. 254
   17th Regt., Co. I .............................. 141
   4$^{th}$ Regt. .......................................... 206
   6th Regt., Co. I ................................ 251
**Westbrook**
   James H. .......................................... 306
**Westmore**
   Mary Ann ........................................ 306
   Richard Henry.................................. 306
**Wharton**
   Benjamin T. ..................................... 306
**Whitaker**
   J.B.................................................... 170
**White**
   Benjamin L. ..................................... 307
   Charles E. ........................................ 307
   Cyrus C. .......................................... 306
   David M. ......................................... 306
   Demarcus......................................... 307
   Edward ............................................ 307
   Elizabeth P....................................... 307
   Elvira A. .......................................... 307
   Emily M. ......................................... 307
   Fountain .......................................... 307
   George W. ....................................... 307
   Harriet P. ......................................... 306
   Harry J............................................. 306

Henry ................................................ 307
James E. ................................ 277, 307
John T. ............................................. 307
Joseph L. ......................................... 307
Mary ................................................ 307
Mary B. ........................................... 307
Mary E. ........................................... 306
Mary Jane ...................................... 307
Mary ................................................ 307
Patrick ............................................. 307
Philip ............................................... 307
Rauna M. ........................................ 306
Richard D. ...................................... 307
Roana .............................................. 307
Roanna ............................................ 306
Susan J. ........................................... 306
Walter .............................................. 307
William ........................................... 307
**Whiteman**
Charles ............................................ 308
**Whitfield**
W.W. ............................................... 103
**Whiting**
John B. ............................................ 308
**Whitlock**
Robert A. ........................................ 308
William W. ..................................... 308
**Whitlow**
Deborah A. ..................................... 308
James L. .......................................... 308
Martha ............................................. 308
**Whitson**
Abraham Shelton ............................ 309
Alethea H. ....................................... 309
Elvira ............................................... 308
Emma .............................................. 309
J.B. .................................................. 309
James ............................................... 308
Lennie C. ........................................ 309
P.H. ................................................. 309
Sarah E. ........................................... 309
Sarah Matilda ................................. 308
Vernon W. ....................................... 309
Vida ................................................. 309
**Whittington**
George F. ........................................ 309
Harriet F. ......................................... 119

**Whitworth**
Prudence ........................................... 57
**Widdifield**
Abigail (Thomas) ........................... 309
George ............................................. 309
George Wooley ............................... 309
**Wigden**
Thomas G. ...................................... 309
**Wiglesworth**
Ed L. ............................................... 309
**Wilbourn**
Cornelia .......................................... 309
Dorah .............................................. 309
Edmonia .......................................... 309
Edna ................................................ 309
Edna J. ............................................ 309
Emery .............................................. 309
Fannie .............................................. 309
Henry .............................................. 309
Samuel ............................................. 309
Thomas ........................................... 309
Thomas W. ...................................... 309
William ........................................... 309
William Robert ............................... 309
**Wilbourne**
Martha A.S. .................................... 215
**Wiley**
Louise ............................................. 235
**Wilhelm**
Henry .............................................. 309
**Wilkes**
Benjamin W. ................................... 309
Berryman ........................................ 310
Catherine ........................................ 309
Elizabeth ......................................... 310
July A.E.M. (Tuck) ......................... 310
Mary C. ........................................... 309
Reuben B. ............................... 234, 310
Susan J. ........................................... 309
William R. ...................................... 309
**Wilkins**
Benjamin ........................................ 310
**Wilkinson**
Ann ................................................. 130
Joseph ............................................. 310
**Willey**
Ira .................................................... 310
**Williams**

Addie .................................................. 310
Adelaide Rebecca .............................. 310
Andrew Jackson ................................ 311
Anna R. ............................................. 311
C. Cornelia ........................................ 243
Charles W. ........................................ 311
Cordelia ............................................ 311
Cordelia F. ........................................ 310
Edward ............................................. 310
Eliza J. .............................................. 311
Elizabeth .......................................... 310
Elizabeth Jane .................................. 294
Fernando ........................................... 311
George W. ........................................ 310
Harriet L. .......................................... 311
Heartwell Y. ..................................... 310
Hugh Lorenzo .................................. 311
Isaac D. ............................................. 310
John James ....................................... 311
John R. ..................................... 233, 311
John W. ............................................ 311
Justice Wright .................................. 311
Letitia A. ............................................ 52
Margaret Sarah ................................. 232
Martha .............................................. 310
Mary A. ............................................ 311
Mary Harrison .................................. 117
Mary V.H. ........................................ 311
Mary V.H. ........................................ 311
R.E. ................................................... 311
Richard C. ........................................ 310
Richard E. ........................................ 311
Richard F. ........................................ 311
Safronia Elizabeth ............................ 311
Sarah A. ............................................ 311
Sarah P. ............................................ 311
Thomas R. ........................................ 311
Virginia ............................................ 311
William H.H. ............................. 61, 311
William Henry ................................. 311
Willieford W. ................................... 311
**Williamson**
   _____ ................................................ 162
   Andrew ........................................... 311
   Anne (Walker) ................................ 311
   Henry Watson ................................. 311
   Lucy Ann ........................................ 239
   Patty S. (Green) ............................... 311
   Thomas ............................................ 311
**Willis**
   Charles ............................................ 104
   Charles S. ................................ 170, 311
   E. 311
   John H. ............................................ 312
   Richard D. ....................................... 111
   Victoria E. ....................................... 311
   William ........................................... 311
**Willman**
   Mary ................................................ 247
**Wills**
   Anne C. ........................................... 312
   Armistead B. .................................... 312
   Christie E. ........................................ 312
   Richard D. ....................................... 312
   Robert S. .......................................... 312
   William ........................................... 312
   William D. ....................................... 312
**Wilson**
   Eliza ................................................ 279
   Elizabeth Ellen ................................ 218
   Frances S. ........................................ 312
   Peter H. ............................................ 312
   Robert K. ......................................... 106
   Saluda A. ......................................... 180
   Samuel G. ........................................ 313
   Samuel W. ....................................... 313
   Sarah Ann ....................................... 233
   Sarah E. ........................................... 211
   Sidney L. ......................................... 265
**Winfield**
   Benjamin F. ..................................... 313
**Winfree**
   Thomas ............................................ 313
**Wingate**
   Mary E. ............................................ 103
**Wingfield**
   Albert G. .......................................... 313
   Charles ............................................ 314
   Melvina ........................................... 314
**Winn**
   James ............................................... 314
   Mary Ann ........................................ 281
   Mary Anne ...................................... 315
**Winston**

Ann L. (Poindexter) ......................... 315
Jennie .............................................. 130
Mary ................................................ 315
Thomas B. ....................................... 315
William James ................................. 315
William S. ........................................ 315
**Winter**
Richard ........................................... 315
**Wisconsin**
Milwaukee Co., Milwaukee ............... 63
**Wisconsin - Infantry**
3rd Regt., Co. H ............................... 88
**Wisconson**
Milwaukee, National Soldiers Home ... 63
**Wolford**
William R. ....................................... 315
**Womack**
Abram N. ......................................... 315
James .............................................. 315
**Wood**
Andrew J. ........................................ 315
Anna C. ........................................... 267
Eliza Jane ......................................... 63
**Woodall**
Eliza Jane ........................................ 275
**Woodhouse**
Emma .............................................. 309
**Woodrow**
Joseph J. .......................................... 315
**Woodruff**
Elizabeth ......................................... 316
Hiram .............................................. 316
Jesse ................................................ 316
**Woods**
Cornelia Maria ................................ 231
**Woodson**
George W. ....................................... 143
Martin R. ......................................... 316
Pocahontas C. .................................. 224
**Woodward**
Hattie L. .......................................... 305
**Wool**
General .................................... 97, 209
John E. .............................................. 78
**Wooten**
Martha Ann ...................................... 60
**Worler**
E.D. .................................................. 54

**Wragg**
Sarah H. ............................................ 85
**Wren**
Albert .............................................. 316
Caldwell .......................................... 316
Catherine ........................................ 316
Catherine (Lindsay) ......................... 316
Charles B. ........................................ 316
Frances ........................................... 316
Frances J. ........................................ 316
Mary V. ........................................... 316
Sarah C. .......................................... 316
William H. ....................................... 316
**Wrenn**
Ada ................................................. 317
Annie B. .......................................... 316
Augustine ........................................ 317
Elizabeth (Mills) .............................. 316
Georgia ........................................... 317
Herbert ........................................... 317
John A. ............................................ 316
L.O. ................................................. 316
Leotha ............................................ 316
Lewis .............................................. 316
Lewis W. ......................................... 316
Lillie ................................................ 316
Martha .................................... 316, 317
Martha E. ........................................ 317
Martha Ella (Hudson) ...................... 317
Martha J. ......................................... 316
Martha J. (Jennings) ........................ 316
Norman ........................................... 317
Olivia .............................................. 316
Roberson Boswell ..................... 95, 316
Robert Lee ...................................... 317
Rosella ............................................ 316
Rozella N. ....................................... 316
Stonewall ........................................ 317
Susan C. .......................................... 317
William M. ...................................... 316
William N. ...................................... 316
**Wright**
John T. ............................................ 317
Sarah Agnes .................................... 204
**Wunderlich**
Isabella ........................................... 182
**Wyatt**

Elizabeth .......................................... 317
John N. ............................................ 317
William C. ........................................ 317
**Wyoming Territory** ............................. 63

## Y
**Yates**
Frances L. ........................................ 317
William M. ...................................... 317
**Yoakley**
Martha ............................................ 308
**Yopp**
William ............................................ 317
**Young**
Catherine A. ..................................... 318

Christopher Clarke ............................ 318
George W. ........................................ 318
John L .............................................. 318
John P ............. 219, 220, 269, 270, 318
John T .............................................. 318
Mary E ............................................. 318
Richard ............................................ 318

## Z
**Zeigler**
Sarah Ann ........................................ 150
**Zinova**
Eleanor ............................................ 146

OFF TO WAR

## Endnotes

[1] *Alexandria Gazette,* January 9, 1847, p. 2, c. 5, Alexandria, VA.
[2] *Richmond Enquirer,* January 5, 1847.
[3] Mexican War Diary of James Lawson Kemper, The Virginia Magazine of History and Biography, v. 74 (1966), p. 425-426.
[4] See testimony of 1st Sgt. William Gravatt in Court-martial of Capt. Robert Scott, Records of the Office of the Judge Advocate General(Army), Record Group 153, EE 454, National Archives & Records Administration, Washington, D.C.
[5] *Alexandria Gazette,* March 14, 1847, p. 2, c. 3, Alexandria, VA.
[6] Records of the Office of the Judge Advocate General(Army), Record Group 153, EE 560, National Archives & Records Administration, Washington, D.C.
[7] *Alexandria Gazette,* March 18, 1847, p.3, c.2, Alexandria, VA.
[8] *Alexandria Gazette,* as reported by the *Cumberland Civilian,* April 8, 1847, p.2, c.4, Alexandria, VA.
[9] Advertisement in Boyd's Directory of the District of Columbia, © 1883, William H. Boyd, Washington, D.C.
[10] *Alexandria Gazette,* March 23, 1847, p. 3, c. 1, Alexandria, VA.
[11] Christian, W. Asbury, D.D., Richmond: Her Past and Present, p. 155, © 1912, L.H. Jenkins, Richmond, VA.
[12] U.S. Census 1860, Hanover Co., VA, p. 394.
[13] Young, William A., Jr., 56th Virginia Infantry, © 1990, H.E. Howard, Inc., Lynchburg, VA.
[14] Mexican War Pension File, WC #214, National Archives and Records Administration, Washington, DC.
[15] U.S. Census 1850, Henrico Co., VA, p. 412.
[16] U.S. Census 1860, Henrico Co., VA, p. 182.
[17] Mexican War Pension File, SC #5231, National Archives and Records Administration, Washington, D.C.
[18] Record of Interments Blandford Cemetery, 1872-1888, p. 188, Blandford Cemetery, Petersburg, VA.
[19] U.S. Census 1860, Dinwiddie Co., VA, p. 412.
[20] Chernault, Tracy, 18th and 20th Battalions of Virginia Heavy Artillery, © 1995, H.E. Howard, Inc., Lynchburg, VA.
[21] Henderson, William D., 12th Virginia Infantry, © 1984, H.E. Howard, Inc., Lynchburg, VA.
[22] Mexican War Pension File, WC #4387, National Archives and Records Administration, Washington, D.C.
[23] Record of Interments Blandford Cemetery, 1872-1888, p. 188, Blandford Cemetery, Petersburg, VA
[24] Letter from P.H. Anderson to John Y. Mason, Secretary of War, July 19, 1847, Regimental Letter Book, 1st Virginia Volunteer Infantry, Record Group 153, National Archives & Records Administration, Washington, D.C
[25] Letter from Col. Hamtramck to Robert Jones, Adjutant General, July 19, 1847, Regimental Letter Book, 1st Virginia Volunteer Infantry, Record Group 153, National Archives & Records Administration, Washington, D.C
[26] Descriptive Roll of Soldiers Discharged…, Record Group 94, Entry 57, National Archives and Records Administration, Wash., D.C.
[27] Mexican War Pension File, WC #8844, National Archives and Records Administration, Washington, D.C.
[28] Mexican War Pension File, SC #84, National Archives and Records Administration, Washington, D.C.
[29] U.S. Census 1850, Montgomery Co., VA, p. 016.
[30] Mexican War Pension File, SC #7790, National Archives and Records Administration, Washington, DC.
[31] U.S. Census 1850, Montgomery Co., VA, p. 016.
[32] U.S. Census 1860, Montgomery Co., VA, p. 577.
[33] Weaver, Jeffrey C., 10th and 19th Battalions of Heavy Artillery, © 1996, H.E. Howard, Inc., Lynchburg, VA.

## VIRGINIA VOLUNTEERS IN MEXICO

[34] Mexican War Pension File, WC #16084, National Archives and Records Administration, Washington, DC.
[35] Letter from T.C. Madison, Asst. Surgeon to George A. Porterfield, Regtl. Adjutant, August 11, 1847, Regimental Letter Book, 1st Virginia Volunteer Infantry, Record Group 153, National Archives & Records Administration, Washington, D.C
[36] Mexican War Pension File SC #9630, Affidavit of Harvey Albertson, National Archives and Records Administration, Washington, D.C.
[37] Mexican War Pension File SC #9630, Affidavits of John Roach and Thomas S. Mahan, National Archives and records Administration, Washington, D.C.
[38] Tombstone, Green Hill Cem., Martinsburg, WV.
[39] Mexican War Pension File, WC #3037, National Archives and Records Administration, Washington, DC.
[40] Proceedings of An Assembly of the Encampments of Knights Templar of the State of Virginia, Held in Richmond, On Friday, being the 16th Day of December, A. L. 1853, A. 0. 736, Printed by C. H. WYNNE, 1854, Richmond, VA. http://www.neocomm.net/~mfulcher/1853.htm
[41] U.S. Census 1860, Berkeley Co., WV, p. 712.
[42] Moore, Robert H., II, Miscellaneous Disbanded Virginia Light Artillery, © 1997, H.E. Howard, Inc., Lynchburg, VA.
[43] U.S. Census 1880, Berkeley Co., WV, p. R038
[44] Norris, J.E., History of the lower Shenandoah Valley, © 1890, Chicago, IL, p.690
[45] Tombstone Inscription.
[46] *Alexandria Gazette*, April 3, 1847, p. 3, c. 1, Alexandria, VA.
[47] Mexican War Pension File, SC #6946, National Archives and Records Administration, Washington, D.C.
[48] Information provided by Barbara A. Reininger, 6783 Starlight Court, Sun Prarie, Wisconsin, 53590, (608) 837-8813. http://freepages.genealogy.rootsweb.com/~barbr/Cont.htm
[49] U.S. Census 1860, Floyd Co., VA.
[50] Mexican War Pension File, SC #6946, National Archives and Records Administration, Washington, D.C.
[51] U.S. Census 1900, Floyd Co., VA, p. 28.
[52] Mexican War Pension File, SC # 72, National Archives and Records Administration, Washington, DC.
[53] U.S. Census 1850, Augusta Co., VA, p. 299.
[54] Robertson, James I., 4th Virginia Infantry, © 1982, H.E. Howard, Inc., Lynchburg, VA.
[55] Mexican War Pension File, SC #22052, National Archives and Records Administration, Washington, D.C.
[56] U.S. Census 1880, Cabell Co., WV, p. S002.
[57] Mexican War Pension File, WC #9675, National Archives and Records Administration, Washington, D.C.
[58] Mexican War Pension File, WC #611, National Archives and Records Administration, Washington, DC.
[59] Records of the Office of the Judge Advocate General(Army), Record Group 153, EE 611, Case 50, National Archives & Records Administration, Washington, D.C.
[60] Mexican War Pension File, WC #611, Affidavits of J.D.K. Sleight and Robert Whittet, National Archives and Records Administration, Washington, DC.
[61] Mexican War Pension WC #13173, National Archives and Records Administration, Washington, D.C.
[62] U.S. Census 1860, Fauquier Co., VA, p. 188.
[63] Wallace, Lee A., Jr., 17th Virginia Infantry, © 1991, H.E. Howard, Inc., Lynchburg, VA.
[64] U.S. Census 1870, Fauquier Co., VA, p. 609.
[65] U.S. Census 1880, Prince William Co., VA, p. 44B.
[66] Mexican War Pension File SC #5530, Application, National Archives and Records Administration, Washington, DC.
[67] Mexican War Pension File WC #13173, Report of C.H. Jonas, Special Examiner 05/13/1888.
[68] Marriage Bond, Augusta Co., VA.
[69] U.S. Census 1850, Augusta Co., VA, p. 397.
[70] Mexican War Pension File, SC #5492, National Archives and Records Administration, Washington, D.C.
[71] Mexican War Pension File, WC #14392, Affidavit of Physician, National Archives and Records Administration, Washington, D.C.

# OFF TO WAR

[72] Muster Roll of Co. L, Record Group 94, Entry 57, National Archives and Records Administration, Wash., D.C.
[73] Record of Interments, Blandford Cemetery, p. 51, Blandford Cemetery, Petersburg, VA.
[74] U.S. Census 1850, Dinwiddie Co., VA.
[75] U.S. Census 1860, Prince George Co., VA, p. 353.
[76] Works Project Administration, Blandford Cemetery Historical Inventory, © 1936/37, Virginia Room, Fairfax City Regional Library.
[77] Trask, Benjamin H., 16th Virginia Infantry, ©1986, H.E. Howard, Inc., Lynchburg, VA.
[78] Weaver, Jeffrey C., Branch, Harrington and Staunton Hill Artillery, © 1997, H.E. Howard, Inc., Lynchburg, VA.
[79] Mexican War Pension File, SC #40, National Archives and Records Administration, Washington, D.C.
[80] Mexican War Pension File, WC #2517, National Archives and Records Administration, Washington, D.C.
[81] U.S. Census 1850, Montgomery Co., VA, p.68.
[82] Davis, Charley L., Giles County, Virginia 1860 Census-Annotated, © 1991, Oakton, VA.
[83] U.S. Census 1880, Clay Co., WV, p. P014.
[84] Information compiled by M. Elaine Jeter (ejeter@concentric.net) Voice: (619) 485-0694; Fax: (619) 485-7908.
[85] Kneebone, John T., Dictionary of Virginia Biography, v. 1, p. 190, © 1998, The Library of Virginia, Richmond, VA.
[86] Mexican War Pension File, SC #37, National Archives and Records Administration, Washington, D.C.
[87] Nine, William G. and Wilson, Ronald G., The Appomattox Paroles April 9-15, 1865, © 1989, H.E. Howard, Inc., Lynchburg, VA
[88] See Loth, Calder, Virginia Landmarks Register, p. 124, © 1986, Virginia Historic Landmarks Board, University of Virginia Press, Charlottesville, VA.
[89] Record of Interments Blandford Cemetery, 1888- 1905, p. 127, Blandford Cemetery, Petersburg, VA.
[90] Mexican War Pension File, WC #13244, National Archives and Records Administration, Washington, D.C.
[91] *Richmond Enquirer*, January 19, 1837, p. 3, c. 6, Richmond, VA.
[92] Christian, W. Asbury, D.D., Richmond: Her Past and Present, p. 140, © 1912, L.H. Jenkins, Richmond, VA.
[93] Records of the Office of the Judge Advocate General(Army), Record Group 153, EE 425, National Archives & Records Administration, Washington, D.C.
[94] Letter to R. Jones, Adjutant General from Col. John F. Hamtramck, August 2, 1847, Regimental Letter Book, 1st Virginia Volunteer Infantry, Record Group 153, National Archives & Records Administration, Washington, D.C
[95] Letter from Col. John F. Hamtramck to Robert Jones, Adjutant General, September 25, 1847, Regimental Letter Book, 1st Virginia Volunteer Infantry, Record Group 153, National Archives & Records Administration, Washington, D.C
[96] U.S. Census 1850, Hanover Co., VA, p. 393.
[97] Official Records of the War of the Rebellion, Series 3, Vol. 5, p. 905, © 1890, U.S. Government Printing Office, Wash., D.C.
[98] U.S. Census 1850, Louisa Co., VA, p. 740.
[99] Order Book – 1834-1835, Fauquier Co., VA, p. 91; Circuit Court Clerks Office, Fauquier Co., Warrenton, VA.
[100] Pipenger, Wesley E., Alexandria, Virginia Death Records 1863-1868 and 1869-1896, © 1995, Family Line Publications, Rear 63 East Main St., Westminster, MD, 21157.
[101] District of Columbia Marriages, Register 1 1811-1858, Washington, D.C.
[102] Boyd's Directory of the District of Columbia, © 1855, p. 6, William H. Boyd, Washington, D.C.
[103] Mexican War Pension Certificate, # WC #3393, National Archives and Records Administration, Washington, D.C.
[104] Mexican War Pension File, SC #7672, National Archives and Records Administration, Washington, DC.
[105] U.S. Census 1850, Lunenburg Co., VA, p. 38.
[106] U.S. Census 1860, Lunenburg Co., VA, p. 1048.

## VIRGINIA VOLUNTEERS IN MEXICO

[107] Rankin, Thomas M., 23rd Virginia Infantry, © 1985, H.E. Howard, Inc., Lynchburg, VA.
[108] Mexican War Pension File, WA #20557, National Archives and Records Administration, Washington, DC.
[109] Marriage Register of Lunenburg Co., VA 1746-1850, p. 67.
[110] Mexican War Pension File, SC #9629, National Archives and Records Administration, Washington, DC.
[111] U.S. Census 1850, Lunenburg Co., VA, p. 41.
[112] U.S. Census 1860, Lunenburg Co., VA, p. 936.
[113] Mexican War Pension File, WC #11672, National Archives and Records Administration, Washington, DC.
[114] U.S. Census 1850, Henrico Co., VA, p. 400.
[115] U.S. Census 1860, Henrico Co., VA, p. 440.
[116] Compiled Confederate Service Records, Record Group No. 109, National Archives, Washington, D.C.
[117] Manarin, Louis H., 15th Virginia Infantry, © 1990, H.E. Howard, Inc., Lynchburg, VA.
[118] Christian, W. Asbury, D.D., Richmond: Her Past and Present, p. 307-308,© 1912, L.H. Jenkins, Richmond, VA.
[119] Hollywood Cemetery Records. Business Records Collection, Microfilm Reel 1018, Library of Virginia, Richmond VA.
[120] U.S. Census 1850, Campbell Co., VA, p. 134.
[121] Bell, Robert T., 11th Virginia Infantry, © 1985, H.E. Howard, Inc., Lynchburg, VA.
[122] Mexican War Pension File, WC #408, National Archives and Records Administration, Washington, DC.
[123] U.S. Census 1860, Floyd Co., VA, p. 519.
[124] Mexican War Pension File, WC #1313, National Archives and Records Administration, Washington, DC.
[125] U.S. Census 1850, Jefferson Co., VA, p. 298.
[126] U.S. Census 1860, Jefferson Co., WV, p. 800.
[127] Last Will & Testament of John Brown, December 2, 1859, Jefferson County Circuit Court Clerks Office, Charlestown, WV.
[128] Wallace Lee A., 5th Virginia Infantry, © 1988, H.E. Howard, Inc., Lynchburg, VA.
[129] U.S. Census 1880, Charles Town, Jefferson Co., WV, p. C016.
[130] Mexican War Pension File, SC #15874, National Archives and Records Administration, Washington, D.C.
[131] Driver, Robert J., Jr., 5th Virginia Cavalry, © 1997, H.E. Howard, Inc., Lynchburg, VA.
[132] Mexican War Pension File, WC #17238, National Archives and Records Administration, Washington, D.C.
[133] Gregory, G. Howard, 53rd Virginia Infantry and 5th Battalion Virginia Infantry, © 1999, H.E. Howard, Inc., Lynchburg, VA.
[134] Marriage Register, Augusta Co., VA.
[135] U.S. Census 1850, Augusta Co., VA, p. 398.
[136] *Staunton Republican Vindicator*, November 24, 1859, p. 2, c. 6, Staunton, VA.
[137] Mexican War Pension File, SC #4301, Survivor Application, National Archives and Records Administration, Washington, D.C.
[138] Mexican War Pension File, SC #4301, Mexican War Discharge, National Archives and Records Administration, Washington, D.C.
[139] Mexican War Pension File, SC #4301, Divorce Decree, National Archives and Records Administration, Washington, D.C.
[140] Records of the Office of the Judge Advocate General(Army), Record Group 153, EE 611, Case 18, National Archives & Records Administration, Washington, D.C.
[141] Mexican War Pension File, WC #1383, National Archives and Records Administration, Washington, D.C.
[142] Record of Interments Blandford Cemetery, 1872-1888, p. 107, Blandford Cemetery, Petersburg, VA
[143] U.S. Census 1870, Dinwiddie Co., VA, p. 221.
[144] Mexican War Pension File, SC #142, National Archives and Records Administration, Washington, D.C.
[145] U.S. Census 1860, Henrico Co., VA, p. 11.

# OFF TO WAR

[146] Letter from John P. Hopkins to Adjutant General Roger Jones, April 24, 1847,Regimental Letter Book, 1st Virginia Volunteer Infantry, Record Group 153, National Archives & Records Administration, Washington, D.C.
[147] Letter from Col. J.F. Hamtramck to Adjt. Gen. Roger Jones, August 1, 1847, Regimental Letter Book, 1st Virginia Volunteer Infantry, Record Group 153, National Archives & Records Administration, Washington, D.C.
[148] Mexican War Pension File, SC #200, National Archives and Records Administration, Washington, DC.
[149] Mexican War Pension Certificate, SC #12648, National Archives and Records Administration, Washington, D.C.
[150] U.S. Census 1850, Augusta Co., VA, p. 296.
[151] U.S. Census 1860, Albemarle Co., VA, p. 646.
[152] U.S. Census 1850, Clarke Co., VA, p. 209.
[153] U.S. Census 1860, Warren Co., VA, p. 988.
[154] Marriage Register, Loudoun Co., VA.
[155] U.S. Census 1860, Loudoun Co., VA, p. 396.
[156] U.S. Census 1850, Dinwiddie Co., VA, p. 372.
[157] U.S. Census 1860, Dinwiddie Co., VA, p. 176.
[158] District of Columbia Marriage Licenses 1811-1858.
[159] Alardice, Bruce S., More Generals in Gray, © 1995, Louisiana State University Press, Baton Rogue, LA.
[160] Records of the Office of the Judge Advocate General(Army), Record Group 153, EE 560, National Archives & Records Administration, Washington, D.C.
[161] Official Records of the War of the Rebellion, Series I, V. 26, Pt. II, p. 25, © 1889, War Department, Washington, D.C.
[162] *Memphis Dailiy Appeal*, Memphis Public Library, History Department, 1850 Peabody Street, Memphis, TN, 38104.
[163] All biographical information from: Warren, Mrs. J.E. "Bankhead Family." Genealogies of Virginia Families From the William and Mary College Quarterly Historical Magazine. Baltimore: Genealogical Publishing Co., 1982. pp. 222-233.
[164] Interment Records of Elmwood Cemetery, 824 South Dudley Street, Memphis, TN, 38104.
[165] Meade, Bishop William, Old Churches Ministers and Families of Virginia, v. 1, p. 404, © 1857, Philadelphia, PA.
[166] Mexican War Pension File, SC #14572, National Archives and Records Administration, Washington, D.C.
[167] Records of the Office of the Judge Advocate General(Army), Record Group 153, FF 74, Case 9, National Archives & Records Administration, Washington, D.C.
[168] Fields, Frank E., Jr., 28th Virginia Infantry, © 1985, H.E. Howard, Inc., Lynchburg, VA.
[169] Scott, Johnny Lee, 60th Virginia Infantry, © 1997, H.E. Howard, Inc., Lynchburg, VA.
[170] Mexican War Pension File, SC #14572, Affidavit of Charles W. Stotham, National Archives and Records Administration, Washington, D.C.
[171] Mexican War Pension File, SC #14572, Declaration of Survivor, March 9, 1887, National Archives and Records Administration, Washington, D.C.
[172] Town of Greenbush, NY Census of 1855, p. 25, Rensselaer Co. Clerk's Office, Rensselaer, NY.
[173] Mexican War Pension File, SC #4600, National Archives and Records Administration, Washington, D.C.
[174] Mexican War Pension File, WC #11212, National Archives and Records Administration, Washington, D.C.
[175] Ruffner, Kevin C., 44th Virginia Infantry, © 1987, H.E. Howard, Inc., Lynchburg, VA.
[176] U.S. Census 1870, Amelia Co., VA, p. 371.
[177] Hadfield, Kathleen H., Historical Notes on Amelia County, Virginia, p. 503, © 1982, Amelia County Historical Society, Amelia, VA.
[178] Mexican War Pension File, SC #3943, National Archives and Records Administration, Washington, D.C.
[179] U.S. Census 1860, Grayson Co., VA, p. 63.

# VIRGINIA VOLUNTEERS IN MEXICO

[180] Bohannon, Keith S., The Giles, Allegheny and Jackson Artillery, © 1990, H.E. Howard Inc., Lynchburg, VA.
[181] Marriage Register #1, pg. 3, Montgomery Co., VA.
[182] U.S. Census 1860, Montgomery Co., VA, p. 588.
[183] U.S. Census 1870, Montgomery Co., VA, p. 17.
[184] Mexican War Pension File, SC #123, National Archives and Records Administration, Washington, DC.
[185] U.S. Census 1860, Frederick Co., VA, p. 400.
[186] U.S. Census 1870, Frederick Co., VA, p. 183.
[187] Mexican War Pension File, WC #10799, National Archives and Records Administration, Washington, DC.
[188] U.S. Census 1870, Washington, D.C., p. 776.
[189] Boyd's Directory of the District of Columbia, © 1874, William H. Boyd, Washington, D.C.
[190] Mexican War Pension File, WC #508, National Archives and Records Administration, Washington, DC.
[191] U.S. Census 1860, Floyd Co., VA, p. 600.
[192] Sherwood, G.L., 54th Virginia Infantry, © 1993, H.E. Howard, Inc., Lynchburg, VA.
[193] U.S. Census 1870, Floyd Co., VA, p. 71.
[194] U.S. Census 1850, Jefferson Co., VA, p. 419.
[195] U.S. Census 1860, Jefferson Co., VA, p. 765.
[196] Mexican War Pension File, SC #5788, National Archives and Records Administration, Washington, DC.
[197] Marriage Register #A, pg. 312, Montgomery Co., VA.
[198] U.S. Census 1850, Montgomery Co., VA, p. 40.
[199] Augusta County, Virginia Marriage Register.
[200] U.S. Census 1850, Augusta Co., VA, p. 244.
[201] U.S. Census 1860, Augusta Co., VA, p. 715.
[202] Hewett, Janet B., The Roster of Confederate Soldiers, 1861-1865, © 1995, Broadfoot Publishing Co., Wilmington, NC.
[203] U.S. Census 1870, Augusta Co., VA, p. 154.
[204] Register of Deaths, Augusta Co., VA, V. I.
[205] U.S. Census 1850, Montgomery Co., VA, p. 33.
[206] Mexican War Pension File, WC #3135, National Archives and Records Administration, Washington, DC.
[207] Marriage Register #A, pg. 321, Montgomery Co., VA.
[208] U.S. Census 1860, Montgomery Co., VA, p. 761.
[209] Mexican War Pension File, SA #173, National Archives and Records Administration, Washington, D.C.
[210] U.S. Census 1850, Norfolk Co., VA, p. 157.
[211] Trask, Benjamin H., 9th Virginia Infantry, © 1984, H.E. Howard, Inc., Lynchburg, VA.
[212] Letter from T.C. Madison, Asst. Surgeon to George A. Porterfield, Regtl. Adjutant, August 11, 1847, Regimental Letter Book, 1st Virginia Volunteer Infantry, Record Group 153, National Archives & Records Administration, Washington, D.C
[213] U.S. Census 1850, Alexandria Co., VA, p. 389.
[214] U.S. Census 1860, Alexandria Co., VA, p. 746.
[215] U.S. Census 1870, Alexandria Co., VA, p. 16.
[216] Mexican War Pension File, SC #165, National Archives and Records Administration, Washington, DC.
[217] U.S. Census 1850, Augusta Co., VA, p. 347.
[218] Death Register Augusta County Register, v. I.
[219] U.S. Census 1850, Augusta Co., VA, p. 311.
[220] Special Census of Union Veterans, Augusta Co., Virginia, National Archives and Records Administration, Washington, DC.
[221] Mexican War Pension File, SA #24207, John H. Steel, alias John G. Hensley, National Archives and Records Administration, Washington, DC.
[222] U.S. Census 1
[223] Mexican War Pension WC #2772, National Archives and Records Administration, Washington, D.C.
[224] Mexican War Pension File, WC #3213, National Archives and Records Administration, Washington, D.C.

# OFF TO WAR

[225] U.S. Census 1850, Goochland Co., VA, 108.
[226] U.S. Census 1860, Augusta Co., VA, 654.
[227] Augusta County Death Register, V. III, 1879-1892.
[228] U.S. Census 1860, Loudoun Co., VA, p. 637.
[229] Marriage Register Loudoun Co., VA.
[230] Mexican War Pension File, WC #3448, National Archives and Records Administration, Washington, DC.
[231] Mexican War Pension File, SC #5499, National Archives and Records Administration, Washington, D.C.
[232] Marriage Register Lunenburg Co., VA.
[233] U.S. Census 1860, Lunenburg Co., VA, p. 973.
[234] U.S. Census 1870, Lunenburg Co., VA, p. 514.
[235] Marriage Register Albemarle Co., VA.
[236] U.S. Census 1860, Albemarle Co., VA, p. 573.
[237] U.S. Census 1870, Albemarle Co., VA, p. 561.
[238] U.S. Census 1850, Montgomery Co., VA, p. 60.
[239] Mexican War Pension File, WC #10827, National Archives and Records Administration, Washington, DC.
[240] Marriage Register #A, pg. 328, Montgomery Co., VA.
[241] U.S. Census 1860, Montgomery Co., VA, p. 708.
[242] U.S. Census 1870, Montgomery Co., VA, p. 100.
[243] Hardesty's Historical & Geographical Encyclopedia, Illustrated, © 1884, H.H. Hardesty & Co., Richmond, VA.
[244] Mexican War Diary of Harvey Black, Virginia Polytechnical Institute & State University, Blacksburg, VA.
[245] U.S. Census 1850, Montgomery Co., VA, p. 003.
[246] U.S. Census 1860, Giles Co., VA p. 871.
[247] U.S. Census 1850, Augusta Co., VA, p. 309.
[248] U.S. Census 1860, Augusta Co., VA, p. 781.
[249] Ayers, Edward L. and Thomas, William G., The Valley of the Shadow, © 1998,The Virginia Center for Digital History Alderman Library, University of Virginia, Charlottesville, VA 22903.
[250] Marriage Register Norfolk Co., VA.
[251] U.S. Census 1850, Norfolk Co., VA, p. 132.
[252] Mexican War Pension File, WC #6252, National Archives and Records Administration, Washington, D.C.
[253] Personal Communication from Mark Hayden rehayden3@home.com
[254] Mexican War Pension File, SC #8888, National Archives and Records Administration, Washington, D.C.
[255] U.S. Census 1850, Caroline Co., VA, p. 304.
[256] U.S. Census 1860, Washington Co., VA, p. 649.
[257] U.S. Census 1870, Wise Co., VA, p. 326.
[258] Addington, Luther F., The Story of Wise Co., VA, © 1956, The Overmountain Press, Johnson City, TN.
[259] Marriage Register Alexandria, VA.
[260] U.S. Census 1870, Fairfax Co., VA, p. 299.
[261] Marriage Register Alexandria, VA.
[262] Records of the Office of the Judge Advocate General(Army), Record Group 153, FF 75, Case 2, National Archives & Records Administration, Washington, D.C.
[263] U.S. Census 1860, Albemarle Co., VA, p. 534.
[264] U.S. Census 1870, Henrico Co., VA, p. 194.
[265] U.S. Census 1850, Essex Co., VA, p. 069.
[266] U.S. Census 1860, Mathews Co., VA, p. 071.
[267] Sherwood, G.L., 59th Virginia Infantry, © 1994, H.E. Howard, Inc., Lynchburg, VA.
[268] U.S. Census 1850, Wake Co., NC, p. 266.

## VIRGINIA VOLUNTEERS IN MEXICO

[269] Mexican War Pension File, WC #944, National Archives and Records Administration, Washington, D.C.
[270] Records of the Office of the Judge Advocate General(Army), Record Group 153, EE 427, Case 14, National Archives & Records Administration, Washington, D.C.
[271] Mexican War Pension File, SC #8059, National Archives and Records Administration, Washington, DC.
[272] U.S. Census 1870, Pittsylvania Co., VA, p. 14.
[273] Mexican War Pension File, WC #14741, National Archives and Records Administration, Washington, DC.
[274] U.S. Census 1860, Lewis Co., VA, p. 002.
[275] Mexican War Pension File, SC #17367, National Archives and Records Administration, Washington, DC.
[276] Interment Records, Fairhaven Memorial Park and Mortuary, 1702 E. Fairhaven, Santa Ana, CA 92705
[277] Records of the Office of the Judge Advocate General(Army), Record Group 153, EE 611, Case 17, National Archives & Records Administration, Washington, D.C.
[278] U.S. Census 1860, Bedford Co., VA, p. 351.
[279] Mexican War Pension File, SC #19599, National Archives and Records Administration, Washington, D.C.
[280] U.S. Census 1850, Montgomery Co., VA, p. 33.
[281] Virginia Military Institute Archives, Lexington, VA.
[282] Fauquier County Minute Book 1857-1859, p. 152, July 28, 1858 *"Benjamin Hellenius Bradford, the son of Helen Bradford and Colonel Benjamin R. Bradford... died in Fauquier Co. in number of years ago unmarried and without issue."*
[283] Death Register 1853-1896, Fauquier Co., VA, Fauquier County Clerk's Office, Warrenton, VA.
[284] U.S. Census 1850, Fauquier Co., VA, p. 207.
[285] Marriage Bond, Amelia Co., VA.
[286] U.S. Census 1850, Amelia Co., VA, p. 47.
[287] Letter from T.C. Madison, Asst. Surgeon to George A. Porterfield, Regtl. Adjutant, August 11, 1847, Regimental Letter Book, 1st Virginia Volunteer Infantry, Record Group 153, National Archives & Records Administration, Washington, D.C
[288] History and Roster of Maryland Volunteers, War of 1861-5, Wilmer, L. Allison, Jarrett, J.H., Vernon, Geo. W. F., © 1898, Gugfenheimer, Weil & Co., Baltimore, MD.
[289] Mexican War Pension Certificate SC #17425, National Archives and Records Administration, Washington, D.C.
[290] U.S. Census 1870, Frio Co., Texas.
[291] U.S. Census 1880, Frio Co., Texas, E.D. 059, p. 011.
[292] Quotation from McHenry Bramblett, Mexican War Pension Certificate SC #17425, National Archives and Records Administration, Washington, D.C.
[293] Mexican War Pension Certificate SC #17425, National Archives and Records Administration, Washington, D.C.
[294] Mexican War Pension File, SC #19755, National Archives and Records Administration, Washington, DC.
[295] U.S. Census 1850, Henrico Co., VA, p. 394.
[296] Mexican War Pension File, WA #15932, National Archives and Records Administration, Washington, DC.
[297] Mexican War Pension File, SC #295, National Archives and Records Administration, Washington, D.C.
[298] Mexican War Pension File, WC #5889, National Archives and Records Administration, Washington, DC.
[299] U.S. Census 1850, Pocahontas Co., VA, p. 293.
[300] Information supplied by Robert T. & Virginia B. Weaver, 5100 John D Ryan Blvd., Apt. #341, San Antonio, TX 78243.
[301] Mexican War Pension File, WC #50, National Archives and Records Administration, Washington, DC.
[302] U.S. Census 1850, Rockbridge Co., VA, p. 403.
[303] Register of Deaths, Volume I, Augusta Co., VA.
[304] Mexican War Pension File, SC #10744, National Archives and Records Administration, Washington, D.C.

305 U.S. Census 1850, Sussex Co., VA, p. 135.
306 U.S. Census 1860, Surrey Co., VA, p. 893.
307 Driver, Robert J., Jr., 1st Battalion Virginia Infantry 39th Battalion Virginia Cavalry, 24th Batalion Virginia Partisan Rangers, © 1996, H.E. Howard, Inc., Lynchburg, VA.
308 U.S. Census 1870, Charles City Co., VA, p. 560.
309 Mexican War Pension File, SC #4597, National Archives and Records Administration, Washington, DC.
310 U.S. Census 1850, Rockingham Co., VA, p. 124.
311 U.S. Census 1860, Rockingham Co., VA, p. 852.
312 Driver, Robert J., Jr., 10th Virginia Cavalry, © 1992, H.E. Howard, Inc., Lynchburg, VA.
313 U.S. Census 1870, Rockingham Co., VA, p. 223.
314 Rockingham Recorder, Vol. I, December 1946, No. 2, Rockingham Historical Society, Harrisonburg, VA.
315 Mexican War Pension File, WC #8956, National Archives and Records Administration, Washington, DC.
316 U.S. Census 1850, Lunenburg Co., VA, p. 003.
317 Register of Marriages, 1850-1872, p. 11, Lunenburg Co., VA, Circuit Court Clerk's Office, Lunenburg Co., VA(Abigail and Mary appear to have been sisters).
318 Register of Marriages, 1850-1872, Lunenburg Co., VA, Circuit Court Clerk's Office, Lunenburg Co., VA.
319 U.S. Census 1870, Lunenburg Co., VA, p. 483(Mary and Abigail appear to have been sisters).
320 Mexican War Pension Certificate, SC #14116, National Archives and Records Administration, Washington, D.C. (see CW Pension application #614539).
321 Marriage Bond, Orange Co., VA, Circuit Court Clerk's Office, Orange, VA.
322 U.S. Census 1850, Caroline Co., VA, p. 303.
323 U.S. Census 1860, Caroline Co., VA, p. 650.
324 Musick, Michael P., 6th Virginia Cavalry, © 1990, H.E. Howard, Inc., Lynchburg, VA.
325 Mexican War Pension SC #6767, National Archives and Records Administration, Washington, D.C.
326 Marriage Certificate, Mexican War Pension WC #9710, National Archives and Records Administration, Washington, D.C.
327 Mexican War Pension WC #9710, National Archives and Records Administration, Washington, D.C.
328 Letter from T.C. Madison, Asst. Surgeon to Lt. Thomas P. August, June 29, 1847, Regimental Letter Book, 1st Virginia Volunteer Infantry, Record Group 153, National Archives & Records Administration, Washington, D.C
329 Mexican War Pension File, SC #11179, Death Certificate, National Archives and Records Administration, Washington, D.C.
330 Mexican War Pension File, SC #11179, National Archives and Records Administration, Washington, D.C.
331 Mexican War Pension File, WC #14941, National Archives and Records Administration, Washington, D.C.
332 *The Daily Express*, January 7, 1857, p. 3, c. 2, Petersburg, VA.
333 Marriage Bond, Fauquier Co., VA.
334 Mexican War Pension Certificate, SC #4044, National Archives and Records Administration, Washington, D.C.
335 U.S. Census 1860, Rappahannock Co., VA, p. 227.
336 U.S. Census 1870, Rappahannock Co., VA, p. 133.
337 Mexican War Pension File, SC #7746, National Archives and Records Administration, Washington, D.C.
338 Mexican War Pension File, WC #13900, National Archives and Records Administration, Washington, D.C.
339 Death Register, King George Co., VA, 1878, ln. 3.
340 U.S. Census 1860, King George Co., VA, p. 411.
341 U.S. Census 1870, King George Co., VA, p. 042.
342 Death Register, King George Co., VA, 1878, ln. 3.

# VIRGINIA VOLUNTEERS IN MEXICO

[343] Mexican War Pension File, WC #3952, National Archives and Records Administration, Washington, D.C.
[344] International Genealogical Index, Film #-1396409.
[345] Information supplied by Lynette Hennigan Denham, 4214 Garton Lane, Pocatelo, ID 83204.
[346] U.S. Census 1850, Henrico Co., VA, p. 243.
[347] Mexican War Pension File, SC #9913, National Archives and Records Administration, Washington, DC.
[348] U.S. Census 1850, Frederick Co., VA, p. 312.
[349] U.S. Census 1860, Nelson Co., VA, p. 785.
[350] U.S. Census 1870, Frederick Co., VA, p. 090.
[351] Marriage Records 1809-1916, Starke County, Ohio.
[352] Record of Interments Blandford Cemetery, 1872-1888, p. 94, Blandford Cemetery, Petersburg, VA.
[353] U.S. Census 1850, Dinwiddie Co., VA, p. 439.
[354] Mexican War Pension File, WC #1123, National Archives and Records Administration, Washington, D.C.
[355] *Petersburg Index & Appeal*, May 1, 1873, p.3, c. 2, Petersburg, VA.
[356] Record of Interments Blandford Cemetery, 1872-1888, p. 94, Blandford Cemetery, Petersburg, VA
[357] Mexican War Pension File, SC #419, National Archives and Records Administration, Washington, DC.
[358] Records of the Office of the Judge Advocate General(Army), Record Group 153, EE 611, Case 30, National Archives & Records Administration, Washington, D.C.
[359] Mexican War Pension File, SC #17691, National Archives and Records Administration, Washington, D.C.
[360] Mexican War Pension WC #2421, National Archives and Records Administration, Washington, D.C.
[361] U.S. Census 1850, Hanover Co., VA, p. 359.
[362] U.S. Census 1860, Hanover Co., VA, p. 431.
[363] U.S. Census 1870, Hanover Co., VA, p. 130.
[364] *Richmond Enquirer*, June 23, 1848, p. 4, c. 7.
[365] U.S. Census 1850, Botetourt Co., VA, p. 144.
[366] Official Records of the War of the Rebellion, Series II, V. 2, p. 1031, © 1880, War Department, Washington, D.C.
[367] Boyd's District of Columbia Directories, Various Issues 1874 – 1892, Washington, DC.
[368] Rock Creek Cemetery Interment Ledger, p. 120, Rock Creek Cemetery, Washington, DC.
[369] Mexican War Pension File, WC #14479, National Archives and Records Administration, Washington, DC.
[370] Mexican War Pension Certificate SC #339, National Archives and Records Administration, Washington, D.C.
[371] U.S. Census 1850, Stafford Co., VA, p. 012.
[372] Record of Interments Blandford Cemetery, 1905-1922, p. 64, Blandford Cemetery, Petersburg, VA
[373] U.S. Census 1850, Dinwiddie Co., VA, p. 374.
[374] U.S. Census 1860, Dinwiddie Co., VA, p. 273.
[375] U.S. Census 1870, Dinwiddie Co., VA, p. 386.
[376] Record of Interments Blandford Cemetery, 1905-1922, p. 64, Blandford Cemetery, Petersburg, VA
[377] Myers, Lorraine F. & Brown, Stuart E., Jr., Some Old Families of Clarke Co., VA, © 1994, Virginia Book Co., Berryville, VA.
[378] Ibid.
[379] Records of the Office of the Judge Advocate General(Army), Record Group 153, EE 611, Case 8, National Archives & Records Administration, Washington, D.C.
[380] Mexican War Pension File, SC #12914, National Archives and Records Administration, Washington, DC.
[381] Tombstone, Harper's Cemetery, Harper's Ferry, WV.
[382] Mexican War Pension File, WC #14927, National Archives and Records Administration, Washington, DC.
[383] Records of the Office of the Judge Advocate General(Army), Record Group 153, EE 553, Case 1, National Archives & Records Administration, Washington, D.C.

# OFF TO WAR

[384] Wayland, John W., A History of Shennandoah Co., VA, © 1976, p. 16, Shennandoah Publishing House, Inc., Strausburg, VA.
[385] U.S. Census 1850, Shennandoah Co., VA, p. 80.
[386] U.S. Census 1860, Jefferson Co., VA, p. 821.
[387] Frye, Dennis E., 2nd Virginia Infantry, © 1984, H.E. Howard, Inc., Lynchburg, VA.
[388] U.S. Census 1880, Jefferson Co., WV, p. B015.
[389] Davis, Charley L., Giles Co., VA 1860 Census - Annotated, © 1991, Oakton, VA.
[390] Scott, J.L., 36th Virginia Infantry, © 1987, H.E. Howard, Inc., Lynchburg, VA.
[391] Mexican War Pension File, SC #9073, National Archives and Records Administration, Washington, DC.
[392] Mexican War Pension File, WC #15304, National Archives and Records Administration, Washington, DC.
[393] U.S. Census 1880, Bucks Co., PA, p. 7A.
[394] Mexican War Pension File, WC #3785, National Archives and Records Administration, Washington, D.C.
[395] Trask, Benjamin H., 61st Virginia Infantry, © 1988, H.E. Howard, Inc., Lynchburg, VA.
[396] Mexican War Pension File, SC #18979, National Archives and Records Administration, Washington, DC.
[397] Mexican War Pension File, WA #15308, National Archives and Records Administration, Washington, DC.
[398] *The Petersburg Daily Republican*, May 10, 1847, p. 4, c. 2, Petersburg, VA.
[399] Records of the Office of the Judge Advocate General(Army), Record Group 153, EE 554, Case 35, National Archives & Records Administration, Washington, D.C.
[400] Records of the Office of the Judge Advocate General(Army), Record Group 153, EE 611, Case 25, National Archives & Records Administration, Washington, D.C.
[401] Mexican War Pension File, SC #13372, National Archives and Records Administration, Washington, D.C.
[402] U.S. Census 1850, Sussex Co., VA, p. 135.
[403] U.S. Census 1860, Sussex Co., VA, p. 474.
[404] Henderson, William D., 41st Virginia Infantry, © 1986, H.E. Howard, Inc., Lynchburg, VA.
[405] Mexican War Pension File, SC #20324, National Archives and Records Administration, Washington, DC.
[406] U.S. Census 1850, Champaign Co., OH, p. 414.
[407] Mexican War Pension File, WC #10936, National Archives and Records Administration, Washington, DC.
[408] U.S. Census 1850, Hanover Co., VA, p. 364.
[409] U.S. Census 1870, Chesterfield Co., VA, p. 248.
[410] U.S. Census 1880, Chesterfield Co., VA, p. 93B.
[411] Mexican War Pension Certificate, SC #18232, National Archives and Records Administration, Washington, D.C.
[412] Record of Interments Blandford Cemetery, 1843-1872, p. 30, Blandford Cemetery, Petersburg, VA
[413] Caroline County Marriage Register, Caroline County Circuit Court Clerks Office, Bowling Green, VA.
[414] Krick, Robert K., 30th Virginia Infantry, © 1983, H.E. Howard, Inc., Lynchburg, VA.
[415] U.S. Census 1870, Cumberland Co., VA, p. 069.
[416] Information provided by Eloise Bringhurst, 310 East 300 North, Pleasant Grove, UT 84062.
[417] Mexican War Pension File, SC #7176, National Archives and Records Administration, Washington, DC.
[418] U.S. Census 1850, Rockingham Co., VA, p. 010.
[419] U.S. Census 1860, Rockingham Co., VA, p. 850.
[420] Mexican War Pension File, WC #12571, National Archives and Records Administration, Washington, DC.
[421] Mexican War Pension File, SC #543, National Archives and Records Administration, Washington, DC.
[422] Mexican War Pension File, WC #9754, National Archives and Records Administration, Washington, DC.
[423] Boyd's Directory of the District of Columbia, © 1890, William H. Boyd, Washington, D.C.

# VIRGINIA VOLUNTEERS IN MEXICO

[424] Mexican War Pension File, SC #1220, National Archives and Records Administration, Washington, D.C.
[425] Mexican War Pension File, WC #9153, National Archives and Records Administration, Washington, D.C.
[426] International Genealogical Index, Film #- 1761083.
[427] Mexican War Pension File, SC #8472, National Archives and Records Administration, Washington, DC.
[428] Marriage Register #A, pg. 410, Montgomery Co., VA.
[429] U.S. Census 1850, Montgomery Co., VA, p. 021.
[430] U.S. Census 1860, Montgomery Co., VA, p. 571.
[431] U.S. Census 1870, Montgomery Co., VA, p. 142.
[432] Mexican War Pension File, SC #4609, National Archives and Records Administration, Washington, DC.
[433] Mexican War Pension File, WC #6728, National Archives and Records Administration, Washington, DC.
[434] U.S. Census 1860, Tazewell Co., VA, p. 894.
[435] Rankin, Thomas M., 37th Virginia Infantry, © 1987, H.E. Howard, Inc., Lynchburg, VA.
[436] Dickinson, Jack L., 16th Virginia Cavalry, © 1989, H.E. Howard, Inc., Lynchburg, VA.
[437] Mexican War Pension File, SC #14533, National Archives and Records Administration, Washington, DC.
[438] Mexican War Pension File, WC #629, National Archives and Records Administration, Washington, D.C.
[439] U.S. Census 1850, Goochland Co., VA, p. 106.
[440] U.S. Census 1860, Berkeley Co., VA, p. 836.
[441] Driver, Robert J., Jr., 1st Virginia Cavalry, © 1991, H.E. Howard, Inc., Lynchburg, VA.
[442] Mexican War Pension File, SC #538, National Archives and Records Administration, Washington, DC.
[443] Marriage Register, Loudoun Co., VA.
[444] U.S. Census 1860, Loudoun Co., VA, p. 625.
[445] Divine, John E., 35th Battalion Virginia Cavalry, © 1985, H.E. Howard, Inc., Lynchburg, VA.
[446] U.C. Census 1870, Loudoun Co., VA, p. 185.
[447] Marriage Register, Loudoun Co., VA.
[448] Mexican War Pension File, WC #13070, National Archives and Records Administration, Washington, DC.
[449] Mexican War Pension File, SC #8101, National Archives and Records Administration, Washington, DC.
[450] Dickinson, Jack L, 8th Virginia Cavalry, © 1986, H.E. Howard, Inc., Lynchburg, VA.
[451] U.S. Census, Frederick Co., VA, p. 164.
[452] Mexican War Pension File, WC #11909, National Archives and Records Administration, Washington, DC.
[453] International Genealogical Index, Film #-0973688.
[454] International Genealogical Index, Film #-1985641.
[455] U.S. Census 1850, Stafford Co., VA, p. 029.
[456] Birth Register Stafford County, pg. 20, ln. 108, Stafford County Clerks Office, Stafford, VA.
[457] U.S. Census 1860, Fauquier Co., VA, p. 131.
[458] U.S. Census 1870, Fauquier Co., VA, p. 415.
[459] Mexican War Pension WC #618, National Archives and Records Administration, Washington, D.C.
[460] International Genealogical Index, Film #-1260992.
[461] U.S. Census 1870, Pulaski Co., VA, p. 040.
[462] Collins, Darrell L., 46th Virginia Infantry, © 1992, H.E. Howard, Inc., Lynchburg, VA.
[463] Mexican War Pension WC #4331, National Archives and Records Administration, Washington, D.C.
[464] Mexican War Pension File, WC #628, National Archives and Records Administration, Washington, D.C.
[465] Cavanaugh, Michael A., 6th Virginia Infantry, © 1988, H.E. Howard, Inc., Lynchburg, VA.
[466] Marriage Bond, Lunenburg Co., VA.
[467] U.S. Census 1850, Jefferson Co., VA, p. 295.
[468] Mexican War Pension File, SC #8407, National Archives and Records Administration, Washington, D.C.

## OFF TO WAR

[469] Mexican War Pension File, WC #15006, National Archives and Records Administration, Washington, D.C.
[470] Weaver, Jeffrey C., 18th and 20th Virginia Battalion Heavy Artillery, © 1995, H.E. Howard, Inc., Lynchburg, VA.
[471] U.S. Census 1870, Louisa Co., VA, p. 377.
[472] Weaver, Jeffrey C., 18th and 20th Virginia Battalion Heavy Artillery, © 1995, H.E. Howard, Inc., Lynchburg, VA.
[473] U.S. Census 1850, Berkeley Co., VA, p. 344.
[474] Mexican War Pension File, SC #9709, National Archives and Records Administration, Washington, D.C.
[475] U.S. Census 1850, Nansemond Co., VA, p. 130.
[476] U.S. Census 1860, Norfolk Co., VA, p. 97.
[477] Mexican War Pension File, WC #12719, National Archives and Records Administration, Washington, D.C.
[478] Mexican War Pension File, SC #16732, National Archives and Records Administration, Washington, DC.
[479] Driver, Robert J., Jr., 14th Virginia Cavalry, © 1988, H.E. Howard, Inc., Lynchburg, VA.
[480] Krick, Robert, 9th Virginia Cavalry, ©1982, H.E. Howard, Inc., Lynchburg, VA.
[481] U.S. Census 1860, Greenbrier Co., VA, p. 305.
[482] U.S Census 1870, Greenbrier Co., WV.
[483] U.S. Census 1880, Monroe Co., WV, p. S043.
[484] Mexican War Pension File, WC #8151, National Archives and Records Administration, Washington, DC.
[485] U.S. Census 1850, Dinwiddie Co., VA, p. 379.
[486] Mexican War Pension File, SC #535, National Archives and Records Administration, Washington, DC.
[487] Marriage Records Knox County, Tennessee 1792-1915.
[488] Mexican War Pension File, WC #13963, National Archives and Records Administration, Washington, DC.
[489] Marriage License Index, Bk. 7, p. 177, Berkeley Co., WV, Circuit Court Clerk's Office, Martinsburg, WV.
[490] U.S. Census 1850, Norfolk Co., VA, p. 147.
[491] U.S. Census 1850, Jefferson Co., VA, p. 300.
[492] International Genealogical Index, Film #- 1761083.
[493] Wallace, Lee A., Jr., A Guide to Virginia Military Organizations 1861-1865, 2nd Edition, © 1986, H.E. Howard, Inc., Lynchburg, VA.
[494] Armstrong, Richard L., 26th Virginia Cavalry, © 1994, H.E. Howard, Inc., Lynchburg, VA.
[495] Vogt, John & Kethley, William, Jr., Brunswick County Marriages, 1750-1853, © Iberian Publishing Co., Athens, GA.
[496] Ibid.
[497] U.S. Census 1850, Brunswick Co., VA, p.
[498] U.S. Census 1860, Brunswick Co., VA, p. 693.
[499] Wise, George, The History of the Seventeenth Virginia Infantry, C.S.A., © 1870, Kelly, Piet & Co., Baltimore, MD.
[500] District of Columbia Marriage Register 1, 1811 - 1858, Washington, D.C.
[501] U.S. Census 1850, Alexandria Co., VA, p. 320.
[502] Hewett, Janet B., Supplement to the Official Records of the Union & Confederate Armies, p. 26-27, © 1995, Broadfoot Publishing Co., Wilmington, NC.
[503] Boyd's Directory of the District of Columbia, © 1863, p. 74, William H. Boyd, Washington, D.C.
[504] Boyd's Directory of the District of Columbia, © 1865, p. 176, William H. Boyd, Washington, D.C.
[505] Boyd's Directory of the District of Columbia, © 1869, p. 211, William H. Boyd, Washington, D.C.
[506] Boyd's Directory of the District of Columbia, © 1870, p. 97, William H. Boyd, Washington, D.C.
[507] U.S. Census 1850, Loudoun Co., VA, p. 166.
[508] District of Columbia Marriage Register 1, 1811 - 1858, Washington, D.C.
[509] Boyd's Directories of the District of Columbia, © 1863-1890, William H. Boyd, Washington, D.C.

# VIRGINIA VOLUNTEERS IN MEXICO

[510] Boyd's Directory of the District of Columbia, © 1869, p. 75, William H. Boyd, Washington, D.C.
[511] Boyd's Directory of the District of Columbia, © 1869, p. 212, William H. Boyd, Washington, D.C.
[512] U.S. Census 1870, Washington, D.C., p. 872.
[513] Boyd's Directory of the District of Columbia, © 1874, William H. Boyd, Washington, D.C.
[514] Mexican War Pension File, WC #5646, National Archives and Records Administration, Washington, D.C.
[515] U.S. Census 1850, Northampton, NC, p. 081.
[516] Gregory, G. Howard, 38th Virginia Infantry, © 1988, H.E. Howard, Inc., Lynchburg, VA.
[517] *Richmond Enquirer*, July 12, 1842, p. 3, c. 6, Richmond, VA.
[518] Records of the Office of the Judge Advocate General(Army), Record Group 153, FF 74, Case 1, National Archives & Records Administration, Washington, D.C.
[519] U.S. Census 1860 Fairfax Co., VA, p. 842.
[520] Fairfax County Secession Voters, Fairfax City Regional Library, Fairfax, VA.
[521] Records of the Commission on Confederate Prisoners, March 28, 1862, p. 153-169, Fairfax City Regional Library, Fairfax, VA.
[522] *Fairfax Herald*, July 28, 1893, Fairfax, VA.
[523] Mexican War Pension WC #2595, National Archives and Records Administration, Washington, D.C.
[524] U.S. Census 1880, Vermilion Co., IL, E.D. 218, p. 018.
[525] Mexican War Pension WC #14437, National Archives and Records Administration, Washington, D.C.
[526] Personal Communication from Susan Allison Willmott, Danville, IL.
[527] Mexican War Pension WC #14437, National Archives and Records Administration, Washington, D.C.
[528] Information provided bt Elke Hall, 500 Tabb Lakes Dr., Yorktown, VA 23693.
[529] Divine, John E., 8th Virginia Infantry, © 1983, H.E. Howard, Inc., Lynchburg, VA.
[530] Mexican War Pension File, SC #16733, National Archives and Records Administration, Washington, DC.
[531] Mexican War Pension File, SC #16733, Affidavit of John Q.A. Dillard, National Archives and Records Administration, Washington, DC.
[532] Mexican War Pension File, SC #16733, Original MW Discharge, National Archives and Records Administration, Washington, DC.
[533] U.S. Census 1850, Amherst Co., VA, p. 139.
[534] Will of William S. Turner, Jr. WB 13, Pg. 31, June 8, 1851, Amherst Co., VA, Circuit Court Clerks, Amherst, VA.
[535] U.S. Census 1860, Amherst Co., VA, p. 277.
[536] Davis, James A., 51st Virginia Infantry, © 1984, H.E. Howard, Inc., Lynchburg, VA.
[537] U.S. Census 1870, Amherst Co., VA, p. 439.
[538] Mexican War Pension File, SC #16733, Letter of D. McC. Weekly, August 15, 1949, National Archives and Records Administration, Washington, DC.
[539] Carmichael, Peter S., The Purcell, Crenshaw and Letcher Artillery, © 1990, H.E. Howard, Inc., Lynchburg, VA.
[540] U.S. Census 1870, James City Co., VA, p. 357.
[541] Donnan Genealogy on the Worldwide Web: http://www.clis.com/donnan/gencom.htm
[542] Mexican War Pension File, SC #692, National Archives and Records Administration, Washington, D.C.
[543] U.S. Census 1850, Dinwiddie Co., VA, p. 422.
[544] U.S. Census 1860, Dinwiddie Co., VA, p. 438.
[545] U.S. Census 1870, Dinwiddie Co., VA, p. 395.
[546] Record of Interments Blandford Cemetery, 1888-1905, p. 44, Blandford Cemetery, Petersburg, VA
[547] Mexican War Pension File, WC #11089, National Archives and Records Administration, Washington, D.C.
[548] *THE FIRST DONNAN FAMILY IN VIRGINIA* (Manuscript) arranged by Henry Quarles Donnan, © December 31, 1929.
[549] Mexican War Pension SC #17219, National Archives and Records Administration, Washington, D.C.
[550] U.S. Census 1850, Dinwiddie Co., VA, p. 347.
[551] U.S. Census 1860, Dinwiddie Co., VA, p.286.
[552] U.S. Census 1870, Dinwiddie Co., VA, p. 274.

# OFF TO WAR

---

[553] Mexican War Pension SC #17219, National Archives and Records Administration, Washington, D.C.
[554] Hewett, Janet B., The Roster of Union Soldiers, 1861-1865, © 1998, Broadfoot Publishing Co., Wilmington, NC.
[555] *The Petersburg Daily Republican*, October 27, 1848, p. 3, c. 1, Petersburg, VA.
[556] Jordan, Weymouth T., Jr., North Carolina Troops 1861-1865, A Roster, V. 4, Infantry, © 1973, North Carolina Archives, Raleigh, North Carolina.
[557] Marriage Register Alexandria Virginia.
[558] U.S. Census 1870, Alexandria, VA, p. 127.
[559] Mexican War Pension File, WC #73, National Archives and Records Administration, Washington, DC.
[560] Crew, R. Thomas, Jr., Grimes' Battery, Grandy's Battery, and Huger's Battery Virginia Artillery, © 1995, H.E. Howard, Inc., Lynchburg, VA.
[561] U.S. Census 1870, Norfolk Co., VA, p. 378.
[562] U.S. Census 1850, Norfolk Co., VA.
[563] International Genealogical Index, Film #-170478.
[564] Marriage Register Rockbridge Co., VA.
[565] U.S. Census 1850, Rockbridge Co., VA, p. 462.
[566] U.S. Census 1870, Rockbridge Co., VA, p. 481.
[567] Marriage Register #A, pg. 311, Montgomery Co., VA.
[568] U.S. Census 1850, Montgomery Co., VA, p. 022.
[569] Marriage Register #1, pg. 1, Montgomery Co., VA.
[570] Marriage Register #A, pg. 312, Montgomery Co., VA.
[571] Marriage Register #1, pg. 1, Montgomery Co., VA.
[572] Votsberger, Margaret Ann, The Dulany's of Welbourne, © 1995, Rockbridge Publishing Co., Berryville, VA.
[573] Fairfax County Minute Book 1858, p. 120, Fairfax County Circuit Court Archives, Fairfax, VA.
[574] U.S. Census 1850, Fairfax Co., VA, p. 186.
[575] Sprouse, Edith M., Fairfax County in 1860: A Collective Biography, © 1996, Maunscript Collection, Fairfax City Regional Library.
[576] U.S. Census 1860, Fairfax Co., VA, p. 843.
[577] Mexican War Pension File, WC #5548, National Archives and Records Administration, Washington, DC.
[578] U.S. Census 1850, Fairfax Co., VA, p. 218.
[579] Record of Interments Blandford Cemetery, 1872-1888, p. 147, Blandford Cemetery, Petersburg, VA
[580] U.S. Census 1850, Dinwiddie Co., VA, p. 430.
[581] Mexican War Pension File, WC #1326, National Archives and Records Administration, Washington, D.C.
[582] *The Daily Express*, May 21, 1857, p. 2, c. 4, Petersburg, VA.
[583] Record of Interments Blandford Cemetery, 1872-1888, p. 147, Blandford Cemetery, Petersburg, VA
[584] Mexican War Pension File, SC #2771, National Archives and Records Administration, Washington, DC.
[585] *Fort Worth Democrat*, July 19, 1873, Ft. Worth, Texas.
[586] Mexican War Pension SC #8084, National Archives and Records Administration, Washington, D.C.
[587] U.S. Census 1860, Alexandria Co., VA, p. 948.
[588] Delauter, Roger U., McNeill's Rangers, © 1986, H.E. Howard, Inc., Lynchburg, VA.
[589] U.S. Census 1870, Alexandria Co., VA, p. 180.
[590] Marriage Register, Alexandria, VA
[591] Mexican War Diary of James Lawson Kemper, Virginia Magazine of History & Biography, v. 74 (1966, p. 425-426.
[592] Mexican War Pension WC #7101, National Archives and Records Administration, Washington, D.C.
[593] U.S. Census 1860, Henrico Co., VA, p. 845.
[594] U.S. Census 1870, Amherst Co., VA, p. 440.
[595] U.S. Census 1850, Franklin Co., VA, p. 059.
[596] U.S. Census 1860, Franklin Co., VA, p. 024.
[597] Adams, Lela C., Marriages of Patrick Co., VA, 1791-1850, © 1972, Bassett, VA.
[598] Marriage License, Alexandria Co.(Arlington Co.), VA

[599] U.S. Census 1860, Alexandria Co., VA, p. 785.
[600] U.S. Census 1870, Alexandria Co., VA, p. 158.
[601] *Alexandria Gazette*, December 31, 1883, Alexandria, VA.
[602] Mexican War Pension File, SC #6050, National Archives and Records Administration, Washington, DC.
[603] Mexican War Pension File, WC #6345, National Archives and Records Administration, Washington, DC.
[604] Marriage Register #A, pg. 312, Montgomery Co., VA.
[605] Mexican War Pension File, WC #156, National Archives and Records Administration, Washington, DC.
[606] Mexican War Pension WC #13790, National Archives and Records Administration, Washington, D.C.
[607] U.S. Census 1850, Henrico Co., VA, p. 340.
[608] Mexican War Pension File, SC #816, National Archives and Records Administration, Washington, DC.
[609] Mexican War Pension File, WC #11807, National Archives and Records Administration, Washington, DC.
[610] Mexican War Pension File, WC #11807, Affidavit of Sallie M. Ellis, National Archives and Records Administration, Washington, DC.
[611] Mexican War Pension File, SC #824, National Archives and Records Administration, Washington, DC.
[612] U.S. Census 1880, Harrison Co., WV, p. 007.
[613] Mexican War Pension File, WC #9431, National Archives and Records Administration, Washington, DC.
[614] Tombstone Inscriptions, Jefferson County, WV, 1687-1980, © 1981, Bee Line Chapter, National Society of Daughters of the American Revolution, Charlestown, WV.
[615] U.S. Census 1860, Ohio Co., VA, p. 456.
[616] U.S. Census 1880, Ohio Co., WV, p. T020.
[617] U.S. Mortality Schedule 1850, WV.
[618] Broyles, Matthew W., Erskine Family Tree, http://www.netlizard.com/matt2/erskine.html#14-1
[619] Mexican War Diary of James Lawson Kemper, Virginia Magazine of History & Biography, v. 74 (1966), p. 407, Richmond, VA.
[620] Dayton, Ruth Woods, Greenbrier Pioneers and Their Homes, p. 290, © 1942, West Virginia Publishing Co., Charleston, WV.
[621] Leonard, Cynthia M., General Assembly of Virginia 1619-1978, © 1978, Library of Virginia, Richmond, VA.
[622] Letter from T.C. Madison, Asst. Surgeon to George A. Porterfield, Regtl. Adjutant, September 27, 1847, Regimental Letter Book, 1st Virginia Volunteer Infantry, Record Group 153, National Archives & Records Administration, Washington, D.C.
[623] Greenbrier County Historical Society, Lewisburg, WV, Reference ZN9.
[624] U.S. Census 1850, Greenbrier Co., VA, p. 271.
[625] U.S. Census 1860, Greenbrier Co., VA, p. 218.
[626] U.S. Census 1850, Norfolk Co., VA, p. 164.
[627] U.S. Census 1870, Norfolk Co., VA, p. 479.
[628] Marriage Register Loudoun Co., VA, Circuit Court Clerk's Office, Leesburg, VA.
[629] Mexican War Pension WC #8910, National Archives and Records Administration, Washington, D.C.
[630] Mexican War Pension File, WC #482, National Archives and Records Administration, Washington, DC.
[631] Mexican War Pension File, SC #19943, National Archives and Records Administration, Washington, DC.
[632] U.S. Census 1850, Jefferson Co., VA, p. 298.
[633] Court Order Book, July 13, 1840, Anthony & Stephen Ewald state intent to become citizens of the U.S., Wythe Co. Clerks Office, Wytheville, VA.
[634] Will of Maria Seagle, August 18, 1857, Will Book 4, pp.305-308, Wythe Co. Clerks Office, Wytheville, VA.
[635] U.S. Census 1850, Wythe Co., VA, p. 279.
[636] U.S. Census 1870, Wythe Co., VA, p. 471.
[637] Mexican War Pension File, SC #2100, National Archives and Records Administration, Washington, DC.
[638] Letter from T. C. Madison, Asst. Surgeon to Lt. Thomas P. August, June 29, 1847, Regimental Letter Book, 1st Virginia Volunteer Infantry, Record Group 153, National Archives & Records Administration, Washington, D.C.

OFF TO WAR

[639] U.S. Census 1850, Preston Co., VA, p. 340.
[640] U.S. Census 1880, Preston Co., WV.
[641] French, S. Bassett, Biographical Sketches, Library of Virginia, Richmond, VA.
[642] Sprouse, Edith M., Fairfax County in 1860: A Collective Biography, © 1996, Manuscript Collection, Fairfax City Regional Library.
[643] Mexican War Pension File, SC #1006, National Archives and Records Administration, Washington, D.C.
[644] *The Petersburg Daily Republican*, December 8, 1848, p. 3, c. 1, Petersburg, VA.
[645] U.S. Census 1850, Dinwiddie Co., VA, p. 492.
[646] U.S. Census 1860, Dinwiddie Co., VA, p. 077.
[647] Mexican War Pension File, WC #2471, National Archives and Records Administration, Washington, DC.
[648] Mexican War Pension File, SC #918, National Archives and Records Administration, Washington, D.C.
[649] Mexican War Pension File, WC #9398, National Archives and Records Administration, Washington, D.C.
[650] Mexican War Pension File, SC #15041, National Archives and Records Administration, Washington, D.C.
[651] Mexican War Pension File, WC #7126, National Archives and Records Administration, Washington, D.C.
[652] U.S. Census 1850, Nelson Co., VA, p. 222.
[653] Mexican War Pension WC #6471, National Archives and Records Administration, Washington, D.C.
[654] U.S. Census 1860, Nelson Co., VA, p. 711.
[655] Jordan, Ervin L., 19th Virginia Infantry, © 1987, H.E. Howard, Inc., Lynchburg, VA.
[656] U.S. Census 1870, Nelson Co., VA, p. 444.
[657] Affidavit of Josiah Faulkner, Mexican War Pension SC #958, National Archives and Records Administration, Washington, D.C.
[658] Mexican War Pension File, SC #915, National Archives and Records Administration, Washington, DC.
[659] U.S. Census 1850, Lunenburg Co., VA, p. 020.
[660] U.S. Census 1860, Lunenburg Co., VA, p. 991.
[661] Boyd's Directory of the District of Columbia, © 1860, p. 71, William H. Boyd, Washington, D.C.
[662] Mexican War Pension WC #14701, National Archives and Records Administration, Washington, D.C.
[663] Boyd's Directories of the District of Columbia, 1863-1907, William H. Boyd, Washington, D.C.
[664] Boyd's Directory of the District of Columbia, © 1863, p. 88, William H. Boyd, Washington, D.C.
[665] Boyd's Directory of the District of Columbia, © 1863, p. 238, William H. Boyd, Washington, D.C.
[666] Boyd's Directory of the District of Columbia, © 1874, William H. Boyd, Washington, D.C.
[667] Mexican War Pension WC #14701, National Archives and Records Administration, Washington, D.C.
[668] Boyd's Directory of the District of Columbia, © 1908, "*Levinia, w. of Richard M.A....,*" William H. Boyd, Washington, D.C.
[669] U.S. Census 1850, Alexandria Co., VA, p. 380.
[670] U.S. Census 1860, Alexandria Co., VA, p. 822.
[671] Alexandria Gazette, December 2, 1878.
[672] Mexican War Pension File, SC #904, National Archives and Records Administration, Washington, D.C.
[673] Virginia Military Order Book, 1846, November 6, 1846, arrested for "gross disrespect to a superior officer," November 12, 1846, dismissed for "breech of arrest," Virginia Military Institute Archives, Lexington, VA.
[674] Letter from Superintendent Francis H. Smith to Slaughter Ficklin, November 7, 1846, Virginia Military Institute Archives, Lexington, VA.
[675] Memoirs of Hon. William McKendree Gwin, California Senator 1850-1855, 1857-1861, Library of Congress, Washington, D.C.
[676] Scott, J.L., 45th Virginia Infantry, © 1989, H.E. Howard, Inc., Lynchburg, VA.
[677] Journals of the Congress of the Confederate States of America, 1861-1865, Friday, September 26, 1862, p. 350.
[678] Ficklin, Walter Homan, A Genealogical History of the Ficklin Family, © 1912, The W.H. Kistler Press, Denver CO.

# VIRGINIA VOLUNTEERS IN MEXICO

[679] Virginia Cavalcade, v.33, no.3, © 1984, p. 114-125 .p. 120, Richmond, VA.
[680] Albemarle Co. Marriage Register, p. 97.
[681] U.S. Census 1850, Albemarle Co., VA, p. 272.
[682] U.S. Census 1860, Augusta Co., VA, p. 780.
[683] Augusta County Marriage Register.
[684] U.S. Census 1850, Augusta Co., VA, p. 303.
[685] U.S. Census 1860, Augusta Co., VA, p. 780.
[686] Driver, Robert J., 52nd Virginia Infantry, © 1986, H.E. Howard, Inc., Lynchburg, VA.
[687] Mexican War Pension SC #16675, National Archives and Records Administration, Washington, D.C.
[688] Affidavit of McKnight & Murphy, Mexican War Pension SC #16675, National Archives and Records Administration, Washington, D.C.
[689] International Genealogical Index, Film #-1903929
[690] Affidavit, Mexican War Pension SC #16675, National Archives and Records Administration, Washington, D.C.
[691] International Genealogical Index, Film #-538522.
[692] Certified Copy of Marriage Record, Mexican War Pension WC #8287, National Archives and Records Administration, Washington, D.C.
[693] *The Petersburg Daily Index*, July 2, 1872, p. 2, c. 4, Petersburg, VA.
[694] Mexican War Pension File, SC #2104, Facsimile from Fitzgerald Family Bible, National Archives and Records Administration, Washington, D.C.
[695] Mexican War Pension File, SC #2104, National Archives and Records Administration, Washington, D.C.
[696] Mexican War Pension File, WC #13782, National Archives and Records Administration, Washington, D.C.
[697] Mexican War Pension File, SC #3047, Affidavit of "brother," Pvt. Layfayette H. Fitzhugh, National Archives and Records Administration, Washington, DC.
[698] Mexican War Pension File, SC #7203, National Archives and Records Administration, Washington, DC.
[699] U.S. Census 1850, Berkeley Co., VA, p. 348.
[700] U.S. Census 1860, Clarke Co., VA, p. 685.
[701] U.S. Census 1870, Clarke Co., VA, p. 450.
[702] Reidenbaugh, Lowell, 27th Virginia Infantry, © 1993, H.E. Howard Inc., Lynchburg, VA.
[703] Register of Deaths 1906-1917, Berkeley County, WV, Circuit Court Clerks Office, Martinsburg, WV.
[704] Clark, Grata Jeter, The Jeter Mosaic, p. 133, © 1987, Arcadia-Clark, Inc., Fort Worth, Texas.
[705] Mexican War Pension SC # 23184, National Archives and Records Administration, Washington, D.C.
[706] U.S. Census 1850, Chesterfield Co., VA, p. 117.
[707] Mexican War Pension WC #7405, National Archives and Records Administration, Washington, D.C.
[708] Confederate Veteran Magazine, © 1896, v. 4, p. 390, Nashville, TN.
[709] Charlotte County Marriage Register, Charlotte Co., VA
[710] U.S. Census 1850, Charlotte Co., VA, p. 048.
[711] U.S. Census 1860, Charlotte Co., VA, p. 210.
[712] Rankin, Thomas M., 22nd Virginia Infantry Battalion, © 1999, H.E. Howard, Inc., Lynchburg, VA.
[713] Lewis County, Virginia Marriage Register Book 6, p. 241.
[714] U.S. Census 1880, Lewis Co., WV, p. C022.
[715] Mexican War Pension File, SC #6752, National Archives and Records Administration, Washington, DC.
[716] Jensen, Les, 32nd Virginia Infantry, © 1990, H.E. Howard, Inc., Lynchburg, VA.
[717] Mexican War Pension File, WC #6204, National Archives and Records Administration, Washington, DC.
[718] Mexican War Pension File, SC #968, National Archives and records Administration, Washington, D.C.
[719] U.S. Census 1870, Greensville Co., VA, p. 385.
[720] Mexican War Pension SA 20672, National Archives and Records Administration, Washington, D.C.
[721] Deposition of James H. Fowler, March 16, 1891, Mexican War Pension SA 20672, National Archives and Records Administration, Washington, D.C.
[722] Mexican War Pension File SC #2288, National Archives and Records Administration, Washington, D.C.
[723] Lunenburg County Marriage Register, p. 31, Lunenburg Co. Circuit Court Clerk's Office.

# OFF TO WAR

[724] Riggs, Susan A., 21st Virginia Infantry, © 1991, H.E. Howard, Inc., Lynchburg, VA.
[725] Krick, Robert, 9th Virginia Cavalry, © 1982, H.E. Howard, Inc., Lynchburg, VA.
[726] Obituary, *The Commercial Appeal*, 01/27/1908, Memphis, TN, Mexican War Pension File WC #18924, National Archives and Records Administration, Washington, D.C.
[727] Death Certificate, Mexican War Pension SC #10910, National Archives and Records Administration, Washington, D.C.
[728] Mexican War Pension SC #10910, National Archives and Records Administration, Washington, D.C.
[729] U.S. Census 1870, Henrico Co., VA, p. 369.
[730] Mexican War Pension File, WC #6261, National Archives and Records Administration, Washington, D.C.
[731] Mexican War Pension File SC #15883, Extract from Family Bible, National Archives and records Administration, Washington, D.C.
[732] U.S. Census 1850, Stafford Co., VA, p. 028.
[733] Records of the Office of the Judge Advocate General(Army), Record Group 153, EE 553, Case 4, National Archives & Records Administration, Washington, D.C.
[734] Mexican War Pension File, SC #2998, National Archives and Records Administration, Washington, DC.
[735] Mexican War Pension SC #2787, National Archives and Records Administration, Washington, D.C.
[736] Christian, W. Asbury, D.D., Richmond: Her Past and Present, p. 163, © 1912, L.H. Jenkins, Richmond, VA.
[737] Albemarle County Bonds & Consent Papers 1850-1853, Circuit Court Clerks Office, Charlottesville, VA.
[738] Christian, W. Asbury, D.D., Richmond: Her Past and Present, p. 197, © 1912, L.H. Jenkins, Richmond, VA.
[739] U.S. Census 1870, Nelson Co., VA, p. 367.
[740] Mexican War Pension WC #5398, National Archives and Records Administration, Washington, D.C.
[741] Cochran, Holly Wanless, Abstracts of Bath County Virginia Will Books 5 and 6 (1843-1875), pps. 115, 126, © 1998, Hollyhock Press, Ashland, OR.
[742] Mexican War Pension File, WC #2536, National Archives and Records Administration, Washington, D.C.
[743] Record of Interments Blandford Cemetery, 1843-1872, p. 346, Blandford Cemetery, Petersburg, VA.
[744] U.S. Census 1850, Henrico Co., VA, p. 399.
[745] *Daily South Side Democrat*, November 4, 1856, p. 2, c. 5, Petersburg, VA.
[746] Record of Interments Blandford Cemetery, 1843-1872, p. 346, Blandford Cemetery, Petersburg, VA.
[747] U.S. Census 1850, Dinwiddie Co., VA, p. 341.
[748] U.S. Census 1870, Dinwiddie Co., VA, p. 209.
[749] U.S. Census 1860, Dinwiddie Co., VA, p. 230.
[750] U.S. Census 1870, Dinwiddie Co., VA, p. 209.
[751] Record of Interments Blandford Cemetery, 1888-1905, p. 12, Blandford Cemetery, Petersburg, VA.
[752] Hubert, Charles F., History of the Fiftieth Regiment, Illinois Volunteer Infantry, In the War of the Union, © 1894, War Veteran Publishing Co., Kansas City, Mo., p. 490.
[753] Hubert, Charles F., History of the Fiftieth Regiment, Illinois Volunteer Infantry, In the War of the Union, © 1894, War Veteran Publishing Co., Kansas City, Mo., p. 491.
[754] Pipenger, Wesley E., District of Columbia Marriages, 1811-1858, © 1994, Family Line Publications, Westminster, MD.
[755] U.S. Census 1850, Elizabeth City Co., VA, p. 056.
[756] U.S. Census 1850, Berkeley Co., VA, p. 343.
[757] U.S. Census 1860, Preston Co., VA, p. 272.
[758] U.S. Census 1880, Taylor Co., WV, p. G018.
[759] Mexican War Pension File, SC #9509, National Archives and Records Administration, Washington, DC.
[760] McIlhany, Edward Washington, Recollections of a '49er, p. 13 &14, © 1908, Hailman Printing Co., Kansas City, MO.
[761] U.S. Census 1860, Jefferson Co., VA, p. 796.
[762] U.S. Census 1880, Jefferson Co., WV, p. C022.

# VIRGINIA VOLUNTEERS IN MEXICO

[763] Register of Deaths, 1881 – 1889, p. 213, Jefferson County, Circuit Court Clerks Office, Charlestown, WV.
[764] Mexican War Pension File, SC #10768, National Archives and Records Administration, Washington, DC.
[765] Official Records of the War of the Rebellion, Series I, V. 2, pp. 456, 556, 558, & Series 1, V. 36, p. 943, © 1880, War Department, Washington, D.C.
[766] Mexican War Pension File, SC #20064, National Archives and Records Administration, Washington, D.C.
[767] Pulaski County Marriage Register, p. 2, ln. 37, Pulaski County Circuit Court Clerks Office, Pulaski, VA.
[768] U.S. Census 1860, Pulaski Co., VA, p. 697.
[769] Robertson, James I., 4th Virginia Infantry, © 1982, H.E. Howard, Inc., Lynchburg, VA.
[770] U.S. Census 1870, Pulaski Co., VA, p. 065.
[771] Pulaski County Marriage Register, p. 21, ln. 11, Pulaski County Circuit Court Clerks Office, Pulaski, VA
[772] Mexican War Pension File, WC #15191, National Archives and Records Administration, Washington, D.C.
[773] Driver, Robert C., Jr., 14th Virginia Cavalry, © 1988, H.E. Howard, Inc., Lynchburg, VA.
[774] Caroline County Marriage Register, Circuit Court Clerks Office, Bowling Green, VA.
[775] U.S. Census 1850, Caroline Co., VA, p. 276.
[776] U.S. Census 1860, Caroline Co., VA, p. 691.
[777] U.S. Census 1870, Caroline Co., VA, p. 242.
[778] Records of the Office of the Judge Advocate General(Army), Record Group 153, EE 427, Case 18, National Archives & Records Administration, Washington, D.C.
[779] U.S. Census 1850, Westmoreland Co., VA, p. 309.
[780] U.S. Census 1860, Westmoreland Co., VA, p. 991.
[781] 48th Virginia Infantry, John D. Chapla, H.E. Howard, Inc., Lynchburg, VA.
[782] Mexican War Pension File, WC #1021, National Archives and Records Administration, Washington, D.C.
[783] Mexican War Pension File, Invalid Claim of Wesley B. Garrett, Affidavit of Claimant, November 13, 1871, National Archives and records Administration, Washington, D.C.
[784] Deposition of Mary Gately, February 20, 1891, Mexican War Pension Certificate WC #7365, National Archives and Records Administration, Washington, D.C
[785] Letter from Patrick Gately to Job Demeree, July 31, 1847, Mexican War Pension Certificate WC #7365, National Archives and Records Administration, Washington, D.C.
[786] Deposition of Mary Gately, February 20, 1891, Mexican War Pension Certificate WC #7365, National Archives and Records Administration, Washington, D.C
[787] Mexican War Pension Certificate WC #7365, National Archives and Records Administration, Washington, D.C
[788] Baptismal record of Margaret Ann Gately, Mexican War Pension Certificate WC #7365, National Archives and Records Administration, Washington, D.C.
[789] Mexican War Pension Certificate WC #7365, National Archives and Records Administration, Washington, D.C.
[790] Mexican War Pension File, SC #7589, National Archives and Records Administration, Washington, D.C.
[791] U.S. Census 1880, Perquimans Co., NC, p. 34B.
[792] Mexican War Pension File, WC #10972, National Archives and Records Administration, Washington, D.C.
[793] Annual Report of the Commissioner of Indian Affairs, 1857- 1859. 36th Congress, 1st Session, Senate Executive Document No. 1, December 1, 1859.
[794] Ligenfelter, Keith, Tehama County Pioneers (Manuscript), Manuscript #110, Keith Lingenfelter Genealogy and Research Collection, Special Collections Department, Meriam Library, California State University, Chico.
[795] *Red Bluff Beacon*, October 17, 1863, Red Bluff, California.

## OFF TO WAR

[796] Ligenfelter, Keith, Tehama County Pioneers (Manuscript), Manuscript #110, Keith Lingenfelter Genealogy and Research Collection, Special Collections Department, Meriam Library, California State University, Chico.
[797] Goodman, David M., A Western Panorama 1849-1865: The Travels, Writings, and Influence of J. Ross Browne, © 1966,: A.H. Clark, Glendale, CA.
[798] Ligenfelter, Keith, Tehama County Pioneers (Manuscript), Manuscript #110, Keith Lingenfelter Genealogy and Research Collection, Special Collections Department, Meriam Library, California State University, Chico.
[799] Report of John C. Caldwell, U.S. Consul at Valparaiso to the Department of State, October 15, 1869, National Archives & Records Administration, Washington, D.C.
[800] *Sacramento Union*, December 18, 1869, Sacramento, CA, reported the death, and commented that "Geiger, some years ago killed a man at Red Bluff, and has since been a fugitive from justice."
[801] Potter, David M., Trail To California: The Overland Journal of Vincent Geiger and Wakeman Bryarly, © 1945, Yale University Press, New Haven and London, 1945.
[802] Mexican War Pension File, WA #10400, National Archives and Records Administration, Washington, D.C.
[803] Brunswick County Marriage Bonds, Circuit Court Clerks Office, Lawrenceville, VA.
[804] U.S. Census 1850, Brunswick Co., VA.
[805] U.S. Census 1860, Brunswick Co., VA, p. 747.
[806] Mexican War Pension File, WA #10400, Affidavit of Robert A. Goodwyn, National Archives and records Administration, Washington, D.C.
[807] U.S. Census 1870, Brunswick Co., VA, p. 124.
[808] Mexican War Pension File, SC #11546, National Archives and Records Administration, Washington, D.C.
[809] Frye, Dennis E., 12$^{th}$ Virginia Cavalry, © 1988, H.E. Howard, Inc., Lynchburg, VA.
[810] Mexican War Pension File, WC #7879, National Archives and Records Administration, Washington, D.C.
[811] Mexican War Pension WC #9582, National Archives and Records Administration, Washington, D.C.
[812] U.S. Census 1870, Pittsylvania Co., VA, p. 403.
[813] Mexican War Pension File, SC #3970, National Archives and Records Administration, Washington, D.C.
[814] U.S. Census 1850, Pulaski Co., VA, p. 224.
[815] U.S. Census 1870, Wythe Co., VA, p. 455.
[816] Mexican War Pension File, WA #12173, National Archives and Records Administration, Washington, D.C.
[817] District of Columbia Marriage Register #1, 1811-1858, Marriage Bureau, Washington, D.C.
[818] Boyd's Directory of the District of Columbia, © 1862, p. 88, William H. Boyd, Washington, D.C.
[819] Mexican War Pension File, SC #5304, National Archives and Records Administration, Washington, D.C.
[820] Marriage Records Ripley County, Missouri, 1833-1921, Recorder of Deeds.
[821] Information provided by Ross Dean Hutson, 17410 Chestnut Dr., Belton, MO, 64012-2824.
[822] Beers History of Warren County, Ohio, © 1882.
[823] Mexican War Pension File, SC #8759, National Archives and Records Administration, Washington, DC.
[824] U.S. Census 1850, Warren Co., OH, p. 211.
[825] History of Warren County (Ohio), p. 740, © 1882. W.H. Beers & Co. Chicago, IL
[826] Cemetery Records of Clinton County, Ohio 1798-1978, p. 163.
[827] Mexican War Pension File, WC #15789, National Archives and Records Administration, Washington, DC.
[828] Mexican War Pension File, WC #4368, National Archives and Records Administration, Washington, DC.
[829] Mexican War Pension File, SC #8624, National Archives and Records Administration, Washington, D.C.
[830] U.S. Census 1850, Augusta Co., VA, p. 217.
[831] U.S. Census 1860, Augusta Co., VA, p. 841.

## VIRGINIA VOLUNTEERS IN MEXICO

[832] Mexican War Pension File, WC #13456, National Archives and Records Administration, Washington, D.C.
[833] U.S. Census 1860, Botetourt Co., VA, p. 176.
[834] U.S. Census 1870, Botetourt Co., VA, p. 569.
[835] Mexican War Pension File, SC #14807, National Archives and Records Administration, Washington, DC.
[836] Mexican War Pension File SC #2108, National Archives and Records Administration, Washington, D.C.
[837] Mexican War Pension File WC #9090, Death Certificate, National Archives & Records Administration, Washington, D.C.
[838] U.S. Census 1850, Dinwiddie Co., VA, p. 486.
[839] U.S. Census 1860, Dinwiddie Co., VA, p. 112.
[840] U.S. Census 1870, Dinwiddie Co., VA, p. 128.
[841] U.S. Census 1870, Dinwiddie Co., VA, p. 153.
[842] U.S. Census 1860, Dinwiddie Co., VA, p. 073.
[843] U.S. Census 1870, Dinwiddie Co., VA, p. 153.
[844] U.S. Census 1850, Brunswick Co., VA, p. 308.
[845] Vogt, John & Kethley, William, Jr., Brunswick County Marriages, 1750-1853, © 1988, Iberian Publishing Co., Athens, GA.
[846] U.S. Census 1860, Brunswick Co., VA, p. 747.
[847] Collins, Darrell L., 46th Virginia Infantry, © 1992, H.E. Howard, Inc., Lynchburg, VA.
[848] U.S. Census 1870, Brunswick Co., VA, p. 125.
[849] Mexican War Pension File, SC #2585, National Archives and Records Administration, Washington, DC.
[850] Lunenburg County Marriage Register, p. 32, Lunenburg Co. Circuit Court Clerk's Office.
[851] U.S. Census 1870, Lunenburg Co., VA, p. 526.
[852] U.S. Census 1850, Nelson Co., VA, p. 302.
[853] U.S. Census 1860, Nelson Co., VA, p. 794.
[854] Mexican War Pension File, WC #6306, National Archives and Records Administration, Washington, DC.
[855] U.S. Census 1850, Augusta Co., VA, p. 292.
[856] Records of the Office of the Judge Advocate General(Army), Record Group 153, EE 611, Case 2, National Archives & Records Administration, Washington, D.C.
[857] Records of the Office of the Judge Advocate General(Army), Record Group 153, EE 611, Case 54, National Archives & Records Administration, Washington, D.C.
[858] Campbell County Marriage Bond, Campbell County Circuit Court Clerks Office.
[859] U.S. Census 1850, Campbell Co., VA, p. 292.
[860] U.S. Census 1850, Campbell Co., VA, p. 116.
[861] U.S. Census 1860, Campbell Co., VA, p. 523.
[862] Mexican War Pension File, SC #3390, National Archives and Records Administration, Washington, DC.
[863] Loudoun County Marriage Register, Loudoun County Circuit Court Clerks Office, Leesburg, VA.
[864] U.S. Census 1870, Loudoun Co., VA, p. 201.
[865] Mexican War Pension File, WC #12442, National Archives and Records Administration, Washington, DC.
[866] Mexican War Pension File, WC #4542, National Archives and Records Administration, Washington, D.C.
[867] Mexican War Pension File, SC #4819, National Archives and Records Administration, Washington, D.C.
[868] U.S. Census 1850, Henrico Co., VA, p. 421.
[869] U.S. Census 1860, Orange Co., VA, p. 674.
[870] U.S. Census 1870, Orange Co., VA, p. 236.
[871] Riggs, David F., 13th Virginia Infantry, © 1988, H.E. Howard, Inc., Lynchburg, VA.
[872] International Genealogy Index, Film #-458379.
[873] U.S. Census 1850, Norfolk Co., VA, p. 096.
[874] International Genealogical Index, Film #-1761077.
[875] Fisher, Therese, Marriages of Caroline Co., VA, 1777-1853, © 1998, Heritage Books, Inc. Bowie, MD.

# OFF TO WAR

[876] U.S. Census 1850, Caroline Co., VA, p. 277.
[877] U.S. Census 1860, Caroline Co., VA, p. 677.
[878] U.S. Census 1870, Caroline Co., VA, p. 234.
[879] Krick, Robert K., 30th Virginia Infantry, © 1983, H.E. Howard, Inc., Lynchburg, VA.
[880] Mexican War Pension File, SC #5569, National Archives and Records Administration, Washington, D.C.
[881] U.S. Census 1850, Mecklenberg Co., VA, p. 117.
[882] U.S. Census 1870, Mecklenberg Co., VA, p. 230.
[883] Alexandria Gazette, November 21, 1855, p. 3.
[884] Mexican War Pension File, SC #16579, National Archives and Records Administration, Washington, D.C.
[885] U.S. Census 1850, Dinwiddie Co., VA, p. 404.
[886] U.S. Census 1860, Dinwiddie Co., VA. p. 430.
[887] U.S. Census 1870, Dinwiddie Co., VA, p. 280.
[888] Mexican War Pension File, WC #2975, National Archives and Records Administration, Washington, D.C.
[889] U.S. Census 1860, Tippecanoe Co., IN, p. 508.
[890] District of Columbia Marriage Licenses, Register 1, 1811-1858, Washington, D.C.
[891] Mexican War Pension File, WC #1961, National Archives and Records Administration, Washington, D.C.
[892] U.S. Census 1850, Norfolk Co., VA, p. 187.
[893] U.S. Census 1850, Norfolk Co., VA, p. 148.
[894] U.S. Census 1860, Norfolk Co., VA, p. 073.
[895] Mexican War Pension File, WC #1575, National Archives and Records Administration, Washington, DC.
[896] U.S. Census 1860, Orange Co., VA, p. 631.
[897] U.S. Census 1870, Orange Co., VA, p. 234.
[898] Johnson, William P., II, Brothers and Cousins: Confederate Soldiers and Sailors of Fairfax Co., VA, © 1995, Iberian Publishing Co., Athens, GA.
[899] U.S. Census 1850, Fairfax Co., VA, p. 130.
[900] U.S. Census 1860, Fairfax Co., VA, p. 872.
[901] Marriage Register, Fairfax Co., VA.
[902] U.S. Census 1870, Fairfax Co., VA, p. 270.
[903] *Fairfax Herald*, June 29, 1906, p. 3, Fairfax, Virginia.
[904] U.S. Census 1860, Fairfax Co., VA.
[905] U.S. Census 1860, Fairfax Co., VA.
[906] Marriage Register Loudoun Co., VA, *Joseph Hains to Mariah Handy, July 29, 1807*, Circuit Court Clerk's Office, Leesburg, VA.
[907] Marriage Register Loudoun Co., VA, Circuit Court Clerk's Office, Leesburg, VA.
[908] Mexican War Pension WC #1407, National Archives and Records Administration, Washington, D.C.
[909] Marriage Certificate, Mexican War Pension WC #2725, National Archives and Records Administration, Washington, D.C.
[910] U.S. Census 1850, Campbell Co., VA, p. 098.
[911] U.S. Census 1860, Campbell Co., VA, p. 327.
[912] U.S. Census 1850, Norfolk Co., VA, p. 221.
[913] U.S. Census 1860, Norfolk Co., VA, p. 664.
[914] U.S. Census 1850, Alexandria Co., VA, p. 317.
[915] U.S. Census 1860, Fairfax Co., VA, p. 783.
[916] U.S. Census 1870, Fairfax Co., VA, p. 325.
[917] Mexican War Pension SC #7013, National Archives and Records Administration, Washington, D.C.
[918] U.S. Census 1850, King George Co., VA, p. 221.
[919] U.S. Census 1860, King George Co., VA, p. 374.
[920] U.S. Census 1870, King George Co., VA, p. 038.
[921] *The Petersburg Republican*, February 5, 1847, p. 3, c. 1, Petersburg, VA

# VIRGINIA VOLUNTEERS IN MEXICO

[922] U.S. Census 1850, Prince George Co., VA, p. 093.
[923] U.S. Census 1860, Surry Co., VA, p. 868.
[924] Mexican War Pension File, WC #2367, National Archives and Records Administration, Washington, DC.
[925] U.S. Census 1860, Brunswick Co., VA, p. 711.
[926] U.S. Census 1850, Nansemond Co., VA.
[927] Malone, Dumas, Dictionary of American Biography, v. 8, p. 216, © 1963, Charles Scribner & Sons, New York, NY.
[928] Cullum, George W., Biographical Register of the Officers and Graduates of the U.S. Military Academy, p. 233, © 1891, Riverside Press, Cambridge, MA.
[929] Records of the Office of the Judge Advocate General(Army), Record Group 153, FF 74, Case 4, National Archives & Records Administration, Washington, D.C.
[930] Letter from Pvt. John A.B. Harding to Col. John F. Hamtramck, June 18, 1847, Regimental Letter Book, 1st Virginia Volunteer Infantry, Record Group 153, National Archives & Records Administration, Washington, D.C
[931] Information provided by George R. Vernon, 6805 SW Sussex, Beaverton, OR 97005.
[932] U.S. Census 1850, Augusta Co., VA, p. 297.
[933] U.S. Census 1860, Augusta Co., VA, p. 753.
[934] U.S. Census 1870, Augusta Co., VA, p. 214.
[935] Mexican War Pension File, SC #1344, National Archives and Records Administration, Washington, D.C.
[936] U.S. Census 1880, Roane Co., WV, p. W039.
[937] Mexican War Pension File, WC #2255, National Archives and Records Administration, Washington, DC.
[938] U.S. Census 1850, Augusta Co., VA, p. 307.
[939] U.S. Census 1860, Augusta Co., VA, p. 797.
[940] U.S. Census 1860, Augusta Co., VA, p. 995.
[941] Record of Interments Blandford Cemetery, 1843-1872, p. 94, Blandford Cemetery, Petersburg, VA.
[942] U.S. Census 1850, Dinwiddie Co., VA, p. 347.
[943] *Daily South Side Democrat*, June 18, 1855, p. 2, c. 5, Petersburg, VA.
[944] Record of Interments Blandford Cemetery, 1843-1872, p. 94, Blandford Cemetery, Petersburg, VA.
[945] U.S. Census 1850, Prince George Co., VA, p. 061.
[946] U.S. Census 1860, Prince George Co., VA, p. 369.
[947] Record of Interments Blandford Cemetery, 1843-1872, p. 210, Blandford Cemetery, Petersburg, VA.
[948] *Daily South Side Democrat*, November 14, 1857, p. 2, c. 3, Petersburg, VA.
[949] Mexican War Pension File, SC #4664, National Archives and Records Administration, Washington, DC.
[950] U.S. Census 1850, Augusta Co., VA, p. 443.
[951] U.S. Census 1860, Highland Co., VA, p. 272.
[952] U.S. Census 1870, Highland Co., VA, p. 180.
[953] Matheny, John C. & Emma R., Vital Records of Highland Co., Virginia, p. 289, © 1986, John C. & Emma R. Matheny, 1718 Glenview Road, Richmond, VA.
[954] Matheny, John C. & Emma R., Vital Records of Highland Co., Virginia, p. 47, © 1986, John C. & Emma R. Matheny, 1718 Glenview Road, Richmond, VA.
[955] U.S. Census 1850, Frederick Co., VA, p. 291.
[956] U.S. Census 1870, Frederick Co., VA, p. 263.
[957] Caroline County Marriage Register, Caroline County Circuit Court Clerks Office, Bowling Green, VA.
[958] Mexican War Pension File, SC #3405, National Archives and Records Administration, Washington, D.C.
[959] Mexican War Pension File, WC #9172, National Archives and Records Administration, Washington, D.C.
[960] International Genealogical Index, Film #- 1059280.
[961] Mexican War Pension SC #10657, National Archives and Records Administration, Washington, D.C.
[962] U.S. Census 1850, Mathews Co., VA, p. 013.
[963] Mexican War Pension WC #7068, National Archives and Records Administration, Washington, D.C.
[964] U.S. Census 1850, Mecklenburg Co., VA, p. 064.

## OFF TO WAR

[965] U.S. Census 1860, Mecklenburg Co., VA, p. 325.
[966] Bell, Landon C., The Old Free State History of Lunenburg County and Southside Virginia, in 2 volumes, p. 154-159, © 1927, William Byrd Press, Richmond, VA.
[967] Records of the Office of the Judge Advocate General(Army), Record Group 153, EE 611, Case 7, National Archives & Records Administration, Washington, D.C.
[968] Marriage Bond, Bedford Co., VA, Circuit Court Clerk's Office, Bedford, VA.
[969] Mexican War Pension File, SC #5108, National Archives and Records Administration, Washington, DC.
[970] U.S. Census 1850, Jefferson Co., VA, p. 418.
[971] U.S. Census 1880, Jefferson County, WV.
[972] Record of Interments Blandford Cemetery, 1843-1872, p. 292, Blandford Cemetery, Petersburg, VA.
[973] U.S. Census 1850, Dinwiddie Co., VA, p. 393.
[974] Mexican War Pension File, SC #11407, National Archives and Records Administration, Washington, DC.
[975] HEATWOLE. History of the Heatwole family, from the beginning of the 17th century to the present time, © 1907, Cornelius J. Heatwole, 1907.
[976] Mexican War Pension File, WC #2039, National Archives and Records Administration, Washington, DC.
[977] U.S. Census 1850, Barbour Co., VA, p. 092.
[978] U.S. Census 1880, Jefferson Co., WV, p. W016.
[979] Mexican War Pension File, SC #20058, National Archives and Records Administration, Washington, DC.
[980] U.S. Census 1870, Augusta Co., VA, p. 226.
[981] Driver, Robert J., 52nd Virginia Infantry, © 1986, H.E. Howard, Inc., Lynchburg, VA.
[982] Mexican War Pension File, WC #13411, National Archives and Records Administration, Washington, DC.
[983] *Martinsburg Gazette*, August 10, 1848, p. 2, 6, Martinsburg, WV.
[984] Mexican War Pension File, SC #3644, National Archives and Records Administration, Washington, DC.
[985] U.S. Census 1880, Jefferson Co., WV, p. C007.
[986] Mexican War Pension File, SC #16503, National Archives and Records Administration, Washington, D.C.
[987] U.S. Census 1850, Augusta Co., VA, p. 301.
[988] U.S. Census 1860, Augusta Co., VA, p. 643.
[989] Mexican War Pension File, WC #4613, National Archives and Records Administration, Washington, D.C.
[990] Mexican War Pension File, SC #7225, National Archives and Records Administration, Washington, D.C.
[991] Mexican War Pension File, WC #11285, National Archives and Records Administration, Washington, D.C.
[992] Mexican War Pension File, SC #1555, National Archives and Records Administration, Washington, D.C.
[993] U.S. Census 1850, Montgomery Co., VA, p. 034.
[994] U.S. Census 1860, Montgomery Co., VA, p. 764.
[995] U.S. Census 1850, Frederick Co., VA, p. 342.
[996] Records of the Office of the Judge Advocate General(Army), Record Group 153, FF 74, Case 7, National Archives & Records Administration, Washington, D.C.
[997] U.S. Census 1850, Alexandria Co., VA, p. 373.
[998] U.S. Census 1860, Fairfax Co., VA, p. 799.
[999] Mexican War Pension File, SC #8181, National Archives and Records Administration, Washington, DC.
[1000] U.S. Census 1850, Jefferson Co., VA, p. 312.
[1001] U.S. Census 1860, Berkeley Co., VA, p. 681.
[1002] U.S. Census 1880, Berkeley Co., WV, p. M041.
[1003] Mexican War Pension File, WC #9818, National Archives and Records Administration, Washington, DC.
[1004] International Genealogical Index, Film #-0820514.

# VIRGINIA VOLUNTEERS IN MEXICO

[1005] Official Records of the War of the Rebellion, Ser. I, V. 29, part 1, pg. 722, © 1890, U.S. Government Printing Office, Wash., D.C.
[1006] Marriage Bonds, Alexandria, VA.
[1007] Death Register, Alexandria (Arlington), Co., VA.
[1008] U.S. Census 1850, Botetourt Co., VA, p. 154.
[1009] Driver, Robert J., Jr., 2nd Virginia Cavalry, © 1995, H.E. Howard, Inc., Lynchburg, VA.
[1010] Stiles, Kenneth L., 4th Virginia Cavalry, © 1985, H.E. Howard, Inc., Lynchburg, VA.
[1011] *Richmond Daily Examiner*, December 27, 1864, p. 2, c. 1.
[1012] Records of the Office of the Judge Advocate General(Army), Record Group 153, EE 611, Case 21, National Archives & Records Administration, Washington, D.C.
[1013] Mexican War Pension File, SC #1195, National Archives and Records Administration, Washington, DC.
[1014] Mexican War Pension File, WC #8839, National Archives and Records Administration, Washington, DC.
[1015] Mexican War Pension File, SC #3802, National Archives and Records Administration, Washington, D.C.
[1016] Wiatt, Alex L., 26th Virginia Infantry, © 1984, H.E. Howard, Inc., Lynchburg, VA.
[1017] U.S. Census 1870, King & Queen Co., VA, p. 377.
[1018] Records of the Office of the Judge Advocate General(Army), Record Group 153, EE 611, Case 46, National Archives & Records Administration, Washington, D.C.
[1019] Mexican War Pension File, WC #6067, National Archives and Records Administration, Washington, DC.
[1020] Marriage Register 1832-1855, Smyth Co., VA, Marion, VA
[1021] U.S. Census 1850, Hanover Co., VA, p. 401.
[1022] Koleszar, Marilyn Brewer, Ashland, Bedford and Taylor Virginia Light Artillery, © 1994, H.E. Howard, Inc., Lynchburg, VA.
[1023] International Genealogical Index, Film #-1553566.
[1024] U.S. Census 1850, Jefferson Co., VA, p. 353.
[1025] Mexican War Pension File, WC #1034, National Archives and Records Administration, Washington, D.C.
[1026] Marriage Register #A, pg. 311, Montgomery Co., VA.
[1027] U.S. Census 1860, Pulaski Co., VA, p. 770.
[1028] U.S. Census 1850, Jefferson Co., VA, p. 353.
[1029] U.S. Census 1850, Norfolk Co., VA, p. 169.
[1030] U.S. Census 1850, New Kent Co., VA, p. 338.
[1031] U.S. Census 1850, Amelia Co., VA, p. 065.
[1032] Mexican War Pension File, WC #1514, National Archives and Records Administration, Washington, DC.
[1033] Records of the Office of the Judge Advocate General(Army), Record Group 153, EE 455, Case 14, National Archives & Records Administration, Washington, D.C.
[1034] U.S. Census 1850, Henrico Co., VA, p. 394.
[1035] Mexican War Pension File, SC #14402, National Archives and Records Administration, Washington, DC.
[1036] U.S. Census 1850, Amherst Co., VA, p. 127B.
[1037] Mexican War Pension File, WC #10013, National Archives and Records Administration, Washington, DC.
[1038] *The Petersburg Republican*, December 29, 1848, p. 3, c. 1, Petersburg, VA.
[1039] U.S. Census 1850, Dinwiddie Co., VA, p. 364.
[1040] Mexican War Pension File, SC #2461, National Archives and Records Administration, Washington, D.C.
[1041] U.S. Census 1850, Augusta Co., VA, p. 212.
[1042] U.S. Census 1860, Augusta Co., VA, p. 833.
[1043] Illinois State Archives, Fulton Co. Marriages, Vol. D, pg. 104, Lic. #200.

# OFF TO WAR

[1044] Mexican War Pension File, SC #16022, National Archives and Records Administration, Washington, DC.
[1045] *Martinsburg Gazette,* July 24, 1845, p. 2, c. 7, Martinsburg, WV.
[1046] Chapla, John, 42nd Virginia Infantry, © 1983, H.E. Howard, Inc., Lynchburg, VA.
[1047] U.S. Census 1880, Berkeley Co., WV, p. R012.
[1048] Mexican War Pension File, WC #14205, National Archives and Records Administration, Washington, DC.
[1049] Marriage Register, District of Columbia.
[1050] U.S. Census 1850, Alexandria Co., VA, p. 325.
[1051] Information provided by Maxcine Lesueur, 1217 East Seahorse Lane, Gilbert, AZ 85234.
[1052] WPA Death Records, Delaware County, Indiana, Delaware County Historical Alliance, 120 E. Washington St. - Muncie, IN 47305.
[1053] Death Certificate of Rhoten Hurst, CH 7, Pg. 13, Delaware County Health Department, 100 W. Main St. Room 207, Muncie, IN 47305
[1054] U.S. Census 1850, Jefferson Co., VA, p. 387.
[1055] Pipenger, Wesley E., District of Columbia Marriage Licenses, Register 1, 1811-1858, © 1994, Family Line Publications, Westminster, MD.
[1056] U.S. Census 1850, Alexandria Co., VA, p. 317.
[1057] U.S. Census 1860, Alexandria Co., VA.
[1058] *Alexandria Gazette,* May 5, 1865, p. 2, Alexandria, VA.
[1059] I'Anson, William H., Doctoral Thesis, *Puerperal Fever or Childbed Fever*, Health Science and Human Services Library, University of Maryland, Baltimore, MD.
[1060] Journals of the Confederate Congress--Thirtieth Day--Tuesday, December 24. 1861, p. 624., Library of Congress, Washington, D.C.
[1061] *Rural Messenger*, January 1, 1876, p. 6, c. 2, Petersburg, VA.
[1062] U.S. Census 1850, Augusta Co., VA, p. 310.
[1063] International Genealogical Index, Film #-1553674.
[1064] Imoboden, Marvin L., Imoboden Family History, http://imboden-m.freeyellow.com/gen3.htm.
[1065] Record of Interments Blandford Cemetery, 1843-1872, p. 286, Blandford Cemetery, Petersburg, VA.
[1066] *The Daily Express*, December 31, 1858, p. 1, c. 5, Petersburg, VA.
[1067] Affidavit of Michael Kipps, Mexican War Pension SC #10885, National Archives and Records Administration, Washington, D.C.
[1068] Affidavit of Dr. C.M. Stiglman, Mexican War Pension SC #10885, National Archives and Records Administration, Washington, D.C.
[1069] Henry County Cemetery Records, Bassett Branch Historical Center, 3964 Fairystone Park Highway, Bassett, Virginia 24055.
[1070] Mexican War Pension WC #13675, National Archives and Records Administration, Washington, D.C.
[1071] Wallace, Lee A., Jr., 17th Virginia Infantry, ©1990, H.E. Howard, Inc., Lynchburg, VA.
[1072] Mexican War Pension File, WC #2636, National Archives and Records Administration, Washington, D.C.
[1073] U.S. Census 1850, Henrico Co., VA, p. 360.
[1074] Mexican War Pension File, WC #2638, National Archives and Records Administration, Washington, D.C.
[1075] Mexican War Pension File, SC # 2821, National Archives and Records Administration, Washington, D.C.
[1076] U.S. Census 1850, Berkeley Co., VA, p. 341.
[1077] Olson, John E., 21st Virginia Cavalry, © 1989, H.E. Howard, Inc., Lynchburg, VA.
[1078] U.S. Census 1850, Alexandria, VA, p. 381.
[1079] U.S. Census 1860, Alexandria, VA, p. 471.
[1080] Alexandria Gazette, February 17, 1872, p. 2.
[1081] Marriage Register, Alexandria, VA.
[1082] *Alexandria Gazette*, December 11, 1896, Alexandria, VA.
[1083] Death Certificate, Caroline Wenzel, 1917, Fairfax Co., VA, Fairfax Co. Circuit Court Archives.
[1084] U.S. Census 1850, Fairfax Co., VA, p. 110.

# VIRGINIA VOLUNTEERS IN MEXICO

[1085] U.S. Census 1860, Fairfax Co., VA, p. 842.
[1086] Fairfax County Secession Voters, Fairfax City Regional Library, Fairfax, VA.
[1087] Letter from T.C. Madison, Asst. Surgeon to Lt. Thomas P. August, June 27, 1847, Regimental Letter Book, 1st Virginia Volunteer Infantry, Record Group 153, National Archives & Records Administration, Washington, D.C
[1088] Mexican War Pension File, WC #1007, National Archives and Records Administration, Washington, D.C.
[1089] U.S. Census 1850, Campbell Co., VA, p. 113.
[1090] Mexican War Pension File, WC #4095, National Archives and Records Administration, Washington, DC.
[1091] Mexican War Pension File, SC #8801, National Archives and Records Administration, Washington, DC.
[1092] Franklin M. Garrett Necrology, Microfilm Roll 19, Frames 118 & 119, Atlanta Historical Society Library, Atlanta, GA.
[1093] U.S. Census 1860, Augusta Co., VA, p. 781.
[1094] U.S. Census 1850, Fayette Co., WV, p. 492.
[1095] U.S. Census 1860, Fayette Co., VA, p. 357.
[1096] Dickinson, Jack L., 8th Virginia Cavalry, © 1986, H.E. Howard, Inc., Lynchburg, VA.
[1097] Record of Interments Blandford Cemetery, 1843-1872, p. 106, Blandford Cemetery, Petersburg, VA.
[1098] Records of the Office of the Judge Advocate General(Army), Record Group 153, EE 611, Case 9, National Archives & Records Administration, Washington, D.C.
[1099] Record of Interments Blandford Cemetery, 1843-1872, p. 106, Blandford Cemetery, Petersburg, VA.
[1100] Mexican War Pension File, SC #8917, National Archives and Records Administration, Washington, D.C.
[1101] Mexican War Pension File, WC #12246, National Archives and Records Administration, Washington, D.C.
[1102] Mexican War Pension File, SC #2848, National Archives and Records Administration, Washington, DC.
[1103] U.S. Census 1850, Jefferson Co., VA, p. 307.
[1104] U.S. Census 1850, Norfolk Co., VA, p. 169.
[1105] Mexican War Pension File, WC #3355, National Archives and Records Administration, Washington, DC.
[1106] Mexican War Pension File, SA #25371, National Archives and Records Administration, Washington, DC.
[1107] U.S. Census 1850, Lunenburg, Co., VA.
[1108] U.S. Census 1860, Lunenburg Co., VA, p. 1018.
[1109] *Daily Express,* December 3, 1856, p. 2, c. 4, Petersburg, VA.
[1110] Mexican War Pension File, WC #5675, National Archives and Records Administration, Washington, D.C.
[1111] Robertson, James I., 18th Virginia Infantry, © 1984, H.E. Howard, Inc., Lynchburg, VA.
[1112] Mexican War Pension File, WC #5675, Letter of William H. Gills, 25th Btln. Va. Inf., 07/04/1888, National Archives and Records Administration, Washington, D.C.
[1113] Records of the Office of the Judge Advocate General(Army), Record Group 153, EE 611, Case 28, National Archives & Records Administration, Washington, D.C.
[1114] U.S. Census 1850, Elizabeth City Co., VA, p. 053.
[1115] Mexican War Pension File, SC #19614, National Archives and Records Administration, Washington, DC.
[1116] Mexican War Pension File, WC #13660, National Archives and Records Administration, Washington, DC.
[1117] Berkeley County, WV Marriage Register, p. 63, Circuit Court Clerks Office, Martinsburg, WV.
[1118] U.S. Census 1880, Berkeley Co., WV, p. R023.
[1119] Mexican War Pension File, SC #19614, Affidavit of J.W. McSherry, M.D., May 12, 1890, National Archives and Records Administration, Washington, DC.
[1120] Register of Deaths 1896-1906, Berkeley County, WV, p. 216, Circuit Court Clerks Office, Martinsburg, WV.

# OFF TO WAR

[1121] Frye, Dennis E., 2nd Virginia Infantry, © 1984, H.E. Howard, Inc., Lynchburg, VA.
[1122] Marriage Register, Goochland Co., VA.
[1123] Mexican War Pension File, SC #17775, National Archives and Records Administration, Washington, D.C.
[1124] U.S. Census 1850, Montgomery Co., VA, p. 04.
[1125] Marriage Register #A, pg. 329, Montgomery Co., VA.
[1126] Mexican War Pension File, WC #7935, National Archives and Records Administration, Washington, D.C.
[1127] Miles, Barry W. Moody K., Marriage Records of Accomack Co., VA, 1854-1895, © 1997, Heritage Books, Inc., Bowie, MD.
[1128] Mexican War Pension File, WC #6940, National Archives and Records Administration, Washington, D.C.
[1129] Mihalyka, Jean Merritt, Gravestone Inscriptions in Northampton Co., VA, © 1984, Virginia State Library, Richmond, VA.
[1130] Woodward, Harold R., Jr., Kemper: The Confederacy's Forgotten Son, c. 1993, Rockbridge Publishing Company, Natural Bridge Station, VA.
[1131] Mexican War Pension File, SC #9258, National Archives and Records Administration, Washington, DC.
[1132] Baird, Nancy C., Early Fauquier County Marriage Bonds 1759-1854, © 1965, Washington, D.C.
[1133] U.S. Census 1850, Doddridge Co., VA, p. 31.
[1134] Letter from Brig. Gen. C. Cushing to Col. John F. Hamtramck, August 16, 1847, Regimental Letter Book, 1st Virginia Volunteer Infantry, Record Group 153, National Archives & Records Administration, Washington, D.C
[1135] Marriage Bond, Augusta Co., VA.
[1136] Letter from 1st Lt. Robert H. Kinney to Col. John F. Hamtramck, June 10, 1847, Regimental Letter Book, 1st Virginia Volunteer Infantry, Record Group 153, National Archives & Records Administration, Washington, D.C.
[1137] U.S. Census 1850, Augusta Co., VA, p. 389.
[1138] U.S. Census 1850, Mineral Co., VA, p. 161.
[1139] Mexican War Pension File, SC #10920, National Archives and Records Administration, Washington, DC.
[1140] Marriage Register #1, pg. 3, Montgomery Co., VA.
[1141] U.S. Census 1860, Montgomery Co., VA, p. 680.
[1142] Marriage License Index, Bk. 5, p. 186, Berkeley Co., WV, Circuit Court Clerk's Office, Martinsburg, WV.
[1143] Mexican War Pension SC #9850, National Archives and Records Administration, Washington, D.C.
[1144] U.S. Census 1850, Fairfax Co., VA, p. 177.
[1145] *Alexandria Gazette*, November 27, 1849, Alexandria, VA.
[1146] U.S. Census 1850, Fairfax Co., VA, p. 177.
[1147] Mexican War Pension WC #6104, National Archives and Records Administration, Washington, D.C.
[1148] U.S. Census 1860, Augusta Co., VA, p. 954.
[1149] *The Petersburg Republican*, July 21, 1848, p. 2, c. 6, Petersburg, VA.
[1150] U.S. Census 1850, Augusta Co., VA, p. 296.
[1151] Mexican War Pension File, WC #5234, National Archives and Records Administration, Washington, D.C.
[1152] U.S. Census 1850, Dinwiddie Co., VA, p. 417.
[1153] U.S. Census 1860, Dinwiddie Co., VA, p. 336.
[1154] Mexican War Pension SC #14536, National Archives and Records Administration, Washington, D.C
[1155] U.S. Census 1870, Frederick Co., VA, p. 014.
[1156] Mexican War Pension WC #9083, National Archives and Records Administration, Washington, D.C.
[1157] Hollingsworth, Pat, 1908 Deaths, Brown County, Kansas, Pat1218@aol.com.
[1158] Mexican War Pension File, WC #2328, National Archives and Records Administration, Washington, D.C.

## VIRGINIA VOLUNTEERS IN MEXICO

[1159] Mexican War Pension File, WC #2328, Physician's Affidavit, National Archives and Records Administration, Washington, D.C.
[1160] Simmons, Samuel William, The Pegram's of Virginia and Their Descendants, 1688-1984, © 1985, :S.W. Simmons., Atlanta, Ga.
[1161] U.S. Census 1860, Dinwiddie Co., VA, p. 080.
[1162] Mexican War Pension File, SC #10813, National Archives and Records Administration, Washington, D.C.
[1163] U.S. Census 1850, Montgomery Co., VA, p. 046.
[1164] Sherwood, W. Cullen, Amherst Artillery, Albemarle Artillery and Sturdivant's Battery, ©1996, H.E. Howard, Inc., Lynchburg, VA.
[1165] Caroline County Marriage Register, Caroline County Circuit Court Clerks Office, Bowling Green, VA.
[1166] U.S. Census 1850, Henrico Co., VA, p. 441.
[1167] Mexican War Pension File, SC #5636, National Archives and Records Administration, Washington, D.C.
[1168] Marriage Register #A, pg. 309, Montgomery Co., VA.
[1169] U.S. Census 1850, Montgomery Co., VA, p. 060.
[1170] U.S. Census 1860, Montgomery Co., VA, p. 655.
[1171] Mexican War Pension File, SC #20163, National Archives and Records Administration, Washington, DC.
[1172] Mexican War Pension File, SC #20163, Copy of a Court Order, City of Richmond, Va. Hustings Court, 12/05/1835, National Archives and Records Administration, Washington, DC.
[1173] Biographical Directory of the United States Congress, http://bioguide.congress.gov/.
[1174] Records of the Office of the Judge Advocate General(Army), Record Group 153, EE 427, Case 22, National Archives & Records Administration, Washington, D.C.
[1175] Biographical Directory of the United States Congress, http://bioguide.congress.gov/.
[1176] U.S. Census 1850, Henrico Co., VA, p. 456.
[1177] U.S. Census 1850, Fairfax Co., VA, p. 178.
[1178] Marriage Register, District of Columbia.
[1179] U.S. Census 1860, Fairfax Co., VA, p. 935.
[1180] Mexican War Pension SC #1241, National Archives and Records Administration, Washington, D.C.
[1181] U.S. Census 1860, Montgomery Co., VA, p. 680.
[1182] Mexican War Pension File, WC #2598, National Archives and Records Administration, Washington, D.C.
[1183] U.S. Census 1860, Montgomery Co., VA, p. 680.
[1184] Mexican War Pension File, SC #12681, National Archives and Records Administration, Washington, DC.
[1185] Marriage Register #1, pg. 3, Montgomery Co., VA.
[1186] Mexican War Pension File, WC #6690, National Archives and Records Administration, Washington, DC.
[1187] *The Petersburg Republican*, January 12, 1849, p. 2, c. 5, Petersburg, VA.
[1188] Mexican War Pension File, SC #20290, National Archives and Records Administration, Washington, D.C.
[1189] Mexican War Pension File, SC #20290, Letter from Charles Loftin to his Pension Attorney, March 11, 1895, National Archives and Records Administration, Washington, D.C.
[1190] Mexican War Pension File, WA #1317, National Archives and Records Administration, Washington, D.C.
[1191] International Genealogical Index, Film #-452847.
[1192] U.S. Census 1850, Bedford Co., VA, p. 174.
[1193] Record of Interments Blandford Cemetery, 1843-1872, p. 94, Blandford Cemetery, Petersburg, VA.
[1194] U.S. Census 1850, Chesterfield Co., VA, p. 161.
[1195] *Daily South Side Democrat*, June 30, 1855, p. 2, c. 6, Petersburg, VA
[1196] U.S. Census 1860, Augusta Co., VA, p. 1097.
[1197] International Genealogical Index, Film #-456430.
[1198] Mexican War Pension File, SA #23772, National Archives and Records Administration, Washington, D.C.

# OFF TO WAR

[1199] Mexican War Pension File, SC #8446, National Archives and Records Administration, Washington, DC.
[1200] Marriage Register #A, pg. 255, Montgomery Co., VA.
[1201] U.S. Census 1850, Henrico Co., VA, p. 249.
[1202] Mexican War Pension File, SC #9686, National Archives and Records Administration, Washington, DC.
[1203] *South Bend Daily Tribune*, July 2, 1896, South Bend, IN.
[1204] Record of Interments Blandford Cemetery, 1888-1905, p. 54, Blandford Cemetery, Petersburg, VA.
[1205] Mexican War Pension File, SC #17924, National Archives and Records Administration, Washington, D.C.
[1206] Mexican War Pension File, WC #9101, National Archives and Records Administration, Washington, D.C.
[1207] Record of Interments Blandford Cemetery, 1888-1905, p. 54, Blandford Cemetery, Petersburg, VA.
[1208] Mexican War Pension File, WC #37, Marriage License, National Archives and Records Administration, Washington, D.C.
[1209] Mexican War Pension File, WC #37, Affidavit of Robert D. Battle, March 11, 1887, National Archives and Records Administration, Washington, D.C.
[1210] Mexican War Pension File, WC #37, Death Certificate, National Archives and Records Administration, Washington, D.C.
[1211] Mexican War Pension File, WC #37, National Archives and Records Administration, Washington, D.C.
[1212] *Craig's Daguerreian Registry The Acknowledged Resource on American Photographers 1839-1860*, www.daguerreotype.com John S. Craig, P.O. Box 1637, Torrington, CT, (860) 496-9791.
[1213] *Philadelphia Ledger*, June 18, 1847, Philadelphia, Pa., Excerpt of letter of Capt. Smith P. Bankhead to the Hon. Robert M. Lee.
[1214] Letter from Col. John F. Hamtramck to General John E. Wool, July 10, 1847; Regimental Letter Book, 1st Virginia Volunteer Infantry, Record Group 153, National Archives & Records Administration, Washington, D.C
[1215] Records of the Office of the Judge Advocate General(Army), Record Group 153, FF 74, Case 13, National Archives & Records Administration, Washington, D.C.
[1216] Mexican War Diary of James Lawson Kemper, Virginia Magazine of History & Biography, v. 74 (1966), p. 407, Richmond, VA.
[1217] Mexican War Pension File, WC #10486, National Archives and Records Administration, Washington, DC.
[1218] U.S. Census 1850, Henrico Co., VA, p. 505.
[1219] Records of the Office of the Judge Advocate General(Army), Record Group 153, EE 611, Case 3, National Archives & Records Administration, Washington, D.C.
[1220] Records of the Office of the Judge Advocate General(Army), Record Group 153, EE 611, Case 53, National Archives & Records Administration, Washington, D.C.
[1221] Records of the Office of the Judge Advocate General(Army), Record Group 153, FF 81, Case 7, National Archives & Records Administration, Washington, D.C.
[1222] International Genealogical Index, Film #- 0013935.
[1223] U.S. Census 1850, Henrico Co., VA, p. 513.
[1224] Records of the Office of the Judge Advocate General(Army), Record Group 153, EE 554, Case 31, National Archives & Records Administration, Washington, D.C.
[1225] Mexican War Pension WA #19135, National Archives and Records Administration, Washington, D.C.
[1226] Records of the Office of the Judge Advocate General(Army), Record Group 153, EE 553, Case 3, National Archives & Records Administration, Washington, D.C.
[1227] U.S. Census 1850, Henrico Co., VA, p. 320.
[1228] U.S. Census 1860, Henrico Co., VA, p. 652.
[1229] Pamphlet, Proceedings of an Annual Assembly of the Grand Commandery of a Knights Templar of the Stat of Virginia, Held in  Richmond, Virginia December 12, 1861, James E. Goode, Main St., Richmond, VA, http://users.sitestar.net/~mfulcher/GCHA.htm
[1230] Mexican War Pension File, SC #7940, National Archives and Records Administration, Washington, D.C.
[1231] Maxwell Genealogy File, Berkeley County Historical Society, Martinsburg, WV.

# VIRGINIA VOLUNTEERS IN MEXICO

[1232] *Martinsburg Gazette*, July 11, 1844, p. 2, c. 7, Martinsburg, WV.
[1233] U.S. Census 1860, Jefferson Co., VA, p. 791.
[1234] Register of Deaths 1887-1896, Berkeley County, WV, p. 136, Circuit Court Clerks Office, Martinsburg, WV.
[1235] Mexican War Pension File, SC #7284, National Archives and Records Administration, Washington, D.C.
[1236] *The Bastrop Advertiser*, November 1, 1873, Bastrop, Texas.
[1237] *The Bastrop Advertiser*, December 20, 1873, Bastrop, Texas.
[1238] *The Bastrop Advertiser*, January 16, 1875, Bastrop, Texas.
[1239] Hewitt, Janet B., The Roster of Confederate Soldiers 1861-1865, © 1996, Broadfoot Publishing Co., Wilmington, NC.
[1240] Record of Interments Blandford Cemetery, 1888-1905, p. 102, Blandford Cemetery, Petersburg, VA.
[1241] *Daily Courier*, October 12, 1870, p. 1, c. 4, Petersburg, VA.
[1242] Record of Interments Blandford Cemetery, 1888-1905, p. 102, Blandford Cemetery, Petersburg, VA.
[1243] Mexican War Pension File, WC #12169, National Archives and Records Administration, Washington, D.C.
[1244] Mexican War Pension File, OW IC #134490, Affidavit of Dennis McCarthy, October 11, 1887, National Archives and Records Administration, Washington, D.C.
[1245] Mexican War Pension File, WC #12169, Letter of daughter, Ella Dodson, December 12, 1913, National Archives and records Administration, Washington, D.C.
[1246] Records of the Office of the Judge Advocate General(Army), Record Group 153, EE 427, Case 4, National Archives & Records Administration, Washington, D.C.
[1247] Mexican War Pension File, SC #5736, National Archives and Records Administration, Washington, DC.
[1248] U.S. Census 1870, Montgomery Co., VA, p. 11.
[1249] Mexican War Pension File, WC #10986, National Archives and Records Administration, Washington, DC.
[1250] Records of the Office of the Judge Advocate General(Army), Record Group 153, EE 611, Case 16, National Archives & Records Administration, Washington, D.C.
[1251] Mexican War Pension File, SC #3988, National Archives and Records Administration, Washington, D.C.
[1252] *The Petersburg Republican*, February 26, 1849, p. 3, c. 1, Petersburg, VA.
[1253] *The Petersburg Republican*, February 1, 1847, p. 4, c. 3, Petersburg, VA.
[1254] *Petersburg Index & Appeal*, August 22, 1874, p. 2, c. 4 & p. 3, c. 2, Petersburg, VA.
[1255] *Petersburg Index & Appeal*, August 24, 1874, p. 3, c. 1, Petersburg, VA
[1256] Record of Interments Blandford Cemetery, 1872-1888, p. 35, Blandford Cemetery, Petersburg, VA.
[1257] Mexican War Pension File WC #589 National Archives and records Administration, Washington, D.C.
[1258] International Genealogical Index, Film #- 2034623.
[1259] U.S. Census 1850, Cumberland Co., VA, p. 283.
[1260] U.S. Census 1850, Frederick Co., VA, p. 361.
[1261] Records of the Office of the Judge Advocate General(Army), Record Group 153, EE 611, Case 35, National Archives & Records Administration, Washington, D.C.
[1262] U.S. Census 1850, Frederick Co., VA, p. 361.
[1263] http://www.rootsweb.com/~wvhampsh/mexw.htm
[1264] Mexican War Pension File, SC #2918, National Archives and Records Administration, Washington, D.C.
[1265] U.S. Census 1860, Augusta Co., VA, p. 608.
[1266] Armstrong, Richard L., 25th Virginia Infantry and 9th Battalion Virginia Infantry, © 1990, H.E. Howard, Inc., Lynchburg, VA.
[1267] U.S. Census 1870, Augusta Co., VA, p. 427.
[1268] Mexican War Pension File, WC #14900, National Archives and Records Administration, Washington, D.C.
[1269] Mexican War Pension File WC #4600 National Archives and Records Administration, Washington, D.C
[1270] Mexican War Pension SC #18489, National Archives and Records Administration, Washington, D.C.

# OFF TO WAR

[1271] Records of the Office of the Judge Advocate General(Army), Record Group 153, EE 553, Case 2, National Archives & Records Administration, Washington, D.C.
[1272] U.S. Census 1850, Cumberland Co., VA, p. 286.
[1273] Mexican War Pension SC #18489, National Archives and Records Administration, Washington, D.C.
[1274] U.S. Census 1850, Henrico Co., VA, p. 387.
[1275] Fairfax County Deed Book E-3, p. 325.
[1276] U.S. Census 1850, Fairfax Co., VA, p. 132.
[1277] Mexican War Pension File, WC #7630, National Archives and Records Administration, Washington, DC.
[1278] U.S. Census 1860, Jefferson Co., VA, p. 934.
[1279] Letter from Col. J.F. Hamtramck to Capt. Irwin McDowell, July 15, 1847, Regimental Letter Book, 1st Virginia Volunteer Infantry, Record Group 153, National Archives & Records Administration, Washington, D.C
[1280] Mexican War Diary of James Lawson Kemper, Virginia Magazine of History & Biography, v. 74 (1966, p. 421, Richmond, VA.
[1281] Records of the Office of the Judge Advocate General(Army), Record Group 153, EE 455, Case 10, National Archives & Records Administration, Washington, D.C.
[1282] Mexican War Pension File, WC #14974, National Archives and Records Administration, Washington, DC.
[1283] Mexican War Pension File, SC #10037, National Archives and Records Administration, Washington, DC.
[1284] U.S. Census 1860, Hampshire Co., WV, p. 312.
[1285] Mexican War Pension File, WC #15160, National Archives and Records Administration, Washington, DC.
[1286] Records of the Office of the Judge Advocate General(Army), Record Group 153, FF 74, Case 12, National Archives & Records Administration, Washington, D.C.
[1287] Mexican War Pension File, WC #261, National Archives and Records Administration, Washington, D.C.
[1288] U.S. Census 1860, Augusta Co., VA, p. 740.
[1289] Death Register, Armistead T. Mills, 07/23/1892, Fairfax Co., VA, Fairfax Co. Circuit Court Clerk's Office.
[1290] U.S. Census 1850, Fairfax Co., VA, p. 191.
[1291] Marriage Register, District of Columbia, 1811-1858, p. 416.
[1292] U.S. Census 1860, Fairfax Co., VA, p. 918.
[1293] Fairfax County Secession Voters, Fairfax City Regional Library, Fairfax, VA.
[1294] U.S. Census 1870, Fairfax Co., VA, p. 401.
[1295] District of Columbia Marriage Register 1, 1858 - 1870, Washington, D.C., v. 1, p. 188.
[1296] U.S. Census 1880, Fairfax Co., VA, p. 378.
[1297] Mexican War Pension SC #2490, National Archives and Records Administration, Washington, D.C.
[1298] Death Register, Armistead T. Mills, 07/23/1892, Fairfax Co., VA, Fairfax Co. Circuit Court Clerk's Office.
[1299] Information provided by Anthony Long, 1110 West Central Ave., Davidsonville Md., 21035.
[1300] U.S. Census 1860, Fairfax Co., VA, p. 915.
[1301] U.S. Census 1850, Henrico Co., VA, p. 259.
[1302] Information supplied by Leonora Margaret & Godfrey Housley, Tualatin, OR.
[1303] Mexican War Pension File, SC #7619, National Archives and Records Administration, Washington, D.C.
[1304] U.S. Census 1850, Montgomery Co., VA, p. 046.
[1305] U.S. Census 1860, Montgomery Co., VA, p. 726.
[1306] Mexican War Pension WC #10988, National Archives and Records Administration, Washington, D.C.
[1307] U.S. Census 1860, Fairfax Co., VA, p. 910.
[1308] Fairfax County Order Book 1858, p. 121, Fairfax County Circuit Court Archives, Fairfax VA.
[1309] Keen, Hugh C. & Mewborn, Horace, 43rd Battalion Virginia Cavalry, Mosby's Command, © 1993, H.E. Howard, Inc. Lynchburg, VA.
[1310] *Alexandria Gazette*, January 13, 1896, Alexandria, VA.

# VIRGINIA VOLUNTEERS IN MEXICO

[1311] Deposition of Lucelia Minor, Mexican War Pension WC #10988, National Archives and Records Administration, Washington, D.C.
[1312] Deposition of Charles King, Mexican War Pension WC #10988, National Archives and Records Administration, Washington, D.C.
[1313] Deposition of Temperence Turberman, Mexican War Pension WC #10988, National Archives and Records Administration, Washington, D.C.
[1314] U.S. Census 1850, Alexandria Co., VA, p. 405.
[1315] U.S. Census 1850, Alexandria Co., VA, p. 405.
[1316] U.S. Census 1860, Alexandria Co., VA, p. 256.
[1317] Death Register, p. 41, Alexandria (Arlington) Co., VA.
[1318] Mexican War Pension WC #4144, National Archives and Records Administration, Washington, D.C.
[1319] Information supplied by Skiles F. Montague, 1016 Main St., Darby, PA, 19023.
[1320] Mexican War Pension WC #492, National Archives and Records Administration, Washington, D.C.
[1321] District of Columbia Marriage Register 1, 1811 - 1858, Washington, D.C.
[1322] Mexican War Pension WC #717, National Archives and Records Administration, Washington, D.C.
[1323] Mexican War Pension SC #19440, National Archives and Records Administration, Washington, D.C.
[1324] Affidavit of Undertaker, Mexican War Pension WC #13241,\ National Archives and Records Administration, Washington, D.C.
[1325] Mexican War Pension File, WC #2290, National Archives and Records Administration, Washington, D.C.
[1326] Fairfax County Chancery Suit, Blackburn v. Blackburn (1838), CCF #4w, Fairfax County Circuit Court Archives, Fairfax, VA.
[1327] Fairfax County Chancery Suit, Moore v. Moore (1858), SCF #224, Fairfax County Circuit Court Archives, Fairfax, VA.
[1328] District of Columbia Marriage Register 1, 1811 - 1858, Washington, D.C.
[1329] U.S. Census 1860, Fairfax Co., VA, p. 882.
[1330] U.S. Census 1870, Fairfax Co., VA, p. 365.
[1331] Boyd's Washington Directories 1893-1897.
[1332] U.S. Census 1850, Fairfax Co., VA, p. 165.
[1333] Mexican War Pension SC #7286, National Archives and Records Administration, Washington, D.C.
[1334] U.S. Census 1860, Fairfax Co., VA, p. 871.
[1335] Record of Interments Blandford Cemetery, 1872-1888, p. 140, Blandford Cemetery, Petersburg, VA.
[1336] Mexican War Pension File, WC #201, National Archives and Records Administration, Washington, D.C.
[1337] Record of Interments Blandford Cemetery, 1872-1888, p. 140, Blandford Cemetery, Petersburg, VA.
[1338] Mexican War Pension File, SC #6114, National Archives and Records Administration, Washington, D.C.
[1339] Marriage Bonds, Mecklenburg Co., VA.
[1340] U.S. Census 1850, Mecklenburg Co., VA, p. 085.
[1341] Mexican War Diary of James Lawson Kemper, Virginia Magazine of History & Biography, v. 74 (1966, p. 427.
[1342] U.S. Census 1850, Buckingham Co., VA, p. 367.
[1343] U.S. Census 1870, Buckingham Co., VA, p. 226.
[1344] Mexican War Pension File, SC #3009, National Archives and Records Administration, Washington, DC.
[1345] U.S. Census 1870, Wythe Co., VA, p. 430.
[1346] U.S. Census 1880, Wythe Co., VA, p. 079.
[1347] *The Petersburg Republican*, July 29, 1843, p. 3, c. 5, Petersburg, VA.
[1348] Records of the Office of the Judge Advocate General(Army), Record Group 153, EE 560, National Archives & Records Administration, Washington, D.C.
[1349] City of Radford Historical Society, Radford, VA.
[1350] U.S. Census 1850, Henrico Co., VA, p. 416.
[1351] Record of Interments Blandford Cemetery, 1843-1872, p. 26, Blandford Cemetery, Petersburg, VA.
[1352] Mexican War Pension SC #19868, National Archives and Records Administration, Washington, D.C.

# OFF TO WAR

[1353] Mexican War Pension File, SC #6844, National Archives and Records Administration, Washington, DC.
[1354] Mexican War Pension File, WA #7130, National Archives and Records Administration, Washington, DC.
[1355] Letter from Col. John F. Hamtramck to Brig. Gen. C. Cushing, July 1847, Regimental Letter Book, 1st Virginia Volunteer Infantry, Record Group 153, National Archives & Records Administration, Washington, D.C
[1356] U.S. Census 1850, Prince George Co., VA, p. 066.
[1357] Information supplied by Skiles F. Montague, 1016 Main Street, Darby, PA, 19023.
[1358] U.S. Census 1850, Essex Co., VA, p. 070.
[1359] Mexican War Pension File, SC #3314, National Archives and Records Administration, Washington, DC.
[1360] U.S. Census 1850, Montgomery Co., VA, p. 058.
[1361] Marriage Register #1, pg. 7, Montgomery Co., VA.
[1362] U.S. Census 1860, Montgomery Co., VA, p. 698.
[1363] U.S. Census 1850, Southampton Co., VA, p. 244a.
[1364] *Daily Index,* March 29, 1872, p. 3, c. 2, Petersburg, VA.
[1365] U.S. Census 1850, Brunswick Co., VA, p. 329.
[1366] U.S. Census 1850, Southampton Co., VA, p. 298.
[1367] Mexican War Pension File, SC #18702, National Archives and Records Administration, Washington, DC.
[1368] U.S. Census 1850, Augusta Co., VA, p. 294.
[1369] U.S. Census 1860, Augusta Co., VA, p. 740.
[1370] U.S. Census 1850, Augusta Co., VA, p. 229.
[1371] Mexican War Pension File, SC #16338, Affidavit of Soldier, National Archives and Records Administration, Washington, D.C.
[1372] Nansemond County Civil War Veterans, Bruce Saunders and Marion Joyner Watson, © Southampton County Historical Society.
[1373] Mexican War Pension WC #2876, National Archives and Records Administration, Washington, D.C.
[1374] District of Columbia Marriage Register 1, 1811 - 1858, Washington, D.C.
[1375] U.S. Census 1870, Washington Co., MS, p. 016.
[1376] Marriage Register, Washington Co., MS, Circuit Court Clerks Office, Washington, MS.
[1377] U.S. Census 1850, Norfolk Co., VA, p. 134.
[1378] Marriage Bond, Bk. 7, p. 17, Berkeley Co., WV, Circuit Court Clerk's Office, Martinsburg, WV.
[1379] *Martinsburg Gazette,* May 30, 1844, p. 3, 1., Martinsburg, WV.
[1380] *Martinsburg Gazette,* March 5, 1846, p. 3, 1., Martinsburg, WV.
[1381] *Martinsburg Gazette,* April 16, 1846, p. 3, 2., Martinsburg, WV.
[1382] International Genealogical Index, Film #-1553420.
[1383] U.S. Census 1860, Campbell Co., VA, p. 516.
[1384] International Genealogical Index, Film #-0820254.
[1385] Marriage Bond, Mecklenburg Co., VA, Circuit Court Clerk's Office, Boydton, VA.
[1386] U.S. Census 1850, Mecklenburg Co., VA, p. 101.
[1387] U.S. Census 1860, Chesterfield Co., VA, p. 425.
[1388] Marriage Register of Lunenburg Co., VA 1746-1850, p. 65.
[1389] U.S. Census 1850, Lunenburg Co., VA, p.12.
[1390] U.S. Census 1860, Lunenburg Co., VA, p. 973.
[1391] Mexican War Pension File, WC #10362, National Archives and Records Administration, Washington, D.C.
[1392] U.S. Census 1850, Campbell Co., VA, p. 084.
[1393] U.S. Census 1860, Campbell Co., VA, p. 337.
[1394] *Martinsburg Gazette,* July 30, 1846, p. 3, 2., Martinsburg, WV.
[1395] U.S. Census 1850, Wythe Co., VA, p. 268.
[1396] U.S. Census 1860, Wythe Co., VA, p. 868.
[1397] Marriage Bonds, Wythe Co., VA.
[1398] U.S. Census 1850, Wythe Co., VA, p. 249.

# VIRGINIA VOLUNTEERS IN MEXICO

[1399] U.S. Census 1880, Wythe Co., VA, p. 113.
[1400] Mexican War Pension File, WC #1604, National Archives and Records Administration, Washington, DC.
[1401] U.S. Census 1850, Augusta Co., VA, p. 301.
[1402] U.S. Census 1860, Augusta Co., VA, p. 751.
[1403] "BOSS RULE." The Handbook of Texas Online.
http://www.tsha.utexas.edu/handbook/online/articles/view/BB/wmb1.html
[1404] "PARR, ARCHER." The Handbook of Texas Online.
http://www.tsha.utexas.edu/handbook/online/articles/view/PP/fpa35.html
[1405] "JIM WELLS COUNTY." The Handbook of Texas Online.
http://www.tsha.utexas.edu/handbook/online/articles/view/JJ/hcj7.html
[1406] U.S. Census 1850, Lunenburg Co., VA, p. 021.
[1407] Mexican War Pension File, WC #1621, National Archives and Records Administration, Washington, D.C.
[1408] U.S. Census 1850, Dinwiddie Co., VA, p. 151.
[1409] Record of Interments Blandford Cemetery, 1843-1872, p. 242, Blandford Cemetery, Petersburg, VA.
[1410] U.S. Census 1860, Sussex Co., VA, p. 486.
[1411] Mexican War Pension File, SC #4453, National Archives and Records Administration, Washington, DC.
[1412] Record of Interments Blandford Cemetery, 1843-1872, p. 54, Blandford Cemetery, Petersburg, VA.
[1413] International Genealogical Index, Film #-0820070.
[1414] U.S. Census 1850, Norfolk Co., VA, p. 171.
[1415] Mexican War Pension File, SC #5412, National Archives and Records Administration, Washington, D.C.
[1416] U.S. Census 1850, Augusta Co., VA, p. 309.
[1417] U.S. Census 1860, Augusta Co., VA, p. 780.
[1418] U.S. Census 1870, Augusta Co., VA, p. 213.
[1419] Letter from Col. John F. Hamtramck to Robert Jones, Adjutant General, September 25, 1847, Regimental Letter Book, 1st Virginia Volunteer Infantry, Record Group 153, National Archives & Records Administration, Washington, D.C
[1420] Letter from Lt. Franklin Pegram to Col. John F. Hamtramck, October 31, 1847, Regimental Letter Book, 1st Virginia Volunteer Infantry, Record Group 153, National Archives & Records Administration, Washington, D.C
[1421] U.S. Census 1850, Dinwiddie Co., VA, p. 349.
[1422] U.S. Census 1850, Augusta Co., VA, p. 377.
[1423] Augusta County Heritage Committee, Augusta Co., VA Heritage Book, 1732-1988, © 1998, Walsworth Publishing Co., Summerville, WV.
[1424] Deposition of Greenberry B. Terrell, March 20, 1894, Mexican War Pension File of Pvt. James T. Pelter, WA #12000, National Archives and Records Administration, Washington, D.C.
[1425] Mexican War Pension File WA #12000, National Archives and records Administration, Washington, D.C.
[1426] U.S. Census 1850, Lee Co., VA, p. 359.
[1427] *The Petersburg Republican*, January 1, 1849, p. 3, c. 1, Petersburg, VA.
[1428] U.S. Census 1850, Dinwiddie Co., VA, p. 344.
[1429] U.S. Census 1860, Amherst Co., VA, p. 420.
[1430] U.S. Census 1870, Norfolk Co., VA, p. 200.
[1431] Lipscomb, Bernard F., Minutes of the One Hundred and Eleventh Session of the Virginia Annual Conference of the Methodist Episcopal Church, South, held at Danville, VA, November 22-30, 1893, © 1893, J.W. Ferguson & Son, Richmond, VA.
[1432] Mexican War Pension File, WC #9092, National Archives and Records Administration, Washington, D.C.
[1433] Record of Interments Blandford Cemetery, 1888-1905, p. 51, Blandford Cemetery, Petersburg, VA.
[1434] Record of Interments Blandford Cemetery, 1843-1872, p. 378, Blandford Cemetery, Petersburg, VA.
[1435] U.S. Census 1860, Dinwiddie Co., VA, p. 167.
[1436] *The Daily Express*, April 4, 1866, p. 2, c. 4, Petersburg, VA.

## OFF TO WAR

[1437] Record of Interments Blandford Cemetery, 1843-1872, p. 378, Blandford Cemetery, Petersburg, VA.
[1438] Mexican War Pension File, WC #3593, National Archives and Records Administration, Washington, D.C.
[1439] Mexican War Pension File, WC #5529, National Archives and Records Administration, Washington, DC.
[1440] U.S. Census 1850, Barbour Co., VA, p. 29.
[1441] U.S. Census 1860, Tucker Co., VA, p. 921.
[1442] U.S. Census 1870, Barbour Co., WV, p. 190.
[1443] U.S. Census 1850, Montgomery Co., VA, p. 049.
[1444] U.S. Census 1850, Caroline Co., VA, p. 225.
[1445] International Genealogical Index, Film #-1058114.
[1446] U.S. Census 1850, Henrico Co., VA, p. 495.
[1447] U.S. Census 1860, Henrico Co., VA, p. 665.
[1448] Mexican War Pension File, SC #9418, National Archives and Records Administration, Washington, DC.
[1449] Tombstone, Woodhouse Cemetery, Walnut Island, Grandy, N.C. (off Rt. 158, Walnut Island Blvd., *SR 1186*, east, to Faris Dr., *SR1189*.)
[1450] Currituck County Marriage Register B, p. 23, Marriage Record of dau. Sarah F. Pitts to Enoch D. Poyner, 12/11/1875, Currituck County Register of Deeds, Currituck Co., NC.
[1451] Mexican War Pension File, SC #15230, National Archives and Records Administration, Washington, D.C.
[1452] U.S. Census 1850, Currituck, NC, p. 177.
[1453] U.S. Census 1860, Princess Anne Co., VA, p. 655.
[1454] U.S. Census 1870, Currituck Co., NC, p. 243.
[1455] The Heritage of Currituck County, p. 358, © 1985, The Albemarle Genealogical Society, Currituck, NC.
[1456] Records of the Office of the Judge Advocate General(Army), Record Group 153, EE 455, Case 13, National Archives & Records Administration, Washington, D.C.
[1457] U.S. Census 1850, Dinwiddie Co., VA, p. 349.
[1458] U.S. Census 1850, Dinwiddie Co., VA, p. 164.
[1459] Mexican War Pension File, WC #2387, National Archives and Records Administration, Washington, DC.
[1460] U.S. Census 1860, Henrico Co., VA, p. 112.
[1461] U.S. Census 1870, Henrico Co., VA, p. 037.
[1462] Mexican War Pension File, SC #3488, National Archives and Records Administration, Washington, D.C.
[1463] U.S. Census 1850, Augusta Co., VA, p. 320.
[1464] U.S. Census 1850, Augusta Co., VA, p. 320.
[1465] U.S. Census 1850, Pulaski Co., VA, p. 697.
[1466] *Richmond Enquirer*, November 16, 1849, p. 2, c. 6, Richmond, VA.
[1467] U.S. Census 1850, Henrico Co., VA, p. 263.
[1468] Christian, W. Asbury, D.D., Richmond: Her Past and Present, p. 448, © 1912, L.H. Jenkins, Richmond, VA.
[1469] Mexican War Pension File, SC #13355, National Archives and Records Administration, Washington, DC.
[1470] *The Petersburg Republican,* September 13, 1847, p. 2, c. 2; January 24, 1848, p. 4, c. 2; January 28, 1848, p. 2, c. 5.
[1471] Record of Interments Blandford Cemetery, 1843-1872, p. 22, Blandford Cemetery, Petersburg, VA.
[1472] Mexican War Pension File, SC #17865, National Archives and Records Administration, Washington, DC.
[1473] Mexican War Pension File, SC #3732, National Archives and Records Administration, Washington, DC.
[1474] A History of Jefferson County, West Virginia, p. 300-01, © 1941 Jefferson Publishing Co., Charlestown, WV.

# VIRGINIA VOLUNTEERS IN MEXICO

[1475] Letter of Col. John F. Hamtramck to Capt. Irvin McDowell, Regimental Letter Book, 1st Virginia Volunteer Infantry, Record Group 153, National Archives & Records Administration, Washington, D.C
[1476] U.S. Census 1850, Berkeley Co., VA, p. 333.
[1477] U.S. Census 1860, Jefferson Co., VA, p. 857.
[1478] U.S. Census 1880, Jefferson Co., WV, p. C004.
[1479] Register of Deaths 1905-1949, p. 158, Jefferson County, Circuit Court Clerks Office, Charlestown, WV.
[1480] Information provided by Kirby Harden, 40 St. Rt. 890, Greenville, KY, 42345.
[1481] U.S. Census 1850, Loudoun Co., VA, p. 185.
[1482] U.S. Census 1860, Clarke Co., VA, p. 634.
[1483] U.S. Census 1850, Clarke Co., VA, p. 432.
[1484] Information provided by Kirby Harden, 40 St. Rt. 890, Greenville, KY, 42345.
[1485] Dayton National Cemetery, VA Medical Center, 4100 West Third Street, Dayton, OH 45428-1008
[1486] U.S. Census 1850, Henrico Co., VA, p. 415.
[1487] *Martinsburg Gazette*, February 25, 1847, p. 2, 5, Martinsburg, WV.
[1488] *Martinsburg Gazette*, August 24, 1848, p. 2, 3, Martinsburg, WV.
[1489] Dorman, John Frederick, The Preston's of Smithfield and Greenfield in Virginia, © 1982, The Filson Club, Louisville, KY.
[1490] U.S. Census 1850, Montgomery Co., VA, p. 005.
[1491] Mexican War Pension File, WC 6086, National Archives and Records Administration, Washington, DC.
[1492] U.S. Census 1860, Montgomery Co., VA, p. 703.
[1493] Driver, Robert C., Jr., 14th Virginia Cavalry, © 1988, H.E. Howard, Inc., Lynchburg, VA.
[1494] *Rural Messenger*, January 30, 1875, p. 35, c. 3, Petersburg, VA.
[1495] *Petersburg Index & Appeal*, November 11, 1875, p. 2, c. 3, Petersburg, VA.
[1496] U.S. Census 1850, Henrico Co., VA, p. 439.
[1497] U.S. Census 1860, Henrico Co., VA, p. 264.
[1498] U.S. Census 1860, Dinwiddie Co., VA, p. 079.
[1499] U.S. Census 1860, Dinwiddie Co., VA, p. 056.
[1500] U.S. Census 1850, Henrico Co., VA, p. 350.
[1501] International Genealogical Index Film #-1903699.
[1502] Mexican War Pension File SC #4854, National Archives and Records Administration, Washington, D.C.
[1503] U.S. Census 1860, Charlotte Co., VA, p. 231.
[1504] U.S. Census 1870, Charlotte Co., VA, p. 166.
[1505] Communication of Dr. A.S. Priddy, copied by Walter M. Priddy, City National Bank Building, Wichita Falls, Texas 76301.
[1506] Mexican War Pension File, WC #8359, National Archives and Records Administration, Washington, D.C.
[1507] Journal of the executive proceedings of the Senate of the United States of America, 1789-1873, Tuesday, December 31, 1811, p. 200.
[1508] Journal of the executive proceedings of the Senate of the United States of America, 1789-1873, Wednesday, February 3, 1813, p. 320.
[1509] Journal of the House of Representatives of the United States, 1789-1873, Monday, December 10, 1832, p. 26.
[1510] *The Warren Sentinel*, August 23, 1907, Front Royal, VA.
[1511] Personal Communication of Adrian Aitichson of Cascade, IA, great-great-grandson of Lt. Col. Thomas B. Randolph. Mr. Aitichson states there is an iron fence surrounding the grave of Thomas B. Randolph but the headstones for all graves have been destroyed. The fence was erected by his grandaughter Minnie Randolph Jones shortly after T.B. Randolph's death. This fact is allegedly documented in an old issue of the Cascade newspaper.
[1512] U.S. Census 1850, Mecklenburg Co., VA, p. 073.
[1513] U.S. Census 1860, Mecklenburg Co., VA, p. 340.

OFF TO WAR

[1514] Bracey, Susan L., Life By The Roaring Roanoke,© 1977, Mecklenburg Bicentennial Commission, Mecklenburg Co., VA.
[1515] Letter from T.C. Madison, Asst. Surgeon to Lt. Thomas P. August, June 27, 1847, Regimental Letter Book, 1st Virginia Volunteer Infantry, Record Group 153, National Archives & Records Administration, Washington, D.C
[1516] U.S. Census 1880, Summers Co., WV, p. G001.
[1517] Mexican War Pension File, WC #2371, National Archives and Records Administration, Washington, D.C.
[1518] U.S. Census 1850, Augusta Co., VA, p. 443.
[1519] U.S. Census 1860, Augusta Co., VA, p. 730.
[1520] Mexican War Pension File, WC #6874, National Archives and Records Administration, Washington, DC.
[1521] U.S. Census 1850, Berkeley Co., VA, p. 387.
[1522] Mexican War Pension WC #4060, National Archives and Records Administration, Washington, D.C.
[1523] U.S. Census 1870, Atchison Co., KS, p. 329.
[1524] Personal Communication of Priscilla Beumee, (Grand niece of soldier), 4212 East Orchard Place, Centennial, CO, 80121-3172. Identifies soldiers middle name "Frederick."
[1525] Deposition of Henry C. Richards, Mexican War Pension SC #11904, National Archives and Records Administration, Washington, D.C.
[1526] Personal Communication of Priscilla Beumee, (G-G-Granddaughter of soldier), 4212 East Orchard Place, Centennial, CO, 80121-3172. Identifies soldiers middle name "Rose."
[1527] Hiatt, Marty and Scott, Craig Robert, Implied Marriages of Fairfax Co., VA, © 1994. Iberian Publishing Co., Athens, Ga.
[1528] U.S. Census 1850, Fairfax Co., VA, p. 130.
[1529] U.S. Census 1850, Ohio Co., VA, p. 055.
[1530] U.S. Census 1850, Mecklenburg Co., VA, p. 105.
[1531] U.S. Census 1870, Prince Edward Co., VA, p. 101.
[1532] Mexican War Pension File, SC #11923, Survivor Claim, National Archives and Records Administration, Washington, D.C.
[1533] Mexican War Pension File, WC #14176, National Archives and Records Administration, Washington, D.C.
[1534] Mexican War Pension File, SC #11923, Affidavit of Claimant, July 27, 1891, National Archives and Records Administration, Washington, D.C.
[1535] Mexican War Pension File, WC #14176, Death Certificate of John Roach, National Archives and Records Administration, Washington, D.C.
[1536] Marriage Bonds, Rockbridge Co., VA.
[1537] U.S. Census 1850, Rockbridge Co., VA, p. 404.
[1538] Death Register Rockbridge Co., VA.
[1539] Mexican War Pension File, SC #3848, National Archives and Records Administration, Washington, DC.
[1540] Mexican War Pension File, SC #3848, Affidavit of David S. Robertson, National Archives and Records Administration, Washington, DC.
[1541] U.S. Census 1850, Norfolk Co., VA, p. 177.
[1542] U.S. Census 1860, Norfolk Co., VA, p. 218.
[1543] The Petersburg Republican, July 14, 1847, p. 3, c. 1, Petersburg, VA.
[1544] Mexican War Pension File, WC #1035, National Archives and Records Administration, Washington, D.C.
[1545] U.S. Census 1850, Chesterfield Co., VA, p. 164.
[1546] U.S. Census 1860, Chesterfield Co., VA, p. 431.
[1547] U.S. Census 1870, Chesterfield Co., VA, p. 240.
[1548] Mexican War Pension File, WC #2498, National Archives and Records Administration, Washington, D.C.
[1549] Scott, James G., and Wyatt, Edward A., IV, Petersburg's Story, A History, © 1960, Titmus Optical Company, Petersburg, VA.
[1550] U.S. Census 1850, Marshall Co., VA.

# VIRGINIA VOLUNTEERS IN MEXICO

[1551] Powell, Scott, History of Marshall County, West Virginia, © 1925, reprinted © 1998, Heritage Books. Bowie, MD.
[1552] Mexican War Pension File, SC #15663, National Archives and Records Administration, Washington, DC.
[1553] U.S. Census 1850, Montgomery Co., VA, p. 057.
[1554] U.S. Census 1860, Montgomery Co., VA, p. 713.
[1555] Mexican War Pension File, WC #11442, National Archives and Records Administration, Washington, DC.
[1556] Mexican War Pension File, SC #14396, National Archives and Records Administration, Washington, DC.
[1557] Marriage Register #A, pg. 311, Montgomery Co., VA.
[1558] U.S. Census 1850, Montgomery Co., VA, p. 008.
[1559] U.S. Census 1860, Montgomery Co., VA, p. 626.
[1560] Mexican War Pension File, WC #10771, National Archives and Records Administration, Washington, DC.
[1561] Information provided by Lyle McAlexander, 6670 Trout Creek Road, Parkdale, OR.
[1562] U.S. Census 1860, Montgomery Co., VA, p. 628.
[1563] Marriage Register, Bedford Co., VA, Circuit Court Clerks Office, Bedford, VA.
[1564] U.S. Census 1860, Bedford Co., VA, p. 309.
[1565] U.S. Census 1870, Wythe Co., VA, p. 391.
[1566] Register of Deaths 1853-1872, p. 8, Jefferson County Circuit Court Clerks Office, Charlestown, WV.
[1567] U.S. Census 1850, Jefferson Co., VA, p. 297.
[1568] U.S. Census 1860, Jefferson Co., VA, p. 802.
[1569] U.S. Census 1850, Henrico Co., VA, p. 393.
[1570] Mexican War Pension File SC #16534, Affidavit of Pensioner, National Archives and records Administration, Washington, D.C.
[1571] U.S. Census 1860, Louisa Co., VA, p. 769.
[1572] Postwar roster of W.J. Hart, Louisa County Circuit Court Clerks Office, Louisa, VA.
[1573] Senior Pastors of the First United Methodist Church, DeKalb, Ill., http://www.firstumc.net/Ministers/History%20of%20Ministers.htm
[1574] Interment Records of Hollywood Memorial Park, 6000 Santa Monica Boulevard, Hollywood, CA. / (323) 469-1181
[1575] Sublett, Charles W., 57th Virginia Infantry, © 1985, H.E. Howard, Inc., Lynchburg, VA.
[1576] Mexican War Pension File, SC #3514, National Archives and Records Administration, Washington, DC.
[1577] Mexican War Pension File, WC #8337, National Archives and Records Administration, Washington, DC.
[1578] U.S. Census 1870, Clay Co., MO.
[1579] *Obituary, Liberty Tribune, June 2, 1876*, Liberty, Missouri.
[1580] Will of Mary A. Schwitzer, Clay County, MO., 1907, Clay County Archives & Historical Library, P.O. Box 99, Liberty, MO.
[1581] Mexican War Pension File, SC #2701, National Archives and Records Administration, Washington, DC.
[1582] *Obituary, Columbus Journal*, August 15, 1894, Columbus, Nebraska.
[1583] Letter from R. Jones, A.G. to Col. J.F. Hamtramck, February 12, 1847, Regimental Letter Book, 1st Virginia Infantry Regiment, Record Group 153, National Archives & Records Administration, Washington, D.C.
[1584] Letter from Col. Hamtramck to Capt. Robert G. Scott, February 16, 1847, Regimental Letter Book, 1st Virginia Regiment, Record Group 153, National Archives & Records Administration, Washington, D.C.
[1585] U.S. Census 1850, Henrico Co., VA, p. 361.
[1586] Spofford, Ainsworth R., Eminent and Representative Men of Virginia and the District of Columbia of the Nineteenth Century, p. 563, © 1893, Brant & Fuller, Madison, WI.
[1587] Mexican War Pension SC #5702, National Archives and Records Administration, Washington, D.C.

# OFF TO WAR

[1588] Records of the Office of the Judge Advocate General(Army), Record Group 153, EE 454, National Archives & Records Administration, Washington, D.C.
[1589] U.S. Census 1850, Henrico Co., VA, p. 332.
[1590] Mexican War Pension WC #12622, National Archives and Records Administration, Washington, D.C.
[1591] Spofford, Ainsworth R., Eminent and Representative Men of Virginia and the District of Columbia of the Nineteenth Century, p. 563, © 1893, Brant & Fuller, Madison, WI.
[1592] Affidavit of J.A. Binford, Mexican War Pension SC #5702, National Archives and Records Administration, Washington, D.C.
[1593] Letter from Annie K. Scott to Sidney L. Wilson, Esq., 12/01/1894, Mexican War Pension WC #12622, National Archives and Records Administration, Washington, D.C.
[1594] U.S. Census 1870, Henrico Co., VA, p. 069.
[1595] Mexican War Pension File, SC #12780, National Archives and Records Administration, Washington, D.C.
[1596] Mexican War Pension File, SC #9452, National Archives and Records Administration, Washington, D.C.
[1597] U.S. Census 1850, Henrico Co., VA, p. 265.
[1598] Mexican War Pension File, WA #10710, National Archives and Records Administration, Washington, D.C.
[1599] Records of the Office of the Judge Advocate General(Army), Record Group 153, EE 611, Case 45, National Archives & Records Administration, Washington, D.C.
[1600] Mexican War Pension File, SC #15576, National Archives and Records Administration, Washington, D.C.
[1601] Record of Interments Blandford Cemetery, 1888-1905, p. 109, Blandford Cemetery, Petersburg, VA.
[1602] U.S. Census 1850, Dinwiddie Co., VA, p. 403.
[1603] U.S. Census 1860, Dinwiddie Co., VA, p. 279.
[1604] U.S. Census 1870, Dinwiddie Co., VA, p. 289.
[1605] Mexican War Pension File, WA #15778, National Archives and Records Administration, Washington, D.C.
[1606] Record of Interments Blandford Cemetery, 1888-1905, p. 109, Blandford Cemetery, Petersburg, VA.
[1607] Mexican War Pension File, SC #8139, National Archives and Records Administration, Washington, D.C.
[1608] Mexican War Pension File, WC #6686, National Archives and Records Administration, Washington, D.C.
[1609] Record of Interments Blandford Cemetery, 1888-1905, p. 27, Blandford Cemetery, Petersburg, VA.
[1610] U.S. Census 1850, Prince George Co., VA, p. 062.
[1611] Mexican War Pension File, SC #4035, National Archives and Records Administration, Washington, D.C.
[1612] U.S. Census 1860, Prince George Co., VA, p. 376.
[1613] Compiled Service Records of Confederate Soldiers, Record Group 109, National Archives and Records Administration, Wash., D.C.
[1614] U.S. Census 1870, Prince George Co., VA, p. 183.
[1615] Mexican War Pension File, SC #4035, Affidavit of Thomas H. Bond, November 25, 1887, National Archives and Records Administration, Washington, D.C.
[1616] Record of Interments Blandford Cemetery, 1888-1905, p. 27, Blandford Cemetery, Petersburg, VA.
[1617] Mexican War Pension File, WA #9959, National Archives and Records Administration, Washington, D.C.
[1618] Mexican War Pension File, SC #11932, National Archives and Records Administration, Washington, DC.
[1619] *Martinsburg Gazette*, February 25, 1847, p. 2, c. 5, Martinsburg, WV.
[1620] Mexican War Pension File, WC #15083, National Archives and Records Administration, Washington, DC.
[1621] U.S. Census 1850, Barbour Co., VA, p. 103.
[1622] U.S. Census 1860, Barbour Co. VA, p. 216.
[1623] U.S. Census 1880, Barbour Co., WV, p. P036.
[1624] Marriage Register #A, pg. 313, Montgomery Co., VA.

## VIRGINIA VOLUNTEERS IN MEXICO

[1625] U.S. Census 1850, Montgomery Co., VA, p. 057.
[1626] U.S. Census 1870, Prince George Co., VA, p. 096.
[1627] Mexican War Pension SC #9752, National Archives and Records Administration, Washington, D.C.
[1628] Mexican War Pension File, WC #441, National Archives and Records Administration, Washington, DC.
[1629] U.S. Census 1850, Jefferson Co., VA, p. 298.
[1630] U.S. Census 1850, Jefferson Co., VA, p. 298.
[1631] Marriages of Jefferson County, Virginia – West Virginia 1801 through 1890, p. 513, Jefferson County Circuit Court Clerks Office, Charlestown, WV.
[1632] U.S. Census 1860, Jefferson Co., VA, p. 809.
[1633] Mexican War Pension File, SC #12253, National Archives and Records Administration, Washington, DC.
[1634] Marriage Register #A, pg. 324, Montgomery Co., VA.
[1635] U.S. Census 1860, Montgomery Co., VA, p. 680.
[1636] Compiled Service Records of Confederate Soldiers, Record Group 109, National Archives and Records Administration, Wash., D.C.
[1637] U.S. Census 1870, Pulaski Co., VA, p. 032.
[1638] Mexican War Pension File, WC #12623, National Archives and Records Administration, Washington, DC.
[1639] Mexican War Pension File, WA #4877, National Archives and Records Administration, Washington, DC.
[1640] Records of the Office of the Judge Advocate General(Army), Record Group 153, EE 455, Case 7, National Archives & Records Administration, Washington, D.C.
[1641] Records of the Office of the Judge Advocate General(Army), Record Group 153, EE 611, Case 13, National Archives & Records Administration, Washington, D.C.
[1642] Mexican War Pension File, SC #9794, National Archives and Records Administration, Washington, D.C.
[1643] U.S. Census 1870, Spotsylvania Co., VA, p. 301.
[1644] U.S. Census 1850, Lunenburg Co., VA, p. 047.
[1645] U.S. Census 1860, Berkeley Co., VA, p. 853.
[1646] *The Petersburg Republican*, February 1, 1847, p. 3, c. 1, Petersburg, VA.
[1647] U.S. Census 1870, Chesterfield Co., VA, p. 372.
[1648] Information provided by Judy Butler Anderson, 4485 S. 2025 W, Roy, UT 84067.
[1649] Mexican War Pension File, SC #13164, National Archives and Records Administration, Washington, DC.
[1650] U.S. Census 1850, Berkeley Co., VA, p. 420.
[1651] U.S. Census 1860, Berkeley Co., VA, p. 909.
[1652] Register of Deaths 1896-1906, Berkeley County, WV, p. 58, Circuit Court Clerks Office, Martinsburg, WV.
[1653] Mexican War Pension File, WC #11676, National Archives and Records Administration, Washington, DC.
[1654] Confederate Veteran Magazine, © 1914,V. 15, p. 371.
[1655] U.S. Census 1860, Dinwiddie Co., VA, p. 345.
[1656] U.S. Census 1870, Dinwiddie Co., VA, p. 383.
[1657] Record of Interments Blandford Cemetery, 1905-1922, p. 8, Blandford Cemetery, Petersburg, VA.
[1658] Mexican War Pension File, SC #12993, National Archives and Records Administration, Washington, DC.
[1659] U.S. Census 1860, Hampshire Co., WV, p. 05.
[1660] U.S. Census 1880, Hardy Co., WV, p. C009.
[1661] Records of the Office of the Judge Advocate General(Army), Record Group 153, EE 611, Case 47, National Archives & Records Administration, Washington, D.C.
[1662] Mexican War Pension File, WC #8624, National Archives and Records Administration, Washington, DC.
[1663] Information provided by Tom Dove, 22 H Queen Victoria Way, Chester MD 21619; www.toad.net/~tdove/Dove_Family/WC_TOC.htm#CNTC

# OFF TO WAR

[1664] Information provided by Laurie McDaniels Howland, Box 167 Clandeboye, Manitoba, R0C 0P0, Canada.
[1665] U.S. Census 1850, Wythe Co., VA, p. 288.
[1666] U.S. Census 1860, Wythe Co., VA, p. 799.
[1667] Obituary *Wytheville Dispatch, July 19, 1877,* Wytheville, Va.
[1668] Mexican War Pension File, WC #603, National Archives and Records Administration, Washington, DC.
[1669] Marriage Bond, Frederick Co., VA.
[1670] U.S. Census 1850, Frederick Co., VA, p. 333.
[1671] U.S. Census 1860, Frederick Co., VA, p. 492.
[1672] U.S. Census 1850, Bedford Co., VA, p. 185.
[1673] U.S. Census 1850, Bedford Co., VA, p. 185.
[1674] Marriage Register, Pittsylvania Co., VA.
[1675] U.S. Census 1860, Pittsylvania Co., VA, p. 509.
[1676] U.S. Census 1870, Pittsylvania Co., VA, p. 409.
[1677] Moore, Robert H., II, The Danville, Eight Star New Market and Dixie Artillery, © 1989, H.E. Howard, Inc., Lynchburg, VA.
[1678] Marriage Register #1, pg. 12, Montgomery Co., VA.
[1679] Marriage Register #A, pg. 312, Montgomery Co., VA.
[1680] U.S. Census 1850, Montgomery Co., VA, p. 022.
[1681] Mexican War Pension File, WC #2756, National Archives and Records Administration, Washington, DC.
[1682] U.S. Census 1870, Montgomery Co., VA, p. 160.
[1683] Marriage Bond, Augusta Co., VA.
[1684] U.S. Census 1850, Augusta Co., VA, p. 439.
[1685] Records of the Office of the Judge Advocate General(Army), Record Group 153, EE 554, Case 25, National Archives & Records Administration, Washington, D.C.
[1686] Mexican War Pension File, WC #4380, National Archives and Records Administration, Washington, DC.
[1687] U.S. Census 1860, Henrico Co., VA, p. 986.
[1688] U.S. Cenusu 1870, Henrico Co., VA, p. 351.
[1689] Mexican War Pension File, WC #3768, National Archives and Records Administration, Washington, DC.
[1690] Mexican War Pension File, SC #4195, National Archives and Records Administration, Washington, DC.
[1691] U.S. Census 1880, Nicholas Co., WV, p. J013.
[1692] Mexican War Pension File, WC #7526, National Archives and Records Administration, Washington, DC.
[1693] International Genealogical Index, Film #-457555.
[1694] Information provided by Fran Peterson, 4046 Splendor Circle, Salt Lake City, UT 84124.
[1695] Mexican War Pension File, SC #6171, National Archives and Records Administration, Washington, D.C.
[1696] U.S. Census 1850, Kanawha Co., VA, p. 143.
[1697] U.S. Census 1860, Kanawha Co., VA, p. 263.
[1698] U.S. Census 1850, Kanawha Co., VA, p. 069.
[1699] U.S. Ceneus 1860, Kanawha Co., VA, p. 303.
[1700] U.S. Census 1850, Rockbridge Co., VA, p. 421.
[1701] U.S. Census 1860, Rockbridge Co., VA, p. 284.
[1702] International Genealogical Index, Film #-2034847.
[1703] U.S. Census 1850, Dinwiddie Co., VA, p. 493.
[1704] U.S. Census 1860, Dinwiddie Co., VA, p. 067.
[1705] Compiled Service Records of Confederate Soldiers, Record Group 109, National Archives and Records Administration, Wash., D.C.
[1706] Mexican War Pension File, SC #4538, National Archives and Records Administration, Washington, D.C.

# VIRGINIA VOLUNTEERS IN MEXICO

[1707] Mexican War Pension File, WC #6213, National Archives and Records Administration, Washington, D.C.
[1708] Wayland, John W., A History of Rockingham Co., VA, © 1912, p. 123, Ruebush-Elkins Company, Dayton, VA.
[1709] Records of the Office of the Judge Advocate General(Army), Record Group 153, EE 554, Case 25, National Archives & Records Administration, Washington, D.C.
[1710] Mexican War Pension File, SC #15718, National Archives and Records Administration, Washington, DC.
[1711] U.S. Census 1880, Nicholas Co., WV, p. K005.
[1712] Mexican War Pension File, WC #12662, National Archives and Records Administration, Washington, DC.
[1713] Wayland, John W., A History of Rockingham Co., VA, © 1912, p. 123, Ruebush-Elkins Company, Dayton, VA.
[1714] Mexican War Pension File, SC #3022, National Archives and Records Administration, Washington, DC.
[1715] Marriage Bond, Goochland Co., VA.
[1716] U.S. Census 1850, Goochland Co., VA, p. 135.
[1717] U.S. Census 1860, Henrico Co., VA, p. 1042.
[1718] U.S. Census 1870, Henrico Co., VA, p. 428.
[1719] Moore, Robert H., II, The Richmond Fayette, Hampden, Thomas, and Blount's Lynchburg Artillery, © 1991, H.E. Howard, Inc., Lynchburg, VA.
[1720] Mexican War Pension File, WC #10005, National Archives and Records Administration, Washington, DC.
[1721] U.S. Census 1860, Campbell Co., VA, p. 222.
[1722] U.S. Census 1870, Campbell Co., VA, p. 005.
[1723] U.S. Census 1850, Alexandria Co., VA, p. 332.
[1724] Mexican War Pension File, SC #19139, National Archives and Records Administration, Washington, DC.
[1725] U.S. Census 1850, Caroline Co., VA, p. 303.
[1726] U.S. Census 1870, Caroline Co., VA, p. 375.
[1727] U.S. Census 1850, Dinwiddie Co., VA, p. 374.
[1728] U.S. Census 1860, Dinwiddie Co., VA, p. 412.
[1729] *The Daily Express*, December 7, 1865, p. 2, c. 2, Petersburg, VA.
[1730] U.S. Census 1870, Dinwiddie Co., VA, p. 190.
[1731] Mexican War Pension File, WC #443, National Archives and Records Administration, Washington, DC.
[1732] U.S. Census 1860, Patrick Co., VA, p. 943.
[1733] U.S. Census 1850, King George Co., VA, p. 235.
[1734] Information provided by Richard B. Spooner, 1918 Bonnie Brae Dr., Lake Oswego, OR 97034.
[1735] *The Daily Index*, April 9, 1872, p. 2, c. 3, Petersburg, VA.
[1736] Mexican War Pension File, SC #6195, National Archives and Records Administration, Washington, DC.
[1737] U.S. Census 1850, Norfolk Co., VA, p. 228.
[1738] Interment Cards Elmwood Cemetery 1875-1990, Microfilm Reel 1900, Library of Virginia, Richmond, VA.
[1739] Affidavits of Poe & Scott, Mexican War Pension SC #13364, National Archives and Records Administration, Washington, D.C.
[1740] U.S. Census 1850, Brunswick Co., VA, p. 311.
[1741] U.S. Census 1850, Henrico Co., VA, p. 418.
[1742] Compiled Service Records of Confederate Soldiers, Record Group 109, National Archives and Records Administration, Wash., D.C.
[1743] International Genealogical Index, Film #-1553824.
[1744] U.S. Census 1860, Montgomery Co., VA, p. 623.
[1745] Marriage Register #A, pg. 317, Montgomery Co., VA.

# OFF TO WAR

[1746] U.S. Census 1860, Montgomery Co., VA, p. 700.
[1747] Records of the Office of the Judge Advocate General(Army), Record Group 153, EE 642, Case 4, National Archives & Records Administration, Washington, D.C.
[1748] Mexican War Pension File, SA #24207, National Archives and Records Administration, Washington, DC.
[1749] U.S. Census 1850, Augusta Co., VA, p. 392.
[1750] *Martinsburg Gazette*, August 24, 1848, p. 2, 3, Martinsburg, WV.
[1751] Marriage Register #A, pg. 309, Montgomery Co., VA.
[1752] U.S. Census 1850, Montgomery Co., VA, p. 047.
[1753] U.S. Census 1860, Montgomery Co., VA, p. 623.
[1754] Lambert, Dobbie E., 25$^{th}$ Virginia Cavalry, © 1994, H.E. Howard, Inc., Lynchburg, VA.
[1755] U.S. Census 1870, Montgomery Co., VA, p. 156.
[1756] Mexican War Pension File, WC #282, National Archives and Records Administration, Washington, DC.
[1757] Mexican War Pension File, SC #8544, National Archives and Records Administration, Washington, DC.
[1758] U.S. Census 1860, Fayette Co., VA, p. 352.
[1759] U.S. Census 1880, Raleigh Co., WV, p. C014.
[1760] Mexican War Pension File, WC #14029, National Archives and Records Administration, Washington, DC.
[1761] *Martinsburg Gazette*, January 6, 1842, p. 3, 4, Martinsburg, WV.
[1762] *Martinsburg Gazette*, March 16, 1843, p. 3, 4., Martinsburg, WV.
[1763] Register of Deaths 1865-1903, Berkeley County, WV, p. 32, Circuit Court Clerks Office, Martinsburg, WV.
[1764] U.S. Census 1850, Brunswick Co., VA, p.
[1765] Mexican War Pension File, SC #1770, National Archives and Records Administration, Washington, DC.
[1766] U.S. Census 1850, Pocahontas Co., VA, p. 298.
[1767] U.S. Census 1850, Greenbrier Co., VA, p. 265.
[1768] U.S. Census 1860, Pocahontas Co., VA, p. 688.
[1769] U.S. Census 1880, Pocahontas Co., WV, p. H013.
[1770] Mexican War Pension File, SC #1834, National Archives and Records Administration, Washington, DC.
[1771] U.S. Census 1870, Shennandoah Co., VA, p. 800.
[1772] Mexican War Pension File, WC #13440, National Archives and Records Administration, Washington, DC.
[1773] Mexican War Pension File, SC #25308, National Archives and Records Administration, Washington, DC.
[1774] Mexican War Pension File, SC #6427, National Archives and Records Administration, Washington, DC.
[1775] U.S. Census 1850, Alexandria Co., VA, p. 382.
[1776] *Alexandria Gazette*, July 30, 1857, p. 3, Alexandria, VA.
[1777] Wife Maria and several other family members are buried in Christ Church Cemetery, Alexandria, VA.
[1778] U.S. Census 1860, Alexandria Co., VA, p. 729.
[1779] Marriage Bonds, Alexandria Co., VA.
[1780] U.S. Census 1850, Alexandria Co., VA, p. 373.
[1781] Information provided by George E. Tabb, 200 W. Fairfax Blvd., Ranson WV 35438-1604.
[1782] U.S. Census 1850, Campbell Co., VA, p. 125.
[1783] U.S. Census 1850, Medina County, Texas, p. 399B.
[1784] *Alexandria Gazette*, July 14, 1851, p. 2, c. 7, Alexandria, VA.
[1785] U.S. Census 1850, Smyth Co., VA, p. 213.
[1786] U.S. Census 1860, Wythe Co., VA, p. 727.
[1787] Mexican War Pension File, WC #1721, National Archives and Records Administration, Washington, DC.

# VIRGINIA VOLUNTEERS IN MEXICO

[1788] Records of the Office of the Judge Advocate General(Army), Record Group 153, EE 455, Case 12, National Archives & Records Administration, Washington, D.C.
[1789] Compiled Service Records of Confederate Soldiers, Record Group 109, National Archives and Records Administration, Wash., D.C.
[1790] International Genealogical Index, Film #-0822009.
[1791] U.S. Census 1850, Pittsylvania Co., VA, p. 130.
[1792] U.S. Census 1860, Lee Co., VA, p. 872.
[1793] U.S. Census 1870, Lee Co., VA, p. 311.
[1794] Mexican War Pension File, SC #13551, National Archives and Records Administration, Washington, DC.
[1795] U.S. Census 1850, Augusta Co., VA, p.
[1796] U.S. Census 1860, Augusta Co., VA, p. 857.
[1797] U.S. Census 1880, Wood Co., WV, p. 067.
[1798] Mexican War Pension File, SC #11052, National Archives and Records Administration, Washington, DC.
[1799] U.S. Census 1850, Montgomery Co., VA, p. 003.
[1800] Marriage Register #A, pg. 325, Montgomery Co., VA.
[1801] U.S. Census 1860, Montgomery Co., VA, p. 569.
[1802] U.S. Census 1870, Montgomery Co., VA, p. 124.
[1803] Mexican War Pension File, WC #2233, National Archives and Records Administration, Washington, DC.
[1804] U.S. Census 1850, Caroline Co., VA, p. 289.
[1805] International Genealogical Index, Film #-1058241.
[1806] Musselman, Homer D., The Caroline Light, Parker and Stafford Light Virginia Artillery, © 1992, H.E. Howard, Inc., Lynchburg, VA.
[1807] U.S. Census 1870, Essex Co., VA, p. 203.
[1808] Mexican War Pension File, WC #4357, National Archives and Records Administration, Washington, DC.
[1809] International Genealogical Index, Film #-1903948.
[1810] U.S. Census 1850, Rockingham Co., VA, p. 052.
[1811] U.S. Census 1860, Augusta Co., VA, p. 1088.
[1812] Mexican War Pension File, SC #3889, National Archives and Records Administration, Washington, DC.
[1813] Deposition of Greenberry B. Terrell, March 20, 1894, Mexican War Pension File of Pvt. James T. Pelter, WA #12000, National Archives and Records Administration, Washington, D.C.
[1814] Mexican War Pension File, SC #19985, National Archives and Records Administration, Washington, DC.
[1815] Letter from Col. John F. Hamtramck to R. Jones, Adjt. Genl., August 2, 1847, Regimental Letter Book, 1st Virginia Volunteer Infantry, Record Group 153, National Archives & Records Administration, Washington, D.C
[1816] Mexican War Pension File, SC #8674, National Archives and Records Administration, Washington, DC.
[1817] Mexican War Pension File, WC #10734, National Archives and Records Administration, Washington, DC.
[1818] Mexican War Pension File, WC #5033, National Archives and Records Administration, Washington, D.C.
[1819] Mexican War Pension WC #11860, National Archives and Records Administration, Washington, D.C.
[1820] International Genealogical Index Film # 456253.
[1821] U.S. Census 1850, Henrico Co., VA, p. 565.
[1822] U.S. Census 1860, Henrico Co., VA, p. 307.
[1823] War of 1812 Pension File, James Thrift, National Archives and Records Administration, Washington, DC.
[1824] Mexican War Pension SC #999, National Archives and Records Administration, Washington, D.C.
[1825] Confederate Veteran Magazine, © 1921, V. 29, p. 304.
[1826] U.S. Census 1900, Webster Co., MO, E.D. 140, p. 008.

## OFF TO WAR

[1827] Mexican War Pension WC #13911, National Archives and Records Administration, Washington, D.C.
[1828] *Alexandria Gazette,* November 13, 1848, Alexandria, VA.
[1829] U.S. Census 1850, Fairfax Co., VA, p. 135.
[1830] Hampton National Cemetery, Cemetery Road at Marshall Avenue, Hampton, VA 23667.
[1831] Mexican War Pension SC #11450, National Archives and Records Administration, Washington, D.C.
[1832] Death Certificate, Mexican War Pension WC #14598, National Archives and Records Administration, Washington, D.C.
[1833] Marriage & Death Notice Clipping, Mexican War Pension WC #14598, National Archives and Records Administration, Washington, D.C.
[1834] Mexican War Pension WC #14598, National Archives and Records Administration, Washington, D.C
[1835] U.S. Census 1860, Henrico Co., VA, p. 782.
[1836] Obituary, *Baltimore Sun, November 2, 1906,* p. 7, Baltimore, Maryland.
[1837] Death Certificate, Mexican War Pension WC #14598, National Archives and Records Administration, Washington, D.C.
[1838] Obituary Clipping, *Baltimore Sun, November 3, 1906,* p. 7, Baltimore, Maryland.
[1839] Mexican War Pension File, WA #4207, National Archives and Records Administration, Washington, DC.
[1840] Mexican War Pension File, SC #1847, National Archives and Records Administration, Washington, D.C.
[1841] U.S. Census 1850, Jefferson Co., VA, p. 311.
[1842] U.S. Census 1850, Fairfax Co., VA, p. 113.
[1843] U.S. Census 1860, Fairfax Co., VA, p. 898.
[1844] Marriage Certificate, Mexican War Pension WC #11605, National Archives and Records Administration, Washington, D.C.
[1845] International Genealogical Index Film #-538057.
[1846] Mexican War Pension File, SC #17458, National Archives and Records Administration, Washington, D.C.
[1847] Marriage Register #A, pg. 315, Montgomery Co., VA.
[1848] Mexican War Pension File, WC 16312, National Archives and Records Administration, Washington, D.C.
[1849] U.S. Census 1850, Sussex Co., VA, p. 135.
[1850] U.S. Census 1860, Dinwiddie Co., VA, p. 361.
[1851] Mexican War Pension File, SC #11744, National Archives and Records Administration, Washington, DC.
[1852] U.S. Census 1850, Elizabeth City Co., VA, p. 041.
[1853] U.S. Census 1850, Chesterfield Co., VA, p. 166.
[1854] U.S. Census 1870, Chesterfield Co., VA, p. 411.
[1855] Mexican War Pension File, SC #1976, National Archives and Records Administration, Washington, D.C.
[1856] Record of Interments Blandford Cemetery, 1843-1872, p. 109, Blandford Cemetery, Petersburg, VA.
[1857] U.S. Census 1850, Dinwiddie Co., VA, p. 372.
[1858] U.S. Census 1850, Norfolk Co., VA, p. 005.
[1859] Mexican War Pension File, WC #3937, National Archives and Records Administration, Washington, DC.
[1860] Records of the Office of the Judge Advocate General (Army), Record Group 153, EE 611, Case 1, National Archives & Records Administration, Washington, D.C.
[1861] U.S. Census 1850, Warren Co., VA, p. 044.
[1862] U.S. Census 1860, Warren Co., VA, p. 959.
[1863] U.S. Census 1870, Fauquier Co., VA, p. 579.
[1864] U.S. Census 1850, Frederick Co., VA, p. 310.
[1865] U.S. Census 1860, Frederick Co., VA, p. 617.
[1866] U.S. Census 1850, Montgomery Co., VA, p. 002.
[1867] U.S. Census 1850, Montgomery Co., VA, p. 002.
[1868] Marriage Register #A, pg. 327, Montgomery Co., VA.
[1869] U.S. Census 1860, Montgomery Co., VA, p. 570.

## VIRGINIA VOLUNTEERS IN MEXICO

[1870] U.S. Census 1870, Montgomery Co., VA, p. 124.
[1871] Mexican War Pension File, WC #833, National Archives and Records Administration, Washington, D.C.
[1872] International Genealogical Index Film # 446162.
[1873] Records of the Office of the Judge Advocate General(Army), Record Group 153, EE 427, Case 1, National Archives & Records Administration, Washington, D.C.
[1874] U.S. Census 1850, Louisa Co., VA, p. 422.
[1875] Marriage Register, 1806-1868, Albemarle Co., VA
[1876] Mexican War Pension File, WC #6192, National Archives and Records Administration, Washington, DC.
[1877] U.S. Census 1850, Albemarle Co., VA, p. 284.
[1878] U.S. Census 1850, Montgomery Co., VA, p. 64.
[1879] U.S. Census 1870, Frederick Co., VA, p. 200.
[1880] Mexican War Pension File WA #11143, Death Certificate of Robert Wallace, National Archives and records Administration, Washington, D.C.
[1881] Mexican War Pension File SC #14245, National Archives and Records Administration, Washington, D.C.
[1882] U.S. Census 1850, Lunenburg Co., VA, p. 020.
[1883] U.S. Census 1870, Brunswick Co., VA, p. 097.
[1884] Mexican War Pension File, SC #15925, National Archives and Records Administration, Washington, DC.
[1885] Kegley, Mary, The Lost Children of Wythe County Virginia, 1790-1878, © 1995, Kegley Books, Wytheville, VA.
[1886] Burke's Presidential Families of the United States of America, © 1981, Burke's Perrage Limited, London, England.
[1887] Brown, Charles, Brown Family Washington Connection, Manuscript, Jefferson County Museum, Charles Town, WV.
[1888] Letter from Lt. Lawrence B. Washington to Col. John F. Hamtramck, July 19, 1847, Regimental Letter Book, 1st Virginia Volunteer Infantry, Record Group 153, National Archives & Records Administration, Washington, DC.
[1889] Letter from Col. John F. Hamtramck to Robert Jones, Adjutant General, September 25, 1847, Regimental Letter Book, 1st Virginia Volunteer Infantry, Record Group 153, National Archives & Records Administration, Washington, D.C
[1890] Brown, Charles, Brown Family Washington Connection, Manuscript, Jefferson County Museum, Charles Town, WV.
[1891] Burke's Presidential Families of the United States of America, © 1981, Burke's Perrage Limited, London, England.
[1892] Letter from Benjamin Waters to Thomas S. Jessup, June 2, 1847, Regimental Letter Book, 1st Virginia Volunteer Infantry, Record Group 153, National Archives & Records Administration, Washington, D.C.
[1893] Letter from G.H. Crossman, Quarter Master to Col. John F. Hamtramck, June 27, 1847, Regimental Letter Book, 1st Virginia Volunteer Infantry, Record Group 153, National Archives & Records Administration, Washington, D.C
[1894] U.S. Census 1850, Dinwiddie Co., VA, p. 440.
[1895] U.S. Census 1860, Dinwiddie Co., VA, p. 044.
[1896] U.S. Census 1870, Dinwiddie Co., VA, p. 446.
[1897] U.S. Census 1850, Chesterfield Co., VA, p. 64.
[1898] U.S. Census 1860, Chesterfield Co., VA, p. 491.
[1899] Crews, Edward R., 14th Virginia Infantry, © 1995, H.E. Howard, Inc., Lynchburg, VA.
[1900] U.S. Census 1850, Frederick Co., VA, p. 283.
[1901] Mexican War Pension File, SC #1601, National Archives and Records Administration, Washington, DC.
[1902] Mexican War Pension SC #5724, National Archives and Records Administration, Washington, D.C.

# OFF TO WAR

[1903] Affidavit of Undertaker, Mexican War Pension WC #9458, National Archives and Records Administration, Washington, D.C.
[1904] Mexican War Pension WC #9458, National Archives and Records Administration, Washington, D.C.
[1905] *The Petersburg Daily Republican,* October 14, 1843, p. 3, c. 3.
[1906] Mexican War Pension File, SC #1986, National Archives and Records Administration, Washington, D.C.
[1907] U.S. Census 1870, Dinwiddie Co., VA, p. 234.
[1908] Record of Interments Blandford Cemetery, 1888-1905, p. 95, Blandford Cemetery, Petersburg, VA.
[1909] Mexican War Pension File, SC #12134, National Archives and Records Administration, Washington, D.C.
[1910] Albemarle County Marriage Register, Charlottesville, VA.
[1911] Confederate Veteran Magazine, © 1905, V. 13, p. 466.
[1912] Obituary, *The Newark Journal*, September 2, 1904, Newark, Arkansas.
[1913] Mexican War Pension File, WA # 17780, National Archives and Records Administration, Washington, D.C.
[1914] Confederate Veteran Magazine, © 1905, V. 13, p. 466.
[1915] U.S. Census 1860, Dinwiddie Co., VA, p. 361.
[1916] U.S. Census 1870, Dinwiddie Co., VA, p. 346.
[1917] U.S. Census 1870, Dinwiddie Co., VA, p. 154.
[1918] District of Columbia Marriage Register 1, 1811 - 1858, Washington, D.C.
[1919] Mexican War Pension SC #11683, National Archives and Records Administration, Washington, D.C.
[1920] U.S. Census 1850, Fairfax Co., VA, p. 184.
[1921] U.S. Census 1870, Fairfax Co., VA, p. 304.
[1922] *The Petersburg Republican*, November 17, 1848, p. 3, c. 1, Petersburg, VA.
[1923] U.S. Census 1850, Dinwiddie Co., VA, p. 429.
[1924] Mexican War Pension File, SC #6226, National Archives and Records Administration, Washington, D.C.
[1925] U.S. Census 1860, Dinwiddie Co., VA, p. 425.
[1926] U.S. Census 1870, Dinwiddie Co., VA, p. 283.
[1927] Record of Interments Blandford Cemetery, 1888-1905, p. 129, Blandford Cemetery, Petersburg, VA.
[1928] Mexican War Pension File, WC #13143, National Archives and Records Administration, Washington, D.C.
[1929] Mexican War Pension File, SC #5470, National Archives and Records Administration, Washington, DC.
[1930] U.S. Census 1850, Nelson Co., VA, p. 287.
[1931] U.S. Census 1860, Nelson Co., VA, p. 698.
[1932] U.S. Census 1870, Nelson Co., VA, p. 405.
[1933] Mexican War Pension File, SC #7653, National Archives and Records Administration, Washington, DC.
[1934] Mexican War Pension File, SC #7653, Affidavit of David M. White, National Archives and Records Administration, Washington, DC.
[1935] U.S. Census 1850, Lunenburg Co., VA, p. 049.
[1936] U.S. Census 1860, Lunenburg Co., VA, p. 956.
[1937] U.S. Census 1870, Lunenburg Co., VA, p. 597.
[1938] Mexican War Pension File, WC #10096, National Archives and Records Administration, Washington, DC.
[1939] Mexican War Pension File, SC #10286, National Archives and Records Administration, Washington, D.C.
[1940] U.S. Census 1860, Dinwiddie Co., VA, p. 009.
[1941] Mexican War Pension File, SC #5979, National Archives and Records Administration, Washington, DC.
[1942] U.S. Census 1860, Augusta Co., VA, p. 805.
[1943] U.S. Census 1870, Augusta Co., VA, p. 221.
[1944] Marriage Register, Washington County, Tenn., Circuit Court Clerk's Office, Jonesborough, Tenn.

# VIRGINIA VOLUNTEERS IN MEXICO

[1945] Affidavit of James L. Whitlow, 04/28/1894, Mexican War Pension SC #15924, National Archives and Records Administration, Washington, D.C.
[1946] Affidavit of Joseph Archer, 07/1902, Mexican War Pension WC #12861, National Archives and Records Administration, Washington, D.C.
[1947] Mexican War Pension File, SC #1804, National Archives and Records Administration, Washington, D.C.
[1948] U.S. Census 1880, Dare Co., NC, p. 70C.
[1949] Mexican War Pension File, WC #11924, National Archives and Records Administration, Washington, D.C.
[1950] International Genealogical Index, Film # 538042.
[1951] U.S. Census 1860, Rockbridge Co., VA, p. 276.
[1952] U.S. Census 1850, Rockbridge Co., VA, p. 550.
[1953] U.S. Census 1850, Lunenburg Co., VA, p. 034.
[1954] U.S. Census 1860, Lunenburg Co., VA, p. 976.
[1955] Sherwood, G.L., 20th and 39th Virginia Infantry, © 1994, H.E. Howard, Inc., Lynchburg, VA.
[1956] Mexican War Pension File, SC #1720, National Archives and Records Administration, Washington, D.C.
[1957] Mexican War Pension File, WC #10659, National Archives and Records Administration, Washington, D.C.
[1958] Mexican War Pension File, SC #1801, National Archives and Records Administration, Washington, D.C.
[1959] *Petersburg Index & Appeal*, April 10, 1874, p. 2, c. 3, Petersburg, VA.
[1960] Mexican War Pension File, WC #12924, National Archives and Records Administration, Washington, D.C.
[1961] Record of Interments Blandford Cemetery, 1843-1872, p. 70, Blandford Cemetery, Petersburg, VA.
[1962] *Daily South Side Democrat*, March 30, 1854, p. 2, c. 3, Petersburg, VA.
[1963] Record of Interments Blandford Cemetery, 1843-1872, p. 70, Blandford Cemetery, Petersburg, VA.
[1964] U.S. Census 1880, Putnam Co., WV, p. C008.
[1965] Mexican War Pension File, WC #6006, National Archives and Records Administration, Washington, DC.
[1966] U.S. Census 1860, Lunenburg Co., VA, p. 1010.
[1967] U.S. Census 1870, Lunenburg Co., VA, p. 594.
[1968] International Genealogical Index, Film # 1553310
[1969] U.S. Census 1860, Norfolk Co., VA, p. 447.
[1970] U.S. Census 1870, Norfolk Co., VA, p. 083.
[1971] Mexican War Pension File, SC #13553, National Archives and Records Administration, Washington, D.C.
[1972] Marriage Register #1, pg. 57, Montgomery Co., VA.
[1973] U.S. Census 1850, Montgomery Co., VA, p. 077.
[1974] Marriage Register #1, pg. 57, Montgomery Co., VA.
[1975] Mexican War Pension File, WC #10714, National Archives and Records Administration, Washington, D.C.
[1976] Mexican War Pension File, SC #15815, National Archives and Records Administration, Washington, DC.
[1977] Mexican War Pension File, WC #10078, National Archives and Records Administration, Washington, DC.
[1978] International Genealogical Index, Film # 1903629.
[1979] U.S. Census 1870, Dinwiddie Co., VA, p.267.
[1980] Mexican War Pension File, SC #6487, National Archives and Records Administration, Washington, D.C.
[1981] Records of the Office of the Judge Advocate General(Army), Record Group 153, EE 553, Case 13, National Archives & Records Administration, Washington, D.C.
[1982] U.S. Census 1860, Sussex Co., VA, p. 461.
[1983] Balfour, Daniel T., 13th Virginia Cavalry, © 1986, H.E. Howard, Inc., Lynchburg, VA.
[1984] Mexican War Pension WC #3347, National Archives and Records Administration, Washington, D.C.

OFF TO WAR

[1985] Harris, Malcom H., M.D., History of Louisa County, Virginia, ©1936, p. 434, The Dietz Press, Richmond, VA.
[1986] U.S. Census 1850, Louisa Co., VA, p. 365.
[1987] U.S. Census 1860, Louisa Co., VA, p. 879.
[1988] U.S. Census 1870, Louisa Co., VA, p. 376.
[1989] U.S. Census 1850, Amelia Co., VA, p. 048.
[1990] *The Daily Index*, November 9, 1869, p.2, c. 2, Petersburg, VA.
[1991] International Genealogical Index, Film # 1621425.
[1992] Mexican War Pension SC #1693, National Archives and Records Administration, Washington, D.C.
[1993] Records of the Office of the Judge Advocate General(Army), Record Group 153, EE 427, Case 2, National Archives & Records Administration, Washington, D.C.
[1994] District of Columbia Marriage Register 1, 1811 - 1858, Washington, D.C.
[1995] U.S. Census 1860, Fairfax Co., VA, p. 992.
[1996] U.S. Census 1850, Campbell Co., VA, p. 076.
[1997] Mexican War Pension WC #11996, National Archives and Records Administration, Washington, D.C.
[1998] U.S. Census 1860, Campbell Co., VA, p. 410.
[1999] U.S. Census 1870, Campbell Co., VA, p. 514.
[2000] Mexican War Pension SC #12136, National Archives and Records Administration, Washington, D.C.
[2001] Mexican War Pension WC #12024, National Archives and Records Administration, Washington, D.C.
[2002] Information provided by John Howard Wren, 1385 Navajo St., Salt Lake City, UT 84104.
[2003] U.S. Census 1870, Alexandria Co., VA, p. 140.
[2004] Boyd's Directory of the District of Columbia, © 1881, William H. Boyd, Washington, D.C.
[2005] Boyd's Directory of the District of Columbia, © 1890, William H. Boyd, Washington, D.C.
[2006] Mexican War Pension WC #12024, National Archives and Records Administration, Washington, D.C.
[2007] Mexican War Pension File, WC #4116, National Archives and Records Administration, Washington, D.C.
[2008] *Petersburg Index & Appeal*, December 30, 1875, p. 3, c. 3, Petersburg, VA.
[2009] Mexican War Pension File, SC #15582, National Archives and Records Administration, Washington, DC.
[2010] Records of the Office of the Judge Advocate General(Army), Record Group 153, EE 455, Case 11, National Archives & Records Administration, Washington, D.C.
[2011] Mexican War Pension File, SC # 16682, National Archives and Records Administration, Washington, D.C.
[2012] Mexican War Pension File, WC #9263, National Archives and Records Administration, Washington, D.C.
[2013] U.S. Census 1850, Norfolk Co., VA, p. 151.

www.ingramcontent.com/pod-product-compliance
Lightning Source LLC
Chambersburg PA
CBHW050425240426
43661CB00055B/2277